1993/47th Annual Edition

EDITED BY KEN WARNER

DBI BOOKS, INC.

ABOUT OUR COVERS

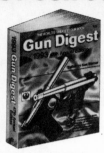

Sturm, Ruger & Co. has been a pioneer in the gun-making industry for over 40 years. They have developed new manufacturing materials and processes specifically for the gun trade, resulting in some of the best gun values on the market today. New stainless steel alloys and efficient investment-casting processes are but two leading examples of Ruger's trailblazing efforts in the field.

Now Ruger has made another breakthrough by combining the best of the gunmaker's art with the latest materials and injection-moulding technology. The result is the new Ruger 22/45 semi-automatic pistol in 22 Long Rifle. Two models are shown here on our covers.

The grip frame is glass-filled, injection-moulded Zytel nylon. This remarkable material is unaffected by saltwater, sweat, oils or bore solvents. The matte black finish won't crack, chip or peel and never needs refinishing. By using this space-age material, Ruger has reduced the overall weight of the new 22/45 grip frame by almost 25 percent from the standard Ruger Mark II pistols, depending on model, and cut back on manufacturing costs, meaning better value for the shooter. Since this composite material is so tough, you needn't worry about marring the grips since they're moulded into the frame—it's all one piece!

Shooters familiar with the 45 ACP M1911 pistol will like the feel of the new Ruger 22/45 because it is similar in grip angle to the ol' 45. The result is a new, but very pleasant, feel and balance for the Ruger 22 pistol. To make things even better, the magazine release button of the 22/45 is on the left side of the frame behind the trigger guard, again similar to the 45 auto.

The barrel and receiver are made of 400-series stainless steel with a brushed satin finish. The bolt is polished chrome-moly steel. Front and rear sights are made of blued steel for good visibility.

The new Ruger 22/45 pistol is offered in three versions: the KP-4 with 4¾-inch tapered barrel and fixed rear sight; the KP-514 with 5¼-inch tapered heavyweight barrel and click-adjustable rear sight for windage and elevation (shown at right on the covers); and the KP-512 using the 5½-inch bull barrel with click-adjustable rear sight for windage and elevation (shown at left on the covers). Each comes in a lockable, fitted plastic box for storage and carry, lock with keys, and a spare magazine.

Improve the tried and true Ruger Standard Auto pistol? It was tough, but the engineers at Sturm, Ruger have done so in great fashion. They've combined the best of the old with the latest that technology has to offer.

Photo by John Hanusin.

GUN DIGEST STAFF
EDITOR-IN-CHIEF
Ken Warner
SENIOR STAFF EDITOR
Harold A. Murtz
ASSOCIATE EDITOR
Robert S.L. Anderson
PRODUCTION MANAGER
John L. Duoba
EDITORIAL/PRODUCTION ASSOCIATE
Jamie L. Puffpaff
ASSISTANT TO THE EDITOR
Lilo Anderson
CONTRIBUTING EDITORS
Bob Bell
Doc Carlson
Dean A. Grennell
Edward A. Matunas
Layne Simpson
Larry S. Sterett
Hal Swiggett
D.A. Warner
J.B. Wood
Don Zutz
EUROPEAN CORRESPONDENT
Raymond Caranta
ELECTRONIC PUBLISHING MANAGER
Nancy J. Mellem
GRAPHIC DESIGN
Jim Billy
MANAGING EDITOR
Pamela J. Johnson
PUBLISHER
Sheldon L. Factor

DBI BOOKS, INC.
PRESIDENT
Charles T. Hartigan
VICE PRESIDENT & PUBLISHER
Sheldon L. Factor
VICE PRESIDENT—SALES
John G. Strauss
TREASURER
Frank R. Serpone

Harlon B. Carter
1913-1991

It's as hard to imagine a bug tough enough to kill Harlon Carter as it is to imagine the gun rights' fight without him, but both of those have come to pass. And it is a sad day.

The complications of cancer finally beat the old warrior, and you have lost a friend because Harlon Carter was the friend of anyone who pulled a trigger in service, sport or competition. Few men are mourned by as many who now mourn Harlon Carter, but then few men deserve to be mourned as he deserves.

Harlon Carter was one of those rare fellows about whom there are many stories, all of them true. We already miss him.

Shooting Sports On TV

Getting big-ticket TV results for low-budget video work is the National Shooting Sports Foundation's latest coup. The Chevy Truck Sportsman's Team Challenge matches, the Summer Biathlon shoots, and a series of video news releases have hit and are hitting Fox, CNN and ESPN as well as individual stations all over the country. Besides presenting sport shooting sympathetically in connection with exciting events, NSSF is able to get hunter-connected wildlife success stories on the tube. Well done.

Three States Now Field A Million

According to NSSF and the U.S. Fish and Wildlife Service, Michigan has joined Pennsylvania and Texas in issuing over a million paid hunting licenses in a single year. Other states on the upswing in 1990: Virginia up 6.6 percent; North Dakota, Iowa and Indiana all up just under 5 percent. That all adds up to $422 million spent on licenses, permits, tags and stamps—and *that* goes straight to wildlife programs.

Crosman Buys Benjamin

Gimbel's may not tell Macy's, as they say, but Crosman is happy about buying Benjamin. Ken Scheele, president of Crosman Corp., says there are no plans to make changes in the products, but he is looking forward to getting into the paintball and slingshot business.

Olympic Shooters Want Out

Saying, in effect, they don't get no respect and not nearly enough money, U.S. shooters in the International disciplines asked the U.S. Olympic Committee to release them from thrall to the NRA. They think they can do better on their own and perhaps they can.

There's glamor on the firing line, the United States Shooting Team believes, and so this is the cover of their Olympic media guide booklet—the gentleman is Skeetshooter Bill Roy; the lady is rifleshooter Launi Meili, who shot in the 1988 Olympics.

Whether or not they could, had not NRA toted 'em this far over the past 90 years or so, is another question, of course.

SHOT Show Does Numbers Again

For the 13th time, NSSF's 1992 SHOT Show was bigger, and filled more space, than ever. Visitors were down just a couple thousand in a *bad* year, but they bought more. So will the 14th Show in Houston do it again? Of course.

Big Ones In Milwaukee

As is their triennial wont, the Boone & Crockett Club gave the world a look at the great harvest from great hunting. This year in Milwaukee there were four new World's Records—a Roo-sevelt elk, a grizzly bear, a muskox and a Rocky Mountain goat—among the 100 trophies on display. It was the 21st North American Big Game Awards program.

Another Fine SCI Rifle

John Bolliger and Shane Thompson select wood for the Grizzly, a 375 H&H Magnum to be first in the Safari Club

International World's Most Dangerous Game series. Decorative motifs will be based on a Dennis Jones sculpture.

James M. Triggs 1924-1992

The hands-down best of firearms illustrators in this century passed away after a long struggle with emphysema and related disorders in June, 1992. Readers of GUN DIGEST knew his work by the many cover illustrations he did over the years, as well as from the extensive review published in the 1992 GUN DIGEST. It will be some time before we see another like Jim Triggs.

CONTENTS

FEATURES

A Modest Proposal by Ken Warner
Wherein the future of hunting is almost assured 6

A Forgotten Rifle by John Wallace
The 1885 Guedes fought with the Boers 8

About the 22 Short by C.E. Harris
Cheap no more, this rimfire round yet has a place 16

Again the Trebuchet by Wilfrid Ward
No peer at all for throwing dead horses 20

More Than An Ace Up His Sleeve... by Stanley C. Crist
What you see ain't always what you get 26

The 30 Carbine by David L. Ward
Nobody likes it but people 28

The Gallinaceous Grade IV by Rob Lucas
A pheasant-killer supreme for 35 years 33

Collecting Hopkins and Allen Guns by Donald R. France
One of the few frontiers left in gun collecting 36

Modern Silenced 22s by Al Paulson
Are in the racks of 40,000 Americans 46

How Good Are Factory Rifles? by Sam Fadala
Out of the box, they're clearly the best ever 60

Blackpowder and Lead Bullets: Where the Sharps Shines by Dennis Bruns
This shooter has his cake and eats it, too 65

Blowback Nines by John Malloy
The history of a concept only now succeeding 70

Arms and the Man by C. Rodney James
How amputees manage their firearms 90

Picking Safari Rifles by Charles Askins
The old pro knows how and tells nearly all 97

The Small Arms Master Plan by Stanley C. Crist
The proud history of recent future military planning 102

The Plight of the French Rifleman by Patrick Constantin
Culture and common sense collide head-on 116

Terry MacFarlane's Souvenir of World War II by Ken Warner
About as nice a piece of soldier art as there is 122

Hunting the Old Ones by Dwain Bland
How to shoot 19th-century style with 19th-century guns 129

The Quiet Rifle by C. Rodney James
It's the 22, of course, but only accurate ones work 138

Custom Guns
This year's artful crop 150

Art of the Engraver
How they're doing it today 151

Collecting Holsters by Bob Arganbright
It's coming, and this is how to get ahead of the game 164

Choke Explained (Once Again) by Don Zutz
Now it's air pressure that shapes the pattern 174

Colt's 455 Model 1911: The First Variation by John Malloy
The British knew a good thing, but didn't use it much 182

Traditional Affordable Air Guns by J.I. Galan
$200 is still big money in the air gun biz 190

A Double Gun Odyssey by Allan H. Pressley
He just never met a repeater he could love 193

Under My Thumb by Lee H. Arten
Is where safeties belong on guns 208

DEPARTMENTS

Expert Reports '93
Shotgun Review by Don Zutz 56
The Guns of Europe by Raymond Caranta 86
Handguns Today: Sixguns and Others by Hal Swiggett 111
Scopes and Mounts by Bob Bell 124
Handloading Update by Dean A. Grennell 134
Handguns Today: Autoloaders by J.B. Wood 146
Rifle Review by Layne Simpson 153
Blackpowder Review by Doc Carlson 161
Utility Guns by Larry S. Sterett 178

Testfire
Grendel's P-30 22 WMR Pistol by J.I. Galan 198
Tar-Hunt's Benchrest Shotgun by Larry S. Sterett 199
Interarms' Mini-Mauser in 7.62x39 by C.E. Harris 200
Ruger's High-Tech 7.62x39 Bolt Gun by Nick Croyle 202
ATIS PM2 Police Pump by Larry S. Sterett 203
Daisy's Power Line 44 by Ladd Fanta 205
Shooting China's New Gang of Four by C.E. Harris 206

One Good Gun
A S&W 1917 Surviving in Nicaragua by Carlos Schmidt 209
A Special Single-Action Colt by Dick Love 212
My "Fake" Double Rifle by Clayton T. Williams 213

Ammunition, Ballistics & Components by Edward A. Matunas 214

Ballistic Tables '93 220

Shooter's Marketplace 225

CATALOG

GUNDEX® 266

Handguns
Autoloaders 273
Competition 300
Double-Action Revolvers 309
Single-Action Revolvers 318
Miscellaneous 323

Rifles—Centerfire
Autoloaders 327
Lever & Slide Action 332
Bolt Actions 337
Single Shots 353
Drillings, Combination Guns,
   Double Rifles 357

Rifles—Rimfire
Autoloaders 360
Lever & Slide Action 364
Bolt Actions & Single Shots 365
Competition Centerfires & Rimfires .. 370

Shotguns
Autoloaders 378
Slide Actions 382
Over/Unders 386
Side-by-Sides 395

Bolt Actions & Single Shots 400
Military & Police 403

Blackpowder Guns
Single Shot Pistols 405
Revolvers 409
Muskets & Rifles 412
Shotguns 424

Air Guns
Handguns 425
Long Guns 430
Paint Ball 443

Warranty Service Center Directory 445

Metallic Sights 457
Chokes and Brakes 460
Scopes and Mounts 461
Spotting Scopes 473
Periodical Publications 475
Arms Library 477
Arms Associations 495

Directory of the Arms Trade
Product Directory 498
Manufacturer's Directory 512

A Modest Proposal

From Ken Warner

To THE EXTENT that what is so joylessly called the "slob hunter" is a problem, I believe what follows here to be a solution. This proposal will also, I am even more happy to say, cut the legs right out from under those thoughtless elitists who support the idea that hunting in the United States should be carried out as it is in Europe and Africa.

We don't have too little game or too little room to hunt it in or too many hunters. What we have is too many shots fired.

Think about that. Suppose it became the norm, or even the law, that one's ammunition load might be—for a whole day in the field—say, three shells for each two upland birds or waterfowl in the legal daily bag, or two centerfire rifle cartridges for each allowed big game animal? For small game and turkeys and varmints, a maximum of two cartridges each—shotshells, or rimfire or centerfire rifle or handgun cartridges—would be ample.

So far as anyone cares to object that additional cartridges might be needed in an emergency, or in order to pursue a wounded bird or animal once the daily ration had been expended, I believe that objection and that perceived need could be met with a sealed package, either one purchased as a sealed package or a package of, for instance, some special handloads sealed by the game authority.

We are already accustomed to having guns illegal for certain tasks. We have state laws disagreeing with each other on the subject in vast and relatively harmless proliferation. Some states forbid rifle cartridges on case length, some on overall length, some on primer system, some on projectile caliber, some on rated energy, and some happy few not at all. We plug five-shot magazines to three shots, and we forbid (Pennsylvania) autoloading rifles and pistols, and demand (Maine) shotgun barrels over 20 inches and deny (Georgia and South Carolina) turkeys death from rifle bullets.

We accept, reasonably cheerfully, all manner of regulation of our field activities. We comply with daily bags, season limits, split seasons, special seasons, gender classifications. We do "Shoot-No Shoot" drill the whole pheasant season and the whole deer season, too, most places. We use steel shot where we must. We get our bag checked, our loads checked, our guns checked whenever a game warden can get to us and thinks he should. We wear, in some states, licenses where game wardens can see them with binoculars. We have a lot of regulation to contend with already.

Thus, this modest proposal: We set out to make careful hunters and good shots by rationing how many rounds they may carry on their persons or in their vehicles. Back at camp or home, they may have ammo by the case, but not out in the bushes.

Indeed, a lot of ammunition someplace will be an absolute necessity, because hunters operating under this eminently reasonable system will practice their shooting and scout their game as never since before the advent of the cartridge. In place of shooting five shots at a can to see if Old Killdeer still functions and carrying 35 rounds to fire at deer, the average guy will fire 30 to 300 shots for zero and practice, carry 10 rounds to camp, and fire just one in the woods—we hope.

Personally, I might say that anyone who has seen me shoot doves might very well break up in giggles at the idea that I would proceed to a dove field with just 24 shells. A wag or two might inquire if I planned an early departure and with some justification. I have seen, in as few as 90 minutes, as many as 30 doves fly on with their hearts shot out.

However, I am willing. There have been a few glory days—seven birds with nine shots once, 17 with one box of shells (overseas) another time—and maybe I'd clean up my act. I'd need to.

I don't think the rifle shooters would suffer much. I'm just back from South Carolina as I write and there I saw seven riflemen take eleven deer with fourteen shots. One deer was hit twice; the others were clean misses, one running, one a try at a head shot. And I have to say that anyone who needs more than two shots to kill a squirrel or rabbit ought to quit spoiling that particular critter's day and go find

This pig took two—one at 200 yards, one up close. It *can* be done, says Warner.

another one. I feel the same way about groundhogs and such—two tries is tops until tomorrow. Guys who peck 10 times at a 400-yard chuck bug me. Very few such follow up their fusillades by hiking over there to check results.

When it comes to ducks and geese, this proposal takes hold where we are all tender. Again, I am willing, and again I'd need to work on a few skills. I really wouldn't mind, though, not since the day I saw eight of the most celebrated shots in America (and me) fire a total of 27 times at a single goose and finally scratch him down. (PS: The downed goose eventually walked away.)

In general, this could have a recruiting poster sort of appeal: "Are you good enough?" and "The woods are looking for a few good men!" are possible slogans. I doubt that would be all it takes, though. It probably would take a provision in the law.

However, we are not talking gun law here. We are talking game regulations. We are talking conservation. We are talking safety, skill, pride, not gun laws.

Suppose, for instance, participation was voluntary? Suppose those willing to play by these rules got an automatic doe tag, or their own early opening day, or their own early season, or head of the line treatment at state game lands or for public blinds? Or all of that? Suppose they had to wear a badge and agree to be checked for extra cartridges? (That's the famous other side of the coin—with every privilege comes, sooner or later, a little pain.) That minor indignity pales beside the potential strip search any Customs agent can order at the border, and indeed seems to look about like what happens routinely to each commercial air traveler every time he or she enters a loading gate area.

Sure, some guys will beat the system. Astronauts carry unauthorized stuff on ten billion dollar space shots. So what? Most won't because, I believe, this is a place where peer pressure might actually work. Where there are no standards, and in this particular regard we have none, peers don't judge. Where there are standards, peers judge harshly indeed. If you don't think so, try to find out why your 15-year-old wears the clothes he or she wears. (Not the clothes you buy—the clothes actually worn.)

In practice, it's simple: You're squirrel hunting and the limit is five so you have ten rounds, plus five under seal. It ain't a great day for you and by 10 AM you have fired ten times and you have a pair of squirrels. That's it. You go home, or go get your fishing rod, or hunt quail, or scout deer, but you and the squirrels are through for the day.

Enforcement is simple, too: If a guy is hunting, he is doing it with at least one of his ten rounds left and no others on him but the sealed pack. If he has more, why he's agreed in advance that he's cheating and—no big deal—he loses his badge and becomes ordinary. He can still hunt, but under slob rules. Maybe he gets his name in the paper. He can ask for a court if he feels there's error, but otherwise he just picks up his badge again after a delay of game, you could call it, or tries to get one next year, or whatever. Of course, if he cheats on the fair play *and* goes over the bag limit, trespasses, shoots out of season—well, he has to handle the rest of it in court.

Putting that in the slob hunter perspective: Where local culture applauds only results, you get pigs at the hunting trough and the most pig wins. When technique counts, it's always some easy talker with a nice smile that gets the girls, and all the pigs just hang out and brag.

So that's it. Modestly, I claim this proposal would change it all, would work. Also modestly, I don't think it has a hope of success in getting a trial because all there is going for it is common sense and one editor.

Unless maybe you'll go along, maybe write to somebody? Not me, mind you—write somebody important. Soon.

Amidst Mausers and British bolt guns, there's a Guedes in ambush as hard-bitten Boers pose for a camera. (From Cape Archives Department, with permission—Print AG1234)

A Forgotten Rifle...

...the 1885 Guedes fought with the Boers

by JOHN WALLACE

WHEN BRITAIN, once in a while, succeeds in avoiding some dramatic historical blunder, it is often because we have made it before. We had something very much like our own Bay of Pigs invasion, for example, and with rather less justification, in the Transvaal in 1895. It was toward an odd memory of that event, and less-known political scandals besides, that my steps led when I wandered into an antique gun shop in Birmingham, and came across a rifle which many lifelong collectors have never seen.

It was a well-made falling block single shot with military sights, bearing the name of the great Steyr arms factory, and the model designation M1885. But there was something quite un-Teutonic about its lines, and to a long-time addict of Frank Barnes' *Cartridges of the World*, the caliber of only 8mm, commonplace only a few years later, was enough to identify it as the Portuguese Guedes, a rifle which Barnes describes as having had a very short life. The rifle was accompanied by a certificate issued by the Birmingham Gun Barrel Proof House, explaining that it could not be proved because ammunition was not available. On this basis, under the local police force's policy at that time, I was able to purchase it freely as an antique.

The Boer War so long ago was not to be my own Guedes' last battle. While working in Saudi Arabia, I applied to my local police force in Scotland for a permit to buy blackpowder for my Kentucky replica. This was refused by the Deputy Chief Constable—soon to be involved with the early stages of the Lockerbie investigation, when his force was castigated under such tragic circumstances by Captain Smith of Pan Am. I wrote to an appeals authority, which is so obscure that my letter was, probably by a genuine accident, redirected to the Home Office, our police ministry. I had been unwise enough to mention that the police had always approved of my leaving my certified firearms at my elderly mother's house in my absence, so why not blackpowder, which has never caused any accident in private hands?

My firearms were promptly seized in a raid on her house, and I was prosecuted for unlawful possession of the

force a round into the chamber, and the rifle is thus better at dealing with a dirty or dented round, or a neck-sized one, than most falling blocks.

Guedes was not alone in realizing the usefulness of this tilting movement. W. Milton Farrow patented an action in the U.S.A. in 1884, and Aydt in Germany in 1885, as the obsolescence of the falling block was becoming obvious, but neither had designs on the military market. The Aydt seems especially relevant, because although a rolling-block-resembling-a-falling-block, like the later Stevens 44, it has a hammer inside the block, very much resembling the Guedes. The Aydt, like the Stevens, was limited by strength to the rather mild cartridges used for schuetzen shooting, and it is arguable that Guedes made the same improvement—gaining strength by swapping a little tilt for a little more

whether this point is oily or dry. The backsight is too close to the eye for comfort by modern standards, and must be left unfocused, rather like half a peepsight. This common feature of European military rifles is probably due to their reliance on youthful conscripts, whose eyes focus better than those of the old soldiers who formed such a valuable part of the British and American armies.

The obvious advantage over the Martini is that the Guedes bore can be cleaned, examined and bore-sighted from the breech. Dirt entering the mechanism would be much more likely to work its way out again, and the lockwork inside the block is very well protected, while the Guedes can easily be dismantled for cleaning. So, in fact, can the military Martini-Henry, but getting it back together is a very much more difficult proposi-

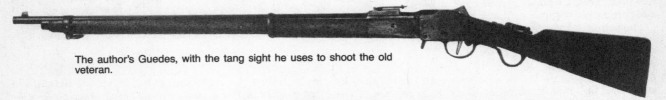

The author's Guedes, with the tang sight he uses to shoot the old veteran.

Guedes at a time when that force, in response to government pressures, reduced its firearm certificate holders by some twelve percent in a few months. Well, I got to be one of the 88 percent, for I won, after a two-day trial at my own expense, and recovered the rifle, which I was most courteously authorized to use after moving to another area where there was a genuine police force. My formal complaint regarding, among other things, corruption, perjury and destruction of evidence, has just passed its first year of investigation and, without interviewing any of the accused officers, who were all retired over a remarkably short period of time, a decision has been taken not to bring criminal charges. But I did it to be more trouble than I was worth, not for dramatic victory. Don't say this article hasn't taught you something.

The Guedes breech mechanism, to return to things of lasting interest, operates in an unusual manner. The falling block slides vertically downward until it disengages from the locking surfaces in the receiver, which are positioned level with the bore. It then becomes free to tilt slightly backward and away from the cartridge head, guided by a short fixed screw in the receiver wall, which slides in a sinuous groove milled in the breechblock side. The reverse movement on closing means that there is some tendency to

slide—which Stevens was to do with its Model 44½. We will probably never know if Aydt inspired Guedes or vice versa, but in 19th-century Europe, it might easily have been that prior publication did not sabotage one's chance of a patent as it does today.

The block houses both hammer and trigger, plus a complex double-ended mainspring, the only spring in the entire rifle except for the leaf spring under the backsight. You should treat this mainspring with the utmost respect if you ever dismantle the Guedes, because it is a long, hard job to make a new one, as I did. The hammer has no exposed spur, since it is self-cocking on the opening stroke of the lever, when its projecting breast contacts a transverse pin. A safety-catch is fitted, sliding transversely in the trigger guard, and seems to be about as reliable as any trigger-locking safety can be, although it must be applied with the finger inside the trigger guard, and a conscript or colonial battalion should have been good for an accidental discharge or two in the process. The trigger pull, however, was vile, with a long, dragging movement, and nothing that can be done will make it really good, since the trigger engages too close to its axis of rotation. The trigger part of the single spring makes sliding contact with the trigger, so the weight of pull varies slightly according to

tion, and the average 19th-century military recruit would have been less accustomed to things mechanical than a modern schoolboy.

The Guedes extractor looks like a potential weakness, since it encloses a full 180 degrees of the case head. Most other falling block rifles had forked extractors which intruded into the chamber at two separate points. A weak case or excessive pressure—of which more later—would tend to force the Guedes extractor against nothing more substantial than its pivot pin. Actual extraction, conversely, is extremely strong and reliable, since the toe of the loading lever operates a sliding actuator, of which the forked rear end drives the extractor. Initially, the upper fork contacts the extractor just below the case rim, giving slow, powerful primary extraction, with little that is likely to go wrong. As the extractor begins to move, however, contact is switched to the lower fork of the actuator, which is much closer to the pivotal axis of the extractor. The latter accelerates sharply so that the case, directed by the high-curving trough in the top of the block, is strongly ejected without any kind of spring or latch. It seems a pity that so many brilliant minds were forced to despair of building anything as simple into the tighter confines of a double-barreled shotgun.

The Guedes was furnished with a

long sword bayonet with a forward-curved yataghan blade. Mine was obtained separately, and most likely was originally supplied with an M1886 Kropatschek, since both used the identical M1885 bayonet. It was side-mounted on the barrel of both rifles, as was common at the time. Muzzleloading rifles, with which many generals would have seen their last frontline service, need a ramrod; and a cleaning rod is still an asset on any blackpowder breechloader. This, it was thought, ruled out a fixed bayonet under the muzzle, a sectional rod having never, apparently, been considered. As a result, the Martini-Henry, and no doubt the Guedes, would shoot twelve to fifteen minutes of angle to one side with the bayonet fixed. This bizarre piece of mental set must have been less than helpful for the last volley before facing the assegais of colonial subjects bent upon self-determination, those who had never read the books that say savages are afraid of gunfire, at any rate.

The sights are of orthodox open military type, graduated to 2000 meters. That would be for the most haphazard volley fire, of course, since quite unpredictable things happen to any small arm bullet at an elevation of almost nine degrees. For the briefest of periods, the Guedes might perhaps have qualified as the finest long-range rifle in the world, outside specialized target shooting. But it was never employed as such, or supplied with comparable ammunition, and its history was to make this academic.

My Guedes bore the stamp "Z.A.R.," which the dealer claimed to stand for "Zuid Afrikaansche Republiek." I wondered at this, since the Republic of South Africa did not exist until very much later, but in my program of research, my first port of call was Mr. D.J. Penn, Keeper of Exhibits and Firearms at the Imperial War Museum in London. He confirmed that this was indeed the mark, as used on other small arms of the independent Boer republic more commonly known as the Transvaal, which together with the Orange Free State was absorbed into the Union of South Africa following the Boer War of 1899. My other main sources were Brigadier-General Ferreira de Lemos of the Museu Militar in Lisbon, and Ms. E.M. Wessels of the War Museum of the Boer Republics in Bloemfontein. To them I owe the pleasure an amateur so seldom encounters in historical research—that of putting together the sources, and a smattering of modern technical knowledge, to unravel a story which I believe nobody in the world knew in its entirety.

Military rifles are proved in battle,

Oom Paul Kruger, however unsophisticated his culture, was seen to outplay Britain's Chamberlain at International Chess in cartoons like this.

and it is hard to over-emphasize the importance of the siege of Plevna in 1877. Here, the Turkish commander Osman Ali Pasha, settling in for a long siege by a much stronger army, disarmed his cavalry and gave their Winchester 1866 carbines to the infantry in the trenches, in addition to their own Martinis, chambered for a slightly slimmer 45-caliber round than the British one. Both weapons were American, Turkey having recently obtained the Martinis from the Providence Tool Company of Rhode Island. Known as the sick man of Europe, the Turks, nonetheless, consistently operated an enlightened policy of small arms acquisition, and in this case they had an exceptionally shrewd and courageous commander. Osman Pasha entrenched his positions, and inflicted enormous losses on the Russian infantry who, being led with the most dismal lack of imagination, were committed to one disastrous frontal attack after another over a period of months. At last, Osman Pasha realized his gallantly held position was no longer tenable, and was forced to surrender after a failed breakout.

There were real lessons to be learned from Plevna. Most European strategists had been dim enough to ignore or underestimate the lessons of the American Civil War, and there had been a comprehensive choice of explanations for the French debacle against Prussia in 1870. But Plevna convinced generals and war ministries that modern musketry ruled the battlefield, and they must forget about close-order infantry maneuvers on open ground, or consign them to the parade ground where they remain fossilized forever. It was obvious that repeating infantry rifles were the indispensable weapons of the future, and that a way must be found to adapt them to something more powerful than the 44 Henry cartridge used in the Winchesters of Plevna. But the best tactical thinkers realized that the real test of a military rifle was not its ultimate long-range capability, but how it would perform when things went drastically wrong, and a man had to fire, usually at close quarters, far greater quantities of ammunition in a short time than any user's manual would recommend. Maxim and Browning both invented automatic guns in the 1880s, and the scene was set for the most logical and consistent evolution toward the Kalashnikov and M-16 of today.

In Portugal, however, Lieutenant L.F. Guedes learned the wrong lesson from Plevna. He appears to have seen it as confirming the accepted belief of the 1870s, that repeaters could perfectly well make do with pistol cartridges, but there was also a need for a long-range infantry weapon which must necessarily be single shot. In fact, his original design, for an 11mm cartridge which resembled and may actually have been the 11mm Gras, would have been a splendid one for the mid-1870s, a rifle which might have got General Custer home again. But it was officially adopted in 1885, when most other European nations were overcoming the problems associated with high-powered repeaters, and an even greater revolution, smokeless powder, was looming nearby on the horizon.

Among small arms designers, there was nothing new or mysterious about the increased ballistic efficiency which could be obtained by a smaller-bore, elongated bullet, and large powder charge in a bottlenecked case. If we consider a given quantity of powder, and hence of gas, it will tend to fill most rapidly a bore of small cross sectional area. The effect will be to run up higher pressure, but drive the bullet at higher velocity. If the bullet is extremely elongated, it will also retain that velocity better, and deliver adequate long-range striking power with flatter trajectory and a light cartridge weight, permitting the soldier to carry more ammunition. Stabilizing that long bullet will demand a faster rifling twist.

loader becomes hard to load, and a breechloader gives excessive pressure, increased barrel heating, and poor accuracy. This effect becomes much more pronounced with a small bore, which has a reduced area for the fouling to form on, and also with fast-twist rifling. The apparent direction of the movement between bullet and bore surfaces is in line with the rifling grooves, but the gas and fouling move in a straight line, so that fast rifling is like a series of corrugations in which the fouling will lodge. The 32 Winchester Special performs quite well with blackpowder, and I have had passable results experimenting with a 303. But both of these use smaller charges than the Guedes, and the 32 Special has slower-twist rifling.

So, military breechloaders at first settled down at around 45-caliber. The 45-70 U.S. Government was among the best for sustained fire, although ballistically inferior to the heavier charge and bullet of the British 577/450 Martini-Henry. There is no better example than the defense of Rorke's Drift in

Martinis kicked viciously, glowed visibly in the dark, and cooked off rounds if held unfired.

Later, the British planned to reduce the caliber of the Martini to .400-inch with rounded Metford rifling which would shed fouling better, and Mauser arrived at a minimum acceptable caliber of 9.5mm for the Model 1871/84 rifles which they supplied to the Turks. But either Lieutenant Guedes or his

The Portuguese arsenal headstamp on this Boer War battlefield relic suggests it was actually a Kropatschek round.

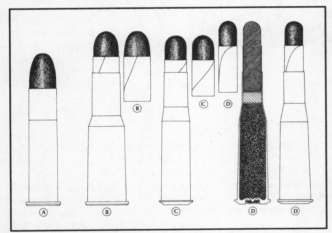

The cartridges of the times: A—U.S. 45-70; B—577/450 Martini-Henry; C—9.5mm Mauser; D—Guedes 8x60R.

Author's shooting cartridges at left, made from 348 Winchester brass and loaded with various bullets; at right is a 19th-century original.

Bannerman's must have had them because this line drawing is from a Bannerman's catalog.

The trouble was, early on, that blackpowder deposits a solid residue of fouling which, with repeated firing, cakes the bore near the chamber throat. The bullet, after forcing its way through all this when it ought to be upsetting to seal the bore, is a loose fit in the cleaner part beyond. A muzzle-

1879, by a hundred British soldiers, whose main force had been massacred while attempting to defend a camp and wagon park with an excessively wide perimeter. Here, in a small and well-fortified position, they fought for ten hours against something over 4000 Zulu warriors, until their uncleaned

superiors took the decision to reduce the caliber of the rifle to 8mm, with conventional rifling and an 11.5-inch twist, while only blackpowder was available.

In fact, smokeless powder, which might with greater reason have been called non-fouling powder, had been used in shotguns for several years, and although nobody had yet controlled its burning rate well enough for use in military rifles, it must have been obvious that such a development was just around the corner. The Portuguese were not to know that Vieille, in France, would make the breakthrough in 1885, under such secrecy that for some years French soldiers were threatened with two years' imprisonment for opening a cartridge, which, one imagines, every one of them therefore did. But either the Portuguese or Steyr must have known that someone in the near future would arrive at this way of breaking the caliber deadlock, and make large stocks of brand-new 11mm rifles an exceedingly embarrassing thing to have.

The production 8x60R Guedes cartridge has a base diameter of .543-inch, which is larger than the modern 300 magnums. But cases made from 348 Winchester, of which mine measure .547-inch rather than the .553-inch Barnes claims, chamber snugly in my rifle. Accurate capacity comparisons depend on the brass thickness, but it should be somewhat more capacious than the 30-06, and might, if it had survived, have provided the basis for an excellent modern single shot or lever-action cartridge. The original load was 71 grains of coarse Rottweil blackpowder, though a modern case may hold less, with a 247-grain lead alloy bullet. Paper-patched bullets would have coped perfectly well with the factory velocity of only about 1706 fps, but what was actually adopted in 1885 was another late and ill-researched bright idea, namely an identical form of patching but using copper foil instead of paper. The foil often failed to detach properly on leaving the muzzle, due no doubt to soldering by friction-generated heat, with disastrous effects on accuracy. A wax pellet between card wads was supposed to lubricate the bore but, in fact, did nothing of the sort and was often picked up intact.

Only fifty prototypes, in which caliber I do not know, were made in Portugal before a contract was placed with Steyr for 40,000 Guedes rifles. We will never know what Steyr thought or said about the caliber reduction, but we know that they carried on with tests during early production, and soon reported extraction difficulties after a large number of shots had been fired. The Portuguese government cancelled the contract in March, 1886, by which time 18,000 rifles had been made. The Steyr company was larger than we can readily imagine, in

an age which no longer depends upon large conscript armies of riflemen. It had been founded in 1869 with nearly eight times the capital of the Mauser brothers two years later, and in 1886 it had a manufacturing capacity of 13,000 rifles per week. Although this may have been taken up mostly with Austria-Hungary's adoption of the straight-pull Mannlicher in the same year, it is feasible that none of the 18,000 Guedes rifles date from 1885. I know of no Guedes with a serial number in five figures, although it is possible that the numbers repeated after reaching 9999.

Steyr was paid 132,000,000 reis of the Portuguese taxpayer's money for the work done, or about $120,000, and they got to keep the rifles. Governments being what they are, the Portuguese were probably relieved to find a more or less honorable way out of having adopted the last single shot military rifle in the world, but they seem not to have connected the problems with the 8mm caliber and blackpowder, which was the propellant initially used in the tube-magazine Kropatscheks which they ordered from Steyr as a replacement. No Guedes rifles appear to have reached the Portuguese military, and there is an interesting contrast between two contemporary military texts which I have seen in photocopied form. The Portuguese Captain Mardel's illustrations were apparently prepared from

a prototype or early design drawings, while Colonel Schmidt, based in Switzerland, appears to have worked from a production rifle.

In the 1890s, the Transvaal enjoyed effective independence under the government of President Krueger, an elderly, humane and extremely astute Biblical patriarch of appalling personal hygiene, who held as an article of faith that the earth was flat, was said to have killed his first Zulu at the

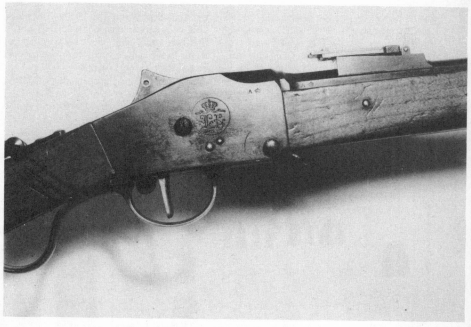

On its right side, the relatively clean Guedes receiver carries the cipher of King Luis I of Portugal.

age of nine, and possessed depths of character which cannot be summarized here. British and other expatriates had become responsible for much of the commerce and technology of what was, basically, a pastoral nation and, by extension, for operating the recently discovered gold field of the Witwatersrand. But the latter activity threatened the Transvaalers with economic and demographic domination by an alien race. So discriminatory taxes were levied, and obstacles placed in the way of the outlanders' acquiring civil rights, although most of the real evidence suggests that few of them cared very much, as long as there was work to be done and fortunes to be made. But these grievances were to be exploited by Cecil B. Rhodes, Prime Minister of the Cape Colony and Godfather of the South African mining industry, who had recently gained control of the diamond mines of the cape, and nursed similar designs on the gold field of the Witwatersrand.

In December, 1895, Rhodes' henchman, Dr. Leander Starr Jameson, was in command of a small force of mounted irregulars on the Transvaal border, present in response to a spontaneous plea for help by the miners, framed in a text which Rhodes was later found to have supplied to them in advance. It seems likely that Rhodes was playing a subtle game, since Joseph Chamberlain, the British Colonial Secretary, would later be all but

pared for a German war in 1914, we probably owe it to Kaiser Wilhelm's ill-considered support for the Boers, which was the first sign that he could be something more menacing than Queen Victoria's grandson. In the event, Boer and British governments did a most admirable job of mending fences. Dr. Jameson was repatriated to the U.K., where he served fourteen months in jail before being released on grounds of ill health. Being a medical

muskets by simple workshop technology, and attempting to cripple a civilized enemy by starving him of arms had barely been thought of. But the likelihood of their being used against British soldiers must undoubtedly have been known, since General Joubert had won the battle of Majuba Hill in the First Boer War of 1881, with Westley Richards monkey-tail capping breechloaders.

General Joubert also contacted one George Evans of Stein and Hunter, the local agents for Alfred Field and Co. of 77 Edmund Street in Birmingham. The firm was a short-lived one, possibly set up as a "front" for someone more respectable, and its name may have been chosen to evoke false associations with the Field falling block rifle. But Edmund Street still exists, just a few yards from the city hall which had been Joseph Chamberlain's first seat of power when he was a successful screw manufacturer. Joubert contracted to buy from them 5000 or less Guedes rifles. Probably the best history of the war, Christopher Pakenham's *The Boar War*, regards this as a blunder of his, but does not appear to appreciate the priority he was instructed to give to early delivery. He was unimpressed by the rifles themselves, which he had reason to know, since the Transvaal had already bought 2700 of them, and the Orange Free State had 1450 in store when war began, possibly because burghers thought accepting one would spoil any chance of getting their hands on a Mauser. In fact, Alfred Field could supply only 2000 more Guedes rifles, suggesting that the factory stocks were exhausted. This means that something over a third of the Guedes rifles reached South Africa, and perhaps much more. While I know that some were used in the Balkans, they must presumably have gone there before General Joubert's partly-fulfilled order, and I have heard rumors that some reached the loyalist Ulster Volunteer Force, then a legal militia, in Northern Ireland in 1914.

The Transvaal consignment was dispatched on the 3rd February, probably directly from the Steyr factory. The Boers paid £2,10 shillings each, or considerably more than the compensation already paid to Steyr for making them in 1886. That was, in fact, quite a lot of money, being around half the ordinary retail price of a new-model Lee-Enfield, which for its purpose was a lot more than twice as good. Since Steyr had presumably covered their costs ten years earlier, it seems likely that Alfred Field made an extremely large

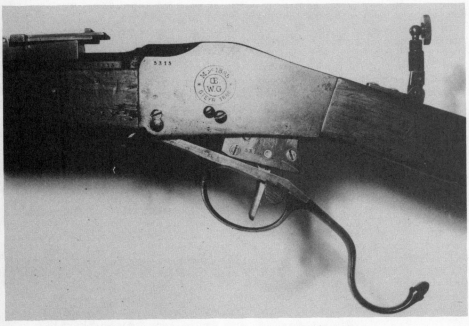

Steyr's mark is on the left side of the receiver. The tang sight is the author's addition.

conclusively shown to have had prior knowledge of the enterprise. Possibly, Rhodes hoped to panic the Boers into more repressive measures, and had been encouraged to expect British intervention in such a case. There is little doubt that by Christmas of 1895 he had realized that an invasion would receive inadequate response among the miners, and had resolved to hold back.

What actually happened, though, is that Jameson, a diminutive, charming, and quite unscrupulous adventurer, led his 500 men in an invasion and advance on Johannesburg. Rhodes is reported to have received the news with the words, "Doctor Jim has upset my applecart." The Boers, of course, were peerless exponents of mounted guerilla warfare, and within a few days the raiders were encircled and taken prisoner, with heavy losses.

In the following weeks, there arose an atmosphere of growing hysteria on both sides, and in much of the foreign press. If Britain was in any way pre-

doctor may have helped, for he certainly seems to have made a successful recovery. War was not to break out until 1899, apparently to pay off a grudge of Chamberlain's. But few people, in January 1896, would have dared imagine it could be so long delayed. It was at that time that the Executive Council of the Transvaal realized that they were desperately short of arms. They instructed their commandant-general, General Joubert, to buy 10,000 rifles with ammunition, and for 5000 of them, priority was to be given to an early delivery date.

Joubert approached the local agents of several firms, including Krag-Jorgensen, and Westley Richards of Birmingham. The Boers were, in fact, to buy a small number of Krags, and a very large number of obsolescent Westley Richards Martinis which were mostly carried by transport driver, etc. Attitudes to gun-running may have been a relic of the days when any country could produce flintlock profit, and probably found it unnecessary to trouble General Joubert with excessive detail regarding the rejection of the rifles by the Portuguese.

Individual Boers appear to have strongly disliked the Guedes, which they termed "Joubert," "Steyr," or "Giddy" rifles. My picture, print number AG1234 of the Cape Archives Department, with whose kind permission it is reproduced, is said to show Boers in ambush at Taaiboschspruit in the Orange Free State, although the postures, and the varied sight settings, suggest that it is posed. By this late date in the war, the few Boers left in the field were hardened and extremely competent guerillas, and their use of captured Lee-Enfields, which at that time had inferior sighting arrangements to the Mauser, was a reluctant expedient, as 7x57 ammunition became hard to obtain. The same may have applied to the single Guedes held by the young Boer in the left foreground. Note that he has chosen to use a tie-on sling, in the same position as one of the holes drilled in the stock of my Guedes for the purpose. The factory sling swivels, on action and nosecap, are suitable for infantry purposes, but not for a horseman.

I do not know if the Boers experienced the jamming reported by Steyr, or if any of their ammunition used blackpowder or the foil-patched bullet. On the outbreak of war, the Transvaal held 10½ million Guedes rounds, as against 17 million Mauser. Some of it was certainly smokeless, although the powders available in the 1890s are not the best propellants for the Guedes. I have seen a photograph of a live Guedes round, which was picked up with the aid of a metal detector on the site of the Boer entrenchments at Magersfontein, and it has a steel-jacketed bullet, similar to those used in the Kropatschek, but too heavily rusted to measure. It is of full 60mm case length, not the 56mm, to which the Kropatschek was reduced soon after its introduction, and yet its Portuguese arsenal 1895 headstamp suggests it was a Kropatschek case.

In fact, published sources regularly confuse the Guedes and Kropatschek versions of the 8x60R Portuguese, copy each other and perpetuate dimensional inaccuracies. My groove diameter slugs out at just under .331-inch, exceptionally close, for a 19th-century rifle, to the published 8.4mm. But this gives nearly double the groove depth of the 30-06, for example. That would be useful with a soft bullet, but not with a steel jacket. So I would not be surprised to find that the Kropatschek

had shallower grooves, and a slightly smaller bullet diameter to suit. If the Boers were simply sold Kropatschek ammunition or bullets, there would then be a danger of bullets stripping in the rifling, and of accelerated bore wear and throat erosion. It would be no more underhanded than supplying the famous "short neck" Mauser round, from reworked 7.65x53 brass, which was widely believed to cause breech explosions.

There are two possible explanations for the jamming reported by Steyr. One is that the breechblock, which is thin walled with a removable sideplate, actually deformed. Any concavity in the breech face would have impeded its initial, entirely downward movement across the cartridge head, or it might have bulged out at the sides, enough to lodge in the receiver. The original Guedes cases, like many of the period, are of A-base design, with a bevel more pronounced than the D.W.M. catalog illustration used by Barnes. This would have concentrated the thrust of the explosion onto a reduced central area, where the thin breech face is not backed up by the sidewalls of the block. But my Guedes, which has seen considerable use, shows no such deformation. Steyr, too, tried to cure the problem by altering the angle of the locking surfaces, and although this was unsuccessful, up to the angle at which involuntary opening took place, it hardly sounds like a response to mechanical weakness.

More likely, I think, is that jamming was caused entirely by the design and softness of the cases, which did not contract after being expanded tight against the chamber walls and breech face. Schmidt's illustration shows a case with thin, beveled head, which would probably have been acceptable in a pistol or 45-70. So would the rather soft brass which was very common, for nobody had ever necked cases down to such an extent, making it unlikely that they understood the fine balance between annealing and work-hardening which is necessary for such an application. According to the 1904 War Office Textbook of Small Arms, chamber pressure of the blackpowder Kropatschek load, at 15.75 long tons per square inch, was identical to the early cordite Lee-Enfields, although it probably fell off more rapidly after an early peak. If we take case design, thinness and softness together with the pressure of a badly fouled Guedes, we have ample explanation for the kind of jamming Steyr encountered.

To use a Guedes today, cases can be made from 450 Nitro Express, prefer-

ably the thick-rimmed Jeffery version, or more easily and cheaply from 348 Winchester. The latter would be ¹⁄₁₀-inch short, which should do no harm if bullets are seated well out; dies for the full-length brass would not crimp the case mouth, but this is unnecessary, especially as the finished rounds do not have to stand pounding in a magazine. RCBS's expander button was under-sized for .330-inch bullets, but I found that my Winchester-made 348 brass-made cases would accept them, with no expander. But you should not do this without making quite sure that the neck of *every* resulting round, with your make and batch of brass, is not a tight fit in the chamber, or dangerous pressures may result. In my brass, .338-inch jacketed bullets sized down with the same die as lead were just one-thousandths larger, because they are more elastic, and this was enough to cause tight chambering. So I ream all my cases with the RCBS reamer die, and use an expander button reduced from .338-inch with emery cloth in a lathe.

Dies can be made by RCBS or North Devon Firearms Services of 3 North St., Braunton, Devon (England), but because of variation and confusion in dimensions, you would be well-advised to send a chamber cast first, made with Cerrosafe alloy or car body repair paste (oil the chamber!), and receive the die maker's assurance that their dies will really match it. Whatever their source, your cases will be valuable to you, and you do not want any more working of the brass than you can help. For an occasional user who has a source of cases, a steel 30 Carbine die, possibly with a little ground off the bottom, may provide a cheap way of neck-sizing. My own fired cases show a slight convexity in the body section, rather like the 8mm Lebel, which may be the result of a swollen chamber, although the condition is benign, causing no extraction difficulties. I have certainly never seen it clearly accounted for in any published dimensions, although it may figure in Mardel's description, which I suspect of being garbled even in Portuguese.

North Eastern Industries (NEI) in Oregon do a splendid 245-grain mould in .330-inch diameter, but great care is necessary in sizing the bullet, which is necessary only to crimp the gas check. Bullet straightness is critical with such a long bullet and a relatively short bearing surface; bullets dipped in melted beeswax will enter the die off center. I size them base first, using softer Saeco lube and a simple NDFS bullet sizing die, with NEI's special top punch grafted onto the top of the ram, but you need a lathe for this. My Rockchucker press easily sizes down .338-inch jacketed bullets with the same die, although I value my rifling too much to fire many of those. It is just possible that Steyr, in 1886, may have been using something quite a bit better than mild steel, but I should hate to count on it. Anyway, there is no need, as a cast gas-check bullet works well at Guedes velocities.

Using blackpowder, the coarsest you can get, fouling is a bearable nuisance, since you will be firing a lot fewer shots than a soldier in a tight corner. Fouling can be reduced by using four or five

The Guedes breechblock with its sideplate off reveals the difficult-to-make mainspring.

grains of shotgun powder closest to the primer; W.W. Greener claims that blackpowder fouling is in liquid form during much of its journey up the bore, so it may be that the shotgun powder, by imparting a higher temperature, prevents it from condensing on the bore. But genuine duplex loads, designed to modify the pressure curve, are best left to 454 Casull enthusiasts, since you never know when one of the constituent powders is going to change its habits. I have never tried Pyrodex, but modest smokeless loads with 4198 or Reloder 7 appear to be safe, if you stop while pressure indicators such as primer deformation still suggest

something considerably gentler than a modern cartridge. I began with 24 grains of Reloder 7, giving about 1525 fps with the NEI bullet, at which it will penetrate two feet of end-grain larch timber. So we have a better big-game cartridge than it sounds, ample for anything that is unlikely to eat you up or squash you flat. Approximate factory ballistics are obtained with 30 grains of Reloder 7, producing very reassuring pressure indications, but I would not go over 28 grains with my sized-down Speer 275-grain semi-spitzers. These give greater, though not alarming, primer deformation, probably due to friction and dimensions rather than weight.

A lighter bullet might be more efficient with smokeless, but you have to decide whether you want to accept the increased freebore before it engages in the rifling, particularly if you use the short 348-based cases, too. If you can find kapok-filled filter tips for rolling cigarettes, these provide consistently measured portions of an excellent inert filler, for no usable smokeless load will come anywhere close to filling the case. What you *must not do* is to use small charges of slow powder, just because the barrel is long and the bullet heavy. That may work very well most of the time, but not always. I know this from the punctured primer which cracked my mainspring, which is always likely to be how the Guedes puts in a protest since the design does not allow a really close-fitting firing pin. The famous freak detonation effect is not necessarily the explanation, since those loads had been chronographing around only 1300 fps. Most firearms discharge before the firing pin has stopped moving forward, increasing its support for the primer, but an undetectably brief hangfire may have resulted in pressure impinging on a stationary or bouncing firing pin. Although I suffered nothing worse than a tingling trigger finger, I don't intend any "next time," just in case that is inconsistent, too.

I fitted an Outdoor Industries tang backsight, partly because the military backsight shoots far too high for most purposes, unless you use the rather rounded notch over its hinge pin. Just once, I placed five NEI bullets in a four-by-two group at 200 yards, but I must have spoken rather nicely to the Guedes beforehand. More often, the groups are wider and inclined to be differently placed from the last time, due probably to that long, thin, full-stocked barrel, secured by bands. Lead bullets have so far proved less consistently accurate than jacketed.

My final discovery was that Dr. Jim, the raider, spent part of his childhood in my home town, Stranraer in Scotland. None of this was mentioned when the same newspaper attacked Doctor Jim after the raid. He became Prime Minister of the Cape Colony in 1908, on a platform of Anglo-Boer reconciliation—did I mention his charm?—so he was the first of many Commonwealth prime ministers to graduate from a British jail. He was given the freedom of the borough when he visited the U.K., but declined to attend the presentation ceremony, pleading other engagements.

General Joubert proved unable to adapt to the modern style of warfare and died of natural causes during the war, but not before he was supplanted by younger generals, some of whom were admired as worthy foes by the British public in time of war, and later became Commonwealth prime ministers in their turn. Cecil Rhodes also died during the war, mourned by thousands who had feared him, perhaps because although an unscrupulous and implacable foe, he had never lacked magnanimity toward a defeated enemy. Chamberlain, technically cleared of implication in the raid by an enquiry which became known as the Lying-in-State in Westminster, was destroyed when his personal feud with the Boer republics degenerated into a morass of incompetence and slaughter, dragging him down from a glowing political future until he is now virtually forgotten. But we remember his son, Neville Chamberlain, whose appeasement of Hitler may have owed much to his father's disastrous brush with military adventurism. That is the trouble with history: Its strands lead in strange and unforeseeable directions, and it takes a brave man to say he has traced them to an end. ●

Bibliography

Barnes, F.C. *Cartridges of the World, 6th Edition.* Northbrook, IL: DBI Books, Inc., 1989.
Mardel, Captain Luiz. *Historia de Arma de Fogo Portatil.* Lisbon: Imprensa Nacional, 1887.
Schmidt, Colonel R. *Les Nouvelles Armes à Feu Portatives adoptees comme Armes de Guerre dans les Etais Modernes.* H. George, Basle, Geneva and Lyons: 1989.
War Office: *Textbook of Small Arms.* London: 1904.

In the old days, it was 50 rats to the box. That's what they liked . . .

About the 22 short

by C.E. HARRIS

I N MANY PLACES, you can no longer find 22 Shorts or CBs on store shelves. If you do, you sure won't be able to buy them at discount; they usually cost more than special-purchase Long Rifle ammo. That's because there is little demand for 22 Shorts and they are a low-profit item. Many shooters never need—and many more wouldn't dare—to shoot a pest in the garden without alarming the neighbors, and don't practice indoors, either, so they think 22 Shorts aren't good for much.

Shorts do have their uses. Suppose your grandpa left you a nice Winchester 1906 pump or a Model 1890 which is chambered for 22 Short only? You don't want to cobble a collectable just to enjoy shooting it once in a while. That would be a good reason to have 22 Shorts around. I know several small game hunters who do just that. Shorts were ideal in their long heyday for the trapper or Big Woods small game hunter who was patient and knew how to stalk, and for Depression-era hunters, young and old. Why else would grandpa have gotten that old rifle in the first place?

However, today's small game hunters face hunting pressure that would frustrate Horace Kephart or Davy

With this much-altered switch-barreled M77/22 Ruger, Harris learned a lot about Shorts.

Crockett. They seldom have the patience or skill to stalk small game within 50 feet. They have to be opportunists who take whatever shots at small game they get, which are often out there in 22 Long Rifle country, beyond 40 yards.

My current interest in 22 Shorts and CBs was renewed because I wanted to shoot quietly in my small suburban basement. My shooting buddies, Bill Bender and Nick Croyle, and

I thereupon decided to test 22 Short ammunition in Bill's Remington 511 bolt-action, the one he had used as a boy. Then we got crazy and went overboard. Ken Warner suggested we find an old Winchester pump chambered for Shorts only. We did that, and also threw in a Depression-era Winchester Model 62 chambered "for Short, Long or Long Rifle" for comparison. We also tested some current sporters which included Bill's new Remington Model

541T, Nick's Ruger M77/22 with original factory barrel, and my Ruger M77/22 which has been modified for "switch-barrel" use. It has several barrels of different rates of rifling twist chambered for both 22 Short and 22 Long Rifle ammunition. We also tested CB Longs, because we wanted to see if they gave better accuracy in Long Rifle chambers than Short ammunition. They don't, but they feed better.

What really does matter, we found, is the *chamber*. The shortened match chamber provided far better groups with Short ammunition than the Long Rifle chamber. Chamber *diameter* is as important as length. The full-up 22 Long Rifle Match chamber has a chamber body close to bullet diameter, and provided good short-range accuracy with Shorts even though bullet jump was considerable. A BSA-Mar-

third the range that Long Rifles will from the same rifle. Within those constraints a Short or CB Long will do the job about as well at 50 feet to 25 yards as a Long Rifle will from 50-70 yards. This is because accuracy, not energy, is the limiting factor in small game hunting effectiveness.

The impact effect of 22 Shorts and Long Rifles is remarkably similar in test media. We tried 2-inch wax blocks (about the thickness of a squirrel) and you could not tell the exit holes apart without a scorecard. Winchester Super-X solids in both 22 Long Rifle and 22 Short made pencil-sized channels. CCI Mini-Mag Short and Long Rifle hollowpoint exit holes were also indistinguishable from each other, trumpeting from a pencil-sized entrance to an exit about an inch in diameter from the 2-inch blocks.

Accuracy nuts find 22 Shorts disappointing. Casual shooters will find them accurate enough if the range is reasonable. The Model 1890 and M62 Winchester 22 pump guns we tested produced 1½- to 2-inch ten-shot groups with open sights at 25 yards. This establishes their practical limit, which would still bag plenty of small game. At 50 yards, they were not accurate enough for small game, but a scope would help.

During the Depression, people bought Shorts because they were cheaper and they worked okay at modest range. Since Shorts aren't cheaper anymore, buy them only if you have a rifle chambered for Shorts only, if you need a quiet load, or if you have a 22 Short handgun.

Our best series of ten-shot, 50-yard groups fired with 22 Short ammunition averaged about an inch, from the switch-barrel Ruger M77/22 bolt-gun with heavyweight barrel, target scope and special 22 Short chamber—not exactly your standard plinker. Most common high-velocity 22 Short ammunition grouped 2 inches or more at 50 yards from the heavy-barrel rifle with scope, and 3-4 inches from ordinary sporters.

At 50 feet, groups were frequently under an inch for ten shots, even with the sporters, when using the better 22 Short ammunition. Only standard-velocity Shorts seemed consistently accurate, though Winchester Super-X solids and CCI Mini-Mag hollowpoints were uniformly good across the board in all the rifles, giving acceptable small game accuracy at short range.

Ammunition quality is an important factor because some brands we tested were clearly superior to others. It may not be practical to test batches,

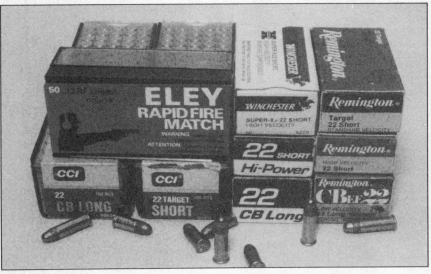

They aren't cheap anymore, but for some jobs 22 Shorts are just the ticket.

The inherent accuracy of 22 Short ammunition, we found, is less affected by barrel twist than by chamber type. We tested for that. Before 1940, slower twists of 20 and 24 inches were used for 22 Short barrels. George Wilson made us two 20-inch twist blanks and Jim Coleman fitted them to my Ruger M77/22. One of these was given the SAAMI-dimensioned match chamber to see how well Long Rifles would shoot in the slow twist. The other one was chambered for 22 Short by stopping a Long Rifle match reamer short so that Short bullet would engrave in the rifling. A used 16-inch twist BSA-Martini 22 Long Rifle target barrel was also set back and rechambered for Shorts in the same manner for comparison.

There was not a significant difference in overall accuracy in comparing 16- and 20-inch-twist 22 Short barrels. The 16-inch-twist barrel is accurate with Shorts, and the slower 20-inch twist provides no miraculous improvement. Most high-velocity Long Rifle ammunition gave normal grouping in the 20-inch twist barrel, and some brands shot quite well, but standard-velocity Long Rifles were unpredictable.

tini Mark II International target rifle with a very snug Long Rifle Match chamber produced some truly amazing groups with Shorts at 50 feet.

The ordinary sporting rifles you see marked "for 22 Short, Long or Long Rifle" usually give poor accuracy with Shorts. There is bullet deformation, misalignment and chamber leading, which all raise hob with accuracy. This assumes you are comparing rifles and sighting systems which are inherently accurate in the first place, such as scoped bolt-guns. In an open-sighted pump gun, which will at best approach an inch at 25 yards if you select ammo it likes, worrying about chambers is like measuring with a micrometer while cutting with an axe.

At 50 yards, most scoped 22 rifles can provide a 1-inch five-shot group on demand with ordinary high-velocity Long Rifles you would buy at your local discount store. Shorts can usually do so at 50 feet, and often will do so in an accurate rifle at 25 yards, but you can determine the latter only by testing. Open-sighted sporters are about as accurate at 25 yards as are scoped ones at 50.

We also decided Shorts or CB Longs give comparable group sizes at one-

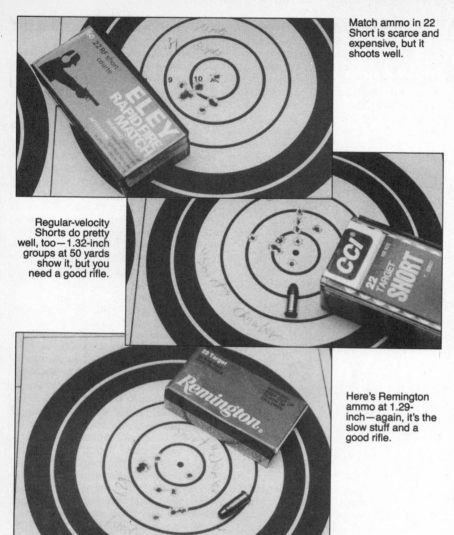

Match ammo in 22 Short is scarce and expensive, but it shoots well.

Regular-velocity Shorts do pretty well, too—1.32-inch groups at 50 yards show it, but you need a good rifle.

Here's Remington ammo at 1.29-inch—again, it's the slow stuff and a good rifle.

Other potential problems with Shorts are visible here—they are, well, so *short*.

but it seemed like everything made by CCI or Winchester was "good," whether CBs, Standard Velocity or High Velocity. Some batches of Remington and Federal CBs shot well in one or more of the rifles, but their high-velocity Shorts seemed inconsistent in our sampling. Standard-velocity Remington Target Shorts I tested were in new-style boxes with the old "U" headstamp, rather than the more common "Rem." I don't know if this has any significance; it's just an observation. Who knows? I know that some ten-year-old Remington High Speed with the same headstamp shot better than new stuff with the "Rem" for which I paid $2.65 per box!

When you want to be sure you are getting accurate 22 Long Rifle ammunition, the usual advice is to buy standard-velocity or match ammo intended for competition. The same advice applies to 22 Shorts, but standard-velocity or target ammo is harder to find. The only target-grade Shorts are made for the International Rapid-Fire Pistol event, which doesn't exactly have the same following as the Bianchi Cup.

We tested some of the best, (or at least the most expensive) 22 Shorts on earth (Eley Green Box at $7 per box!) purely for academic interest. While quite accurate, its performance was not in proportion to its cost. The less expensive American brands of standard-velocity Shorts which are still available—Remington and CCI—are well worth considering. CCI Target Shorts are intended, like Eley Green Box, for the UIT Rapid-Fire Pistol event, but it is priced comparably to CCI Green Tag 22 Long Rifle. While more expensive than your average ammo, it is affordable if you want something you know will be accurate, without having to select individual lots. With other 22 Short ammunition you may have to experiment and test different batches to see what shoots well in your rifle. We found this especially true with CBs, as the CCI and Winchester brands were consistent, but Federals tended to string vertically.

Our testing was limited to the samples we had, and was not comprehensive, and so this isn't to say that other brands are unsatisfactory. With any mass-produced item, manufacturing variations can be expected. That means that if you can, you should shoot a box on paper before you go back and buy the rest of the brick. If all the machines were running happily that day, you could get lucky, but you never know until you try it. ●

Those Were The Days

As a kid, he shot 50 a week, now he's been timed at 50 good shots every 10 minutes.

When I was a boy growing up in the early 1960s, the Virginia countryside we now call "outside the Beltway" was mostly scattered farms and hardwood forests. I was rewarded for potting woodchucks and crows in my mother's garden, and a short walk away were mature stands of oaks and hickories thick with squirrels and other game. Our neighbors were native Southern gentlemen sportsmen, who nurtured our love of the outdoors and encouraged us to enjoy a close-to-the-land lifestyle I remember fondly as somewhere between "The Waltons" and "American Graffiti."

We learned to shoot in an NRA Junior club with our high school rifle team. Our DCM-issue, greased Western Xpert or CIL Canuck (bought at 58 cents a box) was saved for weekend matches either downtown at the NRA range or the South Post of Fort Myer. Back then you could take the black and red A, B & W bus and carry your cased 22 rifle to the range downtown without raising an eyebrow. We were still country boys at heart and were not the least bit embarrassed to be viewed as rednecks by the transient military brats who were our classmates because we could always outshoot them. We plinked all week long in the slow-moving days between hunting seasons.

Life Savers or Necco Wafers at 25 yards offhand, or 50 yards prone, and vanilla wafers offhand at 50 yards or prone at 100, were challenging targets. Our rifle coach made sure we rationed our DCM ammo for organized practice and matches, so our paper route and egg money was used to keep us in plinking ammo. We bought lots of 22 Shorts because they were cheaper than Long Rifles, unlike today. Shorts gave the most fun for the dollar, and had other advantages as well.

Our once-rural neighborhood was gradually falling victim to the developer's chainsaw and bulldozer. We had to depend on quiet shooting. The crack of high-velocity 22s would disturb city folk who had moved into our neighborhood. So we loved standard-velocity shorts when we could get them. Today, I would use CB Longs for this type of shooting, but they were unavailable to us except as exotic and expensive RWS Zimmer Patrone or Eley-Z from the Stoeger catalog.

To those who grew up between the World Wars, the 22 Short also evokes nostalgia. Lud Olson fondly remembers his first 22 rifle, a used Hamilton top-break he got for fifty cents from a local blacksmith in the early 1920s. It was chambered for 22 Longs, but he used only Shorts and BB caps because they were cheaper. Long Rifles keyholed in the Hamilton barrel, which had a slow twist. Only standard-velocity 22s were available, as high-velocity ones didn't appear until the 1930s. The bronze barrel liner of the Hamilton was an advantage in the days of black or Lesmok powder and chlorate primers, but even as a youngster Olson was a good soldier who always cleaned his rifle before nightfall. Lud was never a group shooter or paper puncher, but plinked

a lot of cans and garden pests with his Hamilton. He remembers it was far from a tack driver, but adequate for short range, which is the whole point of using Shorts in the first place.

Bob Sears' parents never objected to him having all the guns he wanted as long as he earned his own money. His first 22 rifle was a Stevens No. 26 Crackshot bought mail order from Montgomery Ward for $4.19 in April, 1939. Standard-velocity Stay-Kleen Shorts (loaded by Federal) were sold at Sears (no relation) and Roebuck for seventeen cents a box. Long Rifles were a quarter. At age 11, Bob made a benchrest by putting pillows on a sawhorse. He sat beside the sawhorse on a kitchen chair, burrowing his hands and the rifle into the pillows. He would put a target on an abandoned barn 100 yards away and try to see how good a group he could get. He remembers his best five-shot groups on a windless day being under three inches with the crude open sights. My, that Stevens must have been wonderful, or else the Shorts they made back in the 1940s were sure better than they are now.

Even at age eleven, Sears had a moderate disdain, which has grown steadily over the years, for can plinkers. Bob tells me the high-speed hollowpoint 22 Short is ideal for shooting small game and pests, such as rats, around the farm. The low noise of the Short wouldn't send the other rats scurrying. Local farmers used to pay him a penny a rat, which kept him in ammunition. Boy, those *were* the days.

C.E. Harris

by WILFRID WARD

A report from the once-medieval front line:

Again The

At Acton Round in Shropshire they play with the mechanical stuff of legend, like this trebuchet.

"DO A PIECE ON Acton Round and its trebuchet for next GUN DIGEST . . . more later," read the editorial command. This cryptic message, I confess, reminded me somewhat of those to Sherlock Holmes, Conan Doyle's great detective. Invariably, Watson, Holmes' biographer, could make nothing of them, but after a few moment's thought by Holmes the indomitable couple would be rushing in a horse cab to a London train terminus, thence to a remote part of the country where the mystery would be solved. I had to play both roles, and eventually, aided by a cutting from the *Wall Street Journal*, and a directory of historic houses, found my goal.

(450/600 pounds). The former followed the course of Napoleon III's experiments and went backwards into a tree. Then in November, 1990, came the high moment when on Guy Fawkes Day (5 November) an effigy of the Pope together with a giant "bomb" of 45 gallons of petrol was thrown. (Fawkes and others had tried to blow up the House of Commons, and eventually died a special death designed by the then-Archbishop of Canterbury.) Though as a Catholic, I could not have condoned such goings on, I confess this must have been a truly remarkable sight. Memories are long in Shropshire, and certainly followed the old 17th century children's rhyme:

Trebuchet

To cut a long story short, early January saw me arriving at the beautiful 18th century manor of Acton Round in the wilds of Shropshire, the home of Mr. Hew Kennedy. Mr. Kennedy has a great interest in things medieval, particularly siege engines. In November, 1989, he and his neighbor, Mr. Richard Barr, had decided to join in partnership to build for themselves the latest, and most effective, of the medieval siege engines: a trebuchet. Initially, a small metal version was created, the design of which was based on pictures from various contemporary sources. This did not work properly, and the scheme went into abeyance. Fortunately, some cousins saw these attempts, and on returning to their home in the North of England decided to construct their own trebuchet on a much larger scale, which was much closer to the original. This used timbers from substantial trees from their forest and, though not so large as the Acton Round version was to become, it was large enough to give full range to the ballistic properties involved. Work at Acton Round continued and, after a year and several near abandonments, the trebuchet was completed in 1990. A considerable part of this success is attributable to the use of a laminated 50-foot beam for the arm, since so large a single piece of timber had been unobtainable. Other beams had broken under the stress.

The first throw was a 120-pound dead sheep. Pianos came next, an upright (350 pounds), followed by a grand

"Please to remember the Fifth of November, Gunpowder, Treason and Plot, For we know no reason, why Gunpowder Treason, should ever be forgot".

It is doubtful whether any spectator at the 1990 celebrations will ever forget them either.

The performances of the trebuchet were varied but after initial difficulties, became more consistent. Some of the principal throws are as follows:

- A 3½ Cwt. (392 pounds) piano went 151 yards.
- A log of similar weight (with better aerodynamics) went 189 yards.
- A 550-pound dead pig traveled 171 yards.
- A 1 Cwt. (112 pounds) weight went 235 yards.
- A dead horse (1344 pounds) went 106 yards.
- A Hillman car (1680 pounds) flew 80 yards but would have gone further had it not become entangled in the machine during launching.

Fortified with these figures, and much other information, I retired to bed in great excitement. I was to have a demonstration next morning.

One must remember that the Kennedy/Barr trebuchet is a modern machine, working on anciently discovered principles, and not a reproduction of its predecessors. It was constructed by modern methods in consultation with a firm of steel erectors. Though wood was used for the arm, it is laminated. The lengths of pine forming the supports are fixed with angled pieces

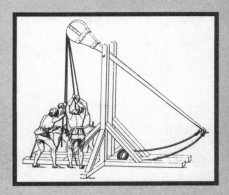

of steel. The weight basket is metal. Thus, the only comparison which can fairly be made is one between the ballistic performance of the ancient and modern machines.

Though there were many siege engines far older than the trebuchet, it was the most powerful and efficient. Historians have tended to lump them together referring to them as ballista or catapults, which is incorrect. One of the difficulties facing the researcher in this field is that most of the relevant works are in Latin or Norman French. Nonetheless, the late Sir Ralph Payne Gallwey had assembled most of the

Serenely sailing to its destiny of flame, an upright piano soars over Shropshire.

The piano and its Molotov cocktail land way out there—a quiet trip ending with a bang.

relevant sources in his, "Treatise on the Siege Engines used in Ancient and Mediaeval Times, for Discharging Great Stones and Arrows." This appeared as Part IV of his work, *The Crossbow* (1903, 2nd. Ed. 1958 The Holland Press, London). Grose's *Military Antiquities* (Vol. 1, p.382, 1801 Edition) offers the following definition of a trebuchet:

> The trebuchet was a machine for throwing stones, for which purpose a sling was sometimes fixed to it; It acted by means of a great weight fastened to the short arm of a lever, which being let fall, raised the end of the long arm with a great velocity.

Dates for the invention vary. Some writers put this as early as the eleventh century; others say the thirteenth century. All are agreed that it came from France. Its superiority over the ballista or the catapult was such that without exaggeration one could call it the Prince of Siege Engines.

Interestingly enough, it is from France that much of our modern knowledge of the subject comes. This is from the *Etudes sur l'Artillerie* prepared to the orders of Napoleon III of France when he was Prince President (Tome 2 Liv. 1 p. 29-41). There, a variety of siege engines are considered, with four types of engine particularly examined and classified as trebuchets by reason of their use of a sling to fling the missile. Moreover, it is stated that the counterweight could be either fixed or mobile *or both*. Users are advised when throwing missiles at night, always to add a burning torch to the stone to be able to gauge the fall exactly. Some, at any rate, seem to have

provision for lateral adjustment, and are said to have been extremely accurate. In calculating the requirements for the recovery of the Holy Land, Mario Santo, who went on the Crusade in 1321, is quoted as referring to trebuchets and arbalests (a form of heavy crossbow), as being equally useful on land or water. Gilles Colonee, who died in 1316, gave the classification to which *L'Etude* refers.

By the fifteenth century we learn how cannon and trebuchets were being used together in sieges. The trebuchet was not confined to Christians and, at the attack on the Isle d'Eubee, Mahomet II used them to throw boulders and putrefying corpses and the like. These were probably copied from those used by the Crusaders in the First Crusade. Although Napoleon's own reproduction trebuchet failed, probably because it was not big enough, this scarce work is an exceptional source for those wishing to pursue this subject. Moreover, although in French, it is the French of the nineteenth century, and so comprehensible to the less scholarly.

Because of their great size, trebu-

Just taken leave of Earth and the arm of the trebuchet, the fated piano begins to fly.

Poised and ready, the 50-foot beam of the Acton Round trebuchet has a malignant, fearsome air on a January morning.

chets were usually built on the spot and, if they were needed elsewhere at the conclusion of an operation, demolished and rebuilt on their new site. The machine itself can best be pictured as a giant seesaw with the board on its side. Instead of being pivoted centrally, the pivot is considerably nearer to one end. Beneath the shorter end a basket hung on a pivot, into which a great weight of sand, rocks or iron was placed. Windlasses were usually employed to wind down the arm against the great counterweight. When it was down, it was secured by means of a giant sear and the missile secured to the sling. On release, the arm swung very quickly to an angle of 45 degrees which was the ideal angle of release for the missile, whereupon it flew off on its own arc.

Although Grose appears to contemplate trebuchets without slings, Payne Gallwey is quite clear that the presence of a sling was the distinguishing mark between it and other engines [p. 314]. The purpose of the sling is to act as an extension of the arm. Lt. Colonel Ben Burrows, Royal Engineers Ltd. expressed the principle as follows:

The purpose of the sling is to increase the radius of gyration of the projectile and hence its linear momentum at the instant of release.

The sling of the Acton Round trebuchet frees itself by unwinding, when the main arm is released. It is only wrapped around a peg on the arm. It thus flies off with the missile. When the engine was being used to throw stones, the sling was like a fairly small net into which the stone was placed with a rope or thong coming from either side. Where a larger object was thrown, the sling was a rope wound around it several times and attached to the arm as described. The projectiles thrown were by no means limited to stones, though in a siege the breaking down of the ramparts was clearly very important. Other uses were the promotion of early forms of germ warfare

by flinging corpses of animals or people into the city to cause disease. The bodies of spies (live or dead) were frequently disposed of in this fashion.

Perhaps, as the supply of spies has clearly dimished since the end of the Cold War and few walled cities would be prepared to receive them, live or dead, these days, the importance of the dead horse for comparative purposes is much greater. Horses have continued to be roughly the same size as their ancestors were. Thus, despite the somewhat inconsistent practices of the ancient authors in matters of weights and measures, one could throw a dead horse, and from the distance it traveled make a direct comparison between the power of modern and medieval trebuchets. Sadly, there is no medieval record of piano throwing.

Nevertheless, that is what Mr. Kennedy did. Next morning, the throw was to take place at 11:30 AM. The site was on the top of a sloping hill above Acton Round Hall. There, a considerable area of open fields made it not only safe for spectators, but gave a good view of the whole operation. A large audience was likely to gather, partly by invitation, and partly of locals. Since no suitable dead animal was available, it was decided that an extra heavy upright piano would go up that day. To add to spectator appeal, a "bomb" of four gallons of petrol would be added.

The first step was for someone—Mr. Barr—to climb about sixty feet to attach a steel rope to the top of the arm of the trebuchet. At the lower end of the arm the weights (five tons of pig iron) rested in their steel box. This, unlike the equivalent in its earlier counterpart, was a direct, non-moving, extension of the arm. The first part of Mr. Barr's climb was by ladder. With the steel rope at his belt he climbed up the arm itself, using a series of rungs made of short metal rods fixed to the arm. From existing pictures, it appears that these are similar to those used to climb the medieval engines. Once the wire was fixed, and Mr. Barr safely returned to ground level, the wire was pulled by a tractor going straight on the line of the center of the

trebuchet. This brought the arm down, leaving the counterweight in mid-air. On reaching the ground, the arm was secured in position by a giant hook-like sear. Ropes straightened; rag bomb fuse lit; the great moment was at hand.

Meanwhile, strays from the audience had been cleared from the danger zones. The great moment came, and the arm was released by the tractor, pulling the sear this time with a rope around a tree. The piano flew at considerable speed, yet with dignity, upon its arc, taking only the sling with it. As it rose the smoke from the bomb increased. Gradually, it slowed as the descent began, and almost before one had time to realize what was happening, it hit the ground some 110 yards away. As it did so, the fall disrupted the petrol drum, and tremendous flames and black smoke belched forth. Perhaps appropriately, and with the use of a little imagination, one could see this as a mushroom-shaped cloud. Soon it was almost all over. The piano had broken up like firewood. The fire had burnt so well that almost all the combustible debris had gone.

Although we were merely playing, one could see how powerful a weapon this was if used at full strength, throwing heavy boulders. As the piano

neared the end of its flight, the audience rushed forward, as though unwilling to believe its eyes that this heavy object had been propelled so far and apparently effortlessly. Black smoke and flames billowed, and then, quite quickly, there was little or nothing left. Not the least remarkable thing to the gun-oriented watcher was the silence of it all before the actual impact.

Much of the detail of the preparations is apparent from my pictures. They do not, however, reproduce the tremendous feeling of excitement and anticipation with which the audience awaited the launch. One feature which must have added to the excitement was the knowledge that some of the earlier throws, like those of the replica trebuchet built by the Emperor Napoleon III, had gone backwards not forwards. Apart from causing subsequent excitement, that incident had severely damaged an oak tree directly behind the engine.

Because of the fixed nature of the apparatus, a great disadvantage of the modern trebuchet is the inability to traverse it. Certainly, if the illustrations from the fourteenth century are correct, and the engines actually worked, this was sometimes got round by mounting them on ships. Likewise

These three—Hew Kennedy at center—and a tractor make the Acton Round trebuchet work.

Every trebuchet in history had its hero for this chore. At Acton Round, his name is Richard Barr.

One of the last pre-throw chores is to set up the gasoline cocktail inside the piano.

The weight box will hold nine tons, but they're using five tons now. The crossarm is no longer in use.

While the tractor tow cable holds the beam down, the Acton Round crew hooks the trigger in place—to be later pulled by the same tractor.

one presumes that an experienced operator could control the length of his throw by varying the weight of the projectile and/or the counterweight. Theoretically, I suppose, the flight of the projectile could have been given a bias or curl by using a missile which was of uneven shape, but this sounds no substitute for traverse. One choice appears to have been bringing a number of trebuchets in the siege train, each of which could concentrate on a particular part of the walls. If this was impossible, dismantling and resiting seems one answer.

Be this as it may, what of the future? Already another enthusiast is considering building a giant crossbow near the same site. Not unnaturally, the partners would like to turn their work to some commercial value. There were even some official experiments to see whether a parachutist could be thrown

and descend by parachute. It was concluded, however, that such an attempt would have been fatal. For his part, Mr. Kennedy would welcome the opportunity to create an even bigger machine, capable of throwing large cars, lorries or even school buses. Although such a creation might eventually give a field day to the lawyers, could it be the basis for a world touring exhibition? Already a visit has been made to America to oversee the building of a trebuchet there, and both radio and television programs have been made on the subject. Where could it all lead?

There is no doubt that the working and development of such machines is a fascinating if time- and money-consuming task. In the days of the eccentric millionaires, one could have imagined men such as Winans vying with each other to produce bigger and more efficient siege engines. Is there room

for a "Trebuchet Club of America," flinging its rocks as far as it can, or even building and rebuilding mock ramparts to be demolished in new record times?

Such a scheme, though not actually productive, would give enjoyment to many (my visit to Acton Round certainly did to me), and competition between members might produce interesting results or even new developments. Somewhat surprisingly, the American source which called the Editor's attention to this matter, and eventually led to my trip north, was the *Wall Street Journal*. As a result, Mr. Kennedy tells me he had a number of inquiries, but that so far, only the supervisory operation which I described has resulted in any definite contract. Those seriously interested can contact Mr. Kennedy at Acton Round Hall, Bridgnorth, Shropshire, England. ●

Acknowledgements

I am indebted to Mr. Hew Kennedy for his hospitality, his introduction to the trebuchet, his provision of both the original books for me to photograph and, above all, to him and Mr. Barr (whose climb risked life and limb) for providing me with a demonstration of their magnificent machine. My researches were greatly aided by Colonel Burrows and the efforts of the librarians of the Joint Oxford and Cambridge Clubs and the London Library. In particular, I am grateful to the latter for permission to reproduce the illustration from Etudes sur l'Artillerie.

MORE THAN AN ACE
UP HIS SLEEVE . . .
by STANLEY C. CRIST

WHAP . . . BAM! Whap . . . BAM! Ed O'Ross, on the set of the 1988 movie *Red Heat,* was practicing with his character's secret weapon. O'Ross convincingly plays the part of Viktor Rosta, a thoroughly rotten scumbag possessed of no socially redeeming characteristics whatsoever. This Russian bad guy apparently misspent part of his youth watching American westerns, for he wears a derringer up his sleeve—a *20mm* derringer—on a spring-propelled track. This unique hideout gun could quite obviously not

be bought at your local gunshop, so master weaponsmith Tim La France (La France Specialties, P.O. Box 178211, San Diego, CA 92177) was asked to design and build it. In the weeks just previous to this request, Tim had built the Podbyrin 9.2mm— a much-modified Desert Eagle—for *Red Heat* star Arnold Schwarzenegger.

There were three requirements for Rosta's hideout gun: It had to be a derringer, have an overly large bore, and ride on a spring-powered track. Within those limits, Tim was allowed com-

plete creative freedom. The numerous Western-style derringers were immediately ruled out because their single-action method of operation would be too slow. Brief consideration was given to the idea of modifying a small-frame revolver to derringer configuration, but this was quickly discarded as being too time-consuming. Finally, at the author's suggestion, a BJT derringer in 38 Special caliber was acquired. This double-barrel stainless pistol is perhaps the prettiest of the centerfire derringers, and aesthetics are of no

(Opposite Page) Ed O'Ross as Viktor Rosta, vile villain of Vladivostok (or someplace), double-crosses a dope dealer in a Chicago bus station men's room.

small concern to Hollywood film-makers. Too, the BJT is a double-action gun, which was vital to getting it into operation quickly and easily. Also of importance, its stainless steel frame would permit a sturdy attachment to the spring mechanism.

Modifying the BJT was a considerably easier proposition than what had been required to create the Podbyrin. Except for some minor reshaping of the trigger guard, all that needed to be done was to saw off the twin 38-caliber barrels and install a single ultra big-bore tube in their place. Careful machining, filing and polishing shaped the new barrel and matched it perfectly to the contours of the rest of the gun.

The really difficult part of the job was developing the spring-powered track system. A lot of thought combined with a goodly amount of cutting, fitting and testing resulted in a stainless steel and aluminum prototype. When the design worked to Tim's satisfaction, the final track was executed—this time built 100 percent of stainless steel in order to have maximum strength and durability. Julia La France—Tim's wife and business manager—constructed the cloth sleeve that serves the dual purpose of providing a method to anchor the track to the shooter's arm and protecting that arm from the metal parts of the track.

It probably should be mentioned that two identical derringers and track assemblies were manufactured. Hollywood—like NASA—is a strong believer in redundancy. Although it is very unlikely that a La France product would fail, filming a movie costs many thousands of dollars per day, so a duplicate gun—even an expensive La France creation—is looked upon as an insurance policy that will allow filming to continue if the original firearm should break.

According to Tim, the 10-gauge bore size was necessary because in one scene the evil Rosta gets the drop on Ivan Danko (Schwarzenegger) who promptly sticks his index finger in the muzzle of the derringer and dares Viktor to shoot. Shades of James Garner and *Support Your Local Sheriff*!

It seems the bad guy wasn't the only one who watched old westerns. Unlike the James Garner movie, Rosta isn't bluffed; he pulls the trigger . . . *and the gun explodes*!! Of course, in real life Captain Danko would have been mi-

Arnold Schwarzenegger portrayed Captain Ivan Danko—Russia's answer to Dirty Harry—shown here with the La France-built Podbyrin 9.2mm pistol.

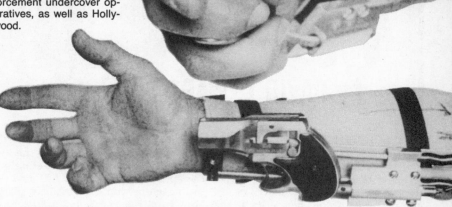

(Right) Now, that's what I call a *big*-bore handgun!

(Below) Viktor's secret weapon, ready for use. La France makes this set-up for collectors and law enforcement undercover operatives, as well as Hollywood.

nus a finger (at the very least), but, that's Hollywood! Alas—or perhaps, fortunately—this scene was not in the film as released to the theaters.

From all outward appearances, a single shot weapon, the manner in which it was modified allowed two rounds of blank ammunition to be chambered and fired. And thanks to the help of film splicing, Viktor manages to shoot as many as three rounds—without reloading—from

this one-shot hideout gun. Still, this is a unique piece of hardware that was interesting to watch in action on the big screen. Along with the 9.2mm Podbyrin—the most powerful handgun in the world (according to Ivan Danko)—this custom derringer showcases La France Specialties' talent for creating the unusual. ●

Credits: *Photos of Arnold Schwarzenegger and Ed O'Ross courtesy of Elaine Oliver of Carolco Pictures.*

The 30 CARBINE

. . . smaller than some, but big enough for most . . .

by DAVID L. WARD

Author and target shot at 50 yards with 1943 IBM Carbine and 110-grain Hornady SP in front of 14.8 grains of IMR 4227. Rifle was capable of respectable accuracy with the right loads.

THE 30 M-1 Carbine has been around now for some fifty years. During that time, it has been called any number of nasty things from worthless to impotent. Other diatribes are simply unprintable here. But if the carbine was so utterly useless and totally disliked, why were so many made (in excess of six million—more than any other weapon in WWII) and why has it seen so much use in combat? And most of all, why is it still so popular even in this day of the more sophisticated and more powerful assault rifle?

The answers to those questions lie in plain view for those who wish to look. The M-1 Carbine performs very well indeed within the parameters for which it was designed. That's the key. It was designed as a light shoulder weapon to replace the 45 ACP and the submachine gun. At distances inside one hundred yards, it handles that task admirably. It is more powerful and more accurate than the 45. Now before you choke on that, look at the energy figures. From an 18-inch barrel, the 30 Carbine musters more than 1950 fps and 900 foot pounds of energy; the 45 manages a little more than 500 fpe, even if you give it 1000 fps from the Thompson SMG.

There's no contest in the accuracy department, either. My IBM Carbine, manufactured in September of 1943, keeps Military Specifications Ball in six to eight inches at 100 yards with iron sights. Try and match that with your issue 45 pistol or Tommy gun.

It is important to keep the M-1 Carbine in perspective. If you wish to compare it to the M-1 Garand or any semi-automatic rifle, assault or otherwise, it fails miserably. It's underpowered and relatively inaccurate, shooting too light a bullet. And that, I suspect, is most of the problem with the carbine for those who used (or maybe never used) it. It started out on the wrong foot, or they did.

Could it be possible that the U.S. Ordnance Department did not provide an adequate explanation of the exact purpose of the carbine for the grunt in the field? I know an inadequate explanation of any topic by our government is hard to fathom, but it could be true. In which case, we begin to see the reason no one could understand why he was issued such a puny toy instead of a Garand. The carbine was never intended to shoot targets at two hundred or three hundred yards, a distance at which many were used, especially in Korea. However, in the up-close-and-personal arena, it offered a lot of controllable firepower and performed as well or better than anything else. Men who fought with them in such a manner generally agree with that statement.

The whole concept that finally emerged as the 30 M-1 Carbine for the U.S. military began after WWI. In the 1920s, both the United States and Germany concluded independently that their main battle cartridges were overly powerful for most combat conditions. The majority of infantry firefights occurred at less than two hundred yards, usually much less. A smaller, less powerful round would offer numerous advantages in weight, cost, and accuracy during rapid-fire and still give adequate killing power in most military situations.

Two possible avenues for development were considered at the time: Increase the power of the submachine gun round to lengthen its useful range or shorten the main battle cartridge and chamber it in a smaller automatic rifle. The Germans opted for the latter and by 1934 had a prototype cartridge based on their full-sized 8mm, but with a case only 33mm long. It delivered a 125-grain bullet at 2247 fps from a 16-inch barrel. Called the 7.92 Kurz, it and the rifle that chambered it were the forerunners of all modern assault weapons. The U.S., meanwhile, opted to do nothing because of the logistics and cost of replacing its whole inventory of shoulder weapons. "Use up what we got"—that's what I always say. Progressive thinking.

By 1940, the idea was resurrected in the U.S. However, the Ordnance Department decided to take a step in the direction of a more powerful pistol cartridge to fit into a lightweight carbine rather than drop the recently developed M-1 Garand. What they got is better than the issue pistol and SMG, while smaller and easier to shoot than the full-sized rifle. Looking at how things developed, this probably was

(Right) Loads for the 30 Carbine: Left to right—Mil. Spec. Ball, Speer 100-grain Plinker, Hornady 110-grain SP, Speer 110-grain HP and Sierra 110-grain HP.

(Left) Standard U.S. WWI small arms cartridges and those that were conceived later. Left to right: 30-06, 45 ACP, 30 Carbine, 7.62 NATO and 5.56 NATO.

the wrong choice, but not necessarily a *bad* choice. The Germans' work on their 7.92 Kurz was kept secret, especially from those who signed the Treaty of Versailles, so the U.S. Ordnance Department was pretty much on its own in the development stages.

Designs were submitted by a number of companies, but the short piston, locked-bolt prototype from Winchester won out and became the Caliber 30 M-1 Carbine as we know it. Winchester based the new cartridge on the obsolete 32 Self-Loading, a nearly worthless semi-rimmed round that sent a 165-grain slug out the barrel at a modest 1450 fps. The bullet was lightened to 100 grains, the pressure bumped, and the velocity consequently increased to 1970 fps from the new rimless case in an 18-inch barrel, a substantial boost in horsepower. The 30 Carbine case measures 32.77mm in length, almost the same as the Kurz, but the smaller diameter and smaller powder capacity force it to give up 300 fps to the German cartridge.

When I asked veterans from WWII or Korea about the performance of the M-1 Carbine in combat, their answers were both interesting and quite similar. Inevitably, the first words out were something like "not worth much" or "didn't kill very well" or, for Korea, "it jammed a lot." But the more they talked, the more they mentioned that for close-in work or night patrols or repelling mass infantry charges it

worked pretty well—lots of firepower when you needed it. And at shorter ranges, the little bullet knocked 'em down quite regularly, multiple hits being somewhat easier to accomplish with the 30 Carbine than with the 45 ACP for the average GI. As for jamming, everything jams when it's frozen or dirty, or both.

Today, the 30 M-1 Carbine is long since retired, at least from the U.S. military, though I expect it is still getting used as a combat arm in a few out-of-the-way places. You could look at the 30 Carbine as a kind of dead end in the evolution of military small arms, much like the woolly mammoth of the Ice Age. It was a good idea at the time, but something better came along and displaced it.

Today, most of the applications for the 30 Carbine are recreational and, as you'll see, for home or self-defense. Currently, AMAC (formerly Iver Johnson) is the only company manufacturing new 30 Carbines for the commercial market. They bought out the Universal people in the mid-1980s and have all of their equipment and materials. AMAC turns out four to five hundred new carbines a month along with one hundred or so improved and revamped Enforcers, a 10.5-inch barreled semi-automatic pistol formerly produced by Universal. They hope to get a stainless steel carbine with a synthetic stock on the market soon. Great for boats and airplanes.

Hollowpoints available for 30 Carbine: Speer 110-grain (left), and Sierra 110-grain. Speer offers lots of exposed lead and gaping hollow area, great for home defense or close-in varmints, while the Sierra is ideal for longer-range varmints.

The 45 ACP at left and 30 Carbine, with 41 and 44 magnums to the right. From an 18-inch barrel, the Carbine round is easily more powerful than the 45 and is very close to the revolver magnums when they are fired in a 6-inch barrel.

On the used market, there are a plethora of carbines, often at very good prices. Buyer beware, however, as some have seen rough duty in the past forty or so years. Others have been refurbished at the factory (or armory, which one I have no idea) and might make pretty nice shooters.

Also, there are carbines in very fine shape selling at a collector's price. Some folks are willing to pay a premium price for a particular manufacturer, often for one with the Winchester headstamp. But Rock-Ola made the fewest carbines at 228,500; followed by Standard Products with 247,155; IBM with 346,500; Quality Hardware with 359,662; National Postal Meter 413,017; Underwood Elliot Fisher 545,616; Saginaw 739,136; Winchester up there with 828,059; and Inland Division of General Motors topping out with 2,625,000 carbines of all types. Prices will vary according to condition, obviously.

Prices also will vary according to the model or variation. The M-1A had the paratrooper folding wire stock. An original in fine condition will set you back a substantial amount. M-2s, designed for select-fire, are around but are subject to federal registration and taxation. For a select-fire weapon, however, they aren't overly expensive, but they do confuse the collector values. Also, there is an M-3 variation that was an M-2 with a receiver grooved for an infra-red sniper scope. I've never run across one, but for the right amount of cash, I'm sure they're available.

Of all the makes and models out there, the one thing they have in com-

mon is they are all shooters in the most basic sense. That is probably the reason the carbine is so popular today: It's fun to shoot and doesn't cost you an arm and a leg to do so. Military Specifications Ball is relatively cheap, as long as you don't burn up several hundred rounds per session.

When I was young, my dad would take my brother and me down to the Missouri River outside Kansas City every so often to do some shooting. We'd bang away with the 22s, having lots of fun but always keeping an eye on the stubby bundle wrapped in an oily, old bedsheet. Finally, Dad would

Light recoil of the 30 Carbine lets everyone enjoy shooting it. Here, author's wife draws a bead on an unsuspecting tin can.

The Carbine, here with an M-1A1 replica folding stock, maps and a modified Camillus Ka-Bar, comprising an ideal and inexpensive survival rifle and kit for airplane, boat or RV.

take out the carbine (brought back from Guadalcanal, or was it New Britain?) which seemed to us like the most powerful rifle in the world. We got to touch off a few rounds, but ammo was limited then, and we never got to shoot it enough. I decided then that I would have one someday. Finally, after waiting too long, I bought the IBM and have enjoyed it ever since.

These days, nearly every major manufacturer of ammo offers a soft-point load in 30 Carbine. That tells you something about this puny round. A lot of folks use it for a lot of hunting. For shooting small game and varmints, there's no question it is very effective out to around one hundred fifty yards—assuming you have mounted the appropriate sights to allow accurate shooting out that far. And I expect quite a few use it for medium game hunting like deer and black bear—sometimes legal, sometimes not. I understand a number of carbines get toted into the swamps in southern states, looking for bear, alligators, and the like.

And why not? Look at the numbers again. The carbine makes 1900 + fps and 900 + fpe of energy with an expanding bullet. A 44 Magnum in a six-inch barrel is similarly potent, and no one hesitates to hunt deer or bear with a 44 Magnum handgun, do they? So what's the matter with the 30 Carbine? As long as it's legal for hunting big game where you are, NOT ONE THING. Just remember to treat it like a long, two-handed pistol and keep your shots less than one hundred

yards, preferably less than seventy-five yards. Hunting in the woods or swamp makes that fairly easy.

Legality brings up two points. First, each state has its own set of rules on minimums for big-game hunting with firearms. Here in Colorado, things are divided into two categories for modern arms: rifles and handguns. Within the rifle category, the poor 30 Carbine is eliminated by a requirement of 1000 fpe residual energy at one hundred yards. No way. It does, however, meet all other requirements. For handguns, though, if you stuff a 120-grain softpoint into it, then it meets the minimums, since there is no downrange energy requirement. Ironic, eh? In all fairness to the Division of Wildlife, all handgun hunters must qualify at a range under state supervision before they may get a big-game license. Still, they would seem to have things backwards.

The second point concerning legality is the assault rifle classification. A straightforward look at the old carbine would seem to place it right in that category. But that is not always the case. Again in Colorado, and Denver in particular, a law was recently passed banning assault-type rifles. It targets weapons designed for magazines of greater than 20-round capacity. AR-15s, AKs, and Uzis, etc. are out. Mini-14s, Auto-Ordnance Thompson semi-automatics, and carbines are OK. Well, almost. For some reason known only to the Denver City Council, Plainfield Carbines are not legal. All others are. But the 30-round magazines

aren't. Unless you're in the suburbs. Or merely passing through the Denver city limits—with it in a case. Anyway, you had best check with your local police department about the whole thing.

Back to ammunition. If you handload, there is considerable flexibility in the 30 Carbine. Besides the full metal jackets and the softpoints, three other very useful bullets out there will add to the carbine's versatility. The Speer 100-grain Plinker is a round-nose, half-jacket bullet designed for moderate velocities. It can be loaded down to near rimfire speeds and still work the action. Great for rabbits, although so is the Military Specifications full metal jacket stuff. Speer also offers its 110-grain Varminter, which has a round-nose style with lots of lead exposed and a huge hollowpoint. If it feeds in your rifle, it would make an outstanding home-defense bullet in front of 14 or 15 grains of W-W 296 or IMR 4227. The third bullet is a 110-grain pointed hollowpoint, ideal for varmints of any persuasion. This last bullet is longer than the round-noses and requires deeper seating, thereby cutting back some on the available powder space. I lost about .5-grain and seated it right on top of the powder. Velocity loss is not bad. This bullet is well worth working up a load or two. It shoots well and definitely damages prairie dogs.

Handloading is pretty straightforward for the 30 Carbine. It headspaces on the case mouth, so there's no crimping allowed. Otherwise, load it just like any straight-walled pistol case. Trim no shorter than 1.286 inches, again because of the headspace. Speaking of trimming, brass is everywhere, some commercial and hordes of G.I. The commercial is a bit lighter with my batch of W-W averaging 69.3 grains and G.I. weighing in at an average of 71.1 grains. It will affect your loads some, so keep an eye on it and don't mix 'em. Also, stick with small-rifle primers; the 30 Carbine pressures are too high for pistol primers.

A number of the faster burning powders work fine for the little 30. The highest velocities come from H110, IMR 4227, 296, and 680. I worked with all but the latter and got good results. I don't see any great need to work up a dozen or so loads for your carbine; I ended up with three, all of which shoot about two inches at 50 yards. If you're interested, they are here.

Loaded with expanding bullets, the 30 Carbine will make an excellent home-defense weapon. With a 15- or 30-round magazine, the question of adequate firepower becomes moot. Almost any member of the family can be taught to shoot it well, unlike a handgun of similar power. And unlike a magnum handgun, the light, expand-

bered for a 30 Carbine case necked to 22. It advertised 3000 fps with a 40-grain full-jacketed bullet, which is not too far from M-16 ballistics. The whole thing could be had in a package with two barrels, one in 30 and one in 22, and at a modest price. Unfortunately, Melvin died as things were getting moving. And according to rumor, his son Ed was killed later in an automobile accident. Either way, the company is out of business, bought out by Plainfield which was bought out by Iver Johnson which was bought out by AMAC. The AMAC people say they could build carbines in 22 or 25 if there was enough demand. On the other hand, how do you know what the demand will be without a rifle to shoot? It's too bad, the rig would have been a dandy. RCBS still offers dies for the 5.7 MMJ, however.

Many others also experimented with necking down the 30 Carbine case. Harold Tucker, of St. Louis, worked with both 22 and 25 calibers. He's out of the business now and was somewhat surprised to have me call and inquire about his work. Apparently, everyone else experimenting with the carbine also has dropped it, since no one I spoke with knew of anyone really working with it. Guy Neil at Hornady has been interested in the 22 version and a 25 version, possibly for silhouette work, but hasn't gotten

HANDLOADING YOUR M-1 CARBINE

Use	Gr. Wgt.	—Bullet— Type	Powder Type	Grains	MV (fps)
Small Game	100	Speer Plinker	4227	13.8	1756
Varmints	110	Sierra Hollowpoint	H110	13.5	1842
Home Defense	100	Hornady Softpoint	4227	14.8	1923

M-1A folding stock turns the 30 Carbine into a compact rifle for boat, trail or RV, or just for a walk around the place.

ing bullet in a 30 Carbine will lose its momentum more rapidly than a heavy, large-caliber bullet, meaning less penetration should you miss your target—perish the thought! As for the big bullet vs. little bullet controversy, if you don't hit a vital spot, the size or weight of the bullet makes little difference, and the carbine is easier to shoot well than a 44 or 45 ACP.

While on the topic of reloading the 30 Carbine, I should mention that some twenty-five years ago there was considerable interest in wildcatting the little case. Remember, this was before the true assault weapons became so popular or even widely available. Everyone liked the carbine but often found the cartridge disappointing.

Enter Melvin Johnson and son Ed. Melvin developed and marketed the 5.7 MMJ Spitfire, a carbine cham-

very far. For everything else, though, modern assault rifles seem to have taken over. Some are about as light and handy, and some are considerably more accurate. Yet the old carbine still has a lot of appeal, and mine is plenty potent and accurate enough for my demands.

Recently, I added a replica of the M-1A1 folding stock to my collection of add-on goodies for the carbine. Although not the answer to a perfect folder, it is well-made (careful, some are not) and makes the carbine even more easily stowable in a car, boat, airplane, or RV. It also just plain looks good. Ram-Line in Wheat Ridge, Colorado, is considering bringing out a synthetic folder for the carbine. If you think that's a good idea, then call 'em and bug 'em about it. While on the topic of stocks, the original on my carbine was quite thick in the area of the

grip, just behind the trigger housing. Some judicious wood removal and contouring makes the weapon considerably more comfortable to shoot.

One other use for the old carbine: It may be one of the best outdoor survival rifles around. It's light; the ammo is light; and it's adequately powerful with softpoints for harvesting food up to the deer class, should you need to. With the folding stock, it is quite compact—measuring about 26 inches folded. Such modest weight and dimensions take up little space in an RV, boat, or airplane.

So it seems that there are a number of uses today for a rifle and cartridge designed fifty years ago. Just remember to look at the 30 M-1 Carbine as a powerful pistol, not as a wimpy rifle. You'll be much happier with it. ●

INTRODUCING THE NEW RUGER 22/45. All the exceptional strength and durability of the legendary Mark II pistol. All the quality and value you expect from Ruger. And a big difference: a rugged, corrosion-free one-piece Zytel grip featuring a grip angle and magazine latch virtually identical to the Government Model 1911. Now you can train, practice, and plink with a pistol chambered for .22 Long Rifle that points and feels like many popular centerfire pistols. Available in three stainless-steel barrel lengths— 5½" bull, 4¾" standard, and 5¼" tapered. Grasp the 22/45 difference today.

Lacey Place
Southport, Connecticut 06490
Entire contents © 1991 by Sturm, Ruger & Company, Inc.
Free instruction manuals for all Ruger firearms are available upon request.

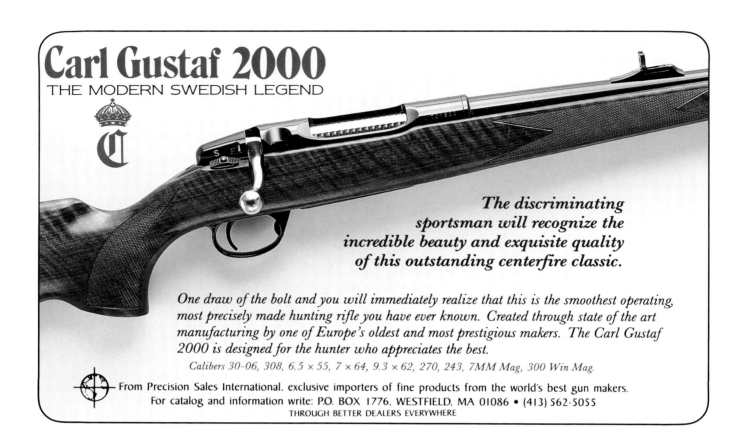

44 MAG

BUY OUR 44 MAG SCOPE AND
SLIP ON THIS GREAT LOOKING JACKET, FREE!

We're giving a sporty, new black, Red Head® jacket ($39.95 value) absolutely free to every hunter smart enough to select our 44 Mag "Daylight Savings" scope.

Dawn or dusk, Simmons' 44 Mag collects more light and stretches the day, thanks to its large, camera-quality 44mm obj. lens. The result? More time in the field. Our 44 Mag is waterproof, fogproof and shock-proof with 1/4 MOA click adjust-ments and non-glare, satin finish. And, as good as all this sounds, it won't cost an arm and a leg.

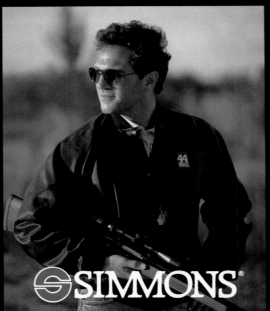

Now we've introduced two brand new versions. A 2-7x44 WA and a 4-12x44 WA with adjustable obj. lens. And we're giving away a slick jacket embroidered with the 44 Mag emblem. It's lined, comes with fitted elastic wrists and waist and snaps up the front. Don't miss out. Because you only get it with our 44 Mag models M1043, M1044 or M1045. Smart hunters like you are going to be snapping them up. (Jacket offer good for purchases made through December 31, 1992.)

SIMMONS®

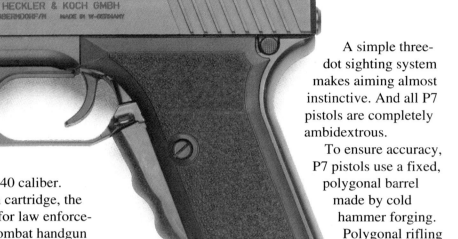
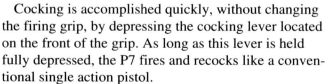

GRADE IV ... a Browning that's dropped over 30,000 ringnecks.

THE GALLINACEOUS

by ROB LUCAS

In the fall of 1990, RSS, serial number 12062 and Capital Gains III, called "Capper," still made a happy team on ringnecks.

Serial Number 12062 was delivered in February, 1958, a silvery-gray and golden walnut thing of beauty. The gun was a near-seamless meld of Grade IV wood and chisel-engraved hardened steel. On each forend side, left and right, were eleven separate edges of figured wood inletted into the front of the B-27 action, uniquely Superposed, flawlessly executed. At 6 pounds, 8 ounces, the 28-inch barrel sets so perfectly counter-balanced with the long-ish butt that the gun rose level and effortlessly in the hands. The action broke with glassy ease and locked back up with a muted tick of the top lever. Engraved in the gold oval mid-way between toe and semi-pistol grip were the initials RSS.

Whereas many a "best" shotgun is conceived for exhibition or politics, an investment bauble immediately locked away unfired in a vault, that is not the case here. For although this over/under was in the Rolls Royce class of sheer elegance, after 33 years of hard, hard use, its appeal is mostly sentimental. We look at the gun and smile, and we can only guess at what it might be worth in dollars.

But this isn't about money, it's about pheasants.

As it happened, the Browning's new owner, Robert S. Sturgis Jr., was neither a politician nor a collector. He was the gun buyer at Marshall Field & Co. He could have had the Purdey, but he picked the Superposed. He chose it over all other designs for its famed reliability. That there were pheasants chiseled into the three action surfaces of his new gun spoke to his fervent hope of shooting lots and lots of them.

Serial number 12062 killed 500 pheasants before 1958 was out.

Long before 1957, the Browning Superposed shotgun was considered too

IN THE SUMMER OF 1957, Robert E. Clark, Sales Manager of the Browning Arms Co. of St. Louis, Missouri, accepted an order for a Grade IV Superposed 20-gauge with a 15-inch length of pull. The order called for two sets of 28-inch barrels, one Imp. Cyl. & Mod., the other Full & Full, with their forends an inch longer than standard. The FN factory built more ostentatious Grade V Midas and gold-inlaid Presentations in 1957, but this 20-gauge was among their upscale best in craftsmanship and quality. The cash price was $835, plus Illinois sales tax.

To put a perspective on that near-thousand-dollar investment: a 1957 Winchester Model 21 De Luxe, custom-stocked, listed for $520; a Purdey hammerless ejector game gun bar-action sidelock, with an extra set of barrels, was under $1,500.

complicated by its few detractors. Browning, so it went, chose to use a barrel lump and hinge pin instead of trunnions, a major design flaw for an over/under, resulting in an action taller than it might have been. And the forend wood arrangement, semi-permanently assembled to the barrels, was a strange concoction at best and extremely expensive if replaced because of all the inletting time. Finally, to work at all, the Superposed depended entirely on the quality of its materials and not the quality of its design.

But even those detractors agreed that the Superposed, as FN built it, was nothing if not reliable and a veritable shooting machine. Handling this particular gun, imagining where it's been from all the scrapes and scratches, one gets a feeling that the Belgian gunsmiths who fit the parts together knew by its long stocking dimensions that it was going to be fired,

cious appetite for Winchester and Remington 2¾-inch, 1-ounce 7½s, thousand upon thousand of the old paper high-brass loads. Through the '70s and middle '80s the Browning launched Winchester and Remington 3-inch 6s, another estimated 15,000 factory loads, all at live birds. Then in 1988 RSS switched back to 7½s, this time new bright-yellow 3-inch ACTIVs he calls "roman candles." There never was any thought to pampering the gun with target loads because it was pretty.

The Browning 20 accounted for 50-150 pheasants a week October to March. Sturgis hunted some pheasants for the pure pleasure of it, just the three of them: himself, his 20-gauge, and a succession of Brittany spaniels named Capitol Gains, field names Capper. He hunted other pheasants because his business required it. He hunted with bankers, vendor executives, and outdoor writers such as R.A. Steindler. He hunted with men like

same banged-up leather takedown case countless thousands of times, the Browning is a long way from elegant. Its deep Grade IV grain still shows through, but the surface wood is scratched and dented and there are heavy scrapes. Along the eleven separate edges inletted into both sides of the action, the wood has shrunk away enough to show a seam. The finish at the buttstock and along the bottom of the pistol grip has simply worn off. The chiseled flying pheasants on the action surfaces are polished nearly flat from so many miles and years of the Sturgis one-hand carry.

There are, however, no splits or cracks in the wood around the action. The complicated Superposed forend iron, and its many inletted surfaces, has withstood the barrel-bending forces of all those thousands of heavy hunting loads without warping or loosening. About the heart of the gun, the B-27 action, after umpteen tons of

That's nearly 35 years of pure hunting wear and tear on Grade IV Browning wood.

The engraving is battered and some of the wood has dried and shrunk from the metal, but serial number 12062 remains a serious shotgun.

not displayed. Grade IV or not, they took extra care that it worked.

Within three years, in 1960, R.S. Sturgis became founder and president of Gander Mountain, Inc., Wilmot, Wisconsin, which today is among the world's largest and most successful outdoor catalog houses. By that time, his Superposed 20 had over a thousand pheasants in its bag. During the next 24 years, the tall and long-armed president of his own company could have swapped the Browning for any high-dollar gun he fancied, but he hunted the Browning. The more he shot it, the more he knew he wanted nothing less. This one over/under shotgun carried him in style through all the years of solitary and occupational pheasant hunting, the '60s, '70s, '80s, and now the 1990s.

Not a single reloaded round has been fired through either barrel in 34 seasons of pheasant hunting. Between 1958 and 1970, the gun had a vora-

Austin Wortley, Jr., Chairman, Penguin/Hoppe's, Inc. The great majority of his birds were harvested at the oldest upland bird club in the state, Oakmount Game Club of McHenry County Illinois, charter date 1944, still owned and operated by the son of the founder, Peter Reiland. While his guests used heavy 12-gauge guns for pheasants, RSS stayed with his bodacious lightweight 20.

Now, after three decades of pheasant hunting, in pheasant weather and pheasant brush, carried in one hand while being rained on, bled on and shed on, leaned against trees and dropped in the grass, from being assembled and broken down out of the

axial and radial force against its antiquated lump and hinge pin, there is nothing to report, except that the top-lever swings a degree or two left of center. The barrels still lock up tight against the breech.

How many pheasants has serial number 12062 killed so far? Mr. Sturgis never thought about it or kept score, not until a nosey writer imposed with the question. (I had to; the Browning wouldn't talk.) RSS is an old school gentleman, the kind who orders food in a restaurant for both himself and his lady and who *never* takes home a doggie bag, even though he has a real doggie. As best we can figure, his Browning has taken him through four

The beautiful grain still shows through the decades of slow daily scrubbing on hunting clothes and brush for much of the year.

distinct gallinaceous phases from great to melancholy.

In the Early Years, RSS recalls signing the tab for 80 pen-raised birds shot with the Browning on a single day, scratch-hunting by himself over Capper from dawn to dusk. Many Early Years shoots were business affairs when he, as president of fledgling Gander Mountain, Inc., and a guest enjoyed a few fast-paced hours harvesting 15-25 pheasants each—once during the workweek, twice on weekends. The Early Years bag was perhaps 350 birds a month for five months times eight years, adding up to 14,000 birds. All shot with the same Browning 20-gauge, and the great percentage with just the under barrel.

In the next dozen Growth Years, when Gander Mountain was adding new stockrooms and new vendors with nearly every catalog, the Browning killed only about 750 birds a year. RSS bought another Superposed, a 12-gauge in Grade II, as competitive Skeet cut into his hunting time. By the recession of 1980, the Skeet Superposed was closing in on three-quarters of a million target rounds fired, and the 20-gauge bird gun had digested

25,000 2¾- and 3-inch heavy hunting loads and brought down nearly that many pheasants.

There were Lean Years in the early '80s—negative Gander growth and very few pheasant afternoons. RSS retained his Oakmount membership, but the Browning stayed broken down in its case. There were lonely Dogless Years after Capitol Gains II died, when the 20-gauge walked half-heartedly "in the easy chair" behind hired guides and strange dogs and popped half-a-dozen birds in ten minutes. About then a new interest stirred things up—skiing in Colorado, Christmas to Memorial Day. The Browning stayed in Illinois.

Total pheasant bag through retirement at Gander Mountain in 1984: 26,000 birds, all shot by same Superposed 20-gauge.

But now the Browning is in its present and happiest gallinaceous phase—bird shooting once again behind the new puppy, Capitol Gains III. It has brought down an average 75 birds a week between October and Christmas for the last five seasons for a final up-to-date grand total pheasant bag of 31,000 birds, give or take a few hens.

The Browning 20-gauge is now 34 years old and RSS near twice that at 66. Both are in good health—no reason to think they won't see the 50,000 mark together at the rate they're going.

In the last week of 1990, RSS followed Capper's nose across a half-frozen drainage ditch, walking carefully on a pair of wobbly sawn logs. The Browning 20-gauge hung from his right arm. He lost his balance and fell in, landing on the seat of his pants in swampy-smelling muck. *Still* in his right hand, a foot below the surface and buried muzzle-to-pad in mud, was his Grade IV Browning 20-gauge loaded with two ACTIV 3-inch 7½s.

"That was the day," he recalls with a rueful smile, "I turned my lovely Browning into a squirt gun." The Browning went up to Gander Mountain just as it had for the past 34 off-seasons for an early disassembly, cleaning, and light oiling.

Shooting at Oakmount Game Club as Mr. Sturgis' guest, I got to watch the Browning in action on eighteen pheasants tossed into 40 acres of sorghum strips. During the morning hunt I saw the shotgun laid, none too gently, on the hood of a Jeep, set aside on a snowbank as Capper retrieved to hand, and used as a cane after a minor spill on the ice. I also noticed RSS' habit of breaking his gun the instant his dog went on point, checking for two loaded chambers, which indicated that if the Superposed had fired 35,000 shells during its life, its action may have been opened and closed 70,000 times.

Capper pointed all the birds and we shot them in a strict gentleman's rotation, 18 pheasants with 22 shots fired. I was nine for twelve on my half using a 12-gauge Model 23, while RSS and the Browning 20 performed as smoothly as Astaire and Rogers, but did need the Modified upper barrel to clout one rooster a second time. My impression was that birds hit with the Browning 20 fell hard.

"Was that ever made in 20-gauge?" RSS inquired politely, looking down at my English-stocked side-by-side.

"I think a few. Collectors grabbed them."

RSS nodded. He broke down his Browning without looking at it and slid the pieces into the takedown case.

"The value of a fine birdgun is in the shooting."

I asked if he'd ever hunted ducks or geese or quail with the Browning and he shook his head.

"Just pheasants. It's a pheasant gun."

That about covers it.

●

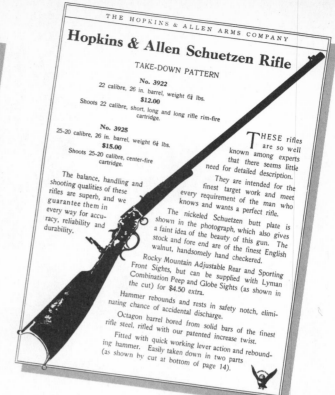

by
DONALD R. FRANCE

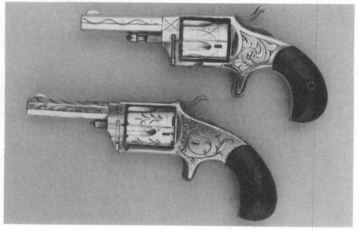

At the top is a Ranger No.2 32 Rimfire with factory engraving, carrying a Mar. 28, 1871 patent date. Below it is an XL No.3, also a 32 with the same date, plus Apr. 27, 1876.

Collecting
Hopkins and

(Opposite page, left) The 6-inch Hopkins & Allen Range Revolver was $5.50 at the turn of the century—22, 32 or 38 caliber.

(Opposite page, right) Your choice of 22 LR or 25-20 in the Hopkins & Allen Schuetzen Rifle, guaranteed in every way.

(Right) Covering all bets, this was the Army Safety Police Revolver, big and formidable looking, in 22, 32 and 38 calibers.

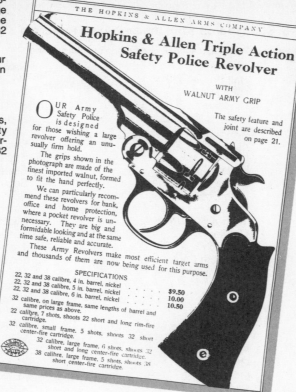

THE HOPKINS & ALLEN ARMS COMPANY

Hopkins & Allen Triple Action Safety Police Revolver

WITH WALNUT ARMY GRIP

The safety feature and joint are described on page 21.

OUR Army Safety Police is designed for those wishing a large revolver offering an unusually firm hold.

The grips shown in the photograph are made of the finest imported walnut, formed to fit the hand perfectly.

We can particularly recommend these revolvers for bank, office and home protection, where a pocket revolver is unnecessary. They are big and formidable looking and at the same time safe, reliable and accurate.

These Army Revolvers make most efficient target arms and thousands of them are now being used for this purpose.

SPECIFICATIONS

22, 32 and 38 calibre, 4 in. barrel, nickel $9.50
22, 32 and 38 calibre, 5 in. barrel, nickel 10.00
22, 32 and 38 calibre, 6 in. barrel, nickel 10.50
32 calibre, on large frame, same lengths of barrel and same prices as above.
22 calibre, 7 shots, shoots 22 short and long rim-fire cartridge.
32 calibre, small frame, 5 shots, shoots 32 short center-fire cartridge.
32 calibre, large frame, 6 shots, shoots 32 short and long center-fire cartridge.
38 calibre, large frame, 5 shots, shoots 38 short center-fire cartridge.

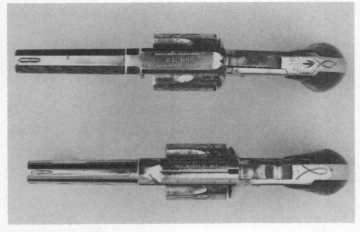

The same two guns, the XL No.3 uppermost, show trim profiles.

IT WAS 35 years ago when, as a boy, I traded my new horse bridle for my first Hopkins & Allen, a 32 RF XL No. 3. That started a collection I'm destined never to be able to complete, for Hopkins and Allen Manufacturing Company was among the most prolific of 19th century manufacturers of differing names and models of firearms.

Hopkins and Allen guns have all along been looked down on by serious firearms collectors. The company was mostly known for its cheap and sometimes gaudy handguns of the 1870s and '80s, often referred to as "Saturday Night Specials." But Hopkins and Allen also made firearms of high quality, especially the line of guns produced for Merwin Hulbert and Co. After 1868, most of the Merwin Hulbert line was made by Hopkins and Allen. It is remarkable that today when the remaining finish of Merwin Hulbert revolvers of 1870-1896 is poor, the actions are usually fairly tight and often in good firing condition. This is less often noted in guns carrying the Hopkins and Allen name. The rifles can be of high or low quality.

Beginning in 1874, firearms for both companies were produced in the same factory. Merwin Hulbert and Company owned a half interest in Hopkins and Allen until an argument with Charles A. Converse in 1874. Converse had made a deal on behalf of H&A with Bacon Arms Company. The conflict ended when Converse sold his interest in H&A to Merwin Hulbert and Company. Joseph Merwin (earlier part of Merwin and Bray) emphasized improved quality and workmanship notably in the line of the fine Merwin Hulbert and Company revolvers. Rifles and shotguns for the two companies were nearly identical except for the name stamped on the barrel. The companies used a number of the same sales and catalog agents offering Merwin Hulbert and Co. firearms, the economical firearms of Hopkins and Allen, plus ammunition by Phoenix.

The period from the Civil War to the turn of the century marked great experimentation and advances in firearm technology. Hopkins and Allen

Allen Guns

Models or Names Stamped on Hopkins and Allen Firearms

(Derived from examination of firearms, research, and reports by other authors)

Acme*
Alex
Alexis*
Alexia
Allen 22 (32)
American Eagle
Americus
ANIT and CHAR (Spanish mfg.)
Aristocrat
Automatic (Revolver)
Bang-up
Bloodhound
Blue Jacket 1, 1½, 2
Blue Whistler
Bonnie Blue (?)
British Bulldog*
Capt. Jack
Cannon Breech
Creedmore No. 1 (22)
Czar*
Defender*
Despatch No. 1
Diamond Arms
Dictator*
Dictator No. 1-2
Double Action No. 6
Double Header
Dreadnought*
Elector
Essex*
Encore
Excelsior*
Expert*
Faultless
Forehand D.A.
Garrison

Governor
Half Breed (32 RF)
Hard Pan*
Hinsdale
Imperial No. 1, 2
Joker
King-Pin
Leader*
Lifelong
Little Pet
Little Scott
Marquis of Lorne*
Metropolitan Police*
Monitor
Monarch*
Mountain Eagle
My Companion
Nero*
No. 3
Non-XL
Never Miss*
New Model Target
Noiseless (rifle)
Old Hickory*
Orient
Paragon
Parole (22)
Pathfinder
Pet
Petrel
Phoenix
Pointer*
Ranger 1, 2, 2½*
Range (?)
Red Hot
Reliable

Reliance
Royal
Russian (Hammer---)
Safety Police (Hammerless)
Scott*
Scout Military Rifle
Schuetzen (rifle)*
Secret Service (Special)
Skeleton Stock Target
Southernor
Spitfire
Striker
Swamp Angel
Terror*
Thames Arms
Tower's Police Safety
Tramps Terror (22)
Union*
Universal Dbl. Action
Western Bulldog
White Jacket
Wonder
XL Bulldog
XL Derringer
XL Double Action
XL Vest Pocket
XL 30 Long
XL Navy
XL Police
XL CR
XL 1, 2, 2½, 3,
   4, 5, 6, 7, 8.
Xpert (22 and 30 only)
You Bet
Victor (?)
1876 Army

*Other makers used this name as well as Hopkins and Allen.
ANIT & CHAR: Were not produced by Hopkins and Allen but a Spanish imitation. AYA Possible. Both Belgian and Spanish. Copies of Merwin Hulbert and Co. revolvers are known to exist in 38 and 32 calibers.

The HOPKINS & ALLEN Single Barrel Breech Loader.

HOPKINS & ALLEN MFG. CO'S SINGLE SHOT GUN, 20 GAUGE.

Using regular
Brass or
Paper Shells.

Weight 5½ lbs.   Length of Barrel 30 inches.

20 GAUGE SHOT SHELL
FOR
XL SHOT GUN.

HOPKINS & ALLEN MFG. CO'S SINGLE SHOT GUN, 12 GAUGE.

Weight 6½ lbs.   Length of Barrel 30 inches. **Choke Bored to do good shooting.**
Using regular Brass or Paper Shells.

Nº 12.

A thumbscrew released the barrel to let this solid frame H&A shotgun pack easier. Otherwise, it was "choke bored to do good shooting."

held or used under license many significant revolver patents of the period, patents listed elsewhere here. Small handguns of the period were effective protection when carried in the coat pocket. Without 20th century antibiotics to fight infections, a wound in the torso, even a small caliber, was often eventually fatal and everyone knew it.

The Hopkins and Allen Arms Company was created by Charles W. Hopkins and Samuel S. Hopkins, along with Charles H. Allen, on June 15, 1868. Charles A. Converse is also said to have joined them. These men had substantial experience as gunsmiths and pistol makers. Their company saw and filled a customer demand for inexpensive handguns of varying qualities. A retailer willing to order a suf-

H&A Rifle Models (Incomplete)

Model No.	Description
722	Takedown 22 (rolling block 18-in. bbl.
822	20-in. bbl. ** (falling block)
832	20-in. bbl.
922	24-in. round bbl.
925	24-in. bbl.
932	32 S&W, 24-in. bbl.
938	38 S&W, 24-in. bbl.
1888	(XL)
1888	Junior 22 L.R.R.F. octagonal bbl.
1889	Belgian Mauser 7.65 mm, rifle (1915)
1889	Belgian Mauser 7.65 mm, carbine (1915)
1922	New Model Junior
1925	New Model Junior 25 cal.
1932	New Model Junior 32 cal.
1938	New Model Jr.
. . . .	
2922	New Model Jr. Takedown, octagonal 24-in. bbl.; checkered
2925	Octagonal 20-in. bbl. Takedown, checkered
2932	Octagonal 20-in. bbl. Takedown, checkered
2938	Octagonal 20-in. bbl. Takedown, checkered
3922	22 Schuetzen Rifle, 26-in. bbl.
3925	25 cal. Schuetzen Rifle
4922	Bolt-action repeating rifle, plain
5022	Bolt-action; better finish, checkered
Noiseless	22 rifle with silencer Scout Military Rifle

* Made with and without hand engraving.
** Choice of two levers, one like a pigtail, the other like the loop lever on Winchesters.

ficient quantity was able to have revolvers manufactured to order stamped with his name as distributor, and we list such known distributors elsewhere here.

Many companies had factories in Norwich, Connecticut. The competition was substantial. In 1888 alone, Hopkins and Allen manufactured 100,000 revolvers. Their Defender revolver *retailed* for a mere 74 cents. By 1884, a customer could choose to pay $13 for a new Colt Lightning, $12.66 for a Merwin Hulbert double-action 38 Automatic revolver, made by Hopkins and Allen, or just $3 for Hopkins and Allen-marked 38's. In 1895, Montgomery Ward Company still advertised Defenders for 74 cents, Blue Jackets for $1.35, and a 22 XL Target Revolver for $3.

Hopkins and Allen's product line kept expanding with the purchase of Bay State Arms in 1887, Forehand Arms Company in 1902 and the W.H. Davenport Firearms Co. in 1909. In 1915, Hopkins and Allen manufacturing rights were sold to Marlin (and later to Numrich Arms Co.) and manufacturing ceased.

People speculate about all the reasons Hopkins and Allen eventually failed. The failure appears due to a number of factors. The company did recover from the burning of the Norwich factory in 1900, though most records appear to have been destroyed. Charles Hopkins, however, died in 1914, and attention diverted to making Model 1899 Mauser rifles for Belgium reduced production of profitable sporting arms, and then Belgium fell to the Germans so the primary customer was gone.

A new Hopkins and Allen Arms Company incorporated in Massachusetts and acquired control of the Norwich, Connecticut, company. It sought $4,250,000 to be raised by a stock offering. The offering claimed "present contracts for foreign governments for rifles assure. . . . handsome profits" and that "other highly profitable contracts pending." The recapitalization failed and so much had been gambled that the company failed. The assets were sold to Marlin-Rockwell. Manufacturing rights were eventually transferred to Numrich Arms Co.

Until recently, there has been little collector interest in Hopkins and Allen. A friend sold literally a pail full of Hopkins and Allen revolvers in the 1960s for $25, but in the 1980s Merwin Hulbert and Co. revolvers began to bring ever-increasing prices. H&A firearms values inflated slower. Many Hopkins and Allen products still go

Shotgun Models (Incomplete)

Model No.	Description
100	
110	10 ga.
112	12 ga. hammerless dbl.
116	16 ga. hammerless dbl.
120*	20 ga. hammerless dbl.
216	12 ga. hammerless dbl.
312	12 ga. hammerless dbl.
316	12 ga. hammerless dbl.
320	20 ga. hammerless dbl.
512	12 ga. hammerless SS
516	16 ga. hammerless SS
520	20 ga. hammerless SS
712	12 ga. hammer SS
720	20 ga. hammer SS
. . . .	
1812	12 ga. safety single gun
1816	16 ga.
2812	12 ga. Better finish, checkered
2816	16 ga. Better finish, checkered
3612	12 ga. Duck gun; auto ejector double w/hammer
3616(?)	16 ga. Double w/hammer (1913)
Double Hammerless	12, 16 ga. (1913)
New Model	12/16/20 ga. Hammer, top-break with steel barrel, checkered pistol grip, forend; ejector
Damascus Cannon	12, 16 ga. (1913) Made with and without ejector
Goose Gun	8, 10, 12 ga. without ejector.

unrecognized or mistaken for those of other manufacturers. Hopkins and Allen revolvers, rifles and shotguns have numerous variations. As common as Hopkins and Allen are, no study of the variations appears ever to have been done. Hopkins and Allen often didn't mark inexpensive revolvers with the company's own name, adding to the confusion. Serial numbers have never been correlated to years of production.

Some Hopkins and Allen revolvers were decorated with gold finish, engraving or colored grips. The grips (and patent dates) often earmark the Hopkins & Allen Revolver. In the 1880s, Hopkins and Allen revolvers were offered with grip choices including wood, rubber, pearl, pearl with "Mexican eagle" design, ivory, amber, agate, carnelian (ruby color), malachite (blue-green color), and jasper (green color).

Identification of a revolver centers

Identified Hopkins and Allen Distributors or Agents

The names of distributors or catalog retailers were sometimes stamped on firearms or cases offered for revolvers.

Company	Catalog Year	Company	Catalog Year
Black & Owen, Detroit		Montgomery Ward & Co., Chicago	1895
E.C. Meacham Arms Co., St. Louis	1884	R. Murdock, American Arms Co.	1895
F.I. Dickenson, Springfield*	(on bbl. of Ranger No. 2)	Alex L. Semple & Co., Louisville	1900-1901
Federal Gun Co.		Sears Roebuck	1903, 1908, 1910 & 1912
Forehand & Wadsworth		Supplee Biddle Hardware Co., Philadelphia (sold Aristocrat)	
Great Western Gunworks, Pittsburgh			
Hartley & Graham, New York	1891	The Essex Repeating Arms Co., Chicago	
C. Henry (marked "C. Henry Model 922")		The Pickering Hardware Co., Cincinnati	
Hibbard, Spencer, Bartlett & Co., Chicago**	1884	Toledo Fire Arms Co., Toledo, Ohio	
Homer Fisher, New York	1880	Van Camp Hardware Co., Indianapolis	
J.A. Richard & Co., Schenectady, New York		Western Gun Works, Chicago (sold Tramp's Terror)	
J.H. Johnston, Pittsburgh	1871		
James Bown & Son, Pittsburgh			
Quintana Bros., Mexico	1876, 1887	Western Reserve Gun Co.	
James P. Fitch, New York (sold Phoenix)		Another likely sales agent was John P. Lovell, of Boston, who sold Merwin Hulbert and Co. firearms.	
Merwin Hulbert and Co.***			

* These names are sometimes found on the frames or barrels of H & A firearms without Hopkins and Allen's own name.
** H S B & Co. may be printed instead of full name.
*** Merwin Hulbert and Co. for years held exclusive distributorship arrangements on Hopkins and Allen firearms.

on accurate observation, proper description and knowledge. Look for:

1. The brand-name, or manufacturer's name, appearing on the firearm.
2. The type of firearm (single shot, revolver, etc.)
3. The serial number (or assembly number) and its location.
4. The caliber.
5. The model (if indicated).
6. The number of chambers.
7. The barrel length.
8. The patent dates (if indicated).
9. Patented features common to a particular manufacturer.
10. A proofmark (foreign maker) on the barrel or receiver, or inspection mark.

Not all of those are useful to identify Hopkins and Allen firearms—for instance, proofmarks and inspection marks. Earlier models have few markings. Start with the markings, caliber, type of frame and cylinder capacity. Barrel lengths are often confusing. Measurement is made from the tip of the barrel to the rear of the barrel just ahead of the cylinder. Grips are positive identification only when other clues are consistent. It is easy to substitute grips.

Collectors can identify Hopkins and Allen firearms by the following:

1. The company name, usually stamped on the top of the barrel or topstrap. The company name changed to "Hopkins & Allen

All carrying 1906 patent dates, this set of three H&A Safety Police guns in 32 and 38 show several variations, including the hammerless option.

Patents Possible on Various Hopkins and Allen Products

Hopkins & Allen used their own and others' patents. Any of the following may be found on their products. Merwin Hulbert and Company used additional patents to those listed.

Date	Patent	Date	Patent
September 24, 1861*	Patent of E. Allen possibly used on F & W DA after 1900	January 19, 1886	Cocking mechanism, breakdown hammerless shotgun. Wm. H. Davenport
May 27, 1862	Curved slot to swing out cylinder. C. Hopkins	March 6, 1886*	(?) F.H. Allen
January 5, 1864	Swing cylinder outward. H.A. Biggs & S.S. Hopkins	October 5, 1886	Improved cam starter for auto ejector on DA break open.
March 28, 1871	Cylinder pin catch and swing release on side of frame. S. Hopkins	October 2, 1888	Set trigger, screw adj., rifle. Wm. H. Davenport
May 28, 1871	Adjustable base pin. S.S. Hopkins	July 2, 1889	Barrel screw. Wm. H. Davenport
January 24, 1874	Cylinder improvement. W.H. Williams	March 12, 1890	(?)
April 21, 1874	M-H Pat.	June 3, 1890	Takedown screw improvement. Wm H. Davenport
December 15, 1874	Single action six-shot revolver with swing out like later M-H. Lever pressed. D. Moore	June 3, 1890	Barrel screw, Wm. H. Armington, Horace A. Briggs
April 27, 1875	Safety notches on cylinder. H. Hopkins	November 25, 1890	(?)
June 29, 1875	Safety catch. C.W. Hopkins	December 9, 1890	Extractor designed to work, interchange barrel. Wm. H. Davenport
March 6, 1877	Cartridge extractor operates when barrel and cylinder move forward. Reduced stuck cartridges. W.A. Hulbert	September 26, 1893	Safety catch on tang of DA hammerless break-open revolver. C.M. Hopkins and J. Boland
March 7, 1877	Sliding loading gate on M-H. W.A. Hulbert	August 2, 1895	(?)
July 17, 1877	Revolver with dovetail catch ahead of trigger. D. Moore (M-H)	November 12, 1895	Cocking device, hammerless shotgun. Wm. H. Davenport
1878	British Patent No. 277	August 11, 1896	Shell extractor on breakdown guns. W. H. Davenport
May (1) 27, 1879	Hammer in solid frame revolver. G.W. Cilley	December 13, 1898	Ejecting device for breakdown rifles. W. H. Davenport
September 25, 1882*	(?) G.W. Cilley	December 5, 1899	Extractor for S.S. hammer shotgun. W. H. Davenport
September 12, 1883	(?)	June 11, 1907	Hammer lock for DA hammerless break-open. J.J. Murphy
April 29, 1884	Sliding side ejector right side, DA revolver. S.S. Hopkins	April 6, 1909	Safety in arm separates from cocking lever. W.H. Gates
January 27, 1885	Folding hammer. S.S. Hopkins	January 11, 1910	Hammer rises on release of trigger pressure. W.H. Gates
June 23, 1885	Takedown screw. S.S. Rifle		
January 5, 1886	Cylinder pin ejector for DA solid top. J. Boland		

Patents were occasionally used by two or more manufacturers and some of the above do not confirm an H&A manufactured firearm.

Arms Company" in 1898. This helps identify the relative time of manufacture.

2. The patent dates utilized by Hopkins and Allen (see list) and often stamped on top of the barrel or topstrap. Patent dates often seen include: March 28, 1871; April 27, 1875; June 29, 1875; May 17, 1879; November 25, 1890; and March 12, 1890.

3. The grip markings. Many, of course, have no markings. A Dog's Head is one example often seen on spur trigger revolver grips. The buttplate of rifles and shotguns were often stamped with an H&A logo. Buttplates may be of stamped metal, cast metal or hard rubber.

4. The model name or distributor's name stamped on the firearm (example: Defender, XL No. 8, Dictator, etc.) We list many of these here.

5. Certain design characteristics consistent with patents used by the company on its revolvers such as:
   - Folding hammer (first offered in 1876).
   - Spring-loaded push-in blade cylinder pin release often on left side of the frame.
   - The 1875-patented safety cylinder with characteristic elevated notches.
   - "Safety Hammer" design used after about 1900 where revolver hammer rests on the top of the frame.
   - Comparison with models appearing in original or reprinted 19th century distributor catalogs can be very helpful. Especially note the locations of screws, studs and the pattern of grips. Hammer shapes may vary, but note general shape.

Numbering on the interesting 1868-

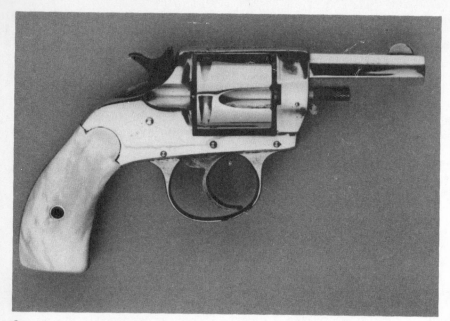

Gem of a Double Action No.6 38, marked "Hopkins & Allen Arms Co.," was made after 1898. (Gard photo)

1900 revolvers hasn't been correlated to years of manufacture. Don't confuse the assembly numbers with the serial number. Usually there is a serial number (and not always on the handle) often under the left grip. The cylinder number (often of three or four digits on front) can be an assembly number usually correlating with the serial number. Most of the Rangers, Defenders, Dictators and Blue Jackets (spur triggers) in the author's collection have three or four digit numbers, apparently assembly numbers which now we identify as a serial number. One later example of an H&A Arms Co. Safety Police 38 has "05" on the ejector, 905 on the cylinder and "6905" under the left grip. Generally, numbers appear in at least two places on revolvers made both before 1898 and after. The numbers seem to usually appear on the front of cylinders before 1898 and the rear of cylinders after 1898. Before 1898, the corresponding number is usually under the left grip.

Among Hopkins and Allen's Most Notable (and Collectable) Products are:

1. The 31-caliber cap and ball revolvers.
2. The Dictator 36-caliber five-shot percussion 4-inch barrel (about 1000 unconverted and 5100 factory converted for 38 RF).
3. The early XL Derringer pistol in 41 caliber.
4. The Xpert single shot derringer (less than 2000).
5. The early seven-shot 22 pocket revolver with part-octagonal and part-round 3-inch barrel (1860s).
6. "Parrot Beak" single shot 22 vest pocket derringer, hammerless with scroll engraving, birds-head grip (several hundred made). Watch for fakes! Offered in blue or nickel with pearl grips.
7. The 1876 Army, XL No. 8, and Navy and Police Models (never used by the military but used by some police departments). Initials engraved such as "D.P.D." on back of butt may indicate the city or department.
8. The Merwin Hulbert and Co. revolvers and rifles; Pocket Armys with an extra 7-inch barrel were available. Pocket and Frontier Army revolvers were marked "Hopkins & Allen Manufacturing Co. Norwich, CONN. USA". Early pocket models of M-H had a Hopkins and Allen patent date.
9. The Schuetzen rifles (22 RF, 25-20 and 38-55 known). Very rare with optional double-set triggers. Some have pistol grip stocks. There is a lady's rifle made after 1902 on the model 1922 frame in 22 LR and 25-20.
10. Triple Action revolver models made after 1900 are fairly common.
11. The Noiseless 22 RF rifle, if complete (Federal law prohibits silencers).
12. Gold-mounted and engraved Czars, etc.
13. Any ANIT & CHAR Spanish imitations or Belgian imitations can be well made or of very poor workmanship. While reported H&A, the Merwin Hulbert-stamped examples are wood gripped and marked on the barrel "ANIT & CHAR. Manufacturers of Fire Arms" in 38 S&W, 44 M-H and 44-40. The author hasn't heard of any examples without M-H designation. Foreign examples should have left-twist rifling instead of right.
14. Single shot target pistols after 1900, especially rare if stamped "Marlin Firearms Corp." (60 made).
15. Cased rifles with one or two extra barrels (first extra is a shotgun barrel) or full-looped levers (like Winchester). Matched 3-barrel sets on medium frame rifle in 16- or 20-gauge, 38 XL or 44 XL shot shells with 22 RF or 32 RF. Some very early "Davenport" style rifles were made in the late 1880s with a "removable floorplate and trigger mechanism"—high quality and desirable.

In general:

Revolvers with ring lanyards or side ejector rods on XLs are uncommon and worth a 50 percent premium. Saddle ring on left of frame possible on M-H carbines of 1880s worth premium.

A blue finish in Ranger, Czar and similar models is rare and worth at least 20-30 percent more than like models with nickel finish. Master engravers including Nimschke, Ulrich, Wolf, Helfrick and Young engraved M-H and may have some marked H&A. This would greatly increase value.

Mediocre engraving on the revolvers of Hopkins & Allen is not uncommon. Engraving appears to have been done late in the finishing process. Intaglio engraving of a coarse nature was done with colored enamel then applied. Gilt was also an option. The enamel is nearly always missing on revolvers seen at gun shows. "Punch Dot" engraving might have red lacquer to resemble small rubies.

Expect dimensional variations. After the fire in 1900, new tooling was necessary resulting in subtle changes in design. "Perch belly" stocks seem about then to appear on some Schuetzens. Similar standard models may not necessarily have interchangeable parts. Just after 1920, Marlin Firearms Corp. built 60 target pistols and 100 38 Safety Police revolvers marked "The Marlin Firearms Corp." on the barrel.

The older 22 models may only have a number in one location (often under the left grip) and can be otherwise unmarked.

No discussion of Hopkins and Allen can be understood without some explanation of Merwin Hulbert and Co. The company distributed other manufacturers' products from about 1871 to about 1896. Their 1887 catalog listed firearms, tackle, bicycles, bats, balls, etc. Hopkins and Allen made most of the firearms. Patents appear to have been shared, as would be expected with the common ownership.

Merwin Hulbert and Co. as "exclusive distributor" for H&A appears to have sold far and wide. Hopkins and Allen is supposed to have bought the company in 1876, according to some unfamiliar with M-H's ownership of H&A since 1874. In the late 1860s, Merwin Hulbert owned half interests in Hopkins and Allen, the American

From the top, we have here a Dictator 32 RF, XL No.2 in 32 RF Short, and an XL Vestpocket 22.

Hopkins and Allen Manufacturing Company
A Brief History

1862 Patent for swing cylinder slot, Chas. W. Hopkins.

1867 Hopkins takes over Bacon factory in Norwich.

1868 Hopkins & Allen Manufacturing Company organized 6/15/68. First products: 31 cap and ball, 36 Dictator (most converted to 38 RF). Soon producing 22 pocket revolver with part-octagonal and part-round 3-inch barrel.

1871 3/28/71: Patent; Samuel S. Hopkins. Producing spur-trigger single-action revolvers including Blue Jacket, XL Vest Pocket, XL Derringer, XL (series), Captain Jack, Ranger No. 2, Swamp Angel and Terror. Use of M-H patents acquired 1870-1874. Producing 1200 revolvers monthly. Merwin Hulbert and Co. began distribution of H&A products in 1871 and continued until about 1896.

1874 Producing XL models. Merwin Hulbert and Co. buys half the company.

1875 4/27/75: Fire pin patent; Henry H. Hopkins.
6/29/75: C.W. Hopkins

1876 Production of M-H single-action Army 44 began. Factory moves to 48 Franklin Street.

1879 5/27/79: Patent.

1880 6/15/80: Patent on folding hammer. Producing Czars, Dictator, Mountain Eagle, Scott.

1884 Catalogs show XL No. 8 Army revolver, 44 Webley.

1885 Folding hammer patented and first produced. Factory now at 132 Franklin St.

1886 Patent for folding hammer spur.

1887 Purchased Bay State Arms Co. (including Davenport patents).

1888 Rifle production begins, including Model 1888 falling block rifle in 22 to 38-55. Production continues to 1892.

Produced 100,000 revolvers in 1888 alone.

1890 Production of Junior single shot rifle and Majestic bicycles began.

1892 XL double-action revolvers in production.

1895 Producing hammer shotgun with 12-, 16-, 20-gauge and 45-70 barrels; Defender, Blue Jacket 22, Czar 22; Automatic Hammerless in 32 and 38.

1896 Hulbert Bros., primary customer and distributor fails.

1898 "Hopkins & Allen Arms Company" name begins. Sells now directly to public.

1900 Production of 922 rifle began. Noiseless, Schuetzen in 25-20, 38-55 and 22 in production. Fire burns Norwich factory. Producton stops until 1902.

1902 Purchased Forehand Arms Co. Production of 822 and 722 began. Triple-action Safety Police model in production; 3922 offered. Employing 600 people.

1906 Until 1915, production of break-open single shot target pistol. Bolt-action 22 rifle produced about this time. Making up to 186 rifle, shotgun, revolver model variations.

1909 Purchased W.H. Davenport Firearms Co.

1913 Producing Cannon Breech shotgun; 8-, 10-, and 12-gauge Goose Gun; hammer and hammerless shotguns.

1914 Contracted to manufacture Model 1899 Mauser bolt action (Belgian). Chas. Hopkins dies; skeleton stock target pistol, Cadet 22 rifle and New Model Vest Pocket Derringer 22 being offered.

1915 Business closed. Production stopped. Assets sold to Marlin-Rockwell. Manufacturing rights sold to Numrich Arms Co.

Common Patent Dates on Various Models

Handguns can often be identified by H&A's common patent dates of March 28, 1871; April 27, 1875; June 29, 1875; May 17, 1879; November 25, 1890; or March 12, 1890. See complete list elsewhere here.

From NRA Firearms Fact Book, 3rd Ed.

Hopkins & Allen. Norwich, Conn. Arms made for Merwin, Hulbert & Co., agents

Common H&A Handgun Logos

Hopkins & Allen. Norwich, Conn. 1868—1915. Pistols and revolvers

H&A

Hopkins & Allen. Norwich, Conn. 1868—1915. Safety Police Cal. .32 revolvers

Hopkins & Allen. Norwich, Conn. Revolvers made for Merwin, Hulbert & Co., agents

Forehand & Wadsworth. Hopkins & Allen. Norwich, Conn. Revolvers bearing either name

Merwin Hulbert and Co. 1868-1896

A firm of promoters and sales agents

1853 Merwin & Bray Co. So known until 1864. Not manufacturers, but distributors, including Prescott and Plant revolvers.

1864 Merwin, Taylor & Simpkins Company. So known until 1868.

1868 Merwin Hulbert & Co. owns 50 percent of three companies, including Hopkins & Allen Manufacturing Company. Most firearms are made by Hopkins & Allen but imitations also by ANIT and CHAR (Spanish manufacturers). Eventually M-H & Co. became H&A's primary distributor.

1874 Purchased H&A outright.

1876 Single-action Army Model 1876 production starts. Tested by Ordnance, 1/22/78. Revolver praised but rejected. Only 32, 38 and 44 calibers are being marketed.

1880 Produced "Smith & Wesson" Model 22s, Double Action Pocket Army with 7-inch extra barrel, Triumph, Double Action Army, Pocket Army and Acme Hammerless revolvers plus rifles. Company in receivership 1880-1881 after Joseph Merwin dies in 1879.

1886 Folding-hammer models first offered starting with XL Bulldog Revolvers. Intaglio engraving and intaglio with gilt offered on most revolver models.

1887 Folding hammer introduced on automatic models. No. 6 off-hand rifle in 38-55 first offered. Also selling XL shotgun in 38 and 44 cals.; No. 1 in 22, 32, and 38; No. 2 in 32; No. 3 in 38; another model rifle & carbine. Mexican eagle grips offered. XL Double Action, XL Bulldog, and Pocket Army revolvers offered.

1892 Name changed to "Hulbert Bros."

1895 Selling Junior rifles 22 and 32 and combined shotgun/rifle 22 or 32 and 12- or 15-gauge. Also target rifle in 32 WCF and 32 RF.

1896 Out of Business.

Common Patent Dates on Various Firearms

Jan. 24, 1874; April 21, 1874; Dec. 15, 1874; Aug. 3, 1875; July 11, 1876; March 6, 1877; April 17, 1877; June 15, 1880; March 14, 1882; Jan. 9, 1883.

Grips offered on XL Revolver models in 1880s (and most other revolvers): rubber, pearl, Mexican eagle (pearl), ivory, amber, agate, carnelian, malachite, jasper.

A Brief History of Ethan Allen to Forehand Arms Company to Hopkins and Allen

1832 Ethan Allen begins producing firearms (Lambert cane gun) as "E. Allen" Grafton, Mass. Grafton-marked firearms are scarce.

1834 Allen obtains patent and produces pepperboxes.

1837 Allen & Thurber. (1837-1842, Grafton, Mass.; later Norwich, Conn).

1842 Moves to Norwich, Conn.; 36 DA percussion added.

1847 Moves to Worcester, Mass.

1854 Allen Thurber & Co., Worcester, Mass.

1856 Allen & Wheelock. Thomas P. Wheelock died in 1863.

1865 E. Allen & Co. until 1871 when E. Allen dies. Sons-in-law Forehand and Wadsworth assumed control of the company in 1871. Seven-shot 22 sidehammer returned to production with 2⁷⁄₁₆-inch octagonal barrel.

1869 Production of cheap spur trigger models begins.

1871 Forehand and Wadsworth producing British Bulldog, Pocket Model, Russian Model, Swamp Angel, Old Model Army, Bulldog, Double Action, Safety Hammer, Terror, side-hammer shotguns, among others, in competition with Hopkins & Allen. Marked "Worcester, Mass."

1877 44 Army revolver production starts.

1880 Wadsworth retires. Name changes to "Forehand Arms Company". Producing Terror 32, Bull Dog 32, 38 and 44, Swamp Angel 41, Improved Double Action 32, 38 and 41, others.

1884 Catalog shows Scotts Top Lever side-hammer shotguns in 10- and 12-gauge, 38 Double Action.

1890 Forehand Arms Company added Double Action, Perfection Automatic. Quality on decline.

1895 Producing hammerless single-barrel 12-gauge, hammerless double shotguns, Automatic Ejector 12-gauge (only) doubles, and numerous revolver models including four DA revolvers in 32 and 38.

1898 Sullivan Forehand dies.

1902 Forehand Arms Company is purchased by Hopkins and Allen.

Common Patent Dates

Sept. 24, 1861; Oct. 22, 1861; Jan. 27, 1871; June 27, 1871; Oct. 28, 1873; April 20, 1875.

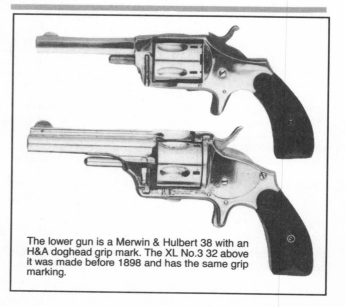

The lower gun is a Merwin & Hulbert 38 with an H&A doghead grip mark. The XL No.3 32 above it was made before 1898 and has the same grip marking.

Other Manufacturers with Same or Similar Name Models

ACME 22 and 32 "Acme" with concealed hammer sold by J. Stevens Arms Co.

ALEXIS In 22 made by Hood Firearms Co., marked "Alexis."

BONNIE BLUE M-H claimed to manufacture about 1877, marked "Bonnie Blue."

BRITISH BULLDOG DA made by Iver Johnson about 1881. Many "Bulldog" guns produced, including L. Ancion Marx of Liege, Belgium; J. Bertrand, Liege, Belgium; Jannsen Fils et Cie, Liege, Belgium. Marked "British Bulldog."

CZAR Made by Hood Firearms Co. in 22. Pat. 1/23/75, marked "Czar." Also, Turner Ross.

DEFENDER Made by Iver Johnson, marked "Defender."

DICTATOR Semi-auto produced (Centaure) by Soc. Anonyme des Fab. d' Armes Reunies, Liege, Belgium.

DREADNOUGHT Revolver produced by Antonio Erasti, Eibar, Spain, and semi-auto by Javier Echaniz of Vergara, Spain.

ESSEX Made by Cresent Firearms for Belknap Hardware, marked "Essex."

EXCELSIOR Made by Bliss & Goodyear—Pat. 4/23/78, marked "Excelsior."

HARDPAN Possibly made by Hood Firearms, marked "Hardpan."

IXL Not H&A product. Made by unknown New York company.

LEADER Made by Crescent.

MARQUIS OF LORNE Made by Ryan.

METROPOLITAN POLICE Also made by Norwich Falls Pistol Co. Sold by Maltby Curtiss Co.

MONARCH Series by Osgood Gun, marked "Monarch."

NERO A 32-cal. "Nero" was made by Rupertus Arms.

NEVERMISS J.M. Marlin Co. made a "Nevermiss."

OLD HICKORY Spur trigger made by Iver Johnson, various calibers.

POINTER Also made by W. Irving Co. New York.

RANGER NO. 2 Made by E.L. Dickinson Co.

REV-O-NOC Made by Crescent. H&A made for Hibbard, Spencer, Bartlett & Co.

SCOTT A model made by W.C. Scott & Son, Birmingham, London (1878), marked "The Scott." Another model by Hood Firearms and "Scott Arms Co."

SECRET SERVICE Made by Iver Johnson.

TERROR Made also by Forehand & Wadsworth (also produced "Electric")

UNION Made in 32 RF by Hood Firearms

XL "XL Shotgun" (also 38 cal.) made by American Metallic Cartridge Co., S. Coventry, Conn., was sold by Merwin Hulbert & Co. "Screw Key" on right side of receiver.

H&A *May* have made a "Red Cloud" and "Red Chieftain" model for Supplee Biddle Hardware Co. and "Red Jacket" Revolver for Hibbard, Spencer, Bartlett & Co. (1884).

H&A Appears to have used name "Acme Arms Company" for private brand revolver sales. J. Stevens Arms Company was a distributor for this brand.

Cartridge Company, and Phoenix Rifle and Ammunition Company.

Hopkins and Allen also produced firearms for Forehand Arms Company, Chichester Rifle Co., The Evans Repeating Rifle Company and probably others. No H&A firearms were made in Mexico, but H&A firearms were sold in Mexico by Quintana Bros.

It is fair to speculate that part of the trouble Merwin Hulbert and Co. had in gaining recognition and acceptance in the market of its own brands of firearms was its association with Hopkins and Allen, who suffered a mediocre reputation earned by its marketing of inexpensive and poorly finished pocket revolvers.

Bibliography

Donald B. Webster, Jr. *Suicide Specials*. 1958.

L.D. Satterlee (ed.). "Ten Old Gun Catalogs." *Gun Digest*, DBI Books, Inc.

Allen W. Terek. "Hopkins & Allen 1868-1915." *Man At Arms*. Nov. 1987.

Paul O. Berg. "The Hopkins & Allen Guns." *The Gun Report*. December, 1961.

Hopkins & Allen Gun Guide & Catalog.

W. Barlow Fors. *Collector's Handbook of U.S. Cartridge Revolvers.*

Dewitt E. Sell. *Collectors Guide to American Cartridge Handguns.* Stackpole Books, Inc.

Norm Flayderman. *Flayderman's Guide to Antique American Firearms . . . and their Values,* 3rd Ed. DBI Books, Inc.

Charles Edward Chapel. *The Gun Collector's Handbook of Values,* 10th Ed.

Charles E. Carder. "Hopkins & Allen Single Shots." *The Gun Report.* July, 1991.

Art Phelps. *The Story of Merwin Hulbert & Co. Firearms.* Taylor Publishing, 1991.

John T. Millard. *A Handbook on the Primary Identification of Revolvers and Semi Automatic Pistols.* Charles C. Thomas Publisher (1974).

James J. Grant, *Boys Single Shot Rifles, More Single Shot Rifles,* Wolfe Publishing, Reprinted 1991.

Numerous old catalogs and Hopkins & Allen and Merwin Hulbert & Co. literature.

Regretfully, the author differs on some details from the dates, models and story of Hopkins & Allen told by others, but believes this version is the most substantiated.

Donald R. France

A collector today can assemble a very interesting and varied (but still inexpensive) collection of H&A 19th century handguns and long guns. The firearms appear to have increasing collector value at least equivalent to inflation. For instance, in about ten years the small XL Vest Pocket single shot pistol has doubled in value. Small frame Merwin Hulbert and Co. revolvers still appear to be "sleepers" among collectors. In selecting firearms to collect, condition is everything. With rare exceptions the finest examples offer more rapid increase in value. ●

The Norrell select-fire, suppressed Ruger 10/22 is superbly engineered and fires at a rate of 750-800 rounds per minute. It's state-of-the-art, but *not* for most citizens.

Ruger 10/22 with SCRC integral suppressor which can be disassembled for cleaning and maintenance. (Walter photo)

MODERN

This High Standard HD Military pistol with integral suppressor is a veteran of the OSS and CIA, and is shown with rare original take-down tool.

Ram-Line Exactor pistol with Precision Arms integral suppressor is very quiet with RWS subsonic ammunition.

SILENCED 22s...

legally possible for most of us

by AL PAULSON

As POPULATION density increases in the United States, it is becoming increasingly difficult to find a place to shoot where the sound of gunfire will not offend someone. Gunshots seem to be the most offensive category of noise pollution for the public at large. The response to this problem in several European countries has been to equip rifles and pistols with silencers.

Contrary to popular belief, silencers provide a viable, fun and *legal* solution to this problem of noise pollution in the United States. About 43,000 Americans use legal silencers for discreet target practice, plinking, and animal control.

My own shooting enjoyment has vastly increased now that I can target practice in my backyard without disturbing the neighbors. As an NRA instructor, I've frequently used silenced 22s to help troublesome students get over their fear of shooting a firearm. The technique even helps experienced people improve their shooting fundamentals, since the exotic qualities of a silenced firearm increase their concentration on what they're doing. Clearly, silencers have a legitimate and useful place in the sporting use of firearms. And have had such a place for nearly a century.

The first successful silencer was marketed in 1909 by Hiram P. Maxim. He dramatically improved his design in 1910, and silencers gradually became relatively common among sport shooters, especially in the northeastern United States. Over the years, I have seen photographs of people quietly target practicing in the yards of homes in beautiful Victorian neighborhoods. Silencers so used provided an innocent and inexpensive source of family fun.

While contemporary movies show silencers being used by villains of the period, I have yet to find a single documented case. Silencers were subjected to the same controls as machineguns in 1934 because game managers feared silencers might be used by poachers. Legal silencers are once again becoming commonplace, we should note, but not one registered silencer has ever been used for an illegal act since 1934, according to government records.

The Gun Control Act of 1934 forced people to destroy their silencers or register them. The original owner had a brief amnesty period in which to register the silencer without cost. If not registered within that period, the silencer became unregisterable contraband, owning which could subject the owner to a big fine and jail sentence. Most owners never got the word in time. Others decided it was too much trouble since each time a registered silencer was sold, the new owner had to pay a $200 transfer tax. That was an incredible amount of money in the depths of the Great Depression. So, few Maxim silencers exist to this day, and these tend to be expensive. Some Maxim models perform well by modern standards. Others do not.

THE AWC Warp 3 suppressor on the Walther TPH pistol was originally developed for government clients who needed a tiny package for discreet diplomacy. (Walter photo)

Silencers slipped into obscurity until World War II, when silenced weapons were used with remarkable success for clandestine and commando operations. Prior to this time, silencers were fitted to the end of a gun's barrel. This design is now commonly referred to as a "muzzle silencer" or "muzzle-can." World War II silencers were commonly built around a highly modified barrel drilled with ports to vent combustion gases into the silencer as near as possible to the chamber. This sort of design is called an "integral silencer."

One of the most effective integral designs of the period was a silenced High Standard HD Military 22 pistol used by OSS operatives on clandestine missions from Berlin to Burma. The pistol was remarkably quiet, even by modern standards. Former OSS personnel formed the nucleus of the Central Intelligence Agency when it was created in 1947, and the silenced HD Military pistols used by the OSS formed the nucleus of the CIA's clandestine armory. Francis Gary Powers had one when his U2 spy plane was shot down over the Soviet Union on May 1, 1960. And CIA operatives used them in Indo-China during the Vietnam era.

Maxim Model 1921 22-caliber suppressor (top), Model 1910 22-caliber suppressor (middle) and Model 1910 44-caliber suppressor (bottom).

While the CIA undoubtedly still has some silenced HD Military pistols in its inventory, High Standard has not manufactured the pistol for some time. It has been replaced by the silenced Ruger 22 pistol for missions where quiet is more important than hitting power. From the Mossad (Israel's intelligence agency) to U.S. Navy SEALs, the silenced Ruger is now reported the favored tool for up-close-and-personal diplomacy. The silenced Ruger is the favorite pistol of sport shooters, as well.

Silencers finally began to reach their military potential during the Vietnam conflict. New silencer designs abounded, and silencers became known by a new and more accurate name: *suppressors*. By then, inflation had rendered the $200 transfer tax much less painful than in 1934. So suppressors once again appeared in the civilian marketplace, largely through the efforts of Mitchell Wer-Bell III and the Military Armament Corporation (MAC).

The company folded in the early 1970s due to a decline in government sales and management problems, and the company's assets were auctioned off. Original MAC suppressors can still be found in the modern marketplace, but they are expensive because of their appeal to collectors. They also tend to provide minimum acceptable sound suppression by modern standards, and they tend to have a limited lifespan—about 200 rounds. While limited lifespan is not a liability to military and clandestine users, lifespan is naturally a major concern for the sport shooter.

For several years, a few post-auction MAC suppressors appeared in the marketplace, and that was it. Then, in 1976, Jonathan Arthur Ciener began manufacturing a new generation of suppressors. He remains the oldest active suppressor manufacturer in the U.S. Ciener's muzzle-cans and integrally suppressed firearms soon became known for performance, workmanship, and outstanding accuracy.

These 22 suppressors cannot, however, be disassembled for cleaning and

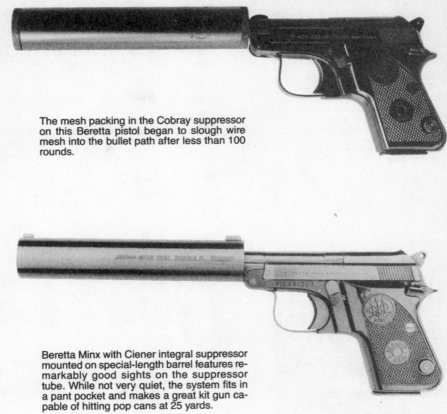

The mesh packing in the Cobray suppressor on this Beretta pistol began to slough wire mesh into the bullet path after less than 100 rounds.

Beretta Minx with Ciener integral suppressor mounted on special-length barrel features remarkably good sights on the suppressor tube. While not very quiet, the system fits in a pant pocket and makes a great kit gun capable of hitting pop cans at 25 yards.

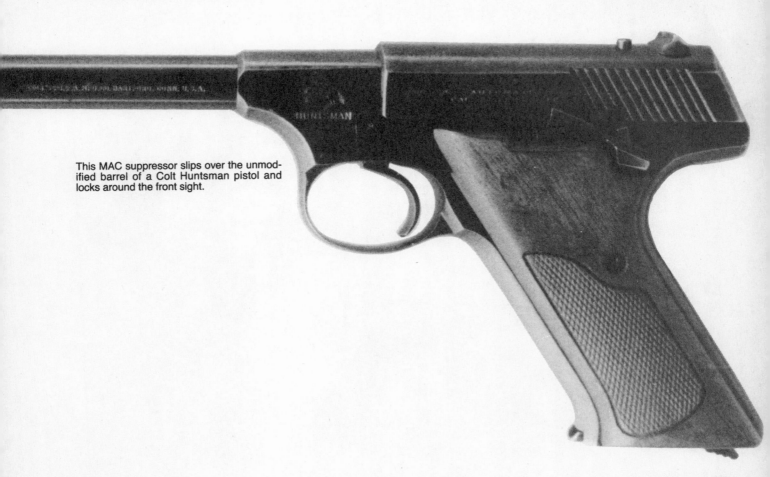

This MAC suppressor slips over the unmodified barrel of a Colt Huntsman pistol and locks around the front sight.

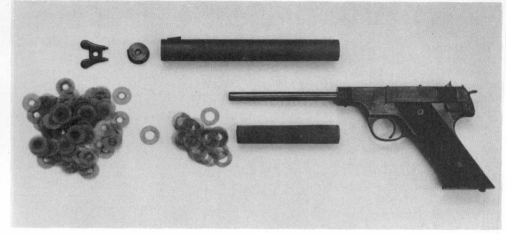

Disassembled High Standard HD Military pistol with spanner, front end cap and suppressor tube, small-hole bronze screen washers, steel washer that separates the two suppressor chambers, large-hole bronze screen washers and rolled bronze screen.

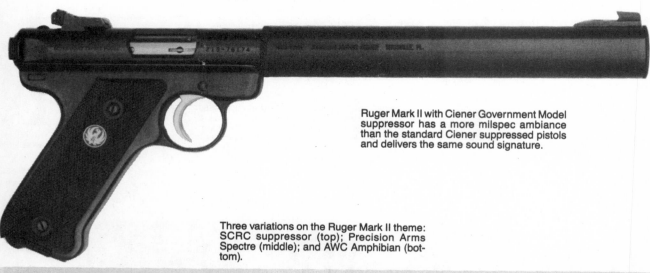

Ruger Mark II with Ciener Government Model suppressor has a more milspec ambiance than the standard Ciener suppressed pistols and delivers the same sound signature.

Three variations on the Ruger Mark II theme: SCRC suppressor (top); Precision Arms Spectre (middle); and AWC Amphibian (bottom).

maintenance. The lifespan of Ciener's 22 supressors should be well in excess of 10,000 rounds. That's several lifetimes—the owner and kids and grandkids and maybe even great-grandkids—for most folks.

But what if you shoot a lot? What if you simply want the security of being able to clean and refurbish your investment so that you know it will last indefinitely? Dr. Phil Dater began designing suppressors in the early 1980s expressly for such people. Each suppressor came with a field manual and specialized tools so the owner could disassemble and maintain it. Dater's integral pistol suppressors should be disassembled, cleaned and repacked (using several dollar's worth of readily available materials) every 500 rounds. His integral rifle suppressors should be disassembled and maintained every 2,000 to 4,000 rounds.

Dater's suppressors were manufactured first by the Automatic Weapons Company (AWC) and then by AWC Systems Technology (also known as AWC for short). Dater's 22 suppressors are now produced by Tim Bixler of South Central Research Corporation (SCRC). Formerly vice president for manufacturing at AWC, Bixler also manufactures excellent suppressors of his own design. AWC has moved on to a new generation of high-performance, radical-design 22 suppressors which are permanently sealed. Many deliver unprecedented sound reduction while maximizing accuracy.

The Amphibian pistol represents the most radical of AWC's new integrally suppressed 22 firearms. The pistol was designed to be carried by U.S. Navy SEALs underwater for special operations. It can be fired without draining the suppressed pistol of water, and it delivers maximum sound reduction if some liquid remains in the suppressor as a coolant. The Amphibian is much quieter than most integrally suppressed 22 *rifles*, yet it achieves this performance with a much smaller volume. This special-purpose pistol may not be as accurate as the other suppressed Ruger pistol which AWC offers, but it is certainly the most sophisticated suppressed 22 on the planet.

An AWC muzzle-can called the Warp 3 was developed when a U.S. government agency wanted a tiny suppressor for the Walther TPH (with special extra-length threaded barrel). The system had to be unusually small for concealed carry when under deep cover. The Warp 3 can also be mated to many other pistols and rifles.

Like the Amphibian, the Warp 3 is designed to be shot wet. Almost un-

Ruger 77/22 with AWC Archangel muzzle suppressor, which can be removed and used on other firearms as well. (Walter photo)

THE LEGAL SILENCER

Silencers and machineguns are tightly controlled but legal under federal law, as long as state or local laws do not prohibit them. The net result is that silencers and machineguns are legal in about two-thirds of the states.

There are three ways to obtain a silencer legally. FFL holders can pay $500 per year for a Class 3 special license which allows an unlimited number of tax-free transfers. Police departments and other government agencies are exempt from federal licenses and transfer taxes. Individuals who are 21 and older, have never been convicted of a felony, and are U.S. citizens can obtain a transfer by paying a one-time $200 tax and surviving an intense background check.

The paperwork required to transfer a silencer or machinegun for individual ownership is somewhat intimidating the first time through. In reality, it merely requires an individual to invest about as much time as it used to take to buy three pounds of sausages in Poland. The simplest way to proceed is to have the manufacturer recommend a Class 3 dealer in your area. The dealer orders the suppressor on the buyer's behalf. Once the Feds have approved transfer of the suppressor to the dealer and he has logged it into his bound book, you can begin the paperwork to transfer the suppressor to you.

The process requires two passport photos, which are attached to two Form 4s provided by the dealer. He'll fill out part, and you'll fill out part. He'll also give you two fingerprint cards. Take these documents to the top law enforcement officer in your community or county. After fingerprinting, this department head must sign both Form 4s, certifying that you are not a bad person as far as he knows. Give the Form 4s and fingerprint cards back to the dealer along with $200 for the one-time-only transfer tax. The dealer submits everything to BATF, which submits the fingerprint cards to the FBI for a two- to three-month background check. Once the FBI clears you, BATF approves the paperwork and returns it to the dealer. You can then take possession.

A photocopy of the approved Form 4 must accompany the suppressor at all times. The original Form 4 should be kept in a safety deposit box or other safe place. The suppressor can be written into your will and passed on as a family heirloom to another generation without incurring an additional transfer tax, but the same paperwork and background checks will be required. Selling or even giving someone the suppressor would require a repeat performance of the paperwork and transfer tax.

If there is no Class 3 dealer in your area, you can fill out the same paperwork through the manufacturer, but delivery must be made through a local conventional FFL holder. This is a recent BATF concession. ○

TABLE 1
Net Sound Reduction in Decibels of Suppressed 22-Caliber Pistols

Pistol	Suppressor	Federal Hi-Power HV LR	Hansen Standard Velocity LR	RWS Subsonic LR
Ruger MK II	Precision Arms	39	38	46
Ruger MK II	AWC RST	23	22	—
Ruger MK II	AWC Amphibian	33	35	41
Ruger MK II	SCRC	23	22	22
High Standard HD Military	OSS/CIA issue	24	—	—
Colt Huntsman	Military Armament Corp.	19	21	20
Walther TPH	AWC Warp 3 dry	16	18	19
Walther TPH	AWC Warp 3 with Break-Free every 10 rounds	24	29	32
Walther TPH	AWC Warp 3 with Break-Free every 3 rounds	34	33	35
Walther TPH	AWC Warp 3 with water every 3 rounds	37	37	37
Walther TPH	AWC Warp 3 with urine every 3 rounds	36	36	35

TABLE 4
Net Sound Reduction in Decibels of Suppressed 22 Short Pocket Pistols

Pistol	Suppressor	CCI Mini Mag Shorts
Beretta 950 BS	SWD BP22	34
Beretta 950 BS	Ciener SBER	19

believable performance is achieved by adding coolant every three shots. The suppressor uses baffles to force the main gas jet away from the bullet and into special environment cells, where some coolant evaporates with each shot, cooling combustion gases and thus robbing them of energy that would be perceived as sound.

While Break-Free is the preferred coolant for the Warp 3 suppressor, any light oil with a high flash point can be used. Water and even shaving gels work, too. SEAL Team 2 has recharged these suppressors in the field with a mixture of water-soluble oil and paraffin, which is carried in little squirt bottles. Perhaps the most interesting suitable fluid is urine, which has a definite advantage wherever fancy lubricant or even water may not be available.

Another manufacturer who caters to those who wish to disassemble and maintain their suppressors is John Norrell. His designs are particularly robust and have a definite milspec ambiance. They may not be as quiet as some competing designs, but they have long maintenance intervals and are particularly well engineered to handle a large volume of particularly dirty ammunition. Norrell's integral 22 suppressors deliver superb engineering and adequate sound reduction.

Norrell's suppressed Ruger pistol should be disassembled and cleaned every 500 rounds. The 18-inch integral rifle suppressor should be disassembled and cleaned every 8,000 rounds, and an 11-inch shorty suppressor (for government agencies) should be cleaned every 4,000 rounds. If you delay cleaning much beyond these limits, disassembly may become impossible,

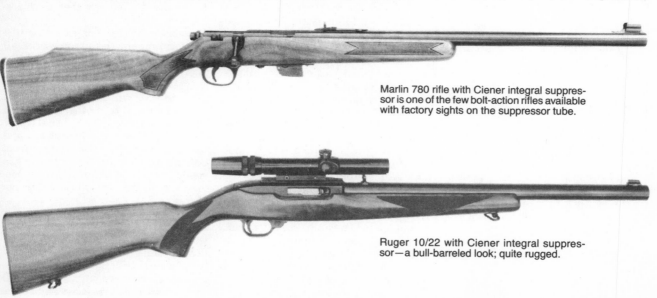

Marlin 780 rifle with Ciener integral suppressor is one of the few bolt-action rifles available with factory sights on the suppressor tube.

Ruger 10/22 with Ciener integral suppressor—a bull-barreled look; quite rugged.

even with the special tools. Norrell's suppressors come with detailed instructions for disassembly, maintenance, operation and troubleshooting.

The newest major player in the civilian and military marketplace is John Leasure of Precision Arms International. While his suppressed Ruger pistol (called the Spectre) is exceptionally quiet, the pick of the Precision Arms litter has to be his incredible suppressed second-generation Ram-Line Exactor pistol. The Exactor has a quieter action than the Ruger. And unlike the Ruger, the Exactor will still function reliably if two coils of the recoil spring are removed to use the superb subsonic Long Rifle hollowpoints made by RWS.

These are the major manufacturers you'll find in the marketplace. While they all produce quality products, performance and price does vary among competing designs. There are numerous small manufacturers as well. Many produce excellent suppressors, including varieties not available from the major manufacturers. Ward Machine, for example, builds invisible suppressors which are housed in the stocks of Ruger 10/22 and Browning takedown rifles. They even produce a silenced 22 rifle inside a Daisy Red Ryder BB gun which looks completely original from the outside!

Other suppressor manufacturers include Blaylock Gun Works, Developmental Concepts, DLO Manufacturing, Fleming Firearms, S&H Arms

TABLE 2
Net Sound Reduction in Decibels of Integrally Suppressed 22-Caliber Rifles

Rifle	Suppressor	Federal Hi-Power HV LR	Hansen Standard Velocity LR	RWS Subsonic LR	Federal Hi-Power CB Longs
Browning Takedown	Ciener	24	23	25	—
Ruger 10/22	AWC R10	23	—	—	—
Ruger 10/22	Norrell	19	—	—	—
Ruger 10/22	SCRC	23	—	—	—
Ruger 10/22	Ciener	22	18	—	—
Marlin 780 Bolt Action	Ciener	19	19	25	23

TABLE 3
Net Sound Reduction in Decibels of 22-Caliber Muzzle-Cans

Gun	Suppressor	Federal Hi-Power HV LR	Hansen Standard Velocity LR	RWS Subsonic LR	Federal Hi-Power CB Longs
Ruger 77/22	Vaime A8	20	20	25	26
Ruger 77/22	AWC Archangel	24	24	25	26
Ruger 77/22	AWC Project C	14	—	24	28
Winchester Model 69	Maxim Model 1921	11	9	25	23
CAR-15 with 22 kit	AWC MK-9 9mm baffles	—	23	—	—
CAR-15 with 22 kit	Larand/Norrell	—	24	—	—

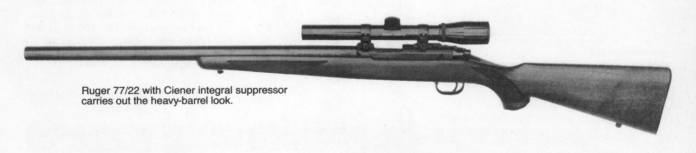

Ruger 77/22 with Ciener integral suppressor carries out the heavy-barrel look.

Walther TPH with special barrel and thread protector, plus AWC Warp 3 suppressor that is so small it is issued with a thread protector that turns the suppressor into a key fob. Now in clandestine service, the Warp 3 provides unprecedented sound suppression in a tiny package to sport shooters as well.

TABLE 5
Sound Signatures in Decibels of Suppressed 22-Caliber Pistols

Pistol	Suppressor	Federal Hi-Power HV LR	Hansen Standard Velocity LR	RWS Subsonic LR	Temperature Degrees Fahrenheit
Ruger MK II	Precision Arms	117	116	108	74-82
Ruger MK II	AWC RST	133	132	—	74-82
Ruger MK II	AWC Amphibian	123	119	113	74-82
Ruger MK II	SCRC	132	132	131	82
High Standard HD Military	OSS/CIA issue	132	—	—	65
Colt Huntsman	Military Armament Corp.	136	133	133	74
Walther TPH	AWC Warp 3 dry	143	139	138	82
Walther TPH	AWC Warp 3 with Break-Free every 10 rounds	135	128	125	74
Walther TPH	AWC Warp 3 with Break-Free every 3 rounds	125	124	122	82
Walther TPH	AWC Warp 3 with water every 3 rounds	122	120	120	82
Walther TPH	AWC Warp 3 with urine every 3 rounds	123	121	122	82

TABLE 8
Sound Signatures in Decibels of Suppressed 22 Short Pocket Pistols

Pistol	Suppressor	CCI Mini Mag Shorts	Temperature Degrees Fahrenheit
Beretta 950 BS	None	154	90
Beretta 950 BS	SWD BP22	120	90
Beretta 950 BS	Ciener SBER	135	90

Manufacturing Company, and Sound Technology. Addresses are listed in the Directory of the Arms Trade here in GUN DIGEST.

How do you choose the best option from the many similar products in the marketplace? You can make such a purchase from a specially licensed dealer who has the experience to recommend a product for your particular needs, show you the product beforehand, and perhaps let you shoot it. *Machine Gun News* (Dept. GD, P.O. Box 761, Hot Springs, AR 71902) critically evaluates suppressors in nearly every issue.

Comparing the performance of suppressors is tricky. Most sound meters, from Radio Shack units to scientific models costing thousands of dollars, fail to properly measure the sound of gunshots because they do not think fast enough—have a fast enough *rise time*—to record the entire event. Only one sound meter has a fast enough rise time: the Bruel and Kjaer Type 2209 Impulse Precision Sound Pressure Meter.

I used this meter (set on A weighting) with a B&K Type 4136 1/4-inch condenser microphone. The microphone was placed one meter away from the front of the suppressor or muzzle, at a 90-degree angle from the bullet flight path. The meter was calibrated just before and just after each test. The ambient temperature was recorded since powder combustion and the speed of sound vary with temperature. Tests were conducted with RWS subsonic, Hansen standard velocity target, and Federal Hi-Power high-velocity LR ammunition. Federal Hi-Power CB Longs were also tried. At least 10 rounds were fired in each test to obtain a valid sample.

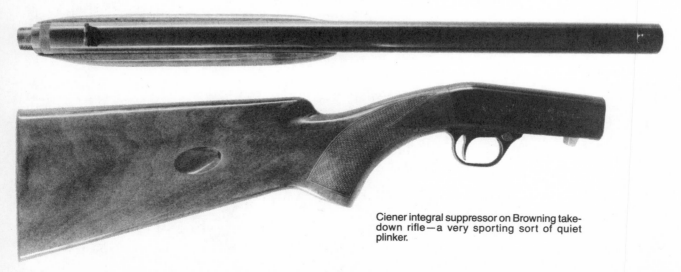

Ciener integral suppressor on Browning takedown rifle—a very sporting sort of quiet plinker.

Tables 1-4 show the net sound reductions produced by suppressed pistols, integrally suppressed rifles, and rifles with muzzle-cans. Tables 5-8 show the actual sound signatures plus the ambient temperature for each test. The data represent two years of research and a lot of frustration. My wife stood in a fog of burned urine mist for more than three hours on a warm afternoon so she could record just one series of experiments on the unique Warp 3 suppressor which was a virtually unique research experience.

None of us has an intuitive grasp of decibels, so let's put those numbers into perspective: The threshold of human hearing is 1 decibel, a quiet conversation is about 56 dB, a 22 CB is about 132 dB, and an M16 is about 165 dB. Seem a bit strange? Well, that may be because this is a logarithmic scale, not a linear one. Thus, a 3 dB decrease in sound means that there is only half the original sound pressure level. A 10 dB decrease is only 1/10th as loud, a 20 dB decrease is 1/100th as loud, and a 30 dB decrease is 1/1000th as loud.

Let's relate that to some data. AWC's Archangel muzzle can decrease the sound signature of a Ruger 77/22 from 132 to 106 decibels when using Federal CB Longs (Table 6). That's a 26 dB reduction (Table 3), which is about 1/400th as loud as the unsuppressed gun. Pulling the trigger on an empty chamber of a Ruger 77/22 produces 112 dB, while the 77/22 firing pin hitting the virgin rim of a once-fired case produces 94 dB.

Fine. The data provide a valid way of comparing the performance of suppressors. But how does this relate to useful performance? An 18 dB reduction probably represents about minimum acceptable performance by modern standards, a 24 dB reduction is very good, and anything over 30 dB is outstanding. A sound signature at 1 meter of 126 dB seems like a pellet rifle, while 118 dB sounds like a BB gun. A sound signature of 110 dB tends to make observers giggle in disbelief.

A suppressed 22 is guaranteed to put the fun back into shooting, open up many new and more convenient places to shoot, and provide an excellent teaching aid for instructors. Suppressors solve the serious problem of noise pollution from gunshots and make shooters better neighbors. Suppressor technology has reached an impressive sophistication, and inflation has rendered the federal transfer tax affordable. Considering all this, the 1990s may be the dawn of the Golden Age of Suppressors. ●

TABLE 6
Sound Signatures in Decibels of Integrally Suppressed 22-Caliber Rifles

Rifle	Suppressor	Federal Hi-Power HV LR	Hansen Standard Velocity LR	RWS Subsonic LR	Federal Hi-Power CB Longs	Temperature Degrees Fahrenheit
Browning Takedown	Ciener	117	116	114	—	72
Ruger 10/22	AWC R10	122	—	—	—	−12
Ruger 10/22	Norrell	126	—	—	—	−12
Ruger 10/22	AWC R10	118	—	—	—	65
Ruger 10/22	Ciener	119C	119C	—	—	28
Marlin 780 Bolt Action	Ciener	124	121	115	111	83

TABLE 7
Sound Signatures in Decibels of 22-Caliber Muzzle-Cans

Guns	Suppressor	Federal Hi-Power HV LR	Hansen Standard Velocity LR	RWS Subsonic LR	Federal Hi-Power CB Longs	Temperature Degrees Fahrenheit
Ruger 77/22	Vaime A8	121	118	113	106	50
Ruger 77/22	AWC Archangel	117	114	113	106	50
Ruger 77/22	AWC Project C	129	—	116	106	75
Winchester Model 69	Maxim Model 1921	130	130	115	110	72
CAR-15 with 22 kit	AWC MK-9 9mm baffles	—	124	—	—	78
CAR-15 with 22 kit	Larand/Norrell	—	123	—	—	78

Silencer Manufacturers

AWC Systems Technology
P.O. Box 41938
Phoenix, AZ 85080-1938
602-780-1050

Blaylock Gun Works
Rt. 3, Box 103-A Lot 25
Victoria, TX 77901
512-573-2744

Ciener, Jonathan Arthur
6850 Riveredge Drive
Titusville, FL 32780
407-268-1921

Developmental Concepts
Rt. 4, New Henderson Road
Clinton, TN 37716
615-945-1428

DLO Manufacturing
415 Howe Avenue
Shelton, CT 06484
203-924-2952

Fleming Firearms
7720 E. 126 Street N.
Collinsville, OK 74021
918-371-3624

John Norrell Arms
2608 Grist Mill Road
Little Rock, AR 72207
501-225-7864

Precision Arms International, Inc.
Rt. 17, Box 456
Saluda, VA 23149
804-758-5233

S&H Arms Manufacturing Company
Rt. 3, Box 689
Berryville, AR 72616
501-545-3511

Sound Technology
P.O. Box 1132
Kodiak, AK 99615
907-486-8448

South Central Research Corporation
P.O. Box 660
Katy, TX 77492-0660
713-492-6332

Ward Machine
5620 Lexington Road
Corpus Christi, TX 78412
512-992-1221

by DON ZUTZ

SHOTGUN REVIEW

IF THERE is a central theme running through the U.S. shotgun scene for 1992, it pivots on the modification of established designs to fit niche markets. With just a few exceptions, there are no spanking-new shotguns around this year. Existing smoothbores have been bobbed for turkey hunting; they've been splattered butt to muzzle by camouflage patterns; some side-by-sides have been given factory-installed choke tubes; others have been the recipients of rifled barrels for slug shooting. A number of gunmakers are finally waking up to the fact that Sporting Clays is here to stay and, suddenly, after the best of America's hunting lies behind it, we are breaking with traditions and making scatterguns weather resistant by the attachment of synthetic stocks and forends.

If there is any consolation in these current practices of altering basic guns for specialized use, it is that the existing guns on which the variations are set were pretty good stuff. Remington's revamping of the Model 11-87, for example, ain't too shabby a project. In many respects, the Remington 11-87 Sporting Clays gun is a new concept which improves responsiveness considerably over the original M11-87. And since the 11-87 is, like its predecessor Model 1100, a natural pointer, this variant of the Remington autoloading family is sure to impact other shotgunning disciplines and hunting as well as Sporting Clays. Indeed, if one truly noteworthy change has

been made in the characteristics of any established shotgun for 1992, it is in the Remington Sporting Clays concept.

Another interesting variation which springs from good stock is the Beretta Model 686

Ultralight Onyx. Made with the same locks, bolts, and low profile as the basic 680 Series, this one has an alloy receiver that helps drop the overall weight to about 5¾ *in 12-gauge!* It carries like a wand but, with 28-inch barrels, retains enough discipline for good upland wingshooting, especially on flushed birds. A sensible hunter won't use robust rounds in it, of course, but high-quality trap loads can get a lot done in the uplands.

A key to the Beretta Ultralight O/U's strength is found in a titanium plate set to act as the standing breech. It'll absorb wear and recoil abuse. For those who like a fancier gun, the Beretta catalog also shows a Model 687EL in the same Ultralight mode with sideplates nicely adorned. But whatever the grade, these feathery Berettas give the upland hunter a 12 that carries like a 410. And what I like about this concept is that the 12-gauge dimensioning provides one with a gripping sensation that is more hand-filling than that found on the equally light but slimmer lesser gauges.

With those two samples leading the way, let's turn to an alphabetized list of other shotguns and shotgun suppliers that have noteworthy news for 1992:

American Arms

Here's where you get the lightest semi-automatic shotguns around, the Franchi 48/AL, which scales about 5½ pounds in 20-gauge and 6½ in 12. During the past year, the 48/AL's recoil-operated system has been changed to a Benelli-like rotary bolt rather than its former Browning long-recoil system.

American Arms still maintains a long list of doubles, both O/U and SxS. The Silver Series of stackbarrels is now available in target grades as well as the traditional lightweight field grades. The target models have long, 2½-inch forcing cones with mildly (0.735-inch) over-bored barrels and can be had ported.

Arrieta

As the price of handmade British doubles soared like a moon-shot rocket, bird-gun fanciers looked to other sources for affordable, yet excellent, side-

Winchester's Model 1300 Series III National Wild Turkey gun has rifle sights and WinCam® laminated stock and forend.

Harrington & Richardson is back with loads of singles, including a 10-gauge Turkey Gun at a modest price, a rifled-barrel slug gun with sights, and the famous old Topper.

Harrington & Richardson's singles mean more young hunters can enjoy the thrills of hunting.

by-sides in game gun styling. Arrieta doubles are attracting considerable attention as a means for filling this price gap. One of the best ever from Iberian gunmakers, the Arrietas are true sidelocks with surprising attention to detail. Several importers work with Arrieta, and the guns are not difficult to obtain on a custom basis.

Benelli

With its 3½-inch 12-gauge chamber, the Benelli Super Black Eagle was the major innovation of 1991. For '92, the Benelli, as handled by Heckler & Koch, has been given a 24-inch rifled slug barrel to extend the SBE's versatility. H&K no longer carries the Renato Gamba guns, as Gamba has decided to go it alone, but H&K does handle the prestigious Heym pieces, which can be had in over/under rifle, combination (rifle/shotgun), or shotgun modes. These are fine Germanic guns with plenty of hand craftsmanship well in evidence.

Beretta

One of the few totally new guns is the Beretta Model A390ST gas-urged autoloader. Sporting a minor humpback on its receiver top, the A390ST has a self-regulating pressure valve so a hunter can just put in the shotshells in any order and shoot! And Beretta is making a Sporting Clays version of the 20-gauge Model A-303, plus the over/under Model 682 is offered in a Sporting Clays version.

Bernardelli

Handled by Magnum Research, Inc., of Minneapolis, Italian-made Bernardelli side-by-sides of the Hemingway model will now be available in 28-gauge. These come in two grades, the Hemingway and the Hemingway Deluxe. Both are boxlocks, but the Deluxe gun has false sideplates, better wood. Interesting for their profiles and features, Hemingways tend to have some things in common with the Churchill XXV guns. Barrels are 25½ inches long and are bored Skeet No. 1 and Skeet No. 2; the splinter forend is relatively long; stock has swan-belly underline.

Browning

In an era when pump guns have been getting cheaper and cheaper, Browning has done a surprise 180-degree turn to bring out a Pigeon Grade BPS with select walnut and gold trim. Also new are a pair of speciality BPS "Game Guns"—the Deer Special and Turkey Special, for which there are matching screw-in choke tubes for slugs (rifled) and ultra-tight turkey clusters. Magnum-grade BPS pumps will now wear the same engraving on their slab-sided receivers as the standard grades, and the reproduction Model 42 410 pump will finally become available.

In autoloaders, the famed ol' Auto-5 has been given a synthetic stock/forend tandem, and with its dull finish becomes part of the Browning "Stalker" concept. The Model A-500G is being cataloged in a Sporting Clays version with 30-inch barrel and 3-inch chamber, but it is difficult to tell it from the field grade A-500G except for the scripted "Sporting Clays" moniker. However, the A-500G does have a high rib for those who like target visibility.

FIAS

Moderately priced FIAS over/

unders are being handled by KBI, Inc. This importer also seems to have the inside track on Russian Baikal shotguns, but availability depends on Russia's being granted most-favored-nation trading privileges.

Gamba (Renato)

Gamba has decided to drop away from importers and handle its own business in the U.S. (Gamba U.S.A., 925 Wilshire Blvd., Santa Monica, CA 90401) These are high-quality guns with big tickets, are something to see and possess good dynamics in target grades.

H&R 1871, Inc.

After some struggles with red ink, Harrington & Richardson is back with new people and a pair of tradenames—New England Firearms and H&R 1871, Inc. The New England items are the lower-priced singles, while the H&R 1871 series has a bit more quality and is based on the grand old Topper design. The lines include junior-sized pieces and run into 10-gauge magnums covered with camo. It's nice to find an active manufacturer in the break-action single shot field, again. Some 3½-inch 12-gauge magnums have screw-in choke tubes.

Ithaca

Ithaca has teamed up with Brenneke to make a rifled Deerslayer that matches the characteristics of Brenneke's new "Golden Slug." This gun is on the proven Ithaca Model 87 frame with a 1:25 rifling twist. The wood is oiled, and the gun is said to deliver exciting groups with the new slug.

Krieghoff International Inc.

Because of demands from the Sporting Clays crowd, Krieghoff has begun putting 32-inch barrels on the K-80 Sporting gun. Otherwise, the K-80 line remains intact.

Lanber

Lanber makes some of the best over/unders ever turned out in Spain. It now has a gas-operated autoloader that has nice lines reminiscent of the Beretta A-303. Some are handled by American Arms, Inc.

Laurona

Another Spanish gunmaker that has established itself stateside, Laurona has beefed up its receivers for 1992 so that rifle barrels can also be affixed. These will be over/under rifle

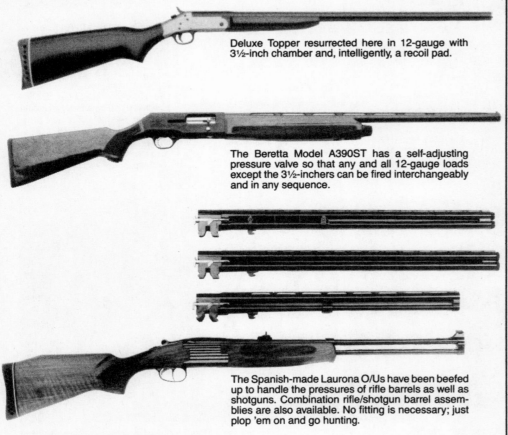

Deluxe Topper resurrected here in 12-gauge with 3½-inch chamber and, intelligently, a recoil pad.

The Beretta Model A390ST has a self-adjusting pressure valve so that any and all 12-gauge loads except the 3½-inchers can be fired interchangeably and in any sequence.

The Spanish-made Laurona O/Us have been beefed up to handle the pressures of rifle barrels as well as shotguns. Combination rifle/shotgun barrel assemblies are also available. No fitting is necessary; just plop 'em on and go hunting.

The Tar-Hunt bolt-action "shotgun" is made for precision slug shooting with a Shaw rifled barrel torqued tightly into a custom-made receiver *a la* benchrest rifles. Other refinements are worked into the rig for optimum accuracy. Two-inch groups have been reported over 100 yards!

assemblies and combination rifle-shotgun units. The added girth on the receiver will take rifle pressures, and the barrels are extra hard.

In straight shotguns, Laurona offers the Silhouette 600-X and Olympic 92-X lines, both in game, trap, and in Sporting Clays configurations. The guns boast anti-rust black chrome and choke tubes with parabolic interior profiles.

Merkel

The great Merkel guns, both side-by-sides and over/unders, are now being distributed by G.S.I., Inc. This franchise has bounced around a lot in the past double decade, but the Merkels are still fine old examples of European gunmaking.

Mossberg

The Mossberg Model 9200 gas-operated autoloader is said to handle all 2¾- and 3-inch 12-gauge loads interchangeably, thanks to one of those self-adjusting pressure-valve systems. Meanwhile, Mossberg's original M5500 semi-auto has been laced with full-coverage camo, and a combo offering finds the regular-finished M5500 available with a 28-inch field barrel and 24-inch rifled barrel with cantilever scope mount.

In pump guns, Mossberg has upgraded the Model 835, calling it the M835 Regal and giving it a high-gloss finish with a dual-comb potential for two different comb heights: one for slug shooting, the other for wingshooting.

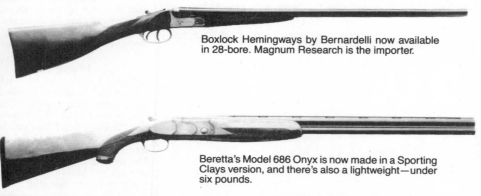

Boxlock Hemingways by Bernardelli now available in 28-bore. Magnum Research is the importer.

Beretta's Model 686 Onyx is now made in a Sporting Clays version, and there's also a lightweight—under six pounds.

Perazzi

Long a premier builder of high-grade competition guns, Perazzi has introduced two new models for 1992, the MX-7 and MX-9. The MX-7 is pointed toward the Sporting Clays and trapshooting arena, while the MX-9 is a higher-priced piece, a trap combo, with an adjustable comb and a new center rib block to change the height of the center bead for pattern placement manipulation.

Precision Sports

A division of the Cortland Line Co., this outfit has assembled a complete array of side-by-sides within reasonable price ranges. For 1992, the 10- and 12-gauge doubles will be given screw-in chokes, which is hardly common in horizontal doubles. The company's American-style M640s have some of the best pointing qualities I've found on lower-priced doubles. Precision Sports is also handling the Bill Hanus "Birdgun II" that can be had with a hard case in 16-, 20-, 28-gauge.

Parker Reproductions

Although the Parker Reproductions are no longer made, a sizable inventory remains and the company is working on a novel plan to supply 16-gauge barrels with some 20-gauge models for a 16, 20 bi-gauge set.

Remington

Besides the light-contour barrels for the 11-87 and 870 as mentioned above, and beyond the new Sporting Clays variant of the 11-87, Remington has added full camouflage treatment to the 11-87 and 870 Special Purpose ("SP") guns. There is also a Special Purpose Synthetic in the 870 line with a 21-inch Turkey barrel and extra-full-choke tube, and a Model 11-87 short-barreled turkey gun which, with 21-inch barrel and total Trebark® camo coverage, has been designated the National Wild Turkey Federation's gun of the year.

The popular M870 Express package has been extended to include a 20-gauge combo pairing a 28-inch field barrel with a Deer barrel with sights. And for mariners and survivalists, the 870 riot piece (18-inch Cylinder barrel) has been finished with an electroless nickel plating inside and out. With its synthetic stock/forend, the M870 Marine Magnum will thwart the impacts of salt water.

The Remington M11-87 Sporting Clays gun has a shortened forend assembly plus a new light-contour barrel for brisk, yet smooth, dynamics. It can also serve as a very effective field gun.

Remington's Model 870 has a light-contour barrel that shaves about a half-pound from the Wingmaster.

The newest Franchi gas-operated autoloader is exclusive this year to Ducks Unlimited as the Banquet Gun.

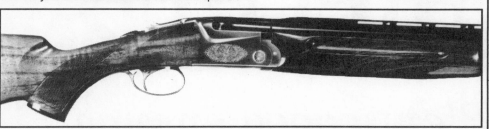

New SKB target guns come with lengthened forcing cones, mildly overbored (0.735-inch) barrels, and a wide step-up competition rib to add weight to the barrel and to disperse rising heat waves.

Shaw 12-gauge rifled barrel and McMillan fiberglass stock. The action and barrel are joined for maximum vibration-free stability according to the same pattern as a benchrest rifle for optimum slug accuracy. The barrel has a 1:36 twist because that's what experience has proved to be right for this rig, which can consistently punch 2-inch groups at 100 yards with certain loads. A boon for deer hunters in agricultural slug-only country, the outfit runs around $1,200 without a scope, but there's a lot of workmanship in each gun.

Tikka

This is the new name for the

complete with a high-sitting ventilated rib, beaver-tailed forearm, and pistol-gripped stock. The barrel is 21 inches. For economy and versatility, T/C 22 rimfire/centerfire barrels can be fitted to same action.

Weatherby

Weatherby continues the Athena and Orion O/Us, expanding the series with a Sporting Clays model that has long cones and a slightly wider bore plus screw-in tubes. There is a trim 28-gauge in the line, and it also has screw-in chokes. Stocked in the Weatherby/California style.

Winchester by U.S. Repeating Arms

Suddenly owned by a French investing group, which also owns Browning, U.S. Repeating Arms has few new shotgun items except a trio of Model 1300 Turkey Guns of various modes. The top dog has a set of open rifle sights for pattern placement with tight-shooting chokes and slugs plus some mechanically applied engraving

The Arrieta doubles offer the lines of British game guns and not the price tag, but still have excellent workmanship.

Ruger

The Ruger Red Label field gun is now made with choice of an English-style (straight) grip or a normal Ruger pistol grip. Formerly, only Orvis had some Rugers made up this way, but now Ruger is spreading the straight-gripped stuff around in both 12- and 20-gauge.

A Red Label Sporting Clays gun is also coming on line with a 30-inch barrel assembly that enlivens the gun by being somewhat lighter than the field-grade gun's 28-inch barrels. Too, the Sporting Clays gun will have longer choke tubes of 2⅞ inches which, the company claims, will lower the recoil thrust.

SKB

After years of absence, side-by-sides are back in the SKB line. So, too, is there an upgraded series of target-grade guns with lengthened forcing cones and overbored barrels. The Sporting Clays guns are made in 12-, 20-, and 28-gauge with a wide, step-up rib that adds to barrel momentum and smoothness while also dispersing rising heat waves. Choke tubes for the target guns have been lengthened in the 12-gauge competition guns for improved patterning. The Model 585 and 685 are good-looking boxlocks; the 885 is a beauty with false sideplates and gorgeous wood.

Tar-Hunt

This one demands a longer explanation than we can give it here. Suffice it to say that the Model RSG-12 is a bolt-action slug gun built on a specially designed and custom-built receiver/bolt assembly with a

Precision Sports handles the Bill Hanus Birdguns as well as myriad SxS models via Parker-Hale of England.

former Valmet shotguns, and the newest product is a Sporting Clays gun. Like all the Valmet rigs, barrels are interchangeable and double rifle rigs can be put on the receiver.

Thompson/Center

Thompson/Center isn't really a shotgun outfit, but there is a snazzy 410 in the Carbine line,

denoting the National Wild Turkey Federation. The intermediate gun of this Series III has a rib rather than sights and is without the engraving, while a third gun is sized for junior hunters and milady as a 20-gauge Turkey piece. All have camo carrying straps and the WinCam® laminated stock/forend fittings. ●

GET COMPLETE DETAILS . . . . .

Our illustrated catalog listings for shotguns now on the market begin on page 378.

by SAM FADALA

How Good Are FACTORY RIFLES?

Plenty good enough and far, far better than they used to be.

The legendary Model 70—right out of the box. How well does it shoot?

"THERE'S A moose. He's bedded down below us," reported Mike Wade, my outfitter. We were on a steep aspen slope at high altitude. I had my Moses Stick with me, a hiking staff I carry in the mountains. I screwed my riflescope up to 10x, steadying the forestock of the Model 70 on the walking stick for solid aim. Most of the moose was blocked by aspens. Only his most northern and southern exposures showed, neither part of anatomy providing a target. There was, however, a narrow lane open to a piece of shoulder. Boom!

"You missed," Mike said. I told him no, the moose just skidded downhill without getting up. We paced the 125 yards to the moose's bed. He wasn't in it. He was piled up ten yards below.

A moose is big, but the target offered on this particular animal was small. Accuracy got that bull. I knew my

Groups are how you tell—measured from the centers of the two farthest-apart bullet holes.

hunting rifle had the ability to deliver a bullet precisely or I wouldn't have shot at all. I can recite a number of similar instances: an elk bedded in the timber with only its head and a couple of inches of neck showing; a mule deer buck across a draw with even less to shoot at.

Accuracy made the difference in tagging these and many other game animals that presented only a patch of vitals to shoot at. But what is accuracy, or more to the point, what is hunting accuracy? Is a four-inch group at 100 yards good enough? A six-inch pattern? It depends. If a shooter can put bullet after bullet into a six-inch circle at 100 yards in the field he's going to take home a lot of venison. Double the distance, double the group size and this hunter will still do all right. Most big game is taken within 200 yards of the hunter anyway, and most big game has a kill zone of at least 12 by 12 inches. By these standards, every big game rifle currently offered makes the accuracy grade, right out of the box—no tuning required, provided neck shots at 200 yards are forbidden. However, in order for a shooter to keep his bullets inside a six-inch circle at 100 yards in the field, the rifle should be capable of a far smaller group size off the bench—two- to three-inch clusters at 100 yards. Many shooters want even greater bullet-placing precision.

The magic accuracy number assigned to bolt-action big game rifles these days is "one"—one minute of angle, which in practical terms means an inch center to center at 100 yards, two inches at 200 yards, three inches at 300 yards, and so forth. But how accurately do rifles shoot out of the box?

That little question led to a lot of benchresting with a great variety of sporting rifles. The results were surprisingly good—not that all test rifles earned a minute-of-angle badge, but all proved that today's factory rifle, coupled with modern factory ammo, provides a hunter with an accuracy edge that pays off when the target is not a deer, but only part of a deer. Out-of-the-box shooting warmed up with an untouched Model 94 carbine chambered for the 30-30. A couple 1.5-inch three-shot groups resulted. But they were flukes and no more realistic than a guy making a half-court shot with a basketball. He can do it once. But can he do it every time? Not likely.

Neither could this scoped carbine shoot a 1.5-inch 100-yard group every time for three shots, three bullet holes being my test for out-of-the-box accuracy. Why three-shot groups? I decided on three-shot strings measured with calipers from the centers of the two farthest apart bullet holes and interpreted to a tenth of an inch, i.e.: ".75-inch center to center." Three-shot groups provide sufficient information without bias. Had I wanted to give the rifles an edge, I would have used "weighted data," whereby ten shots are fired but only the best cluster of five is reported. Weighted data are not an unreasonable idea, because human error is taken into account, the best cluster of five bullet holes out of ten indicating what the rifle *can* do rather than what the shooter *cannot* do. Therefore, three three-shot groups were recorded for a total of nine shots per rifle for each specific load. Variable-power scopes were used, all set at 8x. I looked for a mode, a prevalent group size. Sometimes several three-shot groups were fired before a particular rifle with a particular load provided that mode. A machine rest would have been better, but a clear picture of potential accuracy emerges with repeated shooting.

The Model 94 wasn't a 1.5-incher at 100 yards; it was a 2.5-incher off the bench, on average, with factory fodder. If our only interest were big game sporting rifles limited to 200 yards maximum range on animals of pronghorn size and larger, we'd rise from our cracker barrels, brush off the seats of our pants, shut the damper on the woodburning stove and go home, because a hunter can buy any current sporting rifle, stick a scope on it, purchase a box of factory ammo and never look back.

It isn't that simple, however, if you're interested in seeing how different factory rifles shoot out of the box. There are considerations: action type, barrel weight, overall rifle weight, choice of cartridge, bedding variations of action and barrel, stock style, sights, various ammunition choices and triggers. The action story, I thought, would be simply told like this: "If the goal is bullet grouping without regard for other factors, choose a bolt-action rifle and be happy." Out of the box, best groups do attend the boltgun, in general. But a Ruger No. 1 spoiled the story. Chambered for the 270 Weatherby Magnum cartridge firing factory ammo, this

Two accurate cartridges, the 308 Winchester and the 7mm-08 Remington, which produced excellent groups in these tests.

No. 1 produced .75-inch groups with boring regularity—right out of the box.

The bolt-action rifle did edge the slide-action, semi-auto, lever-action and most single shots; action type alone did not dictate accuracy. Barrel weight was also a deciding factor, even for three-shot groups. This was not directly from the bulk of the barrel or slower barrel heating so much, but from the steadying effect of the heftier tube. A Ruger 77 lightweight rifle, for example, provided ample accuracy, but its own brother, another Model 77, whipped the lightweight model in terms of repeated bullet grouping. I contend the heavier barrel had the accuracy edge because of stability. Precisely the same can be said of rifle weight. A couple flyweights shot remarkable benchrest groups; however, these rifles demanded careful control or they performed poorly. In a side test, I shot accurate super lightweight rifles from the seat of my pants along with heavier rifles in the same caliber. The heavier rifles won all bets once the bench was left behind, even though these particular lightweight rifles were highly accurate from the bench.

Cartridge choice provided a big surprise. Only recently have I conceded that the actual design of the cartridge is important to its accuracy potential. I always held that accuracy is primarily a matter of good bullets out of good barrels, but no longer can I testify against cartridge design in the high court of accuracy. Theory holds that short, fat cartridges are more accurate than long skinny ones. I fired two Winchester Model 70 rifles, both brand new, both fitted with the same 3.5-10x test scope set at 8x. One Model 70 was chambered for the 30-06 Springfield. The other was chambered for the 308 Winchester. The 308 won all bets. Coincidence? Chance? Individual rifle variation? I don't think so. The 308 Winchester cartridge created prize groups in other rifles as well. For example, after obtaining a group size of .60-inch at 100 yards with the 308 Model 70, 22-inch barrel, I tried the same factory RWS Match ammo in a Ruger Model 77 International with 18.5-inch barrel and got the same tiny group from the Ruger, right on the button—.60-inch center-to-center for three shots.

The accuracy/cartridge design octopus held me in its tentacles. I couldn't get away. At one point, I had an out-of-the-box Sako Varminter duking it out with a custom Sako rifle, the latter designed for top-grade accuracy with target barrel and PPC insert (for closer breech tolerances). The factory rifle won—every time. It shouldn't have. The difference, I am certain, lay in the cartridge. The factory single shot bolt-action Sako was chambered for the 22 PPC USA cartridge, while the custom Sako single shot bolt-action rifle was chambered for the 222 Remington. The 222 is a fine cartridge and I'd buy a 222-chambered rifle any time, but the 22 PPC USA round was the winner

in grouping bullets. Groups of .33-inch were common for the 22 PPC USA. Groups in the ½-inch realm were associated with the custom 222 Sako rifle. But even this head-to-head competition didn't surpass the results of testing out-of-the-box rifles chambered for the 308 Winchester round. *In no shootout did a 308 lose to a similar rifle chambered for another round.* Individual rifles may prove to be exceptions because no two rifles are exactly alike. Two rifles would have to have absolutely identical chambers, cartridge lockup dimensions and precisely the barrel specs for a perfect matchup. Two rifles may be almost identical, but never 100 percent identical.

On the other hand, notions about big rounds being inaccurate were extinguished like a match under a faucet. A Weatherby Mark V rifle in 416 Weatherby Magnum, straight out of the box, provided the following results for four three-shot groups: .66-inch, .81-inch, 1.00-inch, 1.25-inch. Two boxes of factory ammo were fired. Not one group over 1.5-inch center-to-center was recorded. So much for big bores lacking accuracy.

Incidentally, two other Mark Vs were tested, both in 257 Weatherby Magnum, 24-inch barrel and 26-inch barrel. Both rifles produced groups under .75-inch with factory ammo with a number of groups falling in the .50-inch column. Mark Vs are accurate.

Bedding of barrel and action provided another winding trail. Rifles that had free-floated barrels shot fine. Rifles that were pressure-pointed shot fine. This follows exactly what Dale Storey, noted gunmaker, and I discovered. We studied barrel bedding for two years, trying to say something definitive. We couldn't. Pressure-pointed test rifles that shot poorly were free-floated for improved accuracy. Free-floated rifles that shot poorly were pressure-pointed for improved accuracy. Conclusion: Excellent out-of-the-box accuracy was shown with factory rifles that had free-floated barrels and

Today's sporting rifle is generally fitted with a scope sight. Scopes were set at 8x for all tests here.

Fadala smoothed triggers and installed scopes for testing—no rebedding, though.

The PCC cartridges, one shown here with the 220 Swift, suggest that cartridge design has a lot to do with rifle accuracy.

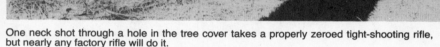

One neck shot through a hole in the tree cover takes a properly zeroed tight-shooting rifle, but nearly any factory rifle will do it.

with factory rifles that had pressure-pointed barrels.

Stock style—one-piece versus two-piece—was addressed, but the letter was marked "lost in the mail." No message was received. The rifles that shot absolutely best wore one-piece stocks, but what about the Ruger No. 1 that provided Scrooge-like groups throughout testing? If two-piece stocks cause poor accuracy, the No. 1 didn't show it.

Sights: Iron-sighted rifles created fatter groups than the same rifle scoped. Nothing new here. Getting all the bullets to land inside of six inches at 100 yards with irons was hard work. I won't accept all blame for these pizza-diet groups because I like irons and use them often on muzzleloaders. But some sights were in effect crude, put on the rifle for reasons of convention, not use. With proper iron sights, results were not so bad. The Ruger 77 International in 308 made me blink with 2.0-inch to 2.5-inch 100-yard groups with factory ammo and iron sights. But when a 2.5-8x Bushnell scope was attached to the same rifle, groups shrank like denim pants in boiling water. Another easy-to-back-up pronouncement: higher magnification provided best groups. The 77 International was temporarily fitted with a straight 4x scope. One session later, that 4x scope was replaced with

a 2.5-8x. Group size decreased as magnification increased—every time.

Specific choice of ammunition was another major factor in out-of-the-box accuracy. Ammo advertised for its accuracy *was*. For example, the surprising .60-inch groups earned by the Model 70 Winchester and Model 77 Ruger both in 308 were fired with RWS Match ammo. Groups with these accurate rifles shooting standard fodder just about doubled in size to about .90-inch center-to-center. I used special accuracy factory ammunition such as Winchester Supreme for part of each test where such ammo was available. Supreme matched my handloads for accuracy. A Browning semi-automatic 30-06 firing Winchester Supreme ammunition provided groups 50 percent tighter than the same rifle firing standard 30-06 ammo. This is not an indictment against standard hunting loads. Obviously, ammunition must be selected with specific bullet performance in mind. I would not use 308 match ammo, for example, on big game, regardless of the extra accuracy. The shooter interested in gaining best accuracy from his out-of-the-box rifle should buy a small supply of different ammo and benchtest *his personal rifle*. Accuracy definitely varies with ammo choice.

Because ammo choices made a sig-

nificant difference in 100-yard accuracy, no rifle was fired with only one type of ammunition, except where there was no choice. I tried to keep things constant and factory all the way, even though this exercise was not a scientific experiment, but only a one-man demonstration.

However, I did fudge on triggers. I cannot say enough good about the modern factory rifle. As for factory ammo, I've shot a lot of it over the years and I've never seen the tight-group results I'm getting now. However, not one factory rifle came with its trigger set at what I felt met the trigger's safe mechanical potential. I can explain why in two words: product liability. The modern trigger is, through design, capable of a crisp and light let-off. Furthermore, I do not like target triggers on hunting rifles. A super lightweight trigger has no place in the big game field. But some of the triggers on some of the test rifles broke at six pounds. These triggers were professionally tuned by a gunsmith for a lighter, crisper release, always with total safety in mind.

Aside from disappointing factory trigger pulls, the various test rifles showed well. The single most accurate rifle out of the box was a Sako Varminter in 6mm PPC USA. Its inclusion was not cheating because that round is

This mule deer, tagged by Nancy Fadala, was dropped at well over 200 yards. The factory Sako 7mm-08 put the bullet right where Mrs. Fadala wanted it.

In this pair of Model 70 7mm Magnums, the custom-made one—restocked, tuned, bedded—shot smaller groups than the one straight from the factory—barely.

legal for big game in many areas. I got two antelope with my test rifle in 6mm PPC USA using handloads with appropriate bullets loaded up to snuff.

What was learned from the factory sporting rifle accuracy shootout? Bolt-action rifles were, as a class, most accurate. The Remington Model 700, for example, especially in 308 Winchester, could be counted on to print under minute-of-angle groups all day, typical of modern bolt-action rifles shooting ammo that the individual rifle happens to like. On the other hand, other action styles provided ample hunting accuracy, particularly a lever-action Browning in 243 Winchester that earned inch-sized 100-yard groups. I also concluded that barrel weight made a difference in rifle control, as well as barrel heat-up with repeated shots, but medium-weight barrels provided ample sporting rifle accuracy.

I also decided that flyweight rifles were fine from the bench, but not as stable as heavier rifles when fired from field positions. Another conclusion: Big bore cartridges are not inaccurate, but there are "accuracy cartridges" that prevail because of their design. As for bedding, tight action/stock fit is desirable, but no proof exists that free-floated barrels on sporting rifles are more accurate than pressure-pointed barrels, across the board, or vice versa. While the one-piece stock probably has the highest potential for providing best accuracy, two-piece stocks on rifles that exhibit close tolerances in all other regards, such as cartridge lockup in the action, can provide fine accuracy. Item: Scopes make a big difference in bullet clustering, as anyone would guess, with high-magnification providing the best chance for tightest groups. Another conclusion: Ammunition advertised as special in regard to accuracy is special. Item: Triggers, while well-designed, are often factory-set to require over five pounds let-off.

Capsulizing the findings of this information one-man shootfest can be accomplished in one sentence: The modern rifle, shooting standard factory ammunition, is capable of better-than-hunting grade accuracy right out of the box without tuning. On the other hand, accuracy may be improved by the professional gunsmith through rebedding an action or altering the barrel/stock relationship or fixing the trigger.

Regardless of this, the hunter is pretty well off with an untouched rifle shooting over-the-counter ammo. Finally, I doubt that store-bought sporting grade rifles and ammo were more accurate during any previous time in history than they are right now. ●

WHERE THE SHARPS SHINES

by DENNIS BRUNS

THE MODEL 1875 is the Sharps rifle that didn't quite happen in the 19th century. It was developed by the Sharps Rifle Company in 1875 as a lightened and simplified version of their popular Model 1874 rifle which, in spite of *its* name, had been more or less in production since 1869 and was based on earlier designs going back 25 years or more. The Model 1874 rifle was a complicated action, difficult to manufacture and unnecessarily heavy, but it was successful.

The Model 1875 was trimmed down to reduce weight for the benefit of target shooters who wanted to use the heaviest possible barrel for better accuracy, while keeping their rifles within the 10-pound weight limit imposed by match rules of the day. The

action was simplified to reduce manufacturing costs and make the Sharps rifles more competitive with those of other manufacturers, particularly the Remington rolling block rifles. Application for a patent on the Model 1875 Sharps action was made in March, 1876, and two Model 1875 Sharps rifles were exhibited at the Philadelphia Centennial Exposition which opened on April 1, 1876. One prototype, a military rifle, was awarded a bronze medal by the Centennial Exposition as one of the best weapons in its class. The fate of this rifle after the exposition closed is unknown. The second prototype, a long-range target rifle, survives today in a private collection.

In the end, the 1875 Sharps was not to be. By July of 1876, the Sharps

Company had decided to drop it. A new action, the Model 1878, or Sharps-Borchardt, was developed to replace the old Model 1874, with production beginning late in 1877. The hammerless Sharps-Borchardt was a good action,

The author with a practice pig. The course of fire is the standard silhouette course at standard ranges, but not all off-hand.

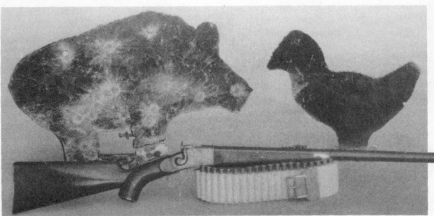

Sharps Long Range Rifle, cartridge belt, and pig and chicken silhouettes.

but it was not as popular with sportsmen as the old Model 1874 it replaced. In an era of riflemen who had learned to shoot using muzzleloaders, then switched to the new-fangled breechloaders, the Sharps-Borchardt probably went a little too far too fast. The Sharps Rifle Manufacturing Company—in hindsight—would probably have been better off making the Model 1875 rifle which, with its side-mounted hammers, would have seemed more like an "honest to God rifle" to the traditionalists of the day.

Several years ago, C. Sharps Arms, of Big Timber, Montana, began making a recreated version of the Model 1875 Sharps. The Model 1875 rifle is

though I have usually been able to make my old conversion Sharps and Trapdoor Springfield rifles deliver two minute of angle accuracy for five-shot groups, and even made a number of minute-of-angle groups when things happen to work out just right.

Since I began shooting the New Model 1875 Sharps rifles though, I have fired enough five-shot groups running minute of angle or better to consider such accuracy normal. The fact is, these rifles will shoot better than I can see using iron sights. Anytime five-shot groups run larger than two inches at 100 yards in good weather, I can start trying to figure out what I've done wrong because I know it's not the rifle.

To date, most of 1875 Sharps rifles

dual-purpose large rifle primers (number WLR, for use with both standard and magnum loads) seem to work best. Federal large rifle or large rifle magnum (#210 or #215) are the next best choice. I don't recommend Winchester large rifle magnum (only) and CCI primers. Pistol primers are easily fired, but seem to produce weak and erratic ignition.

Another characteristic of the NM1875 Sharps action is that it does not have either a rebounding hammer or a firing pin retractor. When the hammer is all the way down, it locks into the top of the breechblock and pushes the tip of the firing pin forward into the chamber where it will strike the bottom of the chamber as the breechblock is lowered. Therefore, the

New Model 1875 Sharps Long Range Rifle with wind-gauge front sight and mid-range tang sight.

doing better the second time around with more than a thousand rifles produced to date. Since the original Model 1875 Sharps never actually went into production, it would not be correct to call new Model 1875 rifles reproductions. Also, the quality of the new rifles is so much better than what has been associated with the term "replica" over the last couple of decades that it seems more appropriate to refer to the new rifles as New Model 1875 Sharps.

For the last two years, I have shot a number of these Model 1875s, courtesy of John Schoffstall, president of C. Sharps Arms. They are beautiful rifles with blued barrels, color case-hardened receivers, and well-fitted walnut stocks. They are rifles a shooter can take pride in and are worthy successors to the hand-crafted Sharps rifles of the last century. However, as a dedicated, paper-punching, steel-clanging target shooter, what has really impressed me about these rifles is their accuracy.

Shooting the New Model 1875 Sharps rifles has forced me to revise my opinion of the accuracy potential of large caliber breechloaders fired with blackpowder and cast bullets. The few accounts that clearly describe the level of accuracy expected from rifles in the 1870s and 1880s indicate that four minutes of angle was considered to be good shooting for a blackpowder breechloader. Modern writers seem to agree with this figure. Until recently, I probably would have too,

have been assembled using Douglas barrels. A few have been fitted with high quality barrels by other makers. This, more than anything else, accounts for the superior accuracy of the new rifles.

In addition, there is a lighter and faster acting hammer than the Model 1874 Sharps from which it was developed. This speeds up lock time and causes less jar to the rifle at the moment of firing. That lock time is more comparable to that of a High Wall Winchester or single-trigger Ballard rifle and faster than the standard set-trigger Ballards.

I have sat with a High Wall Winchester in one hand and a New Model 1875 Sharps in the other, alternatively pulling the trigger of each rifle to compare lock time and couldn't detect any difference. Set triggers are not offered on the New Model 1875 Sharps, but with a little careful stoning, the single trigger can be adjusted to a clean breaking release of two to four pounds if it didn't come that way from the factory. This should be light enough for most purposes.

While the lighter 1875 hammer speeds up lock time, it doesn't deliver as strong a blow to the primer as the heavier 1874 action. Also, there's a striker with a separate firing pin and some of the force of the light hammer blow is lost in the interaction of these parts. As a result, the NM1875 Sharps rifles I've tried shoot best with relatively sensitive primers. Winchester

hammer of a NM1875 Sharps should always be placed on half-cock before the action is opened. This should be an easily formed habit for most shooters. For that matter, it is also a good idea to do this with the Model 1874 Sharps rifles, both originals and replicas. The firing pin retractor on many of these rifles does not function properly due to wear or mismatched parts. One should never open the action of either the Model 1874 or NM1875 Sharps with the hammer on full-cock since there is considerable danger of accidentally touching the trigger and firing the rifle as the action is closed.

Most customers prefer the forend of their NM1875 rifles to be fitted tightly and uniformly against the receiver, so that's the way C. Sharps builds them. However, this is not necessarily the most accurate method of bedding the forend, since it tends to push up on the barrel. One result can be day-to-day variations in point of impact. If this is happening, loosening the two forend screws to reduce pressure on the barrel may improve accuracy.

A better solution is to fit a wood or cardboard shim into the front of the barrel lug recess in the forend so the forend sets back solidly against the breechblock spring lug under the barrel without touching the receiver. The size of the shim can be adjusted to leave a hairline gap about the thickness of heavyweight typing paper between forend and receiver without making any permanent modifications

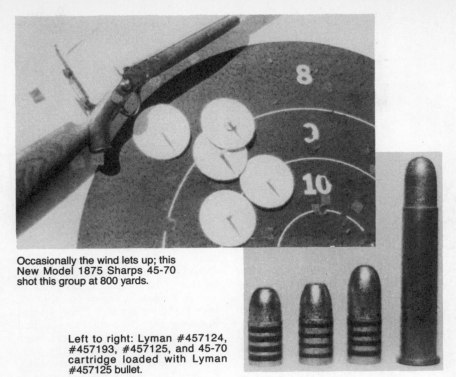

Occasionally the wind lets up; this New Model 1875 Sharps 45-70 shot this group at 800 yards.

Left to right: Lyman #457124, #457193, #457125, and 45-70 cartridge loaded with Lyman #457125 bullet.

to the forend, and without detracting from the overall appearance of the rifle.

Since ammunition companies stopped manufacturing blackpowder cartridges back in the 1920s, shooters who want to fire blackpowder cartridge rifles must, of necessity, be reloaders or pay some custom reloader to make ammunition for them. The NM1875 Sharps, with their greater accuracy potential, require, or perhaps more accurately repay, care in reloading. One cannot just casually slop cartridges together any which way and expect them to produce minute of angle groups, although this sometimes happens. To consistently achieve the full potential, the reloader needs to pay careful attention to such details as bullet seating depth, case neck tension and bullet diameter, orientation, alloy, and quality.

Most New Model 1875 Sharps, particularly those chambered for straight-sided cases, shoot best if the bullet is seated short of the rifling. The NM1875 action has very little capability for forcing overlong cartridges into the chamber anyway, and unless the barrel is wiped out carefully every shot, the build-up of blackpowder fouling will prevent such rounds from chambering.

I find my NM1875 45-70 rifles shoot the smallest groups when using the Lyman #457124, #457193, or #457125 bullets if they are seated so that the mouth of the cartridge case just covers the top grease groove, or about 1⁄16-inch short of the rifling. Most NM1875 45-70 rifles are chambered long enough that these bullets can be seated out with the top grease groove exposed and the upper driving band just touching the rifling, but doing so reduces accuracy. Seating these bullets far enough out so that they are forced a short distance into the rifling as the breechblock is closed often turns groups into patterns. Other bullet designs I have tried also seem to shoot most accurately if the bullet is seated short of the rifling by a similar amount.

In contrast, rifles chambered for the 40-70 bottleneck cartridge seem to shoot best if the bullet is seated far enough out that it is forced against the rifling as the breechblock is closed. Of course, the 40-70 has a reputation for being finicky about ammunition.

The New Model 1875 Sharps rifles are intentionally made with minimum tolerance chambers to improve accuracy. Rifles chambered for the 40-65 Winchester require a special minimum tolerance sizing die which can be purchased from C. Sharps or ordered from the die manufacturer. Tolerances are not quite as close for other cartridges, but problems can develop if the reloader happens to have a maximum tolerance sizing die or tries to load oversized bullets.

On the other hand, cases fired in tight chambers can be reloaded without resizing or with a minimum of re-

sizing which makes them last longer. Fired cases from rifles chambered for 38-55, 38-56, 40-65 Winchester, and 40-70 Sharps Straight are usually a snug fit on properly sized bullets and will shoot accurately if loaded without resizing. Rifles chambered for the 40-70 shoot best if bullets are loaded slip-fit into unsized cases. In this instance, any degree of case neck tightness seems to adversely effect accuracy. Other NM1875 rifles will shoot accurately if bullets are loaded slip-fit into unsized cases. Bullet seating depth is then determined by the powder charge, which should be compressed slightly to the proper depth, either before or as the bullet is seated into the case.

A couple of years ago I discovered (in the middle of a match, of course) that some boxes of my 45-70 blackpowder reloads were scattering shots 12 inches or more vertically at 200 yards while other boxes held to the normal 3 to 4 inches. Bullets, primers, and powders were all the same, but I had been using three different sets of loading dies, depending on where I was doing the reloading. I figured the problem had to be case neck tension—that is, tightness of fit between bullet and case. I shot the rest of my matches that year loading my bullets slip-fit into unsized cases, which reduced case neck tension to a very uniform zero and produced acceptable accuracy.

Eventually, I determined that the NM1875 Sharps I was using shot best if I used the same die set and backed the case sizing die out .35-inch. Running the expander plug of my three-die set into cases neck-sized in this manner leaves them a tight enough fit—on the Lyman #457193 or #457125 bullets—that the bullets can't be pushed into the cases with finger pressure alone; however, a light push on the handle of my loading press will do the job. Ammunition loaded this way is slightly more accurate than if bullets are slip-fit into unsized cases, and I don't have to worry about the bullet falling out if I pick the cartridge up wrong.

Due to manufacturing tolerances, different loading dies will require different adjustments to produce the same results. Also, different rifles and bullet designs may require different amounts of case neck tension to produce best accuracy. In any event, whatever is done should be done consistently. A tight fitting cartridge case can increase velocity by 100 fps over the velocity produced with bullets loaded slip-fit into unsized cases.

I use card wads between powder and

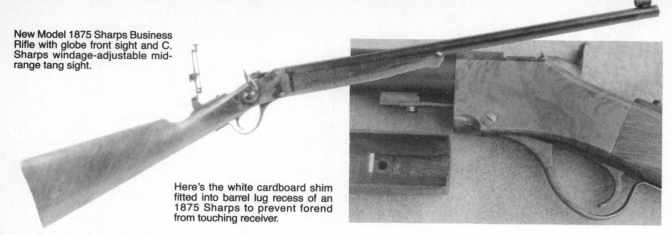

New Model 1875 Sharps Business Rifle with globe front sight and C. Sharps windage-adjustable mid-range tang sight.

Here's the white cardboard shim fitted into barrel lug recess of an 1875 Sharps to prevent forend from touching receiver.

bullet to protect the base of the bullet. Medium-hard alloys on the order of 1:25 or 1:18 tin/lead or 1:3 wheel-weight metal to soft lead seem to produce best accuracy with blackpowder loads at velocities below 1400 fps. I inspect and weigh my bullets. Any bullet with visible casting flaws or weighing more than one-half percent below average weight goes back into the melting pot. I also cast an index mark on my bullet and file index marks on the rims of my cartridge cases. When placing the bullet into the case, the mark on the bullet is lined up with the mark on the case. These marks are then oriented in the same direction when I seat the bullet in my reloading press and when the cartridges are chambered in my rifle. In doing this, it is my hope that any unknown flaw in the bullets or in bullet-case alignment will be oriented the same for each shot and throw the shot off in the same direction and by the same amount, producing better accuracy than if the flaws were oriented randomly.

I prefer to shoot blackpowder cartridge rifles without wiping the barrel out between shots. Instead, I blow slowly through the barrel after every shot using a rubber or plastic tube fitted to the back of a fired case. The moisture in my breath softens the blackpowder fouling so that it is swept out of the barrel as I shoot, rather than building up in accuracy-destroying deposits. I also use a mixture of one part 3Fg to two parts 2Fg blackpowder to reduce fouling. This mixture burns cleaner than 2Fg, but with lower pressure and better accuracy than 3Fg. The burning rate of blackpowder is determined by grain size rather than by chemical composition. Also blackpowder is not progressive burning, so mixing 2Fg and 3Fg to obtain intermediate burning characteristics is not dangerous, as is the case with smokeless powders. In some rifles, particu-larly those chambered for small cases such as the 38-55 or 40-50, powder charges of the cleaner burning 3Fg alone can be used with excellent accuracy. The handloader must balance the benefits of reduced fouling against loss of accuracy caused by increased pressure to determine which powder is best in a particular rifle.

I have always believed that shooting competitions provide a testing ground for rifles, shooters, and ideas. It's one thing to putter around in quiet obscurity, shooting only when the weather happens to be perfect, saving only the best groups, and perhaps mentally editing bad shots out of the record. It's quite another to sign up for a match with tens or even hundreds of other shooters, fire during your assigned relay regardless of weather, and have the results of your efforts, including unexpected wild fliers, posted up for everyone to see. However, it's the best way to find out just how good you, your rifle, and your reloads really are.

The New Model 1875 Sharps rifles, with their high-quality barrels, have the potential to do very well in competition. Much of my experimenting and most of my competition shooting lately have been done with a NM1875 Sharps Long Range rifle chambered for 45-70. This is a top-of-the-line model with 34-inch half-octagon barrel, pistol grip buttstock, wind gauge front and Vernier rear sights, intended primarily for target shooting. I have also done quite a bit of shooting recently with a bottom-of-the-line Business Rifle in 45-70. The use of these two rifles allows me to cross check my loads and ideas.

The Business Rifle, with plain straight-grip stock and heavy round barrel, is not as attractive as the Long Range rifle, but it's still fitted with a Douglas barrel, chambered with the same reamer, and with the same care. Somewhat to my surprise, I find I can usually shoot smaller groups at 100 yards benchrest with the Business Rifle than I can with the Long Range model. Evidently, there's some advantage to using a short heavy barrel. Shooting from crossed sticks at silhouettes or prone at paper targets though, I tend to do better with the Long Range model. Partly this is because I can see the front sight better on the longer barrel and partly it's because the Business Rifle, with steeply sloping straight-grip stock, is harder to hold steady. The basic accuracy is there, but it requires more concentration and effort to achieve it. In a long match this will cost a point or two.

The shooting competitions I most enjoy are the "Black Powder Cartridge Rifle Silhouette" matches which the National Rifle Association started in 1985. These matches combine blackpowder shooting at several hundred yards with targets that go "clang" and fall over when hit. The targets and ranges are the same as for high-power—silhouette chickens at 200 meters; pigs at 300 meters; turkeys at 380 meters; and rams at 500 meters. Rifles must be exposed hammer single shots of pre-1896 American design using traditional metallic sights of the same era. Ammunition is similarly limited to pre-1896 American blackpowder designs loaded with blackpowder or Pyrodex. Smokeless powder and bolt-action rifles are not allowed. The result is a very challenging match using the rifles and technology of the last century rather than those of the next. Results depend more on the ability of the shooter than upon the amount of gimmickry he can afford.

But 19th century or 21st century, a good barrel is still a necessity. During the first four years of BPCRS competition, I used a pair of old rust-pitted conversion Sharps rifles with sights adjustable for elevation but not for windage, and managed to shoot the

Author's notebook shows how the modern blackpowder rifleman has to keep track of his skills and his gear.

second highest score three years out of four. I doubt I could do as well using those rifles now.

With more competitors working hard on rifles, loads, and shooting techniques, the BPCRS National Championships get tougher to win every year. The first match at the NRA Whittington Center range near Raton, New Mexico, in 1985, was won with a score of 32 out of 80 possible in the two-day shoot. The 1990 BPCRS National Championship was won with a score of 53/80. My second place score of 51/80, shot with a NM1875 Sharps Long Range rifle, would have won any previous National, as would the third place score of 50/80. The top three shooters in the 1990 BPCRS Nationals all used rifles fitted with Douglas barrels. A look at the dimensions of the NRA silhouettes and the distances at which they are placed shows that the BPCRS competitor needs a rifle and ammunition capable of grouping into two minutes of angle out to 500 meters if all shots are to even have a chance.

I presently use two loads in my NM1875 45-70 rifles for BPCRS competition. For the 200-meter chickens, which must be shot offhand, I use the Lyman #457193 or #457124 bullets with 65 grains of blackpowder. Velocity runs about 1250 fps. Recoil is mild, giving me less excuse to start flinching. This load can be used out to the 500-meter rams in light rifles so as to keep recoil within comfortable limits, and it also makes a good 200-yard blackpowder schuetzen load for the 45-70.

For the rest of the silhouettes, I use the Lyman #457125 bullet over 68 grains of blackpowder. This powder charge must be compressed before the bullet is seated into the case. Velocity with this load is about 1200 fps. Recoil is bearable in rifles of 10½ pounds or heavier, but some sort of shoulder pad is suggested. This load tends to be un-

pleasant in rifles weighing 9½ pounds or less. The 520-grain bullet is often less accurate at 100 yards than the 400-420-grain bullets, but settles down in flight by 200 yards and bucks the wind better. The 45-68-520 load works fairly well out to 1000 yards for long-range shooting, but groups tend to spread out vertically beyond 600 yards.

I consider the three Lyman bullets mentioned to be about the best of the commercial designs for the 45-70. Lee Precision also makes a 450-grain design (#457-450F) that looks promising. I am inclined to believe that a more sharply pointed bullet of 450 to 480 grains weight might work better for BPCRS competition with the 45-70, particularly if it is designed to seat farther out of the case so as to increase powder capacity by five to ten grains. Lately, I have been testing a custom bullet designed along these lines with promising results. There are few commercial moulds offered in 40-caliber and most of these are too light for BPCRS competition. C. Sharps Arms offers bullet moulds for good 350- and 400-grain designs, or a custom mould can be ordered for a bullet of 380-400 grains.

The New Model 1875 Sharps rifles also perform well in long-range competition. Long-range blackpowder matches out to 1000 yards have been held at the NRA Whittington Center range since 1987. I used a NM1875 Sharps Long Range 45-70 in 1989 to win the match aggregate. For the first two matches in 1987 and 1988, I used a muzzle-loading rifle but didn't do as well. In 1990, the long-range blackpowder matches were held on the Monday following the spring BPCRS match at Raton in April, and again on the Monday following the National BPCRS Championships in September. This "double feature" offers the shooter two different blackpowder

matches for the price of one trip to Raton, and was continued in 1991. I finished up in second place in the aggregates for both of the 1990 long-range blackpowder matches using another NM1875 Sharps Long Range 45-70.

For these matches I used a duplex load consisting of 10 grains of Reloader #7, topped by 55 grains of 2Fg, a card wad, then the Lyman #457125 bullet. This load is approximately equivalent to 90 grains of blackpowder and should not be used in Trapdoor Springfields or other originals with weak blackpowder actions. Muzzle velocity averages about 1380 fps. Accuracy with this load appears to be good, running about 1½ minutes of angle from 200 to 800 yards and opening out to 2½ minutes by 1000 yards. However, at such ranges blackpowder loads are so sensitive to wind that I am seldom able to shoot to the limit of the rifle. I believe a more sharply pointed bullet weighing 540 grains or so, and seated farther out of the case to increase powder capacity, would work better. I have started experimenting with such a bullet with encouraging results.

Other shooters report doing well with NM1875 Sharps rifles at long-range blackpowder matches in Canada, England, and France. The French long-range blackpowder matches are limited to blackpowder only, no duplex loads, and attract shooters from all over Europe. In 1989, four of the top five finishers in the sporting and target breechloader class of the French long-range blackpowder matches used NM1875 Sharps rifles, as did the top two in 1990.

The most common blackpowder cartridge used in Europe is the 45-70, mostly because cases for any other blackpowder cartridge are very difficult to obtain. As I understand it, many of the European long-range blackpowder shooters have their 45-70 rifles chambered with a long tapering throat. This allows them to seat a pointed bullet of 540-550 grains weight well out of the case, leaving room for 80 grains or so of blackpowder.

In all events, the New Model 1875 Sharps rifles now seem to be achieving the success on target ranges and in the field that eluded the original Model 1875 in the last century. In keeping with the Sharps tradition, manufacture and sales of the NM1875 Sharps rifles have recently been reorganized. C. Sharps Arms still builds the rifles, but sales of rifles and accessories are now made through Montana Armory, Inc. Both companies are still in Big Timber, Montana. ●

BLOWBACK
NINES

THE 9MM PARABELLUM (9mm Luger) cartridge was among the early high-pressure pistol cartridges, designed for an extremely strong, locked-breech action. It hardly seems suitable for a straight blowback action, but such pistols have been made and are still being made today.

The cartridge, introduced in 1902, was adopted by the German navy for their Parabellum or Luger pistol of 1904. It became known worldwide following its adoption by the German army for the best-known Luger ever—the famous Pistole 1908 or P08.

The design of the Luger allowed—in fact, required—a high-pressure cartridge. Consider that the entire upper part of the pistol—the barrel, receiver and breechblock, with its toggle lock and contained mechanism—must be moved backward after firing.

At a point, the toggle unlocks, the barrel and receiver stop, and the breechblock continues rearward to eject the fired case. Then, enough residual force must be available from spring compression so that the barreled receiver will return and the breechblock will run forward to chamber the next cartridge.

Obviously, the 9mm Parabellum cartridge had to generate high pressures to make such an action function reliably.

Still, shortly after the introduction of the P08, attempts were made to adapt this cartridge to a blowback design. And real blowback nines arrived on the scene within a few years of 1908. The efforts to make successful blowback pistols chambered for the 9mm Parabellum round spread to a number of countries throughout the world, spanned the intervening decades and continue today.

The first was the German Dreyse. Niklaus von Dreyse (1787-1867) had been the inventor of the famous Prussian "Needle-Gun." He was already long dead when his company was taken over by Rheinische Metallwaren und Maschinenfabrik (later known as "Rheinmetall") in 1891. In 1907, the company brought out its first pistol, a 32-caliber blowback. Because of name recognition and company tradition, the pistol was offered as the "Dreyse," although it had actually been designed by Louis Schmeisser.

A year after the introduction of the Dreyse 32, the German army adopted the 9mm cartridge. Schmeisser began to modify his design for the new army round. He found that the pressure of the cartridge could be contained with an extremely stiff recoil spring. The 9mm Dreyse pistol probably has the strongest recoil spring ever used in a pistol. Because of the heavy spring, it was almost impossible for any but the strongest of men to operate the first prototype.

The solution was the addition of a connector bar along the top of the pistol. The bar was pivoted at the front. When it was lifted at the rear, the slide and recoil spring were disconnected. The slide could then be pulled back easily, compressing only the striker spring. With a cartridge chambered, the connector was pushed back into place, connecting the recoil spring to the slide again.

Dreyse 9mm pistols were offered for commercial sale about 1910. When the World War began in 1914, the Dreyse military 9mm was reportedly considered as a substitute standard for the German army, but was not adopted. Still, a small number were apparently carried by officers as personal sidearms. Production stopped before the end of the war and the total number manufactured was very small—perhaps not more than a few hundred pieces.

The problem with the Dreyse military pistol centered on the spring disconnecting mechanism. Apparently the system worked as designed at first. However, as it was subjected to wear and the strain of firing, the mechanism became unreliable. Old reports suggest that the spring lock could be jarred out of position during shooting. The construction of the pistol would keep the slide from being blown off toward the shooter, but recoil without any spring control could put the pistol out of service.

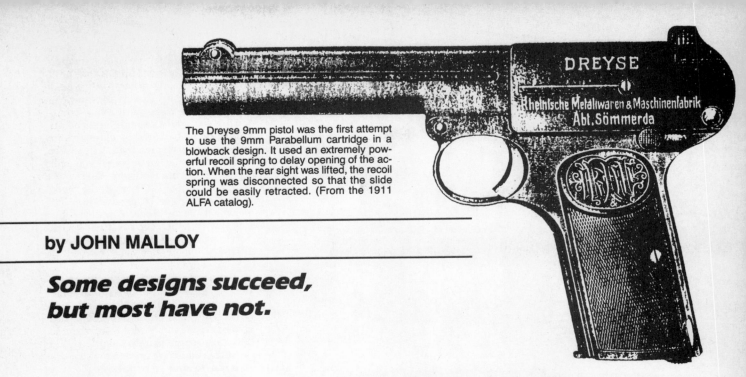

The Dreyse 9mm pistol was the first attempt to use the 9mm Parabellum cartridge in a blowback design. It used an extremely powerful recoil spring to delay opening of the action. When the rear sight was lifted, the recoil spring was disconnected so that the slide could be easily retracted. (From the 1911 ALFA catalog).

by JOHN MALLOY

Some designs succeed, but most have not.

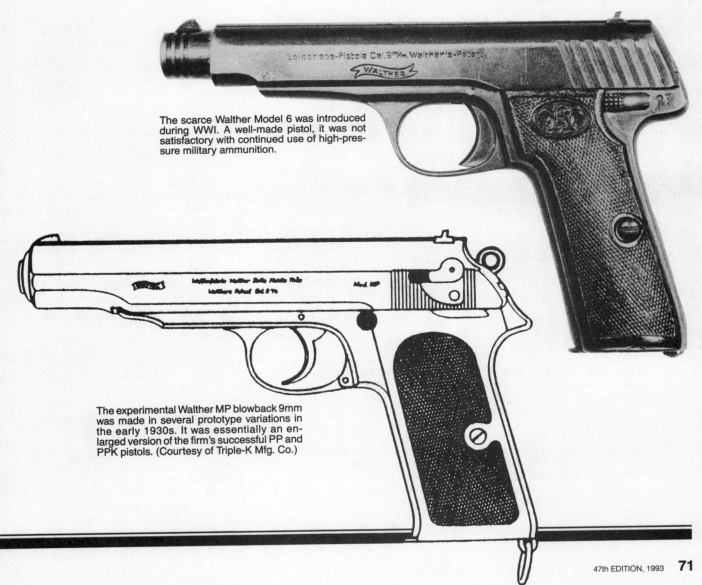

The scarce Walther Model 6 was introduced during WWI. A well-made pistol, it was not satisfactory with continued use of high-pressure military ammunition.

The experimental Walther MP blowback 9mm was made in several prototype variations in the early 1930s. It was essentially an enlarged version of the firm's successful PP and PPK pistols. (Courtesy of Triple-K Mfg. Co.)

The Italian Glisenti of 1910 used a cartridge dimensionally identical to the 9mm Parabellum, but loaded to a much lower power level.

The Beretta Model 1915 blowback pistol cannot be compared to other blowback nines because it was designed for the lower power level of the Glisenti cartridge.

Unfortunately, it was not enough. The Model 6, as were all Walther products of the time, was beautifully made and felt good in the hand. However, neither the weight nor the recoil spring was quite enough, and the pistols could be battered by extensive firing with the service load. They were, however, carried as personal sidearms by some German officers during the war. By early 1917, though, the Model 6 was no longer in production. The blowback 9mm Model 6 was the last pistol with which Carl Walther was directly associated. In 1915, the year of introduction for that pistol, he died. He was 57 years old.

Serial numbers observed or reported range from under 100 to something over 1000. Probably over a thousand, but less than two thousand, specimens of the Model 6 were made. They are scarce pistols today.

At this point, we need to make a side trip, for events were taking place in Italy that require us to be specific about our field of interest.

In 1910, the Italian government had adopted the 9mm Glisenti semi-automatic pistol. The Glisenti was a weak locked-breech design that used a vertical swinging member below the bolt to prop the bolt closed for a short time. The cartridge was dimensionally identical to the 9mm Parabellum, but, because of the weak action, was loaded to a much lower power level. Cartridge collectors today generally refer to it as "9mm Glisenti."

Once the cartridge was adopted, it was inevitable that other Italian designs chambered for it would appear.

In 1915, during World War I, about the same time as the Walther Model 6, the Beretta firm brought out the first in a line of blowback semi-automatic pistols. They included a chambering for the 9mm Glisenti. These pistols, along with later 1919 and 1923 variants, supplemented the Glisenti as Italian military pistols.

The lower power of the 9mm Glisenti cartridge made it easily adaptable to traditional blowback design. To make the story as complete as possible, the Beretta 9mm blowbacks must be mentioned, but they cannot be compared with the others, as they were never meant to be used with cartridges of the Luger power level.

Following Germany's defeat in World War I, manufacture of military pistols in that country was restricted. Walther introduced the Models 7, 8 and 9 as constantly improving pocket pistols. And in 1929, the firm introduced its famous 32-caliber Model PP (Polizei Pistole). Still a blowback pis-

World War I introduced another German 9mm blowback pistol that fared slightly better than the Dreyse—the Walther Model 6.

The Walther firm had been founded in 1886 by Carl Walther and had manufactured sporting rifles and shotguns into the early 1900s. In 1908, the first pistol—the Model 1—was produced. It was a blowback 25-caliber pocket model. Thereafter followed a successful line of small pistols in 25 and 32 calibers. The Model 5 was introduced in 1913, the year before the war began.

The need for more pistols during the early stages persuaded Carl Walther to enlarge his basic blowback design to use the 9mm service cartridge. The

resulting pistol, the Model 6, had a fairly heavy slide and a heavy recoil spring. It also had a feature easy to overlook when considering recoil control—a hammer. The Model 6's hammer is concealed, but the effect was present. The uncocked hammer was held forward by its spring. Because of the short lever arm presented at the point of contact with the slide, it offered considerable initial resistance to the rearward movement of the slide. Once the hammer began to move, resistance fell off rapidly. At the moment of greatest chamber pressure, though, the hammer gave at least some extra control that the striker-fired Dreyse had not had.

tol, the PP introduced the double-action trigger mechanism to the Walther line and ended the system of designating pistol models by number. The new PP was immediately popular, and in 1931 a smaller version, the PPK, came out.

By the early 1930s, Germany had begun to rearm in violation of the Versailles Treaty. A standard 9mm military pistol was wanted to replace the difficult-to-manufacture Luger. Walther, having still made nothing but blowback pistols, drew on the experience of the firm's recent success. The experimental 9mm blowback pistols designed had the appearance of an enlarged PP, with a similar double-action trigger mechanism. Aware of the shortcomings of the Model 6, the company lengthened the barrel from 4¾ to 5 inches, allowing a longer spring and heavier slide. Total weight increased from 33 to 39 ounces.

The pistol—actually several different variations—was designated the Walther Model MP (Militär Pistole). The design still was not able to withstand the continued use of the 9mm Parabellum service ammunition.

Discouraged by the performance of their new blowback 9mm, Walther began development of a locked-breech pistol, retaining the double-action mechanism. This development led to the adoption by the German army, in 1938, of the now-famous Walther P-38. Only a small number of Model MP blowback 9mm pistols were made, and they are very scare today.

While the Germans had produced several unsuccessful pistols in an attempt to field a blowback that would work well with the 9mm Parabellum cartridge, the Spanish did much better with another, slightly more powerful cartridge.

Spain had been the third nation in the world to adopt a semi-automatic pistol. The Bergmann locked-breech pistol of 1903 had been chosen as the official sidearm. Caliber was 9mm Largo (9mm Bergmann-Bayard), a cartridge of the same diameter as the Luger round, but using a case four millimeters longer.

In 1921, a simpler pistol for the same cartridge was adopted. This was the Astra Model 400, designed by the Spanish firm of Esperanza y Unceta. The 400 was a blowback. Its long 6-inch barrel allowed a very long, very strong recoil spring—second only to that of the Dreyse in strength. It also had a slide of substantial weight and a concealed hammer which helped hold the slide forward during the time of highest pressure.

An undetermined number of Llama 9mm Parabellum pistols were made in blowback configuration.

Most parts for the Llama 9mm blowback are the same as those of the locked-breech version. The barrel has no locking notches and no link.

The Astra 400 worked well and was used through the Spanish Civil War. When German forces occupied France in 1940, they purchased about 6000 of the big Astras as substitute standard pistols. However, this gave some soldiers pistols chambered for a nonstandard cartridge.

Now, it has been said that the Astra 400 will function reliably with the shorter 9mm Parabellum cartridge. Without going into the differing opinions on this subject, it seems sufficient to say that the Germans did not find the practice satisfactory.

About 1942 or 1943, the Germans requested that the Astra design be revised, specifically to use the 9mm Parabellum cartridge. The resulting pistol was called the Astra Model 600, although German records refer to it as the Model 600/43.

The redesigned 9mm Parabellum pistol was slightly smaller and lighter than the original 400. Its barrel length of 5¼ inches still allowed a long, strong recoil spring and a fairly heavy slide. The pistol worked well and was accepted by the German army. An acceptance stamp appears on some pistols; apparently the Germans trusted Astra workmanship and it has been reported that not all pistols accepted were stamped.

There were 10,450 reportedly delivered to German forces by late 1944.

Walther Model 6 eventually pooped out, but was still carried by some German officers in WWI.

Disassembly of the Walther Model 6 shows the strong recoil spring used. Inertia of the slide and the act of cocking the hammer also helped delay opening of the action.

Then, after the Allied invasion of Europe, German occupation of the French-Spanish border area ended and the Germans retreated. An order of appoximately 28,000 pistols was not delivered.

A basically good pistol chambered for an increasingly popular cartridge, the Astra 600 stayed in production through World War II and for a short time beyond. A number were sold to the post-war German government for police use. Total number of pistols made was 59,400.

World War II was also responsible for another blowback 9mm Parabellum design. The little-known Tarn pistol was designed by a Polish exile. Development work was carried out at the Swift Rifle Company in London, reportedly by Free Polish engineers ea-

ger to provide arms for a possible reoccupation of Poland. The Tarn used a slide of substantial weight and a strong recoil spring around its fairly long barrel to control the 9mm cartridge.

Several specimens were tested by the British in 1945, with negative results. The pistols were found to be poorly made, the recoil was said to be violent, and it was difficult for the test personnel to pull the slide back.

Only nine Tarn pistols were made, all experimental prototypes with varying features. After the war, the pistols

Collectors may cringe, but the writer fired a Walther Model 6 in 1987, with reduced handloads.

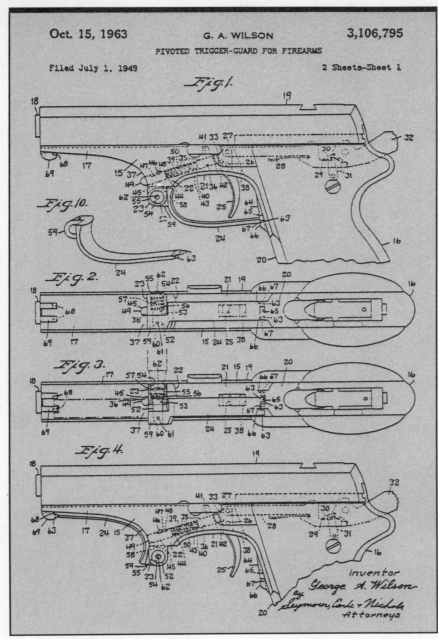

Oct. 15, 1963

G. A. WILSON

3,106,795

PIVOTED TRIGGER-GUARD FOR FIREARMS

Filed July 1, 1949

2 Sheets—Sheet 1

Fig. 1.

Fig. 10.

Fig. 2.

Fig. 3.

Fig. 4.

Inventor
George A. Wilson
By Seymour, Earle & Nichols
Attorneys

Commander. Smith & Wesson offered a new 9mm pistol which became their Model 39. From Canada came the lightweight Inglis, a version of the Browning Hi-Power with an aluminum frame. The final 9mm entry was a new concept—the blowback T3.

The T3 was developed by High Standard Manufacturing Company under a contract with the U.S. Army. It was the first attempt to specifically adapt the 9mm Parabellum cartridge to a short, light pistol of blowback design.

The T3 had a heavy spring around the barrel and an external hammer, both of which aided control of the initial pressure of firing. However, results with the light pistol were not promising until a new chamber design was tried.

An annular cut was made around the circumference of the chamber. On firing, the cartridge case expanded into this cut; the force required to reduce the case back to original size retarded the rearward movement of the slide during the period of highest pressure. This novel method of adapting the 9mm Parabellum round to the blowback design showed considerable potential. The T3, however, did not do particularly well in the tests.

About 1955, the decision was made to retain the 1911A1 45-caliber pistol in service. Work on the T3 was stopped.

It is uncertain just how many T3 pistols were made. All the pistols apparently differed somewhat from each other. Some variations that were begun were never completed. Estimates of finished pistols range from less than a dozen to about two dozen.

Although the T3 project was not successful, the American shooter derived benefits from the test program in the forms of the Colt Commander and the

Text continues, page 79

were acquired by an American importer and sold to collectors.

The years after the war saw new military interest in lighter firearms. The U.S. Army drew up requirements for new weapons, including a new lightweight pistol. For the first time, the 9mm Parabellum cartridge was seriously considered.

A series of tests was begun in 1948. Evaluated against the standard 45-caliber pistol were four 9mm entries. Colt produced a shortened 9mm Government Model that later became the

After WWII, the U.S. Army tested a blowback 9mm pistol, the T3. This is an experimental double-column magazine version that was never finished.

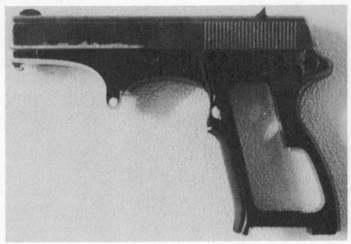

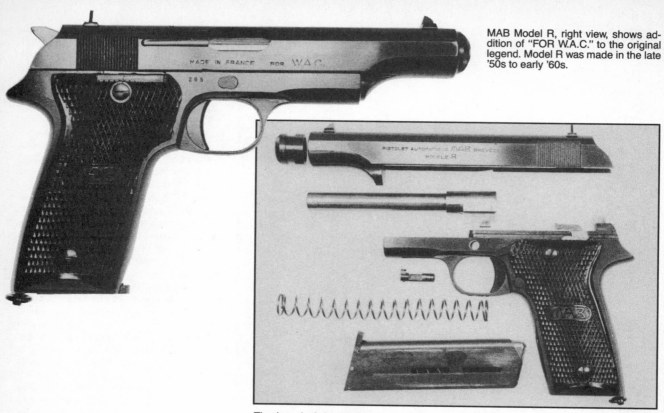

MAB Model R, right view, shows addition of "FOR W.A.C." to the original legend. Model R was made in the late '50s to early '60s.

The barrel of the Model R could move rearward under spring pressure for a short distance, as the slide began to move. The design concept seemed to allow the barrel and slide to move back together, thus gaining some of the benefit of a locked-breech system. The actual effect may be different.

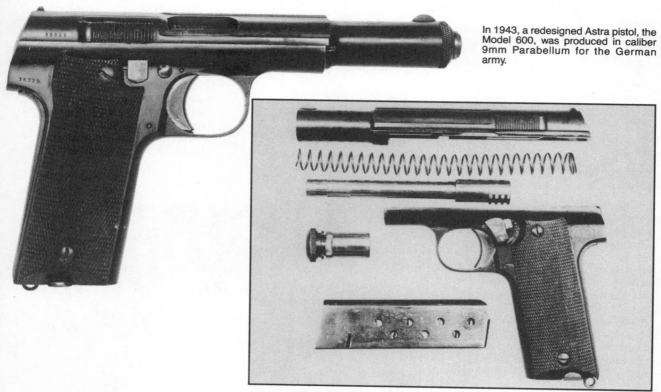

In 1943, a redesigned Astra pistol, the Model 600, was produced in caliber 9mm Parabellum for the German army.

The Astra Model 600 has a very heavy recoil spring. The combined 13-ounce slide and muzzle-cap weight and the energy used to cock the hammer also help control opening of the action.

The rare Bernardelli 9mm Parabellum (9mm Luger) pistol is seldom seen. It was made for a short time during the 1950s.

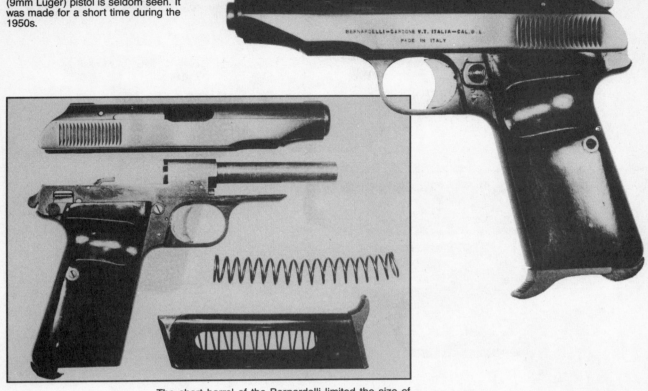

The short barrel of the Bernardelli limited the size of recoil spring that could be used. Recoil buffer can be seen just below the barrel.

The Astra Model 800 Condor was a modification of the WWII Model 600. This specimen was formerly in the Sidney Aberman collection.

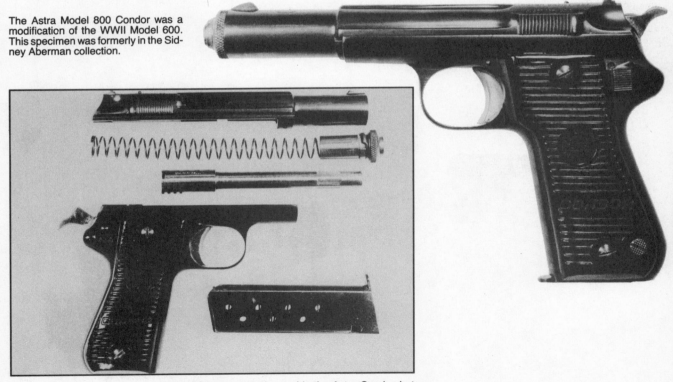

A strong recoil spring is used in the Astra Condor, but the slide is shorter and 1½ ounces lighter than that of the Model 600.

The Heckler & Koch VP70Z was introduced into the U.S. in the early 1970s.

Primary control of recoil in the VP70Z is accomplished by the stiff recoil spring and a 14.5-ounce slide that accounts for 43 percent of the total weight of the pistol.

Robert Malloy demonstrates that the VP70Z is suitable for a traditional one-hand hold. The double-action-only trigger was ahead of its time, and felt recoil is mild.

Smith & Wesson Model 39. These two American pistols, along with the large numbers of World War II souvenir pistols, introduced American shooters to the 9mm. Thus began the popularity of that caliber in the United States.

During the 1950s and 1960s, with western nations updating their arsenals, other 9mm pistols and huge volumes of surplus ammunition came on the market. Surplus ammunition selling at a few cents per round made it desirable to own a 9mm pistol, even if that caliber were not a shooter's first choice. During this post-war period, there was a demand for newly made pistols as well as for the low-priced but serviceable surplus arms. Three new blowback nines were introduced.

One of the new designs, which never really reached the production stage, was the Bernardelli.

The Bernardelli firm of Gardone, Italy, had been in the firearms business since 1865. Their first semi-automatic pistol was a simple but well-made vest-pocket 25. It appeared at the end of the war, in 1945. By the end of the decade, the company had expanded its line to include larger pistols of 22-, 32- and 380-caliber, all of the same basic blowback design.

Observing the popularity of the 9mm Parabellum cartridge, company officials began a project in the 1950s to see if the Bernardelli design could handle the larger cartridge. The resulting 9mm Parabellum pistols were enlarged versions of the basic blowback mechanism. They featured a strong recoil spring around the 3^{15}/$_{16}$-inch barrel, a moderately heavy (11-ounce) slide and an outside hammer with a noticeably stiff mainspring. Buffers on the frame beneath the barrel cushioned the slide at its rearward travel.

These features were not enough. Performance with the full-power cartridge was not satisfactory. Only a small number of the pistols were made, and they are very rare today. The total number produced (which includes several variations, including striker-fired versions) has been estimated at less than 100.

A second design introduced during the 1950s was the Astra Model 800 "Condor." The Spanish manufacturer, by then doing business as Unceta y Cia., sought to capitalize on the good reputation of the Astra Model 600. The wartime Model 600 was redesigned and the resulting pistol was introduced in 1958.

The Model 800 retained the tubular appearance and stiff springs of the wartime pistol, but featured an ex-posed hammer and a slide with a shorter rear portion. The redesigned frame did away with the grip safety and positioned the thumb safety at the rear, behind the left grip.

Although it apparently enjoyed some success in Europe, the Condor pistol never appeared in America in any great quantity. It is reported that a total of slightly more than 11,400 were made before production ended about a decade later, in 1968.

A third 9mm Parabellum blowback design of the '50s was the MAB Model R.

The French firm, Manufacture d'Arms Automatique, of Bayonne, had made 32-caliber pocket pistols from 1933 until 1940. After the occupation, many thousands were made for the Germans during World War II.

In the post-war years, the company expanded its line of small- and medium-size pistols. Included were guns of 22, 32 and 380 calibers. During the mid-1950s, the basic blowback design was modified in an attempt to offer a 9mm Parabellum pistol.

The design was innovative. As might be expected, the overall size was enlarged, and a strong spring and fairly heavy (12-ounce) slide were used. An outside hammer was utilized.

The really novel feature, however, was the barrel mounting. Instead of being fixed to the frame, the barrel was allowed some forward-backward movement. With the slide back, the barrel was pushed to its rearward position by a small coil spring.

With the action closed, the slide, under the influence of the strong recoil spring, pushes the barrel to its forward position. On firing, the barrel (under rearward pressure from its small spring) tends to move back as the slide moves back. MAB engineers apparently hoped this feature would provide at least some of the benefits of a locked-breech system, in which the barrel and slide move back locked together.

The 9mm pistol had a 4¾-inch barrel and weighed about 36 ounces. It was marketed in the United States by Winfield Arms Company of Los Angeles as "Le Militaire." A related company, Western Arms Company, also handled the MAB pistols. To the right-side slide legend of "MADE IN FRANCE" was added an additional stamping, "FOR W.A.C."

The Model R did not sell well. It was introduced in the late '50s and by the early '60s was no longer offered. The pistol is illustrated only for years 1958 through 1963 in the GUN DIGEST catalog sections.

The price remained stable at $62 throughout this period. However, during this time a brand-new commercial Browning Hi-Power (in the same caliber) retailed for $74.50. The lower price was not enough to spur sales of the French pistol.

A demonstration of the Model R does not create a positive impression. There is no manual slide release or manual slide lock. Both these functions are controlled by the magazine. The strange mechanics of the design thus required a good magazine.

After firing, the slide locks open against the magazine follower. When the magazine is withdrawn (with some difficulty, as it is held by the slide under strong spring pressure) an auxiliary lock moves up to retain the slide open.

Inserting a loaded magazine releases this lock, automatically running the slide forward to chamber a round. Inserting an empty magazine will (usually) release the slide a split second before the follower catches it again. Lacking a good magazine, there is virtually no way to release the slide without a partial disassembly of the pistol

These factors, along with the awkward stretch to the thumb safety and the high, sharp sights, probably were enough to dampen most shooters' enthusiasm for the pistol.

Serial numbers of observed specimens range from those in the 200 series to the 1100 series. Experimental turning-barrel locked-breech designs (also, for some reason, designated as Model R) have been reported in the 1500 series. It would seem that the total production of these blowbacks may be somewhere around 1200 to 1400 pieces.

The unusual system of having the barrel follow the slide back without a positive lock was not unique to the French pistol. During 1955-1957, the J. Kimball Arms Company of Detroit, Michigan, made a pistol for the U.S. 30 Carbine cartridge. The barrel also moved back with the slide without a mechanical lock.

However, the Kimball had longitudinal grooves or flutes cut into the chamber. The concept seemed to be that the cartridge case would expand into these grooves and be held to the barrel by friction while being held to the slide by the extractor. The barrel and slide would move rearward together, delaying the blowback action.

It is well known that the Kimball system did not work as planned. A number of guns were damaged by the dangerous recoil, and the company failed within two years.

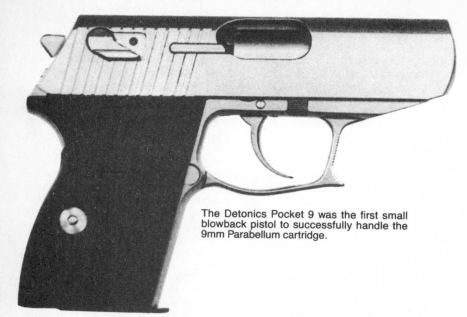

The Detonics Pocket 9 was the first small blowback pistol to successfully handle the 9mm Parabellum cartridge.

almost anyone's definition. Although large and bulky, it is suited to traditional one-hand shooting and holster carry.

The total weight is only about 33 ounces, but 43 percent of that weight is in the slide. It has a very heavy 14.5-ounce slide and a strong recoil spring. The final rearward motion of the slide is stopped against an insert in the takedown latch.

The VP70Z was comfortable to shoot and held 18 rounds. Still, it was not particularly popular. It was expensive, and for the money a shooter got a well-built, but ungainly and clumsy-looking, pistol with a long trigger pull for each shot. So the VP70Z was dropped from production about 1984.

The Spanish firm of Gabilondo, manufacturers of the Llama line, made a 9mm Parabellum blowback pistol during the 1980s.

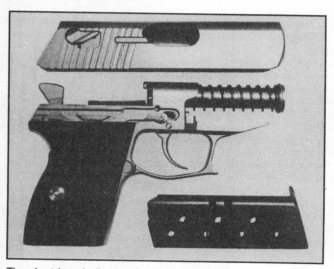

The short barrel allows only a relatively short recoil spring in the Pocket 9. Early models used annular grooves in the chambers to delay the slide opening.

The writer finds that the Pocket 9 works well, but can be a punishing pistol to shoot for an extended period.

What is not so well known is that Kimball made a single prototype pistol to test the system in 9mm Parabellum caliber. The writer examined it a number of years ago, but its location is unknown to me now.

During the late 1960s, the German firm of Heckler & Koch engaged in development of a military firearm that could function as both a pistol and submachine gun. The caliber, naturally, was to be 9mm Parabellum.

Announced about 1970, the VP70 was a large blowback double-action-only pistol. It could be fitted with a shoulder stock. With the stock detached, it was a semi-automatic pistol; with the stock attached, it was capable of three-shot burst fire.

A modified version, the VP70Z, could be used only as a semi-automatic pistol. This version was marketed in the United States, beginning in about 1973 or 1974.

Here we must make another side trip to define the scope of our interest in blowback nines. Other 9mm semi-automatic pistols based on blowback submachine-gun origins have been made and are being made. The Uzi, Wilkinson, Sterling and MAC designs are only a few. They are pistols in the legal sense, but do not lend themselves to natural one-hand use or traditional holster carry. Although they are fun to shoot and useful for special purposes, they will not be considered here.

The VP70Z, however, is a pistol by

The reason for this is unclear. Gabilondo had been making locked-breech pistols of the Colt 1911 design under the Llama name since 1931. Llama locked-breech pistols in 9mm Parabellum caliber had been imported into the United States by Stoeger since about 1952.

With the manufacturing experiences and the machinery already in place, there would seem to be little advantage in switching to a blowback design, since most of the parts of the blowback 9mm are essentially the same as those of its locked-breech brethren. The barrel, however, simply remains stationary in the frame. It does not tip up at the rear to lock into the slide and, indeed, had no locking notches or link. The standard underbarrel recoil spring arrangement of the locked-breech design was used.

While it apparently eliminated some machine work during manufacture, the blowback Llama 9mm was not a success. After a number had been produced, a product advisory was issued, and the blowback pistols were recalled.

Up until the 1980s, all blowback nines reaching the production stage had been full-size military-style pistols. The experimental T3 and the essentially experimental Bernardelli had been unsuccessful attempts to scale down the size.

By the mid-1980s, in spite of cautions from some circles, the 9mm Parabellum cartridge was widely accepted in the United States for police use and personal defense. The niche for a compact 9mm was recognized.

The barrel of this early Pocket 9, in the P2300 serial range, shows annular grooving in the chamber.

Such a pistol would be more easily concealed and could serve as a same-caliber back-up for police officers who carried a nine as a duty pistol.

Two compact blowback designs appeared, the first of which was the Detonics Pocket 9.

Detonics Firearms Industries began in 1976 in Bellevue, Washington. Gradually, the firm became well known for its compact 45-caliber pistol. That pistol was a small locked-breech design based on a modification of the Colt 1911 system.

Detonics had made a few 9mm specimens of its standard compact locked-breech pistol. However, the 9mm was the same size as the 45 and offered few advantages.

A different prototype 9mm Parabellum pistol had been displayed at firearms industry gatherings for several years. In 1985, it was put into production as the Detonics Pocket 9.

A totally new pistol, the Pocket 9 was a blowback. It was made of stainless steel and featured a double-action trigger, ambidextrous safety and recessed sights.

Its short 3-inch barrel did not allow a very heavy slide (only 10.5 ounces) or a very long recoil spring. To control the opening of the action, the Detonics "Chamber-Lok" breech system was used.

A 1984 discussion between the writer and a Detonics representative (prior to the marketing of the Pocket 9) revealed that annular grooves were cut into the chamber walls. The case expanded into these grooves. Moving the case out of the chamber required a

The barrel of this later Pocket 9, in the P3800 serial range, has a smooth, ungrooved chamber.

slight resizing, which delayed the slide opening. This is essentially the same method employed by High Standard during the development work on the T3.

For some reason, Detonics discontinued the "Chamber-Lok" annular grooves during the production of the Pocket 9. A pistol observed in the P2300 serial range has the grooves. One in the P3800 range does not.

Production of the Pocket 9 was short-lived—1986, its second year of production, was also its last.

It is interesting to look at the 1986 Detonics price list. The standard version of the Pocket 9 is there, but two other versions are also listed. The Power 9 is the same pistol with a pol-

ished finish. The Pocket 9 LS is a "long-slide" variant with a 4-inch barrel. I have never seen either.

About the time the Detonics Pocket 9 went out of production, its niche was filled by an Israeli import.

The Sardius SD 9, originally known as the Sirkis SD 9, was the design of Israeli engineer Nehemiah Sirkis. The new compact blowback was imported in small quantities about 1986. By 1987, the SD 9 was handled in the United States by the Maryland firm Armscorp of America and was advertised nationally.

The Sardius is an interesting design. Made to be produced quickly and cheaply, a number of components are derived from heavy stampings. The grips are wrap-around plastic. Obviously designed for close-range undercover use, the trigger is double-action only. However, a manual safety is provided.

The breechblock is a separate piece, but locks solidly into the slide. The short 3-inch barrel did not allow a long, heavy recoil spring, so a new system was used. Four coil springs of different outside diameters are positioned, one inside the other, to operate on the same axis rod below the barrel. The four springs are held captive on their rod and are easily removed as a unit for disassembly.

This combination of springs, resisting the movement of the 10.5-ounce slide/breechblock assembly, serves to delay the breech opening.

The first SD 9 pistols imported into the United States had some mechanical problems. Too, the crudely made European-style catch at the base of the magazine did not find favor with American shooters.

By 1989, a modified Sardius pistol had been introduced. The magazine release of the newer design was at the top of the left grip, where it could be operated by the shooter's right thumb. A trade-in policy was established. The owner of an early SD 9 could return it and step up to the later model for a small fee.

By early 1991, import and distribution of the Sardius SD 9 was being handled by the VWM company of Stafford, Virginia. At the time of this writing, VWM is still distributing the pistol, and a company representative reports that it is popular with law enforcement officers as a back-up pistol.

As we have seen, for a long time—almost three-quarters of a century—all blowback nines produced had been full-size military-type pistols. Then, in the mid-1980s, compact pocket-size pistols in blowback form appeared.

(Above) The Sardius SD 9 was introduced in the late 1980s. It is manufactured in Israel, and heavy stampings are used in its construction.

(Below) SD 9 pistols of current manufacture have the magazine release button at the upper part of the left grip.

Slide opening of the Sardius SD 9 is delayed by four coil springs of different diameters, which are held captive around a common rod.

Although the grip of the Sardius SD 9 has a good shape, the recoil is heavy and the pistol is not pleasant to shoot for an extended period of time.

By the end of that decade, a new type appeared with the introduction of the Maverick.

Although full-size, it had little in common with previous military pistols. Its intended niche seemed to be for personal use as an inexpensive home defense pistol.

In September 1987, the new Maverick blowback 9mm pistol was quietly introduced to the American market. The concept of Ohioan Ed Stallard, the new pistol combined some of the design features of early pocket pistols with a full-power cartridge and late 20th century manufacturing techniques.

Ignoring current trends, the pistol has a single-action trigger mechanism, single-column magazine and thumb safety on the left only. The simple striker firing mechanism also uses the firing pin as an ejector. The design offers few surprises to those familiar with the blowback pocket automatics of many decades ago.

The construction of the pistol, though, is strictly modern. Plastics, easily cast alloys, steel stampings and unbreakable coil springs are used throughout. Roll pins instead of screws are used for assembly—the only screws are the grip screws. The grips themselves retain parts on the side of the frame.

The resulting pistol was made inexpensively and sold at a low price. It was heavy, with a squared-off, boxy shape and a wrinkle paint finish. By traditional standards, it was not particularly handsome, but it was the cheapest new pistol on the market chambered for the 9mm Parabellum cartridge.

Weight was the primary reason for the Maverick's easy handling of the 9mm cartridge. The original version was listed as 48 ounces (about as much as a Smith & Wesson 44 Magnum) and some specimens even ran a few ounces heavier. The 22-ounce slide is a large 43 percent of the total weight of the pistol. The inertia of the massive slide helps keep the case in the chamber longer, giving pressures a chance to drop.

Strangely, the recoil spring is not particularly heavy. Perhaps to make the pistol workable for women and the elderly, spring strength was kept moderate, and prime emphasis was placed on weight.

However, some other subtle techniques were used to control pressures. The rifling is cut only about .002-inch deep, about half the standard practice. This lowers initial resistance to the bullet and helps keep chamber pressure down. In addition, the slide in battery is designed for "zero headspace," allowing the cartridge no play between the chamber shoulder and the breech face. Looseness would have the effect, however slight, of letting the case "slam" back against the slide. Zero headspace allows only a "push" against the slide.

As the new pistols began to sell, the "Maverick" name was called into question in 1988. Although it had been registered by Stallard in Ohio, "Maverick" was registered nationally by a Texas shotgun company. A friendly agreement was reached, and the name of the pistol was changed.

Renaming of the pistol was in keeping with the policy of keeping expenses down. The original pistols bore this legend on the slide:

MAVERICK FIREARMS
MODEL JS-9MM
Mfg. By Stallard Arms Inc.
Mansfield, Oh.

The same die for the legend was kept, but the top line was simply ground off, getting rid of "MAVERICK FIREARMS." The pistol was known thereafter as the "Stallard."

In early 1991, a new grip frame with a curved rear portion was offered, with contoured grips to match the frame shape. The new frames were made of a lighter alloy. The total weight of the pistol went down to about 39 ounces, close to the weight of a Colt 1911. The weight of the slide, relative to the other parts, thus went up.

The version introduced in mid-1991 does away with the wrinkle finish in favor of smooth black or nickel. With little fanfare, the Stallard seems to be finding a market as an acceptable 9mm pistol at a low price.

In any discussion of blowback nines, the question of recoil naturally arises. How much do they kick? What is the recoil really like?

First, a clarification: Any cartridge has a certain recoil energy potential, and this is independent of what kind of arm fires it.

What we are really concerned with is "felt" recoil—the recoil sensed as shock to the shooter's hand. This is influenced, for all pistols, by their weight and the shape of the grips. For semi-automatic pistols, we must add the effects of how rapidly the slide moves back and how abruptly it stops at the end of its travel. We have seen that different designs have addressed these effects in different ways.

Second, a consideration: Shooting any firearm should be safe—for both the shooter and the firearm.

A shooter of a gun of historical or mechanical interest is a custodian of a bit of history. He should be certain of the firearm's condition and use only suitable ammunition. For some of the blowback nines, original ammunition is *not* suitable ammunition.

With these points in mind, let me share a few thoughts:

Your writer has never seen a Dreyse 9mm. In view of the rarity of the pistol and the warnings often repeated in old texts, it would probably be best not to shoot one, even with reduced loads.

The Walther Model 6 is also a scarce item. It is so nicely made, however, that I can well understand a desire to shoot one. Collectors may cringe, but in 1987, my brother, Robert Malloy, and I had the chance to shoot a Model 6. Only light handloads were used. As might be expected, it performed flawlessly. Felt recoil with the reduced loads was moderate. We suspected, though, that full-power 9mm loads might have been hard on both the shooter and the pistol. Parts for these pistols are not available. Think carefully before shooting one.

The Walther MP blowbacks are rare, indeed. I have never seen one, and apparently the few existing specimens are in museums or private collections. One would expect traditional Walther quality and shooting characteristics somewhat better than those of the Model 6. I would love to try one out, but only with reduced loads.

Shooting the Astra 600 is a different story. Due to the heavy spring, heavy slide and hammer-cocking leverage, the rugged Spanish pistols seem to digest any 9mm Parabellum loads without ill effect. The felt recoil is moderate.

A characteristic of the Astra Model 600 seems to be good accuracy. Although the sights are not adjustable, all the 600s I have shot will shoot good groups, close to the aiming point. I have carried mine in the field. For small game and furbearers up to about raccoon or nutria size, it can be very effective.

The same, in general, can be said about the Astra Condor. Accuracy and effectiveness are essentially the same. For field use, the outside hammer can be an advantage. Strangely, though, although it is often considered an improvement of the basic 600 design, the Model 800 Condor is much harder to control during recoil.

A close look at the pistol tells us why. In order to adapt an outside hammer, the rear of the slide was shortened. The slide of the original 600 weighs 13 ounces; that of the 800 only 10.5 ounces. The lighter slide comes back faster and stops harder. In addition, with the hammer and thumb safety moved rearward, the rear frame configuration is different. The web of the hand rides awkwardly low on the grip, making muzzle rise difficult to control.

In 1984 I spent some shooting-range time with a Condor. Accuracy was excellent. However, my notes show recoil as "heavy." Cases were ejected 20-25 feet to the right. Shooting with one hand, the muzzle jump was sometimes bad enough that the thumb tended to push the safety "on" during recoil. Although a good-shooting pistol, the Astra 800 Condor does not offer the control of the 9mm round that its predecessor did.

The Tarn pistol was dropped from consideration by the British due to its "very violent" action. This would indicate that the power level of the military 9mm load was too much for this design to handle. With only nine experimental pieces reported made, the rare Tarn should not be considered a shooter.

The High Standard T3 was made in prototype form only, with almost every specimen slightly different from the others.

Contemporary reports indicated a substantial reduction of felt recoil using the grooved chamber over the plain chamber. Apparently the system was not without problems, however, and final military specifications pointedly required a plain chamber.

About 20 years ago, I had the opportunity of handling what was probably the first working model of the T3. It was then owned by automatic pistol

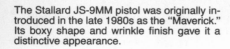

The Stallard JS-9MM pistol was originally introduced in the late 1980s as the "Maverick." Its boxy shape and wrinkle finish gave it a distinctive appearance.

Using a relatively light recoil spring, the JS-9MM pistol depends primarily on massive slide weight to delay opening.

collector Harry F. Klein. It felt good in the hand, and I wondered what it would be like to shoot. The T3 pistols are all historically significant, and their shooting characteristics have been documented. There is hardly any reason that one should be shot now. Still, it certainly would be interesting.

The 9mm Kimball is a one-of-a-kind prototype. I examined it some time ago when it was also owned by Klein. While it would probably perform better than the 30 Carbine Kimballs, its present owner should cherish it as a collection piece only.

The Bernardelli 9mm Parabellum is a rare pistol, and few would get a chance to shoot one. I was fortunate that one was in the possession of my brother, Robert Malloy, in 1987. I shot the pistol only with light handloads. The large frame offered a good grip,

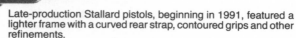

Late-production Stallard pistols, beginning in 1991, featured a lighter frame with a curved rear strap, contoured grips and other refinements.

The grip of the later Stallard pistols is comfortable for extended shooting sessions.

but recoil was heavy, even with the reduced loads. Any positive effect of the recoil buffers must have been slight. I wondered then, since Bernardelli had enlarged the frame beyond pocket pistol size, why they had not made a version with a longer barrel. This would have allowed a heavier slide and stronger spring.

The MAB Model R is a strange pistol. For shooting, the unusual mechanism makes it very difficult to clear a malfunction if one does occur.

Recoil has been described by another shooter as "stiff." I have fired three of these pistols and feel that perhaps that term is not strong enough. Cases go at high speed 20 to 30 feet to the right. My notes indicate that the recoil seems to increase as you shoot; this may just be subjective, though. Certainly, the pistol kicks fiercely with full loads. It is not pleasant to shoot, even with reduced loads.

The Model R's rearward-moving barrel has no positive effect that I could note. Indeed, a suspicion has been growing in my mind that the spring-loaded barrel, contrary to its intended function, may actually give the slide an additional rearward push at the beginning of its cycle.

The Heckler & Koch VP70Z is another strange pistol, but primarily because of its bulk and double-action-only trigger mechanism. As a shooter, it is controllable and actually fun to shoot. The heavy 14.5-ounce slide and strong spring seem to effectively tame the recoil of any standard 9mm loading. A friend of mine described his as a "pussycat."

I have never fired one of the blowback Llama 9mm pistols, but I have examined a specimen. Like the other 1991-styled Llamas, the parts are big and substantial looking. The Louisiana shooter who owns it also has a standard locked-breech Llama 9mm. He could remember little difference between firing the two guns. However, remember that a recall notice was issued on the blowback version. If fired, it should be with mild loads only.

The small Detonics Pocket 9 looks as if it would be brutal to shoot, and most shooters feel it lives up to that appearance. The word most commonly used to describe the recoil is "sharp." Your writer agrees. The pistol I fired (one of the later ungrooved-chamber versions) delivers a hard, sharp blow to the hand with each shot. No one who tried it wanted to shoot it for long. However, the pistol itself does not seem to be affected by the recoil. As a police backup or a personal protection arm, it would be fired very little. For its intended purpose, the heavy recoil is acceptable.

It is possible that the earlier grooved-chamber version would be gentler to shoot. Still, its small size and relatively light weight suggest it would not be pleasant.

Although one owner described the recoil of his Sardius SD 9 as "more like a 44 Magnum," I experienced slightly less felt recoil shooting one than when shooting the Pocket 9. Because the total weight and slide weight of both pistols are almost identical, it may be that the four springs of the Sardius really do make a difference. Or it may be that the larger grip, of different shape, allows a better grasp to help keep the pistol under control.

This is not to say that shooting the SD 9 is pleasant. It is decidedly unpleasant to shoot for any length of time. Again, though, designed for undercover use, it would not be fired much, and the recoil would not be noticed in an emergency situation.

If one's only introduction to blowback nines had been the compact ones just described, trying out the Maverick or Stallard pistols would open a new world.

The tremendous weight of the original pistol just soaks up 9mm recoil. With the recent lighter version, the weight has been principally removed from the frame, not the slide. This means that the weight of the slide has actually increased—relatively—to a full 50 percent of the total weight of the pistol.

With either version, felt recoil is moderate. A variety of commercial loads, military ammunition and handloads were tried, and all were pleasant to shoot. Cases, depending on load, landed 5 to 10 feet away. My 13-year-old son, Patrick, often assists me in trying things out. He considers the Stallard fun to shoot.

The story of blowback nine pistols is an interesting one. Designed specifically for a strong locked-breech action, the 9mm Parabellum cartridge had held an appeal for manufacturers in many countries who have tried to adapt it to the simpler blowback design.

Heavy recoil springs, multiple springs, hammer-cocking leverage, recoil buffers, grooved chambers, fluted chambers, shallow rifling, zero headspace, spring-loaded barrels and heavy slide weight—all these things have been tried. Various combinations of these factors have been used with different pistols.

Some have worked better than others. Some blowback nines had extremely short production runs. Some were essentially experimental, with only one or a few pieces made. Others achieved relatively large-scale production, with thousands or tens of thousands of pistols made.

Through it all, the unlikely combination of the 9mm Parabellum cartridge and the blowback design has endured for over eight decades. Blowback nines may well be with us for some time to come. ●

Special thanks to Robert Malloy, Harry F. Klein, Robert W. Schumacher and the other shooters and collectors who shared their experiences and made their pistols available to the writer.

Selected Bibliography

Antaris, Leonardo M. *Astra Automatic Pistols.* Colorado: Firac Publishing Company, 1988.

Cormach, A.J.R. *German Small Arms.* New York: Exeter Books, 1979.

Ezell, Edward C. *Handguns of the World.* Harrisburg, PA: Stackpole, 1981.

Fjestad, S.P. *Blue Book of Gun Values.* Minneapolis, MN: Blue Book Publications, Inc., 1991.

Hatcher, Julian S. "Kimball Pistol." *American Rifleman,* (October, 1955), p. 74.

Hogg, Ian V., and John Weeks. *Pistols of the World.* San Rafael, CA: Presidio Press, 1978.

Krasne, J.A., editor. *Encyclopedia and Reference Catalog of Auto Loading Guns.* San Diego, CA: Triple K Mfg. Co., 1989.

Magee, Darel. "Big Bore Blow-Back Auto Pistols." *Gun Collector's Digest.* p. 171-177. Northbrook, IL: DBI Books, Inc., 1974.

Petty, Charles E. *High Standard Automatic Pistols, 1932-1950.* Charlotte, NC: American Ordnance Publications, 1976.

Smith, W.H.B. *Book of Pistols and Revolvers.* Harrisburg, PA: Stackpole, 1968.

Whittington, Robert D., III. "Astra Pistols in the German Army." *Guns Magazine,* (November, 1968), p. 41.

Wilson, R.K. *Textbook of Automatic Pistols.* Plantersville, SC: Small Arms Technical Publishing Co., 1943.

by RAYMOND CARANTA

THE GUNS OF EUROPE

THE PAST year cannot be considered as a good one for the whole European economy and for the gun-loving fraternity in particular. The Schengen agreements on future firearms controls still have one year before they are to be enforced in the community, and the governments involved do not rush, not because they are ashamed, but mostly because they cannot find the money required for paying the new employees and computers needed to register all the existing and serviceable fixed-ammunition firearms made since 1870!

Meanwhile, the world industry has released, in one year, about 116 new items in the field of automatic pistols, 50 bolt-action rifles, 42 revolvers, 37 over/unders, 30 side-by-sides, 25 self-loading rifles and about 136 miscellaneous new guns of different other systems, including compressed air and CO_2. Most of those designed in Europe will be exported to the United States, but not all and, among this production from the old continent, the following was selected:

- **Anschütz:** New model 1451 rimfire bolt-action rifle with a stock longer than usual and a simplified action.
- **Ardesa:** Their "Fowler Special Trap" 12-gauge percussion muzzleloader won the World Championship in 1990, while the "Henry Target Rifle" of this reputable gunmaker took a gold medal at the Spanish championship.
- **Arrizabalaga:** This other Spanish manufacturer, established in 1940, makes a fine line of side-by-side shotguns, all fitted with sidelocks.
- **Beretta:** Magnificent "455 EELL Express" side-by-side

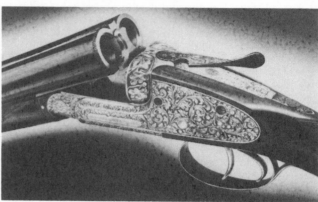

William Powell's Nº 1 sidelock shotgun—an old name once again seen on quality British guns.

A Deluxe version of the Franchi ASSO automatic shotgun with Fronturning patented delayed blowback action.

John Rigby's big game rifle is still chambered in 416 Rigby, unless you'd prefer 458 Winchester Magnum.

The Swiss Ultima Ratio sniper rifle is an impressive piece of ordnance.

express rifle chambered in 375 Holland & Holland Magnum, 458 Winchester Magnum, 470 Nitro Express (3″) or 416 Rigby. The retail price of this masterpiece exceeds $53,000 in France.

- **Blaser:** Has introduced a new 30R Blaser caliber—150- or 180-grain bullets at 3080 and 2800 fps.
- **Chapuis:** Alfa over/unders, Progress side-by-sides and express rifles, Oural folding rifle, Supreme and Imperial express rifles: This year, one of these Imperial rifles has been engraved (a stag in front of the Chambord castle) by a "Best Craftsman of France."
- **Ducros:** A young French gunmaker making, on limited-production basis, high quality side-by-sides and a custom match version of the Colt Python revolver.
- **Ferlib:** Made a pair of fine side-by-sides called "Hommage à Picasso" with modern engraving.
- **Franchi:** Has a fascinating new ASSO delayed blowback automatic shotgun with a patented Fronturning four-lug action.
- **Gamba:** Renato Gamba, the flamboyant gunmaker, offers a nice line of guns, among which we have selected two side-by-sides: a 20-gauge made for the Augusta National Golf Club and a limited series (200 pieces) commemorative model of the bicentenary of the French Revolution, engraved by the master Cesare Giovanelli and the

The Gaucher GN1 silhouette pistol is a sturdy bolt-action model made in St. Etienne in France.

(Right) Renato Gamba's shotgun commemorates the bicentennial of the French Revolution—La Marseillaise evoked in steel.

This match version Python is set up by the French firm Ducros with extended sight radius, orthopedic grip, special hammer, adjustable trigger and front cylinder lock.

French Unique single shot, another international silhouette pistol, comes in several specialized calibers.

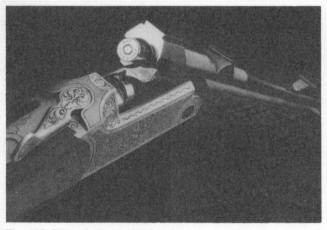

The 30R Blaser caliber is hard-hitting, moves a 150-grain bullet at 3080 fps, the makers say.

The Llama PT2 is a compact twelve-shot selective DA pistol available in 9mm Luger and 40 S&W.

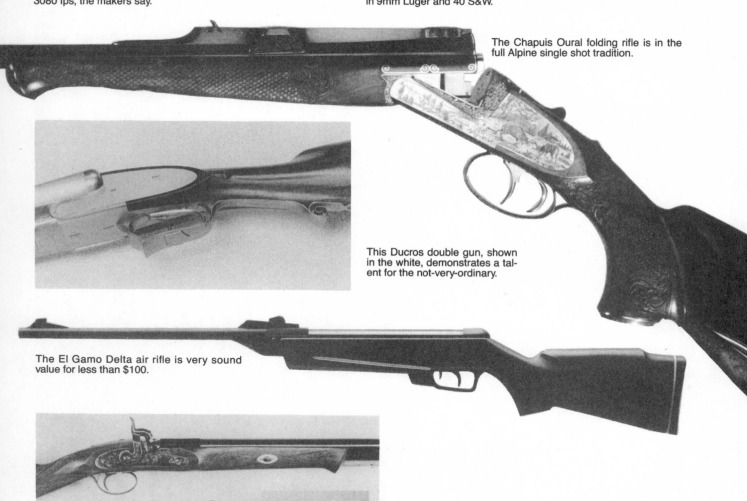

The Chapuis Oural folding rifle is in the full Alpine single shot tradition.

This Ducros double gun, shown in the white, demonstrates a talent for the not-very-ordinary.

The El Gamo Delta air rifle is very sound value for less than $100.

The Fowler Special Trap percussion shotgun made by Ardesa has won a World I.S.U. title.

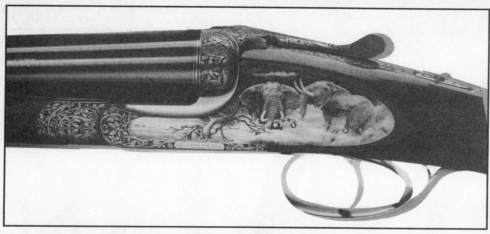

Fighting bull tuskers by Galeazzi enliven Gamba's double 458 built for the Safari Club International.

Beretta's 455 EELL express rifle has detachable sidelocks, can be had in 375 H&H Magnum, 458 Winchester Magnum, 470 Nitro, 416 Rigby and handsome engraving.

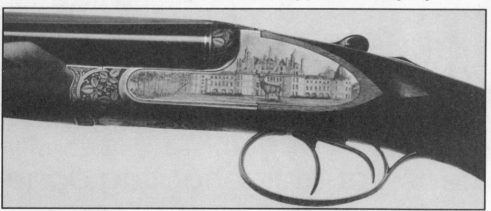

The Chapuis Imperial express rifle with a stag at Chambord engraved by one of France's best.

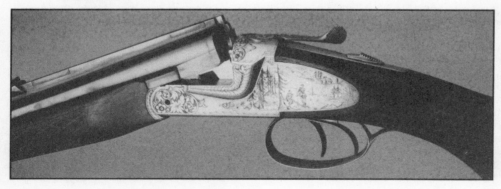

This is the Bivouac express rifle from Gaucher, chambered in classic continental calibers for European shooting.

Maxim N°2 sidelock express rifle in 458 Winchester Magnum, handmade for Safari Club International in 1991.

- **Gamo:** This Spanish specialist of airguns has marketed this year an inexpensive Delta rifle with a barrel sleeved in carbon fibers and an anti-shock polymer stock, at about $100 in France.
- **Gaucher:** The Bivouac side-by-side express rifle is chambered in 9.3x74R, 7x65R and 8x57JRS, and there's a single shot 22 Long Rifle GN1 Silhouette pistol.
- **PMG:** Ultra-modern Ultima Ratio five-shot sniper rifle with half-minute accuracy potential in 308 Winchester, 300 Savage, 7mm-08 Remington, 243 Winchester and 22/243, from the famous Swiss gunmaker Morier.
- **Powell (William):** His N°1 sidelock ejector shotgun is entirely made in England on request for gentlemen, at £19,237.00 (about $40,000) ex works.
- **Rigby (John):** Offers side-by-sides from £14,500 to £16,500, also available in braces at £30,000/34,000 ex works, and bolt-action rifles chambered in 416 Rigby or 458 Winchester Magnum from £2,500 to £4,800 ex works.
- **Rivolier:** Has self-loading Remington Model 7400s, chambered in 35 Whelen exclusively for this French importer; and there's an amazingly light and easy to handle three-barrel shotgun and patented silencers.
- **Unique:** Has a French top-class single shot pistol available in two versions and chambered in 22 Long Rifle, 22 Winchester Magnum, 7x45 TSM (7TCU), 7BR, 357 Magnum and 44 Remington Magnum.
- **Voere:** Its bolt-action rifle— VEC 91—chambered for a new caseless cartridge of 5.7x26UCC caliber—a 55-grain bullet at 3300 fps.
- **Walther:** The compact P88 pistol is fitted with a slide drop-hammer safety. This is a fourteen-shot 9mm Luger, selective double-action pistol, only 7.12-inches long, weighing just 29 ounces. ●

by C. RODNEY JAMES

ARMS AND THE MAN

How amputees get their shooting done . . . anyway.

BEING AN amputee usually comes as a result of some form of trauma. A common reaction to the amputee, on the part of a so-called "normal" person, is often the "My-God-you-poor-bastard-what-happened?" sort and the amputee can tell his tale or not. I usually feel a sense of obligation, to maintain good public relations, but prefer the attitude of my neighbor Harold, the mule rancher, who offers help only when it's asked for and, as he puts it, "talks to me just like I was people."

We upper-extremity-missing per-

(Above) Lady and gentlemen of the nineteenth annual One-Arm Dove Hunt of Olney, Texas. In the center is accountant Joyce Baughns of Dallas, Texas, the first woman participant in the hunt. Founders of the hunt are the two one-armed Jacks—Jack Bishop (far left) and Jack Northrup (far right).

sons have most of the image problems, since a hook doesn't look much like a hand and the mechanical hands available simply aren't worth a damn when it comes to doing things people do with hands of the meat and bone variety. Some of us like to shoot and see no reason to stop simply because of a little

trauma in our lives. But we have a need for some customizing in our shooting rigs. Custom guns are nothing new and enlightened companies such as Smith & Wesson have introduced revolvers with smaller grips for women; Beretta and Ruger have ambidextrous safeties; and Steyr, A-Square, Browning, Remington, Sako, Weatherby and Winchester, among others, offer long guns with stocks and actions for left-handers. Amputees need this and more.

An absence of hands is a major obstacle in handgun shooting, but American ingenuity has a way of rising to the occasion. At age twelve, Jay J. Armes was seriously considering becoming a surgeon, though not at the moment a railroad signal cap he was attempting to dismantle exploded, removing his hands. Armes' second career choice was law enforcement, but both the medical and law enforcement establishments have long held a conservative view regarding the admission of those with disabilities to their ranks. Armes entered law enforcement on his own terms, studying criminology and business to become a licensed private detective. His organization—The Investigators—based in El Paso, Texas, now maintains a worldwide network of operators and has made Armes a multi-millionaire. Armes, however, did not start at that level.

He did his own detective work, soon finding himself in a number of deadly confrontations atypical of those facing most private eyes and much like situations in film and television thrillers. The Charles Bronson film *Breakout* wherein Bronson flies a helicopter into a Mexican prison was based on the actual rescue by Armes, who flew his own chopper. With, at last count, six attempts on his life, Armes needed a

handgun that could be brought into action quickly. His choice was an S&W 38 Chiefs Special revolver, fitted with a clip attachment on the backstrap of the frame, to hold the nonmoving finger of his Hosmer A.P.R.L. hook. The A.P.R.L. voluntary-closing hook is designed so tension on the control cable brings the fingers together, closing the hook, permitting the movable finger to pull the double-action trigger. The amount of grip is controlled by the amount of tension on the cable. Armes, who has had the "Cineplasty" operation—a surgically prepared tunnel through the bicep muscle for placement of a moulded-plastic insert, connected directly to the control cable—is able to get enough grip to climb an elevator cable, and has. As a backup gun, Armes carries a 22 rimfire magnum single shot pistol, built directly into his right prosthesis which has, to date, fired one lethal and, for Armes, lifesaving shot, when he was confronted by a rifle-wielding assailant.

Armes keeps his shooting skills in top form with daily practice in his private indoor range with handguns, machineguns and long guns. Armes fires semi-automatic pistols in the same manner as revolvers, with a clip grip on the back of the frame and the grip safety disconnected. Long guns are

fired in a more conventional manner—gripping the forend with one hook and working the trigger by moving the other hook back against it.

Bill Manning lost his left arm at the shoulder and most of his right hand in combat in Vietnam and is presently Commissioner for the Department of Veterans Affairs for the state of Tennessee. In his spare time, Manning shoots, hunts (with both rifle and bow), races cars and found time to invent a special hook adapted for handgun shooting among other things.

Manning's "Accruhook" features a triangular hole in the nonmoving finger into which fits a beryllium-copper stud, held in place by a bayonet-type locking lever. The studs are offered with round and rectangular bases which can be screwed or bolted into the handles of a variety of tools and appli-

(Above and right) George Moore's Remington Sportsman 58 is fitted with custom stocks and hardware by Steven Goode, who also made identical fittings for Moore's 742. The trigger guard was added after an accidental discharge when a friend bumped the trigger while loading the gun.

(Top right) Bill Combel of Richardson, Texas—a participant since the first hunt—uses a shoulder pod mount, similar to that used by news cameramen, designed with the help of another amputee hunter.

ances, including handguns, assuring a solid grip and a quick release by pressing the lever. The Accruhook is the only commercially-made device of its kind and is available from the United States Manufacturing Company (180 North San Gabriel Blvd., Pasadena, California 91117-0330). The Accruhook operates on a voluntary-opening principle wherein the user pulls on the control cable to open the hook. Closure and grip strength are controlled by rubber tension-bands or springs mounted on the hook. This device works well with single-action revolvers and semi-automatic pistols. The short movement of the hook finger from the bottom of the trigger guard

44 Magnum revolver. A rough-carved set of wood grips are grooved near the bottom to fit the fingers of the Sierra two-load or A.P.R.L. hook, giving this heavy revolver solid support on the right side, allowing use of the left hand for trigger operation.

As George Moore was landing his jet fighter in Vietnam, ground control neglected to mention there was a ditch crossing that particular field. After the plane stopped cartwheeling, Moore spent the next forty-three months in hospitals undergoing amputations and skin grafts, emerging with both legs amputated above the knee, right hand amputated below the elbow and only a partial left hand.

Moore had a degree in public administration and continued his studies in spite of a doctor who told him that someone in Moore's condition had no business in hospital administration. Moore received an M.S. in Public Management from Carnegie-Mellon University, graduating *summa cum laude,* and is now the Assistant Medical Center Director at the Cleveland V.A. Medical Center.

Moore hunted and fished as a boy in Mississippi and continues to this day. Gunsmith Terry Hughes of Glendale, Arizona, crafted a customized 357 Dan Wesson revolver for Moore, who equipped it with a Bushnell Phantom 2.5x scope. The Wesson is uniquely adapted for fitting to a milled aluminum block by virtue of its straight-grip frame. The block is fitted with a Hosmer WD 400 quick-disconnect wrist-unit insert and attaches directly to the right arm socket. The trigger is worked by Moore's left hand, using a cable attachment with a squeeze grip, allowing both double- and single-action fire. Moore has taken about a deer per year at ranges of 150 to 190 yards for the last six years using the Wesson, mostly with iron sights. Though he

to the upper surface of the trigger is not adapted to the long pull of the double-action handgun.

A faulty fuse assembly in a hand grenade cost Roger Weir his right hand in a naval training accident in 1961. On leaving the Navy, Weir went into prosthetic work, then joined the Veterans Administration. He is now Chief of the Prosthetic and Sensory Aids Service at the V.A. Hospital in Huntington, West Virginia.

An avid shooter since his boyhood in upstate New York and past President of the Huntington Rifle and Pistol Club, Weir has combined a study of firearms adaptations with the study and collecting of hooks and mechanical hands. Weir has become a left-handed shooter, to a degree, but has worked out a system for a "two-handed" grip for his Ruger Redhawk

(Above and right) The late Elden Paddock used a shooting vest with a stock boot and a Remington 1100 with a forend grip of a unique and compact design by Ronald Jones.

now hunts with a group, Moore often took to the outdoors alone, stowing his wheelchair in the back of his 1984 Jeep CJ7 Scrambler by means of a Bruno Independent Living Aids "Out Rider" hoist and towing a trailer-mounted Hustler ATV, which he used to traverse the back country. Moore gave up jets, but continued flying a 1968 Ercoupe for ten years. Raising a family, hunting, fishing and working on his farm in Mississippi now occupy his free hours.

Even when I had hands, I was never adept with a handgun and saw little point in pursuing handgun shooting following an accident with homemade explosives that removed my hands at

popped on above my head, but I came up with an idea for a nondestructive version of this system—a block of heavy leather, about 2 inches by 2 inches by about one-inch thick. Under the outer square of leather, a strip of canvas or, better, seat-belt material is placed in the sandwich to form a loop above the long axis of the block and is secured under the first layer of leather on the opposite side. The block is held together by rivets or screws and a ½-inch hole is bored through the center for the hook fingers. The cloth loop created over the top of the block slips over the barrel and forend of the rifle. The size of this loop is critical. It must be made to slip to the point where it will

through the block to engage the oval nut in the track.

Odd as it might seem, those with one arm or hand missing use more in the way of adaptive equipment than bilateral amputees. The reason: If the right hand or arm is missing, most shooters wish to use the left hand and fingers for trigger control, but without shooting on the left side. Most such shooters employ a strategy of moving the trigger to the forend. The methods are many, varied and adapted to the individual shooter on the basis of the type and length of amputation.

For his Ruger 44 Magnum carbine, Roger Weir opted for a pistol grip attachment, built around the grip of a

Roger Weir fires his 44 Ruger Redhawk. Grooved grips fit the hook to offer firm support.

age fifteen. I faced two problems in overcoming the physical aspects of amputation. First was the inability to get a solid grip on anything. Second was learning that my hooks were not hands, but *tools* which now did the work of hands, often in a far different way. For the record, I'm still working on Number Two.

Early attempts at rifle shooting were frustrated by an inability to get a suitable grip on the forend—the hook soon began chewing up the stock. I saw the film *The Best Years Of Our Lives* which contains a sequence of amputee Harold Russell shooting a rifle. The 22 was fitted with a trigger guard screwed into the forend. This gave the front hook solid support, but left holes in the wood—not good for resale of the rifle.

I don't know how or when the light

make a tight fit, which should be the point where the shooter wants to grip the rifle or shotgun. One size will not fit all. I have never detected any adverse effects on accuracy caused by what amounts to a soft barrel band.

For use of this system on Browning and other shotguns with recoiling barrels, I dip the top of a stiff canvas loop in hot paraffin. It can be moulded to the rib of the barrel and after a few shots the paraffin provides enough lubrication for the barrel to slide easily, affording proper ejection, while maintaining a good grip on the sides of the forend. On a rifle such as the 40X Remington, the block can be attached directly to the track used for the movable front sling swivel. The block is drilled vertically. A screw, with a washer under the head, is inserted in the hook hole with the threaded end sticking up

junked 380 pistol of European origin, with a rod to actuate the trigger, running directly under the forend of the carbine. The job was done by Michael Wolak of Watkins Glen, New York.

George Moore selected a Remington 742 Woodsmaster BDL in 30-06 with a Redfield 3-9x variable scope and as a companion autoloader, a Remington Sportsman 58, 12-gauge. Both guns were equipped with identical left-hand pistol grips fitted laterally, to allow Moore to shoot from a wheelchair. The right-hand support is tapped into the receiver just above the spot occupied by the original trigger guard. A universal joint attached to a steel rod gives full flexibility. The distal end is fitted with the same Hosmer quick-disconnect wrist unit as the Dan Wesson revolver. For Moore's convenience the safety was reversed from left to right and fitted with a large button. Moore prefers a trap stock and has both trap and Skeet barrels for the 58. Both are put to use at the local trap and Skeet club where Moore consistently breaks twenty-three of twenty-five in Skeet and trap. The attachments were weighed and measured to fit Moore's body and reach. The customizing, complete with matching high-polish blue finish, is the work of Steven Goode of Torrence, California. Goode, an engineer at T.R.W., builds custom guns as a sideline. He also made Moore a fly rod and spinning rod. Both Moore and Weir have custom hunting knives crafted to fit their respective prostheses and individual needs.

When the late Elden Paddock of Branchport, Yates County, New York lost his right arm at the shoulder in a farm accident, it seemed the end of his hunting and trap shooting. Paddock, however, enlisted gunsmith Ronald Jones of nearby Penn Yan to come up with a solution. Jones made Paddock a leather shooting vest with a boot at the right shoulder, assuring proper placement of the butt of Paddock's Remington 1100, 12-gauge autoloader. The boot had the added advantage of supporting the buttstock, allowing the shooter to rest between shots without having to remove the gun from his shoulder. The trigger is operated by a steel rod through an aluminum guide. A side-mounted grip on the forend is finger-scalloped with a push-button trigger just in front of the left index finger, offering good support with little change in the conventional forend grip. Thus equipped, Paddock was able to continue shooting and, on occasion, break twenty-five straight.

In 1972, in the town of Olney, Texas (population 5,000), County Commissioner Jack Bishop and Community Development Executive Director Jack Northrup were discussing bird hunting over coffee one morning. Known as "the one-armed Jacks"—each having lost an arm through injury—the talk became serious regarding shooting equipment. The discussion expanded to how other amputee shooters cope with their sport and eventually to the establishment of the annual One-Arm Dove Hunt held in Olney the first Friday and Saturday in September after the beginning of dove season—the first weekend after Labor Day.

This year will mark the twentieth annual hunt. Arm amputees are welcome from over the nation, though this unique event is still little known outside of Texas. Participation has grown from a few to over fifty amputees who attended the nineteenth hunt for the large band-tailed pigeon, a swift and difficult target. Spouses, children and friends have become part of the festival, now a community event. Local merchants have contributed ammunition and guns for prizes; area farmers and ranchers furnish hunting sites. There is music, dancing, door prizes, a glove swap, one-arm tales, one-arm talent and a cow chip chunkin' competition pitting amputees against local politicians. (Hey, it's Texas.)

A breakfast, open to all, is served at a charge of ten cents a finger to each diner. If there are enough doves, there is a dove dinner, though of late the scarcity of birds has led to the substitution of hamburgers. Prizes for amputee hunters bringing in the most doves are awarded in both the above- and below-elbow classes, in a competition stiffer than many might think. Bill Richardson—a participant since the first hunt—has won the Illinois State trap shooting championship, the nonresident trap shooting championship in Ohio and several big money

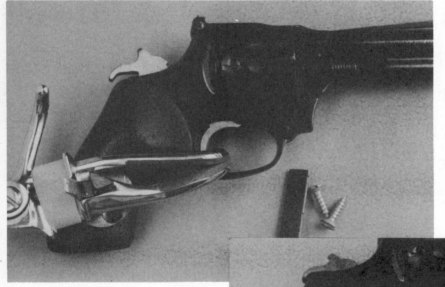

(Above and right) The Accruhook, developed by Bill Manning, uses a bayonet locking system to attach to a stud which can be fitted to a number of devices including handguns. A control cable attached to the thumb of the hook opens the hook raising the attached finger against the trigger of a single-action revolver or semi-automatic. Movement is too limited for use with double-action arms. For the best anchor, a custom grip of a more solid material is recommended.

Weir's 44 Magnum Ruger carbine with custom forearm grip by Michael Wolak.

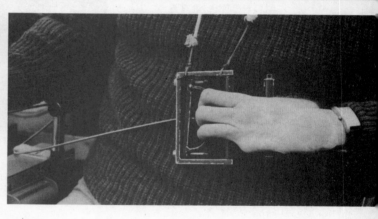

(Above, top right and right) George Moore demonstrates how he bagged about a deer a year with a 357 Magnum. Custom grip for the Dan Wesson is by Terry Hughes. The ATV took Moore through western hunting areas. Squeeze grip for the trigger is operated by Moore's left hand.

The author's forend grip is made of leather, canvas or seatbelt nylon.

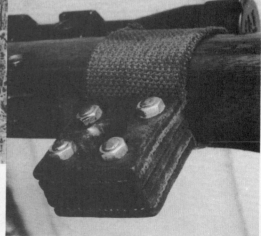

shoots in Las Vegas, besting a considerable number of non-handicapped shooters.

The essence of the dove hunt, however, goes beyond a day's shooting in the field. "It's a lost and lonely feeling to wake up in that hospital missing some parts," commented Ned Robinson, Vice President of the North Texas Amputee support group. "Only another amputee knows where you are coming from." Recent amputees in particular find the hunt not only a source of psychological support, but a valuable meeting to exchange information, ideas and technology, in an atmosphere of relaxed good fellowship where participants range in age from their teens to their seventies, each finding his own path through life's challenges. ●

AUTHOR'S NOTE

Olney, Texas is at the juncture of Texas 79 and Texas 114, 45 miles south of Wichita Falls and 100 miles west of Fort Worth. The One-Arm Dove Hunt Association is a not-for-profit organization. There are no dues or fees for amputees at this time. Active membership is obtained by any amputee making any donation. Honorary membership is open to anyone making a donation. As the activity expands and times are not getting better, there is a real need for a corporate sponsor. Northrup and Bishop have been unsuccessful in finding an arms or ammunition manufacturer to donate a couple of guns for prizes or a case or two of ammunition, which doesn't seem all that much. Interested parties should contact:

One-Arm Dove Hunt Association
P.O. Box 582
Olney, TX 76374
(817) 564-2102/8 AM—5 PM CST
Roger Weir would be interested in hearing from amputees who have devised aids for shooting. He may be reached by letter at 208 West 32nd St., Huntington, WV 25312.

Photo of Jay J. Armes by Fred Honig, reproduced with permission of Macmillan Publishing Company from "Jay J. Armes Investigator" by Jay J. Armes, copyright 1976 by Jay J. Armes. Other photos by the author, Roger Weir and courtesy Mrs. Manly Smith and Jack Bishop.

The author chats with George Moore who holds his Remington 742.

Jay J. Armes needed a gun that could be brought speedily into action. His choice was an S&W Chiefs Special with a backstrap grip fitted to the A.P.R.L. hook.

PICKING SAFARI RIFLES

by CHARLES ASKINS

THE COMPLETE success of the African safari depends far more than most sportsmen realize on the choice of shooting irons. African fauna bears little resemblance to North American game critters and the good old 7mm Magnum falls a little short in many cases. After 30 safaris over the past thirty-five years on all of the Dark Continent, I have formed some pretty solid preferences for guns that will do the job. I'd like to tell you about them.

To begin, it is grievous error to journey off to Northern Rhodesia with only one firearm. Game ranges from the 12-pound dik-dik to the 2000-pound Cape buffalo, and while the 458 Magnum will kill everything in Zimbabwe, it will rob you of a lot of fun if you insist on only the one powder-burner. Better to take a heavy caliber, and the 458 is excellent, but you also need a medium bore. A good gun like the 300 Weatherby Magnum or the 300 Winchester

This buffalo, wounded, charged from 20 feet, was shot in the right nostril at 12 feet. He was dead but still hit the writer.

Magnum. Either will account for game in the 600-1000-pound category and do a most efficient job of bringing the game to ground.

A cardinal rule when selecting the African battery is to always go a little more than slightly over-armed. One time, fully thirty years ago, I journeyed off to Uganda. The country in those days belonged to the British and it was an excellent shooting spot. Winchester had just come along with the 264 Magnum, so nothing would do but that I fetch this brand-new baby into game-rife Uganda. Now the 264 is a

pretty good whitetail gun, but it was way over its depth on the fauna of the area where I hunted. That dinky little 140-grain slug was simply not up to the job. Of course, I had the 458 Magnum, too, but on critters like Uganda kob, I stuck to the 264. It was a disaster!

I was hunting in Africa every year for thirty safaris, one time visiting the continent three times during the twelve months. I usually hunted for thirty days but sometimes only stayed for twenty days. I counted on a trophy for every day I was afield and seldom

did I miss that count. Naturally a feller would get bored if he took over the same pair of shooting irons and I seldom did. The factory models soon wore thin and I got a big kick out of testing numerous wildcat calibers.

A somewhat unusual aspect of the situation was that I never shot a game animal with the 30-06. It wasn't that there was anything wrong with the ancient caliber; it was simply too familiar. Now this is not to say that the '06 would not perform quite satisfactorily on a number of African species. It would, I am sure. Trophies like the eland, greater kudu, oryx, sable and roan antelope and leopard would be suitable game for the Old Reliable. But the bullet should not be less than 180 grains and the 200-grain as a hot handload would be even better.

The second safari, in '59, I again carted along the 458 Magnum for tuskers, buffalo and lion, but I also had

Hunting lions in the Northern Frontier District of Kenya: This zebra was duly hung in a tree as bait.

the 338 Magnum. This was a brand-new loading in those ancient days and neither the rifle—it was the Winchester Model 70—nor the cartridge had ever been in Africa. I am a southpaw and I had a laddy-o named Bob West switch the bolt handle on both the 458 and the 338 to the far side of the fence. The ammo was factory stuff; the 458 drove a 500-grain solid at 4600 foot pounds of muzzle whoosh and the 338 loaded with a 250-grain factory softpoint at 2660 fps indicated 3900 foot pounds of muzzle slam.

I knocked off an 80-pound bull tusker at 50 feet with one shot between ear and eye; and the 338 dropped a seven-foot leopard over the bait at 25 yards. And along with the big cat, there were greater kudu, sable ante-

There are no sighting-in ranges in safari camps. Here the shooter utilizes the hood of the Land Rover.

lope, roan antelope, oryx, hartebeest and wildebeest and a multitude of lesser species, game like waterbuck, bushbuck, sessebe, impala and like trophies.

An interesting peculiarity of African safari hunting is that the professional hunter never has any species of benchrest. Apparently he thinks that the dude hunter arrives in the depth of the bush with his shooting iron perfectly sighted in. After 30 years of shooting over all the better parts of hunting Africa, I have yet to see anything that resembles a place to check out the rifle sights. Knowing this after a lifetime of experience, I go out the first day in camp and drape myself over the hood of the old Land Rover and bang away at an improvised mark.

One time, not too long ago, I did this with a wildcat rifle and a wildcat caliber and about the fifth shot the scope kicked plumb off the rifle. That's right, the recoil was just so unbelievable the mount simply could not take it. The caliber was the 8x68mm, a wildcat of my own concoction, and the rifle was a Remington M700 with Shilen barrel. The fault was neither with the ordnance nor the loading. The trouble was the poorly designed scope mount. I'll not name the make and model, but suffice to say I've shunned that mounting ever since.

What is seldom realized by the brand-new tyro to the African scene is that the walking safari is now behind us. My Old Man and I one time hunted with Charles "Bwana" Cottar in Kenya. The year was 1923, and the safari went on for five weeks. We walked every day, sometimes as much as 20 miles. That marathon is now a thing of the past. The modern professional hunter loads up his client (all dude hunters are now referred to as "cli-

ents") and the veldt is scouted via Land Rover. It is infinitely more pleasant, believe me! Now there are exceptions to this practice. If you elect to go for a bull tusker, then you must walk and 20 miles is not at all unusual.

I put Leupold scopes on all my safari rifles and I set them up in Conetrol mounts. After the disastrous experience with the mounts that could not take the recoil, I have chosen the Conetrol, and regardless of how much kick may be developed, the mount takes it. This, I might add, includes the 460 Weatherby which churns up a mere 80 foot pounds of backward slam!

As for the glass sight, use care you do not choose a scope with too much magnification. I never fire a shot at more than 150 yards, and at this yardage what we are seeking is not magnification but clarity and precision. The best scope I have found, after several hundred trophies brought to bag, is 3½-5x magnification. And the bigger the objective lens the better. I like 40mm and this can be had. I shoot my buffalo (and I have killed 95) at never more than 40 yards and at this distance the target looms up awfully big, believe me. I shoot for the heart and not much magnification is required.

Almost every tyro who makes his first safari fetches along the 375 H&H Magnum. This is a fine load and an excellent caliber for critters like lion, leopard, greater kudu, sable, roan antelope, eland, oryx, hartebeest and similar antelope. But the dear old 375 just cannot cut it when it comes to the most dangerous animal in Africa, the Cape buffalo. Now, I grant you there have been buff shot with the 300-grain

Isiolo, typical hamlet of the Northern Frontier, Kenya, and the last town before the Land Rover safari moves into the bush.

slug, but the truth of the matter is the slug just falls 100 grains short of proper lethality to be recommended for this most difficult animal. Nothing less than 400 grains of hard-nosed punch is needed. My favorite killer is the 416 Magnum with 400 grains of solid—a bullet with no jacket, no lead and no core. I have shot through buffalo bulls from shoulder to shoulder and gone on to wound a second animal. This wounding was unfortunate and I polished off the wounded animal, but the point I am making is that you simply cannot have too much punch in the round you fire on the big ones.

One time Mike Hissey, my favorite professional, and I were in Uganda, this for the second time, and we were spaced out on buffalo. The bag limit

was six in those days and I determined I'd have the full limit. I was shooting the 458 Magnum which is really proper medicine for this most dangerous animal and Hissey, an old hand and a full-time resident of Kenya colony, had an ancient 470 double rifle. It had the usual open sights and had passed through a dozen owners before it came to my hunter.

Once upon a time, mighty close to a century agone, the double gun in calibers like 450, 465, 470, 475 and 476 was the only firearm seen in the hands of safari huntsmen. The old guns killed quite well, you may be sure of that. But when Hissey and I went seeking the mighty bovine in the bush of Uganda, the professional was having plenty of trouble finding cartridges. These had to be purchased in Nairobi and the quantity and quality was a dubious thing.

At any rate, we went a-seeking the

George Parker and Tony Dyer with a 45-inch bull buffalo. The rifle was the 375 Magnum. The days were the old days.

Cape ruffian and we were not long in coming up with a herd of not less than 200 animals. In this sort of crowd, you can easily select the old bulls by their massive horns. I had by this time made enough safaris and shot enough buff to insist on getting up close. I am a heart shooter and I aimed for the shoulder. Hissey and I—with the wind in our favor—crawled on hands and knees to within 40 yards of the big band and then I picked out the biggest bull and shot him spank through the shoulders. The 500-grain 458 slug put him down, but he wouldn't stay supine!

The buffalo floundered for a moment or two and got back on his feet. Whereupon I slammed him with another 500 grains of lethal lead. I had instructed Hissey to shoot, too, after I had gotten in the opener. He poured in his two rounds and this helped, although it did not end the chase. At any rate, and to make a long story short, my professional hunter and I gathered in the full bag of six bulls, but not a single buff was killed with one shot!

In Zambia, much more recently, I was again stalking the country's most dangerous denizen. We came up with a band, I selected a monster bull and, at the usual 40 steps, I pumped 400 grains of hottest lead into his near shoulder. I was, on this occasion, shooting my 416/404 and it dropped the target like he had been struck by nuclear reaction. The only trouble was he bounced back to his feet and took off like a scalded cat.

We got on the sign liberally sprinkled with darkest blood and the professional opined, "He won't go far."

We trailed along for maybe a half-mile and the bull bushed up in some of the most dense mopani. I moved forward, the DuBiel 416 at the ready. At about 20 feet the wounded beast came out of his hidey-hole and he was in full forward gear. Now buffalo, unlike other bovines, do not charge with the head down, the horns at the ready. Instead they come on full speed ahead with the head up and watching the target. The horns are only lowered at the very last instant.

I shot this wounded critter up the right nostril—at 12 feet yet. The bullet reached his brain and he was dead but he did not know it. He was going all out and even though the brain was destroyed he was in high gear and on he came. Just long enough to hit me and I flew one way and my rifle went another. The buff fell partly across my legs and my professional hunter had to get me by the shoulder and pull me out from under the behemoth. The rifle was not harmed and, other than a dozen sore spots, neither was I. Buffalo hunting is never dull, believe me!

Yannie Meyer, a rancher in the Low Veldt of Zimbabwe, owns 54,000 hectares of ranch land. Now a hectare is 2.4 acres so Yannie's holdings are considerable. In this virgin bush he had what the Game Department thought to be some 50,000 of the smaller antelope, stuff like impala, bushbuck, waterbuck and the like. I went over every year for four straight years and I shot Yannie's small buck. I'd go out in the morn and kill five impala, come

(Left) The writer and his long-time professional hunter, Mike Hissey, and a 46-inch sable, good for the Rowland Ward book. The rifle was the 8mm-06.

(Below) An excellent 10-foot lion shot in Botswana by the writer.

(Left) Hunter and trackers string up a kongoni for leopard bait. The carcass must be hung so that the leopard has to lie on the limb and fish for it. If it is too accessible, he will eat it in short order.

back to the ranchhouse, eat a big meal, sleep for 30 minutes and return to the bush and there I'd knock over another five antelope. I'd keep this up for a full two weeks. Within 20 miles of the ranch is the biggest copper mine in all Africa. Here, 15,000 contract workers eat up not only the Askins' contribution but cry for more. I kept this up for four straight years—five bushbuck in the morn and a similar number after noontime. It was richest fun.

The first expedition was with a Sako Hunter, left-hand bolt, in 240 Weatherby. I handloaded a round which drove the bullet of 100 grains at 3000 fps. This was fine except if I occasionally tried to drive the slug through any very considerable amount of brush, it wouldn't always reach the game. I had to watch that one!

The second year I decimated my 140 little bucks with the 270 Weatherby Magnum. The loading was another Askins original using the 150-grain bullet driven by 82 grains H-570, which indicated 3200 fps velocity. This baby was pure poison. I drove the slug through acres of bush and never lost an animal.

Finally, I took over an old favorite of mine, the 8mm-06. This one was made up on the Steyr Model M, left-hand, the wildcat barrel attached by Shilen.

Shooting a 170-grain bullet and 57 grains of MR4064, I realized 3000 fps at the muzzle and simply had a ball. I'd fetched the Steyr along not so much for the multitude on the Yannie Meyer ranch, but to use across all of Zimbabwe. The fourth and last year I decimated the great herds, I again carted along the Steyr.

I've knocked off five African lions, three with the 458 Magnum and the last pair with the 416/404 Magnum. Actually bagging old King Leo ain't all it's cracked to be. You bait the Old Boy, creep into a "hide," as the Limey calls a blind, and await his arrival. One well-placed round is all that is needed. I've accounted for five leopards, too. Again, this is altogether too easy. The bait is strung in a tree; the blind is within 30 yards. Only one word of caution—be double damned sure your first round is a killing one! Nothing on all the African veldt is more

dangerous than a wounded leopard. He'll let you pass and leap on your back and it's pretty sticky right after that.

I have journeyed off to hunt Africa with sometimes as many as five shooting irons—four rifles and a scattergun. I have yet to be given the slightest trouble by any customs officer in any of the hunting states. One time, a few years ago, there was a rebellion brewing and I packed along my favorite handgun, the 45 auto. Again no customs officer raised the slightest alarm.

I have now been through the port of entry of Johannesburg, South Africa, sixteen times. No people can be more friendly, cooperative and helpful. No license, no permit, no entry forms need be filled out. And the same is true of ammunition. I never pack along any great numbers of cartridges, but whether many or few there are never any problems.

Ordinarily, I fly into Jo'burg from either New York or Miami and this is smooth and enjoyable. At times in the past I have pushed off from Athens, Lisbon, Paris and Hamburg, and again there was never any question about the ordnance. One time, however, it was different. I was flying to New Delhi in India and I was traveling on Air India. We touched down at Heathrow in London and I immediately ran into trouble. British customs seized my rifles as I was swapping the Air India ship from New York for the second transport on into India.

"You have no permit for this rifle," they informed me at Heathrow. I went on to New Delhi sans my favorite shooting iron. I had to borrow Percy Dinshaw's old 375 Model 70 to stalk the world's largest buffalo, the mighty gaur. Four months later, Air India of-

The writer with an Angola roan antelope. The roan is as big as the American wapiti. Rifle is a Husqvarna chambered for the 8mm-06.

ficials got my rifles back. By that time, the shikar for gaur was just a memory.

To sum it all, the nimrod who is for Africa should book with the right people, and safari to the right places, of course. And, to get the most juice out of the grandest hunting this earth provides, he should take enough guns, meaning a heavy and a medium, and leave the peashooters home.   ●

Young Masai warrior on the trail. When asked where he was going, he said to his grandparents'. When asked further where his parents were, he said they had been killed. We loaded him in the safari car, spear and all, and took him to his grandparents' kraal.

To learn the meaning of SAMP, PDW, ICW, CSW, SFW and much of military attitude, consult . . .

Revolutionary War PDW—single shot, 58-caliber flintlock.

by STANLEY C. CRIST

The 22-caliber SCAMP was an attempt by Colt to produce a true PDW.

THE SMALL ARMS Master Plan (SAMP)—formulated in September, 1989 at the U.S. Infantry School—outlines the desired characteristics for 21st century infantry weapons. The SAMP envisions a three-member family of small arms—a Personal Defense Weapon (PDW), an Individual Combat Weapon (ICW) and a Crew-Served Weapon (CSW)—in an effort to provide a revolutionary increase in combat power for the individual soldier. This is a laudable goal, but just how closely can reality conform to desire? To answer that question it is necessary to compare the current weaponry state-of-the-art with the characteristics expressed in the SAMP:

The Personal Defense Weapon

The personal defense weapon (as defined by the SAMP) should weigh less than 1.5 pounds, be capable of hands-free carry and possess a high hit probability out to 100 meters. The ammunition should be deadly out to 50 meters, with the ability to defeat body armor.

The personal defense weapon issued by modern armies is—with rare exception—a semi-automatic pistol. This is due to a combination of two factors: tradition and technology. Two centuries ago, the relatively primitive technology limited the infantry arsenal to the muzzle-loading, single shot musket and the muzzle-loading, single

The SMALL ARMS MASTER PLAN

shot pistol. Obviously, only the pistol was sufficiently small and light to serve as what is now called a personal defense weapon, setting edged weapons aside. The invention of the revolver in the middle of the last century gave a significant increase in firepower, but the PDW remained a one-hand gun. Later, with the invention of metallic cartridges and smokeless powder, the way was opened for the development of a much more effective personal defense weapon.

Although the submachine gun came into existence at about the same time as the self-loading pistol, the early submachine gun was much too big and heavy to replace the handgun in the personal defense role. First efforts to get submachine gun firepower in a handgun-size weapon resulted in the machine pistol, nothing more than a standard service pistol modified to fire in the full-auto mode; it was usually equipped with a detachable shoulder stock. The typical machine pistol suf-

fered from excessively high rates of fire, inadequate ammo capacity and lack of controllability, rendering it ineffective at normal combat ranges. As a result, the handgun—which, by the early 1900s had evolved into a magazine-fed, semi-automatic pistol—continued to be the only practical choice for the personal defense requirement.

Shortly before World War I, the United States adopted the 45-caliber M1911 pistol. Rugged, simple and reliable, it was carried by U.S. troops for over 70 years and earned an unequaled reputation for reliability and stopping power. Indeed, the Colt "forty-five" is still considered by many small arms authorities to be the ultimate combat handgun, and some special operations personnel reportedly have resumed using it after experiences in Grenada and Panama led them to question the effectiveness of the 9mm.

After World War II, some elements of the U.S. armed forces began campaigning for a 9mm pistol to replace the 45-caliber M1911A1 then in use. Their reasoning was quite logical: Higher hit probability, greater magazine capacity, less ammunition weight, and NATO-compatibility added up to

a pistol of superior military characteristics. Political and economic factors prevented the adoption of a 9mm handgun until the mid-1980s, when the acquisition of the M9 Beretta gave American soldiers a pistol that possessed the desired qualities.

While accurate and reliable, the double-action M9 is, however, much more complicated than the M1911 it replaced. This complexity is due in part to the double-action mechanism—a design feature that might be unnecessary in a combat weapon—and in part to the multiple safety devices (which are meant to reduce the likelihood of accidental discharges).

An interesting historical note is that Beretta apparently drew heavily from the Walther P38—a World War II German service pistol—when designing what was eventually to become the M9. The double-action mechanism, hammer-dropping safety and straight-line, recoiling barrel and locking block assembly are almost pure Walther in their construction and operation. It is curious that the German army had a double-action 9mm pistol some 40 years before the rest of the world decided it was a good idea. Some consider it a sad state of affairs that the most technologically advanced military establishment on the face of the earth adopted a personal defense weapon based on a 50-year-old design using an 80-year-old cartridge. However, in the realm of conventional handguns, the Beretta does undeniably rank as one of the best.

Long before the M9 pistol was adopted, the submachine gun had been nearly perfected, resulting in PDW alternatives that are overwhelmingly superior to the semi-auto pistol. An American, Gordon Ingram, developed his ultra-compact M10 and M11 submachine guns. While the M10, in 45 and 9mm, was still too big and heavy to replace the pistol, the diminutive 380-caliber M11 was no larger—and only a little heavier—than the 1911 Colt. The M11 was later redesigned by SWD, Inc. to accommodate the more effective 9mm NATO round. With the straight-line stock design, this small submachine gun is much more controllable than machine pistols, although the recoil impulse of the standard 9mm cartridge is nevertheless great enough to cause a high degree of bullet dispersion during full-auto fire. Even so, maximum effective range is still much greater than can be had with the service pistol.

At a weight of four pounds, it would be no great effort to carry the 9mm M11 in a properly designed shoulder holster. As a practical consideration, it

(Left) The ultra-compact M11 SMG looks more like a PDW on firepower.

(Above) The Beretta 9mm is one of the best pistols made for military use, but just one more step toward a PDW.

would have to be loaded with a short, 12-round magazine when holstered, but, backed up with two or three 34-round magazines in a carrying pouch, the soldier would have a personal defense weapon of far greater combat capability than would be had from a semi-automatic pistol and three 15-round magazines.

Steyr of Austria recently unveiled its Tactical Machine Pistol (TMP), a 9mm personal defense weapon that is similar in configuration to the SWD M11. The TMP uses a high-strength synthetic material for the frame, as opposed to the stamped, sheet metal construction of the SWD firearm, and reportedly uses a rotating-bolt, locked-breech method of operation instead of the straight blowback operation more common to weapons of this type.

Interestingly, Steyr has chosen not to equip the TMP with a shoulder stock, expressing the philosophy that speed of engagement is slowed too much when a stock is used. Shooting "from the hip" is a short-range proposition at best, and controllability is certain to be poor when attempting aimed, full-auto fire without a stock. Some combat scenarios may require a "quick-draw" capability; in most situations there is more than enough time to deploy a properly designed shoulder stock, with a corresponding increase in combat effectiveness.

Heckler & Koch, in response to the increasing demand for a personal defense weapon, is marketing the MP5K-PDW. An inventive adaptation of the compact MP5K submachine gun, the MP5K-PDW utilizes the sturdy Choate folding stock to enable accurate, aimed fire. Realizing that many combat operations occur at night, HK has prudently incorporated

a tritium front sight as a standard feature, although leaving a tritium rear sight as an option.

The barrel is slightly longer than that of a standard MP5K, with a threaded muzzle for attachment of a sound suppressor. This is a feature of particular value to crewmen of aircraft downed behind enemy lines; the ability to fire the weapon without detection could easily make the difference between escape and capture.

For pilots of jet fighters and attack helicopters, the leg holster and magazine pouch would allow the six-pound weapon, spare ammo and suppressor to be worn with some degree of comfort while sitting in the cockpit; however, armored vehicle crewmen and other personnel would probably find the shoulder holster to be more convenient. As with the SWD M11, a shorter (15-round) magazine would be necessary in the holstered gun.

A farsighted effort, some years ago, to produce a true personal defense weapon was the Colt SCAMP (Small Caliber Machine Pistol). The SCAMP was innovative in that Colt engineers designed it to meet the specific requirements that they saw as peculiar to the personal defense role, requirements that would—two decades later—be set forth in the Small Arms Master Plan.

First, they determined what characteristics would be desirable for the ammunition. Minimum weight and volume were considered important, and low recoil impulse was vital for maximum controllability. An effective range of 100-150 meters was also wanted, as well as the ability to penetrate the body armor then being introduced onto the battlefield. No readily available cartridge had all the desired characteristics. The standard 9mm

loading possessed the required effective range—but only against unprotected personnel—and was deficient in all other aspects. Commercial 22 rimfire ammo was excellent in regard to having minimum weight, volume and recoil impulse, but lethality and penetration were unacceptably low. The decision was made, therefore, to create a totally new cartridge. It would have a lightweight, small-diameter bullet that would achieve high velocity with low recoil, flat trajectory, optimum effective range and have the capability to defeat body armor.

The machine pistol itself was larger than an M9 Beretta, but still small enough for holster carry. A three-shot burst control was incorporated to balance the desire to maximize hit probability with the need to keep ammo consumption within acceptable limits. In addition to using low-recoil ammunition, controllability was further enhanced by positioning the barrel low in the frame and furnishing a muzzle compensator. As with the Steyr TMP, there was no apparent provision for a folding or telescoping shoulder stock.

The project was eventually shelved by Colt, with only a single prototype built and demonstrated to the U.S. Army. This was regrettable, for it meant that it would be another 20 years before a true personal defense weapon would again receive the attention of armaments manufacturers and the military establishment.

In apparent recognition of the limitations inherent to 9mm weapons and ammunition, Heckler & Koch is developing a small-caliber machine pistol. Using knowledge gained from the perfection of the G11 combat rifle, the HK PDW will use caseless ammo, although with a shorter, lighter bullet

(Left) The SMG as PDW can be small enough for a shoulder holster.

(Right) Fabrique Nationale's P90—the ultimate special operations weapon now, a PDW later? (Courtesy of FN Herstal)

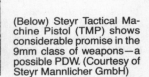

(Left) Two-hand hold, shoulder support and a visible magazine load—great PDW stuff. (Courtesy of FN Herstal)

(Below) Steyr Tactical Machine Pistol (TMP) shows considerable promise in the 9mm class of weapons—a possible PDW. (Courtesy of Steyr Mannlicher GmbH)

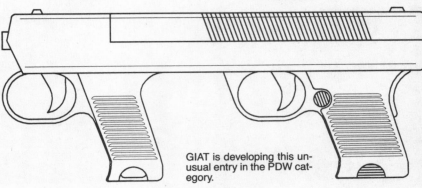

GIAT is developing this unusual entry in the PDW category.

and less propellant. Except for the use of caseless ammunition, it is almost as if the Colt SCAMP were reincarnated, so great are the similarities between the two weapons.

The Colt design fired 42-grain, 22-caliber bullets at 2000 feet per second; HK's will shoot 42-grain, 18-caliber projectiles at 1920 feet per second. Both use large capacity magazines—Colt, 27 rounds; HK, 20 rounds—with 40-round mags optional. Both are machine pistols of nearly the same configuration, size and weight.

It is interesting to note that the German firm seems to be repeating Colt's opting for minimum weight over maximum effectiveness; their weapon is also shown without a folding stock, which is surprising, since they equip the MP5K-PDW with a well-designed stock.

The French firm of GIAT has apparently seen promise in the SCAMP concept, as it is now developing a small-caliber PDW. Although the 5.7mm cartridge it uses is very similar to the Colt-designed round, the weapon itself is unique. While a front pistol grip is not uncommon on small automatic weapons, this design also incorporates a trigger at *both* front and rear grips. Presumably this is to permit the use of different firing postures, but there is no information available from GIAT concerning the design philosophy. A pistol chambered for the 5.7mm round is said to also be under development.

Thus, the semi-automatic pistol was, until recent times, the best available choice for a weapon to be worn continuously. In World War II or Korea, the M9 pistol would have been state-of-the-art. However, combining the 1938 Walther double-action mechanism with the double-column magazine of the 1935 Browning Hi-Power, the M9 seems singularly unimaginative for 1985. The Beretta is an excellent "threat-management tool" for military police use in peacetime and is more than adequate for issue to higher-ranking officers, but ultracompact submachine guns like the M11 and the TMP offer a tremendous improvement in combat capability. Hit probability with a handgun and while under enemy fire is virtually zero beyond point-blank range. A 9mm submachine gun would deliver more usable combat effectiveness. Although standard M882 9mm ball is somewhat lacking in penetration, several options do exist to enhance the ability of 9mm ammunition to defeat body armor.

Although it seems to promise a cost-effective approach, no submachine gun in 9mm caliber can come close to meeting the SAMP guidelines. The M11 weighs almost three times as much as desired, recoil impulse is excessive and hit probability is only about half what is wanted. Perhaps a marriage of the M11/TMP designs with the SCAMP high-velocity, small caliber ammunition can meet the SAMP requirements for hit probability and lethality, but it seems highly unlikely that weight can ever be reduced below about three pounds. The only comparable issue PDW—the Polish PM63, in caliber 9mm Makarov—weighs in at four pounds, and the lightest 9mm NATO service pistol—the Austrian Glock 17—barely makes the 1.5-pound weight limit.

Whatever shape the future PDW takes, it is refreshing to see that the Infantry School refuses to be bound by tradition, seeking instead to spur the development of the Army's first true personal defense weapon.

The Special Operations Weapon

Often classified as PDWs, carbines and most submachine guns are more properly special operations weapons (SOW). A true PDW can be worn on the person virtually 24 hours per day, almost regardless of the activity being performed. Carbines and SMGs will be set aside in order to accomplish any number of duties, be they driving a tank, loading a truck or operating a typewriter. Such weapons are frequently used for personal defense because they are so much more effective than pistols, but they do not truly belong in the personal defense weapon category. Their primary function is to give special operations forces (LRRPs, Rangers, Special Forces, etc.) maximum firepower in a weapon of minimum size and weight.

First introduced in semi-auto form as the U.S. Carbine, Caliber 30, M1 during WWII, the 30 Carbine was in-

The Close Assault Weapon (CAW) was one more step in the evolution of the ICW. Last nomenclature was G11. (Courtesy of Heckler & Koch)

The M16K, produced by La France, is small and light; optical sight improves practical accuracy—but is it CAW or an SOW (Special Operations Weapon)?

The MP5 SMG is the favorite SOW of special forces worldwide now—but never an ICW!

tended to replace the pistol. As the select-fire M2, it became widely available during the Korean conflict. The Carbine was immensely popular with the troops as a basic weapon because of its light weight and large magazine capacity. In the early years of the Vietnam War, the Carbine was often used by Special Forces team members. Its history demonstrates that Carbines are not PDWs.

Classified as a submachine gun because of its pistol-caliber cartridge, it would probably be more appropriate to call the Heckler & Koch MP5 a carbine, due to its general configuration and closed-bolt operation. It is perhaps the most accurate submachine gun available and that factor, combined with utmost reliability, has made it popular with such elite units as the British SAS and the U.S. Army Rangers. The only real negative quality is its weight; the MP5A3 (telescoping-stock version) weighs over seven pounds, with sling and empty magazine.

The smallest and lightest of the M16 variants, the La France M16K made in California would seem to be an ideal choice for special operations use. Even though muzzle velocity of M855 ammunition is reduced to 2400 feet per second by the 8-inch barrel, armor-piercing ability is still much superior to the 9mm. The vortex-type flash suppressor works incredibly well, completely eliminating what would otherwise be an extremely bright muzzle flash. A highly effective silencer has been developed for the weapon (and all other M16 models) for operations requiring stealth, although it necessarily adds to the weight and length. In this class, there is also the Vietnam-era Colt CAR-15.

The Fabrique Nationale P90 is an unusual design with many desirable characteristics for this class of weapon. It is relatively light, very short and boasts an extremely large magazine capacity. It has an integral optical sight and backup iron sights, and cocking handles and other controls are ambidextrous; it is usable by left-handed shooters without modification. It is true that most of these features have appeared on other weapons, thereby making the P90 seem less innovative than it might, at first look, appear. A synthetic "bullpup" stock and compact, integral optical sight were introduced on the Steyr AUG. The longitudinal, transparent plastic magazine was used on the Hill submachine gun of 1952, as was downward ejection through the pistol grip. And the small-caliber, high-velocity cartridge concept was developed by Colt for the SCAMP project. However, Fabrique Nationale is the first to incorporate—and perfect—all of these con-

The M88P, product of a Virginia firm, combines a rifle for long-range accuracy and a shotgun for maximum hit probability at close range—a possible combination SOW-ICW. (Courtesy of Special Service Arms Mfg.)

The USAS-12 delivers massive short-range firepower with a 20-shot drum magazine—a heavy ICW candidate from the SOW ranks. (Courtesy of Gilbert Equipment Co.)

The Franchi SPAS-15 has both pump-action and semi-automatic operation—a semi-SOW, at least. (Courtesy of Luigi Franchi S.p.A.)

cepts into one neat package, creating what may be the ideal close-range combat weapon.

Even with the planned adoption of the three-member family of small arms, special operations forces will almost certainly continue to require special purpose weapons, weapons that are better suited to their mission requirements. The MP5 has an out-standing reputation and is in service with armed forces throughout the world; there is little more that needs to be said about it. The M16K is based on the combat-proven M16 rifle and would seem to be an excellent special operations weapon where commonality with the standard infantry rifle is desired. The P90 *is* state-of-the-art; although there is some debate about the effectiveness of the ultra-lightweight, plastic-core bullets it fires, the concept shows great promise.

The Individual Combat Weapon

The Small Arms Master Plan has set very ambitious goals in the quest for an advanced individual combat weapon. The ICW should be semi-automatic, weigh less than ten pounds

The Chinese Type W87 35mm grenade launcher, with 12-round drum, can be used with integral bipod, rather than a tripod—a CSW now rather than later. (Courtesy of Norinco)

Argentine 12-gauge mini-grenade (right) compared to a U.S. 40mm round.

when fully loaded, be highly effective out to 500 meters against personnel wearing body armor and be able to engage light armored vehicles and slow aircraft. Probable munitions include high explosive/fragmentation and kinetic energy rounds. Also considered desirable is an advanced target acquisition system to reduce aiming and range-estimation errors.

The standard infantry weapon today is a product of evolutionary change—from single shot musket, to single shot rifle, to bolt-action repeating rifle, to semi-automatic rifle, and finally, to select-fire rifle. All of these weapons have one thing in common: Every time they fire they send a single, very small, solid projectile downrange. To hit the target requires correct estimation of range and target speed, as well as achieving a proper sight picture. Under combat stress these tasks become very difficult to accomplish well. As a result, more than 90 percent of those projectiles that are aimed at enemy personnel miss the intended targets. Add in factors such as limited visibility conditions (smoke, fog, darkness, dense foliage, etc.), uneven terrain features and minimal target exposure times, and hit probability approaches zero. A prime example is the incident reported during Operation Desert Storm wherein American and Iraqi infantry engaged in a firefight that lasted more than 15 minutes *. . . without any casualties on either side*!

The individual combat weapon is seen as the solution to these problems. Rifles must be precisely aimed in order to hit the target. The ICW, however, using bursting munitions, needs to be aimed only "close enough."

There is no readily available weapon that even comes close to meeting the SAMP specifications, although the new generation of fighting shotguns does display some of the basic characteristics expected in the individual combat weapon. Buckshot and flechette rounds give a high probability of hitting a moving target out to 100 meters. A recently marketed fin-stabilized slug from France offers rifle-like accuracy out to over 150 meters. More significantly, high explosive ammunition has been developed in this caliber; a 12-gauge "mini-grenade" round has been in production in Argentina for a number of years.

The original Close Assault Weapon (CAW) was created by Heckler & Koch in response to Joint Services Small Arms Program (JSSAP) specifications for an improved combat shotgun. Olin developed the all-brass, "belted"-case ammunition—a high-pressure, high-velocity round designed for increased terminal effect at longer ranges than the standard M162 and M257 12-gauge loads.

At least three anti-personnel rounds were developed: a 9mm load (eight 36-caliber lead pellets at 1600 feet per second), a 7mm load (eight 27-caliber tungsten alloy pellets at 1800 feet per second) and a flechette round (twenty steel darts at 3000 feet per second). Special 6-inch rounds were planned that would have enabled the development of anti-armor and fragmentation munitions. Such extra-length rounds would have to have been single-loaded directly into the chamber. With the termination of the CAW program, H&K and Olin discontinued work on the gun and ammunition.

Ammunition for PDWs and SOWs: 45 ACP, 9mm NATO, 22 SCAMP, 5.7mm SS90, 30 Carbine and 5.56mm NATO.

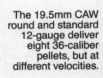
The 19.5mm CAW round and standard 12-gauge deliver eight 36-caliber pellets, but at different velocities.

Teflon-coated KTW round (center) and French Arcane ammunition (right) achieve 50 percent better penetration than standard NATO 9mm ball—PDW and SOW ammo now.

The Gilbert USAS-12 is the only select-fire shotgun currently in production. Made to Mil-Spec standards, it was created with the close assault weapon system specifications as a guideline. With the exception of the cocking handle, configuration and controls are nearly identical to the M16 rifle. A ten-round box magazine is standard, with an optional 20-round drum.

The USAS-12 was designed to employ standard commercial and military 12-gauge shells, which are commonly available throughout the world. The Winchester 000 Buckshot round is nearly as effective as high-pressure ammunition that Olin manufactured for the H&K CAW. Controllability with this ammunition is excellent, due in no small part to the gun's weight; at 12 pounds it is the heaviest military shotgun in production.

The demand for a true combat shotgun was peaking in the mid-1980s, and the SPAS-15 was developed in response. The dual pump-action/semi-automatic operation allows reliable functioning with low-recoil, special purpose munitions as well as standard loads. The folding stock conserves space when transporting the weapon in aircraft or motor vehicles. The lack of full-auto capability is no real handicap for a military shotgun, but the magazine capacity probably should be increased—6 rounds is marginal. In its favor is a loaded weight significantly under its competitors.

The SSAM M88P is the only production (limited production) weapon to date that attempts to achieve effectiveness in both short-range and long-range combat. It does this by combining a rifle and a shotgun in one stock assembly. Although it was originally intended to have semi-automatic operation, current models are pump-action only—a characteristic that limits its desirability for military use. Development is reportedly underway on a version with the rifle chambered for the 5.56mm NATO cartridge.

The Naval Ordnance Station in Louisville, Kentucky, created the Mk 19 Mod 3 40mm automatic grenade launcher that is now in service with all branches of the U.S. military. The Mk 19 Mod 3 is a superb weapon, with a 2200-meter range, but its 75-pound weight limits its usefulness to dismounted infantry. The current infantry weapon, the M203 grenade launcher, is a single shot device with a maximum range of only 400 meters.

In an attempt to give the foot soldier a hand-held weapon of adequate combat capability, NOS Louisville has de-

signed the 40mm Shoulder Fired Weapon (SFW). A pump-action repeater, the SFW holds four rounds (three in the magazine, plus one in the chamber) of specially modified Mk 19 Mod 3 ammunition. These intermediate pressure rounds deliver a maximum range of 1100-1300 meters, making the SFW concept seem very promising. Unfortunately, a three-round magazine is considerably smaller than the ten-round capacity desired by the SAMP. Nor can the weight factor be ignored; the 18-pound weight of the feasibility model could be reduced by the use of graphite composites and other lightweight materials to the 12- to 15-pound range, but that is still far above the SAMP limits.

Weight and magazine capacity notwithstanding, the 40mm SFW is the only weapon on which information is available that has the potential for adoption as the Infantry Combat Weapon. It must be noted, though, that the SFW is still in the development stage and any decision about production depends on the results of continued testing.

Even the best of the 12-gauge fighting shotguns cannot begin to approach the SAMP requirement for a 500-meter effective range, nor is the 18.5mm-caliber likely to permit a useful anti-armor round; there is simply too little payload volume in the 12-gauge shell. It will almost certainly be necessary to develop a weapon/munition in the 25-30mm range in order to carry an adequate explosive charge, and that would seem to dictate a loaded weight (of the ICW) considerably greater than ten pounds.

An advanced target acquisition and fire control is much more feasible. Continuing developments in computer and laser technologies make achievement of this SAMP goal seem not too difficult. For instance, the Army's Communications Electronics Command is funding development of a pocket-sized computer that may transmit visual output from a thermal sight to a helmet-mounted, heads-up display.

It should be possible to field an advanced individual combat weapon by the end of the 20th century. Each of the ICW characteristics expressed in the SAMP can probably be achieved—individually—today. Attempting to combine all of the desired traits into one weapon will require compromise. The Army wants the ultimate infantry weapon; it may become reality.

The Crew-Served Weapon

It is desired that the crew-served

weapon (CSW) be a larger variant of the ICW, with commonality of target acquisition and fire control systems, as well as munitions. The CSW should be effective against personnel out to 2000 meters and light armored vehicles out to 1000 meters. The weight should be no more than 38 pounds, divisible into two 19-pound loads for transport by the two-man crew.

The Type W87 select-fire grenade launcher from Norinco comes close to meeting the guidelines for the CSW. It has an advertised 600-meter effective range, with a maximum range of 1500 meters. Two munitions have been developed for it: a high explosive/fragmentation round and a high explosive dual-purpose round that is said to be able to penetrate 80mm of steel armor. The unique tripod is designed so that the weapon can be used to engage aircraft. In addition to the six-round box magazine, a 12-round drum is available. Carrying weights are 26.4 pounds for the launcher and 17.6 pounds for the tripod.

The conclusions regarding the ICW also apply, but perhaps even more so, to the crew-served weapon. And commonality of munitions, while quite desirable from a logistical viewpoint, hardly seems feasible; why would the same ammunition have *twice* the effective range in the CSW? Especially when that round has been optimized for the individual weapon? It would be rather like expecting the low-velocity grenade of the M203 to travel twice as far if fired in a Mk 19 Mod 3 automatic grenade launcher.

In any case, the CSW is achievable, and the Chinese Type W87 gives a good idea just how closely reality can approach desire.

Is our Small Arms Master Plan an exercise in wishful thinking, or can its visionary goals actually be achieved? Each of the desired specifications can easily be met, using present technology, on an item-by-item basis. Some of the characteristics are even achievable in combination with others. It would be wishful thinking, however, to believe that all of the goals can be accomplished in concert. Fortunately, this fact is recognized in the SAMP with the statement that, "The high goals . . . are meant to be a mark on the wall toward which the developer can strive; not a requirement that the developer must meet."

The Small Arms Master Plan outlines a family of infantry weapons that is nearly perfect, but what can realistically be fielded by the year 2000 will probably be no more than overwhelmingly superior! ●

by **HAL SWIGGETT**

Swiggett's XP-100 Remington 284 Winchester (rechambered from 7mm BR by SSK Industries) is screwed into an H-S Precision synthetic stock. This 12-point whitetail, at about 225 yards, was dropped with a single shot.

HANDGUNS TODAY:

SIXGUNS AND OTHERS

DARK CLOUDS have hovered over our firearms business this past year. There have been, however, a few silver linings. Let's talk about them.

The smallest offering weighs in at 4 ounces. The heaviest encountered tops out a fraction over 6 pounds. Honors for the best catalog go to Smith & Wesson. Why? They dropped 70 or so "numbers." Now it's readable. And understandable.

Two companies have seen fit to chamber the ever-loved 44 Special and both have added a very classy 22 WMR.

All three of the "biggies" (S&W, Colt, Ruger) have succumbed to the "shuck 'em out fast" crowd. One day they will wake up (the crowd), smell the roses, and get back to basics. Many of us know it is much better to hit what we shoot at and do it with an authoritative projectile.

So be it.

American Derringer

That littlest 4-ouncer is a legal (according to Bob Saunders) "Pen" pistol. In 2 seconds it changes from a 4.3-inch "Pen" to a 5.5-inch pistol chambered for 22 Long Rifle. It cocks on opening and has a firing pin block grip safety. Barrel length is 2 inches.

Freedom Arms

Last time around, this Freedom, Wyoming-based company gave us their full-framed big five-shooter in 22 Long Rifle. Two versions: silhouette and

varmint. Now—it should have been expected—there is a 357 Magnum. Same weight. Same revolver. Just different sized holes through its cylinder and barrel. Because it's full-grown, 180-grain sharp-pointed bullets can be loaded. I'm playing with one as this goes in and, for the first time, believe it possible to recommend 357 Magnum (but only this Freedom Arms version) for medium game. Not only can those better bullets be utilized, but the inherent strength of the revolver allows their potential to be developed.

Taurus

A pair of 44 Special five-shot double-action revolvers are offered, from Brazil. Both with heavy barrel, solid rib and full-length ejector shroud. The adjustable sight version is offered with 3-, 4- or 6-inch barrel. With fixed sight drop the 6-incher.

Rimfire enthusiasts will approve of Taurus' Model 941. The reason? It is chambered for 22 WMR. Same features as above: heavy barrel, solid rib, full-length ejector shroud, adjustable sights and, yes, a single flaw. It is offered with only 3- or 4-inch barrels for now.

Rossi

Earlier I had mentioned there were a couple of new 44 Special revolvers. This one is also made in Brazil but by Rossi. It features a 3-inch ribbed barrel with an adjustable rear sight. The five-shot cyl-

Swiggett's original COP 357 Magnum/38 Special has been reincarnated by American Derringer— shown with 22 rimfire and 25 Auto inserts.

American Derringer's 22-caliber Pen pistol straightens out to ride safely in a shirt pocket.

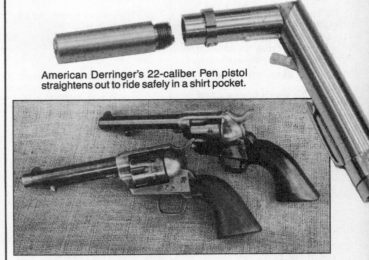

Close-up of Navy Arms "Artillery" (back) revolver and an original 1880 reissued in 1895. The only difference found was the original had inspector initials and serial number on the cylinder, the Navy Arms gun doesn't.

inder is non-fluted. A rubber combat-type grip rounds out this stainless steel 27½-ounce double-action revolver. Also new from Rossi are a pair of rimfire 22s in stainless steel, choice of 22 Long Rifle or 22 WMR.

Navy Arms

Val Forgett's Navy Arms company lists 1873 U.S. Cavalry SAA *and* 1895 U.S. Artillery SAA models with military arsenal markings, color case-hardened frame and walnut stock with the inspector's cartouche. My original Colt is lettered from Colt as being reissued to the military in 1895. Look at the photo to see what "authentic" means.

H&R 1871

It's good to see an old-line name back in production. Harrington & Richardson fell by the wayside a few years back. Was purchased, the line divided into New England Firearms along with H&R. Then fell again. Now it is newly organized under the H&R 1871 banner. Revolvers, for the moment, are offered in three models:

H&R's Sportsman 999 is still a nine-shot top-break with adjustable sights and with 6-inch barrel. I used one of these on my trapline several years immediately after WWII.

Under the New England Firearms banner two solid-frame revolvers are offered. The Ultra Mag 22 WMR is a six-shot with swing-out cylinder and 6-inch heavy barrel. NEF's Lady Ultra is 3 inches of barrel, five-shot and chambered 32 H&R Magnum.

Wesson Firearms

New for this year is the Model 738P, a 38 + P five-shot, double-action stainless steel revolver that is only 6½ inches in length and weighs a tad less than 25 ounces. And there's a Big-Bore Compensator to bring the 445 Super Mag recoil down to more or less 44 Special thumping. Only 1½ inches are added to the length of the standard shroud.

Mitchell Arms

"This time I have a single action that will meet with your approval." That's what the voice said. Looking over my shoulder I found it to come from Don Mitchell.

"Show me."

He did.

Built in the traditional flat-top style, Don's Single Action Army revolver does indeed wear a fully adjustable rear sight. Barrel length is 7½ inches with a serrated ramp front sight.

The caliber?

Forty-four Magnum!

He had me. All I could say was, "You're right!"

There's also a rolling block pistol with half-round, half-octagonal barrel and color case-hardened frame chambered to fire the ever-popular 223 cartridge. Other calibers are 45 Colt, 357 Magnum, 22 WMR and 22 Long Rifle.

Model 629 Classic DX S&W 44 Magnum double action—still cataloged.

Lew Horton has his Smith & Wesson 686 Carry Comp with integral compensator.

S&W's LadySmith 357 Magnum stainless steel revolver—the wheelgun news for this year among the biggies.

European American Armory's Target Grade revolver is available in 22 rimfire and 38 Special/357 Magnum.

Thompson/Center

T/C's first offering was a 10-inch, octagonal barrel, 22 Long Rifle-chambered pistol. Part of their twenty-five-year celebration includes issuing of a 25th Anniversary Contender identical to that first one. It is so identified with etching on both sides of the frame. Should you be able to acquire Catalog 19, this year's edition, both sides of the commemorative are shown on the cover.

Their newest chambering this time around is 375 Winchester, offered in 12-inch Hunter, Super 14 Bull or 14 Hunter. Hunter means deliv-

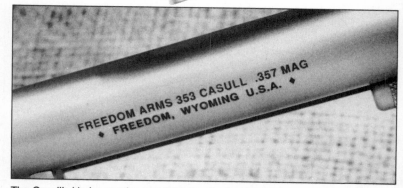

The Casull's kinder, gentler new 357 chambering gets Swiggett's nod for medium game.

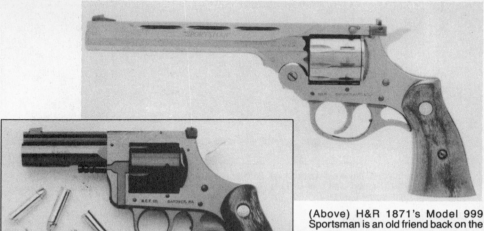

(Above) H&R 1871's Model 999 Sportsman is an old friend back on the scene.

(Left) Lady Ultra from New England Firearms is a 5-shot 32 H&R Magnum.

Wesson Firearms now makes this 5-shot 38 + P in stainless steel. It weighs a bit less than 25 ounces.

Taurus' 44 Special revolvers are offered in stainless (above) or blue, and with 3-, 4- or 6-inch barrels.

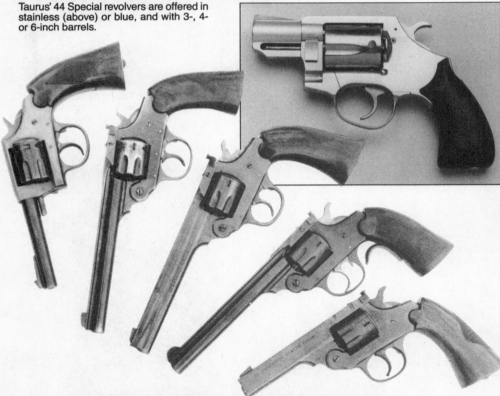

Hal's five Iver Johnson revolvers, left to right: Target Sealed 8, two Super Shot Sealed 8s, Trigger Cocking Single Action and a like-new, delivered in the factory box, 4-inch Super Shot Sealed 8.

ered as a package: pistol with their Muzzle Tamer installed, mounted scope, sling swivel studs and sling. Ready to go. Period.

Competitor

Al Straitiff's Competitor Corporation is in full bloom. His rotary cannon breech single shot pistol automatically cocks on opening and spring power ejects empties. His rotary-style ejector has never before been used in a firearm. All Competitor barrels are interchangeable. Hold on to your hats—Al offers 135 chamberings, from 17 Long Rifle through 300 Win. Mag. to 458 Win. Mag. If you can hold on to it, or even if you can't, Al will build it and sell it to you.

European American Armory

Their line includes double-action and single-action revolvers. The Standard Grade is offered with 2-, 4- or 6-inch barrel in 22 Long Rifle, 22 WMR, 38 Special and 32 H&R Magnum. Fixed sights on all of these DAs, except the 6-inch in 22 LR and 22 WMR which have adjustable sights.

EAA's Tactical Grade 38 Special is offered in two modes: 4-inch with a compensator and 2-inch with bobbed hammer. Both are six-shot. All are blued—including the Target Grade. This one is 6 inches of barrel, wears an adjustable rear sight, features walnut competition-style grip and the frame is drilled and tapped for scope mounting. Chamberings are 22 Long Rifle, 38 Special and 357 Magnum.

SSK

J.D. Jones always comes up with something new. This time it is Black/White Diamond barrel configuration. The name comes from their shape. Looking into the muzzle they are diamond-like in appearance. Color indicates blue or stainless. Not all chamberings will be offered. The reason? Bore diameter on his "biggies" bars them from this one.

Jarrett

On a visit with Kenny and his family for a South Carolina deer hunt, I was offered an XP chambered for 250 Savage Improved topped with a Burris 2½-7x scope and we went to the range. Three cartridges loaded with Nosler 100-grain Ballistic Tips over 41.5 grains of H380, ignited by Federal's 210M pri-

Swiggett centered this ground-hog at about 250 yards with an Ultra Light 223 pistol wearing a 6x Leupold compact scope.

Thompson/Center celebrates their 25th anniversary with this new chambering—the 375 Winchester. Topped with their 2-7x scope, factory 200-grain ammo prints consistent 1½-2-inch groups, some tighter.

Kenny Jarrett's rebarreled and modified XP-100 Remington bolt-action pistol, chambered for 250 Ackley Improved, routinely prints groups like this .415-incher.

SSK Black/White Diamond configuration barrels for Thompson/Center Contender pistols—real eye catchers.

SSK Industries portable benchrest is designed for both rifles and handguns, clamps around the barrel.

Swiggett has used a 30-30 Competitor on a lot of varmint hunts, seldom shoots game without a rest.

M.O.A.'s falling block pistols have a new look, with the lever fit inside the grip front.

M.O.A. is now offering 375, 338, 30 and 7mm wildcat chamberings on a 350 Remington Magnum case. They claim good velocities.

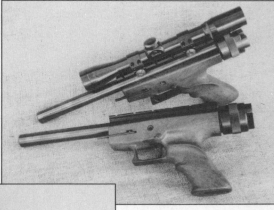

SSP-91 pistols from Magnum Research cock via a lever seen here on the left front forend. Barrels are not interchangeable.

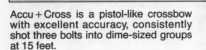

Accu+Cross is a pistol-like crossbow with excellent accuracy, consistently shot three bolts into dime-sized groups at 15 feet.

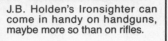

J.B. Holden's Ironsighter can come in handy on handguns, maybe more so than on rifles.

On a dead flat, resourceful Swiggett took an Underwood Pistol Rest out of his boot and made the shot good.

mer, printed .415-inch. No buck of adequate antler proportions presented himself. I lucked out. There would have been no way a miss could have been blamed on the pistol.

Smith & Wesson

Though Colt and Ruger did not, S&W did include a single new revolver in that packet handed to those of us who do our best to keep readers informed. That single entry—their Model 65 (K frame) six-shot 357 Magnum LadySmith. Fixed sights, shrouded ejector rod, 3-inch barrel, rosewood laminate grips and an easy-care frosted stainless finish. It will be delivered in a custom LadySmith, burgundy/silver Bob Allen gun case with a cleaning kit.

Holden Ironsighter

Never could get interested in see-through scope mounts. Seemed to me they were, by nature of their being, uncomfortable to work with. Then I spent a few days with J.B. Holden. We were shooting at some targets at oh-dark-thirty. Try as I would I could not find the target in that scope. J.B. suggested looking through the see-through to line up the revolver then raise up to the scope to shoot. I did and it worked. I'm still not really convinced, but in this particular instance it kept me shooting long after my target couldn't be picked up in the scope. Locate it via the see-through, hold the revolver steady, move my eye up to the scope and fire another round. There is only one way to find out if a see-through will help you. Holden offers them for handguns, rifles and muzzleloaders.

Response to Last Year's "Plea"

I learned one thing. By far, the majority of handgunners are honest folks. Mighty honest. A good many offers came in and I've ended up buying five Iver Johnson revolvers. Three Super Shot Sealed 8s (the model sought), one Target Sealed 8 and one Trigger Cocking Single Action. All in at least fair-to-middlin' condition except one, which is perfect. ●

GET COMPLETE DETAILS . . .

In our catalog pages, coverage of sixguns and others begins on pages 300, 309 and 323.

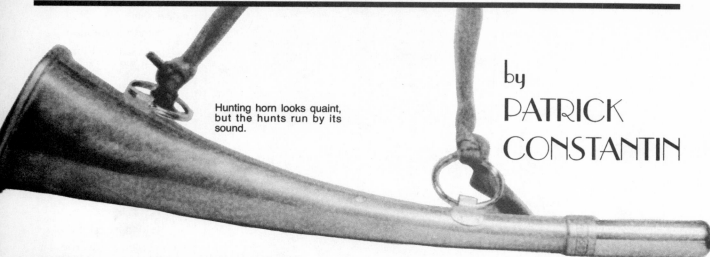

The hunting horn signals . . .

Hunting horn looks quaint, but the hunts run by its sound.

by
PATRICK CONSTANTIN

The Plight of the
FRENCH
RIFLEMAN

I AM A rifleman, which means that I am not merely a rifle user, but an enthusiast: I hunt varmints as well as big game; I shoot in competitive events; I mount my scopes myself; and I zero in all my outfits carefully. It also means that I just can't be bowled over by pumps, autos, lever jobs or multi-barreled German contraptions; to me the rifleman's rifle is the front-locking bolt action. Finally, as a handloader, I find dies that give concentric and consistent ammo more interesting than machinery that cranks out 400 rounds an hour.

All things considered, the man who

is my style of rifleman would probably be happiest and feel most at home in Pennsylvania, in upstate New York, in some states of the West and Midwest or perhaps down under in the Australian outback. It is, alas, my contention that he would be most unhappy and feel least at home in my own country, namely France. Although French shooters can be great experts in one narrow little niche of gun collecting, hunting or competition, only very rarely will one have the reasonably broad range of interests and the modicum of inquisitive spirit without which, in my opinion, no one can call

himself a rifleman in the truest sense of the word.

French hunters fall mainly into two categories: a tiny minority of simon-pure trophy takers who are knowledgeable hunters, but not riflemen in my sense of the word, and a huge majority of seat-of-the-pants shooters, thrill seekers and venison getters. This division of interests is reproduced rather neatly on the map, since big game hunting in France is carried out in two utterly different ways: one is merely a variation on the German style, while the other is the French style proper. We will not devote much space in this article to the former, which takes place chiefly in the most easterly part of the land, roughly the provinces of Alsace and northern Lorraine. Suffice it to say, there, trophy taking is the holy grail and game conservation a matter of religious observance.

The rest of the country, from the Belgian border to the Mediterranean coast, hunts differently. This is indeed one instance of "East is East, etc . . ." The twain, however, do meet on one thing: everywhere in the French hunting picture, extreme regimentation prevails. Nowhere can a hunter simply grab old Betsy and head for the woods. There is no public hunting land open to the individual hunter, and big game hunting on private land is subject

deer family, a good one will weigh all of 65 pounds soaking wet. Quite often, wild boar will be found in the same woods.

All bona fide hunting societies are issued a number of deer tags at the beginning of every season. How many tags are given depends on several factors, the most important being the size of the territory specifically leased by the club for hunting purposes. No tags will be issued on a personal basis to an individual hunter; those tags issued are the collective property of the club. Given this legal layout, it becomes obvious that French-style big game hunting is of necessity a common pursuit, involving a body of men.

Over most of the country, the system means drive-hunting. That form of

being club members. The line of shooters will have to surround a previously chosen area within the woods—how large depends upon their numbers and on how the terrain is configured. As soon as the detailed men have reached their appointed stations, carefully chosen before the morning's drive by the club's president or by a drive captain, the beaters start on their way. Whereas the shooters must get to their stands as stealthily as possible, the beaters are purposefully noisy, and they let their dogs loose at the very moment when the last shooter has reached his station.

The beginning and the end of the drive, as well as the kills, have to be signaled to let everybody in the team keep track of the progress of the operation, which means that everyone must carry a hunting horn. The job of both men and beasts on the moving line is to flush out the deer or the occasional boar from its cover, thus forcing it to cross the standing line of shooters. That tactical setup means that most (like nine out of ten) shots will be taken at game that has been badly spooked and is running hard. Besides, unless your appointed stand happens to be on the edge of a clearing or at the corner of a meadow or open field, your only opportunity to fire will come when a deer jumps across a path. As this takes place in a split second, the sport could be called snap-shooting with a vengeance.

Given the rules of the game, what sort of armament do French hunters use? If we take a typical band of about 25 "shooting" hunters, more than half, say, fourteen, will be carrying shotguns with slugs, since buckshot has been illegal nearly everywhere for fifteen years. Among the rifle toters, two-thirds or so, perhaps eight, will be using autoloaders. That might be six Remington 742s and a couple of Browning BARs. The remaining three will be carrying bolt actions, or an occasional Winchester or Marlin lever job. These proportions may vary slightly according to where you hunt; generally the percentage of shotguns and autoloaders will go down and that of bolt actions will go up as you move northward and eastward.

Very rarely will anyone in the rifle-carrying minority have a scope on his gun. Instead, a peculiar contraption known as a game-drive rib (or *bande de battue* in the vernacular) will often grace the barrel. This is a kind of broad rib, set at a slight angle to the axis of the barrel and extending to half its length. The forward end of that rib is notched and can be used as a rear sight.

This is a relatively open shooting lane in typical French hunts—about three jumps wide.

to many legal restrictions. The readiest solution is nearly always to join a hunting club or society. Most (like 95 percent) of those societies do not own their deer woods, they merely rent them, and the lease has to be periodically renegotiated with the landlord.

Except in some fortunate spots in the east, and in a west-central area known as Sologne, the large European red deer (*Cervus elaphus* for the Latin-minded) is not frequently hunted. The most typical big game animal in the country is the roe deer, locally known as *chevreuil*. It is a *light* member of the

hunting exists in the United States. What makes the French approach special is that dogs are nearly universally used. Another big difference is that there is no wilderness hunting in this country: *all* the woods are open to some form of intensive logging or non-hunting recreational use, which means that they are criss-crossed with paths and dotted with clearings. The paths often form a nearly geometrical grid all over a club's alloted hunting area.

Typically, a drive will begin at the break of dawn. The hunters will be divided into two main groups, the shooters and the beaters, only the former

Being briefed is part of it—fellow in the middle is nattily and traditionally attired, fellow on right is sure to attract jibes for this camo outfit.

(Above) If it's French, there is food, food one sits down to, of course.

(Below) Man holding pen and wad of bills is hunt treasurer checking if every member has fed his fair share into the kitty.

Every shooter seems to have a truckload of excuses and rationalizations for the kind of armament he carries. The majority—slug-gunners—chiefly say that since most of their shots will be taken at running game, they are better served by the same shooting iron they use on bounding hares and flying birds. Those who carry autoloading rifles praise their fast second and third shots and everyone is convinced that scopes are useless for fast action.

My personal opinion is that all those thousands of French hunters *can* be wrong. Especially, I am convinced that a smoothbore loaded with slugs is no longer a *scatter*gun—it has to be aimed, just like a rifle. The "fast second shot" argument of the autoloader boys makes hardly more sense; a deer sprinting across a path in the middle of a wood will hardly ever give you time for more than one *aimed* shot. Besides, semi-autos have slower lock times and mushier triggers than bolt actions, and that ought to be a more important consideration than any second shot when your real aiming and firing time is measured in split seconds.

Are metallic sights the best available? Yes, definitely, if your only alternate choice is a 4x or even a so-called "low power" (such as 2.5x) scope. In fact, the best magnification is 1x, which means none at all. Even if you have a broad, easily seen reticle, and here I agree with our Eastern hunters that the German sort is by far the most practical, any magnification is troublesome because it makes eye relief more critical—a major consideration when your rifle has to be shouldered instantly—while increasing the apparent speed of your target. More difficult to quantify is that queasy, seasick, claustrophobic feeling caused by a restricted field of view within the already confined space of a thick wood.

Yet, when all is said and done, I still do not use iron sights on a big game drive. First, they do have their own drawbacks: three points to align rather than two, and an excessive sensitivity to where the light on your bead comes from. Second, there *is* a device that has all the positive sides of both iron (no magnification) and glass (only two aiming points) sights, the dot of light system. Weaver's discontinued

Quickpoint was an unacknowledged pioneering design, using the sun as its power source; there is the better known Swedish-made Aimpoint which is battery operated; and several other later entries. Few shooters realize these are nothing but miniaturized versions of the reflector gunsights which graced the dashboards of World War II fighter planes. Those were devised to allow a mobile firer to hit a mobile target, so they are among the most logical sights to use on running game. I have myself scored a few pretty spectacular hits on running roe deer with my Aimpoint, yet I have to acknowledge it has a drawback. In dim surroundings, the Aimpoint shooter *must* aim with *both eyes open* if he is to take full advantage of his reflector sight. If he does not, the two-way, or "dichroic" mirror, which is a necessary component of all such sights, will show as a distracting bluish haze between his eye and the target.

If you must close that left eye when aiming however, all is not lost: True low power scopes afford a usable alternative. The keyword here is *true*. The garden variety 2-7s or even 1.5-4s (whose

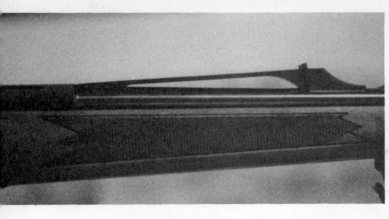

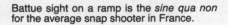
Battue sight on a ramp is the *sine qua non* for the average snap shooter in France.

Four's company: These men are on their way to their stands. All guns *must* be carried slung on the march, for safety reasons.

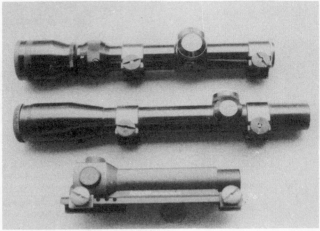
Top to bottom: Tasco 1-3.5x variable scope, Schmidt & Bender 1.25x fixed-power scope, Aimpoint Mark III electronic sight—all used in "aggravated snap-shooting."

real bottom magnification is often more like 1.6x or even 1.75x) are nearly useless on a wildly bounding critter with a dog on its tail. So if you ever decide to hunt roe deer French style, better check that "Magn." column on the left hand side in the "Scopes and Mounts" section of your friendly GUN DIGEST. If you don't, beware the pitfalls, for the really usable scopes are only those with a bottom magnification no higher than 1.25x. I have a fixed 1.256x Schmidt & Bender, which boasts the best anti-reflective coating of any scope I own, and a 1-3.5x Tasco, a true one power at bottom magnification, which feature is a feat of optical engineering in a variable scope.

When we come to the matter of the calibers used by French hunters, we notice that, curiously enough, the most popular centerfire hunting round in this country is the 280 Remington. This is due to the runaway popularity of gas-operated Remington autoloaders and the ban on all rounds that are or have been at any time military issue, so local nimrods have just grabbed what was available in an au-

toloader. Apart from this oddity, the fact that roe deer (which are among the lightest species of big game) and wild boar (which are tough, mean critters, and weigh much more) may be found in the same areas and met on the same hunts, has considerably clouded the caliber picture.

Many hunters are overgunned, some ridiculously so. Indeed the 7mm Remington Magnum, which is already more than enough for boar, has been eclipsed by the much harder kicking 300 Winchester Magnum; if you meet a man toting a BAR in our woods, the odds are it will be chambered for the 300. Another biggie which has found quite a following is the Teutonic 9.3x62, a brute of a round designed before World War I to give German settlers in Africa an affordable lion-busting cartridge. Even the 8x68S dude basher, another hyper-glandular German job that develops about 4500 fpe of muzzle energy and would be a good long-range moose round, has found French takers on animals weighing anywhere from 50 to 300 pounds, and which are rarely shot beyond 75 yards.

The reason so many men are so ab-

surdly overgunned is mostly that they are *not* riflemen. None among the small minority that use a scope zero it in themselves, nor does anybody handload. Precious few ever patronize a range before the season begins, which means that all their shots will be fired from a standing position at fast-moving game in the excitement of the hunt, the ideal condition to do away with the psychological anticipation of the kick and thus greatly minimize felt recoil. Still, a number of hunters choose reasonable calibers, such as the aforementioned 280 for the autoloader boys or its ballistic next of kin, the German 7x64, for the bolt-action users.

Me? I use a handloaded 270 Winchester. My boar load consists of a 150-grain Nosler partition pushed by 58.9 grains of locally made SNPE Vectan Tu 8, and my deer load is a 130 Hornady and 61.6 of Vectan Tu 7. My old paper screen CS 200 chronograph clocked the 130-grainer at 3080 fps and the Powley calculator evaluated pressure at a mild 50,500 psi. The 150 Noslers gave me 2910 fps and 52,000, about par for the course in a rifle with

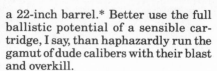

Ye compleat French battue hunter. Attire is neither silent nor designed for comfortable walking. Sole consideration is that it should shield wearer from rain. The scopeless 742 autoloader is also quite typical.

This successful hunter uses *both* a red dot sight and a battue rib. Notice grenade-like effect of the 300 Magnum on roe deer.

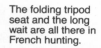

The folding tripod seat and the long wait are all there in French hunting.

A classic boo-boo: This pricey German scope is mounted way too high above the bore for quick shouldering necessary in battue situation.

a 22-inch barrel.* Better use the full ballistic potential of a sensible cartridge, I say, than haphazardly run the gamut of dude calibers with their blast and overkill.

Even if we leave the matter of guns and calibers aside, big game hunting in France remains quite a controversial topic. One school, whose methods and tools I have just described in some detail, regards hunting exclusively in terms of personal enjoyment and adherence to what is regarded as a traditionally French form of the sport, while the other is hyped on trophy taking and game conservation.

Ever since I returned from the U.S. fifteen years ago I have had trouble picking sides. The typical, traditional form of driven game hunt does have enormous drawbacks from a conservationist viewpoint. Letting loose huge numbers of dogs and loud beaters panics the animals badly and breaks down their natural hierarchies, that sort of biological social order which they had established among themselves over a period of time through a kind of trial and error process, and which is vital to their mating, to the rearing of their young and to their common survival generally. Besides, snap-shooting leads to many wounded animals and makes it impossible for the hunter to choose and discriminate before he pulls the trigger.

To redress that sad state of affairs, some hunters have gone all the way to the opposite extreme and have pro-

*Those loads were safe in *my* rifle. I cannot guarantee they would not be dangerous in *yours*.

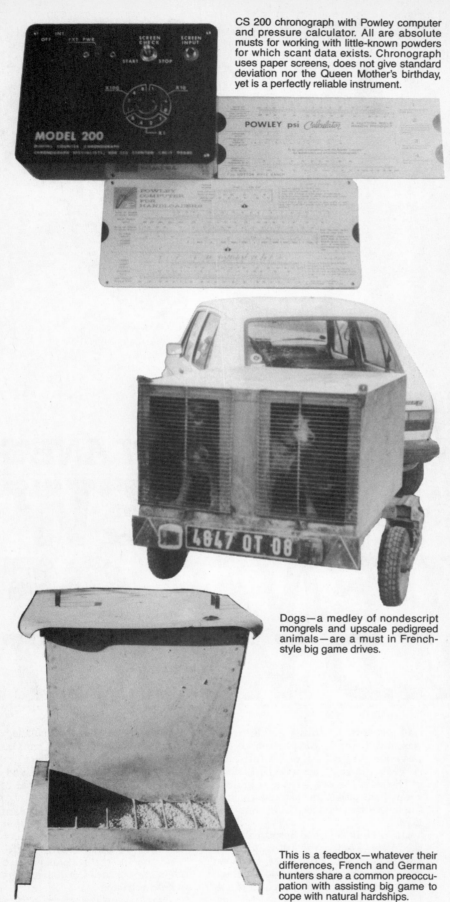

CS 200 chronograph with Powley computer and pressure calculator. All are absolute musts for working with little-known powders for which scant data exists. Chronograph uses paper screens, does not give standard deviation nor the Queen Mother's birthday, yet is a perfectly reliable instrument.

Dogs—a medley of nondescript mongrels and upscale pedigreed animals—are a must in French-style big game drives.

This is a feedbox—whatever their differences, French and German hunters share a common preoccupation with assisting big game to cope with natural hardships.

posed drastic measures, such as adopting nationwide the German system I have hinted at previously, with its Tower of Babel-sized sheltered stands replete with creature comforts, and its ultra-formalized and hyper-finicky culling practices. Here, the ultimate goal becomes the rearing of ever more massive trophy heads (every one of the "good" deer being individually known to the game wardens), and thereby the taking of prize antlers, in a country where American-style wilderness hunting simply does not exist. It becomes a mere form of Rolls-Royce grade—or rather Mercedes-grade— game farming.

German hunters have to take a full-fledged university-level written exam and field test, cramming for which occupies large blocks of their leisure time for several months, before they can receive their complete "Jagdschein" and shoot big game legally.

All the proposed moves in that direction by the trophy collectors and ultra-conservationists have generally enraged the other side and generated equally extreme counter-moves in the opposite direction. The "French tradition" diehards have even managed to have the previously agreed ban on buckshot repealed in one large area of southeastern France, a giant step backward and a disastrous decision conservation-wise. Personally, I call that tussle the battle of the Teutomaniacs versus the stand-patters, and I try not to get embroiled in it. A few moderate hunters believe that a reasonable solution does exist, whereby the drive-hunting system would be reformed rather than abolished. In the milder form they propose, dogs would no longer be used to flush out game and the line of beaters would be silent and more sparse.

Regardless of the outcome of the debate, I do remain optimistic about the future of big game hunting in France. It is backed by a millenium-old tradition, however differently interpreted, and the very violence of the clash among hunters bears witness to a living enthusiasm for the sport. On the other hand, I have serious doubts whether this nation of rifle users, whether they shoot fancy sidelock doubles topped by stove-pipe size German scopes or plain-Jane autoloaders, will ever produce more than a handful of riflemen; being such takes something that goes way beyond a collector's well-lined pocketbook and keen eye for craftsmanship or a pothunter's hard-nosed practicality. It takes a mixture of T.L.C. and active, non-dogmatic curiosity which, so far, has remained in short supply in this land. ●

TERRY MacFARLANE'S NEW SOUVENIR OF WORLD WAR II

DURING World War II, a sergeant in the Army Air Corps whiled away the hours at a series of duty posts in Italy engraving this Beretta. He brought it home and kept it for over 30 years, but its next owner thought it somehow garish and traded it to Terry MacFarlane, who doesn't think it garish at all.

Nor does this writer. It is pure military folk art, as real as a tattoo or a pin-up painted on a fighting airplane. It is a commemorative in the most original of senses. That sergeant, who had jewelers' training, MacFarlane was told, flavored this pistol with the news and the names of his military service, and that included both sides of the war. He was so even-handed, symbolically, that the pistol has meaning for anyone who fought in that theatre.

On its right side, the Beretta carries the insignia of the 3rd, 10th, 34th and 45th U.S. infantry divisions; the Special Service Forces and the 442nd Regimental Combat Team; the patch of the U.S.-Canadian 1st Special Service Force and the "Devil's Brigade;" and insignia of the British Commandos and the U.S. Airborne Pathfinders. There are the U.S. Ranger and Airborne flashes, and General Mark Clark's four stars.

On the left side, the sergeant engraved Marshal Kesselring's name and his batons, along with symbols of the Waffen SS, the Luftwaffe, the Wehrmacht, the Italian Fascist emblem and those of German snipers and moutain troops.

Atop the receiver, there is the patch

of the 15th U.S. Air Force, and along
the exposed barrel flies a P-51, the
Mustang fighter. Along the bottom of
the pistol is an unofficial emblem of
German assault troops, a German
Knight's Cross and the U.S. Congressional Medal of Honor, as well as
the shoulder patch of the U.S. 5th
Army.

So it's a great souvenir of an old war.
And since Terry MacFarlane owns it,
it's *his* new souvenir, his new World
War II souvenir. ●

Ken Warner

by BOB BELL

SCOPES AND MOUNTS

every scope maker I talk to tells me the 3-9x is his best selling model. And there was a time, back in the mid-'50s when Bausch & Lomb brought out their 2½-8x Balvar, that I quite likely would have gone for that one . . . and it's sort of a kissin' cousin to the 3-9x. In fact, there were quite a few years when a 7x61 S&H Magnum wearing a 3-9x Redfield was my favorite shooter.

But eventually I began to notice that I never needed that 9x magnification for big game. So when the 2-7x Redfield came along, I dropped to that, and then later to the 1½-4½x when I realized there was no real need for even 7x on big game. I occasionally killed stuff using that setting, but nothing that a

good 4x couldn't have handled. I just had it so I used it once in awhile. At top power a 2-7x was better on a varmint rifle than a 4x—good enough for chuck shooting to the limit of a 222's effectiveness—but we're talking about a big game scope here.

So I eventually settled on the 1½-4½x class for most of my bigger rifles . . . which is to say, anything from the 7mm-08 up. And that's what I still use most of the time. This size looks nice on a hunting-weight rifle, sits low and close to the receiver as a scope should, is a bit lighter and definitely less bulky than even a 2-7x, and it has all the optics I've ever needed to get the job done. If any big game critter is so far away I can't get a good

E VERY SO OFTEN ye old editor and I sit together in a goose blind or maybe on his back porch in those beautiful West Virginia hills and talk. He contributes most of the dialogue, of course, being the garrulous type, while I tend to be a fella who prefers to put his words down on paper so he can be paid for them. But occasionally ol' KW asks a question which requires a response. Like: "If you were restricted to one scope for all of your big game hunting, what would it be?"

Now, I've been boosting variables for a lot of years, so it might be expected that's the choice I'd make. If I did, I'd be right in synch with the majority of today's hunters, since

Bob Wise agrees a good 4x is logical for most big game hunting and says the Zeiss Diatal C on his Model 70 338 is "the goodest of the good."

Redfield designed this 1-4x for shotgun use, but Bell saw its long eye relief made it the optimum scope choice on a military bolt action, for it can be installed ahead of the unaltered bolt and safety. Mounting system is half Redfield (rear), half Orchard Park Enterprises, and positions scope so low that ocular barely clears action bridge. Tom Stumpf found it worked perfectly on a pair of whitetails last season.

sight picture with a 4½x, it's too far for me to be shooting. And at the other end of the scale, there's that 1½x with its tremendous field and conspicuous reticle—perfect for the tough shots on fast-moving game at close range in thick cover. Somehow, in the real world of hunting, there seem to be lots more of these than the broadside picture book chances at a half-mile, the possibility of which always seems uppermost when someone is buying a scope.

When still hunting, I always have my scope set at 1½x, as that gives the maximum field for the unexpected close-range shot. There's always time to crank it up if I come to a high-country meadow and see something 300 or 400 yards away, but never time to crank it the other way when an elk bursts out of a dense tangle of mountain mahogany at fifteen steps.

It's not, by the way, the power that's the problem up close; it's the lack of field. A 7x scope typically has about a 16-foot field at 100 yards—which gives you about 2½ feet at 15 yards. That doesn't enclose an awful lot of critter. A 1½x scope averages about 70 feet at 100 yards, or 10 + at 15, which at least improves your chances as you can see the whole animal. Admittedly, this is not a typical opportunity either, but such chances do happen. And I keep recalling that at one time I had a string of twenty-two consecutive kills with my scope at 1½x, almost all of them woods shots, the longest at 135 steps. That indicates this power will handle most any big game at ordinary range.

But Ken's question specified a scope for *all* of my big game hunting, so I had to re-think things again. And I concluded that if restricted to only one it would be a straight 4x. "The good ol' 4x," as a longtime hunting pal used to put it. I'll tell you why.

Although it doesn't have the adaptability of a small variable, sacrificing the ultra-short-range efficiency, it tends to handle most chances that arise. For example, in a multiple-deer area awhile back, a pair of driven does crossed in front of me, left to right, flat out running through medium-dense brush. I swung the 308 Ruger Ultralight like a grouse gun, dropped the first, flipped the bolt and dropped the second. The range was only about thirty steps, yet I could plainly see the duplex reticle of my 4x Zeiss right where I wanted it on the shoulder of each deer.

A small variable would have performed as well, of course, but the main reason I'd opt for a straight 4x is there's simply less to go wrong with it. Most of the time, nothing bad happens to a scope while hunting, and when it does, you're usually close to home. So the incident is more of an inconvenience than a real problem. But if you're hundreds of miles back in the bush somewhere, maybe a long paddle and a plane flight from the nearest gunsmith, and something goes wrong with your scope, your hunt might well be over.

There are two inherent problems with variables that straight powers don't have: (1) they're a lot more complicated inside, because it's necessary to move parts to change power, so there's more opportunity for

something to go wrong; and (2) to be able to move those parts there has to be a connecting unit between the external power selector ring and the internal mechanism, and this necessitates a slot through the main tube. Obviously, this increases the chance of leakage—nitrogen out, moisture in—which leads to fogging and other problems. Most manufacturers do a fine job of sealing against such leakage, but this is a problem area which straight power scopes just don't have. And it seems logical to expect that the situation grows worse the more times that power selector ring is turned.

Anyhow, what all this boils down to is that, if I *had* to use only one scope for all my big

game hunting, it would be the best straight 4x I could find.

Now, here's what's new in this year's scopes, presented in random order.

Redfield has a couple of new scopes this year, a 4x40mm Tracker and a 3-9x50mm Golden Five Star. They have the just-introduced Realtree camo finish which makes them nearly invisible in thick cover, especially on a camouflaged gun. Most Redfield scopes are made with either standard black or matte finish too, of course, and some of their mounts have the Realtree camo. The large objectives of these new scopes collect and transmit all the light the human eye can use during legal hunting hours, and provide

large exit pupils for rapid aiming.

Of even more interest to me personally is the little 1-4x shotgun scope which has been around for a couple of years now. It differs significantly from other scopes in this class by having a 6-inch eye relief at all powers. That makes it possible to mount ahead of the unaltered bolt of military rifles such as the '03 Springfield and M98 Mauser, positioning it low enough to almost touch the receiver if the mount permits.

Gunsmith Al Wardrop installed one for me on a restocked M98, using Ralph Avery's (Orchard Park Enterprise) streamlined steel tube to enclose the objective end and a Redfield ring/base on the ac-

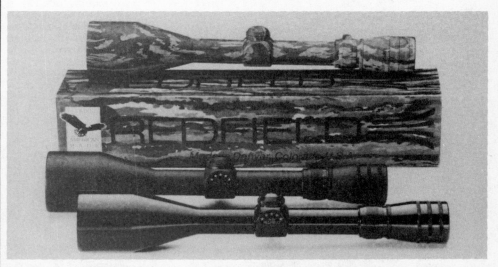

Big objectives and three finish choices mark Redfield's 3-9x 50mm Golden Five Stars, and Redfield can furnish mounts to match the camo pattern, too.

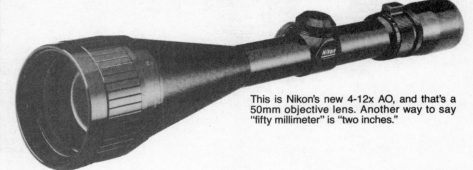

This is Nikon's new 4-12x AO, and that's a 50mm objective lens. Another way to say "fifty millimeter" is "two inches."

The Whitetail Classic from Simmons offers a 3.5-10x power range and, yes, a full 50mm objective lens—your choice of dark or bright finish.

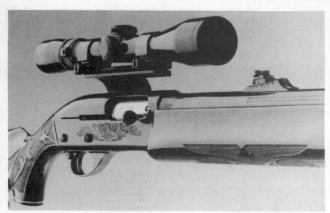

Weaver's Convert-A-Mount for shotguns still mounts easily on repeaters.

tion's receiver ring (not bridge) for the rear installation. This positions the ocular lens just forward of the bolt lift and, of course, permits use of the unaltered military safety. Such mounting should be of interest to anyone who is thinking of buying one of the sturdy WWI or WWII military rifles which have come back on the market again. It requires gunsmith installation (so does the drilling/tapping of mount holes in any military action), but it saves the cost of a new safety and a bolt operation.

If this little 1-4x had been available in the late '40s when the market was flooded with surplus military rifles, Redfield would have sold a million of 'em. There still should be a good demand. You can even put one on a shotgun.

Leupold also has a couple of new scopes. For handgunners, there's the Vari-X 2.5-8 EER (Extended Eye Relief), Leupold's first switch-power pistol scope. It has an enlarged objective for plenty of light even at top power, and eye relief of 12-24 inches. This varies only slightly when magnification is changed from maximum to minimum, an improvement the maker says is due to a breakthrough in the erector lens system.

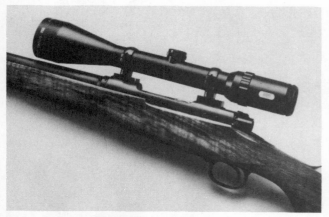

Here we are with Tasco's Titan at 3-12x and a 52mm objective lens, built on a 30mm tube and furnished with rings to match.

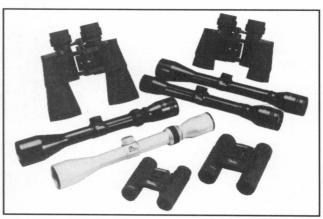

This is a whole line of new scopes by Tasco—the new Golden Antler line from 4x32mm to 2.5-10x with a 44mm objective.

About the size of a standard 4x scope is this Leupold Vari-X III 1.75-6x variable with a 32mm objective.

Shades of long ago—Leupold's Quick-Release scope mounts sport thumb levers as of yore.

A new concept in laser-based optical alignment was developed in conjunction with this scope. Tests on this model were extensive, including 10,000 cycles on the impact machine at 1800g forces, repeated lateral side forces to simulate dropping the firearm/scope combination 4 feet so that the eyepiece shell struck a hard surface, and 6000 cycles of the windage and elevation adjustments through a temperature range from −20 to +150 degrees Fahrenheit.

For riflemen who like small scopes but want a bit more power than the popular 1½-4½x models, there's now a new Vari-X III in 1.75-6x32mm. Boosting the objective diameter from the 20mm typical in a 1-inch tube makes this scope about the size of a normal 4x; however, its exit pupil even at 6x is 5+mm, which means it supplies a beam of light as large as the human eye can admit under any legal shooting conditions. Lenses, as in most Leupolds, have Multicoat 4 coating, to maximize light transmission and reduce glare.

Bushnell has expanded their Trophy line with a large-objective variable which gives a 4-1 magnification range. It's a 2½-10x45mm with amber-coated high contrast optics for top target definition at dawn and dusk. The eyepiece is fast focusing by means of a knurled ring, so the optimum setting can be obtained before the eye can compensate for minor inaccuracies, thus eliminating a problem of fine-threaded eyepieces.

There's also a new 6x40mm Sportview for those deer shooters who prefer to watch the field edges and rights-of-way when the light is poor, and for handgun or shotgun hunters who do their thing at close range, there's a 1x Trophy with "floating" 5-MOA battery-operated red dot for instant target acquisition. Built on a 30mm tube with rings to fit Weaver-style bases, this rig is less than six inches long, under six ounces, has unlimited eye relief, and a 61-foot field. Its usefulness for the brush or swamp hunter is obvious.

Another new Sportview is the 3-9x32mm, which can be focused as close as 10 meters and has resettable ¼-MOA turret adjustments—features which can be useful to silhouette and target shooters.

Bausch & Lomb has several new top-grade spotting scopes and binoculars this year, the Elite series, but reports no new

rifle scopes. Truth is, they have so many now that it would be hard to squeeze another in. For years I've been using their 6-24x on a heavy M700 22-250 and a 12-32x40mm on my No. 1 Ruger 223. I don't know of any better scopes for small critters at long ranges.

Jim Leatherwood, who created the ART (Auto-Ranging Telescopes) used for military sniping and elsewhere, is now having scopes made in Czechoslovakia by the Meopta Co., which for decades produced high quality optical goods for the German and Soviet military. We've seen only one model, marked Leatherwood 4x32, but understand that the company name is New Democracy Inc. (719 Ryan Plaza, Suite 103, Arlington, TX 76011). The reticle is basically a duplex, with tiny reference marks for holdover and windage on the fine central lines. There is also a range scale similar in design to that used in the Soviet Draganov sniping rifle, but of different dimensions. In use, the shooter determines where an 18-inch area of the target fits between two horizontal lines, one of which is curved. He can then read the range in 100-yard units up to 400.

Burris has added one scope to their extensive line, a 2½-10x Signature model. This 4-1 power spread makes it practical to use the same outfit on both big game and varmints if the cartridge is suitable, say 243, 25-06 or whatever. Eyepiece is the Fullfield wide angle, which gives fields of 37-10½ feet, and the objective measures 44mm for plenty of light. Every lens surface has Hi-Lume multi-coating, of course, and adjustments are steel-on-steel ⅛-minute.

Zeiss scopes were aboard a couple of my big game rifles this year, the Diatal C 4x32 on the

New 6x40mm straight Sportview scope by Bushnell provides a 20.5-foot field of view at 100 yards.

This new 3-9x Sportview offers up to 35-foot field of view at 3x and adjusts in ¼-minute resettable adjustments.

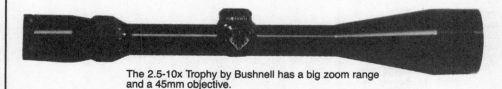

The 2.5-10x Trophy by Bushnell has a big zoom range and a 45mm objective.

Illuminated dot, unlimited eye relief and six-ounce weight of the Bushnell 1x Trophy suit it for shooters who do it close.

The big Burris 2.5-10x Signature has a 44mm objective and, the company says, bigger than usual interior lens systems.

While T.R. Them uses binoculars to get the big picture, Doc Niklaus finds the window-mounted Burris 20x50mm spotter is just the ticket for concentrating on a single pup peeping from a hole a quarter-mile away.

338 and the Z 8x56 on the 7mm Magnum. Both seemed perfect for their jobs, but as it turned out a forest fire ran us out of our first elk camp and snow chased us out of the second, so I didn't fire a shot with the 4x. Things were better with the 8x. Hunting out of Tuktu Hunting & Fishing Club's outcamp at Desbergeres, in northwestern Quebec, I had clean kills on two caribou bulls, a small one for eating, a 50-incher because it was the biggest of some 350 looked at. It rained a lot of the week we were there, with some wet snow in between, but nothing bothered the big Zeiss. It was dry all the way . . . on the inside, that is . . . and crystal clear.

Nikon, too, is offering larger-than-normal objective hunting scopes now, with the introduction of a 3.5-10x50mm and a 4-12x50mm AO (adjustable objective unit). Their lenses are multicoated and internal metal parts are blackened to eliminate light reflection and scattering caused by bright spots. I haven't used either of these yet.

The Nikon I used most in the last year was the 6.5-20x 44mm, which has been aboard my M700 Varmint 223 for two summers. That means it's been the sighting equipment for several thousand shots at least, mostly on prairie dogs. In the Midwest in summertime, lack of light is no problem but mirage often is, especially when bedded down on the ground. That's when I'm grateful for the good power spread on this big variable. If everything is just a glittering shimmer at 20x, I crank it down until things clear

When his Remington needs cleaning or is too hot to hold, Bell switches to his back-up: a heavy No. 1 Ruger, also in 223, topped by a Bausch & Lomb 12-32x40mm. Results are much the same.

Nikon 6.5-20x44mm lets Bell get all the accuracy his heavy-barrel M700 223 can deliver (half-minute is routine). The combination makes things tough on South Dakota prairie dogs—even in sunlight that calls for a shade on the scope and a bandanna over the back of Bell's tender Eastern neck.

up—usually in the 8x-12x bracket. That's still plenty of power for most shots, and there's no detectable change in impact.

Pentax has added a second LightSeeker scope to their line, a 2-8x to accompany the earlier 3-9x. The new model is an inch shorter and an ounce lighter than the earlier one, and due to its lower powers has bigger fields. With 53 feet at 2x, it would be usable even on a dangerous-game rifle, if properly mounted of course. Tube is one-piece construction, internal

zoom tube ocular lenses are said to be 40 percent larger than standard, and all lenses are multicoated. Adjustments are ⅓-MOA.

There's also a new 2½-7x Pentax pistol scope. Built on a 1-inch tube, it has a 36mm objective, up to 28 inches of eye relief at bottom power, 14 at top.

Adjustments are ⅛-MOA.

Swarovski's 1.5-4.5x20mm AL was described here last year. Since then we've had a chance to use it in the field, on a lightweight wildcat 338-caliber based on an opened-up 308 case. It was a perfect choice for this little woods gun, its large field at bottom power (75 feet at 100 yards) making it easy to get on a fast-moving whitetail at snowball distance.

Swarovski's AL (American Line) variables have their reticles in the second focal plane, so they subtend less of the target as power is increased. Hunters who prefer the same subtension at all powers (which is what you get when the reticle is in the first focal plane) can get the European-type Swarovski. With this style there can be no variation in point of impact due to a change in power.

Tasco's extensive optical line has grown still further with one Titan, two World Class, and five new models called the Golden Antlers.

The Titan is a 3-12x with 52mm objective built on a 30mm tube and having five-layer multicoated lenses . . . sort of a big brother to last year's 1.5-6x and 3-9x, which had 42mm objectives. The Quad reticle is located in the first image plane, to eliminate any possible point-of-impact shift. Machined steel rings come with this scope.

The new World Class models are a 3.5-10x with 50mm objective and a straight 4x with 44mm objective. Lenses have three-layer coating and eyepieces are fast-focusing.

The Golden Antler scopes are 4x32mm, 4x40mm, 2.5-10x 44mm, 3-9x32mm, and 3-9x 40mm. All feature wide-view, fully coated optics and the 30/30 reticle.

Simmons also is offering king-size objectives, even exceeding that of their popular 44 Mag model, by going to a 50mm unit on its 3.5-10x Whitetail Classic. This line has one-piece tubes of aircraft aluminum and fully multicoated lenses. These WCs have 360-degree view (full circle, that is) and the Truplex reticle. ●

Gunsmith Al Wardrop likes Redfield's Compact version of the 4-12x Golden Five Star for his short-action 223. He also likes his tripod-mounted Outers rifle rest which makes accurate shooting from the sitting position easy.

HUNTING THE OLD ONES

Nothing gives a hunter the feel of the good ol' days like hunting in old-timey clothes with a muzzleloader.

BY DWAIN BLAND

MANY HUNTERS have asked me what it's like to hunt with grandpa's old gun, because it's well known that I hunt turkeys all over America with old shotguns made back during the 1800s. Some of them, most of them, I should say, tell me they'd like to get themselves one to hunt with. Then they ask: What should I look for in such guns? Where are these old guns found? What do they cost? How do you know if the gun is safe to shoot?

There aren't any stock answers to these questions because each old gun is as different from the next as we are

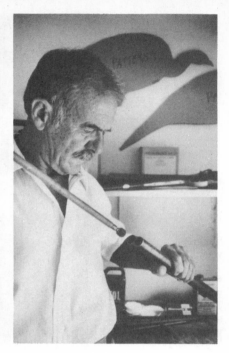

from each other. Each old gun is a thing in itself. Some are rusty; some are in excellent condition. Moreso, when you think how long they've been around.

Take the average family heirloom, great-grandpa's old Betsy: probably rusty inside. Heck knows when it was last cleaned. Or when the locks were last pulled so the gunk could be rubbed from them. Could be it's still loaded. Good many folks kept such guns standing back of the kitchen door, filled and ready to go, 'cause when a big boar coon took a hankering for a chicken dinner there wasn't going to be time for any ladling of a little of this and a little of that.

Nine of ten such old guns are nothing but wall hangers. Never, NEVER ATTEMPT TO SHOOT ONE OF THESE OLD GUNS IF YOU AREN'T WELL VERSED IN BLACKPOWDER FIREARMS. If you want to shoot it, for gosh sakes, take it to a competent *blackpowder* gunsmith, and let him give it a real going-over.

If he says, "Hang it on the wall," HANG IT THERE, AND LEAVE IT.

If he tells you it appears shootable, he'll also add, "You are on your own if you do."

Before we discuss purchasing an antique hunting gun, let's talk about ethics. Many times I've had someone look at a gun I was carrying, then remark, "Oh, you shouldn't have that out here. It should be at home. Or in a museum. You shouldn't hunt with it."

Folks who have traveled this country's backroads needn't be reminded of

Once a person buys an old gun he should make certain it's not loaded, then give it a thorough cleaning, at the same time inspecting it closely. It's wise to send the gun to a reliable *blackpowder* gunsmith who can give it professional care, along with rendering his thoughts on its past and future use.

the thousands of fine old muzzleloaders on display, from tiny mom and pop museums to collections ranging in the hundreds of guns found in public viewing on national levels. Nor does this include the hundreds of thousands of quality firearms stuck away from public view in private collections.

And this is what differentiates an individual seeking a good, old shooter from such collectors. The serious collector ordinarily specializes; some don't, but most do. Perhaps a man collects Kentuckys. I have several times seen an extensive collection of these guns which not only made me drool with anticipation, but gave me the itch just to handle a number of them.

Though I stand before the cases studying the merits of each gun, I've noticed that the average viewer pauses to look at the first ten or twenty, then goes on to other firearms. Such extensive numbers of guns much alike seem a waste to people who feel that these weapons were made for use in home defense and hunting, to provide meat for frontier families. The collector buys the finer guns available, so, ethically, those old-time firearms which *should* be saved for future generations are well preserved in such collections.

Too, the end purpose must be consid-

ered. The collector purchases for personal enjoyment, although this may be no more than owning a piece which may be admired from time to time, handled little, and certainly never fired. The collector buys the best he can afford, hoping to work up in quality, continually selling less desirable guns, and replacing them with those of more merit. On the other hand, a hunter who simply wants to own, and hunt with, a part of the good old days, truly needs only a good, solid shooter; therefore the gun can be a plain, sturdy, unadorned piece.

Hunting ethics must be considered also. Will the old guns kill clean?

Sure. Clean kills, with little or no crippling, are seldom the act of any gun, but lie with the shooter. Modern rifles and shotguns cripple game, the result of hunters not knowing the gun, or how or where it shoots, or if they are utilizing the best load. Sadly, too many do not care.

Time was when the hunters carrying muzzleloaders could be counted on to cripple very little game as these few people were dedicated individuals who knew their guns, then hunted with that knowledge constantly in mind. Today, with so many muzzle-loading seasons, we have a great many hunters afield who have purchased a muzzleloader simply to extend the time they can be in the woods. I knew one who couldn't even load his rifle but had a friend do this. Thankfully, he never fired it the two years prior to when I last saw him, so he kept it loaded from one season to the next. It may yet have that same load stuffed down the barrel.

Ethically, a muzzleloader is fine for hunting. I've always thought that such guns made a better hunter of a person, due to open iron sights, and with the open cylinder choking of the old shotguns. A hunter had to learn to get closer to game, to stalk, or, if he wished to lay an ambush, to learn patience in the endless hours of waiting for the quarry to walk into close gunshot. Besides, so many muzzleloaders are one-shot guns, it becomes a case of making the first shot count, because it's also the last shot.

How do you go about purchasing a fine old shooter, an antique with which you can hunt?

There are any number of places where such guns can be found. Perhaps your local newspaper lists auctions. These are called local auctions, though some may be a hundred miles from where you live. Held in homes, garages, backyards, barns, store buildings, and in auditoriums holding hundreds of people, these are run by an auctioneer who cries the sale. Bids are taken from the audience as each item is offered. These sales can go fast, but you still may have to wait hours for the thing you want to bid on. Auctions are a favored hangout of all types of antique buffs, always hopeful of finding a sleeper, an available antique at a ridiculously low price.

Often you will find auction bills listing items offered at local auctions, at crossroads stores, filling stations, quick-stops, along with other business places. Here in my home state of Oklahoma, settled only since the turn of the century, antique guns are seldom found at these small local sales. Further east or west there are greater chances of old guns being offered at auctions. Many big-city newspapers have auction listings in the classified ads section.

Ordinarily, the guns found at these auctions are, or should be, classed as wall-hangers, too worn, beat up, and decrepit for use. Many aren't even of enough beauty to hang on the fireplace. Many are little more than a hunk of wood with some iron screwed to it. Some have been altered to such uses as lampstands.

Should you read of an auction with some interesting guns being offered, you must get there before sale time, so you can give these a thorough inspection. (We'll go into value later.) Remember, you are strictly on your own and what you see is what you get. If you buy a dud, you are stuck with it. I have been to countless local auctions, many of the old-time farm sales, where lunch is served, the whole thing run under shade trees in the heat of summer, but yet have never found a fine antique muzzleloader. Any number of times I've seen an auction bill listing a gun in excellent condition, or it may say "in good shape," but the person making out the list often wants to make the sale sound like a good one, and you'll not find the merchandise living up to its billing. A person needs to know the market, that is, what a gun is worth, then decide how far he will go toward bidding before that gun is cried for sale.

A completely different type of gun auction are those held each year by the large auction houses such as Christie's, Sotheby-Parke, Richard A. Bourne, James D. Julia, Little John's Antique Arms, and many others. Perhaps you have noticed an upcoming advertisement in the *American Rifleman*, or *The Gun Report*, for one of these huge sales. These organizations offer complete gun collections, often from estates of wealthy gun collectors, museum collections which are being liquidated, and, at times, scores of guns which have been sent them on a consignment basis.

Among gun nuts, this is the "big time" in gun auctions. A sale will attract hundreds, many of them gun dealers, and if a good number of the guns are considered antique quality, you'll find many serious gun collectors among those present.

The auction bill, published prior to the sale, will list all of the guns offered, with a description of each, and, in many instances, an estimate of what the appraiser thinks the guns might bring. The days of the sale will be listed, where it will be held, and also the times and dates for pre-sale inspection. Just the opposite of a small local auction, the guns usually found at this type sale will be quality arms, many in good to excellent condition, but your chances of buying a "sleeper" are between slim and none.

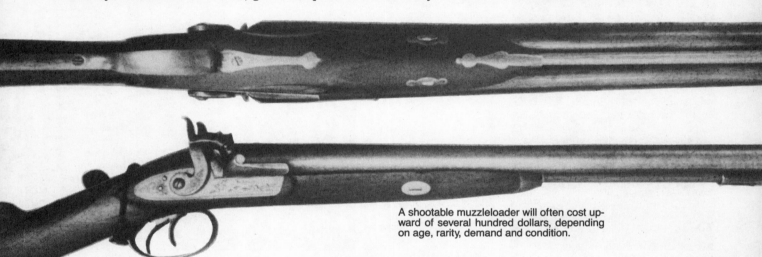

A shootable muzzleloader will often cost upward of several hundred dollars, depending on age, rarity, demand and condition.

For folks who do not live in the area, or cannot attend, catalogs are sometimes offered prior to these sales, listing the guns, condition, etc., and many offer absentee bidding. This makes it possible for anyone to bid on a firearm of his choice even if he cannot attend the sale. I've purchased some fine guns in this manner, and only once did I get one I felt was misrepresented as to its condition. The appraiser must have had an off-moment when he got to the gun, or was distracted, as it had two serious flaws. I could have returned it, but as I wasn't out too many coins, I just ate crow, and later sold it at a small loss. Everyone who is crazy enough to buy antiques, guns or otherwise, is going to someday get stuck; if he doesn't, he either hasn't bought many or he's a liar. It's part of the game. *The Gun Report*, a magazine for gun collectors, is the best source I know to learn of quality auctions of firearms, modern or antique.

Another source is to attend local gun shows; the major shows are also listed in *The Gun Report*. These are often held in convention centers, large auditoriums, or other buildings which will handle huge crowds. These are attended by hundreds of thousands of people across the U.S., everyone from military buffs to serious collectors. Hunters probably make up the bulk of the crowds. Invariably, there are some high-quality gun dealers. Most have retail locations with showrooms exhibiting the firearms they have at present for sale. Reliable veteran antique gun dealers such as Herb Glass, Alan S. Kelley, Ron Ogan, and Eric Vaule will be found at the well-organized gun shows, which are held about the same time of year, and have been for many years. Dates are listed months in ad-

Retail gun dealers, particularly antique gun dealers, are a person's best bet for finding a quality hunting gun. Most are honest, will tell you if they consider a gun shootable, or if it is of such quality that they'd not advise taking such a fine gun afield. Probably the price will also deter a person from using the finer guns for hunting. Dealers invariably have a short free inspection period, and after ordering a gun, you will have three to five days in which to return it, if you don't like the piece, and your money will be refunded.

The well-known Dixie Gun Works, located at Union City, Tennessee, is another source of antique muzzleloaders. These folks offer catalogs for a small fee which list guns-in-stock, along with their descriptions.

The first thing a person needs to know before purchasing an antique

FINE: All original parts; over 30 percent original finish; sharp lettering, numerals and designs on metal and wood; minor marks in wood; good bore.

VERY GOOD: All original parts; none to 30 percent original finish; original metal surfaces smooth with sharp edges; clear lettering, numerals and designs on metal; wood slightly scratched or bruised; bore disregarded for collectors' firearms.

GOOD: Some minor replacement parts; metal smoothly rusted or lightly pitted in places, cleaned or reblued; principal lettering, numerals and designs on metal legible; wood refinished, scratched, bruised or minor cracks repaired; in good working order.

FAIR: Some major parts replaced; minor replacement parts may be required; metal rusted, may be lightly

Local auctions often offer firearms, but seldom good ones for the hunter.

A room like this one at Dixie Gun Works is, of course, a happy hunting ground for shootable old-timers.

vance for those of us who plan on attending, and knowing the quality of the show we can therefore make arrangements to be there.

Smaller local gun shows can also attract many quality dealers, but often these shows will have tables rented by folks who have bought guns down through the years, and decide this is a good way to get rid of them.

Anyone wanting to buy an antique hunting gun must be extremely careful when dealing with unknown dealers, this being another case of "what you see is what you get." Many dealers will tell you honestly that they know nothing about a gun, and are selling it "as is." I've spent hours examining old guns at gun shows, but the few I've bought have all turned out very good. The bore of a gun is most critical, and this is the one area I examine carefully, or as best I can.

gun with which to hunt is the grading system, which is used by the reputable dealers. These are more or less guidelines to follow so that should a dealer offer a gun, and the person wanting one is well versed with the various grades of a gun, the person will have a fairly good idea of what it's like sight unseen.

I've listed the following standards for antique arms, having found these definitions in *Flayderman's Guide to Antique American Firearms . . . and their values*, 5th Edition.

FACTORY NEW: All original parts; 100 percent original finish; in perfect condition in every respect, inside and out.

EXCELLENT: All original parts; over 80 percent original finish; sharp lettering, numerals and designs on metal and wood; unmarred wood; fine bore.

pitted all over, vigorously cleaned or reblued; rounded edges of metal and wood; principal lettering, numerals and designs on metal partly obliterated; wood scratched, bruised, cracked or repaired where broken; in fair working order, or can be easily repaired and placed in working order.

POOR: Major and minor parts replaced; major replacement parts required and extensive restoration needed; metal deeply pitted; principal lettering, numerals and design obliterated; wood badly scratched, bruised and cracked or broken; mechanically inoperative; generally undesirable as a collector's firearm.

These are NRA guidelines, established by that organization as a set of grades for antique guns.

I've usually found shootable guns in the Fine, Very Good, and Good categories. Most guns in the top grades,

Factory New and Excellent, are those which should be kept indoors, either in museums or in private collections.

On examining a gun with which I intend to shoot, the first thing I look at is the bore, hoping there is sufficient metal thickness remaining so the gun will be safe to shoot. I'd never attempt to shoot a gun with barrels which appear to be thin and well worn at the muzzles. Ordinarily, the overall appearance is a giveaway as to how much the gun has been fired. If the gun is pretty well run-down, all the finish is gone from the wood, no browning remains on metal parts, and the area around the breech is worn to a silver smooth polish, you can bet the gun has been shot considerably.

I examine the hammers for hairline cracks. Of course, nipples are also a clue as to recent firing or considerable shooting. But, perhaps these are also

Papers like these and regional and national gun auction announcements are top sources for information on good gun sales.

replacements so this is not a sure-fire clue to how much use the piece has had. The burned areas around nipples indicate amounts of shooting, also.

A potential buyer should examine the stocks closely, particularly those on long rifles, as these are often cracked or broken. The small wrist is extremely susceptible to breakage, and though this delicacy adds tremendously to the beauty of the Kentuckys, many hundreds of these fine old guns have suffered such damage.

Reliable dealers are aware of all of the good, and bad, points of guns which they offer, but some will not point out the bad points. If you don't find them in your inspection, then you've nobody to blame but yourself.

I've often been leery of purchasing old muzzleloaders at gun shows simply because the person with whom I'm dealing isn't known, has perhaps only

a couple of old guns, and therefore will tell me he knows nothing about the gun offered. And, lighting is often poor in such buildings so a good, thorough examination is impossible. Yet, the best old shooter I've owned I bought at such a show.

The price being asked not only reflects the condition of a gun but also its rarity, whether it may be flintlock or caplock, and the amount of fine work, such as engraving, relief carving, or perhaps it's stocked with extra fancy wood. If it's a factory gun perhaps only a few were manufactured, which will hike the price. Demand brings the price up also. Years ago, nobody wanted the old muzzle-loading shotguns. The best could be bought for several hundred dollars, made by famous old makers like Manton, Goucher, Westley Richards, and Purdey. Today, quality antique firearms in

shootable condition can easily run past a thousand dollars. The return to things of our past, to a longing for the feel of our heritage, has brought with it the urge to hunt as they did in the good old days. Not only have there been countless replicas sold, but many hunters have sought out the real thing, an old-time muzzleloader.

If possible, I would always ask a blackpowder gunsmith to go with me if I had located a gun I would like to purchase. And, you'll notice I said, ". . . . a blackpowder gunsmith," as many modern firearms gunsmiths are not well acquainted with muzzleloaders, particularly older guns.

Let the gunsmith examine the barrels, stock, hammers and locks. A shooting gun is no better'n its locks, and a muzzleloader with poor locks is just plain unsafe. Though any gunsmith worth his salt will tell you you

are on your own when you shoot what you've purchased, he will tell you if he thinks the gun is in good enough condition that he'd not be afraid to shoot it. If he wouldn't shoot it, I wouldn't.

I send all of my blackpowder guns, the older ones, to competent blackpowder gunsmiths, have them go over the gun from end to end, then tell me what all needs fixing, and what it'll set me back. And I am fully aware that though a gunsmith may tell me the gun appears safe, and he wouldn't have any qualms about firing it, these old guns could come apart, blowing up in a person's face. Again, buy the best you can. A gun in good condition is less apt to give trouble, and won't cost you further repairs in the long run.

Shooting the old guns is the same as with the new replicas. You practice the same loading sequences, and all of the same rules of safety. If you are squeamish about always being on the safe side, then stick to modern replicas. But, remember, a gun is only as safe as the man makes it. Any firearm can do harm.

Hunting with muzzleloaders has a charm I've yet to find when hunting with modern cartridge busters. Probably it's because I like old things. I write at an old rolltop desk, sit in an old school marm's oak chair. Surrounding me are old Indian pots, animal traps, wooden decoys, and each morning I'd much prefer to put on old clothes. Each to his own.

Few guns can match the beauty of a slender, tiger-striped maple stock of an old Bedford County Kentucky, nor has any gun the feel of an 1800's Westley Richards 10-bore, in side-by-side, with a rich, dark walnut stock, made from the burl with all those fancy curliques showing along the small part, what's known as the wrist to us sootburning hunters.

Truly, beauty is in the eye of the beholder.

No, I'm not a gun collector. I'm a hunter. And an old worn-out guide. And guns are a tool in my trade.

Nor can I help but feel that many of those old-time gunmakers made guns for shooting, some to shoot redskins, some to shoot game. They spent days putting together a fine gun, hunched over a bench in poor light, filing, rasping, boring, all with a keen touch for knowing what looks good, but comes to the shoulder with all the grace of a big eight-point clearing a stone fence.

Some folks will hang their old guns on the wall. Others will put them under lock and key.

My old guns are going hunting.
With me. ●

by **DEAN A. GRENNELL**

HANDLOADING UPDATE

FEW RELATIONSHIPS are as significant and critical as the one between a reloader and the in-house powder/bullet scale. For the past thirty-something years, I have relied upon a Lyman/Ohaus scale. I can't speak for it, of course, but, for my part, I've been comfortably ungruntled with the situation.

Its numbers and graduations are vivid black-on-white, large and easy to distinguish, even in fairly feeble light. Adjusting, checking and zeroing are simple and straightforward procedures. In short, it was—and still is—a component that tends to work upon the solution rather than contributing to the problem. If you don't think a reloader appreciates such support, you must be rather new to the game.

For the past several years, local supermarket checkouts have had electronic scales that weigh produce to the hundredth of a pound. I've often thought how handy that would be around the loading bench, if engineered to suitable sensitivity. There are 7000 grains in one avoirdupois pound and getting things shaved down to ±0.1-grain would involve sensitivity to 1/70,000-pound, i.e., 0.000014285-pound.

On hand is a brochure from **Ohaus Corporation,** 29 Hanover Road, Florham Park, NJ 07932, listing and illustrating a wide assortment of digital-readout scales they offer. Most, if not all, are graduated in the sacred gram and if any read in grains, they have escaped my attention to date. Reloading is one of the few activities that deals with grains as a unit of weight. (I have a reloader friend

by the name of Gerry Gore, operating out of South Africa, who came up with what I regard as the ultimately apropos term for the metric system. He refers to it as Napoleon's Revenge and I'm inclined to drink to that.)

Practically all of the load data available to North American reloaders is given in grains, a unit of measure originally derived from grains of wheat. One grain equals 0.0647989-gram. One gram equals 15.43236 grains and drop as many decimals either way as you feel inclined. Be my Guest, Edgar.

I believe **Blount/RCBS** was the first to put forth an electronic reloader's scale. Maximum capacity was 500 grains; slightly over one ounce (7000 ÷ 16 = 437.5). It operated on an AC adapter or on eight AA batteries (not included). The retail price crowded four C-notes and, what with one thing and the other, I have not as yet worked with the Blount/RCBS electronic scale.

I've found it sometimes pays to wait a bit until prices come down somewhat and conditions stabilize, as it did in this instance. As of the early 1992 catalog, **Lyman** came up with their Model LE-1000 electronic scale with a maximum capacity of 1000 grains. The retail price tag is down to $339.60 for your choice of one that runs off of 115 volt or 220 volt AC juice with the supplied adapter. Either also works with a 9-volt DC battery (not included). As a battery-saving feature, the scale will turn off automatically if not used for five to ten minutes.

You want to determine the weight of something in grams?

No big problem. Merely press down on the mode key and it switches from grains to grams, or vice versa. When first turned on, it reads in grains automatically.

The great virtue of the electronic scale lies in its convenience. Pour a charge of powder into its pan and you get a readout as to its exact weight in a second or three, with no need to juggle counter-poises back and forth, no waiting for the beam to settle down. It's so handy you tend to do a lot more weight

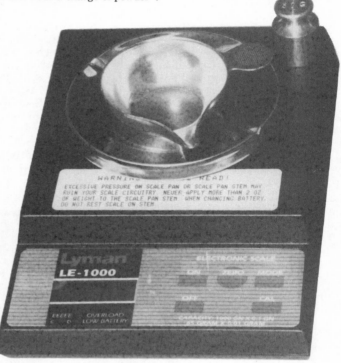

Lyman's LE-1000 electronic scale, at up to $340, is a happy augmentation.

Oehler's personal ballistics lab is yet another wave of the future.

checking and, in reloading, that's all to the good.

Other new Lyman items this year include precision cartridge case length/headspace gauges; a universal inside/outside neck deburring tool that can be used hand-held or on a crank stand; a primer pocket uniforming tool; a flash hole uniformer; a Mag Tumbler with a capacity of nearly three gallons and a smaller Tubby Tumbler with a see-through lid.

There are ten bullet moulds newly added to Lyman's catalog. One is a 200-grain caliber 44 gas-checked, conical-point,

semi-wadcutter, No. 429303, originally introduced in 1958 and brought back by popular demand. The No. 268645 is a 150-grain gas-checked design for 6.5mm. The No. 311664 is a 190-grain gas-checked design for caliber 30 loads. The No. 225646 is a 55-grain gas-checked design for caliber 22 loads. The No. 457643 is a 400-grain plain-base for 45-70 and the like and the No. 454647 is a 285-grain gas-checked design for use in the 454 Casull or in 45 Colt loads.

The other four new moulds are in what Lyman terms their "Devastator" line of hollow-

points. All have comparatively large nasal cavities, tapering inward toward the base. The No. 268645 is a 180-grain for 45 ACP, designated as bullet number 452374 and the mould number, as quoted. You may recall the original 452374 duplicated the profile of the GI hardball load; still in the line, that one's mould number 2660374. The No. 429640 is a gas-checked design for caliber 44 use. The 401638 is a 155-grain bevel-base for 10mm use and the No. 356637 is for 9mm, likewise bevel-based.

The folks at **Blount/RCBS** also have several new bullet

moulds include the 7.62-130-SPL, a 130-grain gas-checked spitzer probably intended for use in the 7.62x39mm. The No. 308-200-SIL is a 200-grain gas-checked design with but one grease groove and nearly all the sidewall of full .309-inch diameter. The No. 45-325-FN-U is a 325-grain for .458-inch sizing and the final letters stand for Flat-Nose Universal.

Likewise new at RCBS is their AmmoMaster press, available in several formats. You can have it as a straight single-station press for conventional loading, or you can set it up to load the caliber 50 Browning Ma-

Here's the Load-Master by Lee—set it up any way you like.

New case length gauges, deburring tools, lots more from Lyman.

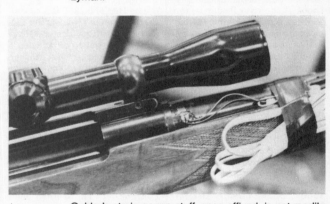

Oehler's strain gauge stuff, once affixed, is not readily removable.

moulds. Their No. 09-147-FN is a 147-grain flat-nose for the 9mm Parabellum. The 40-180-FN is a 180-grain flat-nose for the 10mm. The 44-300-SWC is a 300-grain gas-checked semi-wadcutter for caliber 44 use. The 45-225-CAV is a 225-grain with a truncated cone tip. The CAV stands for Cavalry and it's designed to be sized to .454-inch. The No. 45-300-SWC is a 300-grain gas-checked semi-wadcutter, intended to be sized to .452-inch for use in the 454 Casull.

New RCBS rifle bullet

chine Gun cartridge. For that big boomer, RCBS has the dies and shellholder, Speer has their No. 2491 FMJ/BT bullet at 647 grains, with an awesome ballistic coefficient of .701 and CCI has their No. 35 primer designed for the 50 BMG.

Having acquired a single-station AmmoMaster, you can retrofit it to either a manually indexed progressive or an auto-indexing progressive, complete with the RCBS Powder-Checker and/or their case lube die. They also have a new line of micrometer-adjusted bench-

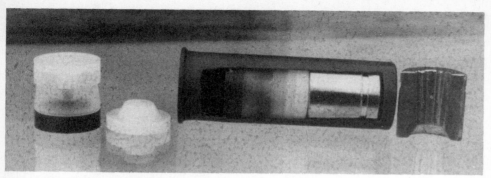

The Wosenitz load revealed—includes a "pusher wad."

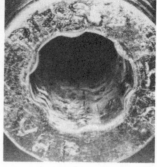

The Wosenitz slug holds rifling in its hollow.

rest bullet seating dies in conjunction with their competition die sets, enabling the fussy reloader to seat bullets for the desired degree of free jump to the leade of the rifling in increments of 0.001-inch; close enough for government work, as they say.

Lee Precision has put in a busy year at the drawing board. Their Load-Master is a massive five-station progressive, with auto-indexing shell plate and removable turrets for a quick die change between calibers. The shell plates are also quick and easy to change, with no tools needed. Available accessories include a case feeder, a case collator for filling the four tubes of the case feeder in ten seconds, a loaded round catcher and a bullet feeder. The last remains under development.

The basic Load-Master retails for $179 or you can get a factory setup Load-Master for $320 in pistol calibers, $310 in rifle calibers. The pistol model has a carbide sizing die, Deluxe Auto-Disk powder measure and a case feeder. The rifle model has Lee Pace-Setter dies, Perfect Powder Measure, Universal Charge Die and case inserter (no case feeder). Large or small primer feeders list for $24.98 each. Shell plates are $29.98 each. The five-hole turrets are $14.98; same prices for the Loaded Round Catcher and/or the Case Collator.

The Lee Perfect Powder Measure is also new to the line since last year. One of its more outstanding features is a soft elastomer wiper that strikes off the metering chamber rather than cutting powder granules. Not only is it quite effortless to operate, even with large-grained extruded powders, but it delivers exceptional drop-to-drop uniformity. Its micrometer stem is graduated in cubic centimeters and the operating manual lists the weights per cu-

bic centimeter for all popular powders, making it possible to work out the trial setting quite closely. Due to variations between lots of powders, it is necessary to verify the final drop weight on a powder scale but the approach is a definite step in the right direction.

Hensley & Gibbs have several new mould designs but, as the copy deadline comes crashing down, I've been unable to shake the details out of Wayne Gibbs. A bit later in the year, they'll have a new catalog and you can put in for a copy by sending a business-length self-addressed stamped envelope to Mrs. Sharon Gibbs, Box 10, Murphy, OR 97533.

The H&G No. 350 is a 44-caliber version of their earlier No. 333 in 38-caliber size. Both are .250-inch front to back, with a single grease groove, flat on both ends. Four of the 38 size can be loaded into a 357 Remington Maximum case and four of the No. 350s can be loaded into a 445 Super Mag, sometimes headstamped 445 Gates. You can get three of the No. 350s into a 44 Magnum case but you'll need one of the Lee Factory Crimp dies to iron out the bulge in its midriff so as to chamber it. There have been numerous requests for H&G to add a similar design in .410-inch diameter for use in the 41 Magnum.

Down at **Oehler Research**, they've whomped up a strain gauge system for measuring breech pressures and recording a trace of the pressure curve. Depending upon your available facilities, it can be fed into a desktop computer or, failing that, a battery-powered laptop or notebook computer. The basic gizmo runs about $700 and the little strain gauges that you epoxy onto the barrel over the chamber are only seven bucks apiece. This strikes me as a highly intriguing development.

Hornady now has the fourth edition of their *Hornady Handbook* out in two volumes. Volume one has all the load data for rifles and handguns, with volume two to supply all the details as to downrange trajectory, remaining velocity and the like. The advantage lies in being able to open both books to the appropriate pages, rather than having to skip back and forth.

The Hornady Apex-91 shotshell loader was illustrated in this report last year, but that proved a trifle premature. It is now docketed to go into production in the spring of 1992.

Back in Cortland, New York, birthplace of the incomparable Cortland apple, **Redding/Saeco** has put in a busy year. New for the coming season are their Straight Line Benchrest Competition bullet seating dies, in which both bullet and cartridge case are aligned to perfection within a close-fitting sleeve before the bullet seating begins. The micrometer seating depth adjustment is infinite—that is to say clickless—and has a provision for you to adjust to zero at your favorite seating depth.

Likewise new from Redding/Saeco is their Competition Model BR-30 powder measure, designed for optimum performance on charge weights between 10 and 50 grains. The diameter of the metering cavity has been reduced and the metering plunger was given a unique hemispherical or cup shape. This creates a metering cavity that resembles the lower portion of a test tube to alleviate irregular powder settling, thus enhancing charge-to-charge uniformity.

Moving on to the line of Redding/Saeco bullet moulds, there are several new designs. In the .313-inch diameter for 32-caliber handguns, there's the No. 326, a 100-grain SWCBB and

This is Lyman's #311664—a 190-grain 30-caliber gas-check design.

the 322A, a 188-grain flat-point. In the .355-inch diameter for 9mmP and 38 Super, there's the No. 924, a 124-grain gas-checked semi-wadcutter and the No. 383, a 140-grain semi-wadcutter. In the .358-inch diameter for use in the 38 Special, there's the No. 053, a 148-grain wadcutter with a crimping groove up front and a single grease groove about midway from nose to tail, with an unbeveled plain base.

Slug loads for shotguns have

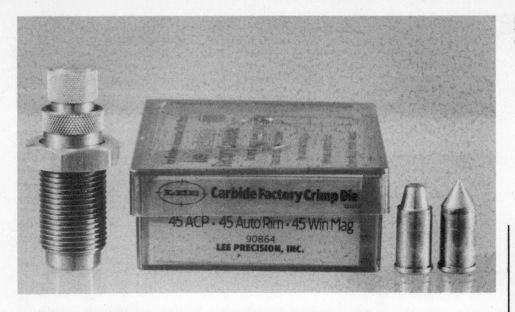
Lee begins to cover a large waterfront—this carbide die produces a factory-style crimp.

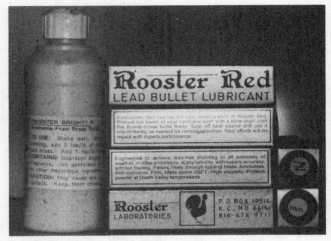
Rooster has lubes and polishes to make nice-looking brass, good-looking bullets.

Data in one, details in the other—Hornady's new manuals make sense.

been the focal point of a lot of attention in recent times. One of the more interesting examples to come to my attention is from **William B. Wosenitz,** 341 No. E. 2nd Court, Dania, FL 33004; 305-923-3748. He has designed, patented and is marketing a Venturi Helix Projectile (VHP) in 12-gauge dimensions that is said to do quite well in smoothbore barrels and considerably better in rifled barrels.

The VHP slug has a tapering, venturi-shaped hollow center with helical "rifling" bands to make the slug spin as it moves through the air. A pusher wad at the rear seals powder gases and falls away as the slug leaves the muzzle. Wosenitz has fired a four-shot group at 100 yards that measures 1¼ inches between centers. That was from a 26-inch rifled barrel. To the present, the VHP slugs are available only in 12-gauge. Weighing five of them on the Lyman scale showed weights from 680.7 to 682.4 grains for an average weight of 681.28 grains.

Wosenitz doesn't quote velocity figures, but furnishes photos of ⁵⁄₁₆-inch aluminum plate the VHP slugs punched through. Fired into wax or damp sand, they expand to double the original diameter. Again, I think this has the sound of interesting possibilities.

Corbin Supply & Manufacturing now can supply draw die sets for making your own bullet jackets in various caliber diameters to lengths of up to .500-inch, using any competent reloading press. Longer jackets require a hydraulic press. According to Dave Corbin, pure copper works just fine as the raw material and he can also supply copper strips of suitable width and thickness. Pricewise, you're looking at about $400 for the hand press tooling, $3500 for the hydraulic tooling. Setting up for additional calibers may cost as little as $160, depending upon specifications. A large package of descriptive literature is available from Corbin for $1.

Midway Arms, Inc., P.O. Box 1483, Columbia, MO 65203 now offers precision-made reloading trays or blocks made of fine-grain hardwood and lightly varnished. Thirteen different sizes are offered, covering cartridges from 25 ACP through 50-70 Government and 50 Sharps. Also new to their line are headspace/maximum length gauges for a great many popular rifle and handgun cartridges, as well as a heater base for lube/sizers to allow the use of high-temperature bullet lubes such as the types available from Rooster Laboratories.

Rooster Laboratories, P.O. Box 19514, Kansas City, MO 64141 can furnish several different formulations of bullet lubricants for use at typical room temperatures or with a heated lube/sizer base. Also new this year is Rooster Bright, an ammonia-free liquid brass polish that can be added to your cleaning medium a short time before putting in the cases. I've used the Rooster Bright and find it puts a nice sparkle on tired brass in a relatively short time.

Bianchi International, 100 Calle Cortez, Temecula, CA 92590, now has plastic storage bags branded Bianchi Blue. Measuring about six by twelve inches, they have a zipper-type closure at one end and the interior is treated with a corrosion preventive compound that keeps ferrous items rust-free for about two years. ●

Author's personal favorites for small game and varmint shooting include the Winchester 52 with standard-weight barrel in 22 Long Rifle with a 6x scope; the Heckler & Koch 300 autoloader in 22 WMR with a 4x scope; and the Winchester '03 autoloader in 22 Winchester Automatic fitted with a tang sight.

THE QUIET RIFLE

No spiteful crack, no big boom for this writer

by C. RODNEY JAMES

THE EAR-SPLITTING crack of a 22-250 or 30-06 has a way of announcing a shooter's presence in the field. The flash and report of a large-caliber rifle or shotgun does not bother many of my shooting acquaintances and, in fact, a few even draw a childlike pleasure from such events. I have come to regard this noise as a necessary evil. The "use enough gun—reach out and get-'em" advocates must be doing their hunting in some other country, or at least *west* of the Mississippi.

There *is* a middle ground whose advocates have included Charles Landis and Henry Stebbins, among others. Their approach to small game and varmint hunting is to get maximum performance from rifles using low-power, low-noise ammunition. That is what this article is about.

From a practical point of view, except possibly signaling for help, firearm noise has no value. It alerts game, annoys land-owners and destroys one's hearing. No offense to the authorities, but silencers (suppressors) can benefit health. Alas, to stay within the law, low noise must be achieved via long barrels and low-power ammunition.

Most shooters generally divided rifles into two discrete types—hunting rifles and precision rifles. The rifle used for small game hunting is lightweight—seldom over seven pounds—and is a repeater with an 18- to 24-inch barrel. The precision rifle is for target shooting. It is a bolt action, usually a single shot, and weighs ten pounds and up, with a 26- to 28-inch barrel. Between these is the "varmint rifle," combining the sporter's magazine with the precision rifle's accuracy. It is this type of rifle that approaches my ideal as a useful shooting tool. Unfortunately, few manufacturers are currently producing such a rifle in the 22 rimfire class.

The 22 Long Rifle has become *the* standard small game cartridge. Most shooters regard the Long Rifle as suitable for squirrels, rabbits and small pests below the size of a woodchuck. In terms of power and accuracy, it is generally considered a fifty-yard cartridge. Fifty yards *is* about the limit, if not *well beyond* the limit in the average, light sporting rifle currently available. The "limit" I speak of is accuracy. The Long Rifle, in its various magnumized forms, is quite capable of reliable killing of woodchucks at ranges of a hundred yards and beyond.

The old rule of thumb regarding suitable accuracy for small game hunting was the ability to group ten consecutive shots in a 1-inch circle. I think this is a good standard, which is why I get annoyed at those three-shot groups and "best five" groups. Five-shot consecutive groups are nearly as good as ten, though experts have demonstrated how five-shot groups can occasionally give skewed results.

That the 22 Long Rifle has fallen into disrepute as a seventy-five- to one-hundred-twenty-five-yard cartridge stems, I believe, from the following conditions: Competitive target shooting with this cartridge at two hundred yards has disappeared. The target rifles used for that shooting are no longer produced. The writers who did that shooting are long dead and their books are out-of-print. This is not to say that supremely accurate target rifles aren't available. They are. Anschutz, Beeman/Feinwerkbau, Tanner and Walther, among others, make rifles for Olympic competition that undoubtedly could pick a fly off a fence post at fifty yards. On the down side, these are *only* suited for Olympic competition. The average price is $2000 and up. They are single shot *only*; and with all their thumbholes, palm rests, butt hooks and adjustable everything, the guns are poorly adapted to hunting, in addition to being about the ugliest things this writer has seen in the gun department.

What is needed to draw the last performance ounce from the 22 Long Rifle in the hunting field, outside of a custom-crafted arm, is to be found in the competition target rifles from the period 1920-1970. These were bolt-action repeaters designed along the lines of early 20th-century military rifles; and, in fact, came into being as small-caliber training rifles for military use. The improvements in rimfire ammunition in the 1920s and '30s led to their use in long-range competition and the civilian equivalent—small game and varmint hunting at long ranges, really long ranges for 22 rimfires.

The 1919 Savage NRA model was the first such rifle on the market, followed by the Model 52 Winchester a year later and by the government-made Model M-1 Springfield in 1922. Both the Savage and the Springfield were gone by WWII. In 1937, Mossberg produced a heavy-barreled, target rifle. It was reworked in several versions, the last being the Model 144 target rifle. Stevens introduced the budget-priced 416 in 1937. And Remington entered the field in 1937 with its Model 37, followed much later by the Model 40-XB rimfire, offered briefly as a repeater. Remington also produced the Model 513, and Winchester the Model 75, as medium-priced target rifles to compete with the Mossberg. There are, lately, more and more "entry level" target models intro-duced, their hunting utility yet to be tested.

In judging the above in accuracy, all were good, but the 52, 37 and 40-XB with heavy barrels would receive my "A" rating for their ability to group ten shots in 1.2 inches at a hundred yards on a regular basis, and often under an inch at that distance. The same rifles with the standard-weight barrel may group a little larger, but weigh nine pounds as opposed to twelve or more for the heavy and extra-heavy "bull" barrel models. A ten-pound, forty-seven-inch rifle may seem a lot to tote around, but no more so than a 12-gauge shotgun, most of which are equal in length, if a bit lighter.

Recent developments, not to mention empirical evidence, have demonstrated that sporting rifles of what might be called "premium quality," and some of very ordinary appearance and cost, have proved to be capable of match or near-match accuracy. The problem in hunting with a five- to six-pound rifle is that steady holding, particularly for high-angle shots, particularly for high-angle shots, requires a muzzle-heavy rifle. A light barrel will wander all over the place, making these shots very difficult.

Those elements, however, that result in an unusually accurate rifle are many, varied and by no means completely understood. Just as every so often a manufacturer comes up with a really great car (remember those Mustangs of the '60s?), so it happens with rifles. Word of mouth and study of test-fire reports in the gun press, assuming they provide adequate data, are a good means of making a first cut to eliminate the dogs. In searching for an exceptionally accurate rifle, it is well to remember that flame-grain walnut stocks, borderless checkering, engraving and highly-polished blue finishes never did much to enhance accuracy.

Accuracy, beyond the cartridge components, is affected mainly by the fit of the bolt or breechblock to the breech; the fit of the cartridge in the chamber and the bullet in the bore; the dimensional consistency of the bore interior, the smoothness of the bore, the type of rifling system and, finally, the balancing of the twist of the rifling in a barrel to the particular bullet to be fired through it at a predetermined velocity. Beyond this is the fit of the barrel and action to the stock. That's a lot to consider.

With the above in mind, the next considerations are to the combinations of bullet, powder and cartridge case to determine which ones are going to give the best results in a particular rifle. It is a known fact that certain rifles will shoot smaller groups, more

Penetration and expansion in solid plywood—harder than white pine, but more uniform. All were fired into ¾-inch plywood slabs stacked face-to-face, at 35 yards, with sandbag rest. All figures are in inches.

BOTTOM ROW, left to right:	Penetration	Expansion	5-shot group
22 Federal HV Short	1.0	.295	.55
22 Winchester HV Long	1.65	.291	1.0
22 CCI HV Long Rifle	2.2	.342	.3
22 CCI Stinger HP (30.5 gr.)	1.5	.372	.45
22 W-W Super Silhouette (42 gr.)	1.8	.360	.9
TOP ROW, left to right:			
22 W-W HV Long Rifle	1.7	.405	.5
22 Remington Viper	1.9	.321	1.2
22 CCI SGB Long Rifle	1.9	.322	.4
22 CCI +V Long Rifle	2.0	.315	.7

Some fatal bullets: 22 Stinger (left) fragmented in the neck of a fox squirrel at 30 yards. CCI HV Long Rifle was flattened by passing through the skull of a woodchuck. The 22 Winchester Automatic upset, then tumbled through a woodchuck and entered the ground. The 22 Winchester Magnum solid has only a slight dent on the nose after passing through a chuck, which needed two follow-up shots.

Thirty-five yard targets: Five-shot group (left) of Navy Arms standard velocity, through a Kimber sporter measures .5-inch. At right is a five-shot .4-inch group of CCI's new small game bullet from a 52 Winchester. Top and bottom groups (five and six shots respectively) are each .7-inch—CCI's new +V Long Rifle in the 52.

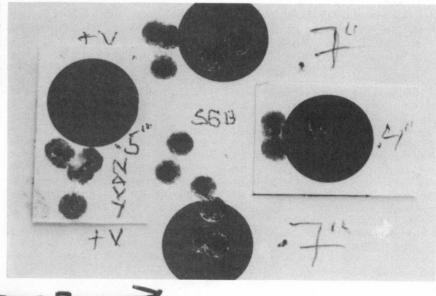

The Kimber sporter is typical of the "premium grade" 22 rifle, often capable of high levels of accuracy.

consistently. The conventional wisdom has been that for 22 rimfire accuracy, the best results are obtained from a bolt-action rifle with a heavy, soft-steel barrel, with a highly polished interior, and a match chamber, free-floated or glass-bedded on a dense wood stock. This combination will outshoot a J.C. Higgins from Sears. It always will . . . nearly.

The premium bolt-action sporters offer better-than-average accuracy, but rarely up to the level of the heavy target rifles, although Kimber rifles have turned in groups under an inch at one hundred yards. Considering their costs—$600 and up—unless light weight is a critical factor, the shooter in search of the best accuracy bang-for-his-buck, would do well to find a good, used 52, 37 or 40-XB which can be had for about the same price.

Even if the Long Rifle were safely reloadable, there would be little point in doing so, in view of the low cost and variety of loadings, bullet weights and styles available for this cartridge. The first improvement in the Long Rifle over the blackpowder ammunition introduced about 1881, came with the target loadings of the mid-1920s. The first "rimfire revolution," however, came in 1926-31 with the introduction of noncorrosive priming and high-velocity loadings that boosted the 40-grain solid and 36-grain hollowpoint bullets from 950-1090 feet per second to 1275-1400 fps, greatly extending range and killing power. The second revolution came in 1976-78 with the introduction of the hyper-velocity loadings generating 1500-1680 fps with 30- to 35-grain bullets. The fact remains, though, that the finest accuracy for this cartridge is achieved when the bullet is traveling about 1050-1120 fps. The problem in scoring hits at *this* velocity is the *high trajectory* of the bullet, requiring the shooter to become an *expert* in range estimation and determining target size, as in typical target ammunition.

Any number of books on small-bore shooting include trajectory and "bullet drop" charts. I never found these of much use, possibly because I am too dense to interpret them properly, or because they are based on averages and not on the particular rifle and ammunition I am using. In order to become skilled in long-range shooting, there are no shortcuts. The best guide to this craft, I have found, is C.S. Landis' 1932 book *22-Calibre Rifle Shooting,* which devotes several chapters to the subject. In brief, the basic idea is to start with an accurate rifle, equipped with a quality scope and ac-

curate ammunition. The next step is to target this ammunition at *known* distances. On average, a standard-velocity loading will shoot reasonably flat to about forty to fifty yards; a high-velocity loading to about sixty yards. The hyper-velocity Stinger will stay flat to about seventy-five. It is a matter of individual preference, but it is generally easier to make precise-hold over/under adjustments at closer ranges than distant ones, and that is where most shots will be taken. Therefore, the optimum range to zero the rifle is at the point where the bullet begins to drop sharply or a bit beyond this if you plan to do a great deal of long-distance shooting. These ranges are about 50-60 yards for the standard-velocity, 60-75 yards for the high-velocity and 75-90 yards for the hyper-velocity loadings. Once the rifle is zeroed, test-shoot the ammunition at intervals of ten yards from a minimum of fifteen yards, or whatever you consider the closest range you might shoot something (this will provide a reference for parallax error), to the maximum accurate range of the rifle—one-inch groups for squirrel-size targets, 2.5-inch groups for woodchuck-size targets. A typical trajectory for a high-velocity loading is shown here, with the rifle zeroed for seventy-five and again at about twenty-five yards.

Once your time and ammunition investment has been made, *write down* the results. This information on a tape strip, attached to the rifle at some convenient point, saves remembering. This data, of course, will be good for one brand and velocity of ammunition *only*. The next step is to become proficient at estimating ranges. One of the best ways is to get out into the country to a spot where you can practice shooting at unknown distances. Once range estimation is no longer a problem, the next step is to move on to "doping" wind drift and mirage effects. I realize this sounds like those "how-to-write-a-novel" formulas that appear in every writing magazine, but the secret lies in doing it long enough until it becomes second nature. About the only useful aid I have found for estimating wind velocity is a Beaufort scale. It is printed in every good dictionary and can be copied on a small card for ready reference. As with range estimation, wind "doping" is an art. I have never

been particularly good at it and avoid taking long shots on windy days.

The lethal range of the Long Rifle cartridge is far beyond its accurate or "effective" range—close to three-fourths of a mile on an adult human, hit in a vital area: Paper ballistics are rather misleading in this respect. While they show what appears to be significant declines in velocities and foot pounds of energy over a hundred yards, author tests with 22 high velocity solid bullets, for penetration in solid plywood, evidenced only a .2-inch decrease between twenty-five and one hundred fifty yards. In ricochet, this lethal range is cut by about half, but is still a considerable distance. Hollowpoints tend to ricochet less than solids, particularly the hyper-velocity ones, but are by no means ricochet proof!

The hyper-velocity loadings, by virtue of their flatter trajectories, make shots to nearly a hundred yards quite possible, with little if any aim adjustment. They are as accurate as the high-velocity loadings and expand more readily. In ricochet, by virtue of being lighter, they have less range. There is a down-side, however. Both high- and hyper-velocity loadings are more susceptible to wind drift than the low-velocity ones. They are also noisier. The Stinger, in particular, makes a

TYPICAL 22 LR HIGH VELOCITY TRAJECTORY

Yards From Muzzle	15	30	40	50	60	70	80	90	100
Inches Above or Below Sightline	−.13	+.39	+.95	+.56	+.50	+.25	−.50	−2.25	−3.75

sharper crack than most. The Remington Yellow Jacket, with its very large cavity, expands with explosive results which are enhanced by the cavity often being filled with bullet lubricant, which behaves as a semifluid. The effect on woodchucks is very lethal. Grackles and starlings are often pulped to the point of being blown in half; so are squirrels, which makes it a poor choice for pot hunting.

A useful loading, now available only as an import, is the standard-velocity hollowpoint, which combines good expansion with low noise, and is a far more effective killer than the solids—standards or target-velocity loadings—that some hunters favor for their superior accuracy. By opening the nose cavity and filling it with paraffin or bullet lubricant, expansion can be enhanced. While on the subject of enhancement, it is a demonstrable fact that just as certain brands and loadings of ammunition will shoot better than others, within a brand, cer-

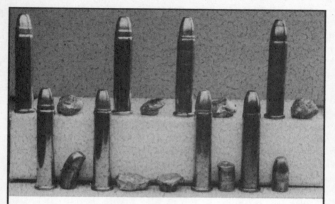

Winchester Rimfire Magnum loadings are coming in greater variety, not all of which are useful. Solid plywood tests at 35 yards through an H&K 300 autoloader. Figures are in inches.

TOP ROW, left to right:	Penetration	Expansion	5-shot group
CCI HP	3.3	.376	.5
CCI + V HP (30.5 gr.)	3.6	.372	.5
Federal HP	2.65	.343	.55
Winchester HP	2.0	.358	.45
BOTTOM ROW, left to right:			
Federal HP (50 gr.)	2.9	—	.35
Federal	2.45	.457 x.335	.3
Federal (2nd bullet/wet newsprint)	11.5	.386	
CCI	5.55	—	.4
Winchester	7.6	—	.4

By virtue of its thin jacket, the Federal 40-grain solid behaves much like a hollowpoint. The slow-moving 50-grain hollowpoint at 1329 fps failed to expand as did hard-jacketed CCI and Winchester bullets—all three are prone to ricochet.

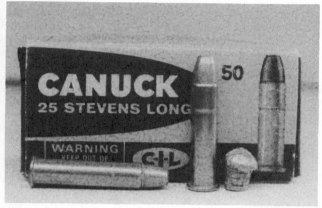

The last of the 25 Stevens came from CIL in Canada about 1971. The bullet on the right penetrated 2.5 inches of plywood at 35 yards, expanding to .356-inch.

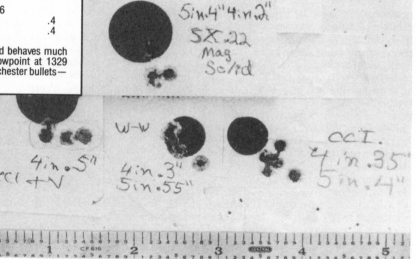

Accuracy of the 22 WMR in both hollow and solidpoint loadings is superb in many rifles including the H&K 300. Thirty-five yard, five-shot groups are Winchester (top and center). CCI + V (four shots, left) and CCI Maxi Mag, right.

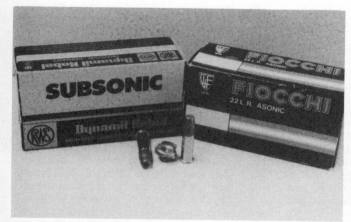

Both R.W.S. and Fiocchi offer low-noise hollowpoint Long Rifle. The bullet in the center penetrated five inches of wet newsprint, expanding to .436-inch.

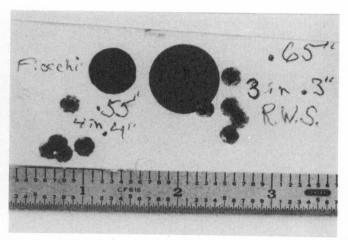

Fiocchi asonic and R.W.S. subsonic—five-shot 35-yard groups measure .55-inch and .65-inch from the Winchester 52.

tain lots (identified by the stamped or printed numbers on the inside box flap) will give superior results. The careful inspection of ammunition, weeding out rounds whose bullets are tipped in the case and have nicks, cuts, dents or uneven fins of lead extending below the case mouth will reduce group sizes.

For other than target work, the solid-bullet loadings offer one advantage—the ability to penetrate bone a little more effectively than hollowpoints. Three attempts have been made to enhance solid bullet effectiveness. The semi-hollowpoint, with a slight nose cavity (.03-inch) came and went in the '70s, when it was found to have little if any effect on bullet expansion. The heavy weight (42-grain), truncated-cone Super Silhouette round, from Winchester, was designed to give more knockdown for metallic silhouette shooting. It was never particularly accurate in any of my rifles, nor did it expand as well as roundpoint, 40-grain high-velocity rounds which were moving faster. The truncated-cone, hyper-velocity rounds at the same weight and velocity as the high-velocity hollowpoints expand no better than the slower high-velocity solid bullets, and accuracy is no better.

The 22 Short, originally the number one pistol cartridge for the Smith & Wesson revolver, was first marketed in 1856. By 1858, Frank Wesson was offering rifles in this chambering. In the post-Civil War era, Winchester, Remington and Stevens made both single shot and repeaters for the Short. The Maynard and Stevens single shots of that era had a reputation for accuracy, even with the load of three grains of blackpowder behind a 30-grain bullet. Smokeless loadings appeared around the turn of the century, and 27-grain hollowpoint hunting ammunition was available around 1910. The use of the Short in carnival and arcade shooting galleries kept rifles for this cartridge current through the 1950s, before video games replaced this sport with buttons and joysticks.

Just as the Long Rifle benefitted from new loadings in 1930, so did the Short, getting a boost from 935-975 fps to 1075-1155 fps, and was offered in match target, standard-velocity, standard, hollowpoint, high-velocity and high-velocity hollowpoint. In the early 1950s, Remington even produced, very briefly, a hyper-velocity loading with a 15-grain sintered-iron bullet with an incredible 1710 fps muzzle velocity. It was named the "Rocket." Intended for gallery use, the bullet would produce a shower of sparks when it struck something hard.

It was not very accurate and the rough iron was erosive to soft barrels. Although the standard-velocity hollowpoint is gone (no great loss), there is still available a good variety of loadings for the 27-grain hollowpoint and the 29-grain solid. The Short qualifies as the most quiet of useful hunting rounds, making a pop a little louder than a pellet rifle. Its small size and mild report belie its deadliness. In solid plywood penetration tests, the high velocity solid will go through 1.5 inches at twenty-five yards, as compared to the high-velocity Long Rifle at 2 inches at that distance. A penetration capability of .5-inch of plywood is enough to cause death in a vital area hit on a person. Documented fatalities with the 22 Short have occurred at 600 yards. The Short does best in a barrel bored for it alone, but is remarkably accurate in some Long Rifle barrels.

The most extensive field-testing of the Short this writer knows of has been by Bob Trowbridge—owner of The Powder Room gun store and target range in Powell, Ohio. It's worth hearing about.

Trowbridge, seventy-two years old, began serious hunting as a boy during the Depression. Meat was expensive and pot hunting was an important source of food. His first rifle was a 32 Stevens, which he traded for a 22 Stevens. The 22 had a broken firing pin, which he replaced with one crafted from a nail. The logic behind the trade was the ammunition. The 32 rimfire Shorts were 27 cents for fifty, the 22 Shorts were 12 cents. The twelve-year-old Trowbridge hunted squirrels in nearby woods and rabbits in the abandoned stone quarries near Dublin, Ohio, where he could occasionally stalk close enough to grab them and save a cartridge. The Shorts finished trapped muskrats and picked off redhorse suckers as they surfaced in the riffles of the, then-unpolluted, Scioto River.

During WWII, Trowbridge served in the infantry, qualifying as expert in every weapon he was entitled to fire. After the war, he did his hunting with a Mossberg 42-M with a Mannlicher-style stock—a variant of the training rifle used for State Guards late in the war. In 1960, he opted for a 550 Remington autoloader, which featured the Williams floating chamber, allowing the interchangeable use of Short, Long and Long Rifle ammunition. Equipped with a 4x Weaver scope, his 550 used Shorts almost exclusively, except for an occasional long shot at a woodchuck.

Standard-velocity Shorts were re-

jected because of their excessively high trajectory. Hollowpoints were eliminated for their lack of precision accuracy. The 550 had a definite preference for Federal and Western ammunition, grouping .5-inch or less at twenty yards. To avoid damage to the bullets in the tubular magazine, the load is kept under fifteen rounds. With the rifle zeroed at forty yards, it zeros again at fifty feet. Trowbridge's approach is to stalk to within sixty yards, aim for the eye and put 29 grains of lead in the squirrel's head. The same approach was equally deadly on three woodchucks last year. Last season, he missed *one* squirrel by failing to compensate for the bullet rise on a close vertical shot. His bag has averaged twelve to fifty squirrels a year for the last thirty years, hunted mostly in nearby woodlots.

The 22 Winchester Magnum Rimfire (WMR) came on the market in 1959, without any rifles. Marlin and Winchester had lever actions out by the early '60s, and arms makers now offer every modern action for it including revolvers, automatic pistols, and even derringers. About the only type of rifle not offered is a heavy-barreled target or varmint rifle, although the Anschutz 1700 22 WMR probably comes the closest. Reports from two shooters recorded in John Lachuk's *Gun Digest Book Of The 22 Rimfire* submitted targets with inch groups at seventy-five yards from a Savage 22 WMR/ 20-gauge over/under, with iron sights. More surprising is a pair of targets fired at one hundred yards, with a J.C. Higgins 42DLM rifle measuring .5-inch for five consecutive shots. The author's Heckler & Koch Model 300 autoloader has turned in .8-inch groups at one hundred yards. The same rifle took a crow at two hundred twenty-five yards with a single shot, with the rifle zeroed for one hundred yards and an estimated 15-inch holdover. The belief that high levels of accuracy can *only* be obtained with bolt-action rifles has been challenged by Heckler & Koch.

It is a shame the 22 WMR is not offered in a match loading, for there's no telling what results might be achieved. Somewhere the WMR got the reputation of being inferior to the Long Rifle in accuracy. Nothing could be farther from the truth. The above results are equal to, if not better than, those obtained from a 52 Winchester using match ammunition, at the same distance. Ballistically, the WMR is about double a Long Rifle and half the 22 Hornet. Originally conceived as a "poor man's varmint cartridge," the WMR may be one of the most useful to

Certain obsolete 22 rimfires are still around and worth the hunt, if you have a gun for them. Left to right, 22 Remington Autoloading; 22 Winchester Automatic; same with roundpoint bullet; 22 Winchester Rim Fire (WRF). The Winchester Automatic will fire *only* in the 03 Winchester autoloader. The Remington and the WRF are compatible with the 22 WRM chamber and useful as low-velocity/low-noise rounds. Thirty-five yard results for plywood penetration, expansion and accuracy with an 03 Winchester and an H&K 300 are as follows:

Cartridge	Penetration	Expansion	5-shot group
22 Remington Autoloading	1.05	.278	1.0
22 Winchester Automatic (flat-point)	2.7	.332	.5
22 Winchester Automatic (round-point)	1.3	.270	.5
22 Winchester Rim Fire	2.4	.339	.3

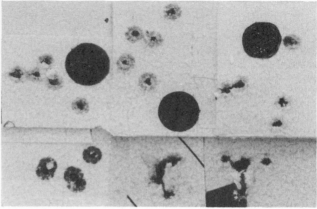

The Long and Short of it: TOP ROW: Three groups of 22 Longs from the 52 Winchester at 35 yards. Left, Remington at .8-inch; center, Federal at .8-inch; and right, Western at 1-inch. BOTTOM ROW: Federal 22 Short through the 52 at 35 yards measures .5-inch. Center and right groups are the same Federal Shorts from Trowbridge, through his 550 Remington autoloader at 50 feet, at .4-inch and .5-inch.

Few centerfires qualify as low-noise cartridges. Left to right: obsolete 22 WCF, 22 Hornet, obsolete 25-50 Stevens, new 25-20 case, 25-20 Winchester, 256 Winchester Magnum, 218 Bee, 221 Remington. The Hornet, 256, 218 and 221 are suitable for down-loading with cast bullets.

Robert Trowbridge, owner of The Powder Room gun shop and target range, with his Remington 550 and Mr. Point Blank—feline ace rodent hunter and sales assistant. The 550 and 22 Shorts have bagged a dozen to fifty squirrels a year for thirty years. Mr. Point Blank does not keep count.

come along since the Long Rifle. Word coming up from the Deep South is that the WMR is good for about everything—squirrels, rabbits, woodchucks, wild turkeys, alligators and small southern deer. Deer hunting with this cartridge is, of course, illegal, but the fact remains that its flat trajectory, tack-driving accuracy and added power make hits in a vital area possible at double or triple Long Rifle range. Grizzly bears have been killed with this cartridge. The WMR is superior in accuracy to the 22 Hornet in many light rifles chambered for that cartridge, giving the WMR an edge though not in trajectory.

The original loadings were 40-grain hollowpoints for varmint shooting and full-metal-jacket solids for small game hunting where the HP proved too destructive. Lately, several variations, some advertised and some not, have come on the market. Winchester's original bullets featured hard jackets applied to lead cores in the conventional manner. CCI and Federal produced bullets with softer, electroplated, copper jackets. In the case of the Federal solid—the thinnest skinned of the lot—the 40-grain solid FMJ bullet will expand on soft targets, while the rest will not.

Federal also fielded a 50-grain bullet in both solid and hollowpoint styles. The fifty was one of those ideas that probably seemed good at the time of inception, but in practice never worked out. Chronographed velocities are in the Long Rifle class. Expansion, even in hard targets such as plywood, is nil while the noise level is the same and recoil is noticeably higher.

In the summer of 1990, CCI introduced a 22 WMR version of the Stinger which features a 30.5-grain hollowpoint called "+V." At an advertised 2200 fps, it is faster than the legendary 5mm Remington Magnum by 100 fps. In hard target (plywood) penetration and expansion tests, the +V went deeper and upset to a greater degree than any magnum hollowpoint tested. What is more, this was

LEARNING FROM OEHLER

Using the new Oehler model 35P chronograph—a sterling piece of equipment—which uses three screens, permitting a double check of each test shot and a built-in printer with a summary function to tally and average up to twenty shots, the following results were obtained on a July day with temperatures in the high 70s and humidity in the 70s. The rifles tested included a Winchester 52B (28-inch barrel) a Ruger 10/22 (18.5-inch barrel) a Winchester 1903 (20-inch barrel) a Winchester 62A (23-inch barrel) a Kimber 82B (22-inch barrel) and an H&K 300 (19-inch barrel). The chronographed figures are averages of five-shot groups, fired after a fouling shot. These are compared with the advertised velocity.

MANUFACTURER VS. ACTUAL VELOCITIES

Cartridge	Manu-facturer	Manuf. MV	Actual MV in 52 Win.	Ruger	Kimber	62 Win.	03 Win.	H&K 300
22 Stinger	CCI	1680	1552	1562	1568	—	—	—
22 Stinger (new loading)	CCI	1640	1642	1566	—	—	—	—
22 +V LR	CCI	1450	1380	1358	1376	—	—	—
22 HV LR	Rem.	1255	1125	1189	—	—	—	—
22 HV LR	CCI	1255	1278	—	—	—	—	—
22 SGB LR	CCI	1235	1245	—	—	—	—	—
22 Asonic	Fio.	—	1020	—	—	—	—	—
22 Yellow J.	Rem.	1500	1421	1404	—	—	—	—
22 Super Sil	W-W	—	1119	—	—	—	—	—
22 Short HV	Fed.	1095	—	—	—	1088	—	—
22 Long HV	W-W	1240	—	—	—	1179	—	—
22 Win Auto	W-W	1055	—	—	—	—	1060	—
22 Rem Auto	Rem.	920	—	—	—	—	—	714
22 WRF	W-W	1450	—	—	—	—	—	1325
22 WMR	W-W	1910	—	—	—	—	—	1721
22 WMR	CCI	1910	—	—	—	—	—	1744
22 WMR 50 gr.	Fed.	1650	—	—	—	—	—	1329
22 WMR +V	CCI	2200	—	—	—	—	—	2157

achieved without sacrificing accuracy—three of four consecutive shots went into .3-inch at thirty-five yards. The single flier spread the group to .5-inch.

Chronographed velocities as published by the ammunition companies are always given with the caveat that they may not be what you will get in "your rifle." My experience has been that they are almost always optimistically high. Air temperature has a significant effect on velocity, with a 20-degree shift in temperature changing velocities to 50 fps higher if the day is warmer and 50 fps lower, if colder. Humidity will also affect velocity by increasing the density of the air and lowering velocities. Barrel length and the tightness of the fit of the bullet in the bore will also play a role, assuming all ammunition components are equal. Within the 22 rimfire class, maximum velocities are claimed in barrels of 18 inches for the 22 Long Rifle and 19 to 20 inches for the 22 WRF and WMR. Longer barrels *sometimes* result in slightly lower velocities, thus noise reduction has its price. Autoloaders of the blowback sort, owing to their slight loss of gas pressure, will supposedly clock slightly lower velocities than locked-breech rifles.

What all of this means is that those rules and figures are to be taken with a grain of salt, if not a spoonful. A few dozen feet per second more or less has no noticeable effect on penetration or expansion. Bullet expansion and cavitation in a living body is affected more by bullet design and material than by minor variations in velocity, i.e. less than 100 fps. The most important concern regarding velocity is its effect on bullet *trajectory*. High trajectories make hitting targets difficult, though by no means impossible, at long ranges. The most annoying problem results from *variations* in velocity within a box or lot of ammunition. This problem is soon evident in "vertical stringing" of shots when the ammunition is targeted. The more distant the target, the greater the problem. *Accuracy* and with it *bullet placement* are by far the most critical factors in sure killing.

There really aren't any quiet centerfires any more, at least as they come from the factory. The 22 Hornet and the 25-20 repeater come about the closest, with the Hornet really too "snappy" to make the cut, although it is a low-recoil cartridge. The Hornet has been loaded down with cast bullets with accurate results, though cast bullets are generally harder than is desirable for hunting or varmint shooting and hollowpoints difficult to make. The 218 Bee, 221 Remington and 256 Winchester Magnum are potential candidates for down-loading, for lower velocities, without sacrificing accuracy, owing to their relatively small case capacities. The only problem with these cartridges is that with the exception of the Hornet, the rifles chambered for them have been light repeaters and few, if any, are capable of high levels of accuracy. There is the option of custom rifles, but only for the wealthy experimenter.

The best of the high-accuracy/low-noise centerfires are the all but forgotten 22 and 25 cartridges for the Winchester, Remington and Stevens single shot rifles from the later part of the last century. The 22 Winchester Centerfire (WCF)—the forerunner of the Hornet—had an excellent record for accuracy and power for small game and varmint use, although the 22 WMR equals its performance. The WCF is easily made from Hornet brass since it is essentially the same.

The 22-15-60, 25-20, and 25-21 Stevens single shot cartridges in heavy- and medium-weight single shot target rifles were capable of groups of an inch or less at one hundred yards. With an 86-grain bullet at 1380-1400 fps velocity, a Remington rolling block in 25-20 Stevens, belonging to a friend, shot, as he put it, "like it had eyes." The Remington could pick off starlings at a hundred yards, using iron sights, with plenty of power for woodchucks at that range. Alas, these cartridges are long gone.

The problem with old cartridges is that even if a rifle for them in good condition can be found, the cartridges are no longer made, thus forcing a shooter to scrounge old brass of dubious quality or locate a source for new brass for handloading, along with obsolete bullet moulds and reloading dies. The 25-20 Stevens case is available from Huntington and may again be produced by El Dorado. Dies are available from 4-D, among others.

There never has been and probably never will be a both ideal and all-purpose load for small game and varmints. To hope for a comeback of the 25-20 or 25-21 Stevens single shot, perhaps in a rimless version, for a nine- to ten-pound bolt rifle is certainly bucking the trend toward "lead squirters" and "hand cannons," but stranger things have happened. The low-noise precision rifle can fill a vital niche in the shooter's armory, if he will take the time to develop the skill to master it. ●

by J. B. WOOD

HANDGUNS TODAY:

AUTOLOADERS

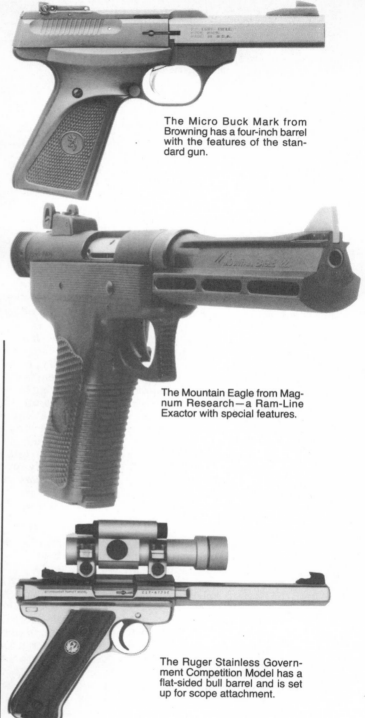

The Micro Buck Mark from Browning has a four-inch barrel with the features of the standard gun.

The Mountain Eagle from Magnum Research—a Ram-Line Exactor with special features.

The Ruger Stainless Government Competition Model has a flat-sided bull barrel and is set up for scope attachment.

At THE RISK of a minor redundancy, I must mention the 40 Smith & Wesson cartridge at the start. Well, it *is* an excellent round, giving "10mm Lite" performance in pistols of 9mm and compact 9mm dimensions. To the guns mentioned last year that offer both 9mm and 40 S&W versions we can add several new pieces.

Among these, there is the new **Beretta** Model 96. It is exactly the same as the Model 92FS, except for the chambering and the dimensional differences necessary for the larger cartridge. Magazine capacity is ten rounds. There is also a Model 96D, in DA-only. For law enforcement, there is the Model 96G, a de-cocker. (In 9mm, there is a new version of the Model 92F called the Centurion, with a compact slide and barrel on a standard-sized frame.)

Ruger has added several new versions of the 45 P90. There is the KP90C, with ambidextrous safety-levers with shorter arcs, and a retracting firing pin. Another version, the KP90DAC, has the same features, with a decock-only lever. The same version is offered in 40 S&W as the KP91DAC. In the 22 pistol department, Ruger now has a version with an injection-moulded Zytel frame that has the same shape and control locations as the old GM-pattern pistol. They call it the 22/45, and it is available in three stainless steel versions, from plinking to serious target configuration.

In the 40 S&W category for **Taurus** are the new Model PT-100 and Model PT-101, the latter number having a fully adjustable rear sight. Both guns are in stainless steel, and both have the new safety system—up for on-safe, horizontal for off-safe, and down for hammer drop. All the other Taurus pistols, the 380 and 9mm Para models, are also now offered in stainless steel.

Accu-Tek, maker of neat little Walther-ish single-action pistols in 25, 32, and 380 ACP, has made some small mechanical changes in the guns, and now offers them in stainless steel in the two larger chamberings and has a DA-only 9mm, the AT-9—in 40 S&W, the AT-40. It can be stainless or black, with 7-round magazine.

Smith & Wesson has dropped several pistols, but announced the Model 915. It is a "basic" 9mm, with fixed sights, 4-inch barrel and straight-backed wrap-around Xenoy grip, a lot like the original Model 59 but with a 15-round magazine. The suggested retail price of $467 will make it a very competitive item.

The innovative **Colt** 9mm Model 2000 has not appeared on the market in any great quantity, but there are new things in the regular large-frame pistols—Delta Elite, Officer's ACP, and the rest. These include flat-topped slides, beavertail grip safeties, combat-style hammers, a relief cut under the guard, and other amenities. Magazine capacity is now

eight rounds on all full-sized models. A new addition to the line is a re-creation of the original military-style pistol, the Model 1991A1. Serial numbers begin where they stopped in 1945.

(Editor's Note: There is another development in large-frame pistols. **China Sports** *has announced production by No-rinco of a Model 1911A1 "built the way Mr. Browning intended." According to the ad, this means drop-forged. No-rinco is the source of a lot of solid and inexpensive guns. KW)*

Designed several years ago in England by David Smith, the Victory MC5 pistol is in production in Florida by **Quality Firearms, Incorporated.** The final design retains its most notable feature—quick conver-

Springfield Armory's Firecat, a compact single action in 9mm and 40 S&W made in the U.S.A.

The Victory MC5 pistol is now being made by QFI in Florida. Convertible calibers include 9mm, 10mm, 45, 40 S&W and 38 Super.

The 380 Bersa Model 86: Matte finish, three-dot sights, and a wrap-around rubber grip.

The Czech Model 52 pistol, now available from Century Arms in 7.62x25mm, the Tokarev round.

sion from 9mm to 45 ACP, 10mm Auto, 40 S&W, and 38 Super. It has selective double action, and can also be carried cocked-and-locked. Also new from QFI is a small stainless 380 pistol, the Model LA380SS.

Now, there is a new 380 **AMT** Back Up. In the same size, the Back Up now has a DA-only trigger system and a six-round magazine. It weighs an ounce more, and is more rounded for better concealment. The prototype I handled had a very smooth trigger pull, and the usual AMT high-precision look.

Browning's BDM 9mm, notable for its selective DA/SA or DA-only firing mechanism, has not reached the market in quantity. There's a new Buck Mark 22 line—the Micro Buck Mark, a compact version with a 4-inch bull barrel.

Ram-Line has announced a compact version of their Exactor, with both barrel and grip shortened, to adapt the pistol to the needs of campers and fishermen. The magazine capacity will be fifteen rounds. I have been shooting a full-sized Target Model Exactor for several months, and its performance is outstanding.

Made for them by Ram-Line, the new Mountain Eagle offered by **Magnum Research** is essentially an Exactor with conventional grip shape, and a barrel configuration like the famed Desert Eagle.

Sigarms is now offering DA-only versions of the P226, P228, and the 40 S&W P229. There is an excellent accessory that has been offered for some time, but a few shooters may have missed it—a "short" trigger for the three guns mentioned above. Smooth-faced, it reduces the DA "reach," and it is relatively inexpensive.

The resurrection of the late lamented Bren Ten is under way, with the slightly re-designed **Peregrine Falcon** offered in 10mm, 45 Auto, and 40 S&W. This is a new company, and the prototypes I have handled were impressive. Remembering one of the main problems of the Bren Ten, a line in the Peregrine brochure brought a smile: "Extra factory-original magazines are available in unlimited quantities."

Springfield Armory has four new pistols they call the "R" series. The Panther is in 9mm, 40 S&W, and 45 ACP, and it is all-steel and double action. The Firecat, in 9mm and 40

S&W, is a compact single action. The Bobcat is a DA 380 ACP, and the Lynx is a single-action 25 ACP. The Panther is the Astra A80; the Bobcat is the Constable; and the Lynx is the Astra Cub. The Firecat is Astra's answer to the Star Firestar, and some may like its "feel" better. All of these are being made by Springfield Armory in Illinois, not in Spain.

The 380 **Grendel** P10 was a nice little DA-only pistol, but some shooters found the top-loading feature to be tedious. Now, there is the Grendel P12. It has all of the same good features, and a detachable 11-round magazine. I have fired a new P12 extensively, and it works every time. There is a slight change in the shape of the polymer grip frame, and it feels better than the P10.

From **Star** in Spain, **Interarms** has the Firestar in a slightly enlarged version in 45 ACP chambering, and a full-sized DA pistol, the Megastar, in 45 ACP. A 10mm version is promised. They also have the Astra A70 in 9mm, a compact single action (see the Springfield Armory Firecat). The Walther TPH is now offered in 25 ACP, and they have the Norinco Model 93 Sportsman, a recreation of the old Colt Woodsman.

Intratec is now producing the little DA-only Protector pistol in 22 LR and 25 ACP, offered in black or satin gray finish. The 22 LR has a 10-round magazine, and the 25 magazine holds 8 rounds. This neat little gun is a modern redesign of the Czech CZ45.

Heckler & Koch now has the P7M10, in 40 S&W chambering. As those familiar with the P7 series will know, the model suffix denotes the magazine capacity—10 rounds. In other news from H&K, all of the P7 pistols are now available in nickel finish. (Finally, the gun used by Hans in the original *Die Hard* film becomes a reality . . .)

In this year, **Mitchell Arms** delivered the first regular-production guns of their American-made stainless steel version of the famed P08 Parabellum. The ones I have examined seem to be exact copies of the old original. Only the miracle of modern machining methods allow it to be offered at the reasonable price of around $700. Mitchell will produce this year a new series based on the Hi-Standard long-gone. Parts will interchange with the old ones, and High Standard servicing will come along.

Action Arms has become the U.S. importer of the CZ75, CZ85, and CZ83 pistols, and these guns are now offered for the first time in America at competitive prices. Meanwhile, in England, **JSL(Hereford) Ltd.** is making a deluxe copy called the Spitfire in stainless steel. This is offered in Standard and Competition versions, in 9mm Para. and 9x21mm. The Spitfire is beautifully made, and it is not in the low-priced category.

While we are in the CZ75 area, I should mention the Tanfoglio pistols offered by **European American Armory**. Now called the Witness, these fine pistols are mechanically updated versions of the TZ75 and TA90 guns sold by F.I.E. and Excam several years ago. The Witness is available in full-sized and compact styles, in 45 ACP, 40 S&W, and 9mm. I shoot a full-sized 40 S&W Witness frequently, and performance is flawless thus far.

My vote for the most impressive new 9mm pistol goes to the **Daewoo** Model DP51 from Korea. Since the prototype of last year, it has had a slight change in the shape of the slide, and the importer is now **Firstshot, Incorporated** of Harrisburg, Pennsylvania. One of the notable features of the DP51 is that the cocked hammer can be pushed to a "down" carry position, and the DA trigger pull is then of single-action weight. Beautiful balance and a short DA trigger reach are other assets, and it is very nicely made. I have fired a regular-production gun, and it works well with all 9mm loads.

If you insist on doing it right, it takes a lot longer. This could be applied to **Desert Industries** (formerly Steel City Arms). This year, they began deliveries of their nice little stainless steel 22 LR and 25 ACP DA pistols. Original production was delayed by a move from Pittsburgh to Las Vegas, Nevada.

Another firm that fits the maxim above is **Wildey**. The big guns have been made in good quantity for more than two years now, and the list of Wildey Magnum chamberings is impressive: 475 W.M., 45 W.M., 357/45 W.M., 11mm W.M., 10mm W.M., and 30 W.M. For those who want custom-loaded rounds in 475 W.M. and 45 W.M., these are available from **Kaswer Custom, Inc.**, 13

The small 380, 32 and 25 pistol from Accu-Tek is now offered in stainless steel.

In 9mm and 40 S&W, the new medium-frame pistol from Accu-Tek is double-action-only and stainless steel.

The new DA-only 380 Back Up from AMT is the same size as the original SA Back Up.

QFI now offers this medium-frame 380 in stainless steel.

The 380 P12 from Grendel has a DA-only trigger system and an 11-round detachable magazine.

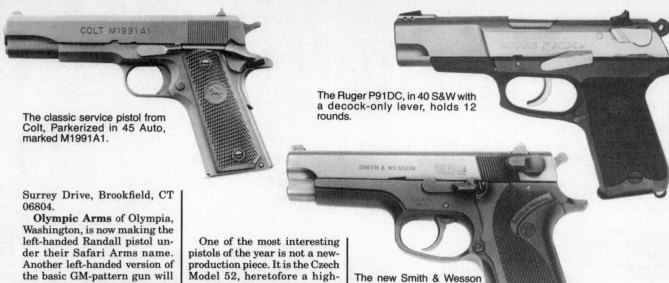

The classic service pistol from Colt, Parkerized in 45 Auto, marked M1991A1.

The Ruger P91DC, in 40 S&W with a decock-only lever, holds 12 rounds.

The new Smith & Wesson Model 915, a no-frills high capacity 9mm at a reasonable price.

Surrey Drive, Brookfield, CT 06804.

Olympic Arms of Olympia, Washington, is now making the left-handed Randall pistol under their Safari Arms name. Another left-handed version of the basic GM-pattern gun will be made by **Rocky Mountain Arms** of Longmont, Colorado, with five chamberings planned. The Rocky Mountain pistol will be in stainless steel with a matte black Teflon finish. This information came from an interesting little paper called the **Lefty Exchange** (Box 1544, Albany, OR 97321).

Except for their limited-production commemorative versions of the Parabellum pistol, **Mauser** of Germany is apparently not making handguns at this time. They are, however, marketing under their Mauser banner the Hungarian 9mm DA and SA versions of the FN Hi-Power. The double actions, full-sized and compact, are the Mauser Model 90. The single action is the Model 80.

The **Claridge Hi-Tec**, reported on in detail last year, is now offered with a fully-integral laser sight, built right into the front of the frame. There is no exposed external wiring. Activation is by a pressure switch on the back of the grip frame. With or without the laser, the Claridge is still one of my favorite pistols.

Another pistol I like a lot, the Argentine **Bersa** 380 marketed by **Eagle Imports**, is now offered in a new version. The Model 86 has all of the good features of the Model 85, plus a wrap-around rubber grip, matte finish, and a three-white-dot sight system. I have fired the Model 86, and the added features are a real advantage.

One of the most interesting pistols of the year is not a new-production piece. It is the Czech Model 52, heretofore a high-priced collector piece in the U.S., and hard to find. Now, from **Century Arms,** the CZ52 is offered for a very reasonable price, and it is a remarkable pistol. It is single action with a unique roller-locked barrel, and its cartridge is in the high-performance category—the 7.62mm Tokarev. I have been trying out one of these in recent weeks, and I am very pleased with it.

Pachmayr is offering a new "Modular-Concept" Signature grip for the Third-Generation Smith & Wesson pistols. The modular design allows different backstraps or a finger-groove side panel to be used. As with all Pachmayr Signature grips, the material is genuine Neoprene. The new grip will fit the S&W Models 5906, 5904, and 4006.

There are two new magazine loaders that deserve to be noted. One is a simple slip-on push-down type, by **Boonie Packer** (Box 12204, Salem, OR 97309). It is notable for its strong construction, ribbed exterior, and for being the first of its type to have a "de-loader" lug on its lower edge. Also, it works with single-column 45 or double-column 9mm magazines. They call it the Ergo (for "ergonomic") Speed Loader. The other loader, for alternate-feed magazines only, is a mechanical type by **C3 Systems** (Box 485, N. Scituate, RI 02857). It uses tray-type "Uni-Clips" that hold up to 30 rounds, and a plunger-type "Rapid-Loader" that strips each row in the clip into the magazine. I have tried this loading system on Uzi and Intratec magazines, and it works. ●

GET COMPLETE DETAILS . . .

Our catalog listings for autoloading pistols now on the market begin on page 273.

The 9mm Daewoo Model DP51, now offered by Firstshot, Inc., is a J.B. Wood favorite.

CUSTOM GUNS

▼ **FRED WELLS**
416 Rigby takedown Mauser—everything but the scope made on the premises.

▼ **JAMES C. TUCKER**
270 Winchester Model 1909 Mauser in English walnut with ebony tip. (Hughes photo)

▼ **JERE D. EGGLESTON**
280 Remington on DWM Mauser action, stocked in English walnut.

▼ **DENNIS ERHARDT**
375 H&H Model 70 with stainless barrel and Turkish walnut stock.

▼ **DON KLEIN**
280 Winchester G33-40 stocked in French walnut with Fisher, Dakota and Talley trimmings.

▼ **VIC OLSON**
45-70 Springfield 1873 done up muzzleloader style in French walnut.

▼ **MAURICE OTTMAR**
9.3x64 Brenneke in BRNO ZG47 action and Turkish walnut with accessories from Burgess and Kehr engraving. (Bolster photo)

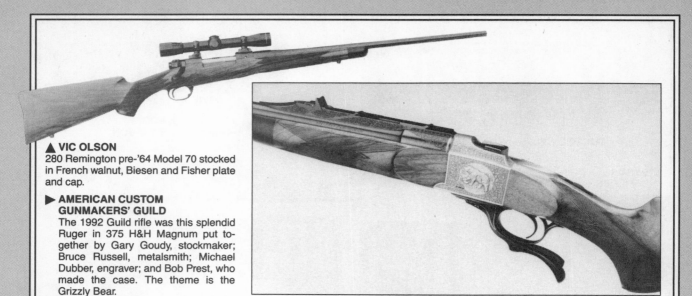

▲ **VIC OLSON**
280 Remington pre-'64 Model 70 stocked in French walnut, Biesen and Fisher plate and cap.

▶ **AMERICAN CUSTOM GUNMAKERS' GUILD**
The 1992 Guild rifle was this splendid Ruger in 375 H&H Magnum put together by Gary Goudy, stockmaker; Bruce Russell, metalsmith; Michael Dubber, engraver; and Bob Prest, who made the case. The theme is the Grizzly Bear.

ART OF THE ENGRAVER

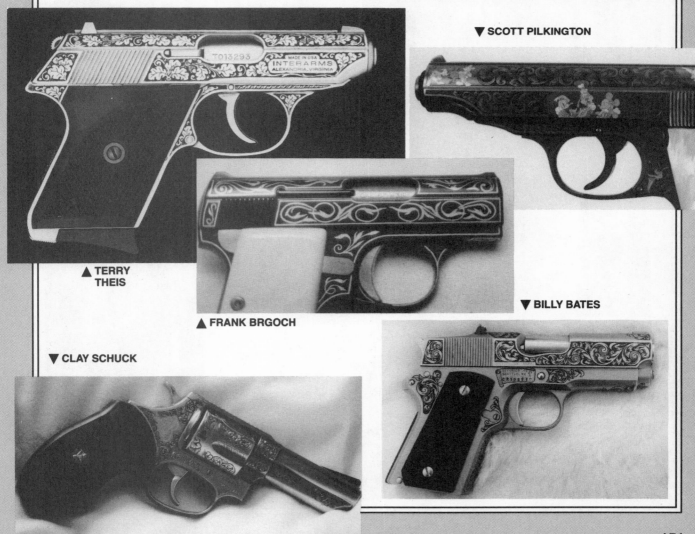

▲ **TERRY THEIS**

▲ **FRANK BRGOCH**

▼ **SCOTT PILKINGTON**

▼ **BILLY BATES**

▼ **CLAY SCHUCK**

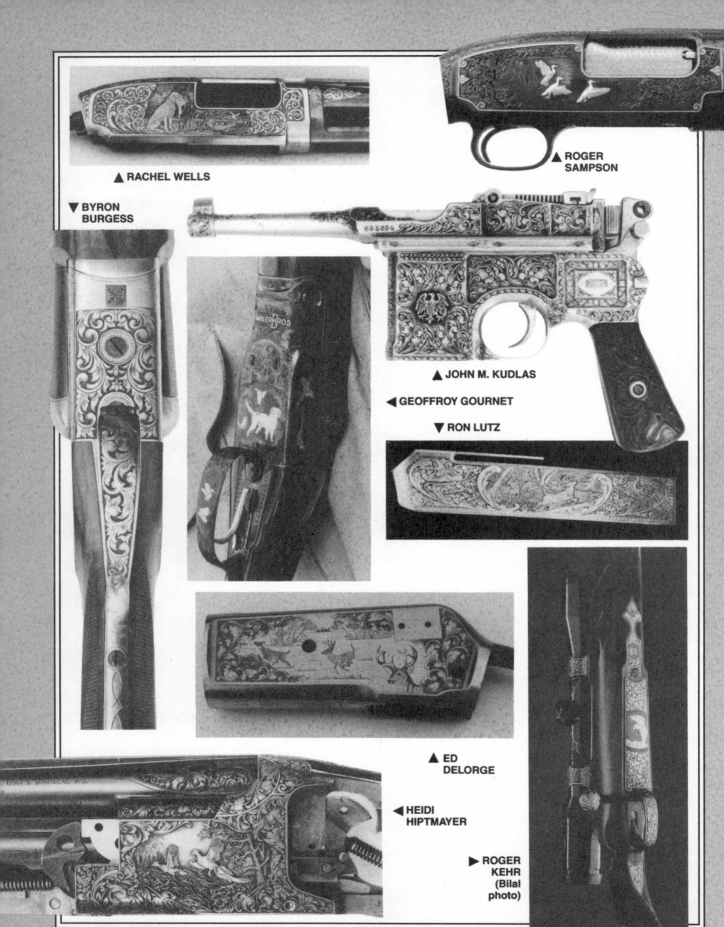

▲ RACHEL WELLS

▲ ROGER SAMPSON

▼ BYRON BURGESS

▲ JOHN M. KUDLAS

◄ GEOFFROY GOURNET

▼ RON LUTZ

▲ ED DELORGE

◄ HEIDI HIPTMAYER

► ROGER KEHR (Bilal photo)

by LAYNE SIMPSON

RIFLE REVIEW

Lots of new stuff for 1992. Three rifle companies have each introduced more interesting models and variations than all combined have during some years in the recent past. Almost totally weatherproof rifles are definitely the thing for buyers to buy and sellers to sell, and this year brings two new ones in stainless steel and synthetic from a couple of majors, along with another coated with electroless nickel. I wonder what Oliver, Eliphalet, and Roy would have to say about them? Moving to the opposite extreme, a rifle once known for its racy styling is now available in a classic version that's so classic it makes your teeth hurt.

I'll do a great deal of shooting in this installment. One rifle, an autoloader in 22 rimfire, consistently puts ten bullets in half an inch at 50 yards. Another rifle, also an autoloader but in 223, averages less than half an inch at 100 yards for five shots. And then there's the king of 30-caliber cartridges; it kicks a 180-grain bullet from a 26-inch barrel at 3500 fps and its hunting-weight barrel seldom fails to snuggle three of them into half minute-of-angle.

You'll see other 22 rimfire rifles in this report, one with a new stainless steel barrel, and a couple of others wearing new laminated wood stocks.

You'll learn about a number of wildcats; you'll discover a new home for an ancient 45 caliber; and you'll learn how to transform an old woods rifle and its even older cartridge into a performer that you might tote into open country.

New varmint rifles with heavy barrels get their share of attention, as well. An old favorite bolt gun with a single shot action is back with a new model number and synthetic stock. Another new model was obviously put together by varmint shooters for varmint shooting and may be the best designed of its breed among standard production rifles.

A lever gun that was introduced long before any of us were here has a new safety, and last but certainly not least, we'll take a brief look at my nomination for the most handsome big game rifle introduced this year.

Now that I have you sitting on the edge of your seats, here's what's new for '92:

Action Arms, Ltd.

Seems like each time I sit down to write a new "Rifle Review," some company has stopped importing BRNO rifles and another company has started. At this very moment (February 10, 1992 at 1:14 PM), Action Arms is the current importer of these Czech-built bolt actions and officials of that company say several models are available. The Model 452 is in 22 rimfire and has five- or ten-round detachable magazines; the slightly bigger Model 527 comes in 22 Hornet, 222 Remington, and 223 Remington. Then there are the Models 600 (standard action), 601 (short action), and 602 (magnum action) rifles in 243 Winchester, 270, 7x57mm Mauser, 308, 30-06, 375 H&H and Winchester's 300- and 458-caliber belted magnums, all with standard Mauser-type box magazines.

A-Square

One thing I like about the folks at A-Square is they offer custom rifles in about every chambering you've heard of and some you probably haven't, and they make the ammunition to go with the rifles. Two new additions to the rifle and ammo line are the 470 Capstick and 375 JRS. On the 375 H&H case, the 470 pushes A-Square 500-grain Dead Tough, Lion Load, or Monolithic Solid bullets along at 2400 fps. The 375 JRS is the 8mm Remington Magnum necked up (or an improved version of the 375 H&H) and is rated at 2700 fps with a 300-grain bullet. For all practical purposes, it is identical to the much older 375 Weatherby Magnum, which means it's a

Happiness is a rainy Alaskan day, foul weather gear that doesn't leak, an all-weather rifle in 358 STA, and an equally wet brown bear.

darned good cartridge. The 470 Capstick and 375 JRS chamberings are also standard options in Winchester Model 70 rifles offered by the U.S. Repeating Arms Co. Custom Shop, which uses A-Square ammo for testing. I haven't tried either cartridge, but have had an A-Square rifle in 450 Ackley Magnum for quite awhile. If time ever permits my doing so, I'll pull its trigger a few times and tell you what happened.

Browning

The first John Browning-designed rifle introduced by Winchester was the Model 1885 single shot. Browning's first lever-action Winchester was the Model 1886. The first '86s were shipped in August of that year and a number of standard variations were eventually introduced: Sporting Rifle (26-inch round, octagon, or half-octagon barrel); Fancy Sporting Rifle (26-inch octagon); Extra Light Weight (22-inch round); and Carbine (22-inch round). For more money, shorter or longer than standard barrel lengths could be had. Before the Model 1886 was discontinued in 1935, almost 160,000 were produced in calibers ranging from the 33 Winchester to the 50-100-450 Express.

Browning (the company) is introducing a replica of the Model 1886 carbine in 1992. It has a 22-inch round barrel in 45-70 caliber, full-length magazine with twin barrel bands, a crescent-style steel buttplate, saddle ring, adjustable rear sight and nonramped blade out front. With an overall length of 40¾ inches, the Browning carbine is rated at 8¼ pounds.

Production of the Grade I version will be limited to a maximum of 7000. It has blued steel and select walnut with a satin finish. The High Grade has better wood and blued steel, except the receiver has a gray finish. Game scenes of mule deer and grizzly bears are highlighted by special gold plating and surrounded by scroll engraving. Only 3000 of these handsome carbines will be built.

Eagle Arms, Inc.

I grew up during the golden era of mail-order surplus firearms with prices that bring tears to our eyes today, and eventually owned and loved a lot of them. Even so, I have never grown exactly fond of today's military-type rifles. My attitude mellowed a bit when I started competing in local USPSA/IPSC three-gun matches as it quickly became evident that I'd either have to use such a rifle or stop playing. Now you know why I've been shooting a Golden Eagle EA-15A2 H-BAR (heavy-barrel) built by Eagle Arms.

The Golden Eagle is a semi-automatic, target grade, civilian version of Uncle Sam's M-16A2, and a virtual clone of the same rifles built by Colt and FN. The one I've been using in competition has the optional weighted buttstock and Hart stainless steel barrel with an extremely heavy contour and 1:9-inch rifling twist. Beneath the handguard, the 20-inch barrel measures 1.175 inches in diameter, steps down to .960-inch just behind the front sight, and steps down again to .735-inch between the front sight and compensator. Fresh from its box the rifle weighed 12¼ pounds.

To see what the Golden Eagle would do on paper, I equipped it with a Leupold 6.5-20x variable and tried nine factory loads from the 100-yard benchrest. Aggregate accuracy for forty-five, five-shot groups was .91-inch. The Black Hills and Hornady 60-grain pointed soft-nose loads won the contest with an average of .66-inch. The rifle also liked Remington's 60-grain match load (.67-inch), as well as the Hornady and Black Hills 52-grain loads (.68- and .75-inch).

I also tried handloads consisting of Berger 52-, 55-, 60-, and 65-grain hollowpoint bullets; W748; Winchester cases; and Remington 7½ primers. Overall cartridge length was 2.270 inches. Five, five-shot groups with the 52-grain bullet measured a remarkably consistent .447-, .454-, .409-, .336-, and .443-inch. The 65-grain Berger came in second with an average of .48-inch. The 55- and 60-grain bullets averaged .52- and .55-inch. Not bad for an autoloading rifle originally designed for shooting big targets in combat rather than tiny groups at the range.

Gibbs Rifle Company

Since Val Forgett III is president of the new (1991) Gibbs Rifle Company, and since Val I is also involved, and since some of the blackpowder and military surplus rifles in the catalog are the same as those either imported or built by Navy Arms, we can probably safely assume that the two companies are somehow affiliated. At any rate, if you want a Midland or Parker-Hale bolt-action centerfire, the folks at Gibbs are the ones to talk to.

According to the catalog, the Midland series of rifles was developed around the 1903 Springfield action, except the floorplate is hinged and a two-position safety is located on the right-hand side of the receiver tang. Three models are offered: 2600 with Monte Carlo-style hardwood stock, 2100 with the same style stock but in walnut, and the 2700 Lightweight with thinner barrel and trimmer walnut stock. Various chamberings are there for the asking: 22-250, 243, 6mm Remington, 270, 6.5x55mm, 7x64mm, 7x57mm, 308 and 30-06. Actions and barreled actions are available.

Gibbs offers a police or military-type sniper rifle. Built around the Parker-Hale Mauser action, the M-85 in 7.62 NATO is used by the elite British S.A.S. force and has been adopted by other Commonwealth countries. This company also imports PMP (not PMC) ammunition in a variety of handgun and rifle calibers.

The Parker-Hale sporting rifle line is also built around a commercial version of the '98 Mauser action. Latest variation is the Scout with laminated wood, muzzlebrake and ten-round detachable box magazine in 243 or 308 calibers. Other models include the 1000 Standard with hardwood stock, the 1100 Lightweight, and the 1200 Super Clip which despite its name really doesn't come with a "clip," but does have a detachable box-type magazine. Calibers are the same as for the Midland series with three exceptions: the Model 1100 African is available in 375 H&H and 458, while the Model 81 African can be bought in 375 or 9.3x62mm Mauser.

Incidentally, I have a Sako FiberClass in 9.3x62mm and think both rifle and cartridge are just great. The case is easily formed from 30-06 brass, and Speer, Barnes, and a few other smaller shops offer good .366-inch bullets. Few of today's hunters are familiar with the "Nine Three," but it was once to German farmers who emigrated to Africa what the Model 94 in 30-30 was to American ranchers who shot the wild out of the West.

Jarrett Rifles, Inc.

An Ultimate Hunter in 280 Improved built around a highly refined Model 700 action, it looked like any other Jarrett rifle. But it wouldn't consistently keep three shots inside half an inch at 100 yards. The second bullet fired from its stainless steel match-grade barrel would almost land in the same hole cut by the first, but the third would almost always increase the group size to about .800-inch. Occasionally, it would land over an inch from its two mates. So, Jarrett junked the $200 barrel (not counting labor cost for its installation) and installed another. Same story; two shots practically in one hole and the third astray. Jarrett next rebedded the barreled action in a new fiberglass stock. Same story. Then he ripped out that bedding and tried again. Same story. Finally, he removed the Leupold scope, carefully clamped the barreled action into his band saw—and sawed it in half, right down through the receiver ring. I've written before that a rifle doesn't leave Jackson, South Carolina, before its time. Some never leave at all.

Another Jarrett Ultimate Hunter I've been playing with was built around a highly modified Model 700 action. It has a McMillan 'glass stock, one of Harold Broughton's No. 4 contour 26-inch match-grade stainless barrels, and weighs 9½ pounds with its Leupold 3.5-10x Vari-X III. It's chambered for a wildcat called the 300 Kong—the 378 Weatherby Magnum case necked down and fire-formed to a bit less body taper and sharper shoulder angle. When the Nosler 180-grain Ballistic Tip is pushed to just under 3500 fps by 114.0 grains of H5010, the rifle consistently puts three of them into less than half an inch at the 100-yard target. The smallest five-shot group I've fired at 500 yards on a relatively breezy day (while resting the rifle over the hood of a Jeep) had a vertical spread of 1.502 inches and a horizontal spread of 4.792 inches. When blasting its propellant gas through a Jarrett

Jay Jarrett holds a custom Jarrett rifle that didn't leave Jackson, South Carolina.

muzzlebrake, recoil of the 300 Kong is much less than with a rifle in 300 Winchester Magnum without a brake. But, believe me, when you burn over 100 grains of powder in a 30-caliber rifle, you make lots of noise.

I took the rifle in 300 Kong on a Colorado elk hunt and stopped off at a gun club in Cortez to check its 100-yard zero. Three shots fired over sandbags landed in a group measuring less than .300-inch. Bob Nosler and Chub Eastman of Nosler Bullets just happened to be peering over my shoulder with spotting scopes as I fired that one. Then and there they both learned at least three things.

Also took an Ultimate Hunter to southeastern Alaska for a go at brown bear in May of '91. The hunt was booked through my pal Keith Atcheson of Jack Atcheson & Sons, Inc. of Butte, Montana. Weighing 7¾ pounds soaking wet, the custom Model 700 wore a 24-inch Lilja barrel with No. 4 contour (.670-inch muzzle diameter) and Mag-na-port's new six-port brake. The 'glass stock was a McMillan Griffin & Howe-style and Armology protected all metal except the stainless steel barrel. It was chambered for

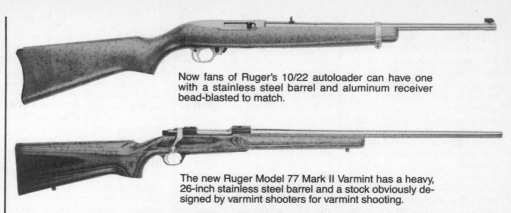

Now fans of Ruger's 10/22 autoloader can have one with a stainless steel barrel and aluminum receiver bead-blasted to match.

The new Ruger Model 77 Mark II Varmint has a heavy, 26-inch stainless steel barrel and a stock obviously designed by varmint shooters for varmint shooting.

Marlin

It had been several years since the 30-30 cartridge and I had ventured afield together. So, when an opportunity to hunt whitetails on Anticosti Island came up, I decided it was time the old antique and I got reacquainted. I would take a Marlin 336CS with its spring-water-clear Bausch & Lomb 1.5-6x variable held in place with George Miller's gorgeous Conetrol mount. Then they told me the island is made up of heavy timber intermixed with open grassy meadows of such vastness one could strain the barrel on a 300 Weatherby Magnum while attempting to

1000 foot pounds at the latter distance. Darned good performance for a woods rifle chambered for a woods cartridge.

More than one cartridge with a spitzer bullet should never be loaded in a tubular magazine so I call these double-shot loads. Since overall cartridge length is short enough to feed through the Marlin, I insert one cartridge in its magazine. When times and circumstances call for it, I lever that cartridge into the chamber and stick another in the magazine, hence, my double-shot loads.

No, I didn't bag a single whitetail with the 30-30. I saw lots of them but kept turning

The 882L shoots seven 22 WMR cartridges before its detachable magazine has to be recharged. Both rifles feature sling swivel studs, rubber buttpad, 22-inch Micro-Groove barrel, gold-plated trigger and adjustable rear sight. The dovetail grooves on their receivers make the mounting of a telescopic sight easy.

Introduced last year, Marlin's Model 2000 target rifle seems to be selling faster than alibis at a congressional hearing. When its price is compared with other rifles of its type, it's easy to see why. Made especially for youngsters, mom and dad like it, too. Haven't shot one yet but probably will before we meet again. If I do, I'll tell you about it.

Precision Sales International

Precision Sales, the Anschutz importer, is now importing the Swedish-built Carl Gustaf 2000 bolt-action centerfire rifle. The 2000, with its triple locking lugs up front, has an extremely smooth bolt travel. Adjustable for pull weights ranging from 3 to 6 pounds, the trigger, along with a roller bearing-type vertical sear, is noted for its crispness. The three-way safety blocks the sear and locks the bolt from rotation, and yet a push on its button allows the bolt to be rotated with the safety on. Chamberings presently available are 243 Winchester, 6.5x55mm Swedish, 270 Winchester, 7x64mm Brenneke, 7mm Remington Magnum, 308 Winchester, 30-06, 300 Winchester Magnum and 9.3x62mm Mauser. Scope mounting bases and rings are also available from Precision Sales.

Remington

There certainly hasn't been any moss growing on the Green

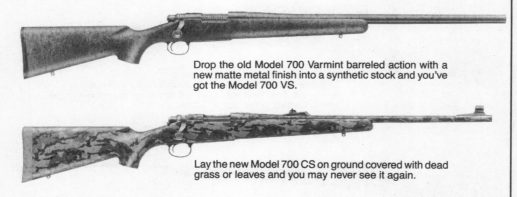

Drop the old Model 700 Varmint barreled action with a new matte metal finish into a synthetic stock and you've got the Model 700 VS.

Lay the new Model 700 CS on ground covered with dead grass or leaves and you may never see it again.

the 358 STA, the 8mm Remington Magnum case necked up and blown out to the improved configuration with 30-degree shoulder. My favorite charge of Hodgdon's H4350 or Hercules' Reloder 19 pushes a 250-grain bullet along at almost 3000 fps. More rain than I ever imagined could fall anytime anywhere fell; I experienced several spine-tingling moments in rough seas in a boat too small to be there; I fired one Nosler Partition and am now looking at a beautiful bear rug. Except for a few lengthy details, that's about all there was to it.

reach the far side with a bullet. Despite that, I stuck by my decision to hunt deer with an 1895-vintage cartridge. But I took along an ace up my sleeve.

My 30-30 handloads pushed the Sierra 125-grain spitzer and Nosler 125-grain Ballistic Tip along at a bit less than 2600 fps. At 300 yards I had no problem keeping five inside 5 inches from benchrest. When zeroed 3 inches high at 100 yards, either brand of bullet landed about eight inches below point of aim at 300. According to the ballistics charts, I would have the capability of delivering just over

down antlers until time was up. I sure had fun developing those double-shot loads, though. And hunting with a lever-action woods gun for a change felt good.

Before leaving the subject of things Marlin, the "L" suffix attached to the Model numbers of the 990L and 882L rifles indicate new laminated wood stocks replete with Monte Carlo-style buttstocks. The former is the old familiar Model 60 autoloader with a tubular magazine that holds fifteen Long Rifle cartridges. When the last shot is fired its bolt remains open.

Giant's feet since we last looked at new rifles. Counting standard production and Custom Shop calibers and variations, the Model 700 possibilities alone exceed 100 for 1992.

Beginning with Remington's new Custom Shop offerings, those who shoot a rifle from the other side will be happy to see the most accurate rifle made in America available with a left-hand action. The 40-XB-LH is now offered in a variety of calibers with single shot or repeating action, Kevlar or wood stock, and with standard or optional 2-ounce trigger. A test group fired in the factory 100-yard tunnel is included with each rifle, and it is not uncommon to see it measure less than half-minute-of-angle for most calibers.

Left-hand versions of the Model 700 Safari Grade rifles are now available with wood or Kevlar stock, the latter with standard or wood-grained finish. I've seen the new finish. You have to really look close to tell that is isn't wood and yet the stock has all the desirable characteristics of a synthetic. The calibers are 8mm Remington Magnum, 375 H&H Magnum, 416 Remington Magnum and 458 Winchester Magnum.

Remington's standard production Model 700 is now available in nine styles: ADL, ADL-LS (laminated walnut), BDL, Varmint, Mountain Rifle, Classic (limited annual production), and new for 1992—the Stainless Synthetic, Varmint Synthetic, and Camo Synthetic. All are quite exciting, but I'm sure more people have been waiting on and asking for the Model 700 SS than for any of the others. Its barreled action is made of 416 stainless steel with a dull matte finish. It has a blind magazine, but I won't be surprised to see an optional hinged floorplate in the near future. The trim synthetic stock is black in color, has moulded checkering at its grip and forend, dull chrome-plated sling swivel studs, a solid recoil pad, and is shaped about like the wood stock of the Mountain Rifle. There are two barrel lengths: 22 inches for the 25-06, 270, 280 and 30-06, and 24 inches for the belted magnums, 7mm Remington, 7mm Weatherby, 300 Winchester and 338 Winchester. The really good news is this one costs about as much more than the Model 700 BDL as you pay for half a box of 280 cartridges.

The new Model 700 CS (Camo Synthetic) has a classic-style synthetic stock and, with the exception of its recoil pad and open sights, is completely coated from muzzle to buttstock with a camouflage pattern. It is quite shocking at first glance, but the longer you look, the more you realize it is the answer to those who yearn for a rifle that will completely disappear from the eyes of game. In fact, if you lay this one down in brown grass or dead leaves, you may never see it again. Model 700 CS long and short action chamberings for 1992 are 22-250, 243, 270, 7mm-08, 280, 308, 30-06 and two belted magnums, 7mm Remington and 300 Weatherby. I'm a bit surprised to not see this one in

Winchester's 300 Magnum.

Last, but certainly not least among new things in green boxes, Remington's 1992 classic cartridge for its limited production Model 700 Classic is the 220 Swift. It has a 24-inch barrel with 1:14 rifling pitch and not many will be made. Buy one of these and you can try Remington's new factory load with its 50-grain bullet at 3780 fps.

Or you can do what I do by loading a 55-grain bullet at about the same velocity with H-380, Reloder 15, or IMR 4064.

Have you tried a Model 700 Mountain Rifle in 257 Roberts? Some say the old cartridge is inaccurate, but my Mountain Rifle obviously isn't aware of it. Its extremely thin 22-inch barrel is a bit picky, and five-shot groups don't measure in the bragging category, but I'm amazed at its three-shot accuracy with some loads when the barrel is allowed to cool down completely between strings. To date, I've tried thirty handloads (mostly with Reloder 19 and 22) with bullet weights ranging from the Sierra and Hornady 75-grain hollowpoints to the Barnes 125-grain pointed soft-nose. Eight loads averaged under an inch. I also tried nine old and new factory loads from Remington, Winchester, Federal and Hornady. With an average of 1.08 inches, Hornady's 117-grain spitzer boattail load was most accurate (in my particular rifle), but Winchester's +P load with the 100-grain Silvertip won the speed contest when it tripped my Oehler

chronograph at a remarkably quick average of 2933 fps. I've yet to try Remington's new 122-grain Extended Range load in this rifle, but it may prove to be just the ticket for open-country hunting of mule deer and caribou.

Ruger

My vote for the most handsome big game rifle introduced in 1992 goes to Ruger's Model 77 Express. It can accurately be described as a scaled-down version of the Model 77 Magnum. Like its bigger mate, the Express has an extremely attractive stock carved from select-grade walnut, with solid recoil pad, contrasting forend tip, steel grip cap, and cut checkering. It also has a quarter-rib integral with the barrel which contains an express-style sight with one stationary and two folding leaves. A band-type sling swivel stud is attached to the barrel out front and a conventional screw-type stud is back on the buttstock. Its safety is Ruger's Mark II-type with three positions. Nominal weight with a 22-inch barrel is 7½ pounds. The calibers have

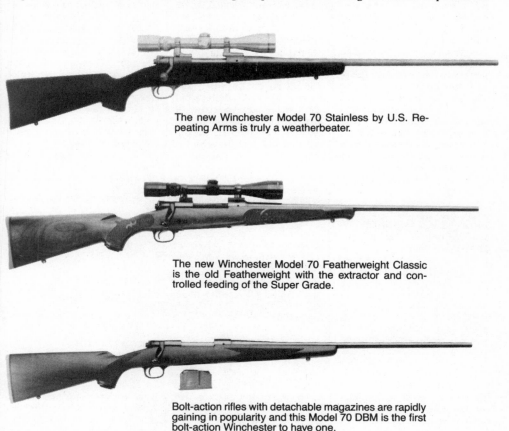

The new Winchester Model 70 Stainless by U.S. Repeating Arms is truly a weatherbeater.

The new Winchester Model 70 Featherweight Classic is the old Featherweight with the extractor and controlled feeding of the Super Grade.

Bolt-action rifles with detachable magazines are rapidly gaining in popularity and this Model 70 DBM is the first bolt-action Winchester to have one.

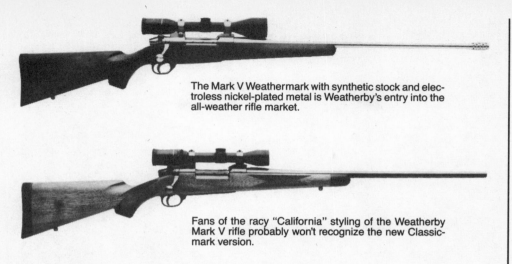

The Mark V Weathermark with synthetic stock and electroless nickel-plated metal is Weatherby's entry into the all-weather rifle market.

Fans of the racy "California" styling of the Weatherby Mark V rifle probably won't recognize the new Classicmark version.

not been finalized as this is written, but some we should eventually see find another home here are the 6.5x55mm Swedish, 270, 7x57mm Mauser, 280, 30-06, 35 Whelen and at least three belted magnums, the 7mm Remington, 300 Winchester and 338 Winchester.

I like a lot of things about Ruger's new Model 77 Mark II Varmint rifle. First there's the heavy, free-floating, 26-inch, 400-series, stainless steel barrel chambered for the 220 Swift. It will last a bit longer than chrome moly and its length squeezes a bit more velocity from the cartridge. The extra couple of inches also puts muzzle blast a bit farther from the ears. Secondly, its laminated wood stock is heavy (as it should be on a varmint rifle made for sitting), stronger and more stable than Mother Nature's version; its extremely wide forend is shaped exactly the way it should be for shooting over a sandbag; and its buttstock with rubber pad is perfectly shaped for shooting from the prone position. In other words, this one was either designed by a varmint shooter or Ruger asked a number of experienced shooters what a varmint rifle should be like before designing it. You can also get one of these in 22-250, 243 or 308.

Savage

Counting all caliber and model variations, the Savage 110 bolt gun is available in fifty variations for 1992, and all come from the factory with safety glasses, foam ear plugs and trigger lock. Following the lead of Remington with its limited edition rifles in classic chamberings each year, Savage has chosen the 7x57mm Mauser for its "One of One Thousand" Model 110WLE (Walnut Limited Edition) rifle for '92. This particular rifle commemorates the 100th anniversary of Paul Mauser's fine little 7mm cartridge. It has a 24-inch barrel without sights and a fancy American walnut stock with cut checkering and sling swivel studs. Only a thousand will be built.

Last year Savage reintroduced the old Model 112R (Repeater) heavy-barrel varmint rifle with a new synthetic stock and renamed it the 112FU. This year the old Model 112V (single shot) with its rigid, solid-bottom receiver is back with a Rynite stock and called the Model 112FVS. Both rifles are available in 223 and 22-250. I've shot a 112FV in 223 with a Burris 12x scope and, even though its forend is too skinny for shooting over sandbags, and its trigger is a bit heavy for precision work, accuracy was darned good for a rifle in its price range. The Black Hills 52- and 55-grain loads averaged 0.61- and 0.72-inch for five shots at 100 yards, while Remington's 60-grain load came in third at 0.83-inch. I fired a ten-shot group at 300 yards with the Black Hills 52-grain load and eight bullets clustered in a group measuring 2.045 inches wide by 1.366 inches high. Two flyers increased group size to 3.183 inches, still plenty close for hitting the vital area of a groundhog as far away as he should be shot with the 223.

I've also shot last year's Model 116FSS with its synthetic stock and stainless steel barreled action. In 30-06, it's a great rifle for sloppy weather hunting. Its other chamberings are 223, 243, 270 and 7mm Remington, 300 Winchester and 338 Winchester Magnums. New for '92 is the 116FCS. Except for its detachable magazine, it is the same as the Model 116FSS. At present it is available only in 270, 30-06, 7mm Remington Magnum and 300 Winchester Magnum.

Sadly enough, the Model 99 lever action appears to be teetering on the brink of discontinuance. It's available in limited quantities for '92 in 243 and 308, but I won't be surprised to see it disappear forever from the Savage catalog within the next few years.

On a more positive note, the 250-3000 and 300 Savage chamberings are available in the Models 110G and 110GNS. The 300 is also available in the Model 110CY which Savage describes as a youth and ladies version with short 12½-inch length of pull.

SSK Industries

The huge family of SSK wildcats has now increased by two. Unlike most of their mates, the new 50-caliber, rebated-rim cartridges were not designed for the T/C Contender. Both are on the shortened 460 Weatherby Magnum case with its belt removed and the rim turned to a nominal diameter .532-inch, same as for belted magnums such as 7mm Remington and 300 Winchester. Forming the case from 416 Rigby in lieu of 460 brass eliminates the necessity of removing the belt in a lathe, but initial cost of A-Square and Federal brass for the Rigby is higher than for the Norma-made Weatherby stuff. To most shooters this is probably a moot point since formed cases as well as handloading dies, 50-caliber bullets and load data are available from SSK.

Two versions are available, 2-inch for the Remington Model Seven and 2½-inch for the Model 700 long action. I have not seen any performance data on the short cartridge, but have been told its longer mate will push a 450-grain bullet along at 2350 fps from a relatively short barrel. That adds up to just over 5500 foot pounds of crunch. Both rifles come with a match-grade barrel, SSK Khrome on all metal and a synthetic stock. Open sights and various scope mounts are optional. Sounds like a perfect recipe for backup work on brown bear in thick, wet Alaskan alder thickets. You can add some African game to this list, too.

Thompson/Center

New magnum chamberings for the TCR single shot rifle are 7mm Remington, 300 Winchester, 338 Winchester, 375 H&H and 416 Remington. The 7mm STW is available only from the Custom Shop. The 7mm and 30-caliber barrels are T/C's 23-inch Light Sporter contour while the larger calibers are in the 25⅞-inch Medium Sporter replete with Muzzle Tamer brake. The new rifles are identified with "MAG" rollmarked on the bottom of their receivers. For details on converting rifles built during past years without the mark for the new magnum barrels, contact the Thompson/Center customer service department.

The TCR is presently available in Deluxe (double trigger) and Hunter (single trigger) styles, both with (depending on caliber) the 23-inch Light Sporter and 25⅞-inch Medium Sporter barrels. Other standard calibers include the 22 Hornet, 222, 223, 22-250, 220 Swift, 243, 270, 7mm-08, 308, 30-06, and 32-40. Shotgun barrel options include 12-gauge 3-inch rifled, 12-gauge 3½-inch, and 10-gauge 3½-inch, the latter two with smooth bore and Full choke constriction.

The 375 Winchester is a new addition to the list of options for the Contender Carbine with 21-inch barrel. It is not available in the 16¼-inch Youth Carbine, but seven other cartridges are.

Ultra Light Arms

For the benefit of those who

may not be aware of it, Ultra Light Arms will chamber its rifles for just about any factory or wildcat cartridge that can be dreamed up. A few that come to mind are the 7mm STW (8mm Remington Magnum case necked down); 358 STA (8mm Remington Magnum case necked up and fire formed to less body taper and a 35-degree shoulder angle); 338-06 (30-06 case necked up); 338-06 Improved; 9.3x62mm Mauser (great old cartridge); 375 Weatherby Magnum (375 H&H Improved); 358 Norma Magnum; 416 Taylor (458 Winchester case necked down); and 416 Remington Magnum.

Ultra Light also chambers its rifles for wildcats of various calibers on the 404 Jeffery (also called 404 Rimless Nitro Express) and 416 Rigby cases. The performance of the 300 Rigby (or whatever Melvin Forbes decides to call it) is about the same as that of the 300 Kong I've been working with. The 378

This Volquartsen custom Ruger 10/22 will keep them all on a squirrel's head at 50 long paces.

The Eagle Arms H-BAR 223 ain't pretty, but it sure is fun to shoot. These five groups were fired at 100 yards with it.

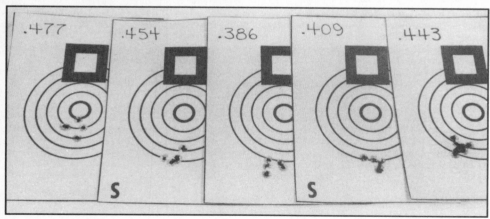

.477   .454   .386   .409   .443

Weatherby Magnum case from which it is formed is nothing more than the Rigby case with a belt and different shoulder angle. When fed over 100 grains of H5010, either cartridge will push a 180-grain bullet from a 26-inch barrel at 3400 to 3500 fps. In other words, they deliver more energy at 300 yards than the 30-06 does at the muzzle.

The Model 70 Featherweight is now available with the old checkered walnut or a new laminated wood stock in a variety of chamberings. A couple of the more interesting are 6.5x 55mm Swedish and 7mm-08 Remington, the latter new for Winchester for '92. A hunting pal recently described the Model 70 Lightweight as a

walnut), Ranger, WinTuff, Trapper and the equally new Trapper Wrangler. A new option for the Ranger is a factory-mounted Bushnell 4x scope. The handy little Trapper with its 16-inch barrel is now available in 30-30, 44 Magnum, 357 Magnum (new) and 45 Colt. The Chuck Connors Wrangler version with its massive "Rifle-

The Winchester Model 1300 shotgun probably doesn't actually fit in here with all these rifles, but since mine wears a scope, has a fully rifled barrel, and shoots quite accurately with slug loads, I'll tell you a bit about it anyhow. Its other barrel is a smoothbore with the WinChoke rifled choke tube. To date, I've burned up about two cases of saboted slug loads, two-thirds Winchester and the rest Federal. At 50 yards, the rifled barrel produced an average of 1.9, 2.4, and 2.9 inches, respectively, with the Winchester 2¾- and 3-inch, and the Federal 2¼-inch loads. At 100 yards the short Winchester and Federal shells averaged 3.3 and 4.4 inches. Change the five averages you've just read to 2.9, 2.9, 2.7, 7.4, and 8.7 inches, and you've got the performance of those loads in the rifled choke tube at the same distances. In other words, there was very little difference in accuracy between the fully rifled barrel and rifled choke tube at 50 yards, but the former was considerably more accurate at 100 yards. When fired from either barrel, the slugs in the three loads

This Marlin Model 882 bolt action in 22 WRM is called Model 882L because it wears a laminated wood stock.

Marlin's 990L autoloader in 22 Long Rifle is the old Model 60 with a new laminated stock.

USRAC

The folks at U.S. Repeating Arms Company have been busy as bees. It is becoming increasingly more difficult to keep up with, for example, the forty-one different caliber and style possibilities of the Model 70.

As its name implies, the new Model 70 Stainless has a stainless steel barreled action with natural gray matte finish. It also has a black synthetic stock consisting of graphite impregnated fiberglass replete with sling swivel studs and solid recoil pad. The barrel lengths are 22 inches (270 and 30-06) and 24 inches (7mm Remington and 300 and 338 Winchester Magnums). Nominal weight is 6¾ pounds, which should put this rifle at around eight pounds with scope, sling, and cartridges.

The Model 70 Sporter is now available in five styles and fifteen calibers, all with 24-inch barrel: Standard (checkered walnut); WinTuff (brown laminated wood); SSM (synthetic stock and matte-finished blued steel); Super Express (checkered walnut in 375 H&H and 458 Winchester Magnum); and new for 1992, the DBM (Detachable Box Magazine). The Sporter DBM has a checkered walnut stock and holds three of 270, 7mm Remington Magnum, 30-06 or 300 Winchester Magnum cartridges in the magazine.

This Parker-Hale Model 1300 Scout from Gibbs has a laminated wood stock, muzzlebrake and 10-round magazine in 243 or 308.

Gibbs introduced this Midland Model 2700 Lightweight built around a modified 1903 Springfield action.

Model 70 Featherweight with a less handsome stock. Be that as it may, this one must be selling as it is now available with three stock options: checkered walnut, checkered WinTuff (brown laminate) and non-checkered WinCam (green laminate). The seven calibers are 223, 22-250, 243, 270, 280, 308 and 30-06.

Shades of the Marlin 336! The Winchester Model 94 now has a transverse safety button in its receiver that blocks the cocked hammer from contact with the firing pin. It is a new feature on all six versions: Standard (plain or checkered

man" style of finger loop comes in 30-30 or 44 Magnum only.

Back during my callow youth, the 32 Winchester Special was quite popular among deer hunters in my neck of the woods, but it was eventually dropped from the Model 94. Being somewhat nostalgic of nature, I'm glad to see it back in the standard-grade carbine. Winchester (the one owned by Olin) loads this cartridge with 170-grain Silvertip and Power Point bullets at 2250 fps. Speer and Hornady still offer bullets as well as load data in their handloading manuals.

were starting to tumble at 200 yards, with group sizes ranging from 18 inches to much worse. Limit this gun and those loads to shots no farther from the muzzle than about 125 yards, and you should bring home the venison.

Volquartsen Custom, Ltd.

Take a look at the letter "e" in the word Digest on the spine of the fine book you're now holding. From the 50-yard benchrest, on a relatively calm day with little to no shifting breezes, I can consistently come mighty close to putting all 50

Browning's new Model 1886 is a limited edition copy of the Winchester Model 86 carbine in 45-70. There's Grade I (above) and the High Grade (below).

For the first time in its 98 years of production, the Winchester Model 94 has a safety on its receiver.

bullets in a box into that "e" from a Ruger 10/22 autoloader. This is not, however, your run-of-mill 10/22. Built by Tom Volquartsen who also specializes in sprinkling accuracy dust on Ruger 77/22 rifles and Mark II pistols, the little carbine has a 17½-inch stainless steel barrel with six lightening flutes, a .920-inch muzzle diameter, and a twenty-eight-port expansion chamber-type integral muzzle-load brake. The extra-wide titanium trigger is much better than one on an autoloader is supposed to be, a consistent 38 ounces with no creep and an adjustable over-travel stop. Volquartsen cuts his own reamers and offers three chamber options: target, match and super match. My test 10/22 had the target chamber. The match-grade barrels he uses must pass an end-to-end bore and groove diameter variation test of no more than 0.0002-inch on the air gauge. Volquartsen's barrels also have undersized bore and groove diameters of .216- and .221-inch, respectively, as opposed to the SAAMI minimum-maximum tolerance ranges of .217-.219 and .222-.224-inch for the 22 rimfire. Measuring 36 inches overall, the little bunny popper weighs 6¼ pounds with its Leupold 3-9x Compact. The receiver and interior surfaces of the flutes on its barrel wore a coat of black Teflon.

Shooting the Volquartsen 10/22 is a lot like eating peanuts—once you start you don't want to stop. The smallest ten-shot group fired at 50 yards was with a particularly accurate lot of Winchester Super Silhouette. Nine bullets snuggled into .299-inch, but a breeze caught me and nudged the tenth aside for .423-inch center-to-center. The fifty-shot average with Winchester's finest was .640-inch. Eley Tenex averaged .511-inch for fifty shots with its smallest ten-shotter measuring .436-inch. Averages with other loads were as follows: CCI Green Tag (.644-inch); Winchester T22 (.709-inch); CCI Pistol Match (.884-inch); and CCI Small Game Bullet (.939-inch). Overall aggregate accuracy for 600 rounds with twelve loads was .975-inch. During the same trips to the range, I fed my Anschutz 54.18MS metallic silhouette gun the same ammunition and pitted it against the 10/22. Its smallest average was .522-inch (Eley Tenex) and its 600-round aggregate was .986-inch. Yep, the autoloader slightly edged out the bolt gun, but for all practical purposes the accuracy of the two was the same. I won't be surprised to see some of these 10/22s show up in competition at the Chevy Truck Team Challenge. For me, though, it's one of the finest little small game rifles I've ever shot.

I also clamped one of Volquartsen's custom Ruger Mark II pistols into my Ransom Rest and sent lots of ten-shot groups toward 50-yard targets. Called the V-2000, it averaged .581-inch for fifty shots with Eley Tenex. Next best was Winchester's Super Silhouette at .717-inch. Overall aggregate for 350 rounds with seven loads was .832-inch.

Weatherby

The Mark V rifle has been factory chambered for a number of cartridges other than the Weatherby belted magnums for the European markets, but the 30-06 was the only non-Weatherby chambering offered in the U.S. Beginning in 1992, the standard production Mark V with its famous California styling is available in 270 Winchester, 7mm Remington Magnum and 375 H&H Magnum. The 270 and 7mm are offered with left- or right-hand action while the 375 is built for right-handers. Quite unusual for a Weatherby rifle is the 22-inch barrel of the 270 and 30-06. The 7mm

and 375 barrels are 24 inches long.

The 375 H&H is also available in a new Mark V variation called the Limited Edition Safari Classic. As its name implies, the rifle has a classic-style stock carved from select-grade American walnut replete with shadow-line cheekpiece, Pachmayr Old English recoil pad and cut checkering. Atop the barrel sits a quarter-rib with fixed and fold-down leaves. Just beyond the forend tip is a barrel band-type sling swivel stud. I'm a bit surprised to not see this one offered in 375 Weatherby Magnum. It's Roy's old improved version of the 375 H&H and is 100 to 200 fps faster. Cases are easily formed by firing 375 H&H factory loads in the 375 Weatherby chamber. A long time favorite of Warren Page, he bagged tons of the world's big game with it.

The Classicmark I is a new standard production version of the Mark V with oil-finished, select-grade Claro walnut, 18-line cut checkering, solid recoil pad and satin-finished blued steel. It is available with left- or right-hand action in nine Weatherby chamberings plus the 270, 7mm Remington Magnum and 30-06. Change the wood to select-grade American walnut, increase the line count of the cut checkering to 22, add a steel grip cap, and you've got the Classicmark II in the same caliber options. These are handsome rifles. They also look exactly like the 416-caliber Mark V with McMillan Griffin & Howe-style fiberglass stock I used on lion, leopard, buffalo and other stuff in Zambia, and reported on in my last "Rifle Review."

Weatherby was the first major company to offer a big game rifle with a synthetic stock (Fibermark), but got behind a bit in the rust-resistant metal department. They're now back in a nose-to-nose race with the competition with the new Mark V Weathermark Alaskan. All metal wears a dull, matte-finished coat of electroless nickel and nestles in a synthetic stock replete with moulded checkering. ●

GET COMPLETE DETAILS . . .

Our fully illustrated cataloging of rifles on the market begins on page 327.

by DOC CARLSON

BLACKPOWDER REVIEW

THINGS CONTINUE to happen in the blackpowder sport that stimulate growth and development. Several states have added muzzle-loading seasons for big game, primarily deer, and the NRA has a new rule book for international-style muzzle-loading shooting and has added long-range (up to 1000 yards) shooting to the single shot blackpowder cartridge discipline currently used in silhouette shooting. All this keeps the manufacturers expanding their lines of products to keep pace with the desires of the buying public.

One of the most controversial additions to the muzzle-loading field a few years ago was the in-line type of rifle, styled very like the modern bolt-action rifle. Aside from that, they load from the front and are ruled by the same limitations of range and velocity.

Modern Muzzleloading Inc., who was among the first to bring the in-line gun on the market, has continued to improve on their design. They have a new brass-lined breech plug that seals against the base of the barrel, effectively eliminating any leakage of powder gasses and fouling into the thread area of the plug—something that has always been a problem with muzzle-loading guns, regardless of their design. It will be standard on all their guns except the new Black Knight, a competitively priced version. The brass-lined and sealed breech plug is available as a retro-fit accessory for the Black Knight and also for their older guns.

The Black Knight rifle, from

Modern Muzzleloading, is U.S.-made, with lower price in mind, and succeeds very well. The gun is of very good quality and priced considerably cheaper than the rest of the line. This gun should find a ready market among hunters out there.

Another innovation from Modern Muzzleloading is an instructional tape to be packed with all their guns. This will allow the purchaser to use his TV and VCR to bring experts right into his living room to tell him firsthand how to load, fire and care for his new acquisition. Considering the current interest in video products, this appears to be a good move.

Gonic Arms, another in-line manufacturer who has been around for some time, continues to improve their offerings also. They are building their in-lines in a wide range of new calibers, using a new trigger system and a new muzzle design to make loading easier. One of the major problems with the slug-shooting type of rifles, which most of the in-line hunting guns are, is starting the bullet easily and straight into the muzzle, especially when the bore becomes fouled after a shot or two. The new counter-bored muzzle on the Gonic guns addresses this problem. The bullet is started into the muzzle much easier and, more important to accuracy, straight with the bore. The ramrod can be used much more efficiently

without having to try to hold the bullet square with the muzzle at the same time that pressure is applied to force it down the barrel. A good idea that will be greatly appreciated by the hunter, I would imagine.

A new name in the in-line group of guns is **White Systems, Inc.** This is the brainchild of Dr. Gary White who some may remember as the head pilot of the Green River Rifle Works, manufacturer of a very traditional muzzle-loading rifle ten years or so ago. The White rifle is well designed and shows the long experience of Dr. White as a hunter of big game. The gun features a side-swing safety similar to the Model 70 Winchester and shoots slugs. The rifle is available in 410-, 451- and 504-caliber. White also makes bullets called the "Super Slug" weighing from 400 to 600 grains. These bullets are patterned after the heavy hunting bullets used in muzzleloaders in the mid-to-late 1800s. This bullet line shoots quite well in any of the other guns that are designed for slug shooting, I'm told.

Connecticut Valley Arms

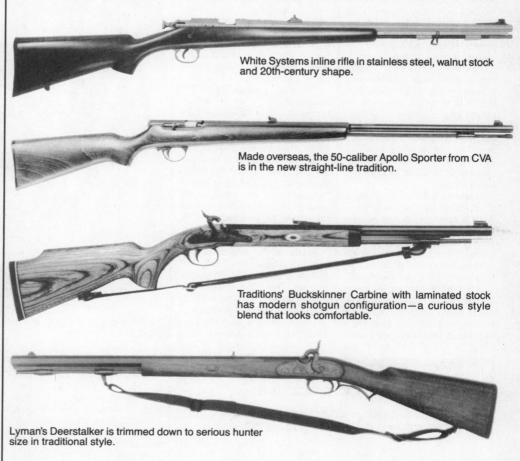

White Systems inline rifle in stainless steel, walnut stock and 20th-century shape.

Made overseas, the 50-caliber Apollo Sporter from CVA is in the new straight-line tradition.

Traditions' Buckskinner Carbine with laminated stock has modern shotgun configuration—a curious style blend that looks comfortable.

Lyman's Deerstalker is trimmed down to serious hunter size in traditional style.

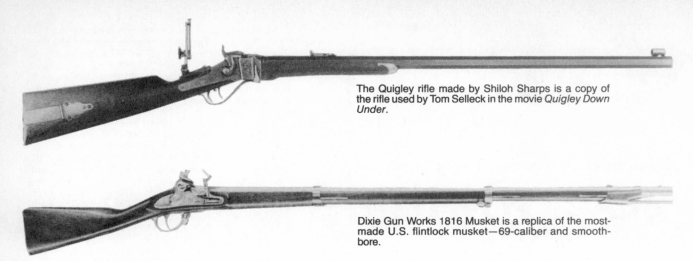

The Quigley rifle made by Shiloh Sharps is a copy of the rifle used by Tom Selleck in the movie *Quigley Down Under.*

Dixie Gun Works 1816 Musket is a replica of the most-made U.S. flintlock musket—69-caliber and smooth-bore.

and **American Arms** are both producing in-line action muzzle-loading rifles that are priced very competitively and show good quality. Both are made overseas and feature slug barrels. Check the catalog section for specifications and pricing on all these guns.

In a more traditional vein, **Lyman** has their Deerstalker model out in a left-hand version—good news for off-side hunters. The guns are available in flint or percussion, 50 or 54 calibers. The Deerstalker is a conventional looking muzzle-loader with a nylon ramrod, darkened hardware, single trigger system and darkly stained wood—all things that the hunter will appreciate. A short carbine version is available in percussion and 50-caliber only. Lyman is also the primary supplier for moulds, loading dies, etc. for many of the black-powder cartridges being shot today.

Traditions, Inc. has added a short rifle—the Buckskinner—with a pistol grip and Monte Carlo laminated stock intended for the hunter. It is available in 50-caliber and either percussion or flint ignition and is sort of a cross between the traditional muzzle-loading rifle and modern types. It is available in right-hand with either 1:66 twist or 1:20 for the slug shooter. A left-hand percussion

version is also in the catalog with a 1:20 twist only.

Euroarms of America, who has had a fine line of Civil War replicas available for some time, has a couple of new guns worthy of note. They have brought back the 1803 Harpers Ferry flintlock rifle that Lewis and Clark used on their trip up the Missouri River. The rifle is made in the correct 54 round ball caliber and the lock has been redesigned from earlier versions to correct some deficiencies. The 1803 was the first U.S. Armory-made rifle. The half-stocked gun is a faithful copy of the original and a good looking gun.

The other gun added to Euroarms line is a very nice replica of the 1841 Mississippi Rifle of Mexican and Civil War fame. This is also made in the 54-caliber round ball of the originals. The form of this gun is basically similar to Civil War muskets, with the exception of being shorter and brass mounted. A very good looking and shooting gun that will be popular with hunters and re-enactors. Percussion, of course.

While on the subject of U.S. muskets, **Dixie Gun Works** has a new Model 1816 flintlock musket. This gun is made in 69-caliber smoothbore, as were the originals, and features the lock plate marked with "Harpers Ferry" and the American eagle

Butler Creek line of sabots and quick loaders for muzzleloaders offers great stuff for hunters.

above "U.S." forward of the hammer. A brass pan and steel hardware compliment the walnut stock to make this a very fine looking replica. This gun had the highest production of any U.S. flintlock musket and many were converted to percussion and used in the Civil War.

Pedersoli is well known as a maker of high quality guns. A

new company, **Flintlocks, Etc.,** has set up to import the entire Pedersoli line of replica guns from Italy. Check the catalog section for their lineup. Some very nice stuff!

If target shooting is your bag, **Austin Sheridan, USA, Inc.** has an exact replica of the J. Sanftl target rifle originally made in Germany in the mid-1800s. The

GET COMPLETE DETAILS . . .

Our catalog listings for muzzle-loading handguns and long guns begin on page 405 and page 412.

replica is made by Paolo Bondini, a well-known Italian maker of fine replica firearms. The gun is rifled with twelve lands and grooves and features a backward-striking hammer on the lock. It comes with both tang peep and dovetailed open sights. It is available as a kit for the first time in the United States from the Sheridan company, which not only saves money for the person who is willing to assemble the rifle, but also allows some alteration during the building to enhance stock fit, etc. This should be well received by target shooters.

We often forget that black-

EC quick reloader from Mt. Alto might wean Carlson from the powderhorn and bullet block.

powder guns are not all muzzleloaders. There is a rebirth of interest in shooting the old blackpowder cartridge guns both for hunting and for use in some of the competitions gaining in popularity around the country. The recent movie, *Quigley Down Under*, starring Tom Selleck, has sparked a lot of interest in the long-range Sharps family of rifles.

Probably the leading maker of these guns on a reproduction basis is **Shiloh Sharps Company**. They have been making the Sharps 1874 series of rifles for some time. This line encompasses the Sharps buffalo rifles used by the hide hunters of the 1870s. The demand is such that, at this printing, they are running a 20-month backlog of orders. Regardless of that, they have brought out the Tom Selleck *Quigley Down Under* rifle, a copy of the rifle that this company made for Selleck's use in the movie. For the person who wants something that is a conversation starter as well as being a beautiful, usable rifle, this might be worth a look. Shiloh can send you dope on this and other rifles that they make.

Another source for blackpowder Sharps-type guns is **Armsport, Inc.** They are importing the Italian-made Sharps in 45-70 caliber with 28-inch barrel in both round and octagon shape. It is also available in carbine style with a 22-inch round barrel which might be of interest to the single shot hunter.

While on the subject of cartridge rifles, **Navy Arms** and Flintlocks Etc. both are importing the Remington Rolling Block Creedmoor rifle. This is a target-type blackpowder cartridge rifle in 45-70 that is intended for use in competitions such as the Black Powder Cartridge Silhouette matches or the Long Range matches shot at 600 to 1000 yards. This rifle is set up with tang-mounted peep sight, globe front sight, heavy barrel and stock cut for long-range target shooting. A nicely made gun and worth a look if blackpowder cartridge shooting is your game.

Incidentally, if you are shooting blackpowder cartridge guns, you should take a look at a bullet lube made by **SPG Bullet Lube Company**. This is the stuff that most of the match shooters in the blackpowder cartridge game are using. It works very nicely to keep fouling soft and improve accuracy.

Brass antique telescope from Selsi Company might be right for the muzzleloader who has everything else.

In the accessory line, **Butler Creek Corp.** has brought back their Poly Patch round ball sabot and the Maxie Patch plastic wad intended to be shot under slug-type bullets. The Poly Patch and Maxie Patch were both on the market some time ago, but were taken off due to some problems with the round ball version. The new Polys are redesigned and the problems have been resolved, so they have

made their reappearance. For those who have been looking for these products the past few years, their reappearance will be good news. The Maxie Patch is especially useful as it guarantees a seal when shooting slug-type bullets. This is absolutely critical to accuracy and is sometimes difficult to achieve with the bullet alone—especially in barrels that were not specifically cut for use with bullet-type projectiles. It's a good product to use routinely under slug bullets in any barrel.

I have examined and used many so-called "quick" reloaders for muzzle-loading guns over the years. They have been something less than quick or handy in most cases. I usually revert to powderhorn and loading block. There is one made by **Mt. Alto Products** that seems to be an answer. Called the E.C. Loader, it holds three extra shots, powder, ball/patch or bullet, and cap. The unit comes with a barrel-centering end that is sized for your particular barrel size. In use, the starter is pulled out until it clicks, the

unit is centered over the bore by the barrel-centering end, the cylinder rotated to bring a loaded chamber over the muzzle and the short starter is pushed down. The powder is dropped when the unit is rotated and the bullet is short started ready to be seated with the ramrod. It takes less time to operate than it does to describe how it works. This one is easy to use and is not so bulky as to be a problem

to carry in the pocket. Should be a usable item for the muzzle-loading hunter.

With the growth of hunting with front-loading guns, the demand for those slug-type bullets has increased. **Hornady** has expanded their line to include saboted bullets using their new, easy-expand pistol bullet. These allow the use of this bullet in muzzle-loading guns of various calibers. The velocity picks up a bit due to the lighter pistol bullet and the bullet is set up to reliably expand at muzzle-loading velocities.

Another pistol-caliber bullet in a plastic sabot for muzzle-loader use is put out by **Modern Muzzleloaders Inc.** Their bullet is pure lead so it gives the same expansion as the bigger, full-size muzzle-loading bullets, but with the potential of higher velocity due to the sub-caliber size of the bullet.

The people who started the slug bullet interest, **Buffalo Bullets**, have expanded their line to include swaged round balls and, glory be, a swaged 58-caliber Minie bullet for the big Civil War muskets, among others. This will be great news to those who shoot this type of bullet in those muskets, either in the hunting field or in re-enactment shots. The Minie bullet is one of the toughest to cast and a lot of them are returned to the melting pot due to imperfections. Shooters, especially those of us with a lazy bent when it comes to casting bullets, will be happy to see this addition.

It is worthy of note that Dixie Gun Works, as well as Navy Arms Company, is bringing in the long brass rifle scopes that were around a few years ago and have been absent for some time. It is good to see these old-time scope sights again available.

What do you give the buck-skinner who has everything? Well, one answer might be a brass telescope carried by **Selsi Company**. It is a solid brass, antique telescoping type and gives 30x magnification. The optics are good and it comes in a wooden box to protect it in your gear. It would look great in any re-enactors outfit and is also a handy "long eye."

This is merely a fast over-sight of the vast amount of blackpowder-oriented products that are on the market for the shooter, collector and hunter. The catalog section of Gun Digest will show you a lot more. Look it over. ●

by BOB ARGANBRIGHT

There are no regulations beyond *Caveat Emptor,* so a lot of people have begun...

COLLECTING HOLSTERS

I REMEMBER MY favorite childhood Christmas. I was about seven years old, and crazy about cowboys. Santa left a Gene Autry cowboy outfit, complete with vest, capgun, gunbelt and holster (real leather), and, as I remember, a lasso. This early fascination with the Hollywood cowboys is perhaps responsible for my association of any handgun with a proper holster for it. In the mid-1950s, while in high school, I was bitten by the Fast Draw bug. This was caused by my interest in the then-new and popular "adult TV western" series, and their emphasis on the Fast Draw abilities of their respective stars.

My first "real" gun was a Hahn 45 BB gun, a beautiful single-action revolver the same size, shape, weight and balance as the famous Colt Single Action Army revolver. This CO_2-powered six-gun was a popular Fast Draw

trainer at that time. Now, all I needed to become a Fast Gun was a gunbelt and Fast Draw holster. But a good one, such as the Arvo Ojala Hollywood version, sold for $39.95, almost three times as much as my six-gun.

About this time, my high school started offering a leather craft class. While I couldn't work it into my schedule, I did arrange for the teacher to order an extra "beginner's kit" for me, and I tried my hand at making my own holsters. While my first attempts were crude, 30 years of persistence and experience have gone by and I can now produce any style holster with professional results.

This interest in holsters inspired me to purchase samples of other holster makers' work for comparison and inspiration, and suddenly I realized I was a "holster collector." Actually, I

have come to realize that I am a general-purpose collector, as I tend to collect anything that interests me, such as guns, handmade knives, art, books, holsters, anything to do with Fast Draw, and anything from the Old West. As I am not the only collector interested in holsters, we will take a closer look at holster collecting. (And for those of you who are wondering: Yes, the leather craft kit did solve my holster problem. I purchased a Tandy Leather Co. "Dee Woolem" Fast Draw holster kit and, once assembled, it was a professional quality fast gun rig.)

While I believe in collecting any holster which one finds interesting, it will help in building an initial collection to choose a theme. The theme may be such things as the maker, the style, the usage, gun type, or even the famous user. For example, in the world of pre-

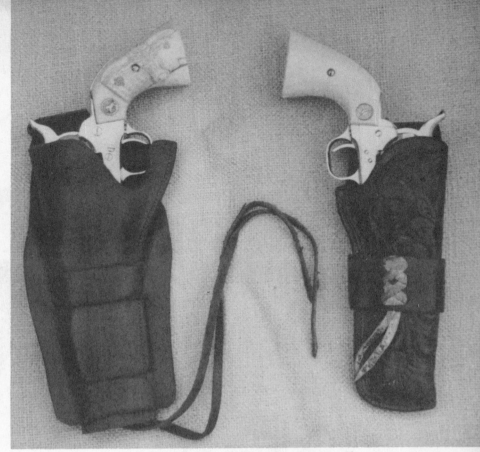

World War II holsters, there were three giants of the industry. These were S.D. Myres of El Paso, Texas; Herman H. Heiser of Denver, Colorado; and George Lawrence Company of Portland, Oregon. All three dated back to pre-20th century, and one could specialize in holsters from any one of these makers. Styles include sporting use (field holsters), police duty rigs, plainclothes police holsters, military holsters and competition holsters.

One might collect unusual holsters such as Berns-Martin break-front "Speed" holsters, or "clamshell" holsters, or swivel holsters and such. Or one may collect only holsters made for a favorite handgun. Also, one could put together a collection of holsters for the milestone handguns, such as the Colt SAA, New Service, Detective Special and Government Model 45 and the Military and Police (M&P), as well as Chief Special and Model 27 from Smith & Wesson.

I must admit I collect along all of these lines. For example, my favorite handgun is the 4¾-inch Colt SAA re-

On the left, an early H.H. Heiser; on the right, a much later Heiser product made closer to the fast-draw ideal.

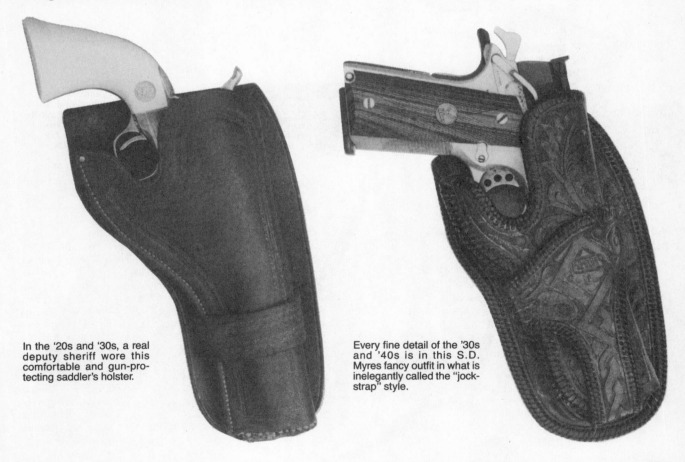

In the '20s and '30s, a real deputy sheriff wore this comfortable and gun-protecting saddler's holster.

Every fine detail of the '30s and '40s is in this S.D. Myres fancy outfit in what is inelegantly called the "jock-strap" style.

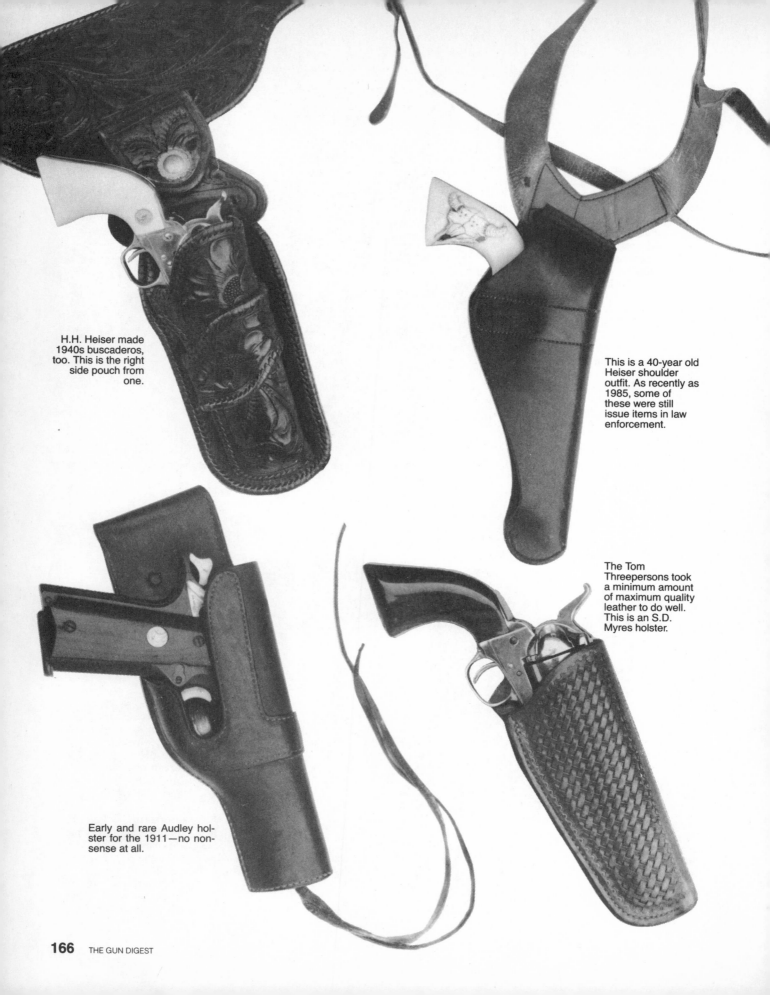

H.H. Heiser made 1940s buscaderos, too. This is the right side pouch from one.

This is a 40-year old Heiser shoulder outfit. As recently as 1985, some of these were still issue items in law enforcement.

The Tom Threepersons took a minimum amount of maximum quality leather to do well. This is an S.D. Myres holster.

Early and rare Audley holster for the 1911—no nonsense at all.

volver. So I have in my collection a new condition S.D. Myres "Threepersons" holster for a 4¾-inch Colt. This holster fits in the category of famous Old West maker, and also in the category of early Fast Draw style, and for a favorite gun. But I also have a Chic Gaylord hip holster for a 3½-inch S&W Model 27. I don't have a gun which will work in this holster, but Gaylord was so important as a holster designer that my collection of famous makers would be incomplete without a sample by Gaylord. Gaylord produced the first of the modern school of holsters in the 1950s and '60s out of his New York City shop. He was the first to use detail moulding to retain the gun, and the

Model 45. And finally, one could collect only custom holsters from custom makers. Let us take a closer look at these different approaches.

Collecting the holsters of the pre-World War II giants will appeal mostly to the collector of antique guns. The collector of blackpowder model Colt SAs, produced prior to 1898, often collects period holsters, and Myres, Heiser and Lawrence were three of the giants. But original holsters from the era are getting scarce and expensive. With the renewed interest in the SA revolver and the popular new cowboy shooting matches, there are several makers specializing in replica Old West-style holsters and cartridge

and a General Patton Commemorative. These beautiful rigs are exact duplicates of holsters and gunbelts which were or could have been used by the people or events commemorated. For example, the O.K. Corral rig is an exact duplicate of an original 1880s-era holster manufactured by the Spangenberg Gunshop of Tombstone, Arizona Territory. It is matched with a correct style money/cartridge belt for the era, and such a rig could have been used by any of the participants in this legendary gunfight.

Antique holsters, though scarce, are still found at gun shows, and I have found them in "junk" boxes in gunshops. While many were cheap mail-

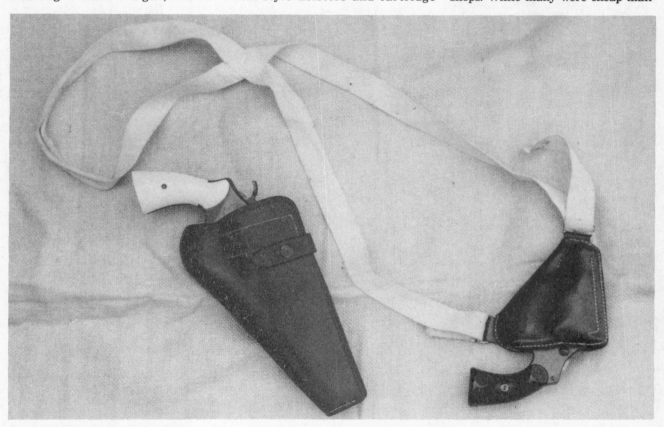

The front-runners for a long time—Berns-Martin upside-down and open-front outfits.

top-of-the-line leather holsters of today are mostly inspired by Gaylord.

Collecting holsters for specific uses includes competition rigs versus hunting rigs. I collect Fast Draw rigs of any time, with an emphasis on the Hollywood makers, such as Bohlin, Ojala, Anderson and Alfonso. Being involved in IPSC/USPSA shooting, I also collect so-called "combat rigs" by Anderson, Alfonso, Bianchi, Sparks, Davis, Blocker and early Rogers synthetics. And these last are all for another favorite handgun, the Colt Government

belts. The most prolific of these is El Paso Saddlery, a firm which dates back to 1889. Also, it should be noted that the George Lawrence Co. is still in business, though they have recently relocated to North Carolina.

While we are looking at the products of El Paso Saddlery, this is a good place to mention the commemorative-type holster. Though John Bianchi, of Bianchi International, offered the first commemorative holster with his John Wayne Commemorative rig, El Paso Saddlery has marketed several commemorative holsters. These include an O.K. Corral Commemorative, a Pat Garret/Billy the Kid Commemorative,

order items, the finer ones will be maker-marked. This stamping usually appears on the face of the holster in a circular form. Maker-marked holsters are more valuable than the unmarked ones, and makers from states with an Old West history bring a premium.

One of the interesting aspects of collecting the old holsters is in researching them. I have an original old holster of Northwestern style with a full skirt and muzzle plug. The muzzle plug was popular in snow country, as it kept snow out of the gun muzzle while one walked through deep snow, or if one took a spill in the snow. This particular

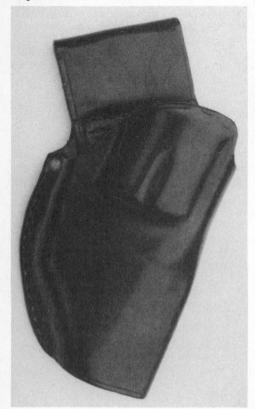

(Below) Legendary Chic Gaylord's way with gun leather—minimum work and a minimum holster—taught them all.

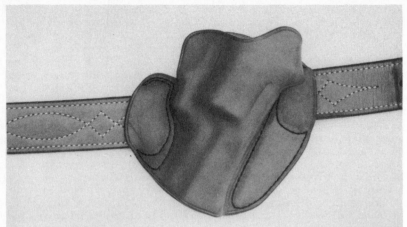

(Above) This Thad Tybka holster for the small of the back shows a lot of design growth, but a lot of Gaylord, too.

(Below) Key to the Baker patent are the two slots on the leading edge which provided a lot of versatility.

(Left) This was all the rage for a while, but better solutions came along and replaced the pop-open clamshell.

old Colt SA holster was used by several different people over the years, as there are two signatures and several cattle brands written on the inside of the skirt. One of the names is "Ed H. Fitch, Deputy Sheriff, Campbell Co, Wy." A letter to the Campbell County Sheriff's Office brought the information that the late Ed Fitch was a Deputy from 1933 to 1934, and had been a long-time rancher in the area. It should be noted that most of these marked Old West holsters were sideline products for saddle makers. While the saddle maker holsters are usually marked with a saddlery name, it is also possible to tell them from the

mail-order holster by the quality of leather used. The mail-order holsters, even when maker-marked, were of a noticably thinner leather than that used by the saddle shops.

There are several "classic" holsters which might form the nucleus of a collection. Since its introduction by S.D. Myres, all major holster makers have produced a "Threepersons"-style holster. Tom Threepersons was a legendary post-World War I gunfighter and lawman ranging from Texas to Canada. Myres made the first "Threepersons" holster to the lawman's specifications, and it became the standard police plainclothes holster. It started

as a western revolver holster (Threepersons' personal holster was for a Colt SAA) and was trimmed of all excess leather, raised higher on the gunbelt and angled slightly gun butt forward to create what is known as the FBI angle. Lawrence makes a version called the "Keith," as used by the late great handgunner Elmer Keith. Two police duty holsters have become classics, both designed pre-World War II. These are the Myres Border Patrol and the Jordan holsters. The Myres Border Patrol model was originally designed by Charles Askins when he was with the U.S. Border Patrol, and it was adopted by them. It is a long-shanked FBI-angled holster which encloses the trigger guard. USBP officer Bill Jordan, a legend in his own right, wasn't satisfied with Askins' design and had a holster made to his specifications. The Jordan version raised the gun higher, trimmed all leather away from the re-

(Left) Andy Anderson made a Victory model for Raquel Welch to wear in "Hannah Caulder" and this was his sizing rig—note numbered notches—of the time.

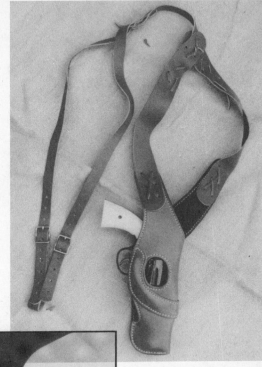

(Right) This is Robert Horton of "Wagon Train" wearing an Arvo Ojala rig like that shown.

(Above) The original Dirty Harry rig for the S&W 44 Magnum Model 29 was a commercial holster.

volver's trigger guard, and stiffened the holsters shank with a metal insert. Jordan's holster was also approved for Border Patrol use, and it became the standard for duty holsters.

Several mechanically interesting classics from pre-World War II include the Audley, the "clamshell," the Berns-Martin "Speed" holster and the very rare Bridgeport swivel plate. The Audley, patented in 1914, was a standard top-draw hip holster for revolvers and auto pistols with a trigger guard lock which secured the gun. At one time, the Audley holster was marketed by the Colt Firearms Company, and it is illustrated in their catalogs. The "clamshell," patented in 1933, hinged down the back and sprang open, like a clamshell, when a release was pressed by inserting the trigger finger through the handgun's trigger guard. The Berns-Martin "Speed" holster was a high-ride break-front hol-

ster, originally designed to carry a long-barreled revolver high on the hip, still easy to draw.

While shoulder holsters might be treated as a topic alone, any classic collection should include a half-breed-style shoulder holster, as produced by Myres, Heiser and Lawrence. These are the skeletonized holsters which include a spring encircling the revolver cylinder to retain the handgun. And the Berns-Martin Lightning holster, the first upside-down shoulder holster, belongs in any classic collection. I understand these were popular with CIA operatives in Vietnam to carry their stainless steel S&W snub revolvers.

The Bridgeport device was patented and submitted to the U.S. Army for testing as a pistol *and carbine* carrier. It is a two-pronged spring clip which fastens to the gunbelt with rivets. It totally replaces the usual holster, and the gun is supported by a mushroom-

headed screw which replaces the hammer screw. The gun may be swiveled and fired without "drawing." Tested and rejected by the U.S. Army, these were sold as surplus. While originals are very expensive, it should be noted that several years ago Bianchi International marketed an exact replica.

Editor Ken Warner has a Dale Myres (not S.D. Myres) shoulder holster which has a bore brush attached in the muzzle end. The handgun sets in the holster with the brush inserted in the bore. The resistance offered by the brush as the gun is drawn provides the only weapon security with this open-top holster. The unique hard plastic "SNIK" was fascinating. Popular during the early days of the International Practical Shooting Confederation, (IPSC) this was a front-draw holster similar to the Berns-Martin. However, the auto pistol was retained in the holster by a

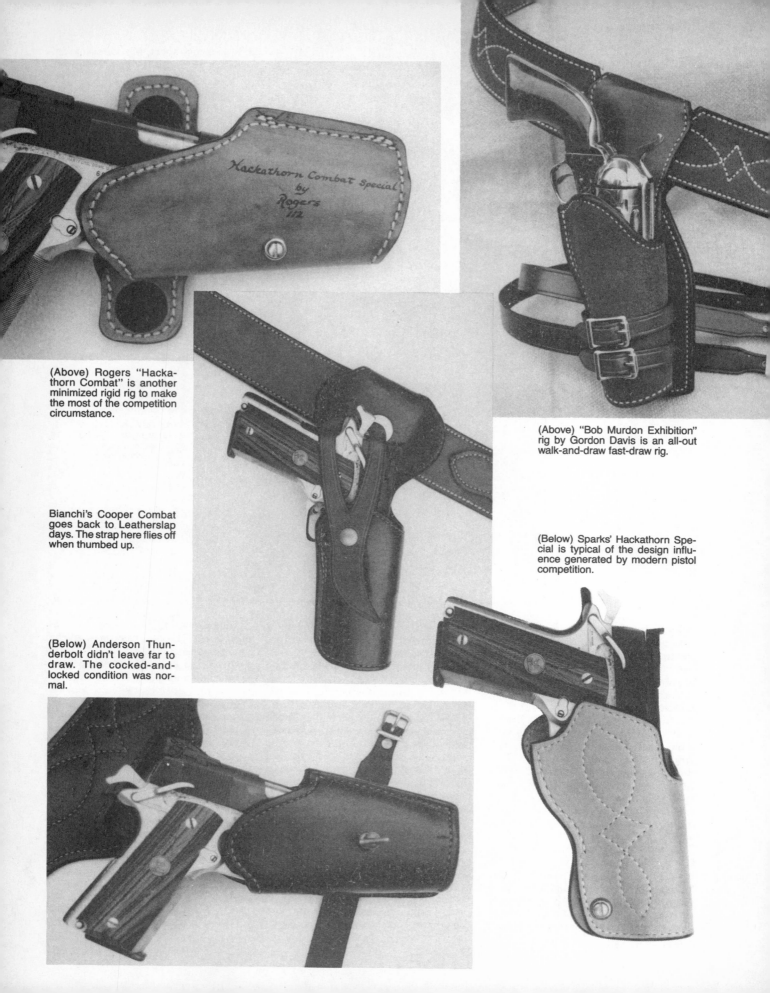

(Above) Rogers "Hackathorn Combat" is another minimized rigid rig to make the most of the competition circumstance.

Bianchi's Cooper Combat goes back to Leatherslap days. The strap here flies off when thumbed up.

(Below) Anderson Thunderbolt didn't leave far to draw. The cocked-and-locked condition was normal.

(Above) "Bob Murdon Exhibition" rig by Gordon Davis is an all-out walk-and-draw fast-draw rig.

(Below) Sparks' Hackathorn Special is typical of the design influence generated by modern pistol competition.

O.K. Corral commemorative (on the belt) with an original holster by an El Paso maker.

Bianchi Bridgeport swivel plate reproduces a device patented in 1882.

plastic tab which fit in the pistol's ejection port. The gun was drawn by pushing it forward with enough force to cam the tab out of the port, at which point the gun would pop out the front of the holster. And finally, the mechanical features collection should include a holster with a thumb-break safety strap. This is a common feature on holsters today, but didn't exist before approximately 1960.

While many of the pre-World War II makers have faded from the scene, they were replaced with new makers who have influenced the direction of holster design. These makers include Gaylord, Seventrees, Bianchi, Safariland, Sparks, Baker, Rogers and Uncle Mike's. These manufacturers are producing, or have produced, the classics of today.

Chic Gaylord was an artist who turned to designing and manufacturing the finest concealment holsters in the world out of a small New York City shop in the late 1950s. Gaylord pioneered lightweight leather with extensive moulding to produce a secure friction fit which has become the standard until recently. Today's product liability and a rash of lawsuits have forced the makers to put "safety straps" on nearly all holsters. Seventrees was the successor to Gaylord. They also specialized in concealment holsters, offering them in horsehide and such exotic leathers as sharkskin.

John Bianchi started making holsters as a hobby while working as a police officer, and his operation has grown into one of the giants of the industry. John was active in the developing combat-shooting sport, and his early line offered several holsters for this then-new sport. My collection includes a Bianchi "Cooper Combat" holster, one of the early steel-lined competition holsters for the Colt Government 45. It is unusual in its "Carl fly-off" safety strap, which encircles the hammer spur of the cocked and locked 45 in such a way that the hammer cannot fall, yet when the safety strap is released it "flies-off" to be completely out of the way for a fast draw. Safariland, originally known as Safari Ltd., patented their exclusive "sight track," which prevents handguns with sharp-edged target front sights from peeling a strip of leather out of the holster each time the handgun is drawn. Safari Ltd. led the way, and most top quality holsters being manufactured today have some type of protection from sharp front sights.

Milt Sparks produced the finest practical combat holsters available and popularized the adjustable tension feature on his hip holsters. The "Hackathorn Special," designed for Ken Hackathorn, well-known firearms authority, has become a modern classic. The finest of inside-the-pants concealment holsters is the Summer Special, also made by Sparks. This is also a modern classic designed by former law officer Bruce Nelson. Nelson has retired from law enforcement and now operates a one-man holster shop, and his holsters are collectibles. Roy Baker, known as the "Pancake Maker," designed and patented the pancake-style holster. Most major makers today produce a similar holster, although only Baker's may have the multiple belt slots in the leading edge which allows one to change the holster angle to wear either strong side or cross-draw. The Baker Pancake is a modern classic.

So far, we have only discussed leather holsters. But the 1970s and 1980s saw the emergence of two new construction types. Both have been successful and the collector will need examples in any general collection. These are the hot moulded (thermal) plastic holster and the padded nylon holster. The hot moulded plastic laminates were pioneered by ex-FBI agent turned holster designer Bill Rogers. My favorite of his line was also a Hackathorn model, the Hackathorn Combat Special for the Colt Government 45. Uncle Mike's pioneered the padded nylon holster, and it has revolutionized the holster industry. One could easily build a collection of nothing but nonleather holsters. These pretty well cover what I consider the modern classics, except for the competition holsters, which are in a class by themselves.

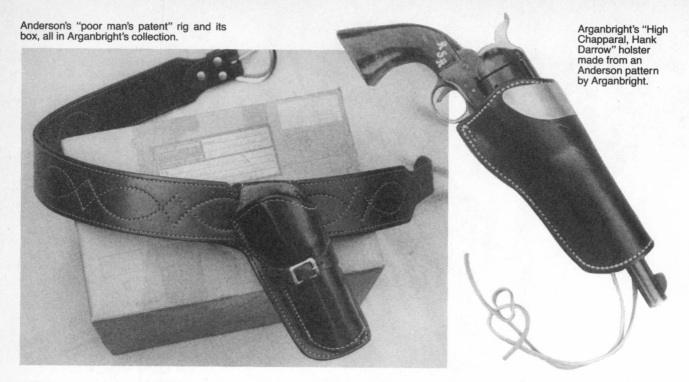

Anderson's "poor man's patent" rig and its box, all in Arganbright's collection.

Arganbright's "High Chapparal, Hank Darrow" holster made from an Anderson pattern by Arganbright.

Competition holsters are of two types: western (Fast Draw) and combat or action rigs. A "rig" is a belt and holster combination, and we will be discussing competition rigs. The western rigs were made by Bohlin, Ojala, Anderson and Alfonso. Ojala and Alfonso are still producing the same style of western rigs. The combat rigs were/are made by Anderson, Alfonso, Bianchi, Blocker, Davis, Hill, Sparks and Safariland. In western rigs, if one wants fancy carving and silver, the rig to find is a Bohlin. Hopalong Cassidy, the Lone Ranger, Gene Autry and Roy Rogers all used Bohlin rigs. If one favors the later TV "adult" westerns and movies, one wants an Ojala or Anderson rig. A beautiful rig which exactly duplicates that worn by Richard Boone in "Have Gun, Will Travel" is available as the "Paladin" direct from Arvo Ojala. Unquestionably a classic in Hollywood western rigs is that worn by Clint Eastwood as the man with no name in his series of spaghetti Westerns. This was an Anderson Walk and Draw (W&D) model with vertical holster rather than the competition muzzle-forward carry. Andy Anderson referred to this as an "Eastwood" rig, and it was available on special order only. While originals are scarce and expensive, Gordon David now offers a beautifully crafted copy, which he catalogs the Rawhide. Any collection of Fast Draw holsters would be incomplete without the favorite of the fanners, an Alfonso Number Two, from Alfonso of Hollywood.

According to Anderson, his most popular combat rig was the open-front model. These were Fast Draw rigs for the Colt Government 45 auto, where the holster was completely open down the front. When a bit more security was required, the front could be closed to different degrees by covering it with snap-attached leather covers. These were the most popular rigs for several years, when "leatherslaps" (live ammo fast draw matches) were common. The best were available from both Anderson's Gunfighter Shop and Alfonso of Hollywood, both located in North Hollywood.

My personal favorite of the classic combat rigs also originated in the Gunfighter Shop. This was the Thunderbolt. Also made for the Colt 45 auto, it was steel-lined, wrapped around from the back with the welt down the front, low cut, and had the first adjustable tension device for securing the gun. When Jeff Cooper was active in combat competition, he used the first Thunderbolt.

I have already mentioned the Hackathorn Special under classics. The Usher International from Gordon Davis was made for world-class combat shooter Jerry Usher and was the holster which made the cross-draw popular in competition for several years. Ted Blocker developed an extreme high-ride competition holster for Mickey Fowler, two-time Bianchi Cup winner, and any collection of combat competition rigs should include a Fowler Speedmaster. First World Com-

bat Champion Ray Chapman designed a competition holster for Bianchi International, which I consider a classic. And today, in 1991, the IPSC/USPSA and action shooters are using the holsters of two makers, Ernie Hill Speed Leather and Safariland. Here we have the best of the old and the wave of the future, with the Hill holster being of steel-lined leather and the Safariland holster is of thermo-laminate construction (hot moulded synthetic).

One might collect rigs as used by the TV and movie stars and celebrities. We have already seen the Bianchi John Wayne Commemorative rig. In addition, Davis Leather Co., El Paso Saddlery and Ted Blocker Holsters offer similar rigs, which they call "the Duke" rigs. We have also seen the Davis "Rawhide." In addition, Davis produces a rig copied after that used by James Drury as "The Virginian" (cataloged as the Virginian), and one like that used by Doug McClure on the same series, cataloged as "the Shiloh." Galco (formerly Jackass Holsters), offers their Miami Classic horizontal-carry shoulder holster, as used by Don Johnson on "Miami Vice." And possibly the most famous of all shoulder rigs, that used by Clint Eastwood as Dirty Harry, was commercially available at one time.

My collection includes a genuine celebrity rig. This is an early Ojala western rig, natural rough-out finish, with no cartridge loops, which makes it a special order. What makes it very special is the name "Robert Horton"

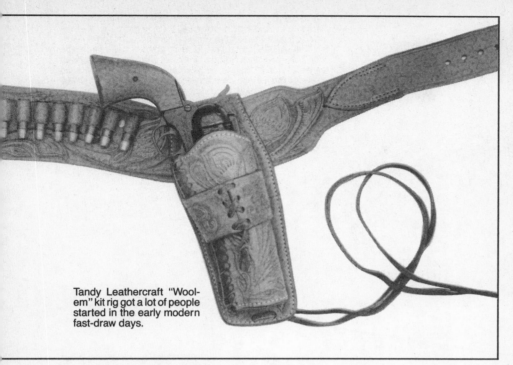

Tandy Leathercraft "Wool-em" kit rig got a lot of people started in the early modern fast-draw days.

stamped in the lining of the gunbelt. This is the rig used by Horton as Flint McCullough, the scout on TV's "Wagon Train" series.

While not owned by a Hollywood celebrity, my Anderson Victory model sizing rig might have been handled and worn by many of them. The sizing rig was unique to the Anderson Gunfighter Shop. A sizing rig was made with an oversized gunbelt, with the size stamped by each hole in the billet (tongue). Andy had a sizing rig for each different model holster which he made. Customers could try on the sizing rigs, and when they found the one they preferred, and placed it around their hips as they wished to wear it, no measurements were needed other than to note the number by the hole the belt was buckled in. I have been fortunate in obtaining several Anderson sizing rigs. Each is stamped in the belt "Property of the Gunfighter Shop, N. Hollywood, CA.," and the model name, such as Victory. Of the several sizing rigs I have or have seen, my favorite is the "Victory" since it might have been worn by Racquel Welch when she was fitted for the Victory rig she wore as lady gunfighter Hannie Caulder in the movie of the same name. Priceless additions to my Hollywood collection are several original Anderson holster patterns. One of these is a Victory-style Fast Draw holster for an 1860 Colt Army percussion revolver. This pattern has the name Johnny Cash hand-written on it by Andy.

A recent addition to my Hollywood collection is a beautiful full hand-carved double holster rig for Colt SAAs made by A.H. Hardy of Beverly Hills, California, and so marked. "Cap" Hardy was a pre-World War II professional exhibition shooter for Peters Cartridge Company. He also manufactured high quality holsters and is mentioned by both Ed McGivern and Elmer Keith in their respective books *Fast & Fancy Revolver Shooting* and *Sixguns*. After relocating to Beverly Hills, Hardy was one of the first of the Hollywood gun coaches. This rig is an early version of a Hollywood rig.

Additional celebrity holsters or rigs (gunbelt and holster) that I know of are an Ojala double rig with twin Colt SAAs, as used by Kevin Costner in the movie *Silverado;* a beautiful full carved and gold filigreed Ojala double, with twin Colt SAAs made for Major Riddle, owner of several casino-hotels in Las Vegas, Nevada, in the late 1950s; the Bob Munden Signature rig from Davis Leather. Bob Munden was listed in the *Guinness Book of World Records* as the fastest man with a gun to ever live. He makes a successful living today as a professional Fast Draw exhibition shooter and has appeared all over the U.S. and in several foreign countries. The Signature rig is an exact duplicate of one he uses, and it has his signature stamped in the face of the belt. At one time, Don Hume, who produces the only authorized Bill Jordan police duty holster, offered a signature version of it.

There are several well-known custom holster makers and any of their holsters are collectibles. The two I am familiar with are Thad Rybka and Ken Null. Rybka's holsters show superb execution and he credits Gaylord and Anderson for design inspiration. Null started by producing the unfilled Seventrees holster order when that firm went out of business, and his line of holsters is similar to Seventrees.

Holster memorabilia can be fascinating. This includes magazine advertisements and holster catalogs. Any pre-World War II holster catalog is very desirable. And catalogs from companies such as Gaylord and Seventrees are rare. Even the early catalogs of such industry giants as Bianchi and Safariland are interesting and hard to locate. I have found it interesting to obtain copies of holster patents, available from the U.S. Patent Office for a small fee. The patent claims for some of them are fascinating.

It has been my experience that one might be able to get along with only one handgun, but never with only one holster for it. If you enjoy the smell of oiled cowhide, the racy look of a SA revolver protruding from a western holster, the Hollywod make-believe of a Dirty Harry drawing his 44 Magnum from his shoulder holster, you may be missing out on the thrill of collecting holsters. While a few of the Hollywood and celebrity rigs are expensive, many collectible holsters are available as inexpensive ($10 or less) used holsters. I have not covered the military holster, as this is a collecting field by itself.

I will close by telling you of my latest holster treasure. Andy Anderson, originally a poor boy from Arkansas, protected his holster designs with what he called "poor man patents." He would take a sample of his holster, with a written description explaining the special features, box it up and send it to himself by registered mail. The unopened box was proof that he had manufactured that particular style of holster on or before the registration date.

Sadly, Andy passed away from a heart attack in June, 1991. I purchased from his estate the very first Walk and Draw AA rig, stamped on the back of the holster "XP-1," for experimental number one. The AA style was Andy's personal favorite of the different models he made, and the XP-1 rig was the sample from his poor man's patent. Collecting may be one way to touch greatness. That's how I feel about my Anderson AA rig and the man who made it. ●

Open Choke

GAS PRESSURE

AIR RESISTANCE (DRAG FACTOR)

The lesser constriction of an open-choked gun lets the wad slam into the exiting shot charge, thus "pancaking" it at the muzzle when the shot charge is trapped between the forward air resistance and the surging powder gases from the rear. This quick spreading of the shot charge soon exposes the pellets individually to air resistance, and they are slowed quicker than if there were other pellets bucking wind ahead of them. As a result, the open-choke patterns scatter and string out further than the Full-choke clusters at 40 yards, because air drag works faster on the greater number of shot individually exposed to the air resistance.

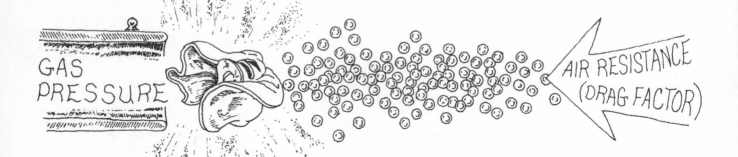

New answers to some old questions
CHOKE EXPLAINED (Once Again)

GAS PRESSURE

AIR RESISTANCE (DRAG FACTOR)

Full Choke

by DON ZUTZ

ANYONE WHO has ever peeled open a shotshell and spilled the pellets into his hand knows there are a lot of 'em at the start. But anyone who has also patterned critically at various ranges with different degrees of choke knows that something happens betwixt the muzzle and the target. Some patterning results show a heavy concentration of shot in the middle, while others spread all over the place; some retain a high percentage of their original shot charge, but others lose over half their pellets en route. And whatever the exact results from a given gun/load combo, there will seldom ever be 100 percent of the pellets still in the 30-inch-diameter patterning circle unless the range is mighty short.

Where do all those pellets go, and what's causing them to act that way?

To the casual hunter or shooter the answer has always been easy. Patterns and pellet flights are the product of "choke." You know what choke is, of course. It's the narrowing and/or other manipulation of the bore diameter and configuration in the muzzle segment for the purpose of dictating the form a shot charge will take as it emerges from confinement and enters free flight. Among the more popularly used chokes, for example, the Full choke will have the most narrow opening, and shot charges coming from it will perforce be swaged down into long, slender strings. At the opposite extreme, the true Cylinder bore will have no constriction, and shot masses coming from it will be shorter and fatter than those launched by the Full choke constriction. Between those extremes are the other working degrees of choke—Improved Cylinder, Skeet #2, Modified, and Improved Modified—all of which give the shot charge a somewhat different frontal area (diameter) at emission. And that frontal area is *the* important thing to remember as we delve into the subject of choke and pellet flights in an effort to understand pattern and shot string development.

For although a shotgun's choke constriction, or lack of it, does indeed influence the way shot charges are formed as they leave the muzzle, there's more to pattern and "tailing" than that. Pellets aren't popped into a vacuum. Once they are free of the barrel/choke confinement, they immediately slam into a strong opposing force—air resistance, alias air drag. Even on a calm day this is no minor obstacle. A high-velocity load of No.6s, for example, comes out of the muzzle doing something around 850-900 *miles* per hour, in which case air becomes a powerful barrier, just as the sonic barrier thwarted aircraft. You get the feel of this pressure when you stick your hand out of the window of a gas buggy tooling along at 65-70 mph, and you really get the idea when you try sticking your arm out of the cockpit of an open biplane doing 150 mph. Now project your speed to 850-900 mph and imagine the impact of air drag! Moreover, your car or airplane keeps pushing and is heavy, whereas a dinky shotgun pellet is obviously lacking continued propulsion and weight, and is, therefore, prone to rapid deceleration.

Okay, so air drag works on shotgun pellets. What does that do other than slow them down? How does air drag influence pattern development and shot strings?

Whereas casual thinking attributes pattern development to the way a choke constriction at the muzzle of a shotgun bunches the shot charge for launching, air drag is the factor that takes over as the shot charge leaves the muzzle. From that instant forward, patterns and shot strings are pretty much the product of air resistance. *In effect, air drag causes a peeling back of the leading layers of shot so that the lower layers of pellets gradually come to the front as the former leading pellets flare outwardly.* Rather than being the first pellets to reach the target, then, the ones that burst from the muzzle first are often, if not always, the pellets which spread and get to the target only after the pellets that started behind them.

That the lower pellets reach the target first is a radical thought, of course. It doesn't seem possible, to an average hunter. Yet by an understanding of air drag and vector analysis, one begins to appreciate the likelihood of just such a pellet-position reversal when the charge gets into free flight. Moreover, the chaps in Remington's plant once ran an experiment that proved the point: They painted pellets in red, white and blue, and then stacked them according to color in a test load which they fired before a high-speed camera set downrange. The resulting color photos showed that the bottom pellets were indeed getting there first! So there's scientific evidence of the phenomenon.

How does it take place, this shot-charge dynamic which has the bottom pellets work to the fore of the in-flight

Patterns are the result of air resistance acting on pellets, with some influence being exerted by the force with which the wad bumps or rams the shot upon exit.

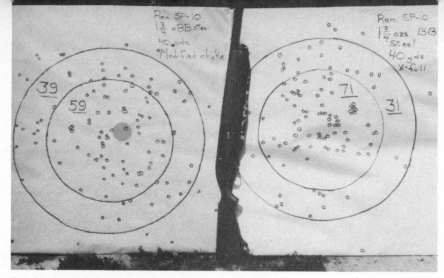

Popular armchair theories aside, steel shot will still give tight patterns from Full- and Extra-Full-choked barrels because of the way shot charges from such snug constrictions encounter air resistance. Modified at left; Full at right.

shot string? It goes something like this, thanks again to the impact of air drag as will be explained:

Let's say the trigger has been pulled and the shot charge has rambled up the bore to the choke constriction. Here the charge is formed into the diameter with which it will hit the air resistance immediately outside the muzzle. Full chokes will emit a narrower shot charge than will Skeet bores or Improved Cylinders, and this diameter does have a bearing upon the eventual in-flight dynamics; however, we'll get back to that shortly. First let's run through a generic happening regardless of the shot charge's diameter at exit.

Whether the shot load comes from a Full choke or a Cylinder bore, the air-drag factor hits the leading pellets like a hammer, slowing them variously depending upon their weight/shape factors and their muzzle velocities. Heavy pellets and ones that remain spherical overcome initial air drag better than pellets which are light and/or deformed. Likewise, air resistance works harder against high-velocity objects than it does against slower ones (which helps explain why the new breed of "lite" target loads with velocities anywhere from 50-150 fps slower than standard target loads can still clobber clay targets so well: The low-velocity "lite" loads retain a higher percentage of their exit velocities than do the speedier charges). Thus, the actual amount of resistance felt by a shot charge can be a complex equation. Suffice it to say here that they are factors. Our role isn't to calculate velocity losses but rather to discuss the influence of air drag on pattern and shot-string development.

As the leading pellets emerge from the muzzle of a shotgun, they are sandwiched between two robust forces. Not only is air restraining them from the front, but trailing pellets are ramming into them from behind. This condition alone can force leading pellets aside and into the fringe of the developing pattern, as the trailing pellets bolt into and through the leading layers.

At this point, a logical question is how can the trailing pellets overtake the leaders? The answer is that they don't encounter the full force of air resistance immediately. They're shielded by the leading layer or two, and they fly in a turbulent condition in which air drag isn't as potent as it is up front on the leaders. In other words, the trailing pellets have the benefit of having somebody ahead of them break trail. It's like geese flying in a wedge so that they don't have to fly straight into the teeth of a high

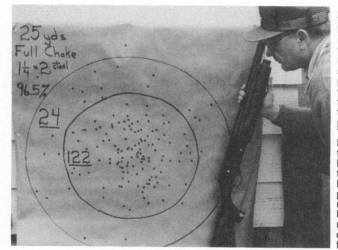

A Full choke drills tight patterns because the narrow muzzle passage puts the pellets out in a long, slender stream so the leading pellets break the wind and give the trailing shot easier travel until the first pellets peel back. Tests indicate the last pellets to come from a Full-choke barrel normally reach the target first, because they are protected from air resistance the longest; hence, they retain more of their original energy the farthest downrange.

wind; the leader breaks through, setting up a minor turbulence for the rest. It's also why you can get better mileage by tailgating an eighteen-wheeler, and why distance runners are often content to run back in the pack throughout much of a race. Thus, the trailing pellets retain more velocity than the leaders for a short distance because they don't feel the impact of air drag fully, until the leaders have peeled back.

Once the leading pellets have flared away, the brunt of air drag hits the pellets that had been directly behind the leaders, and these members, in turn, peel away. The process continues until finally the very last pellets feel the total effects of air drag, at which time they are even with or pulling ahead of the original leading pellets. Thus, air drag causes the slowing of leading pellets, and the action of leading pellets helps produce patterns.

Now for the role of choke constriction in this air drag theory. As mentioned earlier, chokes dictate the di-

ameter of the shot charge as it leaves the gun. This is important because, although the dimensional differences between degrees of choke seem minor, such as just .040-inch between a nominal Cylinder-bored and a Full-choked 12-gauge, the more open chokes (a) allow the passage of a shorter shot string which presents a broader frontal area to immediate air resistance and (b) let the wad and trailing pellets push more vigorously into the leading layers. This ramming from the rear just as the leading shot are being halted by air resistance tends to "pancake" the first layers to exit and direct those early shot away from the bore axis.

The tighter chokes—Improved Modified, Full and Extra-Full—mitigate against an immediate scattering effect by retarding the wad and trailing pellets so that the leading layers of shot can escape without experiencing uncouth slaps on their fannies. This reduced pressure from the rear permits the leading shot from tightly choked guns to fight into air resistance

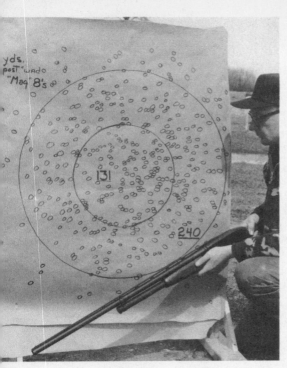

Post wads activate a "spring-away" function which causes pellets to flare out from the core of the cluster, thereby exposing more individual shot to air drag and tending to open the pattern while variously lengthening the shot string.

on their own instead of being rushed into it by the following mass. Moreover, the longer shot strings of tightly choked guns create a situation in which more pellets enjoy the turbulent, lower-drag condition behind the leaders. Photos of shot strings leaving the muzzle prove this: Full-choked strings are stretched out already just ahead of the muzzle, whereas the more open chokes have shorter, more compact charges scant inches ahead of the muzzle.

Between the extremes of Full choke and the most open chokes, various constrictions—Improved Cylinder, Skeet #2 and Modified—put different amounts of pressure on the wad/pellet masses, thus influencing the way in which the emerging ejecta masses encounter air resistance and the way in which the trailing layers and wad impact the leading layers. An Improved Cylinder constriction will encourage easy ejecta passage with the wads pushing into the base pellets and sending them hurtling into the forward layers which are being slowed markedly by air drag, while somewhat tighter modified chokes will retard the wad and lower layers of shot variously so that the upper pellets can escape and get ahead of the ramming action at exit, thereby retaining more shot in the main stream. However, it must be pointed out that eventually the trail-

ing pellets catch up and may pass the leaders even in Full and Modified chokes since, as stated above, air resistance hits the leaders immediately while the trailers have the head wind broken for them over a short distance.

Two more points must be made to substantiate this air drag explanation of shot-charge performance and the influence of choke constrictions. The first is that of shot-string length. Anyone viewing the photos of Full- and open-choked shot charges popping from muzzles will immediately conclude that the Full choke throws the longest in-flight shot string, and that the open-choked guns deliver short, compact shot clouds. But that's not the way it works, folks. Experiments done by Roger Giblin, an electrical engineer at the College of London, indicate that Cylinder bores actually produce longer in-flight shot strings than do Full chokes. This evidence was gathered with impact detectors which measured the time interval between the arrivals of the first and last pellets at thirty and forty yards. Here are the resulting data for 1-ounce lead loads:

In-Flight Shot String Lengths

Yards	Cylinder	Full
30	11.1′ ± 2.5′	7.8′ ± 1.6′
40	17.0′ ± 3.3′	10.9′ ± 1.6′

How can the shot string from a Cylinder bore grow to be nearly six feet longer than one from a Full choke when muzzle-exit photos show the Full-choke load already strung out as it stabs from the muzzle? Air drag is the answer. The individual pellets in an expanding pattern begin to encounter the full effects of air drag sooner than do those of a tighter pattern in which the leaders act as wind breakers; hence, the trailing pellets of a tight pattern retain their starting velocities longer and don't trail out as much, which leads us to a rule of thumb: The tighter and the longer the shot charge on exit, the shorter the in-flight shot string will be. Conversely, the broader and shorter a shot charge is at the muzzle, the longer it will tail out on its way to the target. This may well squelch some ideas that 3- and 3½-inch Magnum loads automatically have lengthy shot strings as well as questioning the idea that Skeet guns and Reverse chokes deliver pancake patterns.

The second point that substantiates the impact of air drag on shot charges is seen in the revised exterior ballistics tables developed by Ed Lowry, a former Winchester ballistician. In a paper published in the December,

1989, issue of the *American Rifleman* ("Shotshell Ballistics Reconsidered," p. 30), Lowry presented data which cocked a skeptical eyebrow at the former shotshell ballistics tables and showed considerable velocity losses between the muzzle and the 3-foot instrumental (coil) velocities published by the industry. In added data offered by Lowry via the National Rifle Association's editorial offices, we find that Lowry's calculations show an actual muzzle velocity of 1302 fps is needed to attain the published velocity of 1200 fps of a standard 3-drams equivalent, 1⅛-ounce trap load. The shot charge in this instance sheds about 100 fps in the first 3-4 feet of its free flight! And the popular 1¼-ounce 12-gauge "duck load" with a published (again 3-foot instrumental) velocity of 1330 fps must be doing 1423 fps at the muzzle to deliver that full 1330 fps when it passes through the chronograph's screens. Thus, if a shot charge can be slowed that much in just a yard or so after leaving the muzzle, the individual pellets can indeed be impacted so that those exposed more directly to the initial resistance of air drag will be arrested more emphatically than those trailing in the wake.

One final point relative to the effects of air drag on pellets was illustrated during the 1968 Olympics when some testing was done to determine the affects of Mexico City's higher elevation on both athletic performances and shotgun patterning. Experiments proved that given gun/load combos gave tighter patterns in the mountains, thanks to the "thinner" air. The leading pellets were less affected by drag; consequently, they slowed down less after emission and weren't bumped into by the greater mass trailing them. And the trailing pellets, once they lost the wind-breaking protection of the leaders, found themselves encountering variously lower drag factors. If you want to shoot patterns to brag about, go climb a mountain!

The subject of shotgun chokes, then, goes well beyond a simple discourse of interior bore tapers and configurations. The entire purpose of the interior dimensions of a choke constriction is to manipulate the pellets for their impact with air resistance. Choke constrictions position the trailing layers of pellets relative to the leading layers, and it is this juxtapositioning that determines how the layers will fare once they come under the heavy pressure of air drag. Chokes form the pellet mass inside the bore; air drag shapes it as soon as the front pellets stick their noses out of the muzzle. ●

by LARRY S. STERETT

UTILITY GUNS

MANY NEW guns, new companies get into the market at the utility or specialty level. Thus, some of the most ingenious designs and new looks and uses come from really small companies; some, we are now finding in a newly scrambled world, from factories once beyond political walls; some are destined to have long market life; some not. Here are our choices of this year's entries:

China Sports

Not many of the Chinese-manufactured arms are original designs, but the ones available are copies of time-tested designs. In handguns, the latest is the Model 88SP, a copy of the double-action 9mm Browning Hi-Power; the previous Model 77B is now called the NP-20, but it is still the "trigger guard cocking" design in 9mm, and the 1911-A1 is just that, a Chinese-produced copy of one of the most famous pistols of all times. Then there is the Makarov Type 59, available in either 9x18mm or 380 ACP, and the Tokarev, NP 15 and NP 15A, available in original 7.62x25 with an extra 38 Super barrel, in 9mm only with an 8-round magazine, and 9mm only with a 13-round magazine.

For rifles, the NHM-90 is an upgraded (more sporterized) Kalashnikov design featuring a Bishop-designed thumbhole stock of huckleberry and a finish that matches the original Chinese forearm. (A 5-round magazine is standard.) The barrel length is just over 16 inches, and there is no longer a bayonet or cleaning rod attached. Caliber is 7.62x39mm. Also new,

pounds compared to 4.5 pounds—it should be a good plinking rifle.

Claridge Hi-Tec

This basic pistol design has been kicking around for nearly a decade, and it has finally arrived. The various models that have been shown over the years have been reduced in number to the S-9, L-9, T-9, and C-9 with barrel lengths of 5, 7.5, 9.5, and 16.25 inches respectively. The L-9 and T-9 models can also be obtained with an integral laser as the ZL-9 and ZT-9 models. The C-9 is a carbine model which is also available as the LEC-9 and ZLEC-9 with a black graphite composite stock. The charging handle is on the left side of the steel upper re-

The new Colt 9mm Sporter Lightweight has a 16-inch barrel, large shell deflector, no bayonet lug and a 5-round magazine.

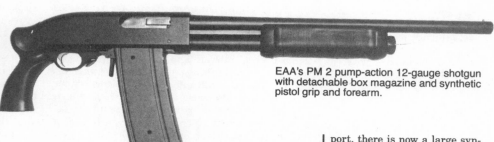

EAA's PM 2 pump-action 12-gauge shotgun with detachable box magazine and synthetic pistol grip and forearm.

and while less utilitarian than the NHM-90, is the EM-322, a bolt-action rimfire rifle that is a copy of the rifle used by the Chinese for Olympic training. It has a barrel length of 18½ inches, and a 5-round detachable box magazine, with two extra magazines fitted into the underside of the Monte Carlo stock. It should be well received, if the model examined is representative of standard production. Along with the EM-322, there may also be an EM-321, a pump-action rimfire repeater with a 9-round tubular magazine capacity. It weighs a bit more than the EM-322—6

ceiver, while the safety is on the left side of the A-356 aluminum alloy lower receiver. Weight of the various models is under four pounds.

Originally advertised as being available in more than a half-dozen chamberings, including the 7.63mm Mauser, the latest Hi-Tec pistols and carbines are available only in 9mm Parabellum, 40 Smith & Wesson, and the 45 ACP. It is still basically the same construction, with only six moving parts, and instant field stripping with the two receiver assemblies hinged at the forward end of the lower receiver.

Colt's Manufacturing

A couple of years back, Colt announced it was discontinuing the AR-15-type sporting rifles in 223, and the 9mm carbine. The rifles are now back, but there have been a few changes. Instead of being called AR-15 Sporter, the label is Colt Sporter, and the bayonet lug has been ground off the bottom of the front sight base. Four models chambered for the 223 Remington cartridge are available—the Lightweight with 16-inch barrel, and the Target Model, Match HBAR, and Competition HBAR, all with 20-inch barrels.

The 9mm is available with a 16-inch barrel, and there have been changes there also. In place of a full-length ejection port, there is now a large synthetic shell deflector at the rear of the port, which in turn requires a portion of the ejection port cover being cut off. (Magazine capacity of the 9mm is 5 rounds.)

The latest 223 Sporter, the Competition HBAR, features a flat-top receiver with integral Weaver-type base for optical sight mounting, and a separate clamp-on carrying handle is provided, complete with the fully adjustable A2 rear sight. Rifling twist on the Competition HBAR is 1 in 9 inches.

European American Armory

Here, the Antonio Zoli line of shotguns is available, but in the utility line, the pump-action

PM2 is the shotgun. It comes in a choice of black or chrome finish, with 20-inch barrel and an overall length of 41 inches. Originally intended to have a folding metal stock, until the Feds got into the act, the PM2 features a black hardwood stock and synthetic forearm. A pistol grip is also available, with the same grip style being introduced by another importer over a decade ago on the regular tubular magazine version of this shotgun. The main feature of the PM2 is the detachable box magazine, which has a capacity of six 12-gauge shells.

Feather Industries

Feather's AT-22 and AT-9 rifles with the sliding stock have been around for several years, but now there are a couple of

field rifle, with detachable 20-round box magazine, reportedly used by A.E.F. aviators during World War I. The Scout has a laminated birchwood stock, a Mauser action fitted with 20-inch barrel having a muzzlebrake, and a 10-round detachable box magazine. The rifle, which has a weight of approximately 8½ pounds, is available in 243 or 308 Winchester.

Heckler & Koch

The M3 Super 90 pump/auto shotgun has been around for a few years, but it is still a good utility gun, featuring a barrel length of 19¾ inches; choice of standard, pistol grip stock or folding stock; 7-round magazine; and standard or ghost ring sights. A new addition in the

pany, which had originally purchased the assets of the Harrington & Richardson firm on its demise. Products with the H&R name are now beginning to reappear. Foremost is one of the premier utility guns of all time, the Topper break-action single-barrel shotgun. Several versions are available, from the 098 in 410 or 20-gauge, each with a 3-inch chamber; the 098 Deluxe in 12-gauge with 28-inch barrel chambered for 3½-inch shells and a screw-in choke system for both lead and steel shot; to the National Wild Turkey Federation 12-gauge with 24-inch interchangeable choke barrel, and a Mossy Oak camouflage. This last version is also available in 10-gauge, under the NEF label, with both chambered for 3½-inch shells. There

is a bit fancy for a utility gun but it will still serve the needs for a durable, simple, time-tested shotgun.

Handgunners wanting a good serviceable revolver chambered for the 22 rimfire cartridges (non-magnum) will welcome the classic top-break Sportsman 999. This 9-shot revolver features automatic shell ejection, adjustable rear sight, double-action mechanism, fluted barrel rib, coil springs, and hardwood stocks. The design is proven, having originated in the U.S.R.A. single-shot target pistol used by the U.S. Army Pistol Team in the era following World War I.

Interarms

Thirty years or more ago, Sako had a rifle chambered for

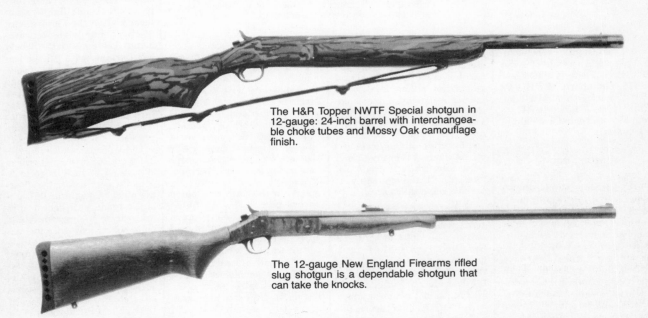

The H&R Topper NWTF Special shotgun in 12-gauge: 24-inch barrel with interchangeable choke tubes and Mossy Oak camouflage finish.

The 12-gauge New England Firearms rifled slug shotgun is a dependable shotgun that can take the knocks.

new versions. In place of the telescoping buttstock assembly, there is now a hi-impact polymer stock that provides a more traditional appearance to what are already excellent utility guns. The new buttstock is also available as a retrofit kit for those shooters owning either the AT-22 or AT-9. The new models are the F2 and F9, and the overall length is 35 inches.

Gibbs Rifle Co.

This Forgett-founded West Virginia company has a good many interesting new products which were formerly manufactured by Parker-Hale, in addition to surplus arms. One of the utility models is the 1300C Scout that is a bit reminiscent of the shortened M1903 Spring-

M1 Super 90 semi-automatic line is the Entry Gun for law enforcement use only. Featuring a 14-inch barrel and 5-round magazine, it has the other features of the regular M1 Super 90 Benelli shotguns with the synthetic pistol grip stock. A new 24-inch E.R. Shaw rifled barrel to be available for the M1 Super 90 shotguns will give this model even more utility. There is also a new Super Black Eagle Custom Slug Gun with custom E.R. Shaw 24-inch rifled barrel.

H&R 1871

In June of 1991, on the 120th anniversary of the founding of Harrington & Richardson, H&R 1871, Inc. purchased the New England Firearms Com-

is also a 10-gauge Topper available under the NEF label, but without the Mossy Oak camouflage, and with a 28-inch Full-choke barrel. Slug shooters haven't been forgotten and the Topper is available with a 24-inch 12-gauge rifled barrel fitted with rifle-type sights.

H&R has not slighted the younger shooters either, and the Topper Classic Youth and Topper Jr. are available in 410, 20- and 28-gauge, and 410 and 20-gauge, respectively. The Classic features an American black walnut stock and forearm with cut checkering, while the Jr. has a hardwood stock without checkering. Both versions have shortened stocks with ventilated rubber recoil pads, and a shortened barrel. The Classic

the 7.62x39mm cartridge. It was based on their small L461 receiver, if the memory is functioning correctly. Apparently it did not sell well, as it soon disappeared from the availability list. Now, Interarms has such a rifle based on the Mini-Mark X Mauser action. With a 20-inch barrel, an overall length of 39¾ inches, and a weight of under 6½ pounds, it would make an ideal "scout" rifle, particularly if fitted with a synthetic stock and a 4x scope. The cartridge is not the 308 Winchester, but it is adequate and has definitely proven itself. For a general utility rifle it would be tough to beat.

Interarms also has the Rossi lever-action carbines chambered for the 357 and 44 Magnum cartridges. These are not long-range cartridges, but the rifles weigh between five and six pounds, with barrel lengths of 16 or 20 inches, depending on the caliber, and they are handy.

The 44 S&W Special cartridge has enjoyed renewed interest since Charter Arms introduced the Bulldog several years ago, and Interarms has a new Rossi so chambered. Tabbed the M720, this new revolver is another handy gun, having a 5-round capacity, 3-inch full ribbed barrel with red

pounds. The magazine is a 10-round detachable box, and the stock is the now-customary thumbhole type.

Kimel Industries

The AP-9 and Mini AP-9 pistols have been around for a few years, but now there's a Target AP-9 pistol with 12-inch barrel and a steel shroud, and the AR-9 9mm Carbine. The barrel lengths on the AP-9 and Mini AP-9 are 5 and 3 inches, respectively. The carbine comes with a barrel length of 16½ inches,

sembles the last of the Savage/Stevens-made break-action single shot shotguns, with the opening lever located at the front of the trigger guard. The outside hammer for manual cocking is there, and so is the automatic ejector when the shotgun is opened.

Barrel lengths range from 25 to 30 inches, depending on the gauge, and chokes are fixed Modified or Full, again depending on the gauge. Available in a choice of 410 or 12-, 16- or 20-gauge, all versions are cham-

Quality Parts/Bushmaster

This firm manufactures semi-automatic versions of the AR-15, and full-auto versions of the M-16. Some of the Bushmaster M16-A2 M4 Carbines saw service with the U.S. military forces during Desert Storm. The E2S Series includes eight different versions, some of which are available only to the military or qualified license holders. In addition, there's the XM15-E2 Target Model that features a 20-inch full diameter

Scattergun Technologies Border Patrol model tactical shotgun for cops has a 14-inch barrel and a 6-round shell capacity. This model is also available with a civilian-legal 18-inch barrel.

insert front sights, rubber combat grips, and a weight of under 28 ounces. There is also a new M515, chambered for the 22 WMR cartridge or the 22 Long Rifle; it has a 4-inch barrel, 6-round capacity and a weight of 30 ounces.

Intratec Firearms

Known for their TEC-9 and TEC-22 in various forms, this firm has the TEC-KOTE finish available on all their arms as an option. This finish is said to be tougher than hard chrome—it is rated at Rockwell C50-53—provides a natural lubricity, and is highly resistant to salt spray corrosion, petroleum distillates, sweat rust, fingerprints, and powder residues; that's providing more utility to any firearm, and is especially desirable for utility arms.

KBI, Inc.

Now that the political scene in the former Iron Curtain countries has changed, we may see some hitherto not-readily-available sporting arms become available. KBI may have the Russian Baikal shotguns available by the time you read this, but they do have the Hungarian SA-85M available now. The SA-85M is a sporterized semi-automatic version of the AKM Kalashnikov rifle as manufactured by FEG of Budapest, Hungary. Featuring a barrel length of just over 16 inches, this rifle has an overall length of just under 35 inches, with an empty weight of 7⅝

steel shroud, and a folding steel stock. Both the pistol and the carbine come with 20-round magazines, although 30-round magazines are available as options, as are flash suppressors and recoil compensators. A lever-type safety is located on the left side of the lower receiver, where it is easily thumb accessible, while a single pin forward of the magazine well permits rapid takedown.

Liberty Arms Works

An assortment of semi-automatic copies of the MAC-10 have been available from a number of companies over the years. One of the latest is the L.A.W. Enforcer. With an overall length of 11 inches and a barrel length of 6¼ inches, the Enforcer tips the scales at an ounce over five pounds, unloaded. Currently available chambered for the 45 ACP cartridge, it uses standard 30-round "grease gun" magazines, and fires from a closed bolt position. A slide-type safety is located on the bottom of the receiver at the right side of the trigger guard. Models chambered for the 9mm and 10mm cartridges are scheduled to be available later.

Magtech

The name may sound new, and so are some of the products, but at least one of them—the Model MT 151—will seem familiar. Manufactured of high-quality ordnance grade steel, with stock and forearm of Brazilian hardwood, the MT 151 re-

bered for 3-inch shells, except the 16 which uses standard length 2¾-inch shells, and is available only with a 28-inch Modified choke barrel. Weights vary from just over five pounds to approximately 6½ pounds, depending on the gauge, barrel length, and stock density. For shooters wanting a knockabout single shot, this bears checking.

Magtech has a repeating 12-gauge, in the form of a pump action tabbed the MT 586P. Constructed of ordnance grade steel with Brazilian hardwood stock and forearm, the 586P features a 19-inch barrel chambered for all 3-inch 12-gauge shells. It has double-action bars, a cross-bolt safety behind the trigger, and an extended magazine tube which will hold eight standard-length 12-gauge shells, or seven 3-inch shells. Solidly constructed, the 586P tips the scales at just over 7¼ pounds.

Magtech offers their version of the excellent Remington bolt-action 22s of yesteryear. With a 21-inch barrel of ordnance steel, as are the receiver and other functioning parts, the MT 122 has a select Brazilian hardwood stock and open sights. The receiver is grooved for tip-off scope mounts, and the action features double extractors, double bolt locking, a red cocking indicator, and a side-lever safety. A six-round detachable box magazine is standard, but a 10-round magazine is available as an option. Weight of the MT 122 is approximately 5¾ pounds.

chrome-lined match barrel having a 1:9 twist of rifling. It's patterned after the Government M-16A2, but with improvements. There is also the Shorty E-2 Carbine, with all the features of the E-2 Target model, less the rear sight system, and having a telescoping buttstock in addition to a choice of 16-inch barrel, or 11.5-inch with 5.5-inch-long permanent suppressor.

The V Match rifle is individually crafted with a choice of 20-, 24-, or 26-inch barrel; a 5-pound trigger let-off; free floating steel handguard; full premium-grade bull barrel with integral flash suppressor; and an upper receiver with the carrying handle removed and a 12-threads-per-screw secured scope mount base installed. Accessories are also available, such as a Harris bipod, scope, laser, etc.

The latest Bushmaster is the E2 Carbine Dissipator. Available with a choice of regular or telescoping buttstock, the Dissipator features a 16-inch match chrome-lined barrel and a full-length M-16A2-style handguard which encloses the lower half of the front sight. The handguard is designed to better dissipate barrel heat by creating a clockwise vacuum moving the heat forward of the front sight before venting. Complete upper receiver assemblies are also available to mount onto regular lower receiver.

Rocky Mountain Arms

This firm produces a series of custom-built pistols and rifles, and modifies others to a customized design. Two of special interest are the Ninja Scout Rifle, which is a specially re-

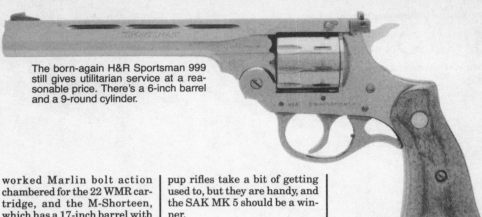

The born-again H&R Sportsman 999 still gives utilitarian service at a reasonable price. There's a 6-inch barrel and a 9-round cylinder.

worked Marlin bolt action chambered for the 22 WMR cartridge, and the M-Shorteen, which has a 17-inch barrel with custom muzzlebrake and front sight, and a hand-honed action. Both rifles have the DuPont Industrial TEFLON-S finish. The Ninja Scout has a 16.5-inch barrel and a special quick takedown system, plus a custom scope mount.

SAK MK 5 Sporting Rifle/Six Enterprises

This "Bullpup" rifle was shown at the '92 SHOT Show, and it should be available by the time you read this. Designed in Australia, and originally intended to be manufactured there, it will be a "Made in America" product, due to the

pup rifles take a bit of getting used to, but they are handy, and the SAK MK 5 should be a winner.

Scattergun Technologies

Shotguns are this firm's business, which is to turn Remington Model 870P Magnum pump actions into practical shotguns or "tactical response" shotguns. There is also one Model 11-87P Magnum autoloader. There are ten models available, based on the 870P receiver, and six of these must be NFA registered, due to having barrel lengths of less than 18 inches; actually the barrel lengths on these short models are either 12.5 or 14 inches, and the magazine capacity ranges from five to seven rounds, depending on the barrel

Stallard Arms/Haskell Mfg.

The semi-automatic blowback 9mm and 45 ACP pistols mentioned last year have been upgraded a bit, and two new versions are available. The trigger guard has been given a bit of a spur at the front as a finger rest, and the stocks have been contoured a bit and have less of the flat-slab shape. The finish is still scratch-resistant black, or nickel, and the barrel length is still 4¾ inches. The two new versions include the JS-40SW chambered for the 40 Smith &

Magtech's MT 151 looks just like the old Savage break-action shotguns. It's to be sold in 410, 20-, 16-, and 12-gauge versions. The slide-action Magtech MT 586P comes only in 12-gauge—there are double-action bars and the 19-inch barrel chambers 3-inch shells.

current problems with foreign-made semi-automatic arms.

It features a one-piece extruded aluminum upper receiver to house the barrel and gas assembly, and a rotating-head bolt assembly similar to the AR 180 design. The lower receiver unit is of glass-filled nylon; it includes the butt, pistol grip, and magazine well. The sights are incorporated into the carrying handle, as is the cocking assembly. A conventional telescopic sight is available as an option.

A 30-round magazine is standard, as is a cross-bolt safety and a barrel length of about 21⅞ inches. Overall length is 31 inches, and the weight without magazine is 8 pounds. Bull-

length, plus a 6-round Side Saddle shell carrier on some models.

Basically, the shotguns are fitted with a new jumbo head safety, new synthetic buttstock and forearm, a new high visibility, non-binding follower, three-way adjustable action sling, and a new set of sights, consisting of a durable ghost ring rear and ramp-type front sight with self-luminous insert. On four of the models—standard, Entry, F.B.I., and Concealment—the forearm contains a pressure-operated high intensity (choice of 5,000 or 11,000 candlepower) flashlight. Other variations include a wooden forearm and pistol grip on the Concealment Model 00, and rubber Pachmayr pistol grip and fore grip on the Concealment Model 02.

Wesson, and the JS-9mm Compact, which will have an inch shorter barrel and one less round in the magazine than the regular JS-9mm, or 7 rounds in place of 8 rounds. The pistols still carry a suggested price tag of under $160. Sights on all versions are fixed and low, making the pistols more of a "point-n-pull" than an "aim-n-shoot" design. The trigger pulls on the pistols examined are heavy, but recoil is not.

Stoeger Arms

Economically priced arms sometimes become more utility oriented than the expensive models, and Stoeger has made some changes in the IGA shotgun line from Brazil. The double trigger side-by-side 12-gauge Uplander is now available with choke tubes in a choice of 26- or 28-inch barrels in ad-

dition to the regular fixed choke models. The ERA 2000 over/under in 12-gauge is also available with choke tubes, as is the 12-gauge over/under Condor I model. Both the ERA 2000 and the Condor I models have a single non-selective trigger, and a choice of 26- or 28-inch barrels. The Reuna single barrel shotgun is available in a choice of 12- or 20-gauge, or 410-bore. One 12-gauge Reuna is available with an interchangeable choke tube, while the other gauges feature fixed chokes. The Reuna has an outside hammer, and the unique method of opening consists of pulling rearward on the trigger guard. Like the majority of the other models by IGA, the Reuna is chambered for 3-inch shells. Hardwood stocks are standard on all IGA shotguns.

Survival Arms

The Armalite AR-7, i.e., Charter Arms AR-7, is now the Survival Arms AR-7. Manufactured in Florida, it is basically the same AR-7 Explorer it has been for a couple of decades. Weighing 2 pounds, 12½ ounces, and available in a choice of three finishes—anti-corrosion black matte, silvertone, and camo—this rimfire rifle has an 8-round magazine. It takes down into two basic units—receiver and barrel assembly—which store, along with the magazine, within the buttstock, and the entire unit floats if dropped overboard.

Winchester

Lever-action rifles have served as utility guns for many years, and Winchester has two new versions of the Model 94—the Wrangler and the Trapper—both with 16-inch barrels and walnut stocks. The Wrangler has a large loop lever and is available in a choice of 30-30 Winchester or 44 Remington Magnum, while the Trapper is available only in 357 Magnum. The finishes are a glossy blue, which is all right, but a matte black would be more suitable for a utility gun. Magazine capacity is nine rounds on the 357 and 44, and five rounds for the time-tested 30-30. According to USRAC, the latest Model 94 actions are even quieter than the older versions, due to closer tolerances on the internal parts, and a new link pin with a set screw to limit lateral travel. The cross-bolt safety also adds to the security of the Model 94, but this was never a rifle known for being accident-prone. ●

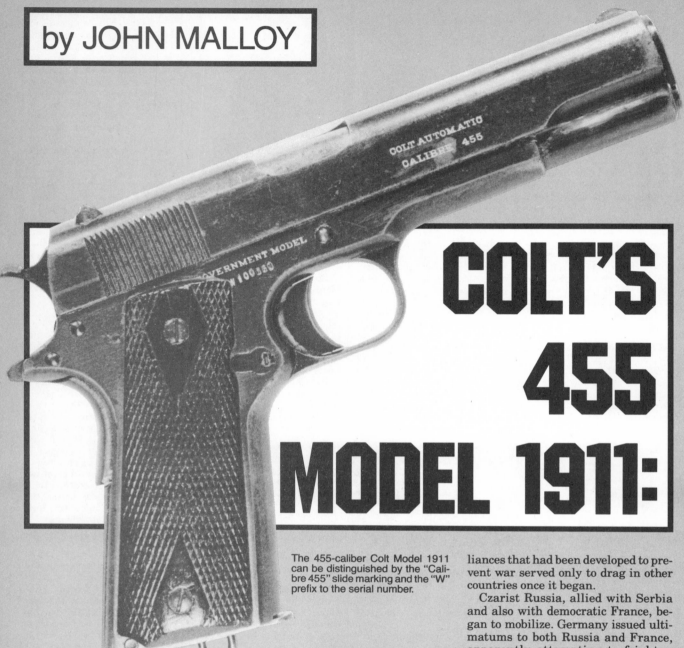

by JOHN MALLOY

COLT'S 455 MODEL 1911:

The 455-caliber Colt Model 1911 can be distinguished by the "Calibre 455" slide marking and the "W" prefix to the serial number.

THE COLT MODEL 1911 is probably the most widely copied pistol ever designed. Outright copies and numerous variations have been made throughout the world.

The traditional caliber has been the original 45 ACP, but variations have been made for a number of calibers down to 22 Long Rifle. Only once has the 1911 design been produced for a cartridge larger than 45. During World War I, Colt manufactured their pistol for the 455 Webley Automatic cartridge.

This self-loading pistol was adopted by Great Britain, giving the British military a substitute standard sidearm actually more reliable than the one it replaced. It was the first caliber variation of Colt's then-new automatic, and turned out to be—by a small margin—the largest caliber for which the 1911 was ever chambered.

With the benefit of hindsight, World War I was almost inevitable. The event that sparked it was the assassination of Archduke Ferdinand of Austria/Hungary by a Serbian. Within a month Austria, supported by Germany, declared war on Serbia. The al-

liances that had been developed to prevent war served only to drag in other countries once it began.

Czarist Russia, allied with Serbia and also with democratic France, began to mobilize. Germany issued ultimatums to both Russia and France, apparently attempting to frighten those countries into a neutral position. This strategy failed, and Germany planned to defeat France before the huge but poorly organized Russian army could be made ready for action. The German army swept into neutral Belgium to attack France.

England was pledged to uphold Belgian neutrality and, at any rate, could not afford to have France's channel ports fall under German domination. British forces went to war against Germany.

The British were poorly prepared for war. The British War Department began programs to increase armament production. One of the actions taken was to arrange for the manufac-

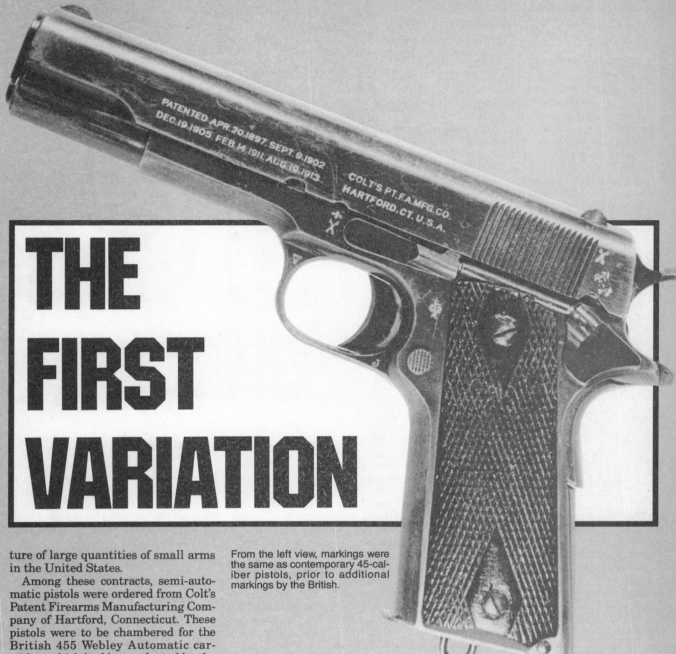

THE FIRST VARIATION

From the left view, markings were the same as contemporary 45-caliber pistols, prior to additional markings by the British.

ture of large quantities of small arms in the United States.

Among these contracts, semi-automatic pistols were ordered from Colt's Patent Firearms Manufacturing Company of Hartford, Connecticut. These pistols were to be chambered for the British 455 Webley Automatic cartridge, which had been adopted by the Royal Navy just a year or so before the outbreak of hostilities.

The United States was officially neutral at that time, but American sympathies were with Britain and France. Under the policy of neutrality, manufacturers could supply arms to any country. However, the British blockade, begun in November, 1914, prevented any great amount of material from going to the Central Powers.

Thus, the pistols were manufactured by Colt and delivered. They saw service in the hands of the Royal Navy and possibly other units. Following the defeat of Germany in November, 1918, they were recalled by the British War

Department. Subsequently reissued to the Royal Air Force in the early 1920s, the 455s remained in British service until after World War II. They were then declared surplus and sold, primarily to American buyers.

The cartridge for which these pistols were chambered is known variously as the 455 Eley, 455 Webley & Scott or 455 Webley Automatic. It has a straight, semi-rimmed case, similar in general dimensions to that of the later 45 ACP. Its blunt, 224-grain bullet at 700 fps was considered an effective man-stopper.

The cartridge was developed much earlier for use in the Webley 1903 self-loading pistol, of which only a few experimental pieces were made. A year or so later, the Webley Model 1904, in caliber 455, did reach production and a small number were sold. This pistol was a real pioneer. If we do not consider the 45-caliber Mars and the 11.35mm Bergmann, which were essentially experimental arms, the Webley 1904 was the first commercial self-loading English pistol and the first large-caliber semi-automatic pistol ever produced anywhere.

Parts of the 455 are the same as those for a 45, but there are a number of small dimensional differences.

The 1904 was beautifully made, but was large, heavy and expensive, and relatively few were sold. Nevertheless, it was one of the first serious attempts to compete with the big-bore stopping power of the revolver. Development continued, with other versions appearing in 1906 and 1909.

By 1912, Webley & Scott had developed what they considered a satisfactory 455 semi-automatic pistol. Opening of the breech was delayed by vertical displacement of the barrel through a system of inclined grooves on the barrel and receiver. The pistol was much lighter and more compact than the 1904. Under the designation "Pistol, Self-Loading, .455, Mark I," it was placed in service in 1913 as the sidearm of the Royal Navy. It was issued to all naval units and to the Royal Marines. The Army retained the 455 Webley revolver. The 1913 pistol, with its 5-inch barrel, weighed a reasonable 39 ounces, and was only 8½ inches long.

However, the precision machining of the inclined tongue-and-groove locking system did not lend itself to relia-ble functioning under adverse conditions. Foreign material such as sand or dirt in the mechanism could put it out of commission. It was thus suitable for service at sea, but not well suited for landing parties. For land use, this questionable functioning made it inferior to the Webley service revolver and the recently adopted pistol of the United States, the 1911 Colt.

The Webley pistol had other drawbacks. The hammer location made cocking difficult. With the shooting hand, the straight angle and protruding grip safety gave the 1913 grip an awkward feel; it did not "point" naturally. The V-type recoil spring under the right grip was a potential source of trouble—if the brittle grip were broken, the spring could be lost, putting the pistol out of service. Nevertheless, under favorable conditions the pistol functioned well, was accurate, and handled a cartridge with good man-stopping characteristics.

By August, 1914, when England entered the war against Germany, fewer than four thousand of these pistols had been made. Webley factories could not increase production of both the Army revolver and the new Navy self-loader; they concentrated on revolver production.

A spur to this decision may have been the fact that, by this time, the new pistol's problem with reliability had begun to show up. During sustained firing, stoppages could be caused just by the powder residue from previous rounds.

The War Department supplemented the Naval pistol supply by obtaining Colt Model 1911 pistols, modified to take the 455 Webley Automatic cartridge. And the choice proved a good one. The Colt pistol was thoroughly reliable, well-suited to handle a large and powerful military cartridge.

Colt introduced the big-bore semi-automatic pistol to the United States in the form of their Model 1905. The cartridge introduced with this pistol was to become known as the 45 Automatic Colt Pistol (45 ACP). The 45 ACP is rimless, slightly shorter and slightly more powerful than the British 455 Webley Automatic round. Still, considering their independent development, the cartridges are surprisingly similar.

Colt's 1905 pistol utilized the Browning double-link locking system that had been introduced with its 38-caliber pistol of 1900. Designed by John M. Browning, locking and unlocking was accomplished by vertical

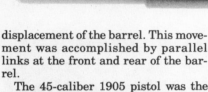

displacement of the barrel. This movement was accomplished by parallel links at the front and rear of the barrel.

The 45-caliber 1905 pistol was the first large-caliber semi-automatic pistol to be commercially manufactured in the United States. With its 5-inch barrel, it was only 8 inches long and weighed about 33 ounces. Light, flat and compact, it was powerful and generally reliable, and stayed in production until replaced by the Model 1911.

The 1905 Colt and the 45 ACP cartridge formed the basis for the 1907 U.S. Army test trials.

These Army trials, which began in 1907 and ended in 1911, were a milestone in the development of the semi-automatic pistol. The end result was the most reliable large-caliber pistol in the world.

The program of tests had been drawn up to determine the type of sidearm best suited to military service. Both revolvers and automatics were subjected to the most extensive testing that had been done to that time. As a result, a 45-caliber revolver was adopted as an interim measure, but field trials continued with Colt and Savage automatics. During these trials, modifications and improvements were made. Both companies submitted redesigned versions for a final series of tests in 1911. John M. Browning made design changes on the new Colt and attended the final tests in person. When the grueling schedule was over, the new Colt had completed the tests, including a six-thousand-round endurance test, without a malfunction. The Colt was adopted on March 29 as "Pistol, Caliber .45, Model 1911."

As adopted, the pistol had a 5-inch barrel and weighed about 38 ounces. The unlocking was still accomplished by downward movement of the barrel, but the barrel had only one link at the rear, with the muzzle supported by a barrel bushing. It had both thumb and grip safeties. For better pointing characteristics, the grip-to-bore angle had been changed from 84 degrees to 74 degrees. The 1911 was offered by Colt to the commercial market, replacing the 1905.

Those Colt 455s issued to the Royal Air Force were handstamped R.A.F. or RAF on the frame forward of the slide release. (Courtesy of Howard J. Nickel)

Probably no other pistol had ever been so thoroughly tested or had such a deserved reputation for reliability. It was the obvious selection for manufacture in 455-caliber when the British began looking for supplementary supplies of pistols.

The similarity in dimensions between the 45 ACP and the 455 Webley Automatic cartridges allowed the Colt 1911 pistol to be readily modified to the British round. In general size and shape, the 455 cartridge resembles the 45 ACP. However, it is semi-rimmed, not rimless. The bullet is blunt and more flattened at the point than that of the 45. The case of the 455 is only slightly longer, but in overall length, the 455 cartridge is actually slightly shorter, due to its flatter bullet. Case body diameters are essentially the same.

In power, the two cartridges were similar. The 455's 224-grain bullet left the muzzle at about 750 feet per second, while the contemporary loading of the 45 used a 230-grain bullet with a muzzle velocity of about 800 feet per second.

The similarity in dimensions and power permitted relatively straightforward production of the 1911 pistol in 455-caliber.

External dimensions remained the same. Visually, the 455 pistol can be distinguished from the 45 only by markings. Legends are generally the same as contemporary commercial 45s, with the exception of the caliber designation "CALIBRE .455" on the right slide and a "W" prefix to the serial number on the right frame. The magazine is marked "CAL .455 ELEY" on its base. Most specimens are found stamped with the broad arrow of the British War Department on

the frame. Those issued to the Royal Air Force have "R.A.F." or "RAF" on the left side of the frame.

That portion of the barrel exposed in the ejection port may be unmarked, or may bear only a proofmark, or the ".455" caliber designation. One observed specimen, however, had this informative legend:

.455″ SL .923
6 GRˢ NPP 10
225″-BULLET

Mechanically, the differences are subtle but are more numerous than might be imagined. Comparison of a 455 pistol with a World War I 45-caliber 1911 revealed these points:

The barrel is the obvious difference, as it must handle the British cartridge. The bore and groove diameters are, respectively, .451-inch and .458-inch, much larger than the corresponding .444-inch and .451-inch of the 45 barrel. The six-groove, left-twist rifling is of the style of the 45. To accommodate the longer case of the 455, the chamber is deeper with less forward shoulder. A groove in the hood allows the cartridge to headspace on the rim. The feed ramp is broader, to accommodate the blunt British bullet.

The barrel is about .005-inch larger in outside diameter, in keeping with its larger bore. Strangely enough, though, the diameter over the chamber is about .005-inch smaller than that of the 45. Another surprise is the width of the link-attachment lug on the underside of the barrel, which is .007-inch smaller than the lug of the 45 barrel. The slide is a close fit to this lug, and a 45 barrel will not go into the 455 slide. These subtle dimensional

larger diameter of the cartridge rim. Thus, a larger magazine-well cut was required in the frame. A 45 magazine will fit loosely in the 455 frame, but a 455 magazine will not go into the 45 frame. The clearance between the frame opening and the widest part of measured magazines turned out to be .012-inch for both the 455 and the 45.

The exact number of 455-caliber

tridge. Correct or not, it is easy to remember. There was some speculation that the serial numbers duplicated numbers assigned to military 45 production. If so, this would place manufacture during late 1914 and 1915. Some authorities, perhaps noting the intriguing similarity of the military serial numbers, have stated that production took place "about 1915." An

Forerunner of the Model 1911, Colt's 1905 pistol introduced the 45 ACP cartridge to America.

Similarity of 45 ACP (left) and 455 Self-Loading cartridges allowed ready modification of the Colt 1911 for the British round.

TABLE 1: Comparison of 455 and 45 ACP cartridges

Cartridge Features	455	45
Case length	.923-inch	.898-inch
Base diameter	.476-inch	.476-inch
Rim diameter	.501-inch	.479-inch
Cartridge length	1.225-inches	1.275-inches
Muzzle velocity	750 fps	810 fps
Bullet weight	224 grs.	230 grs.

idea that the "W" number replaced corresponding numbers in Colt's commercial series production does not seem to be correct.

At any rate, information from British firearms historian Jim Stonley indicates that Colt 455 pistols were in use by British troops by the end of 1916.

Perhaps the most extensive research on the subject for the time was done by Donald F. Bady, author of *Colt Automatic Pistols* (1956, revised 1973). Bady reported that Colt records indicated a total production of 13,510. The first 1500 pistols were reportedly made on Colt commercial frames and numbered within Colt's "C" series, C29001-C30500. (This would indicate production during the year 1916.) After this initial run, the "W" series pistols were shipped, in the range W100001 to about W110700. Thus, the total delivered during the war years would have been about 12,200. Another British contract was supposedly negotiated near the end of the war. If total production of 13,510 is correct, then approximately 1300 pistols may have been delivered from this later contract, probably after the war. Bady

differences may have been planned by Colt to prevent a 45 barrel being installed into a 455 slide when both were assembled concurrently. Of course, 45 barrels were later installed in some surplus 455s; a small amount of file work would probably allow this.

Except for the narrow slot for the barrel lug, the slide exhibits little difference. Either assembled slide will go onto the other frame. The 455 extractor has a different arc because of the larger rim diameter.

The magazine is wider, due to the

Colt 1911 pistols made has not been completely resolved. Likewise, the numbering system used is in some doubt.

For some time, it was thought that all the Colt 455s were in a special serial number range with a "W" prefix, beginning with W100001 and running to about W110000. This indicated a total of about 10,000 pistols produced. The reason for the choice of the "W" prefix is not known. It has been suggested that it represents "Webley," for the developer of the original 455 car-

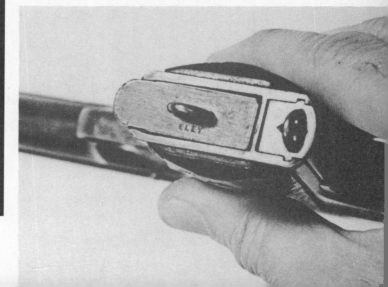

points out that a single pistol in the W124000 range may indicate that the numbers were not continuous with the earlier series, but may have continued after a gap.

The number of postwar pistols may be greater. A collectors' publication recently reported this notation from a Colt shipping book for March/April 1919: "455 Autos 5000 shipped."

As recent collector interest in the 455s increased, other numbers—primarily lower numbers—have come to light. Pistols observed by the writer and reported by collectors include numbers in these series:

W19000
W29000
W40000
W60000-W69000
W71000-W78000
W92000-W99000

Suggestions to account for these lower numbers include early production for trial purposes and early purchase by the British for colonial service. A possibility exists in the later assignment of low numbers to fill gaps in previous series.

At any rate, the dates, the total number and the numbering system of the 1911 455s remain open to some speculation. The subject is of continuing interest to collectors, and information may yet be uncovered that will clear up the uncertainty that still surrounds the numbering of the 455 pistols.

The Webley & Scott 455 Mark I pistol introduced the 455 Self-Loading cartridge into British service in 1913. (Courtesy of Robert C. Blackstone)

Whatever the number, the pistols were ordered to replace the Navy's 1913 Webley and were, logically, used by the Royal Navy. There have been reports that some British and Canadian army units were issued these pistols. While this is possible, it does not seem likely—primarily because of the limited production of the ammunition, which was distributed through naval supply channels. In addition, the Canadians were already using Colt pistols in 45-caliber, and preparations were under way to manufacture 45s under contract in Canada.

There does seem to be documented use of the 455s by the Royal Flying Corps prior to its 1918 reorganization into the Royal Air Force. After World War I, most of the Colt 455s were turned over to the Royal Air Force during the early 1920s, probably beginning in 1923. Most specimens thus have "R.A.F." or "RAF" stamped on the left side of the frame, forward of the slide stop. The stamping was done by hand on a local basis, and may be somewhat irregularly done. No RAF-stamped pistols seem to have been reported in publications with serial numbers under W100000. This may have led to the early idea that numbers began there.

The ammunition for these pistols essentially became obsolete between the

TABLE 2: Comparison of 455 and 45 Pistol Dimensions

Pistol Features	455	45
Barrel:		
Bore diameter	.458-inch	.4515-inch
Groove diameter	.451-inch	.444-inch
Outside diameter	.579-inch	.574-inch
Width over chamber	.683-inch	.688-inch
Width of lug	.355-inch	.362-inch
Slide:		
Inside, at chamber	.725-inch	.731-inch
Frame:		
Magazine well	.573-inch	.559-inch
Magazine:		
Max. width	.561-inch	.547-inch

Magazines for the 1911 455 are stamped "CAL 455" above the lanyard loop and "ELEY" below. The magazine is wider than that of a 45.

wars. Most cartridges in collections are dated as World War I production. Stories have been told that RAF personnel were sometimes issued 45 ACP ammunition to be used in their 455s. The 455 ammunition was actually reintroduced in 1940, but the use of 45 cartridges in the 455 pistols is a real possibility. During the World War II years, the British military had large stores of 45 ACP ammunition acquired for their Thompsons.

The pistols remained in RAF service through the early part of World War II. Stonley reports that they were transferred to Air/Sea Rescue units about 1942. After the war, they were declared surplus, along with large quantities of other British military equipment.

In 1957, the FN Browning 9mm pistol was adopted, and surplus pistols were sold off. The first ad noted that offered the Colt 455s for retail sale was in the March, 1960, *American Rifleman*. The price was $39.95.

When the 455s arrived on these shores, 455 Automatic ammunition was not readily available. To spur sales, some local sellers priced them

lower than 45 Automatics, and ads proclaimed that the 455s "will shoot 45 ACP."

Shooting any cartridge other than the one for which the gun is chambered is not a practice to be generally recommended. The shooter of an old firearm is the custodian of a bit of history and should take care to preserve it. Still, no less an authority than the late Gen. Julian S. Hatcher reported ex-

tensive shooting of 45 ACP ammunition in a 455.

Before considering such a practice, it is wise to examine the relationship of the cartridge to the mechanical parts of the pistol.

The 455 round positions its semi-rim in a groove in the barrel hood to maintain proper headspace. Because the cartridge feeds from the magazine at an angle, there is a large clearance

The 455 cartridge (left) can be approximated by a careful handloader using cases made from 45 Colt, 45 Auto Rim or 451 Detonics brass.

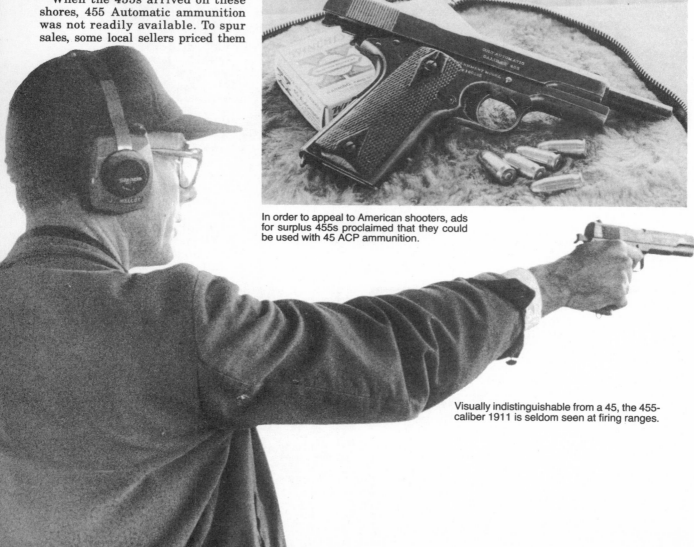

In order to appeal to American shooters, ads for surplus 455s proclaimed that they could be used with 45 ACP ammunition.

Visually indistinguishable from a 45, the 455-caliber 1911 is seldom seen at firing ranges.

between the breech face and the extractor hook. In firing position, the extractor hook is well forward of the semi-rim, making no contact.

When a 45 ACP round is inserted into the 455 chamber, the rimless round slides forward of the hood groove. It would be expected that the shorter case would be held by the extractor against the firing-pin blow, with resulting strain on the hook. However, the case is only .025-inch shorter than that of the 455. In the pistol examined, the clearance between breech face and extractor hook is an even .100-inch, enough to let the 45 cartridge position on the case mouth in the normal manner. The firing pin can easily reach the primer and the case will, of course, move back against the breech face when the cartridge fires. These relationships can be seen from the underside of the assembled slide.

Still, it is something of a surprise to find that 45 ACP cartridges work so well. Both military loads and several varieties of cast-bullet handloads fed and functioned perfectly. Even blunt wadcutters such as Lyman's 452389 and 452309 gave no trouble. The broad feed ramp of the 455 barrel apparently aids the feeding of such bullets.

Accuracy is not particularly good. This is no surprise, considering that the .452-inch bullets are passing through a .458-inch bore, barely riding the tops of the lands. Yet, groups at twenty-five yards proved good enough for informal plinking or emergency short-range defense. "Tipping" of one or more bullets in each five-shot group was evident. Also, three or four shots might form a fairly close group, with the remainder wide. Translated to fifty yards, only three or four shots could be counted on to hit the paper of a conventional fifty-yard bullseye target.

It is possible that erratic ignition may result from different positions—some forward, some rearward—of the cartridges in the chamber. This could add to the detrimental effect of the oversize bore on accuracy.

Accuracy should certainly be better using original 455 cartridges. However, such rounds are now collector's items. Most specimens observed date back to World War I and might not even fire.

It is possible to make ammunition that is close to the original specifications. Modern 45 Colt and 45 Auto-Rim cases can be converted to the semi-rimmed configuration of the 455. In each case, the rim must be turned to .500-inch diameter and an extractor groove cut. Readily done on a lathe, it

can also be accomplished in the ordinary home workshop. Inserting a 45-caliber jacketed bullet into a case will keep the walls from collapsing, and it can be chucked into a ½-inch drill. Carefully filing with a three-cornered file while turning the case will allow thinning the rim and cutting the groove.

The 45 Colt case will be too long and must be trimmed to .923-inch. The 45 Auto-Rim case will be slightly too short, but will headspace on the semi-rim.

Loading is easily accomplished with 45 ACP dies. Among common shellholders, one made for the 45 Colt will be a bit loose but will work.

Another possibility is the use of 451 Detonics Magnum cases. These cases, obtained from Detonics Manufacturing Corporation of Bellevue, WA, are of the general dimensions of the 45 ACP, but are .94-inch long. They can be easily trimmed and used without further modification. Although not semi-rimmed, the case will headspace on the mouth for firing, and will feed and extract reliably. A 45 ACP shellholder can be used, and the cartridge will function through either 455 or 45 magazines.

It is difficult to obtain bullets of the proper diameter. I was fortunate to have access to a mould that cast semi-wadcutter bullets at .457-inch diameter. These bullets were lubricated by hand and used as cast for reloading the modified cases. Groups were noticeably improved. Hollow-base bullets should work well, but a single test with Lyman's 450229 was disappointing.

However, with some experimentation, it should be possible for a careful handloader to produce ammunition that will give excellent accuracy in the Colt 455. Being realistic, though, the exercise is probably academic.

The Colt 1911 455 is a collector's item of some historical interest. Most existing specimens will never be shot, and if they are in mint condition, they probably ought not to be. As with any other collectible firearm, wear and tear will detract from the value. For those owners who just want a few shots to try out a less-than-perfect specimen, 45 ACP cartridges will work well enough.

Considering that their history of production is still indefinite, it is even more difficult to speculate on how many Colt 455s remain in existence. Certainly an appreciable number must have been lost in service during the two World Wars.

Model 1911 455s are occasionally seen at gun shows and in collection

displays. Should you get a chance to examine one, you will be looking at an interesting and seldom-recognized pistol. Produced because of wartime need, it has the distinction of being both the first caliber variation and the largest caliber variation of the Colt Model 1911 series.   ●

SELECTED BIBLIOGRAPHY

Bady, Donald F. *Colt Automatic Pistols*. Alhambra, CA: Bordon, 1973.

Ezell, Edward C. *Handguns of the World*. Harrisburg, PA: Stackpole, 1981.

Goodman, Roy G. "The .455 Webley & Scott Pistol." *American Rifleman*, Vol. 110, No. 5 (May, 1962), pp. 40-43.

Hatcher, Julian S. *Hatcher's Notebook*. Harrisburg, PA: Stackpole, 1962.

Hill, Bob. "Webley's Amazing Autos." *Guns & Ammo*, Vol. 18, No. 3 (March, 1974), pp. 26-29, 82.

Remling, John. "The Webley & Scott .455 Auto Pistol." *Guns*, Vol. XIX, No. 3-6 (June, 1973), pp. 37-39, 64-67.

Smith, W.H.B. and Joseph E. Smith. *Book of Pistols and Revolvers*. Harrisburg, PA: Stackpole, 1968.

Stonley, Jim. "The .455 Automatic Pistol in the British Services, Part One—The Webley .455 Automatic." *Guns Review*, Dec. 1978, pp. 728-732.

Stonley, Jim. "The .455 Automatic Pistol in the British Services, Part Two—Ammunition Troubles and Colt Automatic Purchases." *Guns Review*, Jan. 1979, pp. 20-24.

Stonley, Jim. "The .455 Automatic Pistol in the British Services, Part Three—The Colt .455 Automatic." *Guns Review*, Feb. 1979, pp. 90-92.

Stonley, Jim. "Observed/Reported 'W' Prefix .455 Colt Auto Pistols.": *Auto Mag*, Vol. XIX, Issue 5 (Aug, 1986), p. 105.

Stonley, Jim. ".455 Automatic Pistols in World War I—British Government Contracts." *Guns Review*, March, 1987, pp. 188-190.

Williams, Mason. "Collecting 45s." *Shooting Times*, Vol. 7, No. 4 (April, 1966), pp. 24-29.

Wilson, R.K. *Textbook of Automatic Pistols*. Plantersville, SC: Small Arms Technical Publishing Co., 1943.

Wilson, R.L. *The Colt Heritage*. New York: Simon & Schuster, 1979.

Wood, J.B. "Webley Automatic Pistols." *Shooting Times*, Vol. 10, No. 1 (January, 1969), pp. 44-47, 53-54.

J.I. GALAN REPORTS ON ▸◂ ◂▸ ◂▸ ◂▸ ◂▸ ◂▸ ◂▸ ◂▸

Marksman's #1790 Biathlon Trainer is trim, accurate and affordable.

The Crosman SSP 250 boasts a choice of three different caliber barrels and other features well under $100.

This Chinese-made spring-piston air rifle has a folding stock, credible power and accuracy—retailing for $80.

For quick-shooting combat-style plinking fun, the Daisy Model 45 is a top choice.

(Left) Author puts the Daisy Power Line 920 in 22 through its paces. It's a hard-hitting multi-pump pneumatic with a hardwood stock.

Retailing for around $190, the RWS-Gamo Compact is an outstanding value in a match-grade pellet pistol.

TRADITIONAL AFFORDABLE AIR GUNS

ADULT AIRGUNS come in all types and, quite often, with price tags that can do some serious damage even to an affluent man's wallet. During the last few years the prices of many adult airguns have soared to levels literally unthinkable as recently as a decade ago.

Inflation and other economic factors surely have played a part in this drastic escalation in prices; however, a great deal of the blame must go to the super-sophisticated technology that has in some cases taken over entire segments of the airgun industry. This is particularly true in the area of pre-charged pneumatic guns from England, although a similar situation also applies to most world-class match airguns produced in Germany, which retail for shockingly steep figures.

Just perusing current issues of airgun-related publications, as well as the latest catalogs dealing with many super high-tech airguns from overseas, will give you a clear idea of how much you can expect to pay for really fancy pellet blasters. In the area of British pre-charged pneumatic rifles, for instance, even the most basic model can set you back around $900. And that's without any accessories and/or sights, since most of these pre-charged pneumatics are intended for use with telesights only. The more refined models among the pre-charged genre usually retail for close to $2000, again without any accessories and devoid of sights. By the time you throw in the cost of a good scope sight, air tank, regulator, special charging connector, etc., your bankroll can be rather thin before the first shot is fired.

World-class match airguns from Germany can also punch big holes in checking accounts. Most of these super-accurate, totally recoilless air rifles and air pistols start in the $900 price range also and can run to more than $1,600. Of course, at those price levels you are dealing with impeccable workmanship throughout, as well as Olympic-grade performance, so you generally get the absolute crème de la crème.

All the foregoing looks and sounds impressive— in a scary sort of way— particularly to many newcomers to airgunning. I've had folks comment that it is becoming increasingly difficult to own a "decent" adult airgun in these tough economic times, given the ever-increasing variety of high-priced models available out there. Such a gloomy view of the situation is a bit myopic and ignores the basic fact that you do not have to put mama and the kids on the auction block in order to own an adult airgun of really good quality that will deliver respectable performance.

A large part of the problem is that too many people have forgotten the basic fact that airguns were traditionally supposed to be fun, just reliable and affordable recreational shooting instruments. It seems now many shooters' appreciation of the lower-priced end of the airgun market has been eroded by the barrage of advertising hype extolling the wonders of those expensive high-tech airguns.

I absolutely love to shoot those super-refined, pricey airguns, just like I would love to drive a Rolls Royce or a Ferrari. Top shelf airguns are nothing short of amazing in their sheer beauty and performance. However, I also have a tremendous appreciation for, and derive a great deal of pleasure from, an extensive variety of the more traditional and sometimes fairly inexpensive airguns that are being produced currently. And I am not talking about smooth-bored BB guns. All major American manufacturers of airguns offer comprehensive selections of pellet rifles and pistols that are state-of-the-art when it comes to delivering the most fun for the least possible cash outlay.

Let's say you are looking for a quick-shooting 177 pellet pistol for plinking and informal practice. Well, for less than $60 you can choose either the new Crosman 1008 Repeat Air or the Daisy Power Line 45. The former is an almost exact copy of the 10mm Smith & Wesson selfloader adopted by the FBI, while the latter is a spittin' image of the legendary 45 ACP Colt Government Model. Both guns are powered by a 12-gram CO_2 cartridge, have rifled barrels and produce a MV of 400 fps. The Crosman 1008 carries a straight magazine with capacity for thirteen pellets.

If you prefer a wheelgun instead, those same companies offer outstanding models in 177 caliber that also retail for under $60. The Crosman 357 is a close copy of the sleek Colt Python and is available in different barrel lengths and with six- or ten-shot cylinders. Daisy's Power Line 44 is a stunning look-alike of the big 44 Magnum S&W Model 29 and takes a six-shot pellet cylinder. Again, both models are powered by CO_2 and have a MV of 400 fps or so.

All of these repeaters have common denominators: good value, good performance and lots of fun.

There are quite a few single shot pellet pistols and rifles suitable for paper-punching practice—and sometimes even 10-meter matches—that retail in the $60 to $275 price range. One favorite of mine is the Marksman #1790 Biathlon Trainer, a trim spring-piston barrel-cocking rifle that comes complete with skeletonized stock and match-style diopter sight. For more formal 10-meter events, Daisy offers two outstanding single-pump pneumatic rifles, the Model 853 and the Model 753. Both have Lothar Walther barrels with muzzle weights, full-size wooden stocks and diopter sights. The entry-level Model 853 retails for around $190, while the heavier and somewhat more sophisticated Model 753 goes for $275 or so, which is still far more affordable than $1000-plus for a world-class match air rifle.

In the area of single shot multi-pump pneumatics, American manufacturers also offer quite an array selling for around $100, both rifles and pistols. The Benjamin Air Rifle Co. has the powerful Benjamin/Sheridan Models H and HB pistols in 177-, 20- and 22-caliber, while Crosman has the punchy Models 1377 and 1322 in 177- and 22-caliber, respectively. Hard-hitting and eminently accurate single shot CO_2 pistols are also available from both companies for under $100;

the series E and EB from Benjamin and the SSP 250 from Crosman. Benjamin and Sheridan air rifles are classics in the field of multi-pump pneumatics and currently retail in the $120 to $150 range, depending upon finish grade and sight options.

Crosman and Daisy also offer state-of-the-art multi-pump pneumatic rifles. The Crosman 2100 Classic and 2200 Magnum are superb, while the Daisy Power Line series includes the outstanding 880—which has just celebrated its 20th year in production—and the Models 860, 922, 920 and 970, differing mainly in caliber and stock.

There is a widely held misconcep-

tion that most European adult airguns are prohibitively expensive. Not so at all if you look in the right places. Dynamit Nobel-RWS, Inc., for example, imports a large selection of Diana spring-piston rifles and pistols from Germany, many of which are indeed budget oriented, retailing for up to $250. This lineup includes some magnum-class rifles like the Models 34 and 45, both of which develop a sizzling 1000 fps of MV in 177 caliber and can give a lifetime and more of dependable service with routine maintenance.

Even more affordable is the El Gamo line of adult airguns imported from Spain by Dynamit Nobel-RWS. The new RWS Gamo Hunter 440, for instance, retails for around $205 and can produce up to 1000 fps of muzzle velocity. Other more sedate models from the RWS-Gamo lineup include the underlever-cocking CF-20 at around $190 and the new XP-2000, a barrel cocker, for under $140. In the pistol department, the RWS-Gamo PR-45 and Compact are hard to beat for value in single-pump pneumatics. The Compact is certainly good enough to enter formal 10-meter pistol matches, yet retails for only around $190. One new RWS-Gamo single-stroke pneumatic that is a ton of fun is the AF-10, which can be used as a 15-shot repeater using 4.5mm lead BBs, or as a single shot pellet model. It has a rifled barrel and can produce 430 fps of muzzle velocity. In the spring-piston class, the RWS Gamo Falcon is a super bargain at a suggested retail price of less than $110.

Beeman Precision Arms has always been an importer of some of the top names in European airguns. This company, however, also offers some budget-priced spring-piston rifles and pistols that are long on quality and performance. The Beeman HW30, HW50 and FX-1 rifles, for example, retail for under $200 and have many features found in higher-priced air rifles.

The foregoing, of necessity, has covered only a limited number of the more traditional, budget-oriented airguns, but by now I think that you get the idea. It is not necessary to spend a small fortune in order to enjoy airgun shooting to the fullest. Although there is definitely a place for those top-dollar airguns with fancy propulsion systems and thingamajigs that can consistently shave the whiskers off a mouse at 40 yards, there is also a solid niche for the meat-and-potatoes airguns. In the great majority of cases, the latter perform well enough to give us our money's worth, particularly when the name of the game is uncomplicated shooting fun, pure and simple. ●

The Crosman 357-Eight works as a training gun and a backyard fun gun.

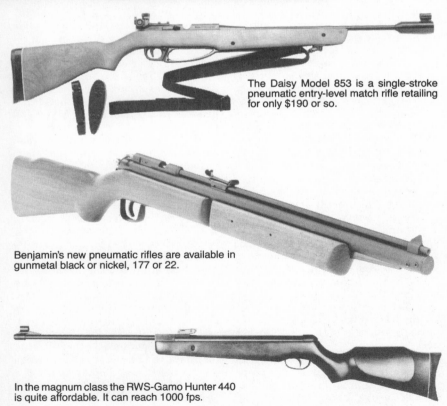

The Daisy Model 853 is a single-stroke pneumatic entry-level match rifle retailing for only $190 or so.

Benjamin's new pneumatic rifles are available in gunmetal black or nickel, 177 or 22.

In the magnum class the RWS-Gamo Hunter 440 is quite affordable. It can reach 1000 fps.

Why Winchester® Engineers Spend Countless Days And Nights Making Something That Will Only Last A Millisecond.

Consistency. That's what it all boils down to. There isn't anything more important when it comes to designing high-quality components.

Primers with superior ignition.

Our engineers know when a bullet comes rifling through the barrel between two and three times the speed of sound, everything's got to perform just right. The brass, the powder, the primer, the bullet, everything. Our engineers also

Shot made the old-fashioned way.

Rifle, shotshell and pistol powders.

Wads that reduce shot deformation.

know if you're going to spend countless hours in the basement reloading shells, they should make sure our components work absolutely perfect. But you won't know just how good they are until you sit down at your workbench and start loading them. You'll be putting 125 years of Winchester know-how into a load that'll be gone in a flash.

The broadest range of cases.

WINCHESTER®
Components Division.

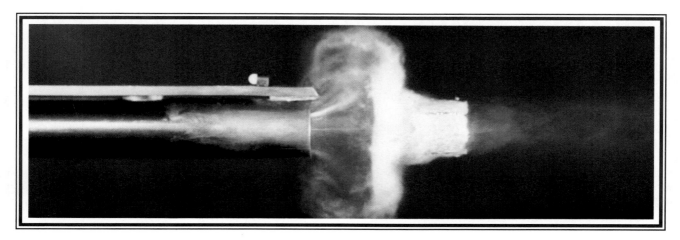

THE SIG SAUER P 226...
Full-Time Safety, Impressive Firepower

Firepower? When your situation demands maximum firepower, the Sig Sauer P 226 will always deliver. Developed specifically for today's law enforcement officer, the Sig Sauer P 226 can deliver 16, 9mm rounds (21 optional) rapid-fire at outstanding accuracy. Adjustable high-contrast sights provide easy target acquisition even when visibility is diminished.

Safe...Always! The unique multiple internal safety and decocking feature make the P 226 the safest gun you can carry under *any* conditions. The loaded and decocked weapon puts the hammer in register with the safety intercept notch, so firing is possible only when the trigger is pulled.

It is the perfect transitional weapon from revolver to semi-automatic. Now being carried by many elite law enforcement agencies in the U.S. and Europe, it has proven itself to be the most efficient, safe and reliable handgun in the world.

Contact us today for the name of your nearest Sigarms dealer. He's anxious to show you the safest ...and most effective gun you can carry.

SIGARMS

SIGARMS, Inc.,
Industrial Drive,
Exeter, NH 03833

THE SIG SAUER P 226...YOUR TACTICAL EDGE!

Leather goods courtesy of Don Hume, Inc.

A Double Gun Odyssey

by ALLAN H. PRESSLEY

The American Arms, Inc., Gentry is typical of medium-priced doubles now on the U.S. market.

I WAS BORN IN 1940 to a father from a farming and hunting family. When I was five, my father started me shooting a 22 rimfire, supporting it over the branch of a small tree. I became a confirmed gun lover.

When I was ten, a friend loaned me his old *Rifleman* magazines to read. I read *Gun Digest,* Stoeger's catalogs, and anything else I could find about guns. I went crazy over the J.P. Sauer doubles that were in the Stoeger catalogs because they had such neat engraving. In 1955, when I was 15, I became a double gun enthusiast because they seemed so much more practical and elegant than other shotguns. I based this on two seasons of hunting with various borrowed shotguns. My hunting experiences since have confirmed this and I remain a confirmed double gun lover. My *Webster's* defines an odyssey as a long wandering or series of travels, and that's what my life with double guns has been.

Nobody I knew as a kid shot formal trap or Skeet or even clays from hand traps. If you mentioned patterning a shotgun, a look of dull stupidity came into their eyes. Every double I saw had 30-inch barrels and was choked Full and Modified. All the automatics, pumps, and singles were invariably Full choked and had 30-inch barrels.

When I would mention that I wanted a double with 26-inch barrels choked Modified and Improved Cylinder, people always said, "It won't be any good for ducks." None of these people ever hunted ducks and, I realized years later, none knew a damn thing about duck hunting.

I bought a used Stoeger Zephyr Model 4E double in 1955. Yes, it had 30-inch barrels and was choked Modified and Full, but that was all I could find that I could afford. The local dime-wielding pundits confirmed the chokes for me! This was the nicest shotgun I could find and I remember paying $80 for it. It was a well-made Spanish sidelock with ejectors and did not have the cheap and crappy engraving so many cheap Spanish doubles had and still have. This gun is shown on page 26 of the 1955 Stoeger catalog. I used it for two seasons with little success. I read John Maynard's "A Shotgun Is a Paintbrush" in the 1957 GUN DIGEST but didn't know much about lead before that. All I knew was that you were supposed to shoot in front of the game. I remember patterning the gun, which my father thought was a waste of time, and I was surprised at how small the patterns were at my typical shooting range.

In 1957 I absolutely had to have a

Winchester Model 52 to shoot small-bore target, so I had to trade the 4E in on a Model 52. In 1958, I found an Ithaca double at the local hardware store for $40, and I bought it—30-inch barrels choked Modified and Full, or so I thought. Years later I found out it was a Flues model made in 1920. Remember, back then, there were almost no gun stores and hardware stores were the only source of guns and ammo in a small town. I didn't do much hunting with this gun, as I went to college in the fall of 1958, and the time needed to get a B.S. in Mechanical Engineering and to search for the wily female took all of my time.

After college I went into the Army and was sent to Germany, where I had asked to go. My CO shot Skeet and had a Browning Superposed Skeet gun. Shooting with him, I learned to lead properly and was able to break 18 out of 25 after a few sessions. The Heidelberg Rod and Gun Club (for U.S. military personnel) charged absurdly low prices for a round of Skeet. We could also get almost any gun for a substantial discount through the Rod and Gun Club. A Browning Superposed was $238 but I only made $355 as a Second Lieutenant. I sold my Ithaca to my Uncle for $40 (I had left it at home) and applied this money to a new gun.

I decided to buy a J.P. Sauer. I could get the plain model, called the Model KIM for $107 or the Model Royal for $157 at the Ramstein Rod and Gun Club. I was going to get a 20-gauge but my CO recommended a 12-gauge. When I looked at them, I found that the 12-gauge KIM and the 20-gauge Royal both weighed the same, around 6-6½ pounds. These were the first light shotguns I ever held. I finally decided to get the 12, but I always regretted not buying the 20. The Royal had double underbolts and a Greener cross bolt and ejectors. The KIM deleted the Greener cross bolt and the ejectors. Both were Anson and Deeley boxlocks. All they had at the Rod and Gun Club were 28-inch guns bored Full and Half. I asked the clerk to look into a gun with 26-inch barrels bored Modified and Improved Cylinder. He found out that Sauer had an agreement with Stoeger to sell 26-inch guns only to Stoeger. I ordered a 28-inch-barreled gun bored Modified and Improved cylinder which had to be special-ordered. When it came, it had a card stating that the right barrel shot 46 percent patterns and the left barrel shot 69 percent patterns in a 30-inch circle at 40 yards using 3.5mm shot. This is 0.138-

inch or equivalent to our #3 shot.

I was a bit disappointed in this; I thought it was awfully tight for both chokes. In later years, I decided that this was the best choke combination for a double if you could only afford one gun. I will discuss later how you can adjust patterns by using different loads and spreader loads. I tried the gun at Skeet but could not do well with it because of the tight chokes. When I returned home, I went hunting with my father-in-law and shot two pheasants the first day. I found out that my father-in-law's Winchester Model 12 had a Modified choke and 28-inch barrel. He said that a Full choke was too tight. He was the only person back then who seemed to have that opinion other than myself and some gun writers.

Then I took a job in Corning, New York, and rapidly found out that the only game birds around that area were ruffed grouse. There were no pheasants to speak of, no quail, and doves were protected. Since I had never hunted waterfowl I didn't think of them. Of necessity, I became a grouse hunter. The grouse season started in early October and ran continuously through January and sometimes February, and you could hunt on Sundays. I hunted almost every Saturday and Sunday through the season. Since my wife had been properly raised by her father and a much older brother who were ardent hunters and fishermen, she thought this was normal behavior.

I did not hit a grouse for two years with the Sauer and knew that my chokes were too tight. I could not afford another double, and I didn't want to get the chokes of the Sauer reamed out. I'm not sure if I even knew that you could have them reamed out back then. An article appeared in the 1966 GUN DIGEST titled "Put and Take Choke" by Francis Sell, who I now regard as one of the best gun writers ever. In the article he discussed how to load spreader loads, using two over shot wads (thin cardboard wads about 0.050-inch thick) to break up the shot column into thirds. I immediately bought some wads and loaded some of these spreader loads, using 3 dram 1⅛-ounce load data with #7½ shot. I patterned them and got between 30 and 35 percent patterns with the right barrel, and 45 percent patterns with the left barrel. The pattern with the right barrel was really big and fairly even. I started hitting grouse and have consistently killed one-third of the grouse I have shot at ever since with that gun and load. Remember, most of the ruffed grouse you shoot at in the Northeast are flushed in thick brush and you have to shoot at them through trees and thick bushes. Perhaps only two percent of the shots you get will be in the clear.

In 1969, Francis Sell wrote an article for *GUNfacts* magazine in which he discussed the fact that pattern densities could be varied by shot size and velocity. The article said that high velocity loads spread more than low velocity loads, and that larger shot patterned tighter than smaller shot. I found this to be true on shooting patterns, and realized that I could make my Sauer shoot anywhere between 30 and 45 percent in the right barrel and between 45 and 75 percent in the left barrel, depending on the loading. Interestingly, I got the tightest patterns with cheap Sears Sport Load shotshells with no shot protectors. This is a phenomenon I saw later on with another gun.

The Sauer had sling swivels on it, and I had bought a German sling to go with it. I found that a sling on a shotgun is incredibly useful. If you are just walking along, and you want to carry the gun easily but be able to shoot fast, use the German sling carry. The gun is slung muzzle down over your left shoulder, bottom forward with your left hand on the forend. This way you can bring the gun up in one smooth, fast motion very quickly. If you need to climb up a steep slope you can sling the gun over your back and climb using both hands. I removed the original swivel bows and drilled them out to accept Jaeger quick-detachable sling swivels. In heavy cover I can take the sling off and put it in my pocket.

In 1969, I started hunting ducks on the Finger Lakes with the Sauer and found it useful for shooting over decoys. The quick handling of the light well-balanced double was very useful in the blind, and my chokes seemed to be just right for any normal shot. I found the sling useful even in this type of hunting. Over the years when I hunt with somebody new, they first laugh when they see a sling on my shotgun. Later, they always show up with a sling on their gun. I strongly recommend a sling on a shotgun for any type of hunting.

I found some loading data for 2¾-dram 1¼-ounce loads and tried them with #9 shot in a spreader load for grouse. This gave me 730 shot in the load, a huge cloud of shot. I finally stopped using it for two reasons. First, grouse hit with it did not seem to go down. Second, I found out by accident that this load had a very severe trajectory. Also, I did not like using 1¼-

With a Sauer named KIM and a dog named Honey, the author scored on grouse in the '70s.

ounce of shot in such a light gun, even though it was only 2¾ dram. I reverted back to my 3 dram-1⅛-#7½ spreader load for grouse.

When I noticed that separate wads were disappearing, I started buying all the wads I could find. They have all gone off the dealers' shelves now. Luckily, I discovered Ballistic Products, Inc., of Long Lake, MN, a few years ago. They have these components for sale if I need more.

In 1969, I acquired a small collection of doubles. In it was an Ithaca #1 NID with a very large aluminum front bead and a small gold center bead. I liked this combination so much that I converted the Sauer to it. Also in the collection were a Syracuse Lefever 16-gauge Durston Special, an L.C. Smith Ideal FWE 12-gauge, and an Ansley Fox A grade 12-gauge.

The Fox had been restocked and

looked good, but the collector value had been ruined. It was an early gun, made in 1908. I decided to make it my duck gun, shooting a heavier shot charge than the 1⅛-ounce charge I had been using in the Sauer. The Fox weighed 8 pounds with 30-inch barrels, but it came up very well because it was so well balanced. The safety did not work properly, and when I took the stock off, I found that the angle at the recoil shoulders was wrong. When everything was tightened up, the stock pulled up against the recoil shoulders and the tang bent, binding the safety. I glass-bedded the end of the stock at the shoulders, just pushing it up against the tang to register it. Then I had to glass-bed the lower tang, and this cured the problem. There is a barely noticeable line of glass-bedding at the recoil shoulders.

I put the two beads and sling swivels on it, and used it for ducks for the next fifteen years with 1½-ounce 2¾-inch magnum shells. I patterned it and found that the right barrel shot from 40 percent with spreaders to 65 percent with 2¾ magnum 2s. The left barrel shot from 60 percent with high brass 6s to 70 percent with 2¾-inch magnum 2s and 4s in modern shot-protected loads.

For duck hunting over decoys, I used high brass 6s in the right barrel for a 50 percent pattern and magnum 4s in the left barrel for a 70 percent pattern. I patterned the left barrel at 45, 50, 55, and 60 yards and learned that I could not kill a duck at over 55 yards, confirming what H.B. Salisbury wrote in "Duck Guns, Loads, and Chokes" in the 5th edition of the GUN DIGEST! This article is highly recommended reading. Experimenting with the decoys, I found that I could just see their beaks at 55 yards, which gave a good ranging reference.

My father-in-law gave me some old Remington and Winchester paper high brass 4 shotshells. These gave beautiful, even, 75 percent patterns out of the left barrel of the Fox, better performance than modern plastic shells with shot cups and buffering material. This gun seems to have extremely thick barrels over the chambers and is somewhat over-bored with the barrels measuring 0.737- and 0.736-inch in diameter. I never tried loading shells to get tighter than 70 percent patterns because I did not think I was a good enough shot and, since the factory buffered loads did not do any better, considered it a waste of time.

Patterning a shotgun is a lot of work. When I read about the Hyde Sport Shop's "Expert Range and Patterning Gauge" I sent for one. It works on the proposal that a specific pattern percentage at 40 yards will have a specific pattern outside diameter at 40 yards and a specific pattern outside diameter at 30 feet. You shoot a pattern at 30 feet and then use a clear plastic overlay to interpret the pattern. The pattern will always be less than 19 inches diameter. A 50-yard slow fire pistol target is 21 inches wide and is just right. This process seems to work okay and is a lot easier to use than shooting patterns at 40 yards, drawing a 30-inch circle and counting the shot holes. When mine finally breaks up I will get some drafting mylar and draw a new one.

In the early '70s, I decided I needed a lighter grouse gun. If the gun came up faster, more grouse would fall, or so went the theory. A Zoli 28-gauge double bored Cylinder and Improved Cylinder showed up at a local gun show. It had 26-inch barrels, weighed 5 pounds, and was a perfect fit with a very short, very straight stock. It shot patterns as marked. It seemed to be the perfect grouse gun. I shot one grouse with it that went up in the open, about five yards away. It got up about three feet in the air when I hit it and fell ten yards away. It had the wad stuck in its breast. This was the answer!

However, after shooting at a number of grouse with this gun, I just didn't seem to be dropping them. After checking the patterns again, I concluded that the ⅞-ounce load was too thin and went back to my faithful Sauer with 3-1⅛-7½ spreader loads. It appeared to be more effective than the 28-gauge even though it took longer to get up. Someday, with the right equipment, I will have to do some experiments with various guns to see what effect gun weight, barrel length, and balance have to do with gun mounting time.

Around this time, I made friends with a local farmer who was also a toolmaker. He had a large collection of good American doubles and he hunted with all of them. We discovered that all of them balanced at 4½ inches in front of the front trigger, no matter what the gun weights or barrel lengths were, or where the hinge pin was located. We concluded that the various makers must have used different densities of wood for the different barrel lengths and weights. I don't see how they could have achieved the balance just by filing the barrels or stock on series production guns. The hinge pins may vary in position but the balance always seems to stay at 4½ inches in front of the front trigger. There is an interesting series of letters on this subject in *GUNfacts* magazine #5, pages 16-17. My friend was a careful and meticulous workman and took all his guns apart to study them. He believed that his Remington doubles were the best made, but he liked the design of the Fox best of all.

At this time I became interested in double-barreled shotgun design. I wrote the NRA and they recommended *The Gun and Its Development* by Greener. I obtained a copy and read it avidly. It was very impressive that this man knew so much about doubles so long ago. As a mechanical engineer I realized that the bolting of an extended rib gun with a bolt engaging the extended rib, such as a Fox or L.C. Smith or a Greener, is far superior to underlug bolting. The moment arm from the hinge pin to the extended rib bolt is about twice as far as the moment arm to a rear underlug. This means that the force on extended rib bolting is half of what it is on a rear underbolt. I particularly like the rotary bolt on the L.C. Smith and Fox. I believe it may achieve the best metal-to-metal contact, without the expensive hand fitting of a best quality handmade gun. Any design is a mass of compromises, but based on what I know, the Ansley Fox design seems to be the best compromise in the field of double gun design. Since nobody has published a book on the Ansley Fox gun at the time of writing, they don't have the recognition that other makes have gotten which have had books published about them.

I realize that many high-grade guns get by on double underlug bolting, but this is because the quality of expensive fitting achieves better contact between the lugs and the bolt. The Winchester Model 21 gets by because the water table is so long and this increases the moment arm between the hinge pin and the bolt. Also, better materials may contribute. However, all things being equal, the extended rib bolting has to be the best. It would be interesting to have a Finite Element Analysis done on the various designs to see how the stresses compare, but that would be expensive.

I sold the L.C. Smith to my friend. Some buffoon had put a recoil pad on it at an extreme angle and it had ferocious down pitch and was unshootable. What a shame that was, it was such a nice gun. At the time, I couldn't afford to have it restocked and I did not think my stocking skills were up to it. This gun had 28-inch barrels and weighed 6½ pounds. It seemed to be choked Modified in both barrels. This doesn't make sense to me—one of the major advantages of a double, in my opinion, is to have two different chokes.

I decided that I needed another double for rough duck hunting when it was raining or when my partner and I floated one of the small rivers in our area. My uncle mentioned that my old Ithaca was getting too heavy for him to carry, (he was well over 70!) and the stock was loose. I gave him the 6½-pound Lefever and took the Ithaca back that I had sold him 10 years before. I found that the wood in the front of the stock was severely degraded from oil soaking. Years before, I learned to store my guns muzzle down for three days after cleaning to let excess oil drain out. I told my uncle to do the same with the Lefever.

After many hours of work, the inside of the front of the Ithaca stock is solid fiberglass with just a thin shell of wood on the outside. The wood was so oil soaked at the front that I could not get epoxy to adhere to the wood to seal two cracks together. I broke off the pieces of wood and cut small flared cavities as a dentist would for a cavity in a tooth, and then worked epoxy into the cavities and put the pieces back on. This is a mechanical attachment rather than an adhesive bond. It doesn't look too bad, only like a cracked stock, but nothing is showing on the surface other than the cracks. The repair has held up through the years and is still solid. I hollowed out the rest of the stock bit by bit and glass bedded it to replace the rotten wood.

I used this gun for rough duck hunting but it is such a clumsy gun. It weighs 8 pounds, has 30-inch barrels, and balances 5½ inches in front of the front trigger. It's almost as bad as a pump or automatic. The Fox and the Ithaca weigh exactly the same on my scale, 8 pounds, have the same length of pull, and the same barrel length of 30 inches, and therefore the same overall length. However, the balance point on the Fox is one inch farther back than the Ithaca, at 4½ inches in front of the front trigger, and that one inch makes all the difference in the world. The Fox comes up like a good gun should and the Ithaca does not.

It may not be just the location of the balance point, but also the amount of weight in the barrels of the Ithaca toward the front. The Fox barrels weigh 3 pounds 10 ounces and the Ithaca barrels weigh 3 pounds 12 ounces. This could have a large felt effect on the rotary moment of inertia. Resting the toe of the butt on a hard surface when the guns are assembled, and weighing just at the muzzles to see what the down force is at the muzzles, the Ithaca weighs 2 ounces more than the Fox, but it's hard to get an accurate weight with my setup. If I do a static analysis, the difference calculates out to 0.174-pound (2.8-ounce), which is probably more accurate than the weighed number. This 0.174-pound at the muzzles makes an enormous difference in the balance. This is not meant to be a condemnation of old Ithaca doubles in general. I have seen many well-balanced ones; it's just that this particular one is not.

Since I had never patterned the gun, I did so and found that it was bored Improved Cylinder and Full, which I have seen on other Ithacas. I remember my uncle saying what a hard shooting gun the Ithaca was. This is probably because he had an Improved Cylinder choke for the first time in his life.

In 1976, I moved to southern New Jersey and made contact with an old duck hunter who had a cabin out on the Meadows, which is land that is under water at high tide. (The cabin was built on pilings.) It's quite an interesting experience to hunt out there. A fellow worker strongly suggested that I not take my good guns out there. He said I needed a cheap throwaway gun on the Meadows because of the salt. He suggested that I buy a cheap pump gun, but I could not do this. Searching the local gun stores, I found a super-cheap Spanish 12-gauge double. You had to open the gun over your knee and the trigger pulls were atrocious. After I got the gun apart, ten hours of work with slip stones got it to open and cock smoothly and with reasonable effort, and got the trigger pulls within reason. The parts of this gun were soft but I would not be shooting it much and I would not cry if it fell into the Delaware Bay. This gun patterned 70 percent left and 60 percent right. I polished the right barrel out so that it would shoot 55 percent patterns. I remember shooting a beautiful double on two ducks right in front of the old man, which impressed him greatly. When I left South Jersey I sold the gun; it had served its intended purpose.

I moved back to upstate New York and resumed grouse hunting with the Sauer and duck hunting with the Fox. I sold the Zoli to fund a new expensive hobby. Several years ago I noticed that my Sauer was loose. It had been shot between 1300 and 1600 times, and all but about 25 shots were 3 dram 1⅛-ounce loads. I don't know if this is the typical life of a 6½-pound 12-gauge Anson & Deeley-style double-barreled shotgun, with only underlug bolting. I started looking for someone who was qualified to repair it—the gun is an old friend and I wanted it in good health.

A few years ago, a friend of mine found a J.P. Sauer 20-gauge Model Royal new in the box at an extremely favorable price. He decided not to get it, so I had him buy it for me. So, 34 years after I started admiring them in the Stoeger catalog and 24 years after I considered buying one, I had my

Dick Ferro holds the goose and the author his A.H. Fox A Grade, his waterfowl gun.

Model Royal 20-gauge. This gun had a plastic trigger guard, meant to look like a typical German horn guard. I don't care for it all that much but at the price of the gun I could live with it.

Two days after I got the gun, while I was admiring it, the trigger guard went "ping" and broke apart. Plastic always breaks, it seems. It was improperly fitted and had a lot of bending and tensile stress on it. Also, perhaps it was damaged during shipping. I fixed it with an internal metal piece but will have to decide what to do about it in the long run. The Sauer factory wants 238 Deutschmarks to fix it, but it will be a problem to get it to Germany.

The gun is marked Full and Half choke but patterns 50 percent in both barrels with Remington factory 2½-⅞-7½s and 40 percent with ⅞-ounce spreader loads. At trap, I did as well with it as I do with a 12-gauge loaded with 1⅛-ounce loads. I shoot trap with the gun down and have somebody else release the trap without warning, to replicate shooting at game. It may be that this gun comes up enough faster to make up for its smaller shot charge and more open choke. Or maybe it's just easier to hit with the open choke.

At a gun show, a friend of mine came up and offered me an AyA boxlock double 12-gauge for $200. I couldn't pass it up at that price. It is a double trigger model, not the single trigger Matador they once sold here, and is like new. He had walked around the gun show trying to sell it. When every interested person found out it was a Spanish double, they made disparaging remarks, not realizing that AyAs were good guns. He couldn't stand the stupid comments any more and just wanted to get rid of it. The gun shoots exactly where it looks, patterns 70 percent left, 55 percent right, and weighs 7 pounds with 28-inch barrels, so it's a little heavy for upland hunting.

I moved again in 1985 and haven't hunted ducks since. I don't know what to do about steel shot. I would like to be ready to hunt ducks again if the opportunity arises. It's becoming clear that I do not dare use steel in my current doubles. Using a pump or automatic is out for me. Parker Reproductions says their gun is okay for steel shot, and Armes de Chasse informs me that the Chapuis is okay for steel shot and the design is very interesting, but I can't afford either of them right now. Precision Sports says their Parker Hale/Ugartecha 10-gauge is okay for steel shot but the gun is very large and heavy. I can not see myself using it in a duck blind. Possibly I can get the AyA bored for steel shot as recommended by Bob LeFever in the "Double Gun Journal." If it cracks the barrels at the chokes, I won't have lost much money.

I finally found someone who came strongly recommended by three different people to work on the Sauer. When he looked at the gun, he said that the looseness was probably caused by the action spreading apart at the hinge pin. He said that in some inexpensive (by his standards, which were very high) German guns the hinge pin was just pressed in, and is not really a threaded flanged bolt that helps to keep the sides from spreading apart. This was great news; I had foreseen a really expensive repair. He fixed the gun and now it's tighter than new.

What have I learned from all this? When you buy a double-barreled shotgun, get a good gun with extended rib bolting, unless it's a very high grade gun from a highly respected maker. If you're not going to shoot it much, I wouldn't pass up a moderate quality gun with double underlugs only, such as my Sauer KIM model, but I would not plan to shoot it much. Get a light gun for upland hunting, and a fairly light gun for duck hunting. Make sure the balance points are correct.

If you reload, which is part of the fun of shooting, don't worry about tight chokes; you can make the gun do what you want by loading spreader loads and by careful selection of factory loads. I use a Lee Load All Jr. which is very cheap and works fine for the little bit of loading that I do. One of the big advantages of a double gun is that you don't need perfectly sized and shaped reloads.

Make sure the gun fits you in comb height unless you want to get into stock bending or add-on pads. I check comb height by closing my eyes and mounting the gun. If, when I open my eyes, I appear to be looking down the rib properly, the gun is probably a good fit. Of course, nothing would be better than to be custom fitted with a try-gun, but that is not an option open to all of us. Remember, the length of pull can be adjusted easily by a competent workman by shortening or adding a recoil pad or spacer. I like the English method of using a piece of ebony for a spacer. I strongly recommend a sling, unless the gun is a collectors item.

Pattern the gun so you know what it is doing; this is critical. You may find patterning confusing at first. Remember that you can get up to 10 percent variation with a specific barrel and load so you will have to shoot several shots and average them. The best way to avoid confusion, and an excessive amount of patterning is to remember:

a. large shot shoots tighter
b. small shot shoots looser
c. lower velocity shoots tighter
d. higher velocity shoots looser
e. spreader loads open up

In patterning three good doubles made between 1908 and 1964, I did not get a Full choke pattern tighter than 70 percent with modern plastic factory loads using shot protectors and buffers. Writers are claiming tighter patterns, but I did not get them. One other advantage of patterning your gun is to make sure that the gun is shooting where you point it.

Read all you can, starting with *The Gun and Its Development,* by Greener, and anything else you can lay your hands on, and learn from those who have gone before you, but do your own testing. *The Modern Shotgun* by Burrard, which is a three-volume set, is a particularly fascinating book and a must read for anybody who likes the technicalities of double guns. It's even better than Greener's book; unfortunately it's now out of print. Buy a good gun, one much better than you think you can afford, when you are young. After 25 years of use, the cost per year will be infinitesimal. Don't buy a gun just because it has neat engraving.

When I picked up my Sauer KIM after its repair, I took my Fox along to have the bores measured. The gunsmith said the chambers looked short to him. When I acquired the gun, I measured the chambers with a scale and believed them to be 2¾ inches long. My collector friend also measured them, and he thought they were 2¾ inches long. The gunsmith gauged them and they turned out to be 2⁹⁄₁₆-inch chambers! I had been shooting the gun for 22 years with short chambers, a testament to the strength of the Fox and my stupidity. The lesson to be learned here is that unless the chambers are marked, have them measured with a proper gauge by somebody who knows what he is doing, as my friend and I did not. The gunsmith reamed the chambers out to 2¾ inches before I left his shop.

What does the future bring? In thinking about all the ruffed grouse I have shot, I have killed the vast majority with one shot, with almost no chances for a second shot. Now, suppose I had a really nice 12-gauge single-barreled shotgun weighing 4½ pounds with a 25-inch barrel, constructed for a 3-inch magnum 1⅞-ounce load of shot, no choke and a rifled section to disperse the shot charge? Such a load would give me 656 7½ shot in a really big pattern, and the gun would come up a little quicker. Of course, such a gun would need an incredibly good recoil pad!

If I could afford it, I would go to Ferlach and have them build me a best grade *kipplauf einzel buchse* (a break-open single-barreled shotgun) with double Kersten bolting, engraved with oak leaves and acorns and grouse scenes, and start a new odyssey. ●

Grendel's P-30 22 WMR Pistol

(Left) The Grendel P-30 is thoroughly state-of-the-art when it comes to materials and overall design.

(Below) The standard P-30 is by no means big. Fully loaded it weighs just 27 ounces.

(Above) Disassembly for cleaning is a cinch. The P-30's simplicity accounts for its utter reliability.

Self-LOADING pistols chambered for the rather potent 22 Winchester Magnum Rimfire cartridge have been as scarce as the proverbial mammaries on a bull. Of course, there have been good reasons for such a dearth of autoloaders that could handle reliably the often underrated and sometimes maligned 22 WMR round.

For openers, the 22 WMR cartridge has a long, thin-walled casing prone to cause higher than normal chamber friction during the chambering and extraction sequence and has, therefore, been considered largely unsuited to basic blowback actions. In addition, that overly long and straight rimmed cartridge with its flat-nosed bullet has also been regarded as generally troublesome when it comes to reliable feeding from a box-type magazine in a selfloader.

There was a special need for an accurate, reliable and economically priced autoloading pistol that could handle the 22 WMR, I have believed, and my long-standing wish has now been satisfactorily answered by Grendel, Inc., a fairly new company based in Rockledge, Florida. The Grendel company has been known, up to now, primarily for its unusual top-loading P-10 pocket-sized autoloader in 380 ACP. Late in 1991, Grendel launched the P-30 model, chambered for the 22 WMR round. This pistol derives its model designation from its huge ammo capacity. That's right, the P-30's magazine stacks a full thirty rounds of 22 WMR.

To begin, the P-30 barrel sleeve/slide unit is cut from solid LaSalle stress-proof steel stock. The steel barrel has a fluted chamber to aid in the extraction of the fired casing and is stationary—press-fitted into the all-steel frame. The latter, in addition, also holds the firing mechanism and forms the ejector and slide rails. Overall, the P-30 measures 8.5 inches, is 5.7 inches high and comes with a 5-inch barrel. The P-30 has a rather large grip/trigger guard that attaches to the frame via eight Allen screws. The grip—as well as the trigger blade, forend and slide extension—are made of glass-reinforced Zytel. The same tough synthetic is used in the construction of the P-30's magazine.

The grip has checkered sides and is large enough to accommodate big hands. I must tell you that I like it and the ample, front-squared trigger guard a lot. The overall heft and balance provide just enough muzzle heaviness to keep that front sight steady on target. Despite its full-size dimensions, the Grendel P-30 manages to weigh only 21 ounces empty, 27 ounces loaded.

The P-30 utilizes the straight blowback system and has a crisp two-stage single-action trigger. Mine lets go at around 3½ pounds. There is an ambidextrous safety, located in the frame, that rotates on the axis of the novel, flat internal hammer. When the safety-lever is pushed up to the "on" position, it both disconnects the trigger and blocks the hammer.

The P-30 is not a target gun. It comes with a basic, though functional, non-adjustable rear sight moulded right out of the slide extension. Up front there is a stout square blade that can be replaced with elements of different heights (available as extras) if the owner wants to change the elevation setting. As it came out of the box, my test gun—which was purchased over the counter at a gun shop—was dead on target out to approximately 50 yards; a graphic example of the 22 WMR round's flat-shooting ability. At 25 yards in fast combat-style shooting, I was consistently able to dump the entire 30-round mag into the "boiler room" area of a silhouette tar-get. I did that time after time. Although the recoil is quite mild, the P-30 produces a decidedly attention-getting blast and muzzle flash. A variety of popular 22 WMR fodder was used in firing a total of 500 rounds or so during tests, without one single stoppage. The P-30 simply digested everything without a hiccup. Those 40-grain pills leave the muzzle of this gun at approximately 1350 fps.

Switching over to a slower firing cadence with more traditional bullseye targets, the pistol printed 10-shot groups averaging just under two inches, also at 25 yards. Not match grade by any means, but quite good enough to take care of just about any deadly serious threat that may arise, whether man or beast. With that 30-round mag fully loaded, the Grendel P-30 is a formidable defense handgun for the home as well as wilderness. In the latter setting it can double to provide small game fare for the table.

Grendel suggests a retail price of $225 for the P-30. The company also offers the model P-30M, a longer-barreled version with a removable muzzle-brake. Although the longer barrel certainly helps the 22 WMR cartridge develop more oomph, I prefer the regular P-30. I am not exaggerating in the least when I say that it is a truly awesome autoloader.

J.I. Galan

Tar-Hunt's Benchrest Shotgun

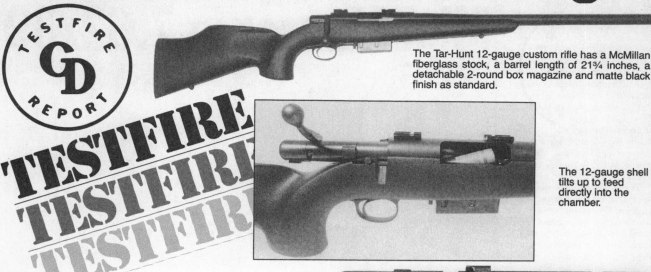

The Tar-Hunt 12-gauge custom rifle has a McMillan fiberglass stock, a barrel length of 21¾ inches, a detachable 2-round box magazine and matte black finish as standard.

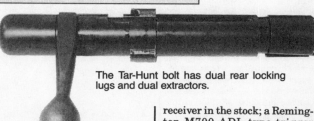

The 12-gauge shell tilts up to feed directly into the chamber.

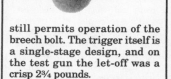

The Tar-Hunt bolt has dual rear locking lugs and dual extractors.

Bolt-action shotguns have been around for at least seven decades, and possibly longer. They have been thought of as utility guns, low in price, slow to operate, and reasonably reliable. They have been generally available in 410, plus 20-, 16-, 12-, and 10-gauge models, some with detachable box magazines, and others with tubes under the barrels. Such shotguns have even been thought of as farmer's guns to keep in the barn, or kid's guns to make the first shot count, and they have been smoothbores.

The Tar-Hunt RSG-12 is not such a shotgun. True, it is a bolt action, it does have a detachable box magazine, and it is relatively slow to operate. It is not a shotgun to keep in the barn, or one with which to start a young shooter; it is not exactly low priced, and it is not a smoothbore. It costs $1200, has a Shaw rifled 12-gauge barrel, a specially designed and manufactured receiver and breech bolt, set up in a black fiberglass McMillan Monte Carlo stock, fitted with a Pachmayr Decelerator rifle pad.

Overall length of the RSG-12 is 41½ inches, with a barrel length of 21¾ inches. It weighs an even 8 pounds without sights. (No sights are provided, but the receiver is drilled and tapped for Weaver-type scope mount bases.)

Rifled 12-bore guns have also been available a long time; they have generally been over/under

or side-by-side guns, intended for use in Africa or India, or, in France, on small game at short ranges. Such have never been overly popular in the U.S., although the past decade has seen an increase of interest, both for deer hunting and slug shoots in organized matches, such as the Diana Match.

The RSG-12 has a matte black finish on all metal parts, except the two-round box magazine which is blued. The barrel is rifled with a right-hand twist of 1:36 inches; it has a countersunk muzzle, and a built-in muzzlebrake is available as an option. The test gun was chambered for standard length 12-gauge shells (2¾ inches) but guns for 3-inch shells may be available later.

Designed for right-handed shooters only, the two-piece breech bolt has dual rear locking lugs that lock into the bridge, instead of the receiver ring. The lugs are large, more than adequate to handle any factory 12-gauge slug loads currently available. Cocking is on the upstroke of the bolt handle, which has a curved shank to clear the eyepiece housing of a scope, and a pear-shaped knob ideally positioned for rapid operation. A shroud covers the cocking piece and twin spring-steel extractors grip opposing sides of the case rim; ejection is to the right rear. A Remington-type lever safety, located behind the bolt handle, locks the trigger when in the on position, but

still permits operation of the breech bolt. The trigger itself is a single-stage design, and on the test gun the let-off was a crisp 2¾ pounds.

The McMillan fiberglass stock features a Monte Carlo comb with semi-rollover cheekpiece. A wide, deep flute on the right side of the nose of the comb resembles that found on a benchrest rifle; this is strictly a right-handed shotgun. The pistol grip is large, and curve of the grip is full, with the distance from the tip of the trigger to the leading edge of the grip base measuring 2⅞ inches. Some shooters may find this a bit tight, but it positions the trigger finger tip directly on the trigger without strain. Circumference of the small of the stock, at its minimum, is an even 6 inches. The entire stock has a black, mottled finish. The length of pull measured 13½ inches, with drops at the comb, heel of the Monte Carlo, and heel of the stock, of 1⁷⁄₁₆, 1¹⁄₁₆, and 2½ inches, respectively. Such a reverse slope on a Monte Carlo tends to move the recoil away from the cheek.

Hex-bolts, located 7¹¹⁄₁₆ inches apart, retain the RSG-12

receiver in the stock; a Remington M700 ADL-type trigger guard is used, and the rear guard bolt screws into the underside of the receiver tang, while a small Phillips screw is used to secure the forward guard tang. The forward guard bolt fits through an escutcheon directly into the underside of the receiver ring. There's a recoil lug between the receiver and the barrel, in the same manner as the Remington M700 family of rifles. Studs for detachable swivels are located on the underside of the forearm and buttstock, should a sling or carrying strap be needed.

The RSG-12 is provided without sights, but drilled and tapped for scope mount bases. Due to the size of the ejection port and the ejection of the empty hulls, Randy Fritz recommends the use of steel scope rings, or reversing the Weaver-type rings so the knobs are on the left side of the receiver; this is to provide clearance for ejection of the 12-gauge hulls.

The test gun was fitted with a 2x Aimpoint. This model, which is adjustable for windage and elevation, allows the bright red dot to be moved so it coincides with the point of impact. The 2x magnification is not high, but it is satisfactory for shotgun use, although a regular 4x or 6x scope would allow for closer holding.

Checking the RSG-12 for accuracy and functioning was done at 50 yards from the bench, using sandbags under the forearm. Federal and Winchester saboted loads were used, along with ACTIV and Federal Hi-Shok. The sabot loads are improved versions of the BRI loads introduced more than 20 years ago. There are slight differences in the actual 50-caliber slugs; Federal uses maroon-colored sabot halves while Winchester uses yellow-colored sabot halves, and there are slight differences in these also.

Three-shot groups were fired, with the smallest obtained using the Winchester 1-ounce load. Group diameter, measured center-to-center, was ¾-inch, with two of the holes overlapping. The largest groups obtained using the Winchester shells measured 1⁷⁄₁₆ inches, center-to-center.

Accuracy with the Federal sabot loads was almost as good, with the smallest group measuring ²⁹⁄₃₂-inch, center-to-center, while the largest measured 1¼ inches. The ACTIV rifled slug load features the Cervo rifled slug, a modification of the Foster design, with more of a cylinder shape and deep hollow point, plus having the hollow base impaled on top of a plastic wad assembly. The smallest three-shot group obtained with the ACTIV load measured 1⁷⁄₁₆ inches, center-to-center, the same as the largest group obtained using the Winchester sabot round. None of the new Brenneke Gold 12-gauge slug loads are available in standard length (2¾ inches), but they would be interesting to try in the RSG-12, if they were available, as the ribs have a reverse twist to engage the rifling in shotgun barrels.

Fired hulls were dropped approximately a pace to the right, depending on the shell brand. Feeding was satisfactory, but every so often a shell would catch on the top of the barrel breech; no particular shell brand seemed to catch more frequently than the others.

The RSG-12 is expensive, but it is also a custom shotgun with a rifled barrel designed to put 12-gauge slugs into the smallest possible group. The craftsmanship is excellent, as is the design. Beyond that, the Tar-Hunt RSG-12 is a bolt-action shotgun with class.

Larry S. Sterett

Interarms' Mini-Mauser in 7.62x39

(Above) Nick Croyle wrings out Interarms cute bolt 7.62x39.

(Left) The firing pin had enough poop for most any primer.

YOU CAN now buy from Interarms an attractive 7.62x 39mm bolt-action sporter my mind's eye could only dream about twenty years ago. Good things are worth waiting for, they say, and the Mini-Mark X is handy, weighs only 6 pounds without scope and measures 39¾ inches overall with 20-inch plain barrel.

From the time I first encountered the 7.62x39mm cartridge, I tried to imagine a light sporting bolt-action for it. While the SKS had obvious sporting potential, being handier and more accurate than an AK, it was and is rather plain and utilitarian. The 7.62x39 is a compact round, equivalent to, but significantly smaller and operating at higher pressures than, the 30-30, just like the 308 Winchester is to the 30-06. It really belonged in a Sako Vixen, I thought.

Although a few 7.62x39 Vixens were made years ago for European sale, the only one I ever saw was tested by Harry Archer and Chuck Lanham in *GUNfacts* magazine about 1970. There was little U.S. market for 7.62x39 sporters until recently because ammo was scarce. The fellow who brought back an SKS was unable to shoot it much because ammo was scarce and expensive.

That situation changed abruptly about 1984 when the great Asian floodgates opened and we were suddenly drowned in a sea of surplus 7.62x39 ammunition which became common as dirt and nearly as cheap. Plentiful surplus ammunition and inexpensive SKSs introduced thousands of Americans to the cartridge and whetted demand for sporters having more sales appeal than the crude military arms. Bolt-guns were only a matter of time. The time is now and Interarms has its Mini-Mark X, hitherto offered in 223.

The Mini-Mark X looks like a typical post-war commercial Mauser sporter, only smaller. A hunter could assemble an entire battery scaled to the cartridges based upon the Mark X and Mini-Mark X series. The place of the 7.62x39 in such a group is obvious as the firearm of choice for short-range varmints, casual plinking with inexpensive surplus ammunition, or for a youngster's light-recoiling first centerfire.

The Mini-Mark X resembles the larger rifles in the Inter-arms line in general appearance, but its action resembles the Sako A1 and earlier L-461 Vixen more than a Mauser 98. The straight-grained walnut stock is well shaped with a tastefully subtle Monte Carlo comb and cheekpiece and is checkered with an 18-line-per-inch bordered point pattern moderately well executed. The barreled action, steel trigger guard and hinged floorplate are polished bright and black oxided. The rifle is practical, handy and attractive.

The hook extractor is dovetailed into a longitudinal slot in the bolt body as in the Belgian Model 89 or Argentine Model 91 Mausers, rather than having the familiar '98 Mauser non-rotating extractor. The Mini-Mark X extractor does not produce the controlled feed of 98-type Mausers, but this is not important given the intended field use of the Mini-Mark X.

Over 300 rounds of surplus Chinese Type PS Ball ammunition known to have "hard" primers were fired, and there were no malfunctions. Another 200 rounds of factory and softpoint bullet handloads were also digested without incident. The three-shot magazine feeds reliably, but the short bolt handle is awkward to operate rapidly from the shoulder, and its flat, checkered underside was uncomfortable when opening the bolt.

The Sako-style guide rib, attached to the bolt body by a rotating collar, and the right locking lug have a groove which engages a slot in the right receiver sidewall, intended to reduce binding of the bolt. On the test rifle the groove in the bolt guide rib was roughly machined, having a series of deep, semi-circular tool marks which caused very rough bolt operation. The roughness was moderated by greasing the bolt guide rib. Bolt operation eased after several hundred cycles of the action, but never approached being smooth until the action rails and bolt guide rib were lapped with a mild abrasive paste.

At first it was not possible to obtain a satisfactory 100-yard zero without shimming the telescope bases. When all 60 minutes of available telescope adjustment was used, point of impact remained a foot high. The stock exerted a great deal of forearm pressure against the light barrel. After removing the barreled action from the stock and using a ½-inch gouge to scrape about 1/16-inch from the barrel channel near the forearm tip, pressure was greatly reduced and a normal point of impact was obtained.

Ten consecutive five-shot groups with Chinese Type PS Ball averaged 2.78 inches, not significantly different from the same ammunition fired in a surplus SKS carbine with issue military sights. A small quantity of commercial softpoint ammunition of various makes was fired with disappointing accuracy—several five-shot groups ranging from 3-5 inches. Similar results were obtained with handloads using 123-grain Speer softpoint bullets and 26.5 grains of Hercules RL-7 powder. However, Sierra 125-grain spitzers of .308-inch diameter averaged under 2 inches, entirely acceptable for so light a rifle.

In an attempt to determine the cause of the inaccuracy, a chamber cast was made. The Mini-Mark X barrel is rifled with four grooves and has a twist of 9½ inches per turn, which is common for this caliber. However, instead of the

---

Interarms Mini-Mark X 7.62x39

Zeiss 10x36 scope, 5-shot groups at 100 yards
Bore diameter .302″, groove diameter .314″, 4-degree leade from .335″ ahead of chamber neck like AKM chamber

	Smallest	Largest	Average
Chinese PS 141-72	1.5	4.9	2.78
125 Sierra 26.5 RL-7	1.25	2.8	1.96

Retest Mini-Mark X after ½″ barrel set-back and rechambering with Lapua-style reamer
0-degree, 45-minute forcing cone from .3114″ ball seat, 35-degree transition from neck to ball seat.

	Smallest	Largest	Average
Chinese PS	0.77	2.51	1.69
Hansen M67 Yugo Ball	1.61	4.97	2.60
125 Sierra 26.5 RL-7	2.14	4.77	3.27

Chinese SKS open sights, 100 yards—for comparison

	Smallest	Largest	Average
PS Ball 141-72	1.9	4.4	3.12

Is Controlled Feeding Still Needed?

The requirement for controlled feeding in military bolt-action rifles was intended to prevent double feeding when panicky conscript troops short-stroked the bolt. Doing so causes a hideous jam in rifles whose extractors are not able to snap over a round which is chambered ahead of the extractor. More important, with the advent of spitzer FMJ bullets for military use, double loading posed risk, though remote, of the point of the double-fed cartridge striking the primer of the one jammed in the chamber, with disastrous results.

Controlled-feed bolt actions such as the Mauser 98 and M1903 Springfield force the cartridge rim under the extractor claw as the round is stripped from the magazine. When the Mauser claw-type extractor is properly fitted, it positively holds the cartridge base against the bolt face, ensuring reliable ignition even if there is

considerable end play of the round in the chamber. The case remains in firm contact with the bolt face through feeding, firing and extraction until the bolt is brought fully to the rear. At the end of the bolt's rearward travel the ejector nose passes through its clearance slot in the left locking lug, striking the cartridge base, pivoting the case off and around the extractor claw and propelling it out at 2:00 o'clock over the right sidewall of the receiver.

The controlled-feed design is still felt desirable among hunters of dangerous game, but this feature is lacking in most modern sporting bolt actions. It has also been deemed unnecessary in all U.S. military rifles which followed the M1903 Springfield. This is because gas operated gun mechanisms operate with far more force and deliberation than a scared 19-year-old who is trying to manipulate the bolt while being shot at. *C.E. Harris*

---

usual .300-inch bore and .310-inch groove with +.002-inch tolerance expected for the 7.62x39, the test rifle had a bore diameter of .302-inch and groove diameter of .314-inch.

The Mini-Mark X chamber resembles those of Yugoslav and Chinese AKM rifles in having no transition from the chamber neck to a conventional ball seat. Instead, it has a 4-degree forcing cone departing abruptly from chamber neck, as shown in the accompanying drawing.

The author has two switch-barrel rifles having several barrels chambered for the 7.62x39 of various barrel groove diameters and twist rates, which produce much better accuracy.

These have a Lapua-style chamber which has a .3114-inch diameter ball seat and a gradual forcing cone of about 1 degree. As an experiment, the barrel of the Interarms rifle was set back ½-inch and rechambered using the Lapua-type reamer, and tested again. After rechambering, the average group size with the Chinese ball ammunition improved dramatically, averaging 1.7 inches for ten consecutive five-shot groups at 100 yards. Accuracy with .308-inch diameter 125-grain Sierras was significantly worse. The reason for this is not clear. The 125-grain softpoint .308 Sierra bullets have given good results in other 7.62x39 rifles with groove diameters from

.308-.312-inch chambered with this reamer. It may be that easing them gradually into a .314-inch barrel was asking too much. Slamming the undersized .308 bullets through the abrupt throat of the original Yugoslav chamber apparently upset the bullet bases enough to fill the large forcing cone.

The Interarms Mini-Mark X shows considerable potential for a utility rifle. I wondered what Jeff Cooper would think of a "Mini Scout Rifle" in 7.62x39? I think I'll try that next! *(Indeed, I insisted—Editor)* Shooters who want a better looking 7.62x39 than the military surplus variety will find the Mini-Mark X has real possibilities.

C.E. Harris

Ruger's High-Tech 7.62x39 Bolt Gun

TESTFIRE
TESTFIRE
TESTFIRE

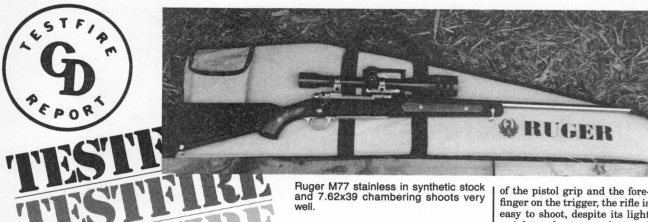

Ruger M77 stainless in synthetic stock and 7.62x39 chambering shoots very well.

Lapua-type chamber is a distinct advantage in the Ruger.

At FIRST glance, the 7.62x39 seems an odd cartridge for a bolt-action rifle. Given a 308 Winchester-sized action and bolt throw, the obvious question to ask is "Why?" The Model 77's magazine has to be blocked for the short cartridge and this precludes loading jacketed bullets heavier than 150 grains out far enough to exploit the available and meager powder capacity.

The resulting rifle is the size and weight of its stablemate in 308 Winchester but possesses the muzzle energy and velocity of a factory 30-30 round fired from a 20-inch carbine. Of course, spitzers can be used in the bolt gun, thus improving downrange performance compared to the blunt bullets which must be used in a tubular magazine 30-30. The 7.62x39 does this at higher pressures, sure, and anybody who tries to load a Savage 340 or Winchester Model 94 30-30 up to 53,000 psi courts serious orthopedic or ophthalmic surgery.

There is an answer and it is that the 7.62x39 is a delightful, homey little cartridge to shoot. It is virtually identical in case capacity to the 30 Herrett, surplus ammo is cheap for practice, the tiny case can be successfully reloaded using almost any rifle powder you have around, and it doesn't require a lot of that. This makes it very inexpensive to reload. It is not as loud as a 30-30, much less a 308 or 243, and its recoil is on a par with a 243. And it is a "thirty," reassuring to people who judge a rifle by the size of the hole in the end of the barrel.

If the 30 Herrett, in 14 inches of pistol barrel, is considered effective on deer, a rimless twin with 22 inches of rifle barrel screwed into a bolt action and weighing only 3 pounds more must certainly be considered effective also. Such a rifle's weight and mild recoil make it attractive to beginning shooters, while it kicks enough like a "big" rifle, and makes enough more noise than a 22, to provide good transition from rimfires to centerfires.

The Ruger Model 77 Mark II is a cute rifle. It weighs 8 pounds even, including a Weaver T6 in the Ruger mounts, so it would weigh 7.5 pounds with any reasonable 4x or compact variable, say a 2-7x. Not a flyweight, but handy nonetheless.

The trigger pull is good for 1992. It registers a consistent 73 ounces on a Schrader gauge and is very controllable, much like a good single-action pull on an Old Model Blackhawk. It exhibits perceptible travel, but is smooth and consistent. Fired properly, by squeezing the trigger between the thumb on top of the pistol grip and the forefinger on the trigger, the rifle is easy to shoot, despite its light weight and attorney-designed trigger. The flat-bottomed forearm, which doesn't look all that great to many, sets up well on the bench and fits easily in the hand in field positions.

I cannot say I actually like the look of the synthetic stock, but it certainly feels and handles well. The pistol grip is like all Ruger/Brownell pistol grips; nicely shaped and great in the hand. Oil wipes right off the non-slip stock surface, Shooter's Choice does not damage it and although Motor Mica (used on the bags) tends to embed in it, it will wipe off with lacquer thinner and that does not damage the finish either. Goncalo Alves wood inserts in the stock are more attractive than green synthetic ones. The fuzzy texture and the thousands of encapsulated air pockets in the moulded stock will make it feel "warm" to the touch in winter, just as does wood. An integral, layered recoil pad soaks up what kick there is in this cartridge.

The stirrup sling swivels are undoubtedly sturdy, but I have never liked storing a rifle or cleaning one with the sling attached. Too many chances of the sling snagging something valuable and dumping it onto the floor. Removing any sling from swivels is an annoyance of the first order. Nor can a favorite sling be switched easily from the Model 77 to another rifle and vice versa.

Stainless alloys formerly were noted for their tendency to gall. Keep the Model 77 bolt lightly greased with Amoco FG or a similar grease formulated for use on stainless steel and it feels and operates just fine. Also grease the cocking surface cam.

The three-position safety will be recognized by anyone who has seen a 77/22, as will be the full-length non-rotating extractor and the positive ejector. The positive ejector may or may not be an improvement, depending upon individual perspective. It can bang up coated cleaning rods, but it will either dump the empties on the bench or toss them well out in the boonies, depending upon how quickly the bolt is cycled. A plunger ejector imparts but one (high) velocity to a withdrawn case or round. Personally, I dislike plunger ejectors and much prefer this one.

The Mark II is not a positive feeding rifle. In all the years I have shot itty-bitty 222 Remington-based ammunition from slam-feed magazines at woodchucks, I have never double-fed a round. I have seen positive-feed actions, with insufficient clearance in the extractor cut or between the extractor and bolt face, fail to pop over a chambered round or fail to pick up fully and jam. Usually, this occurred with cases that had beat-up rims. I have never yet (knock on wood) short-shucked a pump shotgun either. If I were hanging upside down and needed quietly and slowly to feed a round into a chamber, positive feeding would be an advantage, I am certain. Thus far, I have managed to avoid such situations.

The bolt face is not a 7.62x39 (PPC) face. It is a 30-06 face. The extractor, however, is sized for the much smaller 7.62x39 rim groove.

The Lapua chamber, which I believe the Ruger chamber to be very close to, is very forgiving and will handle .308-inch through .311-inch bullets with aplomb and do so with accuracy. My particular lot of Hansen full-jacket ammo had an annoying tendency to partially extrude bullet cores out the base of their jackets and decent accuracy was a sometime achievement. Even at that, we averaged 2.5 inches at 100 yards for the ten five-shot groups. The extruding cores resulted in two other discarded groups exhibiting only four shots. The sample standard deviation agrees with the published coefficient of variation for five-shot groups, which meant our limited sam-

ple was enough to be representative. That got rid of my last sixty rounds of this stuff.

Using Chinese steel-cased and corrosive ball, the Mark II averaged 1.79 inches for ten, five-shot groups, with a standard deviation of 0.53-inch, and the M77 Mark II ignited every one of those hard primers. This is better than average accuracy for military ball, and equals the best 30-caliber service ammunition we have tested (30-06 Ball M2, TW 54 lot 41270).

Ruger, by the way, admonishes shooters to "Use only U.S. commercially manufactured ammunition." There's also a disclaimer for damage or injury when using handloads. A cautionary note regarding hard primers of "certain lots of foreign military ammunition" is also in the gun's enclosed literature.

All that certainly makes for cheap and satisfying shooting. Although stainless steel is more resistant to corrosion than plain carbon steels, the Mark II's stainless action and barrel will corrode eventually if not thoroughly cleaned after using chlorate-primed (corrosive) ammunition. On the other hand, it's a lot simpler to clean than, say, an SKS or Mini Thirty. Using handloads (which, again, Ruger does not recommend) consisting of 125-grain Sierras and 26.5 grains of Hercules RL-7, the test rifle's average for twenty, five-shot groups was 1.55 inches.

The 7.62x39mm round was designed around a .300-inch bore with .310-inch grooves, with the usual tolerance +.002-inch on either dimension. The bore of the test rifle measures .300-inch, as near as can be determined, but the grooves measured .3095-inch. If you were a firearms manufacturer in today's litigious environment, you would cover every possible bet. The manner in which Ruger accomplishes this is enviable in its simplicity and effective in its execution. It works.

If your pickup rifle is a 30 M-1 Carbine, one of the Marlin 94s or an SKS—any of which is at best a four MOA, 100-yard maximum-range shooter—maybe a sturdier rifle which will shoot Chinese ball into groups half those of any reload in the others could be a handy thing. Jim Cowgill certainly thought so. He bought this one because I already had my No. 3 put together.

Nick Croyle

ATIS PM2 Police Pump

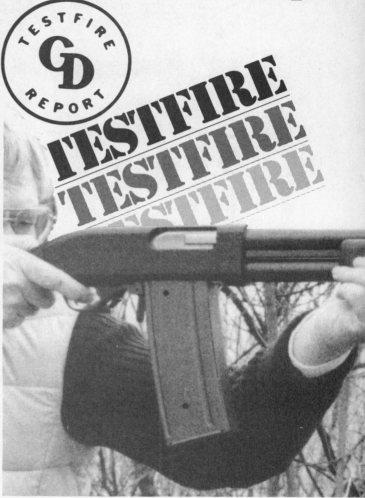

R EPEATING shotguns with detachable box magazines are not new, and, though autoloaders with detachable box magazines have been less common, they have existed for more than 25 years. Now, there's a new pump gun with detachable box magazine. It's manufactured in Italy by ATIS, and distributed in the U.S. by European American Armory as the PM2.

This 12-gauge pump features a barrel length of 19¹¹⁄₁₆ inches and an overall length of 40⅜ inches with the conventional buttstock.

Since the PM2 is slide-operated, the former magazine tube is still present—it will hold five 3-inch 12-gauge shells in re-

serve, or it could be used to hold a small survival kit, or anything else that will fit into a ⅞-inch tube 13 inches long. The contents are readily accessible; simply unscrew what used to be the magazine cap. The forward end of the loading port on the bottom of the receiver has been fitted with a pinned-in-place feed ramp, while the rear of the loading port has been fitted with a magazine release catch housing assembly. This assembly includes a long magazine release which is readily grasped with the thumb as the magazine is grasped for removal or insertion.

The detachable box magazine is of conventional design, with

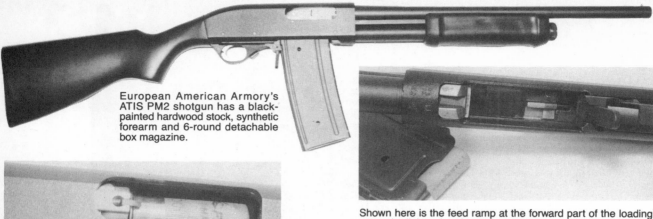

European American Armory's ATIS PM2 shotgun has a black-painted hardwood stock, synthetic forearm and 6-round detachable box magazine.

Shown here is the feed ramp at the forward part of the loading port—the light-colored metal on the left.

Rounds feed directly from the magazine. At the lower left is the magazine release lever.

The PM2 handles well from a standing position, but possibly not from prone.

a detachable floorplate and a domed, highly chromed follower. The PM2 is chambered for 3-inch shells, and the magazine will hold six rounds of these or standard 2¾-inch shells in a single column. Single-column box magazines with a capacity much larger than this become a bit unhandy, although a staggered column design that will feed 12-gauge cartridges is possible.

Insertion of the magazine is easy. Slide the lip on the leading edge of the magazine into the loading port until it slips into the locking groove on the feed ramp. Then simply rotate the magazine toward the rear in a pendulum motion until it snaps into the closed position.

The action release lever extends across the front of the trigger guard, easily accessible with either forefinger. If the action is cocked, pulling the release lever to the rear will permit the slide handle to be pulled back and the breech bolt retracted. If the magazine is loaded, the forward push will chamber a round. When the last round is fired, or the magazine is empty, the follower protrudes upward enough to retard the breech bolt, something which does not normally occur with a tubular magazine pump-action design.

The forearm on the PM2 is synthetic, with ridges fore and aft to serve as hand stops, similar to the forward handstop on a target rifle. It measured 7¹¹⁄₁₆ inches long and has checkered panels on the sides; this checkering was more decorative than functional on the test gun.

The buttstock on the PM2 is of hardwood, painted black, and beneath the buttplate there is a cavity which could be used to store small items, if desired. Such storage requires something to remove the Phillips-head buttplate screws, so if the space is really needed, a quick-change buttpad assembly, such as the new one by Pachmayr, would be ideal. Length of pull on the regular stock was 13½ inches, with drops at the comb and heel of 1⁷⁄₁₆ and 2⁵⁄₁₆ inches, measured from receiver top.

The receiver on the PM2 is of alloy with a baked-on black finish, similar to a rough, no-glare anodizing, while the barrel, magazine, action bars, action tube, and other steel parts have a matte gray-black finish. The breech bolt, which locks directly into the barrel extension, steel-to-steel, has a polished chrome finish. Dual action bars provide extremely smooth action operation, and the location of action release lever is one of the best on any pump-action shotgun available today.

Other than the brass muzzle bead, the PM2 does not have any sights. A ghost ring sight assembly might not be a bad idea, but all such accessories add to the initial cost.

The PM2 was checked out for functioning at 25 yards. Since the test gun had a 0.728-inch bore, and no choke, only a few loads were patterned just to see what it would do. First off was Remington's short magnum containing 1¼ ounces of size 3 steel shot, or an average of 190 pellets per shell by actual count. At 25 yards, the PM2 put an average of 68.9 percent of the size 3 steel pellets inside the 30-inch circle, with 48.9 percent of this total within a 15-inch center circle. The patterns were centered an average of 3¼ inches above and 4¾ inches to the right of the point-of-aim. Next was ACTIV's 3-inch buckshot load containing 41 No. 4 buckshot. At 25 yards it was not difficult to keep all 41 pellets in the 30-inch circle, although strays tended to crowd the edges. Again, the patterns were centered slightly to the right and above the point of aim. The last load checked out was the Cenco rubber pellet load containing nine 30-caliber red rubber pellets. At 25 yards these pellets would not penetrate the second of two layers of corrugated packing cardboard spaced 2 inches apart. The nine pellets stayed within the 30-inch circle, but several times the pellets were not evenly distributed.

A few rounds were put through the PM2 shooting White Flyers, but a Cylinder-bore barrel is not exactly a great clay bird buster. No problems were encountered feeding 2¾- and 3-inch shells during the patterning session, nor the standard length target loads.

The PM2 is an interesting shotgun. Extra magazines are available, so one could be kept loaded with light loads, and another with buckshot, rifled slugs, or whatever. For combat shoots, and even small game hunting, where more than three shots are legal for hunting, the PM2 might be useful. With a synthetic stock it might be even a shotgun the military and police forces could consider, due to the ease with which magazines can be changed.

Larry S. Sterett

Daisy's Power Line 44

A prize for any shooter. Note the addition of a sticker (upper left) to the box face when used to package a nickel-plated Model 144 (shown at bottom) instead of the conventional (blue/black) Model 44.

Maybe IT'S coincidence; maybe it's competition. Both Crosman and Daisy have lately come up with such really neat CO_2 pellet revolvers it's hard to pick one over the other.

I detailed Crosman's Model 357-8GT in GUN DIGEST, 44th Edition, 1990. When I got into Daisy's new Model 44, a look-alike resembling S&W's large-frame 44 Magnum, my toughest job became deciding which to keep.

The standard Daisy Power Line 44 comes with 6-inch barrel. At $10 each, 4- and 8-inch optional, interchangeable barrels are available. These come as a kit with outer barrel shroud, a rifled steel inner shooting barrel, a barrel nut wrench and a barrel spacer gauge. I have the Power Line Model 144, which number designates it as the nickel-plated gun with 8-inch barrel (only) at around $10 more than standard finish. The standard finish is a durable, blue-black coating by electrostatic deposition.

The handsomely nickeled Daisy 144 has a hold on me because of my own penchant for shiny guns. In contrast, Crosman's Model 357-8GT, a Colt Python look-alike, also has 8-inch barrel but not a true plated finish. And neither of these pistols fit into the petite class. Though I called the 357-8 a "Dirty Harry"-size, Daisy's Model 144 is even a shade bulkier at 2 pounds, 10 ounces, empty. The 144's heft is excel-

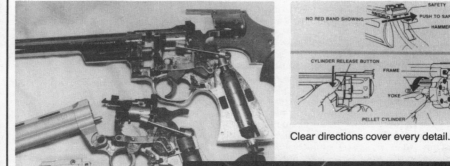

(Above) Similarity of the lockwork in the Daisy 44 (top) and the Crosman 357 is striking. The messy looking lubricant generously applied at key friction points is author's Molykote G paste.

Clear directions cover every detail.

lent with the popular two-hand hold nor does the heavy hammer fall disrupt one's aim—the blow is well absorbed by the gun's mass.

For dry-fire practice, a manual cross-bolt safety blocks the hammer from striking the CO_2 outlet valve stem. Much shooting and long sequences of dry fire with various pellets in place have thus far produced no pellet shifting except when I loaded previously chambered pellets. Regardless, never force the gun

to cock if any added effort should ever be felt, since this would put undue strain on the indexing mechanism.

To provide a needed grip on pellets chambered in the cylinder, the Daisy 144 has three longitudinal ribs in each chamber. One can readily observe the inertial force that hammer fall produces by watching the cylinder move backward 0.008-

inch as the hammer drops during dry fire. That's because, on cocking, the indexing hand rotates the cylinder and positions it forward flush against barrel breach.

My first impression with Daisy's barrel-to-cylinder gap adjustment system was that here's something to play with: i.e., how much would various gaps affect power. However, reducing the gap disrupts the designed smooth operation of cylinder rotation and timing. It is interesting to note that Daisy's method even incorporates a form of spring-loaded cylinder stop and the 0.008-inch gap is almost an industry standard for cartridge revolvers.

In the accuracy department, as expected, results varied with types and pellet brands used. Most airgunners have at some time come face to face with this pellet-to-gun idiosyncrasy. As I gained confidence with the 144, it was heartening to have some groups tighten up to one ragged hole.

The solid-frame Daisy design would, one might think, allow cleaning only from the muzzle end. Fortunately, the barrel and shroud removal feature allows easy disassembly. It could be sinful to stroke a cleaning rod from the 144's muzzle and risk damage to the fine rifling, which is done by Daisy, not Lothar Walther. The gun is all U.S.-made.

Loading CO_2 within the grip is about normal. The 144 provides a spring steel clamp, attached to left grip plate, which snaps and holds into the grip frame, independent of the CO_2 cylinder.

The synthetic rear sights are fully adjustable, and quite precise. Because of a slight tilt, the 144 required a small wedge under the right-hand side to square up with the ramp front sight, as did the earlier Crosman test gun.

The Daisy 144 has a precision-cast, well-fitting sideplate covering the lock work, fastened by two screws. The feel and operation of the trigger mechanism under the plate is much in line with firearms quality.

A good trigger is what invariably separates the match or target gun from the utility and plinker model. The Daisy 144 trigger, out of the box, was somewhat heavy at 5⅛ pounds. After four trials at a fix, it now has a 2¾-pound pull. The double-action pull is commendably low at 10½ pounds.

For a change from single shot monotony, the Daisy 144 offers faster, reliable, repeater action. Lead pellets are difficult to manage with in-line feed magazines, but a revolver cylinder allows maximum individual protection to any variety of pellets. Low cost practice should make this pellet revolver replica a boon to many pistoleros.

Ladd Fanta

Shooting China's New Gang of Four

TESTFIRE GD REPORT

China's gang of four budget-priced rifles are, left to right, the TS-45 air rifle, JW-8 22 bolt action, 7.62x39mm SKS and the 7.62x54R Type 53 carbine.

ARE THE DAYS when a teenager could earn enough money during the summer mowing lawns, or delivering newspapers to buy a first rifle gone forever? The cost of a new airgun, 22 boltgun or high-power hunting rifle is beyond the reach of most kids today, isn't it?

Not if you consider the bargains in plain, basic airguns and firearms being imported from China. Sophisticated shooters will turn up their noses, but when examined seriously, the low-cost imports offer a serviceable starter or extra gun for not much money. The "gang of four" which follow are adequate for the tyro, or as extras to stash in the pickup, or for utility use around the farm.

Let's look at China's "gang of four" basic rifles:
1. **Air rifle, 4.5 mm/177, single shot, side-lever cocking.**
   The TS-45 military-style trainer has a stock and sights similar to the SKS rifle. It is made by Norinco, and imported by Midwest Sport Distributors, Box 129, Fayette, MO 65248. It retails for $42.95, and is a good buy for somebody who is not a dedicated air rifle enthusiast, but wants to have one.
2. **Bolt-action 22 LR, five-**

shot detachable box magazine.

The JW-8 military-style bolt-action trainer is imported as military surplus by Navy Arms. This faithful copy of the famed BRNO design is simple, robust and accurate, and sells in used condition for around $65. These rifles have a well-deserved reputation for accuracy. The JW-15 is the newly manufactured sporter version of the same rifle by Norinco, which is

imported by both Navy Arms and Interarms and sells for $115.
3. **Semi-automatic, 7.62x 39mm, SKS, ten-shot magazine.**
   The ubiquitous SKS is the "gentleman's military rifle." With its non-detachable ten-shot magazine, it escapes the sinister "assault rifle" label. It is a sturdy and dependable workhorse for the pickup or hunting camp and is widely available from numerous sup-

pliers. Used prices are often under $100, and they sell new for $150 and up.

4. **7.62x54R, Type 53 carbine, five-shot magazine.** The Chinese Type 53 is based on the simple but strong Mosin-Nagant action, and is similar to the USSR M1944. The "world's cheapest deer rifle" shoots far better than it looks and can be had in good used condition from Navy Arms for $69.95. (Check current pricing.)

Examining each rifle in turn, let's look at what you get:

The TS-45 air rifle is a 4.5 mm/177-caliber pellet-firing side-lever cocker originally designed for pre-induction military training of school-age youth. Its strong physical resemblance to the SKS is no accident. It is sturdily built, having a light varnished hardwood stock and blued steel parts.

The quality of its exterior finish is utilitarian, in keeping with its military origins—plain but practical. The side-lever cocking mechanism requires only moderate effort. The gun is easy to use, fun to shoot and accurate. The trigger pull is heavy, but quite usable. Its open military-style sights are a bit crude for serious target work, but adequate for plinking and junior training. Velocity of the TS-45 is typical for airguns of the type, about 600-640 fps depending upon pellet weight.

Best accuracy was obtained with Beeman Super Kodiak and RWS Super-H-Point pellets, which do a good job on garden pests at close range. Using the inexpensive Chinese pellets that came with the rifle, five-shot groups at 10 meters (33 feet) averaged an inch. Changing to Beeman Super Kodiak or RWS Super-H-Points, one-inch groups were obtained out to 50 feet, about the maximum useful range of the rifle for pest shooting. This grouping is comparable to CB Longs fired in iron-sighted 22 sporters at the same range. The TS-45 does the same jobs as well and a lot more cheaply.

The TS-45 is ideal for teaching juniors safe gun handling and instructing them in marksmanship fundamentals. I sure wish I'd had one when I was a kid. A single shot air rifle teaches better discipline than the high-capacity BB guns which we used so indiscriminately when I was a boy. The TS-45 is accurate enough to allow adults to hone their skills, and mine gets a lot of use year round for that purpose.

The JW-8 22 bolt action was also designed as a military trainer. It is plain, but sturdy, reliable and highly accurate as light 22 boltguns go. Mine was made in 1968, and came with some exterior dings, but nothing which affected serviceability. I have been delighted. Since I got my JW-8, several friends have also done so, and everyone has been happy.

There is nothing more satisfying than loading a magazine with CCI Green Tag, and setting the sight elevator on 100 meters and shooting a nicely centered 2-inch group with the first pop out of the box. When is the last time you got a rifle that didn't need to be zeroed? I use mine for informal military-style iron-sight, offhand matches and manage to hold my own against the fellows with fancier and more expensive rifles.

The JW-8 receiver is grooved, but apparently for something other than the common Tip-Off rings, which we could not get to fit securely on the military receivers. Nick Croyle drilled and tapped his to take a Weaver 63A base. This works well because you can still use the open sights through the trough of the scope base. I put Unertl blocks on mine, and I have to admit my Unertl Small Game scope looks like it belongs there. (The new JW-15 sporter readily accepts Tip-Off rings for popular scopes.)

Iron sight five-shot groups hover around an inch at 50 yards, which is as good as you can hold. With a scope, you can hang ten shots within an inch at 50 yards with relative ease, if using good ammunition. This is as accurate a 22 as anybody needs if not engaged in formal competition. It's better than the bolt 22 I had as a kid. You can also put the sight elevator all the way up to 200 meters and the graduations are right. If you crack a well-aimed shot at the metallic silhouette chicken you can hear the faint "clink" after the report, and you don't have to walk downrange to set them up nearly as often as you will with your '06.

The 7.62x39 SKS rifle is today's semi-automatic equivalent of a Winchester Model 94 carbine. It is all you could want for a "spare" rifle, being light, handy, simple and reliable. It's not the most accurate rifle around, but a consistent 3-4 inch 100-yard grouper, which is adequate for practical field use. It's easy to shoot and accurate enough to do any iron-sight work just fine. The SKS is a lot of utility rifle for not much money.

Several folks I know picked these up to keep as first center-fire rifles for youngsters. We pass on the following advice. You don't want a new shooter to start right off with a semi-automatic, of course. A manually operated repeater is better and safer. It's a snap to convert the SKS to a straight-pull bolt-action, and, at will, restore normal operation. This is done by removing the handguard and gas cylinder, dropping out the piston rod, and reassembling the rifle without it. This has the advantage of being able to teach the young shooter to load one round at a time, and you don't always have a "hot" rifle which loads itself after each pop. Manual operation discourages new shooters from blazing away and teaches them instead to hold 'em and squeeze 'em, while saving the brass for reloading. The SKS is restored to semi-auto operation by replacing the piston rod once proper fire discipline and safe handling have been instilled. Another tip is to remove the folding bayonet, taking a pound off the rifle.

Surplus 7.62x39 ammo is common as dirt and nearly as cheap. When loaded with softpoint bullets the 7.62x39 cartridge is adequate for varmints or deer up to 100 yards or so. Surplus ammo is so cheap many SKS owners don't even bother to reload. Several friends pull down ball ammo and replace the FMJ slugs with 123-grain Hornady spire points and laugh at my reloading nonsense.

However, I find the SKS is a joy to shoot with cast bullets, and a charge of 15-16 grains of #2400 and the NEI No. 52A bullet works well indeed. The same bullet loaded without the gascheck over 5 grains of Bullseye is a fine small game and plinking load, whereas 2 grains of Bullseye and the 130-grain NEI No. 58, without gascheck, makes a fine 50-foot gallery load for indoor practice. A useful rifle, that SKS.

The Chinese Type 53 7.62x54R bolt-action carbine is based on the Mosin-Nagant action, and similar to the USSR M1944 carbine. For sporting use I recommend the folding bayonet be removed, which is a pound of useless weight. Doing so yields a handy, short rifle with 20.4-inch barrel, not quite as trim as the M1910 and M1938 Russion carbines. It has the heft of a Winchester 94, and ballistics like a 308 Winchester. Surplus military ball ammunition is readily available, and softpoint hunting ammunition is available from Hansen and Norma.

To engage the safety on the Nagant action, grasp the cocking piece, pull it back slightly and rotate it counter-clockwise so that it engages the left rear of the receiver. Simple but effective. The straight bolt handle is felt by many to be awkward to operate, but it is not difficult if you use the same technique used by Finnish soldiers in WWII film clips. The trick to operating a straight bolt handle is to place the palm of your right hand over the receiver bridge with your thumb pressing on the left side of the receiver. The thumb provides additional opening leverage while your first and second fingers grasp the bolt handle. Use a quick rotation of your wrist and work the bolt with a smooth rocking motion. It is possible to operate the rifle rapidly from the shoulder, though it cannot be done with the facility of a good Springfield, of course.

Most of these rifles have seen hard service, but have chrome-lined bores, so even though the outside may be rough, bores remain shootable. A lightly pitted bore will give good hunting accuracy with jacketed bullets as long as the muzzle crown is in good shape. Cast bullets can also be used if of .313-.314-inch diameter, well lubricated, and velocities are kept to about 1600-1800 fps. The NEI No. 52A bullet cast of wheelweights weighs about 166 grains and, when pushed by 16 grains of #2400, will group better than the 3-4 inches you get at 100 yards with ball ammunition, more like the 2½ to 3 inches you can get with softpoints if your eyes are good. I have found the Chinese barrels run large, and bullets intended for the 303 British are more accurate than the 30s.

The Chinese Type 53 may not be the rifle you show off proudly to your friends, but if you want an inexpensive, handy and powerful extra gun, it will get the job done. It isn't fancy, but it works, and besides, if I didn't include it, we wouldn't have a Chinese "gang of four," now would we?

C.E. Harris

Rifles and shotguns with tang safeties make a variety of shooters happy: the grizzled, the collegiate and the Packer fan, shown here, included.

by LEE H. ARTEN

UNDER MY THUMB

I'M NOT MUCH of a Rolling Stones fan, but the title of one of their songs makes a lot of sense to me. The song, "Under My Thumb," has something to do with interpersonal relations. To me, it simply suggests the best place for a safety on a rifle or shotgun.

I'm a fan of the tang safety, but I cheerfully shoot guns with other kinds. Guns without tang safeties get a lot of use in target shooting, plinking, even for some casual hunting.

When I'm hunting seriously these days, I take one of three guns out of the rack. For deer I pick up my Ruger M77 lightweight in 250-3000. Last year, to prove it could be done, I hunted during grouse season with a 12-gauge Mossberg 500 riot gun. The bobbed-off, all-business look of the Mossberg might send the anti-gunners into hysterics, but it worked well on grouse. The third gun, a FIAS 20-gauge over/under has been around longest. It makes a sweet grouse, woodcock and rabbit gun.

At first glance, my 250-3000 and the two shotguns don't seem to have much in common. A closer look, or handling them, reveals that in ready position each one has a safety that fits neatly, conveniently, under the thumb.

In print a while back, someone bad-mouthed tang safeties, the ones on Ruger M77s in particular. I've forgotten the writer's name, but his claim that the Ruger's safety was noisy and made the rifle hard to carry still rankle. He and I must carry rifles differently. I've had no problem with the safety when walking my Ruger around the woods.

Noisy safeties were something that hadn't really worried me until I ran across that article. To see if I'd missed a flaw in my favorite deer rifle, I checked it against a number of other guns. The Ruger tang safety was louder than those on the Mossberg and the FIAS, or the cross-bolt safeties on two Model 12 Winchesters. It was quite a bit quieter than the wing safeties on two semi-sporterized Mauser bolt rifles, and about as quiet as a blackpowder rifle or Marlin 336.

The quietest safeties I found were on the Mossberg, the FIAS, a 1917 Enfield, an M-1 Carbine, and on a single barrel Bronco 410. Two of these were tang safeties. One, on the Enfield, works almost like a tang, although it is set to one side of the bolt. The Carbine's safety is a swinging lever in front of the guard. The Bronco has a cross-bolt type in the frame behind the trigger guard. This informal test took about 10 minutes. It covered many available safety types and indicated any kind of safety can be quiet.

If a safety isn't as noiseless as you'd like, there is often a way to cut down on the clicking and snicking. With most safeties, putting the thumb on one side and a finger on the other and pushing together will slow and partially still the operation. This works, more or less, with all the safeties I've tried, but quiets cross bolts best. I've used the technique in the field, but it is rarely necessary. I shot three deer with the M77 in the last two seasons. I had the wind in my face each time and the deer may not even have heard the safety coming off. If they did hear the click, none paid any attention. No bucks appeared while I hunted with my muzzleloader last season. I did cock the hammer with deer under the sights three times. The does paid no attention to the cocking sound, either.

So far, I've established that tang safeties can be comfortable to use and quiet. Now let's consider simplicity. For me, the tang-type is the simplest safety going, and simplicity is important. I've been hunting for almost 25 years, but I still get a touch of buck fever occasionally. I lost a chance at a deer once because of the fever and a Mauser three-position safety. I've never liked Mauser wings since. Cross-bolt safeties are simple, but the manufacturers keep moving them around. I checked five guns with cross bolts; three had the safety in front of the trigger guard, two had it in back. That can get confusing, especially if you switch guns a lot. (I haven't done it much lately, but in my misspent youth I sometimes used two or three different guns in eight hours of grouse hunting.)

I find tang safeties as simple as any I've used. The only shots I've lost with a tang have come because the FIAS safety also functions as a barrel selector. When I change the firing sequence, the selector will sometimes stop between barrels, keeping either from firing. If I'd learn to set it and forget it, I'd never have a problem.

Besides being simple, tang safeties are also the fastest for me. This is because, despite differences in the size and shape of pistol grips and actions, a tang safety is always in just about the same place. This means that quick safety use, a necessity during grouse season, transfers to the M77 that I carry during deer season. With my three-gun tang-safetied battery, I can go from shotgun to rifle and back without hesitation. Using a tang safety, I never have to stop and wonder where the gun builder left it last time.

Tang safeties are available on Ruger, Browning and Steyr bolt rifles, Ruger single shots, the Savage 99, Mossberg shotguns and most, if not all, double barrel shotguns. Most serious shooters probably have at least one tang-safety-equipped gun. I think shooters who want to be more serious could do worse than to assemble a battery of guns with tang safeties. The only difficulty would be finding a tang safety on a good 22 rifle. The Browning A-Bolt 22 is the only one I'm aware of now.

Tang safeties are fast and easy to find when you need them. Unfortunately, they aren't found in all the places they should be. Versions of the Ruger 77/22 should have tang safeties to match centerfire Ruger 77s. A lever 22 with a tang safety would be the best understudy for the Savage 99, too.

If tang safeties appeared on a couple more good 22 rifles our imperfect world would be just a bit more perfect. Then each gun in a four gun all-around battery would have the safety right where it belongs—under my thumb. ●

One Good Gun

by CARLOS SCHMIDT

A S&W 1917 Surviving In Nicaragua

I WAS HAPPY when my friend Salvador Luna called me to look at some old guns. Being an inveterate gun tinkerer for years before moving to Nicaragua, I had given up hope of locating any legal arms to purchase and use. During the war with the Contras, the Sandinista government distributed many thousands of AK-47s, Moisin-Nagants, SKSs, Makarovs, and Tokarevs to elements of pro-Sandinista groups. Most or all of these weapons are good for shooting people under 100 yards, but are not very good for plinking, reloading, or hunting the small and medium game which abounds in Nicaragua.

"Street" arms are easy to buy, but I wanted a firearm with papers, so I could get a carrying permit and wander the cloud forest and rain forest to my heart's content, searching for the succulent iguana, delicious *guardatinaja* (*Agouti paca*), the fleet-footed *cusuco* (armadillo) and the cotton-tail rabbit. There are also fairly abundant populations of whitetail deer (though much smaller in size than in the U.S.), javelinas, the large and cantankerous white-lipped peccary (on the east coast), and the tapir. Some time ago, I declared a truce with the spotted cats of Nicaragua as they are a thrill to see in the rain forest and I don't like to eat cat meat.

Salvador's offer was to my liking: If I worked on some old pistols, I could pick out a Model 1917 Smith & Wesson 45 revolver if I could find one that would shoot. I arrived at Salvador's home and was led to a room that contained many parts of handguns. Foremost on the floor was a nondescript crate, probably Cuban, that

contained 38 partially dissembled Model 1917s. They were a mixed assembly of whole and partial revolvers that looked like they had been in that box since 1918. No revolver had been used very much as none had cylinders that showed any wear from the cylinder bolt. Four or five revolvers were complete with grips and mainspring. Those had obviously been fired with corrosive priming many, many years ago and had never been cleaned. The cylinders were rusted shut and the handguns could not be opened nor would the trigger raise the hammer more than ¼-inch. Several other revolvers had mainsprings but lacked other parts so they couldn't fire.

Of the 38 handguns, twelve had very good to excellent barrels showing only very slight dots of rust, consistent with Managua's humid climate. Another fifteen had serviceable bores that in all probability would stabilize the 45 ACP military bullet. The last lot of revolvers had barrels that were a deep red in color and would make excellent mini-shotguns, if I could find a twenty-year-old article on how to make shot cartridges for the 45 ACP out of cut-off 7.62 NATO brass.

After separating the 45s into three groups I started to work, pirating, replacing parts, and rebuilding revolvers. The most critical problem was lack of a sufficient number of mainsprings; someone, who knows when or why, partially dissembled the revolvers and removed over half of the mainsprings. Fifty years of caked Cosmoline on the inside of the lockplate was difficult to clean up and I went through two cans of WD-40, easy enough to come by in

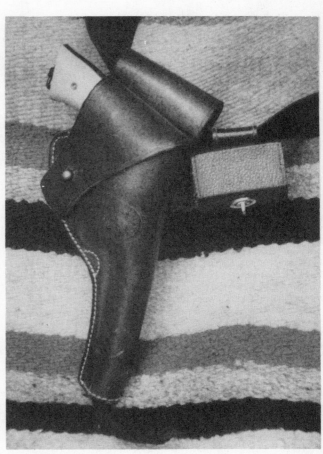

Author found 1917 holster a sensible choice for the 1917 S&W revolver. Could the military have done something right?

the States, but not easy at all to come by in post-revolutionary Nicaragua.

Critical tolerances in revolvers usually include the crane's alignment with the frame, cylinder alignment with the barrel, and the bolt timing with the cylinder. I learned long ago to be very conservative in switching crane and cylinder from one frame to another, so if the crane

was defective on a revolver I left it alone. The fit of the sear contact between the hammer and the trigger is another critical fitting operation, so it is almost always best to substitute the lockwork as a unit rather than in parts. By lifting the complete lockwork from one frame to another, I kept the same interworking of parts and consequently the same trigger pull.

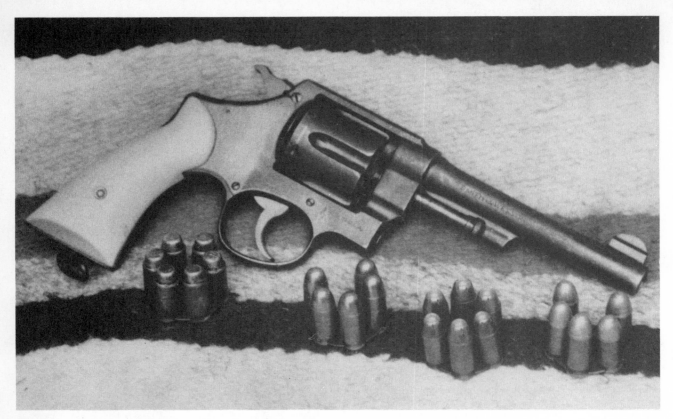

The old gun handles all kinds of loads to fit every Nicaraguan need.

After a few hours I had twelve complete revolvers that worked reasonably well, with very good to excellent bores. I was impressed that all of the revolvers had obviously been carefully hand-fitted and all had a smooth double action with a twelve-pound pull, and not much variation. The single-action trigger pulls on the twelve revolvers were all about three pounds, again with very little variation. All the cylinders were tight, and all of the discoloration on the outside of the guns was from two causes. First, some guns had obviously been rained upon and left to sit in the wooden crate for years, as one side of the revolver would be in perfect condition and the other side would be so deeply pitted that the barrel appeared to have steps or different levels on the outside. The rest of the revolvers appeared to be scratched as if all the handguns had been placed in a gunny sack and tossed around for some time.

Salvador, true to his word, gave me a legal bill of sale for the revolver of my choice, serial number 27670. I subsequently got an unlimited concealed weapons carrying permit with

almost no problem. That old gun had no marks on the cylinder caused by the bolt and had a perfect bore and trigger pull. It had been missing two of the lockplate screws, grips, mainspring and stirrup, and had the lockwork caked with old Cosmoline. The original Parkerizing showed no holster wear. There are many scratches caused from neglect and having all the guns piled together for years. There were no markings showing United States property, only Smith & Wesson commercial markings. It is an old, very slightly used, revolver.

After some scrounging, I located a box of 45 ACP WCC71 ammo and some full-moon clips. I made an almost perfect replica of the 25-yard NRA outdoor timed-fire target and proceeded to the north shore of Lake Managua to try out the old gas pipe. Using a two-hand hold and aiming at six o'clock at the target at 25 yards, the old trooper placed five shots in a two-inch group about an inch to the left of center. That old revolver can shoot. At 50 yards, using a two-hand hold, the sights appear to be dead on at the point of aim; the group was five inches. At 100 yards I had little difficulty hitting 5-gallon cans; apparently the military hardball round is flatter shooting than generally known.

At this point, it can be asked what a Model 1917 Smith & Wesson revolver is doing in Nicaragua. One can only speculate, but the events of 1925 to 1979 may shed some light on that speculation. From 1910 to 1934, Nicaragua had numerous "revolutions," more correctly described as fights among a relatively few families about who should run the show. The United States sent military aid and some Marines sporadically during the 1920s. When Augusto C. Sandino revolted in 1927, President Coolidge and then-President Hoover sent approximately 1500 Marines to subdue Sandino. While the Marines were in Nicaragua, they began instructing and outfitting a local constabulary that was later commanded by Anastasio Somoza Garcia.

From photographs of the era, one can plainly see the small arms carried by both Marines and the constabulary, later called the Guardia Nacional. The Marines carried, as would be expected, the Model 1911A1 45 auto, the Springfield Model 1903, and used the Thompson submachine gun, the Lewis gun, and the Colt water-cooled heavy machinegun. The Nicaraguans, in most photos, carried Krags and Model 1917 revolvers. After the Marines left in 1933 the Nicaraguans be-

came armed with standard U.S. arms.

Somoza was apparently a packrat when it came to military items. It is reported that when the Sandinistas took over in 1979, they found warehouses with all sorts of old crates, many of which were dumped into the ocean. Salvador had the foresight to scrounge what he could, and so I have my S&W 45.

Holsters are a matter on which I hold strong feelings. The three greatest influences on holster developments in the last thirty years have been Arvo Ojala, 007, and Rambo. Arvo Ojala, about 1950, invented the holster and belt that became famous and obligatory in all television and movie westerns. Those not too historically inclined apparently assumed that what was on television was authentic and began buying that type of holster en masse. At best, it looks like a garter belt and the holster fits into a slot in the belt. It looks great but doesn't have any more relation to the Old West than an Edsel. James Bond made things worse with his PPK and Berns-Martin shoulder holster. Since the 1960s, many semi-automatic pistols and rigs have been marketed, all based on a need for concealability and high volume fire at human targets.

Writer finds a good revolver a better tool for small targets at short ranges—so do most shooters.

Writer bags most Nicaraguan game, small to medium, with some emphasis on rocks.

Those arms and holsters and those uses probably exclude 99.5 percent of all handgun owners. What goes for 007 goes even stronger for Rambo guns and rigs. The image sells guns by selling a fantasy of little utility to most people.

For the S&W, I felt I should look for a holster that I could carry on a belt since I wasn't worried about concealability; one that would not allow the handgun to fall out of the holster easily; one that would protect the handgun from the elements; and one that would look appropriate (whatever that means).

Several years ago, I happened to be riding a horse in a particularly desolate desert in the United States. I was looking for Indian rock carvings on that warm October morning and was carrying a Ruger single action in a half-flap holster sold by El Paso Saddlery. It was designed by copying the Model 1917 holster made for the Model 1917 revolver. That holster was not a cross-draw type and carried the revolver on the right side neither tilted backward or forward. The pistol grip was level with the top of the pistol belt and the handgun was secured in the holster by a half-flap that

covered the back of the gun but left the grip free to be grasped easily and relatively quickly.

That holster was genuinely authentic looking, even if I can't recall Richard Boone carrying one on "Have Gun Will Travel." In any event, I was looking at cliff faces while my horse picked his way around some rocks. Old Dobbin walked toward the beginnings of a sand dune that extended up to a rock face perhaps 100 feet in height. I had apparently ridden into an area where prairie rattlers were denning up for the winter. A rattlesnake on the side of that rock face struck at the eye of my horse. My trusty steed reared into the air at least 25 feet (it felt) and launched me into a double backward somersault. I landed flat on my back next to a sand dune and was secure in the knowledge that my trusty Ruger was still in its holster and protected from the sand into which I had fallen. In looking for a holster to acquire for the old S&W, I gravitated toward the Model 1917 holster and have not been at all unhappy with it. It protects the handgun, keeps it readily accessible and doesn't look at all bad.

In Nicaragua, as in the United States, my most numerous victims are rocks. I love to shoot and kill rocks. I don't have to fast-draw and the rock flies

apart if I hit it. Since Nicaragua has no desert but lots of swamps, I expect to shoot some mud clumps, alligators, armadillos, rabbits, iguanas, and, from time to time, a stray fer-de-lance (pit viper). For these uses, the 45 ACP is surprisingly useful. Rather than try to magnumize a 75-year-old revolver, I have tried to make handloads that would not strain anything. I recalled back twenty years when I started shooting a Colt Model 1917 revolver and reloading for it. As with the S&W Model 1917, I was impressed that the old Colt shot G.I. ammo amazingly well and it was much easier to hit small targets with it than the Model 1911A1, probably due to a much better issue trigger and sights and stationary barrel.

Reloading cast bullets, I remembered, was more difficult. Because the rifling in both the Colt and S&W is shallow, cast bullets are not gripped by the rifling very well, especially if they are cast soft. I had good luck with Lyman bullet number 452460, a 200-grain semi-wadcutter that had a long bearing surface in relation to its weight. As long as the bullets were sized to at least 0.452-inch and cast hard, that Colt shot well. I then tried a Keith-style 240-grain semi-wadcutter, number 452423 and again found that that bullet shot well as long as I cast them hard and sized them no smaller than the diameter of the cylinder throats. The light bullets always shot low and the heavy bullets always shot high. Since that old Colt had fixed sights, like the S&W, I had to learn to hold high or low. Relying on my experiences with that old Colt,

I began experimenting with hard-cast bullets and the S&W. Driven to approximately 900 fps by Unique, the 225-grain round-nose cast bullet, made of the hardest, tempered alloy I could cast, one that my fingernail and tooth bounced off with nary a scratch, did everything I wanted from that old trooper. I would have liked to try the Keith cast bullet or number 452460, but I couldn't scrounge them in Nicaragua.

My only complaint is that the smoke generated by Unique and Alox bullet lubricant just doesn't smell as good as the smoke generated by the old, black, Lyman bullet lubricant and Bullseye powder. Sadly, there is no Bullseye in Nicaragua. All jacketed bullets shoot very accurately in the S&W, no soft or .451-inch bullets shoot worth beans, and the 225-grain round-nose cast hard and sized fat is a deadly round for any rock up to at least 25 pounds in weight.

That hard-cast bullet has another utility. Game shot with that bullet, no matter how small or large, does not show any bloodshot meat when the game is cooked. You can eat right up to the bullet hole, something that should not be attempted with many hot loads employing magnum calibers and jacketed, open-pointed bullets. I have found the S&W to be a good shooter and practical sidearm for the savannas and cloud forests of Nicaragua. The only problem now is that I need a long gun. Salvador said that he had located, in an old government warehouse, some very old crates with the word "Krag" painted on them. We'll see, we'll see. ●

by DICK LOVE

A Special Single-Action Colt

I BOUGHT MY first short-action Colt Officer's Model by mistake back in 1960. I was in the Marines then and used to shoot with some pros who were on the base's pistol team. They told me that if I was ever going to do any good with a revolver, I needed an Officer's Model.

In those days, the Colt factory shot a five-round test target with each gun and passed this target on to the customer. What sold me on this particular Officer's Model was the test target. All five rounds were touching, and the group was centered in the X-ring. The weapon had a beautiful single-action let-off, and to be honest, I didn't even think to try the double-action pull. Nobody I knew was firing double action then anyway. I paid $87 and change, standard price for an Officer's Model, and took the revolver home.

It wasn't until a few days later that I noticed the revolver wouldn't fire double action. Pulling the trigger through would rotate the cylinder, but the hammer wouldn't cock and fall. At first, I thought the gun was defective and called the gun shop to complain. The shop's owner sounded surprised and said to bring the Colt in for an exchange.

When I got to the shop, he explained that the gun had been sold by mistake. It had a special shortened hammer fall that gave a faster lock time and was designed for single-action target work only. I thought about this for a few minutes, looked at the test target again, realized the thing was going to be used on targets anyway, and decided to keep it. The owner was a little upset about this, so I asked how much more I owed him for the short action. He growled some and turned away without

answering. I figured what the hell, took my revolver and left.

The old Colt saw a lot of use, but I never approached being good enough for any of the Marine Corps teams. When I left the Corps years later, the revolver went the way of most good things. Money was tight for a new civilian, and I sold the Officer's Model, a Smith & Wesson Model 19 and a 44 Single Action Army to help finance two children and a wife.

In the years since, I'd never seen, read or heard anything of an Officer's Model with a target short action. Then in 1975, I came onto one. John Barclay's gun shop in Van Nuys, California, was selling an Officer's Model in excellent condition that, according to John, had a factory short action. "They didn't make many of these," John said. "It was back in '58 or '59, and they only sent me a few of them." The revolver was iden-

Both of the writer's SA Officer's Models shoot very well, starting with the factory target for his first one.

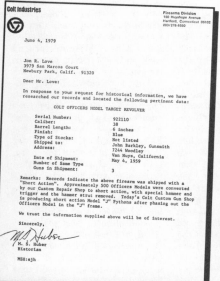

Factory letter establishes that this SA Colt is authentically one of about 500.

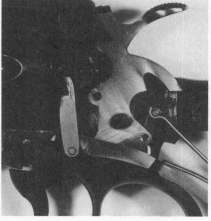

These SA Officer's Models had special hammers and triggers and no hammer struts.

tical to the one I'd owned back at Camp Pendleton.

Prices, though, had gone up. John wanted $200, which was for me a lot of money. But it wasn't the price that decided it. Somehow, less complicated times came to mind. I remembered the good parts of being in the Marine Corps. I thought about the men I had served with and remembered all the hours spent target shooting with friends at the old Las Pulgas range. It came to me that it's not often a man can capture a relic from his past for only $200. I signed the check, smiling.

The test target from the first Officer's Model was found tucked away with some other old papers. Both guns are in the 920,000 serial number range and must have been made about the same time. Trying to find out more about the short action, I wrote the *American Rifleman*'s "Arms Chest" section. The "Arms Chest" expert wrote back that he had never heard of a short-action Colt and felt that my Officer's Model had been modified by a private gunsmith. I was a little disappointed at this and hoped that the *American Rifleman*'s expert had been mistaken.

It turned out that he had. I wrote Colt's Historian, Mr. Martin Huber, and asked for shipping information on the Colt. According to Mr. Huber, the Officer's Model was shipped in 1959 to John Barclay. Further, Mr. Huber wrote that the revolver's short action is indeed a factory modification, and that about five hundred J-frame revolvers had been shipped with this special target feature.

Colt stopped making the Officer's Model more than twenty years ago. Nobody, it seems, is much interested in the 38s anymore. That's probably not really all that bad. I don't know, though. Those old Colts sure were put together.

Browsing through the used gun section of a shop in Encino the other day, I paused over a blue-worn old Colt.

"That's an Officer's Model," the young clerk said. "It's got the same action as a Python. It's a great old gun."

"I know," I told him. "I know." ●

My "Fake" Double Rifle

AFTER THE Second World War, I, like so many others, returned home, married and began to raise a family. One night, early in my marriage, my wife and I went to the movies. Showing was *The Snows of Kilimanjaro*. At that time, I couldn't understand how a hunter could be shooting big game with what I thought to be a shotgun. I hadn't yet seen or heard about double rifles. Soon after, *The American Rifleman* had an article about double rifles and I fell in love with them. As you know, they are very expensive and quite scarce.

Some years later, a gunsmith in California advertised that he was going to build them to order. He also claimed he could rebarrel a shotgun. I was intrigued with the idea and immediately bought a Richland 20-gauge shotgun for this purpose. I mailed it to him the next day without ever firing it. He inquired several times that summer about specifications for the sights and forearm. You may have heard what happened. That fall he disappeared with everything, including my gun and my money.

I was disappointed, but never gave up my dream of a double rifle and started again. I sent letters, made inquiries, etc. One gunsmith replied, stating he didn't normally do that kind of work but was interested in it as a project and a challenge. In his opinion, the best solution was to sleeve the gun.

I took my gun to his shop and he looked it over. It was a Beretta 16-gauge with double underlocking lugs and a cross bolt at the top. He recommended cutting the barrel to 23 inches, building up the extractors and fitting iron sights. The sleeves

The author's 45-70 passes the duck test—it looks like a double rifle, it works like a double rifle and it shoots like a double rifle.

were 45-caliber, chambered for 45-70. It took between six and eight weeks to complete and was beautifully done. When the breech was opened, you had to look closely to tell where it had been sleeved. I was overjoyed and headed right for the rifle range.

When it was new, my double had a two-notch rear sight—right barrel/right notch; left barrel/left notch. It worked out very well and shot into a 4- to 5-inch group at fifty yards with factory loads and handloads of 405-grain bullets. It was a pleasure to shoot and worked perfectly for my purposes.

Several months later, while reading GUN DIGEST, I discovered an article about double rifles. The author said if a double rifle cross-fired, use a heavier bullet and a slower powder. I decided to try it and purchased 100 500-grain bullets. When I loaded them, I used 32 grains of 3031 powder. At our local gun club range, I tried the new loads. Aiming right down the middle, they went 2 to 3 inches

apart. Off came the two-notch sight and the gunsmith installed a three-leaf sight.

Casting my own bullets of wheelweight lead, they came out at 525 grains. Once the powder is loaded, the empty space between the powder and the bullet is filled with Cream of Wheat brand cereal. This leaves the breech cleaner.

I am very happy with my gun even if it is a fake. It is still tight even though I have had it since the early '70s and have shot hundreds of rounds through it. Whenever the lever is opened and the breech is open, it looks like any double-barreled rifle. The Beretta shotgun we started with has stood up beautifully over the years and is a credit to the company that builds them.

Knowing that people who can afford a double-barrel rifle might look down their noses at this gun, I still get a thrill when I open the breech and drop two of those 45-70s into it and pull up and get off two quick shots. I couldn't be happier if the gun was real—the shooting is. ●

by EDWARD A. MATUNAS

AMMUNITION, BALLISTICS AND COMPONENTS

Eﾠ ACH YEAR these pages are devoted to a discussion of ammunition as loaded by the various manufacturers, and to the components assembled by reloaders. At one time, the shooter requiring sufficient accuracy for long-range efforts was, by definition, a reloader. Today, much of our factory ammo is commendable, even remarkable, with respect to accuracy. The likes of Federal's Premium, Remington's Extended Range and Winchester's Supreme ammo lines come to mind when thinking of accuracy.

For hunters desiring near perfection in big game bullet performance, Remington is offering a Safari Grade line of ammo with superbly performing A-Frame bullets as made by Swift. The new Eldorado brand is now available with the Barnes X-Bullet.

Manufacturers, such as CHAA, are also offering custom-grade ammo for multiple purposes. Despite high cost, such ammo is popular with shooters and hunters who want maximum ammo performance without the financial investment and the time required to get into and learn reloading.

On my first safari I shot handloads exclusively. I wanted the best in accuracy and expansion performance possible. I figured reloads were the only way to get what I wanted. Now several safaris later, I am once again preparing to leave for Africa. My ammo for this hunt includes 416 Rigby loaded by

CHAA with Trophy Bonded Bear Claw softpoint and Barnes Solid bullets, Federal 375 H&H Premium grade rounds loaded with Nosler Partitions, Remington 338 Winchester Magnum Safari ammo with Swift A-Frame bullets, and a supply of reloads assembled with the same types of bullets as used in the mentioned factory ammo. Indeed, I could easily have a perfect hunt without the reloads. It's simply a matter of preference now, unless a balky rifle refuses to shoot well with available ammo.

A trend in recent years has been new big-bore cartridges or new loadings for existing heavy game rounds. This year there are no new big calibers to introduce, but there are new loadings for the medium to big bores, one of the most impressive being Remington's use of the Swift A-Frame bullet in the 338 Winchester Magnum and 375 H&H Magnum. Too, new high-tech bullets in new loads from several ammo makers continue another trend.

High-tech designs such as homogeneous rifle bullets of the expanding kind (Barnes' X-Bullet as used by reloaders and in Eldorado and CHAA loadings), slower expanding and deeper penetrating handgun bullets (Winchester's Black Talon), or the large diameter expansion of the Eldorado Starfire handgun bullets, and a lot of other advances continue in the rapidly changing world of ammunition. Almost every bul-

let manufacturer has addressed the genuine need for sophisticated bullets for a great many applications.

As hunters apply the different bullets on various game, it will be evident that the one perfect bullet for all applications still does not, and may never, exist. For example, among the most-proven solid dangerous-game bullets are the homoge-

Ed and a long-tusked wart hog that was bagged with premium grade ammo loaded with Swift A-Frame bullets.

neous bronze types as produced by both A-Square and Barnes. They foul bores a bit more than traditional jacketed bullets, but have a near perfect reputation. Yet, I have evidence of one of these in each brand that bent and deformed under some less-than-usual circumstance. Select bullets for each job carefully and apply them without introducing some change in circumstance in order to ensure success.

We cannot list every single new round of ammunition or every new component introduced since the last issue, let alone all the minor modifications made to preexisting loads and components. To do so would require far more space than is practical to devote to a single topic. Thus, we attempt to choose those items that we feel will stand the test of time. Yet, our crystal ball is probably not nearly as good as we sometimes might like to believe.

Federal Cartridge Company

There are two new-to-the-Premium-ammo-line cartridges loaded with the time-proven Nosler Partition bullets. These are the 7x64mm Brenneke and the 6.5 Swedish Mauser. While not as popular as the 30-30 or 30-06, there are more

than just a few owners of rifles chambered for these cartridges who will appreciate this top-shelf ammo. Undoubtedly, Federal's short-lived association with the importation of Norma ammo has suggested that they can market European cartridges in sufficient quantity to justify the endeavor.

The 7x64mm Brenneke is loaded with a 160-grain Parti-

Can factory ammo shoot accurately? This 1-inch group was fired with premium factory 270 ammo.

tion bullet, while the 6.5 Swedish uses a 140-grain bullet. Full ballistic data for these, and all the other loads discussed in this effort, appear in the average cartridge ballistics tables that follow these pages.

Also new to the Premium brand line are three match grade loads. These are 69-grain hollowpoint for the 223 Remington and 168-grain hollowpoints for the 308 Winchester and 30-06 Springfield. There are new lightweight varmint bullets of 40-grain weight for the 223 Remington and the 22-250 Remington in the Premium line. These will prove extremely frangible even on quarry as small as prairie dogs. A 60-grain lightweight varmint bul-

"Heavy Game Loads"—loads which duplicate usual industry standard velocity loads with a mid-range shot charge weight.

A saboted slug loaded in a 12-gauge 3-inch case is new under the Premium logo. It develops an advertised velocity of 1550 fps. Saboted slugs are becoming popular with many shooters. Still, the best type of slug (sabot or traditional) for any shotgun

New loads in the Safari Grade ammo line are a 338 Winchester Magnum with a 225-grain bullet and a 375 H&H Magnum with a 300-grain bullet, Swift A-Frames both. The Safari logo ammo will have nickel-plated cases.

I have used the Swift A-Frame bullets in 416 to hunt game as small as whitetail deer and as large as eland. These bullets positively expand on the front half and always stay together on the rear half. They are similar to Nosler Partitions in construction, with the added feature of the front core being bonded to the jacket; thus the bullet will retain most of its mass after expansion. Typically, the A-Frame bullets will expand to double diameter and retain as much as 95 percent of their original weight. Loads like these make reloading unnecessary even for the most demanding hunter. Expensive? Yes, but worth every penny when there is a lot riding on the shot.

A new 38 Special load, with standard pressure levels, is a 110-grain Short Jacket Hollow Point. Ballistics are similar to other manufacturers' loads of this type. (See ballistic tables on nearby pages.)

New turkey load packaging includes 10-gauge 3½-inch, 12-gauge 3½-inch, 12-gauge 3-inch, and 12-gauge 2¾-inch shells. Respective shot weights are 2¼ ounces in the 10- and 12-gauge 3½-inch loads. Two ounces of shot for the 12-gauge 3-inch and 1½ ounces for the standard length 12 will be loaded. All of these are Premier line loadings. A 1¼-ounce 12-gauge standard velocity load using #6 shot has been added under the Shur Shot Field load logo.

A 220 Swift load is being added to satisfy the ammo needs of those who will be purchasing Remington's limited run 1993 Classic Model 700 which will be chambered for this cartridge. It will be loaded with a 50-grain bullet.

CHAA, Inc.

For those not yet familiar with the initials CHAA, they stand for Custom Hunting Ammo and Arms. This outfit, run by Ted Greenwood, produces a line of hunting ammunition, assembled with a broad choice of premium or premium plus bullets. As an experienced big game hunter, Ted understands the importance of the best possible bullet for hunting. Thus, he offers Nosler Partition, Nosler Ballistic Tip, Cor-Bon Bonded Core, Trophy Bonded Bear Claw and Barnes Traditional or X-panding bullets. Calibers offered cover almost all popular choices from the 223 Remington through the

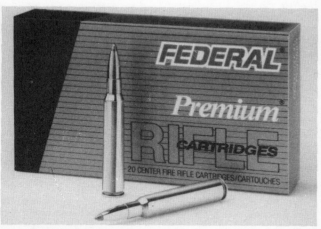

Federal's new Premium package holds some new ammo, like these 7x64mm rounds, and 6.5x55mm as well.

let for the 243 Winchester and a 90-grain 25-06 varmint load are also new Premium centerfire rifle loads. Finally, there is a 120-grain 7-30 Waters Premium load. All of these are loaded with Sierra brand bullets.

The Federal Premium trademark will now be extended to include use on handgun ammo. All of the Hydra-Shok and Nyclad bullets as loaded for the 380 ACP, 9mm Luger, 38 Special, 357 Magnum, 40 S&W, 10mm Auto, and 45 ACP will now carry the Premium brand.

Under the Classic trademark there are three new handgun loads, each having a Federal Hi-Shok hollowpoint bullet. These include the 155-grain 40 S&W, 155-grain 10mm Auto and a 230-grain 45 ACP load. In general, almost all of the loads that used to be sold under the Hi-Power logo will now be sold with the Classic logo. This applies to rifle, handgun, and shotshell ammo. There are a few exceptions which have been upgraded and now are included under the Premium label.

For the American Eagle line of inexpensive ammo, there are two new loads using a 180-grain lead alloy bullet for both the 40 S&W and 10mm Auto. The American Eagle logo shotshell ammo sees the addition of

can be determined only by actual shooting tests with a specific shotgun.

Remington Arms Co.

The Extended Range ammunition line includes six more cartridges now. These are 243 Winchester, 6mm Remington, 257 Roberts, 25-06 Remington, 7mm-08 Remington and 7mm Weatherby Magnum. Both 6mms will be loaded with a 105-grain ER bullet, while both 25s will be loaded with a 122-grain ER bullet. The 7mm-08 is being assembled with a 150-grain ER bullet, while the 7mm Weatherby has a bullet of 165 grains. The Extended Range ammo has been noteworthy for extreme accuracy and therefore appeals to a lot of shooters.

New for large game hunters is Remington's new Safari Grade ammunition line. This line currently includes only loads assembled with the premium-plus grade of Swift A-Frame spitzer softpoint bullets or Barnes Super Solids. The first loads to be incorporated into in this line are the existing three 416 Remington Magmun rounds which include a 350- and 400-grain Swift A-Frame, as well as the 400-grain Barnes solid. These, of course, get the new Safari Grade packaging.

The 10mm Auto with a 155-grain hollowpoint is now included in Federal's Classic handgun loads.

Federal's 3-inch 12-gauge slug is copper-plated.

600 Nitro Express. Barnes Solid bullets are also offered in many calibers. More than seventy standard and not-so-standard cartridges are available under CHAA's Superior Ammunition brand.

The price of this ammo reflects the custom grade bullets used in its assembly. Sure, a seasoned reloader could assemble similar ammo for less, but

New Remington turkey loads in 3½-inch 12- and 10-gauge got out there this year.

not everyone wants to do their own ammo. For these folks premium grade ammo is important, especially when it involves so many first-class choices.

I have had the opportunity to take a hard look at Superior Ammo in caliber 416 Rigby. New virgin Norma cases were used. Loads tested included 400-grain Bear Claw Trophy Bonded softpoint and 400-grain Barnes solids. Packaging was in 10-round (varies with caliber) MTM plastic wallets.

Both loads shot as well as my Ruger 77—always under 2 minutes of angle. The point of impact of the Barnes solid was within 1½-inches of the Bear Claw softpoint at 50 yards. Close enough to allow me to sight in with the expanding bullets and still be able to switch to solids at ranges normal for such loads, without a need to adjust sights.

PMC/Eldorado

PMC ammo has been brought into this country from two Korean plants for many a year. Indeed, it was the PMC paramilitary ammo (now called "Target") that forced the U.S. manufacturers to respond by making similar inexpensive ammo available for plinkers and informal target shooters.

Today, PMC has an ammunition production plant in the Eldorado valley of Nevada. All of the premium grade ammo they sell is loaded in that facility, and it is their goal to manufacture all of their softpoint ammo in this Nevada plant. A spokesman was unable to tell us if the paramilitary ammo was also destined for an eventual shift in production from Korea to the U.S.

The current literature still places the PMC name dominant over the Eldorado name. However, I am told current marketing plans are for the Eldorado name to completely replace the PMC logo. Seems folks there do not simply want to drop the very recognizable PMC logo until they feel that Eldorado has similar recognition.

As mentioned, Eldorado now has several handgun rounds loaded with their new Starfire bullets. This is a unique approach to a hollowpoint variation that provides expansion up to 2½ times bullet diameter. The "hollow" extends to about two-thirds the length of the bullet and has five sharp wedge-shaped ribs on the inside of the cavity. These ribs cause any material entering the point to create forces in the flutes to start dramatic expansion instantaneously. Penetration in 10 percent ballistic gelatin averages about 12 inches—should be enough for rapid incapacitation for most applications. Calibers available are 9mm Luger (115-grain); 38 Special + P (125-grain); 357 Magnum (150-grain); 40 S&W (180-grain); 10mm Auto (180-grain); 44 Magnum (250-grain); and 45 ACP (185-grain). The Starfire loads will be sold under Eldorado's premium brand logo of "Classic" (sound familiar?). All cases will be nickel-plated.

Classic rifle ammo will all be loaded with the Barnes X-Bullet, a homogeneous copper expanding type. (This bullet is described in greater detail under the Barnes bullet section.) Calibers available include 257 Weatherby Magnum (100-grain); 270 Winchester (130- and 150-grain); 270 Weatherby Magnum (130-grain); 7mm Remington Magnum (140- and 160-grain); 7mm Weatherby Magnum (160-grain); 308 Winchester (150- and 165-grain); 30-06 Springfield (150-, 165- and 180-grain); 300 Winchester Magnum (150- and 180-grain); 300 Weatherby Magnum (165- and 180-grain).

The Barnes X-Bullet has been, in the past, a handloader or custom loaded proposition. Its use in a premium line of ammo should allow for a rapid consumer evaluation of its overall performance. This same bullet is also being loaded in Eldorado's Classic Safari Line of ammunition, as is the Barnes homogeneous solid. Loads available are 338 Winchester (225-grain X); 375 H&H (270-grain X and 300-grain solid); 416 Rigby and 416 Remington (both with 350-grain X and 400-grain solid); and 458 Winchester Magnum (400-grain X and 500-grain solid). While PMC/Eldorado does not publish suggested retail prices, their ammo should get to the consumer at about 10 to 15 percent below equivalent other commercial ammo lines.

Of course, Eldorado continues to expand their general line of softpoint ammunition. Added this year are 222 Remington (55-grain softpoint); 22-250 (55-grain FMJ); and loads for the 257, 270, 7mm, and 300 Weatherby Magnum calibers. Also new are a 40 S&W and 10mm Auto with 180-grain hollowpoint.

And for those who shoot the big 50 BMG round, PMC continues to supply it at an affordable price. And mixed in with all the full-metal-case Target ammo is a load for the 6.55x55mm Swedish with a 144-grain bullet.

PMC has been supplying component brass in 200-round packs for some time. Ditto for component bullets. Their new catalog now suggests they will be making available some basic brass for the forming of some oldies but goodies. This might be a way to be able to *safely* use some older firearms. Remember, these cases generally require forming and trimming—thus they are for only the very experienced handloader. The unformed and untrimmed available cases included are shown in a nearby sidebar.

Barnes Bullets

Barnes started making bullets back in 1939. With fifty-plus years in the business they have kept abreast of shooters needs. For a few years now, Barnes has been making available a homogeneous expanding bullet which they call simply "X" bullets. The X-Bullet is a solid copper bullet—no separate jacket or core. As any knowledgeable bullet maker will tell you, one-piece bullets

Remington's Safari Grade Ammo has distinctive packaging. These are 338 Winchester Magnum with 225-grain Swift A-Frame bullets.

are more easily made accurate than bullets assembled from separate components. However, the disadvantage of a solid copper bullet is that it will tend to foul barrels more and it will be a bit longer than one with a dense lead core.

Barnes makes the X-Bullet expand by forming an expansion cavity having four petals on the front end, perhaps best described as a tiny hollowpoint. While hollowpoint bullets have generally failed, in my opinion, as big game bullets, the X-Bullet is gaining a deadly reputation as a bullet that expands well, retains most of its original weight and penetrates deeply. If it has a noticeable shortcoming, its less dense mass sometimes will not allow a traditional bullet weight to be used.

It is no problem to load a 180-grain bullet, or even one of 200 grains, in most 30-caliber cases. But if you are loading a 416 you will be using a 300-, 325-, or 350-grain X-Bullet in place of a traditional 400-grain lead core one. The X-Bullets are all spitzer-shaped, which helps overcome any weight reduction with respect to down-range ballistics.

Accuracy with the half-dozen types of X-Bullets I have used to date has been superb. By the time you read this, I hope to have bashed enough African game to form some personal opinions there. As mentioned earlier, several ammo makers are loading it in premium or custom grade ammo, i.e., Eldorado's Classic and CHAA's Superior ammo. X-Bullets are available from 75-grain .243-inch all the way to 500-grain .458-inch diameter.

Barnes also offers one of the finest true solids available. The traditional large caliber round-nose versions are generally meant for bashing critters of the really tough type. But there are folks who find use for solids

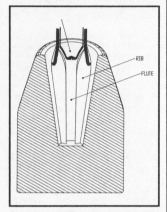

Ribs and flutes in Eldorado Starfire bullet provide rapid expansion.

when hunting critters smaller than Cape buffalo. There are Barnes homogeneous naval bronze round-nose solids in diameters from .600-inch all the way down to .277-inch; and in between there is one designed for a handgun cartridge, i.e. the 44 Magnum. Spitzer solids, also of the same homogeneous bronze, are available in diameters from .224-inch to .375-inch.

Barnes' line of traditional softpoints offers bullets from .224-inch to .475-inch; and in between are a lot of diameters generally available nowhere else. Too, the reloader often has a choice of jacket thickness ranging from 0.030-inch to 0.049-inch. With so much to choose from, Barnes is sure to be pleasing reloaders for another fifty years.

Winchester

Black Talon is Winchester's newest handgun bullet. They say it retains 100 percent of its mass (insuring deep penetration) while expanding to larger diameters. The new bullet will be available in a wide variety of handgun cartridges; the first to be loaded will include 9mm Luger (147-grain), 40 S&W (180-grain), 10mm Auto (200-grain) and 45 ACP (230-grain). The black bullet will be loaded into nickel-plated cases. Plenty of

subsonic handgun loads will be included in the new offerings from Illinois in all the usual popular cartridges.

Turkey loads in the newer 3½-inch 12-gauge shell now include shot sizes #4 and #6 shot at a full 2¼ ounces. These are Grex-buffered and have a velocity of 1150 fps. Also new in the extra-long 12-gauge shotshells is a 00 Buck loading. An 18-pellet 00 Buck 10-gauge 3½-inch load is also new, as is a hollowpoint version of their 12-gauge saboted slugs.

Reloaders will want to get a copy (free) of the 12th edition of the Winchester Ball Powder Data Manual with the included catalog material on all Winchester components. The newer WST, WSL, and WSF shotshell powders are included. The older 452AA and 473AA powders have been discontinued, along with 680.

There is a 16-gauge Double A wad available to the reloader. The new data book is loaded with recipes for the AA com-

Eldorado (PMC to most folks) is enthusiastic about their new Starfire handgun bullets.

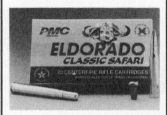

Classic Safari ammo from PMC is all large caliber stuff loaded exclusively with Barnes bullets—either X-Bullet expanding type or homogeneous solids.

pression-formed type cases and this wad.

Handgun data has been noticeably expanded to include lots of loads for the new "shotshell" powders and in areas such as the 9mm Luger, 40 S&W, 10mm Auto and 45 ACP. The new data book is a must if you load Winchester powder.

Nosler

For years Nosler has been busy supplying the superb premium grade Partition hunting

bullets. It would seem Nosler customers love premium bullets, but shun the standard grade plain-vanilla softpoint. The standard line of Solid Base softpoints has been whittled down from twenty-nine choices to a selection of eleven. Perhaps this is the last go with standard bullets for Nosler?

Each year the Partition line expands and this year a 170-grain 30-30 Partition bullet has been added. This is the same bullet Federal has been loading for several years in their Premium 30-30 ammo. The bullet already has a proven track record and it will get the most out of the 30-30. Also new is a 260-grain .375-inch Partition. (I have killed more game with Nosler Partitions than with any other bullet. I never fired a round so doing that gave anything less in the way of performance than as anticipated.)

The Ballistic Tip line of bullets continues to expand rapidly. This year there are four new ones: 6mm, 95-grain; 6.5mm, 100-grain; 7mm, 120-grain; and .338-inch, 200-grain. I have already used up my inventory on each; all are capable of less than minute-of-angle accuracy, shooter and gun being up to the task.

There are also two new handgun bullets from Nosler. Both are .400-inch hollowpoints—a 135- and a 180-grain.

Hercules

No new propellants, but there is an updated Hercules free data booklet. Lots of new shotshell data, including for the 3½-inch 12-gauge shell—up to 2¼-ounce shot charges. More 10-gauge stuff, the new 20-gauge Remington Premier case, and plenty of new target loads. New centerfire cartridge calibers include the 40 S&W, 44-40, 416 Remington and 416 Rigby.

The Hercules data booklet has some loads for cartridges not easily found elsewhere. For example, the 455 Webley and each of the Weatherby Magnums, and the old 348 Winchester.

Accurate

Accurate has another new propellant—2495BR. It is being billed as a medium burning speed suitable for such things as the 6mm BR, 308 Winchester and 30-06 Springfield. The data sheet for 2495BR also list data for the 223 Remington, 225 Winchester, 22-250 Remington, 6mm PPC, 243 Winchester,

6mm Remington, 30-30 Winchester, and 338 Winchester Magnum. The new 2495BR is a single-base extruded-type propellant that the importer suggests has some tendency to muzzle flash in the 30-06 case.

Lyman

During the late 1960s, I was a full-time employee of Lyman. I managed to put together a new lab, and do the data for three reloading handbooks (#44 and 45 Metallic Cartridge and #1 Shotshell) in that time span. Since then, there have been a lot of other handbooks that have come to be. And since then Lyman has produced several new handbooks on cast bullets, shotshell, and metallic cartridges. Remember the saying, "What goes around comes around"? Well, during the last year the Lyman staff and, once again, myself have been hard at work putting together a brand new edition—Metallic Cartridge Reloading Handbook #47.

The new book is big and has a great deal more data than previous editions. Not only have new calibers been added but the data has been expanded for many existing cartridges. Lots of new powders and bullet weights throughout the data section. Equally important is the new style of the handbook. This one is more textbook than any other and every reloader will find it a great asset with some stuff in it not found in any other book. Availability should be about the time this goes to press or shortly after.

As the new text was developed, so were new products to fit specific needs but that's another story. For now, be assured that the new #47 handbook is not simply a rehash of previous editions. It's strong on safety and technical advice, as well as heavy on the servings of data. Buy one—please. Who knows—if it sells well enough Lyman may ask me back to do still another? I could use the money to help finance next year's safari.

Blount

CCI's Blazer ammo has long been a low-cost alternative for the shooter who wants first-class factory ammo but does not care to reload. Blazer uses inexpensive aluminum cases. Hence, ammo gets to the shooter at a very attractive price. Three new Blazer loads have been added this year: 357 Magnum (158-grain), 40 S&W (180-grain), and 45 ACP (230-

Winchester's black bullets penetrate well and offer good expansion without appreciable weight loss.

grain). Each uses a Speer Totally Metal Jacketed (TMJ) bullet.

The 45 ACP load mentioned is the third in a series of loads CCI refers to as Clean-Fire. Each uses a lead and barium-free primer and an electro-chemically plated metal jacket (TMJ) bullet that completely encases the lead bullet core. All this, says Blount, adds up to a

Nosler's Ballistic Tip bullets are popular and accurate. There are four new ones: 6mm 95-grain, 6.5mm 100-grain, 7mm 120-grain and 338 200-grain.

Nosler Partition bullets for the 30-30, exclusively in Federal factory loads for several years, are now available to reloaders who want maximum performance from the cartridge.

lead-free firing point even on indoor ranges.

The TMJ bullet process has also been extended to the manufacturer of hollowpoint, soft-

point, and silhouette designs. Increased accuracy is one of the major advantages of making the bullet jacket from a plating process. High retained bullet weight, after expansion, is another benefit.

Two new handgun component bullets, both 180-grainers are available: .400-inch TMJ and .410-inch hollowpoint. Also, there is a new .500-inch 325-grain hollowpoint. All three use the electro-chemical

The 3½-inch 12-gauge also now comes in 00 buckshot size with 18 pellets; the 10-gauge version counts 18 copper-plated 00s.

jacket forming process that Speer calls Uni-Cor.

Hornady

Lots of new ammo under the Hornady label for this year. Included in the new loadings are 32 ACP, 71-grain FMJ; 44 Remington Magnum, 300-grain XTP; 45 ACP, 200-grain XTP and 230-grain XTP; 303 British, 150- and 174-grain softpoints. New handgun bullets include .357-inch, 180-grain XTP; .400-inch, 180-grain SWC lead; .451-inch, 230-grain XTP. Also new are .416-inch gas checks for cast bullets.

Sierra

Sierra has a new 30-caliber 155-grain HPBT Palma MatchKing bullet. Should be a great choice for 300-yard shooting. The other new rifle bullet for this year is a 6.5mm, .264-inch, 160-grain, semi-pointed flat base bullet. This is their heaviest bullet in this diameter and it is the same weight that gained the original 6.5x54mm Mannlicher-Schoenauer a reputation for being a lot better at

game-taking than its modest ballistics suggested.

All 40 S&W and 10mm Auto fans would delight in another bullet weight to play with. So Sierra has added a 165-grain JHP of their Power Jacket design. These have proven to be reliable expanders.

Garrett Cartridges

Garrett is a custom loader specializing in extremely hard cast-alloy lead bullets. Their 44 Magnum loads are almost legendary. They are now loading jacketed bullets for specialized applications. For example, they have a load that will turn a modern 45-70 into a baby 45-caliber magnum. This ammo is intended only for firearms such as the Ruger No. 1 or Browning single shots.

This hot 45-70 load uses a 400-grain Barnes X-Bullet at a muzzle velocity 2020 fps. That's about 700 fps faster than the original 405-grain ammo, enough to justify a whole new name for the cartridge. I vote for 457 Garrett Magnum. Needless to say, the performance of this round is simply devastating on big game of all kinds.

Another hot 45-70 round is one using a 500-grain jacketed softpoint at 1450 fps—100 fps faster and 100 grains heavier than the traditional load. This one can also be used in the Marlin 1895, Kodiak double rifles and T/C Contender pistols. Accuracy of these loads proved far better than anticipated.

Cook Bullets

Cook custom match grade benchrest bullets stopped being available some time ago. There were those who sorely missed his bullets. They are again being produced by Walter Jankowski of Carrolton, Texas. Jankowski bought Cook's sophisticated machinery and had him supervise its installation and set-up. Phenomenal tolerances are claimed for these bullets, i.e. tangetial squareness of bullet base to axis is 0.0002-inch. Currently a pair of electronic-sensored two-ton hydraulic presses turn out only one bullet (6mm flat base hollowpoint) though others are due to be added.

Hodgdon

Hodgdon's powders are extremely diversified, but still Hodgdon continues to seek new propellants to satisfy a shooter's desire to try new items and gain improvements in results.

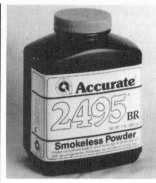

Accurate's newest propellant is 2495BR, a single-base medium-speed type.

Hodgdon's "Clays" is their newest shotshell propellant.

In burning speed, Clays is not unlike Hercules Red Dot—no, don't try to interchange the data for the two. Bulk density is also very similar to Red Dot and this may help in selecting a series of bushings to throw specific charges (always verify thrown weights with a scale). Clays is made in Australia by ADI; and my spies tell me that there is more to come from Hodgdon in the way of new ADI shotshell powders, one of which will also have very wide applications in handgun cartridges.

Improvements in existing powders are also being quietly established. For example, H4198 and H4350 are now being made with a "short" cut. In brief, the lengths of the tubular granulations of both these powders are now shorter than earlier production. This means these powders will now meter more uniformly than ever before. Those who use powder measures will be delighted. Many benchrest shooters have forsaken all other propellants in favor of the new short-

Cook benchrest bullets are once again available for the serious group-shooting set.

grained H4198. Happily, the change in grain geometry has not, according to a Hodgdon spokesman, been accompanied by any change in data requirements. There is a slight, almost imperceptible change in bulk density (about 5 grams per cubic centimeter) and hence powder measure settings may require minor readjustment.

The new Pyrodex Select grade is not simply some marketing ploy to get a few cents

CCI Blazer loads with TMJ bullets are new editions to an already broad offering.

more per pound for this black-powder replacement, as I have heard a few folks comment. Hodgdon is making this powder with a much narrower web, and then applying a special coating to the finished grains. Burning rate is such that it is ideal for heavy muzzle-loading hunting loads.

with Corbin equipment that many folks have started a custom bullet manufacturing business. So many that there is now a book available which lists countless bullet makers. This book also includes a marketing chapter on the custom bullet business. If you need a bullet that no one seems to make, there is a high probability that there is a bullet maker listed who specializes in exactly what you want to find. It's called

used in the U.K., are made in Cyprus by G&L Calibers Ltd. This ammo, which uses a Reifenhauser-style case, is imported into the U.S. by Victory only in target-style loads, i.e. those suitable for sporting clays, Skeet and trap. Shells are color coded, a handy aspect for the sporting clays shooter who uses different loads for differing shots. Cases loaded with 7½ shot are beige in color, those loaded with 8s are red while

and distributing Norma components. They say the Norma MRP powder, and others, have been ordered, will arrive soon, and should reach the retail customer at about $33 per pound—ouch in the wallet! But bench shooters still win matches with Norma 201 and some think it worth every penny.

Conclusion

It is literally time now to conclude this so that I may begin

---

Unformed PMC Cases

- 25-20 Single Shot—2-R Lovell.
- 280 Flanged Nitro Express (rimmed version of 280 Ross) base case.
- 280 Ross base case. Forms 280 Halger, 30 Newton, 303 Mag., 8x68Smm, and 35 Newton.
- 375 H&H base case. Forms 375 Weatherby, 416 Taylor, 458 Lott, etc.
- 375 H&H Flanged base case. Forms 275 and Super 30 Flanged Magnums.
- 404 Jeffery base case. Forms 280 and 333 Jeffery and 460 G&A.
- 405 Winchester 3¼" base case. Forms 35, 38-72, 38-90, 40-72 Winchester; 40-50 and 40-90 Sharps.
- 11mm Mauser base case. Forms 7.7x50Rmm, 9.5x47mm, and 9.5 Turkish.
- 43 Remington Spanish.
- 425 Westley Richards. Forms 11.2x72 Schuler.
- 416 Hoffman (formed cases).
- 416 Rigby (formed cases).
- 45 RCBS 3¼" base case. Forms 40-60 Marlin, 40-70 Bullard, 45-100 Ballard; 45-100 and 45-120 Sharps Straight and a heap of Winchester rounds from 33 to 45-90.
- 450 Straight 3¼" Nitro Express base case. Available in two rim thicknesses of 0.040" standard and 0.060" Jeffery Rim. Forms 333 Rimmed Jeffery, 360 No. 2, 360 Purdey, 450/400BP, 450/400 3", 450/400 3¼", Nitro Express 3¼", and a bunch of others.
- 50 Sharps 3¼" base case. Forms 50-140 3¼" Sharps, 50-90 Sharps, 50-70 Government.
- 500 Nitro Express 3¼" base case. Forms 476 Nitro Express, 470 Nitro Express, 500/465 Nitro Express, 500/450 Nitro Express, 500 Nitro 3".
- 505 Gibbs.
- 577 3" Nitro Express base case. Forms 577 2¼", 577/450 Martini, 577 Snyder.
- 600 Nitro Express (formed cases).

New Speer component handgun bullets are .440-inch 180-grain TMJ; .410-inch 180-grain JHP; and .500-inch 325-grain JHP.

Lots of Custom Bullets

Corbin has been making bullet manufacturing equipment for serious (and some not so serious) folks for many years. It is

World Directory of Custom Bullet Makers and is available from Corbin (503-826-5211) for $24.50.

Victory USA

Victory shotshells, widely

cases holding 9s are light green for all 1⅛-ounce loads. One-ounce loads for 7½, 8, and 9 shot are green, blue and gray respectively. Having shot up a case of this ammo, I can say that it does as it should.

Norma

Norma components and ammunition have been hard to keep up with during the last few decades. The importer/distributer of these items has changed about as frequently as New England weather. Well, OK, it hasn't changed hands every ten minutes, but often enough to keep many folks confused. The last outfit to drop the line was Federal Cartridge Co.

Now I am told there is a new guy on the block—The Paul Company—who is importing

last minute checks of guns and loads before heading southeast to Africa. In a few months I will be back to comment on the application of Remington Safari ammo, CHAA ammo, Federal Premium ammo, and not just a few handloads with respect to their effectiveness on several dozen big game—some mighty big—animals of a varied type. I will be attempting to use some mighty big rounds for appropriate applications; but they will also see use on some diminutive critters. And I will be doing some postmortem bullet penetration and expansion testing to get double or triple the mileage out of each kill. I realize most would find ammo testing a distasteful undertaking, but I promise you I will not back away from my duty. ●

Caliber	Bullet weight grains	-VELOCITY (fps)-					-ENERGY (ft. lbs.)-					-TRAJ. (in.)-				Approx. Price per box
		Muzzle	100 yds.	200 yds.	300 yds.	400. yds.	Muzzle	100 yds.	200 yds.	300 yds.	400 yds.	100 yds.	200 yds.	300 yds.	400 yds.	
17																
17 Remington	25	4040	3284	2644	2086	1606	906	599	388	242	143	+2.0	+1.7	-4.0	-17.0	$15
22																
221 Fireball	50	2800	2137	1580	1180	988	870	507	277	155	109	0.0	-7.0	-28.0	NA	$14
22 Hornet	45	2690	2042	1502	1128	948	723	417	225	127	90	0.0	-7.7	-31.0	NA	$26**
218 Bee	46	2760	2102	1550	1155	961	788	451	245	136	94	0.0	-7.2	-29.0	NA	$44**
222 Remington	50	3140	2602	2123	1700	1350	1094	752	500	321	202	+2.0	-0.4	-11.0	-33.0	$11
222 Remington	55	3020	2562	2147	1773	1451	1114	801	563	384	257	+2.0	-0.4	-11.0	-33.0	$11
22 PPC	52	3400	2930	2510	2130	NA	1335	990	730	525	NA	+2.0	+1.4	-5.0	NA	NA
223 Remington	40	3650	3010	2450	1950	1530	1185	805	535	340	265	+2.0	+1.0	-6.0	-22.0	$12
223 Remington	52/53	3330	2882	2477	2106	1770	1305	978	722	522	369	+2.0	+0.6	-6.5	-21.5	$13
223 Remington	55	3240	2748	2305	1906	1556	1282	922	649	444	296	+2.0	-0.2	-9.0	-27.0	$12
223 Remington	60	3100	2712	2355	2026	1726	1280	979	739	547	397	+2.0	+0.2	-8.0	-24.7	$15
223 Remington	64	3020	2621	2256	1920	1619	1296	977	723	524	373	+2.0	-0.2	-9.3	-23.0	$13
223 Remington	69	3000	2720	2460	2210	1980	1380	1135	925	750	600	+2.0	+0.8	-5.8	-17.5	NA
222 Rem. Mag.	55	3240	2748	2305	1906	1556	1282	922	649	444	296	+2.0	-0.2	-9.0	-27.0	$13
225 Winchester	55	3570	3066	2616	2208	1838	1556	1148	836	595	412	+2.0	+1.0	-5.0	-20.0	$16
224 Wea. Mag.	55	3650	3192	2780	2403	2057	1627	1244	943	705	516	+2.0	+1.2	-4.0	-17.0	$32
22-250 Rem.	40	4000	3320	2720	2200	1740	1420	980	660	430	265	+2.0	+1.8	-3.0	-16.0	$13
22-250 Rem.	53/55	3680	3137	2656	2222	1832	1654	1201	861	603	410	+2.0	+1.3	-4.0	-17.0	$13
22-250 Rem.	60	3600	3195	2826	2485	2169	1727	1360	1064	823	627	+2.0	+2.0	-2.4	-12.3	$19
220 Swift	†50	3780	3158	2617	2135	1710	1586	1107	760	506	325	+2.0	+1.4	-4.4	-17.9	NA
220 Swift	55	3650	3194	2772	2384	2035	1627	1246	939	694	506	+2.0	+2.0	-2.6	-13.4	$19
220 Swift	60	3600	3199	2824	2475	2156	1727	1364	1063	816	619	+2.0	+1.6	-4.1	-13.1	$19
22 Savage H.P	71	2790	2340	1930	1570	1280	1225	860	585	390	190	+2.0	-1.0	-10.4	-35.7	NA
6mm (24)																
6mm BR Rem.	100	2550	2310	2083	1870	1671	1444	1185	963	776	620	+2.5	-0.6	-11.8	NA	$20
6mm PPC	70	3140	2750	2400	2070	NA	1535	1175	895	665	NA	+2.0	+1.4	-5.0	NA	NA
243 Winchester	60	3600	3110	2660	2260	1890	1725	1285	945	680	475	+2.0	+1.8	-3.3	-15.5	$15
243 Winchester	75/80	3350	2955	2593	2259	1951	1993	1551	1194	906	676	+2.0	+0.9	-5.0	-19.0	$15
243 Winchester	85	3320	3070	2830	2600	2380	2080	1770	1510	1280	1070	+2.0	+1.2	-4.0	-14.0	$15
243 Winchester	100	2960	2697	2449	2215	1993	1945	1615	1332	1089	882	+2.5	+1.2	-6.0	-20.0	$15
243 Winchester	†105	2920	2689	2470	2261	2062	1988	1686	1422	1192	992	+2.5	+1.6	-5.0	-18.4	NA
6mm Remington	80	3470	3064	2694	2352	2036	2139	1667	1289	982	736	+2.0	+1.1	-5.0	-17.0	$16
6mm Remington	100	3100	2829	2573	2332	2104	2133	1777	1470	1207	983	+2.5	+1.6	-5.0	-17.0	$16
6mm Remington	†105	3060	2822	2596	2381	2177	2105	1788	1512	1270	1059	+2.5	+1.1	-3.3	-15.0	NA
240 Wea. Mag.	87	3500	3202	2924	2663	2416	2366	1980	1651	1370	1127	+2.0	+2.0	-2.0	-12.0	$32
240 Wea. Mag.*	100	3395	3106	2835	2581	2339	2559	2142	1785	1478	1215	+2.5	+2.8	-2.0	-11.0	$43
25																
25-20 Win.	86	1460	1194	1030	931	858	407	272	203	165	141	0.0	-23.5	NA	NA	$30**
25-35 Win.	117	2230	1866	1545	1282	1097	1292	904	620	427	313	+2.5	-4.2	-26.0	NA	$19
250 Savage	100	2820	2504	2210	1936	1684	1765	1392	1084	832	630	+2.5	+0.4	-9.0	-28.0	$16
257 Roberts	100	2980	2661	2363	2085	1827	1972	1572	1240	965	741	+2.5	-0.8	-5.2	-21.6	$19
257 Roberts	117	2780	2411	2071	1761	1488	2009	1511	1115	806	576	+2.5	-0.2	-10.2	-32.6	$17
257 Roberts	120	2780	2560	2360	2160	1970	2060	1750	1480	1240	1030	+2.5	+1.2	-6.4	-23.6	$17
257 Roberts	†122	2600	2331	2078	1842	1625	1831	1472	1169	919	715	+2.5	0.0	-10.6	-31.4	NA
25-06 Rem.	87	3440	2995	2591	2222	1884	2286	1733	1297	954	686	+2.0	+1.1	-2.5	-14.4	$17
25-06 Rem.	90	3440	3043	2680	2344	2034	2364	1850	1435	1098	827	+2.0	+1.8	-3.3	-15.6	$17
25-06 Rem.	100	3230	2893	2580	2287	2014	2316	1858	1478	1161	901	+2.0	+0.8	-5.7	-18.9	$17
25-06 Rem.	117	2990	2770	2570	2370	2190	2320	2000	1715	1465	1246	+2.5	+1.0	-7.9	-26.6	$17
25-06 Rem.	120	2990	2730	2484	2252	2032	2382	1985	1644	1351	1100	+2.5	+1.2	-5.3	-19.6	$17
25-06 Rem.	†122	2930	2706	2492	2289	2095	2325	1983	1683	1419	1189	+2.5	+1.8	-4.5	-17.5	NA
257 Wea. Mag.	87	3825	3456	3118	2805	2513	2826	2308	1870	1520	1220	+2.0	+2.7	-0.3	-7.6	$32
257 Wea. Mag.	100	3555	3237	2941	2665	2404	2806	2326	1920	1576	1283	+2.5	+3.2	0.0	-8.0	$32
257 Wea. Mag.*	120	3300	3056	2823	2599	2388	2902	2489	2124	1800	1520	+2.5	+2.2	-4.1	-18.4	$47
6.5																
6.5x50mm Jap.	139	2360	2160	1970	1790	1620	1720	1440	1195	985	810	+2.5	-1.0	-13.5	NA	NA
6.5x50mm Jap.	156	2070	1830	1610	1430	1260	1475	1155	900	695	550	+2.5	-4.0	-23.8	NA	NA
6.5x52mm Car.	139	2580	2360	2160	1970	1790	2045	1725	1440	1195	985	+2.5	0.0	-9.9	-29.0	NA
6.5x52mm Car.	156	2430	2170	1930	1700	1500	2045	1630	1285	1005	780	+2.5	-1.0	-13.9	NA	NA
6.5x55mm Swe.	139/†140	2850	2640	2440	2250	2070	2525	2170	1855	1575	1330	+2.5	+1.6	-5.4	-18.9	NA
6.5x55mm Swe.	156	2650	2370	2110	1870	1650	2425	1950	1550	1215	945	+2.5	0.0	-10.3	-30.6	NA
6.5 Rem. Mag.	120	3210	2905	2621	2353	2102	2745	2248	1830	1475	1177	+2.5	+1.7	-4.1	-16.3	Disc.
264 Win. Mag.	140	3030	2782	2548	2326	2114	2854	2406	2018	1682	1389	+2.5	+1.4	-5.1	-18.0	$22
27																
270 Winchester	100	3430	3021	2649	2305	1988	2612	2027	1557	1179	877	+2.0	+1.0	-4.9	-17.5	$17
270 Winchester	130	3060	2776	2510	2259	2022	2702	2225	1818	1472	1180	+2.5	+1.4	-5.3	-18.2	$17
270 Winchester	140	2960	2753	2554	2365	2183	2724	2356	2029	1739	1482	+2.5	+1.6	-4.8	-17.4	$21
270 Winchester	150	2850	2585	2336	2100	1879	2705	2226	1817	1468	1175	+2.5	+1.2	-6.5	-22.0	$17
270 Wea. Mag.	100	3760	3380	3033	2712	2412	3139	2537	2042	1633	1292	+2.0	+2.4	-1.2	-10.1	$32
270 Wea. Mag.	130	3375	3119	2878	2649	2432	3287	2808	2390	2026	1707	+2.5	+2.9	-0.9	-9.9	$32
270 Wea. Mag.*	150	3245	3036	2837	2647	2465	3507	3070	2681	2334	2023	+2.5	+2.6	-1.8	-11.4	$47

CAUTION: PRICES CHANGE, CHECK AT GUNSHOP.

Caliber	Bullet weight grains	VELOCITY (fps) Muzzle	100 yds.	200 yds.	300 yds.	400. yds.	ENERGY (ft. lbs.) Muzzle	100 yds.	200 yds.	300 yds.	400 yds.	TRAJ. (in.) 100 yds.	200 yds.	300 yds.	400 yds.	Approx. Price per box
7mm																
7mm BR	140	2215	2012	1821	1643	1481	1525	1259	1031	839	681	+2.0	-3.7	-20.0	NA	$20
7mm Mauser	139/140	2660	2435	2221	2018	1827	2199	1843	1533	1266	1037	+2.5	0.0	-9.6	-27.7	$17
7mm Mauser	145	2690	2442	2206	1985	1777	2334	1920	1568	1268	1017	+2.5	+0.1	-9.6	-28.3	$17
7mm Mauser	154	2690	2490	2300	2120	1940	2475	2120	1810	1530	1285	+2.5	+0.8	-7.5	-23.5	$17
7mm Mauser	175	2440	2137	1857	1603	1382	2313	1774	1340	998	742	+2.5	-1.7	-16.1	NA	$17
7 x 30 Waters	120	2700	2300	1930	1600	1330	1940	1405	990	685	470	+2.5	-0.2	-12.3	NA	$17.
7mm-08 Rem.	120	3000	2725	2467	2223	1992	2398	1979	1621	1316	1058	+2.0	0.0	-7.6	-22.3	$17
7mm-08 Rem.	140	2860	2625	2402	2189	1988	2542	2142	1793	1490	1228	+2.5	+0.8	-6.9	-21.9	$17
7mm-08 Rem.	†154	2715	2510	2315	2128	1950	2520	2155	1832	1548	1300	+2.5	+1.0	-7.0	-22.7	NA
7x64mm Bren.	154	2820	2610	2420	2230	2050	2720	2335	1995	1695	1430	+2.5	+1.4	-5.7	-19.9	NA
7x64mm Bren.	†160*	2850	2669	2495	2327	2166	2885	2530	2211	1924	1667	+2.5	+1.6	-4.8	-17.8	NA
284 Winchester	150	2860	2595	2344	2108	1886	2724	2243	1830	1480	1185	+2.5	+0.8	-7.3	-23.2	$22
280 Remington	120	3150	2866	2599	2348	2110	2643	2188	1800	1468	1186	+2.0	+0.6	-6.0	-17.9	$17
280 Remington	140	3000	2758	2528	2309	2102	2797	2363	1986	1657	1373	+2.5	+1.4	-5.2	-18.3	$17
280 Remington	150	2890	2624	2373	2135	1912	2781	2293	1875	1518	1217	+2.5	+0.8	-7.1	-22.6	$17
280 Remington	165	2820	2510	2220	1950	1701	2913	2308	1805	1393	1060	+2.5	+0.4	-8.8	-26.5	$17
7x61mm S&H Sup.	154	3060	2720	2400	2100	1820	3200	2520	1965	1505	1135	+2.5	+1.8	-5.0	-19.8	NA
7mm Rem. Mag.	139/140	3175	2923	2684	2458	2243	3133	2655	2240	1878	1564	+2.5	+2.0	-3.4	-14.5	$21
7mm Rem. Mag.	150/154	3110	2830	2085	2320	2085	3221	2667	2196	1792	1448	+2.5	+1.6	-4.6	-16.5	$21
7mm Rem. Mag.	160/162	2950	2730	2520	2320	2120	3090	2650	2250	1910	1600	+2.5	+1.8	-4.4	-17.8	$26
7mm Rem. Mag.	165	2900	2699	2507	2324	2147	3081	2669	2303	1978	1689	+2.5	+1.2	-5.9	-19.0	NA
7mm Rem. Mag.	175	2860	2645	2440	2244	2057	3178	2718	2313	1956	1644	+2.5	+1.0	-6.5	-20.7	$21
7mm Wea. Mag.	140	3225	2970	2729	2501	2283	3233	2741	2315	1943	1621	+2.5	+2.0	-3.2	-14	$21
7mm Wea. Mag.	154	3260	3023	2799	2586	2382	3539	3044	2609	2227	1890	+2.5	+2.8	-1.5	-10.8	$32
7mm Wea. Mag.*	160	3200	3004	2816	2637	2464	3637	3205	2817	2469	2156	+2.5	+2.7	-1.5	-10.6	$47
7mm Wea. Mag.	†165	2950	2747	2553	2367	2189	3188	2765	2388	2053	1756	+2.5	+1.8	-4.2	-16.4	NA
7mm Wea. Mag.	175	2950	2730	2521	2322	2131	3381	2897	2470	2094	1764	+2.5	+1.2	-5.6	-17.6	$32
30																
30 Carbine	110	1990	1567	1236	1035	923	977	600	373	262	208	0.0	-13.5	NA	NA	$27**
303 Savage	190	1890	1612	1372	1183	1055	1507	1096	794	591	469	+2.5	-7.6	NA	NA	$23
30 Remington	170	2120	1822	1555	1328	1153	1696	1253	913	666	502	+2.5	-4.7	-26.3	NA	$18
30-30 Win.	55	3400	2693	2085	1570	1187	1412	886	521	301	172	+2.0	0.0	-10.2	-35.0	$16
30-30 Win.	125	2570	2090	1660	1320	1080	1830	1210	770	480	320	+2.0	-2.6	-19.9	NA	NA
30-30 Win.	150	2390	1973	1605	1303	1095	1902	1296	858	565	399	+2.5	-3.2	-22.5	NA	$13
30-30 Win.	170	2200	1895	1619	1381	1191	1827	1355	989	720	535	+2.5	-5.8	-23.6	NA	$13
300 Savage	150	2630	2354	2094	1853	1631	2303	1845	1462	1143	886	+2.5	-0.4	-10.1	-30.7	$17
300 Savage	180	2350	2137	1935	1754	1570	2207	1825	1496	1217	985	+2.5	-1.6	-15.2	NA	$17
30-40 Krag	180	2430	2213	2007	1813	1632	2360	1957	1610	1314	1064	+2.5	-1.4	-13.8	NA	$17
7.65x53mm Arg.	180	2590	2390	2200	2010	1830	2685	2280	1925	1615	1345	+2.5	0.0	-27.6	NA	NA
307 Winchester	150	2760	2321	1924	1575	1289	2530	1795	1233	826	554	+2.5	-1.5	-13.6	NA	Disc.
307 Wincheste	180	2510	2179	1874	1599	1362	2519	1898	1404	1022	742	+2.5	-1.6	-15.6	NA	$16
7.5x55 Swiss	180	2650	2450	2250	2060	1880	2805	2390	2020	1700	1415	+2.5	+0.6	-8.1	-24.9	NA
308 Winchester	55	3770	3215	2726	2286	1888	1735	1262	907	638	435	+2.0	+1.4	-3.8	-15.8	$19
308 Winchester	150	2820	2533	2263	2009	1774	2648	2137	1705	1344	1048	+2.5	+0.4	-8.5	-26.1	$17
308 Winchester	165	2700	2440	2194	1963	1748	2670	2180	1763	1411	1199	+2.5	0.0	-9.7	-28.5	$18
308 Winchester	168	2680	2493	2314	2143	1979	2678	2318	1998	1713	1460	+2.5	0.0	-8.9	-25.3	$20
308 Winchester	178	2620	2415	2220	2034	1857	2713	2306	1948	1635	1363	+2.5	0.0	-9.6	-27.6	$21
308 Winchester	180	2620	2393	2178	1974	1782	2743	2288	1896	1557	1269	+2.5	-0.2	-10.2	-28.5	$17
30-06 Spfd.	55	4080	3485	2965	2502	2083	2033	1483	1074	764	530	+2.0	+1.9	-2.1	-11.7	$19
30-06 Spfd.	125	3140	2780	2447	2138	1853	2736	2145	1662	1279	953	+2.0	+1.0	-6.2	-21.0	$17
30-06 Spfd.	150	2910	2617	2342	2083	1853	2820	2281	1827	1445	1135	+2.5	+0.8	-7.2	-23.4	$17
30-06 Spfd.	152	2910	2654	2413	2184	1968	2858	2378	1965	1610	1307	+2.5	+1.0	-6.6	-21.3	$21
30-06 Spfd.	165	2800	2534	2283	2047	1825	2872	2352	1909	1534	1220	+2.5	+0.4	-8.4	-25.5	$17
30-06 Spfd.	168	2710	2522	2346	2169	2003	2739	2372	2045	1754	1497	+2.5	+0.4	-8.0	-23.5	$20
30-06 Spfd.	178	2720	2511	2311	2121	1939	2924	2491	2111	1777	1486	+2.5	+0.4	-8.2	-24.6	$21
30-06 Spfd.	180	2700	2469	2250	2042	1846	2913	2436	2023	1666	1362	+2.5	0.0	-9.3	-27.0	$17
30-06 Spfd.	220	2410	2130	1870	1632	1422	2837	2216	1708	1301	988	+2.5	-1.7	-16.0	NA	$18
30 Mag																
308 Norma Mag.	180	3020	2820	2630	2440	2270	3645	3175	2755	2385	2050	+2.5	+2.0	-3.5	-14.8	NA
300 H&H Magnum	180	2880	2640	2412	2196	1990	3315	2785	2325	1927	1583	+2.5	+0.8	-6.8	-21.7	$22
300 H&H Magnum	220	2550	2267	2002	1757	NA	3167	2510	1958	1508	NA	+2.5	-0.4	-12.0	NA	NA
300 Win. Mag.	150	3290	2951	2636	2342	2068	3605	2900	2314	1827	1424	+2.5	+1.9	-3.8	-15.8	$22
300 Win. Mag.	165	3100	2877	2665	2462	2269	3522	3033	2603	2221	1897	+2.5	+2.4	-3.0	-16.9	$24
300 Win. Mag.	178	2980	2769	2568	2375	2191	3509	3030	2606	2230	1897	+2.5	+1.4	-5.0	-17.6	$27
300 Win. Mag.	180	2960	2745	2540	2344	2157	3501	3011	2578	2196	1859	+2.5	+1.2	-5.5	-18.5	$22
300 Win. Mag.	190	2885	2691	2506	2327	2156	3511	3055	2648	2285	1961	+2.5	+1.2	-5.7	-19.0	$27
300 Win. Mag.	200	2830	2680	2530	2380	2240	3560	3180	2830	2520	2230	+2.5	+1.6	-4.7	-17.2	NA
300 Win. Mag.	220	2680	2448	2228	2020	1823	3508	2927	2424	1993	1623	+2.5	0.0	-9.5	-27.5	$23
300 Wea. Mag.	110	3900	3441	3038	2652	2305	3714	2891	2239	1717	1297	+2.0	+2.6	-0.6	-8.7	$32
300 Wea. Mag.	150	3600	3307	3033	2776	2533	4316	3642	3064	2566	2137	+2.5	+3.2	0.0	-8.1	$32
300 Wea. Mag.	†165	3450	3210	3000	2792	2593	4360	3796	3297	2855	2464	+2.5	+3.2	0.0	-7.8	N.A
300 Wea. Mag.	178	3120	2902	2695	2497	2308	3847	3329	2870	2464	2104	+2.5	-1.7	-3.6	-14.7	$39
300 Wea. Mag.*	180	3120	2866	2667	2400	2184	3890	3284	2758	2301	1905	+2.5	+1.7	-3.8	-15.0	$56

AVERAGE CENTERFIRE RIFLE CARTRIDGE BALLISTICS AND PRICES (cont.)

Caliber	Bullet weight grains	Muzzle	VEL 100 yds.	VEL 200 yds.	VEL 300 yds.	VEL 400 yds.	Muzzle	EN 100 yds.	EN 200 yds.	EN 300 yds.	EN 400 yds.	TRAJ 100 yds.	TRAJ 200 yds.	TRAJ 300 yds.	TRAJ 400 yds.	Approx. Price per box
30 Mag (cont.) 300 Wea. Mag.	190	3030	2830	2638	2455	2279	3873	3378	2936	2542	2190	+2.5	+1.6	-4.3	-16.0	$35
300 Wea. Mag.	220	2850	2541	2283	1984	1736	3967	3155	2480	1922	1471	+2.5	+0.4	-8.5	-26.4	$35
31 32-20 Win.	100	1210	1021	913	834	769	325	231	185	154	131	0.0	-32.3	NA	NA	$21**
303 British	†150	2685	2441	2210	1992	1787	2401	1984	1627	1321	1064	+2.5	+0.6	-8.4	-26.2	$19
303 British	180	2460	2124	1817	1542	1311	2418	1803	1319	950	687	+2.5	-1.8	-16.8	NA	$17
7.62x39mm Rus.	123/125	2300	2030	1780	1550	1350	1445	1125	860	655	500	+2.5	-2.0	-17.5	NA	$14
7.62x54mm Rus.	146	2950	2730	2520	2320	NA	2820	2415	2055	1740	NA	+2.5	+2.0	-4.4	-17.7	NA
7.62x54mm Rus.	180	2580	2370	2180	2000	1820	2650	2250	1900	1590	1100	+2.5	0.0	-9.8	-28.5	NA
7.7x58mm Jap.	180	2500	2300	2100	1920	1750	2490	2105	1770	1475	1225	+2.5	0.0	-10.4	-30.2	NA
8x57mm JS Mau.	165	2850	2520	2210	1930	1670	2965	2330	1795	1360	1015	+2.5	+1.0	-7.7	NA	NA
8mm 32 Win.Special	170	2250	1921	1626	1372	1175	1911	1393	998	710	521	+2.5	-3.5	-22.9	NA	$14
8mm Mauser	170	2360	1969	1622	1333	1123	2102	1464	993	671	476	+2.5	-3.1	-22.2	NA	$17
8mm Rem. Mag.	185	3080	2761	2464	2186	1927	3896	3131	2494	1963	1525	+2.5	+1.4	-5.5	-19.7	$27
8mm Rem. Mag.	220	2830	2581	2346	2123	1913	3912	3254	2688	2201	1787	+2.5	+0.6	-7.6	-23.5	$27
33 338 Win. Mag.	200	2960	2658	2375	2110	1862	3890	3137	2505	1977	1539	+2.5	+1.0	-6.7	-22.3	$26
338 Win. Mag.	210	2830	2590	2370	2150	1940	3735	3130	2610	2155	1760	+2.5	+1.4	-6.0	-20.9	NA
338 Win. Mag.	†225	2785	2517	2266	2029	1808	3871	3165	2565	2057	1633	+2.5	+0.4	-8.5	-25.9	$26
338 Win. Mag.	250	2660	2456	2261	2075	1898	3927	3348	2837	2389	1999	+2.5	+0.2	-9.0	-26.2	$26
340 Wea. Mag.*	210	3250	2991	2746	2515	2295	4924	4170	3516	2948	2455	+2.5	1.9	-1.8	-11.8	$56
340 Wea. Mag.*	250	3000	2806	2621	2443	2272	4995	4371	3812	3311	2864	+2.5	+2.0	-3.5	-14.8	$56
338 A-Square	250	3120	2799	2500	2220	1958	5403	4348	3469	2736	2128	+2.5	+2.7	-1.5	-10.5	NA
34 348 Winchester	200	2520	2215	1931	1672	1443	2820	2178	1656	1241	925	+2.5	-1.4	-14.7	NA	$35
357 Magnum	158	1830	1427	1138	980	883	1175	715	454	337	274	0.0	-16.2	-33.1	NA	$24**
35 35 Remington	150	2300	1874	1506	1218	1039	1762	1169	755	494	359	+2.5	-4.1	-26.3	NA	$16
35 Remington	200	2080	1698	1376	1140	1001	1921	1280	841	577	445	+2.5	-6.3	-17.1	-33.6	$15
356 Winchester	200	2460	2114	1797	1517	1284	2688	1985	1434	1022	732	+2.5	-1.8	-17.1	NA	$26
356 Winchester	250	2160	1911	1682	1476	1299	2591	2028	1571	1210	937	+2.5	-3.7	-22.2	NA	$26
358 Winchester	200	2490	2171	1876	1619	1379	2753	2093	1563	1151	844	+2.5	-1.6	-15.6	NA	$28
350 Rem. Mag.	200	2710	2410	2130	1870	1631	3261	2579	2014	1553	1181	+2.5	-0.2	-10.0	-30.1	$29
35 Whelen	200	2675	2378	2100	1842	1606	3177	2510	1958	1506	1145	+2.5	-0.2	-10.3	-31.1	$18
35 Whelen	250	2400	2197	2005	1823	1652	3197	2680	2230	1844	1515	+2.5	-1.2	-13.7	NA	$18
358 Norma Mag.	250	2800	2510	2230	1970	1730	4350	3480	2750	2145	1655	+2.5	+1.0	-7.6	-25.2	NA
9.3 9.3x57mm Mau.	286	2070	1810	1590	1390	1110	2710	2090	1600	1220	955	+2.5	-2.6	-22.5	NA	NA
9.3 x 62mm Mau.	286	2360	2089	1844	1623	NA	3538	2771	2157	1670	1260	+2.5	-1.6	-21.0	NA	NA
9.3 x 64mm	286	2700	2505	2318	2139	1968	4629	3984	3411	2906	2460	+2.5	+2.7	-4.5	-19.2	NA
9.3 x 74Rmm	286	2360	2089	1844	1623	NA	3538	2771	2157	1670	NA	+2.5	-2.0	-11.0	NA	NA
375 38-55 Win.	255	1320	1190	1091	1018	963	987	802	674	587	525	0.0	-23.4	NA	NA	$21
375 Winchester	200	2200	1841	1526	1268	1089	2150	1506	1034	714	527	+2.5	-4.0	-26.2	NA	$23
375 Winchester	250	1900	1647	1424	1239	1103	2005	1506	1126	852	676	+2.5	-6.9	-33.3	NA	$23
375 N.E. 2½"	270	2000	1740	1507	1310	NA	2398	1815	1362	1026	NA	+2.5	-6.0	-30.0	NA	NA
375 Flanged	300	2450	2150	1886	1640	NA	3998	3102	2369	1790	NA	+2.5	-2.4	-17.0	NA	NA
375 H&H Magnum	250	2670	2450	2240	2040	1850	3955	3335	2790	2315	1905	+2.5	-0.4	-10.2	-28.4	NA
375 H&H Magnum	270	2690	2420	2166	1928	1707	4337	3510	2812	2228	1747	+2.5	0.0	-10.0	-29.4	$27
375 H&H Magnum	300	2530	2171	1843	1551	1307	4263	3139	2262	1602	1138	+2.5	-2.0	-16.2	NA	$29
375 Wea. Mag.	300	2700	2420	2157	1911	1685	4856	3901	3100	2432	1891	+2.5	-0.4	-10.7	-	NA
378 Wea. Mag.	270	3180	2976	2781	2594	2415	6062	5308	4635	4034	3495	+2.5	+2.6	-1.8	-11.3	$71
378 Wea. Mag.	300	2929	2576	2252	1952	1680	5698	4419	3379	2538	1881	+2.5	+1.2	-7.0	-24.5	$77
375 A-Square	300	2920	2626	2351	2093	1850	5679	4594	3681	2917	2281	+2.5	+1.4	-6.0	-21.0	NA
40 38-40 Win.	180	1160	999	901	827	764	538	399	324	273	233	0.0	-33.9	NA	NA	$37**
41 450/400-3"	400	2150	1932	1730	1545	1379	4105	3316	2659	2119	1689	+2.5	-4.0	-9.5	-30.3	NA
416 Taylor	400	2350	2117	1896	1693	NA	4905	3980	3194	2547	NA	+2.5	-1.2	-15.0	NA	NA
416 Hoffman	400	2380	2145	1923	1718	1529	5031	4087	3285	2620	2077	+2.5	-1.0	-14.1	NA	NA
416 Rigby	†350	2600	2449	2303	2162	2026	5253	4661	4122	3632	3189	+2.5	-1.8	-10.2	-26.0	NA
416 Rigby	†400	2370	2063	1780	1527	1312	4988	3778	2815	2171	1529	+2.5	-1.7	-17.0	NA	NA
416 Rigby	410	2370	2110	1870	1640	1440	5115	4050	3165	2455	1895	+2.5	-2.4	-17.3	-39.0	NA
416 Rem. Mag.	350	2520	2270	2034	1814	1611	4935	4004	3216	2557	2017	+2.5	-0.8	-12.6	-35.0	$74
416 Rem. Mag.	400	2400	2175	1962	1763	1579	5115	4201	3419	2760	2214	+2.5	-1.5	-14.6	NA	$74
416 Wea. Mag.	400	2700	2397	2115	1852	1613	6474	5104	3971	3047	2310	+2.5	0.0	-10.1	-30.4	$96
425 404 Jeffrey	400	2150	1924	1716	1525	NA	4105	3289	2614	2064	NA	+2.5	-4.0	-22.1	NA	NA
425 Express	400	2400	2160	1934	1725	NA	5115	4145	3322	2641	NA	+2.5	-1.0	-14.0	NA	NA
44 44-40 Win.	200	1190	1006	900	822	756	629	449	360	300	254	0.0	-33.3	NA	NA	$34**
44 Rem. Mag.	240	1760	1380	1114	970	878	1650	1015	661	501	411	0.0	-17.6	NA	NA	$13
444 Marlin	240	2350	1815	1377	1087	941	2942	1753	1001	630	472	+2.5	-15.1	-31.0	NA	$20
444 Marlin	265	2120	1733	1405	1160	1012	2644	1768	1162	791	603	+2.5	-6.0	-32.2	NA	Disc.
45 45-70 Govt.	300	1810	1497	1244	1073	969	2182	1492	1031	767	625	0.0	-14.8	NA	NA	$21
45-70 Govt.	405	1330	1168	1055	977	918	1590	1227	1001	858	758	0.0	-24.6	NA	NA	$21
458 Win. Mag.	350	2470	1990	1570	1250	1060	4740	3065	1915	1205	870	+2.5	-2.5	-21.6	NA	NA
458 Win. Mag.	†400	2450	2295	2146	2002	1865	5330	4678	4089	3560	3080	+2.5	-0.1	-10.3	-29.2	NA
458 Win. Mag.	465	2220	1999	1791	1601	NA	5088	4127	3312	2646	NA	+2.5	-2.0	-17.7	NA	NA
458 Win. Mag.	500	2040	1823	1623	1442	1237	4620	3689	2924	2308	1839	+2.5	-3.5	-22.0	NA	$57
458 Win. Mag.	510	2040	1770	1527	1319	1157	4712	3547	2640	1970	1516	+2.5	-4.1	-25.0	NA	$39

CAUTION: PRICES CHANGE, CHECK AT GUNSHOP.

AVERAGE CENTERFIRE RIFLE CARTRIDGE BALLISTICS AND PRICES (cont.)

	Caliber	Bullet weight grains	-VELOCITY (fps)- Muzzle	100 yds.	200 yds.	300 yds.	400. yds.	-ENERGY (ft. lbs.)- Muzzle	100 yds.	200 yds.	300 yds.	400 yds.	-TRAJ. (in.)- 100 yds.	200 yds.	300 yds.	400 yds.	Approx. Price per box
45 (cont.)	450 N.E.-3¼"	465	2190	1970	1765	1577	NA	4952	4009	3216	2567	NA	+2.5	-3.0	-20.0	NA	NA
	450 N.E.-3¼"	500	2150	1920	1708	1514	NA	5132	4093	3238	2544	NA	+2.5	-4.0	-22.9	NA	NA
	450 No. 2	465	2190	1970	1765	1577	NA	4952	4009	3216	2567	NA	+2.5	-3.0	-20.0	NA	NA
	450 No. 2	500	2150	1920	1708	1514	NA	5132	4093	3238	2544	NA	+2.5	-4.0	-22.9	NA	NA
	458 Lott	465	2380	2150	1932	1730	NA	5848	4773	3855	3091	NA	+2.5	-1.0	-14.0	NA	NA
	458 Lott	500	2300	2062	1838	1633	NA	5873	4719	3748	2960	NA	+2.5	-1.6	-16.4	NA	NA
	450 Ackley Mag	465	2400	2169	1950	1747	NA	5947	4857	3927	3150	NA	+2.5	-1.0	-13.7	NA	NA
	450 Ackley Mag.	500	2320	2081	1855	1649	NA	5975	4085	3820	3018	NA	+2.5	-1.2	-15.0	NA	NA
	460 Short A-Sq.	500	2420	2175	1943	1729	NA	6501	5250	4193	3319	NA	+2.5	-0.8	-12.8	-	NA
	460 Wea. Mag.	500	2700	2404	2128	1869	1635	8092	6416	5026	3878	2969	+2.5	+0.6	-8.9	-28.0	$72
	500/465 N.E.	480	2150	1917	1703	1507	NA	4926	3917	3089	2419	NA	+2.5	-4.0	-22.2	-	NA
475	470 Rigby	500	2150	1912	1693	1494	NA	5132	4058	3182	2478	NA	+2.5	-4.0	-23.0	NA	NA
	470 Nitro Ex.	480	2190	1954	1735	1536	NA	5111	4070	3210	2515	NA	+2.5	-3.5	-20.8	NA	NA
	470 Nitro Ex.	500	2150	1890	1650	1440	1270	5130	3965	3040	2310	1790	+2.5	-4.3	-24.0	NA	NA
	475 No. 2	500	2200	1955	1728	1522	NA	5375	4243	3316	2573	NA	+2.5	-3.2	-20.9	NA	NA
	505 Gibbs	525	2300	2063	1840	1637	NA	6166	4922	3948	3122	NA	+2.5	-3.0	-18.0	NA	NA
50	500 N.E.-3"	570	2150	1928	1722	1533	NA	5850	4703	3752	2975	NA	+2.5	-3.7	-22.0	NA	NA
	500 N.E.-3"	600	2150	1927	1721	1531	NA	6158	4947	3944	3124	NA	+2.5	-4.0	-22.0	NA	NA
58	495 A-Square	570	2350	2117	1896	1693	NA	5850	4703	3752	2975	NA	+2.5	-1.0	-14.5	NA	NA
	495 A-Square	600	2280	2050	1833	1635	NA	6925	5598	4478	3562	NA	+2.5	-2.0	-17.0	NA	NA
	500 A-Square	600	2380	2144	1922	1766	NA	7546	6126	4920	3922	NA	+2.5	-3.0	-17.0	NA	NA
	500 A-Square	707	2250	2040	1841	1567	NA	7947	6530	5318	4311	NA	+2.5	-2.0	-17.0	NA	NA
	577 Nitro Ex.	750	2050	1793	1562	1360	NA	6990	5356	4065	3079	NA	+2.5	-5.0	-26.0	NA	NA

Notes: N.A. in vel. or eng. column = This data not available from manufacturer. N.A.in trajectory column = Bullet has fallen more than 3 feet below line of sight and further hold-over is not practical—in any column means the data was not available at press time. Wea. Mag. = Weatherby Magnum. Spfd. = Springfield. A-Sq. = A-Square. N.E.= Nitro Express. Some manufacturers do not supply suggested retail prices. Others did not get their pricing to us before press time. All pricing can vary dependent on the exact brand and style of ammo selected and/or the retail outlet from which you make your purchase. Pricing has been rounded to the nearest dollar and represent our best estimate of average pricing. * = loads with Nosler Partition bullets. ** = are packed 50 to box, all others are 20 to box. + = special limited production. † = new bullet weight this year.

CENTERFIRE HANDGUN CARTRIDGES—BALLISTICS AND PRICES

Caliber	Bullet Wgt. Grs.	Velocity (fps) MV	50 yds.	100 yds.	Energy (ft. lbs.) ME	50 yds.	100 yds.	Mid-Range Traj. (in.) 50 yds.	100 yds.	Bbl. Lgth. (in.)	Est. Price /box
221 Rem. Fireball	50	2650	2380	2130	780	630	505	0.2	0.8	10½"	$14
25 Automatic	†35	900	813	742	63	51	43	NA	NA	2"	$18
25 Automatic	45	815	730	655	65	55	40	1.8	7.7	2"	$19
25 Automatic	50	760	705	660	65	55	50	2.0	8.7	2"	$16
7.62 Tokarev†	87	1390	NA	NA	365	NA	NA	0.6	NA	4½"	NA
30 Carbine	110	1790	1600	1430	785	625	500	0.4	1.7	10"	$27
32 S&W	88	680	645	610	90	80	75	2.5	10.5	3"	$16
32 S&W Long	98	705	670	635	115	100	90	2.3	10.5	4"	$17
32 Short Colt	80	745	665	590	100	80	60	2.2	9.9	4"	$16
32 Long Colt	82	755	715	675	100	95	85	2.0	8.7	4"	Disc.
32 H&R Magnum	85	1100	1020	930	230	195	165	1.0	4.3	4½"	NA
32 H&R Magnum	95	1030	940	900	225	190	170	1.1	4.7	4½"	NA
32 Automatic	60	970	895	835	125	105	95	1.3	5.4	4"	$22
32 Automatic	71	905	855	810	130	115	95	1.4	5.8	4"	$19
380 Automatic	85/88	990	920	870	190	165	145	1.2	5.1	4"	$23
380 Automatic	90	1000	890	800	200	160	130	1.2	5.5	3-3/4"	$19
380 Automatic	95/†100	955	865	785	190	160	130	1.4	5.9	4"	$19
38 Automatic	130	1040	980	925	310	275	245	1.0	4.7	4½"	Disc.
38 Super Auto +P	115	1300	1145	1040	430	335	275	0.7	3.3	5"	$24
38 Super Auto +P	125/130	1215	1100	1015	425	350	300	0.8	3.6	5"	$20
9mm Luger	88	1500	1190	1010	440	275	200	0.6	3.1	4"	$23
9mm Luger	90	1360	1112	978	370	247	191	NA	NA	4"	$26
9mm Luger	95	1300	1140	1010	350	275	215	0.8	3.4	4"	NA
9mm Luger	115	1155	1045	970	340	280	240	0.9	3.9	4"	$23
9mm Luger	123/125	1110	1030	970	340	290	260	1.0	4.0	4"	$23
9mm Luger	140	935	890	850	270	245	225	1.3	5.5	4"	$23
9mm Luger	147	990	940	900	320	290	265	1.1	4.9	4"	$28
9mm Luger +P	115	1250	1113	1019	399	316	265	0.8	3.5	4"	$25
9mm Federal	115	1280	1130	1040	420	330	280	0.7	3.3	4"V	NA
38 S&W	145	685	650	620	150	135	125	2.4	10.0	4"	$17
38 Short Colt	125	730	685	645	150	130	115	2.2	9.4	6"	$18
38 Special	110	945	895	850	220	195	175	1.3	5.4	4"V	$26
38 (Multi-Ball)	140	830	730	505	215	130	80	2.0	10.6	4"V	$9*
38 Special	148	710	635	565	165	130	105	2.4	10.6	4"V	$18
38 Special	158	755	725	690	200	185	170	2.0	8.3	4"V	$18
38 Special	200	635	615	595	180	170	155	2.8	11.5	4"V	Disc.
38 Special +P	95	1175	1045	960	290	230	195	0.9	3.9	4"V	$27
38 Special +P	110	995	925	870	240	210	185	1.2	5.1	4"V	$22
38 Special +P	125	945	900	860	250	225	205	1.3	5.4	4"V	$22
38 Special +P	129	945	910	870	255	235	215	1.3	5.3	4"V	NA
38 Special +P	†150	884	NA	NA	264	NA	NA	NA	NA	4"V	NA
38 Special +P	158	890	855	825	280	255	240	1.4	6.0	4"V	$19
357 Magnum	110	1295	1095	975	410	290	230	0.8	3.5	4"V	$24
357 (med. Vel.)	125	1220	1075	985	415	315	270	0.8	3.7	4"V	$24
357 Magnum	125	1450	1240	1090	585	425	330	0.6	2.8	4"V	$24
357 (Multi-Ball)	140	1155	830	665	420	215	135	1.2	6.4	4"V	$10*
357 Magnum	140	1360	1195	1075	575	445	360	0.7	3.0	4"V	$24
357 Magnum	145	1290	1155	1060	535	430	360	0.8	3.5	4"V	$29
357 Magnum	†150/158	1235	1105	1015	535	430	360	0.8	3.5	4"V	$24
357 Magnum	180	1145	1055	985	525	445	390	0.9	3.9	4"V	$24
357 Rem. Maximum	158	1825	1590	1380	1170	885	670	0.4	1.7	10½"	$12*
40 S&W	155	1140	1026	958	447	362	309	0.9	4.1	4"	$27
40 S&W	180	985	936	893	388	350	319	1.4	5.0	4"	$31
10mm Automatic	†155	1125	1046	986	436	377	335	0.9	3.9	5"	$22
10mm Automatic	170	1340	1165	1145	680	510	415	0.7	3.2	5"	$31
10mm Automatic	175	1290	1140	1035	650	505	420	0.7	3.3	5½"	$15*
10mm Auto.(FBI)	180	950	905	865	361	327	299	1.5	5.4	4"	$15*
10mm Automatic	180	1030	970	920	425	375	340	1.1	4.7	5"	$15
10mm Automatic	200	1160	1070	1010	495	510	430	0.9	3.8	5"	$16
41 Action Exp.	180	1000	947	903	400	359	326	0.5	4.2	5"	$14*
41 Rem. Magnum	170	1420	1165	1015	760	515	390	0.7	3.2	4"V	$31
41 Rem. Magnum	175	1250	1120	1030	605	490	410	0.8	3.4	4"V	$15*
41 (Med. Vel.)	210	965	900	840	435	375	330	1.3	5.4	4"V	$28
41 Rem. Magnum	210	1300	1160	1060	790	630	525	0.7	3.2	4"V	$13*
44 S&W Special	†180	980	NA	NA	383	NA	NA	NA	NA	6½"	NA
44 S&W Special	200	1035	940	865	475	390	335	1.1	4.9	6½"	$12*
44 S&W Special	240/246	755	725	695	310	285	265	2.0	8.3	6½"	$25
44 Rem. Magnum	180	1610	1365	1175	1035	745	550	0.5	2.3	4"V	$14*
44 Rem. Magnum	200	1400	1192	1053	870	630	492	0.6	NA	6½"	NA
44 Rem. Magnum	210	1495	1310	1165	1040	805	635	0.6	2.5	6½"	$16*
44 (Med. Vel.)	240	1000	945	900	535	475	435	1.1	4.8	6½"	$28
44 R.M.(Jacketed)	240	1180	1080	1010	740	625	545	0.9	3.7	4"V	$13*
44 R.M. (Lead)	240	1350	1185	1070	970	750	610	0.7	3.1	4"V	$28
44 Rem. Magnum	250	1180	1100	1040	775	670	600	0.8	3.6	6½"V	NA
44 Rem. Magnum	†300	1200	1100	1026	959	806	702	NA	NA	7½"	$17
45 Automatic	185	1000	940	890	410	360	325	1.1	4.9	5"	$13*
45 Auto. (Match)	185	770	705	650	245	204	175	2.0	8.7	5"	$27
45 Auto (Match)	200	940	890	840	392	352	312	2.0	8.6	5"	NA
45 Automatic	200	975	917	860	421	372	328	1.4	5.0	5"	NA
45 Automatic	230	830	800	675	355	325	300	1.6	6.8	5"	$10*
45 Automatic	Shot	This data not available									
45 Automatic +P	185	1140	1040	970	535	445	385	0.9	4.0	5"	$28
45 Win. Magnum	230	1400	1230	1105	1000	775	635	0.6	2.8	5"	$13*
45 Auto. Rim	230	810	775	730	335	305	270	1.8	7.4	5½"	Disc.
45 Colt	200	1000	938	889	444	391	351	1.3	4.8	5½"	NA
45 Colt	225	960	890	830	460	395	345	1.3	5.5	5½"	$12*
45 Colt	250/255	860	820	780	410	375	340	1.6	6.6	5½"	$10*
50 Action Exp.	325	1400	1209	1075	1414	1055	835	0.2	2.3	6"	$24*

Notes: Blanks are available in 32 S&W, 38 S&W, and 38 Special. V after barrel length indicates test barrel was vented to produce ballistics similar to a revolver with a normal barrel-to-cylinder gap. Ammo prices are per 50 rounds except when marked with an * which signifies a 20 round box. Not all loads are available from all ammo manufacturers. Listed loads are those made by Remington, Winchester, Federal, and others. DISC. is a discontinued load. Prices are rounded to nearest whole dollar and will vary with brand and retail outlet. † = new bullet, or bullet weight this year.

CAUTION: PRICES CHANGE, CHECK AT GUNSHOP.

RIMFIRE AMMUNITION—BALLISTICS AND PRICES

Cartridge type	Bullet Wt. Grs.	Type	Velocity (fps) 22½" Barrel Muzzle	50 Yds.	100 Yds.	Energy (ft. lbs.) 22½" Barrel Muzzle	50 Yds.	100 Yds.	Velocity (fps) 6" Barrel Muzzle	50 Yds.	Energy (ft lbs) 6" Barrel Muzzle	50 Yds.	Approx. Price Per Box 50 Rds.	100 Rds.
22 Short Blank			Not applicable										3.20	NA
22 CB Short	29	solid	725	667	610	34	29	24	706	—	32	—	10.53 @ 250	
22 Short Match	29	solid	830	752	695	44	36	31	786	—	39	—		N.A.
22 Short Std. Vel.	29	solid	1045	—	810	70	—	42	865	—	48	—	Discontinued	
22 Short High Vel.	29	solid	1095	—	903	77	—	53	—	—	—	—	1.50	N.A.
22 Short H.V. H.P.	27	HP	1120	—	904	75	—	49	—	—	—	—		N.A.
22 CB Long	29	solid	725	667	610	34	29	24	706	—	32	—	2.33	N.A.
22 Long Std. Vel.	29	solid	1180	1038	946	90	69	58	1031	—	68	—		N.A.
22 Long High Vel.	29	solid	1240	—	962	99	—	60	—	—	—	—	2.33	
22 L.R. Match type	40	solid	1070	970	890	100	80	70	940	—	—	—		N.A.
22 L.R. Std. Vel.	40	solid	1138	1047	975	116	97	84	1027	925	93	76	1.87	4.34
22 L.R. High Vel.	40	solid	1255	1110	1017	140	109	92	1060	—	100	—	1.58	3.16
22 L.R. H.V. Sil.	42	solid	1220	—	1003	139	—	94	1025	—	98	—	N.A.	4.72
22 L.R. H.V. H.P.	36/38	HP	1280	1126	1010	131	101	82	1089	—	95	—	1.68	3.36
22 L.R. Shot	—	#11 or #12	1047	—	—	—	—	—	950	—	—	—	4.46	N.A.
22 L.R. Hyper Vel.	36	solid	1410	1187	1056	159	113	89	—	—	—	—	2.80	N.A.
22 L.R. Hyper H.P.	32/33/34	HP	1500	1240	1075	165	110	85	—	—	—	—	2.80	N.A.
22 Win. Mag.	30	HP	2200	1750	1373	322	203	127	1610	—	—	—		N.A.
22 Win. Mag.	40	solid/HP	1910	1490	1326	324	197	156	1428	—	181	—	6.06	N.A.
22 Win. Mag.	50	JHP	1650	—	1280	300	180	—	—	—	—	—	N.A.	N.A.
22 Win. Mag. Shot	—	#11	1126	—	—	—	—	—	—	—	—	—	N.A.	N.A.

Note: The actual ballistics obtained with your firearm can vary considerably from the advertised ballistics. Also ballistics can vary from lot to lot with the same brand and type load. Prices can vary with manufacturer and retail outlet. A — in the price column indicates this size packaging currently unavailable.

SHOTSHELL LOADS AND PRICES

Dram Equivalent	Shot Ozs.	Load Style	Shot Sizes	Brands	Avg. Price /box	Nominal Velocity (fps)
10 Gauge 3½" Magnum						
4½	2¼	premium	BB, 2, 4, 6	Win., Fed., Rem.	$31	1205
4½	2¼	premium	4, 6	Win., Fed.	$13*	1205
4¼	2	high velocity	BB, 2, 4	Rem.	$22	1205
4½	2¼	duplex	4x6	Rem.	$14*	1205
Max	18 pellets	premium	00 buck	Fed., WIN	$7**	1100
Max	54 pellets	premium	4 buck	Win.	$7**	1100
4¼	1¾	steel	T, BBB, BB, 1, 2, 3	Win., Rem.	$26	1260
4¼	1¾	steel duplex	TxBB, BBBx1	Rem.	$12**	1260
4¼	1⅝	steel	F, T, BBB	Win.	$11*	1285
4⅝	1⅝	steel	F, T, BBB	Win., Fed.	$26	1350
Max	1¾	slug, rifled	slug	Fed.	NA	1280
12 Gauge 3½" Magnum						
Max	2¼	premium	4, 6	Fed., Rem., Win.	$6**	1150
Max	18 pellets	premium	00 buck	Fed.	NA	1100
4⅛	1 9/16	steel	F, T, BB, 1, 2	Win., Fed.	$21	1335
4⅛	1 9/16	steel	F, T, BBB	Win.	$9*	1335
12 Gauge 3" Magnum						
4	2	premium	BB, 2, 4, 5, 6	Win., Fed., Rem.	$9*	1175
4	2	duplex	4x6	Rem.	$10	1175
4	1⅞	premium	BB, 2, 4, 6	Win., Fed., Rem.	$20	1210
4	1⅞	duplex	BBx4, 2x4, 2x6, 4x6	Rem.	$9*	1210
4	1⅝	premium	2, 4, 5, 6	Win., Fed., Rem.	$18	1290
4	24 pellets	buffered	1 buck	Win., Fed., Rem.	$5**	1040
4	15 pellets	buffered	00 buck	Win., Fed., Rem.	$5**	1210
4	10 pellets	buffered	000 buck	Win., Fed., Rem.	$5**	1225
4	41 pellets	buffered	4 buck	Win., Fed., Rem.	$5**	1210
Max	1¼	slug, rifled	slug	Fed.	NA	1600
Max	1	slug, rifled	slug, magnum	Rem.	$5**	1760
Max	1	saboted slug	slug	Win.	$9**	N.A.
3⅝	1⅜	steel	F, T, BBB, BB, 1, 2, 3, 4	Win.	$18	1275
3⅝	1⅜	steel duplex	BBBx1, BBx2, 1x3	Rem.	$8*	1275
4	1¼	steel	F, T, BBB, BB, 1, 2, 3, 4, 6	Win.	$8*	1375
4	1¼	steel duplex	BBx1, BBx2, BBx4, 1x3, 2x6	Rem.	$8*	1375
12 gauge 2¾"						
Max	1⅝	magnum	4, 5, 6	Win.	$7*	N.A.
3¾	1½	magnum	BB, 2, 4, 5, 6	Win., Fed., Rem.	$17	1260
3¾	1½	duplex	BBx4, 2x4, 2x6, 4x6	Rem.	$9*	1260
3¾	1¼	high velocity	BB, 2, 4, 5, 6, 7½, 8, 9	Win., Fed., Rem.	$13	1330
3½	1¼	mid velocity	7, 8, 9	Win.	$6	1275
3¼	1¼	std. velocity	6, 7½, 8, 9	Win., Fed., Rem.	$10	1220
3¼	1⅛	std. velocity	4, 6, 7½, 8, 9	Win., Fed., Rem.	$9	1255
3¼	1	std. velocity	6, 7½, 8	Rem., Fed.	$6	1290
3¼	1¼	target	7½, 8, 9	Win., Fed., Rem.	$9	1220
3	1⅛	target	7½, 8, 9, 7½x8	Win., Fed., Rem.	$7	1200
2¾	1⅛	target	7½, 8, 8½, 9, 7½x8	Win., Fed., Rem.	$7	1145
2¼	1⅛	target	7½, 8, 8½, 9	Rem., Fed.	$7	1080
3½	1	target	10	Fed.	NA	1350
3¼	28grams (1oz)	target	7½, 8, 9	Win., Fed., Rem.	$7	1290
2¾	1	target	8½	Fed.	NA	1180
3¾	8 pellets	buffered	000 buck	Win., Fed., Rem.	$4**	1325
4	12 pellets	premium	00 buck	Win., Fed., Rem.	$5**	1290
3¾	9 pellets	buffered	00 buck	Win., Fed., Rem.	$18	1325
3¾	12 pellets	buffered	0 buck	Win., Fed., Rem.	$4**	1275
4	20 pellets	buffered	1 buck	Win., Fed., Rem.	$5**	1075

Dram Equivalent	Shot Ozs.	Load Style	Shot Sizes	Brands	Avg. Price /box	Nominal Velocity (fps)
3¾	16 pellets	buffered	1 buck	Win., Fed., Rem.	$4**	1250
4	34 pellets	premium	4 buck	Win., Fed., Rem.	$5**	1250
3¾	27 pellets	buffered	4 buck	Win., Fed., Rem.	$4**	1325
Max	1	saboted slug	slug	Win., Fed.	$9**	1500
Max	1¼	slug, rifled	slug	Fed.	NA	1520
Max	1	slug, rifled	slug, magnum	Rem.	$5**	1680
Max	1	slug, rifled	slug	Win., Fed., Rem.	$4**	1610
3½	1¼	steel	T, BBB, BB, 1, 2, 3, 4, 5, 6	Win., Fed., Rem.	$17	1300
3½	1¼	steel duplex	BBx2, 1x3	Rem.	$8*	1300
3¾	1⅛	steel	BB, 1, 2, 3, 4, 5, 6	Win., Fed., Rem.	$15	1365
3¾	1⅛	steel duplex	BBx1, BBx2, BBx4, 1x3, 2x6	Rem.	$7*	1365
3¾	1	steel	2, 4, 6	Win., Fed.	$12	1390
16 Gauge 2¾"						
3¼	1¼	magnum	2, 4, 6	Win., Fed., Rem.	$16	1260
3¼	1⅛	high velocity	4, 6, 7½, 8	Win., Fed., Rem.	$12	1295
2¾	1⅛	std. velocity	6, 7½, 8	Fed., Rem.	$9	1185
2½	1	promotional	6, 7½, 8	Win., Fed., Rem.	$6	1165
Max	15/16	steel	2, 4	Fed.	NA	1300
Max	⅞	steel	2, 4	Win.	$15	N.A.
3	12 pellets	buffered	1 buck	Win., Fed., Rem.	$4**	1225
Max	⅘	slug, rifled	slug	Win., Fed., Rem.	$4**	1570
20 Gauge 3" Magnum						
3	1¼	premium	2, 4, 6, 7½	Win., Fed., Rem.	$15	1185
Max	18 pellets	buck shot	2 buck	Fed.	NA	1200
Max	24 pellets	buffered	3 buck	Win.	$5**	N.A.
2¾	20 pellets	buck	3 buck	Rem.	$4**	
3¼	1	steel	1, 2, 3, 4, 5, 6	Win., Fed., Rem.	$15	1330
20 Gauge 2¾"						
2¾	1⅛	magnum	4, 6, 7½	Win., Fed., Rem.	$13	1175
2¾	1	high velocity	4, 5, 6, 7½, 8, 9	Win., Fed., Rem.	$12	1220
2½	1	std. velocity	6, 7½, 8	Rem., Fed.	$9	1165
2½	⅞	promotional	6, 7½, 8	Win., Rem.	$6	1210
2½	⅞	target	8, 9	Win., Fed., Rem.	$8	1200
Max	20 pellets	buffered	3 buck	Win., Fed.	$4	1200
Max	⅝	slug, saboted	slug	Win.	$9**	N.A.
2¾	⅝	slug, rifled	slug	Rem.	$4**	1580
Max	¾	slug, rifled	slug	Win., Fed.	$4**	1570
Max	¾	steel	4, 6	Win., Fed.	$14	1425
28 Gauge 2¾"						
2	1	high velocity	6, 7½, 8	Win.	$12	1125
2¼	¾	high velocity	6, 7½, 8	Win., Fed., Rem.	$11	1295
2	¾	target	9	Win., Fed., Rem.	$10	1200
410 Bore 3"						
Max	11/16	high velocity	4, 5, 6, 7½, 8, 9	Win., Fed., Rem.	$10	1135
410 Bore 2½"						
Max	½	high velocity	4, 6, 7½	Win., Fed., Rem.	$9	1245
Max	⅕	slug, rifled	slug	Win., Fed., Rem.	$3**	1815
1½	½	target	9	Win., Fed., Rem.	$8	1200

NOTES: * = 10 rounds per box. ** = 5 rounds per box. Pricing variations and number of rounds per box can occur with type and brand of ammunition. Listed pricing is for load style and box quantity shown. Not every brand is available in all shot size variations. Some manufacturers do not provide suggested list prices. All prices rounded to nearest whole dollar. The price you pay will vary dependent upon outlet of purchase.

CAUTION: PRICES CHANGE, CHECK AT GUNSHOP.

SHOOTER'S MARKETPLACE

CHOKE TUBE SERVICE/INSTALLATION

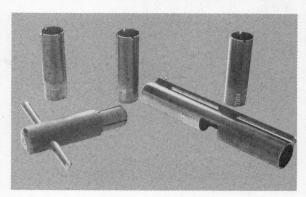

Hastings offers installation of the Briley Long Choke System for any shotgun gauge, all single barrel shotguns and most over/unders and side-by-sides. For double barrel guns, tube series are carefully matched to the barrel wall diameter, and special fixtures and instruments are used to provide a degree of concentricity between bore and choke that will satisfy the most discriminating shooter. Most series are suitable for use with steel shot, but check with them to be sure of the right choice. For barrels that fall short of the minimum wall thickness requirements (many over/unders, side-by-sides and some single barrels), they make special tubes. Give them a call. Screw chokes can be installed in all gauges, including 10, 12, 16, 20, 28, and 410 bore.

HASTINGS BARRELS

NEW TROPHY RIFLESCOPE

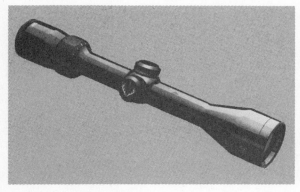

The Bushnell® Trophy® is one riflescope that won't let you down—in the field or on the range. It's the kind of hunting scope that was built for maximum reliability and accuracy with features that matter in the real world.

Every Trophy riflescope features high-contrast, amber-coated optics, fast focus eyepiece, wide-angle field of view, fingertip 1/4-inch click adjustments for easy, accurate sighting-in and rugged fog and waterproof construction.

You can see the entire line of Bushnell and Bausch & Lomb sports optics (riflescopes, binoculars and spotting scopes) at your favorite sporting goods dealer.

Ask about their lifetime limited warranty.

BAUSCH & LOMB SPORTS OPTICS DIVISION

RIFLED SHOTGUN BARRELS

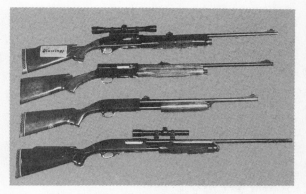

The Hastings Paradox Rifled Slug Barrel, for the shotgun hunter who insists on the accuracy only a rifled bore can provide, is the only off-the-shelf rifled shotgun barrel designed to be an exact replacement on popular makes of shotguns.

Each barrel is produced with a high finish, exacting tolerances and precise contours, and is available in 20" or 24" lengths with either rifle sights or special scope mounts installed.

Hastings Paradox slug barrels are available at fine gunshops, or directly from Hastings. Hastings also manufactures the Choke-Tube II system, integral choke barrels and specialized trap and Skeet barrels, and offers a full range of smithing services. Write or call for more info.

HASTINGS BARRELS

See manufacturers' addresses on page 262.

NEW 2X RED-DOT SIGHT

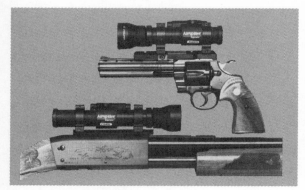

For the first time, Aimpoint has developed a fixed, low-power electronic sight with a floating red dot. The 30mm Aimpoint 5000 2-Power is the only unit with built-in magnification.

The shooter now gets the speed and accuracy of a red dot sight, combined with the advantages of a low-power scope.

Because the magnification is in the objective lens instead of the ocular lens (as with previous screw-in attachments), the dot covers only 1.5" at 200 yards. The 5000 2-Power can be used on all types of firearms and is complete with 30mm rings and all accessories. Suggested retail price for the Aimpoint 5000 2-Power is $399.95. Write Aimpoint direct for more information.

AIMPOINT

NEW HUNTING MAGAZINE

Dedicated to the artistic and workmanlike aspects of the hunt, *Hunting Horizons*, a semi-annual journal, is designed to challenge and entertain, inform and evaluate, transcending the world of the hunter in his environment.

Top writers, trophy-grade photography, as well as superb color graphics on quality gloss paper present the knowledge and lifestyle of great hunting adventures.

Single copy $9.50. Foreign $11.50.

Semi-annual subscription $17.00. Foreign $21.00.

You can write Wolfe Publishing direct, or pick up the phone and give them a call toll-free.

Be sure to mention you saw it in *Shooter's Marketplace*.

WOLFE PUBLISHING COMPANY

PARTITION BULLETS

Hard-hitting and deep penetrating, Nosler Partition® bullets deliver outstanding accuracy, controlled expansion and superior weight retention for any hunting challenge.

Nosler's unique dual core Partition construction and fully tapered jacket result in a bullet that is not only tough enough to withstand the violent impact of high velocity at close range, but will expand reliably at extreme range or on light game.

Partition bullets are available in calibers from .243 through .375 in a variety of weights and configurations.

If you would like to have a current Nosler catalog, just mention that you saw it in *Shooter's Marketplace* and it's yours for free!

NOSLER, INC.

DOUBLE ACTION DERRINGERS

High Standard DA derringers are now being made by the American Derringer Corp. The DA 38 is available in two calibers, 38 Special and 9mm Luger. The DA 38's barrel, receiver, and internal parts are made from high strength stainless steel with aluminum grip frame. Weight is 14.5 oz., the overall length is 4.85" with a barrel length of 3". Satin finish, rosewood grips. The suggested retail price is $250.00.

The DA 22 is available in 22 LR and 22 Mag. and weighs in at 11oz. The overall length is 5" with a 3" barrel length. The finish is blue with rosewood grips. Suggested retail price is $169.95. SPARE PARTS—A limited amount of original High Standard Derringer Parts are available; send $5.00 for list (refundable with purchase).

AMERICAN DERRINGER CORP.

See manufacturers' addresses on page 262.

SHOOTER'S MARKETPLACE

CHECKERING TOOLS

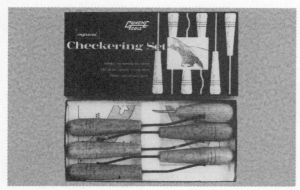

Gunline Checkering Tools are precisely made and come with illustrated instructions and easy to follow sample checkering patterns. Hobbyists and professional gunstockers are still very enthusiastic about the cutting qualities, ease of use and simplicity of design.

Gunline, in business since 1946, offers a full line of replaceable cutters from 16 to 28 lines per inch, medium or fine, 60 to 90 degree, short and long size. Three types of handles are available; one has an offset rear-view feature.

Set prices begin at $24.50 plus $3 for shipping. The illustrated Camp Perry Set of 6 tools ($49.95) provides everything necessary. Call or write for free brochure, prices and order blank.

GUNLINE TOOLS

GATLING GUN PLANS

Now you can own one. These quality blueprints allow scaling to other sizes or calibers (plans are for a 22 rimfire Gatling). Complete 40-page instruction book explains each part and how to make it. Finished Gatling has 10 rifled barrels (12" long) and a 20" overall length. No castings are required. All functioning internal parts. The full-scale drawings are dimensioned and come complete with materials lists and notes describing how RG-G made and assembled the parts.

Original Gatling concepts have been fully adapted to obtainable materials and producible parts. Plans: $39.98.

Send 3x5 self-addressed card to ensure correct shipment.

RG-G INC.

BARREL BEDDING TOOLS

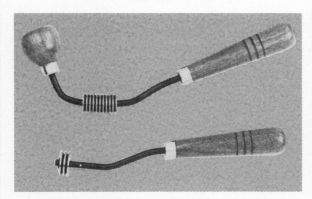

Gunline BBT (Barrel Bedding Tool) has a forward and rear handle for heavy to light duty affording full control of the 11 cushioned cutter discs. The BJ (Barrel Bedder Jr.) style single handle tool is suitable for lighter duty. The GS (Groove Shave) is like the BJ with fewer and larger discs.

Gunline offers a full line of replaceable cutter discs. The BBT is available in $1/2$, $9/16$, $5/8$, $11/16$, $3/4$, $7/8$, 1, $1 1/8$" diameters and retails from $15.95 to $17.50. The BJ Tool Set comes with $1/2$, $5/8$, and $3/4$" (6 each) and retails for $23.75. The GS includes $7/8$, 1 and $1 1/8$" sizes (3 each) and sells for $18.95. Add $3 for shipping and handling.

Call or write for a free brochure, prices and an order blank.

GUNLINE TOOLS

MUZZLELOADING CANNON BLUEPRINTS

These plans are not copies of specific models. They are for strong, well designed, serviceable and attractive cannons. No castings, deep drilling or boring required. Each set of plans consists of fully dimensioned drawings, materials lists, instructions, contour templates and a source list for purchased items. The "Big Guy" features a 2" barrel, copper mount as well as rugged hardwood and solid brass construction.

Simple breech seal allows removal by hand. Complete design package: $18.95. The smaller sundial cannon is equipped with a lens that focuses the noon sun for ignition.

No fuses. All brass. Plans: $13.49. Both sets of plans are available for $26.89.

RG-G, INC.

SHOOTER'S MARKETPLACE

SHOTGUN SADDLE MOUNTS

The new B-Square no-gunsmithing shotgun saddle mounts are now available for most popular 12-gauge shotguns. These mounts straddle the shotgun's receiver and fit tight on top of the gun. All mounts have a standard dovetail and are a "view thru" design so the gun's sights can be used. Any standard dovetail rings can be used with the shotgun mounts.

Available for Remington 870/1100 and 11-87, Mossberg 500, Mossberg 5500, Mossberg 835, Winchester 1400/1300/1200, Ithaca 37/87, and Browning A-5 shotguns.

These no-gunsmithing shotgun mounts sell for $49.95 at your dealer, or call B-Square toll-free.

Be sure to state the model and gauge of your shotgun when ordering.

B-SQUARE COMPANY

SHOTGUN ACCESSORIES

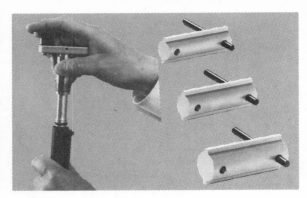

B-Square offers a wide range of shotgun accessories. The "Texas Twister" choke tube speed wrench is currently available for most 12-gauge shotguns. Unlike other wrenches, the "Texas Twister" choke changer incorporates a bore guide to prevent crooked starts and damaged threads. The T-handle is designed to break stubborn tubes loose.

B-Square Remington 870 Fore-end wrench is a must to keep the fore-end wood tight. Available for all gauges.

The speed wrench sells for $29.95 and the fore-end wrench sells for $13.25 at your dealer or call B-Square toll-free.

Be sure to state the model and gauge of your shotgun when ordering.

B-SQUARE COMPANY

NEW LASER & Q.D. MOUNTS

The BSL-1 Laser Sight is compact (2³/₄" long, ³/₄" diameter) and lightweight (2 oz.). It projects a 2" pulsing (not passive) dot at 200 yards (there is no more powerful laser on the market). The BSL-1 is self contained, moisture proof, shock proof, with internal direct beam steering and locking adjustments. The batteries are widely available and can be easily changed. The BSL-1 has a lifetime warranty.

Mounting options include both quick detachable and interchangeable systems to accommodate most popular guns. The BSL-1 mounts over/under the barrel, offset to a scope or quick detachable under the barrel of most popular handguns.

See your local dealer or call their toll free hotline for more information.

B-SQUARE COMPANY

SCREW KITS

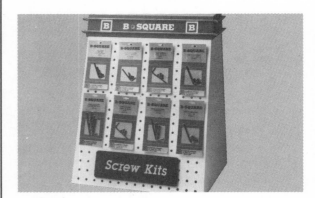

B-Square has become known within the industry as the source for screws—especially those hard to find, "must have" firearms screws we all need at some time.

B-Square screws are available in a variety of sizes and uses. All screw kits include a wrench and the appropriate number of socket head screws plus one extra. Available screw kit categories include base screws, trigger guard/action screws, grip screws, ring screws, plug screws, and Smith & Wesson sideplate screws.

B-Square screw kit display units for retailers are now available. For additional information about display units and/or screw kits, simply call B-Square toll-free.

B-SQUARE COMPANY

See manufacturers' addresses on page 262.

SHOOTER'S MARKETPLACE

GUNSMITH TOOLS

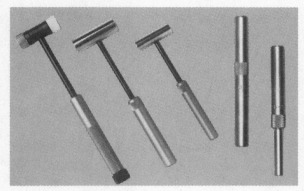

B-Square Brass Hammers and punches are famous for their design and quality. For the professional and the hobby gunsmith, solid brass headed hammers are perfect for dent removal and setting work in machine vises.

They provide the right sensitivity and feel for gunsmithing and other delicate jobs. Hammers are conveniently available in three weights: 2.5 oz., 5 oz., and 10 oz.

B-Square solid brass drifts are for driving out gunsights and large pins without damage. The set of two knurled ¼" diameter and ⅜" diameter punches sell for $9.95 at your dealer or call B-Square toll-free for a catalog featuring their complete line of tools and accessories.

B-SQUARE COMPANY

HANDGUN MOUNTS

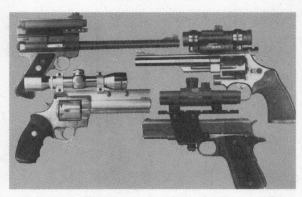

B-Square offers a complete line of no-gunsmithing scope mounts for handguns. All mounts feature a standard dovetail base which accepts any standard dovetail rings (Weaver). Most mounts are available in both blue and stainless finish and feature socket head screws.

As shown above, the Ruger Mark I/II .22 Dovetail, Smith & Wesson K, L, N, Frame, Colt Anaconda, Colt .45 Auto are representative of the diversity of the B-Square line. New mounts are continuously being developed.

For additional information ask your dealer or call B-Square toll-free. They'll be happy to send you a catalog featuring the complete line of mounts and other B-Square products.

B-SQUARE COMPANY

GUN ACCESSORY CATALOGS

Three of the most useful catalogs in the industry can be obtained by writing or calling B-Square (toll free).

MOUNTS CATALOG—B-Square offers over 200 different no-gunsmithing mounting systems for almost every important firearm make and model. Also available are many archery and specialty mounting systems.

LASER CATALOG—The incredible BSL-1 laser sight and interchangeable mounting system has very quickly been established as a standard of excellence in the field.

TOOLS AND ACCESSORIES—B-Square offers innovative tools and shooting accessories for most popular firearms, reloading and shooting games.

B-SQUARE COMPANY

RUGGED "ULTRALIGHT" BIPOD

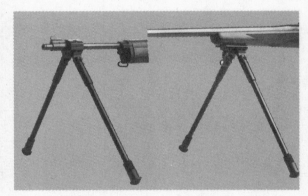

The new B-Square Bipod is currently available in two attachment models—barrel clamp or sporter swivel stud. Bipods feature coil spring "suspension" and extendable legs to 24". They're easy to install and require no gunsmithing or stock alteration. Bipods are designed to swivel 45 degrees for instant leveling on uneven ground.

Sets up quickly—legs simply pull down and lock. When not in use, the legs fold up close against the stock for a clean profile. B-Square bipods are fully machined, no stampings, no protrusions, springs or levers.

B-Square bipods sell for only $59.95 at your dealer or call B-Square toll-free. State type of firearm and barrel diameter when ordering.

B-SQUARE COMPANY

See manufacturers' addresses on page 262.

GLASER SAFETY SLUG AMMUNITION

Glaser Safety Slug's state-of-the-art, professional grade personal defense ammunition is now offered in two bullet styles: *Blue* uses a #12 compressed shot core for maximum ricochet protection and *Silver* uses a #6 compressed shot core for maximum penetration.

The Glaser Safety Slug manufacturing process results in outstanding accuracy with documented groups of less than 1" at 100 yards! This is why Glaser has been a top choice of professional and private law enforcement agencies worldwide for over fifteen years. Currently available in every caliber from 25 ACP through 30-06, including 40 S&W, 10mm, 223 and 7.62x39.

Write for a free brochure.

GLASER SAFETY SLUG, INC.

NEW HOLSTER CATALOG

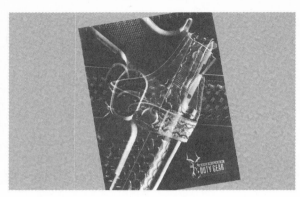

This isn't just any catalog. Safariland's 1992 publication is 112 pages of some of the most comprehensive information ever compiled on law enforcement leather and competition equipment. Computer generated graphics display the products with rich detail, giving you the clearest picture yet of what you'll receive. In short, Safariland will make your buying decisions informed and simple.

You'll see the World Champion 008 Final Option competition holster used by Doug Koenig, Jerry Barnhart and Rob Leatham. What's more, new holsters and accessories designed exclusively for America's elite federal law enforcement agencies are featured in the catalog. Write, call toll free or fax for more information.

SAFARILAND LTD., INC.

NEW ULTRA™ BULLET SEATER

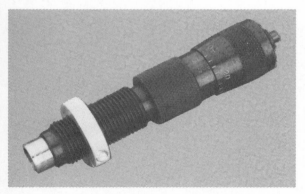

Forster Products has just introduced a new bullet seating die. The adjustment mechanism on the new Ultra™ Die is identical to that on a precision micrometer (.025" bullet movement per revolution). This feature makes it much easier to change seating depths when fine tuning different loads.

Forster's Ultra Die features "clickless" bullet depth adjustment for smooth as silk operation. Case and bullet alignment are insured with Forster's Bench Rest® technology.

The one-piece stem eliminates seating depth consistency problems inherent in bullet seaters with floating stems.

Ultra Dies are available in 51 rifle calibers. Send $1.00 for their 1993 catalog.

FORSTER PRODUCTS

PATENTED RIFLE SLING

The unique, patented design of The Super-Sling® rifle sling permits rapid one-hand adjustment to any desired position. No snaps, buckles, etc., to manipulate when opening or closing The Super-Sling. The infinite one-hand adjustment provides the shooter with a "quick sling" for any shooting position. It greatly improves steady holding of a rifle. The sling is fully assembled with or without detachable swivels.

The Super-Sling is manufactured from superior quality Mil-Spec. type webbing available in 1" or 1¼". A choice of colors/patterns is available: Brown, Tan, Black, Gray, OD Green, Day-Glo Orange, Woodland Camo, Trebark Camo, Realtree Camo, or Arctic White.

THE OUTDOOR CONNECTION, INC.

See manufacturers' addresses on page 262.

ACCESSORY/SERVICE BROCHURE

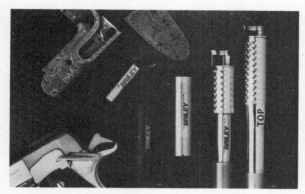

This Houston based firm has always meant fine quality and precision to the avid shotgunner. The Briley tradition of attention to detail and complete customer satisfaction keeps the hunter and competition shooter totally satisfied.

Their brochure describes Briley's line of shotgun and now pistol and revolver services as well. Briley has added a new division for the discerning handgun enthusiast.

Everything from screw-in chokes to competition Skeet tubes to pistol and revolver customizing and accessories. Briley offers an excellent line of both products and services for the shotgunner and handgunner.

Write or call toll free for a free brochure.

BRILEY MFG., INC.

SCREW-IN CHOKES

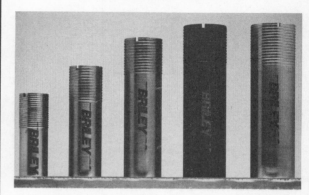

The Briley Screw-in choke is famous for its reliable, uniform patterns and its quality of manufacture. This system allows the shooter the complete choke control necessary to utilize the full spectrum of ammunition available to today's shotgunner.

There are new innovations in chokes as well. The unique "Comp-Choke" gives the shooter not only reliable patterns but also aids in second-shot recovery time by porting gases upward at the muzzle. Total steel-shot compatibility is also available with the screw-in choke system. Even the largest shot sizes are usable through their steel-shot chokes. Turkey hunters as well have exclusive choke designs and constrictions available from Briley.

Write or call toll free for a free brochure

BRILEY MFG., INC.

PISTOL CUSTOMIZING/ACCESSORIES

The newest department at Briley is their fully specialized Pistol Division. Briley can offer the dedicated handgun enthusiast some of the finest modifications, customizing, repair parts and accessories available. Items such as compensators, extended slide releases, thump guards, squared trigger guards and many others are only some of the services available from Briley Pistol Division.

In the future, this division will be manufacturing custom slides, barrels, custom titanium compensators and other unique and ingenious accessories for the discerning handgun shooter and competitor.

As we went to press, Briley advised us that they will also be offering complete, conventional repair services for all makes of handguns.

BRILEY MFG., INC.

CUSTOM SHOTGUN REBARRELLING

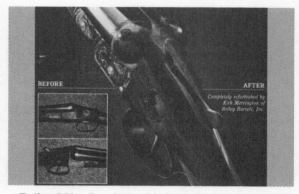

BEFORE AFTER

Completely refurbished by Kirk Merrington of Briley Barrels, Inc.

Briley Mfg., Inc. has added a new custom department that is dedicated to the refurbishing of over/under or side-by-side shotgun barrels. They can, in fact, take a set of unshootable (read that, "worthless") shotgun barrels and fully restore them. Barrels that have been severely dented, rusted or even burst during firing (due to a bore obstruction) can virtually all be saved.

Additionally, Briley can manufacture a set of new barrels (any make) for your gun; they can provide new or custom ribs; and they can completely strip, clean and/or repair your action. Lastly, this new Briley department is offering custom engraving services and complete stock repair & refinishing. Write or call for more details.

BRILEY MFG., INC.

See manufacturers' addresses on page 262.

BLACKPOWDER CATALOG

For over 35 years the Dixie Gun Works catalog has been one of the standards by which other blackpowder catalogs have been measured. At 640-plus pages, it's also the largest blackpowder catalog available.

The 1992 Dixie Gun Works catalog illustrates over 8,000 items, supplies for the hunter, shooter and historical enthusiast. Dixie stocks scarce parts for many military and sporting firearms, antiques and replicas. When it comes to modern blackpowder firearms, Dixie carries a full line of rifles, pistols and shotguns from makers such as Thompson Center, Traditions, Inc., Hatfield, Shiloh, Pedersoli and others. There is also a section dealing with facts and figures designed to improve everyone's knowledge of this fascinating field.

DIXIE GUN WORKS

FLUORITE LENS SPOTTING SCOPE

Kowa Optimed's Prominar spotting scope features the only Fluorite 77mm lens on the market today. The Fluorite lens is unusual in that it offers a sharper image, a wider field of view and increased light-gathering capabilities of no less than 60% over conventional 60mm spotting scopes.

The Prominar would be an ideal choice for the serious varmint hunter, big game hunter or dedicated benchrester.

The Kowa Optimed Prominar comes complete with bayonet mounting for easy eyepiece exchange. There are seven fully interchangeable eyepieces available from the manufacturer. An optional high-quality photo lens coupler is also available.

Write or call for more information.

KOWA OPTIMED, INC.

PROFESSIONAL CUSTOM BULLETS

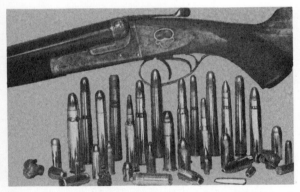

Star Custom Bullets has been making, testing and supplying custom bullets to hunters for nine years, particularly for heavy dangerous game in Africa and Alaska. These superior bullets have been used successfully on elephant, Cape buffalo, lion, bear and other game by hunters, especially professional hunters guiding and "backing up" clients. Star Custom Bullets incorporates ideas through continuing research of actual testing on dangerous game. They offer various solids and soft nose bullets from .22 through .600 N.E. Individual customer specifications may be special ordered.

If you would like to have their current brochure, write and mention you saw it in *Shooter's Marketplace* and they'll send you one free of charge.

PROFESSIONAL HUNTER SUPPLIES

SHOOTERS NEWSPAPER

Established in 1946 *The Shotgun News* is a leader in its field.

It offers some of the finest gun buys in the United States. More than 160,000 persons read, enjoy and profit from its columns 3 times each month.

The Shotgun News has aided thousands of gun enthusiasts locate firearms, both modern and antique—rifles, pistols, shotguns, scopes, etc...all at money saving prices.

The money you save on the purchase of any of the more than 10,000 listings appearing 3 times a month could more than pay for the $20.00 (36 issue) annual subscription cost.

As it says on the cover, it's "the trading post for anything that shoots."

THE SHOTGUN NEWS

See manufacturers' addresses on page 262.

ELECTRONIC SCALE

The RCBS Electronic Scale brings solid state electronic accuracy and convenience to handloaders at a reasonable price.

The LCD digital readings are ideal for weighing bullets and cases and provide the ultimate convenience for checking powder charges.

The scale gives readings in grains; and the range of 0-500 grains is ample for most handloading applications. Can be used at home or at the shooting range.

Comes with an AC adaptor, or operates on 8 AA batteries (not included).

The RCBS Electronic Scale has a two-year warranty against defects in workmanship or materials and carries a suggested retail price of $395.00.

BLOUNT, INC., SPORTING EQUIP. DIV./RCBS PRODUCTS

NEW ELECTRONIC BORE CLEANER

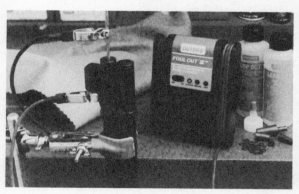

Outers new Foul Out II™ is an electronic bore cleaner that works fast. Set it up, plug it in and an indicator light tells you when the bore is totally free of copper or lead fouling.

The new Outers Foul Out II uses a reverse electro plating process which, through a combination of chemicals and electricity, removes all metal fouling from the bore and bonds it to a stainless steel rod. Foul Out II helps improve accuracy by removing deposits and preventing pitting. It won't harm barrel steel and there is no abrasive motion causing excessive wear. The new Foul Out II runs on either batteries or AC. Suggested retail $89.00.

See your local dealer or write Outers/Weaver for free literature.

BLOUNT, INC.—OUTERS/WEAVER OPERATION

SOMETHING FOR THE LADIES!

TomBoy, Inc., was established by women, for women interested in the sports of hunting and fishing.

TomBoy, Inc., publishes *Tomboy*, the first magazine for women hunters and anglers.

The TomBoy Club is the first women's hunting and fishing club to go nationwide! The TomBoy Club is providing a much needed resource for women who want to learn and experience these sports. Learning resources, outdoor clothing and equipment for women are not readily available because (until now) women have not let their interest in these sports be known. Hence, their logo: "We're Breaking the Silence."

They need your support. Write or call TomBoy, Inc.

TOMBOY, INC.

PRECISION CARTRIDGE MICROMETER

The RCBS "Precision Mic" Cartridge Micrometer is one of the handiest and most innovative new handloading products to come along in several years. For those handloaders seeking the best possible performance from their rifles, it provides a micrometer reading of their chamber dimension and bullet seating depth.

Using a fired case, the gauge gives a precise measurement of the chamber's head-to-shoulder dimension compared to the SAAMI recommendation. The micrometer function of the gauge is also applied to setting bullet seating depth at the optimum position for the best accuracy with the rifle. Available in 17 different calibers. Suggested retail price for each gauge is $37.00. Call or write for more information.

BLOUNT, INC., SPORTING EQUIP. DIV./RCBS PRODUCTS

See manufacturers' addresses on page 262.

SHOOTER'S MARKETPLACE

NEW SERVICE RIFLE PROPELLANT

Accurate Arms Company, Inc., has introduced another extruded powder for the reloader. Accurate 2495BR is a medium-burning propellant specifically for use in service rifle cartridges such as the 308, 30-06, and the 6mm BR Rem. Applications for cast bullets and mid-range loads have also been introduced. Loading data for Accurate 2495BR is in each powder container, as well as the 5th edition of the loading guide.

Here's the current lineup: Nitro 100 for shotshell. No. 2, No. 5, No. 7 and No. 9 for handgun. Plus 1680, 2015BR, 2230, 2460, 2495BR, 2520, 2700, 4350, 3100, and 8700 for rifle.

Write for a free copy of the 5th edition of their loading guide.

ACCURATE ARMS COMPANY, INC.

GUNSMITH SUPPLIES CATALOG

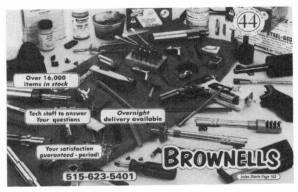

Since 1939, Brownells has been furnishing tools, supplies, fixtures and chemicals to professional gunsmiths and serious hobbyists worldwide. Their 214-page catalog features some of the finest gunsmithing equipment available for rebuilding, repairing, accurizing, engraving, checkering, bluing or building a complete gun. All shipments are made from in-stock inventories, and professional gunsmiths are available for technical support. As Frank Brownell says, "Our products, service, quality and reliability are guaranteed to satisfy 100%—period!"

Catalog free to qualified, full- or part-time gunsmiths and dealers. $3.75 to others—refunded on first $35.00 order. If you don't have your FFL, ask and they'll send free info on the licensing procedures.

BROWNELLS, INC.

KP-33 MAUSER RIFLE ACTIONS

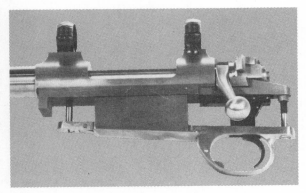

Crandall Tool & Machine Company offers custom Mauser-Type rifle actions, right or left hand, in three magazine lengths:

Short ...... 2.880" .... 1-14 S.A.E. Barrel Thread
Standard ... 3.380" .... 1-14 S.A.E.
Magnum .... 3.780" .... 1$\frac{1}{8}$-12 S.A.E.
416 Rigby ... 3.780" .... 1$\frac{1}{8}$-12 S.A.E.

Crandall features controlled-round feed; external, non-rotating extractor; Mdl. 70 style ejector, bolt stop & 3-position safety; and commercial trigger. Among the options offered are conventional round-ring bridge; single or double square bridge; integral scope mounts; Brevex-style deep box magazine (magnum lengths only). Completed rifles and barreled actions available. Send $2.00 for brochure.

CRANDALL TOOL & MACHINE COMPANY

MULTI-CALIBER SHELL HOLDER

The Quinetics name is familiar to seasoned reloaders. In short, they have a reputation for making quality, reliable products. The Quinetics Automatic Multi-Caliber Shell Holder is one of those good products that seems to get better with age.

Designed to do the job of a fistful of shell holders, the Quinetics offering is easily (read that "conventionally") secured to the ram. You can then go from one caliber to another, pistol and rifle, without changing shell holders. Adjusts automatically to 71 different calibers. It's that simple.

The price is quite reasonable—$13.75. Write, fax or call direct for more information. Dealers and jobbers welcome.

QUINETICS CORPORATION

See manufacturers' addresses on page 262.

RIFLE AND SHOTGUN SLINGS

The Butler Creek sling is an innovative new gun sling that's designed with the hunter's comfort in mind.

Combine the soft, durable features of neoprene and "Comfort Stretch"™ backing...your favorite hunting gun will feel 50% lighter and 100% more comfortable.

The new improved "Non Slip Grip"™ holds the gun snugly in place when carried on the shoulder and forms a solid grip around the shooter's forearm to stabilize barrel weave when shooting off hand.

These very comfortable slings are available in black or camo.

Write or call Butler Creek Corporation for more information.

BUTLER CREEK CORPORATION

DROP-IN CLASSIC STOCKS

Butler Creek Classic Series rifle stocks guarantee superior accuracy and dependability in all adverse weather and hunting conditions.

These stocks are extremely tough and come with a "lifetime warranty."

During the moulding process, extreme care is used to ensure a snug stock-to-metal fit that provides a true "drop in" stock that requires no adjustment, filling or glass bedding.

Butler Creek stocks include swivel studs, contoured butt plate and raised, non-slip checkering. They are available in a fine satin or deluxe textured finish.

Check with your local gun dealer or call for further information on all Butler Creek products.

BUTLER CREEK CORPORATION

10/22 BANANA MAGAZINE LOADER

Butler Creek has introduced the "Hot Lips"® Loader and it's as innovative as the clip it's designed for.

Now you can load your Ruger 10/22 banana magazine at home or in the field. The "Hot Lips" Loader is portable and easy to use; just turn the knob. No more sore thumbs.

You can say goodbye to feeding problems by using the Butler Creek "Hot Lips" banana magazine. The redesigned, separately moulded, self-lubricating, flat feed lip works with all types of 22 ammo.

Combine the new "Hot Lips" Loader and "Hot Lips" magazine and you have the perfect match.

Call or write Butler Creek Corporation for more information.

BUTLER CREEK CORPORATION

QUALITY FOLDING STOCKS

Butler Creek has expanded their offering of quality folding stocks. In addition to "drop in" replacements for Ruger 10/22 and Mini 14/30, they now offer folding stocks for Remington 870, Winchester 1200/1300 and Mossberg 500/590.

Each stock features raised checkering, finger-formed pistol grip and a positive lockup for rock-solid shooting. They are manufactured using today's finest polymer technology. Available in your choice of rugged satin stainless steel or blued steel.

Butler Creek adds swivel studs, quality recoil pad and cheek piece for comfort during sustained shooting. Comes with a "lifetime warranty."

Write Butler Creek Corporation direct or call for more information.

BUTLER CREEK CORPORATION

See manufacturers' addresses on page 262.

SHOOTER'S MARKETPLACE

NEW TWIN TUMBLER

Lyman's new Turbo Twin Tumbler is like two tumblers in one. Large capacity 1200 cleans over 350 pistol cases at one time. Built-in sifter lid for separating media from cases. The 600 Pop Top Bowl System features clear plastic "see thru" lid for inspecting cases as they are being cleaned.

The Twin Tumbler includes both bowl systems which can be used interchangeably for large or small capacity loads.

The 600 system is ideal for rocks or small metal parts deburring.

See your local sporting firearms dealer for a better look at the Twin Tumbler.

For a free catalog, call direct via their toll-free phone number.

LYMAN PRODUCTS CORPORATION

OBSOLETE CARTRIDGE CASES

Red Willow Tool & Armory, Inc. manufactures a complete line of cartridge cases in obsolete and hard to find calibers that range from 6.5mm on up through 4 bore.

The brass is machined from cartridge brass bar stock on state-of-the-art computer-controlled machinery. Their brass is of the highest quality and annealed, ready for use. They can also make custom runs of oddball cases, the minimum order being 200 cases.

Incidentally, Red Willow is also the manufacturer of the Ballard Rifle.

Just give Red Willow Tool & Armory, Inc. a call for more information, or send them your needs by mail or fax.

RED WILLOW TOOL & ARMORY, INC.

HIGH QUALITY KNIVES

Since 1964, A.G. Russell has been one of the best sources for highest quality knives. Not only are there new Morseth knives, handmade since 1934, there are also handmade knives from A.G. Russell and Bob Dozier. A.G. also has knives made to his specs in Germany, Japan and the United States. Pocketknives, hunting knives, outstanding kitchen knives, pocket tools with pliers and many other things to interest the outdoorsman.

A.G. Russell is also one of the best places to buy, sell or trade your handmade or collectible knives and tools.

Over 1,000 handmade knives in stock by the top makers.

Write or call for a *free* catalog.

A.G. RUSSELL KNIVES, INC.

MANUAL TARGETS

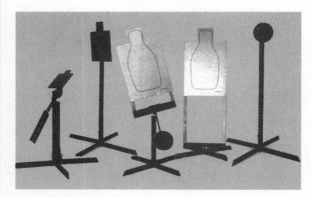

Action Target, a leader in automated target equipment, has introduced their new "PT" line of manual targets.

The PT-Static family is a set of interchangeable parts that can be used to make a variety of targets. Consists of a foot, stand and head. Use the available options to assemble almost any type of target.

The PT-Poppers are simple, versatile, reliable knock-down targets designed for long life. The "hit-zone," which can be easily ordered in a variety of shapes, can be reversed to allow shooting on both surfaces.

Shooting surfaces are made of state-of-the-art $^3/_8$" armor plating. Welded areas are dual-shield welded. Can be ordered for high-power use (223 and 308).

ACTION TARGET, INC.

See manufacturers' addresses on page 262.

NEW SEE-THROUGH SCOPE MOUNT

J.B. Holden Company introduced the patented Ironsighter® "See-Thru" scope mount line in 1967. Today, the Ironsighter two-way sighting option is accepted as standard. The new Wide Ironsighters are their very latest development. The new 700 series Ironsighters are now available for most centerfire, rimfire and muzzleloading rifles as well as many handguns and shotguns.

Holden offers a superior aluminum alloy which is as much as 60% stronger than the materials found in similar products. When combined with solid engineering designs, added metal thickness in high stress areas, and precision-machined contact surfaces, Holden mounts will withstand the heaviest types of use.

J.B. HOLDEN COMPANY

SELF-ADHESIVE RECOIL PAD

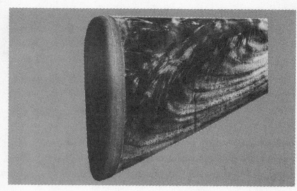

The Add-A-Pad, for rifles or shotguns, can be installed in minutes by simply pressing a pad on the end of the butt, trimming it with a sharp knife, then sanding it to the exact shape of the stock.

Add-A-Pad is made from a shock absorbent blended neoprene with a specially formulated adhesive backing.

The package includes two 1/4-inch and one 1/2-inch pads allowing the use of any one pad or a combination of pads to build a recoil pad up to 1-inch thick. The result is an economical pad which looks professionally installed.

Add-A-Pad costs $10.95 and comes with complete installation instructions.

Call or write for more information.

PALSA OUTDOOR PRODUCTS

NEW BLACK POWDER SCOPE MOUNT

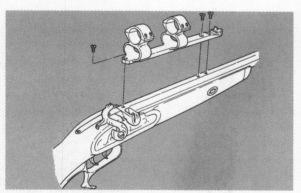

Recent innovations from the J.B. Holden Company include the new Ironsighter® 365, 375 and 385 Black Powder Scope Mounts for popular 1991 and later Thompson/Center rifles. This unique product design, which attaches to factory-drilled holes on the barrel, offers an adjustable rear sight, see-through scope rings and mounting base which are precision machined from a single piece of high strength alloy. The result is a product designed for stability and durability. As the lead product in the recently expanded line of Holden no-gunsmithing black powder scope mounts, each of these new Ironsighters provides superior strength and mounting stability. Write for a catalog and serial number list of drilled and tapped T/C barrels.

J.B. HOLDEN COMPANY

PELLET FIRING CONVERSIONS

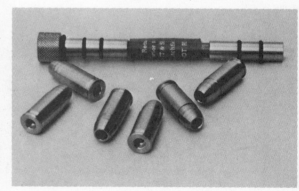

Loch Leven Industries' Convert-a-Pell kit enables the shooter to convert his favorite handgun to shoot inexpensive pellets. Available for any caliber from 380 through 45LC, each Convert-a-Pell kit contains a barrel adapter tube (to convert one's firearm bore to 177 caliber) and six brass "cartridges". No special tools, no disassembly, and no reloading expertise required.

Will not harm bore, action, or component parts of any handgun. A 22 Centerfire rifle version of the Convert-a-Pell kit and complete line of accessories is also available.

You can practice year round, indoors or out, when shooting with Convert-a-Pell. Suggested retail price: Handgun Kit $39.95. Write for more info.

LOCH LEVEN INDUSTRIES

See manufacturers' addresses on page 262.

SHOOTER'S MARKETPLACE

NEW AMMUNITION SERVICE

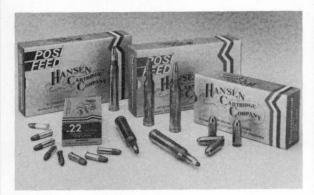

New England Ammunition Company offers a comprehensive selection of Hansen Cartridge Company products. All ammunition has been designed to fit the needs of avid American target shooters, plinkers, hunters and reloaders. It's all new manufactured, non-corrosive, boxer-primed, and fully reloadable. There are over 70 items to choose from.

New England Cartridge Company offers many unique and specialty calibers such as 9mm Makarov full metal jacket and hollow point, as well as such standbys as 30-06 soft point at reasonable prices. Hansen Cartridge Co. ammo is known for its reliability, performance and excellent savings. Write for pricing info and ordering instructions.

NEW ENGLAND AMMUNITION CO.

CUSTOM RIFLE

Jarrett Rifles, Inc. produces and sells an excellent line of sporting firearms. Each Jarrett rifle is made to exacting standards that provide repeatable, consistent accuracy in the field or at the bench. That element, along with innovative chambering, has provided Jarrett with an excellent reputation among the long-range shooting clan.

When you look at a Jarrett rifle don't expect to see a work of art. You'll see a rifle that's designed to be a durable, dependable and accurate shooting tool that's made for the serious hunter and shooter.

Jarrett rifles are built one at a time and are unconditionally guaranteed.

Write or call Jarrett Rifles, Inc. for additional information.

JARRETT RIFLES, INC.

SPORTING CLAYS AND MORE

White Flyer manufactures targets for all clay bird sports including trap, Skeet, sporting clays and International (trap, Skeet & Bunker).

The lineup includes a variety of colors and color combinations to match almost any background or lighting condition. Also available are high visibility "Flash" targets suitable for special shoot-offs, demo shoots, etc.

White Flyer clay targets are available in *Standard* trap and Skeet, as well as *International* trap and Skeet specifications.

White Flyer's Sporting Clay offerings include Pheasant, Rabbit, Midi, Mini and Battue targets.

Dealers can call White Flyer's toll-free number for the name of their local distributor.

WHITE FLYER

TRIPLE ACTION SOLUTION

This is one product solution to gun care and cleaning that offers the triple action of a solvent/lubricant/rust preventive that functions from 450°F to 95° below 0. Continued use of Eezox prevents stiff or jamming actions, lead, brass, copper or plastic wad residue build-up.

According to the manufacturer, scientific tests have shown that Eezox reduces the coefficient of friction by over 50%; and the international standard test for rust prevention (ASTM B-117 - 5% Salt Spray Fog Test) demonstrates its superior performance.

Call Eezox at their toll-free number for additional information. (Dealer/distributor inquiries are invited.)

EEZOX INC.

See manufacturers' addresses on page 262.

LIGHTWEIGHT, COMPACT BINOCULAR

The Swift Instrument 825 Compact Audubon, weighing only 26 ounces and standing just 5" tall, is the ideal glass for field or wood.

This armored, waterproof 7x compact binocular offers a broad field of vision with close focusing to 13 feet.

Its four-lens ocular system and magenta coated optics with multi-coating on the ocular objective lens give a high resolving power that results in an extremely bright image under the most demanding of conditions.

The 825 Compact Audubon is one of the latest in the Swift line-up of internationally famous binoculars.

Write for more information.

SWIFT INSTRUMENTS, INC.

UNIVERSAL RIFLESCOPE

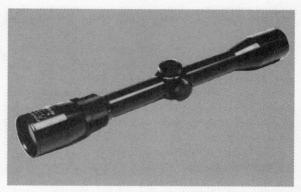

One of the most popular of the Swift Instrument line of riflescopes, the wide angle, waterproof Model 656 features a maximum field of 40 feet at 100 yards at 3x and up to 14 feet at 9x. A maximum R.L.E. of 266 to 30 is provided by the 40mm objective lens. The Model 656 allows the shooter to easily pick up a moving target at the widest field, then zoom in for close up accuracy.

The multi-coated optical system features 11 lens elements and the Quadraplex reticle offers heavy posts to quickly line up the target and fine cross hairs for pin point results.

The Swift Model 656 Riflescope comes attractively gift boxed. Available in regular, matte or silver finish.

Write for more information.

SWIFT INSTRUMENTS, INC.

VARIABLE POWER SPOTTING SCOPE

The 839 Searcher spotting scope from Swift Instruments offers maximum resolution in a compact body with its three-lens achromatic objective and orthoscopic eyepieces.

The variable power rotating head gives you a choice of straight or 45 degree viewing with both 20x and 40x orthoscopic eyepieces. You can also get 30x and 50x eyepieces—they're available from Swift as additional accessories.

The high resolving power of the Searcher makes this spotting scope perfect for tele-photography when adapters are added for your camera.

The Searcher weighs in at only 3 pounds and comes attractively gift boxed. Write Swift Instruments for more information.

SWIFT INSTRUMENTS, INC.

VARIABLE POWER RIFLESCOPE

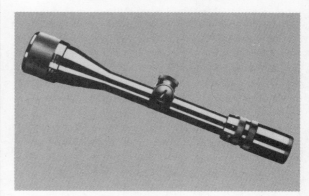

This is an offering that meets the needs of just about anyone looking for a telescopic sight that can do double or even triple duty. The Swift 664 is a 4-12x (40mm objective lens) variable telescopic sight that features parallax adjustment from 5 meters all the way to infinity.

Everyone from big game hunters, to varmint hunters, and on down to air rifle enthusiasts can find a use for the highly versatile Swift 664. It's fogproof, features superb multi-coated lenses, easy external adjustment for windage and elevation, self-centering quadraplex reticle and comes in regular, matte or silver finish. Write Swift Instruments, Inc., directly, and they can provide you with additional information.

SWIFT INSTRUMENTS, INC.

See manufacturers' addresses on page 262.

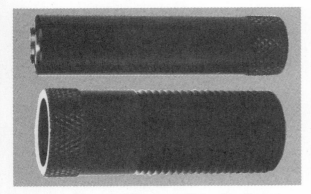

See manufacturers' addresses on page 262.

GUN MAINTENANCE KIT

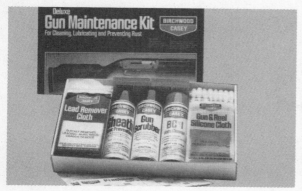

Birchwood Casey has introduced a new kit for cleaning, lubricating and protecting firearms—their Deluxe Gun Maintenance Kit. You get a complete selection of everything needed to keep your guns in top working order. The kit includes: a 9-ounce can of Gun Scrubber®, a 6-ounce can of Sheath® Rust Preventative and a 6-ounce can of BC#1 Bore Cleaner, 14.4x15-inch Gun & Reel Silicone Cloth, 10 Sheath Take-Along Gun Wipes, Lead Remover Polishing Cloth, Precision Squares Paper Targets and Self-Sticking Target Spots. Even gun cleaning patches and swabs are included as additional accessories. Suggested retail price is $21.00.

See your local dealer or write Birchwood Casey direct for a *free* catalog.

BIRCHWOOD LABORATORIES, INC.

LINSEED RUBBING OIL

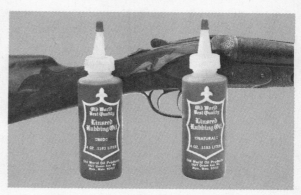

Old World Oil Products has been offering best-quality linseed oil for over a decade. Long recognized as *the* professional gun stock finish, linseed oil brings out the full character and quality of a walnut gun stock.

This superior linseed oil is available in red or amber shades. Serves perfectly for the expert refinishing of old gun lumber or the complete and total enhancement of a brand new gun stock.

This particular product is also ideal when it comes to the maintenance of original, oil-finished stocks.

Each bottle of this excellent linseed oil comes complete with instructions. Simply send $6.00 for your postpaid 4 oz. bottle of red or amber Old World Linseed Oil. No catalogs are available.

OLD WORLD OIL PRODUCTS

TOP QUALITY BULLET LUBE

Rooster Red bullet lubricants are available in a choice of two hardnesses in high-melt, consistently high performance, professional cannelure lubricants. Both are now available in 2"x6" sticks for the commercial reloader, and 1"x4" hollow and solid sticks. With a 230°F melting point, both are proven ideal for indoor and outdoor shooting. Both bond securely to the bullet, thus remain intact during shipping. ZAMBINI is the hard, tough version designed primarily for pistol. Lubesizer must be heated. HVR is softer, but firm.

Designed primarily for high velocity rifle, it's easier to apply, also excellent for pistol.

Prices: 2"x6" sticks $4.00; 1"x4" sticks $135.00 per 100 sticks.

ROOSTER LABORATORIES

NEW RANGE FINDING SCOPE

Shepherd Scopes now have a German design Speed Focus eyepiece that gives you razor sharp images with a twist of the rear ring on the eyepiece. The eyepiece stays rock solid throughout focusing and zooming.

Also new is an adjustable objective lens housing which will accept their new sunshade. The scopes have a new 340 hard matte finish that is extremely scratch resistant.

All scopes have Shepherd's patented dual reticle system that gives you one-shot zeroing, instant range finding, bullet drop and constant visual verification of your original zero.

Call, write or fax the manufacturer direct for a free brochure.

SHEPHERD SCOPE LTD.

See manufacturers' addresses on page 262.

KNIFE SHARPENERS

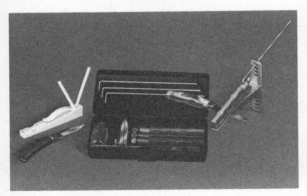

Now anyone can put the sharpest edges on every kind of knife or scissors, even fish hooks, using the patented Lansky Sharpening System and Crock Sticks.

You certainly don't have to be a professional when you use the latest in knife sharpening technology.

Lansky and Crock Stick are two of the world's most respected names in knife sharpening, with sharpeners for every home, field and shop use.

American-made Lansky products are sold worldwide and are catalogued and packaged in 14 different languages.

Send for their free full-color catalog. Please be sure to specify the language of your choice, if other than English, when you order.

LANSKY SHARPENERS & CROCK STICK

TARGET/SIGHT-IN KIT

Insta-Range™ is an extremely simple target and sight-in kit that can be set up anywhere in minutes.

Target folds out to become a rigid self-supporting target stand. Included are: 5 extra targets, bullet hole patches, and sight-in instructions. The extra targets may be placed on the target stand as needed. All materials are contained inside the Insta-Range target when it's folded up, making for a neat, reusable and easy-to-store package.

Priced at just $6.95, the Insta-Range Target and Sight-In Kit is rugged enough to last through many shooting sessions, and it is entirely recyclable and biodegradable.

Call or write Innovision Enterprises for more information.

INNOVISION ENTERPRISES

10/22 TARGET HAMMER

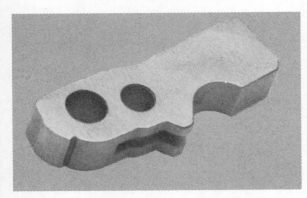

This new target hammer from Volquartsen Custom Ltd. is designed to give the stock Ruger 10/22 a superb "trigger job" by simply installing it in place of the factory hammer. No stoning or fitting is required to the sear or springs.

This hammer may appear similar to the production hammer but is geometrically advanced in the sear engagement area. It is hard plated for superior hardness and lubricity. Trigger pull is reduced to $1\frac{1}{3}$-lb. to $1\frac{3}{4}$-lb. depending on gun.

The target hammer sells for $33.00 plus $4.00 for shipping and handling. Your satisfaction is guaranteed.

To receive a 38-page catalog, send $4.00; however, if you will mention *Shooters Marketplace* that catalog is yours for just $3.00.

VOLQUARTSEN CUSTOM LTD.

COMPUTER SOFTWARE

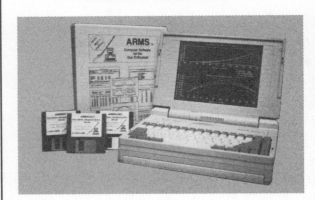

Peripheral Data Systems provides useful computer software for reloaders, shooters and collectors.

ArmsInv: Easily track your collections by type, accessories & serial number. Quickly generates a complete audit trail of any firearm you sell and can quickly provide net profit/loss as well as a bill of sale.

ArmsCalc: A comprehensive software tool that estimates and graphs how a projectile will behave under predetermined circumstances. Graphically compares loads with different bullet types/weights, charges. Gives energy, trajectory, velocity, etc.

Arms load: A comprehensive database for the avid and novice reloader. Easily tracks and catalogs loads. Allows you to produce consistent, high-quality ammo.

Write or call for more info.

PERIPHERAL DATA SYSTEMS

See manufacturers' addresses on page 262.

CARTRIDGES FOR COLLECTORS

Tillinghast's famous *Cartridges for Collectors List* is $2.00 sent prepaid. Lists over 1000 cartridges for sale: Patent Ignition, rimfires, pistol, rifle, shotgun; American and Foreign: books, catalogs. Send $8.00 for the next five Cartridge Lists, a real "bargin." Special—*Antique Ammunition Price Guide #1*, 8½ x 11, 64 pages, well illustrated, Regular: $6.00; Special: $3.50 sent prepaid.

Cartridge list is free with a purchase of the *Antique Ammunition Price Guide #1*. Tillinghast is looking to buy cartridge collections, accumulations, box lots, rare singles of all types.

They also purchase gun catalogs, gun powder tins, as well as gun and ammunition related advertising material.

JAMES C. TILLINGHAST

PISTOL AND RIFLE MAGAZINES

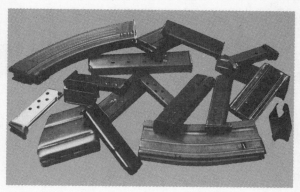

SARCO, Inc., carries an extensive inventory of newly made and surplus magazines for the Colt Model 1911 45 ($4.95), Beretta M92 ($12.00), Taurus M92 ($12.50), Browning Hi-Power ($10.95), Remington Model 513/521 rimfires ($14.95) and Winchester Model 52, 57, 69, 75 ($12.50).

Surplus mags include M-1 Garand (10 for $9.95), AR-15/M-16 30-round ($5.95), FN/FAL 20-round ($3.95), UZI Carbine/SMG 25-round ($4.95), 303 Enfield MKIII ($12.00) and 303 Enfield No.IV ($12.00).

You may order direct, just include $4.00 for shipping and handling.

Send SASE for a complete listing of all magazines in inventory.

No mags over 15 rounds can be sold in New Jersey.

SARCO, INC.

NEW MODULAR-CONCEPT GRIP

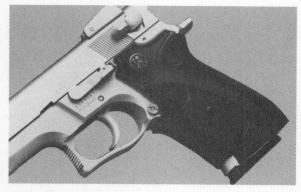

The latest addition to Pachmayr's line of Signature® grips for semi-auto pistols is the Model SW-5904/6, an all-new modular design that allows different backstraps and/or a finger groove front to be fitted.

This latest Pachmayr model puts the gripping power of genuine Neoprene® and their patented wrap-around clam-shell design to work for S&W owners. This combination of CAD/CAM design and material improvements results in better recoil absorption and a gun that "points right."

The Pachmayr SW-5904/6 fits the following Smith & Wesson 3rd Generation model pistols: 5906, 5904 and 4006.

Available for immediate delivery.

PACHMAYR, LTD.

15X LONG-RANGE SCOPE

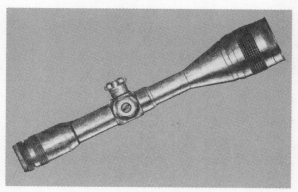

Designed for military and police use, the U.S. Optics SN-1 is a superior long-range telescopic sight. The SN-1 was specifically designed to house an advanced reticle and range finding system, i.e., this is not just a simple modification of an existing, conventional cope sight design. The SN-1 is equipped with superior optics that are fully supported, thereby preventing any loosening of the interior optical elements. It's ruggedly constructed.

The U.S. Optics SN-1 also comes with a calibrated head, 56mm objective lens and ¼-minute adjustment. Options: Custom reticle (your ballistics), solid-state reticle lighting module, mounting system, sun shade and lens covers. Also, 10x, 20x and 36x option. Write for details and prices.

UNITED STATES OPTICS TECHNOLOGIES, INC.

See manufacturers' addresses on page 262.

QUALITY HANDGUN BULLETS

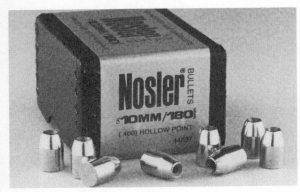

Nosler provides superb handgun bullets for every type of handgunner, and for every kind of shooting, but at a price that helps keep shooting as affordable as it can be.

No matter which Nosler handgun bullet you choose, you're assured the finest in accuracy, consistency and performance. Produced on advanced, fully automated machinery, Nosler is one handgun bullet maker whose product is designed and manufactured to rifle bullet quality standards.

Available in 9mm, .38, 10mm, .41, .44 and .45 calibers, Nosler handgun bullets are offered in a variety of weights and configurations. If you would like a current Nosler catalog, just mention *Shooter's Marketplace*, and it's yours, free!

NOSLER, INC.

ALL-TERRAIN TARGET HOLDER

If you've ever found yourself needing a serious sight check when you're miles away from a formal range, you may want to upgrade your present target system.

The Targ-A-Tote™ target holder was built to let you utilize the nearest safe backstop having a clear view, regardless of terrain type. It accommodates slopes and hard or soft surfaces and can be carried with your target pre-mounted. It comes assembled, and can be set up in one minute. Adjustable legs allow the Targ-A-Tote to be set plumb and stable for precise shooting. All parts can be readily patched or replaced. Write the R-Tech Corporation directly for more information. Mention you saw it in *Shooter's Marketplace*.

R-TECH CORPORATION

FOLDING BIPODS

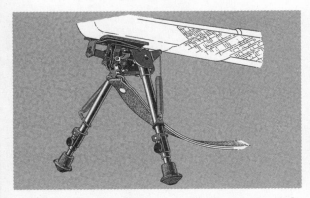

Harris Bipods clamp securely to most stud-equipped bolt-action rifles and are quick-detachable. They will fit some other guns, with adapters. Folding legs have completely adjustable spring-return extensions except for the Model LM. The sling swivel attaches to the clamp. This time-proven design is manufactured with heat-treated steel and hard alloys and has a black anodized finish.

Series S Bipods rotate 45° for instant leveling on uneven ground. Hinged base has tension adjustment and buffer springs to eliminate tremor or looseness in crotch area of the bipod. They are otherwise similar to non-rotating Series 1A2.

Eleven models are available from Harris; and, literature is free.

HARRIS ENGINEERING, INC.

MAGNUM AIR RIFLE CATALOG

Air Rifle Specialists magnum airgun catalog features magnum alloy pellets and accessories. They also have custom-made air rifles and accessories for airgun shooters who want the most power available.

Their pellets are made of a rugged lead alloy so they will retain their shape, but are sufficiently soft enough to produce outstanding accuracy in a high power air rifle.

To order a sample tin of pellets and what they call their "ugly" catalog, send $8.00 net (please specify .177 or .22).

To order their "ugly" catalog only, just send Air Rifle Specialists $2.00.

You'll also receive a $2.00 coupon with your first order.

AIR RIFLE SPECIALISTS

See manufacturers' addresses on page 262.

SHOOTER'S MARKETPLACE

GUNSMITH TOOLS

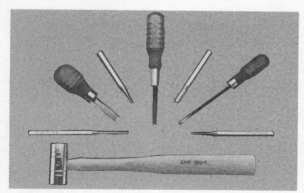

Grace Gunsmith Screwdrivers have hardwood handles and properly heat treated blades that are accurately ground by hand to fit gun screws perfectly. There are three popular sets: HG-8 Standard Set; HG-7 Pistolsmith Set; HG-5 Browning Set.

Grace Brass Hammers are of unmatched quality and have solid CDA 360 brass heads pressed and securely pinned to hickory handles.

Grace Gunsmith Punch Sets include the PS-7 steel pin punches with reverse tapers and the new PS-8 brass pin punches which won't spark or mar your fine firearms.

Grace Gunsmith Tools celebrates 50 years of serving the gunsmith with quality U.S.A.-made products. Write for a free catalog. Dealers and distributors ask for wholesale price list.

GRACE METAL PRODUCTS, INC.

HOME HANDGUN SECURITY

Sportsman's Communicators is offering a new Ready Response Safe Box for home/office handgun storage. It's childproof. It's secure. It can also be opened in 5 seconds—in the dark. Features a telescoping lid, 20 gauge steel welded joints and a concealed piano hinge. Portable? You bet—or pre-drilled for bolting in place. Set your choice of 2,000 combinations in minutes.

Internal foam pads hold gun in place (holds two 6" barrel guns).

Comes in brown or grey—handtooled Deco box in antique brown or ebony also available. Prices: 12"x8"x4" $82.95; 16"x8"x4" $89.95. Deco box (12"x8"x4") $89.95.

Add $6.00 postage and handling.

SPORTSMAN'S COMMUNICATORS

COLORCASE HARDENING

Doug Turnbull of Creekside Gun Shop offers Bone Charcoal Colorcase Hardening. This unique process duplicates the same fine colors that are found on guns manufactured by Parker, L.C. Smith, Colt, Winchester and other celebrated makers. With over 20 years of experience in colorcase work, Turnbull is able to get the natural colors that are notable on fine collectible firearms. No warpage or reassembly problems.

To help complete the restoration work, Rust Blueing of soft-soldered, double-barrels is available for your shotgun. Prepare your parts personally or, with your direction, Turnbull will be glad to give your parts the care in preparation needed to make your project complete. Send $2.00 for color brochure.

DOUG TURNBULL RESTORATION

QUICK RESPONSE SCOPE

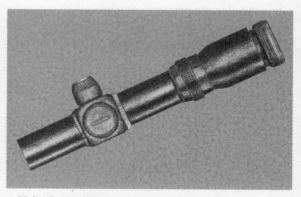

U.S. Optics Technologies, Inc. is offering a new SN-4, 1-4x variable scope that comes with Circle Dot reticle. This system, which offers a wide field of view, allows the shooter to get on target fast and at close ranges. Brightness, lit reticle and a forgiving, long eye relief provides superior low-light shooting capability.

A fine 2-minute dot at high power provides accuracy at extended ranges.

The SN-4 is rugged, versatile and well suited for action rifle competition. Options: 1.5x to 6x; BDC knobs for 223 or 308; duplex reticle and lit reticle module.

For more information, write, call or fax United States Optics Technologies directly.

UNITED STATES OPTICS TECHNOLOGIES, INC.

See manufacturers' addresses on page 262.

NEW AIRGUN DESIGN

Airrow's model Stealth will be offered in a rifled barrel version for 1993. Model designation is (8SRB), and calibers include .177, .22, .25 and the .38. Standard velocities are 1100 fps in all calibers. Barrel lengths range from 17" - 23" in rifled or polygon design.

This new Airrow model Stealth features pneumatic air trigger, variable 1.5x - 5x scope and C.A.R. three-position stock. Additionally, the Airrow model Stealth features all aircraft aluminum and stainless steel construction.

For more information and complete product catalog on this revolutionary new product, contact the manufacturer direct and mention that you read about it in *Shooter's Marketplace*.

AIRROW (SWIVEL MACHINE WORKS, INC.)

NEW RUGGED LASERSIGHT

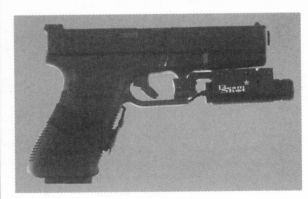

Alpec's Beam Shot™ Lasersight projects a red hot point of laser light right on target. Rugged pistol and rifle mounts are tough enough for combat shooting and mount on all popular pistols. Affordable quality of semiconductor laser technology brings high-tech precision to the experienced shooter.

The Beam Shot mounts easily on all popular pistols and adjusts for windage and elevation by precise X-Y lead screw mechanism. The beam is activated by a removable pressure switch mounted under the shooter's palm. Just hold the weapon in a firm grip and Beam Shot is on target.

It's currently available for most popular semi-auto handguns.

Write for more information.

ALPEC TEAM, INC.

HANDGUN RECOIL BUFFER

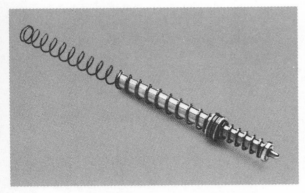

Menck Impact Buffers are designed to replace the recoil spring and guide on Smith & Wesson automatic pistols.

This unique after-market handgun accessory is designed to lessen felt recoil, prevent slide/frame battering and to speed recovery between shots. This is accomplished by a patented all-steel mechanism using field-proven technology with no rubber or plastic pads to wear out.

The Impact Buffer requires only *simple* gunsmithing to install and does not add to the bulk, maintenance, or muzzle flash of the pistol. It's well engineered and made.

For more information, send $2.00 (US) to the manufacturer.

THOMAS W. MENCK, GUNSMITH, INC.

GUN BOOKS & MAGAZINES

Wolfe Publishing offers serious outdoor and gun enthusiasts a line of technical firearms and hunting books, wildlife art prints, as well as two of America's foremost firearms magazines: *Handloader*, the only technical journal in the world devoted to the fine art of loading ammunition, and *Rifle*, considered by many to be the sporting firearms journal for knowledgeable shooters.

If you want to expand your knowledge of firearms and want something a little more than the mass media gun magazines, Wolfe publications and magazines are for you.

Send $1.00 for a catalog listing over 100 books for the Sportsman's Library. Be sure to mention you saw it in *Shooter's Marketplace*.

WOLFE PUBLISHING CO.

See manufacturers' addresses on page 262.

AMERICAN-MADE MUZZLELOADER

Thunder Mountain Arms has created one of the best production muzzleloading plains rifle of its type. Here's why. They use Griffith-designed breeches, tangs, and locks—of 100% hand-fitted steel—with direct channel ignition, carburized wear surfaces, and fully supported fly for durability—plus forged "V" springs for quickness.

Their double set triggers yield a consistently crisp pull—set or unset. Cut-rifled octagonal Green Mountain barrels—.50- or .54-caliber—are 32 inches long and designed for patched balls. Their walnut stocks have a handcrafted oil finish. All furniture is steel and beautifully browned.

All Thunder Mountain Arms products include a limited lifetime warranty.

THUNDER MOUNTAIN ARMS

GENUINE HAWKEN RIFLE KIT

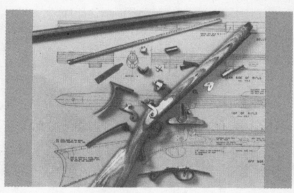

Since the opening of The Hawken Shop in 1815 by Jacob Hawken in St. Louis, they have always offered the finest factory-produced, American-made traditional muzzleloading rifles.

Now The Hawken Shop is manufacturing complete genuine Hawken Rifle kits—some of the most precise and easily assembled kits ever manufactured—using their own locks, Getz cut rifled barrels, and 98% finished half stocks. With each kit The Hawken Shop includes all hardware and wood, complete drawings for completion, plus step-by-step instructions to make finishing your rifle as easy to do as they can possibly make it.

Write, call or fax The Hawken Shop for more information.

THE HAWKEN SHOP

TRIGGER-SAFETY-SPEED LOCK KITS

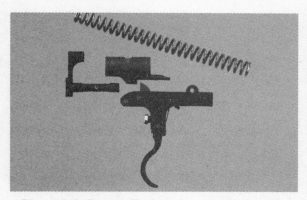

Since 1947, Dayton Traister has supplied quality, adjustable single-stage triggers for Springfields, Enfields and Mausers. They now offer the Mauser '93-96 cock-on-opening conversion. Like their P-14/P-17 conversion, you receive their patented adjustable trigger, new cocking piece and replacement custom-made striker spring—converting your gun from cock-on-closing to cock-on-opening.

The triggers, weighing 2 ounces, are quiet and compact requiring virtually no wood removal from your stock to install.

The Mark II replacement safeties are low-mount design for telescopic sight use. They are one-piece steel, hardened, and tempered. An inserted nylon friction piece ensures quiet, smooth operation.

DAYTON TRAISTER

COMPETITION 'HAWK AND KNIFE COMBO

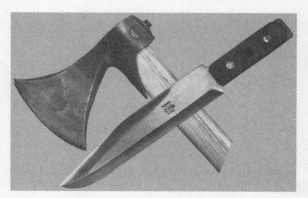

The above tomahawk and knife were specially designed for competition throwing according to NMLRA rules. Knifemaker Harry McEvoy says this tomahawk is the ultimate in throwing design. Its elongated throat lowers throwing stress leverage and impact stress on the handle, reducing breakage. Patented Head-Lok® design secures head to handle better than any other method. Comes with a 'hawk blade cover.

The Hawken "Bowie" has ideal weight and balance for competition throwing. Its semisharp clip edge can be handle *or* blade thrown. Comes with leather belt scabbard.

Their illustrated instruction book *Stick with the Winners* is included with each 'hawk or knife.

THE HAWKEN SHOP

See manufacturers' addresses on page 262.

CAMO PATTERN STOCKS

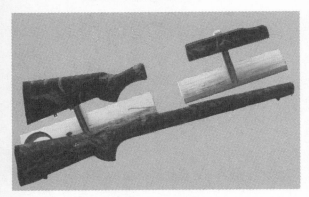

Good news for the hunter who wants a proven camo pattern on his shotgun or rifle stock. Bell & Carlson is now offering Mossy Oak™ Tree Stand™ (top) or Realtree® Brownleaf (bottom) on some of their most popular Carbelite stocks. Textured black, Carbelite Camo and Award Winning woodgrain finishes are also available.

Accurate in every climate, Carbelite stocks have less felt recoil, are stronger than wood, and have a lifetime warranty.

A fully-staffed, experienced service department is available for custom fitting Carbelite stocks to customers' actions.

Contact Bell & Carlson for their free color brochure and model list.

BELL & CARLSON, INC.

CUSTOM BULLET-MAKING SYSTEMS

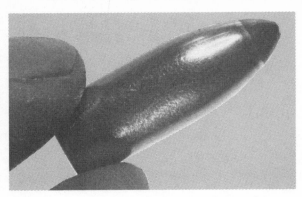

For two decades, Corbin has been the toolmaker behind virtually every custom bullet-making firm in the world, providing ideas, marketing services, swaging dies and presses, components, books and more. Handloaders can make their own jacketed or lead bullets in any weight, diameter, or style from common materials, such as copper strip, tubing or scrap lead, either for hobby use or as a business. Any caliber from .14 airgun to .700 Nitro can be made, *without* molten lead. Corbin offers an "opportunities" kit for $1, explaining how to design, produce, and market custom bullets, and a seven-book library of swaging for $65.

For more information on swaging and custom bullet making, write Corbin direct.

CORBIN MANUFACTURING & SUPPLY, INC.

GUN CARE PRODUCT

Gozon® Gun Metal Guard lubricates and penetrates deep into metal pores, drastically reducing friction and wear. Improves gun performance, prolongs metal life and smooths metal actions. Cleans metal parts. Removes buildup of copper, lead, carbon, sulphur, powder and other harmful residue from firearm bores. Neutralizes acid causing fingerprint contamination. Protects firearms in all-weather and all-terrain conditions against rust and corrosion of metal parts exposed to high humidity, moisture and salt spray conditions. Ideal as an excellent nonflammable metal protector for indoor display and firearms storage. Suggested retail $7.95 for 8 oz. aerosol. Dealer and distributor inquiries welcome, domestic and foreign.

GOZON CORPORATION

LASER/ELECTRONIC SIGHT MOUNTS

Aimtech offers a full line of unique scope, electronic sight and laser mounting systems. Right side auto-pistol mounts, saddle shotgun mounts, double decker bow mounts, see-through muzzleloader mounts as well as their patented revolver and Glock mount are all designed with the convenience of the shooter in mind.

Highest quality computer aided design/manufacture and modern heat treated alloy combine to make them among the best looking, best feeling mounts in the industry.

Available through all major distributors and quality gun dealers.

Write or call the manufacturer for more information or free catalog.

L & S TECHNOLOGIES, INC.

See manufacturers' addresses on page 262.

CUSTOM RELOADING TOOLS

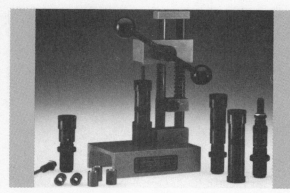

The folks at Custom Products/Neil Jones have twenty years experience in designing and building the most accurate reloading tools available. Their design allows them to custom fit all cartridges including wildcats; and, they are available in ⅞x14 threaded dies and the straight line hand dies preferred by benchrest shooters.

Their micro powder measure is second to none in accuracy and repeatability with even the toughest powders. All tools are designed to do the best job possible with improved accuracy as the goal. Jones will personally assist customers with unusual or difficult handloading problems.

Readers of *Shooter's Marketplace* can send for a free catalog.

CUSTOM PRODUCTS/NEIL JONES

INEXPENSIVE RIFLED SLUG GUN

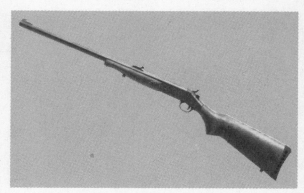

New England Firearms has introduced a 12-gauge rifled slug gun that combines accuracy, power and American-made value. It's currently available in dealers' stores.

The 24" single rifled barrel yields greater accuracy than conventional shotgun barrels at distances of up to 100 yards. Additional features include adjustable rifle sights that increase hit potential with any slug load; sling swivel studs for attachment of a convenient shoulder sling; a transfer safety bar that prevents accidental firing from a blow to the hammer and low-lustre walnut-finish stock and forend.

Deer hunters can count on many years of tough, dependable service with this 12-gauge rifled slug gun. Write for more information.

NEW ENGLAND FIREARMS CO.

SINGLE-TRIGGER CONVERSION

Muzzleloaders Etcetera, Inc. is offering a single-trigger conversion for the T/C Hawken™ and Renegade™ set-trigger rifles. Their trigger and guard assembly offers a large trigger guard that accommodates a gloved finger—especially desirable during cold weather hunting. The conversion is very simple to install and can very easily be removed for re-installation of the set-triggers. No permanent alteration is required. It's available in polished blued steel only.

To order, send $32.50 (includes shipping). Additionally, Muzzleloaders Etcetera, Inc. specializes in quality antiques, arms restoration and appraisal.

Write for more information.

MUZZLELOADERS ETCETERA, INC.

MAGNUM RIMFIRE REVOLVER

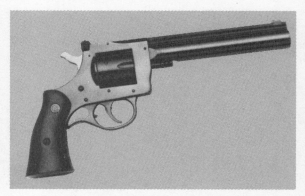

New England Firearms has introduced a new version of its well-known 22 Ultra target revolver, the Ultra Mag™. This new American-made 22 WMR revolver features a solid-frame action with swing-out cylinder, and has a six-shot capacity.

The Ultra Mag uses a 6" heavy target barrel with rebated muzzle and a rib that allows for the mounting of a scope. A fully adjustable rear sight is standard equipment. A smooth single- and double-action trigger, mated with target-quality weight and balance, keeps shots steady. A transfer bar safety prevents accidental discharge from a blow to the hammer. Unbreakable coil springs will provide years of reliable service.

Write for more information.

NEW ENGLAND FIREARMS CO.

See manufacturers' addresses on page 262.

SHOOTER'S MARKETPLACE

CATALOG OFFERING

Established in 1956, Navy Arms continues to be one of the most versatile companies in the firearms field. Primarily known as the founder of the black powder replica industry, Navy Arms Company is also a major importer of military surplus firearms and ammunition.

Navy Arms is now the exclusive distributor of the well-known and popular Parker-Hale line of center-fire and black powder rifles manufactured by Gibbs Rifle Company.

New models for this year include a replica of the Walther Olympia .22 target pistol and a replica of the World War II German G.33/40 chambered for 7.62x39.

Send $2.00 for their full color catalog.

NAVY ARMS COMPANY

CLASSIC REINTRODUCTION

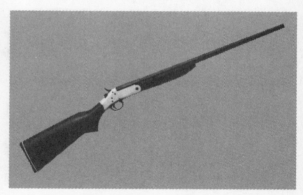

Harrington & Richardson's "Topper 098" shotgun, considered an American classic by veteran shooters, has just been reintroduced by H&R 1871, Inc.

Known for its quality craftsmanship and reasonable pricing, this shotgun is an affordable alternative for hunters of all ages.

The Topper is available in .410, 12-gauge and 20-gauge versions, each with a 3" chamber. The gun carries all the features—plus a few enhancements—which made it one of America's most popular sporting arms: transfer bar safety to prevent accidental firing from a blow to the hammer; nickel-plated frame and blued barrel; black-finished hardwood stock and fore-end; automatic shell ejector; gold-bead front sight and white-line spacer. Write for more info.

H&R 1871, INC.

GUNSTOCK REPAIR & REFINISHING

A & W Repair, Refinishing and Restoration specializes in Browning and other high grade firearms. With 25 years in the firearms industry they offer a variety of services.

Stock refinishing is high-gloss epoxy, a very durable satin finish and European oil finishes. They also do checkering. Metal work includes salt and hot water bluing, graying with edges kept sharp and consistent with original contours.

Their shop is geared to the gun shop or gunsmith who does not have the time or equipment to do this type of restoration work. A & W Repair also welcomes work from individual gun owners.

Write for a free brochure and mention *Shooter's Marketplace*.

A & W REPAIR

CLASSIC TOP-BREAK 22 REVOLVER

Harrington & Richardson has re-introduced the Sportsman 999, a top-break 22 revolver with a nine-shot capacity. The Sportsman 999 combines accuracy, convenience, American-made quality, and a reasonable price. In addition, it offers the following features: automatic shell ejection; fully adjustable sights; smooth double-action trigger; wide target-style hammer spur; transfer safety bar that prevents accidental firing from a blow to the hammer; unbreakable coil springs; fluted barrel ribs for heat dissipation; and walnut finish hardwood grip.

A reliable and accurate handgun, the Sportsman 999 is ideal for hunting, plinking or target shooting. Write for more info.

H&R 1871, INC.

See manufacturers' addresses on page 262.

SHOOTER'S MARKETPLACE

FLEXIBLE AMMO HOLDER

For quick extra shots, Bullet Band™ is designed especially for hunters. Made by Anderson Manufacturing Company, the Bullet Band™ is worn on the arm, wrist or around the stock—hunters need never fumble for ammo again.

All new Bullet Band is made of reinforced neoprene foam and offers unique gripping power not found in elastic products. Hunters need not worry about cartridges falling out—they are always held firmly, and they're easy to get at. Bullet Band holds any full-sized rifle cartridge and is sold two to a pack (wrist and over-the-coat sizes) for a suggested retail of $11.95.

Write Anderson Manufacturing Company direct for more information.

ANDERSON MANUFACTURING CO., INC.

FEATHERWEIGHT BIPOD

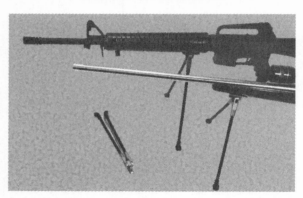

At less than 6 ounces, (half the usual weight), the Glaser/Cherokee bipod offers shooters the ultimate in strength (lifetime guarantee) and beauty. A frontal area 4.5 times smaller than other bipods greatly reduces snag hazards. Uneven terrain is automatically compensated for up to 33 degrees. Deployment and retraction are single, silent, one-hand movements taking less than a second. The bipod easily fits all sporter, varmint and most para-military firearms. The basic mount permits front or rear mounting to the forearm rather than the barrel for target accuracy.

Glaser also offers hidden or quick-detachable custom mounting accessories. Write them for your free brochure.

GLASER SAFETY SLUG, INC.

TRITIUM NIGHT SIGHTS

Trijicon® self-luminous iron sight blades are exceptionally strong and bright night sights for handguns. Sharply defined 3-Dot aiming system improves accuracy potential for both day and nighttime shooting. With inlaid white rings and glowing tritium sapphire dots, Trijicon Night Sights are impervious to cleaning solutions and carry a 10-year warranty against loss of illumination.

Trijicon is a leading supplier to handgun manufacturers, with customers who include: State Police agencies, major city police departments, federal agencies, military special forces.

Over 50 models to choose from for popular handguns and rifles. New adjustable models. Custom models by special order. Made in U.S.A.

TRIJICON, INC.

REFINISHING PRODUCTS

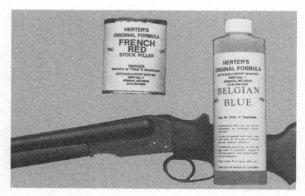

Art's Gun & Sport Shop is a St. Louis based firm that has built a solid reputation with 25 years of experience in high-grade firearm restoration. Over the years, they have discovered some of the finest wood and metal finishing products and now offer them to the gunsmithing trade. Quality rust bluing solutions such as Herter's Original Formula Belgian Blue and wood finish/fillers such as Herter's Original Formula French Red are but two of the excellent products offered.

This outfit's brochure fully details their gunsmithing services and provides instructions on how to successfully rust blue with Belgian Blue.

If you would like to have a brochure, write Art's Gun & Sport Shop direct—the brochure's free.

ART'S GUN & SPORT SHOP, INC.

See manufacturers' addresses on page 262.

NEW SCOPE MOUNT BASE SETS

Kwik-Site bases come in sets, complete with Allen head screws and wrench to speed and ease installation.

Kwik-Site's packaging makes it easy for you to find what you need. Just look for the model (printed on the card) to fit your rifle, shotgun or black powder firearm.

Kwik-Site bases have a bright finish to complement your scope and rings. (By the way, Kwik-Site makes rings to match and they won't scratch your scope when you install them.)

Kwik-Site rings will also fit bases from other manufacturers.

Write the Kwik-Site Company direct for more information, or see your local dealer.

KWIK-SITE CO.

SCOPE RING AND BASE SETS

Kwik-Site is manufacturing a new Combo Pack, Rings and Bases. Their rings are made in two heights (high and low). Kwik-Site Rings & Bases are made in the U.S.A., and feature a brand new mounting system.

Mounting is done in a two-step combination. In step #1, the rings slide over the base; in step #2, the screw is inserted through to the other side of the ring. This makes it virtually impossible for the ring to come loose from the base.

The mounts and rings are made from rugged lightweight aluminum and have a finish that will complement any fine scope.

See your local dealer or write Kwik-Site for more information.

KWIK-SITE CO.

SEE-THRU SCOPE MOUNTS

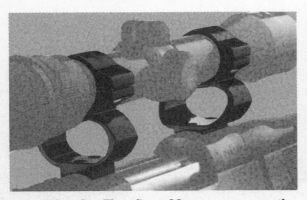

Kwik-Site See-Thru Scope Mounts are among the finest mounts on the market.

With their forward look, they are lowest to the receiver and have the largest viewing area of any see-thru scope mount made today. Popular in dense bush and forest their low profile and wide "see-thru" design gives hunters the immediate option of using iron sights or scope.

Made of high strength bright black anodized aluminum alloy, Kwik-Site mounts install in minutes using supplied allen wrench and screws.

Kwik-Site mounts are available for all popular centerfire rifles, shotguns, muzzleloaders and 22 rimfire rifles.

Write for more info.

KWIK-SITE CO.

NEW SCOPE MOUNTS

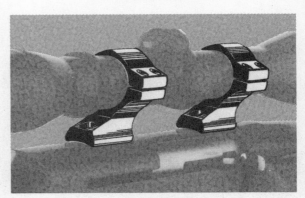

Imperial Bench Rest Kwik-Mounts are another great innovation from Kwik-Site Co.

They are ideal for the hunter who is looking for strong, rigid low mounts for use in open country.

This rugged, lightweight aluminum mount features an integral one-piece base and ring. Installation time is cut in half compared to most popular makes. It uses existing factory holes in the gun's receiver and comes with precision machined allen head screws and wrench. With its bright finish and good looks, it complements the finest scopes and rifles.

Kwik-Site Imperial Bench Rest Mounts are available for all popular rifles.

Write for more info.

KWIK-SITE CO.

PRECISION RIFLE REST

Bald Eagle Precision Machine Co. makes a beautiful rifle rest. It should serve perfectly for the serious benchrester or dedicated varminter. The rest is constructed of aircraft quality aluminum and weighs in at 7 lbs., 12 oz. It's nicely finished with three coats of Imron Clear. Height adjustments are made with a rack and pinion and a mariner wheel. A fourth leg allows lateral movement on the bench. Bald Eagle offers approximately 56 models to choose from, including windage adjustments, right or left hand, cast aluminum or cast iron. "Standard Rest" w/rifle stop and bag seen here.

Prices: $99.95 to $250.00. For more information drop Bald Eagle a line, they'll send you a free brochure.

BALD EAGLE PRECISION MACHINE CO.

NEW DOUBLE-ACTION AUTO

The Model P9R Double Action, Hi-Power Pistol, made in Hungary for Century International, features a S&W type hammer drop safety, hand checkered walnut grips and high luster blue finish. The front sight is fixed, the rear is adjustable. The barrel length is 4.67" and the magazine has a 14-round capacity.

Each P9R Double Action comes complete with spare magazine and cleaning rod.

Write for Century International's free new 24-page catalog containing hundreds of new and surplus rifles, handguns, ammunition, parts and accessories.

Latest products include: Czech, Hungarian and Makarov pistols. Czech, Norinco and Enfield rifles as well as M14 and FAL Sporters.

CENTURY INTERNATIONAL ARMS, INC.

HERTER'S IS BACK

Herter's, a name well-known to the shooting/hunting public, is now back in business and waterfowlers can, once again, get original Herter's decoys. The decoys are *original*—they're made from the original moulds.

Along with the Herter's field and floater decoys, their catalog also features a good selection of Herter's duck and goose calls. Big Foot goose decoys, motion silhouette decoys and hard-to-find waterfowling accessories are also available.

Basically, the new Herter's catalog enables the waterfowler to fill out his spread, complete with calls, weights and other accessories. Call their toll-free number and mention *Shooter's Marketplace*, you'll get that catalog free.

HERTER'S MANUFACTURING, INC.

PROFESSIONAL GUNSMITHING PROGRAM

A comprehensive, apprenticeship-style gunsmith training program that lets you learn in an actual gunsmithing shop. The course covers everything from basic repairs on up to building full-house custom firearms!

You'll get a first-hand view of what really goes on in a gunsmithing business through actual over the counter experience. This course is designed to help you become a competent and independent professional gunsmith trained to the highest standards of craftsmanship. Features state-of-the-art equipment, as well as individual instruction. State approved and certified—approved for eligible veterans. Simply write Professional Gunsmiths of America, Inc. for free school program.

PROFESSIONAL GUNSMITHS OF AMERICA, INC.

See manufacturers' addresses on page 262.

SHOOTER'S MARKETPLACE

FULL-AUTO PUBLICATION

Informative as well as entertaining, *Machine Gun News* is a monthly publication serving gun owners, dealers and collectors nationwide.

You'll find interesting articles and useful reports on fully automatic firearms old and new, as well as timely information on changes and interpretations affecting the full-auto enthusiast.

Advertising, both classified and display, offers hard-to-find firearms, hard-to-find parts, accessories and more.

Machine Gun News is mailed with a protective cover to ensure privacy. To order, just send $29.95 for a one year subscription. Charge card customers may call their order line. Mention you saw it in *Shooter's Marketplace!*

LANE PUBLISHING

ADJUSTABLE DISC APERTURE

When hunting, you are faced with continually changing light conditions. A receiver sight with a fixed aperture is adequate for only one light condition.

The Merit Hunting Disc aperture is instantly adjustable from .025- to .155-inch in diameter, allowing you to maintain a clear sight picture under changing conditions.

The aperture leaves are supported to withstand recoil from heavy calibers and the shank is tapered to provide solid lock-up of the Disc to your receiver sight.

Contact Merit Corporation for a copy of their free brochure describing this and other sighting aids for shooters.

MERIT CORPORATION

GUN DEALER'S BOOK

The *Machine Gun Dealers Bible* fully explains the ins and outs of the Class-3 firearms business. You'll find chapters on dealing with NFA/BATF, doing business, security, traveling, law enforcement, ownership and activities.

Sections on a variety of Title 2 weapons explore and define what is available for purchase. The last chapter contains all of the forms, and deciphers the instructions for completing them. This reference guide incorporates an easy-to-use 3-ring binder that lets you review any topic instantly. Also included is a specially designed bound book for record keeping.

Available directly from the publisher, the *Machine Gun Dealers Bible* sells for $49.95 plus $4.00 for shipping and handling.

LANE PUBLISHING

SHOOTING GLASSES APERTURE

Pistol shooters can now see their sights and target clearly with the Merit Optical Attachment and its instantly adjustable diameter aperture.

An aperture (pinhole) will increase your eyes' depth of field (range of focus) dramatically.

The optical attachment is instantly adjustable from .022- to .156-inch diameter aperture to accommodate different light conditions. The sights and target will be in clear focus.

Additionally, using an aperture distinctly improves the shooter's concentration by actually helping him maintain a consistent position of the head. This device works equally well for bifocals, trifocals or plain lensed shooting glasses.

Contact Merit for a free brochure.

MERIT CORPORATION

See manufacturers' addresses on page 262.

HANDGUN ACCESSORY CATALOG

The handgun accessory field has grown tremendously over the past two decades. and it continues to grow in the 90's.

Ed Brown Products, located in Perry, Missouri, is an outfit that truly specializes in premium quality handgun accessory parts manufacture. Their current catalog carries an excellent lineup of handgun goodies for custom, competition and professional carry use.

While the Ed Brown Products catalog is primarily centered around handgun accessories for the 1911 Government design, the catalog also features Smith & Wesson auto and revolver parts. If you would like one of their catalogs, send $2.00 (refundable with your first order).

ED BROWN PRODUCTS

PRE-FORMED WILDCAT BRASS

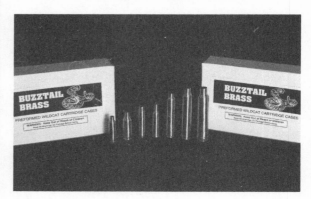

Buzztail Brass currently supplies an extensive selection of pre-formed wildcat brass. In fact, they offer 120 different wildcat calibers, with new additions monthly.

All you need to do is size your selected Buzztail cartridge case in a full-length sizing die, trim the case mouth square, and you're ready to load.

Buzztail Brass actually reduces the cost of handloading hard-to-find brass cases. That really becomes apparent when you consider the cost of specialty forming dies, destroyed cases and, perhaps, the cost of collectible, hard-to-find original ammo—to say nothing about the wear and tear on your gun.

Call or write Buzztail Brass on specific caliber availability for more information.

BUZZTAIL BRASS

POLY-CHOKE® INSTALLATION

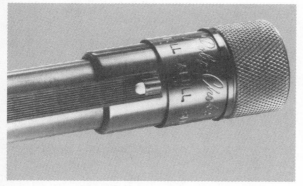

With the Marble Arms Poly-Choke®, there are no noisy choke tubes or wrenches to mess with, no damaged threads to put your shotgun out of action. The choke settings, from Extra Full to Open Cylinder for rifled slugs are permanently installed and instantly at your fingertips. They stand up to steel shot, too. Just twist the knurled sleeve and select your choke.

Available for 12-, 16-, 20- or 28-gauge pumps, autos or singles.

The cost is $75 completely installed for standard model, and $83 for the ventilated model, plus $7 for shipping.

Send either your original or a spare barrel to Marble Arms for installation of a Poly-Choke. Write for a free gun accessories catalog.

MARBLE ARMS

REAMERS & GAUGES

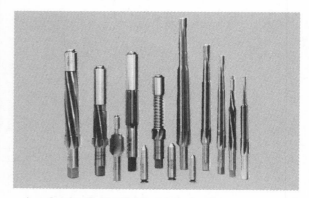

As a leader in the field of chambering reamers and headspace gauges for the gunsmith and serious shooter, Clymer Manufacturing Co., Inc., continues to expand its line of tooling available from stock. Reamers and gauges are offered in all popular rifle, pistol, and shotgun calibers. Many other tools are also available to alter factory-standard firearms to meet an individual shooter's requirements.

Clymer Manufacturing will help the wildcatter in designing a new cartridge and will gladly provide technical assistance in design and manufacture of specialized tooling not normally carried in stock. A 40-page catalog is available for $4.00 (refunded on first $30.00 order).

Call Clymer direct.

CLYMER MANUFACTURING CO., INC.

See manufacturers' addresses on page 262.

SHOOTER'S MARKETPLACE

GUN PARTS CATALOG

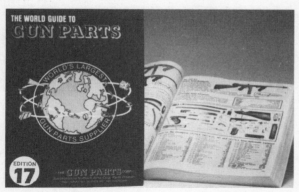

The Gun Parts Corporation, world's largest supplier of gun parts, (formerly Numrich Arms Corp.) is offering a brand new, updated (over 600 pages) 17th Edition Catalog.

You'll find complete listing and pricing of the more than 350 million gun parts they currently have in stock. Over the years, this catalog has become a standard reference for gunsmiths, shooters, collectors and military organizations worldwide.

It consists of machine gun, military, U.S., foreign, commercial and antique gun parts—all of which they stock. This catalog contains hundreds of schematic drawings. To order, simply send $5.95 (Foreign Surface Mail Orders: $10.95. Write direct for Airmail Quote).

THE GUN PARTS CORPORATION

RELOADING DIES

Redding Reloading has built an enviable reputation based on the quality of reloading gear it produces and continues to expand its line of reloading dies that are available from stock.

The latest catalog from Redding lists dies for over 400 different calibers and a whole host of special purpose dies. There are neck-sizing dies, benchrest competition dies, special purpose crimping dies, trim dies, custom made dies and even a section on case forming that lists what you need to form one caliber from another.

If you have something that you've always wanted to shoot or if you're contemplating building up a wildcat, the chances are good that Redding Reloading can supply the dies.

REDDING RELOADING EQUIPMENT

NEW OPTICS WITH UV AND IR COATING

New optical coatings technology is applied to the new Brunton line of Eterna binoculars. The Eterna line offers the shooter one of the most advanced optical systems in the world. Special optical path design allows the user to wear shooting glasses, eyeglasses or sunglasses without getting tunnel vision.

Camera-grade optics are fully multi-coated to reduce reflection. Brunton also adds a revolutionary "ruby" coating which cuts out all of the harmful ultraviolet (UV) and infrared (IR) light. Cuts glare over water or snow.

This superior hunters/shooters optical system provides incredibly clear viewing, crisp detail and improved light transmission.

BRUNTON U.S.A.

PREMIUM BULLET MOULDS

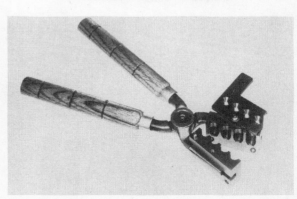

SAECO bullet moulds have long been regarded as a premier name in production bullet moulds by knowledgeable casters.

A few years ago Redding Reloading purchased the remains of the old SAECO Reloading Company and is producing the SAECO line of bullet moulds. The SAECO reputation is now backed by Redding quality so you can be sure that the excellence continues.

Redding has been constantly refining and adding to the line-up of sizes and styles to choose from and offers both two-cavity and four-cavity blocks as standard items. Single-cavity, three-, six- and eight-cavity moulds are also available on special order.

Write or call Redding Reloading for a free catalog of SAECO products.

REDDING RELOADING EQUIPMENT

See manufacturers' addresses on page 262.

SHOOTER'S MARKETPLACE

SCOUT RIFLE

Originating four years ago in response to Col. Jeff Cooper's concept of the general all-purpose rifle, which he calls The Scout Rifle, Clifton Arms initially developed the integral, retractable bipod, and its accompanying state-of-the-art composite stock. Development continued resulting in an integral butt magazine well for storage of cartridges inside the buttstock. Most recent introductions are an all-steel ghost ring rear sight, adjustable for windage and elevation, and an integral-with-the-barrel front sight ramp. Integrating these and other components is the Clifton Scout Rifle. Built on the customer's choice of action, the rifle incorporates all the features specified by Col. Cooper. A comprehensive catalog is available for $4.00.

CLIFTON ARMS, INC.

GUN SCREWDRIVER SET

Made in the USA since 1936, Chapman Manufacturing Company's unique gun screwdriver sets cover an amazing range of screwdriver sizes and applications. Eliminating the need for a bench full of standard units, each part is arranged by order of its size and nests in its own individual compartment affording speedy, one-hand selection.

To ensure the proper tool for the job, Chapman offers the hobbyist a selection of two Gun Screwdriver kits, a companion Adapter Pack G plus a wide range of open stock.

An easy to read informative instruction booklet is included with each kit. All Chapman tools are fully guaranteed.

For more information, write Chapman direct.

THE CHAPMAN MFG. COMPANY

RELOADER'S SUPPLY CATALOG

Huntington Die Specialties is this nation's *foremost* supplier of hard-to-get reloading products plus standard RCBS, CCI, Speer, Bell cases, Sierra bullets and other products. They also manufacture the well-known Huntington Compac Press.

If you're a serious handloader who's looking for something unusual, a beginner who's looking for a place to start, or a dealer who's trying to fill a customer's needs, the Huntington catalog is a must. It's the sort of reloader's "tool" that quickly becomes part of the bench. Both the Retail and Dealer's Catalogs (FFL required) are available from Huntington for $3.00 each.

Don't forget to mention you saw it in *Shooter's Marketplace!*

HUNTINGTON DIE SPECIALTIES

CATALOG & PATCH OFFER

Here's an opportunity to receive a maroon and silver shoulder patch with the new Mitchell Arms gun catalog.

That fully illustrated catalog features some exceptionally fine firearms that range all the way from Bat Masterson's Single Action Army revolver, to an extensive line of combat rifles. You will also receive a pre-production announcement featuring their new line of Mitchell Arms High Standard rimfire target pistols.

Mitchell Arms offers some of the best in exciting guns from the old days, along with today's modern firearms.

Send $5.00 for your Mitchell Arms 1992 catalog and shoulder patch.

MITCHELL ARMS, INC.

See manufacturers' addresses on page 262.

QUICK DETACHABLE MOUNTS

Quick detachable mounts which return to zero accurately offer very practical advantages including the ability to quickly remove a scope while cleaning or repairing a rifle, and the option of carrying a pre-zeroed backup scope while hunting in remote areas.

The Warne quick detachable mounts are an American-made, precision machined product, for a fraction of the price of expensive European detachable systems.

Available in three heights and three diameters (1 inch, 26mm and 30mm), the Warne quick detachable mounts fit a wide variety of rifles and scopes. Suggested retail prices start at $78.50, including bases.

Write Warne Manufacturing directly for more information. Mention you saw it in *Shooter's Marketplace*.

WARNE MANUFACTURING COMPANY

Q.D. DOUBLE LEVER RINGS

The double lever version of the Warne rings features two small opposing levers which operate the spring loaded clamp. The levers mount to the center screw by way of a hexagon collar which allows them to be synchronized in the right position at the same angle.

In rigorous, controlled testing developed by the NRA Technical Staff, with hard-recoiling calibers including 300 Weatherby Magnum, 458 Winchester, and 416 Rigby, repeatability was within plus or minus $1/2$-minute of an angle. The vertically split mounts are superbly sculpted and designed to complement all types of rifles. Each ring is hand polished.

Write Warne Manufacturing directly for more information. Mention you saw it in *Shooter's Marketplace*.

WARNE MANUFACTURING COMPANY

SAKO AND BRNO SCOPE MOUNTS

These vertically split, machined steel mounts fit directly to the receiver dovetails of Sako and BRNO centerfire rifle actions. They fit all lengths of the Sako A Series and BRNO ZKK actions. There are three heights for both 1" and 30mm diameter scopes.

Also available are quick detachable mounts to fit Ruger firearms which feature the integral bases on the receiver. There are several heights including an "extra high" version to accommodate 56mm objective scope lenses on the Model 77 and a "super low" version for lightweight compact scopes. Rings for Ruger firearms are also available for both 1" and 30mm scopes.

Write Warne Manufacturing directly for more information. Mention you saw it in *Shooter's Marketplace*.

WARNE MANUFACTURING COMPANY

Q.D. HANDGUN MOUNT

Here's a new quick detachable scope mount system for the popular Ruger Mark II .22LR pistol. Switch between open sights and back to scope in seconds. Each time the scope returns to the same point of impact.

Installation takes ten minutes—no gunsmithing is required.

The scope mount base, which also holds the original factory rear sight, is attached to the receiver by two screws. The front screw attaches to a barrel band, and the rear screw attaches to a small dovetailed block which fits into the original dovetail slot. Looks very tidy, indeed.

Write Warne Manufacturing directly for more information. Mention you saw it in *Shooter's Marketplace*.

WARNE MANUFACTURING COMPANY

See manufacturers' addresses on page 262.

SHOOTER'S MARKETPLACE

NEW "FULLFIELD" BINOCULARS

Burris recently announced their new Fullfield series of binoculars. They're available in 7x35, 8x40 and 10x50. These ArmourCoated (rubber) binoculars feature precision-ground and fully multicoated BAK 4 high-index prisms that deliver an extremely sharp, crisp image. The 7x35, 8x40 and 10x50 offerings are waterproof.

They all come with ocular dust covers, adjustable neck strap and padded leatherette case.

Also available is the new Mini Binocular in 8x25. Compact, roof prism design will prove ideal for serious hunters.

Fullfield prices range from $287.95 to $348.95. Mini Binocular is $197.95. Send $1.00 for catalog and embroidered patch.

BURRIS COMPANY, INC.

QUALITY GUNSTOCK BLANKS

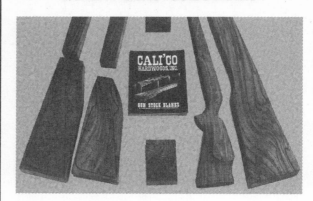

Cali'co Hardwoods has been cutting superior quality shotgun and rifle blanks for over 31 years. Cali'co supplies blanks to many of the major manufacturers—Browning, Weatherby, Ruger, Holland & Holland, to name a few—as well as custom gunsmiths the world over.

Profiled rifle blanks are available, ready for inletting and sanding. Cali'co sells superior California hardwoods in Claro walnut, French walnut, Bastogne, maple and myrtle.

If you want good serviceable blanks or some of the finest exhibition blanks available, give Cali'co Hardwoods a call. Satisfaction guaranteed. A color catalog, retail and dealer price list (FFL required) are free upon request.

CALI'CO HARDWOODS, INC.

NEW SINGLE SHOT PISTOL

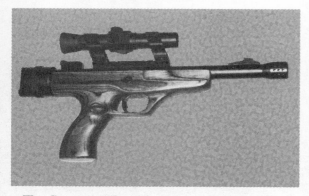

The Competitor® single shot pistol is completely ambidextrous with interchangeable barrels available in over 135 calibers. Competitor barrels can be changed within three minutes.

Competitor Pistols are completely made in the U.S.A., are low cost, strong, reliable, and have a 100% lifetime guarantee.

The complete pistol in black oxide finish, with a 14" barrel, adjustable sights and choice of synthetic or laminated grips, is now available at $364.90, retail.

Standard calibers (includes most rifle calibers) are available for immediate delivery. Contact your local dealers, distributors, or order dealer direct. Write for more information.

COMPETITOR CORPORATION, INC.

CUSTOM PRE-FINISH STOCK

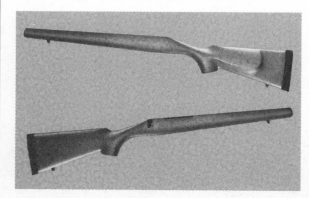

The Custom Pre-Finish stock is a Classic style hunting stock made for most factory barreled actions. Made in a dark gray, textured finish, the Custom Pre-Finish has a standard length of pull and a standard pad.

Weight is a light 1½ pounds.

Inletting is precisely fitted using a duplicate factory action. Add 10-15 minutes to bolt together the rifle with the epoxy compound included, and maximum performance is combined with the stability of synthetics. The Custom Pre-Finish stock is guaranteed for *all* calibers, and highly recommended for magnums.

Write for free stock brochure; or, send $2.00 for catalog.

BROWN PRECISION, INC.

See manufacturers' addresses on page 262.

SHOOTER'S MARKETPLACE

SHOOTING ACCESSORIES

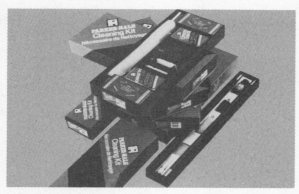

Parker-Hale's famous quality shooting accessories are available in the U.S., imported from England by Precision Sports, a Division of Cortland Line Company. British-made throughout, the following Parker-Hale accessories provide the knowledgeable shooter with a standard of excellence equal to his choice of fine guns:

- Presentation Cleaning Sets
- Nickel Plated Oil Bottles
- Deluxe Wood Shotgun Rods
- Steel Rifle Rods
- Phosphor Bronze Brushes
- Youngs "303" Cleaner
- Express Oil
- Rangoon Oil
- 009 Nitro Solvent
- Snap Caps

Write Precision Sports for a free color catalog.

PRECISION SPORTS

GIBBS RIFLE CATALOG

Gibbs Rifle Company has purchased the rifle and black powder division of Parker-Hale Ltd., as well as the M-85 sniper project. They now manufacture these guns in the United States. Gibbs also makes the Greener Harpoon gun and acts as an American handling agent for W.W. Greener of Birmingham, England.

Gibbs Rifle Company does a large amount of refurbishing of military weapons. A complete polishing, blueing and woodworking facility has been set up for the repair and refinishing of military weapons which Gibbs imports. They also do subcontracting work for other importers and manufacturers.

Send $1.00 for a current, full color, Gibbs Rifle Company catalog.

GIBBS RIFLE COMPANY, INC.

DEHUMIDIFIERS

Buenger Enterprises' GoldenRod is a truly unique dehumidifier designed to handle the worst kind of humidity problems that can occur in any location.

GoldenRod circulates warm, dry convection air currents throughout a gun cabinet on a 24 hour basis, thus preventing any condensation or moisture build-up and thereby stopping rust and corrosion.

The GoldenRod dehumidifier is recommended and sold by the majority of gun safe manufacturers. It is UL listed and made in the U.S.A. The nickel chrome element insures continuous protection. Buenger Enterprises guarantees the dehumidifier for ten years.

Call or write for free descriptive brochures. Dealer inquiries invited.

BUENGER ENTERPRISES

MUZZLELOADER'S STOCK FINISHING KIT

A new kit from Birchwood Casey restores stocks on weathered, old antiques. The Muzzleloader's Stock Finishing Kit features a new Colonial Brown wood stain for that custom reddish-brown color found on so many Early American firearms.

Also included are the traditional Tru-Oil® Gun Stock Finish with its unique blend of linseed and natural oils and Gun Stock Wax which combines the protective and beautifying characteristics of carnauba, beeswax and silicone. The kit contains all essential finishing materials and complete instructions on how to finish your gunstock.

Suggested retail price is $11.60.

See your dealer or write Birchwood Casey direct for a free catalog.

BIRCHWOOD LABORATORIES, INC.

See manufacturers' addresses on page 262.

SIDE BY SIDES

Precision Sports "600" Series doubles are custom-crafted in Spain by master gunmakers of Ugartechea.

Formerly marketed as Parker-Hale, Precision Sports "600" Series doubles in 10, 12, 16, 20, 28 gauges and .410 bore are available in English or American styling and choice of extractors or ejectors.

New models include:

Bill Hanus Birdgun featuring straight-grip stock, single non-selective trigger, ejectors, Skeet 1/Skeet 2 chokes, Churchill style rib, semi-beavertail forend, case-colored receiver, 26" barrels. 16, 20, 28 gauge.

New 640 Slug Gun features pistol grip stock, double trigger, 25" choked IC/IC with rifle sights.

Lifetime Operation Warranty. Write for a free Precision Sports catalog.

PRECISION SPORTS

LEARN GUN REPAIR

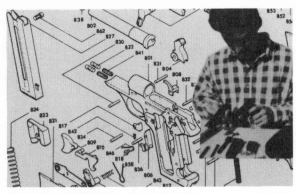

Modern School has been teaching gun repair the home study way since 1946 to over 45,000 students. All courses are nationally accredited and approved for VA/GI benefits. Courses are complete and include all lessons (including how to get your FFL), tool kit, Powley Calculator and Powley Computer, GUN DIGEST, Gun Parts Catalog, mainspring vise, school binders, Brownell's Catalog, pull & drop gauge, trigger pull gauge, two parchment diplomas ready for framing, free consultation service plus much more. Here's how you can get into a career where you can enjoy what you are doing. You can start your own business and make money in your spare time, too. No experience is needed. Write or call for free information. There's no obligation and no salesman will call.

MODERN GUN REPAIR SCHOOL

SHOOTER'S MARKETPLACE
MANUFACTURERS' ADDRESSES

A&W REPAIR *(Pg. 251)*
Attn: Dept. SM'93
2930 Schneider Dr.
Arnold, MO 63010 (314-287-3725)

ACCURATE ARMS COMPANY, INC. *(Pg. 234)*
Attn: Dept. SM'93
Box DB93
McEwen, TN 37101

ACTION TARGET, INC. *(Pg. 236)*
Attn: Dept. SM'93
Box 636
Provo, UT 84603 (801-377-8033;
Fax 801-377-8096)

AIMPOINT *(Pg. 226)*
Attn: Dept. SM'93
580 Herndon Parkway, Suite 500
Herndon, VA 22070 (703-471-6828;
Fax 703-689-0575)

AIR RIFLE SPECIALISTS *(Pg. 244)*
Attn: Dept. SM'93
311 E. Water Street
Elmira, NY 14901 (607-734-7340)

AIRROW (SWIVEL MACHINE WORKS, INC.)
(Pg. 246)
Attn: Dept. SM'93
167 Cherry Street, Suite 286
Milford, CT 06460

ALPEC TEAM, INC. *(Pg. 246)*
Attn: Dept. SM'93
55 Oak Court, Suite 205
Danville, CA 94526 (510-820-1763;
Fax 510-820-8738)

AMERICAN DERRINGER CORP. *(Pg. 226)*
Attn: Dept. SM'93
P.O. Box 8983
Waco, TX 76714 (817-799-9111)

ANDERSON MANUFACTURING CO., INC.
(Pg. 240, 252)
Attn: Dept. SM'93
P.O. Box 2640
Oak Harbor, WA 98277 (206-675-7300)

ART'S GUN & SPORT SHOP, INC. *(Pg. 252)*
Attn: Dept. SM'93
6008 Highway "Y"
Hillsboro, MO 63050

B&C (BELL & CARLSON, INC.) *(Pg. 248)*
Attn: Dept. SM'93
509 North 5th
Atwood, KS 67730 (913-626-3204;
Fax 913-626-9602)

BALD EAGLE PRECISION MACHINE CO. *(Pg. 254)*
Attn: Dept. SM'93
101 Allison Street
Lock Haven, PA 17745 (717-748 6772;
Fax 717-748-4443)

BAUSCH & LOMB SPORTS OPTICS DIV.
(Pg. 225)
Attn: Dept. SM'93
9200 Cody
Overland Park, KS 66214 (800-423-3537)

BIRCHWOOD LABORATORIES, INC.
(Pg. 241, 261)
Attn: Dept. SM'93
7900 Fuller Road
Eden Prairie, MN 55344 (612-937-7933)

BLOUNT, INC., SPORTING EQUIPMENT DIV.
(See Outers Laboratories and RCBS.)

BLUE RIDGE MACHINERY AND TOOLS, INC.
(Pg. 250)
Attn: Dept. SM'93
P.O. Box 536-GD
Hurricane, WV 25526 (800-872-6500;
Fax 304-562-5311)

BRILEY MFG., INC. *(Pg. 231)*
Attn: Dept. SM'93
1085 Gessner, "B"
Houston, TX 77055 (800-331-5718 or
713 932-6995)

ED BROWN PRODUCTS *(Pg. 256)*
Attn: Dept. GD'93
Route 2, Box 2922
Perry, MO 63462 (314-565-3261;
Fax 314-565-2791)

BROWN PRECISION, INC. *(Pg. 260)*
Attn: Dept. SM'93
P.O. Box 270GD
Los Molinos, CA 96055 (916-384-2506)
(Fax/Order Line 800-543-2506)

BROWNELL'S, INC. *(Pg. 234)*
Attn: Dept. SM'93
222 West Liberty
Montezuma, IA 50171 (515-623-5401;
Fax 515-623-3896)

BRUNTON U.S.A. *(Pg. 257)*
Attn: Dept. SM'93
620 East Monroe Ave.
Riverton, WY 82501-4997 (307-856-6559;
Fax 307-856-1840)

B-SQUARE CO. *(Pg. 228, 229)*
Attn: Dept. SM'93
P.O. Box 11281
Ft. Worth, TX 76110-0281 (800-433-2909 or
817-923-0964; Fax 817-926-7012)

BUENGER ENTERPRISES *(Pg. 261)*
Attn: Dept. SM'93
P.O. Box 5286
Oxnard, CA 93031 (800-451-6797;
Fax 805-985-1534)

BURRIS COMPANY, INC. *(Pg. 260)*
Attn: Dept. SM'93
P.O. Box 1747
331 E. 8th St.
Greeley, CO 80632 (303-356-1670;
Fax 303-356-8702)

BUTLER CREEK CORPORATION *(Pg. 235)*
Attn: Dept. SM'93
290 Arden Drive
Belgrade, MT 59714 (406-388-1356;
Fax 406-388 7204)

BUZZTAIL BRASS *(Pg. 256)*
Attn: Dept. SM'93
P.O. Box 656, 10905 Needle Dam Rd.
Keno, OR 97627 (503-884-1072)

CALI'CO HARDWOODS, INC. *(Pg. 260)*
Attn: Dept. SM'93
1648 Airport Blvd.
Windsor, CA 95492 (707-546-4045 or 546-4048;
Fax 707-546 4027)

CENTURY INTERNATIONAL ARMS, LTD.
(Pg. 254)
Attn: Dept. SM'93
48 Lower Newton Street
St. Albans, VT 05478 (802-527-1252)

THE CHAPMAN MANUFACTURING COMPANY
(Pg. 258)
Attn: Dept. SM'93
P.O. Box 250
Route 17 at Sawmill Rd.
Durham, CT 06422 (203-349-9228)

CLIFTON ARMS, INC. *(Pg. 258)*
Attn: Dept. GD-SM
P.O. Box 531258
Grand Prairie, TX 75053 (Fax 214-647-8200)

CLYMER MANUFACTURING CO., INC. *(Pg. 256)*
Attn: Dept. SM'93
1645 West Hamlin Road
Rochester Hills, MI 48309-3368 (313-853-5555;
Fax 313-853-1530)

COMPETITOR CORPORATION INC. *(Pg. 260)*
Attn: Dept. SM'93
293 Townsend Rd., P.O. Box 244
West Groton, MA 01472 (508-448-3521)

CORBIN MANUFACTURING & SUPPLY, INC.
(Pg. 248)
Attn: Dept. SM'93
P.O. Box 2659
White City, OR 97503 (503-826-5211;
Fax 503-826-8669)

CRANDALL TOOL & MACHINE COMPANY
(Pg. 234)
Attn: Dept. SM'93
P.O. Box 569
Cadillac, MI 49601

CUSTOM PRODUCTS/NEIL A. JONES *(Pg. 249)*
Attn: Dept. SM'93
R.D. 1, Box 483-A
Saegertown, PA 16433

DAYTON TRAISTER *(Pg. 247)*
Attn: Dept. SM'93
P.O. Box 593
Oak Harbor, WA 98277 (206-679-4657;
Fax 206-675-1114)

DIXIE GUN WORKS *(Pg. 232)*
Attn: Dept. SM'93
P.O. Box 130
Union City, TN 38261 (800-238-6785;
Fax 901-885-0440)

EEZOX, INC. *(Pg. 238)*
Attn: Dept. SM'93
P.O. Box 772
Waterford, CT 06385 (203-447-8282 or
800-462-3331; Fax 203-447-3484)

FORSTER PRODUCTS *(Pg. 230)*
Attn: Dept. SM'93
82 E. Lanark Ave.
Lanark, IL 61046 (Fax 815-493-2371)

DAVID GENTRY, CUSTOM GUNMAKER *(Pg. 250)*
Attn: Dept. SM'93
314 N. Hoffman
Belgrade, MT 59714 (406-388-GUNS)

GIBBS RIFLE COMPANY, INC. *(Pg. 261)*
Attn: Dept. GD'93
R.R. #2, Box 214, Hoffman Rd.
Cannon Hill Industrial Park
Martinsburg, WV 25401 (304-274-0458)

GLASER SAFETY SLUG, INC. *(Pg. 230, 252)*
Attn: Dept. SM'93
P.O. Box 8223
Foster City, CA 94404 (800-221-3489;
Fax 415-345-0327)

GOZON CORPORATION *(Pg. 248)*
Attn: Dept. SM'93
P.O. Box 6278
Folsom, CA 95630 (Fax 916-983-9500)

GRACE METAL PRODUCTS, INC. *(Pg. 245)*
Attn: Dept. SM'93
P.O. Box 67
Elk Rapids, MI 49629-0067 (616-264-8133)

THE GUN DOCTOR *(Pg. 250)*
Attn: Dept. SM'93
P.O. Box 39242
Downey, CA 90239-0242

GUNLINE TOOLS *(Pg. 227)*
Attn: Dept. SM'93
P.O. Box 478
Placentia, CA 92670 (714-528-5252;
Fax 714-572-4128)

THE GUN PARTS CORPORATION *(Pg. 257)*
Successors to Numrich Arms Parts Division
P.O. Box SM'93
West Hurley, NY 12491 (914-679-2417;
Fax 914-679-5849)

H&R 1871, INC. *(Pg. 251)*
Attn: Dept. SM'93
Industrial Rowe
Gardner, MA 01440

HARRIS ENGINEERING INC. *(Pg. 244)*
Attn: Dept. SM'93
Barlow, KY 42024 (502-334-3633;
Fax 502-334-3000)

HASTINGS BARRELS *(Pg. 225)*
Attn: Dept. SM'93
Box 224
Clay Center, KS 67432 (913-632-3169)

THE HAWKEN SHOP *(Pg. 247)*
Attn: Dept. SM'93
P.O. Box 593
Oak Harbor, WA 98277 (206-679-4657;
Fax 206-675-1114)

HERTER'S MANUFACTURING INC. *(Pg. 254)*
Attn: Dept. SM'93
111 E. Burnett St., P.O. Box 518
Beaver Dam, WI 53916 (800-654-3825;
Fax 414-887-1608)

J.B. HOLDEN COMPANY *(Pg. 237)*
Attn: Dept. SM'93
P.O. Box 320
Plymouth, MI 48170 (313-455-4850;
Fax 313-455-4212)

HUNTINGTON DIE SPECIALTIES *(Pg. 258)*
Attn: Buzz Huntington, Dept. SM'93
P.O. Box 991
Oroville, CA 95965 (916-534-1210)

INNOVISION ENTERPRISES *(Pg. 242)*
Attn: Dept. SM'93
728 Skinner Drive
Kalamazoo, MI 49001 (616-382-1681)

JARRETT RIFLES, INC. *(Pg. 238)*
Attn: Dept. SM'93
383 Brown Road
Jackson, SC 29831 (803-471-3616)

KOWA OPTIMED, INC. *(Pg. 232)*
Attn: Dept. SM'93
20001 S. Vermont Ave.
Torrance, CA 90502 (310-327-1913)

KWIK-SITE CO. *(Pg. 253)*
Attn: Dept. SM'93
5555 Treadwell
Wayne, MI 48184

L&S TECHNOLOGIES, INC. *(Pg. 248)*
Attn: Dept. SM'93
P.O. Box 223
Thomasville, GA 31799 (912-226-4313)

LANE PUBLISHING *(Pg. 255)*
Attn: Dept. SM'93
P.O. Box 759
Hot Springs, AR 71902 (501-623-4951;
Fax 501-623-9832)

LANSKY SHARPENERS & CROCK STICK
(Pg. 242)
Attn: Dept. SM'93
P.O. Box 800
Buffalo, NY 14231 (716-877-7511;
Fax 716-877-6955)

LOCH LEVEN INDUSTRIES *(Pg. 237)*
Attn: Dept. SM'93
P.O. Box 2751
Santa Rosa, CA 95405 (707-573-8735)

LYMAN PRODUCTS CORPORATION *(Pg. 236)*
Attn: Dept. 198
Route 147
Middlefield, CT 06455 (800-22-LYMAN)

MARBLE ARMS CORPORATION *(Pg. 256)*
Attn: Dept. SM'93
P.O. Box 111
Gladstone, MI 49837 (906-428-3710)

THOMAS W. MENCK, GUNSMITH, INC. *(Pg. 246)*
Attn: Dept. GD'93
5703 South 77th Street
Ralston, NE 68127-4201

MERIT CORPORATION *(Pg. 255)*
Attn: C.M. Grant, Dept. SM'93
Box 9044
Schenectady, NY 12309 (518-346-1420)

MITCHELL ARMS, INC. *(Pg. 258)*
Attn: Dept. SM'93
3400 W. MacArthur Blvd. #1
Santa Ana, CA 92704 (714-957-5711)

MODERN GUN REPAIR SCHOOL *(Pg. 262)*
Attn: Dept. GHY93
2538 N. 8th Street, P.O. Box 5338
Phoenix, AZ 85010 (602-990-8346)

MTM MOLDED PRODUCTS COMPANY *(Pg. 250)*
Attn: Dept. SM'93
3370 Oboco Court
Dayton, OH 45414 (513-890-7461;
Fax 513-890-1747)

MUZZLELOADERS ETCETERA, INC. *(Pg. 249)*
Attn: Dept. SM'93
9901 Lyndale Avenue South
Bloomington, MN 55420 (612-884-1161)

NAVY ARMS COMPANY *(Pg. 251)*
Attn: Dept. GD'93
689 Bergen Blvd.
Ridgefield, NJ 07657 (201-945-2500)

NEW ENGLAND AMMUNITION CO. *(Pg. 238)*
Attn: Dept. SM'93
1771 Post Road East, Suite 223
Westport, CT 06880 (203-254-8048)

NEW ENGLAND FIREARMS CO. *(Pg. 249)*
(See H&R 1871, Inc.)

NOSLER, INC. *(Pg. 226, 244)*
Attn: Dept. SM'93
P.O. Box 671
Bend, OR 97709

OLD WORLD OIL PRODUCTS *(Pg. 241)*
Attn: Dept. SM'93
3827 Queen Avenue North
Minneapolis, MN 55412 (612-522-5037)

THE OUTDOOR CONNECTION, INC. *(Pg. 230)*
Attn: Dept. SM'93
201 Douglas, P.O. Box 7751
Waco, TX 76712-7751 (817-772-5575 or
800-533-6076)

OUTERS LABORATORIES, DIV. OF BLOUNT, INC. *(Pg. 233)*
Attn: Dept. SM'93
Route 2
Onalaska, WI 54650 (800-635-7656)

PACHMAYR, LTD. *(Pg. 243)*
Attn: Dept. SM'93
1875 S. Mountain Ave.
Monrovia, CA 91016 (Orders: 800-423-9704;
818-657-7771; Fax 818-358-7251)

PALSA OUTDOOR PRODUCTS *(Pg. 237)*
Attn: Dept. SM'93
P.O. Box 81336
Lincoln, NE 68501 (800-456-9281;
Fax 402-488-2321)

PERIPHERAL DATA SYSTEMS *(Pg. 242)*
Attn: Dept. SM'93
15110 SW Boones Ferry Road #225
P.O. Box 1526
Lake Oswego, OR 97035 (503-697-0533)

PONSNESS/WARREN *(Pg. 240)*
Attn: Dept. SM'93
So. 763 Hwy 41, P.O. Box 8
Rathdrum, ID 83858 (208-687-2231;
Fax 208-687-2233)

PRECISION SPORTS *(Pg. 261, 262)*
Attn: Andy Sonnek, Dept. SM'93
P.O. Box 5588
Cortland, NY 13045-5588 (607-756-2851)

PROFESSIONAL GUNSMITHS OF AMERICA, INC. *(Pg. 254)*
Attn: Dept. SM'93
1301 Franklin
Lexington, MO 64067 (816-259-2636)

PROFESSIONAL HUNTER SUPPLIES *(Pg. 232)*
Attn: Dept. SM'93
P.O. Box 608, 468 Main St.
Ferndale, CA 95536 (707-786-4040;
Fax 707-786-9117)

QUINETICS CORPORATION *(Pg. 234)*
Attn: Dept. SM'93
P.O. Box 13237
San Antonio, TX 78213 (512-684-8561;
Fax 512-684-2912)

RCBS PRODUCTS *(Pg. 233)*
BLOUNT, INC.
Attn: Dept. SM'93
Oro Dam Blvd.
Oroville, CA 95965 (800-533-5000)

REDDING RELOADING, INC. *(Pg. 257)*
Attn: Dept. SM'93
1093 Starr Rd.
Cortland, NY 13045 (607-753-3331;
Fax 607-756-8445)

RED WILLOW TOOL & ARMORY INC. *(Pg. 236)*
Attn: Dept. SM'93
P.O. Box 5, 4004 Hwy. 93 North
Stevensville, MT 59870 (406-777-5401;
Fax 406-777-5402)

R.G.-G., INC. *(Pg. 227)*
Attn: Dept. SM'93 , P.O. Box 1261
Conifer, CO 80433-1261

ROGERS LTD. *(Pg. 240)*
Attn: Dept. SM'93
891 Dixwell Ave.
Hamden, CT 06514 (203-865-8484;
Fax 800-847-7492)

ROOSTER LABORATORIES *(Pg. 241)*
Attn: Dept. SM'93
P.O. Box 412514
Kansas City, MO 64141 (816-474-1622;
Fax 816-474-1307)

R-TECH CORPORATION *(Pg. 244)*
Attn: Dept. GD'93
P.O. Box 1281
Cottage Grove, OR 97424 (503-942-5126)

A.G. RUSSELL KNIVES, INC. *(Pg. 236)*
Attn: Dept. 92DB
1705 Hwy. 71B N
Springdale, AR 72764 (800-255-9034;
Fax 501-751-4520)

SAFARILAND LTD., INC. *(Pg. 230)*
Attn: Dept. SM'93
3120 E. Mission Blvd.
Ontario, CA 91761 (Orders: 800-347-1200;
Fax 800-366-1669)

SARCO, INC. *(Pg. 243)*
Attn: Mag. Dept., SM'93
323 Union Street
Stirling, NJ 07980 (908-647-3800)

SHEPHERD SCOPE LTD. *(Pg. 241)*
Attn: Dept. G.D.A.
Box 189
Waterloo, NE 68069 (402-779-2424;
Fax 402-779-4010)

THE SHOTGUN NEWS *(Pg. 232)*
Attn: D. Clark, Dept. SM'93
P.O. Box 669
Hastings, NE 68902

SPORTSMAN'S COMMUNICATORS *(Pg. 245)*
Attn: Dept. SM'93
588 Radcliffe Ave.
Pacific Palisades, CA 90272

SWIFT INSTRUMENTS, INC. *(Pg. 239)*
Attn: Dept. SM'93
952 Dorchester Ave.
Boston, MA 02125 (617-436-2960;
Fax 617-436-3232)

THUNDER MOUNTAIN ARMS *(Pg. 247)*
Attn: Dept. SM'93
P.O. Box 593
Oak Harbor, WA 98277 (206-679-4657;
Fax 206-675-1114)

JAMES C. TILLINGHAST *(Pg. 243)*
Attn: Dept. GD'93
P.O. Box 270DG
Hancock, NH 03449-270D (603-525-4049)

TOMBOY, INC. *(Pg. 233)*
Attn: Brandy Church, Dept. SM'93
P.O. Box 846
Dallas, OR 97338 (503-623-8405)

TRIJICON, INC. *(Pg. 252)*
Attn: Dept. SM'93
P.O. Box 2130
Farmington Hills, MI 48333 (313-553-4960;
Fax 313-553-6129)

DOUG TURNBULL RESTORATION *(Pg. 245)*
Attn: Dept. SM'93
6562 County Rd. 30
Holcomb, NY 14469 (716-657-6338)

UNITED STATES OPTICS TECHNOLOGIES, INC. *(Pg. 243, 245)*
Attn: Ben Williams, Dept. SM'93
15936 Downey Ave.
Paramount, CA 90723 (310-220-2616;
Fax 310-220-2627)

VOLQUARTSEN CUSTOM LTD. *(Pg. 242)*
Attn: Dept. SM'93
Rt. 1, Box 33A, P.O. Box 271
Carroll, IA 51401 (712-792-4238;
Fax 712-792-2542)

WALKER ARMS CO., INC. *(Pg. 240)*
Attn: Dept. SM'93
499 County Road 820
Selma, AL 36701 (Service: 205-872-6231 or
Parts: 205-875-8056)

WARNE MANUFACTURING COMPANY *(Pg. 259)*
Attn: Dept. SM'93
9039 SE Jannsen Road
Clackamas, OR 97015 (503-657-5590;
Fax 503-657-5695)

WHITE FLYER *(Pg. 238)*
Div. of Reagent Chemical & Research, Inc.
Attn: Dept. SM'93
9139 W. Redfield Road
Peoria, AZ 85381 (800-647-2898)

WOLFE PUBLISHING CO. *(Pg. 226, 246)*
Attn: Dept. SM'93
6471 Airpark Drive
Prescott, AZ 86301 (800-899-7810)

1993
GUN DIGEST
Complete Compact
CATALOG

GUNDEX® 266-272

Autoloading Handguns 273-300
Competition Handguns 300-308
Double-Action Revolvers 309-317
Single-Action Revolvers 318-322
Miscellaneous Handguns 323-327
Centerfire Rifles—Autoloaders 327-332
Centerfire Rifles—Lever & Slide . . . 332-337
Centerfire Rifles—Bolt Action 337-353
Centerfire Rifles—Single Shot 353-357
Drillings, Combination Guns, Double
   Rifles 357-359
Rimfire Rifles—Autoloaders 360-363
Rimfire Rifles—Lever & Slide 364
Rimfire Rifles—Bolt Actions & Single
   Shots 365-369
Competition Rifles—Centerfire &
   Rimfire 370-377
Shotguns—Autoloaders 378-382
Shotguns—Slide Actions 382-386
Shotguns—Over/Unders 386-394
Shotguns—Side By Sides 395-399

Shotguns—Bolt Actions & Single Shots 400-402
Shotguns—Military & Police 403-405
Blackpowder Single Shot Pistols . . . 405-408
Blackpowder Revolvers 409-412
Blackpowder Muskets & Rifles 412-423
Blackpowder Shotguns 424-425
Air Guns—Handguns 425-430
Air Guns—Long Guns 430-442
Air Guns—Paint Ball Guns 443-444

Warranty Service Center Directory 445

Metallic Sights 457
Chokes & Brakes 460
Scopes & Mounts 461
Spotting Scopes 473
Periodical Publications 475
Arms Library 477
Arms Associations 495

Directory of the Arms Trade
   Product Directory 498
   Manufacturers' Directory 512

GUNDEX

GUNDEX®

A listing of all the guns in the catalog, by name and model, alphabetically and numerically.

A

A.A. Arms AP9 Auto Pistol, 273
A.A. Arms AP9 Target Auto Pistol, 273
A.A. Arms AR9 Semi-Automatic Rifle, 327
A.A. Arms Mini AP9 Auto Pistol, 273
Accu-Tek AT-9 Auto Pistol, 273
Accu-Tek AT-25AL Auto Pistol, 273
Accu-Tek AT-25SS Auto Pistol, 273
Accu-Tek AT-25SSB Auto Pistol, 273
Accu-Tek AT-32SS Auto Pistol, 273
Accu-Tek AT-32SSB Auto Pistol, 273
Accu-Tek AT-40 Auto Pistol, 273
Accu-Tek AT-40B Auto Pistol, 273
Accu-Tek AT-380SS Auto Pistol, 273
Accu-Tek AT-380SSB Auto Pistol, 273
Air Arms SM 100 Air Rifle, 430
Air Arms NJR 100 Air Rifle, 430
Air Arms TM 100 Air Rifle, 430
Air Arms XM 100 Air Rifle, 430
Airrow Model 8S1P Stealth Air Rifle, 431
Airrow Model 8SRB Stealth Air Rifle, 431
Alpine Custom Grade Bolt-Action Rifle, 337
Alpine Supreme Grade Bolt-Action Rifle, 337
American Arms Brittany Double Shotgun, 395
American Arms CX-22 DA Auto Pistol, 274
American Arms Derby Side-by-Side Shotgun, 395
American Arms Gentry Double Shotgun, 395
American Arms Grulla #2 Double Shotgun, 395
American Arms Hawkeye Percussion Rifle, 412
American Arms P-98 Auto Pistol, 273
American Arms PK-22 DA Auto Pistol, 274
American Arms PX-22 Auto Pistol, 274
American Arms PX-25 Auto Pistol, 274
American Arms Regulator Single Actions, 318
American Arms Silver I O/U Shotgun, 386
American Arms Silver II O/U Shotgun, 386
American Arms Silver Lite O/U Shotgun, 386
American Arms Silver Skeet O/U Shotgun, 386
American Arms Silver Sporting O/U Shotgun, 386
American Arms Silver Trap O/U Shotgun, 386
American Arms Spectre DA Auto Pistol, 274
American Arms TS/SS 10 Double Shotgun, 395
American Arms TS/SS 12 Double Shotgun, 395
American Arms WS/OU 10 O/U Shotgun, 397
American Arms WS/OU 12 O/U Shotgun, 387
American Arms WS/SS 10 Double Shotgun, 395
American Arms/Franchi Black Magic 48/AL Shotgun, 378
American Arms/Franchi Falconet 2000 O/U Shotgun, 386
American Arms/Franchi LAW-12 Shotgun, 403
American Arms/Franchi SPAS-12 Shotgun, 403
American Arms/Franchi Sporting 2000 O/U Shotgun, 386
American Derringer COP 357 Derringer, 323
American Derringer DA 38 Model Derringer, 323
American Derringer Lady Derringer, 323
American Derringer Mini COP 357 Derringer, 323
American Derringer Model 1 Derringer, 323
American Derringer Model 3 Derringer, 323
American Derringer Model 4 Derringer, 323
American Derringer Model 6 Derringer, 323
American Derringer Model 7 Derringer, 323
American Derringer Model 10 Lightweight Derringer, 323
American Derringer Semmerling LM-4 Pistol, 324
American Derringer Texas Commemorative Derringer, 323
AMT 45 ACP Hardballer Long Slide, 275
AMT 45 ACP Hardballer Pistol, 275
AMT Automag II Auto Pistol, 274
AMT Automag III Auto Pistol, 274
AMT Automag IV Auto Pistol, 275
AMT Backup Auto Pistol, 275
AMT Backup Double Action Only Pistol, 275
AMT Javelina Auto Pistol, 275
AMT Lightning 25/22 Rifle, 360
AMT Lightning Small Game Hunting Rifle, 360
AMT On Duty DA Auto Pistol, 275
Anschutz 54.18 REP Deluxe Silhouette Rifle, 371
Anschutz 54.18 Silhouette Rifle, 371
Anschutz 54.18 Standard Silhouette Rifle, 371
Anschutz 54.18MSL Silhouette Rifle, 371
Anschutz 64-MS, 64-MS Left-Hand Silhouette Rifle, 370
Anschutz 525 Deluxe Auto Rifle, 360
Anschutz 1403B Biathlon Rifle, 370
Anschutz 1416D Classic Left-Hand Bolt-Action Rifle, 365
Anschutz 1416D/1516D Deluxe Bolt-Action Rifles, 365
Anschutz 1418D/1518D Deluxe Bolt-Action Rifles, 365
Anschutz 1700 FWT Bolt-Action Rifle, 365
Anschutz 1700 Meistergrade Bolt-Action RF Rifle, 365
Anschutz 1700D Bavarian Bolt-Action CF Rifle, 338
Anschutz 1700D Bavarian Bolt-Action RF Rifle, 365
Anschutz 1700D Bavarian Meistergrade CF Bolt-Action Rifle, 338
Anschutz 1700D Classic Bolt-Action CF Rifle, 337
Anschutz 1700D Classic Bolt-Action RF Rifle, 365
Anschutz 1700D Classic Meistergrade Bolt-Action CF Rifle, 337
Anschutz 1700D Custom Bolt-Action CF Rifle, 338
Anschutz 1700D Custom Bolt-Action RF Rifle, 365
Anschutz 1700D Custom Meistergrade Bolt-Action Rifle, 338
Anschutz 1700D Graphite Custom Bolt-Action RF Rifle, 365
Anschutz 1700D Meistergrade Bolt-Action RF Rifle, 365
Anschutz 1700D Meistergrade Custom Bolt-Action RF Rifle, 365
Anschutz 1803D Intermediate Match Rifle, 370
Anschutz 1808D RT Super Match 54 Target Rifle, 370
Anschutz 1827B Biathlon Rifle, 370
Anschutz 1903D Match Rifle, 370
Anschutz 1907 Match Rifle, 371
Anschutz 1907-L Match Rifle, 371
Anschutz 1910 Super Match II Rifle, 371
Anschutz 1911 Match Rifle, 370
Anschutz 1911-L Match Rifle, 370
Anschutz 1913 Super Match Rifle, 371
Anschutz 1913-L Super Match Rifle, 371
Anschutz 2002 Match Air Rifle, 431
Anschutz 2002D RT Running Target Air Rifle, 431
Anschutz Achiever Bolt-Action Rifle, 365
Anschutz Exemplar Bolt-Action Pistol, 324
Anschutz Super Match 54 Target Model 2007 Rifle, 370
Anschutz Super Match 54 Target Model 2013 Rifle, 370
Arieta Model 557 Double Shotgun, 396
Arieta Model 570 Double Shotgun, 396
Arieta Model 578 Double Shotgun, 396
Arieta Model 600 Imperial Double Shotgun, 396
Arieta Model 801 Double Shotgun, 396
Arieta Model 802 Double Shotgun, 396
Arieta Model 803 Double Shotgun, 396
Arieta Model 871 Double Shotgun, 396
Arieta Model 872 Double Shotgun, 396
Arieta Model 873 Double Shotgun, 396
Arieta Model 874 Double Shotgun, 396
Arieta Model 875 Double Shotgun, 396
Arieta Model Imperial Tiro Double Shotgun, 396
Arieta Sidelock Double Shotguns, 396
Arizaga Model 31 Double Shotgun, 395
Armoury R140 Hawken Percussion Rifle, 412
Armscor Model 14D Deluxe Bolt-Action Rifle, 365
Armscor Model 14P Bolt-Action Rifle, 365
Armscor Model 20C Auto Rifle, 360
Armscor Model 20P Auto Rifle, 360
Armscor Model 50S Auto Rifle, 360
Armscor Model 1400 SC Super Classic Bolt-Action Rifle, 366
Armscor Model 1400LW Classic Lightweight Bolt-Action Rifle, 365
Armscor Model 1500 SC Super Classic Bolt-Action Rifle, 366
Armscor Model 1500LW Bolt-Action Rifle, 365
Armscor Model 1500S Bolt-Action Rifle, 366
Armscor Model 1600 Auto Rifle, 360
Armscor Model 2000SC Auto Rifle, 360
Armscor Model AK22 Auto Rifle, 360
Armsport 1050 Series Double Shotguns, 395
Armsport 1863 Sharps Rifle, Carbine, 412
Armsport 1866 Sharps Rifle, Carbine, 353
Armsport 2700 Goose Gun O/U Shotgun, 387
Armsport 2700 Series O/U Shotgun, 387
Armsport 2705 O/U Shotgun, 387
Armsport 2730/2731 O/U Shotgun, 387
Armsport 2733/2735 O/U Shotgun, 387
Armsport 2741 O/U Shotgun, 387
Armsport 2742 Sporting Clays O/U Shotgun, 387
Armsport 2744 Sporting Claus O/U Shotgun, 387
Armsport 2750 Sporting Clays O/U Shotgun, 387
Armsport 2751 Sporting Clays O/U Shotgun, 387
Armsport 2900 Tri-Barrel Shotgun, 387
Armsport Single Barrel Shotgun, 400
Army 1851 Percussion Revolver, 409
Army 1860 Percussion Revolver, 409
ARS AR6 Repeating Air Rifle, 431
ARS/Farco CO_2 Air Shotgun, 431
A-Square Caesar Bolt-Action Rifle, 337
A-Square Hannibal Bolt-Action Rifle, 337
Astra A70 Auto Pistol, 275
Auto-Ordnance 27 A-1 Thompson, 328
Auto-Ordnance 40 S&W 1911A1 Pistol, 276
Auto-Ordnance 45 ACP General Pistol, 276
Auto-Ordnance 1911A1 Auto Pistol, 276
Auto-Ordnance 1927A1C, 328
Auto-Ordnance 1927A1 Lightweight Rifle, 328
Auto-Ordnance 1927A5 Pistol, 328
Auto-Ordnance 1927A3 Auto Rifle, 360
Auto-Ordnance Thompson M1, 328
Auto-Ordnance ZG-51 Pit Bull Pistol, 276
AyA Boxlock Double Shotguns, 396
AyA Matador Double Shotgun, 396
AyA Model 1 Double Shotgun, 396
AyA Model 2 Double Shotgun, 396
AyA Model 4 Deluxe Double Shotgun, 396
AyA Model 4 Double Shotgun, 396
AyA Model 53 Double Shotgun, 396
AyA Model 56 Doubel Shotgun, 396
AyA Model XXV Boxlock Double Shotgun, 396
AyA Model XXV Sidelock Double Shotgun, 396
AyA Sidelock Double Shotguns, 396

B

Baby Bretton O/U Shotgun, 387
Baby Dragoon 1848, 1849 Pocket, Wells Fargo Revolvers, 409
Baby Eagle Auto Pistol, 276
Barrett Light-Fifty Model 82 Auto Rifle, 328
Barrett Model 90 Bolt-Action Rifle, 338
Beeman/Harper Aircane, 434
Beeman Adder Air Pistol, 425
Beeman Air Hunter Air Rifle, 431
Beeman Air Wolf Air Rifle, 431
Beeman Carbine Model C1, 434
Beeman Classic Magnum Air Rifle, 432
Beeman Crow Magnum Air Rifle, 432
Beeman FX-1 Air Rifle, 433
Beeman Gamekeeper Air Rifle, 432
Beeman HW70 Air Pistol, 426
Beeman HW70A Air Pistol, 426
Beeman Manitou FT Match Air Rifle, 432
Beeman P1 Magnum Air Pistol, 425
Beeman P2 Match Air Pistol, 426
Beeman R1 Air Carbine, 434
Beeman R1 Air Rifle, 434
Beeman R1 Laser Air Rifle, 434
Beeman R7 Air Rifle, 434
Beeman R8 Air Rifle, 434
Beeman R10 Air Rifles, 435
Beeman RX-1 Gas-Spring Magnum Air Rifle, 434
Beeman Super 7 Air Rifle, 432
Beeman UL-7 Air Rifle, 432
Beeman Wolf Pup Air Rifle, 431
Beeman Wolverine Air Pistol, 426
Beeman/Feinwerkbau 65 MKI Air Pistol, 426
Beeman/Feinwerkbau 65 MKII Air Pistol, 426
Beeman/Feinwerkbau 100 Air Pistol, 426
Beeman/Feinwerkbau 300-S Mini-Match Air Rifle, 433
Beeman/Feinwerkbau 300-S Series Match Air Rifle, 432
Beeman/Feinwerkbau 2600 Target Rifle, 371
Beeman/Feinwerkbau C5 CO_2 Rapid Fire Air Pistol, 426
Beeman/Feinwerkbau C20 CO_2 Air Pistol, 426
Beeman/Feinwerkbau C25 CO_2 Air Pistol, 426
Beeman/Feinwerkbau C60 CO_2 Air Rifle, 433
Beeman/Feinwerkbau Mini C60 CO_2 Air Rifle, 433
Beeman/Feinwerkbau Model 601 Air Rifle, 433
Beeman/Feinwerkbau Model 601 Running Target Air Rifle, 433
Beeman/HW30 Air Rifle, 433
Beeman/HW50 Light/Sporter Target Air Rifle, 433
Beeman/HW55 Target Air Rifle, 433
Beeman/HW55MM Target Air Rifle, 433
Beeman/HW55SM Target Air Rifle, 433
Beeman/HW55T Target Air Rifle, 433
Beeman/HW77 Air Rifle and Carbine, 434
Beeman/HW 60J Bolt-Action Rifle, 338
Beeman/HW 60J-ST Bolt-Action Rifle, 366
Beeman/HW 660 Match Rifle, 371
Beeman/Weihrauch HW 60 Target Rifle, 371
Benelli Black Eagle Competition Auto Shotgun, 378
Benelli M1 Super 90 Auto Shotgun, 403
Benelli M1 Super 90 Field Auto Shotgun, 378
Benelli M1 Super 90 Slug Auto Shotgun, 378
Benelli M3 Super 90 Pump/Auto Shotgun, 403
Benelli Montefeltro Super 90 Shotgun, 378
Benelli Super Black Eagle Auto Shotgun, 378
Benelli Super Black Eagle Slug Shotgun, 378
Benjamin CO_2 Air Rifles, 435
Benjamin Model 392 Air Rifle, 435
Benjamin Model 392W Air Rifle, 435
Benjamin Model 397 Air Rifle, 435
Benjamin Model 397W Air Rifle, 435
Benjamin Model G392 Air Rifle, 435
Benjamin Model G392W Air Rifle, 435
Benjamin Model G397 Air Rifle, 435
Benjamin Model G397W Air Rifle, 435
Benjamin Model GS392W Air Rifle, 435
Benjamin Model GS393 Air Rifle, 435
Benjamin Model GS397 Air Rifle, 435
Benjamin Model GS397W Air Rifle, 435
Benjamin Model S392 Air Rifle, 435
Benjamin Model S392W Air Rifle, 435
Benjamin Model S397 Air Rifle, 435
Benjamin Model S397W Air Rifle, 435
Benjamin Pneumatic Air Rifles, 435
Benjamin/Sheridan CO_2 Pellet Pistols, 427
Benjamin/Sheridan E17 Pellet Pistol, 427
Benjamin/Sheridan E20 Pellet Pistol, 427
Benjamin/Sheridan EB17 Pellet Pistol, 427
Benjamin/Sheridan EB20 Pellet Pistol, 427
Benjamin/Sheridan H17 Pellet Pistol, 427
Benjamin/Sheridan H20 Pellet Pistol, 427
Benjamin/Sheridan HB17 Pellet Pistol, 427
Benjamin/Sheridan HB20 Pellet Pistol, 427
Benjamin/Sheridan Pneumatic Pellet Pistols, 427
Beretta 80 Series DA Pistols, 276
Beretta 390 Field Auto Shotgun, 379
Beretta 626 Onyx Double Shotgun, 397
Beretta 627 EELL Double Shotgun, 397
Beretta 627 EL Double Shotgun, 397
Beretta 682 Pigeon Silver O/U Shotgun, 388
Beretta 682 Skeet O/U Shotgun, 388
Beretta 682 Sporting Combo O/U Shotgun, 388
Beretta 682 Sporting O/U Shotgun, 388
Beretta 682 Super Skeet O/U Shotgun, 388
Beretta 682 Super Sport O/U Shotgun, 388
Beretta 682 Super Trap O/U Shotgun, 388
Beretta 682 Trap Combo Set Shotguns, 388
Beretta 682 Trap Mono Shotgun, 388
Beretta 682 Trap O/U Shotgun, 388
Beretta 682 Trap Top Single Shotgun, 388
Beretta 686 EL O/U Shotgun, 387
Beretta 686 English Course Sporting O/U Shotgun, 388
Beretta 686 Field O/U Shotgun, 387
Beretta 686 L Silver O/U Shotgun, 387
Beretta 686 Onyx O/U Shotgun, 387
Beretta 686 Onyx Sporting O/U Shotgun, 388
Beretta 686 Sporting Combo O/U Shotgun, 388
Beretta 686 Sporting O/U Shotgun, 388
Beretta 686 Ultralight O/U Shotgun, 387
Beretta 687 EELL O/U Shotgun, 387

Beretta 687 EELL Skeet O/U Shotgun, 388
Beretta 687 EELL Sporter O/U Shotgun, 388
Beretta 687 EELL Trap O/U Shotgun, 388
Beretta 687 EL O/U Shotgun, 387
Beretta 687 English Course Sporting O/U Shotgun, 388
Beretta 687 L Field O/U Shotgun, 387
Beretta 687 Sporting Combo O/U Shotgun, 388
Beretta 687 Sporting O/U Shotgun, 388
Beretta A-303 Auto Shotgun, 379
Beretta A-303 Sporting Clays Shotgun, 379
Beretta A-303 Upland Auto Shotgun, 379
Beretta A-303 Youth Shotgun, 379
Beretta ASE 90 Competition O/U Shotgun, 387
Beretta ASE 90 Pigeon, Trap, Skeet O/U Shotgun, 387
Beretta ASE 90 Sporting Clays O/U Shotgun
Beretta ASE 90 Sporting O/U Shotgun, 388
Beretta Express SSO O/U Double Rifle, 357
Beretta Model 21 Auto Pistol, 277
Beretta Model 21 EL Auto Pistol, 277
Beretta Model 84F DA Pistol, 276
Beretta Model 85F DA Pistol, 276
Beretta Model 86 Pistol, 276
Beretta Model 87 DA Auto Pistol, 276
Beretta Model 89 Sport Pistol, 276
Beretta Model 89 Target Pistol, 301
Beretta Model 92D Pistol, 277
Beretta Model 92F Stainless Pistol, 277
Beretta Model 92F-EL Pistol, 276
Beretta Model 92F-EL Stainless Pistol, 277
Beretta Model 92FC Pistol, 276
Beretta Model 92FCM Pistol, 276
Beretta Model 92FS Pistol, 276
Beretta Model 92FS Pistol, 276
Beretta Model 96 Centurion Pistol, 276
Beretta Model 96 Pistol, 277
Beretta Model 96D Pistol, 277
Beretta Model 96F Compact Pistol, 277
Beretta Model 96F Pistol, 277
Beretta Model 452 EELL Double Shotgun, 396
Beretta Model 452 Sidelock Double Shotgun, 396
Beretta Model 455 SxS Express Rifle, 357
Beretta Model 950 BS Pistol, 277
Beretta Model 1201F Auto Shotgun, 379
Beretta Model 1201FP3 Auto Shotgun, 403
Beretta Over/Under Field Shotguns, 387
Beretta Series 682 Competition O/U Shotguns, 388
Beretta SO5, SO6, SO9 O/U Shotguns, 388
Beretta Sporting Clays Shotguns, 388
Beretta SSO6 Express Double Rifle, 357
Beretta SSO6 Gold Express Double Rifle, 357
Beretta SxS Field Shotguns, 397
Bernardelli Brescia Hammer Double Shotgun, 396
Bernardelli Express VB Double Rifle, 357
Bernardelli Hemingway Deluxe Double Shotgun, 396
Bernardelli Hemingway Lightweight Double Shotgun, 396
Bernardelli Model Italia Double Shotgun, 396
Bernardelli Model Italia Extra Double Shotgun, 396
Bernardelli S. Uberto 2E Double Shotgun, 396
Bernardelli Series Roma 3E Double Shotgun, 396
Bernardelli Series Roma 3EM Double Shotgun, 396
Bernardelli Series Roma 4E Double Shotgun, 396
Bernardelli Series Roma 4EM Double Shotgun, 396
Bernardelli Series Roma 6E Double Shotgun, 396
Bernardelli Series Roma 6EM Double Shotgun, 396
Bernardelli Series S. Uberto Double Shotguns, 396
Bernardelli System Holland H. Double Shotgun, 396
Bernardelli System Holland H. VB Gold Double Shotgun, 396
Bernardelli System Holland H. VB Liscio Double Shotgun, 396
Bernardelli System Holland H. VB Lusso Double Shotgun, 396
Bersa Model 23 Auto Pistol, 277
Bersa Model 83 Auto Pistol, 277
Bersa Model 85 Auto Pistol, 277
Bersa Model 86 Auto Pistol, 277
BF Single Shot Pistol, 300
Black Watch Scotch Pistol, 405
Blaser R84 Bolt-Action Rifle, 338
Bostonian Percussion Rifle, 412
BRNO 537 Sporter Bolt-Action Rifle, 338
BRNO CZ 75 Auto Pistol, 277
BRNO CZ 83 Auto Pistol, 278
BRNO CZ 85 Auto Pistol, 278
BRNO CZ 85 Combat Auto Pistol, 278
BRNO ZKB-527 Fox Bolt-Action Rifle, 338
BRNO ZKK-600 Bolt-Action Rifle, 338
BRNO ZKK-601 Bolt-Action Rifle, 338
BRNO ZKK-602 Bolt-Action Rifle, 338
BRNO ZKM-452 Deluxe Bolt-Action Rifle, 366
BRNO ZKM-452 Standard Bolt-Action Rifle, 366
Browning A-500G Auto Shotgun, 379
Browning A-500G Buck Special Shotgun, 379
Browning A-500G Sporting Clays Shotgun, 379
Browning A-500R Auto Shotgun, 380
Browning A-500R Buck Special Shotgun, 380
Browning A-Bolt 22 Bolt-Action Rifle, 366
Browning A-Bolt 22 Gold Medallion Bolt-Action Rifle, 366
Browning A-Bolt Composite Stalker Bolt-Action Rifle, 339
Browning A-Bolt Gold Medallion Bolt-Action Rifle, 339
Browning A-Bolt Hunter Bolt-Action Rifle, 338
Browning A-Bolt Left-Hand Bolt-Action Rifle, 339
Browning A-Bolt Medallion Bolt-Action Rifle, 338
Browning A-Bolt Micro Medallion Bolt-Action Rifle, 339
Browning A-Bolt Short Action Hunter Bolt-Action Rifle, 339
Browning A-Bolt Short Action Medallion Bolt-Action Rifle, 339
Browning A-Bolt Stainless Stalker Bolt-Action Rifle, 339
Browning Auto-5 Buck Special Shotgun, 379
Browning Auto-5 Light 12 and 20, Sweet 16 Auto Shotgun, 379
Browning Auto-5 Magnum 12 Shotgun, 379
Browning Auto-5 Magnum 20 Shotgun, 379
Browning Auto-5 Magnum Stalker Shotgun, 379
Browning Auto-5 Stalker Shotgun, 379
Browning Auto-22 Grade VI Rifle, 361
Browning Auto-22 Rifle, 361
Browning BDA-380 DA Pistol, 279
Browning BDM DA Auto Pistol, 278
Browning BL-22 Grade I Lever-Action Rifle, 364
Browning BL-22 Grade II Lever-Action Rifle, 364
Browning BPS Buck Special Pump Shotgun, 382
Browning BPS Game Gun Deer Special Pump Shotgun, 382
Browning BPS Game Gun Turkey Special Pump Shotgun, 382
Browning BPS Ladies, Youth Pump Shotgun, 382
Browning BPS Pigeon Grade Pump Shotgun, 382
Browning BPS Pump Shotgun, 382
Browning BPS Stalker Pump Shotgun, 382
Browning BPS Upland Special Pump Shotgun, 382
Browning BT-99 Competition Trap Special Shotgun, 400
Browning BT-99 Plus Micro Shotgun, 400
Browning BT-99 Plus Trap Shotgun, 400
Browning Buck Mark 22 Auto Pistol, 278
Browning Buck Mark Field 5.5 Pistol, 301
Browning Buck Mark Plus Auto Pistol, 278
Browning Buck Mark Silhouette Pistol, 301
Browning Buck Mark Target 5.5 Gold Pistol, 301
Browning Buck Mark Target 5.5 Pistol, 301
Browning Buck Mark Unlimited Match Pistol, 301
Browning Buck Mark Varmint Pistol, 278
Browning Citori O/U Grade I Hunting O/U Shotgun, 388
Browning Citori O/U Grade I Lightning O/U Shotgun, 388
Browning Citori O/U Grade I Skeet Shotgun, 389
Browning Citori O/U Grade I Trap Shotgun, 389
Browning Citori O/U Grade III Hunting O/U Shotgun, 388
Browning Citori O/U Grade III Lightning O/U Shotgun, 388
Browning Citori O/U Grade III Skeet Shotgun, 389
Browning Citori O/U Grade III Trap Shotgun, 389
Browning Citori O/U Grade VI Hunting O/U Shotgun, 388
Browning Citori O/U Grade VI Skeet Shotgun, 389
Browning Citori O/U Grade VI Trap Shotgun, 389
Browning Citori O/U Gran Lightning O/U Shotgun, 388
Browning Citori O/U GTI Sporting Clays O/U Shotgun, 389
Browning Citori O/U Model Skeet Shotguns, 389
Browning Citori O/U Shotgun, 388
Browning Citori O/U Trap Shotgun, 389
Browning Citori Plus Trap Combo O/U Shotgun, 389
Browning Citori Plus Trap Shotgun, 389
Browning Hi-Power Auto Pistol, 278
Browning Hi-Power HP-Practical Pistol, 278
Browning High-Power Semi-Auto Rifle, 328
Browning Lightning Sporting Clays O/U Shotgun, 388
Browning Magnum Semi-Auto Rifle, 328
Browning Micro Buck Mark Auto Pistol, 278
Browning Micro Buck Mark Plus Pistol, 278
Browning Micro Citori Lightning O/U Shotgun, 388
Browning Model 42 Pump Shotgun, 382
Browning Model 52 Bolt-Action Rifle, 366
Browning Model 81 BLR Lever-Action Rifle, 332
Browning Model 81 Long Action BLR Rifle, 332
Browning Model 1885 Single Shot Rifle, 353
Browning Model 1886 High Grade Carbine, 332
Browning Model 1886 Lever-Action Rifle, 332
Browning Special Sporting Clays, 389
Browning Superlight Citori Grade I O/U Shotgun, 388
Browning Superlight Citori Grade III O/U Shotgun, 388
Browning Superlight Citori Grade VI O/U Shotgun, 388
Browning Superlight Citori O/U Shotgun, 388
Bryco Model 38 Auto Pistol, 279
Bryco Model 48 Auto Pistol, 279
BSA Supersport Air Rifle, 435
BSA Scorpion Air Pistol, 427
BSA Superstar Air Rifle, 435

C

Cabanas Espronceda Bolt-Action Rifle, 366
Cabanas Leyre Bolt-Action Rifle, 366
Cabanas Master Bolt-Action Rifle, 366
Cabanas Mini 82 Youth Bolt Action Rifle, 366
Cabanas Model R83 Bolt-Action Rifle, 366
Cabanas Phaser Bolt-Action Rifle, 366
Cabanas Pony Youth Bolt-Action Rifle, 366
Cabanas Varmint Bolt-Action Rifle, 366
Cabela's 12-Gauge Percussion Shotgun, 424
Cabela's Accura 9000 Muzzleloader Rifle, 412
Cabela's Blue Ridge Rifle, 413
Cabela's Hawken's Hunter Rifle, 413
Cabela's Multi-Choke Percussion Shotgun, 424
Cabela's Paterson Revolver, 409
Cabela's Swivel-Barrel Percussion Rifle, 413
Cabela's Taos Percussion Rifle, 413
Cabela's Traditional Hawken's Rifle, 413
Calico Model 110 Auto Pistol, 279
Calico Model M-100 Auto Carbine, 361
Calico Model M-105 Sporter, 351
Calico Model M-900 Carbine, 328
Calico Model M-950 Auto Pistol, 279
Calico Model M-951 Tactical Carbine, 328
Calico Model M-951-S Tactical Carbine, 328
Carl Gustaf 2000 Bolt-Action Rifle, 340
Century Centurion 14 Sporter Bolt-Action Rifle, 339
Century Enfield Sporter #4 Bolt-Action Rifle, 339
Century Gun Distributor Model 100 Single Action, 318
Century International FAL Sporter Rifle, 328
Century International M-14 Semi-Auto Rifle, 328
Century Mauser 98 Sporter Bolt-Action Rifle, 339
Century Model P9R Auto Pistol, 279
Century Swedish Sporter #38 Bolt-Action Rifle, 339
Chapuis O/U Shotgun, 389
Chapuis RGExpress Double Rifle, 357
Chapuis Side-by-Side Shotgun, 397
Charleville Flintlock Pistol, 405
Chipmunk Single Shot Rifle, 367
Churchill Auto Shotgun, 380
Churchill Monarch O/U Shotgun, 389
Churchill Turkey Auto Shotgun, 380
Churchill Windsor IV O/U Shotgun, 389
Cimarron 1860 Henry Rifle, 332
Cimarron 1866 Winchester Replicas, 332
Cimarron 1873 30" Express Rifle, 333
Cimarron 1873 Frontier Six Shooter, 318
Cimarron 1873 Peacemaker Repro Single Action, 318
Cimarron 1873 Short Rifle, 333
Cimarron 1873 Single Action Army Revolver, 318
Cimarron 1873 Sporting Rifle, 333
Cimarron 1875 Remington Single Action, 318
Cimarron 1890 Remington Revolver, 318
Cimarron U.S. Cavalry Model Single Action, 318
Claridge Hi-Tec C Carbine, 329
Claridge Hi-Tec Model ALEC-9 Carbine, 329
Claridge Hi-Tec Model L Pistol, 279
Claridge Hi-Tec Model LEC-9 Carbine, 329
Claridge Hi-Tec Model S Pistol, 279
Claridge Hi-Tec Model T Pistol, 279
Claridge Hi-Tec Model ZL-9 Pistol, 279
Claridge Hi-Tec Model ZT-9 Pistol, 279
Colt 10mm Delta Elite Auto Pistol, 280
Colt All American Model 2000 DA Pistol, 280
Colt Anaconda Revolver, 309
Colt Army Police Percussion Revolver, 409
Colt Combat Commander Auto Pistol, 281
Colt Combat Elite Mk IV/Series 80 Pistol, 280
Colt Delta Gold Cup Auto Pistol, 301
Colt Double Eagle Mk II/Series 90 DA Combat Commander Pistol, 280
Colt Double Eagle Mk II/Series 90 DA Pistol, 280
Colt Double Eagle Officer's ACP Pistol, 280
Colt Gold Cup National Match Mk IV/Series 80 Pistol, 301
Colt Government Model 380 Pistol, 281
Colt Government Model Mk IV/Series 80 Pistol, 280
Colt King Cobra Revolver, 309
Colt Lightweight Commander Mk IV/Series 80 Pistol, 281
Colt Model 1991 A1 Auto Pistol, 280
Colt Mustang 380 Pistol, 281
Colt Mustang Plus II Pistol, 281
Colt Mustang Pocketlite Pistol, 281
Colt Officer's ACP Mk IV/Series 80 Pistol, 281
Colt Pocketlite 380 Pistol, 281
Colt Python Revolver, 309
Colt Single Action Army, 318
Colt Sporter Competition HBAR Range Selected Rifle, 372
Colt Sporter Competition HBAR Rifle, 372
Colt Sporter Lightweight Rifle, 329
Colt Sporter Match HBAR Rifle, 372
Colt Sporter Target Model Rifle, 372
Competitor Single Shot Pistol, 301
Confederate Navy Percussion Revolver, 410
Cook & Brother Confederate Carbine, 413
Coonan 357 Magnum Model B Pistol, 281
Coonan 357 Magnum Pistol, 281
Cooper Arms Model 36, 38 Sporter Rifles, 367
Cooper Arms Model TRP-1 ISU Standard Rifle, 372
Cosmi Auto Shotgun, 380
Crosman Auto Air II Air Pistol, 427
Crosman Model 357 Air Pistol, 427
Crosman Model 760 Pumpmaster Air Rifle, 436
Crosman Model 781 Single Pump Air Rifle, 436
Crosman Model 782 Black Diamond Air Rifle, 436
Crosman Model 788 BB Scout Air Rifle, 436
Crosman Model 1008 Repeat Air Pistol, 427
Crosman Model 1322, 1377 Air Pistols, 427
Crosman Model 1357 Air Pistol, 427
Crosman Model 1389 Backpacker Air Rifle, 436
Crosman Model 2100 Classic Air Rifle, 436
Crosman Model 2200 Magnum Air Rifle, 436
Crosman Model SSP250 Air Pistol, 428
Crucelegui Hermanos Model 150 Double Shotgun, 397
CVA 1858 Remington Target Revolver, 411
CVA Apollo 90 Percussion Carbine, 413
CVA Apollo 90 Percussion Rifle, 413
CVA Apollo 90 Shadow Percussion Rifle, 413
CVA Apollo 90 Sporter Percussion Rifle, 413
CVA Bushwacker Percussion Rifle, 414
CVA Classic Turkey Percussion Double Shotgun, 424
CVA Colonial Pistol, 406
CVA Colt Sheriff's Model Revolver, 410
CVA Express Percussion Rifle, 413
CVA Frontier Flintlock Percussion Rifle, 414
CVA Frontier Hunter Carbine, 414
CVA Frontier Percussion Carbine, 414
CVA Hawken Deerslayer Rifle/Carbine, 414
CVA Hawken Percussion Rifle, 414
CVA Hawken Pistol, 406
CVA Kentucky Hunter Percussion Rifle
CVA Kentucky Percussion Rifle, 414
CVA Mountain Rifle, 414
CVA Pennsylvania Long Rifle, 414
CVA Philadelphia Derringer, 406
CVA Plainsman Percussion Rifle, 414
CVA Pocket Remington Revolver, 409
CVA Remington Bison Revolver, 411
CVA Siber Pistol, 406
CVA Squirrel Rifle, 415
CVA St. Louis Hawken Percussion Rifle, 414
CVA Stalker Rifle/Carbine, 414
CVA Third Model Colt Dragoon Revolver, 409
CVA Tracker Carbine, 415
CVA Trapper Percussion Shotgun, 424
CVA Trophy Carbine, 415
CVA Vest Pocket Derringer, 406
CVA Wells Fargo Model Revolver, 409

D

Daewoo DP51 Auto Pistol, 281
Daisy 1938 Red Ryder Classic Air Rifle, 436
Daisy Model 91 Match Air Pistol, 428
Daisy Model 188 Air Pistol, 428
Daisy Model 840 Air Rifle, 436

Daisy Model 1894 Air Rifle, 437
Daisy/Power Line 44 Air Pistol, 428
Daisy/Power Line 45 Air Pistol, 428
Daisy/Power Line 93 Air Pistol, 428
Daisy/Power Line 130 Air Rifle, 437
Daisy/Power Line 645 Air Pistol, 428
Daisy/Power Line 693 Air Pistol, 428
Daisy/Power Line 717 Pellet Pistol, 428
Daisy/Power Line 747 Pellet Pistol, 428
Daisy/Power Line 753 Target Air Rifle, 437
Daisy/Power Line 853 Air Rifle, 437
Daisy/Power Line 860 Pump-Up Air Rifle, 437
Daisy/Power Line 880 Pump-Up Air Rifle, 437
Daisy/Power Line 922 Air Rifle, 437
Daisy/Power Line CO_2 1200 Air Pistol, 429
Daisy/Power Line Eagle 7856 Pump-Up Air Rifle, 437
Daisy/Power Line Match 777 Pellet Pistol, 429
Daisy/Youth Line Air Rifles, 437
Daisy/Youth Line Model 95 Air Rifle, 437
Daisy/Youth Line Model 105 Air Rifle, 437
Daisy/Youth Line Model 111 Air Rifle, 437
Dakota 22 Sporter Bolt-Action Rifle, 367
Dakota 76 22 Sporter Bolt-Action Rifle, 340
Dakota 76 Classic Bolt-Action Rifle, 339
Dakota 76 Rigby African Bolt-Action Rifle, 340
Dakota 76 Safari Bolt-Action Rifle, 340
Dakota 76 Short Action Rifle, 339
Dakota 1875 Outlaw Revolver, 319
Dakota 1890 Police Revolver, 319
Dakota Hartford Artillery Single-Action Revolver, 319
Dakota Hartford Cavalry Single-Action Revolver, 319
Dakota Hartford Single-Action Revolver, 319
Dakota New Model Single-Action Revolver, 319
Dakota Single Shot Rifle, 354
Daly, Charles, Field Grade O/U Shotgun, 389
Daly, Charles, Lux O/U Shotgun, 389
Daly, Charles, Model DSS Double Shotgun, 397
Davis D-38 Derringer, 324
Davis Derringers, 324
Davis P-32 Auto Pistol, 282
Davis P-380 Auto Pistol, 282
Desert Eagle Magnum Pistol, 282
Desert Industries Big Twenty Shotgun, 400
Desert Industries Double Deuce Pistol, 282
Desert Industries G-90 Single Shot Rifle, 354
Desert Industries Two Bit Special Pistol, 282
Desert Industries War Eagle Pistol, 282
Dixie 1863 Springfield Musket, 415
Dixie 1873 Carbine, 333
Dixie Abilene Pistol, 406
Dixie Brass Frame Derringer, 406
Dixie Delux Cub Rifle, 415
Dixie Engraved 1873 Rifle, 333
Dixie Hawken Rifle, 415
Dixie Lincoln Derringer, 406
Dixie Magnum Percussion Shotgun, 424
Dixie Pennsylvania Pistol, 406
Dixie Screw Barrel Pistol, 406
Dixie Squirrel Rifle, 415
Dixie Tennessee Mountain Rifle, 415
Dixie Third Model Dragoon Revolver, 409
Dixie Tornado Target Pistol, 407
Dixie U.S. Model 1816 Flintlock Musket, 415
Dixie U.S. Model 1861 Springfield Musket, 415
Dixie Wyatt Earp Percussion Revolver, 410
D Max Auto Carbine, 329
D Max Auto Pistol, 282

E

E.A.A. Big Bore Bounty Hunter Revolver, 319
E.A.A. Bounty Hunter Revolver, 319
E.A.A. European 380/DA Auto Pistol, 282
E.A.A. European EA22T Target Auto Pistol, 301
E.A.A. European Model Auto Pistol, 282
E.A.A. PM2 Pump Shotgun, 403
E.A.A. Standard Grade Revolvers, 309
E.A.A. Tactical Grade Revovlers, 309
E.A.A. Target Grade Revolvers, 302
E.A.A. Witness Carry Comp DA Auto Pistol, 283
E.A.A. Witness Compact DA Auto Pistol, 283
E.A.A. Witness DA Auto Pistol, 283
E.A.A. Witness Gold Team Auto Pistol, 302
E.A.A. Witness Silver Team Auto Pistol, 302
E.A.A./Antonio Zoli Express E Double Rifle, 358
E.A.A./Antonio Zoli Express EM Double Rifle, 358
E.A.A./Antonio Zoli Express Rifle, 358
Eagle Arms EA-15 Action Master Auto Rifle, 329
Eagle Arms EA-15 Auto Rifle, 329
Eagle Arms EA-15 E1, E2 Carbines, 329
Eagle Arms EA-15 Golden Eagle Auto Rifle, 329
Eagle Arms EA-15 H-BAR Auto Rifle, 329
El Gamo 126 Super Match Target Air Rifle, 438
E.M.F. 1860 Henry Rifle, 333
E.M.F. 1866 Yellowboy Lever Actions, 333
E.M.F. 1873 Lever-Action Rifle, 333
Erma ER Match Revolvers, 302
Erma ER-777 Sporting Revolver, 309
Erma ESP 85A Competition Pistol, 302
Erma ESP 85A Sporting Model Pistol, 283
Euroarms Buffalo Carbine, 415
Euroarms Duck Percussion Shotgun, 424

F

Famas Semi-Auto Air Rifle, 438
FAS 601 Match Pistol, 302
FAS 602 Match Pistol, 302
FAS 603 Match Pistol, 302
Faucher GP Silhouette Pistol, 303
Feather AT-9 Semi-Auto Carbine, 329
Feather AT-22 Semi-Auto Carbine, 361
Feather Guardian Angel Pistol, 324
Feather Model F2 Semi-Auto Carbine, 361
Federal Engineering XC220 Auto Carbine, 361
Federal Engineering XC900/XC450 Auto Carbines, 330
Federal Ordnance M14SA Target Rifle, 372
FEG GKK-92C Auto Pistol, 283
FEG MBK-9HP Auto Pistol, 283
FEG MBK-9HPC Auto Pistol, 283
FEG PJK-9HP Auto Pistol, 283
FEG PMK-380 Auto Pistol, 283
FEG SA-85M Autoloading Rifle, 330
Ferlib Model F VI Double Shotgun, 397
Ferlib Model F VII Double Shotgun, 397
Ferlib Model F VII SC Double Shotgun, 397
Ferlib Model F VII SP Sideplate Double Shotgun, 397
Finnish Lion Standard Target Rifle, 372
Francotte, Auguste, Bolt-Action Rifle, 340
Francotte, Auguste, Boxlock Double Rifle, 358
Francotte, Auguste, Boxlock Double Shotgun, 397
Francotte, Auguste, Sidelock Double Rifle, 358
Francotte, Auguste, Sidelock Double Shotgun, 397
Freedom Arms Casull Model 252 Silhouette Revolver, 302
Freedom Arms Casull Model 252 Varmint Revolver, 302
Freedom Arms Casull Model 353 Premier Grade Revolver, 319
Freedom Arms Casull Model 353 Revolver, 319
Freedom Arms 454 Casull Field Grade Revolver, 319
Freedom Arms 454 Casull Premier Revolver, 319
French-Style Dueling Pistol, 406

G

Galil Sporter Rifle, 330
Gamba Daytona Competition O/U Shotgun, 389
Garbi Model 100 Double Shotgun, 397
Garbi Model 101 Double Shotgun, 397
Garbi Model 103A, B Double Shotguns, 397
Garbi Model 200 Double Shotgun, 397
GAT Air Pistol, 429
GAT Air Rifle, 438
Gaucher GN1 Silhouette Pistol, 324
Glock 17 Auto Pistol, 284
Glock 17 Competition Pistol, 303
Glock 17L Auto Pistol, 284
Glock 19 Auto Pistol, 284
Glock 20 Auto Pistol, 284
Glock 21 Auto Pistol, 284
Glock 22 Auto Pistol, 284
Glock 23 Auto Pistol, 284
Gonic GA-87 M/L Rifle, 416
Grendel P-12 Auto Pistol, 284
Grendel P-30 Auto Pistol, 284
Grendel P-30L Auto Pistol, 284
Grendel P-31 Auto Pistol, 284
Grendel R-31 Auto Carbine, 361
Griswold & Gunnison Percussion Revolver, 410
GZ Carbon Series 2000 Constant-Air Paint Ball Pistol, 443
GZ Carbon Series 2000 Paint Ball Pistol, 443
GZ Carbon Series 2000 PRO Model Paint Ball Pistol, 443
GZ Series 1000 Paint Ball Pistol, 443

H

Haenel Model 110 Air Rifle, 438
Haenel Model 120 Air Rifle, 438
Haenel Model 120S Air Rifle, 438
Haenel Model 410 Air Rifle, 438
Haenel Model 600 Air Rifle, 438
Haenel Model 800 Air Rifle, 438
Haenel Model 900 Match Rifle, 372
Hammerli Model 150 Free Pistol, 303
Hammerli Model 152 Match Pistol, 303
Hammerli Model 208 Target Pistol, 303
Hammerli Model 208s Match Pistol, 303
Hammerli Model 211 Target Pistol, 303
Hammerli Model 212 Auto Pistol, 285
Hammerli Model 280 Target Pistol, 303
Hanus, Bill, Birdgun Double Shotguns, 398
Harper's Ferry 1803 Flintlock Rifle, 416
Harper's Ferry 1806 Pistol, 407
Harrington & Richardson N.W.T.F. Turkey Mag Shotgun, 400
Harrington & Richardson Sportsman 999 Revolver, 310
Harrington & Richardson Topper Classic Youth Shotgun, 400
Harrington & Richardson Topper Deluxe Model 098 Shotgun, 400
Harrington & Richardson Topper Junior Model 098 Shotgun, 400
Harrington & Richardson Topper Model 098 Shotgun, 400
Haskell JS-45 Auto Pistol, 285
Hatfield Mountain Rifle, 416
Hatfield Squirrel Rifle, 416
Hatfield Uplander Black Widow Grade VI Double Shotgun, 398
Hatfield Uplander Golden Quail Grade IV Double Shotgun, 398
Hatfield Uplander Grade II Double Shotgun, 398
Hatfield Uplander Royale Grade VII Double Shotgun, 398
Hatfield Uplander Super Pigeon Grade III Double Shotgun, 398
Hatfield Uplander Top Hat Grade VIII Double Shotgun, 398
Hatfield Uplander Woodcock Grade V Double Shotgun, 398
Hawken Percussion Pistol, 407
Hawken Rifle, 416
Heckler & Koch P7K3 Auto Pistol, 285
Heckler & Koch P7M8 Auto Pistol, 285
Heckler & Koch P7M10 Auto Pistol, 285
Heckler & Koch P7M13 Auto Pistol, 285
Heckler & Koch PSG-1 Marksman Rifle, 372
Heckler & Koch SP89 Auto Pistol, 285
Heckler & Koch SR9 Rifle, 330
Heckler & Koch SR9(T) Target Rifle, 330
Helwan "Brigadier" Auto Pistol, 285
Heym Magnum Express Bolt-Action Rifle, 340
Heym Model 22S Safety Combo Gun, 358
Heym Model 33 Boxlock Drilling, 358
Heym Model 37 Sidelock Drilling, 358
Heym Model 37B Double Rifle Drilling, 358
Heym Model 55B/55SS O/U Double Rifle, 358
Heym Model 55BF O/U Combo Gun, 358
Heym Model 88B SxS Double Rifle, 358
Heym Model 88B-SS SxS Double Rifle, 358
Heym SR 20 Alpine Series Bolt-Action Rifle, 340
Heym SR 20 Classic Series Bolt-Action Rifle, 340
Heym SR 20 Classic Sportsman Series Bolt-Action Rifle, 340
Heym SR 20 Trophy Series Bolt-Action Rifle, 340
High Standard Derringer, 324
Howa Heavy Barrel Varmint Bolt-Action Rifle, 341
Howa M1500 Trophy Bolt-Action Rifle, 341

I

Iberia Firearms JS-40 Auto Pistol, 286
Intratec Protec-22 Auto Pistol, 286
Intratec Protec-25 Auto Pistol, 286
Intratec TEC-22T Auto Pistol, 286
Intratec TEC-22TK Auto Pistol, 286
Intratec TEC-DC9 Auto Pistol, 286
Intratec TEC-DC9K Auto Pistol, 286
Intratec TEC-DC9M Auto Pistol, 286
Intratec TEC-DC9MK Auto Pistol, 286
Intratec TEC-DC9MS Auto Pistol, 286
Intratec TEC-DC9S Auto Pistol, 286
Israeli Kareen Auto Pistol, 286
Ithaca Model 87 Basic Field Combo Pump Shotgun, 383
Ithaca Model 87 Deerslayer Deluxe Combo Pump Shotgun, 383
Ithaca Model 87 Deerslayer II Rifled Shotgun, 383
Ithaca Model 87 Deerslayer Pump Shotgun, 383
Ithaca Model 87 Deluxe Pump Shotgun, 383
Ithaca Model 87 Hand Grip Pump Shotgun, 403
Ithaca Model 87 M&P DSPS Pump Shotgun, 403
Ithaca Model 87 Supreme Pump Shotgun, 383
Ithaca Model 87 Turkey Gun. 383
Ithaca X-Caliber Single Shot Pistol, 325
Ithaca-Navy Hawken Rifle, 416

J

Jennings J-22 Auto Pistol, 287
Jennings J-25 Auto Pistol, 287
Jericho 941 Auto Pistol, 286
Iver Johnson 50th Anniversary M-1 Carbine, 330
Iver Johnson Compact 25 ACP Pistol, 287
Iver Johnson Enforcer Auto Pistol, 287
Iver Johnson M-1 Carbine, 330
Iver Johnson Model 5100A1 Long-Range Rifle, 341
JSL Spitfire Auto Pistol, 286

K

Kassnar Grade I O/U Shotgun, 390
KDF K-15 American Bolt-Action Rifle, 341
Kentuckian Rifle and Carbine, 417
Kentucky Flintlock Pistol, 407
Kentucky Flintlock Rifle, 416
Kentucky Percussion Pistol, 407
Kentucky Percussion Rifle, 416
Kintrek Model KBP-1 Auto Rifle, 361
Knight MK-85 BK-92 Black Knight Rifle, 416
Knight MK-85 Grand American Rifle, 416
Knight MK-85 Grizzly PLB Rifle, 416
Knight MK-85 Grizzly PLB Stainless Rifle, 416
Knight MK-85 Hunter Rifle, 416
Knight MK-85 Light Knight Rifle, 416
Knight MK-85 Predator Rifle, 416
Knight MK-85 Stalker Rifle, 416
Kodiak MK. III Percussion Double Rifle, 417
Kodiak Mk. IV Double Rifle, 358
Korth Revolver, 310
Krico Model 260 Auto Rifle, 362
Krico Model 300 Deluxe Bolt-Action Rifle, 367
Krico Model 300 Standard Bolt-Action Rifle, 367
Krico Model 300 Stutzen Bolt-Action Rifle, 367
Krico Model 300A SA Bolt-Action Rifle, 367
Krico Model 360 S2 Biathlon Rifle, 373
Krico Model 360S Biathlon Rifle, 373
Krico Model 400 Match Rifle, 373
Krico Model 500 Kricotronic Match Rifle, 373
Krico Model 600 Bolt-Action Rifle, 341
Krico Model 600 Match Rifle, 373
Krico Model 600 Sniper Rifle, 373
Krico Model 700 Bolt-Action Rifle, 341
Krico Model 700 Deluxe Bolt-Action Rifle, 341
Krico Model 700 Deluxe S Bolt-Action Rifle, 341
Krico Model 700 Stutzen Bolt-Action Rifle, 341
Krieghoff K-80 Four-Barrel Skeet Set O/U Shotgun, 390
Krieghoff K-80 International Skeet O/U Shotgun, 390
Krieghoff K-80 Live Bird O/U Shotgun, 390
Krieghoff K-80 O/U Trap Shotguns, 390
Krieghoff K-80 Single Barrel Trap Shotgun, 401
Krieghoff K-80 Skeet O/U Shotgun, 390
Krieghoff K-80 Skeet Special O/U Shotgun, 390
Krieghoff K-80 Sporting Clays O/U Shotgun, 390
Krieghoff K-80 Trap Combo Shotgun, 390
Krieghoff K-80 Trap Unsingle Shotgun, 390
Krieghoff K-80/RT O/U Shotguns, 390
Krieghoff KS-5 Special Shotgun, 401
Krieghoff KS-5 Trap Shotgun, 401
Krieghoff Neptun Drilling, 359
Krieghoff Teck O/U Combo Gun, 359
Krieghoff Trumpf Drilling, 359
Krieghoff Ulm O/U Combo Gun, 359

L

Lakefield Arms Mark I Bolt-Action Rifle, 367
Lakefield Arms Mark I-Y Bolt-Action Rifle, 367
Lakefield Arms Mark II Bolt-Action Rifle, 367
Lakefield Arms Mark II-Y Bolt-Action Rifle, 367
Lakefield Arms Model 64B Auto Rifle, 362

Lakefield Arms Model 90B Target Rifle, 373
Lakefield Arms Model 91T Target Rifle, 373
Lakefield Arms Model 92S Silhouette Rifle, 373
L.A.R. Grizzly Win Mag 8", 10" Pistols, 287
L.A.R. Grizzly Win Mag 44 Mag Mk IV Pistol, 287
L.A.R. Grizzly Win Mag Mk I Pistol, 287
Laurona Model 83 MG O/U Shotguns, 391
Laurona Model 84 Super Trap O/U Shotgun, 391
Laurona Model 85 MS Super Pigeon O/U Shotgun, 391
Laurona Model 85 MS Super Trap O/U Shotgun, 391
Laurona Model 85 S Super Skeet O/U Shotgun, 391
Laurona Model 85 Super Game O/U Shotgun, 391
Laurona Silhouette 300 Sporting Clays O/U Shotgun, 390
Laurona Silhouette 300 Trap O/U Shotgun, 390
Laurona Silhouette Ultra-Magnum O/U Shotgun, 390
Laurona Super Model O/U Shotguns, 391
LeMat Army Model Revolver, 410
LeMat Cavalry Model Revolver, 410
LeMat Naval-Style Revolver, 410
LePage Percussion Dueling Pistol, 407
Ljutic LM-6 Deluxe O/U Shotgun, 391
Ljutic LM-6 Super Deluxe O/U Shotgun, 391
Ljutic LTX Super Deluxe Mono Gun Shotgun, 401
Ljutic Mono Gun Single Barrel Shotgun, 401
Ljutic Recoilless Space Gun Shotgun, 401
Llama Comanche III Revolver, 310
Llama Compact Frame Auto Pistol, 287
Llama Large Frame Auto Pistol, 288
Llama M-82 DA Auto Pistol, 288
Llama M-87 9mm Comp Pistol, 303
Llama Small Frame Auto Pistol, 287
Llama Super Comanche IV Revolver, 310
London Armory 2-Band Enfield 1858 Rifle, 417
London Armory 3-Band Enfield Rifle, 417
London Armory Enfield Musketoon, 417
Lorcin Auto Pistol, 288
Lorcin L-32 Auto Pistol, 288
Lorcin L-380 Auto Pistol, 288
Lyman Deerstalker Custom Carbine, 417
Lyman Deerstalker Rifle, 417
Lyman Great Plains Rifle, 418
Lyman Plains Pistol, 407
Lyman Trade Rifle, 417

M

Magnum Research SSP-91 Single Shot Pistol, 325
Magtech Model MT-22C Bolt-Action Rifle, 367
Magtech Model MT-66 Auto Rifle, 362
Magtech Model MT-151 Single Shot Shotgun, 401
Magtech Model MT-586P Pump Shotgun, 404
Mandall/Cabanas Pistol, 325
Mark X American Field Series Bolt-Action Rifle, 341
Mark X Viscount Bolt-Action Rifle, 341
Marksman 17 Air Pistol, 429
Marksman Model 28 International Air Rifle, 439
Marksman Model 40 International Air Rifle, 439
Marksman Model 55T Air Rifle, 439
Marksman Model 56-FTS Field Target Air Rifle, 439
Marksman Model 56-S Silhouette Air Rifle, 439
Marksman Model 59T Air Rifle, 439
Marksman Model 60 Air Rifle, 439
Marksman Model 61 Air Carbine, 439
Marksman Model 70T Air Rifle, 439
Marksman Model 71 Air Rifle, 439
Marksman Model 72 Air Rifle, 439
Marksman Model 1010 Repeater Air Pistol, 429
Marksman Model 1010X Repeater Air Pistol, 429
Marksman Model 1015 Special Editon Air Pistol, 429
Marksman Model 1740 Air Rifle, 439
Marksman Model 1750 BB Biathlon Repeater Air Rifle, 439
Marksman Model 1780 Air Rifle, 439
Marksman Model 1790 Biathlon Trainer Air Rifle, 439
Marksman/Anschutz Model 380 Match Air Rifle, 438
Marlin Model 9 Camp Carbine, 330
Marlin Model 9N Camp Carbine, 330
Marlin Model 15YN "Little Buckaroo" Bolt-Action Rifle, 368
Marlin Model 25MN Bolt-Action Rifle, 368
Marlin Model 25N Bolt-Action Rifle, 368
Marlin Model 30AS Lever-Action Carbine, 333
Marlin Model 39AS Golden Lever-Action Rifle, 364
Marlin Model 39TDS Lever-Action Carbine, 364
Marlin Model 45 Carbine, 330
Marlin Model 55 Goose Gun Bolt-Action Shotgun, 401
Marlin Model 60 Self-Loading Rifle, 362
Marlin Model 70HC Auto Rifle, 362
Marlin Model 70P Papoose Auto Rifle, 362
Marlin Model 336CS Lever-Action Carbine, 333
Marlin Model 444S Lever-Action Sporter, 334
Marlin Model 880 Bolt-Action Rifle, 368
Marlin Model 881 Bolt-Action Rifle, 368
Marlin Model 882 Bolt-Action Rifle, 368
Marlin Model 883 Bolt-Action Rifle, 368
Marlin Model 990L Self-Loading Rifle, 362
Marlin Model 995 Self-Loading Rifle, 362
Marlin Model 1894CL Classic Lever-Action Carbine, 334
Marlin Model 1894CS Lever-Action Carbine, 334
Marlin Model 1894S Lever-Action Carbine, 334
Marlin Model 1895SS Lever-Action Rifle, 334
Marlin Model 2000 Target Rifle, 374
Marocchi Avanza O/U Shotgun, 391
Marocchi Avanza Sporting Clays O/U Shotgun, 391
Mauser Model 66 Bolt-Action Rifle, 341
Mauser Model 80 SA Auto Pistol, 288
Mauser Model 86-SR Specialty Rifle, 374
Mauser Model 90 DA Auto Pistol, 288
Mauser Model 99 Bolt-Action Rifle, 342
Mauser Model 201 Bolt-Action Rifle, 368
Mauser Model 201 Luxus Bolt-Action Rifle, 368
Maverick Model 88 Bullpup Shotgun, 404
Maverick Models 88, 91 Pump Shotguns, 383
Maximum Single Shot Pistol, 325
McMillan 300 Phoenix Long Range Rifle, 374
McMillan Classic Stainless Sporter Bolt-Action Rifle, 342
McMillan Combo M-87/M-88 50-Cal. Rifle, 374
McMillan Long Range Rifle, 374
McMillan M-86 Sniper Rifle, 374
McMillan M-89 Sniper Rifle, 374
McMillan National Match Rifle, 374
McMillan Signature Alaskan Bolt-Action Rifle, 342
McMillan Signature Classic Sporter Bolt-Action Rifle, 342
McMillan Signature Jr. Long Range Pistol, 304
McMillan Signature Super Varminter Bolt-Action Rifle, 342
McMillan Signature Titanium Mountain Rifle, 342
McMillan Talon Safari Bolt-Action Rifle, 342
McMillan Talon Sporter Bolt-Action Rifle, 342
McMillan Wolverine Auto Pistol, 304
Merkel Model 8 Double Shotgun, 398
Merkel Model 47E Double Shotgun, 398
Merkel Model 47S Double Shotgun, 398
Merkel Model 147E Double Shotgun, 398
Merkel Model 147S Double Shotgun, 398
Merkel Model 200E O/U Shotgun, 391
Merkel Model 201E O/U Shotgun, 391
Merkel Model 203E O/U Shotgun, 391
Merkel Over/Under Shotguns, 391
Merkel Side-by-Side Double Shotguns, 398
Mini-Mark X Bolt-Action Rifle, 341
Mississippi Model 1841 Percussion Rifle, 423
Mitchell Arms 1858 Henry Replica, 334
Mitchell Arms 1866 Winchester Replica, 334
Mitchell Arms 1873 Winchester Replica, 334
Mitchell Arms AK-22 Semi-Auto Rifle, 362
Mitchell Arms Bat Masterson Single-Action Revolver, 320
Mitchell Arms CAR-15/22 Auto Rifle, 363
Mitchell Arms Citation II Auto Pistol, 288
Mitchell Arms Galil/22 Auto Rifle, 362
Mitchell Arms M-16A-1/22 Auto Rifle, 363
Mitchell Arms MAS/22 Auto Rifle, 363
Mitchell Arms Olympic I.S.U. Auto Pistol, 304
Mitchell Arms Pistol Parabellum '08, 288
Mitchell Arms PPS/22 Auto Rifle, 363
Mitchell Arms Rolling Block Target Pistol, 325
Mitchell Arms Sharpshooter Auto Pistol, 288
Mitchell Arms Single-Action Army Revolvers, 320
Mitchell Arms Sport-King Auto Pistol, 289
Mitchell Arms Trophy II Auto Pistol, 288
Model 85 Paint Ball Machine Pistol, 443
Model 1885 High Wall Rifle, 354
Moore, Charles, Flintlock Pistol, 407
Moore & Patrick Flint Dueling Pistol, 407
Mossberg Model 500, 590 Mariner Pump Shotguns, 404
Mossberg Model 500 Bantam Pump Shotgun, 384
Mossberg Model 500 Camo Combo Pump Shotgun, 384
Mossberg Model 500 Camo Pump Shotgun, 384
Mossberg Model 500 Ghost-Ring Shotgun, 404
Mossberg Model 500 Intimidator Shotgun, 404
Mossberg Model 500 Muzzleloader Combo Pump Shotgun, 383
Mossberg Model 500 Security Shotguns, 404
Mossberg Model 500 Sporting Combo Pump Shotgun, 383
Mossberg Model 500 Sporting Pump Shotgun, 383
Mossberg Model 500 Trophy Slugster Pump Shotgun, 383
Mossberg Model 500 Turkey Model Pump Shotgun, 384
Mossberg Model 590 Ghost-Ring Shotgun, 404
Mossberg Model 590 Intimidator Shotgun, 404
Mossberg Model 590 Pump Shotgun, 404
Mossberg Model 835 N.W.T.F. 1992 Edition Pump Shotgun, 384
Mossberg Model 835 Regal Ulti-Mag Pump Shotgun, 384
Mossberg Model 835 Special Value Pump Shotgun, 384
Mossberg Model 5500 MKII Auto Shotgun, 380
Mossberg Model 9200 Regal Auto Shotgun, 380
Mossberg Model HS 410 Pump Shotgun, 404
Mountain Eagle Auto Pistol, 289
Mowrey 1 N 30 Conical Rifle, 418
Mowrey Percussion Shotgun, 424
Mowrey Plains Rifle, 418
Mowrey Silhouette Rifle, 418
Mowrey Squirrel Rifle, 418
Murray, J.P., 1862-1864 Cavalry Carbine, 418

N

Navy 1851 Percussion Revolver, 410
Navy 1861 Percussion Revolver, 409
Navy Arms 1763 Charleville Musket, 418
Navy Arms 1777 Charleville Musket, 418
Navy Arms 1816 M.T. Wickham Musket, 418
Navy Arms 1862 C.S. Richmond Musket, 418
Navy Arms 1863 Springfield Musket, 418
Navy Arms 1866 Yellowboy Rifle, 335
Navy Arms 1873 Single-Action Revolver, 320
Navy Arms 1873 Sporting Rifle, 335
Navy Arms 1873 U.S. Cavalry Model Revolver, 320
Navy Arms 1873 Winchester-Style Carbine, 335
Navy Arms 1873 Winchester-Style Rifle, 335
Navy Arms 1895 U.S. Artillery Model Revolver, 320
Navy Arms #2 Creedmoor Rifle, 354
Navy Arms D. Henry Carbine, 335
Navy Arms Deluxe 1858 Remington-Style Revolver, 410
Navy Arms Fowler Percussion Shotgun, 425
Navy Arms Henry Trapper Rifle, 335
Navy Arms Iron Frame Henry Rifle, 335
Navy Arms Japanese Matchlock Rifle, 418
Navy Arms LePage Dueling Pistol, 407
Navy Arms Military Henry Rifle, 335
Navy Arms Mortimer Flintlock Rifle, 419
Navy Arms Mortimer Flintlock Shotgun, 425
Navy Arms Mountain Pistol, 408
Navy Arms Pennsylvania Long Rifle, 419
Navy Arms Rolling Block Buffalo Rifle, 354
Navy Arms Sharps Cavalry Carbine, 354
Navy Arms Sharps Percussion Carbine, 419
Navy Arms Sharps Plains Rifle, 354
Navy Arms Smith Carbine, 419
Navy Arms Steel Shot Magnum Percussion Shotgun, 424
Navy Arms T&T Percussion Shotgun, 425
Navy Arms Tryon Creedmoor Target Model Rifle, 423
Navy Arms TT-Olympia Auto Pistol, 289
Navy Arms TU-33/40 Carbine, 343
Navy Arms TU-Navy Arms TU-33/40 Bolt-Action Carbine, 368
Navy Arms TU-Navy Arms TU-KKW Sniper Rifle, 368
Navy Arms TU-Navy Arms TU-KKW Training Rifle, 368
New Advantage Arms Derringer, 325
New England Firearms Handi-Rifle, 354
New England Firearms Lady Ultra Revolver, 310
New England Firearms N.W.T.F. Shotgun, 402
New England Firearms R92, R73 Revolvers, 310
New England Firearms Standard Pardner Shotgun, 401
New England Firearms Standard Pardner Youth Shotgun, 401
New England Firearms Tracker II Slug Shotgun, 402
New England Firearms Tracker Slug Shotgun, 402
New England Firearms Turkey and Goose Gun Shotgun, 401
New England Firearms Ultra Revolver, 310
New Generation Snake Charmer Shotgun, 402
New Model 1858 Army Percussion Revolver, 410
New Model 1858 Army Target Model Revolver, 410
Norinco 88SP Auto Pistol, 289
Norinco JW-15 Bolt-Action Rifle, 369
Norinco JW-27 Bolt-Action Rifle, 369
Norinco M93 Sportsman Auto Pistol, 289
Norinco M1911 Auto Pistol, 290
Norinco MAK 90 Semi-Auto Rifle, 331
Norinco Model 22 ATD Auto Rifle, 363
Norinco NP-15 Tokarev Auto Pistol, 289
Norinco NP-15A Auto Pistol, 289
Norinco NP-20 Auto Pistol, 289
Norinco Type 59 Makarov DA Pistol, 289
Norinco Type EM-332 Bolt-Action Rifle, 369
North American Arms Black Widow Revolver, 320
North American Arms Mini-Master Revolvers, 320
North American Arms Mini-Revolvers, 320

O

Olympic Arms CAR Series Carbines, 331
Olympic Arms International Match Rifle, 375
Olympic Arms K-4 AR-15 Rifle, 331
Olympic Arms Multimatch Rifle, 375
Olympic Arms Service Match Rifle, 375
Olympic Arms Ultramatch Rifle, 375

P

Pachmayr Dominator Pistol, 325
Para-Ordnance P12.45 Auto Pistol, 290
Para-Ordnance P12.45C Auto Pistol, 290
Para-Ordnance P13.45 Auto Pistol, 290
Para-Ordnance P14.45 Auto Pistol, 290
Para-Ordnance P14.45C Auto Pistol, 290
Parker Auto Pistol, 289
Parker Reproductions A-1 Special Double Shotgun, 398
Parker Reproductions D Grade Double Shotgun, 398
Parker Reproductions Double Shotgun, 398
Parker, W., Flintlock Pistol, 408
Parker-Hale Enfield 1853 Musket, 419
Parker-Hale Enfield 1861 Musketoon, 419
Parker-Hale Enfield Pattern 1858 Naval Rifle, 419
Parker-Hale Limited Edition Whitworth Sniping Rifle, 419
Parker-Hale M-85 Sniper Rifle, 375
Parker-Hale M-87 Target Rifle, 375
Parker-Hale Model 81 Classic African Bolt-Action Rifle, 343
Parker-Hale Model 81 Classic Bolt-Action Rifle, 343
Parker-Hale Model 1000 Bolt-Action Rifle, 343
Parker-Hale Model 1100 Lightweight Bolt-Action Rifle, 343
Parker-Hale Model 1100M African Magnum Bolt-Action Rifle, 343
Parker-Hale Model 1200 Super Bolt-Action Rifle, 343
Parker-Hale Model 1200 Super Clip Bolt-Action Rifle, 343
Parker-Hale Model 1300C Scout Bolt-Action Rifle, 343
Parker-Hale Model 2100 Midland Bolt-Action Rifle, 344
Parker-Hale Model 2600 Midland Bolt-Action Rifle, 344
Parker-Hale Model 2700 Midland Lightweight Bolt-Action Rifle, 344
Parker-Hale Model 2800 Midland Bolt-Action Rifle, 344
Parker-Hale Three-Band Volunteer Rifle, 419
Parker-Hale Volunteer Rifle, 419
Parker-Hale Whitworth Military Target Rifle, 419
Pennsylvania Full-Stock Rifle, 420
Perazzi DB81 Special O/U Shotgun, 391
Perazzi Grand American 88 Special O/U Shotgun, 391
Perazzi Mirage Special Sporting O/U Shotgun, 391
Perazzi Mirage Special Four-Gauge Skeet Shotgun, 391
Perazzi Mirage Special Skeet O/U Shotgun, 391
Perazzi MX3 Special Combo Shotgun, 391
Perazzi MX3 Special Single, O/U Shotguns, 391
Perazzi MX7 O/U Shotgun, 392
Perazzi MX8 Special Combo Shotgun, 391
Perazzi MX8 Special Single Shotguns, 391
Perazzi MX8/MX8 Special Trap, Skeet O/U Shotguns, 391
Perazzi MX12 Hunting O/U Shotgun, 392
Perazzi MX12C Hunting O/U Shotgun, 392
Perazzi MX20 Hunting O/U Shotgun, 392
Perazzi MX20C Hunting O/U Shotgun, 392
Perazzi TM1 Special Single Trap Shotgun, 402
Perazzi TMX Special Single Trap Shotgun, 402
Peregrine Falcon Auto Pistol, 290
Perugini-Visini Model Selous Double Rifle, 359
Perugini-Visini Victoria-D Double Rifle, 359
Perugini-Visini Victoria-M Double Rifle, 359
Peters Stahl PSP-07 Combat Compensator Pistol, 304
Phelps Eagle I Revolver, 320
Phelps Heritage I Revolver, 320
Phoenix Arms Raven Auto Pistol, 290
Piotti King Extra Double Shotgun, 398
Piotti King No. 1 Double Shotgun, 398
Piotti Lunik Double Shotgun, 398
Piotti Piuma Double Shotgun, 398
Pocket Police 1862 Percussion Revolver, 411

Precision Sports Model 600 Series Double Shotguns, 399
Precision Sports Model 640 Slug Gun Double Shotgun, 399
Precision Sports Model 640A Double Shotgun, 399
Precision Sports Model 640E Double Shotgun, 399
Precision Sports Model 640M Double Shotgun, 399
Precision Sports Model 645A Bi-Gauge Double Shotgun, 399
Precision Sports Model 645A Double Shotgun, 399
Precision Sports Model 645E Bi-Gauge Double Shotgun, 399
Precision Sports Model 645E Double Shotgun, 399
Precision Sports Model 645E-XXV Double Shotgun, 399
Precision Sports Model 650A Double Shotgun, 399
Precision Sports Model 650E Double Shotgun, 399
Precision Sports Model 655A Double Shotgun, 399
Precision Sports Model 655E Double Shotgun, 399
PSP-25 Auto Pistol, 290

Q

QFI Model LA380 Auto Pistol, 290
QFI Model LA380SS Auto Pistol, 290
QFI Model SA25 Auto Pistol, 290
QFI Plains Rider Single-Action Revolver, 320
QFI RP Series Revolvers, 310
QFI Tigress 25 Auto Pistol, 290
QFI Victory MC5 Auto Pistol, 291
QFI Western Ranger Revolver, 320
Quality Parts Shorty E-2 Carbine, 375
Quality Parts V Match Rifle, 375
Quality Parts XM15-E2 Target Model Rifle, 375
Queen Anne Flintlock Pistol, 408

R

Rahn Deer Series Bolt-Action Rifle, 344
Rahn Elk Series Bolt-Action Rifle, 344
Rahn Himalayan Series Bolt-Action Rifle, 344
Rahn Safari Series Bolt-Action Rifle, 344
Ram-Line Exactor Target Pistol, 304
Ranger Alpha Auto Pistol, 304
Ranger AMBO Auto Pistol, 291
Ranger EXT Auto Pistol, 291
Ranger G.I. Model Auto Pistol, 291
Ranger Lite Auto Pistol, 291
Ranger Supercomp Auto Pistol, 304
Reb 1860 Percussion Revolver, 410
Red Willow Armory Ballard No. 5 Pacific Rifle, 355
Red Willow Armory Ballard No. 8 Union Hill Rifle, 355
Red Willow Armory Ballard No. 1½ Hunting Rifle, 355
Remington 11-87 Magnum Turkey (SPS-T) Shotgun, 381
Remington 11-87 N.W.T.F. Auto Shotgun, 381
Remington 11-87 Premier Auto Shotgun, 380
Remington 11-87 Premier Skeet Auto Shotgun, 380
Remington 11-87 Premier Trap Shotgun, 381
Remington 11-87 Special Purpose Deer Gun, 381
Remington 11-87 Special Purpose Magnum Shotgun, 381
Remington 11-87 Special Purpose Synthetic Camo Shotgun, 381
Remington 11-87 Special Purpose Synthetic Shotgun, 380
Remington 11-87 Sporting Clays Auto Shotgun, 380
Remington 40-XB KS Target Rifle, 376
Remington 40-XB Rangemaster Target Centerfire Rifle, 376
Remington 40-XBBR KS Target Rifle, 376
Remington 40-XC KS National Match Course Rifle, 376
Remington 40-XR KS Rimfire Position Rifle, 376
Remington 40-XR Rimfire Custom Sporter, 369
Remington 90-T Super Single Shotgun, 402
Remington 541-T Bolt-Action Rifle, 369
Remington 552BDL Speedmaster Rifle, 363
Remington 572BDL Fieldmaster Pump Rifle, 364
Remington 700 ADL Bolt-Action Rifle, 344
Remington 700 ADL/LS Bolt-Action Rifle, 344
Remington 700 BDL Bolt-Action Rifle, 344
Remington 700 BDL Custom Grade Bolt-Action Rifle, 344
Remington 700 BDL Left-Hand Bolt-Action Rifle, 345
Remington 700 BDL Varmint Special Bolt-Action Rifle, 344
Remington 700 Camo Synthetic Bolt-Action Rifle, 345
Remington 700 Classic Bolt-Action Rifle, 345
Remington 700 Custom KS Mountain Rifle, 345
Remington 700 Mountain Rifle, 345
Remington 700 Safari Bolt-Action Rifle, 345
Remington 700 Safari Custom KS Bolt-Action Rifle, 344
Remington 700 Stainless Synthetic Bolt-Action Rifle, 344
Remington 700 Varmint Synthetic Bolt-Action Rifle, 344
Remington 870 20-Ga. Deer Gun Pump Shotgun, 384
Remington 870 Express Combo Pump Shotgun, 385
Remington 870 Express Pump Shotgun, 385
Remington 870 Express Rifle-Sighted Deer Gun Pump Shotgun, 384
Remington 870 Express Turkey Pump Shotgun, 385
Remington 870 Express Youth Pump Shotgun, 385
Remington 870 High Grade Pump Shotguns, 385
Remington 870 LW-20 Pump Shotgun, 384
Remington 870 Magnum-Turkey SPS-T Pump Shotgun, 385
Remington 870 Marine Magnum Pump Shotgun, 384
Remington 870 Special Field Pump Shotgun, 385
Remington 870 Special Purpose Deer Gun Pump Shotgun, 384
Remington 870 Special Purpose Magnum Pump Shotgun, 385
Remington 870 Special Purpose Synthetic Camo Pump Shotgun, 384
Remington 870 TC Trap Pump Shotgun, 384
Remington 870 Wingmaster Deer Gun Pump Shotgun, 384
Remington 870 Wingmaster Pump Shotgun, 384
Remington 870 Wingmaster Small Gauge Pump Shotguns, 384
Remington 870P Police Pump Shotgun, 405
Remington 1100 20-Ga. Deer Gun Shotgun, 381
Remington 1100 LT-20 Auto Shotgun, 381
Remington 1100 LT-20 Tournament Skeet Shotgun, 381
Remington 1100 LT-20 Youth Shotgun, 381
Remington 1100 Special Field Shotgun, 381
Remington 7400 Auto Carbine, 331
Remington 7400 Auto Rifle, 331
Remington 7600 Slide-Action Carbine, 335
Remington 7600 Slide-Action Rifle, 335
Remington Model Seven Bolt-Action Rifle, 345
Remington Model Seven Custom KS Bolt-Action Rifle, 345
Remington SP-10 Magnum Auto Shotgun, 381
Remington SP-10 Magnum Turkey Combo Shotgun, 381
Remington Texas Percussion Revolver, 410
Remington XP-100 Custom HB Long Range Pistol, 326
Remington XP-100 Silhouette Pistol, 304
Remington XP-100 Varmint Special Pistol, 326
Remington XP-100R KS Repeater Pistol, 326
Remington-Style Rolling Block Carbine, 355
Rizzini Boxlock Double Shotgun, 399
Rizzini Sidelock Double Shotgun, 399
Rogers & Spencer Percussion Revolver, 411
Rossi M92 SRC Saddle-Ring Carbine, 335
Rossi M92 SRS Puma Short Carbine, 335
Rossi Model 59 SA Pump Rifle, 364
Rossi Model 62 SA Pump Rifle, 364
Rossi Model 62 SAC Pump Carbine, 364
Rossi Model 65 SRC Saddle-Ring Carbine, 335
Rossi Model 68 Revolver, 311
Rossi Model 68/2 Revolver, 311
Rossi Model 88 Stainless Revolver, 311
Rossi Model 88/2 Stainless Revolver, 311
Rossi Model 515 Revolver, 311
Rossi Model 720 Revolver, 311
Rossi Model 851 Revolver, 311
Rossi Model 971 Revolver, 311
RPM XL Single Shot Pistol, 326
Ruger 10/22 Auto Sporter, 363
Ruger 10/22 Autoloading Carbine, 363
Ruger 22/45 Mark II Auto Pistol, 292
Ruger 44 Old Army Percussion Revolver, 411
Ruger 77/22 Rimfire Bolt-Action Rifle, 369
Ruger 77/22R Rimfire Bolt-Action Rifle, 369
Ruger 77/22RF Rimfire Bolt-Action Rifle, 369
Ruger 77/22RM Rimfire Bolt-Action Rifle, 369
Ruger 77/22RP Rimfire Bolt-Action Rifle, 369
Ruger 77/22RS Rimfire Bolt-Action Rifle, 369
Ruger 77/22RSM Rimfire Bolt-Action Rifle, 369
Ruger 77/22RSP Rimfire Bolt-Action Rifle, 369
Ruger Bisley Single-Action Revolver, 321
Ruger Bisley Small Frame Revolver, 321
Ruger Blackhawk Revolver, 321
Ruger BN31 Revolver, 321
Ruger BN34 Revolver, 321
Ruger BN34X Revolver, 321
Ruger BN36 Revolver, 321
Ruger BN36X Revolver, 321
Ruger BN41 Revolver, 321
Ruger BN42 Revolver, 321
Ruger BN45 Revolver, 321
Ruger BP-7 Percussion Revolver, 411
Ruger GP-100 Revolvers, 311
Ruger GP-141 Revolver, 311
Ruger GP-160 Revolver, 311
Ruger GP-161 Revolver, 311
Ruger GPF-330 Revolver, 311
Ruger GPF-331 Revolver, 311
Ruger GPF-340 Revolver, 311
Ruger GPF-341 Revolver, 311
Ruger GPF-830 Revolver, 311
Ruger GPF-831 Revolver, 311
Ruger GPF-840 Revolver, 311
Ruger GPF-841 Revolver, 311
Ruger K77/22RMP Rimfire Bolt-Action Rifle, 369
Ruger K77/22RSMP Bolt-Action Rifle, 369
Ruger K77/22RSP Rimfire Bolt-Action Rifle, 369
Ruger K-Mini-14/5 Rifle, 331
Ruger K-Mini-14/5R Ranch Rifle, 331
Ruger KBN34 Revolver, 321
Ruger KBN36 Revolver, 321
Ruger KBP-7 Percussion Revolver, 411
Ruger KGP-141 Revolver, 311
Ruger KGP-160 Revolver, 311
Ruger KGP-161 Revolver, 311
Ruger KGPF-330 Revolver, 311
Ruger KGPF-331 Revolver, 311
Ruger KGPF-340 Revolver, 311
Ruger KGPF-341 Revolver, 311
Ruger KGPF-830 Revolver 311
Ruger KGPF-831 Revolver, 311
Ruger KGPF-840 Revolver, 311
Ruger KGPF-841 Revolver, 311
Ruger KM77MKIIRP Bolt-Action Rifle, 346
Ruger KMK 4 Standard Auto Pistol, 292
Ruger KMK 6 Standard Auto Pistol, 292
Ruger KMK-514 Target Model Auto Pistol, 305
Ruger KMK-678 Target Model Auto Pistol, 305
Ruger KMK-678G Government Target Model Auto Pistol, 305
Ruger KMK-678GC Stainless Government Competition Model 22 Pistol, 305
Ruger KP85CMKII Automatic Pistol, 291
Ruger KP89DCC Automatic Pistol, 291
Ruger KP90C Automatic Pistol, 291
Ruger KP91DAC Decocker Automatic Pistol, 292
Ruger KP91DAO Double-Action Only Pistol, 292
Ruger KS45N Revolver, 321
Ruger KS47N Revolver, 321
Ruger KS47NH Revolver, 321
Ruger KS411N Revolver, 321
Ruger KSP-221 Revolver, 311
Ruger KSP-240 Revolver, 311
Ruger KSP-241 Revolver, 311
Ruger KSP-321 Revolver, 311
Ruger KSP-331 Revolver, 311
Ruger KSP-821 Revolver, 311
Ruger KSP-831 Revolver, 311
Ruger KSP-921 Revolver, 311
Ruger KSP-931 Revolver, 311
Ruger KSP-3231 Revolver, 311
Ruger KSRH-7 Revolver, 312
Ruger KSRH-9 Revolver, 312
Ruger M77 Mark II All-Weather Stainless Bolt-Action Rifle, 346
Ruger M77 Mark II Bolt-Action Rifle, 346
Ruger M77 Mark II Deluxe Bolt-Action Rifle, 345
Ruger M77 Mark II Magnum Bolt-Action Rifle, 346
Ruger M77EXPMKII Bolt-Action Rifle, 345
Ruger M77MKIILR Bolt-Action Rifle, 346
Ruger M77MKIIR Bolt-Action Rifle, 346
Ruger M77MKIIRL Bolt-Action Rifle, 346
Ruger M77MKIIRS Bolt-Action Rifle, 346
Ruger M77NV Varmint Rifle, 346
Ruger M77R Bolt-Action Rifle, 346
Ruger M77RL Ultra Light Bolt-Action Rifle, 346
Ruger M77RLS Ultra Light Carbine, 346
Ruger M77RS Bolt-Action Rifle, 346
Ruger M77RSI International Carbine, 346
Ruger M77RSM MkII Bolt-Action Rifle, 346
Ruger Mark II Bull Barrel Pistol, 305
Ruger Mark II Government Target Model Pistol, 305
Ruger Mark II Standard Auto Pistol, 292
Ruger Mark II Target Model Auto Pistol, 305
Ruger Mini Thirty Rifle, 331
Ruger Mini-14/5 Autoloading Rifle, 331
Ruger Mini-14/5 Rifle, 331
Ruger Mini-14/5R Ranch Rifle, 331
Ruger MK 4 Standard Auto Pistol, 292
Ruger MK 6 Standard Auto Pistol, 292
Ruger MK-514 Target Model Auto Pistol, 305
Ruger MK-678 Target Model Auto Pistol, 305
Ruger MK-678G Government Target Model Pistol, 305
Ruger No. 1 RSI International Rifle, 355
Ruger No. 1A Light Sporter Rifle, 355
Ruger No. 1B Single Shot Rifle, 355
Ruger No. 1H Tropical Rifle, 355
Ruger No. 1S Medium Sporter Rifle, 355
Ruger No. 1V Special Varminter Rifle, 355
Ruger P85 Mark II Automatic Pistol, 291
Ruger P85CMKII Automatic Pistol, 291
Ruger P85DCC Decocker Automatic Pistol, 291
Ruger P89 Double-Action Only Pistol, 291
Ruger P89DCC Automatic Pistol, 291
Ruger P90 Automatic Pistol, 291
Ruger P90 Decocker Automatic Pistol, 291
Ruger P90DAC Decocker Automatic Pistol, 291
Ruger P91 Decocker Automatic Pistol, 292
Ruger P91 Double-Action Only Pistol, 292
Ruger Red Label English Field O/U Shotgun, 392
Ruger Red Label O/U Shotgun, 392
Ruger Redhawk Revolver, 312
Ruger S45N Revolver, 321
Ruger S47N Revolver, 321
Ruger S411N Revolver, 321
Ruger Single-Six Revolver, 321
Ruger SP-101 Revolvers, 311
Ruger Stainless Government Competition Model 22 Pistol, 305
Ruger Super Blackhawk Hunter Revolver, 321
Ruger Super Blackhawk Revolver, 321
Ruger Super Redhawk Revolver, 312
Ruger Super Single-Six Convertible Revolver, 321
RWS Gamo AF-10 Air Pistol, 430
RWS Gamo CF-20 Air Rifle, 441
RWS Gamo Delta Air Rifle, 441
RWS Gamo Expomatic 2000 Air Rifle, 441
RWS Gamo Falcon Air Pistol, 430
RWS Gamo Hunter 440 Air Rifle, 441
RWS Gamo PR-45 Air Pistol, 430
RWS/Diana Model 5G Air Pistol, 429
RWS/Diana Model 6G, 6GS Air Pistols, 429
RWS/Diana Model 6M Match Air Pistol, 429
RWS/Diana Model 10 Match Air Pistol, 430
RWS/Diana Model 24 Air Rifle, 440
RWS/Diana Model 24C Air Rifle, 440
RWS/Diana Model 26 Air Rifle, 440
RWS/Diana Model 28 Air Rifle, 440
RWS/Diana Model 34 Air Rifle, 440
RWS/Diana Model 36 Air Carbine, 440
RWS/Diana Model 36 Air Rifle, 440
RWS/Diana Model 36 Muzzlebrake Air Rifle, 440
RWS/Diana Model 36S Air Rifle, 440
RWS/Diana Model 38 Air Rifle, 440
RWS/Diana Model 45 Air Rifle, 440
RWS/Diana Model 52 Air Rifle, 440
RWS/Diana Model 70 Match Air Rifle, 440
RWS/Diana Model 72 Air Rifle, 440
RWS/Diana Model 75 T01 Match Air Rifle, 440
RWS/Diana Model 75S T01 Air Rifle, 440
RWS/Diana Model 100 Match Air Rifle, 441

S

Safari Arms Enforcer Auto Pistol, 292
Safari Arms G.I. Auto Pistol, 292
Safari Arms Matchmasater Pistol, 305
Sako Deluxe Lightweight Bolt-Action Rifle, 347
Sako FiberClass Sporter Bolt-Action Rifle, 347
Sako Hunter Bolt-Action Rifle, 347
Sako Hunter Left-Hand Bolt-Action Rifle, 347
Sako Hunter Left-Hand Deluxe Bolt-Action Rifle, 347
Sako Hunter LS Bolt-Action Rifle, 347
Sako Mountain-Style Carbine, 347
Sako Safari Grade Bolt-Action Rifle, 347
Sako Super Deluxe Sporter Bolt-Action Rifle, 347
Sako Varmint Heavy Barrel Bolt-Action Rifle, 347
San Marco 10-Ga. Deluxe O/U Shotgun, 393
San Marco 10-Ga. O/U Shotgun, 393
San Marco 12-Ga. Wildfowler Deluxe O/U Shotgun, 392
San Marco 12-Ga. Wildfowler O/U Shotgun, 392
San Marco Field Special O/U Shotgun, 392

GUNDEX

Sauer 90 458 Safari Bolt-Action Rifle, 348
Sauer 90 Bolt-Action Rifle, 348
Sauer 90 Lux Bolt-Action Rifle, 348
Sauer 90 Supreme Bolt-Action Rifle, 348
Savage 24F O/U Combination Gun, 359
Savage 24F-12T Turkey Gun, 359
Savage 99C Lever-Action Rifle, 336
Savage 110CY Youth/Ladies Bolt-Action Rifle, 348
Savage 110F Bolt-Action Rifle, 348
Savage 110FNS Bolt-Action Rifle, 348
Savage 110FP Police Bolt-Action Rifle, 349
Savage 110FXP3 Bolt-Action Rifle, 348
Savage 110G Bolt-Action Rifle, 348
Savage 110GC Bolt-Action Rifle, 348
Savage 110GLNS Bolt-Action Rifle, 348
Savage 110GNS Bolt-Action Rifle, 348
Savage 110GV Varmint Bolt-Action Rifle, 348
Savage 110GXP3 Bolt-Action Rifle, 348
Savage 110WLE One of One Thousand Limited Edition, 348
Savage 112FV Varmint Bolt-Action Rifle, 348
Savage 112FVS Varmint Bolt-Action Rifle, 348
Savage 114CU Classic Ultra Bolt-Action Rifle, 348
Savage 116FCS Bolt-Action Rifle, 348
Savage 116FSS Bolt-Action Rifle, 348
Savage 312 Field O/U Shotgun, 393
Savage 312SC Sporting Clays O/U Shotgun, 393
Savage 312T Trap O/U Shotgun, 393
Second Model Brown Bess Carbine, 420
Second Model Brown Bess Musket, 420
Seecamp LWS 32 DA Pistol, 292
Sharp Model U-FP CO_2 Pistol, 430
Sharps 1874 Old Reliable Rifle, 355
Sharps Percussion Rifles, 420
Sharps, C., Arms New Model 1874 Old Reliable Rifle, 355
Sharps, C., Arms New Model 1875 Business Rifle, 355
Sharps, C., Arms New Model 1875 Carbine, 355
Sharps, C., Arms New Model 1875 Classic Sharps Rifle, 356
Sharps, C., Arms New Model 1875 Rifle, 355
Sharps, C., Arms New Model 1875 Saddle Rifle, 355
Sharps, C., Arms New Model 1875 Sporting Rifle, 355
Sharps, C., Arms New Model 1875 Target & Long Range Rifle, 356
Sheridan CO_2 Air Rifles, 441
Sheridan CO_2 F9 Air Rifle, 441
Sheridan CO_2 FBW9 Air Rifle, 441
Sheridan CO_2 FW9 Air Rifle, 441
Sheridan CO_2 Model FB9 Air Rifle, 441
Sheridan P68-AT Paint Ball Pistol, 443
Sheridan Paint Pistol, 443
Sheridan Pneumatic (Pump-Up) Air Rifles, 441
Sheridan Pneumatic Model C9 Air Rifle, 441
Sheridan Pneumatic Model CB9 Air Rifle, 441
Sheridan Pneumatic Model CBW9 Air Rifle, 441
Sheridan Pneumatic Model CW9 Air Rifle, 441
Sheridan VM68-Magnum Paint Ball Pistol, 443
Sheridan VM68 Paint Ball Pistol, 444
Sheriff Model 1851 Percussion Revolver, 411
Shiloh Sharps 1863 Military Carbine, 420
Shiloh Sharps 1863 Military Rifle, 420
Shiloh Sharps 1863 Sporting Rifle, 420
Shiloh Sharps 1874 Business Rifle, 356
Shiloh Sharps 1874 Carbine, 356
Shiloh Sharps 1874 Hartford Model Rifle, 356
Shiloh Sharps 1874 Long Range Express Rifle, 356
Shiloh Sharps 1874 Military Carbine, 356
Shiloh Sharps 1874 Military Rifle, 356
Shiloh Sharps 1874 Montana Roughrider Rifle, 356
Shiloh Sharps 1874 Saddle Rifle, 356
Shiloh Sharps 1874 Sporting Rifle No. 1, 356
Shiloh Sharps 1874 Sporting Rifle No. 3, 356
Shiloh Sharps The Jaeger Rifle, 356
SIG P-210-2 Auto Pistol, 292
SIG P-210-5 Target Auto Pistol, 292
SIG P-210-6 Auto Pistol, 292
SIG Sauer P220 "American" Auto Pistol, 293
SIG Sauer P225 DA Auto Pistol, 293
SIG Sauer P226 DA Auto Pistol, 293
SIG Sauer P228 DA Auto Pistol, 293
SIG Sauer P229 DA Auto Pistol, 293
SIG Sauer P230 DA Auto Pistol, 293
SKB Model 505 Deluxe O/U Shotgun, 392
SKB Model 505 Skeet Set O/U Shotgun, 392
SKB Model 505 Sporting Clays O/U Shotgun, 392
SKB Model 505 Trap, Skeet O/U Shotguns, 392
SKB Model 605 O/U Shotgun, 392
SKB Model 605 Skeet Set O/U Shotgun, 392
SKB Model 605 Sporting Clays O/U Shotgun, 392
SKB Model 605 Trap, Skeet O/U Shotguns, 392
SKB Model 885 Field Set O/U Shotgun, 392
SKB Model 885 Skeet O/U Shotgun, 392
SKB Model 885 Sporting Clays O/U Shotgun, 392
SKB Model 885 Trap Combo Shotgun, 392
SKB Model 885 Trap O/U Shotgun, 392
SKB Model 1300 Upland Mag Shotgun, 381
SKB Model 1900 Auto Shotgun, 381
SKB Model 1900 Trap Shotgun, 381
Smith & Wesson 4500 Series Pistols, 294
Smith & Wesson 5900 Series Auto Pistols, 295
Smith & Wesson Model 6904/6906 DA Pistols, 295
Smith & Wesson Model 10 M&P Heavy Barrel Revolver, 312
Smith & Wesson Model 10 M&P Revolver, 312
Smith & Wesson Model 13 H.B. M&P Revolver,312
Smith & Wesson Model 14 Full Lug Revolver, 312
Smith & Wesson Model 15 Combat Masterpiece Revolver, 312
Smith & Wesson Model 16 Full Lug Revolver, 312
Smith & Wesson Model 17 K-22 Full Lug Revolver, 312
Smith & Wesson Model 19 Combat Magnum Revolver, 313
Smith & Wesson Model 27 Revolver, 313
Smith & Wesson Model 29 Classic DX Revolver, 313
Smith & Wesson Model 29 Classic Revolver, 313
Smith & Wesson Model 29 Magnum Revolver, 313
Smith & Wesson Model 36 Chiefs Special Revolver, 313
Smith & Wesson Model 36-LS LadySmith Revolver, 313
Smith & Wesson Model 37 Airweight Revolver, 313
Smith & Wesson Model 38 Bodyguard Revolver, 314
Smith & Wesson Model 41 Target Pistol, 305
Smith & Wesson Model 49 Bodyguard Revolver, 314
Smith & Wesson Model 52 38 Master Auto Pistol, 305
Smith & Wesson Model 57 Revolver, 314
Smith & Wesson Model 60 3" Full Lug Revolver, 313
Smith & Wesson Model 60 Chiefs Special Stainless Revolver, 313
Smith & Wesson Model 60-LS LadySmith Revolver, 313
Smith & Wesson Model 63 22/32 Kit Gun Revolver, 314
Smith & Wesson Model 64 M&P Revolver, 314
Smith & Wesson Model 65 Revolver, 312
Smith & Wesson Model 65LS LadySmith Revolver, 314
Smith & Wesson Model 66 Stainless Combat Magnum Revolver, 314
Smith & Wesson Model 422 Auto Pistol, 293
Smith & Wesson Model 586 Distinguished Combat Magnum Revolver, 314
Smith & Wesson Model 617 Full Lug Revolver, 312
Smith & Wesson Model 622 Auto Pistol, 293
Smith & Wesson Model 625-2 Revolver, 314
Smith & Wesson Model 629 Classic DX Revolver, 313
Smith & Wesson Model 629 Classic Revolver, 313
Smith & Wesson Model 629 Magnum Revolver, 313
Smith & Wesson Model 632 Revolver, 315
Smith & Wesson Model 640 Centennial Revolver, 315
Smith & Wesson Model 642 Centennial Airweight Revolver, 315
Smith & Wesson Model 648 K-22 Masterpiece MRF Revolver, 312
Smith & Wesson Model 649 Bodyguard Revolver, 314
Smith & Wesson Model 651 Revolver, 315
Smith & Wesson Model 657 Revolver, 314
Smith & Wesson Model 686 Distinguished Combat Magnum Revolver, 314
Smith & Wesson Model 915 Auto Pistol, 294
Smith & Wesson Model 940 Centennial Revolver, 315
Smith & Wesson Model 1006 DA Auto Pistol, 295
Smith & Wesson Model 1066 DA Auto Pistol, 295
Smith & Wesson Model 1076 DA Auto Pistol, 295
Smith & Wesson Model 1076-NS DA Auto Pistol, 295
Smith & Wesson Model 1086 DA Auto Pistol, 295
Smith & Wesson Model 2206 Auto Pistol, 293
Smith & Wesson Model 2214 Sportsman Pistol, 294
Smith & Wesson Model 3913 LadySmith Pistol, 294
Smith & Wesson Model 3913-NL Auto Pistol, 294
Smith & Wesson Model 3913/3914 Auto Pistols, 294
Smith & Wesson Model 3953/3954 DA Pistols, 294
Smith & Wesson Model 4006 DA Auto Pistol, 295
Smith & Wesson Model 4013/4014, 4053/4054 Pistols, 294
Smith & Wesson Model 4026 DA Auto Pistol, 294
Smith & Wesson Model 4046 DA Auto Pistol, 295
Smith & Wesson Model 4506 Auto Pistol, 294
Smith & Wesson Model 4516 Auto Pistol, 294
Smith & Wesson Model 4566 DA Auto Pistol, 294
Smith & Wesson Model 4576 DA Auto Pistol, 294
Smith & Wesson Model 4586 DA Auto Pistol, 294
Smith & Wesson Model 5903 Auto Pistol, 295
Smith & Wesson Model 5904 Auto Pistol, 295
Smith & Wesson Model 5906 Auto Pistol, 295
Smith & Wesson Model 5926 Auto Pistol, 295
Smith & Wesson Model 5946 Auto Pistol, 295
Snake Charmer II Shotgun, 402
Spiller & Burr Percussion Revolver, 411
Splatmaster 102 Marking Pistol, 444
Splatmaster Rapide Comp Semi-Auto Paint Ball Pistol, 444
Splatmaster Rapide Semi-Auto Paint Ball Pistol, 444
Sportarms Model 66 Revolver, 315
Sportarms Model HS21S Single-Action Revolver, 321
Sportarms Model 213 Tokarev Pistol, 295
Springfield Armory 1911A1 Auto Pistol, 296
Springfield Armory 1911A1 Bullseye Wadcutter Pistol, 306
Springfield Armory 1911A1 Champion Pistol, 296
Springfield Armory 1911A1 Compact Pistol, 296
Springfield Armory 1911A1 Custom Carry Gun, 296
Springfield Armory 1911A1 Factory Comp Pistol, 296
Springfield Armory 1911A1 N.M. Hardball Pistol, 306
Springfield Armory 1911A2 S.A.S.S. Pistol, 326
Springfield Armory BM-59 Alpine Model Rifle, 332
Springfield Armory BM-59 Alpine Paratrooper Rifle, 332
Springfield Armory BM-59 Italian Model Rifle, 332
Springfield Armory BM-59 Nigerian Mark IV Rifle, 332
Springfield Armory BM-59 Rifle, 332
Springfield Armory Bobcat Auto Pistol, 297
Springfield Armory Custom P9 "World Cup" Pistol, 306
Springfield Armory Entry Level Wadcutter Pistol, 306
Springfield Armory Firecat Auto Pistol, 297
Springfield Armory Lynx Auto Pistol, 297
Springfield Armory M6 Scout Rifle/Shotgun, 359
Springfield Armory M-1A Bush Rifle, 331
Springfield Armory M-1A National Match Rifle, 331
Springfield Armory M-1A Rifle, 331
Springfield Armory M-1A Super Match Rifle, 331
Springfield Armory M-1A Super Match Rifle, 376
Springfield Armory M-21 Law Enforcement Rifle, 376
Springfield Armory P9 DA Auto Pistol, 296
Springfield Armory P9 Factory Comp Pistol, 296
Springfield Armory P9 Ultra LSP Long Slide Pistol, 296
Springfield Armory Panther Auto Pistol, 297
Springfield Armory Product Improved 1911A1 Defender Pistol, 296
Springfield Armory Trophy Master Competition Pistol, 306
Springfield Armory Trophy Master Distinguished Pistol, 306
Springfield Armory Trophy Master Expert Pistol, 306
Stallard JS-9MM Auto Pistol, 297
Star Firestar Auto Pistol, 297
Star Firestar M45 Auto Pistol, 297
Star Megastar 45 ACP Auto Pistol, 297
Star Model 31P Auto Pistol, 298
Star Model 31PK Auto Pistol, 298
Sterling HR81-17 Air Rifle, 442
Sterling HR81-20 Air Rifle, 442
Sterling HR81-22 Air Rifle, 442
Sterling HR83-17 Air Rifle, 442
Sterling HR83-20 Air Rifle, 442
Sterling HR83-22 Air Rifle, 442
Sterling Spring Piston Air Rifles, 442
Steyr A.U.G. Autoloading Rifle, 332
Steyr CO_2 Match Air Rifle Model 91, 442
Steyr CO_2 Match Pistol, 430
Steyr CO_2 Running Target Air Rifle, 442
Steyr-Mannlicher Luxus Model L, M, S Bolt-Action Rifles, 349
Steyr-Mannlicher Match UIT Rifle, 377
Steyr-Mannlicher Model M Professional Bolt-Action Rifle, 349
Steyr-Mannlicher Sporter Models SL, L, M, S, S/T Bolt-Action Rifles, 349
Steyr-Mannlicher SSG P-I Rifle, 376
Steyr-Mannlicher SSG P-III Rifle, 377
Steyr-Mannlicher SSG P-IV Rifle, 377
Stoeger/IGA Coach Gun Double Shotgun, 399
Stoeger/IGA Condor O/U Shotgun, 393
Stoeger/IGA Double Shotgun, 399
Stoeger/IGA Reuna Single Barrel Shotgun, 402
Stoeger/IGA Single Barrel Shotgun, 402
Sundance BOA Suto Pistol, 298
Sundance Model A-25 Auto Pistol, 298
Survival Arms AR-7 Explorer Rifle, 363

T

Tactical Response TR-870 Border Patrol Pump Shotgun, 405
Tactical Response TR-870 FBI Model Pump Shotgun, 405
Tactical Response TR-870 K-9 Model Pump Shotgun, 405
Tactical Response TR-870 Military Model Pump Shotgun, 405
Tactical Response TR-870 Patrol Model Pump Shotgun, 405
Tactical Response TR-870 Pump Shotguns, 405
Tactical Response TR-870 Urban Sniper Model Pump Shotgun, 405
Tanner 50 Meter Free Rifle, 377
Tanner 300 Meter Free Rifle, 377
Tanner Standard UIT Rifle, 377
Taurus Model 65 Revolver, 315
Taurus Model 66 Revolver, 315
Taurus Model 73 Sport REvolver, 315
Taurus Model 76 Revolver, 315
Taurus Model 80 Revolver, 315
Taurus Model 82 Heavy Barrel Revolver, 316
Taurus Model 83 Revolver, 316
Taurus Model 85 Revolver, 316
Taurus Model 85CH Revolver, 316
Taurus Model 86 Revolver, 316
Taurus Model 94 Revolver, 316
Taurus Model 96 Revolver, 316
Taurus Model 441/431 Revolvers, 316
Taurus Model 669 Revolver, 316
Taurus Model 689 Revolver, 316
Taurus Model 741 Revolver, 315
Taurus Model 941 Revolver, 317
Taurus Model PT-58 Auto Pistol, 298
Taurus Model PT-22/PT-25 Auto Pistols, 298
Taurus Model PT-92 Auto Pistol, 298
Taurus Model PT-92C Compact Auto Pistol, 298
Taurus Model PT-99 Suto Pistol, 298
Taurus Model PT-100 Auto Pistol, 299
Taurus Model PT-101 Auto Pistol, 299
Techni-Mec Model 610 O/U Shotgun, 393
Techni-Mec Model SPL 640 Folding O/U Shotgun, 393
Techni-Mec Model SR 690 Trap, Skeet O/U Shotguns, 393
Techni-Mec Model SR 692 EM O/U Shotgun, 393
Techni-Mec Model SR 692 Slug O/U Shotgun, 393
Techni-Mec Model SR 694 O/U Shotgun, 393
Techni-Mec Model SR 695 O/U Shotgun, 393
Techni-Mec Model SR 702 O/U Shotgun, 393
Techni-Mec Model SR 802 O/U Shotgun, 393
Texas Longhorn Arms Cased Set, 322
Texas Longhorn Arms Grover's Improved No. Five Revolver, 322
Texas Longhorn Arms Right-Hand Single-Action Revolver, 322
Texas Longhorn Arms Sesquicentennial Model Revolver, 322
Texas Longhorn Arms South Texas Army Limited Edition Revolver, 322
Texas Longhorn Arms Texas Border Special Revolver, 322
Texas Longhorn Arms "The Jezebel" Pistol, 326
Texas Longhorn Arms West Texas Flat Top Target Revolver, 322
Texas Paterson 1836 Percussion Revolver, 411
Texas Remington Revolving Carbine, 363
Theoben Classic Air Rifle, 442
Theoben Eliminator Air Rifle, 442
Theoben Grand Prix Air Rifle, 442
Theoben Imperator FT Air Rifle, 442
Theoben Imperator SLR 88 Air Rifle, 442
Thompson/Center Big Boar Rifle, 420
Thompson/Center Contender Carbine, 357
Thompson/Center Contender Carbine Survival System, 357
Thompson/Center Contender Carbine Youth Model, 357
Thompson/Center Contender Hunter Package, 327
Thompson/Center Contender Pistol, 327
Thompson/Center Hawken Rifle, 420
Thompson/Center High Plains Sporter Rifle, 420
Thompson/Center New Englander Percussion Shotgun, 425
Thompson/Center New Englander Rifle, 421
Thompson/Center Pennsylvania Hunter Carbine, 421
Thompson/Center Pennsylvania Hunter Rifle, 421

Thompson/Center Renegade Hunter Rifle, 421
Thompson/Center Renegade Rifle, 421
Thompson/Center Scout Pistol, 408
Thompson/Center Scout Rifle, 420
Thompson/Center Super 14 Contender Pistol, 306
Thompson/Center Super 16 Contender Pistol, 306
Thompson/Center TCR '87 Hunter Shotgun, 402
Thompson/Center TCR '87 Single Shot Rifle, 356
Thompson/Center Tree Hawk Carbine, 421
Thompson/Center Tree Hawk Percussion Shotgun, 425
Thompson/Center White Mountain Carbine, 421
Thunder Five Revolver, 317
Tikka Bolt-Action Rifle, 349
Tikka Model 412S Combo Gun, 359
Tikka Model 412S Double Rifle, 359
Tikka Model 412S Field Grade O/U Shotgun, 393
Tikka Model 412S Sporting Clays O/U Shotgun, 393
Tikka Premium Grade Bolt-Action Rifles, 349
Tikka Varmint/Continental Bolt-Action Rifle, 349
Tikka Whitetail/Battue Bolt-Action Rifle, 349
Timber Wolf Pump Rifle, 336
Tippmann Model 68-Special Paint Ball Gun, 444
Tippmann Model SL-68 II Pump Paint Ball Gun, 444
TMI Single Shot Pistol, 307
Traditions Buckskinner Carbine, 421
Traditions Frontier Carbine, 422
Traditions Frontier Rifle, 422
Traditions Frontier Scout Rifle, 422
Traditions Hawken Rifle, 422
Traditions Hawken Woodsman Rifle, 422
Traditions Hunter Rifle, 422
Traditions Pennsylvania Rifle, 422
Traditions Pioneer Pistol, 408
Traditions Pioneer Rifle/Carbine, 422
Traditions Trapper Pistol, 408
Traditions Trophy Rifle, 422
Traditions William Parker Pistol, 408
Trail Guns Kodiak 10-Ga. Percussion Shotgun, 425
Tryon Percussion Rifle, 423
Tryon Trailblazer Rifle, 422

U

Uberti 1st Model Dragoon Revolver, 412
Uberti 2nd Model Dragoon Revolver, 412
Uberti 3rd Model Dragoon Revolver, 412
Uberti 1861 Navy Percussion Revolver, 410
Uberti 1862 Pocket Navy Percussion Revolver, 411
Uberti 1866 Sporting Rifle, 336
Uberti 1866 Yellowboy Carbine, 336
Uberti 1873 Buckhorn Single-Action Revolver, 322
Uberti 1873 Carbine, 336
Uberti 1873 Cattleman Single Actions, 322
Uberti 1873 Sporting Rifle, 336
Uberti 1875 SA Army Outlaw Revolver, 322
Uberti 1890 Army Outlaw Revolver, 322
Uberti Henry Carbine, 336
Uberti Henry Rifle, 336
Uberti Henry Trapper Carbine, 336
Uberti Rolling Block Baby Carbine, 357
Uberti Rolling Block Target Pistol, 327
Uberti Santa Fe Hawken Rifle, 423
Ugartechea 10-Gauge Magnum Double Shotgun, 399
Ultra Light Arms Model 24 Bolt-Action Rifle, 350
Ultra Light Arms Model 24 Left-Hand Bolt-Action Rifle, 350
Ultra Light Arms Model 28 Bolt-Action Rifle, 350
Ultra Light Arms Model 20 Bolt-Action Rifle, 350
Ultra Light Arms Model 20 Left-Hand Bolt-Action Rifle, 350
Ultra Light Arms Model 20 REB Hunter's Pistol, 327
Ultra Light Arms Model 90 Muzzleloader Rifle, 423
Unique D.E.S. 32U Rapid Fire Match Pistol, 307
Unique D.E.S. 69U Target Pistol, 307
Unique Model 2000-U Match Pistol, 307
Uzi Pistol, 299

V

Voere Model 2115 Auto Rifle, 363
Voere Model 2155, 2165 Bolt-Action Rifles, 350
Voere Model 2185 Auto Rifle, 332
Voere Model 2185 Match Rifle, 377

W

Walker 1847 Percussion Revolver, 412
Walther CG90 Air Rifle, 442
Walther CP3 Air Pistol, 430
Walther GSP Match Pistol, 307
Walther GSP-C Match Pistol, 307
Walther LG90 Match Air Rifle, 442
Walther OSP Rapid-Fire Match Pistol, 307
Walther P-5 Auto Pistol, 299
Walther P-5 Compact Auto Pistol, 299
Walther P-38 Auto Pistol, 299
Walther P-88 Auto Pistol, 300
Walther PP Auto Pistol, 299
Walther PPK American Auto Pistol, 299
Walther PPK/S American Auto Pistol, 299
Walther TPH Auto Pistol, 300
Walther UIT Match Rifle, 377
Weatherby Athena Grade V O/U Shotgun, 394
Weatherby Athena Over/Under Shotguns, 394
Weatherby Athena Single Barrel Trap Shotgun, 402
Weatherby Classicmark I Bolt-Action Rifle, 351
Weatherby Classicmark II Bolt-Action Rifle, 351
Weatherby Euromark Bolt-Action Rifle, 351
Weatherby Fibermark Alaskan Bolt-Action Rifle, 350
Weatherby Fibermark Bolt-Action Rifle, 350
Weatherby Lazermark V Bolt-Action Rifle, 350
Weatherby Mark V Bolt-Action Rifle, 350
Weatherby Mark V Crown Custom Action Rifle, 350
Weatherby Mark V Safari Grade Custom Grade Rifles, 350
Weatherby Orion I Field O/U Shotgun, 394
Weatherby Orion II Field O/U Shotgun, 394
Weatherby Orion II Skeet O/U Shotgun, 394
Weatherby Orion II Sporting Clays O/U Shotgun, 394
Weatherby Orion II Trap Shotgun, 394
Weatherby Orion III Field O/U Shotgun, 394
Weatherby Orion Over/Under Shotguns, 394
Weatherby Orion Sporting Clays O/U Shotgun, 394
Weatherby Vanguard Classic I Bolt-Action Rifle, 351
Weatherby Vanguard Classic II Bolt-Action Rifle, 351
Weatherby Vanguard VGX Deluxe Bolt-Action Rifle, 351
Weatherby Vanguard Weatherguard Bolt-Action Rifle, 351
Weatherby Weathermark Alaskan Bolt-Action Rifle, 351
Weatherby Weathermark Bolt-Action Rifle, 351
Wesson Firearms Action Cup/PPC Revolvers, 308
Wesson Firearms Model 8-2 Revolver, 317
Wesson Firearms Model 9-2 Revolver, 317
Wesson Firearms Model 14-2 Revolver, 317
Wesson Firearms Model 15 Gold Series Revolver, 317
Wesson Firearms Model 15-2 Revolver, 317
Wesson Firearms Model 22 Revolver, 317
Wesson Firearms Model 22 Silhouette Revolver, 307
Wesson Firearms Model 32M Revolver, 317
Wesson Firearms Model 40 Silhouette Revolver, 308
Wesson Firearms Model 41V Revolver, 317
Wesson Firearms Model 44V Revolver, 317
Wesson Firearms Model 45V REvolver, 317
Wesson Firearms Model 322/7322 Target Revolver, 308
Wesson Firearms Model 445 Supermag Revolver, 308
Wesson Firearms Model 714-2 Revolver, 317
Wesson Firearms Model 738P Revolver, 317
White Systems Super 91 Percussion Rifle, 423
White Systems Whitetail Percussion Rifle, 423
Whitworth Safari Express Bolt-Action Rifle, 351
Wichita Classic Bolt-Action Rifle, 342
Wichita Classic Silhouette Pistol, 308
Wichita International Pistol, 308

Wichita Master Pistol, 327
Wichita Silhouette Pistol, 308
Wichita Silhouette Rifle, 377
Wichita Varmint Bolt-Action Rifle, 352
Wildey Automatic Pistol, 300
Wilkinson Linda Auto Pistol, 300
Wilkinson Sherry Auto Pistol, 300
Wilkinson Terry Carbine, 332
Winchester Model 70 DBM Bolt-Action Rifle, 352
Winchester Model 70 Featherweight Bolt-Action Rifle, 352
Winchester Model 70 Featherweight Classic Bolt-Action Rifle, 353
Winchester Model 70 Featherweight WinTuff Bolt-Action Rifle, 352
Winchester Model 70 Heavy Barrel Varmint Bolt-Action Rifle, 352
Winchester Model 70 Lightweight Bolt-Action Rifle, 353
Winchester Model 70 Sharpshooter Bolt-Action Rifle, 353
Winchester Model 70 SHB Bolt-Action Rifle, 352
Winchester Model 70 Sporter Bolt-Action Rifle, 352
Winchester Model 70 Sporter WinTuff Bolt-Action Rifle, 352
Winchester Model 70 SSM Sporter Bolt-Action Rifle, 352
Winchester Model 70 Stainless Bolt-Action Rifle, 352
Winchester Model 70 Super Express Magnum Bolt-Action Rifle, 353
Winchester Model 70 Super Grade Bolt-Action Rifle, 353
Winchester Model 94 Big Bore Side Eject Rifle, 337
Winchester Model 94 Ranger Side Eject Rifle, 336
Winchester Model 94 Side Eject Rifle, 336
Winchester Model 94 Trapper Side Eject Carbine, 336
Winchester Model 94 Wrangler Side Eject Carbine, 337
Winchester Model 1300 8-Shot Pistol Grip Security Shotguns, 405
Winchester Model 1300 Defender Pump Shotgun, 405
Winchester Model 1300 Ladies/Youth Pump Shotgun, 386
Winchester Model 1300 N.W.T.F. #1 Pump Shotgun, 386
Winchester Model 1300 Ranger Combo, Deer Gun Pump Shotguns, 385
Winchester Model 1300 Ranger Ladies/Youth Pump Shotgun, 386
Winchester Model 1300 Ranger Pump Shotgun, 386
Winchester Model 1300 Slug Hunter Deer Gun Pump Shotgun, 385
Winchester Model 1300 Slug Hunter Pump Shotgun, 385
Winchester Model 1300 Stainless Marine Pump Shotgun, 405
Winchester Model 1300 Turkey Gun Pump Shotgun, 385
Winchester Model 1300 Walnut Pump Shotgun, 385
Winchester Model 1300 Whitetails Unlimited Pump Shotgun, 385
Winchester Model 1400 Semi-Auto Shotgun, 382
Winchester Model 1400 Walnut Slug Hunter Shotgun, 382
Winchester Model 9422 Lever-Action Rifle, 364
Winchester Model 9422 Magnum Lever-Action Rifle, 364
Winchester Ranger Bolt-Action Rifle, 353

Z

Zanoletti, Pietro, Model 2000 Field O/U Shotgun, 394
Zoli, A., Rifle-Shotgun O/U Combo, 359
Zoli Model AZ-1900 Classic Bolt-Action Rifle, 353
Zoli Savana Double Rifle, 359
Zoli Silver Falcon O/U Shotgun, 394
Zoli Silver Fox Double Shotgun, 399
Zoli Woodsman O/U Shotgun, 394
Zoli Z90 Mono-Trap Shotgun, 402
Zoli Z90 Skeet O/U Shotgun, 394
Zoli Z90 Sporting Clays O/U Shotgun, 394
Zoli Z90 Trap O/U Shotgun, 394
Zouave Percussion Rifle, 423

Includes models suitable for several forms of competition and other sporting purposes.

A.A. ARMS AP9 AUTO PISTOL
Caliber: 9mm Para., 20-shot magazine.
Barrel: 5".
Weight: 3.5 lbs. **Length:** 11.8" overall.
Stocks: Checkered plastic.
Sights: Adjustable post front in ring, fixed open rear.
Features: Matte blue/black or nickel finish. Lever safety blocks trigger and sear. Fires from closed bolt. Introduced 1988. Made in U.S. Available from Kimel Industries.
Price: Matte blue/black $264.00
Price: Nickel finish $274.00
Price: Mini AP9 (3" barrel) $258.00
Price: Nickel finish $268.00
Price: Target AP9 (12" bbl., grooved forend), blue $279.00

A.A. Arms AP9

ACCU-TEK MODEL AT-9 AUTO PISTOL
Caliber: 9mm Para., 7-shot magazine.
Barrel: 3.2".
Weight: 28 oz. **Length:** 6.25" overall.
Stocks: Black checkered nylon.
Sights: Blade front, rear adjustable for windage; three-dot system.
Features: Stainless steel construction. Double action only. Firing pin block with no external safeties. Lifetime warranty. Introduced 1992. Made in U.S. by Accu-Tek.
Price: Satin stainless $270.00
Price: Black finish over stainless $275.00

Accu-Tek AT-9

Accu-Tek AT-40 Auto Pistol
Same as the Model AT-9 except chambered for 40 S&W. Introduced 1992.
Price: Stainless $270.00
Price: Black finish over stainless (AT-40B) $275.00

ACCU-TEK MODEL AT-380SS AUTO PISTOL
Caliber: 380 ACP, 5-shot magazine.
Barrel: 2.75".
Weight: 20 oz. **Length:** 5.6" overall.
Stocks: Grooved black composition.
Sights: Blade front, rear adjustable for windage.
Features: Stainless steel frame and slide. External hammer; manual thumb safety; firing pin block, trigger disconnect. Lifetime warranty. Introduced 1992. Made in U.S. by Accu-Tek.
Price: Satin stainless $170.00
Price: Black finish over stainless (AT-380SSB) $175.00

Accu-Tek AT-380SS

Accu-Tek Model AT-32SS Auto Pistol
Same as the AT-380SS except chambered for 32 ACP. Introduced 1990.
Price: Satin stainless $164.00
Price: Black finish over stainless (AT-32SSB) $169.00

Accu-Tek Model AT-25SS/AT-25AL Auto Pistols
Similar to the AT-380SS except chambered for 25 ACP with 7-shot magazine. Also available with aluminum frame and slide with 11-oz. weight (AT-25AL). Introduced 1991.
Price: Satin stainless $147.00
Price: Black finish over stainless (AT-25SSB) $152.00
Price: Satin aluminum (AT-25AL) $152.00

AMERICAN ARMS MODEL P-98 AUTO PISTOL
Caliber: 22 LR, 8-shot magazine.
Barrel: 5".
Weight: 25 oz. **Length:** 8⅛" overall.
Stocks: Grooved black polymer.
Sights: Blade front, rear adjustable for windage.
Features: Double action with hammer-block safety, magazine disconnect safety. Alloy frame. Has external appearance of the Walther P-38 pistol. Introduced 1989. Made in U.S. by American Arms, Inc.
Price: $219.00

American Arms P-98

CAUTION: PRICES CHANGE, CHECK AT GUNSHOP.

AMERICAN ARMS MODEL PX-22/PX-25 AUTO PISTOLS
Caliber: 22 LR or 25 ACP, 7-shot magazine.
Barrel: 2.85".
Weight: 15 oz. **Length:** 5.39" overall.
Stocks: Black checkered plastic.
Sights: Fixed.
Features: Double action; 7-shot magazine. Polished blue finish. Introduced 1989. Made in U.S. From American Arms, Inc.
Price: PX-22 . . . . $189.00
Price: PX-25 . . . . $199.00

American Arms PX-22

AMERICAN ARMS MODEL CX-22 DA AUTO PISTOL
Caliber: 22 LR, 8-shot magazine.
Barrel: 3⅓".
Weight: 22 oz. **Length:** 6⅓" overall.
Stocks: Checkered black polymer.
Sights: Blade front, rear adjustable for windage.
Features: Double action with manual hammer-block safety, firing pin safety. Alloy frame. Has external appearance of Walther PPK. Blue/black finish. Introduced 1990. Made in U.S. by American Arms, Inc.
Price: $189.00

AMERICAN ARMS MODEL PK22 DA AUTO PISTOL
Caliber: 22 LR, 8-shot magazine.
Barrel: 3.3".
Weight: 22 oz. **Length:** 6.3" overall.
Stocks: Checkered plastic.
Sights: Fixed.
Features: Double action. Polished blue finish. Slide-mounted safety. Made in the U.S. by American Arms, Inc.
Price: $199.00

American Arms Spectre

AMERICAN ARMS SPECTRE DA PISTOL
Caliber: 9mm Para., 30-shot; 40 S&W, 25-shot; 45 ACP, 30-shot magazine.
Barrel: 6".
Weight: 4 lbs., 8 oz. **Length:** 13.75".
Stocks: Black nylon.
Sights: Post front adjustable for windage and elevation, fixed U-notch rear.
Features: Triple action blowback fires from closed bolt; ambidextrous safety and decocking levers; matte black finish; magazine loading tool. For standard velocity ammunition only. From American Arms, Inc.
Price: 9mm, 40 S&W $389.00
Price: 45 ACP $409.00

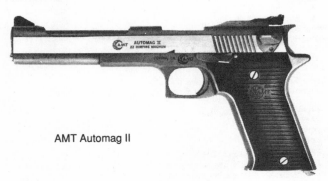

AMT Automag II

AMT AUTOMAG II AUTO PISTOL
Caliber: 22 WMR, 9-shot magazine (7-shot with 3⅜" barrel).
Barrel: 3⅜", 4½", 6".
Weight: About 23 oz. **Length:** 9⅜" overall.
Stocks: Grooved carbon fiber.
Sights: Blade front, Millett adjustable rear.
Features: Made of stainless steel. Gas-assisted action. Exposed hammer. Slide flats have brushed finish, rest is sandblast. Squared trigger guard. Introduced 1986. From AMT.
Price: $375.95

AMT AUTOMAG III PISTOL
Caliber: 30 Carbine, 9mm Win. Mag., 8-shot magazine.
Barrel: 6⅜".
Weight: 43 oz. **Length:** 10½" overall.
Stocks: Carbon fiber.
Sights: Blade front, Millett adjustable rear.
Features: Stainless steel construction. Hammer-drop safety. Slide flats have brushed finish, rest is sandblasted. Introduced 1989. From AMT.
Price: $629.99

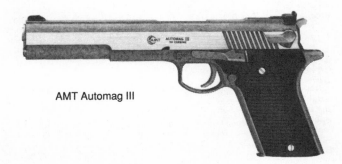

AMT Automag III

CAUTION: PRICES CHANGE, CHECK AT GUNSHOP.

AMT AUTOMAG IV PISTOL
Caliber: 10mm Magnum, 45 Winchester Magnum, 6-shot magazine.
Barrel: 6.5" (45), 8⅝" (10mm).
Weight: 46 oz. **Length:** 10.5" overall with 6.5" barrel.
Stocks: Carbon fiber.
Sights: Blade front, Millett adjustable rear.
Features: Made of stainless steel with brushed finish. Introduced 1990. Made in U.S. by AMT.
Price: **$675.95**

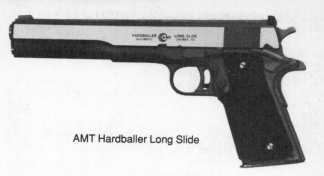

AMT Hardballer Long Slide

AMT 45 ACP HARDBALLER LONG SLIDE
Caliber: 45 ACP.
Barrel: 7". **Length:** 10½" overall.
Stocks: Wrap-around rubber.
Sights: Fully adjustable rear sight.
Features: Slide and barrel are 2" longer than the standard 45, giving less recoil, added velocity, longer sight radius. Has extended combat safety, serrated matte rib, loaded chamber indicator, wide adjustable trigger. From AMT.
Price: **$649.99**

AMT 45 ACP HARDBALLER
Caliber: 45 ACP.
Barrel: 5".
Weight: 39 oz. **Length:** 8½" overall.
Stocks: Wrap-around rubber.
Sights: Adjustable.
Features: Extended combat safety, serrated matte slide rib, loaded chamber indicator, long grip safety, beveled magazine well, adjustable target trigger. All stainless steel. From AMT.
Price: **$625.95**
Price: Government model (as above except no rib, fixed sights) . . **$575.95**

AMT Backup DAO

AMT BACKUP AUTO PISTOL
Caliber: 380 ACP, 5-shot magazine.
Barrel: 2½".
Weight: 18 oz. **Length:** 5" overall.
Stocks: Carbon fiber.
Sights: Fixed, open, recessed.
Features: Concealed hammer, blowback operation; manual and grip safeties. All stainless steel construction. Smallest domestically-produced pistol in 380. From AMT.
Price: **$256.95**

AMT Backup Double Action Only Pistol
Similar to the standard Backup except has double-action-only mechanism, enlarged trigger guard, slide is rounded ar rear. Has 6-shot magazine. Introduced 1992. From AMT.
Price: **$285.95**

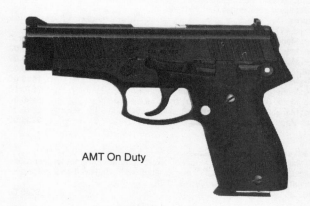

AMT On Duty

AMT ON DUTY DA PISTOL
Caliber: 9mm Para., 15-shot; 40 S&W, 11-shot; 45 ACP, 9-shot magazine.
Barrel: 4½".
Weight: 32 oz. **Length:** 7¾" overall.
Stocks: Smooth carbon fiber.
Sights: Blade front, rear adjustable for windage; three-dot system.
Features: Choice of DA with decocker or double action only. Inertia firing pin, trigger disconnector safety. Aluminum frame with steel recoil shoulder, stainless steel slide and barrel. Introduced 1991. Made in the U.S. by AMT.
Price: 9mm, 40 S&W **$529.95**
Price: 45 ACP **$569.99**

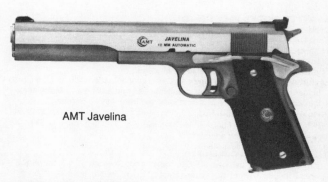

AMT Javelina

AMT JAVELINA 10MM PISTOL
Caliber: 10mm Auto, 8-shot magazine.
Barrel: 7".
Weight: 40 oz. **Length:** 10½" overall.
Stock: Wraparound rubber.
Sights: Blade front, Millett adjustable rear.
Features: All stainless construction. Brushed finish. Introduced 1989. From AMT.
Price: **$675.95**

ASTRA A70 AUTO PISTOL
Caliber: 9mm Para., 8-shot; 40 S&W, 6-shot magazine.
Barrel: 3.5".
Weight: 29.3 oz. **Length:** 6.5" overall.
Stocks: Checkered composition.
Sights: Blade front, rear adjustable for windage.
Features: All steel frame and slide. Serrated grip straps and trigger guard. Matte blue finish. Introduced 1992. Imported from Spain by Interarms.
Price: Blue, 9mm Para. **$415.00**
Price: Blue, 40 S&W **$440.00**
Price: Chrome, 9mm Para. **$440.00**
Price: Chrome, 40 S&W **$465.00**

CAUTION: PRICES CHANGE, CHECK AT GUNSHOP.

AUTO-ORDNANCE 1911A1 AUTOMATIC PISTOL
Caliber: 9mm Para., 38 Super, 9-shot; 10mm, 45 ACP, 7-shot magazine.
Barrel: 5".
Weight: 39 oz. **Length:** 8½" overall.
Stocks: Checkered plastic with medallion.
Sights: Blade front, rear adjustable for windage.
Features: Same specs as 1911A1 military guns—parts interchangeable. Frame and slide blued; each radius has non-glare finish. Made in U.S. by Auto-Ordnance Corp.
Price: 45 cal. $368.95
Price: 9mm, 38 Super $404.25
Price: 10mm (has three-dot combat sights, rubber wrap-around grips) $404.25
Price: 45 ACP General (Parkerized) $410.50

Auto-Ordnance ZG-51 Pit Bull Auto
Same as the 1911A1 except has 3½" barrel, weighs 36 oz. and has an over-all length of 7¼". Available in 45 ACP only; 7-shot magazine. Introduced 1989.
Price: $404.25

Auto-Ordnance 40 S&W 1911A1
Similar to the standard 1911A1 except has 4½" barrel giving overall length of 7¾", and weighs 37 oz. Has three-dot combat sight system, black rubber wrap-around grips, 8-shot magazine. Introduced 1991.
Price: $415.95

BERETTA MODEL 80 SERIES DA PISTOLS
Caliber: 380 ACP, 13-shot magazine (8-shot for M85F); 22 LR, 7-shot (M87).
Barrel: 3.82".
Weight: About 23 oz. (M84/85); 20.8 oz. (M87). **Length:** 6.8" overall.
Stocks: Glossy black plastic (wood optional at extra cost).
Sights: Fixed front, drift-adjustable rear.
Features: Double action, quick takedown, convenient magazine release. Introduced 1977. Imported from Italy by Beretta U.S.A.
Price: Model 84F (380 ACP) $525.00
Price: Model 84F wood grips $555.00
Price: Model 84F nickel finish $600.00
Price: Model 85F nickel finish, 8-shot $550.00
Price: Model 85F plastic grips, 8-shot $485.00
Price: Model 85F wood grips, 8-shot $510.00
Price: Model 87, 22 LR, 7-shot magazine, wood grips $490.00
Price: Model 87 Long Barrel, 22 LR, single action $510.00
Price: Model 89 Sport Wood, single action, 22 LR $735.00

Beretta Model 86
Similar to the 380-caliber Model 85 except has tip-up barrel for first-round loading. Barrel length is 4.33", overall length of 7.33". Has 8-shot magazine, walnut or plastic grips. Introduced 1989.
Price: $555.00

BERETTA MODEL 92FS PISTOL
Caliber: 9mm Para., 15-shot magazine.
Barrel: 4.9".
Weight: 34 oz. **Length:** 8.5" overall.
Stocks: Checkered black plastic; wood optional at extra cost.
Sights: Blade front, rear adjustable for windage.
Features: Double action. Extractor acts as chamber loaded indicator, squared trigger guard, grooved front- and backstraps, inertia firing pin. Matte finish. Introduced 1977. Made in U.S. and imported from Italy by Beretta U.S.A.
Price: With plastic grips $625.00
Price: With wood grips $645.00

Beretta Model 92FC Pistol
Similar to the Beretta Model 92FS except has cut down frame, 4.3" barrel, 7.8" overall length, 13-shot magazine, weighs 31.5 oz. Introduced 1989.
Price: With plastic grips $625.00
Price: With wood grips $645.00

Beretta Model 92F-EL Pistol
Same as the standard Model 92FS except has gold trim on the safety levers, trigger, magazine release and grip screws. Top of barrel has the Beretta logo with gold inlay, the slide has P. Beretta signature engraved in gold inlay. Figured walnut grips are contoured and have the Beretta logo deeply engraved. High polish blued finish on barrel, slide and frame. Introduced 1991.
Price: $700.00

Auto-Ordnance 1911A1

BABY EAGLE AUTO PISTOL
Caliber: 9mm Para., 40 S&W, 41 A.E.
Barrel: 4.37".
Weight: 33 oz. **Length:** 8.12" overall.
Stocks: High-impact black polymer.
Sights: Blade front, rear adjustable for windage; three-dot system.
Features: Double-action mechanism; polygonal rifling; ambidextrous safety. Introduced 1992. Imported by Magnum Research.
Price: 9mm Para., 40 S&W, 41 A.E. $569.00
Price: Conversion kit, 9mm Para. to 41 A.E. $239.00

Beretta Model 84F

Beretta Model 92FS

Beretta Model 92FCM Pistol
Similar to the Model 92FC except has thinner grip, straight 8-shot magazine. Weighs 30.8 oz., has 1.25" overall width. Introduced 1989.
Price: With plastic grips $625.00

Beretta Models 92FS/96 Centurion Pistols
Same as the Model 92FS and 96 except uses slide and barrel (4.3") of the Compact versions. Trijicon or three-dot sight systems. Plastic or wood grips. Introduced 1992.
Price: Model 92FS Centurion, three-dot sights, plastic grips $625.00
Price: As above, Trijicon sights, plastic grips $690.00
Price: Model 96 Centurion, three-dot sights, plastic grips $640.00

CAUTION: PRICES CHANGE, CHECK AT GUNSHOP.

Beretta Model 92D Pistol

Same as the Model 92FS except double action only and has bobbed hammer, no external safety. Introduced 1992.
Price: With plastic grips, three-dot sights **$585.00**
Price: As above with Trijicon sights **$650.00**

Beretta Model 92F Stainless Pistol

Same as the Model 92FS except has stainless steel barrel and slide, and frame of aluminum-zirconium alloy. Has three-dot sight system. Introduced 1992.
Price: **$755.00**
Price: Model 92F-EL Stainless (gold trim, engraved barrel, slide, frame, gold-finished safety-levers, trigger, magazine release, grip screws) . **$1,240.00**

Beretta Model 96 Auto Pistol

Same as the Model 92F except chambered for 40 S&W. Ambidextrous triple safety mechanism with passive firing pin catch, slide safety/decocking lever, trigger bar disconnect. Has 10-shot magazine; Compact version has 9-shot. Available with Trijicon or three-dot sights. Introduced 1992.
Price: Model 96F, plastic grips **$640.00**
Price: Model 96F Compact **$640.00**
Price: Model 96D, double action only, three-dot sights **$605.00**
Price: As above, Trijicon sights **$670.00**

BERETTA MODEL 950 BS AUTO PISTOL

Caliber: 22 Short, 6-shot; 25 ACP, 8-shot.
Barrel: 2.5".
Weight: 9.9 oz. (22 Short, 10.2 oz.) **Length:** 4.5" overall.
Stocks: Checkered black plastic.
Sights: Fixed.
Features: Single action, thumb safety; tip-up barrel for direct loading/unloading, cleaning. From Beretta U.S.A.
Price: Blue, 22, 25 . . . . **$180.00**
Price: Nickel, 22, 25 . . . . **$210.00**
Price: Engraved **$260.00**
Price: Matte blue, 25 ACP only **$150.00**

BERSA MODEL 83, 85 AUTO PISTOL

Caliber: 380 ACP, 13-shot magazine.
Barrel: 3.5".
Weight: 25.75 oz. **Length:** 6.6" overall.
Stocks: Walnut with stippled panels.
Sights: Blade front, notch rear adjustable for windage; three-dot system.
Features: Double action; firing pin and magazine safeties. Available in blue or nickel. Introduced 1989. Distributed by Eagle Imports, Inc.
Price: Blue **$324.95**
Price: Nickel **$383.95**
Price: Model 83 (as above, except 7-shot magazine), blue **$274.95**
Price: Model 83, nickel **$306.95**

BERSA MODEL 86 AUTO PISTOL

Caliber: 380 ACP, 13-shot magazine.
Barrel: 3.5".
Weight: 22 oz. **Length:** 6.6" overall.
Stocks: Wraparound textured rubber.
Sights: Blade front, rear adjustable for windage; three-dot system.
Features: Double action; firing pin and magazine safeties; combat-style trigger guard. Matte blue or satin nickel. Introduced 1992. Distributed by Eagle Imports, Inc.
Price: Matte blue **$366.95**
Price: Satin nickel **$399.95**

BRNO CZ 75 AUTO PISTOL

Caliber: 9mm Para., 15-shot magazine.
Barrel: 4.7".
Weight: 34.3 oz. **Length:** 8.1" overall.
Stocks: Polymer.
Sights: Square post front, rear adjustable for windage; three-dot system.
Features: Double action; blued finish. Imported from Czechoslovakia by Action Arms Ltd.
Price: Mil-spec black finish **$525.00**
Price: Matte blue **$549.00**
Price: High-polish blue **$569.00**

Beretta Model 92D

Beretta Model 21 Pistol

Similar to the Model 950 BS. Chambered for 22 LR and 25 ACP. Both double action. 2.5" barrel, 4.9" overall length. 7-round magazine on 22 cal.; 8-round magazine on 25 cal.; 22 cal. available in nickel finish. Both have walnut grips. Introduced in 1985.
Price: 22-cal. **$235.00**
Price: 22-cal., nickel finish **$260.00**
Price: 25-cal. **$235.00**
Price: 25-cal., nickel finish **$260.00**
Price: EL model, 22 or 25 . . . . **$285.00**
Price: Matte blue, 22 or 25 . . . . **$185.00**

BERSA MODEL 23 AUTO PISTOL

Caliber: 22 LR, 10-shot magazine.
Barrel: 3.5".
Weight: 24.5 oz. **Length:** 6.6" overall.
Stocks: Walnut with stippled panels.
Sights: Blade front, notch rear adjustable for windage; three-dot system.
Features: Double action; firing pin and magazine safeties. Available in blue or nickel. Introduced 1989. Distributed by Eagle Imports, Inc.
Price: Blue **$274.95**
Price: Nickel **$306.95**

Bersa Model 85

Bersa Model 86

BRNO CZ 83 DOUBLE-ACTION PISTOL
Caliber: 380 ACP, 13-shot magazine.
Barrel: 3.8".
Weight: 26.2 oz. **Length:** 6.8" overall.
Stocks: Checkered polymer.
Sights: Square post front, rear adjustable for windage; three-dot system.
Features: Double action; ambidextrous magazine release and safety. Polished and matte blue combination. Imported from Czechoslovakia by Action Arms Ltd.
Price: **$429.00**

BROWNING BDM DA AUTO PISTOL
Caliber: 9mm Para., 15-shot magazine.
Barrel: 4.73"
Weight: 31 oz. **Length:** 7.85" overall.
Stocks: Moulded black composition; checkered, with thumbrest on both sides.
Sights: Low profile removable blade front, rear screw adjustable for windage.
Features: Mode selector allows switching from DA pistol to "revolver" mode via a switch on the slide. Decocking lever/safety on the frame. Two redundant, passive, internal safety systems. All steel frame; matte black finish. Introduced 1991. Made in the U.S. From Browning.
Price: **$514.95**

BRNO CZ 85 Auto Pistol
Same gun as the CZ 75 except has ambidextrous slide release and safety-levers, contoured composition grips, matte finish on top of slide. Introduced 1986.
Price: Mil-spec black finish **$565.00**
Price: Matte blue **$585.00**
Price: High-polish blue **$619.00**

BRNO CZ 85 Combat Auto Pistol
Same as the CZ 85 except has combat-style trigger guard; mil-spec black finish only; lanyard ring hammer. Introduced 1992.
Price: **$685.00**

Browning BDM

Browning Micro Buck Mark

Browning Micro Buck Mark
Same as the standard Buck Mark and Buck Mark Plus except has 4" barrel. Available in blue or nickel. Has 16-click Pro Target rear sight. Introduced 1992.
Price: Blue **$224.95**
Price: Nickel **$259.95**
Price: Micro Buck Mark Plus **$269.95**

Browning Buck Mark Varmint

Browning Hi-Power HP

BROWNING BUCK MARK 22 PISTOL
Caliber: 22 LR, 10-shot magazine.
Barrel: 5½".
Weight: 32 oz. **Length:** 9½" overall.
Stocks: Black moulded composite with skip-line checkering.
Sights: Ramp front, Browning Pro Target rear adjustable for windage and elevation.
Features: All steel, matte blue finish or nickel, gold-colored trigger. Buck Mark Plus has laminated wood grips. Made in U.S. Introduced 1985. From Browning.
Price: Buck Mark, blue **$224.95**
Price: Buck Mark, nickel finish with contoured rubber stocks **$259.95**
Price: Buck Mark Plus **$269.95**

Browning Buck Mark Varmint
Same as the Buck Mark except has 9⅞" heavy barrel with .900" diameter and full-length scope base (no open sights); walnut grips with optional forend, or finger-groove walnut. Overall length is 14", weight is 48 oz. Introduced 1987.
Price: **$334.95**

BROWNING HI-POWER 9mm AUTOMATIC PISTOL
Caliber: 9mm Para., 13-shot magazine.
Barrel: 4²¹⁄₃₂".
Weight: 32 oz. **Length:** 7¾" overall.
Stocks: Walnut, hand checkered, or black Polyamide.
Sights: ⅛" blade front; rear screw-adjustable for windage and elevation. Also available with fixed rear (drift-adjustable for windage).
Features: External hammer with half-cock and thumb safeties. A blow on the hammer cannot discharge a cartridge; cannot be fired with magazine removed. Fixed rear sight model available. Ambidextrous safety available only with matte finish, moulded grips. Imported from Belgium by Browning.
Price: Fixed sight model, walnut grips **$509.95**
Price: 9mm with rear sight adj. for w. and e., walnut grips **$554.95**
Price: Mark III, standard matte black finish, fixed sight, moulded grips, ambidextrous safety **$469.95**
Price: Silver chrome, adjustable sight, Pachmayr grips **$564.95**

Browning Hi-Power HP-Practical Pistol
Similar to the standard Hi-Power except has silver-chromed frame with blued slide, wrap-around Pachmayr rubber grips, round-style serrated hammer and removable front sight, fixed rear (drift-adjustable for windage). Introduced 1991.
Price: **$549.95**

Browning BDA-380

BROWNING BDA-380 DA AUTO PISTOL
Caliber: 380 ACP, 13-shot magazine.
Barrel: 3¹³⁄₁₆".
Weight: 23 oz. **Length:** 6¾" overall.
Stocks: Smooth walnut with inset Browning medallion.
Sights: Blade front, rear drift-adjustable for windage.
Features: Combination safety and de-cocking lever will automatically lower a cocked hammer to half-cock and can be operated by right- or left-hand shooters. Inertia firing pin. Introduced 1978. Imported from Italy by Browning.
Price: Blue **$564.95**
Price: Nickel **$594.95**

Bryco Model 48

BRYCO MODEL 48 AUTO PISTOLS
Caliber: 22 LR, 32 ACP, 380 ACP, 6-shot magazine.
Barrel: 4".
Weight: 19 oz. **Length:** 6.7" overall.
Stocks: Polished resin-impregnated wood.
Sights: Fixed.
Features: Safety locks sear and slide. Choice of satin nickel, bright chrome or black Teflon finishes. Announced 1988. From Jennings Firearms.
Price: 22 LR, 32 ACP **$139.00**
Price: 380 ACP **$139.00**

Consult our Directory pages for the location of firms mentioned.

BRYCO MODEL 38 AUTO PISTOLS
Caliber: 22 LR, 32 ACP, 380 ACP, 6-shot magazine.
Barrel: 2.8".
Weight: 15 oz. **Length:** 5.3" overall.
Stocks: Polished resin-impregnated wood.
Sights: Fixed.
Features: Safety locks sear and slide. Choice of satin nickel, bright chrome or black Teflon finishes. Introduced 1988. From Jennings Firearms.
Price: 22 LR, 32 ACP **$109.95**
Price: 380 ACP **$129.95**

CALICO MODEL M-950 AUTO PISTOL
Caliber: 9mm Para., 50- or 100-shot magazine.
Barrel: 7.5".
Weight: 2.25 lbs. (empty). **Length:** 14" overall (50-shot magazine).
Stocks: Glass-filled polymer.
Sights: Post front adjustable for windage and elevation, fixed notch rear.
Features: Helical feed 50- or 100-shot magazine. Ambidextrous safety, static cocking handle. Retarded blowback action. Glass-filled polymer grip. Introduced 1989. From Calico.
Price: **$587.90**

Calico Model M-950

CALICO MODEL 110 AUTO PISTOL
Caliber: 22 LR, 100-shot magazine.
Barrel: 6".
Weight: 3.7 lbs. (loaded). **Length:** 17.9" overall.
Stocks: Moulded composition.
Sights: Adjustable post front, notch rear.
Features: Aluminum alloy frame; flash suppressor; pistol grip compartment; ambidextrous safety. Uses same helical-feed magazine as M-100 Carbine. Introduced 1986. Made in U.S. From Calico.
Price: **$248.90**

CENTURY MODEL P9R PISTOL
Caliber: 9mm Para., 14-shot magazine.
Barrel: 4.6".
Weight: 35 oz. **Length:** 8" overall.
Stocks: Checkered.
Sights: Blade front, rear drift adjustable for windage.
Features: Double action with hammer-drop safety. Polished blue finish. Comes with spare magazine. Imported from Hungary by Century International Arms.
Price: **$349.95**

CLARIDGE HI-TEC MODEL S, L, T PISTOLS
Caliber: 9mm Para., 18-shot magazine.
Barrel: 5" (S model); 7.5" (L model); 9.5" (T model).
Weight: 3 lbs., 2 oz. (L model). **Length:** 15.1" overall (L model).
Stocks: Moulded composition.
Sights: Adjustable post front in ring, open rear adjustable for windage.
Features: Aluminum or stainless frame. Telescoping bolt; floating firing pin. Safety locks the firing pin. Also available in 40 S&W and 45 ACP. Made in U.S. by Claridge Hi-Tec, Inc.
Price: Model S (5") **$419.50**
Price: Model L (7.5") **$466.50**
Price: Model T (target, 9.5") **$466.50**
Price: Model ZL-9 (7.5" with laser sight) **$776.50**
Price: Model ZT-9 (9.5" with laser sight) **$776.50**

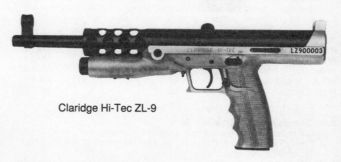

Claridge Hi-Tec ZL-9

COLT ALL AMERICAN MODEL 2000 DA AUTO
Caliber: 9mm Para., 15-shot magazine.
Barrel: 4.5".
Weight: 29 oz. (polymer frame); 33 oz. (aluminum frame). **Length:** 7.5" overall.
Stocks: Checkered polymer.
Sights: Ramped blade front, rear drift-adjustable for windage. Three dot system.
Features: Double-action only. Moulded polymer or aluminum frame, blued steel slide. Internal striker block safety. Introduced 1991. Made in U.S. by Colt's Mfg. Co., Inc.
Price: Polymer frame $575.00
Price: Aluminum frame . . . . **NA**

Colt All American 2000

COLT MODEL 1991 A1 AUTO PISTOL
Caliber: 45 ACP, 7-shot magazine.
Barrel: 5".
Weight: 38 oz. **Length:** 8.5" overall.
Stocks: Checkered black composition.
Sights: Ramped blade front, fixed square notch rear, high profile.
Features: Parkerized finish. Continuation of serial number range used on original G.I. 1911-A1 guns. Comes with one magazine and moulded carrying case. Introduced 1991.
Price: $499.95

COLT GOVERNMENT MODEL MK IV/SERIES 80
Caliber: 38 Super, 9-shot; 40 S&W, 45 ACP, 8-shot magazine.
Barrel: 5".
Weight: 38 oz. **Length:** 8½" overall.
Stocks: Rubber combat.
Sights: Ramp front, fixed square notch rear; three-dot system.
Features: Grip and thumb safeties and internal firing pin safety, long trigger.
Price: 45 ACP, blue $639.95
Price: 45 ACP, stainless $679.95
Price: 45 ACP, bright stainless $749.95
Price: 38 Super, blue $649.95
Price: 38 Super, stainless $684.95
Price: 38 Super, bright stainless $754.95
Price: 40 S&W, stainless $679.95

Colt Model 1991 A1

Colt 10mm Delta Elite
Similar to the Government Model except chambered for 10mm auto cartridge. Has three-dot high profile front and rear combat sights, rubber combat stocks with Delta medallion, internal firing pin safety, and new recoil spring/buffer system. Introduced 1987.
Price: Blue $704.95
Price: STS $714.95
Price: BSTS $784.95

Colt Combat Elite MK IV/Series 80
Similar to the Government Model except in 45 ACP only, has stainless frame with ordnance steel slide and internal parts. High profile front, rear sights with three-dot system, extended grip safety, beveled magazine well, rubber combat stocks. Introduced 1986.
Price: $774.95

Colt Government Model

COLT DOUBLE EAGLE MKII/SERIES 90 DA PISTOL
Caliber: 10mm, 40 S&W, 45 ACP, 8-shot magazine.
Barrel: 4½", 5".
Weight: 39 ozs. **Length:** 8½" overall.
Stocks: Black checkered Xenoy thermoplastic.
Sights: Blade front, rear adjustable for windage. High profile three-dot system. Colt Accro adjustable sight optional.
Features: Made of stainless steel with matte finish. Checkered and curved extended trigger guard, wide steel trigger; decocking lever on left side; traditional magazine release; grooved frontstrap; bevelled magazine well; extended grip guard; rounded, serrated combat-style hammer. Announced 1989.
Price: $695.95
Price: As above, except Accro adjustable sight $725.95
Price: 10mm $715.95
Price: 10mm, Accro sight $745.95
Price: Combat Comm., 45, 4½" bbl. $695.95
Price: Combat Comm., 40 S&W, 4½" bbl. $695.95

Colt Double Eagle MkII

Colt Double Eagle Officer's ACP
Similar to the regular Double Eagle except 45 ACP only, 3½" barrel, 34 oz., 7¼" overall length. Has 5¼" sight radius. Also offered in Lightweight version weighing 25 oz. Introduced 1991.
Price: Standard or Lightweight $695.95

CAUTION: PRICES CHANGE, CHECK AT GUNSHOP.

COLT GOVERNMENT MODEL 380

Caliber: 380 ACP, 7-shot magazine.
Barrel: 3¼".
Weight: 21¾ oz. **Length:** 6" overall.
Stocks: Checkered composition.
Sights: Ramp front, square notch rear, fixed.
Features: Scaled-down version of the 1911A1 Colt G.M. Has thumb and internal firing pin safeties. Introduced 1983.
Price: Blue **$419.95**
Price: Nickel **$469.95**
Price: Stainless **$449.95**
Price: Pocketlite 380, blue **$419.95**

Colt Government Pocketlite

Colt Mustang Plus II

Similar to the 380 Government Model except has the shorter barrel and slide of the Mustang. Introduced 1988.
Price: Blue **$419.95**
Price: Stainless **$449.95**

Colt Mustang 380, Mustang Pocketlite

Similar to the standard 380 Government Model. Mustang has steel frame (18.5 oz.), Pocketlite has aluminum alloy (12.5 oz.). Both are ½" shorter than 380 G.M., have 2¾" barrel. Introduced 1987.
Price: Mustang 380, blue **$419.95**
Price: As above, nickel **$469.95**
Price: As above, stainless **$449.95**
Price: Mustang Pocketlite, blue **$419.95**
Price: Mustang Pocketlite STS/N **$449.95**

Colt Combat Commander

COLT OFFICER'S ACP MK IV/SERIES 80

Caliber: 45 ACP, 6-shot magazine.
Barrel: 3½".
Weight: 34 oz. (steel frame); 24 oz. (alloy frame). **Length:** 7¼" overall.
Stocks: Rubber combat.
Sights: Ramp blade front with white dot, square notch rear with two white dots.
Features: Trigger safety lock (thumb safety), grip safety, firing pin safety; long trigger; flat mainspring housing. Also available with lightweight alloy frame and in stainless steel. Introduced 1985.
Price: Blue **$639.95**
Price: L.W., matte finish **$639.95**
Price: Stainless **$679.95**
Price: Bright stainless **$749.95**

COLT COMBAT COMMANDER AUTO PISTOL

Caliber: 38 Super, 9-shot; 45 ACP, 8-shot.
Barrel: 4¼".
Weight: 36 oz. **Length:** 7¾" overall.
Stocks: Rubber combat.
Sights: Fixed, glare-proofed blade front, square notch rear; three-dot system.
Features: Long trigger; arched housing; grip and thumb safeties.
Price: 45, blue **$639.95**
Price: 45, stainless **$689.95**
Price: 38 Super, blue **$649.95**

Coonan 357 Magnum

Colt Lightweight Commander MK IV/Series 80

Same as Commander except high strength aluminum alloy frame, rubber combat grips, weight 27½ oz. 45 ACP only.
Price: Blue **$639.95**

COONAN 357 MAGNUM PISTOL

Caliber: 357 Mag., 7-shot magazine.
Barrel: 5".
Weight: 42 oz. **Length:** 8.3" overall.
Stocks: Smooth walnut.
Sights: Open, adjustable.
Features: Unique barrel hood improves accuracy and reliability. Many parts interchange with Colt autos. Has grip, hammer, half-cock safeties. From Coonan Arms.
Price: Model B (linkless barrel, interchangeable ramp front sight, new rear sight) **$699.00**

Daewoo DP51

DAEWOO DP51 AUTO PISTOL

Caliber: 9mm Para., 13-shot magazine.
Barrel: 4.1".
Weight: 28.2 oz. **Length:** 7.48" overall.
Stocks: Checkered composition.
Sights: Blade front, square notch rear drift adjustable for windage.
Features: Patented tri-action mechanism. Ambidextrous manual safety and magazine catch, half-cock and firing pin block. Alloy frame, squared trigger guard. Matte black finish. Introduced 1991. Imported from Korea by Firstshot.
Price: **$499.99**

DAVIS P-32 AUTO PISTOL
Caliber: 32 ACP, 6-shot magazine.
Barrel: 2.8".
Weight: 22 oz. **Length:** 5.4" overall.
Stocks: Laminated wood.
Sights: Fixed.
Features: Choice of black Teflon or chrome finish. Announced 1986. Made in U.S. by Davis Industries.
Price: **$87.50**

DAVIS P-380 AUTO PISTOL
Caliber: 380 ACP, 5-shot magazine.
Barrel: 2.8".
Weight: 22 oz. **Length:** 5.4" overall.
Stocks: Black composition.
Sights: Fixed.
Features: Choice of chrome or black Teflon finish. Introduced 1991. Made in U.S. by Davis Industries.
Price: **$98.00**

Davis P-32

Desert Eagle Magnum

D Max Auto

Desert Industries Double Deuce

E.A.A. EUROPEAN MODEL AUTO PISTOLS
Caliber: 22 LR, 10-shot; 32 ACP or 380 ACP, 7-shot magazine.
Barrel: 3.88".
Weight: 26 oz. **Length:** 7⅜" overall.
Stocks: European hardwood.
Sights: Fixed blade front, rear drift-adjustable for windage.
Features: Chrome or blue finish; magazine, thumb and firing pin safeties; external hammer; safety-lever takedown. Imported from Italy by European American Armory.
Price: Blue **$225.00**
Price: Blue/chrome **$249.00**
Price: Chrome **$249.00**
Price: Blue/gold **$260.00**
Price: Ladies Model **$299.00**

D MAX AUTO PISTOL
Caliber: 9mm Para., 10mm Auto, 40 S&W, 45 ACP, 30-shot magazine.
Barrel: 6" (8", 10" optional).
Weight: 5 lbs. **Length:** 13.75" overall.
Stocks: Smooth walnut grip and forend.
Sights: Post front, open rear adjustable for windage and elevation.
Features: Blowback semi-auto with trigger-block safety. Fires from closed bolt. Side-feed magazine. Max-Coat finish. Drilled and tapped for scope base. Made in the U.S. by D Max Industries.
Price: **$539.00**

DESERT EAGLE MAGNUM PISTOL
Caliber: 357 Mag., 9-shot; 41 Mag., 44 Mag., 8-shot; 50 Magnum, 7-shot.
Barrel: 6", 10", 14" interchangeable.
Weight: 357 Mag.—52 oz. (alloy), 62 oz. (steel); 41 Mag., 44 Mag.—56 oz. (alloy), 66.9 oz. (stainless). **Length:** 10¼" overall (6" bbl.).
Stocks: Wraparound soft rubber.
Sights: Blade on ramp front, combat-style rear. Adjustable available.
Features: Rotating three-lug bolt; ambidextrous safety; combat-style trigger guard; adjustable trigger optional. Military epoxy finish. Satin, bright nickel, hard chrome, polished and blued finishes available. Imported from Israel by Magnum Research, Inc.
Price: 357, 6" bbl., standard pistol **$789.00**
Price: As above, alloy frame **$789.00**
Price: As above, stainless steel frame **$839.00**
Price: 41 Mag., 6", standard pistol **$799.00**
Price: 41 Mag., alloy frame **$799.00**
Price: 41 Mag., stainless steel frame **$849.00**
Price: 44 Mag., 6", standard pistol **$839.00**
Price: As above, alloy frame **$839.00**
Price: As above, stainless steel frame **$889.00**
Price: 50 Magnum, 6" bbl., standarad pistol **$1,189.00**

DESERT INDUSTRIES WAR EAGLE PISTOL
Caliber: 9mm Para., 14-shot magazine; 10mm, 13-shot; 40 S&W, 14-shot; 45 ACP, 12-shot.
Barrel: 4".
Weight: 35.5 oz. **Length:** 7.5" overall.
Stocks: Rosewood.
Sights: Fixed.
Features: Double action; matte-finished stainless steel; slide mounted ambidextrous safety. Announced 1986. From Desert Industries, Inc.
Price: **$795.00**

DESERT INDUSTRIES DOUBLE DEUCE, TWO BIT SPECIAL PISTOLS
Caliber: 22 LR, 6-shot; 25 ACP, 5-shot.
Barrel: 2½".
Weight: 15 oz. **Length:** 5½" overall.
Stocks: Rosewood.
Sights: Special order.
Features: Double action; stainless steel construction with matte finish; ambidextrous slide-mounted safety. From Desert Industries, Inc.
Price: 22 . . . . **$399.95**
Price: 25 (Two-Bit Special) **$399.95**

E.A.A. European 380/DA Pistol
Similar to the standard European except in 380 ACP only, with double-action trigger mechanism. Available in blue, chrome or blue/chrome finish. Introduced 1992. From European American Armory.
Price: Blue **$275.00**
Price: Chrome **$299.00**
Price: Blue/chrome **$299.00**

E.A.A. Witness Sport

ERMA SPORTING PISTOL MODEL ESP 85A
Caliber: 22 LR, 8-shot; 32 S&W Long, 5-shot.
Barrel: 6".
Weight: 39.9 oz. **Length:** 10" overall.
Stocks: Checkered walnut with thumbrest. Adjustable target stocks optional.
Sights: Interchangeable blade front, micro. rear adjustable for windage and elevation.
Features: Interchangeable caliber conversion kit available; adjustable trigger, trigger stop. Imported from Germany by Precision Sales Int'l. Introduced 1988.
Price: 22 LR **$1,228.00**
Price: 32 S&W Long **$1,284.00**
Price: 22 LR, chrome **$1,449.00**
Price: 22 LR conversion unit **$689.00**
Price: 32 S&W conversion unit **$746.00**

FEG GKK-92C AUTO PISTOL
Caliber: 9mm Para., 14-shot magazine.
Barrel: 4".
Weight: 34 oz. **Length:** 7.33" overall.
Stocks: Hand-checkered walnut.
Sights: Blade front, rear adjustable for windage.
Features: Double action; slide-mounted safety; hooked trigger guard; finger-grooved frontstrap. Polished blue finish. Introduced 1992. Imported from Hungary by K.B.I., Inc.
Price: **$379.00**
Price: MBK-9HP (as above except 4.67" bbl., smooth frontstrap) . . **$349.00**
Price: MBK-9HPC (compact version) **$359.00**

FEG PJK-9HP AUTO PISTOL
Caliber: 9mm Para., 13-shot magazine.
Barrel: 4.75".
Weight: 32 oz. **Length:** 8" overall.
Stocks: Hand-checkered walnut.
Sights: Blade front, rear adjustable for windage.
Features: Single action; polished blue or hard chrome finish; rounded combat-style serrated hammer. Comes with two magazines and cleaning rod. Imported from Hungary by K.B.I., Inc.
Price: Blue **$329.00**
Price: Hard chrome **$435.00**

FEG PMK-380

E.A.A. WITNESS DA AUTO PISTOL
Caliber: 9mm Para., 16-shot magazine; 40 S&W, 12-shot magazine; 41 Action Express, 11-shot magazine; 45 ACP, 10-shot magazine.
Barrel: 4.72".
Weight: 35.33 oz. **Length:** 8.10" overall.
Stocks: Checkered rubber.
Sights: Undercut blade front, open rear adjustable for windage.
Features: Double-action trigger system; squared-off trigger guard; frame-mounted safety. Introduced 1991. Imported from Italy by European American Armory.
Price: 9mm, blue **$550.00**
Price: 9mm, satin chrome **$595.00**
Price: 9mm, blue slide, chrome frame **$595.00**
Price: 9mm Compact, blue, 13-shot **$550.00**
Price: As above, blue slide, chrome frame, or all-chrome **$595.00**
Price: 40 S&W or 41 A.E., blue **$595.00**
Price: As above, blue slide, chrome frame, or all-chrome **$650.00**
Price: 40 S&W or 41 A.E. Compact, 8-shot, blue **$595.00**
Price: As above, blue slide, chrome frame, or all-chrome **$650.00**
Price: 45 ACP, blue **$695.00**
Price: As above, blue slide, chrome frame, or all-chrome **$750.00**
Price: 45 ACP Compact, 8-shot, blue **$695.00**
Price: As above, blue slide, chrome frame or all-chrome **$750.00**
Price: 9mm/40 S&W Combo, blue, compact or full size **$825.00**
Price: As above, blue/chrome, compact or full size **$875.00**
Price: 9mm/40 S&W/41 A.E. Tri Caliber, blue, compact or full size . **$995.00**
Price: As above, blue/chrome **$1,050.00**
Price: 9mm or 40 S&W Carry Comp, blue **$775.00**
Price: As above, blue/chrome **$825.00**
Price: As above, 45 ACP **$1,010.00**

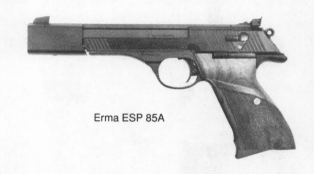

Erma ESP 85A

FEG PJK-9HP

FEG PMK-380 AUTO PISTOL
Caliber: 380 ACP, 7-shot magazine.
Barrel: 4".
Weight: 21 oz. **Length:** 7" overall.
Stocks: Checkered black nylon with thumbrest.
Sights: Blade front, rear adjustable for windage.
Features: Double action; anodized aluminum frame, polished blue slide. Comes with two magazines, cleaning rod. Introduced 1992. Imported from Hungary by K.B.I., Inc.
Price: **$199.00**

CAUTION: PRICES CHANGE, CHECK AT GUNSHOP.

Glock 17

GLOCK 17 AUTO PISTOL
Caliber: 9mm Para., 17-shot magazine.
Barrel: 4.49".
Weight: 21.9 oz. (without magazine). **Length:** 7.28" overall.
Stocks: Black polymer.
Sights: Dot on front blade, white outline rear adjustable for windage.
Features: Polymer frame, steel slide; double-action trigger with "Safe Action" system; mechanical firing pin safety, drop safety; simple takedown without tools; locked breech, recoil operated action. Adopted by Austrian armed forces 1983. NATO approved 1984. Imported from Austria by Glock, Inc.
Price: With extra magazine, magazine loader, cleaning kit **$579.95**
Price: Model 17L (6" barrel) **$768.25**

Glock 19 Auto Pistol
Similar to the Glock 17 except has a 4" barrel, giving an overall length of 6.85" and weight of 20.99 oz. Magazine capacity is 15 rounds. Fixed or adjustable rear sight. Introduced 1988.
Price: **$579.95**

Glock 20 10mm Auto Pistol
Similar to the Glock Model 17 except chambered for 10mm Automatic cartridge. Barrel length is 4.60", overall length is 7.59", and weight is 26.3 oz. (without magazine). Magazine capacity is 15 rounds. Fixed or adjustable rear sight. Comes with an extra magazine, magazine loader, cleaning rod and brush. Introduced 1990. Imported from Austria by Glock, Inc.
Price: **$638.49**

Glock 21 Auto Pistol
Similar to the Glock 17 except chambered for 45 ACP, 13-shot magazine. Overall length is 7.59", weight is 25.2 oz. (without magazine). Fixed or adjustable rear sight. Introduced 1991.
Price: **$638.49**

Glock 23 Auto Pistol
Similar to the Glock 19 except chambered for 40 S&W, 13-shot magazine. Overall length is 6.85", weight is 20.6 oz. (without magazine). Fixed or adjustable rear sight. Introduced 1990.
Price: **$579.95**

Glock 22 Auto Pistol
Similar to the Glock 17 except chambered for 40 S&W, 15-shot magazine. Overall length is 7.28", weight is 22.3 oz. (without magazine). Fixed or adjustable rear sight. Introduced 1990.
Price: **$579.95**

GRENDEL P-12 AUTO PISTOL
Caliber: 380 ACP, 11-shot magazine.
Barrel: 3".
Weight: 13 oz. **Length:** 5.3" overall.
Stocks: Checkered DuPont ST-800 polymer.
Sights: Fixed.
Features: Double action only with inertia safety hammer system. All steel frame; grip forms magazine well and trigger guard. Introduced 1992. Made in U.S. by Grendel, Inc.
Price: Blue **$175.00**
Price: Electroless nickel **$195.00**

Glock 23

CONSULT
SHOOTER'S MARKETPLACE
Page 225, This Issue

Grendel P-12

GRENDEL P-30 AUTO PISTOL
Caliber: 22 WMR, 30-shot magazine.
Barrel: 5", 8".
Weight: 21 oz. (5" barrel). **Length:** 8.5" overall (5" barrel).
Stocks: Checkered Zytel.
Sights: Blade front, fixed rear.
Features: Blowback action with fluted chamber; ambidextrous safety, reversible magazine catch. Scope mount available. Introduced 1990.
Price: With 5" barrel **$225.00**
Price: With removable muzzlebrake (Model P-30M) **$235.00**
Price: With 8" barrel (Model P-30L) **$280.00**

GRENDEL P-31 AUTO PISTOL
Caliber: 22 WMR, 30-shot magazine.
Barrel: 11".
Weight: 48 oz. **Length:** 17.5" overall.
Stocks: Checkered black Zytel grip and forend.
Sights: Blade front adjustable for windage and elevation, fixed rear.
Features: Blowback action with fluted chamber. Ambidextrous safety. Matte black finish. Muzzlebrake. Scope mount optional. Introduced 1991. Made in the U.S. by Grendel, Inc.
Price: **$345.00**

Grendel P-31

CAUTION: PRICES CHANGE, CHECK AT GUNSHOP.

HAMMERLI MODEL 212 AUTO PISTOL
Caliber: 22 LR, 8-shot magazine.
Barrel: 4.9".
Weight: 31 oz.
Stocks: Checkered walnut.
Sights: Blade front, rear adjustable for windage only.
Features: Polished blue finish. Imported from Switzerland by Beeman, Mandall and Hammerli Pistols USA.
Price: About **$1,650.00**

Hammerli Model 212

Haskell JS-45

HASKELL JS-45 CALIBER PISTOL
Caliber: 45 ACP, 7-shot magazine.
Barrel: 4.5".
Weight: 44 oz. **Length:** 7.95" overall.
Stocks: Checkered acetal resin.
Sights: Fixed; low profile.
Features: Internal drop-safe mechanism; all aluminum frame. Introduced 1991. From MKS Supply, Inc.
Price: Matte black **$149.95**
Price: Brushed nickel **$159.95**

HECKLER & KOCH P7M8 AUTO PISTOL
Caliber: 9mm Para., 8-shot magazine.
Barrel: 4.13".
Weight: 29 oz. **Length:** 6.73" overall.
Stocks: Stippled black plastic.
Sights: Blade front, adjustable rear; three dot system.
Features: Unique "squeeze cocker" in frontstrap cocks the action. Gas-retarded action. Squared combat-type trigger guard. Blue finish. Compact size. Imported from Germany by Heckler & Koch, Inc.
Price: P7M8, blued **$999.00**
Price: P7M8, nickel **$1,039.00**
Price: P7M13 (13-shot capacity, ambidextrous magazine release, forged steel frame), blued **$999.00**
Price: P7M13, nickel **$1,299.00**

Heckler & Koch P7M10

Heckler & Koch P7M10 Auto Pistol
Similar to the P7M8 except chambered for 40 S&W with 10-shot magazine. Weighs 43 oz., overall length is 6.9". Introduced 1992. Imported from Germany by Heckler & Koch, Inc.
Price: Blue **$1,259.00**
Price: Nickel **$1,299.00**

Heckler & Koch P7K3 Auto Pistol
Similar to the P7M8 and P7M13 except chambered for 22 LR or 380 ACP, 8-shot magazine. Uses an oil-filled buffer to decrease recoil. Introduced 1988.
Price: **$999.00**
Price: 22 LR conversion unit **$524.00**

HECKLER & KOCH SP89 AUTO PISTOL
Caliber: 9mm Para., 15- or 30-shot magazine.
Barrel: 4.5".
Weight: 4.4 lbs. **Length:** 12.8" overall.
Stocks: Black high-impact plastic.
Sights: Post front, diopter rear adjustable for windage and elevation.
Features: Semi-auto pistol inspired by the HK94. Has special flash-hider forend. Introduced 1989. Imported from Germany by Heckler & Koch, Inc.
Price: **$1,299.00**

Consult our Directory pages for the location of firms mentioned.

Heckler & Koch SP89

HELWAN "BRIGADIER" AUTO PISTOL
Caliber: 9mm Para., 8-shot magazine.
Barrel: 4.5".
Weight: 32 oz. **Length:** 8" overall.
Stocks: Grooved plastic.
Sights: Blade front, rear adjustable for windage.
Features: Polished blue finish. Single-action design. Cross-bolt safety. Imported by Interarms.
Price: **$248.33**

IBERIA FIREARMS JS-40 S&W AUTO
Caliber: 40 S&W, 8-shot magazine.
Barrel: 4.5".
Weight: 44 oz. **Length:** 7.95" overall.
Stocks: Checkered acetal resin.
Sights: Fixed; low profile.
Features: Internal drop-safe mechansim; all aluminum frame. Introduced 1991. From MKS Supply, Inc.
Price: Matte black **$149.95**
Price: Brushed nickel **$159.95**

Iberia JS-40

INTRATEC TEC-DC9 AUTO PISTOL
Caliber: 9mm Para., 32-shot magazine.
Barrel: 5".
Weight: 50 oz. **Length:** 12½" overall.
Stock: Moulded composition.
Sights: Fixed.
Features: Semi-auto, fires from closed bolt; firing pin block safety; matte blue finish. Made in U.S. by Intratec.
Price: **$260.00**
Price: TEC-DC9S (as above, except stainless) **$353.00**
Price: TEC-DC9K (finished with TEC-KOTE) **$290.00**

Intratec TEC-DC9M Auto Pistol
Similar to the TEC-DC9 except smaller. Has 3" barrel, weighs 44 oz.; 20-shot magazine. Made in U.S. by Intratec.
Price: **$239.00**
Price: TEC-DC9MS (as above, stainless) **$330.00**
Price: TEC-DC9MK (finished with TEC-KOTE) **$270.00**

Intratec TEC-DC9

INTRATEC PROTEC-22, 25 AUTO PISTOLS
Caliber: 22 LR, 10-shot; 25 ACP, 8-shot magazine.
Barrel: 2½".
Weight: 14 oz. **Length:** 5" overall.
Stocks: Wraparound composition in gray, black or driftwood color.
Sights: Fixed.
Features: Double-action only trigger mechanism. Choice of black, satin or TEC-KOTE finish. Announced 1991. Made in U.S. by Intratec.
Price: 22 or 25, black finish **$99.95**
Price: 22 or 25, satin or TEC-KOTE finish **$104.95**

INTRATEC TEC-22T AUTO PISTOL
Caliber: 22 LR, 30-shot magazine.
Barrel: 4".
Weight: 30 oz. **Length:** 11³⁄₁₆" overall.
Stocks: Moulded composition.
Sights: Protected post front, front and rear adjustable for windage and elevation.
Features: Ambidextrous cocking knobs and safety. Matte black finish. Accepts any 10/22-type magazine. Introduced 1988. Made in U.S. by Intratec.
Price: **$157.00**
Price: TEC-22TK (as above, TEC-KOTE finish) **$178.95**

ISRAELI KAREEN AUTO PISTOL
Caliber: 9mm Para., 13-shot magazine.
Barrel: 4.75".
Weight: 32 oz. **Length:** 8" overall.
Stocks: Textured composition.
Sights: Blade front, rear adjustable for windage.
Features: Blued steel frame. Introduced 1969. Imported from Israel by J.O. Arms & Ammunition.
Price: About **$425.00**

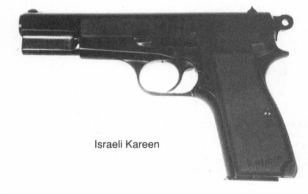

Israeli Kareen

JERICHO 941 AUTO PISTOL
Caliber: 9mm, 16-shot magazine.
Barrel: 4⅜".
Weight: 33 oz. **Length:** 8⅛" overall.
Stocks: High impact black polymer.
Sights: Blade front, rear adjustable for windage; three tritium dots.
Features: Double action; all steel construction; polygonal rifling; ambidextrous safety. Introduced 1990. Produced in Israel by Israel Military Industries; distributed by K.B.I., Inc.
Price: **$599.00**

Jericho 941

JSL SPITFIRE AUTO PISTOL
Caliber: 9mm Para., 15-shot magazine.
Barrel: 4.3".
Weight: 40 oz. **Length:** 8.85" overall.
Stocks: Textured composition.
Sights: Blade front, full adjustable rear.
Features: Stainless steel construction. Double-action mechanism with ambidextrous safety. Introduced 1992. Imported from England by Rogers Ltd. International.
Price: **$1,998.99**

CAUTION: PRICES CHANGE, CHECK AT GUNSHOP.

IVER JOHNSON COMPACT 25 ACP
Caliber: 25 ACP.
Barrel: 2".
Weight: 9.3 oz.
Stocks: Checkered composition.
Sights: Fixed.
Features: Ordnance steel construction with bright blue slide, matte blue frame, color case-hardened trigger. Comes in jewelry-type presentation box. Introduced 1991. From Iver Johnson.
Price: **$199.95**

Iver Johnson Compact

IVER JOHNSON ENFORCER AUTO
Caliber: 30 M-1 Carbine, 15- or 30-shot magazine, or 9mm Para.
Barrel: 10½".
Weight: 4 lbs. **Length:** 18½" overall.
Stocks: American walnut with metal handguard.
Sights: Gold bead ramp front. Peep rear.
Features: Accepts 15- or 30-shot magazines. From Iver Johnson.
Price: 30 M-1 . . . . **$416.50**
Price: 9mm Para. **$448.95**

Jennings J-25

JENNINGS J-22, J-25 AUTO PISTOLS
Caliber: 22 LR, 25 ACP, 6-shot magazine.
Barrel: 2½".
Weight: 13 oz. (J-22). **Length:** 4¹⁵⁄₁₆" overall (J-22).
Stocks: Walnut on chrome or nickel models; grooved black Cycolac or resin-impregnated wood on Teflon model.
Sights: Fixed.
Features: Choice of bright chrome, satin nickel or black Teflon finish. Introduced 1981. From Jennings Firearms.
Price: J-22, about **$75.00**
Price: J-25, about **$89.95**

L.A.R. Grizzly Win Mag

L.A.R. GRIZZLY WIN MAG MK I PISTOL
Caliber: 357 Mag., 357/45, 10mm, 44 Mag., 45 Win. Mag., 45 ACP, 7-shot magazine.
Barrel: 5.4", 6.5".
Weight: 51 oz. **Length:** 10½" overall.
Stocks: Checkered rubber, non-slip combat-type.
Sights: Ramped blade front, fully adjustable rear.
Features: Uses basic Browning/Colt 1911A1 design; interchangeable calibers; beveled magazine well; combat-type flat, checkered rubber mainspring housing; lowered and back-chamfered ejection port; polished feed ramp; throated barrel; solid barrel bushings. Available in satin hard chrome, matte blue, Parkerized finishes. Introduced 1983. From L.A.R. Mfg., Inc.
Price: 45 Win. Mag. **$893.00**
Price: 357 Mag. **$920.00**
Price: Conversion units (357 Mag.) **$221.00**
Price: As above, 45 ACP, 10mm, 45 Win. Mag.,
357/45 Win. Mag. **$207.00**

L.A.R. Grizzly Win Mag 8" & 10"
Similar to the standard Grizzly Win Mag except has lengthened slide and either 8" or 10" barrel. Available in 45 Win. Mag., 45 ACP, 357/45 Grizzly Win. Mag., 10mm or 357 Magnum. Introduced 1987.
Price: 8", 45 ACP, 45 Win. Mag., 357/45 Grizzly Win. Mag. **$1,313.00**
Price: As above, 10" **$1,375.00**
Price: 8", 357 Magnum **$1,337.50**
Price: As above, 10" **$1,400.00**

L.A.R. Grizzly 44 Mag MK IV
Similar to the Win. Mag. Mk I except chambered for 44 Magnum, has beavertail grip safety. Matte blue finish only. Has 5.4" or 6.5" barrel. Introduced 1991. From L.A.R. Mfg., Inc.
Price: **$920.00**

LLAMA SMALL FRAME AUTO PISTOLS
Caliber: 22 LR, 32, 380.
Barrel: 3¹¹⁄₁₆".
Weight: 23 oz. **Length:** 6½" overall.
Stocks: Checkered plastic, thumbrest.
Sights: Fixed front, adjustable notch rear.
Features: Ventilated rib, manual and grip safeties. Imported from Spain by Stoeger Industries.
Price: Blue **$325.00**
Price: Satin chrome, 22 LR or 380 . . . . **$399.00**
Price: Duo-Tone (satin chrome frame, blue slide), 380 only **$385.00**

Llama Small Frame

LLAMA COMPACT FRAME AUTO PISTOL
Caliber: 9mm Para., 9-shot, 45 ACP, 7-shot.
Barrel: 4⁵⁄₁₆".
Weight: 37 oz.
Stocks: Smooth walnut.
Sights: Blade front, rear adjustable for windage.
Features: Scaled-down version of the Large Frame gun. Locked breech mechanism; manual and grip safeties. Introduced 1985. Imported from Spain by Stoeger Industries.
Price: Blue **$385.00**
Price: Satin chrome **$499.00**
Price: Duo-Tone (satin chrome frame, blue slide) **$475.00**

LLAMA LARGE FRAME AUTO PISTOL
Caliber: 38 Super, 45 ACP.
Barrel: 5".
Weight: 40 oz. **Length:** 8½" overall.
Stocks: Checkered walnut.
Sights: Fixed.
Features: Grip and manual safeties, ventilated rib. Imported from Spain by Stoeger Industries.
Price: Blue **$385.00**
Price: Satin chrome, 45 ACP only **$499.00**
Price: Duo-Tone (satin chrome frame, blue slide) **$475.00**

Llama Large Frame

LLAMA M-82 DA AUTO PISTOL
Caliber: 9mm Para., 15-shot magazine.
Barrel: 4¼".
Weight: 39 oz. **Length:** 8" overall.
Stocks: Matte black polymer.
Sights: Blade front, rear drift adjustable for windage. High visibility three-dot system.
Features: Double-action mechanism; ambidextrous safety. Introduced 1987. Imported from Spain by Stoeger Industries.
Price: **$975.00**

Llama M-82

LORCIN AUTO PISTOL
Caliber: 25 ACP, 7-shot magazine.
Barrel: 2¼".
Weight: 13.5 oz. **Length:** 4.75" overall.
Stocks: Smooth composition.
Sights: Fixed.
Features: Available in choice of finishes: black and gold, chrome and satin, chrome or black. Introduced 1989. From Lorcin Engineering.
Price: **$79.95**

LORCIN L-32, L-380 AUTO PISTOLS
Caliber: 32 ACP, 380 ACP, 7-shot magazine.
Barrel: NA.
Weight: 22 oz. **Length:** NA.
Stocks: Grooved composition.
Sights: Fixed.
Features: Black or chrome finish with black grips. Introduced 1992. From Lorcin Engineering.
Price: 32 ACP **$85.00**
Price: 380 ACP **$95.00**

Lorcin 25 ACP

MAUSER MODEL 80 SA AUTO PISTOL
Caliber: 9mm Para., 13-shot magazine.
Barrel: 4.67".
Weight: 31.7 oz. **Length:** 8" overall.
Stocks: Checkered beechwood.
Sights: Blade front, rear adjustable for windage.
Features: Uses basic Hi-Power design. Polished blue finish. Introduced 1992. Imported from Germany by Precision Imports, Inc.
Price: **$416.00**

Mauser Model 90 DA Auto Pistols
Similar to the Mauser Model 80 except has double-action trigger system. Has 14-shot magazine, weighs 35.2 oz. Introduced 1992. Imported from Germany by Precision Imports, Inc.
Price: Model 90 DA **$467.00**
Price: Model 90 DA Compact (4.13" bbl., 7.4" overall, 33.5 oz.) . . . **$502.00**

MITCHELL PISTOL PARABELLUM '08 AUTO
Caliber: 9mm Para., 8-shot magazine.
Barrel: 4".
Weight: 29.6 oz. **Length:** 9.6" overall.
Stocks: Checkered walnut.
Sights: Blade front, fixed rear.
Features: Recreation of the American Eagle Parabellum pistol in stainless steel. Chamber loaded indicator. Made in U.S. From Mitchell Arms, Inc.
Price: **$695.00**

MITCHELL ARMS SHARPSHOOTER AUTO PISTOL
Caliber: 22 LR, 10-shot magazine.
Barrel: 5.5" bull.
Weight: 42 oz. **Length:** 10.25" overall.
Stocks: Checkered walnut with thumbrest.
Sights: Ramp front, slide-mounted square notch rear adjustable for windage and elevation.
Features: Military grip. Slide lock; smooth gripstraps; push-button takedown. Announced 1992. From Mitchell Arms, Inc.
Price: Blued . . . . **NA**

MITCHELL ARMS TROPHY II AUTO PISTOL
Caliber: 22 LR, 10-shot magazine.
Barrel: 5.5" bull, 7.25" fluted.
Weight: 44.5 oz. (5.5" barrel). **Length:** 9.75" overall (5.5" barrel).
Stocks: Checkered walnut with thumbrest.
Sights: Undercut ramp front, click-adjustable frame-mounted rear.
Features: Grip duplicates feel of military 45; positive action magazine latch; front- and backstraps stippled. Trigger adjustable for pull, over-travel; gold-filled roll marks, gold-plated trigger, safety, magazine release; push-button barrel takedown. Available in blue or stainless steel. Announced 1992. From Mitchell Arms, Inc.
Price: . . . . **NA**

Mitchell Arms Citation II Auto Pistol
Same as the Trophy II except has nickel-plated trigger, safety and magazine release, and has silver-filled roll marks. Available in blue or stainless steel. Announced 1992. From Mitchell Arms, Inc.
Price: . . . . **NA**

MITCHELL ARMS SPORT-KING AUTO PISTOL
Caliber: 22 LR, 10-shot magazine.
Barrel: 4.5", 6.75".
Weight: 39 oz. (4.5" barrel).**Length:** 9" overall (4.5" barrel).
Stocks: Checkered black plastic.
Sights: Blade front, rear adjustable for windage.
Features: Military grip; standard trigger; push-button barrel takedown. All stainless steel. Announced 1992. From Mitchell Arms, Inc.
Price: . . . . **NA**

NAVY ARMS TT-OLYMPIA PISTOL
Caliber: 22 LR.
Barrel: 4.6".
Weight: 28 oz. **Length:** 8" overall.
Stocks: Checkered hardwood.
Sights: Blade front, rear adjsutable for windage.
Features: Reproduction of the Walther Olympia pistol. Polished blue finish. Introduced 1992. Imported by Navy Arms.
Price: **$300.00**

Norinco NP-20

NORINCO NP-15 TOKAREV AUTO PISTOL
Caliber: 7.62x25mm, 38 Super, 8-shot magazine.
Barrel: 4.5".
Weight: 29 oz. **Length:** 7.7" overall.
Stocks: Grooved black plastic.
Sights: Fixed.
Features: Matte blue finish. Imported from China by China Sports, Inc.
Price: . . . . **NA**
Price: NP-15A (9mm Para., 13-shot magazine) . . . . **NA**

NORINCO TYPE 59 MAKAROV DA PISTOL
Caliber: 9x18mm, 380 ACP, 8-shot magazine.
Barrel: 3.5".
Weight: 21 oz. **Length:** 6.3" overall.
Stocks: Checkered plastic.
Sights: Blade front, adjustable rear.
Features: Blue finish. Double action. Introduced 1990. Imported from China by China Sports, Inc.
Price: . . . . **NA**

Parker Auto

MOUNTAIN EAGLE AUTO PISTOL
Caliber: 22 LR, 15-shot magazine.
Barrel: 6.5".
Weight: 21 oz. **Length:** 10.6" overall.
Stocks: One-piece impact-resistant polymer in "conventional contour"; checkered panels.
Sights: Serrated ramp front with interchangeable blades, rear adjustable for windage and elevation; interchangeable blades.
Features: Injection moulded grip frame, alloy receiver; hybrid composite barrel replicates shape of the Desert Eagle pistol. Flat, smooth trigger. Introduced 1992. From Magnum Research.
Price: **$199.00**

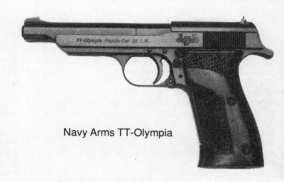

Navy Arms TT-Olympia

NORINCO 88SP AUTO PISTOL
Caliber: 9mm Para., 13-shot magazine.
Barrel: 4.5".
Weight: 34 oz. **Length:** 7.75" overall.
Stocks: Checkered composition.
Sights: Blade front, rear adjustable for windage.
Features: Double action. Matte blue finish. Imported from China by China Sports, Inc.
Price: . . . . **NA**

NORINCO NP-20 AUTO PISTOL
Caliber: 9mm Para., 8-shot magazine.
Barrel: 5".
Weight: 34 oz. **Length:** 7.5" overall.
Stocks: Checkered wood.
Sights: Blade front, adjustable rear.
Features: Uses trigger guard cocking, gas-retarded recoil action. Front of trigger guard can be used to cock the action with the trigger finger. Introduced 1989. Imported from China by China Sports, Inc.
Price: . . . . **NA**

> Consult our Directory pages for the location of firms mentioned.

NORINCO M93 SPORTSMAN AUTO PISTOL
Caliber: 22 LR, 10-shot magazine.
Barrel: 4.6".
Weight: 26 oz. **Length:** 8.6" overall.
Stocks: Checkered composition.
Sights: Blade front, rear adjustable for windage.
Features: All steel construction with blue finish, Introduced 1992. Imported from China by Interarms.
Price: **$225.00**

PARKER AUTO PISTOL
Caliber: 10mm Auto, 8-shot; 40 S&W, 8-shot; 45 ACP, 7-shot.
Barrel: 3⅜", 5", 7".
Weight: 29 oz. to 44 oz. **Length:** 6⅜" (3⅜" barrel).
Stocks: Grooved composition.
Sights: Fixed or Millett adjustable.
Features: Single action. Made of stainless steel. Introduced 1990. Made in the U.S. by Wyoming Arms Mfg. Corp.
Price: 3⅜" barrel, fixed sights only **$399.00**
Price: 5" barrel, fixed **$399.00**
Price: 5" barrel, adjustable sights **$424.00**
Price: 7" barrel, adjustable sights, 10mm, 40 S&W, 45 ACP **$449.00**

NORINCO M1911 AUTO PISTOL
Caliber: 45 ACP, 7-shot magazine.
Barrel: 5".
Weight: 39 oz. **Length:** 8.5" overall.
Stocks: Checkered wood.
Sights: Blade front, rear adjustable for windage.
Features: Matte blue finish. Comes with two magazines. Imported from China by China Sports, Inc.
Price: . . . . **NA**

Para-Ordnance P14.45

PARA-ORDNANCE P14.45 AUTO PISTOL
Caliber: 45 ACP, 13-shot magazine.
Barrel: 5".
Weight: 28 oz. (alloy frame). **Length:** 8.5" overall.
Stocks: Textured composition.
Sights: Blade front, rear adjustable for windage. High visibility three-dot system.
Features: Available with alloy, steel or stainless steel frame with black finish (silver or stainless gun). Steel and stainless steel frame guns weigh 38 oz. (P14.45), 35 oz. (P13.45), 33 oz. (P12.45). Grooved match trigger, rounded combat-style hammer. Double column, high-capacity magazine gives 14-shot total capacity (P14.45). Beveled magazine well. Manual thumb, grip and firing pin lock safeties. Solid barrel bushing. Introduced 1990. Made in Canada by Para-Ordnance.
Price: P14.45 . . . . **$716.25**
Price: P13.45 (12-shot magazine, 4¼" bbl., 25 oz., alloy) . . . **$716.25**
Price: P12.45 (11-shot magazine, 3½" bbl., 24 oz., alloy) **$708.75**
Price: P14.45C steel frame **$716.25**
Price: P12.45C steel frame **$708.75**

PEREGRINE FALCON AUTO PISTOL
Caliber: 10mm, 40 S&W, 10-shot magazine, 45 ACP, 8-shot magazine.
Barrel: 5".
Weight: 37.5 oz. **Length:** 8.5" overall.
Stocks: Black Du Pont Zytel with stipple finish.
Sights: Post front, rear adjustable for windage and elevation; Tri-Square system.
Features: Double-action with passive firing pin lock, decocking lever, ambidextrous thumb safety levers; reversible magazine release; beveled magazine well; stainless steel magazine. Black slide, stainless frame. Announced 1990. Made in U.S. by Peregrine Industries.
Price: 10mm, 40 S&W, 45 ACP **$795.00**

Phoenix Arms Model Raven

PHOENIX ARMS MODEL RAVEN AUTO PISTOL
Caliber: 25 ACP, 6-shot magazine.
Barrel: 2⁷/₁₆".
Weight: 15 oz. **Length:** 4¾" overall.
Stocks: Smooth walnut, ivory-colored or black slotted plastic.
Sights: Ramped front, fixed rear.
Features: Available in blue, nickel or chrome finish. Made in U.S. Available from Phoenix Arms.
Price: **$69.95**

Peregrine Falcon

QFI Model LA380C

PSP-25 AUTO PISTOL
Caliber: 25 ACP, 6-shot magazine.
Barrel: 2⅛".
Weight: 9.5 oz. **Length:** 4⅛" overall.
Stocks: Checkered black plastic.
Sights: Fixed.
Features: All steel construction with polished finish. Introduced 1990. Made in the U.S. under F.N. license; distributed by K.B.I., Inc.
Price: Blue **$249.00**
Price: Hard chrome **$329.99**

QFI MODEL LA380 PISTOL
Caliber: 380 ACP.
Barrel: 3⅛".
Weight: 25 oz. **Length:** 6¼" overall.
Stocks: Smooth European walnut.
Sights: Blade front, rear adjustable for windage.
Features: Single action. External hammer, magazine safety with hammer, trigger and firing pin block. Available in blue, chrome and Lady models. Introduced 1991. Made in U.S. by QFI.
Price: Blue **$146.95**
Price: As above, chrome (LA380C) **$169.95**
Price: Model LA380SS (as above except stainless steel) **$219.95**

QFI MODEL SA25 PISTOL
Caliber: 25 ACP, 6-shot magazine.
Barrel: 2.5".
Weight: 12 oz. **Length:** 4⅝" overall.
Stocks: Smooth walnut.
Sights: Fixed.
Features: External hammer; fast simple takedown. Introduced 1991. Made in U.S.A. by QFI.
Price: Blue **$54.95**
Price: Chrome with pearlite grips **$64.95**
Price: 24K gold and bright blue frame, smooth walnut grips **$104.95**
Price: Tigress 25, blue frame, gold slide, ivory polymer grips, case . **$154.95**

QFI VICTORY MC5 AUTO PISTOL

Caliber: 9mm Para., 17-shot magazine.
Barrel: 4.5", 6", 7.5".
Weight: 45 oz. **Length:** 8.5" overall (4.5" barrel).
Stocks: High impact black plastic.
Sights: Ramped front, rear adjustable for windage.
Features: Single and double action; ambidextrous multi-function safety. Easy interchangeability from 9mm Para. to 45 ACP, 40 S&W, 38 Super or 10mm by changing barrel and magazine. Announced 1992. From QFI.
Price: 9mm $465.00
Price: Conversion kits $180.00

Ranger EXT Auto Pistol

Similar to the Ranger G.I. model except has Millett high-profile fixed sights, checkered walnut grips, extended grip safety, thumb safety, slide and magazine releases. Introduced 1987. From Federal Ordnance, Inc.
Price: $459.95

Ranger Lite Auto Pistol

Similar to the Ranger EXT except has frame of aluminum alloy giving weight of 32 oz. Has wraparound rubber grips, high-profile Millett fixed sights, extended grip and thumb safeties, slide and magazine releases, lightened speed trigger. Black anodized frame, blued steel slide. Introduced 1990. From Federal Ordnance, Inc.
Price: 45 ACP only $454.95

Ranger AMBO Auto Pistol

Similar to the Ranger EXT except has ambidextrous slide release and safety. Introduced 1987. From Federal Ordnance, Inc.
Price: $479.95

RUGER P85 MARK II AUTOMATIC PISTOL

Caliber: 9mm Para., 15-shot magazine.
Barrel: 4.50".
Weight: 32 oz. **Length:** 7.84" overall.
Stocks: Grooved black Xenoy composition.
Sights: Square post front, square notch rear adjustable for windage, both with white dot inserts.
Features: Double action with ambidextrous slide-mounted safety-levers. Slide is 4140 chrome moly steel or 400-series stainless steel, frame is a lightweight aluminum alloy. Ambidextrous magazine release. Blue or stainless steel. Introduced 1986; stainless introduced 1990.
Price: P85CMKII, blue, with extra magazine and magazine loading tool, plastic case $410.00
Price: KP85CMKII, stainless, with extra magazine and magazine loading tool, plastic case $452.00

Ruger P85DCC Decocker Automatic Pistol

Similar to the standard P85 except has ambidextrous decocking levers in place of the regular slide-mounted safety. The decocking levers move the firing pin inside the slide where the hammer can not reach it, while simultaneously blocking the firing pin from forward movement—allows shooter to decock a cocked pistol without manipulating the trigger. Conventional thumb decocking procedures are therefore unnecessary. Blue or stainless steel. Introduced 1990.
Price: P89DCC, blue with extra magazine and loader, plastic case . $410.00
Price: KP89DCC, stainless, with extra magazine, plastic case . . . $452.00

Ruger P89 Double-Action Only Automatic Pistol

Same as the KP85 Mk II except operates only in the double-action mode. Has a bobbed, spurless hammer, gripping grooves on each side of the rear of the slide; no external safety or decocking lever. An internal safety prevents forward movement of the firing pin unless the trigger is pulled. Available in 9mm Para., stainless steel only. Introduced 1991.
Price: With lockable case, extra magazine, magazine loading tool . $452.00

Ruger P90 Decocker Automatic Pistol

Similar to the P90 except has a manual decocking system. The ambidextrous decocking levers move the firing pin inside the slide where the hammer can not reach it, while simultaneously blocking the firing pin from forward movement—allows shooter to decock a cocked pistol without manipulating the trigger. Available only in stainless steel. Overall length 7.87", weight 34 oz. Introduced 1991.
Price: P90DAC with lockable case, extra magazine, and magazine loading tool $488.65

RANGER G.I. MODEL AUTO PISTOL

Caliber: 45 ACP, 7-shot magazine.
Barrel: 5".
Weight: 38 oz. **Length:** 8½" overall.
Stocks: Checkered plastic.
Sights: Blade front, rear drift adjustable for windage.
Features: Made in U.S. from 4140 steel and other high-strength alloys. Barrel machined from a forged billet. Introduced 1988. From Federal Ordnance, Inc.
Price: Standard model $439.95

Ranger EXT

Ruger P85 Mark II

Ruger KP90C

RUGER P90 AUTOMATIC PISTOL

Caliber: 45 ACP, 7-shot magazine.
Barrel: 4.50".
Weight: 33.5 oz. **Length:** 7.87" overall.
Stocks: Grooved black Xenoy composition.
Sights: Square post front, square notch rear adjustable for windage, both with white dot inserts.
Features: Double action with ambidextrous slide-mounted safety-levers which move the firing pin inside the slide where the hammer can not reach it, while simultaneously blocking the firing pin from forward movement. Stainless steel only. Introduced 1991.
Price: KP90C with lockable case, extra magazine $488.65

RUGER P91 DECOCKER AUTOMATIC PISTOL

Caliber: 40 S&W, 11-shot magazine.
Barrel: 4.50".
Weight: 33 oz. **Length:** 7.87" overall.
Stocks: Grooved black Xenoy composition.
Sights: Square post front, square notch rear adjustable for windage, both with white dot inserts.
Features: Ambidextrous slide-mounted decocking levers move the firing pin inside the slide where the hammer can not reach it while simultaneously blocking the firing pin from forward movement. Allows shooter to decock a cocked pistol without manipulating the trigger. Conventional thumb decocking procedures are therefore unnecessary. Stainless steel only. Introduced 1991.
Price: KP91DAC with lockable case, extra magazine, and magazine loading tool **$488.65**

Ruger P91 Double Action Only Automatic Pistol

Same as the KP91DAC except operates only in the double-action mode. Has a bobbed, spurless hammer, gripping grooves on each side at the rear of the slide, no external safety or decocking levers. An internal safety prevents forward movement of the firing pin unless the trigger is pulled. Available in 40 S&W, stainless steel only. Introduced 1992.
Price: KP91DAO with lockable case, extra magazine, and magazine loading tool **$488.65**

Ruger KP91DAC

Ruger 22/45 Mark II

RUGER MARK II STANDARD AUTO PISTOL

Caliber: 22 LR, 10-shot magazine.
Barrel: 4¾" or 6".
Weight: 36 oz. (4¾" bbl.). **Length:** 8⁵⁄₁₆" (4¾" bbl.).
Stocks: Checkered plastic.
Sights: Fixed, wide blade front, square notch rear adjustable for windage.
Features: Updated design of the original Standard Auto. Has new bolt hold-open latch. 10-shot magazine, magazine catch, safety, trigger and new receiver contours. Introduced 1982.
Price: Blued (MK 4, MK 6) **$236.00**
Price: In stainless steel (KMK 4, KMK 6) **$314.25**

Ruger 22/45 Mark II Pistol

Similar to the other 22 Mark II autos except has grip frame of Zytel that matchs the angle and magazine latch of the Model 1911 45 ACP pistol. Available in 4¾" standard, 5¼" tapered and 5½" bull barrel. Introduced 1992.
Price: KP4 (4¾" barrel) **$264.00**
Price: KP514 (5¼" barrel) **$314.00**
Price: KP512 (5½" barrel) **$314.00**

Consult our Directory pages for the location of firms mentioned.

Safari Arms Enforcer

SEECAMP LWS 32 STAINLESS DA AUTO

Caliber: 32 ACP Win. Silvertip, 6-shot magazine.
Barrel: 2", integral with frame.
Weight: 10.5 oz. **Length:** 4⅛" overall.
Stocks: Glass-filled nylon.
Sights: Smooth, no-snag, contoured slide and barrel top.
Features: Aircraft quality 17-4 PH stainless steel. Inertia-operated firing pin. Hammer fired double-action only. Hammer automatically follows slide down to safety rest position after each shot—no manual safety needed. Magazine safety disconnector. Polished stainless. Introduced 1985. From L.W. Seecamp.
Price: **$375.00**

SIG P-210-2 AUTO PISTOL

Caliber: 7.65mm or 9mm Para., 8-shot magazine.
Barrel: 4¾".
Weight: 31¾ oz. (9mm). **Length:** 8½" overall.
Stocks: Checkered black composition.
Sights: Blade front, rear adjustable for windage.
Features: Lanyard loop; matte finish. Conversion unit for 22 LR available. Imported from Switzerland by Mandall Shooting Supplies.
Price: P-210-2 Service Pistol **$3,000.00**

SAFARI ARMS ENFORCER PISTOL

Caliber: 45 ACP, 6-shot magazine.
Barrel: 3.8"
Weight: 35 oz. (standard); 27 oz. (lightweight). **Length:** 7.7" overall.
Stocks: Smooth walnut with etched black widow spider logo.
Sights: Ramped blade front, rear adjustable for windage and elevation.
Features: Ambidextrous extended safety, extended slide release; Commander-style hammer; beavertail grip safety; throated, ported, tuned, with cone-shaped barrel. Choice of ordnance steel, stainless, or alloy. From Safari Arms, Inc.
Price: **$710.00**

Safari Arms G.I. Pistol

Similar to the Safari Arms Matchmaster pistol (see Competition Handguns section) except has G.I. slide and 5" G.I. chrome-lined barrel on a Safari steel frame unit. Has beavertail grip safety and Commander hammer, extended slide release, checkered grips. Matte black finish. Introduced 1991. From Safari Arms, Inc.
Price: **$425.00**

SIG P-210-6 AUTO PISTOL

Caliber: 9mm Para., 8-shot magazine.
Barrel: 4¾".
Weight: 36.2 oz. **Length:** 8½" overall.
Stocks: Checkered black plastic; walnut optional.
Sights: Blade front, micro. adjustable rear for windage and elevation.
Features: Adjustable trigger stop; target trigger; ribbed frontstrap; sandblasted finish. Conversion unit for 22 LR consists of barrel, recoil spring, slide and magazine. Imported from Switzerland by Mandall Shooting Supplies.
Price: P-210-6 . . . . **$3,200.00**
Price: P-210-5 Target **$3,500.00**

SIG SAUER P220 "AMERICAN" AUTO PISTOL
Caliber: 9mm, 38 Super, 45 ACP, (9-shot in 9mm and 38 Super, 7 in 45).
Barrel: 4⅜".
Weight: 28¼ oz. (9mm). **Length:** 7¾" overall.
Stocks: Checkered black plastic.
Sights: Blade front, drift adjustable rear for windage.
Features: Double action. De-cocking lever permits lowering hammer onto locked firing pin. Squared combat-type trigger guard. Slide stays open after last shot. Imported from Germany by SIGARMS, Inc.
Price: "American," blue (side-button magazine release, 45 ACP only) **$780.00**
Price: 45 ACP, blue, Siglite night sights **$880.00**
Price: K-Kote finish **$850.00**
Price: K-Kote, Siglite night sights **$950.00**

SIG Sauer P220 "American"

SIG SAUER P225 DA AUTO PISTOL
Caliber: 9mm Para., 8-shot magazine.
Barrel: 3.8".
Weight: 26 oz. **Length:** 7³⁄₃₂" overall.
Stocks: Checkered black plastic.
Sights: Blade front, rear adjustable for windage. Optional Siglite night sights.
Features: Double action. De-cocking lever permits lowering hammer onto locked firing pin. Square combat-type trigger guard. Shortened, lightened version of P220. Imported from Germany by SIGARMS, Inc.
Price: **$775.00**
Price: With Siglite night sights **$875.00**
Price: K-Kote finish **$845.00**
Price: K-Kote with Siglite night sights **$945.00**

SIG Sauer P226 DA Auto Pistol
Similar to the P220 pistol except has 15-shot magazine, 4.4" barrel, and weighs 26½ oz. 9mm only. Imported from Germany by SIGARMS, Inc.
Price: Blue **$805.00**
Price: With Siglite night sights **$905.00**
Price: Blue, double-action only **$805.00**
Price: Blue, double-action only, Siglite night sights **$905.00**
Price: K-Kote finish **$875.00**
Price: K-Kote, Siglite night sights **$975.00**
Price: K-Kote, double-action only **$875.00**
Price: K-Kote, double-action only, Siglite night sights **$975.00**

SIG Sauer P228 DA Auto Pistol
Similar to the P226 except has 3.86" barrel, with 7.08" overall length and 3.35" height. Chambered for 9mm Para. only, 13-shot magazine. Weight is 29.1 oz. with empty magazine. Introduced 1989. Imported from Germany by SIGARMS, Inc.
Price: Blue **$805.00**
Price: Blue, with Siglite night sights **$905.00**
Price: Blue, double-action only **$805.00**
Price: Blue, double-action only, Siglite night sights **$905.00**
Price: K-Kote finish **$875.00**
Price: K-Kote, Siglite night sights **$975.00**
Price: K-Kote, double-action only **$875.00**
Price: K-Kote, double-action only, Siglite night sights **$975.00**

SIG Sauer P228

SIG Sauer P229 DA Auto Pistol
Similar to the P228 except chambered for 40 S&W with 12-shot magazine. Has 3.86" barrel, 7.08" overall length and 3.35" height. Weight is 30.5 oz. Introduced 1991. Imported from Germany by SIGARMS, Inc.
Price: Blue **$875.00**
Price: Blue, double-action only **$875.00**

SIG SAUER P230 DA AUTO PISTOL
Caliber: 32 ACP, 8-shot; 380 ACP, 7-shot.
Barrel: 3¾".
Weight: 16 oz. **Length:** 6½" overall.
Stocks: Checkered black plastic.
Sights: Blade front, rear adjustable for windage.
Features: Double action. Same basic action design as P220. Blowback operation, stationary barrel. Introduced 1977. Imported from Germany by SIGARMS, Inc.
Price: Blue **$510.00**
Price: In stainless steel (P230 SL) **$595.00**

SIG Sauer P230

Smith & Wesson Model 2206 Auto
Similar to the Model 422/622 except made entirely of stainless steel with non-reflective finish. Weight is 35 oz. with 4½" barrel, 39 oz. with 6" barrel. Other specs are the same. Introduced 1990.
Price: With fixed sight **$299.00**
Price: With adjustable sight **$355.00**

SMITH & WESSON MODEL 422, 622 AUTO
Caliber: 22 LR, 10-shot magazine.
Barrel: 4½", 6".
Weight: 22 oz. (4½" bbl.). **Length:** 7½" overall (4½" bbl.).
Stocks: Checkered plastic (Field), checkered walnut (Target).
Sights: Field—serrated ramp front, fixed rear; Target—Patridge front, adjustable rear.
Features: Aluminum frame, steel slide, brushed blue finish; internal hammer. Introduced 1987. Model 2206 introduced 1990.
Price: Blue, 4½", 6", fixed sight **$214.00**
Price: As above, adjustable sight **$267.00**
Price: Stainless (Model 622), 4½", 6", fixed sight **$259.00**
Price: As above, adjustable sight **$311.00**

Smith & Wesson Model 2214 Sportsman Auto

Similar to the Model 422 except has 3" barrel, 8-shot magazine; dovetail Patridge front sight with white dot, fixed rear with two white dots; matte blue finish, black composition grips with checkered panels. Overall length 6⅛", weight 18 oz. Introduced 1990.

Price: **$245.00**

SMITH & WESSON MODEL 915 DA AUTO PISTOL

Caliber: 9mm Para., 15-shot magazine.
Barrel: 4".
Weight: 28.5 oz. **Length:** 7.5" overall.
Stocks: One-piece Xenoy, wraparound with straight backstrap.
Sights: Post front with white dot, fixed rear.
Features: Alloy frame, blue carbon steel slide. Slide-mounted decocking lever. Introduced 1992.
Price: **$467.00**

Smith & Wesson Model 2214

SMITH & WESSON MODEL 3913/3914 DOUBLE ACTIONS

Caliber: 9mm Para., 8-shot magazine.
Barrel: 3½".
Weight: 26 oz. **Length:** 6¹³⁄₁₆" overall.
Stocks: One-piece Delrin wraparound, textured surface.
Sights: Post front with white dot, Novak LoMount Carry with two dots, adjustable for windage.
Features: Aluminum alloy frame, stainless slide (M3913) or blue steel slide (M3914). Bobbed hammer with no half-cock notch; smooth .304" trigger with rounded edges. Straight backstrap. Extra magazine included. Introduced 1989.
Price: Model 3913 . . . . **$585.00**
Price: Model 3914 . . . . **$528.00**

Smith & Wesson Model 3913 LadySmith Auto

Similar to the standard Model 3913/3914 except has frame that is upswept at the front, rounded trigger guard. Comes in frosted stainless steel with matching gray grips. Grips are ergonomically correct for a woman's hand. Novak LoMount Carry rear sight adjustable for windage, smooth edges for snag resistance. Extra magazine included. Introduced 1990.
Price: **$603.00**

Smith & Wesson Model 3953/3954 DA Pistols

Same as the Models 3913/3914 except double-action only. Model 3953 has stainless slide with alloy frame; Model 3954 has blued steel slide. Overall length 7"; weight 25.5 oz. Extra magazine included. Introduced 1990.
Price: Model 3953 . . . . **$585.00**
Price: Model 3954 . . . . **$528.00**

Smith & Wesson Model 915

SMITH & WESSON MODEL 4013/4014, 4053/4054 AUTOS

Caliber: 40 S&W, 7-shot magazine.
Barrel: 3½".
Weight: 26 oz. **Length:** 7" overall.
Stocks: One-piece Xenoy wraparound with straight backstrap.
Sights: Post front with white dot, fixed Novak LoMount Carry rear with two white dots.
Features: Models 4013/4014 are traditional double action; Models 4053/4054 are double-action only; Models 4013, 4053 have stainless slide on alloy frame; 4014, 4054 have blued steel slide. Introduced 1991.
Price: Models 4013, 4053 . . . . **$686.00**
Price: Models 4014, 4054 . . . . **$629.00**

SMITH & WESSON MODEL 4026 DA AUTO

Caliber: 40 S&W, 11-shot magazine.
Barrel: 4".
Weight: 39 oz. **Length:** 7.5" overall.
Stocks: Xenoy one-piece wraparound.
Sights: Post front with white dot, Novak LoMount Carry rear with two white dots.
Features: Stainless steel. Has spring-loaded, frame-mounted decocking lever, magazine disconnector safety and firing pin safety. Matte finish. Bobbed hammer, smooth trigger. Introduced 1992.
Price: **$724.00**

Smith & Wesson Model 3913-NL Pistol

Same as the 3913/3914 LadySmith autos except without the LadySmith logo and it has a slightly modified frame design. Right-hand safety only. Has stainless slide on alloy frame; extra magazine included. Introduced 1990.
Price: **$585.00**

Smith & Wesson Model 4506

SMITH & WESSON MODEL 4500 SERIES AUTOS

Caliber: 45 ACP, 7-shot magazine (M4516), 8-shot magazine (M4506).
Barrel: 3¾" (M4516), 5" (M4506).
Weight: 34½ oz. (4516). **Length:** 7⅛" overall (4516).
Stocks: Delrin one-piece wraparound, arched or straight backstrap on M4506, straight only on M4516.
Sights: Post front with white dot, adjustable or fixed Novak LoMount Carry on M4506, fixed Novak LoMount Carry only on M4516.
Features: M4506 has serrated hammer spur; M4516 has bobbed hammer. Both guns in stainless only. Extra magazine included. Introduced 1989.
Price: Model 4506, fixed sight **$735.00**
Price: Model 4506, adjustable sight **$765.00**
Price: Model 4516 . . . . **$735.00**
Price: Model 4566 (stainless, 4¼", traditional DA, ambidextrous safety) **$735.00**
Price: Model 4576 (stainless, 4¼", traditional DA with decocking lever) **$762.00**
Price: Model 4586 (stainless, 4¼", DA only) **$735.00**

Smith & Wesson Model 1006 Double-Action Auto

Similar to the Model 4506 except chambered for 10mm auto with 9-shot magazine. Available with either Novak LoMount Carry fixed rear sight with two white dots or adjustable micrometer-click rear with two white dots. All stainless steel construction; one-piece Delrin stocks with straight backstrap; curved backstrap available as option. Has 5" barrel, 8½" overall length, weighs 38 oz. with fixed sight. Rounded trigger guard with knurling. Extra magazine included. Introduced 1990.

Price: With fixed sight $747.00
Price: With adjustable sight $773.00

Smith & Wesson Model 1006

Smith & Wesson Model 1066 Auto Pistol

Similar to the Model 1006 except has 4¼" barrel, fixed sight, ambidextrous safety. Extra magazine included. Introduced 1990.

Price: $730.00

Smith & Wesson Model 1076 Auto

Same as the Model 1006 except has frame-mounted decocking lever, fixed sight only; traditional double-action mechanism. Extra magazine included. Introduced 1990.

Price: $755.00
Price: Model 1076-NS (as above with night sights) $825.00

Smith & Wesson Model 1086 DA Pistol

Same as the Model 1006 except is double-action only, fixed sight; satin stainless; straight backstrap. Model 1086 has 4¼" barrel. Extra magazine included. Introduced 1990.

Price: $730.00

Smith & Wesson Model 4046 DA Pistol

Similar to the Model 4006 except is double-action only. Has a semi-bobbed hammer, smooth trigger, 4" barrel; Novak LoMount Carry rear sight, post front with white dot. Overall length is 7½", weight 39 oz. Extra magazine included. Introduced 1991.

Price: $708.00
Price: With fixed night sights $812.00

SMITH & WESSON MODEL 4006 DA AUTO

Caliber: 40 S&W, 11-shot magazine.
Barrel: 4".
Weight: 36 oz. **Length:** 7½" overall.
Stocks: Xenoy wraparound with checkered panels.
Sights: Replaceable post front with white dot, Novak LoMount Carry fixed rear with two white dots, or micro. click adjustable rear with two white dots.
Features: Stainless steel construction with non-reflective finish. Straight backstrap. Extra magazine included. Introduced 1990.

Price: With adjustable sights $736.00
Price: With fixed sight $708.00
Price: With fixed night sights $812.00

Smith & Wesson Model 5946

SMITH & WESSON MODEL 5900 SERIES AUTO PISTOLS

Caliber: 9mm Para., 15-shot magazine.
Barrel: 4".
Weight: 28½ to 37½ oz. (fixed sight); 29 to 38 oz. (adj. sight). **Length:** 7½" overall.
Stocks: Xenoy wraparound with curved backstrap.
Sights: Post front with white dot, fixed or fully adjustable with two white dots.
Features: All stainless, stainless and alloy or carbon steel and alloy construction. Smooth .304" trigger, .260" serrated hammer. Extra magazine included. Introduced 1989.

Price: Model 5903 (stainless, alloy frame, traditional DA, adjustable sight, ambidextrous safety) $686.00
Price: As above, fixed sight $655.00
Price: Model 5904 (blue, alloy frame, traditional DA, adjustable sight, ambidextrous safety) $639.00
Price: As above, fixed sight $610.00
Price: Model 5906 (stainless, traditional DA, adjustable sight, ambidextrous safety) $704.00
Price: As above, fixed sight $672.00
Price: With fixed night sights $808.00
Price: Model 5926 (as above, stainless) $697.00
Price: Model 5946 (as above, stainless frame and slide) $672.00

Smith & Wesson Model 6904

Smith & Wesson Model 6904/6906 Double-Action Autos

Similar to the Models 5904/5906 except with 3½" barrel, 12-shot magazine (20-shot available), fixed rear sight, .260" bobbed hammer. Extra magazine included. Introduced 1989.

Price: Model 6904, blue $578.00
Price: Model 6906, stainless $637.00
Price: Model 6946 (stainless, DA only, fixed sights) $637.00
Price: With fixed night sights $741.00

SPORTARMS TOKAREV MODEL 213

Caliber: 9mm Para., 8-shot magazine.
Barrel: 4.5".
Weight: 31 oz. **Length:** 7.6" overall.
Stocks: Grooved plastic.
Sights: Fixed.
Features: Blue finish, hard chrome optional. 9mm version of the famous Russian Tokarev pistol. Made in China by Norinco. Imported by Sportarms of Florida. Introduced 1988.

Price: Blue, about $196.95
Price: Hard chrome, about $226.95

SPRINGFIELD ARMORY 1911A1 AUTO PISTOL
Caliber: 9mm Para., 9-shot; 38 Super, 10-shot; 40 S&W, 45 ACP, 8-shot.
Barrel: 5".
Weight: 35.06 oz. **Length:** 8.59" overall.
Stocks: Checkered walnut.
Sights: Fixed low-profile combat-style.
Features: Beveled magazine well. All forged parts, including frame, barrel, slide. All new production. Introduced 1990. From Springfield Armory.

Price: 9mm, 45, Parkerized	$499.00
Price: 9mm, 45, blued	$539.00
Price: 45 only, Duotone (blue slide, hard chrome frame)	$599.00
Price: 45 only, stainless	$769.00
Price: 40 S&W, Parkerized	$649.00
Price: 40 S&W, blued	$689.00
Price: 38 Super, Parkerized	$599.00
Price: 38 Super, blued	$629.00

Springfield Armory 1911A1

Springfield Armory 1911A1 Custom Carry Gun
Similar to the standard 1911A1 except has fixed three-dot low profile sights, Videki speed trigger, match barrel and bushing; extended thumb safety, beavertail grip safety; beveled, polished magazine well, polished feed ramp and throated barrel; match Commander hammer and sear, tuned extractor; lowered and flared ejection port; Shok Buff, full-length spring guide rod; walnut grips. Comes with two magazines with slam pads, plastic carrying case. Available in 9mm Para., 9x21, 38 Super, 10mm, 40 S&W, 45 ACP. Introduced 1992. From Springfield Armory Custom Shop.
Price: 9mm Para., blue or Parkerized $1,200.00

Springfield Armory 1911A1 Factory Comp

SPRINGFIELD ARMORY P9 DA PISTOL
Caliber: 9mm Para., 15-shot magazine; 40 S&W, 11-shot; 45 ACP, 10-shot.
Barrel: 4.72".
Weight: 32.16 oz. **Length:** 8.1" overall.
Stocks: Checkered walnut.
Sights: Blade front, open rear drift-adjustable for windage; three-dot system.
Features: Patterned after the CZ-75. Frame-mounted thumb safety. Magazine catch can be switched to opposite side. Commander hammer. Introduced 1989.

Price: 9mm, Parkerized	$519.00
Price: 9mm, blued	$549.00
Price: 9mm, stainless	$599.00
Price: 40 S&W, Parkerized	$549.00
Price: 40 S&W, blued	$569.00
Price: 40 S&W, stainless	$629.00
Price: 45 ACP, Parkerized	$549.00
Price: 45 ACP, blued	$579.00
Price: 45 ACP, stainless	$629.00

Springfield Armory P9 Factory Comp Pistol
Similar to the standard P9 except comes with dual-port compensator system, extended sear safety, extended magazine release, fully adjustable rear sight, extra-slim competition wood grips. Stainless or bi-tone (stainless and blue). Weighs 33.92 oz., overall length is 9.625" with 5.50" barrel. Introduced 1992.

Price: 9mm, bi-tone	$779.00
Price: 9mm, stainless	$799.00
Price: 40 S&W, bi-tone	$809.00
Price: 40 S&W, stainless	$819.00
Price: 45 ACP, bi-tone	$819.00
Price: 45 ACP, stainless	$829.00

Springfield Armory 1911A1 Factory Comp
Similar to the standard 1911A1 except comes with bushing-type dual-port compensator, adjustable rear sight, extended thumb safety, Videki speed trigger, and beveled magazine well. Checkered walnut grips standard. Available in 38 Super or 45 ACP, blue only. Introduced 1992.
Price: 38 Super $869.00
Price: 45 ACP $839.00

Springfield Armory 1911A1 Champion Pistol
Similar to the standard 1911A1 except slide and barrel are ½" shorter. Has low-profile three-dot sight system. Comes with Commander hammer and walnut stocks. Available in 45 ACP only; blue or stainless. Introduced 1989.
Price: Blue $609.00
Price: Stainless $749.00

Springfield Armory 1911A1 Compact Pistol
Similar to the Champion model except has a shortened slide with 4.025" barrel, 7.75" overall length. Magazine capacity is 7 shots. Has Commander hammer, checkered walnut grips. Available in 45 ACP only. Introduced 1989.
Price: Blued $609.00
Price: Stainless $749.00

Springfield Armory Product Improved 1911A1 Defender Pistol
Similar to the 1911A1 Champion except has tapered cone dual-port compensator system, rubberized grips. Has reverse recoil plug, full-length recoil spring guide, serrated frontstrap, extended thumb safety, Commander-style hammer with modified grip safety to match and a Videki speed trigger. Duotone finish. Introduced 1991.
Price: 40 S&W or 45 ACP $999.00

Springfield Armory P9 Ultra LSP Long Slide Pistol
Same as the standard P9 except has 5.03" ported barrel, 8.38" overall length and weighs 34.56 oz. Rubber stocks. IPSC approved. Introduced 1990.

Price: 9mm, Parkerized	$609.00
Price: 9mm, Blued	$639.00
Price: 9mm, bi-tone (blue/stainless)	$689.00
Price: 9mm, stainless	$769.00
Price: 40 S&W, Parkerized	$639.00
Price: 40 S&W, blued	$669.00
Price: 40 S&W, bi-tone	$719.00
Price: 40 S&W, stainless	$799.00
Price: 45 ACP, Parkerized	$709.00
Price: 45 ACP, blued	$739.00
Price: 45 ACP, bi-tone	$779.00
Price: 45 ACP, stainless	$859.00

Springfield Armory P9 Standard

CAUTION: PRICES CHANGE, CHECK AT GUNSHOP.

Springfield Armory Bobcat

Springfield Armory Lynx

Springfield Armory Panther

SPRINGFIELD ARMORY BOBCAT AUTO PISTOL
Caliber: 380 ACP, 13-shot magazine.
Barrel: 3.52".
Weight: 21.92 oz. **Length:** 6.6" overall.
Stocks: Textured composition.
Sights: Blade front, rear adjustable for windage.
Features: Double-action mechanism with slide-mounted, ambidextrous decocker; frame-mounted slide stop; button magazine release; Commander hammer. Matte blue finish. Introduced 1991. From Springfield Armory.
Price: **$449.00**

SPRINGFIELD ARMORY FIRECAT AUTO PISTOL
Caliber: 9mm Para., 8-shot; 40 S&W, 7-shot magazine.
Barrel: 3.51".
Weight: 25.76 oz. **Length:** 6.52" overall.
Stocks: Checkered walnut.
Sights: Low profile blade front, fixed rear; three-dot system.
Features: Single-action mechanism, all steel construction. Has firing pin block safety and frame-mounted thumb safety; frame-mounted slide stop; button magazine release; checkered front and rear straps, checkered and squared trigger guard; Commander hammer. Matte blue only. Introduced 1991. From Springfield Armory, Inc.
Price: 9mm Para. **$489.00**
Price: 40 S&W **$519.00**

SPRINGFIELD ARMORY LYNX AUTO PISTOL
Caliber: 25 ACP, 7-shot magazine.
Barrel: 2.23".
Weight: 10.56 oz. **Length:** 4.43" overall.
Stocks: Checkered composition.
Sights: Blade front, rear adjustable for windage; three-dot system.
Features: All steel construction; frame-mounted thumb safety/slide stop; Commander hammer; magazine safety. Matte blue finish. Introduced 1991. From Springfield Armory.
Price: **$249.00**

SPRINGFIELD ARMORY PANTHER AUTO PISTOL
Caliber: 9mm Para., 15-shot; 40 S&W, 11-shot; 45 ACP, 9-shot magazine.
Barrel: 3.79".
Weight: 28.96 oz. **Length:** 7.04" overall.
Stocks: Narrow profile checkered walnut.
Sights: Low profile blade front, rear adjustable for windage; three-dot system.
Features: Double-action mechanism with hammer drop and firing pin safeties; serrated front and rear straps; serrated slide top; Commander hammer; frame-mounted slide stop; button magazine release. Matte blue finish. Introduced 1991. From Springfield Armory, Inc.
Price: 9mm Para., 40 S&W, 45 ACP **$609.00**

STALLARD JS-9MM AUTO PISTOL
Caliber: 9mm Para., 8-shot magazine.
Barrel: 4.5".
Weight: 41 oz. **Length:** 7.72" overall.
Stocks: Textured acetal plastic.
Sights: Fixed, low profile.
Features: Single-action design. Scratch-resistant, non-glare blue finish. Introduced 1990. From MKS Supply, Inc.
Price: Matte black **$139.95**
Price: Brushed nickel **$149.95**

STAR FIRESTAR AUTO PISTOL
Caliber: 9mm Para., 7-shot; 40 S&W, 6-shot.
Barrel: 3.39".
Weight: 30.35 oz. **Length:** 6.5" overall.
Stocks: Checkered rubber.
Sights: Blade front, fully adjustable rear; three-dot system.
Features: Low-profile, combat-style sights; ambidextrous safety. Available in blue or weather-resistant Starvel finish. Introduced 1990. Imported from Spain by Interarms.
Price: Blue, 9mm **$431.67**
Price: Starvel finish 9mm **$461.67**
Price: Blue, 40 S&W **$456.67**
Price: Starvel finish, 40 S&W **$486.67**

Star Firestar M45 Auto Pistol
Similar to the standard Firestar except chambered for 45 ACP with 6-shot magazine. Has 3.6" barrel, weighs 35 oz., 6.85" overall length. Reverse-taper Acculine barrel. Introduced 1992. Imported from Spain by Interarms.
Price: Blue **$491.67**
Price: Starvel finish **$521.67**

Star Firestar

STAR MEGASTAR 45 ACP AUTO PISTOL
Caliber: 10mm, 45 ACP, 12-shot magazine.
Barrel: 4.6".
Weight: 47.6 oz. **Length:** 8.44" overall.
Stocks: Checkered composition.
Sights: Blade front, adjustable rear.
Features: Double-action mechanism; steel frame and slide; reverse-taper Acculine barrel. Introduced 1992. Imported from Spain by Interarms.
Price: Blue, 10mm **$658.33**
Price: Starvel finish, 10mm **$688.33**
Price: Blue, 45 ACP **$658.33**
Price: Starvel finish, 45 ACP **$688.33**

STAR MODEL 31P & 31PK DOUBLE-ACTION PISTOLS

Caliber: 9mm Para., 15-shot magazine.
Barrel: 3.86".
Weight: 30 oz. **Length:** 7.6" overall.
Stocks: Checkered black plastic.
Sights: Square blade front, square notch rear click-adjustable for windage and elevation.
Features: Double or single action; grooved front- and backstraps and trigger guard face; ambidextrous safety cams firing pin forward; removable backstrap houses the firing mechanism; Model 31P has steel frame; Model PK is alloy. Introduced 1984. Imported from Spain by Interarms.
Price: Model 31P, 40 S&W, blue, steel frame **$610.00**
Price: Model 31P, 40 S&W, Starvel finish, steel frame **$640.00**
Price: Model 31P, 9mm, blue, steel frame, ... **$550.00**
Price: Model 31P, 9mm, Starvel finish, steel frame **$580.00**
Price: Model 31PK, 9mm only, blue, alloy frame **$550.00**

Star Model 31P

SUNDANCE MODEL A-25 AUTO PISTOL

Caliber: 25 ACP, 7-shot magazine.
Barrel: 2.5".
Weight: 16 oz. **Length:** 4⅞" overall.
Stocks: Grooved black ABS or simulated smooth pearl; optional pink.
Sights: Fixed.
Features: Manual rotary safety; button magazine release. Bright chrome or black Teflon finish. Introduced 1989. Made in U.S. by Sundance Industries, Inc.
Price: **$79.95**

SUNDANCE BOA AUTO PISTOL

Caliber: 25 ACP, 7-shot magazine.
Barrel: 2½".
Weight: 16 oz. **Length:** 4⅞".
Stocks: Grooved ABS or smooth simulated pearl; optional pink.
Sights: Fixed.
Features: Patented grip safety, manual rotary safety; button magazine release; lifetime warranty. Bright chrome or black Teflon finish. Introduced 1991. Made in the U.S. by Sundance Industries, Inc.
Price: **$95.00**

Sundance BOA

TAURUS MODEL PT 22/PT 25 AUTO PISTOLS

Caliber: 22 LR, 9-shot (PT 22); 25 ACP, 8-shot (PT 25).
Barrel: 2.75".
Weight: 12.3 oz. **Length:** 5.25" overall.
Stocks: Smooth Brazilian hardwood.
Sights: Blade front, fixed rear.
Features: Double action. Tip-up barrel for loading, cleaning. Blue only. Introduced 1992. Made in U.S. by Taurus International.
Price: 22 LR or 25 ACP **$182.00**

TAURUS MODEL PT58 AUTO PISTOL

Caliber: 380 ACP, 12-shot magazine.
Barrel: 4.01".
Weight: 30 oz. **Length:** 7.2" overall.
Stocks: Brazilian hardwood.
Sights: Integral blade on slide front, notch rear adjustable for windage. Three-dot system.
Features: Double action with exposed hammer; inertia firing pin. Introduced 1988. Imported by Taurus International.
Price: Blue **$423.00**
Price: Satin nickel **$454.00**
Price: Stainless steel **$481.00**

TAURUS MODEL PT 92 AUTO PISTOL

Caliber: 9mm Para., 15-shot magazine.
Barrel: 4.92".
Weight: 34 oz. **Length:** 8.54" overall.
Stocks: Brazilian hardwood.
Sights: Fixed notch rear. Three-dot sight system.
Features: Double action, exposed hammer, chamber loaded indicator. Inertia firing pin. Imported by Taurus International.
Price: Blue **$473.00**
Price: Blue, Deluxe Shooter's Pak (extra magazine, case) **$501.00**
Price: Nickel **$511.00**
Price: Nickel, Deluxe Shooter's Pak (extra magazine, case) **$539.00**
Price: Stainless steel **$538.00**
Price: Stainless, Deluxe Shooter's Pak (extra magazine, case) . . . **$564.00**

Taurus PT 92C

Taurus PT 92C Compact Pistol

Similar to the PT-92 except has 4.25" barrel, 13-shot magazine, weighs 31 oz. and is 7.5" overall. Available in stainless steel, blue or satin nickel. Introduced 1991. Imported by Taurus International.
Price: Blue **$473.00**
Price: Blue, Deluxe Shooter's Pak (extra magazine, case) **$501.00**
Price: Nickel **$511.00**
Price: Nickel, Deluxe Shooter's Pak (extra magazine, case) **$539.00**
Price: Stainless steel **$538.00**
Price: Stainless, Deluxe Shooter's Pak (extra magazine and case) . **$564.00**

Taurus PT 99 Auto Pistol

Similar to the PT-92 except has fully adjustable rear sight, smooth Brazilian walnut stocks and is available in stainless steel, polished blue or satin nickel. Introduced 1983.
Price: Blue **$512.00**
Price: Blue, Deluxe Shooter's Pak (extra magazine, case) **$540.00**
Price: Nickel **$554.00**
Price: Nickel, Deluxe Shooter's Pak (extra magazine, case) **$583.00**
Price: Stainless steel **$582.00**
Price: Stainless, Deluxe Shooter's Pak (extra magazine, case) . . . **$609.00**

TAURUS PT 100 AUTO PISTOL
Caliber: 40 S&W, 11-shot magazine.
Barrel: 5".
Weight: 34 oz.
Stocks: Smooth Brazilian hardwood.
Sights: Fixed front, drift-adjustable rear. Three-dot combat.
Features: Double action, exposed hammer. Ambidextrous hammer-drop safety; inertia firing pin; chamber loaded indicator. Introduced 1991. Imported by Taurus International.
Price: Blue **$482.00**
Price: Blue, Deluxe Shooter's Pak (extra magazine, case) **$510.00**
Price: Nickel **$521.00**
Price: Nickel, Deluxe Shooter's Pak (extra magazine, case) . . . **$548.00**
Price: Stainless **$547.00**
Price: Stainless, Deluxe Shooter's Pak (extra magazine, case) . . . **$575.00**

Taurus PT101

Taurus PT 101 Auto Pistol
Same as the PT 100 except has micro-click rear sight adjustable for windage and elevation, three-dot combat-style. Introduced 1991.
Price: Blue **$522.00**
Price: Blue, Deluxe Shooter's Pak (extra magazine, case) **$549.00**
Price: Nickel **$569.00**
Price: Nickel, Deluxe Shooter's Pak (extra magazine, case) . . . **$592.00**
Price: Stainless **$592.00**
Price: Stainless, Deluxe Shooter's Pak (extra magazine, case) . . . **$623.00**

UZI® PISTOL
Caliber: 9mm Para.
Barrel: 4.5".
Weight: 3.8 lbs. **Length:** 9.5" overall.
Stocks: Black plastic.
Sights: Post front with white dot, open rear click-adjustable for windage and elevation, two white dots.
Features: Semi-auto blowback action; fires from closed bolt; floating firing pin. Comes in a moulded plastic case with 20-round magazine; 25- and 32-round magazines available. Imported from Israel by Action Arms. Introduced 1984.
Price: **$595.00**

Uzi Pistol

WALTHER PP AUTO PISTOL
Caliber: 22 LR, 15-shot; 32 ACP, 380 ACP, 7-shot magazine.
Barrel: 3.86".
Weight: 23½ oz. **Length:** 6.7" overall.
Stocks: Checkered plastic.
Sights: Fixed, white markings.
Features: Double action; manual safety blocks firing pin and drops hammer; chamber loaded indicator on 32 and 380; extra finger rest magazine provided. Imported from Germany by Interarms.
Price: 22 LR **$900.00**
Price: 32 . . . . **$1,000.00**
Price: 380 . . . . **$1,075.00**
Price: Engraved models . . . . **On Request**

Walther PPK/S American

Walther PPK/S American Auto Pistol
Similar to Walther PP except made entirely in the United States. Has 3.27" barrel with 6.1" length overall. Introduced 1980.
Price: 380 ACP only **$585.00**
Price: As above, stainless **$585.00**

Walther PPK American Auto Pistol
Similar to Walther PPK/S except weighs 21 oz., has 6-shot capacity. Made in the U.S. Introduced 1986.
Price: Stainless, 380 ACP only **$585.00**
Price: Blue, 380 ACP only **$585.00**

WALTHER P-38 AUTO PISTOL
Caliber: 9mm Para., 8-shot.
Barrel: 4¹⁵⁄₁₆".
Weight: 28 oz. **Length:** 8½" overall.
Stocks: Checkered plastic.
Sights: Fixed.
Features: Double action; safety blocks firing pin and drops hammer. Matte finish standard, polished blue, engraving and/or plating available. Imported from Germany by Interarms.
Price: **$950.00**
Price: Engraved models . . . . **On Request**

Walther P-38

Walther P-5 Auto Pistol
Latest Walther design that uses the basic P-38 double-action mechanism. Caliber 9mm Para., barrel length 3½"; weight 28 oz., overall length 7".
Price: **$1,233.00**
Price: P-5 Compact **$1,660.00**

WALTHER MODEL TPH AUTO PISTOL
Caliber: 22 LR, 25 ACP, 6-shot magazine.
Barrel: 2¼".
Weight: 14 oz. **Length:** 5⅜" overall.
Stocks: Checkered black composition.
Sights: Blade front, rear drift-adjustable for windage.
Features: Made of stainless steel. Scaled-down version of the Walther PP/PPK series. Made in U.S. Introduced 1987. From Interarms.
Price: Blue of stainless steel, 22 or 25 . . . . **$445.00**

WALTHER P-88 AUTO PISTOL
Caliber: 9mm Para., 15-shot magazine.
Barrel: 4".
Weight: 31½ oz. **Length:** 7⅜" overall.
Stocks: Checkered black composition.
Sights: Blade front, rear adjustable for windage and elevation.
Features: Double action with ambidextrous decocking lever and magazine release; alloy frame; loaded chamber indicator; matte finish. Imported from Germany by Interarms.
Price: **$1,550.00**

Walther TPH

Wildey Auto

Wilkinson "Sherry"

WILDEY AUTOMATIC PISTOL
Caliber: 10mm Wildey Mag., 11mm Wildey Mag., 45 Win. Mag., 475 Wildey Mag., 357 Wildey Mag., 7-shot magazine.
Barrel: 5", 6", 7", 8", 10", 12" (45 Win. Mag.); 8", 10", 12" (all other cals.). Interchangeable.
Weight: 64 oz. (5" barrel). **Length:** 11" overall (7" barrel).
Stocks: Hardwood.
Sights: Ramp front with interchangeable red, orange, black (high and low) blades, fully adjustable rear. Scope base available.
Features: Gas-operated action. Made of stainless steel. Has three-lug rotary bolt. Double action. Polished and matte finish. Made in U.S. by Wildey, Inc.
Price: . . . . **$1,175.00 to $1,495.00**

WILKINSON "SHERRY" AUTO PISTOL
Caliber: 22 LR, 8-shot magazine.
Barrel: 2⅛".
Weight: 9¼ oz. **Length:** 4⅜" overall.
Stocks: Checkered black plastic.
Sights: Fixed, groove.
Features: Cross-bolt safety locks the sear into the hammer. Available in all blue finish or blue slide and trigger with gold frame. Introduced 1985.
Price: **$169.95**

WILKINSON "LINDA" AUTO PISTOL
Caliber: 9mm Para., 31-shot magazine.
Barrel: 8⁵⁄₁₆".
Weight: 4 lbs., 13 oz. **Length:** 12¼" overall.
Stocks: Checkered black plastic pistol grip, maple forend.
Sights: Protected blade front, aperture rear.
Features: Fires from closed bolt. Semi-auto only. Straight blowback action. Cross-bolt safety. Removable barrel. From Wilkinson Arms.
Price: **$412.00**

HANDGUNS—COMPETITION HANDGUNS

Models specifically designed for classic competitive shooting sports.

BF SINGLE SHOT PISTOL
Caliber: Standard—22 LR, 7mm SuperMag, 7-30 Waters, 32-20, (.308) Win., 30-30 Win., 357 Mag., 357 SuperMag (Maximum). Many other special chamberings on request.
Barrel: 10", 12", 14".
Weight: 46 oz. (10" bbl.).
Stocks: Plain and finger-grooved, ambidextrous; oil-finished walnut.
Sights: Burris Patridge front on ramp, Williams or RPM open rear with target knobs, adjustable for windage and elevation. Drilled and tapped for scope mount.
Features: Falling block short-stroke action, automatic case ejection. Wilson or Douglas air-gauged match-grade barrel. Flat black oxide finish. Introduced 1988. Made in U.S. by E.A. Brown Mfg.
Price: 10" barrel, no sights **$499.95**
Price: 12" barrel, no sights **$562.50**
Price: 14" barrel, no sights **$593.75**
Price: 10" barrel, Williams sights **$537.50**
Price: 12" barrel, Williams sights **$599.95**

CONSULT
Shooter's Marketplace
Page 225, This Issue

Price: 14" barrel, Williams sights **$631.25**
Price: 10" barrel, RPM sights **$581.25**
Price: 12" barrel, RPM sights **$643.75**
Price: 14" barrel, RPM sights **$674.95**

CAUTION: PRICES CHANGE, CHECK AT GUNSHOP.

BERETTA MODEL 89 TARGET PISTOL

Caliber: 22 LR, 8-shot magazine.
Barrel: 6"
Weight: 41 oz. **Length:** 9.5" overall.
Stocks: Target-type walnut with thumbrest.
Sights: Interchangeable blade front, fully adjustable rear.
Features: Single-action target pistol. Matte blue finish. Imported from Italy by Beretta U.S.A.
Price: $735.00

Beretta Model 89

BROWNING BUCK MARK SILHOUETTE

Caliber: 22 LR, 10-shot magazine.
Barrel: 9⅞".
Weight: 53 oz. **Length:** 14" overall.
Stocks: Smooth walnut stocks and forend, or finger-groove walnut.
Sights: Post-type hooded front adjustable for blade width and height; Pro Target rear fully adjustable for windage and elevation.
Features: Heavy barrel with .900" diameter; 12½" sight radius. Special sighting plane forms scope base. Introduced 1987. Made in U.S. From Browning.
Price: $379.95

Browning Buck Mark Target 5.5

Same as the Buck Mark Silhouette except has a 5½" barrel with .900" diameter. Has hooded sights mounted on a scope base that accepts an optical or reflex sight. Rear sight is a Browning fully adjustable Pro Target, front sight is an adjustable post that customizes to different widths, and can be adjusted for height. Contoured walnut grips with thumbrest, or finger-groove walnut. Matte blue finish. Overall length is 9⅝", weight is 35½ oz. Has 10-shot magazine. Introduced 1990. From Browning.
Price: $359.95
Price: Target 5.5 Gold (as above with gold anodized frame and top rib) $379.95

Browning Buck Mark Field 5.5

Same as the Target 5.5 except has hoodless ramp-style front sight and low profile rear sight. Matte blue finish, contoured or finger-groove walnut stocks. Introduced 1991.
Price: $359.95

COLT GOLD CUP NATIONAL MATCH MK IV/SERIES 80

Caliber: 45 ACP, 8-shot magazine.
Barrel: 5", with new design bushing.
Weight: 39 oz. **Length:** 8½".
Stocks: Rubber combat with silver-plated medallion.
Sights: Patridge-style front, Colt-Elliason rear adjustable for windage and elevation, sight radius 6¾".
Features: Arched or flat housing; wide, grooved trigger with adjustable stop; ribbed-top slide, hand fitted, with improved ejection port.
Price: Blue $819.95
Price: Stainless $874.95
Price: Bright stainless $940.95
Price: Delta Gold Cup (10mm, stainless) $899.95

COMPETITOR SINGLE SHOT PISTOL

Caliber: 22 LR through 50 Action Express, including belted magnums.
Barrel: 14" standard; 10.5" silhouette; 16" optional.
Weight: About 59 oz. (14" bbl.). **Length:** 15.12" overall.
Stocks: Ambidextrous; synthetic (standard) or laminated or natural wood.
Sights: Ramp front, adjustable rear.
Features: Rotary canon-type action cocks on opening; cammed ejector; interchangeable barrels, ejectors. Adjustable single stage trigger, sliding thumb safety and trigger safety. Matte blue finish. Introduced 1988. From Competitor Corp., Inc.
Price: 14", standard calibers, synthetic grip $364.90
Price: Extra barrels, from $132.95

E.A.A. EUROPEAN EA22T TARGET AUTO

Caliber: 22 LR, 12-shot.
Barrel: 6".
Weight: 40 oz. **Length:** 9.10" overall.
Stocks: Checkered walnut, with thumbrest.
Sights: Blade on ramp front, rear adjustable for windage and elevation.
Features: Blue finish. Finger-rest magazine. Imported by European American Armory Corp.
Price: $399.00

Browning Buck Mark Unlimited Match

Same as the Buck Mark Silhouette except has 14" heavy barrel. Conforms to IHMSA 15" maximum sight radius rule. Introduced 1991.
Price: $449.95

Browning Buck Mark Target 5.5

Colt Gold Cup National Match

E.A.A. European EA22T

E.A.A. TARGET GRADE REVOLVERS
Caliber: 22 LR, 8-shot, 38 Special, 357 Mag., 6-shot.
Barrel: 6".
Weight: 50.2 oz. **Length:** 11.8" overall.
Stocks: Walnut, competition style.
Sights: Blade front with three interchangeable blades, fully adjustable rear.
Features: Adjustable trigger with trigger stop and trigger shoe; frame drilled and tapped for scope mount; target hammer. Comes with barrel weights, plastic carrying box. Introduced 1991. Imported from Germany by European American Armory.
Price: **$499.00**

E.A.A. WITNESS GOLD TEAM AUTO
Caliber: 9mm Para., 9x21, 40 S&W, 41 A.E., 45 ACP.
Barrel: 5.1".
Weight: 41.6 oz. **Length:** 9.6" overall.
Stocks: Checkered walnut, competition style.
Sights: Square post front, fully adjustable rear.
Features: Triple-chamber compensator; competition SA trigger; extended safety and magazine release; competition hammer; beveled magazine well; beavertail grip. Hand-fitted major components. Hard chrome finish. Match-grade barrel. From E.A.A. Custom Shop. Introduced 1992. From European American Armory.
Price: **$2,195.00**

ERMA ER MATCH REVOLVERS
Caliber: 22 LR, 32 S&W Long, 6-shot.
Barrel: 6".
Weight: 47.3 oz. **Length:** 11.2" overall.
Stocks: Stippled walnut, adjustable match-type.
Sights: Blade front, micrometer rear adjustable for windage and elevation.
Features: Polished blue finish. Introduced 1989. Imported from Germany by Precision Sales International.
Price: 22 LR or 32 S&W Long **$1,345.00**

ERMA ESP 85A COMPETITION PISTOL
Caliber: 22 LR, 8-shot; 32 S&W, 5-shot magazine.
Barrel: 6".
Weight: 39 oz. **Length:** 10" overall.
Stocks: Match-type of stippled walnut; adjustable.
Sights: Interchangeable blade front, micrometer adjustable rear with interchangeable leaf.
Features: Five-way adjustable trigger; exposed hammer and separate firing pin block allow unlimited dry firing practice. Blue or matte chrome; right- or left-hand. Introduced 1988. Imported from Germany by Precision Sales International.
Price: 22 LR **$1,345.00**
Price: 22 LR, left-hand **$1,375.00**
Price: 22 LR, matte chrome **$1,578.00**
Price: 32 S&W **$1,400.00**

FAS 601 Match Pistol
Similar to Model 602 except has different match stocks with adjustable palm shelf, 22 Short only for rapid fire shooting; weighs 40 oz., 5.6" bbl.; has gas ports through top of barrel and slide to reduce recoil; slightly different trigger and sear mechanisms. Imported from Italy by Nygord Precision Products.
Price: **$1,150.00**

FREEDOM ARMS CASULL MODEL 252 SILHOUETTE
Caliber: 22 LR, 5-shot cyclinder.
Barrel: 9.95".
Weight: 63 oz. **Length:** NA
Stocks: Black micarta, western style.
Sights: 1/8" Patridge front, Iron Sight Gun Works silhouette rear, click adjustable for windage and elevation.
Features: Stainless steel. Built on the 454 Casull frame. Two-point firing pin, lightened hammer for fast lock time. Trigger pull is 3 to 5 lbs. with pre-set overtravel screw. Introduced 1991. From Freedom Arms.
Price: Silhouette Class **$1,295.00**
Price: Extra fitted 22 WMR cylinder **$206.75**

Freedom Arms Casull Model 252 Varmint
Similar to the Silhouette Class revolver except has 7.5" barrel, weighs 59 oz., has black and green laminated hardwood grips, and comes with brass bead front sight, express shallow V rear sight with windage and elevation adjustments. Introduced 1991. From Freedom Arms.
Price: Varmint Class **$1,248.00**
Price: Extra fitted 22 WMR cylinder **$206.75**

E.A.A. Witness Gold Team

E.A.A. Witness Silver Team Auto
Similar to the Wittness Gold Team except has double-chamber compensator, paddle magazine release, checkered walnut grips, double-dip blue finish. Comes with Super Sight or drilled and tapped for scope mount. Built for the intermediate competition shooter. Introduced 1992. From European American Armory Custom Shop.
Price: 9mm Para., 9x21, 40 S&W, 41 A.E. **$1,195.00**

Erma ER Match

FAS 602 MATCH PISTOL
Caliber: 22 LR, 5-shot.
Barrel: 5.6".
Weight: 37 oz. **Length:** 11" overall.
Stocks: Walnut wraparound; sizes small, medium or large, or adjustable.
Sights: Match. Blade front, open notch rear fully adjustable for windage and elevation. Sight radius is 8.66".
Features: Line of sight is only $^{11}/_{32}$" above centerline of bore; magazine is inserted from top; adjustable and removable trigger mechanism; single lever takedown. Full 5-year warranty. Imported from Italy by Nygord Precision Products.
Price: **$1,050.00**

FAS 603 Match Pistol
Similar to the FAS 602 except chambered for 32 S&W with 5-shot magazine; 5.3" barrel; 8.66" sight radius; overall length 11.0"; weighs 42.3 oz. Imported from Italy by Nygord Precision Products.
Price: **$1,150.00**

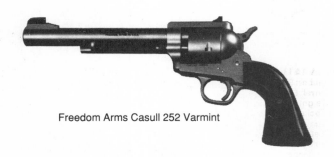

Freedom Arms Casull 252 Varmint

Glock 17L

HAMMERLI MODEL 150 FREE PISTOL

Caliber: 22 LR, single shot.
Barrel: 11.3".
Weight: 43 oz. **Length:** 15.35" overall.
Stocks: Walnut with adjustable palm shelf.
Sights: Sight radius of 14.6". Micro rear sight adjustable for windage and elevation.
Features: Single shot Martini action. Cocking lever on left side of action with vertical operation. Set trigger adjustable for length and angle. Trigger pull weight adjustable between 5 and 100 grams. Guaranteed accuracy of .78", 10 shots from machine rest. Imported from Switzerland by Beeman, Hammerli Pistols USA, and Mandall Shooting Supplies.
Price: About . . . . **$1,980.00 to $2,217.00**

HAMMERLI MODEL 208s PISTOL

Caliber: 22 LR, 8-shot magazine.
Barrel: 5.9".
Weight: 37.5 oz. **Length:** 10" overall.
Stocks: Walnut, target-type with thumbrest.
Sights: Blade front, open fully adjustable rear.
Features: Adjustable trigger, including length; interchangeable rear sight elements. Imported from Switzerland by Beeman, Hammerli Pistols USA, Mandall Shooting Supplies.
Price: About . . . . **$1,665 to $1,955.00**

HAMMERLI MODEL 208, 211 TARGET PISTOLS

Caliber: 22 LR.
Barrel: 5.9", 6-groove.
Weight: 37.6 oz. (45 oz. with extra heavy barrel weight). **Length:** 10".
Stocks: Walnut. Adjustable palm rest (208), 211 has thumbrest grip.
Sights: Match sights, fully adjustable for windage and elevation (click adjustable). Interchangeable front and rear blades.
Features: Semi-automatic, recoil operated. 8-shot clip. Slide stop. Fully adjustable trigger (2¼ lbs. and 3 lbs.). Extra barrel weight available. Imported from Switzerland by Mandall Shooting Supplies, Beeman.
Price: Model 208, approx. (Mandall) **$1,755.00**
Price: Model 211, approx. (Mandall) **$1,650.00**
Price: Model 208 (Beeman) **$1,955.00**

Hammerli 280

LLAMA M-87 9MM COMP

Caliber: 9mm Para., 14-shot magazine.
Barrel: 6".
Weight: 47 oz. **Length:** 9.5" overall.
Stocks: Polymer composition.
Sights: Patridge front, fully adjustable rear.
Features: A match-ready Comp pistol. Built-in ported compensator, over-size magazine and safety releases, fixed barrel bushing, bevelled magazine well, extended trigger guard. Introduced 1989. Imported by Stoeger Industries.
Price: **$1,450.00**

GAUCHER GP SILHOUETTE PISTOL

Caliber: 22 LR, single shot.
Barrel: 10".
Weight: 42.3 oz. **Length:** 15.5" overall.
Stocks: Stained hardwood.
Sights: Hooded post on ramp front, open rear adjustable for windage and elevation.
Features: Matte chrome barrel, blued bolt and sights. Other barrel lengths available on special order. Introduced 1991. Imported by Mandall Shooting Supplies.
Price: **$323.00**

GLOCK 17L COMPETITION AUTO

Caliber: 9mm Para., 17-shot magazine.
Barrel: 6.02".
Weight: 23.3 oz. **Length:** 8.7" overall.
Stocks: Black polymer.
Sights: Blade front with white dot, fixed or adjustable rear.
Features: Polymer frame, steel slide; double-action trigger with "Safe Action" system; mechanical firing pin safety, drop safety; simple takedown without tools; locked breech, recoil operated action. Introduced 1989. Imported from Austria by Glock, Inc.
Price: **$768.25**

HAMMERLI MODEL 152 MATCH PISTOL

Caliber: 22 LR.
Barrel: 11.2".
Weight: 46.9 oz. **Length:** 16.9" overall.
Stocks: Match.
Sights: Changeable post front, micrometer rear.
Features: Electronic trigger. Introduced 1990. Imported from Switzerland by Beeman, Hammerli Pistols USA, Mandall Shooting Supplies.
Price: About . . . . **$2,105.00 to $2,333.00**

Hammerli 208s

HAMMERLI MODEL 280 TARGET PISTOL

Caliber: 22 LR, 6-shot; 32 S&W Long WC, 5-shot.
Barrel: 4.5".
Weight: 39.1 oz. (32). **Length:** 11.8" overall.
Stocks: Walnut match-type with stippling, adjustable palm shelf.
Sights: Match sights, micrometer adjustable; interchangeable elements.
Features: Has carbon-reinforced synthetic frame and bolt/barrel housing. Trigger is adjustable for pull weight, take-up weight, let-off, and length, and is interchangeable. Interchangeable metal or carbon fiber counterweights. Sight radius of 8.8". Comes with barrel weights, spare magazine, loading tool, cleaning rods. Introduced 1990. Imported from Switzerland by Beeman, Hammerli Pistols USA and Mandall Shooting Supplies.
Price: 22-cal., about . . . . **$1,505.00 to $1,895.00**
Price: 32-cal., about . . . . **$1,650.00 to $1,655.00**

Llama M-87 Comp

McMILLAN SIGNATURE JR. LONG RANGE PISTOL
Caliber: Any suitable caliber.
Barrel: To customer specs.
Weight: 5 lbs.
Stock: McMillan fiberglass.
Sights: None furnished; comes with scope rings.
Features: Right- or left-hand McMillan benchrest action of titanium or stainless steel; single shot or repeater. Comes with bipod. Introduced 1992. Made in U.S. by McMillan Gunworks, Inc.
Price: **$2,370.00**

McMillan Wolverine

McMILLAN WOLVERINE AUTO PISTOL
Caliber: 9mm Para., 10mm Auto, 38 Wadcutter, 38 Super, 45 Italian, 45 ACP.
Barrel: 6".
Weight: 45 oz. **Length:** 9.5" overall.
Stocks: Pachmayr rubber.
Sights: Blade front, fully adjustable rear; low profile.
Features: Integral compensator; round burr-style hammer; extended grip safety; checkered backstrap; skeletonized aluminum match trigger. Many finish options. Announced 1992. Made in U.S. by McMillan Gunworks, Inc.
Price: Combat or Competition Match **$1,500.00**

MITCHELL ARMS OLYMPIC I.S.U. AUTO PISTOL
Caliber: 22 Short, 10-shot magazine.
Barrel: 6.75" round tapered, with stabilizer.
Weight: 40 oz. **Length:** 11.25" overall.
Stocks: Checkered walnut with thumbrest.
Sights: Undercut ramp front, frame-mounted click adjustable square notch rear.
Features: Integral stabilizer with two removable weights. Trigger adjustable for pull and over-travel; blue finish; stippled front and backstraps; push-button barrel takedown. Announced 1992. From Mitchell Arms.
Price: . . . . **NA**

PETERS STAHL PSP-07 COMBAT COMPENSATOR PISTOL
Caliber: 45 ACP, 7-shot, or 10mm Auto, 8-shot magazine.
Barrel: 6".
Weight: 45 oz. **Length:** 10" overall.
Stocks: Pachmayr Presenation rubber.
Sights: Interchangeable blade front, fully adjustable Peters Stahl rear.
Features: Linkless barrel with polygonal rifling and integral PS competition compensator; semi-extended PS slide stop and thumb safety; rearward extended magazine release; adjustable Videcki trigger; Wilson stainless beavertail grip safety; Pachmayr rubber mainspring housing. Introduced 1989. Imported from Germany by Federal Ordnance.
Price: 45 ACP **$2,599.95**
Price: 10mm Auto **$2,650.95**

Ram-Line Exactor Target

RAM-LINE EXACTOR TARGET PISTOL
Caliber: 22 LR, 15-shot magazine.
Barrel: 8.0".
Weight: 23 oz. **Length:** 12.3" overall.
Stocks: One-piece injection moulded in conventional contour; checkered side panels, ridged front and backstraps.
Sights: Ramp front with interchangeable .125" blade, rear adjustable for windage and elevation.
Features: Injection moulded grip frame, alloy receiver; hybrid composite barrel. Constant force sear spring gives 2.5-lb. trigger pull. Adapt-A-Barrel allows mounting weights, flashlight. Drilled and tapped receiver for scope mounting. Jewelled bolt. Comes with carrying case, test target. Introduced 1990. Made in U.S. by Ram-Line, Inc.
Price: **$279.97**

RANGER ALPHA AUTO PISTOL
Caliber: 38 Super, 9-shot; 10mm Auto, 8-shot; 45 ACP, 7-shot.
Barrel: 5", 6", ported or unported.
Weight: 42 oz. **Length:** 8.5" overall.
Stocks: Wraparound rubber.
Sights: Interchangeable front, fully adjustable Peters Stahl rear.
Features: Peters Stahl linkless barrel system, polygonal rifling; extended grip safety, thumb safety, slide release, magazine release. High polish blue finish. Introduced 1990. From Federal Ordnance.
Price: 5" unported, 38 Super, 45 . . . . **$999.95**
Price: 5" ported, 38 Super, 45 . . . . **$1,015.95**
Price: 5" unported, 10mm **$1,015.95**
Price: 5" ported, 10mm **$1,024.95**
Price: 6" unported, 38 Super, 45 . . . . **$1,015.95**
Price: 6" ported, 38 Super, 45 . . . . **$1,024.95**
Price: 6" ported, 10mm **$1,049.95**

RANGER SUPERCOMP AUTO PISTOL
Caliber: 10mm Auto, 8-shot; 45 ACP, 7-shot magazine.
Barrel: 6".
Weight: 42 oz. **Length:** 9.4" overall.
Stocks: Wraparound rubber.
Sights: Ramped blade front, fully adjustable, low-profile Ranger rear.
Features: Uses Peters Stahl linkless barrel system with polygonal rifling and integral competition compensator; extended grip safety, thumb safety, slide release, magazine release; lightened speed trigger; full-length recoil spring guide; lowered ejection port; beveled magazine well; ramped and throated barrel. Blued slide, electroless nickel frame. Introduced 1990. From Federal Ordnance.
Price: 10mm **$1,399.95**
Price: 45 ACP **$1,389.95**

Remington XP-100 Silhouette

REMINGTON XP-100 SILHOUETTE PISTOL
Caliber: 7mm BR Remington, 35 Remington, single shot.
Barrel: 14½".
Weight: 4½ lbs. **Length:** 21¼" overall.
Stocks: Brown nylon, one piece, checkered grip.
Sights: None furnished. Drilled and tapped for scope mounts.
Features: Universal grip fits right or left hand; match-type grooved trigger, two-position thumb safety.
Price: 7mm BR Rem. **$427.00**
Price: 35 Rem. **$441.00**

CAUTION: PRICES CHANGE, CHECK AT GUNSHOP.

Ruger Government Target

RUGER MARK II TARGET MODEL AUTO PISTOL
Caliber: 22 LR, 10-shot magazine.
Barrel: 5¼", 6⅞".
Weight: 42 oz. **Length:** 11⅛" overall.
Stocks: Checkered hard plastic.
Sights: .125" blade front, micro-click rear, adjustable for windage and elevation. Sight radius 9⅜".
Features: Introduced 1982.
Price: Blued (MK-514, MK-678) **$294.50**
Price: Stainless (KMK-514, KMK-678) **$373.00**

Ruger Mark II Government Target Model
Same gun as the Mark II Target Model except has 6⅞" barrel, higher sights and is roll marked "Government Target Model" on the right side of the receiver below the rear sight. Identical in all aspects to the military model used for training U.S. armed forces except for markings. Comes with factory test target. Introduced 1987.
Price: Blued (MK-678G) **$340.50**
Price: Stainless (KMK-678G) **$411.29**

Ruger Mark II Bull Barrel
Same gun as the Target Model except has 5½" or 10" heavy barrel (10" meets all IHMSA regulations). Weight with 5½" barrel is 42 oz., with 10" barrel, 52 oz.
Price: Blued (MK-512, MK-10) **$294.50**
Price: Stainless (KMK-512, KMK-10) **$373.00**

Ruger Stainless Government Competition Model 22 Pistol
Similar to the Mark II Government Target Model stainless pistol except has 6⅞" slab-sided barrel; the receiver top is drilled and tapped for a Ruger scope base adaptor of blued, chromemoly steel; comes with Ruger 1" stainless scope rings with integral bases for mounting a variety of optical sights; has checkered laminated grip panels with right-hand thumbrest. Has blued open sights with 9¼" radius. Overall length is 11⅛", weight 44 oz. Introduced 1991.
Price: KMK-678GC **$425.00**

Safari Arms Matchmaster

SAFARI ARMS MATCHMASTER PISTOL
Caliber: 45 ACP, 7-shot magazine.
Barrel: 5"; National Match, stainless steel.
Weight: 44 oz. **Length:** 8.7" overall.
Stocks: Smooth walnut with etched scorpion logo.
Sights: Ramped blade front, rear adjustable for windage and elevation.
Features: Beavertail grip safety, extended safety, extended slide release, Commander-style hammer; throated, ported, tuned. Finishes: Parkerized matte black, or stainless steel. Available from Safari Arms, Inc.
Price: **$690.00**

Smith & Wesson Model 41

> Consult our Directory pages for the location of firms mentioned.

SMITH & WESSON MODEL 41 TARGET
Caliber: 22 LR, 10-shot clip.
Barrel: 5½", 7".
Weight: 44 oz. **Length:** 9" overall.
Stocks: Checkered walnut with modified thumbrest, usable with either hand.
Sights: ⅛" Patridge on ramp base; S&W micro-click rear adjustable for windage and elevation.
Features: ⅜" wide, grooved trigger; adjustable trigger stop.
Price: S&W Bright Blue, satin matted top area **$738.00**

SMITH & WESSON MODEL 52 38 MASTER AUTO
Caliber: 38 Special (for mid-range W.C. with flush-seated bullet only), 5-shot magazine.
Barrel: 5".
Weight: 40 oz. with empty magazine. **Length:** 8⅝" overall.
Stocks: Checkered walnut.
Sights: ⅛" Patridge front, S&W micro-click rear adjustable for windage and elevation.
Features: Top sighting surfaces matte finished. Locked breech, moving barrel system; checked for 10-ring groups at 50 yards. Coin-adjustable sight screws. Dry-firing permissible if manual safety on.
Price: S&W Bright Blue **$890.00**

Smith & Wesson Model 52

SPRINGFIELD ARMORY 1911A1 BULLSEYE WADCUTTER PISTOL
Caliber: 38 Super, 10mm, 40 S&W, 45 ACP.
Barrel: 5", 6".
Weight: 45 oz. **Length:** 8.59" overall (5" barrel).
Stocks: Checkered walnut.
Sights: Bo-Mar rib with undercut blade front, fully adjustable rear.
Features: Built for wadcutter loads only. Has full-length recoil spring guide rod, fitted Videki speed trigger with 3.5-lb. pull; match Commander hammer and sear; beavertail grip safety; lowered and flared ejection port; tuned extractor; fitted slide to frame; Shok Buff; beveled and polished magazine well; checkered front strap and steel mainspring housing (flat housing standard); removable grip scope mount; polished and throated National Match barrel and bushing. All except 45 ACP have supported chambers. Comes with two magazines with slam pads, plastic carrying case, test target. Introduced 1992. From Springfield Armory Custom Shop.
Price: 38 Super, blue, 5" **$1,840.00**
Price: As above, 6" **$1,869.00**
Price: 10mm, 40 S&W, blue, 5" **$1,989.00**
Price: As above, 6" **$2,013.00**
Price: 45 ACP, blue, 5" **$1,640.00**
Price: As above, 6" **$1,669.00**
Price: 45 ACP, blue, 6", ported **$1,720.00**

Springfield Armory Trophy Master Competition Pistol
Similar to the 1911A1 Entry Level Wadcutter Pistol except has brazed, serrated improved ramp front sight; extended ambidextrous thumb safety; match Commander hammer and sear; serrated rear slide; Pachmay flat mainspring housing; extended magazine release; beavertail grip safety; full-length recoil spring guide; Pachmayr wrap-around grips. All except 45 ACP have supported chamber. Comes with two magazines with slam pads, plastic carrying case. Introduced 1992. From Springfield Armory Custom Shop.
Price: 9x21, 38 Super, blue, 5" **$1,700.00**
Price: 10mm, 40 S&W, blue, 5" **$1,835.00**
Price: 45 ACP, blue, 5" **$1,569.00**

Springfield Armory Trophy Master Distinguished Pistol
Has all the features of the 1911A1 Trophy Master Expert except is full-house pistol with Bo-Mar low-mounted adjustable rear sight with hidden rear leaf; full-length recoil spring guide rod and recoil spring retainer; checkered magazine well/mainspring housing matched to beveled magazine well (Smith & Alexander, flat, standard); flattened and checkered trigger guard; serrated top of slide and compensator; cocking serrations on front of slide; walnut grips. All except 45 ACP have supported chamber. Hard chrome finish. Comes with five magazines with slam pads, plastic carrying case. From Springfield Armory Custom Shop.
Price: 9x21, 38 Super **$2,749.00**
Price: 10mm, 40 S&W **$2,869.00**
Price: 45 ACP **$2,569.00**

SPRINGFIELD ARMORY CUSTOM P9 "WORLD CUP"
Caliber: 9x21, 17-shot; 40 S&W, 12-shot magazine.
Barrel: 5½".
Weight: About 36 oz.
Stocks: Checkered walnut match style.
Sights: Blade front, BoMar adjustable, low mounted.
Features: Match barrel with tapered cone dual-port compensator; full-length recoil rod system; reverse recoil plug; improved custom extractor; extended ambidextrous thumb safety; beavertail grip safety; square trigger guard; checkered front- and backstraps; extended magazine release; aluminum match trigger with overtravel stop, single-action only; match-grade Commander hammer. Comes with three magazines, carrying case. Introduced 1991. From Springfield Armory.
Price: **$2,935.00**

Springfield Armory Entry Level Wadcutter Pistol
Similar to the 1911A1 Bullseye Wadcutter Pistol except has low-mounted Bo-Mar adjustable rear sight, undercut blade front; match throated barrel and bushing; polished feed ramp; lowered and flared ejection port; fitted Videki speed trigger with tuned 3.5-lb. pull; fitted slide to frame; Shok Buff; arched steel mainspring housing; Pachmayr grips. Comes with two magazines with slam pads, plastic carrying case, test target. Introduced 1992. From Springfield Armory Custom Shop.
Price: 38 Super (with supported chamber) **$1,249.00**
Price: 10mm (with supported chamber) **$1,440.00**
Price: 40 S&W (with supported chamber) **$1,440.00**
Price: 45 ACP, blue, 5" only **$1,049.00**

Springfield Armory 1911A1 N.M. Hardball Pistol
Similar to the 1911A1 Entry Level Wadcutter Pistol except has Bo-Mar adjustable rear sight with undercut front blade; fitted match Videki trigger with 4-lb. pull; fitted slide to frame; throated National Match barrel and bushing, polished feed ramp; Shok Buff; tuned extractor; Herrett walnut grips. Comes with one magazine, plastic carrying case, test target. Introduced 1992. From Springfield Armory Custom Shop.
Price: 45 ACP, blue **$1,000.00**

Springfield Armory Trophy Master Expert Pistol
Similar to the 1911A1 Trophy Master Competition Pistol except has S.A. dual-chamber tapered cone compensator on match barrel with dovetailed front sight; lowered and flared ejection port; fully tuned for reliability. All except 45 ACP have supported chamber. Comes with two magazines, plastic carrying case. Introduced 1992. From Springfield Armory Custom Shop.
Price: 9x21, 38 Super, Duotone finish **$1,960.00**
Price: 10mm, 40 S&W, Duotone finish **$2,095.00**
Price: 45 ACP, Duotone finish **$1,829.00**

Springfield Armory P9 "World Cup"

THOMPSON/CENTER SUPER 14 CONTENDER
Caliber: 22 LR, 222 Rem., 223 Rem., 7mm TCU, 7-30 Waters, 30-30 Win., 35 Rem., 357 Rem. Maximum, 44 Mag., 10mm Auto, 445 Super Mag., single shot.
Barrel: 14".
Weight: 45 oz. **Length:** 17¼" overall.
Stocks: T/C "Competitor Grip" (walnut and rubber).
Sights: Fully adjustable target-type.
Features: Break-open action with auto safety. Interchangeable barrels for both rimfire and centerfire calibers. Introduced 1978.
Price: **$415.00**
Price: Extra barrels, blued **$195.00**

Thompson/Center Super 16 Contender
Same as the T/C Super 14 Contender except has 16¼" barrel. Rear sight can be mounted at mid-barrel position (10¾" radius) or moved to the rear (using scope mount position) for 14¾" radius. Overall length is 20¼". Comes with T/C Competitor Grip of walnut and rubber. Available in 22 LR, 22 WMR, 223 Rem., 7-30 Waters, 30-30 Win., 35 Rem., 44 Mag., 45-70 Gov't. Also available with 16" vent rib barrel with internal choke, caliber 45 Colt/410 shotshell.
Price: **$420.00**
Price: 45-70 Gov't **$440.00**
Price: Extra 16" barrels (blued) **$200.00**
Price: As above, 45-70 . . . . **$220.00**
Price: Super 16 Vent Rib (45-410) **$450.00**
Price: Extra vent rib barrel **$230.00**

Thompson/Center Super 14 Contender

CAUTION: PRICES CHANGE, CHECK AT GUNSHOP.

TMI SINGLE SHOT PISTOL

Caliber: 22 LR, 223, 7mm TCU, 7mm Int., 30 Herrett, 357 Maximum, 41 Mag., 44 Mag., 454 Casull, 375 Super Mag. Others on special order.
Barrel: 10.5", 14".
Weight: NA **Length:** NA.
Stocks: Smooth walnut with thumbrest.
Sights: Ramp front, open adjustable rear.
Features: Interchangeable barrels of blue ordnance or bright stainless steel; ventilated barrel shroud; receiver has integral scope mount. Introduced 1987. From TMI Products.
Price: With 10.5" bbl. **$562.50**
Price: With 14" bbl. **$578.50**
Price: Extra barrels, 10.5", standard calibers **$93.75**
Price: Special calibers, add **$62.50**

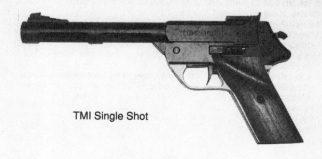

TMI Single Shot

Unique D.E.S. 69U

Unique Model 2000-U

WALTHER GSP MATCH PISTOL

Caliber: 22 LR, 32 S&W wadcutter (GSP-C), 5-shot.
Barrel: 5¾".
Weight: 44.8 oz. (22 LR), 49.4 oz. (32). **Length:** 11.8" overall.
Stocks: Walnut, special hand-fitting design.
Sights: Fixed front, rear adjustable for windage and elevation.
Features: Available with either 2.2 lb. (1000 gm) or 3 lb. (1360 gm) trigger. Spare mag., bbl. weight, tools supplied in Match Pistol Kit. Imported from Germany by Interarms.
Price: GSP, with case **$1,750.00**
Price: GSP-C, with case **$1,810.00**
Price: 22 LR conversion unit for GSP-C (no trigger unit) . . . **$1,000.00**
Price: 22 Short conversion unit for GSP-C (with trigger unit) . **$1,420.00**
Price: 32 S&W conversion unit for GSP-C (no trigger unit) . . . **$1,330.00**
Price: GSP Jr. (4.5" bbl., case) **$1,810.00**

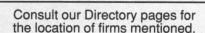

> Consult our Directory pages for the location of firms mentioned.

Walther OSP Rapid-Fire Pistol

Similar to Model GSP except 22 Short only, stock has adjustable free-style hand rest.
Price: **$2,160.00**

UNIQUE D.E.S. 32U RAPID FIRE MATCH

Caliber: 32 S&W Long wadcutter.
Barrel: 5.9".
Weight: 40.2 oz.
Stocks: Anatomically shaped, adjustable stippled French walnut.
Sights: Blade front, micrometer click rear.
Features: Trigger adjustable for weight and position; dry firing mechanism; slide stop catch. Optional sleeve weights. Introduced 1990. Imported from France by Nygord Precision Products.
Price: Right-hand, about **$1,150.00**
Price: Left-hand, about **$1,215.00**

UNIQUE D.E.S. 69U TARGET PISTOL

Caliber: 22 LR, 5-shot magazine.
Barrel: 5.91".
Weight: 35.3 oz. **Length:** 10.5" overall.
Stocks: French walnut target-style with thumbrest and adjustable shelf; hand-checkered panels.
Sights: Ramp front, micro. adj. rear mounted on frame; 8.66" sight radius.
Features: Meets U.I.T. standards. Comes with 260-gram barrel weight; 100, 150, 350-gram weights available. Fully adjustable match trigger; dry-firing safety device. Imported from France by Nygord Precision Products.
Price: Right-hand, about **$1,075.00**
Price: Left-hand, about **$1,115.00**

UNIQUE MODEL 2000-U MATCH PISTOL

Caliber: 22 Short, 5-shot magazine.
Barrel: 5.9".
Weight: 43 oz. **Length:** 11.3" overall.
Stocks: Anatomically shaped, adjustable, stippled French walnut.
Sights: Blade front, fully adjustable rear; 9.7" sight radius.
Features: Light alloy frame, steel slide and shock absorber; five barrel vents reduce recoil, three of which can be blocked; trigger adjustable for position and pull weight. Comes with 340-gram weight housing, 160-gram available. Introduced 1984. Imported from France by Nygord Precision Products.
Price: Right-hand, about **$1,250.00**
Price: Left-hand, about **$1,265.00**

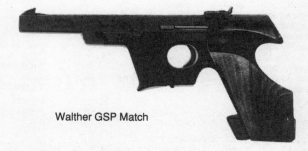

Walther GSP Match

WESSON FIREARMS MODEL 22 SILHOUETTE REVOLVER

Caliber: 22 LR, 6-shot.
Barrel: 10", regular vent or vent heavy.
Weight: 53 oz.
Stocks: Combat style.
Sights: Patridge-style front, .080" narrow notch rear.
Features: Single action only. Available in blue or stainless. Introduced 1989. From Wesson Firearms Co., Inc.
Price: Blue, regular vent **$430.00**
Price: Blue, vent heavy **$448.00**
Price: Stainless, regular vent **$458.00**
Price: Stainless, vent heavy **$485.00**

WESSON FIREARMS ACTION CUP/PPC REVOLVERS
Caliber: 38 Spec., 357 Mag., 6-shot.
Barrel: Extra heavy 6" bull shroud with removable underweight.
Weight: 4 lbs., 7 oz. (PPC, with weight).
Stocks: Pachmayr Gripper.
Sights: Tasco Pro Point II on Action Cup; Aristocrat with three-position rear on PPC model.
Features: Competition tuned with narrow trigger, chamfered cylinder chambers. Action Cup available in stainless only, PPC in bright blue or stainless. Introduced 1989.
Price: Action Cup **$913.00**
Price: PPC, blue **$780.00**
Price: PPC, stainless **$857.00**

Wesson Firearms Model 445 Supermag Revolver
Similar size and weight as the Model 40 revolvers. Chambered for the 445 Supermag cartridge, a longer version of the 44 Magnum. Barrel lengths of 4", 6", 8", 10". Contact maker for complete price list. Introduced 1989. From Wesson Firearms Co., Inc.
Price: 4", vent heavy, blue **$539.00**
Price: As above, stainless **$615.00**
Price: 8", vent heavy, blue **$594.00**
Price: As above, stainless **$662.00**
Price: 10", vent heavy, blue **$615.00**
Price: As above, stainless **$683.00**
Price: 8", vent slotted, blue **$575.00**
Price: As above, stainless **$632.00**
Price: 10", vent slotted, blue **$597.00**
Price: As above, stainless **$657.00**

WESSON FIREARMS MODEL 322/7322 TARGET REVOLVER
Caliber: 32-20, 6-shot.
Barrel: 2.5", 4", 6", 8", standard, vent, vent heavy.
Weight: 43 oz. (6" VH). **Length:** 11.25" overall.
Stocks: Checkered walnut.
Sights: Red ramp interchangeable front, fully adjustable rear.
Features: Brigh blue or stainless. Introduced 1991. From Wesson Firearms Co., Inc.
Price: 6", blue **$355.00**
Price: 6", stainless **$384.00**
Price: 8", vent, blue **$397.00**
Price: 8", stainless **$425.00**
Price: 6", vent heavy, blue **$405.00**
Price: 6", vent heavy, stainless **$433.00**
Price: 8", vent heavy, blue **$415.00**
Price: 8", vent heavy, stainless **$451.00**

WICHITA SILHOUETTE PISTOL
Caliber: 308 Win. F.L., 7mm IHMSA, 7mm-308.
Barrel: 14¹⁵⁄₁₆".
Weight: 4½ lbs. **Length:** 21⅜" overall.
Stock: American walnut with oil finish. Glass bedded.
Sights: Wichita Multi-Range sight system.
Features: Comes with left-hand action with right-hand grip. Round receiver and barrel. Fluted bolt, flat bolt handle. Wichita adjustable trigger. Introduced 1979. From Wichita Arms.
Price: Center grip stock **$1,150.00**
Price: As above except with Rear Position Stock and target-type Lightpull trigger **$1,150.00**

WICHITA INTERNATIONAL PISTOL
Caliber: 22 LR, 22 WMR, 32 H&R Mag., 357 Super Mag., 357 Mag., 7R, 7mm Super Mag., 7-30 Waters, 30-30 Win., single shot.
Barrel: 10", 10½", 14".
Weight: 3 lbs. 2 oz. (with 10", 10½" barrels).
Stocks: Walnut grip and forend.
Sights: Patridge front, adjustable rear. Wichita Multi-Range sight system optional.
Features: Made of stainless steel. Break-open action. Grip dimensions same as Colt 45 Auto. Drilled and tapped for furnished see-thru rings. Extra barrels are factory fitted. Introduced 1983. Available from Wichita Arms.
Price: International 10" **$550.00**
Price: International 14" **$585.00**
Price: Extra barrels, 10" **$325.00**
Price: Extra barrels, 14" **$355.00**

WESSON FIREARMS MODEL 40 SILHOUETTE
Caliber: 357 Maximum, 6-shot.
Barrel: 4", 6", 8", 10".
Weight: 64 oz. (8" bbl.). **Length:** 14.3" overall (8" bbl.).
Stocks: Smooth walnut, target-style.
Sights: ⅛" serrated front, fully adjustable rear.
Features: Meets criteria for IHMSA competition with 8" slotted barrel. Blue or stainless steel. Made in U.S. by Wesson Firearms Co., Inc.
Price: Blue, 4" **$488.00**
Price: Blue, 6" **$508.00**
Price: Blue, 8" **$525.00**
Price: Blue, 10" **$543.00**
Price: Stainless, 4" **$550.00**
Price: Stainless, 6" **$569.00**
Price: Stainless, 8" slotted **$595.00**
Price: Stainless, 10" **$609.00**

Wesson Firearms Model 40

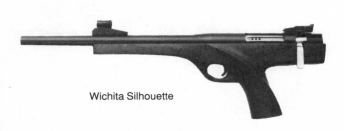

Wichita Silhouette

WICHITA CLASSIC SILHOUETTE PISTOL
Caliber: All standard calibers with maximum overall length of 2.800".
Barrel: 11¼".
Weight: 3 lbs., 15 oz.
Stocks: AAA American walnut with oil finish, checkered grip.
Sights: Hooded post front, open adjustable rear.
Features: Three locking lug bolt, three gas ports; completely adjustable Wichita trigger. Introduced 1981. From Wichita Arms.
Price: **$2,950.00**

Wichita International

CAUTION: PRICES CHANGE, CHECK AT GUNSHOP.

Includes models suitable for hunting and competitive courses for fire, both police and international.

COLT ANACONDA REVOLVER
Caliber: 44 Rem. Magnum, 6-shot.
Barrel: 4", 6", 8".
Weight: 53 oz. (6" barrel). **Length:** 11⅝" overall.
Stocks: Combat-style black neoprene with finger grooves.
Sights: Red insert front, adjustable white outline rear.
Features: Stainless steel; full-length ejector rod housing; ventilated barrel rib; offset bolt notches in cylinder; wide spur hammer. Introduced 1990.
Price: **$539.95**

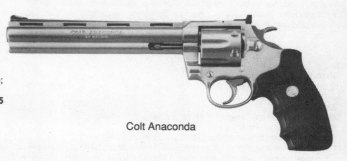

Colt Anaconda

COLT KING COBRA REVOLVER
Caliber: 357 Magnum, 6-shot.
Barrel: 2½", 4", 6", 8" (STS); 2½", 4", 6", 8" (BSTS); 2½", 4", 6" (blue).
Weight: 42 oz. (4" bbl). **Length:** 9" overall (4" bbl.).
Stocks: Checkered rubber.
Sights: Red insert ramp front, adjustable white outline rear.
Features: Full-length contoured ejector rod housing, barrel rib. Introduced 1986.
Price: STS, 2½", 4", 6", 8" **$434.95**
Price: BSTS, 2½", 4", 6", 8" **$469.95**
Price: Blue, 2½", 4", 6" **$409.95**

Colt Python

COLT PYTHON REVOLVER
Caliber: 357 Magnum (handles all 38 Spec.), 6-shot.
Barrel: 2½", 4", 6" or 8", with ventilated rib.
Weight: 38 oz. (4" bbl.). **Length:** 9¼" (4" bbl.).
Stocks: Rubber wraparound.
Sights: ⅛" ramp front, adjustable notch rear.
Features: Ventilated rib; grooved, crisp trigger; swing-out cylinder; target hammer.
Price: Royal blue, 2½", 4", 6", 8" **$775.95**
Price: Stainless, 2½", 4", 6", 8" **$864.95**
Price: Bright stainless, 2½", 4", 6", 8" **$894.95**

Colt King Cobra

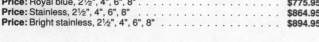

E.A.A. Standard Grade

E.A.A. STANDARD GRADE REVOLVERS
Caliber: 22 LR, 22 LR/22 WMR, 8-shot; 32 H&R Mag., 7-shot; 38 Special, 6-shot.
Barrel: 4", 6" (22 rimfire); 2" (32 H&R Mag.); 2", 4" (38 Special).
Weight: 38 oz. (22 rimfire, 4"). **Length:** 8.8" overall (4" bbl.).
Stocks: Hardwood with finger grooves.
Sights: Blade front, fixed or adjustable on rimfires; fixed only on 32, 38.
Features: Swing-out cylinder; hammer block safety; blue finish. Introduced 1991. Imported from Germany by European American Armory.
Price: 22 LR 4", 32 H&R 2", 38 Special 2" **$250.00**
Price: 38 Special, 4" **$275.00**
Price: 22 LR, 6" **$295.00**
Price: 22 LR/22 WMR combo, 4" **$350.00**
Price: As above, 6" **$375.00**

E.A.A. Tactical Grade Revolvers
Similar to the Standard Grade revolvers except in 38 Special only, 2" or 4" barrel, fixed sights. Compensator on 4", bobbed hammer (DA only) on 2" model. Introduced 1991. Imported from Germany by European American Armory.
Price: 2", bobbed hammer **$275.00**
Price: 4", compensator **$350.00**

ERMA ER-777 SPORTING REVOLVER
Caliber: 22 LR, 32 S&W, 357 Mag., 6-shot.
Barrel: 4", 5½".
Weight: 43.3 oz. **Length:** 9½" overall (4" barrel).
Stocks: Stippled walnut service-type.
Sights: Interchangeable blade front, micro-adjustable rear for windage and elevation.
Features: Polished blue finish. Adjustable trigger. Imported from Germany by Precision Sales Int'l. Introduced 1988.
Price: **$1,200.00**
Price: ER-772 (22 LR), ER-773 (32 S&W) **$1,265.00**

Erma ER-777

HARRINGTON & RICHARDSON SPORTSMAN 999 REVOLVER

Caliber: 22 Short, Long, Long Rifle, 9-shot.
Barrel: 4", 6".
Weight: 30 oz. (4" barrel). **Length:** NA.
Stocks: Walnut-finished hardwood.
Sights: Blade front adjustable for elevation, rear adjustable for windage.
Features: Top-break loading; polished blue finish; automatic shell ejection. Reintroduced 1992. From H&R 1871, Inc.
Price: **$229.95**

Harrington & Richardson Sportsman 999

KORTH REVOLVER

Caliber: 22 LR, 22 Mag., 32 H&R Mag., 32 S&W Long, 357 Mag., 9mm Parabellum.
Barrel: 3", 4", 6".
Weight: 33 to 38 oz. **Length:** 8" to 11" overall.
Stocks: Checkered walnut, sport or combat.
Sights: Blade front, rear adjustable for windage and elevation.
Features: Four interchangeable cylinders available. Major parts machined from hammer-forged steel; cylinder gap of .002". High polish blue finish. Presentation models have gold trim. Imported from Germany by Mandall Shooting Supplies.
Price: With two cylinders **$3,300.00**

LLAMA COMANCHE III REVOLVERS

Caliber: 357 Mag.
Barrel: 4", 6".
Weight: 28 oz. **Length:** 9¼" (4" bbl.).
Stocks: Checkered walnut.
Sights: Fixed blade front, rear adjustable for windage and elevation.
Features: Ventilated rib, wide spur hammer. Satin chrome finish available. Imported from Spain by Stoeger Industries.
Price: Blue finish **$339.00**
Price: Satin chrome **$395.00**

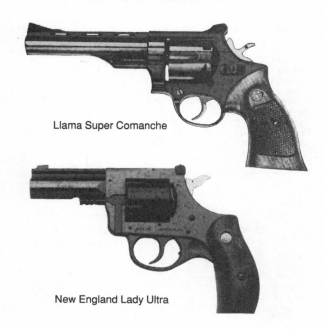

Llama Super Comanche

Llama Super Comanche IV Revolver

Similar to the Comanche except: large frame, 44 Mag. with 6", 8½" barrel, 6-shot cylinder; smooth, extra wide trigger; wide spur hammer; over-size walnut, target-style grips. Weight is 3 lbs., 2 oz. Blue finish only.
Price: 44 Mag. **$440.00**

NEW ENGLAND FIREARMS R92, R73 REVOLVERS

Caliber: 22 LR, 9-shot; 32 H&R Mag., 5-shot.
Barrel: 2½", 4".
Weight: 26 oz. (22 LR, 2½"). **Length:** 8½" overall (4" bbl.).
Stocks: Walnut-finished American hardwood with NEF medallion.
Sights: Fixed.
Features: Choice of blue or nickel finish. Introduced 1988. From New England Firearms Co.
Price: 22 LR **$114.95**
Price: 32 H&R Mag. **$129.95**

New England Lady Ultra

NEW ENGLAND FIREARMS LADY ULTRA REVOLVER

Caliber: 32 H&R Mag., 5-shot.
Barrel: 3".
Weight: 31 oz. **Length:** 7.25" overall.
Stocks: Walnut-finished hardwood with NEF medallion.
Sights: Blade front, fully adjustable rear.
Features: Swing-out cylinder; polished blue finish. Comes with lockable storage case. Introduced 1992. From New England Firearms Co.
Price: **$149.95**

NEW ENGLAND FIREARMS ULTRA REVOLVER

Caliber: 22 LR, 9-shot; 22 WMR, 6-shot.
Barrel: 6".
Weight: 36 oz. **Length:** 10⅝" overall.
Stocks: Walnut-finished hardwood with NEF medallion.
Sights: Blade front, fully adjustable rear.
Features: Blue finish. Bull-style barrel with recessed muzzle, high "Lustre" blue/black finish. Introduced 1989. From New England Firearms.
Price: **$149.95**
Price: Ultra Mag 22 WMR **$149.95**

QFI "RP Series"

QFI "RP SERIES" REVOLVERS

Caliber: 22 LR, 22 WMR, 22 LR/WMR combo, 32 S&W, 32S&W Long, 32 H&R Mag., 38 Spec., 6-shot.
Barrel: 2" or 4".
Weight: 23 oz. (2" barrel). **Length:** 6¼" overall (2" barrel).
Stocks: Magnum-style round butt; checkered plastic.
Sights: Ramp front, fixed square notch rear.
Features: One-piece solid frame; checkered hammer spur, serrated trigger; blue finish. Introduced 1991. Made in U.S. by QFI.
Price: . . . . **$104.95 to $129.95**

Rossi Model 68

ROSSI MODEL 515 REVOLVER
Caliber: 22 LR, 22 WMR, 6-shot.
Barrel: 4".
Weight: 30 oz. **Length:** 9" overall.
Stocks: Checkered Brazilian hardwood.
Sights: Red insert front on ramp, fully adjustable square notch rear.
Features: All stainless steel construction; shrouded ejector rod. Introduced 1992. Imported from Brazil by Interarms.
Price: **$248.33**

ROSSI MODEL 720 REVOLVER
Caliber: 44 Special, 5-shot.
Barrel: 3".
Weight: 27.5 oz. **Length:** 8" overall.
Stocks: Checkered rubber, combat style.
Sights: Red insert front on ramp, fully adjustable rear.
Features: All stainless steel construction; solid barrel rib; full ejector rod shroud. Introduced 1992. Imported from Brazil by Interarms.
Price: **$310.00**

ROSSI MODEL 851 REVOLVER
Caliber: 38 Special, 6-shot.
Barrel: 3" or 4".
Weight: 27.5 oz. (3" bbl.). **Length:** 8" overall (3" bbl.).
Stocks: Checkered Brazilian hardwood.
Sights: Blade front with red insert, rear adjustable for windage.
Features: Medium-size frame; stainless steel construction; ventilated barrel rib. Introduced 1991. Imported from Brazil by Interarms.
Price: **$263.33**

ROSSI MODEL 971 REVOLVER
Caliber: 357 Mag., 6-shot.
Barrel: 2½", 4", 6", heavy.
Weight: 36 oz. **Length:** 9" overall.
Stocks: Checkered Brazilian hardwood.
Sights: Blade front, fully adjustable rear.
Features: Full-length ejector rod shroud; matted sight rib; target-type trigger, wide checkered hammer spur. Introduced 1988. Imported from Brazil by Interarms.
Price: 4", stainless **$298.33**
Price: 6", stainless **$298.33**
Price: 4", blue **$263.33**
Price: 2½", stainless **$303.33**

RUGER SP-101 REVOLVER
Caliber: 22 LR, 32 H&R Mag., 6-shot, 9mm Para., 38 Special +P, 357 Mag., 5-shot.
Barrel: 2¼", 3¹⁄₁₆", 4".
Weight: 2¼"—25 oz.; 3¹⁄₁₆"—27 oz.
Sights: Adjustable on 22, 32, fixed on others.
Stocks: Ruger Santoprene Cushioned Grip with Xenoy inserts.
Features: Incorporates improvements and features found in the GP-100 revolvers into a compact, small frame, double-action revolver. Full-length ejector shroud. Stainless steel only. Introduced 1988.
Price: KSP-821 (2½", 38 Spec.) **$408.00**
Price: KSP-831 (3¹⁄₁₆", 38 Spec.) **$408.00**
Price: KSP-221 (2¼", 22 LR) **$408.00**
Price: KSP-240 (4", 22 LR) **$408.00**
Price: KSP-241 (4" heavy bbl., 22 LR) **$408.00**
Price: KSP-3231 (3¹⁄₁₆", 32 H&R) **$408.00**
Price: KSP-921 (2¼", 9mm Para.) **$408.00**
Price: KSP-931 (3¹⁄₁₆", 9mm Para.) **$408.00**
Price: KSP-321 (2¼", 357 Mag.) **$408.00**
Price: KSP-331 (3¹⁄₁₆", 357 Mag.) **$408.00**

ROSSI MODEL 68 REVOLVER
Caliber: 38 Spec.
Barrel: 2", 3".
Weight: 22 oz.
Stocks: Checkered wood.
Sights: Ramp front, low profile adjustable rear.
Features: All-steel frame, thumb latch operated swing-out cylinder. Introduced 1978. Imported from Brazil by Interarms.
Price: 38, blue, 3" **$210.00**
Price: M68/2 (2" barrel), wood or rubber grips **$220.00**
Price: 3", nickel **$215.00**

ROSSI MODEL 88 STAINLESS REVOLVER
Caliber: 32 S&W, 38 Spec., 5-shot.
Barrel: 2", 3".
Weight: 22 oz. **Length:** 7.5" overall.
Stocks: Checkered wood, service-style.
Sights: Ramp front, square notch rear drift adjustable for windage.
Features: All metal parts except springs are of 440 stainless steel; matte finish; small frame for concealability. Introduced 1983. Imported from Brazil by Interarms.
Price: 3" barrel **$240.00**
Price: M88/2 (2" barrel), wood or rubber grips **$255.00**

Rossi Model 971

Ruger SP-101

RUGER GP-100 REVOLVERS
Caliber: 38 Special, 357 Magnum, 6-shot.
Barrel: 3", 3" heavy, 4", 4" heavy, 6", 6" heavy.
Weight: 3" barrel—35 oz., 3" heavy barrel—36 oz., 4" barrel—37 oz., 4" heavy barrel—38 oz.
Sights: Fixed; adjustable on 4" heavy, 6", 6" heavy barrels.
Stocks: Ruger Santoprene Cushioned Grip with Goncalo Alves inserts.
Features: Uses action and frame incorporating improvements and features of both the Security-Six and Redhawk revolvers. Full length and short ejector shroud. Satin blue and stainless steel. Introduced 1988.
Price: GP-141 (357, 4" heavy, adj. sights, blue) **$413.50**
Price: GP-160 (357, 6", adj. sights, blue) **$413.50**
Price: GP-161 (357, 6" heavy, adj. sights, blue) **$413.50**
Price: GPF-330 (357, 3"), GPF-830 (38 Spec.) **$397.00**
Price: GPF-331 (357, 3" heavy), GPF-831 (38 Spec.) **$397.00**
Price: GPF-340 (357, 4"), GPF-840 (38 Spec.) **$397.00**
Price: GPF-341 (357, 4" heavy), GPF-841 (38 Spec.) **$397.00**
Price: KGP-141 (357, 4" heavy, adj. sights, stainless) **$446.50**
Price: KGP-160 (357, 6", adj. sights, stainless) **$446.50**
Price: KGP-161 (357, 6" heavy, adj. sights, stainless) **$446.50**
Price: KGPF-330 (357, 3", stainless), KGPF-830 (38 Spec.) **$430.00**
Price: KGPF-331 (357, 3" heavy, stainless), KGPF-831 (38 Spec.) **$430.00**
Price: KGPF-340 (357, 4", stainless), KGPF-840 (38 Spec.) **$430.00**
Price: KGPF-341 (357, 4" heavy, stainless), KGPF-841 (38 Spec.) . . **$430.00**

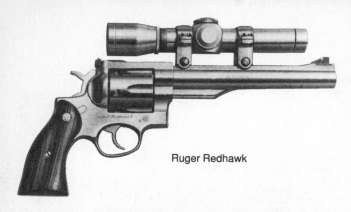

Ruger Redhawk

SMITH & WESSON Model 10 M&P REVOLVER
Caliber: 38 Special, 6-shot.
Barrel: 2", 4".
Weight: 30½ oz. **Length:** 9¼" overall.
Stocks: Checkered walnut, Service. Round or square butt.
Sights: Fixed, ramp front, square notch rear.
Price: Blue $346.00

Smith & Wesson Model 10 38 M&P Heavy Barrel
Same as regular M&P except: 4" heavy ribbed bbl. with ramp front sight, square rear, square butt, wgt. 33½ oz.
Price: Blue $346.00

SMITH & WESSON MODEL 13 H.B. M&P
Caliber: 357 and 38 Special, 6-shot.
Barrel: 3" or 4".
Weight: 34 oz. **Length:** 9⁵⁄₁₆" overall (4" bbl.).
Stocks: Checkered walnut, Service.
Sights: ⅛" serrated ramp front, fixed square notch rear.
Features: Heavy barrel, K-frame, square butt (4"), round butt (3").
Price: Blue $353.00
Price: Model 65, as above in stainless steel $368.00

SMITH & WESSON MODEL 14 FULL LUG REVOLVER
Caliber: 38 Special, 6-shot.
Barrel: 6", full lug.
Weight: 47 oz. **Length:** 11⅛" overall.
Stocks: Combat-style Morado with square butt.
Sights: Pinned Patridge front, adjustable micrometer click rear.
Features: Has .500" target hammer, .312" smooth combat trigger. Polished blue finish. Reintroduced 1991. Limited production.
Price: $425.00

SMITH & WESSON MODEL 15 COMBAT MASTERPIECE
Caliber: 38 Special, 6-shot.
Barrel: 4".
Weight: 32 oz. **Length:** 9⁵⁄₁₆" (4" bbl.).
Stocks: Checkered walnut. Grooved tangs.
Sights: Front, Baughman Quick Draw on ramp, micro-click rear, adjustable for windage and elevation.
Price: Blued $375.00

SMITH & WESSON MODEL 16 FULL LUG REVOLVER
Caliber: 32 Magnum, 6-shot.
Barrel: 6", full lug.
Weight: 42 oz. **Length:** 9⅛" overall.
Stocks: Square butt Goncalo Alves, combat-style.
Sights: Patridge-style front, adjustable micrometer click rear.
Features: Polished blue finish. Has .500" target hammer, .400" serrated trigger. Introduced 1990.
Price: $419.00

Smith & Wesson Model 648 K-22 Masterpiece MRF
Similar to the Model 17 except made of stainless steel and chambered for 22 WMR cartridge. Available with 6" full-lug barrel only, combat-style square butt grips, combat trigger and semi-target hammer. Introduced 1991.
Price: $416.00

RUGER REDHAWK
Caliber: 44 Rem. Mag., 6-shot.
Barrel: 5½", 7½".
Weight: About 54 oz. (7½" bbl.). **Length:** 13" overall (7½" barrel).
Stocks: Square butt Goncalo Alves.
Sights: Interchangeable Patridge-type front, rear adjustable for windage and elevation.
Features: Stainless steel, brushed satin finish, or blued ordnance steel. Has a 9½" sight radius. Introduced 1979.
Price: Blued, 44 Mag., 5½", 7½" $458.50
Price: Blued, 44 Mag., 7½", with scope mount, rings $496.50
Price: Stainless, 44 Mag., 5½", 7½" $516.75
Price: Stainless, 44 Mag., 7½", with scope mount, rings $557.25

Ruger Super Redhawk Revolver
Similar to the standard Redhawk except has a heavy extended frame with the Ruger Integral Scope Mounting System on the wide topstrap. The wide hammer spur has been lowered for better scope clearance. Incorporates the mechanical design features and improvements of the GP-100. Choice of 7½" or 9½" barrel, both with ramp front sight base with Redhawk-style Interchangeable Insert sight blades, adjustable rear sight. Comes with Ruger "Cushioned Grip" panels of Santoprene with Goncalo Alves wood panels. Satin polished stainless steel, 44 Magnum only. Introduced 1987.
Price: KSRH-7 (7½"), KSRH-9 (9½") $589.00

Smith & Wesson Model 65

Smith & Wesson Model 15

SMITH & WESSON MODEL 17 K-22 FULL LUG
Caliber: 22 LR, 6-shot.
Barrel: 4", 6", 8⅜".
Weight: 39 oz. (6" bbl.). **Length:** 11⅛" overall.
Stocks: Square butt Goncalo Alves, combat-style.
Sights: Patridge front with 6", 8⅜", serrated on 4", S&W micro-click rear adjustable for windage and elevation.
Features: Grooved tang, polished blue finish, full lug barrel. Introduced 1990.
Price: 4" $394.00
Price: 6" $432.00
Price: 8⅜" $444.00

Smith & Wesson Model 617 Full Lug Revolver
Similar to the Model 17 Full Lug except made of stainless steel. Has semi-target .375" hammer, .312" smooth combat trigger on 4"; 6" available with either .312" smooth combat trigger or .400" serrated trigger and .500" target hammer. Introduced 1990.
Price: 4" $416.00
Price: 6", semi-target hammer, combat trigger $416.00
Price: 6", target hammer, target trigger $421.00

SMITH & WESSON MODEL 19 COMBAT MAGNUM
Caliber: 357 Magnum and 38 Special, 6-shot.
Barrel: 2½", 4", 6".
Weight: 36 oz. **Length:** 9⁹⁄₁₆" (4" bbl.).
Stocks: Checkered Goncalo Alves, target. Grooved tangs.
Sights: Front ⅛" Baughman Quick Draw on 2½" or 4" bbl., Patridge on 6" bbl., micro-click rear adjustable for windagae and elevation.
Features: Also available in nickel finish.
Price: S&W Bright Blue, adj. sights, from **$369.00**

Smith & Wesson Model 27

SMITH & WESSON MODEL 27 357 MAGNUM REVOLVER
Caliber: 357 Magnum and 38 Special, 6-shot.
Barrel: 6".
Weight: 45½ oz. **Length:** 11⁵⁄₁₆" overall.
Stocks: Checkered walnut, Magna. Grooved tangs and trigger.
Sights: Serrated ramp front, micro-click rear, adjustable for windage and elevation.
Price: **$440.00**

Smith & Wesson Model 629

SMITH & WESSON MODEL 29 44 MAGNUM REVOLVER
Caliber: 44 Magnum, 44 Special or 44 Russian, 6-shot.
Barrel: 4", 6", 8⅜".
Weight: 47 oz. (6" bbl.), 44 oz. (4" bbl.). **Length:** 11⅜" overall (6" bbl.).
Stocks: Oversize target-type, checkered Goncalo Alves. Tangs and target trigger grooved, checkered target hammer.
Sights: ⅛" red ramp front, micro-click rear, adjustable for windage and elevation.
Price: S&W Bright Blue, 4", 6" **$501.00**
Price: 8⅜" bbl., blue **$512.00**
Price: Model 629 (stainless steel), 4", 6" **$530.00**
Price: Model 629, 8⅜" barrel **$548.00**

Smith & Wesson Model 29, 629 Classic Revolvers
Similar to the standard Model 29 and 629 except has full-lug 5", 6½" or 8⅜" barrel; chamfered front of cylinder; interchangable red ramp front sight with adjustable white outline rear; Hogue square butt Santoprene grips with S&W monogram; the frame is drilled and tapped for scope mounting. Factory accurizing and endurance packages. Overall length with 5" barrel is 10½"; weight is 51 oz. Introduced 1990.
Price: Model 29 Classic, 5", 6½" **$540.00**
Price: As above, 8⅜" **$551.00**
Price: Model 629 Classic (stainless), 5", 6½" **$569.00**
Price: As above, 8 ⅜" **$588.00**

Smith & Wesson Model 629 Classic DX

Smith & Wesson Model 29, 629 Classic DX Revolvers
Similar to the Classic Hunters except offered only with 6½" or 8⅜" full-lug barrel; comes with five front sights: 50-yard red ramp; 50-yard black Patridge; 100-yard black Patridge with gold bead; 50-yard black ramp; and 50-yard black Patridge with white dot. Comes with Morado combat-type grips with Cornuba wax finish and Hogue combat-style square butt conversion grip. Introduced 1991.
Price: Model 29 Classic DX, 6½" **$713.00**
Price: As above, 8⅜" **$728.00**
Price: Model 629 Classic DX, 6½" **$755.00**
Price: As above, 8⅜" **$780.00**

Smith & Wesson Model 60 3"

SMITH & WESSON MODEL 36 CHIEFS SPECIAL & AIRWEIGHT
Caliber: 38 Special, 5-shot.
Barrel: 2", 3".
Weight: 19½ oz. (2" bbl.); 13½ oz. (Airweight). **Length:** 6½" (2" bbl. and round butt).
Stocks: Checkered walnut, round or square butt.
Sights: Fixed, serrated ramp front, square notch rear.
Price: Blue, standard Model 36, 2", 3" **$351.00**
Price: As above, nickel, 2" only **$363.00**
Price: Blue, Airweight Model 37, 2" only **$372.00**
Price: As above, nickel, 2" only **$363.00**

Smith & Wesson Model 60 Chiefs Special Stainless
Same as Model 36 except: 2" bbl. and round butt only.
Price: Stainless steel **$386.00**

Smith & Wesson Model 60 3" Full-Lug Revolver
Similar to the Model 60 Chief's Special except has 3" full-lug barrel, adjustable micrometer click black blade rear sight; rubber Uncle Mike's Custom Grade combat grips. Overall length 7½"; weight 24½ oz. Introduced 1991.
Price: **$410.00**

Smith & Wesson Model 36-LS LadySmith

Smith & Wesson Model 36-LS, 60-LS LadySmith
Similar to the standard Model 36. Available with 2" or 3" barrel. The 2" comes with smooth, contoured rosewood grips with the S&W monogram; 3" has smooth, finger-grooved Goncalo Alves grips. Each has a speedloader cutout. Comes in a fitted carry/storage case. Introduced 1989.
Price: Model 36-LS **$384.00**
Price: Model 60-LS (as above except in stainless) **$434.00**

SMITH & WESSON MODEL 38 BODYGUARD
Caliber: 38 Special, 5-shot.
Barrel: 2".
Weight: 14½ oz. **Length:** 6⁵⁄₁₆" overall.
Stocks: Checkered walnut.
Sights: Fixed serrated ramp front, square notch rear.
Features: Alloy frame; internal hammer.
Price: Blue $394.00
Price: Nickel $405.00

Smith & Wesson Model 49

Smith & Wesson Model 49, 649 Bodyguard Revolvers
Same as Model 38 except steel construction, weight 20½ oz.
Price: Blued, Model 49 . . . . $373.00
Price: Stainless, Model 649 . . . . $424.00

SMITH & WESSON MODEL 57, 657 41 MAGNUM REVOLVERS
Caliber: 41 Magnum, 6-shot.
Barrel: 6".
Weight: 48 oz. **Length:** 11⅜" overall.
Stocks: Oversize target-type checkered Goncalo Alves.
Sights: ⅛" red ramp front, micro-click rear adjustable for windage and elevation.
Price: S&W Bright Blue, 6" $444.00
Price: Stainless, Model 657, 6" $473.00
Price: As above, 8⅜" $490.00

SMITH & WESSON MODEL 63, 22/32 KIT GUN
Caliber: 22 LR, 6-shot.
Barrel: 2", 4".
Weight: 24 oz. (4" bbl.). **Length:** 8⅜" (4" bbl. and round butt).
Stocks: Checkered walnut, round or square butt.
Sights: Front, serrated ramp, micro-click rear, adjustable for windage and elevation.
Features: Stainless steel construction.
Price: 4" $418.00
Price: 2" round butt $418.00

SMITH & WESSON MODEL 64 STAINLESS M&P
Caliber: 38 Special, 6-shot.
Barrel: 2", 3", 4".
Weight: 34 oz. **Length:** 9⁵⁄₁₆" overall.
Stocks: Checkered walnut, Service style.
Sights: Fixed, ⅛" serrated ramp front, square notch rear.
Features: Satin finished stainless steel, square butt.
Price: $383.00

Smith & Wesson Model 65LS

SMITH & WESSON MODEL 65LS LADYSMITH
Caliber: 357 Magnum, 6-shot.
Barrel: 3".
Weight: 31 oz. **Length:** 7.94" overall.
Stocks: Rosewood, round butt.
Sights: Serrated ramp front, fixed notch rear.
Features: Stainless steel with frosted finish. Smooth combat trigger, service hammer, shrouded ejector rod. Comes with soft case. Introduced 1992.
Price: $434.00

SMITH & WESSON MODEL 66 STAINLESS COMBAT MAGNUM
Caliber: 357 Magnum and 38 Special, 6-shot.
Barrel: 2½", 4", 6".
Weight: 36 oz. **Length:** 9⁹⁄₁₆" overall.
Stocks: Checkered Goncalo Alves target.
Sights: Front, Baughman Quick Draw on ramp, micro-click rear adjustable for windage and elevation.
Features: Satin finish stainless steel.
Price: From . . . . $420.00 to $468.00

SMITH & WESSON MODEL 586, 686 DISTINGUISHED COMBAT MAGNUMS
Caliber: 357 Magnum.
Barrel: 4", 6", full shroud.
Weight: 46 oz. (6"), 41 oz. (4").
Stocks: Goncalo Alves target-type with speed loader cutaway.
Sights: Baughman red ramp front, four-position click-adjustable front, S&W micrometer click rear (or fixed).
Features: Uses new L-frame, but takes all K-frame grips. Full-length ejector rod shroud. Smooth combat-type trigger, semi-target type hammer. Trigger stop on 6" models. Also available in stainless as Model 686. Introduced 1981.
Price: Model 586, blue, 4", from $417.00
Price: Model 686, stainless, from $439.00
Price: Model 586, 6", adjustable front sight, blue $417.00
Price: Model 686, 6", adjustable front sight $479.00
Price: As above, 8⅜" $470.00

Smith & Wesson Model 586

SMITH & WESSON MODEL 625-2 REVOLVER
Caliber: 45 ACP, 6-shot.
Barrel: 5".
Weight: 46 oz. **Length:** 11.375" overall.
Stocks: Pachmayr SK/GR Gripper rubber.
Sights: Patridge front on ramp, S&W micrometer click rear adjustable for windage and elevation.
Features: Stainless steel construction with .400" semi-target hammer, .312" smooth combat trigger; full lug barrel. Introduced 1989.
Price: $535.00

Smith & Wesson Model 625-2

CAUTION: PRICES CHANGE, CHECK AT GUNSHOP.

SMITH & WESSON MODEL 640, 940 CENTENNIAL
Caliber: 38 Special, 9mm Para., 5-shot.
Barrel: 2", 3".
Weight: 20 oz. **Length:** 6⁵⁄₁₆" overall.
Stocks: Round butt Goncalo Alves.
Sights: Serrated ramp front, fixed notch rear.
Features: Stainless steel version of the original Model 40 but without the grip safety. Fully concealed hammer, snag-proof smooth edges. Model 640 introduced 1990; Model 940 introduced 1991.
Price: Model 640 (38 Special) **$424.00**
Price: Model 940 (9mm Para., rubber grips) **$429.00**

Smith & Wesson Model 640 Centennial

Smith & Wesson Model 642 Centennial Airweight
Similar to the Model 640 Centennial except has a clear-anodized alloy frame giving weight of 15.8 oz. Chambered for 38 Special, 2" or 3" stainless barrel; stainless cylinder; concealed hammer; Uncle Mike's Custom Grade Santoprene grips. Fixed square notch rear sight, serrated ramp front. Introduced 1990.
Price: **$410.00**

SMITH & WESSON MODEL 651 REVOLVER
Caliber: 22 WMR, 6-shot cylinder.
Barrel: 4".
Weight: 24½ oz. **Length:** 8¹¹⁄₁₆" overall.
Stocks: Checkered service Morado; square butt.
Sights: Red ramp front, adjustable micrometer click rear.
Features: Stainless steel construction with semi-target hammer, smooth combat trigger. Reintroduced 1991. Limited production.
Price: **$412.00**

SPORTARMS MODEL HS38S REVOLVER
Caliber: 38 Special, 6-shot.
Barrel: 3", 4".
Weight: 31.3 oz. **Length:** 8" overall (3" barrel).
Stocks: Checkered hardwood; round butt on 3" model, target-style on 4".
Sights: Blade front, adjustable rear.
Features: Polished blue finish; ventilated rib on 4" barrel. Made in Germany by Herbert Schmidt; Imported by Sportarms of Florida.
Price: About **$150.00**

TAURUS MODEL 66 REVOLVER
Caliber: 357 Magnum, 6-shot.
Barrel: 3", 4", 6".
Weight: 35 oz.
Stocks: Checkered Brazilian hardwood.
Sights: Serrated ramp front, micro-click rear adjustable for windage and elevation. Red ramp front with white outline rear on stainlees models only.
Features: Wide target-type hammer spur, floating firing pin, heavy barrel with shrouded ejector rod. Introduced 1978. Imported by Taurus International.
Price: Blue **$274.00**
Price: Nickel **$289.00**
Price: Stainless steel **$348.00**
Price: Model 65 (similar to M66 except has a fixed rear sight and ramp front), blue, 3" or 4" only **$249.00**
Price: Model 65, satin nickel, 3" or 4" only **$264.00**

TAURUS MODEL 76 REVOLVER
Caliber: 32 H&R Magnum, 6-shot.
Barrel: 6", heavy, solid rib.
Weight: 34 oz.
Stocks: Checkered Brazilian hardwood.
Sights: Patridge-type front, micro-click rear adjustable for windage and elevation.
Features: Target hammer, adjustable target trigger. Blue only. Introduced 1991. Imported by Taurus International.
Price: **$308.00**
Price: Model 741 (as above except 4" bbl., blue) **$239.00**
Price: Model 741, satin nickel **$276.00**

TAURUS MODEL 80 STANDARD REVOLVER
Caliber: 38 Spec., 6-shot.
Barrel: 3" or 4".
Weight: 30 oz. (4" bbl.). **Length:** 9¼" overall (4" bbl.).
Stocks: Checkered Brazilian hardwood.
Sights: Serrated ramp front, square notch rear.
Features: Imported by Taurus International.
Price: Blue **$216.00**
Price: Satin nickel **$231.00**

Smith & Wesson Model 632 Revolver
Similar to the Model 642 Centennial Airweight except chambered for 32 H&R Magnum with 6-shot cylinder. Has alloy frame, stainless cylinder, yoke and 2" barrel only. Weight is 15.5 oz. Introduced 1991.
Price: **$410.00**

Smith & Wesson Model 651

Taurus Model 66

TAURUS MODEL 73 SPORT REVOLVER
Caliber: 32 H&R Mag., 6-shot.
Barrel: 3", heavy.
Weight: 22 oz. **Length:** 8¼" overall.
Stocks: Checkered Brazilian hardwood.
Sights: Ramp front, notch rear.
Features: Imported by Taurus International.
Price: Blue **$223.00**
Price: Satin nickel **$243.00**

Taurus Model 76

Taurus Model 80

TAURUS MODEL 82 HEAVY BARREL REVOLVER

Caliber: 38 Spec., 6-shot.
Barrel: 3" or 4", heavy.
Weight: 34 oz. (4" bbl.). **Length:** 9¼" overall (4" bbl.).
Stocks: Checkered Brazilian hardwood.
Sights: Serrated ramp front, square notch rear.
Features: Imported by Taurus International.
Price: Blue **$216.00**
Price: Satin nickel **$231.00**

TAURUS MODEL 85 REVOLVER

Caliber: 38 Spec., 5-shot.
Barrel: 2", 3".
Weight: 21 oz.
Stocks: Checkered Brazilian hardwood.
Sights: Ramp front, square notch rear.
Features: Blue, satin nickel finish or stainless steel. Introduced 1980. Imported by Taurus International.
Price: Blue **$237.00**
Price: Satin nickel, 3" only **$257.00**
Price: Stainless steel **$297.00**

Taurus Model 85CH Revolver

Same as the Model 85 except has 2" barrel only and concealed hammer. Smooth Brazilian hardwood stocks. Introduced 1991. Imported by Taurus International.
Price: Blue **$237.00**
Price: Stainless **$297.00**

TAURUS MODEL 86 REVOLVER

Caliber: 38 Spec., 6-shot.
Barrel: 6" only.
Weight: 34 oz. **Length:** 11¼" overall.
Stocks: Oversize target-type, checkered Brazilian hardwood.
Sights: Patridge front, micro-click rear adjustable for windage and elevation.
Features: Blue finish with non-reflective finish on barrel. Imported by Taurus International.
Price: **$308.00**

TAURUS MODEL 94 REVOLVER

Caliber: 22 LR, 9-shot cylinder.
Barrel: 3", 4".
Weight: 25 oz.
Stocks: Checkered Brazilian hardwood.
Sights: Serrated ramp front, click-adjustable rear for windage and elevation.
Features: Floating firing pin, color case-hardened hammer and trigger. Introduced 1989. Imported by Taurus International.
Price: Blue **$249.00**
Price: Stainless **$296.00**

TAURUS MODEL 441/431 REVOLVERS

Caliber: 44 Special, 5-shot.
Barrel: 3", 4", 6".
Weight: 40.4 oz. (6" barrel). **Length:** NA.
Stocks: Checkered Brazilian hardwood.
Sights: Serrated ramp front, micrometer click rear adjustable for windage and elevation.
Features: Heavy barrel with solid rib and full-length ejector shroud. Introduced 1992. Imported by Taurus International.
Price: Blue **$290.00**
Price: Stainless **$364.00**
Price: Model 431 (fixed sights), blue **$265.00**
Price: Model 431 (fixed sights), stainless **$331.00**

TAURUS MODEL 669 REVOLVER

Caliber: 357 Mag., 6-shot.
Barrel: 4", 6".
Weight: 37 oz., (4" bbl.).
Stocks: Checkered Brazilian hardwood.
Sights: Serrated ramp front, micro-click rear adjustable for windage and elevation.
Features: Wide target-type hammer, floating firing pin, full-length barrel shroud. Introduced 1988. Imported by Taurus International.
Price: Blue **$284.00**
Price: Stainless **$356.00**

TAURUS MODEL 83 REVOLVER

Caliber: 38 Spec., 6-shot.
Barrel: 4" only, heavy.
Weight: 34 oz.
Stocks: Oversize checkered Brazilian hardwood.
Sights: Ramp front, micro-click rear adjustable for windage and elevation.
Features: Blue or nickel finish. Introduced 1977. Imported by Taurus International.
Price: Blue **$228.00**
Price: Satin nickel **$241.00**

Taurus Model 85CH

Taurus Model 86

TAURUS MODEL 96 REVOLVER

Caliber: 22 LR, 6-shot.
Barrel: 6".
Weight: 34 oz. **Length:** NA.
Stocks: Checkered Brazilian hardwood.
Sights: Patridge-type front, micrometer click rear adjustable for windage and elevation.
Features: Heavy solid barrel rib; target hammer; adjustable target trigger. Blue only. Imported by Taurus International.
Price: **$308.00**

Taurus Model 441

Taurus Model 689 Revolver

Same as the Model 669 except has full-length ventilated barrel rib. Available in blue or stainless steel. Introduced 1990. From Taurus International.
Price: Blue, 4" or 6" **$295.00**
Price: Stainless, 4" or 6" **$370.00**

TAURUS MODEL 941 REVOLVER
Caliber: 22 WMR, 8-shot.
Barrel: 3", 4".
Weight: 27.5 oz. (4" barrel). **Length:** NA.
Stocks: Checkered Brazilian hardwood.
Sights: Serrated ramp front, rear adjustable for windage and elevation.
Features: Solid rib heavy barrel with full-length ejector rod shroud. Blue or stainless steel. Introduced 1992. Imported by Taurus International.
Price: Blue **$274.00**
Price: Stainless **$326.00**

Taurus Model 941

THUNDER FIVE REVOLVER
Caliber: 45 Colt/410 shotshell, 2" and 3"; 5-shot cylinder.
Barrel: 2".
Weight: 48 oz. **Length:** 9" overall.
Stocks: Pachmayr checkered rubber.
Sights: Fixed.
Features: Double action with ambidextrous hammer-block safety; squared trigger guard; internal draw bar safety. Made of chrome moly steel, with matte blue finish. Announced 1991. From Tapco, Inc.
Price: **$379.00**

Wesson Model 14-2

WESSON FIREARMS MODEL 8-2 & MODEL 14-2
Caliber: 38 Special (Model 8-2); 357 (14-2), both 6-shot.
Barrel: 2½", 4", 6", 8"; interchangeable.
Weight: 30 oz. (2½"). **Length:** 9¼" overall (4" bbl.).
Stocks: Checkered, interchangeable.
Sights: ⅛" serrated front, fixed rear.
Features: Interchangeable barrels and grips; smooth, wide trigger; wide hammer spur with short double-action travel. Available in stainless or Brite blue. Contact Wesson Firearms for complete price list.
Price: Model 8-2, 2½", blue **$267.00**
Price: As above except in stainless **$311.00**
Price: Model 714-2 Pistol Pac, stainless **$517.00**

Wesson Firearms Model 9-2, 15-2 & 32M Revolvers
Same as Models 8-2 and 14-2 except they have adjustable sight. Model 9-2 chambered for 38 Special, Model 15-2 for 357 Magnum. Model 32M is chambered for 32 H&R Mag. Same specs and prices as for 15-2 guns. Available in blue or stainless. Contact Wesson Firearms for complete price list.
Price: Model 9-2 or 15-2, 2½", blue **$338.00**
Price: As above except in stainless **$366.00**

Wesson Model 32M

Wesson Firearms Model 15 Gold Series
Similar to the Model 15 except has smoother action to reduce DA pull to 8-10 lbs.; comes with either 6" or 8" vent heavy slotted barrel shroud with bright blue barrel. Shroud is stamped "Gold Series" with the Wesson signature engraved and gold filled. Hammer and trigger are polished bright; rosewood grips. New sights with orange dot Patridge front, white triangle on rear blade. Introduced 1989.
Price: 6" **$544.00**
Price: 8" **$554.00**

WESSON FIREARMS MODEL 22 REVOLVER
Caliber: 22 LR, 22 WMR, 6-shot.
Barrel: 2½", 4", 6", 8", 10"; interchangeable.
Weight: 36 oz. (2½"). 44 oz. (6"). **Length:** 9¼" overall (4" barrel).
Stocks: Checkered; undercover, service or over-size target.
Sights: ⅛" serrated, interchangeable front, white outline rear adjustable for windage and elevation.
Features: Built on the same frame as the Wesson 357; smooth, wide trigger with over-travel adjustment, wide spur hammer, with short double-action travel. Available in Brite blue or stainless steel. Contact Wesson Firearms for complete price list.
Price: 2½" bbl., blue **$338.00**
Price: As above, stainless **$366.00**
Price: With 4", vent. rib, blue **$370.00**
Price: As above, stainless **$398.00**
Price: Stainless Pistol Pac, 22 LR, blue **$637.00**

Wesson Model 22

WESSON FIREARMS MODEL 41V, 44V, 45V REVOLVERS
Caliber: 41 Mag., 44 Mag., 45 Colt, 6-shot.
Barrel: 4", 6", 8", 10"; interchangeable.
Weight: 48 oz. (4"). **Length:** 12" overall (6" bbl.).
Stocks: Smooth.
Sights: ⅛" serrated front, white outline rear adjustable for windage and elevation.
Features: Available in blue or stainless steel. Smooth, wide trigger with adjustable over-travel; wide hammer spur. Available in Pistol Pac set also. Contact Wesson Firearms for complete price list.
Price: 41 Mag., 4", vent **$413.00**
Price: As above except in stainless **$462.00**
Price: 44 Mag., 4", blue **$431.00**
Price: As above except in stainless **$507.00**
Price: 45 Colt, 4", vent **$431.00**
Price: As above except in stainless **$507.00**

Wesson Model 738P

WESSON FIREARMS MODEL 738P REVOLVER
Caliber: 38 Special +P, 5-shot.
Barrel: 2".
Weight: 24.6 oz. **Length:** 6.5" overall.
Stocks: Pauferro wood or rubber.
Sights: Blade front, fixed notch rear.
Features: Designed for +P ammunition. Stainless steel construction. Introduced 1992. Made in U.S. by Wesson Firearms Co., Inc.
Price: **$270.00**

Both classic six-shooters and modern adaptations for hunting and sport.

AMERICAN ARMS REGULATOR SINGLE ACTIONS
Caliber: 357 Mag. 44-40, 45 Colt.
Barrel: 4¾", 7½".
Weight: 32 oz. (4¾" barrel) **Length:** 8⅛" overall (4¾" barrel).
Stocks: Smooth walnut.
Sights: Blade front, groove rear.
Features: Blued barrel and cylinder, brass trigger guard and backstrap; Deluxe model has blued trigger guard and backstrap. Introduced 1992. Imported from Italy by American Arms, Inc.
Price: Regulator, single cylinder **$299.00**
Price: Regulator, dual cylinder (44-40/44 Spec. or 45 Colt/45 ACP) . **$349.00**
Price: Deluxe, single cylinder **$369.00**
Price: Deluxe, dual cylinder (44-40/44 Spec. or 45 Colt/45 ACP) . . **$399.00**

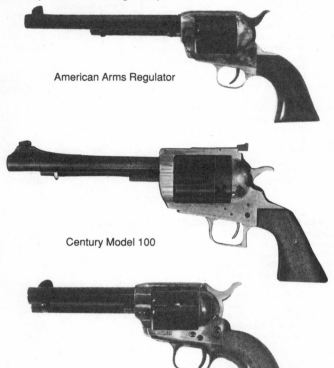
American Arms Regulator

Century Model 100

CENTURY GUN DIST. MODEL 100 SINGLE ACTION
Caliber: 30-30, 375 Win., 444 Marlin, 45-70, 50-70.
Barrel: 6½" (standard), 8", 10", 12".
Weight: 6 lbs. (loaded). **Length:** 15" overall (8" bbl.).
Stocks: Smooth walnut.
Sights: Ramp front, Millett adjustable square notch rear.
Features: Highly polished high tensile strength manganese bronze frame, blue cylinder and barrel; coil spring trigger mechanism. Calibers other than 45-70 start at $1,500.00. Contact maker for full price information. Introduced 1975. Made in U.S. From Century Gun Dist., Inc.
Price: 6½" barrel, 45-70 . . . . **$1,250.00**

CIMARRON U.S. CAVALRY MODEL SINGLE ACTION
Caliber: 45 Colt.
Barrel: 7½".
Weight: 42 oz. **Length:** 13½" overall.
Stocks: Walnut.
Sights: Fixed.
Features: Has "A.P. Casey" markings; "U.S." plus patent dates on frame, serial number on backstrap, trigger guard, frame and cylinder, "APC" cartouche on left grip; color case-hardened frame and hammer, rest charcoal blue. Exact copy of the original. Imported by Cimarron Arms.
Price: **$459.00**

Cimarron 1873 Peacemaker

CIMARRON 1873 PEACEMAKER REPRO
Caliber: 22 LR, 22 WMR, 38 WCF, 357 Mag., 44 WCF, 44 Spec., 45 Colt.
Barrel: 4¾", 5½", 7½".
Weight: 39 oz. **Length:** 10" overall (4" barrel).
Stocks: Walnut.
Sights: Blade front, fixed or adjustable rear.
Features: Uses "old model" blackpowder frame with "Bullseye" ejector or New Model frame. Imported by Cimarron Arms.
Price: Peacemaker, 4¾" barrel **$429.00**
Price: Frontier Six Shooter, 5½" barrel **$429.00**
Price: Single Action Army, 7½" barrel **$429.00**

Cimarron Artillery Model Single Action
Similar to the U.S. Cavalry model except has 5½" barrel, weighs 39 oz., and is 11½" overall. U.S. markings and cartouche, case-hardened frame and hammer; 45 Colt only.
Price: **$459.00**

CIMARRON 1875 REMINGTON
Caliber: 357 Mag., 44-40, 45 Colt, 6-shot.
Barrel: 7½".
Weight: 44 oz. **Length:** 13¾" overall.
Stocks: Smooth walnut.
Sights: Blade front, notch rear.
Features: Replica of the 1875 Remington S.A. Army revolver. Brass trigger guard, color case-hardened frame, rest blued, or nickel finish. Imported by Cimarron Arms.
Price: **$389.95**

Cimarron 1875 Remington

CIMARRON 1890 REMINGTON REVOLVER
Caliber: 357 Mag., 44-40, 45 Colt, 6-shot.
Barrel: 5½".
Weight: 37 oz. **Length:** 12½" overall.
Stocks: American walnut.
Sights: Blade front, groove rear.
Features: Replica of the 1890 Remington single action. Brass trigger guard, rest is blued, or nickel finish. Lanyard ring in butt. Imported by Cimarron Arms.
Price: **$389.95**

COLT SINGLE ACTION ARMY REVOLVER
Caliber: 44-40, 45 Colt, 6-shot.
Barrel: 4¾", 5½", 7½".
Weight: 40 oz. (4¾" barrel). **Length:** 10¼" overall (4¾" barrel).
Stocks: American walnut.
Sights: Blade front, notch rear.
Features: Available in full nickel finish with nickel grip medallions, or Royal Blue with color case-hardened frame, gold grip medallions. Reintroduced 1992.
Price: **$1,119.95**

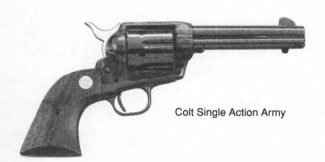
Colt Single Action Army

DAKOTA 1875 OUTLAW REVOLVER
Caliber: 357, 44-40, 45 Colt.
Barrel: 7½".
Weight: 46 oz. **Length:** 13½" overall.
Stocks: Smooth walnut.
Sights: Blade front, fixed groove rear.
Features: Authentic copy of 1875 Remington with firing pin in hammer; color case-hardened frame, blue cylinder, barrel, steel backstrap and brass trigger guard. Also available in nickel, factory engraved. Imported by E.M.F.
Price: All calibers **$465.00**
Price: Nickel **$550.00**
Price: Engraved **$600.00**
Price: Engraved Nickel **$710.00**

Dakota 1890 Police Revolver
Similar to the 1875 Outlaw except has 5½" barrel, weighs 40 oz., with 12½" overall length. Has lanyard ring in butt. No web under barrel. Calibers 357, 44-40, 45 Colt. Imported by E.M.F.
Price: All calibers **$470.00**
Price: Nickel **$560.00**
Price: Engraved **$620.00**
Price: Engraved nickel **$725.00**

E.A.A. BIG BORE BOUNTY HUNTER SA REVOLVERS
Caliber: 357 Mag., 41 Mag., 44-40, 44 Mag., 45 Colt, 6-shot.
Barrel: 5", 7".
Weight: 2.5 lbs. **Length:** 11" overall (5" barrel).
Stocks: Smooth walnut.
Sights: Blade front, grooved topstrap rear.
Features: Transfer bar safety; three position hammer; hammer forged barrel. Introduced 1992. Imported by European American Armory.
Price: Blue **$425.00**
Price: Color case-hardened frame **$440.00**
Price: Blue with gold-plated grip frame **$440.00**
Price: Gold-plated **$499.00**

FREEDOM ARMS PREMIER 454 CASULL
Caliber: 44 Mag., 45 Colt/45 ACP (optional cylinder), 454 Casull, 5-shot.
Barrel: 3", 4¾", 6", 7½", 10".
Weight: 50 oz. **Length:** 14" overall (7½" bbl.).
Stocks: Impregnated hardwood.
Sights: Blade front, notch or adjustable rear.
Features: All stainless steel construction; sliding bar safety system. Hunter Pak includes 7½" gun, sling and studs, aluminum carrying case with tool and cleaning kit. Lifetime warranty. Made in U.S.A.
Price: Field Grade (matte finish, polymer grips), adjustable sights, 4¾", 6", 7½", 10" **$1,063.00**
Price: Field Grade, fixed sights, 4¾" only **$1,000.00**
Price: Field Grade, 44 Rem. Mag., adjustable sights, 7½", 10" only **$1,063.00**
Price: Premier Grade (brush finish, impregnated hardwood grips) adjustable sights, 4¾", 6", 7½", 10" **$1,340.00**
Price: Premier Grade, fixed sights, 7½" only **$1,263.00**
Price: Premier Grade, 44 Rem. Mag., adjustable sights, 7½", 10" only **$1,340.00**
Price: Premier Grade, U.S. Deputy Marshall (3" barrel, no ejector, adjustable sights, medallion in left hardwood grip) **$1,509.00**
Price: As above, fixed sights **$1,432.00**
Price: Premier Grade Hunter Pak, black micarta grips, 2x Leupold scope, Leupold rings and base, no front sight base **$1,558.45**
Price: Premier Grade Hunter Pak, adjustable sight, black micarta grips **$1,653.90**
Price: Field Grade Hunter Pak, polymer grips, 2x Leupold scope, Leupold rings and base, no front sight base **$1,269.15**
Price: Field Grade Hunter Pak, polymer grips, low-profile adjustable sight **$1,342.15**
Price: Fitted 45 ACP or 45 Colt cylinder, add **$206.75**

Freedom Arms Casull Model 353 Revolver
Similar to the Premier 454 Casull except chambered for 357 Magnum with 5-shot cylinder; 7½" or 9" barrel. Weighs 59 oz. with 7½" barrel. Standard model has adjustable sights, matte finish, Pachmayr grips, 7½" or 9" barrel; Silhouette has 9" barrel, Patridge front sight, Iron Sight Gun Works Silhouette adjustable rear, Pachmayr grips, trigger over-travel adjustment screw. All stainless steel. Introduced 1992.
Price: Standard **$1,063.00**
Price: Premier Grade (brushed finish, impregnated hardwood grips, Premier Grade sights(7½", 9" **$1,340.00**
Price: Silhouette **$1,131.00**

DAKOTA HARTFORD SINGLE-ACTION REVOLVERS
Caliber: 22 LR, 357 Mag., 32-20, 38-40, 44-40, 44 Spec., 45 Colt.
Barrel: 4¾", 5½", 7½".
Weight: 45 oz. **Length:** 13" overall (7½" barrel).
Stocks: Smooth walnut.
Sights: Blade front, fixed rear.
Features: Identical to the origianl Colts with inspector cartouche on left grip, original patent dates and U.S. markings. All major parts serial numbered using original Colt-style lettering, numbering. Bullseye ejector head and color case-hardening on frame and hammer. Introduced 1990. From E.M.F.
Price: **$600.00**
Price: Cavalry or Artillery **$655.00**
Price: Nickel plated **$760.00**
Price: Cattlebrand engraved nickel **$1,150.00**
Price: Scroll engraved **$840.00**
Price: Scroll engraved nickel **$1,000.00**

Dakota New Model Single-Action Revolvers
Similar to the standard Dakota except has color case-hardened forged steel frame, black nickel backstrap and trigger guard. Calibers 357 Mag., 44-40, 45 Colt only.
Price: **$490.00**
Price: Nickel **$636.00**

E.A.A. Big Bore Bounty Hunter

E.A.A. Bounty Hunter

E.A.A. BOUNTY HUNTER REVOLVER
Caliber: 22 LR, 22 WMR, 6-shot cylinder.
Barrel: 4¾", 6", 9".
Weight: 32 oz. **Length:** 10" overall (4¾" barrel).
Stocks: European hardwood.
Sights: Blade front, rear adjustable for windage.
Features: Available in blue or blue/gold finish. Introduced 1991. From European American Armory Corp.
Price: 4¾", blue **$115.00**
Price: 4¾", blue, 22 LR/22 WMR combo **$135.00**
Price: 4¾", blue/gold, 22 LR/22 WMR combo **$145.00**
Price: 6", blue, 22 LR/22 WMR combo **$140.00**
Price: 6", blue/gold, 22 LR/22 WMR combo **$150.00**
Price: 9", blue, 22 LR/22 WMR combo **$155.00**
Price: 9", blue/gold, 22 LR/22 WMR combo **$165.00**

Freedom 454 Field Grade

MITCHELL SINGLE-ACTION ARMY REVOLVERS

Caliber: 357 Mag., 44-40, 44 Mag., 45 ACP, 45 Colt, 6-shot.
Barrel: 4¾", 5½", 6", 7½".
Weight: NA. **Length:** NA.
Stocks: One-piece walnut.
Sights: Serrated ramp front, fixed or adjustable rear.
Features: Color case-hardened frame, brass or steel backstrap/trigger guard; hammer-block safety. Bright nickel-plated model and dual cylinder models available. Contact importer for complete price list. Imported by Mitchell Arms, Inc.
Price: Cowboy, 4¾", Army 5½", Cavalry 7½", blue, 357, 44-40, 45 Colt, 45 ACP **$389.00**
Price: As above, nickel **$429.00**
Price: 45 Colt/45 ACP dual cyl., blue **$439.00**
Price: As above, nickel **$479.00**
Price: Bat Masterson model, 45 Colt, 4¾", nickel **$429.00**

Mitchell Single-Action

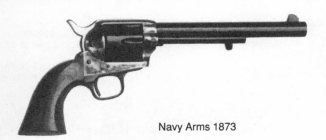

Navy Arms 1873

NAVY ARMS 1873 SINGLE-ACTION REVOLVER

Caliber: 44-40, 45 Colt, 6-shot cylinder.
Barrel: 3", 4¾", 5½", 7½".
Weight: 36 oz. **Length:** 10¾" overall (5½" barrel).
Stocks: Smooth walnut.
Sights: Blade front, groove in topstrap rear.
Features: Blue with color case-hardened frame, or nickel. Introduced 1991. Imported by Navy Arms.
Price: Blue **$345.00**
Price: Nickel **$410.00**
Price: 1873 U.S. Cavalry Model (7½", 45 Colt, arsenal markings) . . **$495.00**
Price: 1895 U.S. Artillery Model (as above, 5½" barrel) **$495.00**

North American Mini

NORTH AMERICAN MINI-REVOLVERS

Caliber: 22 LR, 22 WMR, 5-shot.
Barrel: 1⅛", 1⅝".
Weight: 4 to 6.6 oz. **Length:** 3⅝" to 6⅛" overall.
Stocks: Laminated wood.
Sights: Blade front, notch fixed rear.
Features: All stainless steel construction. Polished satin and matte finish. Engraved models available. From North American Arms.
Price: 22 LR, 1⅛" bbl. **$162.50**
Price: 22 LR, 1⅝" bbl. **$162.50**
Price: 22 WMR, 1⅝" bbl. **$182.50**
Price: 22 WMR, 1⅛" or 1⅝" bbl. with extra 22 LR cylinder **$217.50**

NORTH AMERICAN MINI-MASTER

Caliber: 22 LR, 22 WMR, 5-shot cylinder.
Barrel: 4".
Weight: 10.7 oz. **Length:** 7.75" overall.
Stocks: Checkered hard black rubber.
Sights: Blade front, white outline rear adjustable for elevation, or fixed.
Features: Heavy vent barrel; full-size grips. Non-fluted cylinder. Introduced 1989.
Price: Adjustable sight, 22 WMR or 22 LR **$265.50**
Price: As above with extra WMR/LR cylinder **$300.50**
Price: Fixed sight, 22 WMR or 22 LR **$255.50**
Price: As above with extra WMR/LR cylinder **$290.50**

PHELPS HERITAGE I, EAGLE I REVOLVERS

Caliber: 444 Marlin, 45-70, 6-shot.
Barrel: 8" or 12", 16" (45-70).
Weight: 5½ lbs. **Length:** 19½" overall (12" bbl.).
Stocks: Smooth walnut.
Sights: Ramp front, adjustable rear.
Features: Single action; polished blue finish; safety bar. From Phelps Mfg. Co.
Price: 8", 45-70 or 444 Marlin, about **$865.00**
Price: 12", 45-70 or 444 Marlin, about **$890.00**

North American Black Widow Revolver

Similar to the Mini-Master except has 2" Heavy Vent barrel. Built on the 22 WMR frame. Non-fluted cylinder, black rubber grips. Available with either Millett Low Profile fixed sights or Millett sight adjustable for elevation only. Overall length 5⅞", weight 8.8 oz. From North American Arms.
Price: Adjustable sight, 22 LR or 22 WMR **$233.50**
Price: As above with extra WMR/LR cylinder **$268.50**
Price: Fixed sight, 22 LR or 22 WMR **$223.50**
Price: As above with extra WMR/LR cylinder **$258.50**

QFI Western Ranger

QFI WESTERN RANGER REVOLVER

Caliber: 22 LR, 22 LR/22 WMR.
Barrel: 3¼", 4¾", 6½", 9".
Weight: 31 oz. (4¾" bbl.). **Length:** 10" overall.
Stocks: American walnut.
Sights: Blade front, notch rear.
Features: Single action, blue/black finish. Introduced 1991. Made in the U.S. by QFI.
Price: 22 LR, 3¼" or 4¾" **$104.95**
Price: As above, convertible (22 LR/22 WMR) **$119.95**
Price: 22 LR, 6½" **$104.95**
Price: As above, convertible (22 LR/22 WMR) **$119.95**
Price: 22 LR, 9" **$111.95**
Price: As above, convertible (22 LR/22 WMR) **$139.95**

CAUTION: PRICES CHANGE, CHECK AT GUNSHOP.

QFI PLAINS RIDER SINGLE-ACTION REVOLVER

Caliber: 22 LR, 22 LR/22 WMR, 6-shot.
Barrel: 3", 4¾", 6½", 9".
Weight: 35 oz. (6½" barrel). **Length:** 11" overall (6½" barrel).
Stocks: Black composition.
Sights: Blade front, fixed rear.
Features: Blue/black finish. Available with extra cylinder. Introduced 1991. From QFI.
Price: 22 LR, 3", 4¾", 6½" $99.95
Price: As above, combo $125.95
Price: 22 LR, 9" $110.95
Price: As above, combo $146.95

Ruger Blackhawk

Ruger Bisley

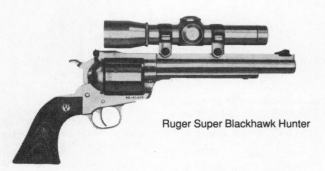

Ruger Super Blackhawk Hunter

Ruger SSM Single-Six

Ruger Bisley Small Frame Revolver

Similar to the Single-Six except frame is styled after the classic Bisley "flat-top." Most mechanical parts are unchanged. Hammer is lower and smoothly curved with a deeply checkered spur. Trigger is strongly curved with a wide smooth surface. Longer grip frame designed with a hand-filling shape, and the trigger guard is a large oval. Adjustable dovetail rear sight; front sight base accepts interchangeable square blades of various heights and styles. Has an unfluted cylinder and roll engraving. Weight about 41 oz. Chambered for 22 LR and 32 H&R Mag., 6½" barrel only. Introduced 1985.
Price: $328.75

RUGER BLACKHAWK REVOLVER

Caliber: 30 Carbine, 357 Mag./38 Spec., 41 Mag., 44 Mag., 45 Colt, 6-shot.
Barrel: 4⅝" or 6½", either caliber; 7½" (30 Carbine, 45 Colt only).
Weight: 42 oz. (6½" bbl.). **Length:** 12¼" overall (6½" bbl.).
Stocks: American walnut.
Sights: ⅛" ramp front, micro-click rear adjustable for windage and elevation.
Features: Ruger interlock mechanism, independent firing pin, hardened chrome moly steel frame, music wire springs throughout.
Price: Blue, 30 Carbine (7½" bbl.), BN31 . . . . $315.00
Price: Blue, 357 Mag. (4⅝", 6½"), BN34, BN36 . . . . $328.00
Price: Blue, 357/9mm Convertible (4⅝", 6½"), BN34X, BN36X . . . $343.50
Price: Blue, 41 Mag., 45 Colt (4⅝", 6½"), BN41, BN42, BN45 . . . $328.00
Price: Stainless, 357 Mag. (4⅝", 6½"), KBN34, KBN36 . . . . $404.00

Ruger Bisley Single-Action Revolver

Similar to standard Blackhawk except the hammer is lower with a smoothly curved, deeply checkered wide spur. The trigger is strongly curved with a wide smooth surface. Longer grip frame has a hand-filling shape. Adjustable rear sight, ramp-style front. Has an unfluted cylinder and roll engraving, adjustable sights. Chambered for 32 H&R Mag., 357, 41, 44 Mags. and 45 Colt; 7½" barrel; overall length of 13". Introduced 1985.
Price: $391.00

RUGER SUPER BLACKHAWK

Caliber: 44 Magnum, 6-shot. Also fires 44 Spec.
Barrel: 5½", 7½", 10½".
Weight: 48 oz. (7½" bbl.), 51 oz. (10½" bbl.). **Length:** 13⅜" overall (7½" bbl.).
Stocks: American walnut.
Sights: ⅛" ramp front, micro-click rear adjustable for windage and elevation.
Features: Ruger interlock mechanism, non-fluted cylinder, steel grip and cylinder frame, square back trigger guard, wide serrated trigger and wide spur hammer.
Price: Blue (S45N, S47N, S411N) $378.50
Price: Stainless (KS45N, KS47N, KS411N) $413.75
Price: Stainless KS47NH Hunter with scope rings, 7½" $479.50

RUGER SUPER SINGLE-SIX CONVERTIBLE

Caliber: 22 LR, 6-shot; 22 WMR in extra cylinder.
Barrel: 4⅝", 5½", 6½", or 9½" (6-groove).
Weight: 34½ oz. (6½" bbl.). **Length:** 11¹³⁄₁₆" overall (6½" bbl.).
Stocks: Smooth American walnut.
Sights: Improved Patridge front on ramp, fully adjustable rear protected by integral frame ribs.
Features: Ruger interlock mechanism, transfer bar ignition, gate-controlled loading, hardened chrome moly steel frame, wide trigger, music wire springs throughout, independent firing pin.
Price: 4⅝", 5½", 6½", 9½" barrel $281.00
Price: 5½", 6½" bbl. only, stainless steel $354.00

Ruger SSM Single-Six Revolver

Similar to the Super Single-Six revolver except chambered for 32 H&R Magnum (also handles 32 S&W and 32 S&W Long). Weight is about 34 oz. with 6½" barrel. Barrel lengths: 4⅝", 5½", 6½", 9½". Introduced 1985.
Price: $270.00

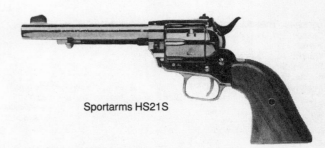

Sportarms HS21S

SPORTARMS MODEL HS21S SINGLE ACTION

Caliber: 22 LR or 22 LR/22 WMR combo, 6-shot.
Barrel: 5½".
Weight: 33.5 oz. **Length:** 11" overall.
Stocks: Smooth hardwood.
Sights: Blade front, rear drift adjustable for windage.
Features: Available in blue with imitation stag or wood stocks. Made in Germany by Herbert Schmidt; Imported by Sportarms of Florida.
Price: 22 LR, blue, "stag" grips, about $80.00
Price: 22 LR/22 WMR combo, blue, wood stocks, about $110.00

TEXAS LONGHORN ARMS GROVER'S IMPROVED NO. FIVE
Caliber: 44 Magnum, 6-shot.
Barrel: 5½".
Weight: 44 oz. **Length:** NA.
Stocks: Fancy AAA walnut.
Sights: Square blade front on ramp, fully adjustable rear.
Features: Music wire coil spring action with double locking bolt; polished blue finish. Handmade in limited 1,200-gun production. Grip contour, straps, over-sized base pin, lever latch and lockwork identical copies of Elmer Keith design. Lifetime warranty to original owner. Introduced 1988.
Price: **$985.00**

TEXAS LONGHORN ARMS RIGHT-HAND SINGLE ACTION
Caliber: All centerfire pistol calibers.
Barrel: 4¾".
Weight: NA. **Length:** NA.
Stocks: One-piece fancy walnut, or any fancy AAA wood.
Sights: Blade front, grooved topstrap rear.
Features: Loading gate and ejector housing on left side of gun. Cylinder rotates to the left. All steel construction; color case-hardened frame; high polish blue; music wire coil springs. Lifetime guarantee to original owner. Introduced 1984. From Texas Longhorn Arms.
Price: South Texas Army Limited Edition—handmade, only 1,000 to be produced; "One of One Thousand" engraved on barrel **$1,500.00**

Texas Longhorn Arms Sesquicentennial Model Revolver
Similar to the South Texas Army Model except has ¾-coverage Nimschke-style engraving, antique golden nickel plate finish, one-piece elephant ivory grips. Comes with handmade solid walnut presentation case, factory letter to owner. Limited edition of 150 units. Introduced 1986.
Price: **$2,500.00**

Texas Longhorn Arms Texas Border Special
Similar to the South Texas Army Limited Edition except has 3½" barrel, bird's-head style grip. Same special features. Introduced 1984.
Price: **$1,500.00**

Texas Longhorn Arms West Texas Flat Top Target
Similar to the South Texas Army Limited Edition except choice of barrel length from 7½" through 15"; flat-top style frame; ⅛" contoured ramp front sight, old model steel micro-click rear adjustable for windage and elevation. Same special features. Introduced 1984.
Price: **$1,500.00**

UBERTI 1873 CATTLEMAN SINGLE ACTIONS
Caliber: 38 Spec., 357 Mag., 44 Spec., 44-40, 45 Colt/45 ACP, 6-shot.
Barrel: 4¾", 5½", 7½"; 44-40, 45 Colt also with 3".
Weight: 38 oz. (5½" bbl.). **Length:** 10¾" overall (5½" bbl.).
Stocks: One-piece smooth walnut.
Sights: Blade front, groove rear; fully adjustable rear available.
Features: Steel or brass backstrap, trigger guard; color case-hardened frame; blued barrel, cylinder. Imported from Italy by Uberti USA.
Price: Steel backstrap, trigger guard, fixed sights **$410.00**
Price: Brass backstrap, trigger guard, fixed sights **$365.00**

UBERTI 1875 SA ARMY OUTLAW REVOLVER
Caliber: 357 Mag., 44-40, 45 Colt, 6-shot.
Barrel: 7½".
Weight: 44 oz. **Length:** 13¾" overall.
Stocks: Smooth walnut.
Sights: Blade front, notch rear.
Features: Replica of the 1875 Remington S.A. Army revolver. Brass trigger guard, color case-hardened frame, rest blued. Imported by Uberti USA.
Price: **$405.00**
Price: Nickel-plated **$450.00**

UBERTI 1890 ARMY OUTLAW REVOLVER
Caliber: 357 Mag., 44-40, 45 Colt, 6-shot.
Barrel: 5½".
Weight: 37 oz. **Length:** 12½" overall.
Stocks: American walnut.
Sights: Blade front, groove rear.
Features: Replica of the 1890 Remington single action. Brass trigger guard, rest is blued. Imported by Uberti USA.
Price: **$410.00**
Price: Nickel-plated **$455.00**

Texas Longhorn Grover's No. Five

Texas Longhorn Border Special

Uberti Cattleman

Texas Longhorn Arms Cased Set
Set contains one each of the Texas Longhorn Right-Hand Single Actions, all in the same caliber, same serial numbers (100, 200, 300, 400, 500, 600, 700, 800, 900). Ten sets to be made (#1000 donated to NRA museum). Comes in hand-tooled leather case. All other specs same as Limited Edition guns. Introduced 1984.
Price: **$5,750.00**
Price: With ¾-coverage "C-style" engraving **$7,650.00**

Uberti 1873 Buckhorn Single Action
A slightly larger version of the Cattleman revolver. Available in 44 Magnum or 44 Magnum/44-40 convertible, otherwise has same specs.
Price: Steel backstrap, trigger guard, fixed sights **$410.00**
Price: Convertible (two cylinders) **$460.00**

Uberti 1875 Army

CAUTION: PRICES CHANGE, CHECK AT GUNSHOP.

Specially adapted single-shot and multi-barrel arms.

American Derringer Model 1

AMERICAN DERRINGER MODEL 3
Caliber: 38 Special.
Barrel: 2.5".
Weight: 8.5 oz. **Length:** 4.9" overall.
Stocks: Rosewood.
Sights: Blade front.
Features: Made of stainless steel. Single shot with manual hammer block safety. Introduced 1985. From American Derringer Corp.
Price: **$120.00**

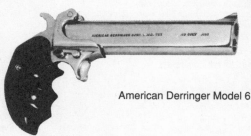

American Derringer Model 6

American Derringer Model 7
Similar to Model 1 except made of high strength aircraft aluminum. Weighs 7½ oz., 4.82" o.a.l., rosewood stocks. Available in 22 LR, 32 H&R Mag., 380 ACP, 38 Spec., 44 Spec. Introduced 1986.
Price: 22 LR or 38 Spec. **$212.50**
Price: 380 ACP **$199.95**
Price: 32 H&R Mag. **$202.50**
Price: 44 Spec. **$500.00**

American Derringer Texas Commemorative
A Model 1 Derringer with solid brass frame, stainless steel barrel and rosewood grips. Available in 38 Speical, 44-40 Win., or 45 Colt. Introduced 1987.
Price: 38 Spec. **$215.00**
Price: 44-40 or 45 Colt **$320.00**

AMERICAN DERRINGER DA 38 MODEL
Caliber: 9mm Para., 38 Spec., 357 Mag.
Barrel: 3".
Weight: 14.5 oz. **Length:** 4.8" overall.
Stocks: Rosewood, walnut or other hardwoods.
Sights: Fixed.
Features: Double-action only; two-shots. Manual safety. Made of satin-finished stainless steel and aluminum. Introduced 1989. From American Derringer Corp.
Price: 38 Spec. **$245.00**
Price: 9mm Para. **$257.00**
Price: 357 Mag. **$300.00**

American Derringer Mini COP Derringer
Similar to the COP 357 except chambered for 22 WMR. Barrel length of 2.85", overall length of 4.95", weight is 16 oz. Double action with automatic hammer-block safety. Made of stainless steel. Grips of rosewood, walnut or other hardwoods. Introduced 1990. Made in U.S. by American Derringer Corp.
Price: **$312.50**

AMERICAN DERRINGER MODEL 1
Caliber: 22 LR, 22 WMR, 30 Luger, 30-30 Win., 32 ACP, 380 ACP, 38 Spec., 9mm Para., 357 Mag., 357 Maximum, 10mm, 40 S&W, 41 Mag., 38-40, 44-40 Win., 44 Spec., 44 Mag., 45 Colt, 45 ACP, 410-bore (2½").
Barrel: 3".
Weight: 15½ oz. (38 Spec.). **Length:** 4.82" overall.
Stocks: Rosewood, Zebra wood.
Sights: Blade front.
Features: Made of stainless steel with high-polish or satin finish. Two-shot capacity. Manual hammer block safety. Introduced 1980. Available in almost any pistol caliber. Contact the factory for complete list of available calibers and prices. From American Derringer Corp.
Price: 22 LR or WMR **$237.50**
Price: 38 Spec. **$215.00**
Price: 357 Maximum **$265.00**
Price: 357 Mag. **$247.00**
Price: 9mm, 380, ... **$208.00**
Price: 10mm, 40 S&W **$250.00**
Price: 44 Spec. **$320.00**
Price: 44-40 Win., 45 Colt, 45 Auto Rim **$320.00**
Price: 30-30, 41, 44 Mags., 45 Win. Mag. **$375.00**
Price: 45-70, single shot **$312.00**
Price: 45 Colt, 410, 2½" **$320.00**
Price: 45 ACP, 10mm Auto **$250.00**
Price: 125th Anniversary model (brass frame, stainless bbl., 44-40, 45 Colt, 38 Spec.) **$320.00**
Price: Alaskan Survival model (45-70 upper, 410-45 Colt lower) . . . **$387.50**

American Derringer Model 4
Similar to the Model 1 except has 4.1" barrel, overall length of 6", and weighs 16½ oz.; chambered for 3" 410-bore shotshells or 45 or 44 Magnum Colt. Can be had with 45-70 upper barrel and 3" 410-bore or 45 Colt bottom barrel. Made of stainless steel. Manual hammer block safety. Introduced 1985.
Price: 3" 410/45 Colt (either barrel) **$350.00**
Price: 3" 410/45 Colt or 45-70 (Alaskan Survival model) **$387.50**
Price: 44 Magnum with oversize grips **$422.00**

American Derringer Model 6
Similar to the Model 1 except has 6" barrels chambered for 3" 410 shotshells or 45 Colt, rosewood stocks, 8.2" o.a.l. and weighs 21 oz. Shoots either round for each barrel. Manual hammer block safety. Introduced 1986.
Price: High polish or satin finish **$387.50**
Price: Gray matte finish **$350.00**

American Derringer Model 10 Lightweight
Similar to the Model 1 except frame is of aluminum, giving weight of 10 oz. Available in 45 Colt or 45 ACP only. Matte gray finish. Introduced 1989.
Price: 45 Colt **$320.00**
Price: 45 ACP **$250.00**
Price: Model 11 (38 Spec., aluminum bbls., wgt. 11 oz.) **$205.00**

American Derringer Lady Derringer
Same as the Model 1 except has tuned action, is fitted with scrimshawed synthetic ivory grips; chambered for 32 H&R Mag. and 38 Spec.; 22 LR, 22 WMR, 380 ACP, 357 Mag., 9mm Para., 45 ACP, 45 Colt/410 shotshell available at extra cost. Deluxe Grade is highly polished; Deluxe Engraved is engraved in a pattern similar to that used on 1880s derringers. All come in a French fitted jewelry box. Introduced 1991.
Price: Deluxe Grade **$250.00**
Price: Deluxe Engraved Grade **$695.00**

> Consult our Directory pages for the location of firms mentioned.

AMERICAN DERRINGER COP 357 DERRINGER
Caliber: 38 Spec. or 357 Mag., 4-shot.
Barrel: 3.14".
Weight: 16 oz. **Length:** 5.53" overall.
Stocks: Rosewood.
Sights: Fixed.
Features: Double-action only. Four shots. Made of stainless steel. Introduced 1990. Made in U.S. by American Derringer Corp.
Price: **$375.00**

American Derringer Semmerling

AMERICAN DERRINGER SEMMERLING LM-4
Caliber: 9mm Para., 7-shot magazine; 45 ACP, 5-shot magazine.
Barrel: 3.625".
Weight: 24 oz. **Length:** 5.2" overall.
Stocks: Checkered plastic on blued guns, rosewood on stainless guns.
Sights: Open, fixed.
Features: Manually-operated repeater. Height is 3.7", width is 1". Comes with manual, leather carrying case, spare stock screws, wrench. From American Derringer Corp.
Price: Blued **$1,750.00**
Price: Stainless steel **$1,875.00**

Anschutz Exemplar Hornet

ANSCHUTZ EXEMPLAR BOLT-ACTION PISTOL
Caliber: 22 LR, 5-shot; 22 Hornet, 5-shot.
Barrel: 10", 14".
Weight: 3½ lbs. **Length:** 17" overall.
Stock: European walnut with stippled grip and forend.
Sights: Hooded front on ramp, open notch rear adjustable for windage and elevation.
Features: Uses Match 64 action with left-hand bolt; Anschutz #5091 two-stage trigger set at 9.85 oz. Receiver grooved for scope mounting; open sights easily removed. Introduced 1987. Imported from Germany by PSI.
Price: 22 LR **$480.00**
Price: 22 LR, left-hand **$492.50**
Price: 22 LR, 14" barrel **$509.50**
Price: 22 Hornet (no sights, 10" bbl.) **$822.00**

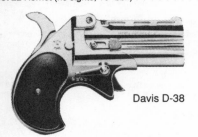

Davis D-38

DAVIS DERRINGERS
Caliber: 22 LR, 22 WMR, 25 ACP, 32 ACP.
Barrel: 2.4".
Weight: 9.5 oz. **Length:** 4" overall.
Stocks: Laminated wood.
Sights: Blade front, fixed notch rear.
Features: Choice of black Teflon or chrome finish; spur trigger. Introduced 1986. Made in U.S. by Davis Industries.
Price: **$64.90**

DAVIS D-38 DERRINGER
Caliber: 38 Special.
Barrel: 2.75".
Weight: 11.5 oz. **Length:** 4.65" overall.
Stocks: Textured black synthetic.
Sights: Blade front, fixed notch rear.
Features: Alloy frame, steel-lined barrels, steel breech block. Plunger-type safety with integral hammer block. Chrome or black Teflon finish. Introduced 1992. Made in U.S. by Davis Industries.
Price: **$89.90**

Feather Guardian Angel

FEATHER GUARDIAN ANGEL PISTOL
Caliber: 22 LR/22 WMR.
Barrel: 2".
Weight: 12 oz. **Length:** 5" overall.
Stocks: Black composition.
Sights: Fixed.
Features: Uses a pre-loaded two-shot drop-in "magazine." Stainless steel construction; matte finish. From Feather Industries. Introduced 1988.
Price: **$119.95**

GAUCHER GN1 SILHOUETTE PISTOL
Caliber: 22 LR, single shot.
Barrel: 10".
Weight: 2.4 lbs. **Length:** 15.5" overall.
Stock: European hardwood.
Sights: Blade front, open adjustable rear.
Features: Bolt action, adjustable trigger. Introduced 1990. Imported from France by Mandall Shooting Supplies.
Price: About **$319.95**
Price: Model GP Silhouette **$380.00**

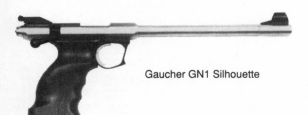

Gaucher GN1 Silhouette

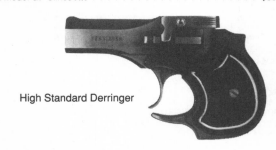

High Standard Derringer

HIGH STANDARD DERRINGER
Caliber: 22 LR, 22 WMR, 2-shot.
Barrel: 3.5".
Weight: 11 oz. **Length:** 5.12" overall.
Stocks: Black composition.
Sights: Fixed.
Features: Double action, dual extraction. Hammer-block safety. Blue finish. Introduced 1990. Made in U.S. by American Derringer Corp.
Price: **$157.00**

Ithaca X-Caliber

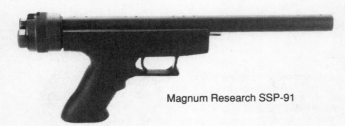

Magnum Research SSP-91

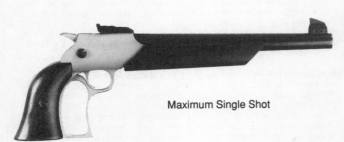

Maximum Single Shot

New Advantage Derringer

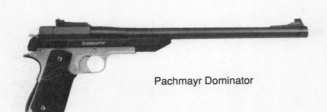

Pachmayr Dominator

ITHACA X-CALIBER SINGLE SHOT
Caliber: 22 LR, 44 Mag.
Barrel: 10", 15".
Weight: 3¼ lbs. **Length:** 15" overall (10" barrel).
Stocks: Goncalo Alves grip and forend on Model 20; American walnut on Model 30.
Sights: Blade on ramp front; Model 20 has adjustable, removable target-type rear. Drilled and tapped for scope mounting.
Features: Dual firing pin for RF/CF use. Polished blue finish.
Price: 22 LR, 10", 44 Mag., 10" or 15" **$270.00**
Price: 22 LR/44 Mag. combo, 10" and 15" **$365.00**
Price: As above, both 10" barrels **$365.00**

MAGNUM RESEARCH SSP-91 SINGLE SHOT PISTOL
Caliber: 22 LR, 22 WMR, 22 Hornet, 223, 22-250, 243, 6mm BR, 7mm BR, 7mm-08, 30-30, 308, 30-06, 357 Mag., 35 Rem., 358 Win., 44 Mag., 444 Marlin.
Barrel: 14", interchangable.
Weight: 4lbs., 2 oz. **Length:** 15" overall.
Stocks: Composition, with thumbrest.
Sights: None furnished; drilled and tapped for scope mounting and open sights. Open sights optional.
Features: Cannon-type rotating breech with spring-activated ejector. Ordnance steel with matte blue finish. Cross-bolt safety. External cocking lever on left side of gun. Introduced 1991. Made by Ordnance Technology, Inc. Available from Magnum Research, Inc.
Price: Complete pistol **$299.00**
Price: Barreled action only **$229.00**
Price: Scope base **$12.95**
Price: Adjustable open sights **$29.95**

MANDALL/CABANAS PISTOL
Caliber: 177, pellet or round ball; single shot.
Barrel: 9".
Weight: 51 oz. **Length:** 19" overall.
Stock: Smooth wood with thumbrest.
Sights: Blade front on ramp, open adjustable rear.
Features: Fires round ball or pellets with 22 blank cartridge. Automatic safety; muzzlebrake. Imported from Mexico by Mandall Shooting Supplies.
Price: **$139.95**

MAXIMUM SINGLE SHOT PISTOL
Caliber: 22 LR, 22 Hornet, 22 BR, 223 Rem., 22-250, 6mm BR, 6mm-223, 243, 250 Savage, 6.5mm-35, 7mm TCU, 7mm BR, 7mm-35, 7mm INT-R, 7mm-08, 7mm Rocket, 7mm Super Mag., 30 Herrett, 30 Carbine, 308 Win., 7.62 x 39, 32-20, 357 Mag., 357 Maximum, 358 Win., 44 Mag.
Barrel: 8¾", 10½", 14".
Weight: 61 oz. (10½" bbl.); 78 oz. (14" bbl.). **Length:** 15", 18½" overall (with 10½" and 14" bbl., respectively).
Stocks: Smooth walnut stocks and forend.
Sights: Ramp front, fully adjustable open rear.
Features: Falling block action; drilled and tapped for M.O.A. scope mounts; integral grip frame/receiver; adjustable trigger; Douglas barrel (interchangeable). Introduced 1983. Made in U.S. by M.O.A. Corp.
Price: Stainless receiver, blue barrel **$566.00**
Price: Stainless receiver, stainless barrel **$616.00**
Price: Extra blued barrel **$149.00**
Price: Extra stainless barrel **$202.00**
Price: Scope mount **$52.00**

NEW ADVANTAGE ARMS DERRINGER
Caliber: 22 LR, 22 WMR, 4-shot.
Barrel: 2½".
Weight: 15 oz. **Length:** 4½" overall.
Stocks: Smooth walnut.
Sights: Fixed.
Features: Double-action mechanism, four barrels, revolving firing pin. Rebounding hammer. Blue or stainless. Reintroduced 1989. From New Advantage Arms Corp.
Price: 22 LR, 22 WMR, blue **$199.00**
Price: As above, stainless **$219.00**

PACHMAYR DOMINATOR PISTOL
Caliber: 22 Hornet, 223, 7mm-06, 308, 35 Rem., 44 Mag., single shot.
Barrel: 10½" (44 Mag.), 14" all other calibers.
Weight: 4 lbs. (14" barrel). **Length:** 16" overall (14" barrel).
Stocks: Pachmayr Signature system.
Sights: Optional sights or drilled and tapped for scope mounting.
Features: Bolt-action pistol on 1911A1 frame. Comes as complete gun. Introduced 1988. From Pachmayr.
Price: Either barrel $524.50

MITCHELL ARMS ROLLING BLOCK TARGET PISTOL
Caliber: 22 LR, 22 WMR, 357 Mag., 45 Colt, 223 Rem., single shot.
Barrel: 9.875", half-round, half-octagon.
Weight: 44 oz. **Length:** 14" overall.
Stocks: Walnut grip and forend.
Sights: Blade front, fully adjustable rear.
Features: Replica of the 1871 rolling block target pistol. Brass trigger guard, color case-hardened frame, blue barrel. Imported from Italy by Mitchell Arms, Inc.
Price: **$395.00**

RPM XL SINGLE SHOT PISTOL

Caliber: 22 LR, 22 WMR, 225 Win., 25 Rocket, 6.5 Rocket, 32 H&R Mag., 357 Max., 357 Mag., 30-30 Win., 30 Herrett, 357 Herrett, 41 Mag., 44 Mag., 454 Casull, 375 Win., 7mm UR, 7mm Merrill, 30 Merrill, 7mm Rocket, 270 Ren, 270 Rocket, 270 Max., 45-70.

Barrel: 8" slab, 10¾", 12", 14" bull; .450" wide vent. rib, matted to prevent glare.

Weight: About 60 oz. **Length:** 12¼" overall (10¾" bbl.).

Stocks: Smooth Goncalo with thumb and heel rest.

Sights: Front .100" blade, Millett rear adjustable for windage and elevation. Hooded front with interchangeable post optional.

Features: Polished blue finish, hard chrome optional. Barrel is drilled and tapped for scope mounting. Cocking indicator visible from rear of gun. Has spring-loaded barrel lock, positive hammer block thumb safety. Trigger adjustable for weight of pull and over-travel. For complete price list contact RPM.

Price: Regular ¾" frame, right-hand action $807.50
Price: As above, left-hand action $832.50
Price: Wide ⅞" frame, right-hand action $857.50
Price: Extra barrel, 8", 10¾" $287.50
Price: Extra barrel, 12", 14" $357.50

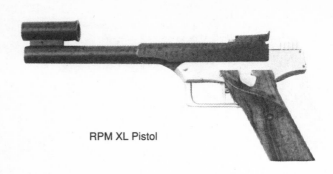

RPM XL Pistol

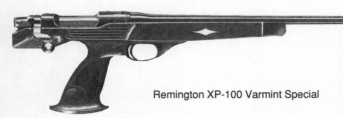

Remington XP-100 Varmint Special

REMINGTON XP-100 VARMINT SPECIAL

Caliber: 223 Rem., single shot.

Barrel: 14½".

Weight: 60 oz. **Length:** 21¼" overall.

Stock: Black nylon one-piece, checkered grip with white spacers.

Sights: Tapped for scope mount.

Features: Fits left or right hand, is shaped to fit fingers and heel of hand. Grooved trigger. Rotating thumb safety, cavity in forend permits insertion of up to five 38-cal. 130-gr. metal jacketed bullets to adjust weight and balance. Included is a black vinyl, zippered case.

Price: Including case, about $419.00

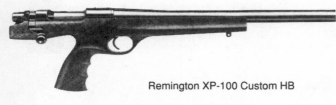

Remington XP-100 Custom HB

Remington XP-100 Custom HB Long Range Pistol

Similar to the XP-100 "Varmint Special" except chambered for 223 Rem., 22-250, 7mm-08 Rem., 35 Rem., 250 Savage, 6mm BR, 7mm BR, 308. Offered with standard 14½" barrel with adjustable rear leaf and front bead sights, or with heavy 15½" barrel without sights. Custom Shop 14½" barrel, Custom Shop English walnut stock in right- or left-hand configuration. Action tuned in Custom Shop. Weight is under 4½ lbs. (heavy barrel, 5½ lbs.). Introduced 1986.

Price: Right- or left-hand $945.00

Remington XP-100R KS

Remington XP-100R KS Repeater Pistol

Similar to the Custom Long Range Pistol except chambered for 223 Rem., 22-250, 7mm-08 Rem., 250 Savage, 308, 350 Rem. Mag., and 35 Rem., and has a blind magazine holding 5 rounds (7mm-08 and 35), or 6 (223 Rem.). Comes with a rear-handle, synthetic stock of Du Pont Kevlar to eliminate the transfer bar between the forward trigger and rear trigger assembly. Fitted with front and rear sling swivel studs. Has standard-weight 14½" barrel with adjustable leaf rear sight, bead front. The receiver is drilled and tapped for scope mounts. Weight is about 4½ lbs. Introduced 1990. From Remington Custom Shop.

Price: $800.00

SPRINGFIELD ARMORY 1911A2 S.A.S.S. PISTOL

Caliber: 22 LR, 223, 243, 7mm BR, 7mm-08, 308, 357 Mag., 358 Win., 44 Mag., single shot.

Barrel: 10.7" or 14.9".

Weight: 4 lbs. 2 oz. (14.9" bbl.). **Length:** 17.2" overall (14.9" barrel); 13" with 10.7" barrel.

Stocks: Rubberized wraparound.

Sights: Blade on ramp front, fully adjustable open rear. Drilled and tapped for scope mounting.

Features: Uses standard 1911A1 frame with a break-open top half interchangeable barrel system. Available as complete gun or as conversion unit only (requires fitting). Introduced 1989.

Price: Complete pistol, 15" bbl. $749.00
Price: As above, 10¾" bbl. $749.00
Price: Conversion unit, 15" bbl. $399.00
Price: As above, 10¾" $399.00

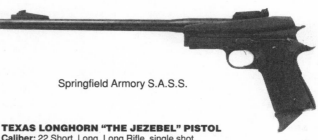

Springfield Armory S.A.S.S.

TEXAS LONGHORN "THE JEZEBEL" PISTOL

Caliber: 22 Short, Long, Long Rifle, single shot.

Barrel: 6".

Weight: 15 oz. **Length:** 8" overall.

Stocks: One-piece fancy walnut grip (right- or left-hand), walnut forend.

Sights: Bead front, fixed rear.

Features: Handmade gun. Top-break action; all stainless steel; automatic hammer block safety; music wire coil springs. Barrel is half-round, half-octagon. Announced 1986. From Texas Longhorn Arms.

Price: About $250.00

T/C Contender

THOMPSON/CENTER CONTENDER

Caliber: 7mm TCU, 30-30 Win., 22 LR, 22 WMR, 22 Hornet, 223 Rem., 270 Ren, 7-30 Waters, 32-20 Win., 357 Mag., 357 Rem. Max., 44 Mag., 10mm Auto, 445 Super Mag., 45/410, single shot.
Barrel: 10", tapered octagon, bull barrel and vent. rib.
Weight: 43 oz. (10" bbl.). **Length:** 13¼" (10" bbl.).
Stocks: T/C "Competitor Grip." Right or left hand.
Sights: Under-cut blade ramp front, rear adjustable for windage and elevation.
Features: Break-open action with automatic safety. Single-action only. Interchangeable bbls., both caliber (rim & centerfire), and length. Drilled and tapped for scope. Engraved frame. See T/C catalog for exact barrel/caliber availability.
Price: Blued (rimfire cals.) $405.00
Price: Blued (centerfire cals.) $405.00
Price: Extra bbls. (standard octagon) $185.00
Price: 45/410, internal choke bbl. $205.00

Thompson/Center Contender Hunter Package
Package contains the Contender pistol in 223, 7-30 Waters, 30-30, 375 Win., 357 Rem. Maximum, 35 Rem., 44 Mag. or 45-70 with 12" or 14" barrel with T/C's Muzzle Tamer, a 2.5x Recoil Proof Long Eye Relief scope with lighted reticle, q.d. sling swivels with a nylon carrying sling. Comes with a suede leather case with foam padding and fleece lining. Introduced 1990. From Thompson/Center Arms.
Price: 12" barrel $685.00
Price: 14" barrel $695.00

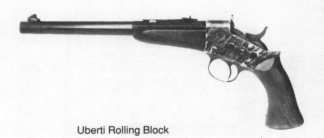

Uberti Rolling Block

UBERTI ROLLING BLOCK TARGET PISTOL
Caliber: 22 LR, 22 WMR, 22 Hornet, 357 Mag., single shot.
Barrel: 9⅞", half-round, half-octagon.
Weight: 44 oz. **Length:** 14" overall.
Stocks: Walnut grip and forend.
Sights: Blade front, fully adjustable rear.
Features: Replica of the 1871 rolling block target pistol. Brass trigger guard, color case-hardened frame, blue barrel. Imported by Uberti USA.
Price: $380.00

Ultra Light Model 20

ULTRA LIGHT ARMS MODEL 20 REB HUNTER'S PISTOL
Caliber: 22-250 thru 308 Win. standard. Most silhouette calibers and others on request. 5-shot magazine.
Barrel: 14", Douglas No. 3.
Weight: 4 lbs.
Stock: Composite Kevlar, graphite reinforced. Du Pont Imron paint in green, brown, black and camo.
Sights: None furnished. Scope mount included.
Features: Timney adjustable trigger; two-position, three-function safety; benchrest quality action; matte or bright stock and metal finish; right- or left-hand action. Shipped in hard case. Introduced 1987. From Ultra Light Arms.
Price: $1,500.00

Wichita Master

WICHITA MASTER PISTOL
Caliber: 6mm BR, 7mm BR, 243, 7mm-08, 22-250, 308, 3 or 5-shot magazine.
Barrel: 13", 14.875".
Weight: 4.5 lbs. (13" barrel). **Length:** NA.
Stock: American walnut with oil finish; glass bedded.
Sights: Hooded post front, open adjustable rear.
Features: Comes with left-hand action with right-hand grip. round receiver and barrel. Wichita adjustable trigger. Introduced 1991. From Wichita Arms.
Price: $1,500.00

CENTERFIRE RIFLES—AUTOLOADERS

Includes models for hunting, adaptable to and suitable for certain competition.

A.A. ARMS AR9 SEMI-AUTOMATIC RIFLE
Caliber: 9mm Para., 20-shot magazine.
Barrel: 16¼".
Weight: 6.5 lbs. **Length:** 33" overall.
Stock: Folding buttstock, checkered plastic grip.
Sights: Adjustable post front in ring, fixed open rear.
Features: Fires from closed bolt; lever safety blocks trigger and sear; vented barrel shroud. Matte blue/black or nickel finish. Introduced 1991. Made in U.S. From Kimel Industries.
Price: Blue/black finish $369.00

A.A. Arms AR9

Thompson M1

Auto-Ordnance Thompson M1

Similar to the Model 27 A-1 except is in the M-1 configuration with side cocking knob, horizontal forend, smooth unfinned barrel, sling swivels on butt and forend. Matte black finish. Introduced 1985.

Price: **$712.50**

CONSULT
SHOOTER'S MARKETPLACE
Page 225, This Issue

AUTO-ORDNANCE 27 A-1 THOMPSON

Caliber: 45 ACP, 30-shot magazine.
Barrel: 16".
Weight: 11½ lbs. **Length:** About 42" overall (Deluxe).
Stock: Walnut stock and vertical forend.
Sights: Blade front, open rear adjustable for windage.
Features: Recreation of Thompson Model 1927. Semi-auto only. Deluxe model has finned barrel, adjustable rear sight and compensator; Standard model has plain barrel and military sight. From Auto-Ordnance Corp.
Price: Deluxe **$735.00**
Price: 1927A5 Pistol (M27A1 without stock; wgt. 7 lbs.) **$704.00**
Price: 1927A1C Lightweight model **$707.00**

BARRETT LIGHT-FIFTY MODEL 82 A-1 AUTO

Caliber: 50 BMG, 10-shot detachable box magazine.
Barrel: 29".
Weight: 28.5 lbs. **Length:** 57" overall.
Stock: Composition with Sorbothane recoil pad.
Sights: Open, iron and 10x scope.
Features: Semi-automatic, recoil operated with recoiling barrel. Three-lug locking bolt; muzzlebrake. Self-leveling bipod. Fires same 50-cal. ammunition as the M2HB machinegun. Introduced 1985. From Barrett Firearms.
Price: From **$6,750.00**

Browning High-Power

Browning Magnum Semi-Auto Rifle

Same as the standard caliber model, except weighs 8⅜ lbs., 45" overall, 24" bbl., 3-round mag. Cals. 7mm Mag., 300 Win. Mag., 338 Win. Mag.
Price: Grade 1, with sights **$679.95**
Price: Grade 1, no sights **$663.95**

BROWNING HIGH-POWER SEMI-AUTO RIFLE

Caliber: 243, 270, 280, 30-06, 308.
Barrel: 22" round tapered.
Weight: 7⅜ lbs. **Length:** 43" overall.
Stock: French walnut p.g. stock and forend, hand checkered.
Sights: Adj. folding-leaf rear, gold bead on hooded ramp front, or no sights.
Features: Detachable 4-round magazine. Receiver tapped for scope mounts. Trigger pull 3½ lbs. Imported from Belgium by Browning.
Price: Grade 1, with sights **$632.95**
Price: Grade 1, no sights **$616.95**

CALICO MODEL M-900 CARBINE

Caliber: 9mm Para., 50- or 100-shot magazine.
Barrel: 16.1".
Weight: 3.7 lbs. (empty). **Length:** 28½" overall (stock collapsed).
Stock: Sliding steel buttstock.
Sights: Post front adjustable for windage and elevation, fixed notch rear.
Feature: Helical feed 50- or 100-shot magazine. Ambidextrous safety, static cocking handle. Retarded blowback action. Glass-filled polymer grip. Introduced 1989. From Calico.
Price: **$636.90**

Calico Model M-951

Calico Model M-951 Tactical Carbine

Similar to the M-900 Carbine except has an adjustable forward grip, long compensator, and 16.1" barrel. 9mm Para., 50- or 100-shot magazine. Introduced 1990. Made in U.S. by Calico.
Price: **$682.90**
Price: M-951-S (as above except fixed buttstock) **$696.90**

Century M-14

CENTURY INTERNATIONAL FAL SPORTER RIFLE

Caliber: 308 Win.
Barrel: 20.75".
Weight: 9 lbs., 13 oz. **Length:** 41.125" overall.
Stock: Bell & Carlson thumbhole sporter.
Sights: Protected post front, adjustable aperture rear.
Features: Matte blue finish; rubber butt pad. From Century International Arms.
Price: **$749.95**

CENTURY INTERNATIONAL M-14 SEMI-AUTO RIFLE

Caliber: 308 Win., 20-shot magazine.
Barrel: 22".
Weight: 8.25 lbs. **Length:** 40.8" overall.
Stock: Walnut with rubber recoil pad.
Sights: Protected blade front, fully adjustable aperture rear.
Features: Gas-operated; forged receiver; Parkerized finish. Imported from China by Century International Arms.
Price: **$437.95**

CLARIDGE HI-TEC C CARBINE
Caliber: 9mm Para., 18-shot magazine.
Barrel: 16.1".
Weight: 4 lbs., 9 oz. **Length:** 31.7" overall.
Stock: Walnut.
Sights: Adjustable post front in ring, open rear adjustable for windage.
Features: Aluminum or stainless frame. Telescoping bolt, floating firing pin. Safety locks the firing pin. Sight radius of 20.1". Accepts same magazines as Claridge Hi-Tec pistols. Can be equipped with scope or Aimpoint sight. Also available in 40 S&W and 45 ACP. Made in U.S. From Claridge Hi-Tec, Inc.
Price: $525.50
Price: Model LEC-9 (as above with graphite composite stock) . . . $579.00
Price: Model ZLEC-9 (as above with laser sight) $898.50

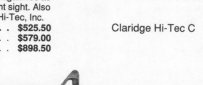
Claridge Hi-Tec C

Colt Sporter Lightweight

COLT SPORTER LIGHTWEIGHT RIFLE
Caliber: 9mm Para., 223 Rem., 5-shot magazine.
Barrel: 16".
Weight: 6.7 lbs. (223); 7.1 lbs. (9mm Para.). **Length:** 34.5" overall extended.
Stock: Composition stock, grip, forend.
Sights: Post front, rear adjustable for windage and elevation.
Features: 5-round detachable box magazine, flash suppressor, sling swivels. Forward bolt assist included. Introduced 1991.
Price: $859.95

D MAX AUTO CARBINE
Caliber: 9mm Para., 10mm Auto, 40 S&W, 45 ACP 30-shot magazine.
Barrel: 16.25".
Weight: About 7.5 lbs. **Length:** 38.5".
Stock: Walnut butt, grip, forend.
Sights: Post front, open rear adjustable for windage and elevation. Aperture rear optional.

Features: Blowback semi-auto fires from closed bolt; trigger-block safety. Side-feed magazine. Integral optical sight base. Max-Coat finish. Made in U.S. by D Max Industries.
Price: $579.00

Eagle Arms EA-15

EAGLE ARMS EA-15 AUTO RIFLE
Caliber: 223 Rem., 30-shot magazine.
Barrel: 20".
Weight: About 7 lbs. **Length:** 39" overall.
Stock: Black composition; trapdoor-style buttstock.
Sights: Post front, fully adjustable rear.
Features: Upper and lower receivers have push-type pivot pin for easy takedown. Receivers hard coat anodized. E2-style forward assist mechanism. Integral raised M-16A2-type fence around magazine release button. Introduced 1989. Made in U.S. by Eagle Arms, Inc.
Price: $800.00

Eagle Arms EA-15 Action Master Auto Rifle
Same as the EA-15 Standard Model except has a one-piece international-style upper receiver for scope mounting, no front sight; solid aluminum handguard tube; free-floating 20" Douglas Premium fluted barrel; muzzle compensator; NM trigger group and bolt carrier group. Weighs about 8 lbs., 5 oz. Introduced 1991. Made in U.S. by Eagle Arms, Inc.
Price: $1,075.00

Eagle Arms EA-15 E2 H-BAR Auto Rifle
Same as the EA-15 Golden Eagle except has 20" standard heavy match barrel with 1:9" twist. Weighs about 8 lbs., 9 oz. Introduced 1989. Made in U.S. by Eagle Arms, Inc.
Price: $890.00
Price: With standard sights $895.00

Eagle Arms EA-15 Golden Eagle Auto Rifle
Same as the EA-15 Standard Model except has E2-style National Match rear sight with ½-MOA adjustments, elevation-adjustable NM front sight with set screw; 20" Douglas Premium extra-heavy match barrel with 1:9" twist; NM trigger group and bolt carrier group. Weight about 12 lbs., 12 oz. Introduced 1991. Made in U.S. by Eagle Arms, Inc.
Price: $1,075.00

Eagle Arms EA-15 E1, E2 Carbines
Same as the EA-15 Standard Model except has collapsible carbine-type buttstock, 16" heavy carbine barrel. Weighs about 5 lbs., 14 oz. (E1), 6 lbs., 2 oz. (E2). Introduced 1989. Made in U.S. by Eagle Arms, Inc.
Price: E1 Carbine $845.00
Price: E2 Carbine (.73" dia. bbl., NM sights) $895.00

Feather Model F9

FEATHER AT-9 SEMI-AUTO CARBINE
Caliber: 9mm Para., 25-shot magazine.
Barrel: 17".
Weight: 5 lbs. **Length:** 35" overall (stock extended); 26½" (closed).
Stock: Telescoping wire, composition pistol grip.
Sights: Hooded post front, adjustable aperture rear.
Features: Semi-auto only. Matte black finish. From Feather Industries. Announced 1988.
Price: $499.95
Price: Model F9 (fixed stock) $534.95

Federal XC900

FEDERAL ENGINEERING XC900/XC450 AUTO CARBINES
Caliber: 9mm Para., 32-shot; 45 ACP, 16-shot magazine,
Barrel: 16.5" (with flash hider).
Weight: 8 lbs. **Length:** 34.5" overall.
Stock: Quick-detachable tube steel.
Sights: Hooded post front, Williams adjustable rear; sight bridge grooved for scope mounting.
Features: Quick takedown; all-steel Heli-arc welded construction; internal parts industrial hard chromed. Made in U.S. by Federal Engineering Corp.
Price: Includes receiver cap, sling, swivels **$639.00**

GALIL SPORTER RIFLE
Caliber: 223, 308, 5-shot magazine.
Barrel: 16.1" (223), 18.5" (308).
Weight: 8.7 lbs. **Length:** 40.5" overall (223).
Stock: Hardwood thumbhole.
Sights: Hooded post front, flip-type adjustable rear.
Features: Black-finished wood and metal. Comes with 5-shot magazine. Introduced 1991. From Action Arms Ltd.
Price: **$950.00**

FEG SA-85M AUTOLOADING RIFLE
Caliber: 7.62x39, 10-shot magazine.
Barrel: 16.3".
Weight: 7 lbs., 10 oz. **Length:** 34.7" overall.
Stock: Hardwood handguard and thumbhole buttstock.
Sights: Cylindrical post front, tangent rear adjustable for windage and elevation.
Features: Matte finish. Chrome-lined barrel. Imported from Hungary by K.B.I., Inc.
Price: **$549.00**

H&K SR9

HECKLER & KOCH SR9 RIFLE
Caliber: 308 Win., 5-shot magazine.
Barrel: 19.7", bull.
Weight: 11 lbs. **Length:** 42.4" overall.
Stock: Kevlar reinforced fiberglass with thumbhole; wood grain finish.
Sights: Post front, aperture rear adjustable for windage and elevation.
Features: A redesigned version of the HK91 rifle. Comes standard with bull barrel with polygonal rifling. Uses HK clawlock scope mounts. Introduced 1990. Imported from Germany by Heckler & Koch, Inc.
Price: **$1,369.00**

Heckler & Koch SR9(T) Target Rifle
Same as the SR9 rifle except has MSG90 adjustable buttstock, trigger group from the PSG1 Marksman's Rifle, and the PSG1 contoured pistol grip with palm shelf. Introduced 1992. Imported from Germany by Heckler & Koch, Inc.
Price: **$1,799.00**

Iver Johnson M-1 Carbine

Iver Johnson 50th Anniversary M-1 Carbine
Same as the standard Iver Johnson 30-caliber M-1 Carbine except has deluxe walnut stock with red, white and blue circular enameled American flag embedded in the stock, and gold-filled roll-engraving with the words "50th Anniversary 1941-1991" on the slide. Parkerized finish. Introduced 1991. From Iver Johnson Arms.
Price: **$384.95**

IVER JOHNSON M-1 CARBINE
Caliber: 30 U.S. Carbine, or 9mm Para.
Barrel: 18" four-groove.
Weight: 6½ lbs. **Length:** 35½" overall.
Stock: Glossy-finished hardwood or walnut; collapsible wire.
Sights: Click-adjustable peep rear.
Features: Gas-operated semi-auto carbine. 15-shot detachable magazine. Made in U.S.A.
Price: 30 cal., Parkerized finish, hardwood stock, metal handguard . **$349.95**
Price: 30 cal., Parkerized finish, walnut stock and handguard **$384.95**
Price: 9mm, hardwood stock, metal handguard **$365.00**
Price: 9mm, walnut stock and handguard **$399.00**
Price: 30 cal., collapsible wire stock **$443.00**
Price: 9mm, collapsible wire stock **$448.95**

Marlin Model 45

MARLIN MODEL 9 CAMP CARBINE
Caliber: 9mm Para., 12-shot magazine.
Barrel: 16½", Micro-Groove® rifling.
Weight: 6¾ lbs. **Length:** 35½" overall.
Stock: Walnut-finished hardwood; rubber buttpad; Mar-Shield® finish; swivel studs.
Sights: Ramp front with orange post, cutaway Wide-Scan™ hood, adjustable open rear.
Features: Manual bolt hold-open; Garand-type safety, magazine safety; loaded chamber indicator; receiver drilled, tapped for scope mounting. Introduced 1985.
Price: **$363.50**
Price: Model 9N (nickel-Teflon finish) **$410.01**

Marlin Model 45 Carbine
Similar to the Model 9 except chambered for 45 ACP, 7-shot magazine. Introduced 1986.
Price: **$363.50**

CAUTION: PRICES CHANGE, CHECK AT GUNSHOP.

Olympic CAR-310

OLYMPIC ARMS CAR SERIES CARBINES
Caliber: 223, 30-shot; 9mm Para., 34-shot; 45 ACP, 16-shot; 10mm, 40 S&W, 16-shot; 7.62x39mm, 18-shot.
Barrel: 16".
Weight: 6½ lbs. **Length:** 35" overall (stock extended).
Stock: Telescoping butt.
Sights: Post front adjustable for elevation, rear adjustable for windage.
Features: Based on the AR-15 rifle. Has A2 Stowaway pistol grip. Introduced 1975. Made in U.S. by Olympic Arms, Inc.
Price: CAR-15, 223 caliber **$639.95**
Price: CAR-9, 9mm Para. **$712.95**
Price: CAR-45, 45 ACP **$719.95**
Price: CAR-40, 40 S&W **$719.95**
Price: CAR-310, 10mm **$791.95**
Price: 7.62x39mm . . . . **NA**

OLYMPIC ARMS K-4 AR-15 RIFLE
Caliber: 223, 30-shot magazine.
Barrel: 20".
Weight: 8 lbs. **Length:** 39" overall.
Stock: Full-length black composition; M-16 style.
Sights: Post front adjustable for elevation, peep-style rear adjustable for windage. E-2-style sight system optionally available.
Features: Heavy match-grade barrel; trapdoor in buttstock and A-2 stow-away pistol grip. Introduced 1975. Made in U.S. by Olympic Arms, Inc.
Price: **$679.95**

NORINCO MAK 90 SEMI-AUTO RIFLE
Caliber: 7.62x39, 5-shot magazine.
Barrel: 16.25".
Weight: 8 lbs., 2 oz. **Length:** 35.5" overall.
Stock: Walnut-finished thumbhole with recoil pad.
Sights: Adjustable post front, open adjustable rear.
Features: Chrome-lined barrel; forged receiver; black oxide finish. Comes with extra magazine, oil bottle, cleaning kit, sling. Imported from China by Century International Arms.
Price: **$293.95**

Remington 7400

REMINGTON 7400 AUTO RIFLE
Caliber: 243 Win., 270 Win., 280 Rem., 308 Win. and 30-06, 4-shot magazine.
Barrel: 22" round tapered.

Weight: 7½ lbs. **Length:** 42" overall.
Stock: Walnut, deluxe cut checkered p.g. and forend. Satin or high-gloss finish.
Sights: Gold bead front sight on ramp; step rear sight with windage adjustable.
Features: Redesigned and improved version of the Model 742. Positive cross-bolt safety. Receiver tapped for scope mount. 4-shot clip mag. Introduced 1981.
Price: About **$503.00**
Price: Carbine (18½" bbl., 30-06 only) **$503.00**

Ruger Mini-14/5R

RUGER MINI-14/5 AUTOLOADING RIFLE
Caliber: 223 Rem., 5-shot detachable box magazine.
Barrel: 18½".
Weight: 6.4 lbs. **Length:** 37¼" overall.
Stock: American hardwood, steel reinforced.
Sights: Ramp front, fully adjustable rear.
Features: Fixed piston gas-operated, positive primary extraction. New buffer system, redesigned ejector system. Ruger S100RH scope rings included. 20-, 30-shot magazine available to police departments and government agencies only.
Price: Mini-14/5R, Ranch Rifle, blued, scope rings **$530.00**
Price: K-Mini-14/5R, Ranch Rifle, stainless, scope rings **$580.00**
Price: Mini-14/5, blued, no scope rings **$491.50**
Price: K-Mini-14/5, stainless, no scope rings **$542.00**

Ruger Mini Thirty Rifle
Similar to the Mini-14 Ranch Rifle except modified to chamber the 7.62x39 Russian service round. Weight is about 7 lbs., 3 oz. Has 6-groove barrel with 1-10" twist, Ruger Integral Scope Mount bases and folding peep rear sight. Detachable 5-shot staggered box magazine. Blued finish. Introduced 1987.
Price: Blue **$530.00**
Price: Stainless **$580.00**

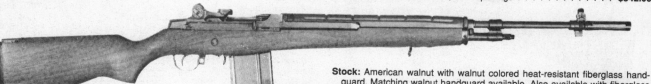

Springfield M-1A

SPRINGFIELD ARMORY M-1A RIFLE
Caliber: 7.62mm NATO (308), 243 Win., 5-, 10- or 20-shot box magazine.
Barrel: 25¹/₁₆" with flash suppressor, 22" without suppressor.
Weight: 8¾ lbs. **Length:** 44¼" overall.

Stock: American walnut with walnut colored heat-resistant fiberglass handguard. Matching walnut handguard available. Also available with fiberglass stock.
Sights: Military, square blade front, full click-adjustable aperture rear.
Features: Commercial equivalent of the U.S. M-14 service rifle with no provision for automatic firing. From Springfield Armory.
Price: Standard M-1A rifle, about **$1,129.00**
Price: National Match about **$1,499.00**
Price: Super Match (heavy premium barrel) about **$1,799.00**
Price: M1A-A1 Bush Rifle, walnut stock, about **$1,229.00**

CAUTION: PRICES CHANGE, CHECK AT GUNSHOP.

SPRINGFIELD ARMORY BM-59
Caliber: 7.62mm NATO (308 Win.), 20-shot box magazine.
Barrel: 19.3".
Weight: 9¼ lbs. **Length:** 43.7" overall.
Stock: Walnut, with trapped rubber buttpad.
Sights: Military square blade front, click adjustable peep rear.
Features: Full military-dress Italian service rifle. Available in selective fire or semi-auto only. Refined version of the M-1 Garand. Accessories available include: folding Alpine stock, muzzlebrake/flash suppressor/grenade launcher combo, bipod, winter trigger, grenade launcher sights, bayonet, oiler. Extremely limited quantities. Introduced 1981.
Price: Standard Italian model, about **$1,440.00**
Price: Alpine model, about **$1,572.00**
Price: Alpine Paratrooper model, about **$1,840.00**
Price: Nigerian Mark IV model, about **$1,572.00**

VOERE MODEL 2185 AUTO RIFLE
Caliber: 243, 6.5x55, 270, 308, 30-06, 7x57, 7x64, 8x57, 9.3x62, 7mm Rem. Mag., 300 Win. Mag., 2-shot magazine.
Barrel: 20".
Weight: 7.75 lbs. **Length:** 43.5" overall.
Stock: European walnut.
Sights: Blade front, open adjustable rear. Drilled and tapped for scope mounting.
Features: Gas-operated action; two-stage trigger; cocking indicator inside trigger guard. Introduced 1992. Imported from Austria by Rahn Gun Works, Inc.
Price: . . . . **NA**

STEYR A.U.G. AUTOLOADING RIFLE
Caliber: 223 Rem.
Barrel: 20".
Weight: 8½ lbs. **Length:** 31" overall.
Stock: Synthetic, green. One-piece moulding houses receiver group, hammer mechanism and magazine.
Sights: 1.5x scope only; scope and mount form the carrying handle.
Features: Semi-automatic, gas-operated action; can be converted to suit right- or left-handed shooters, including ejection port. Transparent 30- or 42-shot magazines. Folding vertical front grip. Introduced 1983. Imported from Austria by Gun South, Inc. **Available on limited basis only to law enforcement officers.**
Price: . . . . **NA**

WILKINSON TERRY CARBINE
Caliber: 9mm Para., 31-shot magazine.
Barrel: 16³⁄₁₆".
Weight: 6 lbs., 3 oz. **Length:** 30" overall.
Stock: Maple stock and forend.
Sights: Protected post front, aperture rear.
Features: Semi-automatic blowback action fires from a closed breech. Bolt-type safety and magazine catch. Ejection port has automatic trap door. Receiver equipped with dovetail for scope mounting. Made in U.S. From Wilkinson Arms.
Price: **$485.92**

CENTERFIRE RIFLES—LEVER & SLIDE

Both classic arms and recent designs in American-style repeaters for sport and field shooting.

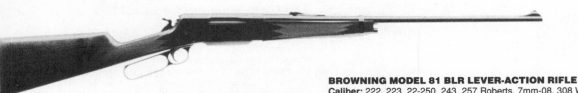

Browning Long Action BLR

Browning Model 81 Long Action BLR
Similar to the standard Model 81 BLR except has long acton to accept 30-06, 270 and 7mm Rem. Mag. Barrel lengths are 22" for 30-06 and 270, 24" for 7mm Rem. Mag. Has six-lug rotary bolt; bolt and receiver are full-length fluted. Fold-down hammer at half-cock. Weight about 8½ lbs., overall length 42½" (22" barrel). Introduced 1991.
Price: **$529.95**

BROWNING MODEL 81 BLR LEVER-ACTION RIFLE
Caliber: 222, 223, 22-250, 243, 257 Roberts, 7mm-08, 308 Win. or 358 Win., 4-shot detachable magazine.
Barrel: 20" round tapered.
Weight: 6 lbs., 15 oz. **Length:** 39¾" overall.
Stock: Checkered straight grip and forend, oil-finished walnut.
Sights: Gold bead on hooded ramp front; low profile square notch adj. rear.
Features: Wide, grooved trigger; half-cock hammer safety. Receiver tapped for scope mount. Recoil pad installed. Imported from Japan by Browning.
Price: With sights **$499.95**

Browning 1886 Carbine

Browning Model 1886 High Grade Carbine
Same as the standar Model 1886 Carbine except has high grade walnut with cut-checkered grip and forend and gloss finish. Receiver and lever are grayed steel. Receiver has scroll engraving and game scenes of mule deer and grizzly bear highlighted by a special gold plating and engraving process. Limited to 3000 guns. Introduced 1992.
Price: **$1,175.00**

CIMARRON 1860 HENRY REPLICA
Caliber: 44 WCF, 13-shot magazine.
Barrel: 24¼" (rifle), 22" (carbine).
Weight: 9½lbs. **Length:** 43" overall (rifle).
Stock: European walnut.
Sights: Bead front, open adjustable rear.
Features: Brass receiver amd buttplate. Uses original Henry loading system. Faithful to the original rifle. Introduced 1991. Imported by Cimarron Arms.
Price: **$799.95**

BROWNING MODEL 1886 LEVER-ACTION CARBINE
Caliber: 45-70, 8-shot magazine.
Barrel: 22".
Weight: 8 lbs., 3 oz. **Length:** 40.75" overall.
Stock: Satin-finished select walnut with metal crescent buttplate.
Sights: Blade front, open adjustable rear.
Features: Recreation of the original gun. Full-length magazine, classic-style forend with barrel band, saddle ring. Polished blue finish. Limited to 7000 guns. Introduced 1992. Imported from Japan by Browning.
Price: **$749.95**

CIMARRON 1866 WINCHESTER REPLICAS
Caliber: 22 LR, 22 WMR, 38 Spec., 44 WCF.
Barrel: 24¼" (rifle), 19" (carbine).
Weight: 9 lbs. **Length:** 43" overall (rifle).
Stock: European walnut.
Sights: Bead front, open adjustable rear.
Features: Solid brass receiver, buttplate, forend cap. Octagonal barrel. Faithful to the original Winchester '66 rifle. Introduced 1991. Imported by Cimarron Arms.
Price: Rifle **$689.95**
Price: Carbine **$649.95**

Cimarron 1873 Short

Cimarron 1873 30"

Dixie 1873

CIMARRON 1873 SHORT RIFLE
Caliber: 22 LR, 22 WMR, 357 Magnum, 44-40, 45 Colt.
Barrel: 20" tapered octagon.
Weight: 7.5 lbs. **Length:** 39" overall.
Stock: Walnut.
Sights: Bead front, adjustable semi-buckhorn rear.
Features: Has half "button" magazine. Original-type markings, including caliber, on barrel and elevator and "Kings" patent. From Cimarron Arms.
Price: **$799.95**

CIMARRON 1873 30" EXPRESS RIFLE
Caliber: 22 LR, 22 WMR, 357 Mag., 38-40, 44-40, 45 Colt.
Barrel: 30", octagonal.
Weight: 8½ lbs. **Length:** 48" overall.
Stock: Walnut.
Sights: Blade front, semi-buckhorn ramp rear. Tang sight optional.
Features: Color case-hardened frame; choice of modern blue-black or charcoal blue for other parts. Barrel marked "Kings improvement." From Cimarron Arms.
Price: **$819.95**

Cimarron 1873 Sporting Rifle
Similar to the 1873 Express except has 24" barrel with half-magazine.
Price: **$799.95**
Price: 1873 Saddle Ring Carbine, 19" barrel **$729.95**

DIXIE ENGRAVED 1873 RIFLE
Caliber: 44-40, 11-shot magazine.
Barrel: 20", round.
Weight: 7¾ lbs. **Length:** 39" overall.
Stock: Walnut.
Sights: Blade front, adjustable rear.
Features: Engraved and case-hardened frame. Duplicate of Winchester 1873. Made in Italy. From Dixie Gun Works.
Price: **$995.00**
Price: Plain, blued carbine **$875.00**

E.M.F. 1866 YELLOWBOY LEVER ACTIONS
Caliber: 38 Spec., 44-40.
Barrel: 19" (carbine), 24" (rifle).
Weight: 9 lbs. **Length:** 43" overall (rifle).
Stock: European walnut.
Sights: Bead front, open adjustable rear.
Features: Solid brass frame, blued barrel, lever, hammer, buttplate. Imported from Italy by E.M.F.
Price: Rifle **$848.00**
Price: Carbine **$825.00**

E.M.F. MODEL 73 LEVER-ACTION RIFLE
Caliber: 357 Mag., 44-40, 45 Colt.
Barrel: 24".
Weight: 8 lbs. **Length:** 43¼" overall.
Stock: European walnut.
Sights: Bead front, rear adjustable for windage and elevation.
Features: Color case-hardened frame (blue on carbine). Imported by E.M.F.
Price: Rifle **$1,050.00**
Price: Carbine, 19" barrel **$1,020.00**

E.M.F. 1860 HENRY RIFLE
Caliber: 44-40 or 44 rimfire.
Barrel: 24.25".
Weight: About 9 lbs. **Length:** About 43.75" overall.
Stock: Oil-stained American walnut.
Sights: Blade front, rear adjustable for elevation.
Features: Reproduction of the original Henry rifle with brass frame and buttplate, rest blued. From E.M.F.
Price: Standard **$1,100.10**

> Consult our Directory pages for the location of firms mentioned.

Marlin Model 336CS

MARLIN MODEL 336CS LEVER-ACTION CARBINE
Caliber: 30-30 or 35 Rem., 6-shot tubular magazine.
Barrel: 20" Micro-Groove®.
Weight: 7 lbs. **Length:** 38½" overall.
Stock: Select American black walnut, capped p.g. with white line spacers. Mar-Shield® finish; rubber buttpad; swivel studs.
Sights: Ramp front with Wide-Scan™ hood, semi-buckhorn folding rear adjustable for windage and elevation.
Features: Hammer-block safety. Receiver tapped for scope mount, offset hammer spur; top of receiver sand blasted to prevent glare.
Price: **$392.90**

Marlin Model 30AS Lever-Action Carbine
Same as the Marlin 336CS except has walnut-finished hardwood p.g. stock, 30-30 only, 6-shot. Hammer-block safety. Adjustable rear sight, brass bead front.
Price: **$334.50**

Marlin Model 1894S

Marlin Model 1894CS Carbine

Similar to the standard Model 1894S except chambered for 38 Special/357 Magnum with full-length 9-shot magazine, 18½" barrel, hammer-block safety, brass bead front sight. Introduced 1983.

Price: **$441.95**

MARLIN MODEL 1895SS LEVER-ACTION RIFLE

Caliber: 45-70, 4-shot tubular magazine.
Barrel: 22" round.
Weight: 7½ lbs. **Length:** 40½" overall.
Stock: American black walnut, full pistol grip. Mar-Shield® finish; rubber buttpad; q.d. swivel studs.

MARLIN MODEL 1894S LEVER-ACTION CARBINE

Caliber: 44 Special/44 Magnum, 10-shot tubular magazine.
Barrel: 20" Micro-Groove®.
Weight: 6 lbs. **Length:** 37½" overall.
Stock: American black walnut, straight grip and forend. Mar-Shield® finish. Rubber rifle buttpad; swivel studs.
Sights: Wide-Scan™ hooded ramp front, semi-buckhorn folding rear adjustable for windage and elevation.
Features: Hammer-block safety. Receiver tapped for scope mount, offset hammer spur, solid top receiver sand blasted to prevent glare.

Price: **$441.95**

Sights: Bead front with Wide-Scan™ hood, semi-buckhorn folding rear adjustable for windage and elevation.
Features: Hammer-block safety. Solid receiver tapped for scope mounts or receiver sights; offset hammer spur.

Price: **$476.45**

Marlin Model 1894CL

Marlin Model 1894CL Classic

Similar to the 1894CS except chambered for 218 Bee, 25-20 and 32-20 Win. Has 6-shot tubular magazine. 22" barrel with 6-groove rifling, brass bead front sight, adjustable semi-buckhorn folding rear. Hammer-block safety. Weighs 6¼ lbs., overall length of 38¾". Bee has rubber rifle butt pad, swivel studs. Introduced 1988.

Price: **$474.25**

MARLIN MODEL 444SS LEVER-ACTION SPORTER

Caliber: 444 Marlin, 5-shot tubular magazine.
Barrel: 22" Micro-Groove®.
Weight: 7½ lbs. **Length:** 40½" overall.
Stock: American black walnut, capped p.g. with white line spacers, rubber rifle buttpad. Mar-Shield® finish; swivel studs.
Sights: Hooded ramp front, folding semi-buckhorn rear adjustable for windage and elevation.
Features: Hammer-block safety. Receiver tapped for scope mount; offset hammer spur.

Price: **$476.45**

Mitchell 1858 Henry

MITCHELL 1858 HENRY REPLICA

Caliber: 44-40, 13-shot magazine.
Barrel: 24¼" (rifle), 22" (carbine).
Weight: 9.5 lbs. **Length:** 43" overall (rifle).
Stock: European walnut.
Sights: Bead front, open adjustable rear.
Features: Brass receiver and buttplate. Uses original Henry loading system. Faithful to the original rifle. Introduced 1990. Imported by Mitchell Arms, Inc.

Price: **$975.00**

Mitchell 1873

MITCHELL 1873 WINCHESTER REPLICA

Caliber: 44-40, 45 Colt, 13-shot.
Barrel: 24¼" (rifle), 19" (carbine).
Weight: 9.5 lbs. **Length:** 43" overall (rifle).
Stock: European walnut.
Sights: Bead front, open adjustable rear.
Features: Color case-hardened steel receiver. Faithful to the original Model 1873 rifle. Introduced 1990. Imported by Mitchell Arms, Inc.

Price: **$895.00**

MITCHELL 1866 WINCHESTER REPLICA

Caliber: 38 Spec., 44-40, 13-shot.
Barrel: 24¼" (rifle); 19" (carbine).
Weight: 9 lbs. **Length:** 43" overall (rifle).
Stock: European walnut.
Sights: Bead front, open adjustable rear.
Features: Solid brass receiver, buttplate, forend cap. Octagonal barrel. Faithful to the original Winchester '66 rifle. Introduced 1990. Imported by Mitchell Arms, Inc.

Price: **$799.00**

CAUTION: PRICES CHANGE, CHECK AT GUNSHOP.

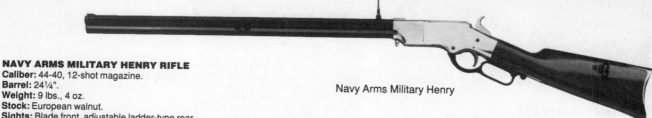

Navy Arms Military Henry

NAVY ARMS MILITARY HENRY RIFLE
Caliber: 44-40, 12-shot magazine.
Barrel: 24¼".
Weight: 9 lbs., 4 oz.
Stock: European walnut.
Sights: Blade front, adjustable ladder-type rear.
Features: Brass frame, buttplate, rest blued. Recreation of the model used by cavalry units in the Civil War. Has full-length magazine tube, sling swivels; no forend. Introduced 1991. Imported from Italy by Navy Arms.
Price: **$875.00**

Navy Arms Iron Frame Henry
Similar to the Military Henry Rifle except receiver is blued or color case-hardened steel. Introduced 1991. Imported by Navy Arms.
Price: **$895.00**

NAVY ARMS 1866 YELLOWBOY RIFLE
Caliber: 44-40, 12-shot magazine.
Barrel: 24", full octagon.
Weight: 8½ lbs. **Length:** 42½" overall.
Stock: European walnut.

Navy Arms Henry Trapper
Similar to the Military Henry Rifle except has 16½" barrel, weighs 7½ lbs. Brass frame and buttplate, rest blued. Introduced 1991. Imported from Italy by Navy Arms.
Price: **$875.00**

Navy Arms D. Henry Carbine
Similar to the Military Henry rifle except has 22" barrel, weighs 8 lbs., 12 oz., is 41" overall; no sling swivels. Caliber 44-40. Introduced 1992. Imported from Italy by Navy Arms.
Price: **$875.00**

Sights: Blade front, adjustable ladder-type rear.
Features: Brass frame, forend tip, buttplate, blued barrel, lever, hammer. Introduced 1991. Imported from Italy by Navy Arms.
Price: **$710.00**
Price: Carbine, 19" barrel **$685.00**

Navy Arms 1873 Winchester-Style

Navy Arms 1873 Sporting Rifle
Similar to the 1873 Winchester-Style rifle except has checkered pistol grip stock, 30" octagonal barrel (24" available). Introduced 1992. Imported by Navy Arms.
Price: **$895.00**

NAVY ARMS 1873 WINCHESTER-STYLE RIFLE
Caliber: 44-40, 45 Colt, 12-shot magazine.
Barrel: 24".
Weight: 8¼ lbs. **Length:** 43" overall.
Stock: European walnut.
Sights: Blade front, buckhorn rear.
Features: Color case-hardened frame, rest blued. Full-octagon barrel. Introduced 1991. Imported by Navy Arms.
Price: **$840.00**
Price: Carbine, 19" barrel **$815.00**

Remington 7600

REMINGTON 7600 SLIDE ACTION
Caliber: 243, 270, 280, 30-06, 308, 35 Whelen.
Barrel: 22" round tapered.

Weight: 7½ lbs. **Length:** 42" overall.
Stock: Cut-checkered walnut p.g. and forend, Monte Carlo with full cheekpiece. Satin or high-gloss finish.
Sights: Gold bead front sight on matted ramp, open step adjustable sporting rear.
Feature: Redesigned and improved version of the Model 760. Detachable 4-shot clip. Cross-bolt safety. Receiver tapped for scope mount. Also available in high grade versions. Introduced 1981.
Price: About **$480.00**
Price: Carbine (18½" bbl., 30-06 only) **$480.00**

Rossi SRC Carbine

ROSSI M92 SRC SADDLE-RING CARBINE
Caliber: 38 Spec./357 Mag., 44 Spec./44-40, 44 Mag., 10-shot magazine.
Barrel: 20".
Weight: 5¾ lbs. **Length:** 37" overall.
Stock: Walnut.
Sights: Blade front, buckhorn rear.
Features: Recreation of the famous lever-action carbine. Handles 38 and 357 interchangeably. Has high-relief puma medallion inlaid in the receiver. Introduced 1978. Imported by Interarms.
Price: **$331.67**
Price: 44 Spec./44 Mag. (Model 65) **$348.33**

Rossi M92 SRS Puma Short Carbine
Similar to the standard M92 except has 16" barrel, overall length of 33", in 38/357 only. Puma medallion on side of receiver. Introduced 1986.
Price: **$331.67**

CAUTION: PRICES CHANGE, CHECK AT GUNSHOP.

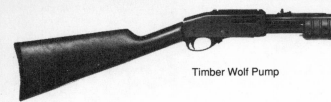

Timber Wolf Pump

Weight: 6.1 lbs. **Length:** 37" overall.
Stock: Walnut.
Sights: Blade front, adjustable rear.
Features: Push-button safety on trigger guard; takedown; adjustable stock; integral scope mount on receiver. Blue finish. Introduced 1989. Imported from Israel by Action Arms Ltd. (357 only) and Springfield Armory. (44 Mag. only).
Price: 357 Mag., blue (Action Arms) $319.00
Price: 357 Mag., satin chrome (Action Arms) $379.00
Price: 44 Mag., about $429.00

TIMBER WOLF PUMP RIFLE
Caliber: 38 Spec./357 Mag., 10-shot magazine; 44 Mag., 10-shot magazine.
Barrel: 18.5".

Savage 99C

Weight: 7.75 lbs. **Length:** 42.75" overall.
Stock: Walnut with checkered p.g. and forend, Monte Carlo comb.
Sights: Hooded ramp front, adjustable ramp rear sight. Tapped for scope mounts.
Features: Grooved trigger, top tang slide safety locks trigger and lever. Brown rubber buttpad, q.d. swivel studs, push-button magazine release.
Price: $620.00

SAVAGE 99C LEVER-ACTION RIFLE
Caliber: 243 or 308 Win., detachable 4-shot magazine.
Barrel: 22", chromemoly steel.

UBERTI 1866 SPORTING RIFLE
Caliber: 22 LR, 22 WMR, 38 Spec., 44-40, 45 Colt.
Barrel: 24¼", octagonal.
Weight: 8.1 lbs. **Length:** 43¼" overall.
Stock: Walnut.

Sights: Blade front adjustable for windage, rear adjustable for elevation.
Features: Frame, buttplate, forend cap of polished brass, balance charcoal blued. Imported by Uberti USA.
Price: $780.00
Price: Yellowboy Carbine (19" round bbl.) $720.00

UBERTI 1873 SPORTING RIFLE
Caliber: 22 LR, 22 WMR, 38 Spec., 357 Mag., 44-40, 45 Colt.
Barrel: 24¼", 30", octagonal.
Weight: 8.1 lbs. **Length:** 43¼" overall.
Stock: Walnut.
Sights: Blade front adjustable for windage, open rear adjustable for elevation.
Features: Color case-hardened frame, blued barrel, hammer, lever, buttplate, brass elevator. Also available with pistol grip stock ($100.00 extra). Imported by Uberti USA.
Price: $900.00
Price: 1873 Carbine (19" round bbl.) $890.00
Price: 1873 "Trappers Model" carbine (16" bbl.) $850.00

Uberti 1873 Rifle

UBERTI HENRY RIFLE
Caliber: 44-40.
Barrel: 24¼", half-octagon.
Weight: 9.2 lbs. **Length:** 43¾" overall.
Stock: American walnut.
Sights: Blade front, rear adjustable for elevation.
Features: Frame, elevator, magazine follower, buttplate are brass, balance blue (also available in polished steel). Imported by Uberti USA.
Price: $895.00
Price: Henry Carbine (22¼" bbl.) $900.00
Price: Henry Trapper (16", 18" bbl.) $900.00

Winchester Model 94 Side Eject Checkered Walnut

> Consult our Directory pages for the location of firms mentioned.

Winchester Model 94 Ranger Side Eject Lever-Action Rifle
Same as Model 94 Side Eject except has 5-shot magazine, American hardwood stock and forend, post front sight. Introduced 1985.
Price: $287.00
Price: With 4x32 Bushnell scope, mounts $338.00

Winchester Model 94 Trapper Side Eject
Same as the Model 94 except has 16" barrel, 5-shot magazine in 30-30, 9-shot in 357 Magnum, 44 Magnum/44 Special, 45 Colt. Has stainless steel claw extractor, saddle ring, hammer spur extension, walnut wood.
Price: 30-30 . . . . $325.00
Price: 357 Mag., 44 Mag./44 Spec., 45 Colt $344.00

WINCHESTER MODEL 94 SIDE EJECT LEVER-ACTION RIFLE
Caliber: 30-30, 7x30 Waters, 32 Win. Spec., 6-shot tubular magazine.
Barrel: 16", 20".
Weight: 6½ lbs. **Length:** 37¾" overall.
Stock: Straight grip walnut stock and forend.
Sights: Hooded blade front, semi-buckhorn rear. Drilled and tapped for scope mount. Post front sight on Trapper model.
Features: Solid frame, forged steel receiver; side ejection, exposed rebounding hammer with automatic trigger-activated transfer bar. Introduced 1984.
Price: Checkered walnut $352.00
Price: No checkering, walnut $325.00
Price: With WinTuff laminated hardwood stock, 30-30 only $352.00

Winchester 94 Wrangler

Winchester Model 94 Wrangler Side Eject
Same as the Model 94 except has 16" barrel and large loop lever for large and/or gloved hands. Has 9-shot capacity (5-shot for 30-30), stainless steel claw extractor. Available in 30-30, 44 Magnum/44 Special. Reintroduced 1992.
Price: 30-30 . . . . **$341.00**
Price: 44 Magnum/44 Special **$359.00**

WINCHESTER MODEL 94 BIG BORE SIDE EJECT
Caliber: 307 Win., 356 Win., 6-shot magazine.
Barrel: 20".
Weight: 7 lbs. **Length:** 38⅝" overall.
Stock: American walnut. Satin finish.
Sights: Hooded ramp front, semi-buckhorn rear adjustable for windage and elevation.
Features: All external metal parts have Winchester's deep blue finish. Rifling twist 1:12". Rubber recoil pad fitted to buttstock. Introduced 1983. From U.S. Repeating Arms Co.
Price: **$352.00**

CENTERFIRE RIFLES—BOLT ACTION

Includes models for a wide variety of sporting and competitive purposes and uses.

Alpine Rifle

ALPINE BOLT-ACTION RIFLE
Caliber: 22-250, 243 Win., 270, 30-06, 308, 7mm Rem. Mag., 8mm, 5-shot magazine (3 for magnum).
Barrel: 23" (std. cals.), 24" (mag.).

Weight: 7½ lbs.
Stock: European walnut. Full p.g. and Monte Carlo; checkered p.g. and forend; rubber recoil pad; white line spacers; sling swivels.
Sights: Ramp front, open rear adjustable for windage and elevation.
Features: Made by Firearms Co. Ltd. in England. Imported by Mandall Shooting Supplies.
Price: Custom Grade **$395.00**
Price: Supreme Grade **$425.00**

A-SQUARE CAESAR BOLT-ACTION RIFLE
Caliber: 7mm Rem. Mag., 30-06, 300 Win. Mag., 300 H&H, 300 Wea. Mag., 8mm Rem. Mag., 338 Win. Mag., 340 Wea. Mag., 9.3x62, 9.3x64, 375 Wea. Mag., 375 H&H, 375 JRS, 416 Hoffman, 416 Rem. Mag., 416 Taylor, 425 Express, 458 Win. Mag., 458 Lott, 450 Ackley, 470 Capstick.
Barrel: 20" to 26" (no-cost customer option).
Weight: 8½ to 11 lbs.
Stock: Claro walnut with hand-rubbed oil finish; classic style with A-Square Coil-Chek® features for reduced recoil; flush detachable swivels. Customer

choice of length of pull.
Sights: Choice of three-leaf express, forward or normal-mount scope, or combination (at extra cost).
Features: Matte non-reflective blue, double cross-bolts, steel and fiberglass reinforcement of wood from tang to forend tip; three-position positive safety; three-way adjustable trigger; expanded magazine capacity. Right- or left-hand. Introduced 1984. Made in U.S. by A-Square Co., Inc.
Price: **$2,250.00**

A-Square Hannibal

A-SQUARE HANNIBAL BOLT-ACTION RIFLE
Caliber: 7mm Rem. Mag., 30-06, 300 Win. Mag., 300 H&H, 300 Wea. Mag., 8mm Rem. Mag., 338 Win. Mag., 340 Wea. Mag., 338 A-Square Mag., 9.3x62, 9.3x64, 375 H&H, 375 Wea. Mag., 375 JRS, 375 A-Square Mag., 378 Wea. Mag., 416 Taylor, 416 Rem. Mag., 416 Hoffman, 416 Rigby, 416 Wea. Mag., 404 Jeffery, 425 Express, 458 Win. Mag., 458 Lott, 450 Ackley, 460 Short A-Square Mag., 460 Wea. Mag., 470 Capstick, 495 A-Square Mag., 500 A-Square Mag.

Barrel: 20" to 26" (no-cost customer option).
Weight: 9 to 11¾ lbs.
Stock: Claro walnut with hand-rubbed oil finish; classic style with A-Square Coil-Chek® features for reduced recoil; flush detachable swivels. Customer choice of length of pull. Available with synthetic stock.
Sights: Choice of three-leaf express, forward or normal-mount scope, or combination (at extra cost).
Features: Matte non-reflective blue, double cross-bolts, steel and fiberglass reinforcement of wood from tang to forend tip; Mauser-style claw extractor; expanded magazine capacity; two-position safety; three-way target trigger. Right-hand only. Introduced 1983. Made in U.S. by A-Square Co., Inc.
Price: Walnut stock **$2,195.00**
Price: Synthetic stock **$2,395.00**

Anschutz 1700D Classic

ANSCHUTZ 1700D CLASSIC RIFLES
Caliber: 22 Hornet, 5-shot clip; 222 Rem., 3-shot clip.
Barrel: 24", ¹³⁄₁₆" dia. heavy.

Weight: 7¾ lbs. **Length:** 43" overall.
Stock: Select European walnut with checkered pistol grip and forend.
Sights: Hooded ramp front, folding leaf rear; drilled and tapped for scope mounting.
Features: Adjustable single stage trigger. Receiver drilled and tapped for scope mounting. Introduced 1988. Imported from Germany by Precision Sales International.
Price: **$1,360.00**
Price: Meistergrade (select stock, gold engraved trigger guard) . . **$1,559.00**

Anschutz 1700D Custom Rifles

Similar to the Classic models except have roll-over Monte Carlo cheekpiece, slim forend with Schnabel tip, Wundhammer palm swell on pistol grip, rosewood grip cap with white diamond insert. Skip-line checkering on grip and forend. Introduced 1988. Imported from Germany by PSI.
Price: **$1,389.00**
Price: Meistergrade (select stock, gold engraved trigger guard) . . **$1,588.00**

BARRETT MODEL 90 BOLT-ACTION RIFLE

Caliber: 50 BMG, 5-shot magazine.
Barrel: 29".
Weight: 22 lbs. **Length:** 35" overall.
Stock: Sorbothane recoil pad.

BEEMAN/HW 60J BOLT-ACTION RIFLE

Caliber: 222 Rem.
Barrel: 22.8".
Weight: 6.5 lbs. **Length:** 41.7" overall.
Stock: Walnut with cheekpiece; cut checkered p.g. and forend.
Sights: Hooded blade on ramp front, open rear.
Features: Polished blue finish; oil-finished wood. Imported from Germany by Beeman. Introduced 1988.
Price: **$889.50**

ANSCHUTZ 1700D BAVARIAN BOLT-ACTION RIFLE

Caliber: 22 Hornet, 222 Rem., detachable clip.
Barrel: 24".
Weight: 7¼ lbs. **Length:** 43" overall.
Stock: European walnut with Bavarian cheek rest. Checkered p.g. and forend.
Sights: Hooded ramp front, folding leaf rear.
Features: Uses the improved 1700 Match 54 action with adjustable trigger. Drilled and tapped for scope mounting. Introduced 1988. Imported from Germany by Precision Sales International.
Price: **$1,360.00**
Price: Meistergrade (select stock, gold engraved trigger guard) . . **$1,559.00**

Sights: Scope optional.
Features: Bolt-action, bullpup design. Disassembles without tools; extendable bipod legs; match-grade barrel; high efficiency muzzlebrake. Introduced 1990. From Barrett Firearms Mfg., Inc.
Price: From **$3,650.00**

Beeman/HW 60J

Blaser R84

BRNO ZKB 527 FOX BOLT-ACTION RIFLE

Caliber: 22 Hornet, 222 Rem., 223 Rem., 5-shot magazine.
Barrel: 23½".
Weight: 6 lbs., 11 oz. **Length:** 42½" overall.
Stock: Turkish walnut, with Monte Carlo.
Sights: Hooded front, open adjustable rear.
Features: Detachable box magazine; adjustable double-set triggers, grooved receiver. Imported from Czechoslovakia by Action Arms Ltd.
Price: **$565.00**
Price: 223 Rem. **$579.00**

BRNO ZKK 600, 601, 602 BOLT-ACTION RIFLES

Caliber: 30-06, 270 (M600); 223, 243 (M601); 300 Win. Mag., 375 H&H, 458 Win. Mag. (M602), 5-shot magazine.
Barrel: 23½" (M600, 601); 25" (M602).
Weight: 6 lbs., 3 oz. to 9 lbs., 4 oz. **Length:** 43" overall (M601).
Stock: Walnut.
Sights: Hooded ramp front, open folding leaf adjustable rear.
Features: Adjustable set trigger (standard trigger included); grooved receiver;

BRNO 537 SPORTER BOLT-ACTION RIFLE

Caliber: 270, 308, 30-06.
Barrel: 23.6".
Weight: 7 lbs., 9 oz. **Length:** 44.7" overall.
Stock: Checkered walnut.

BLASER R84 BOLT-ACTION RIFLE

Caliber: Std. cals.—22-250, 243, 6mm Rem., 25-06, 270, 280, 30-06; magnum cals.—257 Wea., 264 Win. Mag., 7mm Rem. Mag., 300 Win. Mag., 300 Wea., 338 Win. Mag., 375 H&H.
Barrel: 23" (24" in magnum cals.).
Weight: 7-7¼·lbs. **Length:** Std. cals.—41" overall (23" barrel).
Stock: Two-piece Turkish walnut. Solid black buttpad.
Sights: None furnished. Comes with low-profile Blaser scope mountings.
Features: Interchangeable barrels (scope mountings on barrel), and magnum/standard caliber bolt assemblies. Left-hand models available in all calibers. Imported from Germany by Autumn Sales, Inc.
Price: Right-hand, standard or magnum calibers **$2,250.00**
Price: Left-hand, standard or magnum calibers **$2,300.00**
Price: Interchangeable barrels, standard or magnum calibers **$575.00**

easy-release floorplate; sling swivels. Imported from Czechoslovakia by Action Arms Ltd.
Price: ZKK 600 Standard **$519.00**
Price: As above, Monte Carlo stock **$649.00**
Price: ZKK 601 Standard **$519.00**
Price: As above, Monte Carlo stock **$569.00**
Price: ZKK 602, Monte Carlo stock **$829.00**
Price: As above, Standard stock **$779.00**
Price: As above, 458 Win. Mag. **$795.00**

Sights: Hooded ramp front, adjustable folding leaf rear.
Features: Shrouded bolt design; American-style safety; grooved receiver; sling swivels. Introduced 1992. Imported from Czechoslovakia by Action Arms Ltd.
Price: **$595.00**

Browning A-Bolt Hunter

BROWNING A-BOLT RIFLE

Caliber: 25-06, 270, 30-06, 280, 7mm Rem. Mag., 300 Win. Mag., 338 Win. Mag., 375 H&H Mag.
Barrel: 22" medium sporter weight with recessed muzzle; 26" on mag. cals.
Weight: 6½ to 7½ lbs. **Length:** 44¾" overall (magnum and standard); 41¾" (short action).

Stock: Classic style American walnut; recoil pad standard on magnum calibers.
Features: Short-throw (60°) fluted bolt, three locking lugs, plunger-type ejector; adjustable trigger is grooved and gold-plated. Hinged floorplate, detachable box magazine (4 rounds std. cals., 3 for magnums). Slide tang safety. Medallion has glossy stock finish, rosewood grip and forend caps, high polish blue. Introduced 1985. Imported from Japan by Browning.
Price: Medallion, no sights **$584.95**
Price: Hunter, no sights **$499.95**
Price: Hunter, with sights **$563.95**
Price: Medallion, 375 H&H Mag., with sights **$682.95**

CAUTION: PRICES CHANGE, CHECK AT GUNSHOP.

Browning Micro Medallion

Browning A-Bolt Left Hand
Same as the Medallion model A-Bolt except has left-hand action and is available only in 270, 30-06, 7mm Rem. Mag., 375 H&H. Introduced 1987.
Price: **$609.95**
Price: 375 H&H, with sights **$707.95**

Browning A-Bolt Stainless Stalker
Similar to the Hunter model A-Bolt except receiver is made of stainless steel; the rest of the exposed metal surfaces are finished with a durable matte silver-gray. Graphite-Fiberglass composite textured stock. No sights are furnished. Available in 270, 30-06, 7mm Rem. Mag., 375 H&H. Introduced 1987.
Price: **$651.95**
Price: Composite Stalker (as above, checkered stock) **$514.95**
Price: Left-hand, no sights **$671.95**
Price: 375 H&H, with sights **$749.95**
Price: 375 H&H, left-hand, with sights **$771.95**

Browning A-Bolt Micro Medallion
Similar to the standard A-Bolt except is a scaled-down version. Comes with 20" barrel, shortened length of pull (13⁵⁄₁₆"); three-shot magazine capacity; weighs 6 lbs., 1 oz. Available in 243, 308, 7mm-08, 257 Roberts, 223, 22-250. Introduced 1988.
Price: No sights **$584.95**

Browning A-Bolt Gold Medallion
Similar to the standard A-Bolt except has select walnut stock with brass spacers between rubber recoil pad and between the rosewood grip cap and forend tip; gold-filled barrel inscription; palm-swell pistol grip, Monte Carlo comb, 22 lpi checkering with double borders; engraved receiver flats. In 270, 30-06, 7mm Rem. Mag. only. Introduced 1988.
Price: **$794.95**

Browning A-Bolt Short Action
Similar to the standard A-Bolt except has short action for 22 Hornet, 223, 22-250, 243, 257 Roberts, 7mm-08, 284 Win., 308 chamberings. Available in Hunter or Medallion grades. Weighs 6½ lbs. Other specs essentially the same. Introduced 1985.
Price: Medallion, no sights **$584.95**
Price: Hunter, no sights **$499.95**
Price: Hunter, with sights **$563.95**

Century Swedish #38

CENTURY SWEDISH SPORTER #38
Caliber: 6.5x55 Swede, 5-shot magazine.
Barrel: 24".
Weight: NA. **Length:** 44.1" overall.
Stock: Walnut-finished European hardwood with checkered p.g. and forend; Monte Carlo comb.
Sights: Blade front, adjustable rear.
Features: Uses M38 Swedish Mauser action; comes with Holden Ironsighter see-through scope mount. Introduced 1987. From Century International Arms.
Price: About **$212.95**

CENTURY CENTURION 14 SPORTER
Caliber: 7mm Rem. Mag., 300 Win. Mag., 5-shot magazine.
Barrel: 24".
Weight: NA. **Length:** 43.3" overall.
Stock: Walnut-finished European hardwood. Checkered p.g. and forend. Monte Carlo comb.
Sights: None furnished.
Features: Uses modified Pattern 14 Enfield action. Drilled and tapped; scope base mounted. Blue finish. From Century International Arms.
Price: About **$237.95**
Price: With Bell & Carlson black fiberglass stock **$287.95**

CENTURY ENFIELD SPORTER #4
Caliber: 303 British, 10-shot magazine.
Barrel: 25.2".
Weight: 8 lbs., 5 oz. **Length:** 44.5" overall.
Stock: Beechwood with checkered p.g. and forend, Monte Carlo comb.
Sights: Blade front, adjustable aperture rear.
Features: Uses Lee-Enfield action; blue finish. Trigger pinned to receiver. Introduced 1987. From Century International Arms.
Price: **$199.95**

CENTURY MAUSER 98 SPORTER
Caliber: 243, 270, 308, 30-06.
Barrel: 24".
Weight: NA. **Length:** 44" overall.
Stock: Black synthetic.
Sights: None furnished. Scope base installed.
Features: Mauser 98 action; bent bolt handle for scope use; low-swing safety; matte black finish; blind magazine. Introduced 1992. From Century International Arms.
Price: . . . . **NA**

CONSULT **Shooter's MARKETPLACE** Page 225, This Issue

Dakota 76 Classic

Dakota 76 Short Action Rifles
A scaled-down version of the standard Model 76. Standard chamberings are 22-250, 243, 6mm Rem., 250-3000, 7mm-08, 308, others on special order. Short Classic Grade has 21" barrel; Alpine Grade is lighter (6½ lbs.), has a blind magazine and slimmer stock. Introduced 1989.
Price: Short Classic **$2,150.00**
Price: Alpine **$1,995.00**

DAKOTA 76 CLASSIC BOLT-ACTION RIFLE
Caliber: 257 Roberts, 270, 280, 30-06, 7mm Rem. Mag., 338 Win. Mag., 300 Win. Mag., 375 H&H, 458 Win. Mag.
Barrel: 23".
Weight: 7½ lbs. **Length:** NA.
Stock: Medium fancy grade walnut in classic style. Checkered p.g. and forend; solid buttpad.
Sights: None furnished; drilled and tapped for scope mounts.
Features: Has many features of the original Model 70 Winchester. One-piece rail trigger guard assembly; steel grip cap. Adjustable trigger. Many options available. Left-hand rifle available at same price. Introduced 1988. From Dakota Arms, Inc.
Price: **$2,150.00**

Dakota 76 Safari

Dakota 416 Rigby African
Similar to the 76 Safari except chambered for 404 Jeffery, 416 Rigby, 416 Dakota, 450 Dakota, 4-round magazine, select wood, two stock cross-bolts. Has 24" barrel, weight of 9-10 lbs. Ramp front sight, standing leaf rear. Introduced 1989.
Price: **$3,500.00**

DAKOTA 22 SPORTER BOLT-ACTION RIFLE
Caliber: 22 LR, 22 Hornet, 5-shot magazine.
Barrel: 22".
Weight: About 6.5 lbs. **Length:** NA.
Stock: Claro or English walnut in classic design; 13.5" length of pull. Choice of grade. Point panel hand checkering. Swivel studs. Black butt pad.

AUGUSTE FRANCOTTE BOLT-ACTION RIFLES
Caliber: 243, 270, 7x64, 30-06, 308, 300 Win. Mag., 338, 7mm Rem. Mag., 375 H&H, 458 Win. Mag.; others on request.
Barrel: 23½" to 26½".
Weight: 8 to 10 lbs.
Stock: Fancy European walnut. To customer specs.
Sights: To customer specs.
Features: Basically a custom gun, Francotte offers many options. Imported from Belgium by Armes de Chasse.
Price: . . . . **$9,000.00** to **$15,000.00**

DAKOTA 76 SAFARI BOLT-ACTION RIFLE
Caliber: 338 Win. Mag., 300 Win. Mag., 375 H&H, 458 Win. Mag.
Barrel: 23".
Weight: 8½ lbs. **Length:** NA.
Stock: Fancy walnut with ebony forend tip; point-pattern with wraparound forend checkering.
Sights: Ramp front, standing leaf rear.
Features: Has many features of the original Model 70 Winchester. Barrel band front swivel, inletted rear. Cheekpiece with shadow line. Steel grip cap. Introduced 1988. From Dakota Arms, Inc.
Price: Wood stock **$2,950.00**

Sights: None furnished; comes with mount bases.
Features: Combines features of Winchester 52 and Dakota 76 rifles. Full-sized receiver; rear locking lugs and bolt machined from bar stock. Trigger and striker-blocking safety; adjustable trigger. Introduced 1992. From Dakota Arms, Inc.
Price: **$995.00**

CARL GUSTAF 2000 BOLT-ACTION RIFLE
Caliber: 243, 6.5x55, 7x64, 270, 308, 30-06, 7mm Rem. Mag., 300 Win. Mag., 3-shot detachable magazine.
Barrel: 24".
Weight: 7.5 lbs. **Length:** 44 " overall.
Stock: Select European walnut with hand-rubbed oil finish; Monte Carlo cheekpiece; Wundhammar swell pistol grip; 18 l.p.i. checkering.
Sights: Optional. Drilled and tapped for scope mounting.
Features: Three-way adjustable single-stage, roller bearing trigger; three-position safety; triple front locking lugs; free-floating barrel; swivel studs. Comes with factory test target. Introduced 1991. Imported from Sweden by Precision Sales International.
Price: Without sights **$1,875.00**
Price: With sights **$1,985.00**

Heym SR 20 Alpine

Heym SR 20 Alpine Series Carbine
Similar to the Trophy Series except available in 243, 270, 7x57, 308, 30-06, 6.5x55, 7x64, 8x57JS with 20" barrel, open sights; full-length "Mountain rifle" stock with steel forend cap, steel grip cap. Introduced 1989. Imported from Germany by Heckler & Koch, Inc.
Price: **$2,335.00**

Heym SR 20 Classic Safari Rifle
Similar to the Trophy Series except in 404 Jeffery, 425 Express, 458 Win. Mag. 24" barrel; has large post front sight, three-leaf express rear; barrel-mounted ring-type front q.d. swivel, q.d. rear; double-lug recoil bolt in stock. Introduced 1989. Imported from Germany by Heckler & Koch, Inc.
Price: **$2,725.00**
Price: For left-hand rifle, add **$450.00**

HEYM SR 20 TROPHY SERIES RIFLE
Caliber: 243, 7x57, 270, 308, 30-06, 7mm Rem. Mag., 338 Win. Mag., 375 H&H; other calibers on request.
Barrel: 22" (standard cals.); 24" (magnum cals.).
Weight: About 7 lbs.
Stock: AAA-grade European walnut with cheekpiece, solid rubber buttpad, checkered grip and forend, oil finish, rosewood grip cap.
Sights: German silver bead ramp front, open rear on quarter-rib. Drilled and tapped for scope mounting.
Features: Octagonal barrel, barrel-mounted q.d. swivel, standard q.d. rear swivel. Imported from Germany by Heckler & Koch, Inc.
Price: **$2,450.00**
Price: For left-hand rifle, add **$450.00**

Heym SR 20 Classic Sportsman Series Rifle
Similar to the Trophy Series except has round barrel without sights. Imported from Germany by Heckler & Koch, Inc. Introduced 1989.
Price: Standard calibers **$2,285.00**
Price: Magnum calibers **$2,415.00**

Heym Express

HEYM MAGNUM EXPRESS SERIES RIFLE
Caliber: 338 Lapua Mag., 375 H&H, 378 Wea. Mag., 416 Rigby, 500 Nitro Express 3", 460 Wea. Mag., 500 A-Square, 450 Ackley, 600 N.E.
Barrel: 24".
Weight: About 9.9 lbs. **Length:** 45¼" overall.

Stock: Classic English design of AAA-grade European walnut with cheekpiece, solid rubber buttpad, steel grip cap.
Sights: Adjustable post front on ramp, three-leaf express rear.
Features: Modified magnum Mauser action, Timney single trigger; special hinged floorplate; barrel-mounted q.d. swivel, q.d. rear; vertical double recoil lug in rear of stock. Introduced 1989. Imported from Germany by Heckler & Koch, Inc.
Price: **$6,245.00**
Price: For left-hand rifle, add **$575.00**
Price: 600 Nitro Express **$10,900.00**

CAUTION: PRICES CHANGE, CHECK AT GUNSHOP.

HOWA M1500 TROPHY BOLT-ACTION RIFLE
Caliber: 223, 22-250, 243, 270, 30-06, 308, 7mm Rem. Mag., 300 Win. Mag., 338 Win. Mag.
Barrel: 22" (24" in magnum calibers).
Weight: 7½-7¾ lbs. **Length:** 42" overall (42½" for 270, 30-06, 7mm).
Stock: American walnut with Monte Carlo comb and cheekpiece; 18 lpi checkering on p.g. and forend.
Sights: Hooded ramp gold bead front, open round-notch rear adjustable for windage and elevation. Drilled and tapped for scope mounts.
Features: Trigger guard and magazine box are a single unit with a hinged floorplate. Comes with q.d. swivel studs. Composition non-slip buttplate with white spacer. Magnum models have rubber recoil pad. Introduced 1979. Imported from Japan by Interarms.
Price: **$528.33**
Price: 7mm Rem. Mag., 300 Win. Mag., 338 Win. Mag. **$548.33**

KDF K15 AMERICAN BOLT-ACTION RIFLE
Caliber: 25-06, 257 Wea. Mag., 270, 270 Wea. Mag., 7mm Rem. Mag., 30-06, 300 Win. Mag., 300 Wea. Mag., 338 Win. Mag., 340 Wea. Mag., 375 H&H, 411 KDF Mag., 416 Rem. Mag., 458 Win. Mag.; 4-shot magazine for standard calibers, 3-shot for magnums.
Barrel: 22" standard, 24" optional.
Weight: About 8 lbs. **Length:** 44" overall (24" barrel).
Stock: Laminated standard; Kevlar composite or AAA walnut in classic, schnabel or thumbhole styles optional.
Sights: None furnished; optional. Drilled and tapped for scope mounting.
Features: Three-lug locking design with 60° bolt lift; ultra-fast lock time; fully adjustable trigger. Options available. Introduced 1991. Made in U.S. by KDF, Inc.
Price: Standard calibers **$1,950.00**
Price: Magnum calibers **$2,000.00**

KRICO MODEL 600 BOLT-ACTION RIFLE
Caliber: 222, 223, 22-250, 243, 308, 5.6x50 Mag., 4-shot magazine.
Barrel: 23.6".
Weight: 7.9 lbs. **Length:** 43.7" overall.
Stock: European walnut with Monte Carlo comb.
Sights: None furnished; drilled and tapped for scope mounting.
Features: Rubber recoil pad, sling swivels, checkered grip and forend. Polished blue finish. Imported from Germany by Mandall Shooting Supplies.
Price: **$1,295.00**

Howa Heavy Barrel Varmint Rifle
Similar to the Trophy model except has heavy 24" barrel, available in 223, 308 and 22-250 only, Parkerized finish. No sights furnished; drilled and tapped for scope mounts. Introduced 1989. Imported from Japan by Interarms.
Price: **$565.00**

IVER JOHNSON MODEL 5100A1 LONG-RANGE RIFLE
Caliber: 50 BMG.
Barrel: 29", fully fluted, free-floating.
Weight: 36 lbs. **Length:** 51.5" overall.
Stocks: Composition. Adjustable drop and comb.
Sights: None furnished. Optional Leupold Ultra M1 16x scope.
Features: Bolt-action long-range rifle. Adjustable trigger. Rifle breaks down for transport, storage. From Iver Johnson.
Price: **$5,000.00**

KRICO MODEL 700 BOLT-ACTION RIFLES
Caliber: 17 Rem., 222, 222 Rem. Mag., 223, 5.6x50 Mag., 243, 308, 5.6x57 RWS, 22-250, 6.5x55, 6.5x57, 7x57, 270, 7x64, 30-06, 9.3x62, 6.5x68, 7mm Rem. Mag., 300 Win. Mag., 8x68S, 7.5 Swiss, 9.3x64, 6x62 Freres.
Barrel: 23.6" (std. cals.); 25.5" (mag. cals.).
Weight: 7 lbs. **Length:** 43.3" overall (23.6" bbl.).
Stock: European walnut, Bavarian cheekpiece.
Sights: Blade on ramp front, open adjustable rear.
Features: Removable box magazine; sliding safety. Drilled and tapped for scope mounting. Imported from Germany by Mandall Shooting Supplies.
Price: Model 700 . . . . **$995.00**
Price: Model 700 Deluxe S **$1,495.00**
Price: Model 700 Deluxe **$1,025.00**
Price: Model 700 Stutzen (full stock) **$1,295.00**

> Consult our Directory pages for the location of firms mentioned.

Mark X Viscount

Mark X Viscount Rifle
Same gun and features as the Mark X American Field except has stock of European hardwood. Imported from Yugoslavia by Interarms. Reintroduced 1987.
Price: **$539.00**
Price: 7mm Rem. Mag., 300 Win. Mag. **$559.00**

Mini-Mark X Rifle
Scaled-down version of the Mark X American Field. Uses miniature M98 Mauser-system action, chambered for 223 Rem. and 7.62x39; 20" barrel. Overall length of 39¾", weight 6.35 lbs. Drilled and tapped for scope mounting.

MARK X AMERICAN FIELD SERIES
Caliber: 22-250, 243, 25-06, 270, 7x57, 7mm Rem. Mag., 308 Win., 30-06, 300 Win. Mag.
Barrel: 24".
Weight: 7 lbs. **Length:** 45" overall.
Stock: Genuine walnut stock, hand checkered with 1" sling swivels.
Sights: Ramp front with removable hood, open rear sight adjustable for windage and elevation.
Features: Mauser-system action. One-piece trigger guard with hinged floorplate, drilled and tapped for scope mounts and receiver sight, hammer-forged chrome vanadium steel barrel. Imported from Yugoslavia by Interarms.
Price: With adj. trigger, sights **$665.00**
Price: 7mm Rem. Mag., 300 Win. Mag. **$685.00**

Checkered hardwood stock. Adjustable trigger. Introduced 1987. Imported from Yugoslavia by Interarms.
Price: **$500.00**

Mauser Model 66

MAUSER MODEL 66 BOLT-ACTION RIFLE
Caliber: 243, 270, 308, 30-06, 5.6x57, 6.5x57, 7x64, 9.3x62, 7mm Rem. Mag., 300 Wea. Mag., 300 Win. Mag., 6.5x68, 8x68S, 9.3x64, 375 H&H, 458 Win. Mag. Three-shot magazine.
Barrel: 21" (Stutzen); 24" (standard cals.); 26" (magnum cals.).

Weight: 7.5 to 9.3 lbs. **Length:** 39" overall (std. cals.).
Stock: Hand-checkered European walnut, hand-rubbed oil finish. Rosewood forend and grip caps.
Sights: Blade front on ramp, open rear adjustable for windage and elevation.
Features: Telescopic short-stroke action; interchangeable, free-floated, medium-heavy barrels. Mini-claw extractor; adjustable single-stage trigger; internal magazine. Introduced 1989. Imported from Germany by Precision Imports, Inc.
Price: With Monte Carlo stock **$1,998.00**
Price: Stutzen (full-length stock) **$2,104.00**
Price: Safari model **$2,332.00**

Mauser Model 99

Stock: Hand-checkered European walnut with rosewood grip cap.
Sights: None furnished. Drilled and tapped for scope mounting.
Features: Accuracy bedding with free-floated barrel, three front-locking bolt lugs, 60° bolt throw. Fastest lock time of any sporting rifle. Adjustable single-stage trigger. Silent safety locks bolt, sear, trigger. Introduced 1989. Imported from Germany by Precision Imports, Inc.

Price: Classic stock, oil finish, std. cals.	**$1,267.00**
Price: As above, magnum cals.	**$1,320.00**
Price: Classic stock, high luster finish, std. cals.	**$1,426.00**
Price: As above, magnum cals.	**$1,479.00**
Price: Monte Carlo stock, oil finish, std. cals.	**$1,267.00**
Price: As above, magnum cals.	**$1,320.00**
Price: Monte Carlo stock, high luster, std. cals.	**$1,426.00**
Price: As above, magnum cals.	**$1,479.00**

MAUSER MODEL 99 BOLT-ACTION RIFLE
Caliber: 243, 25-06, 270, 308, 30-06, 5.6x57, 6.5x57, 7x57, 7x64 (standard cals.); 7mm Rem. Mag., 257 Wea. Mag., 270 Wea. Mag., 300 Wea. Mag., 300 Win. Mag., 338 Win. Mag., 375 H&H, 8x68S, 9.3x64 (magnum cals.); removable 4-shot magazine (std. cals.), 3-shot (magnum cals.).
Barrel: 24" (std.), 26" (mag.).
Weight: About 8 lbs. **Length:** 44" overall (std. cals.).

McMillan Signature Sporter

McMILLAN SIGNATURE CLASSIC SPORTER
Caliber: 22-250, 243, 6mm Rem., 7mm-08, 284, 308 (short action); 25-06, 270, 280 Rem., 30-06, 7mm Rem. Mag., 300 Win. Mag., 300 Wea. (long action); 338 Win. Mag., 340 Wea., 375 H&H (magnum action).
Barrel: 22", 24", 26".
Weight: 7 lbs. (short action).
Stock: McMillan fiberglass in green, beige, brown or black. Recoil pad and 1" swivels installed. Length of pull up to 14¼".
Sights: None furnished. Comes with 1" rings and bases.
Features: Uses McMillan right- or left-hand action with matte black finish. Trigger pull set at 3 lbs. Four-round magazine for standard calibers; three for magnums. Aluminum floorplate. Fiberglass and wood stocks optional. Introduced 1987. From McMillan Gunworks, Inc.
Price: **$2,299.00**

McMillan Signature Super Varminter
Similar to the Classic Sporter except has heavy contoured barrel, adjustable trigger, field bipod and special hand-bedded fiberglass stock (Fibergrain optional). Chambered for 223, 22-250, 220 Swift, 243, 6mm Rem., 25-06, 7mm-08 and 308. Comes with 1" rings and bases. Introduced 1989.
Price: **$2,370.00**

McMillan Alaskan

McMillan Signature Alaskan
Similar to the Classic Sporter except has match-grade barrel with single leaf rear sight, barrel band front, 1" detachable rings and mounts, steel floorplate, electroless nickel finish. Has wood Monte Carlo stock with cheekpiece, palm-swell grip, solid buttpad. Chambered for 270, 280 Rem., 30-06, 7mm Rem. Mag., 300 Win. Mag., 300 Wea., 358 Win., 340 Wea., 375 H&H. Introduced 1989.
Price: **$3,225.00**

McMillan Signature Titanium Mountain Rifle
Similar to the Classic Sporter except action made of titanium alloy, barrel of chromemoly steel. Stock is of graphite reinforced fiberglass. Weight is 5½ lbs. Chambered for 270, 280 Rem., 30-06, 7mm Rem. Mag., 300 Win. Mag. Fibergrain stock optional. Introduced 1989.
Price: **$2,995.00**

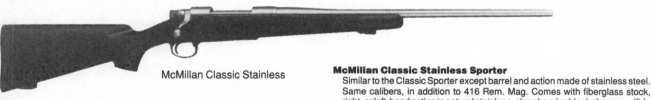

McMillan Classic Stainless

McMillan Classic Stainless Sporter
Similar to the Classic Sporter except barrel and action made of stainless steel. Same calibers, in addition to 416 Rem. Mag. Comes with fiberglass stock, right- or left-hand action in natural stainless, glass bead or black chrome sulfide finishes. Introduced 1990. From McMillan Gunworks, Inc.
Price: **$2,450.00**

McMILLAN TALON SAFARI RIFLE
Caliber: 300 Win. Mag., 300 Wea. Mag., 338 Win. Mag., 300 H&H, 340 Wea. Mag., 375 H&H, 404 Jeffery, 416 Rem. Mag., 458 Win. Mag. (Safari Magnum); 378 Wea. Mag., 416 Rigby, 416 Wea. Mag., 460 Wea. Mag. (Safari Super Magnum).
Barrel: 24".
Weight: About 9-10 lbs. **Length:** 43" overall.
Stock: McMillan fiberglass Safari.
Sights: Barrel band front ramp, multi-leaf express rear.
Features: Uses McMillan Safari action. Has q.d. 1" scope mounts, positive locking steel floorplate, barrel band sling swivel. Match-grade barrel. Matte black finish standard. Introduced 1989. From McMillan Gunworks, Inc.
Price: Talon Safari Magnum **$3,570.00**
Price: Talon Safari Super Magnum **$4,120.00**

McMILLAN TALON SPORTER RIFLE
Caliber: 25-06, 270, 280 Rem., 30-06 (Long Action); 7mm Rem. Mag., 300 Win. Mag., 300 Wea. Mag., 300 H&H, 338 Win. Mag., 340 Wea. Mag., 375 H&H, 416 Rem. Mag.
Barrel: 24" (standard).
Weight: About 7½ lbs. **Length:** NA.
Stock: Choice of walnut or McMillan fiberglass.
Sights: None furnished; comes with rings and bases. Open sights optional.
Features: Uses pre-'64 Model 70-type action with cone breech, controlled feed, claw extractor and three-position safety. Barrel and action are of stainless steel; chromemoly optional. Introduced 1991. From McMillan Gunworks, Inc.
Price: **$2,541.00**

Navy Arms TU-33/40

NAVY ARMS TU-33/40 CARBINE
Caliber: 7.62x39mm, 4-shot magazine.
Barrel: 20.75".

Weight: 9 lbs. **Length:** NA.
Stock: Hardwood.
Sights: Hooded barleycorn front, military V-notch adjustable rear.
Features: Miniature Mauser-style action. Comes with leather sling. Introduced 1992. Imported by Navy Arms.
Price: .... **NA**

Parker-Hale 81 Classic

PARKER-HALE MODEL 81 CLASSIC RIFLE
Caliber: 22-250, 243, 6mm Rem., 270, 6.5x55, 7x57, 7x64, 308, 30-06, 300 Win. Mag., 7mm Rem. Mag., 4-shot magazine.
Barrel: 24".
Weight: About 7¾ lbs. **Length:** 44½" overall.
Stock: European walnut in classic style with oil finish, hand-cut checkering; palm-swell pistol grip, rosewood grip cap.
Sights: Drilled and tapped for open sights and scope mounting. Scope bases included.
Features: Uses Mauser-style action; one-piece steel, Oberndorf-style trigger guard with hinged floorplate; rubber buttpad; quick-detachable sling swivels. Introduced 1984. Made by Gibbs Rifle Co., distributed by Navy Arms.
Price: **$900.00**

Parker-Hale Model 81 Classic African Rifle
Similar to the Model 81 Classic except chambered only for 375 H&H and 9.3x62. Has adjustable trigger, barrel band front swivel, African express rear sight, engraved receiver. Classic-style stock has a solid buttpad, checkered pistol grip and forend. Introduced 1986. Made by Gibbs Rifle Co., distributed by Navy Arms.
Price: **$1,050.00**

Parker-Hale Model 1100 Lightweight Rifle
Similar to the Model 81 Classic except has slim barrel profile, hollow bolt handle, alloy trigger guard/floorplate. The Monte Carlo stock has a schnabel forend, hand-cut checkering, swivel studs, palm-swell pistol grip. Comes with hooded ramp front sight, open Williams rear adjustable for windage and elevation. Same calibers as Model 81. Overall length is 43", weight 6½ lbs., with 22" barrel. Introduced 1984. Made by Gibbs Rifle Co., distributed by Navy Arms.
Price: **$595.00**

Parker-Hale Model 1000 Rifle
Similar to the Model 81 Classic except has walnut Monte Carlo stock, 22" barrel (24" in 22-250), weighs 7.25 lbs. Not available in 300 Win. Mag. Introduced 1992. Made by Gibbs Rifle Co., distributed by Navy Arms.
Price: **$495.00**
Price: Model 1000 Clip (detachable magazine) **$535.00**

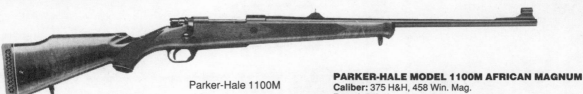

Parker-Hale 1100M

PARKER-HALE MODEL 1200 SUPER RIFLE
Caliber: 22-250, 243, 6mm, 25-06, 270, 6.5x55, 7x57, 7x64, 308, 30-06, 8mm Mauser (standard action); 7mm Rem. Mag., 300 Win. Mag. (1200M Super Magnum).
Barrel: 24".
Weight: About 7½ lbs. **Length:** 44½" overall.
Stock: European walnut, rosewood grip and forend tips, hand-cut checkering; roll-over cheekpiece; palm-swell pistol grip; ventilated recoil pad; wraparound checkering.
Sights: Hooded post front, open rear.
Features: Uses Mauser-style action with claw extractor; gold-plated adjustable trigger; silent side safety locks trigger, sear and bolt; aluminum trigger guard. Introduced 1984. Made by Gibbs Rifle Co., distributed by Navy Arms.
Price: **$595.00**

PARKER-HALE MODEL 1100M AFRICAN MAGNUM
Caliber: 375 H&H, 458 Win. Mag.
Barrel: 24".
Weight: 9.5 lbs. **Length:** NA.
Stock: Checkered walnut with reinforcing lugs.
Sights: Hooded ramp front, shallow V open rear.
Features: Mauser-style 98 action with steel trigger guard, special lengthened steel magazine. Drilled and tapped for scope mounts. Made by Gibbs Rifle Co., distributed by Navy Arms.
Price: **$930.00**

Parker-Hale Model 1200 Super Clip Rifle
Same as the Model 1200 Super except has a detachable steel box magazine and steel trigger guard. Introduced 1984. Made by Gibbs Rifle Co., distributed by Navy Arms.
Price: **$640.00**

Parker-Hale 1300C

PARKER-HALE MODEL 1300C SCOUT RIFLE
Caliber: 243, 308, 10-shot magazine.
Barrel: 20".
Weight: 8.5 lbs. **Length:** 41" overall.
Stock: Checkered laminated birch.
Sights: None furnished. Drilled and tapped for scope mounting.
Features: Detachable magazine; muzzle brake; polished blue finish. Introduced 1992. Made by Gibbs Rifle Co., distributed by Navy Arms.
Price: **$595.00**

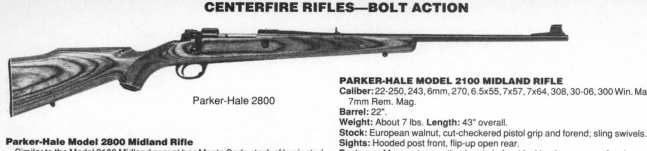

Parker-Hale 2800

Parker-Hale Model 2800 Midland Rifle
Similar to the Model 2100 Midland except has Monte Carlo stock of laminated birch. Not available in 300 Win. Mag. Made by Gibbs Rifle Co., distributed by Navy Arms.
Price: **$385.00**

RAHN DEER SERIES BOLT-ACTION RIFLE
Caliber: 25-06, 308, 270.
Barrel: 24".
Weight: NA. **Length:** NA.
Stock: Circassian walnut with rosewood forend and grip caps, Monte Carlo cheekpiece, semi-schnabel forend; hand checkered.
Sights: Bead front, open adjustable rear. Drilled and tapped for scope mount.
Features: Free-floating barrel; rubber recoil pad; one-piece trigger guard with hinged, engraved floorplate; 22 rimfire conversion insert available. Introduced 1986. From Rahn Gun Works, Inc.
Price: **$1,400.00**
Price: With custom stock made to customer specs **$1,450.00**

Rahn Safari Series Rifle
Similar to the "Deer Series" except chambered for 308 Norma Mag., 300 Win. Mag., 8x68S, 9x64. Choice of Cape buffalo, rhino or elephant engraving. Gold oval nameplate with three initials. Introduced 1986.
Price: **$1,675.00**
Price: With stock made to customer specs **$1,725.00**

Rahn Elk Series

PARKER-HALE MODEL 2100 MIDLAND RIFLE
Caliber: 22-250, 243, 6mm, 270, 6.5x55, 7x57, 7x64, 308, 30-06, 300 Win. Mag., 7mm Rem. Mag.
Barrel: 22".
Weight: About 7 lbs. **Length:** 43" overall.
Stock: European walnut, cut-checkered pistol grip and forend; sling swivels.
Sights: Hooded post front, flip-up open rear.
Features: Mauser-type action has twin front locking lugs, rear safety lug, and claw extractor; hinged floorplate; adjustable single-stage trigger; silent side safety. Introduced 1984. Made by Gibbs Rifle Co., distributed by Navy Arms.
Price: **$375.00**
Price: Model 2600 (hardwood stock, no white spacers) **$360.00**

Parker-Hale Midland Model 2700 Lightweight Rifle
Similar to the Model 2100 Midland except has tapered lightweight barrel, aluminum trigger guard, lightened stock. Receiver drilled and tapped for scope mounting. Weighs 6.5 lbs. Not available in 300 Win. Mag. Introduced 1992. Made by Gibbs Rifle Co., distributed by Navy Arms.
Price: **$415.00**

Rahn Himalayan Series Rifle
Similar to the "Deer Series" except chambered for 5.6x57 or 6.5x68S, short stock of walnut or fiberglass, and floorplate engravings of a yak with scroll border. Introduced 1986.
Price: **$1,550.00**
Price: With walnut stock made to customer specs **$1,600.00**

Rahn Elk Series Rifle
Similar to the "Deer Series" except chambered for 6x56, 30-06, 7mm Rem. Mag. and has elk head engraving on floorplate. Introduced 1986.
Price: **$1,500.00**
Price: With stock made to customer specs **$1,550.00**

Remington 700 BDL

Remington 700 BDL Bolt-Action Rifle
Same as the 700 ADL except chambered for 222, 223 (short action, 24" barrel), 22-250, 25-06, 6mm Rem. (short action, 22" barrel), 243, 270, 7mm-08, 280, 300 Savage, 30-06, 308; skip-line checkering; black forend tip and grip cap with white line spacers. Matted receiver top, quick-release floorplate. Hooded ramp front sight; q.d. swivels.
Price: About **$519.00**
Also available in 17 Rem., 7mm Rem. Mag., 300 Win. Mag. (long action, 24" barrel), 338 Win. Mag., 35 Whelen (long action, 22" barrel). Overall length 44½", weight about 7½ lbs.
Price: About **$545.00**
Price: Custom Grade, about **$2,186.00**

REMINGTON 700 ADL BOLT-ACTION RIFLE
Caliber: 243, 270, 308, 30-06 and 7mm Rem. Mag.
Barrel: 22" or 24" round tapered.
Weight: 7 lbs. **Length:** 41½" to 43½" overall.
Stock: Walnut. Satin-finished p.g. stock with fine-line cut checkering, Monte Carlo.
Sights: Gold bead ramp front; removable, step-adj. rear with windage screw.
Features: Side safety, receiver tapped for scope mounts.
Price: About **$439.00**
Price: 7mm Rem. Mag., about **$465.00**
Price: Model 700 ADL/LS (laminated stock, 243, 270, 30-06 only) . . **$485.00**
Price: As above, 7mm Rem. Mag. **$512.00**

Remington 700 BDL Varmint Special
Same as 700 BDL, except 24" heavy bbl., 43½" overall, weighs 9 lbs. Cals. 222, 223, 22-250, 243, 6mm Rem., 7mm-08 Rem. and 308. No sights.
Price: About **$552.00**

Remington 700 Varmint Synthetic

Remington 700 Varmint Synthetic Rifle
Similar to the 700 BDL Varmint Special except has composite stock reinforced with DuPont Kevlar, fiberglass and graphite. Has aluminum bedding block that runs the full length of the receiver. Free-floating barrel. Metal has black matte finish; stock has textured black and gray finish and swivel studs. Available in 223, 22-250, 308. Introduced 1992.
Price: **$625.00**

Remington 700 Safari

Similar to the 700 BDL except custom finished and tuned. In 8mm Rem. Mag., 375 H&H, 416 Rem. Mag. or 458 Win. Magnum calibers only with heavy barrel. Hand checkered, oil-finished stock in classic or Monte Carlo style with recoil pad installed. Delivery time is about 5 months.

Price: About **$953.00**
Price: Classic stock, left-hand **$1,012.00**
Price: Safari Custom KS (Kevlar stock), right-hand **$1,098.00**
Price: As above, left-hand **$1,157.00**
Price: Custom KS wood-grained stock, right-hand **$1,205.00**
Price: As above, left-hand **$1,264.00**

Remington 700 BDL Left Hand

Same as 700 BDL except mirror-image left-hand action, stock. Available in 22-250, 243, 308, 270, 30-06 only.

Price: About **$572.00**
Price: 7mm Rem. Mag., 338 Win. Mag., about **$604.00**

Reminton 700 Stainless Synthetic

Remington 700 Stainless Synthetic Rifle

Similar to the 700 BDL except has stainless barrel, bolt and receiver with synthetic stock profiled like the Mountain Rifle, with blind magazine, corrosion-resistant follower, black textured finish, checkered pistol grip and forend, swivel studs. Matte-finished metal. Introduced 1992.

Price: 25-06, 270, 280, 30-06 . . . . **$532.00**
Price: 7mm Wea. Mag., 7mm Rem. Mag., 300 Win. Mag.,
338 Win. Mag. **$559.00**

Remington 700 Custom KS Mountain Rifle

Similar to the 700 "Mountain Rifle" except custom finished with Kevlar reinforced resin synthetic stock. Available in both left- and right-hand versions. Chambered for 270 Win., 280 Rem., 30-06, 7mm Rem. Mag., 300 Win. Mag., 300 Wea. Mag., 35 Whelen, 338 Win. Mag., 8mm Rem. Mag., 375 H&H, all with 24" barrel only. Weight is 6 lbs., 6 oz. Introduced 1986.

Price: Right-hand **$949.00**
Price: Left-hand **$1,008.00**
Price: Stainless **$1,082.00**
Price: With wood-grained Kevlar stock, right-hand **$1,056.00**
Price: As above, left-hand **$1,114.00**

Remington 700 Mountain Rifle

Similar to the 700 BDL except weighs 6¾ lbs., has a 22" tapered barrel. Redesigned pistol grip, straight comb, contoured cheekpiece, satin stock finish, fine checkering, hinged floorplate and magazine follower, two-position thumb safety. Chambered for 243, 257 Roberts, 270 Win., 7x57, 7mm-08, 25-06, 280 Rem., 30-06, 308, 4-shot magazine. Overall length is 42½". Introduced 1986.

Price: About **$519.00**

Remington 700 Camo Synthetic

Remington 700 Camo Synthetic Rifle

Similar to the 700 BDL except has synthetic stock and the stock and metal (except bolt and sights) are fully camouflaged in Mossy Oak Bottomland camo. Comes with swivel studs, open adjustable sights. Available in 22-250, 243, 7mm-08, 270, 280, 30-06, 308, 7mm Rem. Mag., 300 Wea. Mag. Introduced 1992.

Price: Standard calibers **$563.00**
Price: Magnum calibers **$589.00**

REMINGTON 700 CLASSIC RIFLE

Caliber: 220 Swift only, 5-shot magazine.
Barrel: 24".
Weight: About 7¾ lbs. **Length:** 44½" overall.
Stock: American walnut, 20 lpi checkering on p.g. and forend. Classic styling. Satin finish.
Sights: None furnished. Receiver drilled and tapped for scope mounting.
Features: A "classic" version of the M700 ADL with straight comb stock. Fitted with rubber recoil pad. Sling swivel studs installed. Hinged floorplate. Limited production in 1992 only.

Price: About **$519.00**

Remington Model Seven Custom KS

Similar to the standard Model Seven except has custom finished stock of lightweight Kevlar aramid fiber and chambered for 223 Rem., 7mm-08, 308, 35 Rem. and 350 Rem. Mag. Barrel length is 20", weight 5¾ lbs. Comes with iron sights and is drilled and tapped for scope mounting. Special order through Remington Custom Shop. Introduced 1987.

Price: **$949.00**

Remington Model Seven

REMINGTON MODEL SEVEN BOLT-ACTION RIFLE

Caliber: 223 Rem. (5-shot); 243, 7mm-08, 6mm, 308 (4-shot).
Barrel: 18½".
Weight: 6¼ lbs. **Length:** 37½" overall.
Stock: Walnut, with modified schnabel forend. Cut checkering.
Sights: Ramp front, adjustable open rear.
Features: Short-action design; silent side safety; free-floated barrel except for single pressure point at forend tip. Introduced 1983.

Price: About **$519.00**

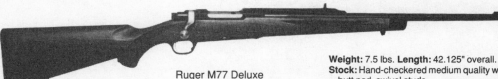

Ruger M77 Deluxe

RUGER M77 MARK II DELUXE RIFLE

Caliber: 270, 30-06, 7mm Rem. Mag., 300 Win. Mag., 4-shot magazine.
Barrel: 22", with integral steel rib; barrel-mounted front swivel stud.

Weight: 7.5 lbs. **Length:** 42.125" overall.
Stock: Hand-checkered medium quality walnut with steel grip cap, black rubber butt pad, swivel studs.
Sights: Ramp front, open rear adjustable for windage and elevation mounted on rib.
Features: Mark II action with three-position safety, stainless steel bolt, steel trigger guard, hinged steel floorplate. Introduced 1991.

Price: M77EXPMKII **$1,550.00**

RUGER M77 MARK II RIFLE

Caliber: 223, 243, 6mm Rem., 270, 308, 30-06, 7mm Rem. Mag., 300 Win. Mag., 4-shot magazine.
Barrel: 20", 22"; 24" (magnums).
Weight: About 7 lbs. **Length:** 39¾" overall.
Stock: Hand-checkered American walnut; swivel studs, rubber butt pad.
Sights: None furnished. Receiver has Ruger integral scope mount base, comes with Ruger 1" rings. Some models have iron sights.
Features: Short action with new trigger and three-position safety. New trigger guard with redesigned floorplate latch. Left-hand model available. Introduced 1989.
Price: M77MKIIR (no sights, 223, 243, 6mm Rem., 308) **$557.81**
Price: M77MKIIRS (open sights, 243, 308) **$616.35**
Price: M77MKIIRL (short action, 20" bbl., 6, 223, 243, 308) . . . **$592.46**
Price: M77MKIILR (long action, left-hand, 270, 30-06, 7mm Rem. Mag., 300 Win. Mag.) **$573.56**

Ruger M77RLS Ultra Light Carbine

Similar to the Model 77RL Ultra Light except has 18½" barrel, Ruger Integral Scope Mounting System, iron sights, and hinged floorplate. Available in 270, 30-06. Weight is 6 lbs., overall length 38⅞". Introduced 1987.
Price: **$592.46**

Ruger M77RL Ultra Light

Similar to the standard M77 except weighs only 6 lbs., chambered for 270, 30-06, 257; barrel tapped for target scope blocks; has 20" Ultra Light barrel. Overall length 40". Ruger's steel 1" scope rings supplied. Introduced 1983.
Price: **$592.46**

Ruger M77 All-Weather

Ruger M77 Mark II All-Weather Stainless Rifle

Similar to the wood-stock M77 Mark II except all metal parts are of stainless steel, and has an injection-moulded, glass-fiber-reinforced Du Pont Zytel stock. Chambered for 223, 243, 270, 308, 30-06, 7mm Rem. Mag., 300 Win. Mag., 338 Win. Mag. Has the fixed-blade-type ejector, three-position safety, and new trigger guard with patented floorplate latch. Comes with Integral Scope Base Receiver and 1" Ruger scope rings, built-in sling swivel loops. Introduced 1990.
Price: KM77MKIIRP **$558.00**

Ruger M77RSI International

Ruger M77RSI International Carbine

Same as the standard Model 77 except has 18½" barrel, full-length Mannlicher-style stock, with steel forend cap, loop-type steel sling swivels. Integral-base receiver, open sights, Ruger 1" steel rings. Improved front sight. Available in 250-3000, 270, 30-06. Weighs 7 lbs. Length overall is 38⅜".
Price: **$623.44**

RUGER M77 MARK II MAGNUM RIFLE

Caliber: 375 H&H, 4-shot magazine; 416 Rigby, 458 Win. Mag., 3-shot magazine.
Barrel: 26", with integral steel rib.
Weight: 9.25 lbs. (375); 10.25 lbs. (416, 458). **Length:** 40.5" overall.
Stock: Circassian walnut with hand-cut checkering, swivel studs, steel grip cap, rubber butt pad.

Sights: Ramp front, three leaf express on serrated integral steel rib. Rib also serves as base for front scope ring.
Features: Uses an enlarged Mark II action with three-position safety, stainless bolt, steel trigger guard and hinged steel floorplate. Controlled feed. Introduced 1989.
Price: M77RSM MKII **$1,550.00**

Ruger M77R

Ruger M77RS Bolt-Action Rifle

Similar to Ruger 77R except has open sights. Calibers 270, 30-06, 7mm Rem. Mag., 300 Win. Mag., 338 Win. Mag., 35 Whelen, with 22" barrel (24" in magnum calibers). Weight about 7 lbs. Integral-base receiver, Ruger 1" rings and open sights.
Price: **$616.35**

RUGER M77R BOLT-ACTION RIFLE

Caliber: 22-250, 220 Swift (Short Stroke action); 270, 7x57, 257 Roberts, 280 Rem., 30-06, 25-06, 7mm Rem. Mag., 300 Win. Mag., 338 Win. Mag.
Barrel: 22" round tapered (24" in 220 Swift and magnum action calibers).
Weight: 6¾ lbs. **Length:** 42" overall (22" barrel).
Stock: Hand checkered American walnut, p.g. cap, sling swivel studs and rubber butt pad.
Sights: None supplied; comes with Ruger 1" scope rings.
Features: Integral scope mount bases, diagonal bedding system, hinged floorplate, adjustable trigger, tang safety.
Price: With Ruger steel scope rings, no sights (M77R) **$557.81**

Ruger M77NV Varmint

RUGER M77NV VARMINT

Caliber: 22-250, 220 Swift, 243, 308.
Barrel: 26" heavy stainless steel with matte finish.
Weight: Approx. 9.25 lbs. **Length:** Approx. 44" overall.
Stock: Laminated American hardwood with flat forend, steel swivel studs; no checkering or grip cap.
Sights: Integral scope mount bases in receiver.
Features: Ruger diagonal bedding system. Ruger steel 1" scope rings supplied. Fully adjustable trigger. Steel floorplate and trigger guard. New version introduced 1992.
Price: **$623.44**

CAUTION: PRICES CHANGE, CHECK AT GUNSHOP.

Sako Hunter

Sako Hunter Left-Hand Rifle
Same gun as the Sako Hunter except has left-hand action, stock with dull finish. Available in medium, long and magnum actions. Introduced 1987.
Price: Standard calibers, 22-250 to 7mm-08 . . . . **$1,055.00**
Price: Magnum calibers **$1,100.00**
Price: 375 H&H, 416 Rem. Mag. **$1,115.00**
Price: Deluxe, standard calibers, 25-06, 30-06 . . . . **$1,430.00**
Price: Deluxe, magnum calibers **$1,445.00**
Price: Deluxe, 375 H&H, 416 Rem. Mag. **$1,460.00**
Price: Long action, 25-06, 270, 280, 30-06 . . . . **$1,085.00**

SAKO HUNTER RIFLE
Caliber: 17 Rem., 222 PPC, 222, 223, 6mm PPC (short action); 22-250, 243, 7mm-08, 308 (medium action); 25-06, 270, 30-06, 7mm Rem. Mag., 300 Win. Mag., 338 Win. Mag., 375 H&H Mag., 300 Wea. Mag., 416 Rem. Mag. (long action).
Barrel: 22" to 24" depending on caliber.
Weight: 5¾ lbs. (short); 6¼ lbs. (med.); 7¼ lbs. (long).
Stock: Hand-checkered European walnut.
Sights: None furnished. Scope mounts included.
Features: Adj. trigger, hinged floorplate. Imported from Finland by Stoeger.
Price: 17 Rem. **$975.00**
Price: 222, 223, 22-250, 243, 308, 7mm-08 . . . . **$975.00**
Price: Long action cals. (except magnums) **$1,000.00**
Price: Magnum cals. **$1,020.00**
Price: 375 H&H, 416 Rem. Mag., from **$1,035.00**
Price: 300 Wea. **$1,035.00**
Price: 22 PPC, 6mm PPC, Hunter **$1,245.00**
Price: As above, Deluxe **$1,565.00**

Sako Hunter LS

Sako Safari Grade Bolt Action
Similar to the Hunter except available in long action, calibers 338 Win. Mag. or 375 H&H Mag. or 416 Rem. Mag. only. Stocked in French walnut, checkered 20 lpi, solid rubber buttpad; grip cap and forend tip; quarter-rib "express" rear sight, hooded ramp front. Front sling swivel band-mounted on barrel.
Price: **$2,625.00**

Sako Hunter LS Rifle
Same gun as the Sako Hunter except has laminated stock with dull finish. Chambered for same calibers. Also available in left-hand version. Introduced 1987.
Price: Medium action **$1,190.00**
Price: Long action, from **$1,155.00**
Price: Magnum cals., from **$1,175.00**
Price: 375 H&H, 416 Rem. Mag., from **$1,185.00**

Sako Mannlicher

Sako FiberClass Sporter
Similar to the Hunter except has a black fiberglass stock in the classic style, with wrinkle finish, rubber buttpad. Barrel length is 23", weight 7 lbs., 2 oz. Comes with scope mounts. Introduced 1985.
Price: 22-250, 243, 308, 7mm-08 . . . . **$1,275.00**
Price: 25-06, 270, 280 Rem., 30-06 . . . . **$1,310.00**
Price: 7mm Rem. Mag., 300 Win. Mag., 338 Win. Mag. **$1,325.00**
Price: 375 H&H, 416 Rem. Mag. **$1,340.00**

Sako Mannlicher-Style Carbine
Same as the Hunter except has full "Mannlicher" style stock, 18½" barrel, weighs 7½ lbs., chambered for 243, 25-06, 270, 308 and 30-06, 7mm Rem. Mag., 300 Win. Mag., 338 Win. Mag., 375 H&H. Introduced 1977. From Stoeger.
Price: 243, 308 . . . . **$1,130.00**
Price: 270, 30-06 . . . . **$1,165.00**
Price: 338 Win. Mag., 375 H&H **$1,180.00**
Price: 375 H&H **$1,200.00**

Sako Deluxe Lightweight

Sako Super Deluxe Sporter
Similar to Deluxe Sporter except has select European walnut with high-gloss finish and deep-cut oak leaf carving. Metal has super high polish, deep blue finish. Special order only.
Price: **$2,790.00**

Sako Deluxe Lightweight
Same action as Hunter except has select wood, rosewood p.g. cap and forend tip. Fine checkering on top surfaces of integral dovetail bases, bolt sleeve, bolt handle root and bolt knob. Vent. recoil pad, skip-line checkering, mirror finish bluing.
Price: 17 Rem., 222, 223, 22-250, 243, 308, 7mm-08 . . . . . . **$1,325.00**
Price: 25-06, 270, 280 Rem., 30-06 . . . . **$1,365.00**
Price: 7mm Rem. Mag., 300 Win. Mag., 338 Win. Mag. **$1,380.00**
Price: 300 Wea., 375 H&H, 416 Rem. Mag. **$1,395.00**

Sako Heavy Barrel

Sako Varmint Heavy Barrel
Same as std. Super Sporter except has beavertail forend; available in 17 Rem., 222, 223 (short action), 22 PPC, 6mm PPC (single shot), 22-250, 243, 308, 7mm-08 (medium action). Weight from 8¼ to 8½ lbs., 5-shot magazine capacity.
Price: 17 Rem., 222, 223 (short action) **$1,110.00**
Price: 22-250, 243, 308 (medium action) **$1,110.00**
Price: 22 PPC, 6mm PPC (single shot) **$1,330.00**

Sauer 90

SAUER 90 BOLT-ACTION RIFLE
Caliber: 270, 25-06, 30-06, 7mm Rem. Mag., 300 Win. Mag., 300 Wea. Mag., 338 Win., 375 H&H, 458 Win. Mag., 4-shot magazine for standard calibers, 3-shot for magnums.
Barrel: 24" (standard calibers), 26" (magnum calibers).
Weight: 7.25 to 8 lbs. **Length:** 44" overall (24" barrel).

Stock: Monte Carlo style with sculptured cheekpiece, hand-checkered grip and forend, rosewood grip cap and forend tip. Lux is European walnut with oil finish, Supreme is American walnut with high-gloss lacquer finish.
Sights: None furnished; drilled and tapped for scope mount.
Features: Rear bolt cam activated locking lug action with 65° bolt lift, fully adjustable gold-plated trigger, chamber-loaded signal pin, cocking indicator, tang-mounted slide safety. Detachable box magazine. Introduced 1986. Imported from Germany by G.U., Inc.
Price: Lux or Supreme **$1,495.00**
Price: With engraving LVL I **$2,495.00**
Price: With engraving LVL II **$3,095.00**
Price: With engraving LVL III **$3,395.00**
Price: With engraving LVL IV **$3,995.00**
Price: 458 Safari **$1,995.00**

Savage 110G

Savage 110GXP3 Bolt-Action Rifle
Similar to the 110G except comes with 3-9x32 scope, rings and bases, Savage/Pathfinder leather sling, Uncle Mike's swivels, gun lock, ear plugs, safety glasses and sight-in target. Available in 223, 22-250, 243, 270, 308, 30-06, 7mm Rem. Mag., 300 Win. Mag. Introduced 1991.
Price: **$375.00**

Savage 110CY Youth/Ladies Rifle
Similar to the Savage 110G except has walnut-finished hardwood stock with 12½" length of pull, and is chambered for 243 and 300 Savage. Comes with gun lock, ear plugs, sight-in target and shooting glasses. Introduced 1991.
Price: **$350.00**

Savage 110WLE One of One Thousand Limited Edition Rifle
Similar to the Savage 110G except is chambered for 7x57mm Mauser only, and comes with high-luster #2 fancy-grade American walnut stock with cut checkering, swivel studs, and recoil pad. Highly polished barrel; the bolt has a laser-etched Savage logo. Included are gun lock, ear plugs, sight-in target and shooting glasses. Introduced 1992.
Price: About **$475.00**

Savage 116FSS Bolt-Action Rifle
Similar to the Savage 110F except made of stainless steel. Has black DuPont Rynite stock. Drilled and tapped for scope mounts; no open sights supplied. In 223, 243, 30-06, 270, 7mm Rem. Mag., 300 Win. Mag., 338 Win. Mag.; 22" barrel for 30-06, 270; 24" for magnums. Introduced 1991.
Price: **$500.00**
Price: Model 116FCS (as above with removable box magazine; cals. 30-06, 270, 7mm Rem. Mag., 300 Win. Mag. only) **$525.00**

SAVAGE 110G BOLT-ACTION RIFLE
Caliber: 22-250, 223, 250 Savage, 25-06, 7mm-08, 270, 308, 30-06, 243, 5-shot; 7mm Rem. Mag., 300 Win. Mag., 338 Win. Mag., 4-shot.
Barrel: 22" round tapered, 24" for magnum.
Weight: 6¾ lbs. **Length:** 42⅜" (22" barrel).
Stock: Walnut-finished checkered hardwood with Monte Carlo; hard rubber buttplate.
Sights: Ramp front, step adjustable rear.
Features: Top tang safety, receiver tapped for scope mount. Full-floating barrel; adjustable trigger. Introduced 1989.
Price: **$340.00**
Price: Left-hand, 30-06, 270, 7mm Rem. Mag. only, M110GLNS . . **$400.00**
Price: Model 110GNS (no sights) **$340.00**
Price: Model 110FNS (no sights, black composite stock) **$370.00**
Price: Model 110GC (removable box magazine, 30-06, 270, 7mm Rem. Mag., 300 Win. Mag.) **$375.00**

Savage 110FXP3 Bolt-Action Rifle
Same as the Savage 110F except has black composite stock and comes with a 3-9x32 scope, Kwik-Site rings and bases, Savage/Pathfinder leather sling, Uncle Mike's swivels, gun lock, ear plugs, shooting glasses and sight-in target. Chambered for 223, 22-250, 308, 243, 30-06, 270, 7mm Rem. Mag., 300 Win. Mag. Introduced 1991.
Price: **$390.00**

Savage 110F Bolt-Action Rifle
Similar to the Model 110G except has a black Du Pont Rynite stock with black buttpad, swivel studs, removable open sights. Same calibers as the 110G except 250 Savage, 25-06, 7mm-08. Introduced 1988.
Price: Right-hand only **$360.00**

Savage 110GV Varmint Rifle
Similar to the Model 110G except has medium-weight varmint barrel, no sights, receiver drilled and tapped for scope mounting. Calibers 22-250, 223 only. Introduced 1989.
Price: **$400.00**

Savage 112FV Varmint

Savage 112FV Varmint Rifle
Similar to the Savage 110G except has 26" heavy barrel, chambered for 223 and 22-250, and comes with a DuPont Rynite stock. Drilled and tapped for

scope mounts. Weight is 9 lbs. Included are gun lock, ear plugs, sight-in target and shooting glases. Reintroduced 1991.
Price: **$360.00**
Price: Model 112FVS (single shot) **$360.00**

Savage 114CU

Savage 114CU Classic Ultra Rifle
Similar to the Savage 110G except comes with adjustable sights, a straight American walnut stock with high-gloss finish, cut checkering, grip cap and recoil pad. Removable box magazine hold five rounds (four for magnums). Chambered for 270, 30-06, 7mm Rem. Mag. and 300 Win. Mag. Introduced 1991.
Price: **$520.00**

Savage 110FP Police

SAVAGE 110FP POLICE RIFLE
Caliber: 223, 308, 4-shot magazine.
Barrel: 24", heavy.

Weight: 9 lbs. **Length:** 45.5" overall.
Stock: Black Rynite composition.
Sights: None furnished. Receiver drilled and tapped for scope mounting.
Features: Matte finish on all metal parts. Double swivel studs on the forend for sling and/or bipod mount. Introduced 1990. From Savage Arms.
Price: **$500.00**

Steyr Sporter Model M

STEYR-MANNLICHER SPORTER MODELS SL, L, M, S, S/T
Caliber: 222 Rem., 222 Rem. Mag., 223 Rem., 5.6x50 Mag. (Model SL); 5.6x57, 243, 308, 22-250, 6mm Rem. (Model L); 6.5x57, 270, 7x64, 30-06, 9.3x62, 6.5x55, 7.5 Swiss, 7x57, 8x57 JS (Model M); 6.5x68, 7mm Rem. Mag., 300 Win. Mag., 8x68S, 9.3x64, 375 H&H, 458 Win. Mag. (Model S).
Barrel: 20" (full-stock), 23.6" (half-stock), 26" (magnums).
Weight: 6.8 to 7.5 lbs. **Length:** 39" (full-stock), 43" (half-stock).
Stock: Hand-checkered European walnut. Full Mannlicher or standard half-stock with Monte Carlo comb and rubber recoil pad.
Sights: Ramp front, open adjustable rear.
Features: Choice of single- or double-set triggers. Detachable 5-shot rotary magazine. Drilled and tapped for scope mounting. Model M actions available in left-hand models; S (magnum) actions available in half-stock only. Imported by GSI, Inc.

Price: Models SL, L, M, half-stock **$1,618.00**
Price: As above, full-stock **$1,743.00**
Price: Models SL, L Varmint, 26" heavy barrel . . . **$1,743.00**
Price: Model M left-hand, half-stock (270, 30-06, 7x64) **$1,743.00**
Price: As above, full-stock (270, 7x57, 7x64, 30-06) **$1,868.00**
Price: Model S Magnum **$1,743.00**
Price: Model S/T, 26" heavy barrel (375 H&H, 9.3x64, 458 Win. Mag.) **$1,868.00**

Steyr Luxus M

Steyr-Mannlicher Luxus Model L, M, S
Similar to the Sporter series except has single set trigger, detachable steel 3-shot, in-line magazine, rear tang slide safety. Calibers: 5.6x57, 243, 308 (Model L); 6.5x57, 270, 7x64, 30-06, 9.3x62, 6.5x55, 7.5 Swiss (Model M); 6.5x68, 7mm Rem. Mag., 300 Win. Mag., 8x68S (Model S). S (magnum) calibers available in half-stock only. Imported by GSI, Inc.
Price: Model L, M, half-stock **$2,118.00**
Price: As above, full-stock **$2,243.00**
Price: Model S (magnum) **$2,243.00**

Steyr-Mannlicher Model M Professional Rifle
Similar to the Sporter series except has black ABS Cycolac stock, Parkerized finish. Chambered for 6.5x57, 270, 7x64, 30-06, 9.3x62. Has 23.6" barrel, weighs 7.5 lbs. Also available in left-hand version. Imported by GSI, Inc.
Price: **$1,368.00**

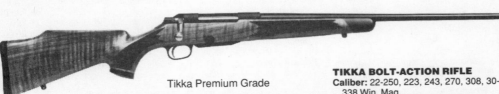

Tikka Premium Grade

TIKKA BOLT-ACTION RIFLE
Caliber: 22-250, 223, 243, 270, 308, 30-06, 7mm Rem. Mag., 300 Win. Mag., 338 Win. Mag.
Barrel: 22½" (std. cals.), 24½" (magnum cals.).
Weight: 7⅛ lbs. **Length:** 43" overall (std. cals.).
Stock: European walnut with Monte Carlo comb, rubber buttpad, checkered grip and forend.
Sights: None furnished.
Features: Detachable four-shot magazine (standard calibers), three-shot in magnums. Receiver dovetailed for scope mounting. Introduced 1988. Imported from Finland by Stoeger Industries.
Price: Standard calibers **$835.00**
Price: Magnum calibers **$860.00**

Tikka Premium Grade Rifles
Similar to the standard grade Tikka except has stock with roll-over cheekpiece, select walnut, rosewood grip and forend caps. Hand-checkered grip and forend. Highly polished and blued barrel. Introduced 1990. Imported from Finland by Stoeger.
Price: Standard calibers **$1,030.00**
Price: Magnum calibers **$1,070.00**

Tikka Whitetail/Battue

Tikka Whitetail/Battue Rifle
Similar to the standard Tikka rifle except has 20½" barrel with raised quarter-rib with wide V-shaped sight for rapid sighting. Chambered for 308, 270, 30-06, 7mm Rem. Mag., 300 Win. Mag., 338 Win. Mag. Made in Finland by Sako. Introduced 1991. Imported by Stoeger.
Price: 308, 270, 30-06 . . . . **$860.00**
Price: 7mm Rem. Mag., 300 Win. Mag., 338 Win. Mag. **$895.00**

Tikka Varmint/Continental Rifle
Similar to the standard Tikka rifle except has heavy barrel, extra-wide forend. Chambered for 22-250, 223, 243, 308. Introduced 1991. Made in Finland by Sako. Imported by Stoeger.
Price: **$1,090.00**

Ultra Light Model 20

Ultra Light Arms Model 28 Rifle

Similar to the Model 20 except in 264, 7mm Rem. Mag., 300 Win. Mag., 338 Win. Mag. Uses 24" Douglas Premium No. 2 contour barrel. Weighs 5½ lbs., 45" overall length. KDF or ULA recoil arrestor built in. Any custom feature available on any ULA product can be incorporated.

Price: Right-hand **$2,900.00**
Price: Left-hand **$3,000.00**

VOERE MODEL 2155, 2165 BOLT-ACTION RIFLE

Caliber: 22-250, 270, 308, 243, 30-06, 7x64, 5.6x57, 6.5x55, 8x57 JRS, 7mm Rem. Mag., 300 Win. Mag., 8x68S, 9.3x62, 9.3x64, 6.5x68.
Stock: European walnut, hog-back style; checkered pistol grip and forend.
Sights: Ramp front, open adjustable rear.
Features: Mauser-type action with 5-shot detachable box magazine; double-set or single trigger; drilled and tapped for scope mounting. Imported from Austria by L. Joseph Rahn. Introduced 1984.

ULTRA LIGHT ARMS MODEL 20 RIFLE

Caliber: 17 Rem., 22 Hornet, 222 Rem., 223 Rem. (Model 20S); 22-250, 6mm Rem., 243, 257 Roberts, 7x57, 7x57 Ackley, 7mm-08, 284 Win., 308 Savage. Improved and other calibers on request.
Barrel: 22" Douglas Premium No. 1 contour.
Weight: 4½ lbs. **Length:** 41½" overall.
Stock: Composite Kevlar, graphite reinforced. Du Pont imron paint colors—green, black, brown and camo options. Choice of length of pull.
Sights: None furnished. Scope mount included.
Features: Timney adjustable trigger; two-position three-function safety. Benchrest quality action. Matte or bright stock and metal finish. 3" magazine length. Shipped in a hard case. From Ultra Light Arms, Inc.

Price: Right-hand **$2,400.00**
Price: Model 20 Left Hand (left-hand action and stock) **$2,500.00**
Price: Model 24 (25-06, 270, 280 Rem., 30-06,
3⅜" magazine length) **$2,500.00**
Price: Model 24 Left Hand (left-hand action and stock) **$2,600.00**

Price: M2165, standard calibers, single trigger **$1,056.00**
Price: As above, double-set triggers **$1,056.00**
Price: M2165, magnum calibers, single trigger **$1,100.00**
Price: As above, double-set triggers **$1,100.00**
Price: M2165, classic stock, single trigger **$1,056.00**
Price: As above, double-set triggers **$950.00**
Price: M2155 (as above, no jeweling, military safety, single trigger) . **$798.00**
Price: As above, double triggers **$876.00**

Weatherby Mark V

Weatherby Lazermark V Rifle

Same as standard Mark V except stock has extensive laser carving under cheekpiece on butt, p.g. and forend. Introduced 1981.

Price: 240 Wea. thru 300 Wea., 24" bbl., right- or left-hand **$1,355.00**
Price: As above, 26" bbl., right-hand or 300 W.M. left-hand **$1,383.00**
Price: 340 Wea., right- or left-hand **$1,383.00**
Price: 378 Wea., right- or left-hand **$1,565.00**
Price: As above, 26" **$1,727.00**
Price: As above, 26" **$1,811.00**

Weatherby Fibermark

Weatherby Fibermark Alaskan Rifle

Similar to the Weatherby Fibermark rifle except all metal parts are plated with electroless nickel for corrosion resistance. Available in 270 Wea. Mag., 7mm Wea. Mag., 300 Wea. Mag., 340 Wea. Mag. Introduced 1991.

Price: From . . . . **$1,556.00** to **$1,584.00**

Weatherby Mark V Crown Custom Rifles

Uses hand-honed, engraved Mark V barreled action with fully-checkered bolt knob, damascened bolt and follower. Floorplate is engraved "Weatherby Custom." Super fancy walnut stock with inlays and stock carving. Gold monogram with name or initials. Right-hand only. Available in 240, 257, 270, 7mm, 300 Wea. Mag. or 30-06. Introduced 1989.

Price: From . . . . **$3,533.00** to **$4,933.00**
Price: For 340 Wea. Mag., add **$20.00**

WEATHERBY MARK V BOLT-ACTION RIFLE

Caliber: All Weatherby cals., plus 22-250, 270, 30-06, 7mm Rem. Mag., 375 H&H.
Barrel: 24" or 26" round tapered.
Weight: 6½-10½ lbs. **Length:** 43¼"-46½" overall.
Stock: Walnut, Monte Carlo with cheekpiece, high luster finish, checkered p.g. and forend, recoil pad.
Sights: Optional (extra).
Features: Cocking indicator, adjustable trigger, hinged floorplate, thumb safety, quick detachable sling swivels.

Price: Cals. 224 and 22-250, 26" bbl., right-hand only **$1,233.00**
Price: Cals. 240, 257, 270, 7mm, 30-06 and 300 (24" bbl.)
right- or left-hand **$1,225.00**
Price: With 26" No. 2 contour bbl., right-hand or 300 W.M. left only **$1,255.00**
Price: Cal. 340 (26" bbl.), right- or left-hand **$1,255.00**
Price: Cal. 378 (26" bbl.), right- or left-hand **$1,440.00**
Price: 416 Wea. Mag., 26" **$1,596.00**
Price: 460 Wea. Mag., 26" **$1,681.00**

Weatherby Fibermark Rifle

Same as the standard Mark V except the stock is of fiberglass; finished with a non-glare black wrinkle finish and black recoil pad; receiver and floorplate have low luster blue finish; fluted bolt has a satin finish. Available in left-hand only, 22", 24" or 26" barrel, 240 Wea. Mag. through 340 Wea. Mag. calibers. Introduced 1983.

Price: 240 Wea. Mag. through 300 Wea. Mag., 24" bbl. **$1,376.00**
Price: 300, 340, Wea. Mag. **$1,494.00**
Price: 270 Win., 30-06, 22" bbl. **$1,376.00**

Weatherby Mark V Safari Grade Custom Rifles

Uses the Mark V barreled action. Stock is of European walnut with satin oil finish, rounded ebony tip and cap, black presentation recoil pad, no white spacers, and pattern #16 fine-line checkering. Matte finish bluing, floorplate is engraved "Weatherby Safari Grade"; 24" barrel. Standard rear stock swivel, barrel band front swivel. Has quarter-rib rear sight with a stationary leaf and one folding shallow V leaf. Front sight is a hooded ramp with brass bead. Right- or left-hand. Allow 8-10 months delivery. Introduced 1985.

Price: 300 W.M. **$3,301.00**
Price: 340 W.M. **$3,321.00**
Price: 378 W.M. **$3,481.00**
Price: 416 W.M. **$3,534.00**
Price: 460 W.M. **$3,574.00**

CAUTION: PRICES CHANGE, CHECK AT GUNSHOP.

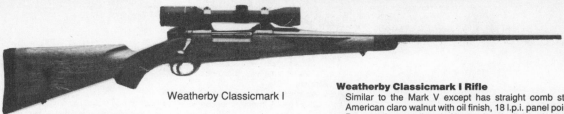

Weatherby Classicmark I

Weatherby Weathermark Rifle
Similar to the Classicmark rifle except has impregnated-color black composite stock with raised point checkering. Uses the Mark V action. Weighs 7.5 lbs. Right-hand only. Introduced 1992.
Price: 240, 257, 270, 7mm, 300 Wea. Mags., 7mm Rem. Mag.,
24" bbl. **$1,000.00**
Price: 240, 257, 270, 7mm, 300, 340 Wea. Mags, 26" bbl. **$1,027.00**
Price: 270 Win., 30-06, 22" bbl. **$1,000.00**

Weatherby Weathermark Alaskan Rifle
Same as the Weathermark except all metal plated with electroless nickel. Available in right-hand only. Introduced 1992.
Price: 240, 257, 270, 7mm, 300 Wea. Mags., 7mm Rem. Mag.,
24" bbl. **$1,180.00**
Price: 240, 257, 270, 7mm, 300, 340 Wea. Mags., 26" bbl. **$1,207.00**
Price: 270 Win., 30-06, 22" bbl. **$1,180.00**

Weatherby Classicmark II Rifle
Similar to the Classicmark I except has deluxe hand-selected American walnut stock with straight comb, shadow-line cheekpiece and rounded forend, 22 l.p.i. wraparound point checkering, oil finish, steel grip cap, Old English recoil pad, satin-finished metal. Uses the Mark V action. Available in right-hand version only. Introduced 1992.
Price: 240, 257, 270, 7mm, 300 Wea. Mags., 7mm Rem. Mag.,
24" bbl. **$1,775.00**
Price: 240, 257, 270, 7mm Wea. Mag., 26" bbl. **$1,803.00**
Price: 270 Win., 30-06, 22" bbl. **$1,775.00**
Price: 300, 340 Wea. Mag., 26" bbl. **$1,803.00**
Price: 378 Wea. Mag., 26" bbl. **$1,976.00**
Price: 416 Wea. Mag., 26" bbl. **$2,128.00**
Price: 460 Wea. Mag., 26" bbl. **$2,207.00**
Price: Safari Classic 375 H&H **$2,693.00**

Weatherby Classicmark I Rifle
Similar to the Mark V except has straight comb stock of hand-selected American claro walnut with oil finish, 18 l.p.i. panel point checkering and a 1" Presentation recoil pad. All metal satin finished. Uses the Mark V action. Available in right- or left-hand versions. Introduced 1992.
Price: 240, 257, 270, 7mm, 300 Wea. Mags., 7mm Rem. Mag., 24" bbl., right-
or left-hand **$1,175.00**
Price: 240, 257, 270, 7mm Wea. Mags., 26" bbl., right-hand only . **$1,203.00**
Price: 270 Win., 30-06, 22" bbl., right- or left-hand **$1,175.00**
Price: 300, 340 Wea. Mag., 26" bbl., right- or left-hand **$1,203.00**
Price: 378 Wea. Mag., 26" bbl., right- or left-hand **$1,373.00**
Price: 416 Wea. Mag., 26" bbl., right- or left-hand **$1,525.00**
Price: 460 Wea. Mag., 26" bbl., right- or left-hand **$1,605.00**

Weatherby Vanguard Classic II Rifle
Similar to the Classicmark I except has rounded forend with black tip, black grip cap with walnut diamond inlay, 20 lpi checkering. Solid black recoil pad. Oil-finished stock. Available in 22-250, 243, 270, 7mm Rem. Mag., 30-06, 300 Win. Mag., 338 Win. Mag., 270 Wea. Mag., 300 Wea. Mag. Introduced 1989.
Price: **$750.00**

WEATHERBY EUROMARK BOLT-ACTION RIFLE
Caliber: All Weatherby calibers except 224, 22-250.
Barrel: 24" or 26" round tapered.
Weight: 6½ to 10½ lbs. **Length:** 44¼" overall (24" bbl.).
Stock: Walnut, Monte Carlo with extended tail, fine-line hand checkering, satin oil finish, ebony forend tip and grip cap with maple diamond, solid buttpad.
Sights: Optional (extra).
Features: Cocking indicator; adjustable trigger; hinged floorplate; thumb safety; q.d. sling swivels. Introduced 1986.
Price: With 24" barrel (240, 257, 270, 7mm, 30-06, 300), right-
or left-hand **$1,257.00**
Price: 26" No. 2 contour barrel, right- or left-hand (300 only) . . . **$1,285.00**
Price: 340 Wea. Mag., 26", right- or left-hand **$1,285.00**
Price: 378 Wea. Mag., right- or left-hand **$1,469.00**
Price: 416 Wea. Mag., 26", right- or left-hand **$1,632.00**
Price: 460 Wea. Mag., 26", right- or left-hand **$1,708.00**

Weatherby Vanguard VGX

Weatherby Vanguard Weatherguard Rifle
Has a forest green or black wrinkle-finished synthetic stock. All metal is matte blue. Has a 24" barrel, weighs 7½ lbs., measures 44½". In 223, 243, and 308; 40½" in 270, 7mm-08, 7mm Rem. Mag., 30-06. Accepts same scope mount bases as Mark V action. Introduced 1989.
Price: Right-hand only **$495.00**

WEATHERBY VANGUARD VGX DELUXE RIFLE
Caliber: 22-250, 243, 270, 270 Wea. Mag., 7mm Rem. Mag., 30-06, 300 Win. Mag., 300 Wea. Mag., 338 Win. Mag.; 5-shot magazine (3-shot for magnums).
Barrel: 24", No. 2 contour.
Weight: 7⅞-8½ lbs. **Length:** 44½" overall (22-250, 243 are 44").
Stock: Walnut with high luster finish; rosewood grip cap and forend tip.
Sights: Optional, available at extra cost.
Features: Fully adjustable trigger; side safety; rubber recoil pad. Introduced 1989. Imported from Japan by Weatherby.
Price: **$750.00**

Weatherby Vanguard Classic I Rifle
Similar to the Vanguard VGX Deluxe except has a "classic" style stock without Monte Carlo comb, no forend tip. Has distinctive Weatherby grip cap. Satin finish on stock. Available in 223, 243, 270, 7mm-08, 7mm Rem. Mag., 30-06, 308; 24" barrel. Introduced 1989.
Price: **$568.00**

Whitworth Safari Express

WHITWORTH SAFARI EXPRESS RIFLE
Caliber: 375 H&H, 458 Win. Mag.
Barrel: 24".
Weight: 7½-8 lbs. **Length:** 44".
Stock: Classic English Express rifle design of hand checkered, select European walnut.
Sights: Three-leaf open sight calibrated for 100, 200, 300 yards on ¼-rib, ramp front with removable hood.
Features: Solid rubber recoil pad, barrel-mounted sling swivel, adjustable trigger, hinged floorplate, solid steel recoil cross bolt. From Interarms.
Price: 375, 458, with express sights **$900.00**

Wichita Classic

WICHITA CLASSIC RIFLE

Caliber: 17-222, 17-222 Mag., 222 Rem., 222 Rem. Mag., 223 Rem., 6x47; other calibers on special order.
Barrel: 21⅛".
Weight: 8 lbs. **Length:** 41" overall.
Stock: AAA Fancy American walnut. Hand-rubbed and checkered (20 lpi). Hand-inletted, glass bedded, steel grip cap. Pachmayr rubber recoil pad.
Sights: None. Drilled and tapped for scope mounting.
Features: Available as single shot or repeater. Octagonal barrel and Wichita action, right- or left-hand. Checkered bolt handle. Bolt is hand-fitted, lapped and jeweled. Adjustable trigger is set at 2 lbs. Side thumb safety. Firing pin fall is ³⁄₁₆". Non-glare blue finish. From Wichita Arms.
Price: Single shot **$2,950.00**

WICHITA VARMINT RIFLE

Caliber: 222 Rem., 222 Rem. Mag., 223 Rem., 22 PPC, 6mm PPC, 22-250, 243, 6mm Rem., 308 Win.; other calibers on special order.
Barrel: 20⅛".
Weight: 9 lbs. **Length:** 40⅛" overall.
Stock: AAA Fancy American walnut. Hand-rubbed finish, hand checkered, 20 lpi pattern. Hand-inletted, glass bedded, steel grip cap. Pachmayr rubber recoil pad.
Sights: None. Drilled and tapped for scope mounts.
Features: Right- or left-hand Wichita action with three locking lugs. Available as a single shot or repeater with 3-shot magazine. Checkered bolt handle. Bolt is hand fitted, lapped and jeweled. Side thumb safety. Firing pin fall is ³⁄₁₆". Non-glare blue finish. From Wichita Arms.
Price: Single shot **$2,250.00**

Winchester Model 70 Sporter

Winchester Model 70 SSM Sporter

Same as the Model 70 Sporter except has black composite, graphite-impregnated stock and matte-finished metal. Available in 270, 30-06, 7mm Rem. Mag., 300 Win. Mag., 338 Win. Mag. Weighs about 7.8 lbs. Comes with scope bases and rings. Introduced 1992.
Price: **$554.00**

Winchester Model 70 Sporter WinTuff

Same as the Model 70 Sporter except has classic-style brown laminated stock with sculpted cheekpiece, diamond point checkering, sling swivel studs, and contoured rubber recoil pad. Available in 270, 30-06, 7mm Rem. Mag., 300 Win. Mag., 300 Wea. Mag., 338 Win Mag. Weighs about 7.8 lbs. Comes with scope bases and rings. Introduced 1992.
Price: **$540.00**

Winchester Model 70 DBM Rifle

Same as the Model 70 Sporter except has detachable box magazine. Available in 270, 30-06, 7mm Rem. Mag., 300 Win. Mag. with 24" barrel. Introduced 1992.
Price: **$569.00**

WINCHESTER MODEL 70 SPORTER

Caliber: 22-250, 223, 243, 25-06, 270, 270 Wea., 30-06, 264 Win. Mag., 7mm Rem. Mag., 300 H&H, 300 Win. Mag., 300 Wea. Mag., 338 Win. Mag., 3-shot magazine.
Barrel: 24".
Weight: 7¾ lbs. **Length:** 44½" overall.
Stock: American walnut with Monte Carlo cheekpiece. Cut checkering and satin finish.
Sights: Optional hooded ramp front, adjustable folding leaf rear. Drilled and tapped for scope mounting.
Features: Three-position safety, stainless steel magazine follower; rubber buttpad, epoxy bedded receiver recoil lug. From U.S. Repeating Arms Co.
Price: With sights **$540.00**
Price: With bases and rings **$540.00**

Winchester Model 70 Stainless Rifle

Same as the Model 70 Sporter except has stainless steel barrel and action with matte gray finish, black composite stock impregnated with fiberglass and graphite, contoured rubber recoil pad. Available in 270, 30-06, (22" barrel), 7mm Rem. Mag., 300 Win. Mag. (24" barrel), 3- or 5-shot magazine. Weighs 6.75 lbs. Introduced 1992.
Price: **$576.00**

> Consult our Directory pages for the location of firms mentioned.

Winchester Model 70 Varmint

Winchester Model 70 SHB (Synthetic Heavy Barrel)

Same as the Model 70 Heavy Barrel Varmint except has black synthetic stock with checkering, matte blue finish. Available in 308 Win. only. Weighs 9 lbs. Introduced 1992.
Price: **$563.00**

Winchester Model 70 Heavy Barrel Varmint

Similar to the Model 70 Sporter except has heavy 26" barrel with counter-bored muzzle. Available in 22-250, 223, 243 and 308. Receiver bedded in sporter-style stock. Has rubber buttpad. Receiver drilled and tapped for scope mounting. Weight about 9 lbs., overall length 46". Introduced 1989.
Price: **$563.00**

Winchester Model 70 Featherweight

Winchester Model 70 Featherweight

Available with standard action in 270 Win., 280 Rem., 30-06, 7mm Rem. Mag., 300 Win. Mag., short action in 22-250, 223, 243, 6.5x55, 7mm-08, 308; 22" tapered. Featherweight barrel; classic-style American walnut stock with Schnabel forend, wraparound checkering fashioned after early Model 70 custom rifle patterns. Red rubber buttpad, sling swivel studs. Weighs 6¾ lbs. (standard action), 6½ lbs. (short action). Introduced 1984.
Price: **$540.00**

Winchester Model 70 WinTuff

Winchester Model 70 Featherweight WinTuff
Same as the Model 70 Featherweight except has brown laminated stock. Available in 22-250, 223, 243, 270, 308, 30-06. Weighs 6.75-7 lbs. Comes with scope bases and rings. Introduced 1992.
Price: **$540.00**

WINCHESTER MODEL 70 LIGHTWEIGHT RIFLE
Caliber: 270, 280, 30-06 (standard action); 22-250, 223, 243, 308 (short action), both 5-shot magazine, except 6-shot in 223.
Barrel: 22".
Weight: 6¼ lbs. **Length:** 40½" overall (std.), 40" (short).
Stock: American walnut with satin finish, deep-cut checkering.
Sights: None furnished. Drilled and tapped for scope mounting.
Features: Three position safety; stainless steel magazine follower; hinged floorplate; sling swivel studs. Introduced 1984.
Price: Walnut **$471.00**
Price: With WinTuff laminated stock **$471.00**
Price: With WinCam green laminated stock, 270, 30-06 only **$471.00**

WINCHESTER MODEL 70 SUPER EXPRESS MAGNUM
Caliber: 375 H&H Mag., 458 Win. Mag., 3-shot magazine.
Barrel: 24" (375), 22" (458).
Weight: 8½ lbs.
Stock: American walnut with Monte Carlo cheekpiece. Wraparound checkering and finish.
Sights: Hooded ramp front, open rear.
Features: Two steel cross bolts in stock for added strength. Front sling swivel stud mounted on barrel. Contoured rubber buttpad. From U.S. Repeating Arms Co.
Price: About **$816.00**

ZOLI MODEL AZ-1900 CLASSIC BOLT-ACTION RIFLE
Caliber: 243, 6.5x55, 270, 308, 30-06, 7mm Rem. Mag., 300 Win. Mag.
Barrel: 21" (24" on 7mm Rem. Mag., 300 Win. Mag.).
Weight: 7.25 lbs. **Length:** 41.75" overall (21" bbl.).
Stock: Checkered Turkish circassian walnut. Model AZ-1900M has Bell & Carlson synthetic stock.

Winchester Model 70 Featherweight Classic
Same as the Model 70 Featherweight except has claw controlled-round feeding system; action is bedded in a standard-grade walnut stock. Available in 270, 280 Rem., 30-06. Drilled and tapped for scope mounts; comes with rings and bases. Weighs 7.25 lbs. Introduced 1992.
Price: **$749.00**

Winchester Ranger Rifle
Similar to Model 70 Lightweight except chambered only for 223, 243, 270, 30-06, with 22" barrel. American hardwood stock, no checkering, composition butt-plate. Metal has matte blue finish. Introduced 1985.
Price: **$427.00**
Price: Ranger Ladies/Youth, 243, 308 only, scaled-down stock . . . **$443.00**

WINCHESTER MODEL 70 SHARPSHOOTER
Caliber: 308 Win., 300 Win. Mag.
Barrel: 24" (308), 26" (300 Win. Mag.).
Weight: 11 lbs. **Length:** 44.5" overall (24" barrel).
Stock: McMillan A-2 target style; glass bedded; recoil pad, swivel studs.
Sights: None furnished; comes with bases and rings.
Features: Hand-honed and fitted action, Schneider barrel. Matte blue finish. Introduced 1992. From U.S. Repeating Arms Co. **$1,495.00**

WINCHESTER MODEL 70 SUPER GRADE
Caliber: 270, 30-06, 5-shot magazine; 7mm Rem. Mag., 300 Win. Mag., 338 Win. Mag., 3-shot magazine.
Barrel: 24".
Weight: About 7¾ lbs. **Length:** 44½" overall.
Stock: Walnut with straight comb, sculptured cheekpiece, wraparound cut checkering, tapered forend, solid rubber buttpad.
Sights: None furnished; comes with scope bases and rings.
Features: Controlled round feeding with stainless steel claw extractor, bolt guide rail, three-position safety; all steel bottom metal, hinged floorplate, stainless magazine follower. Introduced 1990. From U.S. Repeating Arms Co.
Price: **$997.00**

Sights: Open sights supplied with gun but not mounted. Drilled and tapped for scope mounts.
Features: Polished blue finish, oil-finished stock. Engine-turned bolt. Introduced 1989. Imported from Italy by European American Armory.
Price: **$1,295.00**
Price: Model AZ-1900M (synthetic stock) **$1,195.00**

CENTERFIRE RIFLES—SINGLE SHOT

Classic and modern designs for sporting and competitive use.

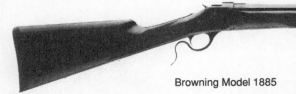

Browning Model 1885

BROWNING MODEL 1885 SINGLE SHOT RIFLE
Caliber: 223, 22-250, 30-06, 270, 7mm Rem. Mag., 45-70.
Barrel: 28".
Weight: About 8½ lbs. **Length:** 43½" overall.
Stock: Walnut with straight grip, schnabel forend.
Sights: None furnished; drilled and tapped for scope mounting.
Features: Replica of J.M. Browning's high-wall falling block rifle. Octagon barrel with recessed muzzle. Imported from Japan by Browning. Introduced 1985.
Price: **$771.95**

ARMSPORT 1866 SHARPS RIFLE, CARBINE
Caliber: 47-70.
Barrel: 28", round or octagonal.
Weight: 8.10 lbs. **Length:** 46" overall.
Stock: Walnut.
Sights: Blade front, folding adjustable rear. Tang sight set optionally available.
Features: Replica of the 1866 Sharps. Color case-hardened frame, rest blued. Imported by Armsport.
Price: **$840.00**
Price: With octagonal barrel **$890.00**
Price: Carbine, 22" round barrel **$820.00**

Dakota Single Shot

DESERT INDUSTRIES G-90 SINGLE SHOT RIFLE
Caliber: 22-250, 220 Swift, 223, 6mm, 243, 25-06, 257 Roberts, 270 Win., 270 Wea. Mag., 280, 7x57, 7mm Rem. Mag., 30-06, 300 Win. Mag., 300 Wea. Mag., 338 Win. Mag., 375 H&H, 45-70, 458 Win. Mag.
Barrel: 20", 22", 24", 26"; light, medium, heavy.
Weight: About 7.5 lbs.
Stock: Walnut.
Sights: None furnished. Drilled and tapped for scope mounting.
Features: Cylindrical falling block action. All steel construction. Blue finish. Announced 1990. From Desert Industries, Inc.
Price: $525.00

DAKOTA SINGLE SHOT RIFLE
Caliber: Most rimmed and rimless commercial calibers.
Barrel: 23".
Weight: 6 lbs. **Length:** 39½" overall.
Stock: Medium fancy grade walnut in classic style. Checkered grip and forend.
Sights: None furnished. Drilled and tapped for scope mounting.
Features: Falling block action with under-lever. Top tang safety. Removable trigger plate for conversion to single set trigger. Introduced 1990. Made in U.S. by Dakota Arms.
Price: $2,150.00
Price: Barreled action $1,550.00
Price: Action only $1,300.00

Navy Arms Creedmoor

Navy Arms #2 Creedmoor Rifle
Similar to the Navy Arms Buffalo Rifle except has 30" tapered octagon barrel, checkered full-pistol grip stock, blade front sight, open adjustable rear sight and Creedmoor tang sight. Introduced 1991. Imported by Navy Arms.
Price: $695.00

NAVY ARMS ROLLING BLOCK BUFFALO RIFLE
Caliber: 45-70.
Barrel: 26", 30".
Stocks: Walnut.
Sights: Blade front, adjustable rear.
Features: Reproduction of classic rolling block action. Available with full-octagon or half-octagon-half-round barrel. Color case-hardened action. From Navy Arms.
Price: $510.00

Navy Sharps Plains Rifle

Navy Arms Sharps Cavalry Carbine
Similar to the Sharps Plains Rifle except has 22" barrel, overall length of 39", and weighs 7¾ lbs. Has blade front sight, military ladder-style rear, barrel band on forend. Color case-hardened action, rest blued. Introduced 1991. Imported by Navy Arms.
Price: $650.00

NAVY ARMS SHARPS PLAINS RIFLE
Caliber: 45-70.
Barrel: 28½".
Weight: 8 lbs., 10 oz. **Length:** 45¾" overall.
kStock: Checkered walnut butt and forend.
Sights: Blade front, open rear adjustable for windage.
Features: Color case-hardened action, rest blued. Introduced 1991. Imported by Navy Arms.
Price: $650.00

NEW ENGLAND FIREARMS HANDI-RIFLE
Caliber: 22 Hornet, 223, 243, 30-30, 30-06, 45-70.
Barrel: 22".
Weight: 7 lbs.
Stock: Walnut-finished hardwood.
Sights: Ramp front, folding rear. Drilled and tapped for scope mount; 223, 243, 30-06 have no open sights, come with scope mounts.
Features: Break-open action with side-lever release. The 243 and 30-06 have recoil pad and Monte Carlo stock for shooting with scope. Swivel studs on all

New England Handi-Rifle

models. Blue finish. Introduced 1989. From New England Firearms.
Price: 243, 30-06 . . . . $199.95
Price: 22 Hornet, 223, 30-30, 45-70 . . . . $189.95

Model 1885 High Wall

MODEL 1885 HIGH WALL RIFLE
Caliber: 30-40 Krag, 32-40, 38-55, 40-65 WCF, 45-70.

Barrel: 26" (30-40), 28" all others. Douglas Premium #3 tapered octagon.
Weight: NA. **Length:** NA.
Stock: Premium American black walnut.
Sights: Marble's standard ivory bead front, #66 long blade flat top rear with reversible notch and elevator.
Features: Recreation of early octagon top, thick-wall High Wall with coil spring action. Tang drilled, tapped for High Wall tang sight. Receiver, lever, hammer and breechblock color case-hardened. Introduced 1991. Available from Montana Armory, Inc.
Price: $1,095.00

CAUTION: PRICES CHANGE, CHECK AT GUNSHOP.

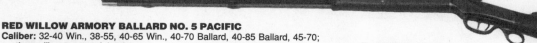

RED WILLOW ARMORY BALLARD NO. 5 PACIFIC

Caliber: 32-40 Win., 38-55, 40-65 Win., 40-70 Ballard, 40-85 Ballard, 45-70; other calibers on special order.
Barrel: 30", tapered octagon.
Weight: 10-11.5 lbs. **Length:** NA.
Stock: Oil-finished American walnut with crescent butt, schnabel forend.
Sights: Blade front, buckhorn rear.
Features: Exact recreation of the Ballard No. 5 Pacific; double-set triggers; under-barrel wiping rod; drilled and tapped for tang sight; ring lever. Mid- and long range sights, fancy wood, single trigger optionally available. Made in U.S. Introduced 1992. From Red Willow Tool & Armory, Inc.
Price: Standard model **$1,530.00**

Red Willow No. 5

Red Willow Armory Ballard No. 1½ Hunting Rifle

Similar to the Ballard No. 5 Pacific except has 30" medium-heavy tapered round barrel, no wiping rod, weighs 9 lbs. Has S-type lever, single trigger. Same calibers as No. 5 Pacific. Options include mid- and long range tang sights, Swiss tube with bead of Lyman globe front, fancy wood, double-set triggers, custom rifles. Introduced 1992. From Red Willow Tool & Armory, Inc.
Price: Standard model **$1,125.00**

Red Willow Armory Ballard No. 8 Union Hill Rifle

Similar to the Ballard No. 5 Pacific except has 30" part round-part octagon barrel; weighs 10 lbs. Oil-finished checkered American walnut stock with cheek rest, pistol grip, nickeled off-hand-style buttplate. Swiss tube sight with bead front, drilled and tapped for tang sight. Exact recreation of the original, with double-set triggers. Options include mid- and long range tang sights, Lyman globe front, fancy wood, single trigger, buckhorn rear sight, customs. Made in U.S. Introduced 1992. From Red Willow Tool & Armory, Inc.
Price: Standard model **$2,212.00**

REMINGTON-STYLE ROLLING BLOCK CARBINE

Caliber: 45-70.
Barrel: 30", octagonal.
Weight: 11¾ lbs. **Length:** 46½" overall.
Stock: Walnut.
Sights: Blade front, adjustable rear.
Features: Color case-hardened receiver, brass trigger guard, buttplate and barrel band, blued barrel. Imported from Italy by E.M.F.
Price: **$820.00**

Ruger No. 1B

Ruger No. 1H Tropical Rifle

Similar to the No. 1B Standard Rifle except has Alexander Henry forend, adjustable folding leaf rear sight on quarter-rib, ramp front with dovetail gold bead, 24" heavy barrel. Calibers 375 H&H (weight about 8¼ lbs.), 416 Rigby, and 458 Win. Mag. (weight about 9 lbs.).
Price: No. 1H **$634.00**
Price: Barreled action **$429.50**

RUGER NO. 1B SINGLE SHOT

Caliber: 220 Swift, 22-250, 223, 243, 6mm Rem., 25-06, 257 Roberts, 270, 280, 30-06, 7mm Rem. Mag., 300 Win. Mag., 338 Win. Mag., 270 Wea., 300 Wea.
Barrel: 26" round tapered with quarter-rib; with Ruger 1" rings.
Weight: 8 lbs. **Length:** 43⅜" overall.
Stock: Walnut, two-piece, checkered p.g. and semi-beavertail forend.
Sights: None, 1" scope rings supplied for integral mounts.
Features: Under-lever, hammerless falling block design has auto ejector, top tang safety.
Price: **$634.00**
Price: Barreled action **$429.50**

Ruger No. 1S Medium Sporter

Similar to the No. 1B Standard Rifle except has Alexander Henry-style forend, adjustable folding leaf rear sight on quarter-rib, ramp front sight base and dovetail-type gold bead front sight. Calibers 7mm Rem. Mag., 338 Win. Mag., 300 Win. Mag. with 26" barrel, 45-70 with 22" barrel. Weight about 7½ lbs. In 45-70.
Price: No. 1S **$634.00**
Price: Barreled action **$429.50**

Ruger No. 1A Light Sporter

Similar to the No. 1B Standard Rifle except has lightweight 22" barrel, Alexander Henry-style forend, adjustable folding leaf rear sight on quarter-rib, dovetailed ramp front with gold bead. Calibers 243, 30-06, 270 and 7x57. Weight about 7¼ lbs.
Price: No. 1A **$634.00**
Price: Barreled action **$429.50**

Ruger No. 1 International

Ruger No. 1 RSI International

Similar to the No. 1B Standard Rifle except has lightweight 20" barrel, full-length Mannlicher-style forend with loop sling swivel, adjustable folding leaf rear sight on quarter-rib, ramp front with gold bead. Calibers 243, 30-06, 270 and 7x57. Weight is about 7¼ lbs.
Price: No. 1 RSI **$656.00**
Price: Barreled action **$429.50**

Ruger No. 1V Special Varminter

Similar to the No. 1B Standard Rifle except has 24" heavy barrel. Semi-beavertail forend, barrel tapped for target scope block, with 1" Ruger scope rings. Calibers 22-250, 220 Swift, 223, 25-06. Weight about 9 lbs.
Price: No. 1V **$634.00**
Price: Barreled action **$429.50**

SHARPS 1874 OLD RELIABLE

Caliber: 45-70.
Barrel: 28", octagonal.
Weight: 9¼ lbs. **Length:** 46" overall.
Stock: Checkered walnut.
Sights: Blade front, adjustable rear.
Features: Double set triggers on rifle. Color case-hardened receiver and butt-plate, blued barrel. Imported from Italy by E.M.F.
Price: Rifle or carbine **$950.00**
Price: Military rifle, carbine **$860.00**
Price: Sporting Rifle **$860.00**

C. SHARPS ARMS NEW MODEL 1874 OLD RELIABLE

Caliber: 40-50, 40-70, 40-90, 45-70, 45-90, 45-100, 45-110, 45-120, 50-70, 50-90, 50-140.
Barrel: 26", 28", 30" tapered octagon.
Weight: About 10 lbs. **Length:** NA.
Stock: American black walnut; shotgun butt with checkered steel buttplate; straight grip, heavy forend with schnabel tip.
Sights: Blade front, buckhorn rear. Drilled and tapped for tang sight.
Features: Recreation of the Model 1874 Old Reliable Sharps Sporting Rifle. Double set triggers. Reintroduced 1991. Made in U.S. by C. Sharps Arms. Available from Montana Armory, Inc.
Price: **$995.00**

C. Sharps 1875 Sporting

C. SHARPS ARMS NEW MODEL 1875 RIFLE
Caliber: 22LR, 32-40 & 38-55 Ballard, 38-56 WCF, 40-65 WCF, 40-90 3¼", 40-90 2⅝", 40-70 2¹⁄₁₀", 40-70 2¼", 40-70 2½", 40-50 1¹¹⁄₁₆", 40-50 1⅞", 45-90, 45-70, 45-100, 45-110, 45-120. Also available on special order only in 50-70, 50-90, 50-140.
Barrel: 24", 26", 30" (standard); 32", 34" optional.
Weight: 8-12 lbs.
Stocks: Walnut, straight grip, shotgun butt with checkered steel buttplate.
Sights: Silver blade front, Rocky Mountain buckhorn rear.
Features: Recreation of the 1875 Sharps rifle. Production guns will have case colored receiver. Available in Custom Sporting and Target versions upon request. Announced 1986. From C. Sharps Arms Co. and Montana Armory, Inc.
Price: 1875 Carbine (24" tapered round bbl.) **$725.00**
Price: 1875 Saddle Rifle (26" tapered oct. bbl.) **$825.00**
Price: 1875 Sporting Rifle (30" tapered oct. bbl.) **$850.00**
Price: 1875 Business Rifle (28" tapered round bbl.) **$775.00**

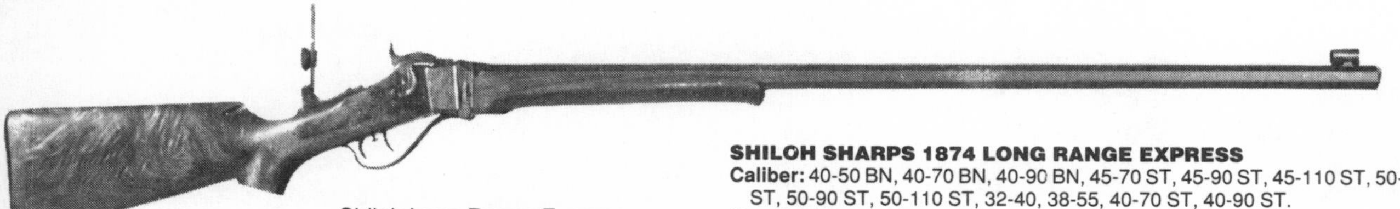

C. Sharps Arms 1875 Classic Sharps
Similar to the New Model 1875 Sporting Rifle except has 26", 28" or 30" full octagon barrel, crescent buttplate with toe plate, Hartford-style forend with cast German silver nose cap. Blade front sight, Rocky Mountain buckhorn rear. Weight is 10 lbs. Introduced 1987. From C. Sharps Arms Co. and Montana Armory, Inc.
Price: $1,075.00

C. Sharps Arms New Model 1875 Target & Long Range
Similar to the New Model 1875 except available in all listed calibers except 22 LR; 34" tapered octagon barrel; globe with post front sight, Long Range Vernier tang sight with windage adjustments. Pistol grip stock with cheek rest; checkered steel buttplate. Introduced 1991. From C. Sharps Arms Co. and Montana Armory, Inc.
Price: $1,165.00

Shiloh Long Range Express

Shiloh Sharps 1874 Business Rifle
Similar to No. 3 Rifle except has 28" heavy round barrel, military-style buttstock and steel buttplate. Weight about 9½ lbs. Calibers 40-50 BN, 40-70 BN, 40-90 BN, 45-70 ST, 45-90 ST, 50-70 ST, 50-100 ST, 32-40, 38-55, 40-70 ST, 40-90 ST.
Price: **$830.00**
Price: 1874 Carbine (similar to above except 24" round bbl., single trigger—double set avail.) **$830.00**
Price: 1874 Saddle Rifle (similar to Carbine except has 26" octagon barrel, semi-fancy shotgun butt) **$895.00**

Shiloh Sharps 1874 Military Rifle
Has 30" round barrel. Iron block front sight and Lawrence-style rear ladder sight. Military butt, buttplate, patchbox assembly optional; three barrel bands; single trigger (double set available). Calibers 40-50x1¹¹⁄₁₆" BN, 40-70x2¹⁄₁₀" BN, 40-90 BN, 45-70x2¹⁄₁₀" ST, 50-70 ST.
Price: **$975.00**

Shiloh Sharps 1874 Montana Roughrider
Similar to the No. 1 Sporting Rifle except available with half-octagon or full-octagon barrel in 24", 26", 28", 30", 34" lengths; standard supreme or semi-fancy wood, shotgun, pistol grip or military-style butt. Weight about 8½ lbs. Calibers 30-40, 30-30, 40-50x1¹¹⁄₁₆" BN, 40-70x2¹⁄₁₀" BN, 45-70x2¹⁄₁₀" ST. Globe front and tang sight optional.
Price: Standard supreme **$840.00**
Price: Semi-fancy **$920.00**

SHILOH SHARPS 1874 LONG RANGE EXPRESS
Caliber: 40-50 BN, 40-70 BN, 40-90 BN, 45-70 ST, 45-90 ST, 45-110 ST, 50-70 ST, 50-90 ST, 50-110 ST, 32-40, 38-55, 40-70 ST, 40-90 ST.
Barrel: 34" tapered octagon.
Weight: 10½ lbs. **Length:** 51" overall.
Stock: Oil-finished semi-fancy walnut with pistol grip, shotgun-style butt, traditional cheek rest and accent line. Schnabel forend.
Sights: Globe front, sporting tang rear.
Features: Recreation of the Model 1874 Sharps rifle. Double set triggers. Made in U.S. by Shiloh Rifle Mfg. Co.
Price: **$965.00**
Price: Sporting Rifle No. 1 (similar to above except with 30" bbl., blade front, buckhorn rear sight) **$940.00**
Price: Sporting Rifle No. 3 (similar to No. 1 except straight-grip stock, standard wood) **$840.00**
Price: 1874 Hartford model **$975.00**

Shiloh Sharps The Jaeger
Similar to the Montana Roughrider except has half-octagon 26" lightweight barrel, 30-30 only. Standard supreme black walnut.
Price: **$895.00**

Shiloh Sharps 1874 Military Carbine
Has 22" round barrel with blade front sight and full buckhorn ladder-type rear. Military-style buttstock with barrel band on military-style forend. Steel buttplate, saddle bar and ring. Standard supreme grade only. Weight is about 8½ lbs. Calibers 40-70 BN, 45-70, 50-70. Introduced 1989.
Price: **$835.00**

Thompson/Center TCR '87

THOMPSON/CENTER TCR '87 SINGLE SHOT RIFLE
Caliber: 22 Hornet, 222 Rem., 223 Rem., 22-250, 243 Win., 270, 308, 7mm-08, 30-06, 32-40 Win., 12-ga. slug. Also 10-ga. and 12-ga. field barrels.
Barrel: 23" (standard), 25⅞" (heavy).
Weight: About 6¾ lbs. **Length:** 39½" overall.
Stock: American black walnut, checkered p.g. and forend.

Sights: None furnished.
Features: Break-open design with interchangeable barrels. Single-stage trigger. Cross-bolt safety. Made in U.S. by T/C. Introduced 1983.
Price: With Medium Sporter barrel (223, 22-250, 7mm-08, 308, 32-40 Win.) **$595.00**
Price: With Light Sporter barrel (22 Hornet, 222, 223, 22-250, 243, 270, 7mm-08, 308, 30-06) **$595.00**
Price: 12-ga. slug barrel **$275.00**
Price: Extra Medium or Light Sporter barrel **$250.00**
Price: 10-, 12-ga. field barrels **$250.00**

T/C Contender Carbine

THOMPSON/CENTER CONTENDER CARBINE
Caliber: 22 LR, 22 Hornet, 223 Rem., 7mm T.C.U., 7x30 Waters, 30-30 Win., 357 Rem. Maximum, 35 Rem., 44 Mag., 410, single shot.
Barrel: 21".
Weight: 5 lbs., 2 oz. **Length:** 35" overall.
Stock: Checkered American walnut with rubber buttpad. Also with Rynite stock and forend.
Sights: Blade front, open adjustable rear.
Features: Uses the T/C Contender action. Eleven interchangeable barrels available, all with sights, drilled and tapped for scope mounting. Introduced 1985. Offered as a complete Carbine only.
Price: Rifle calibers **$450.00**
Price: Extra barrels, rifle calibers, each **$205.00**
Price: 410 shotgun **$470.00**
Price: Extra 410 barrel **$230.00**
Price: Rynite stock, forend **$415.00**
Price: As above, 21" vent. rib smoothbore 410 bbl. **$440.00**

Thompson/Center Contender Carbine Survival System
Combines the Rynite-stocked Contender Carbine with two 16¼" barrels—one chambered for 223 Rem., the other for 45 Colt/410 bore. The frame/buttstock assembly store in the camouflage Cordura case, measuring 25½"x6¾". Introduced 1991.
Price: **$595.00**

Thompson/Center Contender Carbine Youth Model
Same as the standard Contender Carbine except has 16¼" barrel, shorter buttstock with 12" length of pull. Comes with fully adjustable open sights. Overall length is 29", weight about 4 lbs., 9 oz. Available in 22 LR, 22 WMR, 223 Rem., 7x30 Waters, 30-30, 35 Rem., 44 Mag. Also available with 16¼", rifled vent. rib barrel chambered for 45/410.
Price: **$415.00**
Price: With 45/410 barrel **$445.00**
Price: Extra barrels **$200.00**
Price: Extra 45/410 barrel **$230.00**
Price: Extra 45-70 barrel **$220.00**

> Consult our Directory pages for the location of firms mentioned.

Uberti Rolling Block

UBERTI ROLLING BLOCK BABY CARBINE
Caliber: 22 LR, 22 WMR, 22 Hornet, 357 Mag., single shot.
Barrel: 22".
Weight: 4.8 lbs. **Length:** 35½" overall.
Stock: Walnut stock and forend.
Sights: Blade front, fully adjustable open rear.
Features: Resembles Remington New Model No. 4 carbine. Brass trigger guard and buttplate; color case-hardened frame, blued barrel. Imported by Uberti USA.
Price: **$460.00**

DRILLINGS, COMBINATION GUNS, DOUBLE RIFLES

Designs for sporting and utility purposes worldwide.

Beretta 455EELL Express

BERETTA MODEL 455 SxS EXPRESS RIFLE
Caliber: 375 H&H, 458 Win. Mag., 470 NE, 500 NE 3", 416 Rigby.
Barrel: 23½" or 25½".
Weight: 11 lbs.
Stock: European walnut with hand-checkered grip and forend.
Sights: Blade front, folding leaf V-notch rear.
Features: Sidelock action with easily removable sideplates; color case-hardened finish (455), custom big game or floral motif engraving (455EELL). Double triggers, recoil pad. Introduced 1990. Imported from Italy by Beretta U.S.A.
Price: Model 455 . . . . **$36,750.00**
Price: Model 455EELL **$47,000.00**

BERETTA EXPRESS SSO O/U DOUBLE RIFLES
Caliber: 375 H&H, 458 Win. Mag., 9.3x74R.
Barrel: 25.5".
Weight: 11 lbs.
Stock: European walnut with hand-checkered grip and forend.
Sights: Blade front on ramp, open V-notch rear.
Features: Sidelock action with color case-hardened receiver (gold inlays on SSO6 Gold). Ejectors, double triggers, recoil pad. Introduced 1990. Imported from Italy by Beretta U.S.A.
Price: SSO6 . . . . **$20,300.00**
Price: SSO6 Gold **$23,060.00**

CHAPUIS RGEXPRESS DOUBLE RIFLE
Caliber: 30-06, 7x65R, 8x57 JRS, 9.3x74R.
Barrel: 23.6".
Weight: 8-9 lbs. **Length:** NA.
Stock: Deluxe walnut with Monte Carlo comb, oil finish.
Sights: Bead on ramp front, adjustable express rear on quarter-rib.
Features: Boxlock action with long trigger guard, automatic ejectors, double hook Blitz system action with coil springs; coin metal finish; trap grip cap for extra front sight. Imported from France by Armes de Chasse.
Price: About . . . . **$7,000.00 to $8,500.00**

BERNARDELLI EXPRESS VB DOUBLE RIFLE
Caliber: 9.3x74R.
Barrel: 25½".
Weight: About 7.9 lbs.
Stock: Select walnut with cheekpiece, long beavertail-schnabel forend; hand checkered grip and forend. Pistol grip or straight English.
Sights: Bead on ramp front, quarter-rib with leaf rear.
Features: Coin-finished or color case-hardened boxlock action with automatic ejectors, double or single trigger; hand-cut rib. Introduced 1990. Imported from Italy by Magnum Research.
Price: $7,033.00
Price: With single trigger $7,240.00

E.A.A./ANTONIO ZOLI EXPRESS RIFLE

Caliber: 7.65R, 30-06, 9.3x74R.
Barrel: 25.5".
Weight: About 8 lbs. **Length:** 40.5" overall.
Stock: Fancy European walnut with raised cheekpiece, fine-line checkering.
Sights: Bead front, adjustable express rear on quarter-rib.
Features: Boxlock action; engraved coin-finished frame; double-set triggers; selective automatic ejectors; rubber recoil pad; sling swivels. Imported from Italy by European American Armory.
Price: Express Model **$4,495.00**
Price: Express E (better engraving) **$4,995.00**
Price: Express EM (elaborate engraving, extra-fancy wood) . . . **$5,495.00**

AUGUSTE FRANCOTTE SIDELOCK DOUBLE RIFLES

Caliber: 243, 7x64, 7x65R, 8x57JRS, 270, 30-06, 9.3x74R, 375 H&H, 470 N.E.; others on request.
Barrel: 23½" to 26".
Weight: 7.61 lbs. (medium calibers), 11.1 lbs. (mag. calibers).
Stock: Fancy European walnut; dimensions to customer specs. Straight or pistol grip style. Checkered butt, oil finish.
Sights: Bead on ramp front, leaf rear on quarter-rib; to customer specs.
Features: Custom made to customer's specs. Special extractor for rimless cartridges; back-action sidelocks; double trigger with hinged front trigger. Automatic or free safety. Wide range of options available. Imported from Belgium by Armes de Chasse.
Price: . . . . **$30,000.00 to $36,000**

HEYM MODEL 22S SAFETY COMBO GUN

Caliber/Gauge: 16- or 20-ga. (2¾", 3"), 12-ga. (2¾") over 22 Hornet, 22 WMR, 222 Rem., 223, 243 Win., 5.6x50R, 5.6x52R, 6.5x55, 6.5x57R, 7x57R, 8x57 JRS.
Barrel: 24", solid rib.
Weight: About 5½ lbs.
Stock: Dark European walnut, hand-checkered p.g. and forend. Oil finish.
Sights: Silver bead ramp front, folding leaf rear.
Features: Tang-mounted cocking slide, floating rifle barrel, single-set trigger. Base supplied for quick-detachable scope mounts. Patented rocker-weight

HEYM MODEL 33 BOXLOCK DRILLING

Caliber/Gauge: 5.6x50R Mag., 5.6x52R, 6.5x55, 6.5x57R, 7x57R, 7x65R, 8x57JRS, 9.3x74R, 243, 308, 30-06; 16x16 (2¾"), 20x20 (3").
Barrel: 25" (Full & Mod.).
Weight: About 6½ lbs. **Length:** 42" overall.
Stock: Dark European walnut, checkered p.g. and forend; oil finish.

HEYM MODEL 55B/55SS O/U DOUBLE RIFLE

Caliber: 7x65R, 308, 30-06, 8x57JRS, 9.3x74R.
Barrel: 25".
Weight: About 8 lbs., depending upon caliber. **Length:** 42" overall.
Stock: Dark European walnut, hand-checkered p.g. and forend. Oil finish.
Sights: Silver bead ramp front, open V-type rear.
Features: Boxlock or full sidelock; Kersten double cross bolt, cocking indicators; hand-engraved hunting scenes. Options available include interchangeable barrels, Zeiss scopes in claw mounts, deluxe engravings and stock carving, etc. Imported from Germany by Heckler & Koch, Inc.
Price: Model 55B boxlock **$12,435.00**
Price: Model 55SS sidelock **$15,820.00**
Price: Interchangeable shotgun barrels, add **$3,130.00**
Price: Interchangeable rifle barrels, add **$4,950.00**

HEYM MODEL 88B SIDE-BY-SIDE DOUBLE RIFLE

Caliber: 30-06, 8x57JRS, 9.3x74R, 375 H&H.
Barrel: 25".
Weight: 7½ lbs. (std. cals.), 8½ lbs. (mag.). **Length:** 42" overall.
Stock: Fancy French walnut, classic North American design.
Sights: Silver bead post on ramp front, fixed or three-leaf express rear.
Features: Action has complete coverage hunting scene engraving. Available as boxlock or with q.d. sidelocks. Imported from Germany by Heckler & Koch, Inc.
Price: Boxlock . . . . **$10,700.00 to $17,560.00**
Price: Sidelock, Model 88B-SS, from **$15,400.00**

AUGUSTE FRANCOTTE BOXLOCK DOUBLE RIFLE

Caliber: 243, 270, 30-06, 7x64, 7x65R, 8x57JRS, 9.3x74R, 375 H&H, 470 N.E.; other calibers on request.
Barrel: 23.5" to 26".
Weight: NA. **Length:** NA.
Stock: Deluxe European walnut to customer specs; pistol grip or straight grip with Francotte cheekpiece; checkered butt; oil finish.
Sights: Bead front on long ramp, quarter-rib with fixed V rear.
Features: Side-by-side barrels; Anson & Deeley boxlock action with double triggers (front hinged), manual safety, floating firing pins and gas vent safety screws. Splinter or beavertail forend. English scroll engraving; coin finish or color case-hardening. Many options available. Imported from Belgium by Armes de Chasse.
Price: From about . . . . **$20,000.00 to $25,000.00**

HEYM MODEL 37B DOUBLE RIFLE DRILLING

Caliber/Gauge: 7x65R, 30-06, 8x57JRS, 9.3x74R; 20-ga. (3").
Barrel: 25" (shotgun barrel choked Full or Mod.).
Weight: About 8½ lbs. **Length:** 42" overall.
Stock: Dark European walnut, hand-checkered p.g. and forend. Oil finish.
Sights: Silver bead front, folding leaf rear. Available with scope and Suhler claw mounts.
Features: Full sidelock construction. Greener-type cross bolt, double under lugs, cocking indicators. Imported from Germany by Heckler & Koch, Inc.
Price: Model 37B double rifle drilling **$14,275.00**
Price: Model 37B Deluxe (hunting scene engraving) **$17,780.00**

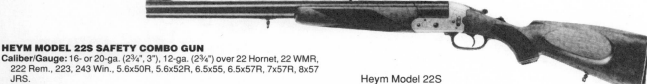

Heym Model 22S

system automatically uncocks gun if accidentally dropped or bumped hard. Imported from Germany by Heckler & Koch, Inc.
Price: Model 22SZ **$2,860.00**

Sights: Silver bead front, folding leaf rear. Automatic sight positioner. Available with scope and Suhler claw mounts.
Features: Boxlock action with Greener-type cross bolt and safety, double under lugs. Double-set triggers. Plastic or steel trigger guard. Engraving coverage varies with model. Imported from Germany by Heckler & Koch, Inc.
Price: Model 33 Standard **$8,865.00**
Price: Model 33 Deluxe (hunting scene engraving) **$9,240.00**

Heym Model 37 Sidelock Drilling

Similar to Model 37 Double Rifle Drilling except has 12x12, 16x16 or 20x20 over 5.6x50R Mag., 5.6x52R, 6.5x55, 6.5x57R, 7x57R, 7x65R, 8x57JRS, 9.3x74R, 243, 308 or 30-06. Rifle barrel is manually cocked and uncocked.
Price: Model 37 with border engraving **$11,285.00**
Price: As above with engraved hunting scenes **$17,325.00**

Heym Model 55BF O/U Combo Gun

Similar to Model 55B O/U rifle except chambered for 12-, 16-, or 20-ga. (2¾" or 3") over 5.6x50R, 222 Rem., 223 Rem., 5.6x52R, 243, 6.5x57R, 270, 7x57R, 7x65R, 308, 30-06, 8x57JRS, 9.3x74R. Has solid rib barrel. Available with interchangeable shotgun and rifle barrels.
Price: Model 55BF boxlock **$7,900.00**

Kodiak Mk. IV

KODIAK MK. IV DOUBLE RIFLE

Caliber: 45-70.
Barrel: 24".
Weight: 10 lbs. **Length:** 42½" overall.
Stock: European walnut with semi-pistol grip.
Sights: Ramp front with bead, adjustable two-leaf rear.
Features: Exposed hammers, color case-hardened locks. Rubber recoil pad. Introduced 1988. Imported from Italy by Trail Guns Armory.
Price: About **$1,895.00**

KRIEGHOFF TECK O/U COMBINATION GUN
Caliber/Gauge: 12, 16, 20/22 Hornet, 222, 243, 270, 30-06, 308 and standard European calibers. O/U rifle also available in 458 Win. on special order.
Barrel: 25" on double rifle combo, 28" on O/U shotgun. Optional free-floating rifle barrel available.
Weight: 7-7½ lbs.
Stock: Hand-checkered European walnut with German-style grip and cheek-piece.
Sights: White bead front on shotgun, open or folding on rifle or combo.
Features: Boxlock action with non-selective single trigger or optional single/double trigger. Greener cross bolt. Ejectors standard on all but O/U rifle. Top tang safety. Light scroll engraving. Imported from Germany by Krieghoff International, Inc.
Price: From . . . . $7,995.00 to $9,500.00
Price: Ulm (full sidelock model), from . . . . $14,950.00 to 18,606.00

PERUGINI-VISINI MODEL SELOUS SIDELOCK DOUBLE RIFLE
Caliber: 30-06, 7mm Rem. Mag., 7x65R, 9.3x74R, 270 Win., 300 H&H, 338 Win., 375 H&H, 458 Win. Mag., 470 Nitro.
Barrel: 22"-26".
Weight: 7¼ to 10½ lbs., depending upon caliber. **Length:** 41" overall (24" bbl.).
Stocks: Oil-finished walnut, checkered grip and forend; cheekpiece.
Sights: Bead on ramp front, express rear on quarter-rib.
Features: True sidelock action with ejectors; sideplates are hand detachable; comes with leather trunk case. Introduced 1983. Imported from Italy by Wm. Larkin Moore.
Price: $24,000.00

KRIEGHOFF TRUMPF DRILLING
Caliber/Gauge: 12, 16, 20/22 Hornet, 222 Rem., 243, 270, 30-06, 308. Standard European calibers also available.
Barrel: 25". Shot barrels choked Imp. Mod. & Full. Optional free-floating rifle barrel available.
Weight: About 7½ lbs.
Stock: Hand-checkered European walnut with German-style grip and cheek-piece. Oil finish.
Sights: Bead front, automatic pop-up open rear.
Features: Boxlock action with double or optional single trigger, top tang shotgun safety. Fine, light scroll engraving. Imported from Germany by Krieghoff International, Inc.
Price: $8,875.00
Price: Neptun (full sidelock drilling), from $19,750.00

Perugini-Visini Victoria Double Rifles
A boxlock double rifle which shares many of the same features of the Selous model. Calibers 7x65R, 30-06, 9.3x74R, 375 H&H Mag., 458 Win. Mag., 470; double triggers; automatic ejectors. Many options available, including an extra 20-ga. barrel set.
Price: Victoria-M (7x65R, 30-06, 9.3x74R), from about $6,800.00
Price: Victoria-D (375, 458, 470), from about $12,500.00

Savage 24F-12T

SAVAGE 24F O/U COMBINATION GUN
Caliber/Gauge: 22 Hornet, 223, 30-30 over 12 (24F-12) or 22 LR, 22 Hornet, 223, 30-30 over 20-ga. (24F-20); 3" chambers.
Action: Takedown, low rebounding visible hammer. Single trigger, barrel selector spur on hammer.
Barrel: 24" separated barrels; 12-ga. has Full, Mod., Imp. Cyl. choke tubes, 20-ga. has fixed Mod. choke.
Weight: 7 lbs. **Length:** 40½" overall.
Stock: Black Rynite composition.
Sights: Ramp front, rear open adjustable for elevation. Grooved for tip-off scope mount.
Features: Removable butt cap for storage and accessories. Introduced 1989.
Price: 24F-12 . . . . $400.00
Price: 24F-20 . . . . $400.00

Savage 24F-12T Turkey Gun
Similar to Model 24F except has camouflage Rynite stock and Full, Imp. Cyl., Mod. choke tubes. Available only in 22 Hornet or 223 over 12-gauge with 3" chamber. Introduced 1989.
Price: $420.00

Springfield M6 Scout

SPRINGFIELD ARMORY M6 SCOUT RIFLE/SHOTGUN
Caliber: 22 LR over 410-bore.
Barrel: 18.25".
Weight: 4.5 lbs. **Length:** 32" overall.
Stock: Steel, folding, with storage for 15 22 LR, four 410 shells.
Sights: Blade front, military aperture for 22; V-notch for 410.
Features: All-metal construction. Designed for quick disassembly and minimum maintenance. Folds for compact storage. Introduced 1982; reintroduced 1991. Made in U.S. by Springfield Armory.
Price: $249.00

TIKKA MODEL 412S COMBINATION GUN
Caliber/Gauge: 12 over 222, 308.
Barrel: 24" (Imp. Mod.).
Weight: 7⅝ lbs.
Stock: American walnut, with recoil pad. Monte Carlo style. Standard measurements 14"x1⅜"x2"x2⅜".
Sights: Blade front, flip-up-type open rear.
Features: Barrel selector on trigger. Hand-checkered stock and forend. Barrels are screw-adjustable to change bullet point of impact. Barrels are interchangeable. Introduced 1980. Imported from Italy by Valmet.
Price: $1,255.00
Price: Extra barrels, from $720.00

TIKKA MODEL 412S DOUBLE RIFLE
Caliber: 9.3x74R.
Barrel: 24".
Weight: 8⅝ lbs.
Stock: American walnut with Monte Carlo style.
Sights: Ramp front, adjustable open rear.
Features: Barrel selector mounted in trigger. Cocking indicators in tang. Recoil pad. Valmet scope mounts available. Introduced 1980. Imported from Italy by Valmet.
Price: With ejectors, 9.3x74R $1,470.00

A. ZOLI RIFLE-SHOTGUN O/U COMBO
Caliber/Gauge: 12-ga. over 222, 308 or 30-06.
Barrel: Combo—24"; shotgun—28" (Mod. & Full).
Weight: About 8 lbs. **Length:** 41" overall (24" bbl.).
Stock: European walnut.
Sights: Blade front, flip-up rear.
Features: Available with German claw scope mounts on rifle/shotgun barrels. Comes with set of 12/12 (Mod. & Full) barrels. Imported from Italy by Mandall Shooting Supplies.
Price: With two barrel sets $1,695.00
Price: As above with claw mounts, scope $2,495.00

ZOLI SAVANA DOUBLE RIFLE
Caliber: 7x65R, 30-06, 9.3x74R.
Barrel: 25.5".
Weight: NA. **Length:** NA.
Stock: Premium grade French walnut with full pistol grip, cheekpiece.
Sights: Gold bead front, fixed V-notch rear in quarter-rib.
Features: Anson & Deeley boxlock action with choice of single or double triggers. Bushed firing pins, cocking indicators. Silvered, engraved frame. Imported from Italy by European American Armory.
Price: Savana E $6,495.00
Price: Savana EM (deluxe wood, engraving) $6,995.00

Designs for hunting, utility and sporting purposes, including training for competition.

AMT Lightning Hunting II

AMT LIGHTNING 25/22 RIFLE
Caliber: 22 LR, 30-shot magazine.
Barrel: 18", tapered or bull.
Weight: 6 lbs. **Length:** 26½" (folded), 37" (open).
Stock: Folding stainless steel.
Sights: Ramp front, fixed rear.
Features: Made of stainless steel with matte finish. Receiver dovetailed for scope mounting. Extended magazine release. Standard or "bull" barrel. Youth stock available. Introduced 1984. From AMT.
Price: **$295.95**

AMT Lightning Small-Game Hunting Rifle II
Same as the Lightning 25/22 except has conventional stock of black fiberglass-filled nylon, checkered at the grip and forend, and fitted with Uncle Mike's swivel studs. Removable recoil pad provides storage for ammo, cleaning rod and survival knife. No iron sights—receiver grooved for scope mounting. Has a 22" full-floating target weight barrel, weighs 6¾ lbs., overall length of 40½", 10-shot rotary magazine. Introduced 1987; 22 WMR introduced 1992. From AMT.
Price: **$299.99**
Price: As above, 22 WMR **$359.99**

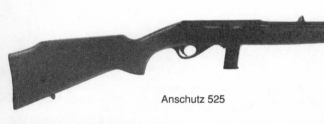

Anschutz 525

ANSCHUTZ 525 DELUXE AUTO
Caliber: 22 LR, 10-shot clip.
Barrel: 24".
Weight: 6½ lbs. **Length:** 43" overall.
Stock: European hardwood; checkered pistol grip, Monte Carlo comb, beavertail forend.
Sights: Hooded ramp front, folding leaf rear.
Features: Rotary safety, empty shell deflector, single stage trigger. Receiver grooved for scope mounting. Introduced 1982. Imported from Germany by PSI.
Price: **$519.00**

Armscor Model AK22

ARMSCOR MODEL AK22 AUTO RIFLE
Caliber: 22 LR, 15- and 30-shot magazine.
Barrel: 18.5".
Weight: 7 lbs. **Length:** 36" overall.
Stock: Plain mahogany.
Sights: Post front, open rear adjustable for windage and elevation.
Features: Resembles the AK-47. Matte black finish. Introduced 1987. Imported from the Philippines by Ruko Products.
Price: About **$229.00**
Price: With folding steel stock, about **$259.00**

Armscor Model 2000SC

ARMSCOR MODEL 20P AUTO RIFLE
Caliber: 22 LR, 15-shot magazine.
Barrel: 21".
Weight: 6.5 lbs. **Length:** 39.75" overall.
Stock: Walnut-finished mahogany.
Sights: Hooded front, rear adjustable for elevation.
Features: Receiver grooved for scope mounting. Blued finish. Introduced 1990. Imported from the Philippines by Ruko Products.
Price: About **$99.00**
Price: With checkered stock **$119.00**
Price: Model 20C (carbine-style stock, steel barrel band, buttplate) . **$139.00**
Price: Model 2000SC (as above except has checkered stock, fully adjustable sight, rubber buttpad, forend tip), about **$279.00**
Price: Model 50S (similar to Model 20P except has ventilated barrel shroud, and 30-shot magazine) **$179.00**

ARMSCOR MODEL 1600 AUTO RIFLE
Caliber: 22 LR, 15-shot magazine.
Barrel: 19.5".
Weight: 6 lbs. **Length:** 38" overall.
Stock: Mahogany.
Sights: Post front, aperture rear.
Features: Resembles Colt AR-15. Matte black finish. Introduced 1987. Imported from the Philippines by Ruko Products.
Price: About **$159.00**
Price: M1600R (as above except has retractable buttstock, ventilated forend), about **$179.00**

AUTO-ORDNANCE 1927A-3
Caliber: 22 LR, 10-, 30- or 50-shot magazine.
Barrel: 16", finned.
Weight: About 7 lbs.
Stock: Walnut stock and forend.
Sights: Blade front, open rear adjustable for windage and elevation.
Features: Recreation of the Thompson Model 1927, only in 22 Long Rifle. Alloy receiver, finned barrel.
Price: **$487.50**

Browning Auto-22

Browning Auto-22 Grade VI

Same as the Grade I Auto-22 except available with either grayed or blued receiver with extensive engraving with gold-plated animals: right side pictures a fox and squirrel in a woodland scene; left side shows a beagle chasing a rabbit. On top is a portrait of the beagle. Stock and forend are of high-grade walnut with a double-bordered cut checkering design. Introduced 1987.
Price: Grade VI, blue or gray receiver $708.95

CALICO MODEL M-100 CARBINE

Caliber: 22 LR, 100-shot magazine.
Barrel: 16".
Weight: 5.7 lbs. (loaded). **Length:** 35.8" overall (stock extended).
Stock: Folding steel.
Sights: Post front adjustable for elevation, notch rear adjustable for windage.
Features: Uses alloy frame and helical-feed magazine; ambidextrous safety; removable barrel assembly; pistol grip compartment; flash suppressor; bolt stop. Made in U.S. From Calico.
Price: $350.90

Feather Model F2

Grendel R-31

Kintrek KBP-1

KINTREK MODEL KBP-1 AUTO RIFLE

Caliber: 22 LR, 17-shot magazine.
Barrel: 25".

BROWNING AUTO-22 RIFLE

Caliber: 22 LR, 11-shot.
Barrel: 19¼".
Weight: 4¾ lbs. **Length:** 37" overall.
Stock: Checkered select walnut with p.g. and semi-beavertail forend.
Sights: Gold bead front, folding leaf rear.
Features: Engraved receiver with polished blue finish; cross-bolt safety; tubular magazine in buttstock; easy takedown for carrying or storage. Imported from Japan by Browning.
Price: Grade I $344.95

Calico Model M-105 Sporter

Calico Model M-105 Sporter

Similar to the M-100 except has hand-rubbed wood buttstock and forend. Weight is 4¾ lbs. Introduced 1987.
Price: $380.90

FEATHER AT-22 SEMI-AUTO CARBINE

Caliber: 22 LR, 20-shot magazine.
Barrel: 17".
Weight: 3.25 lbs. **Length:** 35" overall (stock extended).
Stock: Telescoping wire; composition pistol grip.
Sights: Protected post front, adjustable aperture rear.
Features: Removable barrel. Length when folded is 26". Matte black finish. From Feather Industries. Introduced 1986.
Price: $249.95
Price: Model F2 (fixed stock) $279.95

FEDERAL ENGINEERING XC220 AUTO CARBINE

Caliber: 22 LR, 30-shot magazine.
Barrel: 16.5" (with flash hider).
Weight: 7.25 lbs. **Length:** 34.5" overall.
Stock: Quick-detachable tube steel.
Sights: Hooded post front, Williams adjustable rear; sight bridge grooved for scope mounting.
Features: Quick takedown; all-steel heli-arc welded construction; internal parts industrial hard chromed. Made in U.S. by Federal Engineering Corp.
Price: Includes receiver cap, sling, swivels $459.00

GRENDEL R-31 AUTO CARBINE

Caliber: 22 WMR, 30-shot magazine.
Barrel: 16".
Weight: 4 lbs. **Length:** 23.5" overall (stock collapsed).
Stock: Telescoping tube, Zytel forend.
Sights: Post front adustable for windage and elevation, aperture rear.
Features: Blowback action with fluted chamber; ambidextrous safety. Steel receiver. Matte black finish. Muzzle brake. Scope mount optional. Introduced 1991. Made in U.S. by Grendel, Inc.
Price: $385.00

Weight: 5.5 lbs. **Length:** 31½" overall.
Stock: Solid black synthetic with smooth pebble finish.
Sights: Post front, fully adjustable aperture rear. Drilled and tapped for scope mount.
Features: Bullpup design. Has grip safety and trigger-blocking safeties. Ejects empties out through bottom of stock. Bolt hold-open operated by grip safety. Matte black finish. Introduced 1991. Made in U.S. by Kintrek, Inc.
Price: $249.00

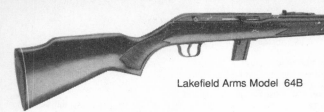

Lakefield Arms Model 64B

KRICO MODEL 260 AUTO RIFLE
Caliber: 22 LR, 5-shot magazine.
Barrel: 19.6".
Weight: 6.6 lbs. **Length:** 38.9" overall.
Stock: Beech.
Sights: Blade on ramp front, open adjustable rear.
Features: Receiver grooved for scope mounting. Sliding safety. Imported from Germany by Mandall Shooting Supplies.
Price: **$700.00**

LAKEFIELD ARMS MODEL 64B AUTO RIFLE
Caliber: 22 LR, 10-shot magazine.
Barrel: 20".
Weight: 5½ lbs. **Length:** 40" overall.
Stock: Walnut-finished hardwood with Monte Carlo-type comb, checkered grip and forend.
Sights: Bead front, open adjustable rear. Receiver grooved for scope mounting.
Features: Thumb-operated rotating safety. Blue finish. Side ejection, bolt hold-open device. Introduced 1990. Made in Canada by Lakefield Arms Ltd.
Price: About **$129.95**

Magtech Model MT-66

MAGTECH MODEL MT-66 AUTO RIFLE
Caliber: 22 LR, 14-shot tubular magazine.
Barrel: 19⅝" (six groove).

Weight: 4¼ lbs. **Length:** 38½" overall.
Stock: Moulded black nylon with checkered pistol grip and forend.
Sights: Blade front, open adjustable rear.
Features: Tube magazine loads through buttplate; top tang safety; receiver grooved for scope mounts. Introduced 1991. Imported from Brazil by Magtech Recreational Products, Inc.
Price: About **$119.95**

Marlin Model 990L

Marlin Model 990L Self-Loading Rifle
Similar to the Model 60 except has laminated hardwood stock with black rubber rifle butt pad and swivel studs, gold-plated steel trigger. Ramp front sight with brass bead and Wide-Scan hood, adjustable semi-buckhorn folding rear. Weighs 5.75 lbs. Introduced 1992. From Marlin.
Price: **$209.45**

MARLIN MODEL 60 SELF-LOADING RIFLE
Caliber: 22 LR, 14-shot tubular magazine.
Barrel: 22" round tapered.
Weight: About 5½ lbs. **Length:** 40½" overall.
Stock: Walnut-finished Monte Carlo, full pistol grip; Mar-Shield® finish.
Sights: Ramp front, open adjustable rear.
Features: Matted receiver is grooved for scope mount. Manual bolt hold-open; automatic last-shot bolt hold-open.
Price: **$144.50**

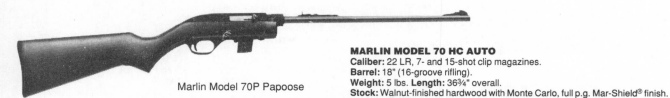

Marlin Model 70P Papoose

MARLIN MODEL 995 SELF-LOADING RIFLE
Caliber: 22 LR, 7-shot clip magazine.
Barrel: 18" Micro-Groove®.
Weight: 5 lbs. **Length:** 36¾" overall.
Stock: American black walnut, Monte Carlo-style, with full pistol grip. Checkered p.g. and forend; white buttplate spacer; Mar-Shield® finish.
Sights: Ramp bead front with Wide-Scan™ hood; adjustable folding semi-buckhorn rear.
Features: Receiver grooved for scope mount; bolt hold-open device; cross-bolt safety. Introduced 1979.
Price: **$193.20**

MITCHELL AK-22 SEMI-AUTO RIFLE
Caliber: 22 LR, 20-shot magazine; 22 WMR, 10-shot magazine.
Barrel: 18".
Weight: 6½ lbs. **Length:** 36" overall.
Stock: European walnut.
Sights: Post front, open adjustable rear.
Features: Replica of the AK-47 rifle. Wide magazine to maintain appearance. Imported from Italy by Mitchell Arms, Inc.
Price: 22 LR **$349.95**
Price: 22 WMR **$349.95**

MARLIN MODEL 70 HC AUTO
Caliber: 22 LR, 7- and 15-shot clip magazines.
Barrel: 18" (16-groove rifling).
Weight: 5 lbs. **Length:** 36¾" overall.
Stock: Walnut-finished hardwood with Monte Carlo, full p.g. Mar-Shield® finish.
Sights: Ramp front, adjustable open rear. Receiver grooved for scope mount.
Features: Receiver top has serrated, non-glare finish; cross-bolt safety; manual bolt hold-open.
Price: **$164.15**

Marlin Model 70P Papoose
Similar to the Model 70 HC except is a takedown model with easily removable barrel—no tools needed. Has 16¼" Micro-Groove® barrel, walnut-finished hardwood stock, ramp front, adjustable open rear sights, cross-bolt safety. Takedown feature allows removal of barrel without tools. Overall length is 35¼", weight is 3¼ lbs. Receiver grooved for scope mounting. Comes with zippered case. Introduced 1986.
Price: **$181.95**

MITCHELL GALIL/22 AUTO RIFLE
Caliber: 22 LR, 20-shot magazine; 22 WMR, 10-shot magazine.
Barrel: 18".
Weight: 6.5 lbs. **Length:** 36" overall.
Stock: European walnut butt, grip, forend; also with folding stock.
Sights: Post front adjustable for elevation, rear adjustable for windage.
Features: Replica of the Israeli Galil rifle. Introduced 1987. Imported by Mitchell Arms, Inc.
Price: 22 LR, fixed or folding stock **$349.95**
Price: 22 WMR, fixed or folding stock **$349.95**

CAUTION: PRICES CHANGE, CHECK AT GUNSHOP.

MITCHELL MAS/22 AUTO RIFLE

Caliber: 22 LR, 20-shot magazine.
Barrel: 18".
Weight: 7½ lbs. **Length:** 28.5" overall.
Stock: Walnut butt, grip and forend.
Sights: Adjustable post front, flip-type aperture rear.
Features: Bullpup design resembles French armed forces rifle. Top cocking lever, flash hider. Introduced 1987. Imported by Mitchell Arms, Inc.
Price: 22 LR $349.95

Mitchell CAR-15/22 Semi-Auto Rifle

Similar to the M-16 A-1/22 rifle except has 16¾" barrel, telescoping butt, giving an overall length of 32" when collapsed. Adjustable post front sight, adjustable aperture rear. Scope mount available. Has 15-shot magazine. Replica of the CAR-15 rifle. Introduced 1990. Imported by Mitchell Arms, Inc.
Price: $349.95

MITCHELL PPS/50 RIFLE

Caliber: 22 LR, 20-shot magazine (50-shot drum optional).
Barrel: 16½".
Weight: 5½ lbs. **Length:** 33½" overall.
Stock: Walnut.
Sights: Blade front, adjustable rear.
Features: Full-length perforated barrel shroud. Matte finish. Introduced 1989. Imported by Mitchell Arms, Inc.
Price: With 20-shot "banana" magazine $349.95
Price: With 50-shot drum magazine $419.95

MITCHELL M-16A-1/22 RIFLE

Caliber: 22 LR, 15-shot magazine.
Barrel: 20.5".
Weight: 7 lbs. **Length:** 38.5" overall.
Stock: Black composition.
Sights: Adjustable post front, adjustable aperture rear.
Features: Replica of the AR-15 rifle. Full width magazine. Comes with military-type sling. Introduced 1990. Imported by Mitchell Arms, Inc.
Price: 22 LR $349.95

Norinco Model 22 ATD

NORINCO MODEL 22 ATD RIFLE

Caliber: 22 LR, 11-shot magazine.
Barrel: 19.4".

Weight: 4.6 lbs. **Length:** 36.6" overall.
Stock: Checkered hardwood.
Sights: Blade front, open adjustable rear.
Features: Browning-design takedown action for storage, transport. Cross-bolt safety. Tube magazine loads through buttplate. Blue finish with engraved receiver. Introduced 1987. Imported from China by Interarms.
Price: $158.33

Ruger K10/22RB

Ruger 10/22 Auto Sporter

Same as 10/22 Carbine except walnut stock with hand checkered p.g. and forend; straight buttplate, no barrel band, has sling swivels.
Price: Model 10/22 DSP $254.50

RUGER 10/22 AUTOLOADING CARBINE

Caliber: 22 LR, 10-shot rotary magazine.
Barrel: 18½" round tapered.
Weight: 5 lbs. **Length:** 37¼" overall.
Stock: American hardwood with p.g. and bbl. band.
Sights: Brass bead front, folding leaf rear adjustable for elevation.
Features: Detachable rotary magazine fits flush into stock, cross-bolt safety, receiver tapped and grooved for scope blocks or tip-off mount. Scope base adaptor furnished with each rifle.
Price: Model 10/22 RB (blue) $201.50
Price: Model K10/22RB (bright finish stainless barrel) $236.00

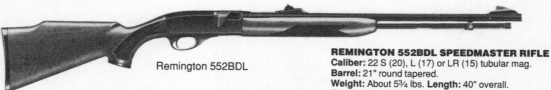

Remington 552BDL

TEXAS REMINGTON REVOLVING CARBINE

Caliber: 22 LR.
Barrel: 21".
Weight: 5¾ lbs. **Length:** 36" overall.
Stock: Smooth walnut.
Sights: Blade front, rear adjustable for windage and elevation.
Features: Brass frame, buttplate and trigger guard, blued cylinder and barrel. Introduced 1991. Imported from Italy by E.M.F.
Price: $420.00

REMINGTON 552BDL SPEEDMASTER RIFLE

Caliber: 22 S (20), L (17) or LR (15) tubular mag.
Barrel: 21" round tapered.
Weight: About 5¾ lbs. **Length:** 40" overall.
Stock: Walnut. Checkered grip and forend.
Sights: Bead front, step open rear adjustable for windage and elevation.
Features: Positive cross-bolt safety, receiver grooved for tip-off mount.
Price: About $213.00

> Consult our Directory pages for the location of firms mentioned.

VOERE MODEL 2115 AUTO RIFLE

Caliber: 22 LR, 8- or 15-shot magazine.
Barrel: 18.1".
Weight: 5.75 lbs. **Length:** 37.7" overall.
Stock: Walnut-finished beechwood with cheekpiece; checkered pistol grip and forend.
Sights: Post front with hooded ramp, leaf rear.
Features: Clip-fed autoloader with single stage trigger, wing-type safety. Imported from Austria by L. Joseph Rahn. Introduced 1984.
Price: Model 2115 . . . . $500.00
Price: Model 2114S (as above except no cheekpiece, checkering or white line spacers at grip, buttplate) $430.00

SURVIVAL ARMS AR-7 EXPLORER RIFLE

Caliber: 22 LR, 8-shot magazine.
Barrel: 16".
Weight: 2.5 lbs. **Length:** 34.5" overall; 16.5" stowed.
Stock: Moulded Cycolac; snap-on rubber butt cap.
Sights: Square blade front, aperture rear adjustable for elevation.
Features: Takedown design stores barrel and action in hollow stock. Light enough to float. Black, Silvertone or camouflage finish. Reintroduced 1992. From Survival Arms, Inc.
Price: $150.00
Price: Black finish with telescoping stock, 25-shot magazine $200.00
Price: Black finish with wood stock $150.00

Classic and modern models for sport and utility, including training.

Browning BL-22

BROWNING BL-22 LEVER-ACTION RIFLE
Caliber: 22 S (22), L (17) or LR (15), tubular magazine.
Barrel: 20" round tapered.

Weight: 5 lbs. **Length:** 36¾" overall.
Stock: Walnut, two-piece straight grip Western style.
Sights: Bead post front, folding-leaf rear.
Features: Short throw lever, half-cock safety, receiver grooved for tip-off scope mounts. Imported from Japan by Browning.
Price: Grade I **$301.50**
Price: Grade II (engraved receiver, checkered grip and forend) . . . **$343.50**

Marlin Model 39AS Golden

MARLIN MODEL 39AS GOLDEN LEVER-ACTION RIFLE
Caliber: 22 S (26), L (21), LR (19), tubular magazine.
Barrel: 24" Micro-Groove®.

Weight: 6½ lbs. **Length:** 40" overall.
Stock: American black walnut with white line spacers at p.g. cap and buttplate; Mar-Shield® finish. Swivel studs; rubber buttpad.
Sights: Bead ramp front with detachable Wide-Scan™ hood, folding rear semi-buckhorn adjustable for windage and elevation.
Features: Hammer-block safety; rebounding hammer. Takedown action, receiver tapped for scope mount (supplied), offset hammer spur; gold-plated steel trigger.
Price: **$394.05**

MARLIN 39TDS CARBINE
Caliber: 22 S (16), 22 L (12), 22 LR (11).
Barrel: 16½" Micro-Groove®.
Weight: 5¼ lbs. **Length:** 32⅝" overall.
Stock: American black walnut with straight grip; short forend with blued tip. Mar-Shield® finish.
Sights: Ramp front with Wide-Scan™ hood, adjustable semi-buckhorn folding rear.
Features: Takedown style, comes with carrying case. Hammer-block safety, rebounding hammer; blued metal, gold-plated steel trigger. Introduced 1988.
Price: With case **$418.95**

NORINCO EM-321 PUMP RIFLE
Caliber: 22 LR, 9-shot magazine.
Barrel: 19.5".
Weight: 6 lbs. **Length:** 37" overall.
Stock: Hardwood.
Sights: Blade front, open folding rear.
Features: Blue finish; grooved slide handle. Imported from China by China Sports, Inc.
Price: . . . . **NA**

REMINGTON 572BDL FIELDMASTER PUMP RIFLE
Caliber: 22 S (20), L (17) or LR (14), tubular magazine.
Barrel: 21" round tapered.
Weight: 5½ lbs. **Length:** 42" overall.
Stock: Walnut with checkered p.g. and slide handle.

Sights: Blade ramp front; sliding ramp rear adjustable for windage and elevation.
Features: Cross-bolt safety; removing inner magazine tube converts rifle to single shot; receiver grooved for tip-off scope mount.
Price: About **$224.00**

Rossi Model 62 SAC

Rossi Model 62 SAC Carbine
Same as standard model except 22 LR only, has 16¼" barrel. Magazine holds slightly fewer cartridges.
Price: Blue **$215.00**
Price: Nickel **$231.67**

ROSSI MODEL 62 SA PUMP RIFLE
Caliber: 22 LR, 22 WMR.
Barrel: 23", round or octagonal.
Weight: 5¾ lbs. **Length:** 39¼" overall.
Stock: Walnut, straight grip, grooved forend.
Sights: Fixed front, adjustable rear.
Features: Capacity 20 Short, 16 Long or 14 Long Rifle. Quick takedown. Imported from Brazil by Interarms.
Price: Blue **$215.00**
Price: Nickel **$231.67**
Price: Blue, with octagonal barrel **$240.00**
Price: 22 WMR, as Model 59 . . . . **$265.00**

Winchester Model 9422

Winchester Model 9422 Magnum Lever-Action Rifle
Same as the 9422 except chambered for 22 WMR cartridge, has 11-round mag. capacity.
Price: Walnut **$381.00**
Price: With WinCam green stock **$381.00**
Price: With WinTuff brown laminated stock **$381.00**

WINCHESTER MODEL 9422 LEVER-ACTION RIFLE
Caliber: 22 S (21), L (17), LR (15), tubular magazine.
Barrel: 20½".
Weight: 6¼ lbs. **Length:** 37⅛" overall.
Stock: American walnut, two-piece, straight grip (no p.g.).
Sights: Hooded ramp front, adjustable semi-buckhorn rear.
Features: Side ejection, receiver grooved for scope mounting, takedown action. From U.S. Repeating Arms Co.
Price: Walnut **$367.00**
Price: With WinTuff laminated stock **$367.00**

Includes models for a variety of sports, utility and competitive shooting.

Anschutz Achiever

ANSCHUTZ ACHIEVER BOLT-ACTION RIFLE
Caliber: 22 LR, single shot adaptor.
Barrel: 19½".
Weight: 5 lbs. **Length:** 35½" to 36⅔" overall.

Stock: Walnut-finished hardwood with adjustable buttplate, vented forend, stippled pistol grip. Length of pull adjustable from 11⅞" to 13".
Sights: Hooded front, open rear adjustable for windage and elevation.
Features: Uses Mark 2000-type action with adjustable two-stage trigger. Receiver grooved for scope mounting. Designed for training in junior rifle clubs and for starting young shooters. Introduced 1987. Imported from Germany by Precision Sales International.
Price: **$395.00**
Price: Sight Set #1 . . . . **$67.00**

Anschutz 1416D/1516D

Anschutz 1418D/1518D Deluxe Rifles
Similar to the 1416D/1516D rifles except has full-length Mannlicher-style stock, shorter 19¾" barrel. Weighs 5½ lbs. Stock has mahogany schnabel tip. Model 1418D chambered for 22 LR, 1518D for 22 WMR. Imported from Germany by Precision Sales International.
Price: 1418D **$1,029.00**
Price: 1518D **$1,049.00**

ANSCHUTZ 1700D CLASSIC RIFLES
Caliber: 22 LR, 5-shot clip.
Barrel: 23½", ¹³⁄₁₆" dia. heavy.
Weight: 7¾ lbs. **Length:** 42½" overall.
Stock: Select European walnut with checkered pistol grip and forend.
Sights: Hooded ramp front, folding leaf rear; drilled and tapped for scope mounting.
Features: Adjustable single stage trigger. Receiver drilled and tapped for scope mounting. Introduced 1988. Imported from Germany by Precision Sales International.
Price: 22 LR **$1,199.00**
Price: As above, Meistergrade (select walnut, gold engraved trigger guard), add **$199.00**

Anschutz 1700 FWT Bolt-Action Rifle
Similar to the Anschutz Custom except has McMillan fiberglass stock with Monte Carlo, roll-over cheekpiece, Wundhammer swell, and checkering. Comes without sights but the receiver is drilled and tapped for scope mounting. Has 22" barrel, single stage #5095 trigger. Weighs 6.25 lbs. Introduced 1989.
Price: With fiberglass stock **$1,189.00**
Price: As above, with Fibergrain stock **$1,399.00**

ANSCHUTZ 1700D BAVARIAN BOLT-ACTION RIFLE
Caliber: 22 LR, 5-shot clip.
Barrel: 24".
Weight: 7¼ lbs. **Length:** 43" overall.
Stock: European walnut with Bavarian cheek rest. Checkered p.g. and forend.
Sights: Hooded ramp front, folding leaf rear.

ANSCHUTZ 1416D/1516D DELUXE RIFLES
Caliber: 22 LR (1416D), 5-shot clip; 22 WMR (1516D), 4-shot clip.
Barrel: 22½".
Weight: 6 lbs. **Length:** 41" overall.
Stock: European walnut; Monte Carlo with cheekpiece, schnabel forend, checkered pistol grip and forend.
Sights: Hooded ramp front, folding leaf rear.
Features: Uses Model 1403 target rifle action. Adjustable single stage trigger. Receiver grooved for scope mounting. Imported from Germany by Precision Sales International.
Price: 1416D, 22 LR **$679.00**
Price: 1516D, 22 WMR **$699.00**
Price: 1416D Classic left-hand **$698.00**

Anschutz 1700D Custom Rifles
Similar to the Classic models except have roll-over Monte Carlo cheekpiece, slim forend with schnabel tip, Wundhammer palm swell on pistol grip, rosewood grip cap with white diamond insert. Skip-line checkering on grip and forend. Introduced 1988. Imported from Germany by Precision Sales International.
Price: 22 LR **$1,237.00**
Price: Custom 1700 Meistergrade (select walnut, gold engraved trigger guard), add **$199.00**

Anschutz 1700D Graphite Custom Rifle
Similar to the Model 1700D Custom except has McMillan graphite reinforced stock with roll-over cheekpiece. Has 22" barrel. No sights furnished, but drilled and tapped for scope mounting. Comes with embroidered sling, Michael's quick-detachable swivels. Introduced 1991.
Price: **$1,229.00**

Features: Uses the Improved 1700 Match 54 action with adjustable 5096 trigger. Drilled and tapped for scope mounting. Introduced in 1988. Imported from Germany by Precision Sales International.
Price: 22 LR **$1,237.00**
Price: Custom 1700D Meistergrade (select walnut, gold engraved trigger guard), add **$199.00**

Armscor Model 14D

ARMSCOR MODEL 14P BOLT-ACTION RIFLE
Caliber: 22 LR, 10-shot magazine.
Barrel: 23".

Weight: 7 lbs. **Length:** 41.5" overall.
Stock: Walnut-finished mahogany.
Sights: Bead front, rear adjustable for elevation.
Features: Receiver grooved for scope mounting. Blued finish. Introduced 1987. Imported from the Philippines by Ruko Products.
Price: About **$109.00**
Price: Model 14D Deluxe (checkered stock) **$129.00**

CAUTION: PRICES CHANGE, CHECK AT GUNSHOP.

Armscor Model 1500 SC Super Classic
Similar to the Model 1500S except has hand-checkered American walnut stock with Monte Carlo and cheekpiece, contrasting wood forend tip and grip cap, red rubber recoil pad, engine-turned bolt. Introduced 1990.
Price: $299.00
Price: In 22 LR, as Model 1400 SC $289.00

BEEMAN/HW 60J-ST BOLT-ACTION RIFLE
Caliber: 22 LR.
Barrel: 22.8".
Weight: 6.5 lbs. **Length:** 41.7" overall.
Stock: Walnut with cheekpiece, cut checkered p.g. and forend.
Sights: Hooded blade on ramp front, open rear.
Features: Polished blue finish; oil-finished walnut. Imported from Germany by Beeman. Introduced 1988.
Price: $585.00

BRNO ZKM-452 DELUXE BOLT-ACTION RIFLE
Caliber: 22 LR, 5-shot magazine.
Barrel: 23.6".
Weight: 6.9 lbs. **Length:** 42.6" overall.
Stock: Checkered walnut.

Browning A-Bolt 22

Browning A-Bolt Gold Medallion
Similar to the standard A-Bolt except stock is of high-grade walnut with brass spacers between stock and rubber recoil pad and between the rosewood grip cap and forend. Medallion-style engraving covers the receiver flats, and the words "Gold Medallion" are engraved and gold filled on the right side of the barrel. High gloss stock finish. Introduced 1988.
Price: No sights $496.95

Browning Model 52

BROWNING MODEL 52 BOLT-ACTION RIFLE
Caliber: 22 LR, 5-shot magazine.
Barrel: 24".

Cabanas Master

Cabanas Leyre Bolt-Action Rifle
Similar to Master model except 44" overall, has sport/target stock.
Price: $149.95
Price: Model R83 (17" barrel, hardwood stock, 40" o.a.l.) $79.95
Price: Mini 82 Youth (16½" barrel, 33" o.a.l., 3½ lbs.) $69.95
Price: Pony Youth (16" barrel, 34" o.a.l., 3.2 lbs.) $69.95

CABANAS PHASER RIFLE
Caliber: 177.
Barrel: 19".
Weight: 6 lbs., 12 oz. **Length:** 42" overall.
Stock: Target-type thumbhole.
Sights: Blade front, open fully adjustable rear.
Features: Fires round ball or pellets with 22 blank cartridge. Imported from Mexico by Mandall Shooting Supplies.
Price: $159.95

Armscor Model 1500 Rifle
Similar to the Model 14P except chambered for 22 WMR. Has 21.5" barrel, double lug bolt, checkered stock, weighs 6.5 lbs. Introduced 1987.
Price: About $159.00

BRNO ZKM 452 STANDARD BOLT-ACTION RIFLE
Caliber: 22 LR, 5- or 10-shot magazine.
Barrel: 25".
Weight: 6 lbs., 9 oz. **Length:** 43½" overall.
Stock: Beechwood.
Sights: Hooded bead front, open rear adjustable for elevation.
Features: Blue finish; oiled stock; grooved receiver. Imported from Czechoslovakia by Action Arms Ltd.
Price: $279.00

Sights: Hooded bead front, open rear adjustable for windage and elevation.
Features: Blue finish; grooved receiver; oiled stock; sling swivels. Introduced 1992. Imported from Czechoslovakia by Action Arms Ltd.
Price: $309.00

BROWNING A-BOLT 22 BOLT-ACTION RIFLE
Caliber: 22 LR, 22 WMR, 5-shot magazines standard.
Barrel: 22".
Weight: 5 lbs., 9 oz. **Length:** 40¼" overall.
Stock: Walnut with cut checkering, rosewood grip cap and forend tip.
Sights: Offered with or without open sights. Open sight model has ramp front and adjustable folding leaf rear.
Features: Short 60-degree bolt throw. Top tang safety. Grooved for 22 scope mount. Drilled and tapped for full-size scope mounts. Detachable magazines. Gold-colored trigger preset at about 4 lbs. Imported from Japan by Browning. Introduced 1986.
Price: A-Bolt 22, no sights $374.95
Price: A-Bolt 22, with open sights $384.95
Price: A-Bolt 22 WMR, no sights $429.95
Price: As above, with sights $439.95

Weight: 7 lbs. **Length:** NA.
Stock: High-grade walnut with oil-like finish. Cut-checkered grip and forend, metal grip cap, rosewood forend tip.
Sights: None furnished. Drilled and tapped for scope mounting or iron sights.
Features: Recreation of the Winchester Model 52C Sporter with minor safety improvements. Duplicates the adjustable Micro-Motion trigger system. Button release magazine. Only 5000 made. Introduced 1991. Imported from Japan by Browning.
Price: $499.95

CABANAS MASTER BOLT-ACTION RIFLE
Caliber: 177, round ball or pellet; single shot.
Barrel: 19½".
Weight: 8 lbs. **Length:** 45½" overall.
Stocks: Walnut target-type with Monte Carlo.
Sights: Blade front, fully adjustable rear.
Features: Fires round ball or pellet with 22-cal. blank cartridge. Bolt action. Imported from Mexico by Mandall Shooting Supplies. Introduced 1984.
Price: $159.95
Price: Varmint model (has 21½" barrel, 4½ lbs., 41" o.a.l., varmint-type stock) $119.95

Cabanas Espronceda IV Bolt-Action Rifle
Similar to the Leyre model except has full sporter stock, 18¾" barrel, 40" overall length, weighs 5½ lbs.
Price: $134.95

Chipmunk Rifle

CHIPMUNK SINGLE SHOT RIFLE
Caliber: 22, S, L, LR, single shot.
Barrel: 16⅛".

Weight: About 2½ lbs. **Length:** 30" overall.
Stocks: American walnut, or camouflage.
Sights: Post on ramp front, peep rear adjustable for windage and elevation.
Features: Drilled and tapped for scope mounting using special Chipmunk base ($9.95). Made in U.S. Introduced 1982. From Oregon Arms.
Price: Standard $149.95
Price: Deluxe (better wood, checkering) $199.95

COOPER ARMS MODEL 36, 38 SPORTER RIFLES
Caliber: 22 LR, 22 Cooper Magnum Centerfire, 5-shot magazine.
Barrel: 22".
Weight: 8 lbs. **Length:** 41¾" overall.
Stock: AA Claro walnut, hand-checkered (Standard grade); AA fancy French walnut or AAA Claro walnut with beaded Monte Carlo cheekpiece, hand-checkering (Custom grade).
Sights: None furnished; optional.

Features: Action has three front locking lugs, 45-degree bolt rotation; fully adjustable single stage trigger; Wiseman/McMillan competition barrel; swivel studs, Pachmayr buttpad, oil-finished wood. Introduced 1991. Made in U.S. by Cooper Arms.
Price: Model 36 Custom (22 LR) $795.00
Price: Model 36 Standard (22 LR) $695.00
Price: Model 38 Custom (22 Cooper Centerfire Magnum) $995.00
Price: Model 38 Standard (22 Cooper Centerfire Magnum) $895.00

Dakota 22 Sporter

DAKOTA 22 SPORTER BOLT-ACTION RIFLE
Caliber: 22 LR, 22 Hornet, 5-shot magazine.
Barrel: 22".

Weight: About 6.5 lbs. **Length:** NA.
Stock: Claro or English walnut in classic design; 13.6" length of pull. Choice of grade. Point panel hand checkering. Swivel studs. Black butt pad.
Sights: None furnished; comes with mount bases.
Features: Combines features of Winchester 52 and Dakota 76 rifles. Full-sized receiver; rear locking lug and bolt machined from bar stock. Trigger and striker-blocking safety; adjustable trigger. Introduced 1992. From Dakota Arms, Inc.
Price: $995.00

KRICO MODEL 300 BOLT-ACTION RIFLES
Caliber: 22 LR, 22 WMR, 22 Hornet.
Barrel: 19.6" (22 RF), 23.6" (Hornet).
Weight: 6.3 lbs. **Length:** 38.5" overall (22 RF).
Stock: Walnut-stained beech.
Sights: Blade on ramp front, open adjustable rear.
Features: Double triggers, sliding safety. Checkered grip and forend. Imported from Germany by Mandall Shooting Supplies.
Price: Model 300 Standard $700.00
Price: Model 300 Deluxe $795.00
Price: Model 300 Stutzen (walnut full-length stock) $825.00
Price: Model 300 SA (walnut Monte Carlo stock) $750.00

LAKEFIELD ARMS MARK I BOLT-ACTION RIFLE
Caliber: 22 LR, single shot.
Barrel: 20½".
Weight: 5½ lbs. **Length:** 39½" overall.
Stock: Walnut-finished hardwood with Monte Carlo-type comb, checkered grip and forend.
Sights: Bead front, open adjustable rear. Receiver grooved for scope mounting.
Features: Thumb-operated rotating safety. Blue finish. Rifled or smooth bore. Introduced 1990. Made in Canada by Lakefield Arms Ltd.
Price: About $117.95
Price: Mark I-Y (Youth), 19" barrel, 37" overall, 5 lbs. $117.95

LAKEFIELD ARMS MARK II BOLT-ACTION RIFLE
Caliber: 22 LR, 10-shot magazine.
Barrel: 20½".
Weight: 5½ lbs. **Length:** 39½" overall.
Stock: Walnut-finished hardwood with Monte Carlo-type comb, checkered grip and forend.
Sights: Bead front, open adjustable rear. Receiver grooved for scope mounting.
Features: Thumb-operated rotating safety. Blue finish. Introduced 1990. Made in Canada by Lakefield Arms Ltd.

Lakefield Arms Mark II Left-Hand

Price: About $124.95
Price: Mark II-Y (youth), 19" barrel, 37" overall, 5 lbs. $124.95
Price: Mark II left-hand $137.95
Price: Mark II-Y (youth) left-hand $137.95

Magtech Model MT-22C

MAGTECH MODEL MT-22C BOLT-ACTION RIFLE
Caliber: 22 S, L, LR, 6- and 10-shot magazines.
Barrel: 21" (six-groove).
Weight: 5¾ lbs. **Length:** 39" overall.
Stock: Brazilian hardwood.
Sights: Blade front, open rear adjustable for windage and elevation.
Features: Sliding wing-type safety; double extractors; red cocking indicator; receiver grooved for scope mount. Introduced 1991. Imported from Brazil by Magtech Recreational Products, Inc.
Price: About $119.95

Marlin Model 880

Marlin Model 25N Bolt-Action Repeater
Similar to Marlin 880, except walnut-finished p.g. stock, adjustable open rear sight, ramp front.
Price: **$153.55**

Marlin Model 25MN Bolt-Action Rifle
Similar to the Model 25N except chambered for 22 WMR. Has 7-shot clip magazine, 22" Micro-Groove® barrel, walnut-finished hardwood stock. Introduced 1989.
Price: **$175.40**

Marlin Model 882L

Marlin Model 883 Bolt-Action Rifle
Same as Marlin 882 except tubular magazine holds 12 rounds of 22 WMR ammunition.
Price: **$214.85**
Price: Model 883N (nickel-Teflon finish) **$266.95**

MAUSER MODEL 107 BOLT-ACTION RIFLE
Caliber: 22 LR, 5-shot magazine.
Barrel: 21.6".
Weight: 5.1 lbs. **Length:** 40" overall.
Stock: Walnut-stained beechwood with Monte Carlo, checkered grip and forend; sling swivels.
Sights: Hooded blade front, adjustable open rear.
Features: Dual extractors, 60-degree bolt throw; steel trigger guard and floorplate. Grooved receiver for scope mounting. Satin blue finish. Introduced 1992. Imported from Germany by Precisiion Imports, Inc.
Price: **$370.00**

MAUSER MODEL 201 BOLT-ACTION RIFLE
Caliber: 22 LR, 22 WMR, 5-shot magazine.
Barrel: 21".
Weight: About 6.5 lbs. **Length:** 40" overall.
Stock: Walnut-stained beech with Monte Carlo comb and cheekpiece. Checkered grip and forend.
Sights: Available with or without sights.
Features: Hammer forged medium-heavy, free-floated barrel. Bolt has two front locking lugs, dual extractors. Adjustable trigger. Safety locks bolt, sear and trigger. Receiver accepts rail mounts and is drilled and tapped for scope

MARLIN MODEL 880 BOLT-ACTION RIFLE
Caliber: 22 LR; 7-shot clip magazine.
Barrel: 22" Micro-Groove®.
Weight: 5½ lbs. **Length:** 41".
Stock: Monte Carlo American black walnut with checkered p.g. and forend. Rubber buttpad, swivel studs. Mar-Shield® finish.
Sights: Wide-Scan™ ramp front, folding semi-buckhorn rear adjustable for windage and elevation.
Features: Receiver grooved for scope mount. Introduced 1989.
Price: **$211.65**

Marlin Model 881 Bolt-Action Rifle
Same as the Marlin 880 except tubular magazine, holds 17 Long Rifle, 19 Long, 25 Short cartridges. Weighs 6 lbs.
Price: **$220.45**

Marlin Model 882 Bolt-Action Rifle
Same as the Marlin 880 except 22 WMR cal. only with 7-shot clip magazine; weight about 6 lbs. Comes with swivel studs.
Price: **$233.30**
Price: Model 882L (laminated hardwood stock) **$247.35**

MARLIN MODEL 15YN "LITTLE BUCKAROO"
Caliber: 22 S, L, LR, single shot.
Barrel: 16¼" Micro-Groove;rm.
Weight: 4¼ lbs. **Length:** 33¼" overall.
Stock: One-piece walnut-finished hardwood with Monte Carlo; Mar-Shield® finish.
Sights: Ramp front, adjustable open rear.
Features: Beginner's rifle with thumb safety, easy-load feed throat, red cocking indicator. Receiver grooved for scope mounting. Introduced 1989.
Price: **$147.85**

mounting. Introduced 1989. Imported from Germany by Precision Imports, Inc.
Price: 22 LR with sights **$549.00**
Price: As above, no sights **$529.00**
Price: 22 WMR with sights **$599.00**
Price: As above, no sights **$579.00**
Price: Luxus, 22 LR with sights **$726.00**
Price: As above, no sights **$685.00**
Price: Luxus, 22 WMR with sights **$781.00**
Price: As above, no sights **$750.00**

Navy Arms TU-KKW Training

NAVY ARMS TU-KKW TRAINING RIFLE
Caliber: 22 LR, 5-shot detachable magazine.
Barrel: 26".
Weight: 8 lbs. **Length:** 44" overall.
Stock: Walnut-stained hardwood.
Sights: Blade front, open rear adjustable for elevation; military style.
Features: Replica of the German WWII training rifle. Polished blue metal. Bayonet lug, cleaning rod, takedown disk in butt. Introduced 1991. Imported by Navy Arms.
Price: **$200.00**

Navy Arms TU-33/40 Carbine
Similar to the TU-KKW Training Rifle except has 20.75" barrel, weighs 7.5 lbs. Based on Mauser G.33/40 mountain carbine. Introduced 1992. Imported by Navy Arms.
Price: **$200.00**

Navy Arms TU-KKW Sniper Trainer
Same as the TU-KKW except comes with Type 89 2.75x scope with quick-detachable mount system. Introduced 1992. Imported by Navy Arms.
Price: **$275.00**

Norinco JW-27

NORINCO JW-27 BOLT-ACTION RIFLE
Caliber: 22 LR, 5-shot magazine.
Barrel: 22.75".
Weight: 5 lbs., 14 oz. **Length:** 41.75" overall.
Stock: Walnut-finished hardwood with checkered grip and forend.
Sights: Dovetailed bead on blade front, fully adjustable rear.
Features: Receiver grooved for scope mounting. Blued finish. Introduced 1992. Imported from China by Century International Arms.
Price: **$105.95**

REMINGTON 581-S SPORTSMAN RIFLE
Caliber: 22 S, L or LR, 5-shot clip magazine.
Barrel: 24" round.
Weight: 4¾ lbs. **Length:** 42⅜" overall.
Stock: Walnut-finished hardwood, Monte Carlo with p.g.
Sights: Bead post front, screw adjustable open rear.
Features: Sliding side safety, wide trigger, receiver grooved for tip-off scope mounts. Comes with single shot adaptor. Reintroduced 1986.
Price: About **$196.00**

NORINCO JW-15 BOLT-ACTION RIFLE
Caliber: 22 LR, 5-shot detachable magazine.
Barrel: 24".
Weight: 5 lbs., 12 oz. **Length:** 41¾" overall.
Stock: Walnut-stained hardwood.
Sights: Hooded blade front, open rear drift adjustable for windage.
Features: Polished blue finish; sling swivels; wing-type safety. Introduced 1991. Imported by Interarms, Navy Arms.
Price: About **$110.00**

NORINCO TYPE EM-332 BOLT-ACTION RIFLE
Caliber: 22 LR, 5-shot magazine.
Barrel: 18.5".
Weight: 4.5 lbs. **Length:** 41.5" overall.
Stock: Hardwood.
Sights: Blade front on ramp, open adjustable rear.
Features: Has magazine holder on side of butt that holds two extra magazines. Blue finish. Introduced 1990. Imported from China by China Sports, Inc.
Price: . . . . **NA**

Remington 40-XR Custom

REMINGTON 40-XR RIMFIRE CUSTOM SPORTER
Caliber: 22 LR.
Barrel: 24".
Weight: 10 lbs. **Length:** 42½" overall.
Stock: Full-sized walnut, checkered p.g. and forend.
Sights: None furnished; drilled and tapped for scope mounting.
Features: Custom Shop gun. Duplicates Model 700 centerfire rifle.
Price: Grade I **$2,186.00**

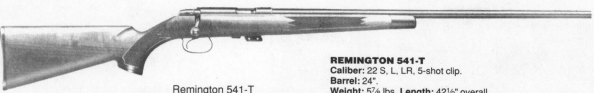

Remington 541-T

REMINGTON 541-T
Caliber: 22 S, L, LR, 5-shot clip.
Barrel: 24".
Weight: 5⅞ lbs. **Length:** 42½" overall.
Stock: Walnut, cut-checkered p.g. and forend. Satin finish.
Sights: None. Drilled and tapped for scope mounts.
Features: Clip repeater. Thumb safety. Reintroduced 1986.
Price: About **$356.00**

CONSULT
SHOOTER'S MARKETPLACE
Page 225, This Issue

Ruger K77/22RSP

RUGER 77/22 RIMFIRE BOLT-ACTION RIFLE
Caliber: 22 LR, 10-shot rotary magazine; 22 WMR, 9-shot rotary magazine.
Barrel: 20".
Weight: About 5¾ lbs. **Length:** 39¾" overall.
Stock: Checkered American walnut or injection-moulded fiberglass-reinforced Du Pont Zytel with Xenoy inserts in forend and grip, stainless sling swivels.
Sights: Brass bead front, adjustable folding leaf rear or plain barrel with 1" Ruger rings.
Features: Mauser-type action uses Ruger's 10-shot rotary magazine. Three-position safety, simplified bolt stop, patented bolt locking system. Uses the dual screw barrel attachment system of the 10/22 rifle. Integral scope mount-

ing system with 1" Ruger rings. Blued model introduced in 1983. Stainless steel model and blued model with the synthetic stock introduced in 1989.
Price: 77/22R (no sights, rings, walnut stock) **$402.00**
Price: 77/22RS (open sights, rings, walnut stock) **$424.00**
Price: 77/22RP (no sights, rings, synthetic stock) **$330.75**
Price: 77/22RSP (open sights, rings, synthetic stock) **$353.00**
Price: K77/22RP (stainless, no sights, rings, synthetic stock) . . . **$397.00**
Price: K77/22RSP (stainless, open sights, rings, synthetic stock) . . **$419.00**
Price: 77/22RM (22 WMR, blue, walnut stock) **$402.00**
Price: K77/22RSMP (22 WMR, stainless, open sights, rings, synthetic stock) **$445.20**
Price: K77/22RMP (22 WMR, stainless, synthetic stock) **$419.00**
Price: 77/22RSM (22 WMR, blue, open sights, rings, walnut stock) . **$424.00**

Includes models for classic American and ISU target competition and other sporting and competitive shooting.

ANSCHUTZ 64-MS, 64-MS LEFT SILHOUETTE
Caliber: 22 LR, single shot.
Barrel: 21½", medium heavy; ⅞" diameter.
Weight: 8 lbs. **Length:** 39½" overall.
Stock: Walnut-finished hardwood, silhouette-type.
Sights: None furnished. Receiver drilled and tapped for scope mounting.
Features: Uses Match 64 action. Designed for metallic silhouette competition. Stock has stippled checkering, contoured thumb groove with Wundhammer swell. Two-stage #5091 trigger. Slide safety locks sear and bolt. Introduced 1980. Imported from Germany by Precision Sales International.
Price: 64-MS $889.00
Price: 64-MS Left $948.00

ANSCHUTZ 1827B BIATHLON RIFLE
Caliber: 22 LR, 5-shot magazine.
Barrel: 21½".
Weight: 8½ lbs. with sights. **Length:** 42½" overall.
Stock: Walnut-finished hardwood; cheekpiece, stippled pistol grip and forend.
Sights: Globe front specially designed for Biathlon shooting, micrometer rear with hinged snow cap.
Features: Uses Match 54 action and nine-way adjustable trigger; adjustable wooden buttplate, Biathlon butthook, adjustable hand-stop rail. **Special Order Only.** Introduced 1982. Imported from Germany by Precision Sales International.
Price: Right-hand $2,284.00
Price: With Fortner straight-pull bolt $3,550.00
Price: As above, left-hand $3,880.00

ANSCHUTZ 1808D RT SUPER MATCH 54 TARGET
Caliber: 22 LR, single shot.
Barrel: 32½".
Weight: 9.4 lbs. **Length:** 50½" overall.
Stock: Walnut-finished European hardwood. Heavy beavertail forend; adjustable cheekpiece and buttplate. Stippled grip and forend.

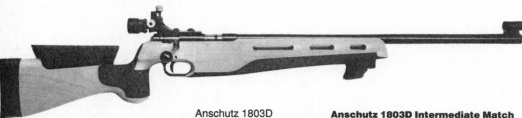

Anschutz 1803D

ANSCHUTZ 1911 MATCH RIFLE
Caliber: 22 LR, single shot.
Barrel: 27¼" round (1" dia.).
Weight: 11 lbs. **Length:** 46" overall.
Stock: Walnut-finished European hardwood; American prone style with Monte Carlo, cast-off cheekpiece, checkered p.g., beavertail forend with swivel rail and adjustable swivel, adjustable rubber buttplate.
Sights: None. Receiver grooved for Anschutz sights (extra). Scope blocks.
Features: Two-stage #5018 trigger adjustable from 2.1 to 8.6 oz. Extremely fast lock time. Imported from Germany by Precision Sales International.
Price: Right-hand, no sights $2,049.00
Price: M1911-L (true left-hand action and stock) $2,188.00

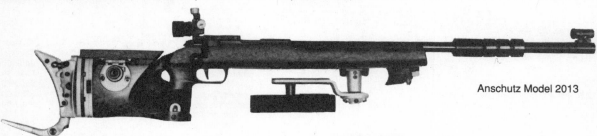

ANSCHUTZ SUPER MATCH 54 TARGET MODEL 2013
Caliber: 22 LR.
Barrel: 19.75" (26" with tube installed).
Weight: 12.5 lbs. **Length:** NA.
Stock: European walnut; target adjustable.

ANSCHUTZ 1403B BIATHLON RIFLE
Caliber: 22 LR, 5-shot magazine.
Barrel: 21½".
Weight: 8½ lbs. **Length:** 42½" overall.
Stock: Blonde-finished European hardwood. Stippled pistol grip.
Sights: Globe front with snow cap and muzzle cover, optional micrometer peep rear with spring-hinged snow cap.
Features: Uses Match 64 Target action with three-way adjustable two-stage trigger; slide safety. Comes with five magazines. Adjustable buttplate. Introduced 1991. Imported from Germany by Precision Sales International.
Price: $997.50

ANSCHUTZ 1903D MATCH RIFLE
Caliber: 22 LR, single shot.
Barrel: 25", ¾" diameter.
Weight: 8.6 lbs. **Length:** 43¾" overall.
Stock: Walnut-finished hardwood with adjustable cheekpiece; stippled grip and forend.
Sights: None furnished.
Features: Uses Anschutz Match 64 action and #5091 two-stage trigger. A medium weight rifle for intermediate and advanced Junior Match competition. Introduced 1987. Imported from Germany by Precision Sales International.
Price: Right-hand $1,049.00
Price: Left-hand $1,115.00
Price: #6823 sight set $266.00

Sights: None furnished. Grooved for scope mounting.
Features: Designed for Running Target competition. Nine-way adjustable single-stage trigger, slide safety. Introduced 1991. Imported from Germany by Precision Sales International.
Price: Right-hand $1,729.00

Anschutz 1803D Intermediate Match
Similar to the Model 1903D except has blonde-finished European hardwood stock, buttplate and cheekpiece have fewer adjustments. Takes Anschutz #6825 sight set (optional). Weight is 9.5 lbs. Introduced 1991.
Price: $1,012.00
Price: #6825 sight set $246.00

Anschutz Super Match 54 Target Model 2007
Similar to the Model 2013 except has ISU Standard design European walnut stock. Sights optional. Introduced 1992. Imported from Germany by Precision Sales International.
Price: $2,526.00

Anschutz Model 2013

Sights: Optional.
Features: Improved Super Match 54 action, #5018 trigger give fastest consistent lock time for a production target rifle. Barrel is micro-honed; trigger has nine point of adjustment, two stages. Slide safety. Comes with test target. Introduced 1992. Imported from Germany by Precision Sales International.
Price: $3,577.00

CAUTION: PRICES CHANGE, CHECK AT GUNSHOP.

Anschutz 1913

Anschutz 1910 Super Match II
Similar to the Super Match 1913 rifle except has a stock of European hardwood with tapered forend and deep receiver area. Hand and palm rests not included. Uses Match 54 action. Adjustable hook buttplate and cheekpiece. Sights not included. Introduced 1982. Imported from Germany by Precision Sales International.
Price: Right-hand **$2,589.00**
Price: Left-hand **$2,767.00**

Anschutz 1913 Super Match Rifle
Same as the Model 1911 except European walnut International-type stock with adjustable cheekpiece, adjustable aluminum hook buttplate, adjustable hand stop, weight 15½ lbs., 46" overall. Imported from Germany by Precision Sales International.
Price: Right-hand, no sights **$2,899.00**
Price: M1913-L (left-hand action and stock) **$3,094.00**

Anschutz 1907 Match Rifle
Same action as Model 1913 but with ⅞" diameter 26" barrel. Length is 44½" overall, weight 10 lbs. Blonde wood finish with vented forend. Designed for ISU requirements; suitable for NRA matches.
Price: Right-hand, no sights **$1,739.00**
Price: M1907-L (true left-hand action and stock) **$1,849.00**

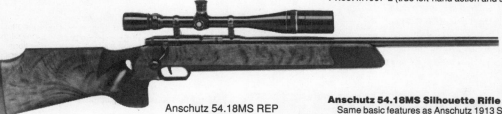

Anschutz 54.18MS REP

Anschutz 54.18MS REP Deluxe Silhouette Rifle
Same basic action and trigger specifications as the Anschutz 1913 Super Match but with removable 5-shot clip magazine, 22" barrel extendable to 30" using optional extension and weight set. Receiver drilled and tapped for scope mounting. Silhouette stock with thumbhole grip is of fiberglass with walnut wood Fibergrain finish. Introduced 1990. Imported from Germany by Precision Sales International.
Price: 54.18MS REP Deluxe **$1,789.00**
Price: 54.18MS Standard with fiberglass stock **$1,999.00**

Anschutz 54.18MS Silhouette Rifle
Same basic features as Anschutz 1913 Super Match but with special metallic silhouette European hardwood stock and two-stage trigger. Has 22" barrel; receiver drilled and tapped.
Price: **$1,465.00**
Price: 54.18MSL (true left-hand version of above) **$1,539.00**

BEEMAN/HW 660 MATCH RIFLE
Caliber: 22 LR.
Barrel: 26".
Weight: 10.7 lbs. **Length:** 45.3" overall.
Stock: Match-type walnut with adjustable cheekpiece and buttplate.
Sights: Globe front, match aperture rear.
Features: Adjustable match trigger; stippled p.g. and forend; forend accessory rail. Imported from Germany by Beeman. Introduced 1988.
Price: **$889.50**

Beeman/FWB 2600

BEEMAN/FEINWERKBAU 2600 TARGET RIFLE
Caliber: 22 LR, single shot.
Barrel: 26.3".
Weight: 10.6 lbs. **Length:** 43.7" overall.
Stock: Laminated hardwood and hard rubber.

Sights: Globe front with Interchangeable Inserts; micrometer match aperture rear.
Features: Identical smallbore companion to the Beeman/FWB 600 air rifle. Free floating barrel. Match trigger has fingertip weight adjustment dial. Introduced 1986. Imported from Germany by Beeman.
Price: Right-hand **$1,398.00**
Price: Left-hand **$1,575.00**
Price: Free rifle, right-hand **$1,998.00**
Price: Free rifle, left-hand **$2,150.00**

Beeman/HW 60

BEEMAN/WEIHRAUCH HW 60 TARGET RIFLE
Caliber: 22 LR, single shot.
Barrel: 26.8".

Weight: 10.8 lbs. **Length:** 45.7" overall.
Stock: Walnut with adjustable buttplate. Stippled p.g. and forend. Rail with adjustable swivel.
Sights: Hooded ramp front, match-type aperture rear.
Features: Adjustable match trigger with push-button safety. Left-hand version also available. Introduced 1981. Imported from Germany by Beeman.
Price: Right-hand **$798.00**
Price: Left-hand **$878.95**

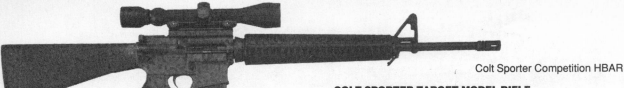

Colt Sporter Competition HBAR

COLT SPORTER TARGET MODEL RIFLE

Caliber: 223 Rem., 5-shot magazine.
Barrel: 20".
Weight: 7.5 lbs. **Length:** 39" overall.
Stock: Composition stock, grip, forend.
Sights: Post front, aperture rear adjustable for windage and elevation.
Features: Five-round detachable box magazine, standard-weight barrel, flash suppressor, sling swivels. Has forward bolt assist. Military matte black finish. Model introduced 1991.
Price: **$879.95**

Colt Sporter Competition HBAR Range Selected Rifle

Same as the Sporter Competition HBAR #R6700 except is range selected for accuracy, and comes with 3-9x rubber armored scope, scope mount, carrying handle with iron sights, Cordura nylon carrying case. Introduced 1992.
Price: Model R6700CH **$1,459.95**

Colt Sporter Match HBAR Rifle

Similar to the Target Model except has heavy barrel, 800-meter rear sight adjustable for windage and elevation. Introduced 1991.
Price: **$919.95**

Colt Sporter Competition HBAR Rifle

Similar to the Sporter Target except has flat-top receiver with integral Weaver-type base for scope mounting. Counter-bored muzzle, 1:9" rifling twist. Introduced 1991.
Price: Model R6700 . . . . **$969.95**

COOPER ARMS MODEL TRP-1 ISU STANDARD RIFLE

Caliber: 22 LR, single shot.
Barrel: 24".
Weight: 8.5 lbs. **Length:** 40.5" overall.
Stock: Walnut, competition style with adjustable cheekpiece and buttpad.

Sights: None furnished; accepts Anschutz sight packages.
Features: Action has three front locking lugs, 45-degree bolt rotation; fully adjustable single stage trigger; hand-lapped match grade Wiseman/McMillan barrel. Introduced 1991. Made in U.S. by Cooper Arms.
Price: **$795.00**

Federal Ordnance M14SA

FINNISH LION STANDARD TARGET RIFLE

Caliber: 22 LR, single shot.
Barrel: 27⅝".
Weight: 10½ lbs. **Length:** 44⁹⁄₁₆" overall.
Stock: French walnut, target style.
Sights: Globe front, International micrometer rear.
Features: Optional accessories: palm rest, hook buttplate, forend stop and swivel assembly, buttplate extension, five front sight aperture inserts, three rear sight apertures, Allen wrench. Adjustable trigger. Imported from Finland by Mandall Shooting Supplies.
Price: Without sights **$695.00**
Price: Sight set **$195.00**

HAENEL MODEL 900 MATCH RIFLE

Caliber: 22 LR.
Barrel: 25.9".
Weight: 10.8 lbs. **Length:** 44.6" overall.
Stock: Match-type beech with stippled grip and forend, adjustable comb and

FEDERAL ORDNANCE M14SA TARGET RIFLE

Caliber: 7.62mm NATO (308 Win.).
Barrel: 22".
Weight: 9 lbs., 8 oz. **Length:** 48" overall.
Stock: Fiberglass or wood.
Sights: G.I., fully adjustable for windage and elevation.
Features: Civilian version of the M-14 service rifle. All metal has Parkerized finish. Introduced 1988. From Federal Ordnance.
Price: With fiberglass stock **$749.95**
Price: With walnut stock, forend **$839.95**
Price: With black textured stock **$749.95**

butt pad.
Sights: Match-type globe front, fully adjustable aperture rear.
Features: Adjustable trigger; polished blue finish. Sight radius adjustable from 31.1" to 32.6". Introduced 1992. Imported from Germany by GSI, Inc.
Price: **$749.00**

Heckler & Koch PSG-1

HECKLER & KOCH PSG-1 MARKSMAN RIFLE

Caliber: 308, 5- and 20-shot magazines.
Barrel: 25.6", heavy.
Weight: 17.8 lbs. **Length:** 47.5" overall.
Stock: Matte black high impact plastic, adjustable for length, pivoting butt cap, vertically-adjustable cheekpiece; target-type pistol grip with adjustable palm shelf.

Sights: Hendsoldt 6x42 scope.
Features: Uses HK-91 action with low-noise bolt closing device; special forend with T-way rail for sling swivel or tripod. Gun comes in special foam-fitted metal transport case with tripod, two 20-shot and two 5-shot magazines, cleaning rod. Imported from Germany by Heckler & Koch, Inc. Introduced 1986.
Price: **$8,859.00**

CAUTION: PRICES CHANGE, CHECK AT GUNSHOP.

Krico Model 360S Biathlon

KRICO MODEL 360S BIATHLON RIFLE
Caliber: 22 LR, 5-shot magazine.
Barrel: 21.25".
Weight: 9.26 lbs. **Length:** 40.55" overall.
Stock: Walnut with high comb, adjustable buttplate.
Sights: Globe front, fully adjustable Diana 82 match peep rear.
Features: Straight-pull action with 17.6-oz. match trigger. Comes with five magazines (four stored in stock recess), muzzle/sight snow cap. Introduced 1991. Imported from Germany by Mandall Shooting Supplies.
Price: **$1,695.00**

KRICO MODEL 360 S2 BIATHLON RIFLE
Caliber: 22 LR, 5-shot magazine.
Barrel: 21.25".
Weight: 9 lbs., 15 oz. **Length:** 40.55" overall.
Stock: Biathlon design of black epoxy-finished walnut with pistol grip.
Sights: Globe front, fully adjustable Diana 82 match peep rear.
Features: Pistol-grip-activated action. Comes with five magazines (four stored in stock recess), muzzle/sight snow cap. Introduced 1991. Imported from Germany by Mandall Shooting Supplies.
Price: **$1,595.00**

KRICO MODEL 400 MATCH RIFLE
Caliber: 22 LR, 22 Hornet, 5-shot magazine.
Barrel: 23.2" (22 LR), 23.6" (22 Hornet).
Weight: 8.8 lbs. **Length:** 42.1" overall (22 RF).
Stock: European walnut, match type.
Sights: None furnished; receiver grooved for scope mounting.
Features: Heavy match barrel. Double-set or match trigger. Imported from Germany by Mandall Shooting Supplies.
Price: **$950.00**

KRICO MODEL 500 KRICOTRONIC MATCH RIFLE
Caliber: 22 LR, single shot.
Barrel: 23.6".
Weight: 9.4 lbs. **Length:** 42.1" overall.
Stock: European walnut, match type with adjustable butt.
Sights: Globe front, match micrometer aperture rear.
Features: Electronic ignition system for fastest possible lock time. Completely adjustable trigger. Barrel has tapered bore. Imported from Germany by Mandall Shooting Supplies.
Price: **$3,950.00**

KRICO MODEL 600 SNIPER RIFLE
Caliber: 222, 223, 22-250, 243, 308, 4-shot magazine.
Barrel: 23.6".
Weight: 9.2 lbs. **Length:** 45.2" overall.
Stock: European walnut with adjustable rubber buttplate.
Sights: None supplied; drilled and tapped for scope mounting.
Features: Match barrel with flash hider; large bolt knob; wide trigger shoe. Parkerized finish. Imported from Germany by Mandall Shooting Supplies.
Price: **$2,645.00**

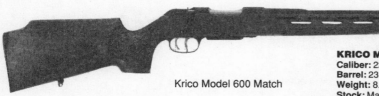

Krico Model 600 Match

KRICO MODEL 600 MATCH RIFLE
Caliber: 222, 223, 22-250, 243, 308, 5.6x50 Mag., 4-shot magazine.
Barrel: 23.6".
Weight: 8.8 lbs. **Length:** 43.3" overall.
Stock: Match stock of European walnut with cheekpiece.
Sights: None furnished; drilled and tapped for scope mounting.
Features: Match stock with vents in forend for cooling, rubber recoil pad, sling swivels. Imported from Germany by Mandall Shooting Supplies.
Price: **$1,250.00**

Lakefield Model 90B

LAKEFIELD ARMS MODEL 91T TARGET RIFLE
Caliber: 22 LR, single shot.
Barrel: 25".
Weight: 8 lbs. **Length:** 43⅝" overall.
Stock: Target-type, walnut-finished hardwood.
Sights: Target front with inserts, peep rear with ¼-minute click adjustments.
Features: Comes with shooting rail and hand stop. Also available as 5-shot repeater as Model 91-TR. Introduced 1991. Made in Canada by Lakefield Arms.
Price: Model 91T **$419.95**
Price: Model 91-TR (repeater) **$444.95**

LAKEFIELD ARMS MODEL 90B TARGET RIFLE
Caliber: 22 LR, 5-shot magazine.
Barrel: 21".
Weight: 8¼ lbs. **Length:** 39⅝" overall.
Stock: Natural finish hardwood with clip holder, carrying and shooting rails, butt hook, hand stop.
Sights: Target front with inserts, peep rear with ¼-minute click adjustments.
Features: Biathlon-style rifle with snow cap muzzle protector. Comes with five magazines. Introduced 1991. Made in Canada by Lakefield Arms.
Price: About **$519.95**

Lakefield Model 92S

Lakefield Arms Model 92S Silhouette Rifle
Similar to the Model 90B except has high-comb target-type stock of walnut-finished hardwood. Comes without sights, but receiver is drilled and tapped for scope base. Weight about 8 lbs. Introduced 1992. Made in Canada by Lakefield Arms.
Price: **$354.95**

Marlin Model 2000

MAUSER MODEL 86-SR SPECIALTY RIFLE
Caliber: 308 Win., 9-shot detachable magazine.
Barrel: 25.6", fluted, 1:12 twist.
Weight: About 10.8 lbs. **Length:** 47.7" overall.
Stock: Laminated wood, fiberglass, or special match thumbhole wood. All have rail in forend and adjustable recoil pad.
Sights: None furnished. Competition metallic sights or scope mount optional.
Features: Match barrel with muzzlebrake. Action has two front bolt locking lugs. Action bedded in stock with free-floated barrel. Match trigger adjustable as single or two-stage; fully adjustable for weight, slack, and position. Silent safety locks bolt, firing pin. Introduced 1989. Imported from Germany by Precision Imports, Inc.
Price: With fiberglass stock **$4,400.00**
Price: With match thumbhole stock **$4,650.00**

McMILLAN COMBO M-87/M-88 50-CALIBER RIFLE
Caliber: 50 BMG, single shot.
Barrel: 29", with muzzlebrake.
Weight: About 21½ lbs. **Length:** 53" overall.
Stock: McMillan fiberglass.
Sights: None furnished.
Features: Right-handed McMillan stainless steel receiver, chromemoly barrel with 1:15 twist. Introduced 1987. From McMillan Gunworks, Inc.
Price: **$4,000.00**
Price: M-87R (5-shot repeater) "Combo" **$4,270.00**

MARLIN MODEL 2000 TARGET RIFLE
Caliber: 22 LR, single shot.
Barrel: 22" heavy, Micro-Groove® rifling, match chamber, recessed muzzle.
Weight: 8 lbs. **Length:** 41" overall.
Stock: High-comb fiberglass/Kevlar with stipple finish grip and forend.
Sights: Hooded Lyman front with seven aperture inserts, fully adjustable Lyman target rear peep.
Features: Stock finished with royal blue enamel. Buttplate adjustable for length of pull, height and angle. Aluminum forend rail with stop and quick-detachable swivel. Two-stage target trigger; red cocking indicator. Five-shot adaptor kit available. Introduced 1991. From Marlin.
Price: **$543.75**

McMILLAN NATIONAL MATCH RIFLE
Caliber: 7mm-08, 308, 5-shot magazine.
Barrel: 24", stainless steel.
Weight: About 11 lbs. (std. bbl.). **Length:** 43" overall.
Stock: Modified ISU fiberglass with adjustable buttplate.
Sights: Barrel band and Tompkins front; no rear sight furnished.
Features: McMillan repeating action with clip slot, Canjar trigger. Match-grade barrel. Available in right-hand only. Fibergrain stock, sight installation, special machining and triggers optional. Introduced 1989. From McMillan Gunworks, Inc.
Price: **$2,598.00**

McMillan Long Range

McMILLAN 300 PHOENIX LONG RANGE RIFLE
Caliber: 300 Phoenix.
Barrel: 28".
Weight: 12.5 lbs. **Length:** NA.
Stock: Fiberglass with adjustable cheekpiece, adjustable butt plate.
Sights: None furnished; comes with rings and bases.
Features: Matte black finish; textured stock. Introduced 1992. Made in U.S. by McMillan Gunworks, Inc.
Price: **$2,995.00**

McMILLAN LONG RANGE RIFLE
Caliber: 300 Win. Mag., 7mm Rem. Mag., 300 Phoenix, 338 Lapua, single shot.
Barrel: 26", stainless steel, match-grade.
Weight: 14 lbs. **Length:** 46½" overall.
Stock: Fiberglass with adjustable buttplate and cheekpiece. Adjustable for length of pull, drop, cant and cast-off.
Sights: Barrel band and Tompkins front; no rear sight furnished.
Features: Uses McMillan solid bottom single shot action and Canjar trigger. Barrel twist 1:12. Introduced 1989. From McMillan Gunworks, Inc.
Price: **$2,598.00**

McMillan M-86

McMILLAN M-89 SNIPER RIFLE
Caliber: 308 Win., 5-shot magazine.
Barrel: 28" (with suppressor).
Weight: 15 lbs., 4 oz.
Stock: McMillan fiberglass; adjustable for length; recoil pad.
Sights: None furnished. Drilled and tapped for scope mounting.
Features: Uses McMillan repeating action. Comes with bipod. Introduced 1990. From McMillan Gunworks, Inc.
Price: Standard (non-suppressed) **$2,200.00**

McMILLAN M-86 SNIPER RIFLE
Caliber: 308, 30-06, 4-shot magazine; 300 Win. Mag., 300 Phoenix, 3-shot magazine.
Barrel: 24", McMillan match-grade in heavy contour.
Weight: 11¼ lbs. (308), 11½ lbs. (30-06, 300). **Length:** 43½" overall.
Stock: Specially designed McHale fiberglass stock with textured grip and forend, recoil pad.
Sights: None furnished.
Features: Uses McMillan repeating action. Comes with bipod. Matte black finish. Sling swivels. Introduced 1989. From McMillan Gunworks, Inc.
Price: **$1,895.00**
Price: 300 Phoenix **$2,445.00**

Olympic International

Olympic Arms International Match Rifle
Similar to the Ultramatch Rifle except comes with globe front sight, fully adjustable aperture rear, standard trigger set at 4.5 to 5 lbs pull. Introduced 1991. Made in U.S. by Olympic Arms, Inc.
Price: **$1,179.95**

OLYMPIC ARMS ULTRAMATCH RIFLE
Caliber: 223, 30-shot magazine.
Barrel: 20", stainless steel; 1:10" twist, 1:8.5" on request.
Weight: 9 lbs. (add 1¾ lbs for steel handguard). **Length:** 39½" overall.
Stock: Black composition; match aluminum or steel handguard.
Sights: None supplied; includes scope mounts.
Features: Uses international match AR-15-type upper receiver; set trigger; Max-hard surfacing on upper and lower receivers. Introduced 1987. Made in U.S. by Olympic Arms, Inc.
Price: **$1,152.95**

Olympic Service Match

OLYMPIC ARMS MULTIMATCH RIFLE
Caliber: 223, 30-shot magazine.
Barrel: 16" Ultramatch; free-floated with aluminum handguard.
Weight: 7½ lbs. **Length:** 35½" overall.
Stock: Composition AR-15A2 butt, or collapsible aluminum buttstock.
Sights: Choice of E-2 fully adjustable system or International Match upper receiver for low mounting of scope.
Features: Built on AR-15-type action. Has stainless steel free-floating barrel with aluminum handguard. Introduced 1991. Made in U.S. by Olympic Arms, Inc.
Price: **$916.95**

OLYMPIC ARMS SERVICE MATCH RIFLE
Caliber: 223, 30-shot magazine.
Barrel: 20" Ultramatch.
Weight: 8¾ lbs. **Length:** 39½" overall.
Stock: Black composition A2 standard stock.
Sights: Post front, fully adjustable aperture rear.
Features: Conforms to all DCM standards. Uses Olympic Arms E2 upper receiver, lined A2-style handguards, standard trigger, choice of A1 or A2 flash suppressor. Introduced 1989. Made in U.S. by Olympic Arms, Inc.
Price: **$899.95**

Parker-Hale M-85

PARKER-HALE M-85 SNIPER RIFLE
Caliber: 308 Win., 10-shot magazine.
Barrel: 24¼".
Weight: 12½ lbs (with scope). **Length:** 45" overall.
Stock: McMillan fiberglass (several color patterns available).
Sights: Post front adjustable for windage, fold-down rear adjustable for elevation.
Features: Comes with quick-detachable bipod, palm stop with rail; sling swivels; matte finish. Made by Gibbs Rifle Co., distributed by Navy Arms.
Price: Less scope **$1,950.00**

PARKER-HALE M-87 TARGET RIFLE
Caliber: 308 Win., 243, 6.5x55, 308, 30-06, 300 Win. Mag. (other calibers on request), 5-shot detachable box magazine.
Barrel: 26" heavy.
Weight: About 10 lbs. **Length:** 45" overall.
Stock: Walnut target-style, adjustable for length of pull; solid buttpad; accessory rail with hand-stop. Deeply stippled grip and forend.
Sights: None furnished. Receiver dovetailed for Parker-Hale "Roll-Off" scope mounts.
Features: Mauser-style action with large bolt knob. Parkerized finish. Introduced 1987. Made by Gibbs Rifle Co., distributed by Navy Arms.
Price: **$1,500.00**

Quality Parts Shorty E-2 Carbine
Same as the XM15-E2 Target Model except has 16" barrel and telescoping buttstock. Standard sights. From Quality Parts Co.
Price: **$690.00**
Price: E-2 Carbine Dissipator (as above except has M-16A2 handguard for better cooling), E-2 sight, standard or telescoping stock **$770.00**
Price: As above with A-1 sights, standard or telescoping stock . . . **$720.00**

QUALITY PARTS V MATCH RIFLE
Caliber: 223, 30-shot magazine.
Barrel: 20", 24", 26"; 1:9" twist.
Weight: NA. **Length:** NA.
Stock: Composition.
Sights: None furnished; comes with scope mount base installed.
Features: Hand-built match gun. Barrel is .950" outside diameter with counterbored crown: integral flash suppressor; upper receiver has brass deflector; free-floating steel handguard accepts laser sight, flashlight, bipod; 5-lb. trigger pull. From Quality Parts Co.
Price: From **$1,200.00**

> Consult our Directory pages for the location of firms mentioned.

QUALITY PARTS XM-15-E2 TARGET MODEL RIFLE
Caliber: 223, 30-shot magazine.
Barrel: 20", 24", 26"; 1:7" or 1:9" twist; heavy.
Weight: NA. **Length:** NA.
Stock: Black composition.
Sights: Adjustable post front, adjustable aperture rear.
Features: Patterned after Colt M-16A2. Chrome-lined barrel with manganese phosphate exterior. Has E-2 lower receiver with push-pin. From Quality Parts Co.
Price: 20" match heavy barrel **$740.00**
Price: 24" match heavy barrel **$750.00**
Price: 26" match heavy barrel **$760.00**

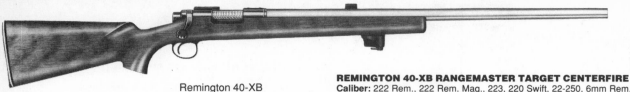

Remington 40-XB

REMINGTON 40-XC KS NATIONAL MATCH COURSE RIFLE
Caliber: 7.62 NATO, 5-shot.
Barrel: 24", stainless steel.
Weight: 11 lbs. without sights. **Length:** 43½" overall.
Stock: Kevlar, position-style, with palm swell, handstop.
Sights: None furnished.
Features: Designed to meet the needs of competitive shooters firing the national match courses. Position-style stock, top loading clip slot magazine, anti-bind bolt and receiver, bright stainless steel barrel. Meets all ISU Army Rifle specifications. Adjustable buttplate, adjustable trigger.
Price: About **$1,281.00**

REMINGTON 40-XBBR KS
Caliber: 22 BR Rem., 222 Rem., 222 Rem. Mag., 223, 6mmx47, 6mm BR Rem., 7.62 NATO (308 Win.).
Barrel: 20" (light varmint class), 24" (heavy varmint class).
Weight: 7¼ lbs. (light varmint class); 12 lbs. (heavy varmint class).
Length: 38" (20" bbl.), 42" (24" bbl.).

REMINGTON 40-XB RANGEMASTER TARGET CENTERFIRE
Caliber: 222 Rem., 222 Rem. Mag., 223, 220 Swift, 22-250, 6mm Rem., 243, 25-06, 7mm BR Rem., 7mm Rem. Mag., 30-338 (30-7mm Rem. Mag.), 300 Win. Mag., 7.62 NATO (308 Win.), 30-06, single shot.
Barrel: 27¼".
Weight: 11¼ lbs. **Length:** 47" overall.
Stock: American walnut or Kevlar with high comb and beavertail forend stop. Rubber non-slip buttplate.
Sights: None. Scope blocks installed.
Features: Adjustable trigger pull. Receiver drilled and tapped for sights.
Price: Standard s.s., stainless steel barrel, about **$1,056.00**
Price: Left-hand **$1,114.00**
Price: Model 40-XB KS **$1,205.00**
Price: Left-hand **$1,264.00**
Price: Extra for repeater model (KS) **$88.00**
Price: Extra for 2-oz. trigger **$147.00**

Stock: Kevlar.
Sights: None. Supplied with scope blocks.
Features: Unblued stainless steel barrel, trigger adjustable from 1½ lbs. to 3½ lbs. Special 2-oz. trigger at extra cost. Scope and mounts extra.
Price: With Kevlar stock **$1,281.00**
Price: Extra for 2-oz. trigger, about **$147.00**

Remington 40-XR KS

REMINGTON 40-XR KS RIMFIRE POSITION RIFLE
Caliber: 22 LR, single shot.
Barrel: 24", heavy target.
Weight: 10 lbs. **Length:** 43" overall.
Stock: Kevlar. Position-style with front swivel block on forend guide rail.
Sights: Drilled and tapped. Furnished with scope blocks.
Features: Meets all ISU specifications. Deep forend, buttplate vertically adjustable, wide adjustable trigger.
Price: About **$1,205.00**

Springfield M-1A Match

SPRINGFIELD ARMORY M-21 LAW ENFORCEMENT
Caliber: 243, 7mm-08, 308 Win.
Barrel: 22", Douglas heavy, air-gauged.
Weight: 11.81 lbs. **Length:** 44¼" overall.
Stock: Heavy walnut with adjustable comb, ventilated recoil pad. Glass bedded.
Sights: National Match front and rear.
Features: Refinement of the standard M-1A rifle. Has specially knurled shoulder for new figure-eight operating rod guide. Comes with one 20-round magazine. Introduced 1987. From Springfield Armory, Inc.
Price: **$2,101.00**

SPRINGFIELD ARMORY M-1A SUPER MATCH
Caliber: 243, 7mm-08, 308 Win.
Barrel: 22", heavy Douglas Premium, or Hart stainless steel.
Weight: About 10 lbs. **Length:** 44.31" overall.
Stock: Heavy walnut competition stock with longer pistol grip, contoured area behind the rear sight, thicker butt and forend, glass bedded.
Sights: National Match front and rear.
Features: Has figure-eight-style operating rod guide. Introduced 1987. From Springfield Armory, Inc.
Price: About **$1,799.00**

Steyr-Mannlicher SSG P-I

STEYR-MANNLICHER SSG P-I RIFLE
Caliber: 243, 308 Win.
Barrel: 25.6".
Weight: 8.6 lbs. **Length:** 44.5" overall.

Stock: ABS Cycolac synthetic half-stock. Removable spacers in butt adjusts length of pull from 12¾" to 14".
Sights: Hooded blade front, folding leaf rear.
Features: Parkerized finish. Choice of interchangeable single- or double-set triggers. Detachable 5-shot rotary magazine (10-shot optional). Receiver grooved for Steyr and Bock Quick Detach mounts. Imported from Austria by GSI, Inc.
Price: Synthetic half-stock **$1,634.00**
Price: SSG-PII (as above except has large bolt knob, heavy bbl., no sights, forend rail). **$1,783.00**

CAUTION: PRICES CHANGE, CHECK AT GUNSHOP.

Steyr-Mannlicher SSG P-IV

STEYR-MANNLICHER MATCH UIT RIFLE
Caliber: 308 Win., 10-shot magazine.
Barrel: 25.5".
Weight: 10 lbs. **Length:** 44" overall.
Stock: Walnut with stippled grip and forend. Special UIT Match design.
Sights: Walther globe front, Walther peep rear.
Features: Double-pull trigger adjustable for let-off point, slack, weight of first-stage pull, release force and length; buttplate adjustable for height and length. Meets UIT specifications. Introduced 1984. Imported from Austria by GSI, Inc.
Price: **$4,562.00**

Steyr-Mannlicher SSG P-IV Rifle
Similar to the SSG P-I except has 16.75" heavy barrel with flash hider. Available in 308 only. ABS Cycolac synthetic stock in green or black. Introduced 1992. Imported from Austria by GSI, Inc.
Price: **$2,082.00**

Steyr-Mannlicher SSG P-III Rifle
Similar to the SSG P-I except has 26" heavy barrel, diopter match sight bases. Available in 308 only. Has H-S Precision Pro-Series stock (black only). Introduced 1992. Imported from Austria by GSI, Inc.
Price: **$2,529.00**

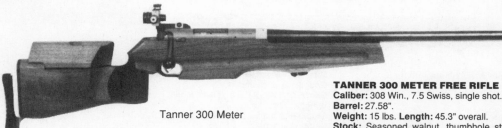

Tanner 300 Meter

TANNER STANDARD UIT RIFLE
Caliber: 308, 7.5mm Swiss, 10-shot.
Barrel: 25.9".
Weight: 10.5 lbs. **Length:** 40.6" overall.
Stock: Match style of seasoned nutwood with accessory rail; coarsely stippled pistol grip; high cheekpiece; vented forend.
Sights: Globe front with interchangeable inserts, Tanner micrometer-diopter rear with adjustable aperture.
Features: Two locking lug revolving bolt encloses case head. Trigger adjustable from ½ to 6½ lbs.; match trigger optional. Comes with 300-meter test target. Imported from Switzerland by Mandall Shooting Supplies. Introduced 1984.
Price: About **$4,700.00**

TANNER 50 METER FREE RIFLE
Caliber: 22 LR, single shot.
Barrel: 27.7".
Weight: 13.9 lbs. **Length:** 44.4" overall.
Stock: Seasoned walnut with palm rest, accessory rail, adjustable hook buttplate.
Sights: Globe front with interchangeable inserts, Tanner micrometer-diopter rear with adjustable aperture.
Features: Bolt action with externally adjustable set trigger. Supplied with 50-meter test target. Imported from Switzerland by Mandall Shooting Supplies. Introduced 1984.
Price: About **$4,000.00**

TANNER 300 METER FREE RIFLE
Caliber: 308 Win., 7.5 Swiss, single shot.
Barrel: 27.58".
Weight: 15 lbs. **Length:** 45.3" overall.
Stock: Seasoned walnut, thumbhole style, with accessory rail, palm rest, adjustable hook butt.
Sights: Globe front with interchangeable inserts, Tanner-design micrometer-diopter rear with adjustable aperture.
Features: Three-lug revolving-lock bolt design; adjustable set trigger; short firing pin travel; supplied with 300-meter test target. Imported from Switzerland by Mandall Shooting Supplies. Introduced 1984.
Price: About **$4,900.00**

VOERE MODEL 2185 MATCH RIFLE
Caliber: 308, 30-06, 7x64, 5-shot magazine.
Barrel: 20".
Weight: 11 lbs. **Length:** 45.2" overall.
Stock: Match-type laminated wood with glass bedding. Adjustable cheekpiece and buttplate.
Sights: Hooded post front, aperture rear.
Features: Gas-operated action; free-floating barrel; blue finish. Introduced 1992. Imported from Austria by Rahn Gun Works, Inc.
Price: . . . . **NA**

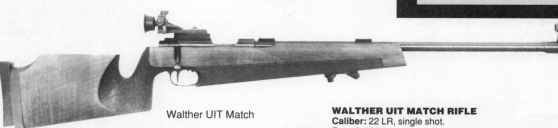

Walther UIT Match

WICHITA SILHOUETTE RIFLE
Caliber: All standard calibers with maximum overall cartridge length of 2.800".
Barrel: 24" free-floated Matchgrade.
Weight: About 9 lbs.
Stock: Metallic gray fiberthane with ventilated rubber recoil pad.
Sights: None furnished. Drilled and tapped for scope mounts.
Features: Legal for all NRA competitions. Single shot action. Fluted bolt, 2-oz. Canjar trigger; glass-bedded stock. Introduced 1983. From Wichita Arms.
Price: **$2,250.00**
Price: Left-hand **$2,400.00**

WALTHER UIT MATCH RIFLE
Caliber: 22 LR, single shot.
Barrel: 25½".
Weight: 16.5 lbs. **Length:** 46" overall.
Stock: Walnut, adjustable for length and drop; forend guide rail for sling or palm rest.
Sights: Globe-type front, fully adjustable aperture rear. Scope mount bases included.
Features: Conforms to both NRA and UIT requirements. Fully adjustable trigger. Left-hand stock available on special order. Imported from Germany by Interarms.
Price: **$1,400.00**

Includes a wide variety of sporting guns and guns suitable for various competitions.

American Arms/Franchi 48/AL

AMERICAN ARMS/FRANCHI BLACK MAGIC 48/AL
Gauge: 12 or 20, 2¾" chamber.
Barrel: 24" rifled, 24", 26", 28" (Franchoke Imp. Cyl., Mod., Full choke tubes).
Vent. rib.
Weight: 5.2 lbs. (20-gauge). **Length:** NA
Stock: 14¼"x1⅝"x2½". Walnut with checkered grip and forend.
Features: Recoil-operated action. Chrome-lined bore; cross-bolt safety. Imported from Italy by American Arms, Inc.
Price: $579.00
Price: 12-ga., 24" rifled slug, open sights $599.00

Benelli M1 Super 90 Field

Benelli M1 Super 90 Slug Shotgun
Similar to the M1 Super 90 Field except comes with 19¾" barrel (Cyl. choke) giving 41" overall length and weight of 6 lbs., 13 oz. Has 3" chamber, 7-shot magazine capacity, matte black finish. Standard buttstock of high-impact polymer. Rifle sights standard, ghost ring sighting system available. Imported from Italy by Hecker & Koch, Inc.
Price: With rifle sights $699.00
Price: With ghost ring sight system $749.00

BENELLI M1 SUPER 90 FIELD AUTO SHOTGUN
Gauge: 12, 3" chamber.
Barrel: 21", 24", 26", 28" (choke tubes).
Weight: 7 lbs., 4 oz.
Stock: High impact polymer.
Sights: Metal bead front.
Features: Sporting version of the military & police gun. Uses the rotating Montefeltro bolt system. Ventilated rib; blue finish. Comes with set of five choke tubes. Imported from Italy by Heckler & Koch, Inc.
Price: $799.00

Benelli Montefeltro Super 90

Consult our Directory pages for the location of firms mentioned.

Benelli Montefeltro Super 90 Shotgun
Similar to the M1 Super 90 except has checkered walnut stock with high-gloss finish. Uses the Montefeltro rotating bolt system with a simple inertia recoil design. Full, Imp. Mod, Mod., Imp. Cyl. choke tubes. Weight is 7-7½ lbs. Finish is matte black. Introduced 1987.
Price: 21", 24", 26", 28" $799.00
Price: Left-hand, 26", 28" $849.00

BENELLI BLACK EAGLE COMPETITION AUTO SHOTGUN
Gauge: 12, 3" chamber.
Barrel: 26", 28" (Full, Mod., Imp. Cyl., Imp. Mod., Skeet choke tubes). Mid-bead sight.
Weight: 7.1 to 7.6 lbs. **Length:** 49⅝" overall (26" barrel).
Stock: European walnut with high-gloss finish. Special competition stock comes with drop adjustment kit.
Features: Uses the Montefeltro rotating bolt inertia recoil operating system with a two-piece steel/aluminum etched receiver (bright on lower, blue upper). Drop adjustment kit allows the stock to be custom fitted without modifying the stock. Black lower receiver finish, blued upper. Introduced 1989. Imported from Italy by Heckler & Koch, Inc.
Price: $1,059.00

BENELLI SUPER BLACK EAGLE SHOTGUN
Gauge: 12, 3½" chamber.
Barrel: 26", 28" (Imp. Cyl., Mod., Imp. Mod., Full choke tubes).
Weight: 7 lbs., 5 oz. **Length:** 49⅝" overall (28" barrel).
Stock: European walnut with satin or gloss finish. Adjustable for drop.
Sights: Bead front.
Features: Uses Montfeltro inertia recoil bolt system. Fires all 12-gauge shells from 2¾" to 3½" magnums. Introduced 1991. Imported from Italy by Heckler & Koch, Inc.
Price: $1,059.00

Benelli Slug Gun

Benelli Super Black Eagle Slug Gun
Similar to the Benelli Super Black Eagle except has 24" E.R. Shaw Custom rifled barrel with 3" chamber, and comes with scope mount base. Uses the Montefeltro inertia recoil bolt system. Matte-finish receiver. Weight is 7.5 lbs., overall length 45.5". Introduced 1992. Imported from Italy by Heckler & Koch, Inc.
Price: .... NA

CAUTION: PRICES CHANGE, CHECK AT GUNSHOP.

Beretta 390

BERETTA 390 FIELD AUTO SHOTGUN
Gauge: 12, 3" chamber.
Barrel: 24", 26", 28", 30", Mobilchoke choke tubes.
Weight: About 7 lbs.
Stock: Select walnut. Adjustable drop and cast.
Features: Gas-operated action with self-compensating valve allows shooting all loads without adjustment. Alloy receiver, reversible safety; chrome-plated bore; floating vent. rib. Matte-finish models for turkey/waterfowl also available. Introduced 1992. Imported from Italy by Beretta U.S.A.
Price: $775.00
Price: Model 390 Field (matte finish) $775.00

BERETTA A-303 AUTO SHOTGUN
Gauge: 20, 2¾" or 3" chamber.
Barrel: 26", 28", Mobilchoke choke tubes.
Weight: About 6½ lbs., 20-gauge; about 7½ lbs., 12-gauge.
Stock: American walnut; hand-checkered grip and forend.
Features: Gas-operated action, alloy receiver, magazine cut-off, push-button safety. Mobilchoke models come with three interchangeable flush-mounted screw-in choke tubes. Imported from Italy by Beretta U.S.A. Introduced 1983.
Price: Mobilchoke, 20-ga. $755.00
Price: 12-ga. trap with standard trap stock $735.00
Price: 12- or 20-ga., Skeet $735.00
Price: A-303 Youth Gun, 20-ga., 2¾" or 3" chamber, 24" barrel .. $735.00
Price: A-303 Sporting Clays with Mobilchoke, 12 or 20 .... $835.00

Beretta A-303 Upland Model
Similar to the field A-303 except 12- or 20-gauge, has 24" vent. rib barrel with Mobilchoke choke tubes, 2¾" chamber, straight English-style stock. Introduced 1989.
Price: $735.00

BERETTA MODEL 1201F AUTO SHOTGUN
Gauge: 12, 3" chamber.
Barrel: 24", 26", 28" vent. rib with Mobilchoke choke tubes.
Weight: 7 lbs., 4 oz.
Stock: Special strengthened technopolymer, matte black finish. Adjustable butt

and recoil pad.
Features: Resists abrasion and adverse effects of water, salt and other damaging materials associated with tough field conditions. Imported from Italy by Beretta U.S.A. Introduced 1988.
Price: $625.00

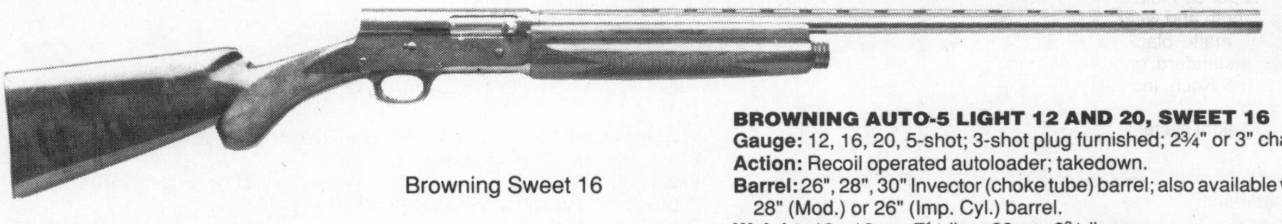

Browning Sweet 16

BROWNING AUTO-5 LIGHT 12 AND 20, SWEET 16
Gauge: 12, 16, 20, 5-shot; 3-shot plug furnished; 2¾" or 3" chamber.
Action: Recoil operated autoloader; takedown.
Barrel: 26", 28", 30" Invector (choke tube) barrel; also available with Light 20-ga. 28" (Mod.) or 26" (Imp. Cyl.) barrel.
Weight: 12-, 16-ga. 7¼ lbs.; 20-ga. 6⅜ lbs.
Stock: French walnut, hand checkered half-p.g. and forend. 14¼"x1⅝"x2½".
Features: Receiver hand engraved with scroll designs and border. Double extractors, extra bbls. Interchangeable without factory fitting; mag. cut-off; cross-bolt safety. Imported from Japan by Browning.
Price: Light 12, 20, Sweet 16, vent. rib., Invector ... $719.95
Price: Extra Invector barrel $249.95
Price: Light 12 Buck Special $724.95
Price: 3" Magnum Buck Special $747.95
Price: Extra fixed-choke barrel (Light 20 only) .. $194.95
Price: 12, 16, 20 Buck Special barrel $254.95

Browning Auto-5 Stalker
Similar to the Auto-5 Light and Magnum models except has matte blue metal finish and black graphite-fiberglass stock and forend. Stock is scratch and impact resistant and has checkered panels. Light Stalker has 2¾" chamber, 26" or 28" vent. rib barrel with Invector choke tubes, weighs 8 lbs., 1 oz. (26"). Magnum Stalker has 3" chamber, 28" or 30" vent. rib barrel with Invector choke tubes, weighs 8 lbs., 11 oz. (28"). Introduced 1992.
Price: Light Stalker $719.95
Price: Magnum Stalker $742.95

Browning Auto-5 Magnum 12
Same as standard Auto-5 except chambered for 3" magnum shells (also handles 2¾" magnum and 2¾" HV loads). 28" Mod., Full; 30" and 32" (Full) bbls. Comes with Invector choke tubes. 14"x1⅝"x2½" stock. Recoil pad. Wgt. 8¾ lbs.
Price: With Invector choke tubes $742.95
Price: Extra Invector barrel $249.95

Browning Auto-5 Magnum 20
Same as Magnum 12 except 26" or 28" barrel with Invector choke tubes. With ventilated rib, 7½ lbs.
Price: Invector only $742.95
Price: Extra Invector barrel $249.95

Browning A-500G

BROWNING A-500G AUTO SHOTGUN
Gauge: 12, 3" chamber.
Barrel: 26", 28", 30", Invector choke tubes. Ventilated rib.
Weight: 7 lbs., 14 oz. (26" bbl.). **Length:** 47½" overall.
Stock: 14⅜"x1½"x2". Select walnut with gloss finish, rounded pistol grip. Recoil pad standard.
Features: Gas-operated action with four-lug rotary bolt, cross-bolt safety. Interchangeable barrels. High-polish blue finish with light engraving on receiver and "A-500G" in gold color. Patented gas metering system to handle all loads. Built-in buffering system to absorb recoil, reduce stress on internal parts. Introduced 1990. Imported by Browning.
Price: $639.95
Price: Extra Invector barrels $249.95
Price: A-500G Buck Special $672.95
Price: 24" Buck Special barrel $282.95

Browning A-500G Sporting Clays
Same as the standard A-500G except has 28" or 30" Invector choke barrel, receiver has semi-gloss finish with "Sporting Clays" in gold lettering. Introduced 1992.
Price: $639.95

BROWNING A-500R AUTO SHOTGUN

Gauge: 12 only, 3" chamber.
Barrel: 24" Buck Special, 26", 28", 30" with Invector choke tubes.
Weight: 7 lbs., 7 oz. (30" bbl.). **Length:** 49½" overall (30" bbl.).
Stock: 14¼"x1½"x2½"; select walnut with gloss finish; checkered p.g. and forend; black vent., recoil pad.
Sights: Metal bead front.
Features: Uses a short-recoil action with four-lug rotary bolt and composite and coil spring buffering system. Shoots all loads without adjustment. Has a magazine cut-off, Invector chokes. Introduced 1987. Imported from Belgium by Browning.
Price: $559.95
Price: A-500R Buck Special $592.95
Price: Extra Invector barrel $199.95
Price: 24" Buck Special barrel $232.95

COSMI AUTOMATIC SHOTGUN

Gauge: 12 or 20, 2¾" or 3" chamber.
Barrel: 22" to 34". Choke (including choke tubes) and length to customer specs. Boehler steel.
Weight: About 6¼ lbs. (20-ga.).
Stock: Length and style to customer specs. Hand-checkered exhibition grade circassian walnut standard.
Features: Hand-made, essentially a custom gun. Recoil-operated auto with tip-up barrel. Made completely of stainless steel (lower receiver polished); magazine tube in buttstock holds 7 rounds. Double ejectors, double safety system. Comes with fitted leather case. Imported from Italy by Incor, Inc.
Price: From $7,400.00

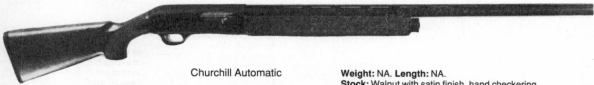

Churchill Automatic

CHURCHILL AUTOMATIC SHOTGUN

Gauge: 12, 2¾" or 3" chamber, 5-shot magazine.
Barrel: 24", 25", 26", 28" (choke tubes).

Weight: NA. **Length:** NA.
Stock: Walnut with satin finish, hand checkering.
Features: Gas-operated action, magazine cut-off, non-glare metal finish. Gold-colored trigger. Introduced 1990. Imported by Ellett Bros.
Price: $549.95
Price: Turkey, 25" bbl. $569.95

Mossberg Model 9200

MOSSBERG MODEL 9200 REGAL SEMI-AUTO SHOTGUN

Gauge: 12, 3" chamber.
Barrel: 24" (rifled bore), 28" (Accu-Choke tubes); vent. rib.

Weight: About 7.5 lbs. **Length:** 48" overall (28" bbl.).
Stock: Walnut with high-gloss finish.
Features: Shoots all 2¾" or 3" loads without adjustment. Alloy receiver, ambidextrous top safety. Introduced 1992.
Price: $373.00

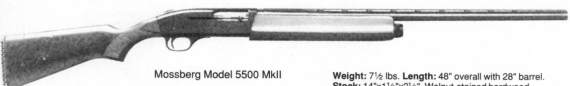

Mossberg Model 5500 MkII

MOSSBERG MODEL 5500 MKII SEMI-AUTO SHOTGUN

Gauge: 12, 2¾" and 3" chamber.
Barrel: 26", 28" (2¾" chamber, ACCU-II tubes—Imp. Cyl., Mod., Full); 24" (3" chamber, ACCU-II tubes—Imp. Cyl., Mod., Full (both vent. rib).

Weight: 7½ lbs. **Length:** 48" overall with 28" barrel.
Stock: 14"x1½"x2½". Walnut-stained hardwood.
Features: Combo or single barrel versions available. Gas-operated action. Blue or camo finish. Mossberg Cablelock included. Introduced 1988.
Price: From about $376.00
Price: Camo, 28", from about $393.00
Price: With N.T.W.F. Mossy Oak finish $428.00

Remington 11-87 Sporting Clays

REMINGTON 11-87 PREMIER SHOTGUN

Gauge: 12, 3" chamber.
Barrel: 26", 28", 30" Rem Choke tubes. Light Contour barrel.
Weight: About 8¼ lbs. **Length:** 46" overall (26" bbl.).
Stock: Walnut with satin or high-gloss finish; cut checkering; solid brown buttpad; no white spacers.
Sights: Bradley-type white-faced front, metal bead middle.
Features: Pressure compensating gas system allows shooting 2¾" or 3" loads interchangeably with no adjustments. Stainless magazine tube; redesigned feed latch, barrel support ring on operating bars; pinned forend. Introduced 1987.
Price: $607.00
Price: Left-hand $665.00
Price: Premier Cantilever Deer Barrel, scope rings, sling, swivels, Monte Carlo stock $678.00

Remington 11-87 Premier Skeet

Similar to 11-87 Premier except Skeet dimension stock with cut checkering, satin finish, two-piece buttplate; 26" barrel with Skeet or Rem Chokes (Skeet, Imp. Skeet). Gas system set for 2¾" shells only. Introduced 1987.
Price: $663.00
Price: Left-hand $728.00

REMINGTON 11-87 SPORTING CLAYS

Gauge: 12, 2¾" chamber
Barrel: 26", 28", vent. rib, Rem Choke (Skeet, Imp. Cyl., Mod., Full); Light Contour barrel. Medium height rib.
Weight: 7.5 lbs. **Length:** 46.5" overall (26" barrel).
Stock: 14³⁄₁₆"x1½"x2¼". Walnut, with cut checkering; sporting clays butt pad.
Features: Top of receiver, barrel and rib have matte finish; shortened magazine tube and forend; lengthened forcing cone; ivory bead front sight; competition trigger. Special no-wrench choke tubes marked on the outside. Comes in two-barrel fitted hard case. Introduced 1992.
Price: $718.00

Remington 11-87 Synthetic Camo

Remington 11-87 Special Purpose Magnum
Similar to the 11-87 Premier except has dull stock finish, Parkerized exposed metal surfaces. Bolt and carrier have dull blackened coloring. Comes with 26" or 28" barrel with Rem Chokes, padded Cordura nylon sling and q.d. swivels. Introduced 1987.
Price: $607.00
Price: With synthetic stock and forend (SPS) $607.00
Price: Magnum-Turkey with synthetic stock (SPS-T) $620.00

Remington 11-87 Premier Trap
Similar to 11-87 Premier except trap dimension stock with straight or Monte Carlo combs; select walnut with satin finish and Tournament-grade cut checkering; 30" barrel with Rem Chokes (Trap Full, Trap Extra Full, Trap Super Full). Gas system set for 2¾" shells only. Introduced 1987.
Price: With straight stock, Rem Choke $670.00
Price: With Monte Carlo stock $685.00
Price: Left-hand, straight stock $737.00
Price: Left-hand, Monte Carlo stock $753.00

Remington 11-87 Special Purpose Synthetic Camo
Similar to the 11-87 Special Purpose Magnum except has synthetic stock and all metal (except bolt and trigger guard) and stock covered with Mossy Oak Bottomland camo finish. In 12-gauge only, 26", 28" vent. rib, Rem Choke. Comes with camo sling, swivels. Introduced 1992.
Price: $673.00

Remington 11-87 N.W.T.F. Auto
Same as the Remington 11-87 Special Purpose Magnum with synthetic stock except has complete brown Trebark camouflage finish. Has 21" vent. rib barrel with Rem Choke turkey barrel, Imp. Cyl. and Turkey Extra-Full tubes. Comes with camo sling, swivels. Introduced 1992.
Price: $673.00

Remington 11-87 Special Purpose Deer Gun
Similar to the 11-87 Special Purpose Magnum except has 21" barrel with rifle sights, rifled and Imp. Cyl. choke tubes. Gas system set to handle all 2¾" and 3" slug, buckshot, high velocity field and magnum loads. Not designed to function with light 2¾" field loads. Introduced 1987.
Price: $587.00
Price: With cantilever scope mount, rings $640.00

Remington SP-10

Remington SP-10 Magnum Turkey Combo
Combines the SP 10 with 26" or 30" vent. rib barrel, plus extra 22" rifle-sighted barrel with Mod., Full, Extra-Full Turkey Rem Choke tubes. Comes with camo sling, swivels. Introduced 1991.
Price: $1,066.00

REMINGTON SP-10 MAGNUM AUTO SHOTGUN
Gauge: 10, 3½" chamber, 3-shot magazine.
Barrel: 26", 30" (Full and Mod. Rem Chokes).
Weight: 11 to 11¼ lbs. **Length:** 47½" overall (26" barrel).
Stock: Walnut with satin finish. Checkered grip and forend.
Sights: Metal bead front.
Features: Stainless steel gas system with moving cylinder; ⅜" ventilated rib. Receiver and barrel have matte finish. Brown recoil pad. Comes with padded Cordura nylon sling. Introduced 1989.
Price: $933.00

Remington 1100 Special Field

Remington 1100 Special Field
Similar to standard Model 1100 except 12- and 20-ga. only, comes with 21" Rem Choke barrel. LT-20 version 6½ lbs.; has straight-grip stock, shorter forend, both with cut checkering. Comes with vent. rib only; matte finish receiver without engraving. Introduced 1983.
Price: 12- and 20-ga., 21" Rem Choke, about $589.00

Remington 1100 20-Gauge Deer Gun
Same as 1100 except 20-ga. only, 21" barrel (Imp. Cyl.), rifle sights adjustable for windage and elevation; recoil pad with white spacer. Weight 7¼ lbs.
Price: About $532.00

SKB Model 1900 Auto Shotgun
Similar to the Model 1300 except has engraved bright-finish receiver, grip cap, gold-plated trigger. Introduced 1988.
Price: Field $545.00
Price: Slug (22" barrel, rifle sights) $545.00

SKB Model 1900 Trap
Similar to the Model 1900 Field except in 12-gauge only (2¾" chamber), 30" barrel with Inter Choke tubes and 9.5mm wide raised rib. Introduced 1988.
Price: $545.00

REMINGTON 1100 LT-20 AUTO
Gauge: 20, 28, 410.
Barrel: 25" (Full, Mod.), 26", 28" with Rem Chokes.
Weight: 7½ lbs.
Stock: 14"x1½"x2½". American walnut, checkered p.g. and forend.
Features: Quickly interchangeable barrels. Matted receiver top with scroll work on both sides of receiver. Cross-bolt safety.
Price: With Rem Chokes, 20-ga. about $589.00
Price: 28 and 410 . . . . $633.00
Price: Youth Gun LT-20 (21" Rem Choke) $576.00
Price: 20-ga., 3" magnum $589.00

Remington 1100 LT-20 Tournament Skeet
Same as the 1100 except 26" barrel, special Skeet boring, vent. rib, ivory bead front and metal bead middle sights. 14"x1½"x2½" stock. 20-, 28-, 410-ga. Weight 7½ lbs., cut checkering, walnut, new receiver scroll.
Price: Tournament Skeet (28, 410), about $670.00
Price: Tournament Skeet (20), about $670.00

SKB MODEL 1300 UPLAND MAG SHOTGUN
Gauge: 12, 2¾" or 3"; 20, 3".
Barrel: 22" (Slug), 26", 28" (Inter Choke tubes).
Weight: 6½ to 7¼ lbs. **Length:** 48¼" overall (28" barrel).
Stock: 14½"x1½"x2½". Walnut, with hand-checkered grip and forend.
Sights: Metal bead front.
Features: Gas operated with Universal Automatic System. Blued receiver. Magazine cut-off system. Introduced 1988. Imported from Japan by GU, Inc.
Price: Field $495.00
Price: Slug (22" bbl., rifle sights) $495.00

Winchester Model 1400

WINCHESTER MODEL 1400 SEMI-AUTO SHOTGUN
Gauge: 12 and 20, 2¾" chamber.
Barrel: 22", 26", 28" vent. rib with Winchoke tubes (Imp. Cyl., Mod., Full).
Weight: 7¾ lbs. **Length:** 48⅝" overall.
Stock: Walnut-finished hardwood, finger-grooved forend with deep cut checkering. Also available with walnut stock.
Sights: Metal bead front.
Features: Cross-bolt safety, front-locking rotary bolt, black serrated buttplate, gas-operated action. From U.S. Repeating Arms Co., Inc.
Price: Ranger, vent. rib with Winchoke $341.00
Price: As above with walnut stock (1400 Walnut) $378.00
Price: Deer barrel combo $394.00

Winchester Model 1400 Walnut "Slug Hunter"
Similar to the Model 1400 except in 12-ga. only with smooth bore 22" barrel, with adjustable open sights. Comes with Imp. Cyl. and Sabot choke tubes. Receiver is drilled and tapped for scope mounting, has threaded steel inserts and comes with bases. Walnut stock and forend with cut checkering. Introduced 1990. From U.S. Repeating Arms Co., Inc.
Price: $420.00

SHOTGUNS—SLIDE ACTIONS

Includes a wide variety of sporting guns and guns suitable for competitive shooting.

Browning BPS 10-Ga.

BROWNING BPS PUMP SHOTGUN
Gauge: 10, 12, 3½" chamber; 12 or 20, 3" chamber (2¾" in target guns), 5-shot magazine.
Barrel: 10-ga.—24" Buck Special, 28", 30", 32" Invector; 12-, 20- ga.—22", 24", 26", 28", 30", 32" (Imp. Cyl., Mod. or Full). Also available with Invector choke tubes, 12- or 20-ga.; Upland Special has 22" barrel with Invector tubes. BPS 3½" has back-bored barrel.
Weight: 7 lbs., 8 oz. (28" barrel). **Length:** 48¾" overall (28" barrel).
Stock: 14¼"x1½"x2½". Select walnut, semi-beavertail forend, full p.g. stock.
Features: Bottom feeding and ejection, receiver top safety, high post vent. rib. Double action bars eliminate binding. Vent. rib barrels only. All 12- and 20-gauge guns with 3" chamber available with fully engraved receiver flats at no extra cost. Each gsuge has its own unique game scene. Introduced 1977. Imported from Japan by Browning.
Price: 10-ga., Hunting, Invector $584.95
Price: 12-ga., 3½" Mag., Hunting, Invector PLUS $584.95
Price: 12-ga., Hunting $442.95
Price: 12-, 20-ga., Upland Special, Invector $442.95
Price: 10-ga. and 3½" 12-ga. Mag., Buck Special $589.95
Price: 12-ga. Buck Special $448.95

Browning BPS Stalker Pump Shotgun
Same gun as the standard BPS except all exposed metal parts have a matte blued finish and the stock has a durable black finish with a black recoil pad. Available in 10-ga. (3½") and 12-ga. with 3" or 3½" chamber, 22", 28", 30" barrel with Invector choke system. Introduced 1987.
Price: 12-ga., 3" chamber $442.95
Price: 10-, 12-ga., 3½" chamber $584.95

Browning BPS Pump Shotgun (Ladies and Youth Model)
Same as BPS Upland Special except 20-ga. only, 22" Invector barrel, stock has pistol grip with recoil pad. Length of pull is 13¼". Introduced 1986.
Price: $442.95

Browning BPS Pigeon Grade Pump shotgun
Same as the standard BPS except has select high grade walnut stock and forend, and gold-trimmed receiver. Available in 12-gauge only with 26" or 28" vent. rib barrels. Introduced 1992.
Price: $599.95

Browning BPS Game Gun Turkey Special
Similar to the standard BPS except has satin-finished walnut stock and dull-finished barrel and receiver. Receiver is drilled and tapped for scope mounting. Rifle-style stock dimensions and swivel studs. Has Extra-Full Turkey choke tube. Introduced 1992.
Price: $469.95

Browning BPS Game Deer

Browning BPS Game Gun Deer Special
Similar to the standard BPS except has newly designed receiver/magazine tube/barrel mounting system to eliminate play, heavy 20.5" barrel with rifle-type sights with adjustable rear, solid receiver scope mount, "rifle" stock dimensions for scope or open sights, sling swivel studs. Gloss-finish wood with checkering, polished blue metal. Introduced 1992.
Price: $489.95

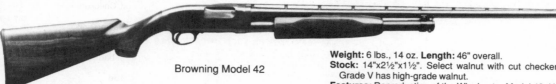

Browning Model 42

Weight: 6 lbs., 14 oz. **Length:** 46" overall.
Stock: 14"x2½"x1½". Select walnut with cut checkering, semi-gloss finish; Grade V has high-grade walnut.
Features: Reproduction of the Winchester Model 42. Has high post floating rib with grooved sighting plane; cross-bolt safety in trigger guard; polished blue finish. Limited to 6000 Grade I and 6000 Grade V guns. Introduced 1991. Imported from Japan by Browning.
Price: Model 42, Grade I $799.95
Price: Model 42, Grade V $1,360.00

BROWNING MODEL 42 PUMP SHOTGUN
Gauge: 410-bore, 3" chamber.
Barrel: 26" (Full).

CAUTION: PRICES CHANGE, CHECK AT GUNSHOP.

Ithaca Model 87 Supreme

ITHACA MODEL 87 SUPREME PUMP SHOTGUN
Gauge: 12, 20, 3" chamber, 5-shot magazine.
Barrel: 26" (Imp. Cyl., Mod., Full tubes), 28" (Mod.), 30" (Full). Vent. rib.
Weight: 6¾ to 7 lbs.
Stock: 14"x1½"x2¼". Full fancy-grade walnut, checkered p.g. and slide handle.
Sights: Raybar front.
Features: Bottom ejection, cross-bolt safety. Polished and blued engraved receiver. Reintroduced 1988. From Ithaca Acquisition Corp.
Price: **$819.00**
Price: M87 Camo Vent. (28", Mod. choke tube, camouflage finish) . **$524.00**
Price: M87 Field **$458.00**

ITHACA MODEL 87 DEERSLAYER SHOTGUN
Gauge: 12, 20, 3" chamber.
Barrel: 20", 25" (Special Bore), or rifled bore.
Weight: 6 to 6¾ lbs.
Stock: 14"x1½"x2¼". American walnut. Checkered p.g. and slide handle.
Sights: Raybar blade front on ramp, rear adjustable for windage and elevation, and grooved for scope mounting.
Features: Bored for slug shooting. Bottom ejection, cross-bolt safety. Reintroduced 1988. From Ithaca Acquisition Corp.
Price: **$391.00**
Price: Deluxe Combo (12- and 20-ga. barrels) **$549.00**
Price: Deluxe **$429.00**
Price: Field Deerslayer **$407.00**

Ithaca Model 87 Deluxe Pump Shotgun
Similar to the Model 87 Supreme Vent. Rib except comes with choke tubes in 25", 26", 28" (Mod.), 30" (Full). Standard-grade walnut.
Price: **$495.00**

Ithaca Deerslayer II Rifled Shotgun
Similar to the Deerslayer except has rifled 25" barrel and checkered American walnut stock and forend with high-gloss finish and Monte Carlo comb. Solid frame construction. Introduced 1988.
Price: 12 or 20 . . . . **$525.00**

Ithaca Model 87 Basic Field Combo
Similar to the Model 87 Supreme except comes with 28" (choke tubes) and 20" or 25" (Deer, Special Bore) barrels. Oil-finished wood, no checkering, blued trigger.
Price: **$427.00**
Price: As above except with rifled barrel **$459.00**

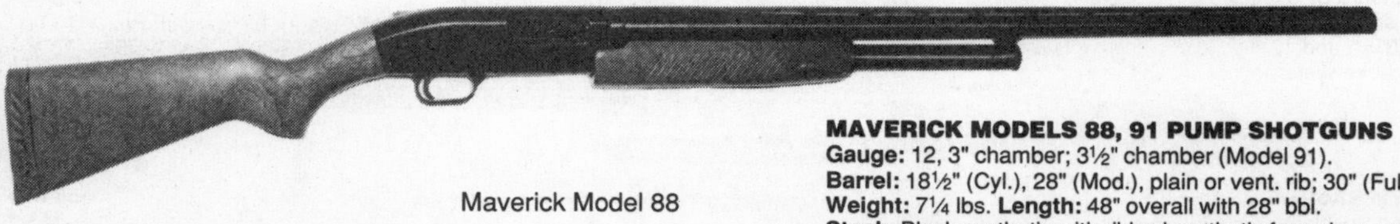

Ithaca Model 87 Turkey Gun
Similar to the Model 87 Supreme except comes with 24" (fixed Full or Full choke tube) barrel, either Camoseal camouflage or matte blue finish, oiled wood, blued trigger.

Price: With fixed choke, blue **$409.00**
Price: With choke tube, blue **$420.00**
Price: With fixed choke, Camoseal **$515.00**
Price: With choke tube, Camoseal **$525.00**

Maverick Model 88

CONSULT **Shooter's Marketplace** Page 225, This Issue

MAVERICK MODELS 88, 91 PUMP SHOTGUNS
Gauge: 12, 3" chamber; 3½" chamber (Model 91).
Barrel: 18½" (Cyl.), 28" (Mod.), plain or vent. rib; 30" (Full), plain or vent. rib.
Weight: 7¼ lbs. **Length:** 48" overall with 28" bbl.
Stock: Black synthetic with ribbed synthetic forend, or wood.
Sights: Bead front.
Features: Alloy receiver with blue finish; cross-bolt safety in trigger guard; interchangeable barrels. Rubber recoil pad. Mossberg Cablelock included. Introduced 1989. From Maverick Arms, Inc.
Price: Model 88, synthetic stock, 18½", 28", 30" plain bbl. **$193.00**
Price: Model 88, synthetic stock, 28", 30" vent. rib **$211.00**
Price: Model 88, wood stock, 28" vent. rib, three choke tubes **$224.00**
Price: Model 88, synthetic stock, 24" with rifle sights **$211.00**
Price: Model 88, synthetic stock, Combo 18½", 28" plain bbl. **$218.00**
Price: Model 88, synthetic stock, Combo 18½" (plain), 28" (vent. rib) **$235.00**
Price: Model 88, wood stock, Combo 18½" (plain), 28" (vent. rib with three choke tubes) **$252.00**
Price: Model 91, synthetic stock, 28" plain bbl. with one Full steel shot choke tube **$239.00**
Price: As above, vent. rib bbl. **$256.00**

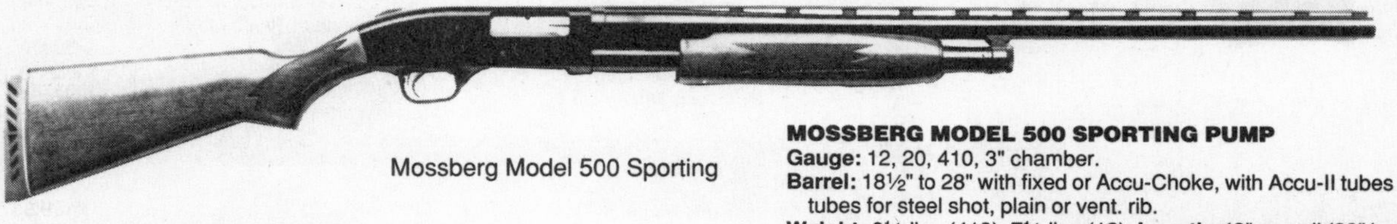

Mossberg Model 500 Sporting

MOSSBERG MODEL 500 TROPHY SLUGSTER
Gauge: 12, 3" chamber.
Barrel: 24", rifled bore. Plain (no rib).
Weight: 7¼ lbs. **Length:** 44" overall.
Stock: 14" pull, 1⅜" drop at heel. Walnut; Dual Comb design for proper eye positioning with or without scoped barrels. Recoil pad and swivel studs.
Features: Ambidextrous thumb safety, twin extractors, dual slide bars. Comes with scope mount. Mossberg Cablelock included. Introduced 1988.
Price: Rifled bore, with scope mount **$320.00**
Price: Rifled bore, rifle sights **$294.00**

MOSSBERG MODEL 500 SPORTING PUMP
Gauge: 12, 20, 410, 3" chamber.
Barrel: 18½" to 28" with fixed or Accu-Choke, with Accu-II tubes or Accu-Steel tubes for steel shot, plain or vent. rib.
Weight: 6¼ lbs. (410), 7¼ lbs. (12). **Length:** 48" overall (28" barrel).
Stock: 14"x1½"x2½". Walnut-stained hardwood. Checkered grip and forend.
Sights: White bead front, brass mid-bead.
Features: Ambidextrous thumb safety, twin extractors, disconnecting safety, dual action bars. Mossberg Cablelock included. From Mossberg.
Price: From about **$253.00**
Price: Sporting Combos (field barrel and Slugster barrel), from . . . **$324.00**

Mossberg Model 500 Muzzleloader Combo
Same as the Model 500 Sporting Pump except comes with 28" vent. rib Accu-Choke barrel with Imp. Cyl., Mod. and Full choke tubes and 24" fully rifled 50-caliber muzzle-loading barrel and ramrod. Uses #209 standard primer. Introduced 1992.
Price: **$399.00**

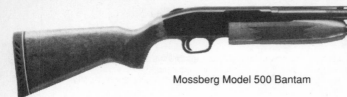

Mossberg Model 500 Bantam

Mossberg Model 500 Camo Pump

Same as the Model 500 Sporting Pump except 12-gauge only and entire gun is covered with special camouflage finish. Receiver drilled and tapped for scope mounting. Comes with q.d. swivel studs, swivels, camouflage sling, Mossberg Cablelock.

Price: From about $293.00
Price: Camo Combo (as above with extra Slugster barrel), from about **$334.00**

Mossberg Model 500 Bantam Pump

Same as the Model 500 Sporting Pump except 20-gauge only, 22" vent. rib Accu-Choke barrel with three choke tubes; has 1" shorter stock, reduced length from pistol grip to trigger, reduced forend reach. Introduced 1992.

Price: $273.00

Mossberg Turkey Model 500 Pump

Same as the Model 500 Sporting Pump except has overall OFM camo finish, Ghost-Ring sights, Accu-Choke barrel with Imp. Cyl., Mod., Full, Extra-Full lead shot choke tubes, 24" barrel, swivel studs, camo sling. Introduced 1992.

Price: $346.00

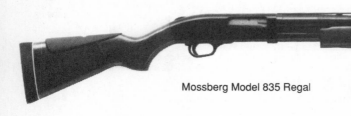

Mossberg Model 835 Regal

Mossberg Special Value Model 835 Pump Shotgun

Same as the Model 835 Regal except has walnut-stained hardwood stock and comes only with Modified choke tube. Introduced 1992.

Price: $278.00

MOSSBERG MODEL 835 REGAL ULTI-MAG PUMP

Gauge: 12, 3½" chamber.
Barrel: 24", 28", Accu-Mag with four choke tubes for steel or lead shot.
Weight: 7¾ lbs. **Length:** 48½" overall.
Stock: 14"x1½"x2½". Dual Comb. Walnut-stained hardwood or camo synthetic; both have recoil pad.
Sights: White bead front, brass mid-bead.
Features: Shoots 2¾", 3" or 3½" shells. Backbored barrel to reduce recoil, improve patterns. Ambidextrous thumb safety, twin extractors, dual slide bars. Mossberg Cablelock included. Introduced 1988.
Price: Blue, wood stock $373.00
Price: Camo finish, synthetic stock $400.00
Price: National Wild Turkey Federation 1992 Edition (Realtree camo) $428.00

Remington 870 Wingmaster

Remington 870 Special Purpose Deer Gun

Similar to the 870 Wingmaster except available with 20" barrel with rifled and Imp. Cyl. choke tubes; rifle sights or cantilever scope mount with rings. Metal has black, non-glare finish, satin finish on wood. Recoil pad, detachable sling of camo Cordura nylon. Introduced 1989.

Price: With rifle sights, Monte Carlo stock $439.00
Price: With scope mount and rings, Monte Carlo stock $497.00

Remington 870 TC Trap

Same as the Model 870 except 12-ga. only, 30" Rem Choke, vent. rib barrel, Ivory front and white metal middle beads. Special sear, hammer and trigger assembly. 14⅜"x1½"x1⅞" stock with recoil pad. Hand fitted action and parts. Weight 8 lbs.

Price: Model 870TC Trap, Rem Choke, about $613.00
Price: TC Trap with Monte Carlo stock, about $628.00

REMINGTON 870 WINGMASTER

Gauge: 12, 3" chamber.
Barrel: 26", 28", 30" (Rem Chokes). Light Contour barrel.
Weight: 7¼ lbs. **Length:** 46½" overall (26" bbl.).
Stock: 14"x2½"x1". American walnut with satin or high-gloss finish, cut-checkered p.g. and forend. Rubber buttpad.
Sights: Ivory bead front, metal mid-bead.
Features: Double action bars; cross-bolt safety; blue finish. Available in right- or left-hand style. Introduced 1986.
Price: $460.00
Price: Left-hand (28" only) $519.00
Price: Deer Gun (rifle sights, 20" bbl.) $412.00
Price: Deer Gun, left-hand, Monte Carlo stock $495.00
Price: LW-20 20-ga., vent. rib, 26", 28" (Rem Choke) $455.00

Remington 870 Wingmaster Small Gauges

Same as the standard Model 870 Wingmaster except chambered for 20-ga. (2¾" and 3"), 28-ga., and 410-bore. The 20-ga. available with 26", 28" vent. rib barrel with Rem Choke tubes, high-gloss or satin wood finish; 28 and 410 available with 25" Full or Mod. fixed choke, satin finish only.

Price: 20-ga. $451.00
Price: 20-ga. Deer Gun, rifle sights $412.00
Price: 28 and 410 . . . . $498.00

Remington 870 SPS Camo

Remington 870 Marine Magnum

Similar to the 870 Wingmaster except all metal is plated with electroless nickel and has black synthetic stock and forend. Has 18" plain barrel (Cyl.), bead front sight, 7-shot magazine. Introduced 1992.

Price: $439.00

Remington 870 Special Purpose Synthetic Camo

Similar to the 870 Special Purpose Magnum except has synthetic stock and all metal (except bolt and trigger guard) and stock covered with Mossy Oak Bottomland camo finish. In 12-gauge only, 26", 28" vent. rib, Rem Choke. Comes with camo sling, swivels. Introduced 1992.

Price: $425.00

Remington 870 Express Rifle-Sighted Deer Gun

Same as the Model 870 Express except comes with 20" barrel with fixed Imp. Cyl. choke, open iron sights, Monte Carlo stock. Introduced 1991.

Price: $260.00
Price: With fully rifled barrel $289.00

CAUTION: PRICES CHANGE, CHECK AT GUNSHOP.

Remington 870 SPS-T Turkey

Remington Model 870 Express Youth Gun
Same as the Model 870 Express except comes with 12½" length of pull, 21" barrel with Mod. Rem Choke tube. Hardwood stock with low-luster finish. Introduced 1991.
Price: **$264.00**

Remington 870 Special Purpose Magnum
Similar to the Model 870 except chambered only for 12-ga., 3" shells, vent. rib. 26" or 28" Rem Choke barrel. All exposed metal surfaces are finished in dull, non-reflective black. Wood has an oil finish. Comes with padded Cordura 2" wide sling, quick-detachable swivels. Chrome-lined bores. Dark recoil pad. Introduced 1985.
Price: About **$451.00**
Price: With synthetic stock, forend (SPS) **$359.00**
Price: Magnum-Turkey (synthetic stock, forend) SPS-T **$372.00**

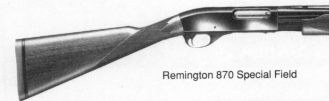

Remington 870 Special Field

Remington 870 High Grades
Same as 870 except better walnut, hand checkering. Engraved receiver and barrel. Vent. rib. Stock dimensions to order.
Price: 870D, about **$2,389.00**
Price: 870F, about **$4,921.00**
Price: 870F with gold inlay, about **$7,381.00**

Remington 870 Express Turkey
Same as the Model 870 Express except comes with 3" chamber, 21" vent. rib turkey barrel and Extra-Full Rem Choke Turkey tube; 12-ga. only. Introduced 1991.
Price: **$277.00**

Remington 870 Special Field
Similar to the standard Model 870 except comes with 21" barrel only, 3" chamber, choked Imp. Cyl., Mod., Full and Rem Choke; 12-ga. weighs 6¾ lbs., LW-20 weighs 6 lbs.; has straight-grip stock, shorter forend, both with cut checkering. Vent. rib barrel only. Introduced 1984.
Price: 12- or 20-ga., Rem Choke, about **$451.00**

Remington 870 Express
Similar to the 870 Wingmaster except has a walnut-toned hardwood stock with solid, black recoil pad and pressed checkering on grip and forend. Outside metal surfaces have a black oxide finish. Comes with 26" or 28" vent. rib barrel with a Mod. Rem Choke tube. Introduced 1987.
Price: 12 or 20 .... **$264.00**
Price: Express Combo (with extra 20" Deer barrel), 12 or 20 ... **$359.00**
Price: Express 20-ga., 28" with Mod. Rem Choke tubes ... **$264.00**
Price: 410-bore **$289.00**

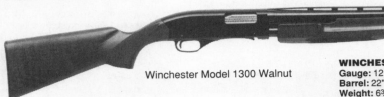

Winchester Model 1300 Walnut

Winchester Model 1300 Turkey Gun
Similar to the standard Model 1300 Featherweight except 12-ga. only, 30" barrel with Mod., Full and Extra Full Winchoke tubes, matte finish wood and metal. Comes with recoil pad, Cordura sling and swivels.
Price: With WinCam green camo laminated stock, about **$414.00**
Price: National Wild Turkey Federation Series III **$436.00**

WINCHESTER MODEL 1300 WALNUT PUMP
Gauge: 12 and 20, 3" chamber, 5-shot capacity.
Barrel: 22", 26", 28", vent. rib, with Full, Mod., Imp. Cyl. Winchoke tubes.
Weight: 6⅜ lbs. **Length:** 42⅝" overall.
Stock: American walnut, with deep cut checkering on pistol grip, traditional ribbed forend; high luster finish.
Sights: Metal bead front.
Features: Twin action slide bars; front-locking rotary bolt; roll-engraved receiver; blued, highly polished metal; cross-bolt safety with red indicator. Introduced 1984. From U.S. Repeating Arms Co., Inc.
Price: **$362.00**
Price: Model 1300 Ladies/Youth, 22" vent. rib **$358.00**

Winchester Model 1300 Slug Hunter Deer

Winchester Model 1300 Slug Hunter Deer Gun
Same as the Model 1300 except has rifled 22" barrel, WinTuff laminated stock or walnut, rifle-type sights. Introduced 1990.
Price: Walnut stock **$427.00**
Price: Brown laminated stock **$427.00**
Price: Whitetails Unlimited model **$449.00**

Winchester Model 1300 Ranger Pump Gun Combo & Deer Gun
Similar to the standard Ranger except comes with two barrels: 22" (Cyl.) deer barrel with rifle-type sights and an interchangeable 28" vent. rib Winchoke barrel with Full, Mod. and Imp. Cyl. choke tubes. Drilled and tapped; comes with rings and bases. Available in 12- and 20-gauge 3" only, with recoil pad. Introduced 1983.
Price: Deer Combo with two barrels **$354.00**
Price: 12- or 20-ga., 22" (Cyl.) **$299.00**
Price: 12-ga., 22" rifled barrel **$320.00**
Price: 12-ga., 22" (Imp. Cyl., rifled sabot tubes) **$332.00**
Price: Combo 12-ga. with 18" (Cyl.) and 28" (Mod. tube) ... **$354.00**
Price: Rifled Deer Combo (22" rifled and 28" vent. rib barrels, 12 or 20-ga.) **$375.00**

Winchester Model 1300 Slug Hunter
Similar to the Model 1300 except in 12-ga. only with smooth bore 22" barrel, with adjustable open sights. Comes with Imp. Cyl. and Sabot choke tubes. Receiver is drilled and tapped for scope mounting, and comes with bases. Walnut stock and forend with cut checkering. Introduced 1990. From U.S. Repeating Arms Co., Inc.
Price: **$437.00**

Winchester 1300 Ranger

Winchester Model 1300 Ranger Ladies/Youth Pump Gun
Similar to the standard Ranger except chambered only for 3" 20-ga., 22" vent. rib barrel with Winchoke tubes (Full, Mod., Imp. Cyl.). Weighs 6½ lbs., measures 41⅝" o.a.l. Stock has 13" pull length and gun comes with discount certificate for full-size stock. Introduced 1983. From U.S. Repeating Arms Co., Inc.
Price: Vent. rib barrel, Winchoke $303.00
Price: With walnut stock $358.00
Price: National Wild Turkey Federation #1 . . . . $411.00

WINCHESTER MODEL 1300 RANGER PUMP GUN
Gauge: 12 or 20, 3" chamber, 5-shot magazine.
Barrel: 26", 28" vent. rib with Full, Mod., Imp. Cyl. Winchoke tubes.
Weight: 7 to 7¼ lbs.
Length: 48⅝" to 50⅝" overall.
Stock: Walnut-finished hardwood with ribbed forend.
Sights: Metal bead front.
Features: Cross-bolt safety, black rubber recoil pad, twin action slide bars, front-locking rotating bolt. From U.S. Repeating Arms Co., Inc.
Price: Vent. rib barrel, Winchoke, about $286.00

SHOTGUNS—OVER/UNDERS

Includes a variety of game guns and guns for competitive shooting.

American Arms/Franchi Falconet

AMERICAN ARMS/FRANCHI FALCONET 2000 O/U
Gauge: 12, 2¾" chambers.
Barrel: 26" (Imp. Cyl., Mod., Full Franchoke tubes).

AMERICAN ARMS/FRANCHI SPORTING 2000 O/U
Gauge: 12, 2¾" chambers.
Barrel: 28" (Skeet, Imp. Cyl., Mod., Full Franchoke tubes).
Weight: 7.75 lbs.
Stock: Checkered walnut.

Weight: 6 lbs.
Stock: Checkered walnut; 14¼" length of pull.
Sights: White flourescent bead front.
Features: Silvered boxlock action with gold-plated game scene; single selective trigger; automatic selective ejectors. Reintroduced 1992. Imported from Italy by American Arms, Inc.
Price: $1,439.00

Sights: White flourescent bead front.
Features: Blued boxlock action with single selective mechanical trigger, automatic selective ejectors; ported barrels. Introduced 1992. Imported from Italy by American Arms, Inc.
Price: $1,679.00

American Arms Silver

American Arms Silver II Shotgun
Similar to the Silver I except 26" barrel (Imp. Cyl., Mod., Full choke tubes, 12- and 20-ga.), 28" (Imp. Cyl., Mod., Full choke tubes, 12-ga. only), 26" (Imp. Cyl. & Mod. fixed chokes, 28 and 410), 26" two-barrel set (Imp. Cyl. & Mod., fixed, 28 and 410); automatic selective ejectors. Weight is about 6 lbs., 15 oz. (12-ga., 26").
Price: $649.00
Price: Two-barrel set (28, 410) $999.00

AMERICAN ARMS SILVER I O/U
Gauge: 12, 20, 28, 410, 3" chamber (28 has 2¾").
Barrel: 26" (Imp. Cyl. & Mod., all gauges), 28" (Mod. & Full, 12, 20).
Weight: About 6¾ lbs.
Stock: 14⅛"x1⅜"x2⅜". Checkered walnut.
Sights: Metal bead front.
Features: Boxlock action with scroll engraving, silver finish. Single selective trigger, extractors. Chrome-lined barrels. Manual safety. Rubber recoil pad. Introduced 1987. Imported from Italy and Spain by American Arms, Inc.
Price: 12- or 20-gauge $499.00
Price: 28 or 410 . . . . $559.00

American Arms Silver Skeet O/U
Similar to the Silver II except has 26" ported barrels with elongated forcing cones, raised target-type vent. rib with two bead sights. Stock dimensions: 14⅜"x1⅜"x2⅜". Weighs 7 lbs., 6 oz. Comes with Skeet, Skeet, Imp. Cyl., Mod. choke tubes. Introduced 1992. Imported by American Arms, Inc.
Price: $839.00

AMERICAN ARMS SILVER SPORTING O/U
Gauge: 12, 2¾" chambers.
Barrel: 28" (Skeet, Imp. Cyl., Mod., Full choke tubes).
Weight: 7⅜ lbs. **Length:** 45½" overall.
Stock: 14⅜"x1½"x2⅜". Figured walnut, cut checkering; Sporting Clays quick-mount buttpad.
Sights: Target bead front.
Features: Boxlock action with single selective trigger, automatic selective ejectors; special broadway channeled rib; vented barrel rib; chrome bores. Chrome-nickel finish on frame, with engraving. Introduced 1990. Imported from Spain by American Arms, Inc.
Price: $849.00

American Arms Silver Lite O/U
Similar to the Silver I except has lightweight alloy receiver with blue finish and engraving. Available in 12- or 20-gauge only. Single selective trigger, automatic selective ejectors. Comes with 26" barrel with Imp. Cyl., Mod., Full choke tubes. Introduced 1990. Imported by American Arms, Inc.
Price: $749.00

American Arms Silver Trap O/U
Similar to the Silver II except has 30" ported barrels with elongated forcing cones, raised target-type vent. rib with two sight beads. Stock dimensions: 14⅜"x1½"x1⅝". Weight is 7 lbs., 12 oz. Comes with Mod., Imp. Mod., Full, Full choke tubes. Introduced 1992. Imported by American Arms, Inc.
Price: $849.00

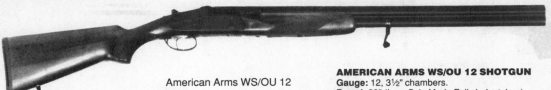

American Arms WS/OU 12

American Arms WT/OU 10 Shotgun

Similar to the WS/OU 12 except chambered for 10-gauge 3½" shell, 26" (Full & Full, choke tubes) barrel. Single selective trigger, extractors. Non-reflective finish on wood and metal. Imported by American Arms, Inc.

Price: **$859.00**

ARMSPORT 2700 O/U GOOSE GUN

Gauge: 10, 3½" chambers.
Barrel: 28" (Full & Imp. Mod.), 32" (Full & Full).
Weight: About 9.8 lbs.
Stock: European walnut.

AMERICAN ARMS WS/OU 12 SHOTGUN

Gauge: 12, 3½" chambers.
Barrel: 28" (Imp. Cyl., Mod., Full choke tubes).
Weight: 6 lbs., 15 oz. **Length:** 46" overall.
Stock: 14⅛"x1⅛"x2⅜". European walnut with cut checkering, black vented recoil pad, matte finish.
Features: Boxlock action with single selective trigger, automatic selective ejectors; chrome bores. Matte metal finish. Imported by American Arms, Inc.
Price: **$659.00**

Features: Boss-type action; double triggers; extractors. Introduced 1986. Imported from Italy by Armsport.
Price: Fixed chokes **$1,190.00**
Price: With choke tubes **$1,299.00**

Armsport M2730

ARMSPORT 2900 TRI-BARREL SHOTGUN

Gauge: 12, 3" chambers.
Barrel: 28" (Imp., Mod., Full).
Weight: 7¾ lbs.
Stock: European walnut.
Features: Has three barrels. Top-tang barrel selector; double triggers; silvered, engraved frame. Introduced 1986. Imported from Italy by Armsport.
Price: **$3,400.00**

ARMSPORT 2700 SERIES O/U

Gauge: 10, 12, 20, 28, 410.
Barrel: 26" (Imp. Cyl. & Mod.); 28" (Mod. & Full); vent. rib.
Weight: 8 lbs.
Stock: European walnut, hand-checkered p.g. and forend.
Features: Single selective trigger, automatic ejectors, engraved receiver. Imported by Armsport. Contact Armsport for complete list of models.
Price: M2733/2735 (Boss-type action, 12, 20, extractors) **$790.00**
Price: M2741 (as above with ejectors) **$825.00**
Price: M2730/2731 (as above with single trigger, screw-in chokes) . **$975.00**
Price: M2705 (410 bore, 26" Imp. & Mod., double triggers) **$785.00**
Price: M2742 Sporting Clays (12-ga., 28", choke tubes) **$930.00**
Price: M2744 Sporting Clays (20-ga., 26", choke tubes) **$930.00**
Price: M2750 Sporting Clays (12-ga., 28", choke tubes, sideplates) **$1050.00**
Price: M2751 Sporting Clays (20-ga., 26", choke tubes, sideplates) **$1050.00**

BABY BRETTON OVER/UNDER SHOTGUN

Gauge: 12 or 20, 2¾" chambers.
Barrel: 27½" (Cyl., Imp. Cyl., Mod., Full choke tubes).
Weight: About 5 lbs.
Stock: Walnut, checkered pistol grip and forend, oil finish.
Features: Receiver slides open on two guide rods, is locked by a large thumb

Baby Bretton

lever on the right side. Extractors only. Light alloy barrels. Imported from France by Mandall Shooting Supplies.
Price: **$895.00**

Beretta ASE 90 Trap

BERETTA OVER/UNDER FIELD SHOTGUNS

Gauge: 12, 20, 28, and 410 bore, 2¾", 3" and 3½" chambers.
Barrel: 26" and 28" (Mobilchoke tubes).
Stock: Close-grained walnut.
Features: Highly-figured, American walnut stocks and forends, and a unique, weather-resistant finish on barrels. The 686 Onyx bears a gold P. Beretta signature on each side of the receiver. Imported from Italy by Beretta U.S.A.
Price: 686 Onyx **$1,355.00**
Price: 686 two bbl. set **$2,085.00**
Price: 686 Field **$1,355.00**
Price: 686L Silver (12, 20, polished silver receiver) . **$1,385.00**
Price: 686EL (engraved sideplates, hard case) . . **$2,200.00**
Price: 687L Field **$1,870.00**
Price: 687 EL (gold inlays, sideplates) **$3,180.00**
Price: 687 EELL (engraved sideplates) . . . . **$4,625.00** to **$5,130.00**

BERETTA ASE 90 COMPETITION O/U SHOTGUN

Gauge: 12, 2¾" chambers.
Barrel: 28" (Pigeon, Sporting Clays, Skeet), 30" (Sporting Clays, Trap), Mobilchoke choke tubes on Sporting Clays, Trap; fixed chokes on Trap, Skeet, Pigeon.
Weight: About 8 lbs., 6 oz.
Stock: High grade walnut.
Features: Has drop-out trigger assembly, wide ventilated top and side ribs, hard-chrome bores. Competition-style receiver with coin-silver finish, gold inlay Pietro Beretta initials. Comes with hard case. Introduced 1992. Imported from Italy by Beretta U.S.A.
Price: Pigeon, Trap, Skeet **$8,070.00**
Price: Sporting Clays **$8,140.00**

BERETTA MODEL 686 ULTRALIGHT O/U

Gauge: 12, 2¾" chambers.
Barrel: 26", 28", Mobilchoke choke tubes.
Weight: About 5 lbs., 13 oz.
Stock: Select American walnut with checkered grip and forend.
Features: Low-profile aluminum alloy receiver with titanium breech face insert. Matte black receiver finish with gold P. Beretta signature inlay. Single selective trigger; automatic safety. Introduced 1992. Imported from Italy by Beretta U.S.A.
Price: **$1,525.00**

Beretta Model SO6 EELL

BERETTA MODEL SO5, SO6, SO9 SHOTGUNS
Gauge: 12, 2¾" chambers.
Barrel: To customer specs.
Stock: To customer specs.

BERETTA SPORTING CLAYS SHOTGUNS
Gauge: 12 and 20, 2¾" chambers.
Barrel: 28", 30", Mobilchoke.
Stock: Close-grained walnut.
Sights: Luminous front sight and center bead.
Features: Equipped with Beretta Mobilchoke flush-mounted screw-in choke tube system. Models vary according to grade, from field-grade Beretta 686 Sporting with its floral engraving pattern, to competition-grade Beretta 682 Sporting with its brushed satin finish and adjustable length of pull to the 687 Sporting with intricately hand-engraved game scenes, fine line, deep-cut checkering. Imported from Italy by Beretta U.S.A.
Price: 682 Sporting, 30" (with case) **$2,605.00**
Price: 682 Super Sport, 28", 30", tapered rib **$2,760.00**

Features: SO5—Trap, Skeet and Sporting Clays models SO5 and SO5 EELL; SO6—SO6 and SO6 EELL are field models. SO6 has a case-hardened or silver receiver with contour hand engraving. SO6 EELL has hand-engraved receiver in a fine floral or "fine English" pattern or game scene, with bas-relief chisel work and gold inlays. SO6 and SO6 EELL are available with sidelocks removable by hand. Imported from Italy by Beretta U.S.A.
Price: SO5 Trap, Skeet, Sporting **$12,300.00**
Price: SO5 Combo, two-bbl. set **$15,836.00**
Price: SO6 Trap, Skeet, Sporting **$16,600.00**
Price: SO6 EELL Field, custom specs **$27,300.00**
Price: SO9 (12, 20, 28, 410, 26", 28", 30", any choke) **$29,250.00**

Price: 682 Sporting 20-gauge **$2,605.00**
Price: 682 Sporting Combo, 28" and 30" **$3,470.00**
Price: 686 Sporting **$1,940.00**
Price: 686 Onyx Sporting **$1,940.00**
Price: 686 English Course Sporting, 2¾" chambers, 28" **$2,015.00**
Price: 686 Sporting Combo, 28" and 30" **$2,605.00**
Price: 687 Sporting **$2,560.00**
Price: 687 Sporting (20-gauge) **$2,560.00**
Price: 687 EELL Sporter (hand engraved sideplates, deluxe wood) **$4,705.00**
Price: 687 English Course Sporting, 2¾" chambers, 28" **$2,630.00**
Price: 687 Sporting Combo, 28" and 30" **$3,410.00**
Price: ASE 90 Sporting **$8,140.00**

Beretta 682 Competition

BERETTA SERIES 682 COMPETITION OVER/UNDERS
Gauge: 12, 2¾" chambers.
Barrel: Skeet—26" and 28"; trap—30" and 32", Imp. Mod. & Full and Mobilchoke; trap mono shotguns—32" and 34" Mobilchoke; trap top single guns—32" and 34" Full and Mobilchoke; trap combo sets—from 30" O/U, 32" unsingle to 32" O/U, 34" top single.
Stock: Close-grained walnut, hand checkered.
Sights: Luminous front sight and center bead.
Features: Trap Monte Carlo stock has deluxe trap recoil pad. Various grades

available; contact Beretta U.S.A. for details. Imported from Italy by Beretta U.S.A.
Price: 682 Skeet **$2,520.00**
Price: 682 Trap **$2,495.00**
Price: 682 Trap Mono shotguns **$3,400.00**
Price: 682 Trap Top Single shotguns **$2,650.00**
Price: 682 Trap Combo sets . . . . **$3,340.00 to $3,400.00**
Price: 682 Pigeon Silver **$2,760.00**
Price: 687 EELL Trap . . . . **$4,610.00 to $5,815.00**
Price: 687 EELL Skeet (4-bbl. set) **$8,040.00**
Price: 682 Super Skeet (adjustable comb and butt pads, bbl. porting) **$2,915.00**
Price: 682 Super Trap (adjustable comb and butt pad, bbl. porting) . . . . **$2,885.00 to $3,865.00**

Browning Citori Gran Lightning

Browning Superlight Citori Over/Under
Similar to the standard Citori except available in 12, 20 with 24", 26" or 28" Invector barrels, 28 or 410 with 26" barrels choked Imp. Cyl. & Mod. or 28" choked Mod. & Full. Has straight grip stock, schnabel forend tip. Superlight 12 weighs 6 lbs., 9 oz. (26" barrels); Superlight 20, 5 lbs., 12 oz. (26" barrels). Introduced 1982.
Price: Grade I only, 28 or 410 . . . . **$1,160.00**
Price: Grade III, Invector, 12 or 20 . . . . **$1,180.00**
Price: Grade III, 28 or 410 . . . . **$1,845.00**
Price: Grade VI, Invector, 12 or 20 . . . . **$2,415.00**
Price: Grade VI, 28 or 410 . . . . **$2,575.00**
Price: Grade I Invector, 12 or 20 . . . . **$1,155.00**
Price: Grade I Invector, Upland Special (24" bbls.), 12 or 20 . . . **$1,155.00**

Browning Lightning Sporting Clays
Similar to the Citori Lightning with rounded pistol grip and classic forend. Has high post tapered rib or lower hunting-style rib with 30" back-bored Invector Plus barrels, ported or non-ported, 3" chambers. Gloss stock finish, radiused recoil pad. Has "Lightning Sporting Clays Edition" engraved and gold filled on receiver. Introduced 1989.
Price: Low-rib, ported **$1,270.00**
Price: High-rib, ported **$1,330.00**

BROWNING CITORI O/U SHOTGUN
Gauge: 12, 20, 28 and 410.
Barrel: 26", 28" (Mod. & Full, Imp. Cyl. & Mod.), in 28 and 410. Also offered with Invector choke tubes. Lightning 3½" has Invector PLUS back-bored barrels.
Weight: 6 lbs., 8 oz. (26" 410) to 7 lbs., 13 oz. (30" 12-ga.).
Length: 43" overall (26" bbl.).
Stock: Dense walnut, hand checkered, full p.g., beavertail forend. Field-type recoil pad on 12-ga. field guns and trap and Skeet models.
Sights: Medium raised beads, German nickel silver.
Features: Barrel selector integral with safety, automatic ejectors, three-piece takedown. Imported from Japan by Browning. Contact Browning for complete list of models and prices.
Price: Grade I, Hunting, Invector, 12 and 20 . . . . **$1,110.00**
Price: Grade III, Hunting, Invector, 12 and 20 . . . . **$1,645.00**
Price: Grade VI, Hunting, Invector, 12 and 20 . . . . **$2,360.00**
Price: Grade I, Hunting, 28 and 410, fixed chokes **$1,000.00**
Price: Grade III, Lightning, 28 and 410, fixed chokes **$1,830.00**
Price: Grade VI, 28 and 410, high post rib, fixed chokes **$2,560.00**
Price: Grade I, Lightning, Invector, 12, 20 . . . . **$1,140.00**
Price: Grade I, Hunting, 28", 30" only, 3½", Invector Plus **$1,180.00**
Price: Grade III, Lightning, Invector, 12, 20 . . . . **$1,675.00**
Price: Grade VI, Lightning, Invector, 12, 20 . . . . **$2,400.00**
Price: Gran Lightning, 26", 28", Invector **$1,560.00**

Browning Micro Citori Lightning
Similar to the standard Citori 20-ga. Lightning except scaled down for smaller shooter. Comes with 24" barrels with Invector choke system, 13¾" length of pull. Weighs about 6 lbs., 3 oz. Introduced 1991.
Price: **$1,170.00**

CAUTION: PRICES CHANGE, CHECK AT GUNSHOP.

Browning Citori GTI

Browning Special Sporting Clays

Similar to the GTI except has full pistol grip stock with palm swell, gloss finish, 28", 30" or 32" barrels with back-bored Invector Plus chokes (ported or non-ported); high post tapered rib. Also available as 28" and 30" two-barrel set. Introduced 1989.
Price: With ported barrels **$1,330.00**

Browning Citori O/U Trap Models

Similar to standard Citori except 12 gauge only; 30", 32" ported or non-ported (Full & Full, Imp. Mod. & Full, Mod. & Full) or Invector Plus, 34" single barrel in Combo Set (Full, Imp. Mod., Mod.), or Invector model; Monte Carlo cheek piece (14⅜"x1⅜"x1⅜"x2"); fitted with trap-style recoil pad; conventional target rib and high post target rib.
Price: Grade I, Invector Plus, ported bbls. **$1,915.00**
Price: As above, non-ported bbls. **$1,890.00**
Price: Grade I, Invector, high post target rib . . . **$1,250.00**
Price: Grade III, Invector, high post target rib . . **$1,785.00**
Price: Grade VI, Invector, high post target rib . . **$2,520.00**
Price: Grade I, Invector Plus Ported **$1,315.00**
Price: Grade III, Invector Plus Ported **$1,820.00**
Price: Grade IV, Invector Plus Ported **$2,555.00**

Browning Citori Plus Trap Combo

Same as the Citori Plus Trap except comes with 34" single barrel with the 32" O/U model, or 32" or 34" single with the 30" O/U model. Introduced 1992.
Price: With fitted luggage case **$3,275.00**

CHAPUIS OVER/UNDER SHOTGUN

Gauge: 12, 16, 20.
Barrel: 22", 23.6", 26.8", 27.6", 31.5", chokes to customer specs.
Weight: 5 to 8 lbs. **Length:** NA.
Stock: French walnut, straight English or pistol grip.
Features: Double hook blitz system boxlock action with automatic ejectors or extractors. Long trigger guard (most models), choice of raised solid rib, vent. rib or ultra light rib. Imported from France by Armes de Chasse.
Price: About . . . . **$4,000.00 to $5,000.00**

Browning Citori GTI Sporting Clays

Similar to the Citori Hunting except has semi-pistol grip with slightly grooved, semi-beavertail forend, satin-finish stock, radiused rubber buttpad. Has three interchangeable trigger shoes, trigger has three length of pull adjustments. Wide 13mm vent. rib, 28" or 30" barrels (ported or non-ported) with Invector Plus choke tubes. Ventilated side ribs. Introduced 1989.
Price: With ported barrels **$1,350.00**

Browning Citori O/U Skeet Models

Similar to standard Citori except 26", 28" (Skeet & Skeet) only; stock dimensions of 14⅜"x1½"x2", fitted with Skeet-style recoil pad; conventional target rib and high post target rib.
Price: Grade I Invector (high post rib) **$1,250.00**
Price: Grade I, 28 and 410 (high post rib) **$1,250.00**
Price: Grade III, 12 and 20 (high post rib) **$1,785.00**
Price: Grade VI, 12 and 20 (high post rib) **$2,520.00**
Price: Four barrel Skeet set—12, 20, 28, 410 barrels, with case, Grade I only **$4,160.00**
Price: Grade III, four-barrel set (high post rib) . . . **$4,780.00**
Price: Grade VI, four-barrel set (high post rib) . . . **$5,355.00**
Price: Grade I, three-barrel set **$2,890.00**
Price: Grade III, three-barrel set **$3,360.00**
Price: Grade VI, three-barrel set **$4,125.00**

Browning Citori Plus Trap Gun

Similar to the Grade I Citori Trap except comes only with 30" barrels with .745" over-bore, Invector Plus choke system with Full, Imp. Mod. and Mod. choke tubes; high post, ventilated, tapered, target rib for adjustable impact from 3" to 12" above point of aim. Available with or without ported barrels. Select walnut stock has high-gloss finish, Monte Carlo comb, modified beavertail forend and is fully adjustable for length of pull, drop at comb and drop at Monte Carlo. Has Browning Recoil Reduction System. Introduced 1989.
Price: Grade I, with ported barrel **$1,915.00**
Price: Grade I, non-ported barrel **$1,870.00**

CHURCHILL WINDSOR IV OVER/UNDER SHOTGUNS

Gauge: 12, 20, 28, 410, 3" chambers.
Barrel: 12 ga.—26", 28" (ICT choke tubes); 20 ga.—26" (ICT choke tubes).
Stock: European walnut, checkered pistol grip, gloss finish.
Features: Boxlock action with silvered, engraved finish; single selective trigger; automatic ejectors. Imported by Ellett Bros. Introduced 1984.
Price: **$689.95**

Churchill Sporting Clays

Churchill Sporting Clays O/U

Similar to the Windsor IV except in 12-gauge only with 28" ported barrels with choke tubes (Skeet, Skeet, Imp. Cyl., Mod.). Automatic ejectors, raised target-style vent. rib, white front target bead, brass middle. Black rubber recoil pad. Weighs about 7.5 lbs. Introduced 1992. Imported by Ellett Bros.
Price: **$899.95**

CHARLES DALY FIELD GRADE O/U

Gauge: 12 or 20, 3" chambers.
Barrel: 12- and 20- ga.—26" (Imp. Cyl. & Mod.), 12-ga.—28" (Mod. & Full).
Weight: 6 lbs., 15 oz. (12-ga.); 6 lbs., 10 oz. (20-ga.). **Length:** 43½" overall (26" bbl.).
Stock: 14⅛"x1⅜"x2⅜". Walnut with cut-checkered grip and forend. Black, vent. rubber recoil pad. Semi-gloss finish.
Features: Boxlock action with manual safety; extractors; single selective trigger. Color case-hardened receiver with engraving. Introduced 1989. Imported from Europe by Outdoor Sports Headquarters.
Price: **$475.00**

Charles Daly Lux Over/Under

Similar to the Field Grade except available in 12, 20, 28, 410-bore, has automatic selective ejectors, antique silver finish on frame, and has choke tubes for Imp. Cyl., Mod. and Full. Introduced 1989.
Price: **$699.00**

CHURCHILL MONARCH OVER/UNDER SHOTGUNS

Gauge: 12 or 20, 3" chambers.
Barrel: 26" (Imp. Cyl. & Mod.), 28" (Mod. & Full). Chrome-lined.
Weight: About 7 lbs.
Stock: European walnut with checkered p.g. and forend.
Features: Single selective trigger; blued receiver; vent. rib. Introduced 1986. Imported by Ellett Bros.
Price: **$519.95**

GAMBA DAYTONA COMPETITION OVER/UNDER

Gauge: 12, 20, 2¾" or 3" chambers.
Barrel: Skeet—26¾", 28" (Skeet & Skeet); Trap—30" (Imp. Mod. & Full), 32" (Mod. & Full); Sporting—28" (Mod. & Full), 30" (Imp. Mod. & Full); Monotrap—32" (Full).
Weight: 7.7 to 8.6 lbs.
Stock: Hand-checkered select walnut with oil finish.
Features: Boxlock action with detachable trigger mechanism; Boss-type locking system; automatic ejectors; anatomical single trigger, optional single selective, release or adjustable trigger. Black or chrome frame. Imported from Italy by Gamba U.S.A.
Price: Trap, 12- or 20-ga. **$4,995.00**
Price: Skeet, 12-ga. **$4,995.00**
Price: Pigeon, 12-ga. **$4,995.00**
Price: Sporting, 12-ga. **$4,995.00**
Price: American Trap, 12-ga. **$5,395.00**
Price: Engraved Grades . . . . . . **$9,390.00 to $13,195.00**
Price: Sideplate Grades . . . . . **$11,500.00 to $11,900.00**
Price: Sidelock Grades . . . . . . **$23,995.00 to $26,995.00**

Kassnar Grade I

KASSNAR GRADE I O/U SHOTGUN
Gauge: 12, 20, 28, 410, 3" chambers.
Barrel: 26" (Imp. Cyl. & Mod.), 28" (Mod. & Full), 28" (choke tubes).
Weight: 6.5 to 7.5 lbs.
Stock: European walnut with checkered grip and forend.
Features: Boxlock action with single selective trigger; blued and engraved receiver; vent. rib. Imported by K.B.I., Inc.
Price: . . . . **$500.00 to $750.00**

Krieghoff K-80 Sporting Clays

KRIEGHOFF K-80 SKEET SHOTGUN
Gauge: 12, 2¾" chambers.
Barrel: 28" (Skeet & Skeet, optional Tula or choke tubes).
Weight: About 7¾ lbs.
Stock: American Skeet or straight Skeet stocks, with palm-swell grips. Walnut.
Features: Satin gray receiver finish. Selective mechanical trigger adjustable for position. Choice of ventilated 8mm parallel flat rib or ventilated 8-12mm tapered flat rib. Introduced 1980. Imported from Germany by Krieghoff International, Inc.
Price: Standard, Skeet chokes **$5,875.00**
Price: As above, Tula chokes **$6,175.00**
Price: Lightweight model (weighs 7 lbs.), Standard **$5,875.00**
Price: Two-Barrel Set (tube concept), 12-ga., Standard **$10,400.00**
Price: Skeet Special (28", tapered flat rib, Skeet & Skeet choke tubes) **$6,250.00**

KRIEGHOFF K-80 LIVE BIRD SHOTGUN
Gauge: 12, 2¾" chambers.
Barrel: 28", 30" (Imp. Mod. & Super Full or choke tubes), 29" optional (Imp. Mod. & Special Full).
Weight: About 8 lbs.
Stock: Four stock dimensions available. Checkered walnut.
Features: Steel receiver with satin gray finish, engraving. Selective mechanical trigger adjustable for position. Ventilated step rib. Free-floating barrels. Comes with aluminum case. Introduced 1980. Imported from Germany by Krieghoff International, Inc.
Price: Standard grade **$6,145.00**

KRIEGHOFF K-80 SPORTING CLAYS O/U
Gauge: 12.
Barrel: 28" or 30" with choke tubes.
Weight: About 8 lbs.
Stock: #3 Sporting stock designed for gun-down shooting.
Features: Choice of standard or lightweight receiver with satin nickel finish and classic scroll engraving. Selective mechanical trigger adjustable for position. Choice of tapered flat or 8mm parallel flat barrel rib. Free-floating barrels. Aluminum case. Imported from Germany by Krieghoff International, Inc.
Price: Standard grade with five choke tubes **$6,795.00**

Krieghoff K-80 International Skeet
Similar to the Standard Skeet except has ½" ventilated Broadway-style rib, special Tula chokes with gas release holes at muzzle. International Skeet stock. Comes in fitted aluminum case.
Price: Standard grade **$6,575.00**

Krieghoff K-80 Four-Barrel Skeet Set
Similar to the Standard Skeet except comes with barrels for 12, 20, 28, 410. Comes with fitted aluminum case.
Price: Standard grade **$13,400.00**

Krieghoff K-80/RT Shotguns
Same as the standard K-80 shotguns except has a removable internally selective trigger mechanism. Can be considered an option on all K-80 guns of any configuration. Introduced 1990.
Price: RT (removable trigger) option on K-80 guns, add **$1,850.00**
Price: Extra trigger mechanisms **$1,450.00**

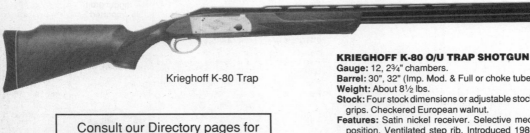

Krieghoff K-80 Trap

Consult our Directory pages for the location of firms mentioned.

KRIEGHOFF K-80 O/U TRAP SHOTGUN
Gauge: 12, 2¾" chambers.
Barrel: 30", 32" (Imp. Mod. & Full or choke tubes).
Weight: About 8½ lbs.
Stock: Four stock dimensions or adjustable stock available; all have palm-swell grips. Checkered European walnut.
Features: Satin nickel receiver. Selective mechanical trigger, adjustable for position. Ventilated step rib. Introduced 1980. Imported from Germany by Krieghoff International, Inc.
Price: K-80 O/U (30", 32", Imp. Mod. & Full), from **$6,145.00**
Price: K-80 Unsingle (32", 34", Full), Standard, from **$6,900.00**
Price: K-80 Combo (two-barrel set), Standard, from **$8,850.00**

Laurona 300 Sporting Clays

Laurona Silhouette 300 Trap
Same gun as the Silhouette 300 Sporting Clays except has 29" barrels, trap stock dimensions of 14⅜"x17⁄16"x1⅝", weighs 7 lbs., 15 oz. Available with flush or knurled Multichokes.
Price: **$1,310.00**

LAURONA SILHOUETTE 300 SPORTING CLAYS
Gauge: 12, 2¾" or 3" chambers.
Barrel: 28", 29" (Multichoke tubes, flush-type or knurled).
Weight: 7 lbs., 12 oz.
Stock: 14⅜"x1⅜"x2½". European walnut with full pistol grip, beavertail forend. Rubber buttpad.
Features: Selective single trigger, automatic selective ejectors. Introduced 1988. Imported from Spain by Galaxy Imports.
Price: **$1,250.00**
Price: Silhouette Ultra-Magnum, 3½" chambers **$1,265.00**

CAUTION: PRICES CHANGE, CHECK AT GUNSHOP.

Laurona Super 85 MS Pigeon

Features: Boxlock action, silvered with engraving. Automatic selective ejectors; choke tubes available on most models; single selective or twin single triggers; black chrome barrels. Has 5-year warranty, including metal finish. Imported from Spain by Galaxy Imports.

LAURONA SUPER MODEL OVER/UNDERS
Gauge: 12, 20, 2¾" or 3" chambers.
Barrel: 26", 28" (Multichoke), 29" (Multichokes and Full).
Weight: About 7 lbs.
Stock: European walnut. Dimensions vary according to model. Full pistol grip.

Price: Model 83 MG, 12- or 20-ga. **$1,215.00**
Price: Model 84S Super Trap (fixed chokes) **$1,340.00**
Price: Model 85 Super Game, 12- or 20-ga. **$1,215.00**
Price: Model 85 MS Super Trap (Full/Multichoke) **$1,390.00**
Price: Model 85 MS Super Pigeon **$1,370.00**
Price: Model 85 S Super Skeet, 12-ga. **$1,300.00**

Ljutic LM-6

Stock: To customer specs. Oil finish, hand checkered.
Features: Custom-made gun. Hollow-milled rib, pull or release trigger, pushbutton opener in front of trigger guard. From Ljutic Industries.

LJUTIC LM-6 DELUXE O/U SHOTGUN
Gauge: 12.
Barrel: 28" to 34", choked to customer specs for live birds, trap, International Trap.
Weight: To customer specs.

Price: Super Deluxe LM-6 O/U **$14,995.00**
Price: Over/under Combo (interchangeable single barrel, two trigger guards, one for single trigger, one for doubles) **$21,995.00**
Price: Extra over/under barrel sets, 29"-32" **$5,995.00**

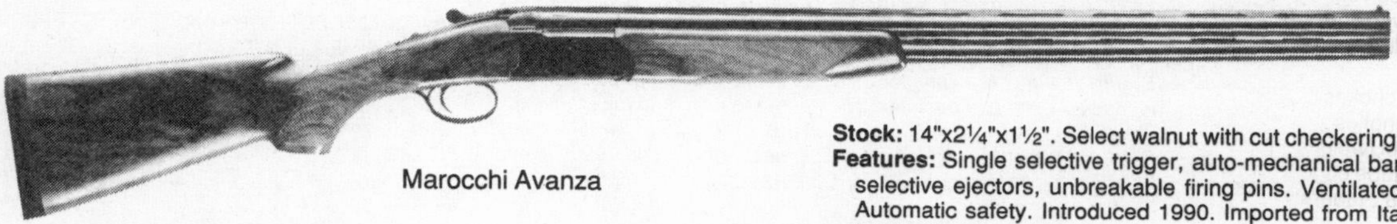

Marocchi Avanza

Stock: 14"x2¼"x1½". Select walnut with cut checkering. Recoil pad.
Features: Single selective trigger, auto-mechanical barrel cycling, automatic selective ejectors, unbreakable firing pins. Ventilated top and middle ribs. Automatic safety. Introduced 1990. Imported from Italy by Precision Sales International.

MAROCCHI AVANZA O/U SHOTGUN
Gauge: 12 and 20, 3" chambers.
Barrel: 26" (Imp. Cyl. & Mod. or Imp. Cyl., Mod., Full Interchokes); 28" (Mod. & Full or Imp. Cyl. Mod., Full Interchokes).
Weight: 6 lbs., 6 oz. to 6 lbs., 13 oz.

Price: 12-ga., 26" or 28", fixed chokes **$725.00**
Price: As above, with Interchokes **$769.00**
Price: 20-ga., 26" or 28", fixed chokes **$768.00**
Price: As above, with Interchokes **$814.00**
Price: Sporting Clays (12-ga. only, 28" Interchokes, trigger adj. for length) **$839.00**

MERKEL OVER/UNDER SHOTGUNS
Gauge: 12, 16, 20, 28, 410, 2¾", 3" chambers.
Barrel: 26", 26¾", 28" (standard chokes).
Weight: 6 to 7 lbs.
Stock: European walnut. Straight English or pistol grip.
Features: Models 200E and 201E are boxlocks, 203E and 303E are sidelocks. All have auto. ejectors, articulated front triggers. Auto. safety, selective and non-selective triggers optional. Imported from Germany by GSI, Inc.

Price: 200E, about **$2,995.00**
Price: 201E, about **$3,695.00**
Price: 203E (sidelock), about **$7,895.00**

PERAZZI MX8/MX8 SPECIAL TRAP, SKEET
Gauge: 12, 2¾" chambers.
Barrel: Trap—29½" (Imp. Mod. & Extra Full), 31½" (Full & Extra Full). Choke tubes optional. Skeet—27⅝" (Skeet & Skeet).
Weight: About 8½ lbs. (Trap); 7 lbs., 15 oz. (Skeet).
Stock: Interchangeable and custom made to customer specs.
Features: Has detachable and interchangeable trigger group with flat V springs. Flat 7/16" ventilated rib. Many options available. Imported from Italy by Perazzi U.S.A., Inc.

Price: From **$7,000.00**
Price: MX8 Special (adj. four-position trigger), from **$7,400.00**
Price: MX8 Special Single (32" or 34" single barrel, step rib), from **$7,000.00**
Price: MX8 Special Combo (o/u and single barrel sets), from . . . **$9,850.00**

Perazzi Grand American 88 Special
Similar to the MX8 except has tapered 7/16"x5/16" high ramped rib. Choked Imp. Mod. & Full, 29½" barrels.
Price: From **$7,000.00**
Price: Special Single (32" or 34" single barrel), from **$7,000.00**
Price: DB81 Special, from **$7,700.00**

Perazzi Mirage Special Skeet Over/Under
Similar to the MX8 Skeet except has adjustable four-position trigger, Skeet stock dimensions.
Price: From **$7,400.00**

PERAZZI MIRAGE SPECIAL SPORTING O/U
Gauge: 12, 2¾" chambers.
Barrel: 27⅝", 28⅜" (Imp. Mod. & Extra Full).
Weight: 7 lbs., 12 oz.
Stock: Special specifications.
Features: Has single selective trigger; flat 7/16"x5/16" vent. rib. Many options available. Imported from Italy by Perazzi U.S.A., Inc.
Price: **$7,780.00**

Perazzi MX3 Special

Perazzi MX3 Special Single, Over/Under
Similar to the MX8 Special except has an adjustable four-position trigger, high 7/16"x5/16" rib, weighs 8½ lbs. Choked Mod. & Full.
Price: From **$6,500.00**
Price: MX3 Special Single (32" or 34" single barrel), from **$6,500.00**
Price: MX3 Special Combo (o/u and single barrel sets), from . . . **$8,550.00**

Perazzi Mirage Special Four-Gauge Skeet
Similar to the Mirage Sporting model except has Skeet dimensions, interchangeable, adjustable four-position trigger assembly. Comes with four barrel sets in 12, 20, 28, 410, flat 5/16"x5/16" rib.
Price: From **$16,800.00**
Price: MX3 Special Set, from **$15,400.00**

PERAZZI MX12 HUNTING OVER/UNDER
Gauge: 12, 2¾" chambers.
Barrel: 26", 27⅝", 28⅜", 29½" (Mod. & Full); choke tubes available in 27⅝", 29½" only (MX12C).
Weight: 7 lbs., 4 oz.
Stock: To customer specs; Interchangeable.
Features: Single selective trigger; coil springs used in action; schnabel forend tip. Imported from Italy by Perazzi U.S.A., Inc.
Price: From **$7,000.00**
Price: MX12C (with choke tubes), from **$7,380.00**

Perazzi MX7 Over/Under Shotgun
Based on the MX12 coil spring, fixed trigger mechanism, but has trigger selector on top. Flat and rounded receiver similar to the MX3, with thicker

Perazzi MX20C

Perazzi MX20 Hunting Over/Under
Similar to the MX12 except 20-ga. frame size. Available in 20, 28, 410 with 2¾" or 3" chambers. 26" standard, and choked Mod. & Full. Weight is 6 lbs., 6 oz.
Price: From **$7,300.00**
Price: MX20C (as above, 20-ga. only, choke tubes), from **$7,730.00**

frame. The 28⅜" barrels have side ribs and screw-in chokes. An optional 29½" barrel set is offered. Introduced 1992.
Price: **$5,450.00**

RUGER RED LABEL O/U SHOTGUN
Gauge: 12 and 20, 3" chambers.
Barrel: 26", 28" (Skeet, Imp. Cyl., Full, Extra-Full, Mod. screw-in choke tubes). Proved for steel shot.
Weight: About 7 lbs. (20-ga.); 7½ lbs. (12-ga.). **Length:** 43" overall (26" barrels).
Stock: 14"x1½"x2½". Straight grain American walnut. Checkered pistol grip and forend, rubber butt pad.
Features: Single selective mechanical trigger, selective automatic ejectors; serrated free-floating vent. rib. Comes with two Skeet, one Imp. Cyl., one Mod., one Full choke tube and wrench; Extra-Full tube available at extra cost. Made in U.S. by Sturm, Ruger & Co.
Price: Red Label with pistol grip stock **$1,157.50**
Price: English Field with straight-grip stock **$1,157.50**

Ruger English Field

Ruger Sporting Clays O/U Shotgun
Similar to the Red Label except 12-gauge only, 30" barrels back-bored to .744" diameter with stainless steel choke tubes. Weight is 7.75 lbs., overall length 47". Stock dimensions of 14⅛"x1½"x2½". Free-floating serrated vent. rib with brass front and mid-rib beads. No barrel side spacers. Comes with two Skeet, one Imp. Cyl., one Mod. choke tubes. Full and Extra-Full available at extra cost. Introduced 1992.
Price: **$1,285.00**

SKB 505 Deluxe

SKB Model 605 Over/Under Shotgun
Similar to the Model 505 Deluxe except has gold-plated trigger, semi-fancy American walnut stock, jeweled barrel block and fine engraving in silvered receiver, top lever, and trigger guard.
Price: Field **$1,195.00**
Price: Two-barrel Field Set (12 & 20 or 28 & 410) **$1,695.00**
Price: Trap, Skeet **$1,195.00**
Price: Two-barrel trap combo **$1,595.00**
Price: Sporting Clays **$1,245.00**
Price: Skeet Set (20, 28, 410) **$2,395.00**

SKB Model 885 Over/Under Trap, Skeet, Sporting Clays
Similar to the Model 605 except has engraved sideplates, top lever and trigger guard, semi-fancy American walnut stock.
Price: Field, Skeet/Trap **$1,595.00**

SKB MODEL 505 DELUXE OVER/UNDER SHOTGUN
Gauge: 12, 2¾" or 3"; 20, 3"; 28, 2¾"; 410, 3".
Barrel: 12-ga.—26", 28", 30", 32", 34" (Inter-Choke tube); 20-ga.—26", 28" (Inter-Choke tube); 28—26", 28" (Inter-Choke tube); 410—26", 28" (Imp. Cyl. & Mod., Mod. & Full).
Weight: 6.6 to 8.5 lbs. **Length:** 43" to 51⅜" overall.
Stock: 14⅛"x1½"x2³⁄₁₆". Hand checkered walnut with high-gloss finish. Target stocks available in standard and Monte Carlo.
Sights: Metal bead front (field), target style on Skeet, trap, Sporting Clays.
Features: Boxlock action; silver nitride finish with game scene engraving; manual safety, automatic ejectors, single selective trigger. Introduced 1987. Imported from Japan by G.U., Inc.
Price: Field **$995.00**
Price: Two-barrel Field Set (12 & 20 or 28 & 410) **$1,495.00**
Price: Trap, Skeet **$995.00**
Price: Two-barrel trap combo **$1,395.00**
Price: Sporting Clays model **$1,045.00**
Price: Skeet Set (20, 28, 410) **$2,195.00**

Price: Skeet Set (20, 28, 410) **$2,995.00**
Price: Trap Combo **$2,195.00**
Price: Field Set **$2,195.00**
Price: Sporting Clays **$1,645.00**

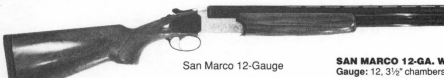

San Marco 12-Gauge

San Marco Field Special O/U Shotgun
Similar to the 12-ga. Wildfowler except in 12-, 20- and 28-gauge with 3" chambers, 26" (Imp. Cyl. & Mod.) or 28" (Full & Mod.) barrels. Stock dimensions of 14¼"x1½"x1½". Weight of 5½ to 6 lbs. Engraved, silvered receiver, vented top and middle ribs, single trigger. Introduced 1990. Imported from Italy by Cape Outfitters.
Price: **$695.00**

SAN MARCO 12-GA. WILDFOWLER SHOTGUN
Gauge: 12, 3½" chambers.
Barrel: 28" (Mod. & Mod., Full & Mod.), vented top and middle ribs.
Weight: 7 lbs., 12 oz.
Stock: 15"x1½"x2¼". Walnut, with checkered grip and forend.
Features: Chrome-lined bores with long forcing cones; single non-selective trigger; extractors on Standard, automatic ejectors on Deluxe; silvered, engraved action. Waterproof wood finish. Introduced 1990. Imported from Italy by Cape Outfitters.
Price: Standard **$595.00**
Price: Deluxe **$695.00**

CAUTION: PRICES CHANGE, CHECK AT GUNSHOP.

SAN MARCO 10-GAUGE O/U SHOTGUN

Gauge: 10, 3½" chambers.
Barrel: 28" (Mod. & Mod.), 32" (Mod. & Full). Chrome lined.
Weight: 9 to 9½ lbs.
Stock: 15"x1⅜"x2⅛". Walnut.
Features: Solid ⅜" barrel rib. Long forcing cones. Double triggers, extractors;

Deluxe grade has automatic ejectors. Engraved receiver with game scenes, matte finish. Waterproof finish on wood. Introduced 1990. Imported from Italy by Cape Outfitters.
Price: Standard grade **$795.00**
Price: Deluxe grade **$895.00**

Savage 312 Field

SAVAGE 312 FIELD O/U SHOTGUN

Gauge: 12, 3".
Barrel: 26", 28" (Imp. Cyl., Mod., Full choke tubes).
Weight: 7 lbs. **Length:** 43" overall (26" barrel).
Stock: Checkered walnut with ventilated recoil pad.
Features: Single trigger; satin chrome finished frame. Ventilated top and middle ribs. Introduced 1990. From Savage Arms.
Price: **$680.00**

Savage 312T Trap Over/Under Shotgun

Similar to the Model 312 Field gun, except has 30" barrels (Full, Mod. choke tubes), measures 47" overall, weighs 7¼ lbs., and has checkered walnut Monte Carlo stock with rubber recoil pad. Introduced 1990. From Savage Arms.
Price: **$700.00**

Savage 312SC Sporting Clays Shotgun

Similar to the Model 312F Field gun except has 28" barrels (Skeet 1, Skeet 2, Mod., Imp. Cyl., Mod., Full choke tubes), curved target-type recoil pad. Receiver marked with "Sporting Clays" on each side. Introduced 1990. From Savage Arms.
Price: **$720.00**

Stoeger/IGA Condor

STOEGER/IGA CONDOR OVER/UNDER SHOTGUN

Gauge: 12, 20, 3" chambers.
Barrel: 26" (Full & Full, Imp. Cyl. & Mod.), 28" (Mod. & Full), or with choke tubes.

Weight: 6¾ to 7 lbs.
Stock: 14½"x1½"x2½". Oil-finished hardwood with checkered pistol grip and forend.
Features: Manual safety, single trigger, extractors only, ventilated top rib. Introduced 1983. Imported from Brazil by Stoeger Industries.
Price: **$525.00**
Price: With choke tubes **$565.00**

Techni-Mec Model SPL 640

TECHNI-MEC MODEL SPL 640 FOLDING O/U

Gauge: 12, 16, 20, 28, 2¾" chambers; 410, 3" chambers.
Barrel: 26" (Mod. & Full).
Weight: 5½ lbs.
Stock: European walnut.
Features: Gun folds in half for storage, transportation. Chrome-lined barrels; ventilated rib; photo-engraved silvered receiver. Imported from Italy by L. Joseph Rahn. Introduced 1984.
Price: Double triggers **$425.00**
Price: Single trigger **$450.00**

TECHNI-MEC MODEL SR 692 EM OVER/UNDER

Gauge: 12, 16, 20, 2¾" or 3" chambers.
Barrel: 26", 28", 30" (Mod., Full, Imp. Cyl., Cyl.).
Weight: 6½ lbs.
Stock: 14½"x1½"x2½". European walnut with checkered grip and forend.
Features: Boxlock action with dummy sideplates, fine game scene engraving; single selective trigger; automatic ejectors available. Contact importer for data on complete line. Imported from Italy by L. Joseph Rahn. Introduced 1984.
Price: **$1,225.00**
Price: Slug gun **$1,000.00**
Price: SR 690 Trap, Skeet **$1,125.00**
Price: SRL 694 Trap, Skeet **$1,600.00**
Price: SRL 695 Trap, Skeet **$1,800.00**
Price: SRL 702 Trap, Skeet **$2,000.00**
Price: SRL 802 Trap, Skeet **$1,400.00**

TECHNI-MEC MODEL 610 OVER/UNDER

Gauge: 10, 3½" chambers.
Barrel: 32" (Imp. Mod. & Full).
Stocks: Hand-checkered walnut.
Features: Single selective trigger; silvered engraved frame, blued barrels. Rubber recoil pad. Introduced 1991. Imported from Italy by Mandall Shooting Supplies.
Price: **$1,200.00**

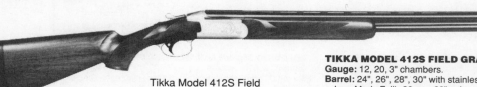

Tikka Model 412S Field

TIKKA MODEL 412S FIELD GRADE OVER/UNDER

Gauge: 12, 20, 3" chambers.
Barrel: 24", 26", 28", 30" with stainless steel screw-in chokes (Imp. Cyl, Mod., Imp. Mod., Full); 20-ga., 28" only.
Weight: About 7¼ lbs.
Stock: American walnut. Standard dimensions—13⁹⁄₁₀"x1½"x2⅖". Checkered p.g. and forend.
Features: Free interchangeability of barrels, stocks and forends into double rifle model, combination gun, etc. Barrel selector in trigger; auto. top tang safety; barrel cocking indicators. Introduced 1980. Imported from Italy by Stoeger.
Price: Model 412S (ejectors) **$1,155.00**
Price: Model 412S Sporting Clays, 12-ga., 28", choke tubes . . . **$1,270.00**

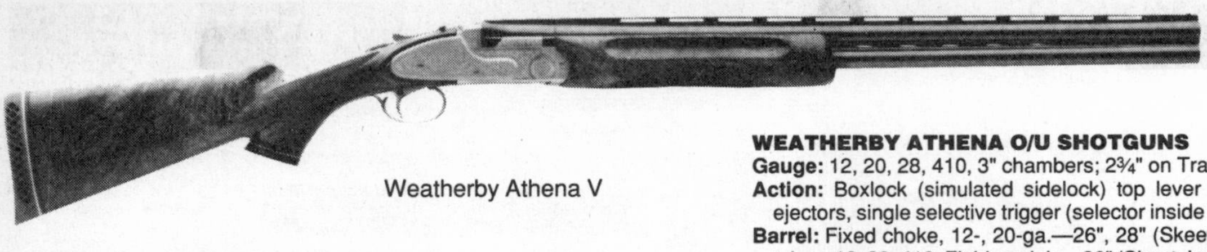

Weatherby Athena V

WEATHERBY ORION O/U SHOTGUNS

Gauge: 12, 20, 410, 3" chambers; 28, 2¾" chambers.
Barrel: Fixed choke, 12, 20, 28, 410—26", 28", 30" (Imp. Cyl. & Mod., Full & Mod., Skeet & Skeet); IMC Multi-Choke, 12, 20, Field models—26" (Imp. Cyl., Mod., Full, Skeet), 28" (Imp. Cyl., Mod., Full), 30" (Mod., Full); O/U Trap models—30", 32" (Imp. Mod., Mod., Full); Single bbl. Trap—32", 34" (Imp. Mod., Mod., Full).
Weight: 6½ to 9 lbs.
Stock: American walnut, checkered grip and forend. Rubber recoil pad. Dimensions for Field and Skeet models, 14¼"x1½"x2½".
Features: Selective automatic ejectors, single selective mechanical trigger. Top tang safety, Greener cross bolt. Orion I has plain blued receiver, no engraving; Orion II has engraved, blued receiver; Orion III has silver-gray receiver with engraving. Imported from Japan by Weatherby.
Price: Orion I, Field, 12 or 20, IMC **$1,050.00**
Price: Orion II, Field, 12 or 20, IMC **$1,202.00**
Price: Orion II, Field, 28 or 410, fixed chokes **$1,202.00**
Price: Orion II, Skeet, 12 or 20, fixed chokes **$1,216.00**
Price: Orion II, Trap, 12, IMC **$1,264.00**
Price: Orion III, Field, 12 or 20, IMC **$1,344.00**

WEATHERBY ATHENA O/U SHOTGUNS

Gauge: 12, 20, 28, 410, 3" chambers; 2¾" on Trap gun.
Action: Boxlock (simulated sidelock) top lever break-open. Selective auto ejectors, single selective trigger (selector inside trigger guard).
Barrel: Fixed choke, 12-, 20-ga.—26", 28" (Skeet & Skeet); IMC Multi-Choke tubes, 12, 20, 410, Field models—26" (Skeet, Imp. Cyl., Mod.), 28" (Imp. Cyl., Mod., Full), 30" (12-ga. only. Full, Mod., Full); O/U Trap models—30", 32" (Mod., Imp. Mod., Full).
Weight: 12-ga., 7⅜ lbs.; 20-ga. 6⅞ lbs.
Stock: American walnut, checkered p.g. and forend (14¼"x1½"x2½").
Features: Mechanically operated trigger. Top tang safety, Greener cross bolt, fully engraved receiver, recoil pad installed. IMC models furnished with three interchangeable flush-fitting choke tubes. Imported from Japan by Weatherby. Introduced 1982.
Price: Skeet, fixed choke **$1,965.00**
Price: 12- or 20-ga., IMC Multi-Choke, Field **$1,950.00**
Price: IMC Multi-Choke Trap **$1,975.00**
Price: Athena Grade V (more elaborate engraving), 12 and 20 . . **$2,450.00**
Price: Extra IMC Multi-Choke tubes **$20.00**

Weatherby Orion Sporting Clays

Similar to the standard Orion except in 12-gauge only with 28" barrels, IMC choke tubes with elongated forcing cones. Blued receiver with two 24 karat gold clay targets on the bottom of the receiver. Has a raised rib with center and front beads. Special stock dimensions of 14¼"x2¼"x1½"; rounded buttpad. Introduced 1991.
Price: **$1,436.00**

Weatherby Orion II Sporting Clays

PIETRO ZANOLETTI MODEL 2000 FIELD O/U

Gauge: 12 only.
Barrel: 28" (Mod. & Full).
Weight: 7 lbs.
Stock: European walnut, checkered grip and forend.
Sights: Gold bead front.
Features: Boxlock action with auto ejectors, double triggers; engraved receiver. Imported from Italy by Mandall Shooting Supplies. Introduced 1984.
Price: **$895.00**

ZOLI SILVER FALCON OVER/UNDER

Gauge: 12 or 20, 3" chambers.
Barrel: 12 ga.—26", 28"; 20 ga.—26"; Imp. Cyl., Mod., Imp. Mod., Full choke tubes.
Weight: 6.25 to 7.25 lbs.
Stock: 14¼"x2⅛"x1⁵⁄₁₆". Oil-finished Turkish circassian walnut.
Features: Boxlock action with silver finish, floral engraving; single selective trigger, automatic ejectors. Introduced 1989. Imported from Italy by European American Armory.
Price: **$1,495.00**

ZOLI Z90 TRAP GUN

Gauge: 12, 2¾" chambers.
Barrel: 29½" or 32". Comes with Mod., Imp. Mod. and Full choke tubes.
Weight: 8.5 lbs.
Stock: 14½"x2⅛"x1½"x1½". Checkered Turkish circassian walnut with Monte Carlo, recoil pad, oil finish.
Features: Boxlock action with automatic selective ejectors, single selective trigger adjustable for pull length; step-type vent. rib and vent. center rib. Introduced 1989. Imported from Italy by European American Armory.
Price: **$2,195.00**

Zoli Z90 Skeet Gun

Similar to the Z90 Trap except has 28" barrels with fixed Skeet & Skeet chokes, 14¼"x2¼"x1½" stock dimensions (drop at heel also available at 2⅛", 2⅜" or 2½"). Weighs 7.75 lbs. Available in 12-gauge only. Introduced 1989. Imported from Italy by European American Armory.
Price: **$2,195.00**

Weatherby Orion II Sporting Clays O/U

Similar to the Orion II Field except in 12-gauge only with 2¾" chambers, 28", 30" barrels with Imp. Cyl., Mod., Full chokes. Stock dimensions are 14¼"x1½"x2¼"; weight 7.5 to 8 lbs. Matte finish, competition center vent. rib, mid-barrel and enlarged front beads. Rounded recoil pad. Receiver finished in silver nitride with acid-etched, gold-plate clay pigeon monogram. Barrels have lengthened forcing cones. Introduced 1992.
Price: **$1,436.00**

ZOLI Z90 SPORTING CLAYS SHOTGUN

Gauge: 12, 2¾" chambers.
Barrel: 28". Comes with four choke tubes—two Skeet, one each Imp. Cyl. and Mod.
Weight: 7.25 lbs.
Stock: 14¼"x2⅛"x1½". Turkish circassian walnut with checkered grip and forend; oil finish.
Features: Sidelock action with silvered and engraved frame, single selective trigger, selective automatic ejectors. Schnabel forend tip; solid rubber butt pad. Introduced 1989. Imported from Italy by European American Armory.
Price: **$2,195.00**

ZOLI WOODSMAN OVER/UNDER SHOTGUN

Gauge: 12, 3" chambers.
Barrel: 23" (five choke tubes furnished—two each Cyl., plus Imp. Cyl., Mod., Full).
Weight: 6.75 lbs.
Stock: 14½"x2⁵⁄₁₆"x1⅜". Turkish circassian walnut with skip-line checkering, rubber butt pad; oil finish.
Sights: Rifle-type sights on raised rib. Folding leaf rear, bead front.
Features: Boxlock action with silvered and engraved frame, single selective trigger, automatic selective ejectors. Introduced 1989. Imported from Italy by European American Armory.
Price: **$1,495.00**

CAUTION: PRICES CHANGE, CHECK AT GUNSHOP.

Variety of models for utility and sporting use, including some competitive shooting.

American Arms Brittany

AMERICAN ARMS BRITTANY SHOTGUN
Gauge: 12, 20, 3" chambers.
Barrel: 12-ga.—27"; 20-ga.—25" (Imp. Cyl., Mod., Full choke tubes).
Weight: 6 lbs., 7 oz. (20-ga.).
Stock: 14⅛"x1⅜"x2⅜". Hand-checkered walnut with oil finish, straight English-style with semi-beavertail forend, or pistol grip stock with gloss finish.
Features: Boxlock action with case-color finish, engraving; single selective trigger, automatic selective ejectors; rubber recoil pad. Introduced 1989. Imported from Spain by American Arms, Inc.
Price: Straight grip or pistol grip $689.00

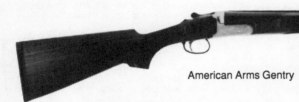

American Arms Gentry

AMERICAN ARMS GENTRY DOUBLE SHOTGUN
Gauge: 12, 20, 28, 410, 3" chambers except 16, 28, 2¾".
Barrel: 26" (Imp. Cyl. & Mod., all gauges), 28" (Mod., & Full, 12 and 20 gauges).
Weight: 6¼ to 6¾ lbs.
Stock: 14⅛"x1⅜"x2⅜". Hand-checkered walnut with semi-gloss finish.
Sights: Metal bead front.
Features: Boxlock action with English-style scroll engraving, color case-hardened finish. Double triggers, extractors. Independent floating firing pins. Manual safety. Five-year warranty. Introduced 1987. Imported from Spain by American Arms, Inc.
Price: 12, 16 or 20 . . . . $559.00
Price: 28 or 410 . . . . $599.00

American Arms Derby Side-by-Side
Has sidelock action with English-style engraving on the sideplates. Straight-grip, hand-checkered walnut stock with splinter forend, hand-rubbed oil finish. Single non-selective trigger, automatic selective ejectors. Same chokes, rib, barrel lengths as the Gentry. Has 5-year warranty. From American Arms, Inc.
Price: 12- or 20-ga. $929.00

American Arms Grulla

AMERICAN ARMS GRULLA #2 DOUBLE SHOTGUN
Gauge: 12, 20, 28, 410.
Barrel: 12-ga.—28" (Mod. & Full); 26" (Imp. Cyl. & Mod.), all gauges.
Weight: 5 lbs., 13 oz. to 6 lbs., 4 oz.
Stock: Select walnut with straight English grip, splinter forend; hand-rubbed oil finish; checkered grip, forend, butt.
Features: True sidelock action with double triggers, detachable locks, automatic selective ejectors, cocking indicators, gas escape valves. Color case-hardened receiver with scroll engraving. English-style concave rib. Introduced 1989. Imported from Spain by American Arms, Inc.
Price: 12, 20, 28, 410 . . . . $2,798.00
Price: Two-barrel sets $3,658.00

AMERICAN ARMS WS/SS 10
Gauge: 10, 3½" chambers.
Barrel: 32" (Full & Full). Flat rib.
Weight: 10 lbs., 13 oz.
Stock: 14⁵⁄₁₆"x1⅜"x2⅜". Hand-checkered walnut with beavertail forend, full pistol grip, dull finish, rubber recoil pad.
Features: Boxlock action with double triggers and extractors. All metal has Parkerized finish. Comes with camouflaged sling, sling swivels, 5-year warranty. Introduced 1987. Imported from Spain by American Arms, Inc.
Price: $599.00

American Arms TS/SS 12 Side-by-Side
Similar to the WS/SS 10 except in 12-ga. with 3½" chambers, 26" barrels with Imp. Cyl., Mod., Full choke tubes, single selective trigger, extractors. Comes with camouflage sling, swivels, 5-year warranty. From American Arms, Inc.
Price: $599.00

American Arms TS/SS 10 Double Shotgun
Similar to the WS/SS 10 except has 26" (Full & Full choke tubes) barrels, raised solid rib. Double triggers, extractors. All metal and wood has matte finish. Imported by American Arms, Inc.
Price: $599.00

ARMSPORT 1050 SERIES DOUBLE SHOTGUNS
Gauge: 12, 20, 410, 28, 3" chambers.
Barrel: 12-ga.—28" (Mod. & Full); 20-ga.—26" (Imp. & Mod.); 410—26" (Full & Full); 28-ga.—26" (Mod. & Full).
Weight: About 6¾ lbs.
Stock: European walnut.
Features: Chrome-lined barrels. Boxlock action with engraving. Imported from Italy by Armsport.
Price: 12, 20 . . . . $785.00
Price: 28, 410 . . . . $860.00

Arizaga Model 31

ARIZAGA MODEL 31 DOUBLE SHOTGUN
Gauge: 12, 16, 20, 28, 410.
Barrel: 26", 28" (standard chokes).
Weight: 6 lbs., 9 oz. **Length:** 45" overall.
Stock: Straight English style or pistol grip.
Features: Boxlock action with double triggers; blued, engraved receiver. Imported by Mandall Shooting Supplies.
Price: $550.00

ARRIETA SIDELOCK DOUBLE SHOTGUNS
Gauge: 12, 16, 20, 28, 410.
Barrel: Length and chokes to customer specs.
Weight: To customer specs.
Stock: 14½"x1½"x2½" (standard dimensions), or to customer specs. Straight English with checkered butt (standard), or pistol grip. Select European walnut with oil finish.
Features: Essentially a custom gun with myriad options. Holland & Holland-pattern hand-detachable sidelocks, selective automatic ejectors, double triggers (hinged front) standard, single selective optional. Most have self-opening action. Finish and engraving to customer specs. Imported from Spain by Wingshooting Adventures.
Price: Model 557, auto ejectors, from **$2,750.00**
Price: Model 570, auto ejectors, from **$3,050.00**
Price: Model 578, auto ejectors, from **$3,600.00**
Price: Model 600 Imperial, self-opening, from **$4,990.00**
Price: Model 601 Imperial Tiro, self-opening, from . . . **$5,750.00**
Price: Model 801, from **$7,950.00**
Price: Model 802, from **$7,950.00**
Price: Model 803, from **$5,850.00**
Price: Model 871, auto ejectors, from **$4,290.00**
Price: Model 872, self-opening, from **$9,790.00**
Price: Model 873, self-opening, from **$6,850.00**
Price: Model 874, self-opening, from **$7,950.00**
Price: Model 875, self-opening, from **$13,950.00**

AYA BOXLOCK SHOTGUNS
Gauge: 12, 16, 20, 28, 410.
Barrel: 26", 27", 28", depending upon gauge.
Weight: 5 to 7 lbs.
Stock: European walnut.
Features: Anson & Deeley system with double locking lugs; chopper lump barrels; bushed firing pins; automatic safety and ejectors; articulated front trigger. Imported by Armes de Chasse.
Price: Model XXV, 12 or 20 . . . . **$3,300.00**
Price: Model 4 Deluxe, 12, 16, 20, 28, 410 . . . . **$3,500.00**
Price: Model 4, 12, 16, 20, 28, 410 . . . . **$2,000.00**

AYA SIDELOCK DOUBLE SHOTGUNS
Gauge: 12, 16, 20, 28, 410.
Barrel: 26", 27", 28", 29", depending upon gauge.
Weight: NA.
Stock: Figured European walnut; cut checkering; oil finish.
Features: Sidelock actions with double triggers (articulated front), automatic safety, automatic ejectors, cocking indicators, bushed firing pins, replaceable hinge pins, chopper lump barrels. Many options available. Imported by Armes de Chasse.
Price: Model 1, 12 or 20, exhibition-quality wood **$7,000.00**
Price: Model 2, 12, 16, 20, 28, 410 . . . . **$3,700.00**
Price: Model 53, 12, 16, 20 . . . . **$5,300.00**
Price: Model 56, 12 only **$8,200.00**
Price: Model XXV, 12 or 20, Churchill-type rib **$4,300.00**
Price: Matador, 12 or 20, single selective trigger, pistol grip stock . **$2,000.00**

Bernardelli Brescia

BERNARDELLI SERIES S. UBERTO DOUBLES
Gauge: 12, 20, 28, 2¾" or 3" chambers.
Barrel: 25⅝", 26¾", 28", 29½" (Mod. & Full).
Weight: 6 to 6½ lbs.
Stock: 14³⁄₁₆"x2³⁄₈"x1⁹⁄₁₆" standard dimensions. Select walnut with hand checkering.
Features: Anson & Deeley boxlock action with Purdey locks, choice of extractors or ejectors. Uberto 1 has color case-hardened receiver, Uberto 2 and F.S. silvered and differ in amount and quality of engraving. Custom options available. Imported from Italy by Magnum Research.
Price: S. Uberto 2E **$1,924.00**
Price: As above with single trigger **$2,005.00**

Bernardelli System Holland H. Side-by-Side
True sidelock action. Available in 12-gauge only, reinforced breech, three round Purdey locks, automatic ejectors, folding right trigger. Model VB Liscio has color case-hardened receiver and sideplates with light engraving. VB and VB Tipo Lusso are silvered and engraved.
Price: VB Liscio **$10,757.00**
Price: VB Lusso **$14,377.00**
Price: VB Gold **$57,992.00**

BERNARDELLI BRESCIA HAMMER DOUBLE SHOTGUN
Gauge: 12, 20, 2¾" or 3"; 16, 2¾".
Barrel: 25½" (Cyl. & Mod., Imp. Cyl. & Imp. Mod.), 26¾" (Imp. Cyl. & Imp. Mod., Mod. & Full), 28" (Mod. & Full), 29½" (Imp. Mod. & Full).
Weight: About 7 lbs.
Stock: Straight English grip. Checkered European walnut.
Features: Color case-hardened boxlock action. Introduced 1990. Imported from Italy by Magnum Research.
Price: **$2,482.00**
Price: Model Italia, fully engraved **$2,844.00**
Price: Model Italia Extra **$7,861.00**

Bernardelli Series Roma Shotguns
Similar to the Series S. Uberto Models except with dummy sideplates to simulate sidelock action. In 12-, 16-, 20-, 28-gauge, 25½", 26¾", 28", 29" barrels. Straight English or pistol grip stock. Chrome-lined barrels, boxlock action, double triggers, ejectors, automatic safety. Checkered butt. Special choke combinations, barrel lengths optional.
Price: Roma 3E, about **$1,986.00**
Price: Roma 4E (12, 20, 28), about **$2,276.00**
Price: Roma 6E (12, 20, 28), about **$2,482.00**
Price: Roma 3EM with ejectors, about **$2,067.00**
Price: Roma 4EM with ejectors (12, 20, 28), about **$2,354.00**
Price: Roma 6EM with ejectors (12, 20, 28), about **$2,563.00**

Bernardelli Hemingway

Consult our Directory pages for the location of firms mentioned.

BERETTA MODEL 452 SIDELOCK SHOTGUN
Gauge: 12, 2¾" or 3" chambers.
Barrel: 26", 28", 30", choked to customer specs.
Weight: 6 lbs., 13 oz.
Stock: Dimensions to customer specs. Highly figured walnut; Model 452 EELL has walnut briar.
Features: Full sidelock action with English-type double bolting; automatic selective ejectors, manual safety; double triggers, single or single non-selective trigger on request. Essentially custom made to specifications. Model 452 is coin finished without engraving; 452 EELL is fully engraved. Imported from Italy by Beretta U.S.A.
Price: 452 . . . . **$22,470.00**
Price: 452 EELL **$30,680.00**

BERNARDELLI HEMINGWAY LIGHTWEIGHT DOUBLES
Gauge: 12, 20, 2¾" or 3"; 16, 28, 2¾".
Barrel: 23½" to 28" (Cyl. & Imp. Cyl. to Mod. & Full).
Weight: 6¼ lbs.
Stock: Straight English grip of checkered European walnut.
Features: Silvered and engraved boxlock action. Folding front trigger on double-trigger models. Ejectors. Imported from Italy by Magnum Research.
Price: Hemingway, 12 or 20 . . . . **$2,172.00**
Price: With single trigger **$2,253.00**
Price: Deluxe, with sideplates **$2,482.00**
Price: As above, single trigger **$2,563.00**

Beretta 627 EL

CHAPUIS SIDE-BY-SIDE SHOTGUN
Gauge: 12, 16, 20.
Barrel: 22", 23.6", 26.8", 27.6", 31.5", chokes to customer specs.
Weight: 5 to 10 lbs. **Length:** NA.
Stock: French walnut, straight English or pistol grip.
Features: Double hook Blitz system center sidelock action with notched action zone, automatic ejectors or extractors. Long trigger guard (most models), choice of raised solid rib, vent. rib or ultra light rib. Imported from France by Armes de Chasse.
Price: About . . . . $4,000.00 to $5,000.00

CRUCELEGUI HERMANOS MODEL 150 DOUBLE
Gauge: 12, 16 or 20, 2¾" chambers.
Action: Greener triple cross bolt.
Barrel: 20", 26", 28", 30", 32" (Cyl. & Cyl., Full & Full, Mod. & Full, Mod. & Imp. Cyl., Imp. Cyl. & Full, Mod. & Mod.).
Weight: 5 to 7¼ lbs.
Stock: Hand-checkered walnut, beavertail forend.
Features: Double triggers; color case-hardened receiver; sling swivels; chrome-lined bores. Imported from Spain by Mandall Shooting Supplies.
Price: $450.00

BERETTA SIDE-BY-SIDE FIELD SHOTGUNS
Gauge: 12 and 20, 3", 3½" chambers.
Barrel: 26" and 28" (Mobilchoke tubes).
Stock: Close-grained American walnut.
Features: Front and center beads on a raised ventilated rib. Onyx has P. Beretta signature on each side of the receiver, while a gold gauge marking is inscribed atop the rib. Imported from Italy by Beretta U.S.A.
Price: 626 Onyx $1,870.00
Price: 627 EL (gold inlays, sideplates) $3,270.00
Price: 627 EELL (engraved sideplates, pistol grip or straight English stock) $5,405.00

CHARLES DALY MODEL DSS DOUBLE
Gauge: 12, 20, 3" chambers.
Barrel: 26", choke tubes.
Weight: 6 lbs., 13 oz. (12-ga.). **Length:** 44.5" overall.
Stock: 14⅛"x1⅜"x2⅜". Figured walnut; pistol grip; cut checkering; black rubber recoil pad; semi-beavertail forend.
Features: Boxlock action with automatic selective ejectors, automatic safety, gold single trigger. Engraved, silvered frame. Introduced 1990. Imported by Outdoor Sports Headquarters.
Price: $675.00

FERLIB MODEL F VII DOUBLE SHOTGUN
Gauge: 12, 16, 20, 28, 410.
Barrel: 25" to 28".
Weight: 5½ lbs. (20-ga.).
Stock: Oil-finished walnut, checkered straight grip and forend.
Features: Boxlock action with fine scroll engraving, silvered receiver. Double triggers standard. Introduced 1983. Imported from Italy by Wm. Larkin Moore.
Price: F.VI $5,000.00
Price: F.VII $5,700.00
Price: F.VII SC $7,200.00
Price: F.VII SP Sideplate $10,100.00

Francotte Boxlock

AUGUSTE FRANCOTTE BOXLOCK SHOTGUN
Gauge: 12, 16, 20, 28 and 410-bore, 2¾" or 3" chambers.
Barrel: 26" to 29", chokes to customer specs.
Weight: NA. **Length:** NA.
Stock: Deluxe European walnut to customer specs. Straight or pistol grip; checkered butt; oil finish; splinter or beavertail forend.
Sights: Bead front.
Features: Anson & Deeley boxlock action with double locks, double triggers (front hinged), manual or automatic safety, Holland & Holland ejectors. English scroll engraving, coin finish or color case-hardening. Many options available. Imported from Belgium by Armes de Chasse.
Price: From about . . . . $16,000.00 to $20,000.00

AUGUSTE FRANCOTTE SIDELOCK SHOTGUN
Gauge: 12, 16, 20, 28 and 410-bore, 2¾" or 3" chambers.
Barrel: 26" to 29", chokes to customer specs.
Weight: NA. **Length:** NA.
Stock: Deluxe European walnut to customer specs. Straight or pistol grip; checkered butt; oil finish; splinter or beavertail forend.
Sights: Bead front.
Features: True Holland & Holland sidelock action with double locks, double triggers (front hinged), manual or automatic safety, Holland & Holland ejectors. English scroll engraving, coin finish or color case-hardening. Many options available. Imported from Belgium by Armes de Chasse.
Price: From about . . . . $20,000.00 to $25,000.00

Garbi Model 100

Garbi Model 101 Side-by-Side
Similar to the Garbi Model 100 except is hand engraved with scroll engraving, select walnut stock. Better overall quality than the Model 100. Imported from Spain by Wm. Larkin Moore.
Price: $4,500.00

Garbi Model 103A, B Side-by-Side
Similar to the Garbi Model 100 except has Purdey-type fine scroll and rosette engraving. Better overall quality than the Model 101. Model 103B has nickel-chrome steel barrels, H&H-type easy opening mechanism; other mechanical details remain the same. Imported from Spain by Wm. Larkin Moore.
Price: Model 103A, from $6,100.00
Price: Model 103B, from $8,300.00

GARBI MODEL 100 DOUBLE
Gauge: 12, 16, 20, 28.
Barrel: 26", 28", choked to customer specs.
Weight: 5½ to 7½ lbs.
Stock: 14½"x2¼"x1½". European walnut. Straight grip, checkered butt, classic forend.
Features: Sidelock action, automatic ejectors, double triggers standard. Color case-hardened action, coin finish optional. Single trigger; beavertail forend, etc. optional. Five other models are available. Imported from Spain by Wm. Larkin Moore.
Price: From $3,900.00

Garbi Model 200 Side-by-Side
Similar to the Garbi Model 100 except has heavy-duty locks, magnum proofed. Very fine Continental-style floral and scroll engraving, well figured walnut stock. Other mechanical features remain the same. Imported from Spain by Wm. Larkin Moore.
Price: $8,400.00

HATFIELD UPLANDER SHOTGUN

Gauge: 20, 3" chambers.
Barrel: 26" (Imp. Cyl. & Mod.).
Weight: 5¾ lbs.
Stock: Straight English style, special select XXX fancy maple. Hand-rubbed oil finish. Splinter forend.
Features: Double locking under-lug boxlock action; color case-hardened frame; single non-selective trigger. Grades differ in engraving, finish, gold work. Introduced 1988. From Hatfield.

Price: Grade II Uplander	**$2,500.00**
Price: Grade III Uplander Super Pigeon	**$3,500.00**
Price: Grade IV Uplander Golden Quail	**$5,500.00**
Price: Grade V Uplander Woodcock	**$6,900.00**
Price: Grade VI Uplander Black Widow	**$7,900.00**
Price: Grade VII Uplander Royale	**$7,900.00**
Price: Grade VIII Uplander Top Hat	**$17,500.00**

Hatfield Uplander

BILL HANUS BIRDGUN DOUBLES

Gauge: 16, 20, 28.
Barrel: 26" (Skeet & Skeet).
Weight: About 6¼ lbs. (16-ga.).
Stock: Hand-checkered walnut; straight grip, semi-beavertail forend.
Features: Color case-hardened boxlock action; raised Churchill rib; single non-selective trigger; auto ejectors, auto safety. Introduced 1991. Imported by Precision Sports.

Price: 16-, 20-ga.	**$1,269.95**
Price: 28-ga.	**$1,399.95**

MERKEL SIDE-BY-SIDE SHOTGUNS

Gauge: 12, 20, 2¾" or 3" chambers.
Barrel: 26", 26¾", 28" (standard chokes).
Weight: 6 to 7 lbs.
Stock: European walnut. Straight English or pistol grip.
Features: Models 8, 47E, 147E, 76E are boxlocks; others are sidelocks. All have double triggers, double lugs and Greener cross-bolt locking and automatic ejectors. Choking and patterning for steel shot (by importer). Upgraded wood, engraving, etc. optional. Imported from Germany by GSI, Inc.

Price: Model 8, about	**$995.00**
Price: Model 47E, about	**$1,365.00**

Merkel 47E Double

Price: Model 147E, about	**$1,695.00**
Price: Model 47S, about	**$3,595.00**
Price: Model 147S, about	**$4,495.00**

PARKER REPRODUCTION SIDE-BY-SIDE SHOTGUN

Gauge: 12, 20, 28, 2¾" or 3" chambers.
Barrel: 26" (Imp. Cyl. & Mod., 2¾" chambers), Skeet & Skeet available, 28" (Mod. & Full).
Weight: About 6¾ lbs. (12-ga.), 6½ lbs. (20-ga.), 5½ lbs. (28-ga.).
Stock: Fancy American walnut, checkered grip and forend. Straight stock or pistol grip, splinter or beavertail forend; 28 lpi checkering.
Features: Reproduction of the original Parker—parts interchangeable with

original. Double or single selective trigger; checkered skeleton buttplate; selective ejectors; bores hard chromed, excluding choke area. Two-barrel sets available. Hand engraved scroll and scenes on case-hardened frame. Fitted leather trunk included. Limited production. Introduced 1984. Made by Winchester in Japan. Imported by Parker Div. of Reagent Chemical.

Price: D Grade, one-barrel set	**$3,370.00**
Price: A-1 Special, two-barrel set	**$11,200.00**

Piotti King No. 1

PIOTTI KING NO. 1 SIDE-BY-SIDE

Gauge: 12, 16, 20, 28, 410.
Barrel: 25" to 30" (12-ga.), 25" to 28" (16, 20, 28, 410). To customer specs. Chokes as specified.

Piotti Lunik Side-by-Side

Similar to the Piotti King No. 1 except better overall quality. Has Renaissance-style large scroll engraving in relief, gold crown in top lever, gold name and gold crest in forend. Best quality Holland & Holland-pattern sidelock ejector double with chopper lump (demi-bloc) barrels. Other mechanical specifications remain the same. Imported from Italy by Wm. Larkin Moore.

Price:	**$18,700.00**

Weight: 6½ lbs. to 8 lbs. (12-ga. to customer specs.).
Stock: Dimensions to customer specs. Finely figured walnut; straight grip with checkered butt with classic splinter forend and hand-rubbed oil finish standard. Pistol grip, beavertail forend, satin luster finish optional.
Features: Holland & Holland pattern sidelock action, automatic ejectors. Double trigger with front trigger hinged standard; non-selective single trigger optional. Coin finish standard; color case-hardened optional. Top rib; level, file-cut standard; concave, ventilated optional. Very fine, full coverage scroll engraving with small floral bouquets, gold crown in top lever, name in gold, and gold crest in forend. Imported from Italy by Wm. Larkin Moore.

Price:	**$17,500.00**

Piotti King Extra Side-by-Side

Similar to the Piotti King No. 1 except highest quality wood and metal work. Choice of either bulino game scene engraving or game scene engraving with gold inlays. Engraved and signed by a master engraver. Exhibition grade wood. Other mechanical specifications remain the same. Imported from Italy by Wm. Larkin Moore.

Price:	**$27,300.00**

Piotti Piuma

PIOTTI PIUMA SIDE-BY-SIDE

Gauge: 12, 16, 20, 28, 410.
Barrel: 25" to 30" (12-ga.), 25" to 28" (16, 20, 28, 410).

Weight: 5½ to 6¼ lbs. (20-ga.).
Stock: Dimensions to customer specs. Straight grip stock with walnut checkered butt, classic splinter forend, hand-rubbed oil finish are standard; pistol grip, beavertail forend, satin luster finish optional.
Features: Anson & Deeley boxlock ejector double with chopper lump barrels. Level, file-cut rib, light scroll and rosette engraving, scalloped frame. Double triggers with hinged front standard, single non-selective optional. Coin finish standard, color case-hardened optional. Imported from Italy by Wm. Larkin Moore.

Price:	**$10,700.00**

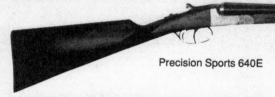

Precision Sports 640E

PRECISION SPORTS MODEL 600 SERIES DOUBLES

Gauge: 10, 3½" chambers; 12, 16, 20, 2¾" chambers; 28, 410, 3" chambers.
Barrel: 25", 26", 27", 28" (Imp. Cyl. & Mod., Mod. & Full).
Weight: 12-ga., 6¾-7 lbs.; 20-ga., 5¾-6 lbs.
Stock: 14½"x1½"x2½". Hand-checkered walnut with oil finish. "E" (English) models have straight grip, splinter forend, checkered butt. "A" (American) models have p.g. stock, beavertail forend, buttplate.
Features: Boxlock action; silvered, engraved action; automatic safety; ejectors or extractors. E-models have double triggers, concave rib (XXV models have Churchill-type rib); A-models have single, non-selective trigger, raised matte rib. Made in Spain by Ugartechea. Imported by Precision Sports. Introduced 1986.

Price: 640E (12, 16, 20; 26", 28"), extractors $849.95
Price: 640E (28, 410 only), extractors $939.95
Price: 640A (12, 16, 20; 26", 28"), extractors $964.95
Price: 640A (28, 410 only), ejectors $1,109.95
Price: 640M "Big Ten" (10-ga. 26", 30", 32", Full & Full) . . $999.95
Price: 640 Slug Gun (12, 25", Imp. Cyl. & Imp. Cyl.) $1,119.95
Price: 645E (12, 16, 20; 26", 28"), with ejectors $1,089.95
Price: 645E (28, 410), with ejectors $1,149.95
Price: 645A (12, 16, 20; 26", 28"), with ejectors $1,199.95
Price: 645A (28, 410), ejectors $1,309.95
Price: 645E-XXV (12, 16, 20; 25"), with ejectors $1,099.95
Price: 645E-XXV (28, 410), with ejectors $1,199.95
Price: 645E Bi-Gauge (20/28), ejectors $1,619.95
Price: 645A Bi-Gauge (20/28), ejectors $1,749.95
Price: 650E (12), extrators, choke tubes $919.95
Price: 650A (12), extrators, choke tubes $1,039.95
Price: 655E (12), ejectors, choke tubes $1,149.95
Price: 655A (12), ejectors, choke tubes $1,259.95

RIZZINI BOXLOCK SIDE-BY-SIDE

Gauge: 12, 20, 28, 410.
Barrel: 25" to 30" (12-ga.), 25" to 28" (20, 28, 410).
Weight: 5½ to 6¼ lbs. (20-ga.).
Stock: Dimensions to customer specs. Straight grip stock with checkered butt, classic splinter forend, hand-rubbed oil finish are standard; pistol grip, beavertail forend, satin luster finish optional.

Features: Anson & Deeley boxlock ejector double with chopper lump barrels. Level, file-cut rib, light scroll and rosette engraving, scalloped frame. Double triggers with hinged front standard, single non-selective optional. Coin finish standard, color case-hardened optional. Imported from Italy by Wm. Larkin Moore.
Price: 12-, 20-ga., from $19,900.00
Price: 28, 410 bore, from $22,000.00

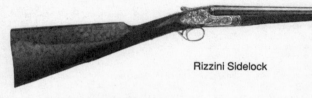

Rizzini Sidelock

RIZZINI SIDELOCK SIDE-BY-SIDE

Gauge: 12, 20, 28, 410.
Barrel: 25" to 30" (12-ga.), 25" to 28" (20, 28, 410). To customer specs. Chokes as specified.
Weight: 6½ lbs. to 8 lbs. (12-ga. to customer specs).

Stock: Dimensions to customer specs. Finely figured walnut; straight grip with checkered butt with classic splinter forend and hand-rubbed oil finish standard. Pistol grip, beavertail forend, satin luster finish optional.
Features: Holland & Holland pattern sidelock action, auto ejectors. Double triggers with front trigger hinged standard; non-selective single trigger optional. Coin finish standard; color case-hardened optional. Top rib level, file cut standard; concave, ventilated optional. Very fine, full coverage scroll engraving with small floral bouquets, gold crown in top lever, name in gold, and gold crest in forend. Imported from Italy by Wm. Larkin Moore.
Price: 12-, 20-ga., from $31,500.00
Price: 28, 410 bore, from $35,300.00

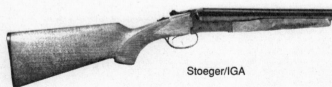

Stoeger/IGA

STOEGER/IGA SIDE-BY-SIDE SHOTGUN

Gauge: 12, 20, 28, 2¾" chambers; 410, 3" chambers.
Barrel: 26" (Full & Full, 410 only, Imp. Cyl. & Mod.), 28" (Mod. & Full).
Weight: 6¾ to 7 lbs.
Stock: 14½"x1½"x2½". Oil-finished hardwood. Checkered pistol grip and forend.
Features: Automatic safety, extractors only, solid matted barrel rib. Double triggers only. Introduced 1983. Imported from Brazil by Stoeger Industries.
Price: $415.00
Price: Coach Gun, 12, 20, 410, 20" bbls. $357.00

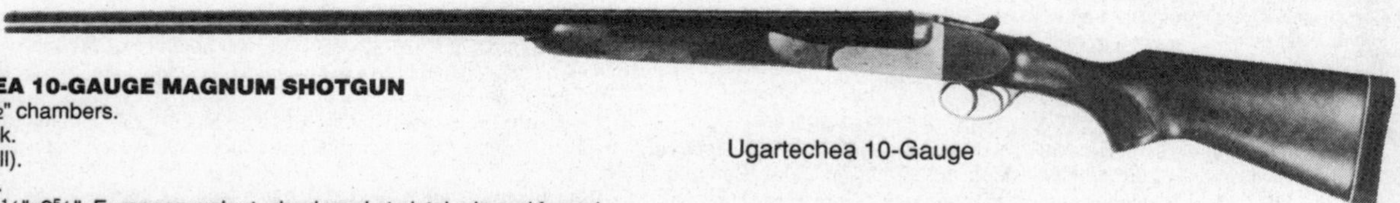

UGARTECHEA 10-GAUGE MAGNUM SHOTGUN

Gauge: 10, 3½" chambers.
Action: Boxlock.
Barrel: 32" (Full).
Weight: 11 lbs.
Stock: 14½"x1½"x2⅝". European walnut, checkered at pistol grip and forend.
Features: Double triggers; color case-hardened action, rest blued. Front and center metal beads on matted rib; ventilated rubber recoil pad. Forend release has positive Purdey-type mechanism. Imported from Spain by Mandall Shooting Supplies.
Price: $599.95

Ugartechea 10-Gauge

ZOLI SILVER FOX SIDE-BY-SIDE SHOTGUN

Gauge: 12 or 20, 3" chambers.
Barrel: 12 ga.—26" (Imp. Cyl. & Mod.), 28" (Mod. & Full); 20 ga.—26" (Imp. Cyl. & Mod.).
Weight: 6.25 to 7.25 lbs.
Stock: 14½"x2⁵⁄₁₆"x1½". Select Turkish circassian walnut with straight grip, splinter forend, oil finish; solid recoil pad.
Features: Boxlock action with single tirgger, selective ejectors, polished, engraved, silver receiver. "Best Grade" gun. Introduced 1989. Imported from Italy by European American Armory.
Price: Either gauge $2,995.00

Variety of designs for utility and sporting purposes, as well as for competitive shooting.

Armsport Single

ARMSPORT SINGLE BARREL SHOTGUN
Gauge: 20, 3" chamber.
Barrel: 26" (Mod.).
Weight: About 6½ lbs.
Stock: Hardwood with oil finish.
Features: Chrome-lined barrel, manual safety, cocking indicator. Opening lever behind trigger guard. Imported by Armsport.
Price: **$100.00**

Browning BT-99 Plus

Browning BT-99 Plus Micro
Similar to the standard BT-99 Plus except scaled down for smaller shooters. Comes with 30" barrel with adjustable rib system and buttstock with adjustable length of pull range of 13½" to 14". Also has Browning's recoil reducer system, ported barrels, Invector Plus choke system and back-bored barrel. Weight is about 8 lbs., 6 oz. Introduced 1991.
Price: With ported barrel **$1,780.00**
Price: With non-ported barrel **$1,765.00**

Browning BT-99 Plus Trap Gun
Similar to the Grade I BT-99 except comes only with 34" barrel with .745" over bore, Invector Plus choke system with Full, Imp. Mod. and Mod. choke tubes; high post, ventilated, tapered, target rib adjustable from 3" to 12" above point of aim. Available with or without ported barrel. Select walnut stock has

BROWNING BT-99 COMPETITION TRAP SPECIAL
Gauge: 12, 2¾" chamber.
Action: Top lever break-open, hammerless.
Barrel: 32" or 34" with ¹¹⁄₃₂" wide high post floating vent. rib. Comes with Invector Plus choke tubes; .745" overbore.
Weight: 8 lbs. (32" bbl.).
Stock: French walnut; hand-checkered, full pistol grip, full beavertail forend; recoil pad. Trap dimensions with M.C. 14⅜"x1⅜"x1⅜"x2".
Sights: Ivory front and middle beads.
Features: Gold-plated trigger with 3½-lb. pull, deluxe trap-style recoil pad, automatic ejector, no safety. Available with either Monte Carlo or standard stock. Imported from Japan by Browning.
Price: Grade I Invector, Plus Ported barrels **$1,200.00**

high-gloss finish, Monte Carlo comb, modified beavertail forend and is fully adjustable for length of pull, drop at comb and drop at Monte Carlo. Has Browning Recoil Reduction System. Introduced 1989.
Price: Grade I, with ported barrel **$1,780.00**
Price: Grade I, non-ported barrel **$1,765.00**

DESERT INDUSTRIES BIG TWENTY SHOTGUN
Gauge: 20, 2¾" chamber.
Barrel: 19" (Cyl.).
Weight: 4¾ lbs. **Length:** 31¾" overall.
Stock: Fixed wire, with buttplate. Walnut forend and grip.
Stock: Bead front.
Features: Single shot action of all steel construction. Blue finish. Announced 1990. From Desert Industries, Inc.
Price: **$189.95**

Harrington & Richardson Topper Classic Youth Shotgun
Similar to the Topper Junior 098 except available in 20-gauge (3", Mod.), 410-bore (Full) with 3" chamber; 28-gauge, 2¾" chamber (Mod.); all have 22" barrel. Stock is American black walnut with cut-checkered pistol grip and forend. Ventilated rubber recoil pad with white line spacers. Blued barrel, blued frame. Introduced 1992. From H&R 1871, Inc.
Price: **$139.95**

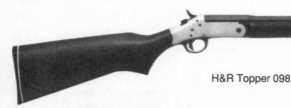

H&R Topper 098

Harrington & Richardson Topper Deluxe Model 098
Similar to the standard Topper 098 except 12-gauge only with 3½" chamber, 28" barrel with choke tube (comes with Mod. tube, others optional). Satin nickel frame, blued barrel, black-finished wood. Introduced 1992. From H&R 1871, Inc.
Price: **$124.95**

HARRINGTON & RICHARDSON TOPPER MODEL 098
Gauge: 12, 20, 410, 3" chamber.
Barrel: 12 ga.—28" (Mod.); 20 ga.—26" (Mod.); 410 bore—26" (Full).
Weight: 5-6 lbs.
Stock: Black-finish hardwood with full pistol grip; semi-beavertail forend.
Sights: Gold bead front.
Features: Break-open action with side-lever release, automatic ejector. Satin nickel frame, blued barrel. Reintroduced 1992. From H&R 1871, Inc.
Price: **$109.95**
Price: Topper Junior 098 (as above except 22" barrel, 20-ga. (Mod.), 410-bore (Full), 12½" length of pull) **$114.95**

H&R N.W.T.F. Turkey

Harrington & Richardson N.W.T.F Turkey Mag
Similar to the Topper 098 except covered with Mossy Oak camouflage. Chambered for 12-gauge 3½" chamber, 24" barrel (comes with Turkey Full choke tube, others available); weighs 6 lbs., overall length 40". Comes with Mossy Oak sling, swivels, studs. Introduced 1992. From H&R 1871, Inc.
Price: **$159.95**

CAUTION: PRICES CHANGE, CHECK AT GUNSHOP.

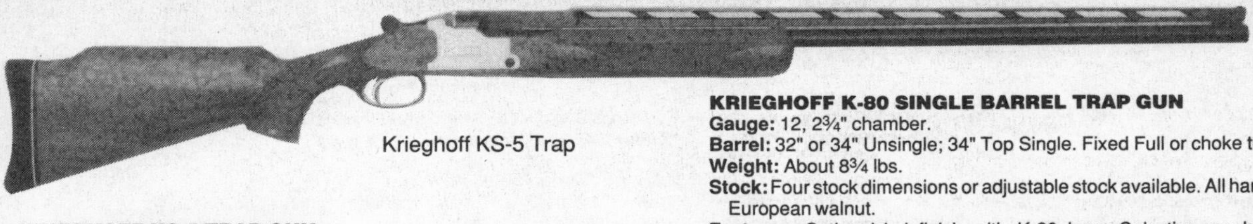

Krieghoff KS-5 Trap

KRIEGHOFF KS-5 TRAP GUN
Gauge: 12, 2¾" chamber.
Barrel: 32", 34"; Full choke or choke tubes.
Weight: About 8½ lbs.
Stock: Choice of high Monte Carlo (1½"), low Monte Carlo (1⅜") or factory adjustable stock. European walnut.
Features: Ventilated tapered step rib. Adjustable trigger or optional release trigger. Choice of blue or nickeled receiver. Comes with fitted aluminum case. Introduced 1988. Imported from Germany by Krieghoff International, Inc.
Price: Fixed choke, cased $3,250.00
Price: With choke tubes $3,630.00

KRIEGHOFF K-80 SINGLE BARREL TRAP GUN
Gauge: 12, 2¾" chamber.
Barrel: 32" or 34" Unsingle; 34" Top Single. Fixed Full or choke tubes.
Weight: About 8¾ lbs.
Stock: Four stock dimensions or adjustable stock available. All hand-checkered European walnut.
Features: Satin nickel finish with K-80 logo. Selective mechanical trigger adjustable for finger position. Tapered step vent. rib. Adjustable point of impact on Unsingle.
Price: Standard grade full Unsingle $6,700.00
Price: Standard grade full Top Single $6,550.00
Price: RT (removable trigger) option, add $1,850.00

Krieghoff KS-5 Special
Same as the KS-5 except the barrel has a fully adjustable rib and adjustable stock. Rib allows shooter to adjust point of impact from 50%/50% to nearly 90%/10%. Introduced 1990.
Price: $4,150.00

Ljutic Mono Gun

LJUTIC MONO GUN SINGLE BARREL
Gauge: 12 only.
Barrel: 34", choked to customer specs; hollow-milled rib, 35½" sight plane.
Weight: Approx. 9 lbs.
Stock: To customer specs. Oil finish, hand checkered.
Features: Totally custom made. Pull or release trigger; removable trigger guard contains trigger and hammer mechanism; Ljutic pushbutton opener on front of trigger guard. From Ljutic Industries.
Price: With standard, medium or Olympic rib, custom 32"-34" bbls. $4,495.00
Price: As above with screw-in choke barrel $4,695.00

LJUTIC LTX SUPER DELUXE MONO GUN
Super Deluxe version of the standard Mono Gun with high quality wood, extra-fancy checkering pattern in 24 lpi, double recessed choking. Available in two weights: 8¼ lbs. or 8¾ lbs. Extra light 33" barrel; medium-height rib. Introduced 1984. From Ljutic Industries.
Price: $5,595.00
Price: With three screw-in choke tubes $5,995.00

LJUTIC RECOILLESS SPACE GUN SHOTGUN
Gauge: 12 only, 2¾" chamber.
Barrel: 30" (Full). Screw-in or fixed-choke barrel.
Weight: 8½ lbs.
Stock: 14½" to 15" pull length; universal comb; medium or large p.g.

Sights: Vent. rib.
Features: Pull trigger standard, release trigger available; anti-recoil mechanism. Revolutionary new design. Introduced 1981. From Ljutic Industries.
Price: From $5,995.00

Magtech Model MT-151

MAGTECH MODEL MT-151 SINGLE SHOT SHOTGUN
Gauge: 12, 20, 410, 3" chamber; 16, 2¾" chamber.

Barrel: 12-ga.—28" (Mod.), 30" (Full); 16-ga.—28" (Mod.); 20-ga.—26" (Mod.), 28" (Full); 410—25", 28" (Full).
Weight: About 5¾ lbs.
Stock: Brazilian hardwood, beavertail forend.
Features: Trigger guard opener button. Exposed hammer. Three-piece takedown. Introduced 1991. Imported from Brazil by Magtech Recreational Products, Inc.
Price: About $99.95

Marlin Model 55

MARLIN MODEL 55 GOOSE GUN BOLT ACTION
Gauge: 12 only, 2¾" or 3" chamber.

Action: Bolt action, thumb safety, detachable two-shot clip. Red cocking indicator.
Barrel: 36" (Full).
Weight: 8 lbs. **Length:** 56¾" overall.
Stock: Walnut-finished hardwood, p.g., ventilated recoil pad. Swivel studs, MarShield® finish.
Features: Brass bead front sight, U-groove rear sight.

NEW ENGLAND FIREARMS STANDARD PARDNER
Gauge: 12, 20, 410, 3" chamber; 16, 28, 2¾" chamber.
Barrel: 12-ga.—28" (Full, Mod.); 16-ga.—28" (Full); 20-ga.—26" (Full, Mod.); 28-ga.—26" (Mod.); 410-bore—26" (Full).
Weight: 5-6 lbs. **Length:** 43" overall (28" barrel).
Stock: Walnut-finished hardwood with full pistol grip.
Sights: Bead front.
Features: Transfer bar ignition; break-open action with side-lever release. Introduced 1987. From New England Firearms.
Price: $99.95
Price: Youth model (20-ga., 22" barrel) $104.95

NEW ENGLAND FIREARMS TURKEY AND GOOSE GUN
Gauge: 10, 3½" chamber.
Barrel: 28" (Full).
Weight: 9.5 lbs. **Length:** 44" overall.
Stock: American hardwood with walnut, or matte camo finish; ventilated rubber recoil pad.
Sights: Bead front.
Features: Break-open action with side-lever release; ejector. Matte finish on metal. Introduced 1992. From New England Firearms.
Price: Walnut-finish wood $149.95
Price: Camo finish, sling and swivels $159.95

New England Slug

New England Firearms N.W.T.F. Shotgun

Similar to the Turkey/Goose Gun except completely covered with Mossy Oak comouflage finish; interchangeable choke tubes (comes with Turkey Full, others optional); comes with Mossy Oak sling. Introduced 1992. From New England Firearms.

Price: $199.95

PERAZZI TM1 SPECIAL SINGLE TRAP

Gauge: 12, 2¾" chambers.
Barrel: 32" or 34" (Extra Full).
Weight: 8 lbs., 6 oz.
Stock: To customer specs; interchangeable.

Remington 90-T

REMINGTON 90-T SUPER SINGLE SHOTGUN

Gauge: 12, 2¾" chamber.
Barrel: 30", 32", 34", fixed choke or Rem Choke tubes; ported or non-ported. Medium-high tapered, ventilated rib; white Bradley-type front bead, stainless center bead.

Snake Charmer II

SNAKE CHARMER II SHOTGUN

Gauge: 410, 3" chamber.

STOEGER/IGA SINGLE BARREL SHOTGUN

Gauge: 12, 2¾" chamber; 20, 410, 3" chamber.
Barrel: 12-ga.—26" (Imp. Cyl.), 28" (Full); 20-ga.—26" (Full); 410 bore—26" (Full).
Weight: 5¼ lbs.
Stock: 14"x1½"x2½". Brazilian hardwood.

Thompson/Center Hunter

WEATHERBY ATHENA SINGLE BARREL TRAP

Gauge: 12, 2¾" chamber.
Barrel: 32", 34" (Full, Mod., Imp. Mod., Multi-Choke tubes).
Weight: About 8½ lbs. **Length:** 49½" overall with 32" barrel.
Stock: 14⅜"x1⅜"x1¾"x1¾". American walnut with checkered p.g. and forend.
Sights: White front, brass middle bead.
Features: Engraved, silvered sideplate receiver; ventilated rubber recoil pad. Can be ordered with an extra over/under barrel set. Introduced 1988. Imported from Japan by Weatherby.
Price: $1,975.00
Price: Combo $2,616.00

NEW ENGLAND FIREARMS TRACKER SLUG GUN

Gauge: 12, 20, 3" chamber.
Barrel: 24" (Cyl.).
Weight: 6 lbs. **Length:** 40" overall.
Stock: Walnut-finished hardwood with full pistol grip, recoil pad.
Sights: Blade front, fully adjustable rifle-type rear.
Features: Break-open action with side-lever release; blued barrel, color case-hardened frame. Introduced 1992. From New England Firearms.
Price: Tracker $124.95
Price: Tracker II (as above except fully rifled bore) $129.95

Features: Tapered and stepped high rib; adjustable four-position trigger. Also available with choke tubes. Imported from Italy by Perazzi U.S.A., Inc.
Price: From $5,500.00
Price: TMX Special Single (as above except special high rib), from $5,700.00

Weight: About 8¾ lbs.
Stock: 14⅜"x1⅜" (or 1½" or 1¼")x1½". Choice of drops at comb, pull length available plus or minus 1". Figured American walnut with low-luster finish, checkered 18 lpi; black vented rubber recoil pad. Cavity in forend and buttstock for added weight.
Features: Barrel is over-bored with elongated forcing cones. Removable sideplates can be ordered with engraving; drop-out trigger assembly. Metal has non-glare matte finish. Available with extra barrels in different lengths, chokes, extra trigger assemblies and sideplates, porting, stocks. Introduced 1990. From Remington.
Price: Depending on options $2,995.00

Barrel: 18¼".
Weight: About 3½ lbs. **Length:** 28⅝" overall.
Stock: ABS grade impact resistant plastic.
Features: Thumbhole-type stock holds four extra rounds. Stainless steel barrel and frame. Reintroduced 1989. From Sporting Arms Mfg., Inc.
Price: $139.00
Price: New Generation Snake Charmer (as above except with black carbon steel bbl.) $129.00

Sights: Metal bead front.
Features: Exposed hammer with half-cock safety; extractor; blue finish. Introduced 1987. Imported from Brazil by Stoeger Industries.
Price: $112.00
Price: Reuna model (12-ga., Full choke tube) $132.00

THOMPSON/CENTER TCR '87 HUNTER SHOTGUN

Gauge: 10, 12, 3½".
Barrel: 25" (Full).
Weight: 8 lbs.
Stock: Uncheckered walnut.
Sights: Bead front.
Features: Uses same receiver as TCR '87 rifle models, and stock has extra ⁷⁄₁₆" drop at heel. Choke designed for steel shot. Introduced 1989. From Thompson/Center.
Price: $595.00

ZOLI Z90 MONO-TRAP GUN

Gauge: 12, 2¾" chamber.
Barrel: 32" or 34" (choke tubes).
Weight: 8.5 lbs.
Stock: 14½"x2⅛"x1¼"x1¼". Checkered Turkish circassian walnut with Monte Carlo; oil finish.
Features: Boxlock action with automatic ejector; trigger adjustable for length of pull; step-type vent. rib with two sight beads. Matte blue finish on receiver. Introduced 1989. Imported from Italy by European American Armory.
Price: $2,195.00

CAUTION: PRICES CHANGE, CHECK AT GUNSHOP.

Designs for utility, suitable for and adaptable to competitions and other sporting purposes.

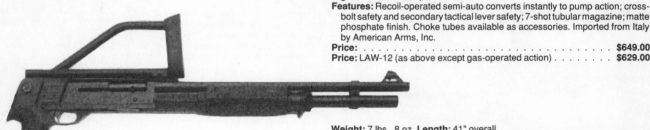

American Arms/Franchi SPAS-12

AMERICAN ARMS/FRANCHI SPAS-12 SHOTGUN
Gauge: 12, 2¾" chamber.
Barrel: 21½" (Cyl.), with muzzle protector.
Weight: 8¾ lbs. **Length:** 41" overall.
Stock: Black nylon with full pistol grip.
Sights: Blade front, aperture rear.
Features: Recoil-operated semi-auto converts instantly to pump action; cross-bolt safety and secondary tactical lever safety; 7-shot tubular magazine; matte phosphate finish. Choke tubes available as accessories. Imported from Italy by American Arms, Inc.
Price: **$649.00**
Price: LAW-12 (as above except gas-operated action) **$629.00**

Benelli M3 Super 90

BENELLI M3 SUPER 90 PUMP/AUTO SHOTGUN
Gauge: 12, 3" chamber, 7-shot magazine.
Barrel: 19¾" (Cyl.).

Weight: 7 lbs., 8 oz. **Length:** 41" overall.
Stock: High-impact polymer with sling loop in side of butt; rubberized pistol grip on optional SWAT stock. Also folding stock and standard stock models.
Sights: Post front, buckhorn rear adjustable for windage.
Features: Combination pump/auto action. Alloy receiver with inertia recoil rotating locking lug bolt; matte finish; automatic shell release lever. Introduced 1989. Imported by Heckler & Koch, Inc.
Price: **$899.00**
Price: With Ghost Ring sight system **$949.00**
Price: With folding stock **$999.00**

Benelli M1 Super 90

Benelli M1 Super 90
Similar to the M3 Super 90 except is semi-automatic only, has overall length of 39¾" and weighs 7 lbs., 4 oz. Introduced 1986.
Price: Slug Gun with standard stock **$699.00**
Price: With pistol grip stock (Defense) **$749.00**
Price: With ghost ring sight system **$749.00**

Beretta Model 1201FP3

BERETTA MODEL 1201FP3 AUTO SHOTGUN
Gauge: 12, 3" chamber.
Barrel: 20" (Cyl.).
Weight: 7.3 lbs. **Length:** NA
Stock: Special strengthened technopolymer, matte black finish.
Stock: Fixed rifle type.
Features: Has 6-shot magazine. Introduced 1988. Imported from Italy by Beretta U.S.A.
Price: **$660.00**

E.A.A. PM2 PUMP SHOTGUN
Gauge: 12, 6-shot.
Barrel: 20".
Weight: 6.8 lbs. **Length:** 41" overall.
Stock: Black-finished wood butt, composite forend.
Features: Removable box magazine, dual action bars, cross-bolt safety. Black or chrome finish. Introduced 1991. From European American Armory.
Price: Black finish **$675.00**
Price: Matte chrome **$750.00**
Price: Black with night sights **$795.00**

ITHACA MODEL 87 M&P DSPS SHOTGUNS
Gauge: 12, 3" chamber, 5- or 8-shot magazine.
Barrel: 20" (Cyl.).
Weight: 7 lbs.
Stock: Walnut.
Sights: Bead front on 5-shot, rifle sights on 8-shot.
Features: Parkerized finish; bottom ejection; cross-bolt safety. Reintroduced 1988. From Ithaca Acquisition Corp.
Price: M&P, 5-shot **$407.00**
Price: DSPS, 8-shot **$407.00**
Price: DSPS, 5-shot, nickel **$510.00**

Ithaca Model 87 Hand Grip Shotgun
Similar to the Model 87 M&P except has black polymer pistol grip and slide handle with nylon sling. In 12- or 20-gauge, 18½" barrel (Cyl.), 5-shot magazine. Reintroduced 1988.
Price: **$391.00**

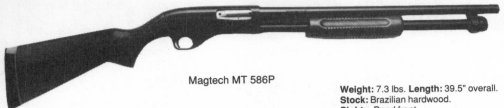

Magtech MT 586P

MAGTECH MT 586P PUMP SHOTGUN
Gauge: 12, 3" chamber, 7-shot magazine (8-shot with 2¾" shells).
Barrel: 19" (Cyl.).
Weight: 7.3 lbs. **Length:** 39.5" overall.
Stock: Brazilian hardwood.
Sights: Bead front.
Features: Dual action slide bars, cross-bolt safety. Blue finish. Introduced 1991. Imported from Brazil by Magtech Recreational Products.
Price: About **$219.00**

Maverick Model 88

MAVERICK MODEL 88 BULLPUP SHOTGUN
Gauge: 12, 3" chamber; 6-shot magazine.
Barrel: 18½" (Cyl.).
Weight: 9½ lbs. **Length:** 26½" overall.
Stock: Bullpup design of high-impact plastics.
Sights: Fixed, mounted in carrying handle.
Features: Uses the Model 88 pump shotgun action. Cross-bolt and grip safeties. Mossberg Cablelock included. Introduced 1991. From Maverick Arms.
Price: **$282.00**

Mossberg 500 Security

Mossberg Model 500, 590 Intimidator Shotguns
Similar to the Model 500 or 590 Security with synthetic stock except has integral Laser Sight built into the forend. Mossberg Cablelock included. Introduced 1990.
Price: Model 500, blue, 6-shot **$505.00**
Price: Model 500, Parkerized, 6-shot **$526.00**
Price: Model 590, blue, 9-shot **$555.00**
Price: Model 590, Parkerized, 9-shot **$601.00**

MOSSBERG MODEL 500 SECURITY SHOTGUNS
Gauge: 12, 3" chamber.
Barrel: 18½", 20" (Cyl.).
Weight: 7 lbs.
Stock: Walnut-finished hardwood or synthetic field.
Sights: Metal bead front.
Features: Available in 6- or 8-shot models. Top-mounted safety, double action slide bars, swivel studs, rubber recoil pad. Blue, Parkerized, Marinecote finishes. Pistol grip kit and Mossberg Cablelock included. **Price list not complete—contact Mossberg for full list.**
Price: From about **$246.00**
Price: Combo (as above except also comes with an extra field barrel), from about **$300.00**

Mossberg HS 410

Mossberg Model 500, 590 Ghost-Ring Shotguns
Similar to the Model 500 Security except has adjustable blade front, adjustable Ghost-Ring rear sight with protective "ears." Model 500 has 18.5" (Cyl.) barrel, 6-shot capacity; Model 590 has 20" (Cyl.) barrel, 9-shot capacity. Both have synthetic field stock. Mossberg Cablelock included. Introduced 1990. From Mossberg.
Price: Model 500, blue **$300.00**
Price: As above, Parkerized **$348.00**
Price: Model 590, blue **$359.00**
Price: As above, Parkerized **$406.00**

Mossberg Model HS 410 Shotgun
Similar to the Model 500 Security pump except chambered for 410, 3" shells; has pistol grip forend, thick recoil pad, muzzle brake and has special spreader choke on the 18.5" barrel. Overall length is 37.5", weight is 6.25 lbs. Blue finish; synthetic field stock. Also available with integral Laser Sight forend. Mossberg Cablelock and video included. Introduced 1990.
Price: HS 410 . . . . **$253.00**
Price: HS 410 Laser **$424.00**

Mossberg Model 590

Mossberg Model 500, 590 Mariner Pump
Similar to the Model 500 or 590 Security except all metal parts finished with Marinecote, a Teflon and metal coating to resist rust and corrosion. Synthetic field stock; pistol grip kit included. Mossberg Cablelock included.
Price: 6-shot **$336.00**
Price: 9-shot **$401.00**

MOSSBERG MODEL 590 SHOTGUN
Gauge: 12, 3" chamber.
Barrel: 20" (Cyl.).
Weight: 7¼ lbs.
Stock: Synthetic field or Speedfeed.
Sights: Metal bead front.
Features: Top-mounted safety, double slide action bars. Comes with heat shield, bayonet lug, swivel studs, rubber recoil pad. Blue, Parkerized or Marinecote finish. Mossberg Cablelock included. From Mossberg.
Price: Blue, synthetic stock **$305.00**
Price: Parkerized, synthetic stock **$349.00**
Price: Blue, Speedfeed stock **$319.00**
Price: Parkerized, Speedfeed stock **$366.00**

CAUTION: PRICES CHANGE, CHECK AT GUNSHOP.

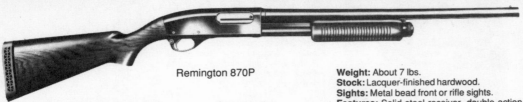

Remington 870P

REMINGTON 870P POLICE SHOTGUN
Gauge: 12, 3" chamber.
Barrel: 18", 20" (Police Cyl.), 20" (Imp. Cyl.).

Weight: About 7 lbs.
Stock: Lacquer-finished hardwood.
Sights: Metal bead front or rifle sights.
Features: Solid steel receiver, double action slide bars. Blued or Parkerized finish.
Price: 18" or 20", bead sight, about **$356.00**
Price: 20", rifle sights, about **$383.00**

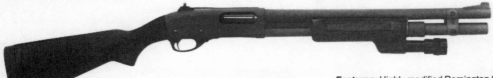

Tactical Response TR-870

TACTICAL RESPONSE TR-870 SHOTGUN
Gauge: 12, 3" chamber, 7-shot magazine.
Barrel: 18" (Cyl.).
Weight: 9 lbs. **Length:** 38" overall.
Stock: Fiberglass-filled polypropolene with non-snag recoil absorbing butt pad. Nylon tactical forend houses flashlight.
Sights: Trak-Lock ghost ring sight system. Front sight has tritium insert.

Features: Highly modified Remington 870P with Parkerized finish. Comes with nylon three-way adjustable sling, high visibility non-binding follower, Jumbo Head safety, and Side Saddle extended 6-shot shell carrier on left side of receiver. Introduced 1991. From Scattergun Technologies, Inc.
Price: Standard model **$695.00**
Price: FBI model, 5-shot **$665.00**
Price: Patrol model, 5-shot, no Side Saddle **$525.00**
Price: Border Patrol model, 7-shot, standard forend **$555.00**
Price: Military model, 7-shot, bayonet lug **$655.00**
Price: K-9 model, 7-shot **$755.00**
Price: Urban Sniper, 7-shot, rifled bbl., Burris Scout scope, Rem. 11-87 action **$1,095.00**

Winchester Defender

Winchester Model 1300 Stainless Marine Pump Gun
Same as the Defender except has bright chrome finish, stainless steel barrel, rifle-type sights only. Phosphate coated receiver for corrosion resistance.
Price: About **$436.00**

Winchester 8-Shot Pistol Grip Pump Security Shotguns
Same as regular Defender Pump but with pistol grip and forend of high-impact resistant ABS plastic with non-glare black finish. Introduced 1984.
Price: Pistol Grip Defender, about **$257.00**

WINCHESTER MODEL 1300 DEFENDER PUMP GUN
Gauge: 12, 20, 3" chamber, 5- or 8-shot capacity.
Barrel: 18" (Cyl.).
Weight: 6¾ lbs. **Length:** 38⅝" overall.
Stock: Walnut-finished hardwood stock and ribbed forend, or synthetic; or pistol grip.
Sights: Metal bead front.
Features: Cross-bolt safety, front-locking rotary bolt, twin action slide bars. Black rubber buttpad. From U.S. Repeating Arms Co.
Price: 8-shot, wood or synthetic stock **$257.00**
Price: 5-shot, wood stock **$257.00**

BLACKPOWDER SINGLE SHOT PISTOLS—FLINT & PERCUSSION

Black Watch Pistol

BLACK WATCH SCOTCH PISTOL
Caliber: 577 (.500" round ball).
Barrel: 7", smoothbore.
Weight: 1½ lbs. **Length:** 12" overall.
Stock: Brass.
Sights: None.
Features: Faithful reproduction of this military flintlock. From Dixie Gun Works, E.M.F.
Price: . . . . **$148.00 to $310.00**

Dixie Charleville

CHARLEVILLE FLINTLOCK PISTOL
Caliber: 69 (.680" round ball).
Barrel: 7½".
Weight: 48 oz. **Length:** 13½" overall.
Stock: Walnut.
Sights: None.
Features: Brass frame, polished steel barrel, iron belt hook, brass buttcap and backstrap. Replica of original 1777 pistol. Imported by Dixie Gun Works, E.M.F., Navy Arms.
Price: . . . . **$189.00 to $325.00**

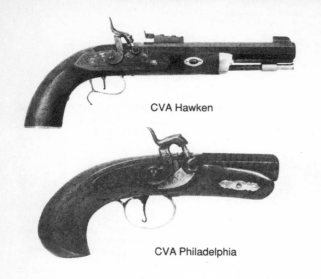

CVA Hawken

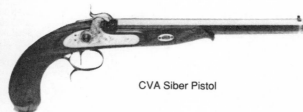

CVA Philadelphia

CVA Siber Pistol

DIXIE ABILENE DERRINGER
Caliber: 41.
Barrel: 2½", six-groove rifling.
Weight: 8 oz. **Length:** 6½" overall.
Stock: Walnut.
Features: All steel version of Dixie's brass-framed derringers. Blued barrel, color case-hardened frame and hammer. Shoots .395" patched ball. Comes with wood presentation case. From Dixie Gun Works.
Price: $81.50
Price: Kit form $51.95

Dixie Brass Frame

DIXIE BRASS FRAME DERRINGER
Caliber: 41.
Barrel: 2½".
Weight: 7 oz. **Length:** 5½" overall.
Stock: Walnut.
Features: Brass frame, color case-hardened hammer and trigger. Shoots .395" round ball. Engraved model available. From Dixie Gun Works.
Price: Plain model $69.95
Price: Engraved model $95.50
Price: Kit form, plain model $53.95

DIXIE PENNSYLVANIA PISTOL
Caliber: 44 (.430" round ball).
Barrel: 10" (⅞" octagon).
Weight: 2½ lbs.
Stock: Walnut-stained hardwood.
Sights: Blade front, open rear drift-adjustable for windage; brass.
Features: Available in flint only. Brass trigger guard, thimbles, nosecap, wedgeplates; high-luster blue barrel. Imported from Italy by Dixie Gun Works.
Price: Finished $149.95
Price: Kit $119.95

CVA COLONIAL PISTOL
Caliber: 45.
Barrel: 6¾", octagonal, rifled. **Length:** 12¾" overall.
Stock: Selected hardwood.
Features: Case-hardened lock, brass furniture, fixed sights. Steel ramrod. Available in percussion only. Imported by CVA.
Price: Finished $119.95
Price: Kit $84.95

CVA HAWKEN PISTOL
Caliber: 50.
Barrel: 9¾"; ¹⁵⁄₁₆" flats.
Weight: 50 oz. **Length:** 16½" overall.
Stock: Select hardwood.
Sights: Beaded blade front, fully adjustable open rear.
Features: Color case-hardened lock, polished brass wedge plate, nose cap, ramrod thimbles, trigger guard, grip cap. Hooked breech. Imported by CVA.
Price: $164.95
Price: Kit $104.95

CVA PHILADELPHIA DERRINGER PISTOL
Caliber: 45.
Barrel: 3⅛".
Weight: 16 oz. **Length:** 7" overall.
Stock: Select hardwood.
Sights: Fixed.
Features: Engraved wedge plates. Imported by CVA.
Price: $89.95
Price: Kit form $79.95

CVA SIBER PISTOL
Caliber: 45.
Barrel: 10½".
Weight: 34 oz. **Length:** 15½" overall.
Stock: High-grade French walnut, checkered grip.
Sights: Barleycorn front, micro-adjustable rear.
Features: Reproduction of pistol made by Swiss watchmaker Jean Siber in the 1800s. Precision lock and set-trigger give fast lock time. Has engraved, polished steel barrel, trigger guard. Imported by CVA.
Price: $439.95

CVA VEST POCKET DERRINGER
Caliber: 44.
Barrel: 2½", brass.
Weight: 7 oz.
Stock: Two-piece walnut.
Features: All brass frame with brass ramrod. A muzzle-loading version of the Colt No. 3 derringer. Imported by CVA.
Price: Finished $61.95
Price: Kit $59.95

DIXIE SCREW BARREL PISTOL
Caliber: .445".
Barrel: 2½".
Weight: 8 oz. **Length:** 6½" overall.
Stock: Walnut.
Features: Trigger folds down when hammer is cocked. Close copy of the originals once made in Belgium. Uses No. 11 percussion caps. From Dixie Gun Works.
Price: $89.00
Price: Kit $74.95

DIXIE LINCOLN DERRINGER
Caliber: 41.
Barrel: 2", 8 lands, 8 grooves.
Weight: 7 oz. **Length:** 5½" overall.
Stock: Walnut finish, checkered.
Sights: Fixed.
Features: Authentic copy of the "Lincoln Derringer." Shoots .400" patched ball. German silver furniture includes trigger guard with pineapple finial, wedge plates, nose, wrist, side and teardrop inlays. All furniture, lockplate, hammer, and breech plug engraved. Imported from Italy by Dixie Gun Works.
Price: With wooden case $285.95
Price: Kit (not engraved) $89.95

FRENCH-STYLE DUELING PISTOL
Caliber: 44.
Barrel: 10".
Weight: 35 oz. **Length:** 15¾" overall.
Stock: Carved walnut.
Sights: Fixed.
Features: Comes with velvet-lined case and accessories. Imported by Mandall Shooting Supplies.
Price: $295.00

Dixie Tornado

Dixie Harper's Ferry

KENTUCKY FLINTLOCK PISTOL
Caliber: 44, 45.
Barrel: 10⅛".
Weight: 32 oz. **Length:** 15½" overall.
Stock: Walnut.
Sights: Fixed.
Features: Specifications, including caliber, weight and length may vary with importer. Case-hardened lock, blued barrel; available also as brass barrel flint Model 1821. Imported by Cabela's (44, 50), Navy Arms (44 only), The Armoury, E.M.F.
Price: . . . . $145.00 to $207.00
Price: Brass barrel (E.M.F.) $265.00
Price: In kit form, from . . . . $90.00 to $112.00
Price: Single cased set (Navy Arms) $300.00
Price: Double cased set (Navy Arms) $515.00

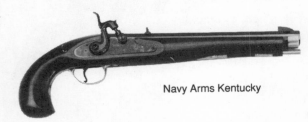

Navy Arms Kentucky

Lyman Plains Pistol

CHARLES MOORE FLINTLOCK PISTOL
Caliber: 45.
Barrel: 10", octagonal.
Weight: 36 oz. **Length:** 15" overall.
Stock: Checkered hardwood.
Sights: Blade front, fixed notch rear.
Features: German silver trigger guard, rest blued. Imported from Italy by E.M.F.
Price: $400.00

MOORE & PATRICK FLINT DUELING PISTOL
Caliber: 45.
Barrel: 10", rifled.
Weight: 32 oz. **Length:** 14½" overall.
Stock: European walnut, checkered.
Sights: Fixed.
Features: Engraved, silvered lockplate, blue barrel. German silver furniture. Imported from Italy by Dixie Gun Works.
Price: $335.00

DIXIE TORNADO TARGET PISTOL
Caliber: 44 (.430" round ball).
Barrel: 10", octagonal, 1:22 twist.
Stocks: Walnut, target-style. Left unfinished for custom fitting. Walnut forend.
Sights: Blade on ramp front, micro-type open rear adjustable for windage and elevation.
Features: Grip frame style of 1860 Colt revolver. Improved model of the Tingle and B.W. Southgate pistol. Trigger adjustable for pull. Frame, barrel, hammer and sights in the white, brass trigger guard. Comes with solid brass, walnut-handled cleaning rod with jag and nylon muzzle protector. Introduced 1983. From Dixie Gun Works.
Price: $215.50

HARPER'S FERRY 1806 PISTOL
Caliber: 58 (.570" round ball).
Barrel: 10".
Weight: 40 oz. **Length:** 16" overall.
Stock: Walnut.
Sights: Fixed.
Features: Case-hardened lock, brass-mounted browned barrel. Replica of the first U.S. Gov't.-made flintlock pistol. Imported by Navy Arms, Dixie Gun Works, E.M.F.
Price: . . . . $225.00 to $405.00
Price: Kit (Dixie) $184.95

HAWKEN PERCUSSION PISTOL
Caliber: 54.
Barrel: 9", octagonal.
Weight: 40 oz. **Length:** 14" overall.
Stock: Checkered walnut.
Sights: Blade front, fixed notch rear.
Features: German silver trigger guard, blued barrel. Imported from Italy by E.M.F.
Price: $370.00

Kentucky Percussion Pistol
Similar to flint version but percussion lock. Imported by Cabela's, The Armoury, E.M.F., Navy Arms, CVA (50-cal.).
Price: . . . . $141.95 to $250.00
Price: Brass barrel (E.M.F.) $275.00
Price: In kit form (CVA, Armoury) $97.95
Price: Single cased set (Navy Arms) $290.00
Price: Double cased set (Navy Arms) $495.00

LE PAGE PERCUSSION DUELING PISTOL
Caliber: 45.
Barrel: 10", rifled.
Weight: 40 oz. **Length:** 16" overall.
Stock: Walnut, fluted butt.
Sights: Blade front, notch rear.
Features: Double-set triggers. Blued barrel; trigger guard and buttcap are polished silver. Imported by Dixie Gun Works, E.M.F.
Price: . . . . $259.95 to $400.00

LYMAN PLAINS PISTOL
Caliber: 50 or 54.
Barrel: 8", 1:30 twist, both calibers.
Weight: 50 oz. **Length:** 15" overall.
Stock: Walnut half-stock.
Sights: Blade front, square notch rear adjustable for windage.
Features: Polished brass trigger guard and ramrod tip, color case-hardened coil spring lock, spring-loaded trigger, stainless steel nipple, blackened iron furniture. Hooked patent breech, detachable belt hook. Introduced 1981. From Lyman Products.
Price: Finished $214.95
Price: Kit $179.95

NAVY ARMS LE PAGE DUELING PISTOL
Caliber: 44.
Barrel: 9", octagon, rifled.
Weight: 34 oz. **Length:** 15" overall.
Stock: European walnut.
Sights: Adjustable rear.
Features: Single-set trigger. Polished metal finish. From Navy Arms.
Price: Percussion $475.00
Price: Single cased set, percussion $685.00
Price: Double cased set, percussion $1,290.00
Price: Flintlock, rifled $550.00
Price: Flintlock, smoothbore (45-cal.) $550.00
Price: Flintlock, single cased set $760.00
Price: Flintlock, double cased set $1,430.00

Navy Arms Mountain

Dixie W. Parker

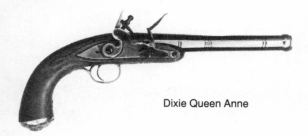

Dixie Queen Anne

NAVY ARMS MOUNTAIN PISTOL
Caliber: 50.
Barrel: 10", octagonal, rifled.
Weight: 36 oz. **Length:** 15½" overall.
Stock: European walnut.
Sights: Blade front, notch rear adjustable for windage.
Features: Color case-hardened lock, blued barrel, brass furniture. Imported by Navy Arms.
Price: Flintlock $225.00
Price: Percussion $215.00

W. PARKER FLINTLOCK PISTOL
Caliber: 45.
Barrel: 11", rifled.
Weight: 40 oz. **Length:** 16½" overall.
Stock: Walnut.
Sights: Blade front, notch rear.
Features: Browned barrel, silver-plated trigger guard, finger rest, polished and engraved lock. Double-set triggers. Imported by Dixie Gun Works.
Price: $208.00

QUEEN ANNE FLINTLOCK PISTOL
Caliber: 50 (.490" round ball).
Barrel: 7½", smoothbore.
Stock: Walnut.
Sights: None.
Features: Browned steel barrel, fluted brass trigger guard, brass mask on butt. Lockplate left in the white. Made by Pedersoli in Italy. Introduced 1983. Imported by Dixie Gun Works, Navy Arms.
Price: From Dixie $166.50
Price: From Navy Arms $200.00
Price: Kit (Dixie Gun Works only) $138.50

TRADITIONS WILLIAM PARKER PISTOL

THOMPSON/CENTER SCOUT PISTOL
Caliber: 45, 50 and 54.
Barrel: 12", interchangeable.
Weight: 4 lbs., 6 oz. **Length:** NA.
Stocks: American black walnut stocks and forend.
Sights: Blade on ramp front, fully adjustable Patridge rear.
Features: Patented in-line ignition system with special vented breech plug. Patented trigger mechanism consists of only two moving parts. Interchangeable barrels. Wide grooved hammer. Brass trigger guard assembly. Introduced 1990. From Thompson/Center.
Price: 45-, 50- or 54-cal. $315.00
Price: Extra barrel, 45-, 50- or 54-cal. $140.00

Thompson/Center Scout

Traditions William Parker

Consult our Directory pages for the location of firms mentioned.

Caliber: 45 and 50.
Barrel: 10⅜", ¹⁵/₁₆" flats; polished steel.
Weight: 40 oz. **Length:** 17½" overall.
Stock: Walnut with checkered grip.
Sights: Brass blade front, fixed rear.
Features: Replica dueling pistol with 1:18" twist, hooked breech. Brass wedge plate, trigger guard, cap guard; separate ramrod. Double-set triggers. Polished steel barrel, lock. Imported by Traditions, Inc.
Price: $252.00

TRADITIONS PIONEER PISTOL
Caliber: 45.
Barrel: 9⅝", ¹³/₁₆" flats.
Weight: 36 oz. **Length:** 15" overall.
Stock: Beech.
Sights: Blade front, fixed rear.
Features: V-type mainspring; 1:18" twist. Single trigger. German silver furniture, blackened hardware. From Traditions, Inc.
Price: $169.00
Price: Kit $119.00

Traditions Pioneer

TRADITIONS TRAPPER PISTOL
Caliber: 45, 50.
Barrel: 9¾", ⅞" flats.
Weight: 2¾ lbs. **Length:** 16" overall.
Stock: Beech.
Sights: Blade front, adjustable rear.
Features: Double-set triggers; brass buttcap, trigger guard, wedge plate, forend tip, thimble. From Traditions, Inc.
Price: $170.00
Price: Kit $130.00

Army 1851

Dixie 1860 Army

BABY DRAGOON 1848, 1849 POCKET, WELLS FARGO

Caliber: 31.
Barrel: 3", 4", 5"; seven-groove, RH twist.
Weight: About 21 oz.
Stock: Varnished walnut.
Sights: Brass pin front, hammer notch rear.
Features: No loading lever on Baby Dragoon or Wells Fargo models. Unfluted cylinder with stagecoach holdup scene; cupped cylinder pin; no grease grooves; one safety pin on cylinder and slot in hammer face; straight (flat) mainspring. From Armsport, Dixie Gun Works, Uberti USA, Cabela's.
Price: 6" barrel, with loading lever (Dixie Gun Works) **$185.00**
Price: 3", 4", 5½", 6" (Uberti USA) **$295.00**
Price: As above, silver-plated (Uberti USA) **$240.00**
Price: 1849 Pocket (Cabela's) **$179.95**

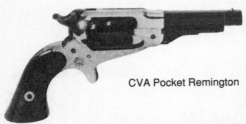

CVA Pocket Remington

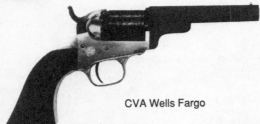

CVA Wells Fargo

Dixie Third Model Dragoon

ARMY 1851 PERCUSSION REVOLVER

Caliber: 44, 6-shot.
Barrel: 7½".
Weight: 45 oz. **Length:** 13" overall.
Stocks: Walnut finish.
Sights: Fixed.
Features: 44-caliber version of the 1851 Navy. Imported by The Armoury, Armsport.
Price: **$129.00**

ARMY 1860 PERCUSSION REVOLVER

Caliber: 44, 6-shot.
Barrel: 8".
Weight: 40 oz. **Length:** 13⅝" overall.
Stocks: Walnut.
Sights: Fixed.
Features: Engraved Navy scene on cylinder; brass trigger guard; case-hardened frame, loading lever and hammer. Some importers supply pistol cut for detachable shoulder stock, have accessory stock available. Imported by Cabela's, E.M.F., CVA, Navy Arms, The Armoury, Cimarron, Dixie Gun Works (half-fluted cylinder, not roll engraved), Euroarms of America (brass or steel model), Armsport, Mitchell, Uberti USA.
Price: About . . . . $92.95 to **$235.00**
Price: Single cased set (Navy Arms) **$250.00**
Price: Double cased set (Navy Arms) **$400.00**
Price: 1861 Navy: Same as Army except 36-cal., 7½" bbl., wgt. 41 oz., cut for shoulder stock; round cylinder (fluted avail.), from E.M.F., CVA (brass frame, 44-cal.), Cabela's, Mitchell . . . . $99.95 to **$249.00**
Price: Steel frame kit (E.M.F., Mitchell, Navy, Euroarms) **$125.00 to $187.00**
Price: Colt Army Police, fluted cyl., 5½", 36-cal. (Cabela's) **$96.95**

CABELA'S PATERSON REVOLVER

Caliber: 36, 5-shot cylinder.
Barrel: 7½".
Weight: 24 oz. **Length:** 11½" overall.
Stocks: One-piece walnut.
Sights: Fixed.
Features: Recreation of the 1836 gun. Color case-hardened frame, steel backstrap; roll-engraved cylinder scene. Imported by Cabela's.
Price: **$199.95**

CVA POCKET REMINGTON

Caliber: 31.
Barrel: 4", octagonal.
Weight: 15½ oz. **Length:** 7½" overall.
Stocks: Two-piece walnut.
Sights: Post front, grooved topstrap rear.
Features: Spur trigger, brass frame with blued barrel and cylinder. Introduced 1984. Imported by CVA.
Price: Finished **$125.95**

CVA WELLS FARGO MODEL

Caliber: 31.
Barrel: 4", octagonal.
Weight: 28 oz. (with extra cylinder). **Length:** 9" overall.
Stocks: Walnut.
Sights: Post front, hammer notch rear.
Features: Brass frame and backstrap; blue finish. Comes with extra cylinder. Imported by CVA.
Price: Brass frame, finished **$125.95**

DIXIE THIRD MODEL DRAGOON

Caliber: 44 (.454" round ball).
Barrel: 7⅜".
Weight: 4 lbs., 2½ oz.
Stocks: One-piece walnut.
Sights: Brass pin front, hammer notch rear, or adjustable folding leaf rear.
Features: Cylinder engraved with Indian fight scene. This is the only Dragoon replica with folding leaf sight. Brass backstrap and trigger guard; color case-hardened steel frame, blue-black barrel. Imported by Dixie Gun Works.
Price: **$149.95**

CVA Third Model Colt Dragoon

Similar to the Dixie Third Dragoon except has 7½" barrel, weighs 4 lbs., 6 oz., blade front sight. Overall length of 14". 44-caliber, 6-shot.
Price: **$229.95**

GRISWOLD & GUNNISON PERCUSSION REVOLVER

Caliber: 36 or 44, 6-shot.
Barrel: 7½".
Weight: 44 oz. (36-cal.). **Length:** 13" overall.
Stocks: Walnut.
Sights: Fixed.
Features: Replica of famous Confederate pistol. Brass frame, backstrap and trigger guard; case-hardened loading lever; rebated cylinder (44-cal. only). Rounded Dragoon-type barrel. Imported by Navy Arms (as Reb Model 1860), E.M.F.
Price: About $229.00
Price: Single cased set (Navy Arms) $195.00
Price: Double cased set (Navy Arms) $315.00
Price: Reb 1860 (Navy Arms) $100.00
Price: As above, kit $80.00

LE MAT CAVALRY MODEL REVOLVER

Caliber: 44/65.
Barrel: 6¾" (revolver); 4⅞" (single shot).
Weight: 3 lbs., 7 oz.
Stocks: Hand-checkered walnut.
Sights: Post front, hammer notch rear.
Features: Exact reproduction with all-steel construction; 44-cal. 9-shot cylinder, 65-cal. single barrel; color case-hardened hammer with selector; spur trigger guard; ring at butt; lever-type barrel release. From Navy Arms.
Price: Cavalry model (lanyard ring, spur trigger guard) . . . $595.00
Price: Army model (round trigger guard, pin-type barrel release) . . $595.00
Price: Naval-style (thumb selector on hammer) $595.00

Uberti 1851 Squareback

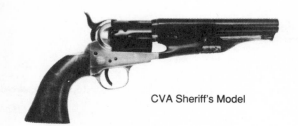

CVA Sheriff's Model

NEW MODEL 1858 ARMY PERCUSSION REVOLVER

Caliber: 36 or 44, 6-shot.
Barrel: 6½" or 8".
Weight: 40 oz. **Length:** 13½" overall.
Stocks: Walnut.
Sights: Blade front, groove-in-frame rear.
Features: Replica of Remington Model 1858. Also available from some importers as Army Model Belt Revolver in 36-cal., a shortened and lightened version of the 44. Target Model (Uberti USA, Navy Arms) has fully adjustable target rear sight, target front, 36 or 44. Imported by Cabela's, CVA (as 1858 Remington Army), Dixie Gun Works, Navy Arms, The Armoury, E.M.F., Euroarms of America (engraved, stainless and plain), Armsport, Mitchell, Uberti USA.
Price: Steel frame, about . . . . $140.00 to $224.95
Price: Steel frame kit (Euroarms, Navy Arms) . . $115.95 to $150.00
Price: Single cased set (Navy Arms) $240.00
Price: Double cased set (Navy Arms) $390.00
Price: Stainless steel Model 1858 (Euroarms, Uberti USA, Cabela's, Navy Arms, Armsport) . . . . $220.00 to $325.00
Price: Target Model, adjustable rear sight (Cabela's, Euroarms, Uberti USA, Navy Arms, E.M.F.) . . . . $95.95 to $300.00
Price: Brass frame (CVA, Cabela's, Navy Arms) . . . $169.95 to $212.95
Price: As above, kit (CVA, Dixie Gun Works, Navy Arms) $145.00 to $188.95
Price: Remington "Texas" (Mitchell) $199.00

DIXIE WYATT EARP REVOLVER

Caliber: 44.
Barrel: 12" octagon.
Weight: 46 oz. **Length:** 18" overall.
Stocks: Two-piece walnut.
Sights: Fixed.
Features: Highly polished brass frame, backstrap and trigger guard; blued barrel and cylinder; case-hardened hammer, trigger and loading lever. Navy-size shoulder stock ($45) will fit with minor fitting. From Dixie Gun Works.
Price: $130.00

Le Mat Cavalry Model

NAVY MODEL 1851 PERCUSSION REVOLVER

Caliber: 36, 44, 6-shot.
Barrel: 7½".
Weight: 44 oz. **Length:** 13" overall.
Stocks: Walnut finish.
Sights: Post front, hammer notch rear.
Features: Brass backstrap and trigger guard; some have 1st Model squareback trigger guard, engraved cylinder with navy battle scene; case-hardened frame, hammer, loading lever. Imported by The Armoury, Cabela's, Mitchell, Navy Arms, E.M.F., Dixie Gun Works, Euroarms of America, Armsport, CVA (36-cal. only), Uberti USA.
Price: Brass frame . . . . $139.95 to $229.00
Price: Steel frame . . . . $130.00 to $285.00
Price: Silver-plated backstrap, trigger guard (Uberti USA) $249.00
Price: Kit form . . . . $110.00 to $123.95
Price: Engraved model (Dixie Gun Works) $139.95
Price: Single cased set, steel frame (Navy Arms) $235.00
Price: Double cased set, steel frame (Navy Arms) $375.00
Price: Confederate Navy (Cabela's) $69.95

Uberti 1861 Navy Percussion Revolver

Similar to 1851 Navy except has round 7½" barrel, rounded trigger guard, German silver blade front sight, "creeping" loading lever. Available with fluted or round cylinder. Imported by Uberti USA.
Price: Steel backstrap, trigger guard, cut for stock $295.00

CVA Colt Sheriff's Model

Similar to the Uberti 1861 Navy except has 5½" barrel, brass or steel frame, semi-fluted cylinder. In 36-caliber only.
Price: Brass frame, finished $149.95
Price: 1861 Navy, steel frame, 36-cal. $219.95
Price: As above, brass frame, 44-cal. $139.95
Price: As above, kit $124.95
Price: Brass frame (Armsport) $155.00
Price: Steel frame (Armsport) $193.00

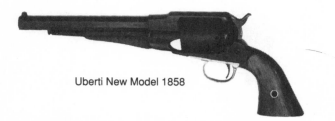

Uberti New Model 1858

NAVY ARMS DELUXE 1858 REMINGTON-STYLE REVOLVER

Caliber: 44.
Barrel: 8".
Weight: 2 lbs., 13 oz.
Stocks: Smooth walnut.
Sights: Dovetailed blade front.
Features: First exact reproduction—correct in size and weight to the original, with progressive rifling; highly polished with blue finish, silver-plated trigger guard. From Navy Arms.
Price: Deluxe model $350.00

CVA Remington Bison

POCKET POLICE 1862 PERCUSSION REVOLVER
Caliber: 36, 5-shot.
Barrel: 4½", 5½", 6½", 7½".
Weight: 26 oz. **Length:** 12" overall (6½" bbl.).
Stocks: Walnut.
Sights: Fixed.
Features: Round tapered barrel; half-fluted and rebated cylinder; case-hardened frame, loading lever and hammer; silver or brass trigger guard and backstrap. Imported by CVA (5½" only), Navy Arms (5½" only), Uberti USA (5½", 6½" only).
Price: About . . . . $143.95 to $279.00
Price: Single cased set with accessories (Navy Arms) $350.00
Price: Kit (CVA) $139.95
Price: With silver-plated backstrap, trigger guard (Uberti USA) . . . $245.00

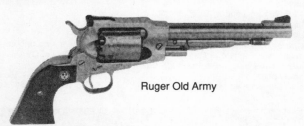

Ruger Old Army

RUGER 44 OLD ARMY PERCUSSION REVOLVER
Caliber: 44, 6-shot. Uses .457" dia. lead bullets.
Barrel: 7½" (6-groove, 16" twist).
Weight: 46 oz. **Length:** 13¾" overall.
Stocks: Smooth walnut.
Sights: Ramp front, rear adjustable for windage and elevation.
Features: Stainless steel; standard size nipples, chrome-moly steel cylinder and frame, same lockwork as in original Super Blackhawk. Also available in stainless steel. Made in USA. From Sturm, Ruger & Co.
Price: Stainless steel (Model KBP-7) $428.00
Price: Blued steel (Model BP-7) $335.50

SPILLER & BURR REVOLVER
Caliber: 36 (.375" round ball).
Barrel: 7", octagon.
Weight: 2½ lbs. **Length:** 12½" overall.
Stocks: Two-piece walnut.
Sights: Fixed.
Features: Reproduction of the C.S.A. revolver. Brass frame and trigger guard. Also available as a kit. From Dixie Gun Works, Mitchell, Navy Arms.
Price: . . . . $89.95 to $199.00
Price: Kit form $95.00
Price: Single cased set (Navy Arms) $220.00
Price: Double cased set (Navy Arms) $350.00

Texas Paterson

UBERTI 1862 POCKET NAVY PERCUSSION REVOLVER
Caliber: 36, 5-shot.
Barrel: 5½", 6½", octagonal, 7-groove, LH twist.
Weight: 27 oz. (5½" barrel). **Length:** 10½" overall (5½" bbl.).
Stocks: One-piece varnished walnut.
Sights: Brass pin front, hammer notch rear.
Features: Rebated cylinder, hinged loading lever, brass or silver-plated backstrap and trigger guard, color-cased frame, hammer, loading lever, plunger and latch, rest blued. Has original-type markings. From Uberti USA.
Price: With brass backstrap, trigger guard $299.00

CVA Remington Bison
Similar to the CVA 1858 Remington Target except has 10¼" octagonal barrel, 44-caliber, brass frame.
Price: Finished $239.95
Price: From Armsport $222.00

CVA 1858 Remington Target
Similar to the New Model 1858 Remington except has ramped blade front sight, adjustable rear.
Price: $234.95

Euroarms Rogers & Spencer

ROGERS & SPENCER PERCUSSION REVOLVER
Caliber: 44.
Barrel: 7½".
Weight: 47 oz. **Length:** 13¾" overall.
Stocks: Walnut.
Sights: Cone front, integral groove in frame for rear.
Features: Accurate reproduction of a Civil War design. Solid frame; extra large nipple cut-out on rear of cylinder; loading lever and cylinder easily removed for cleaning. From Euroarms of America (standard blue, engraved, burnished, target models), Navy Arms.
Price: . . . . $160.00 to $240.00
Price: Nickel-plated $215.00
Price: Engraved (Euroarms) $286.00
Price: Kit version $95.00
Price: Target version (Euroarms, Navy Arms) $250.00
Price: Brushed satin chrome (Navy Arms) $230.00
Price: Burnished London Gray (Euroarms, Navy Arms) $250.00

SHERIFF MODEL 1851 PERCUSSION REVOLVER
Caliber: 36, 44, 6-shot.
Barrel: 5".
Weight: 40 oz. **Length:** 10½" overall.
Stocks: Walnut.
Sights: Fixed.
Features: Brass backstrap and trigger guard; engraved navy scene; case-hardened frame, hammer, loading lever. Imported by E.M.F.
Price: Steel frame $172.00
Price: Brass frame $140.00

TEXAS PATERSON 1836 REVOLVER
Caliber: 36 (.376" round ball).
Barrel: 7½".
Weight: 42 oz.
Stocks: One-piece walnut.
Sights: Fixed.
Features: Copy of Sam Colt's first commercially-made revolving pistol. Has no loading lever but comes with loading tool. From Dixie Gun Works, Navy Arms, Uberti USA.
Price: About . . . . $310.00 to $380.00
Price: With loading lever (Uberti USA) $425.00
Price: Engraved (Navy Arms) $450.00

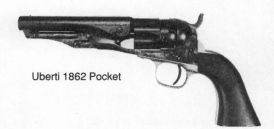

Uberti 1862 Pocket

BLACKPOWDER REVOLVERS

Uberti 1st Model Dragoon

UBERTI 1st MODEL DRAGOON
Caliber: 44.
Barrel: 7½", part round, part octagon.
Weight: 64 oz.
Stocks: One-piece walnut.
Sights: German silver blade front, hammer notch rear.
Features: First model has oval bolt cuts in cylinder, square-back flared trigger guard, V-type mainspring, short trigger. Ranger and Indian scene roll-engraved on cylinder. Color case-hardened frame, loading lever, plunger and hammer; blue barrel, cylinder, trigger and wedge. Available with old-time charcoal blue or standard blue-black finish. Polished brass backstrap and trigger guard. From Uberti USA.
Price: $315.00

Uberti 3rd Model Dragoon Revolver
Similar to the 2nd Model except for oval trigger guard, long trigger, modifications to the loading lever and latch. Imported by Uberti USA.
Price: Military model (frame cut for shoulder stock, steel backstrap) $320.00
Price: Civilian (brass backstrap, trigger guard) $315.00

Uberti 2nd Model Dragoon Revolver
Similar to the 1st Model except distinguished by rectangular bolt cuts in the cylinder.
Price: $315.00

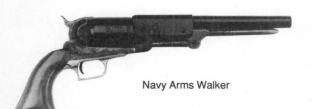

Navy Arms Walker

WALKER 1847 PERCUSSION REVOLVER
Caliber: 44, 6-shot.
Barrel: 9".
Weight: 84 oz. **Length:** 15½" overall.
Stocks: Walnut.
Sights: Fixed.
Features: Case-hardened frame, loading lever and hammer; iron backstrap; brass trigger guard; engraved cylinder. Imported by Cabela's, CVA, Navy Arms, Dixie Gun Works, Uberti USA, E.M.F., Cimarron.
Price: About . . . . $195.00 to $350.00
Price: Single cased set (Navy Arms) $375.00

BLACKPOWDER MUSKETS & RIFLES

Armoury R140 Hawken

ARMOURY R140 HAWKEN RIFLE
Caliber: 45, 50 or 54.
Barrel: 29".
Weight: 8¾ to 9 lbs. **Length:** 45¾" overall.
Stock: Walnut, with cheekpiece.
Sights: Dovetail front, fully adjustable rear.
Features: Octagon barrel, removable breech plug; double set triggers; blued barrel, brass stock fittings, color case-hardened percussion lock. From Armsport, The Armoury.
Price: . . . . $225.00 to $245.00

BOSTONIAN PERCUSSION RIFLE
Caliber: 45.
Barrel: 30", octagonal
Weight: 7¼ lbs. **Length:** 46" overall.
Stock: Walnut.
Sights: Blade front, fixed notch rear.
Features: Color case-hardened lock, brass trigger guard, buttplate, patchbox. Imported from Italy by E.M.F.
Price: $285.00

AMERICAN ARMS HAWKEYE RIFLE
Caliber: 50, 54.
Barrel: 22", 1:28" twist.
Weight: 6.75 lbs. **Length:** 41.5" overall.
Stock: Walnut; contemporary styling with rubber recoil pad.
Sights: Blade on ramp front, fully adjustable open rear.
Features: Striker-fired in-line ignition system; modern trigger; dual safety systems. Drilled and tapped for scope mounts. Introduced 1992. Imported from Italy by American Arms, Inc.
Price: Blued $279.00
Price: Stainless steel $419.00

ARMSPORT 1863 SHARPS RIFLE, CARBINE
Caliber: 45, 54.
Barrel: 28", round.
Weight: 8.4 lbs. **Length:** 46" overall.
Stock: Walnut.
Sights: Blade front, folding adjustable rear. Tang sight set optionally available.
Features: Replica of the 1863 Sharps. Color case-hardened frame, rest blued. Imported by Armsport.
Price: $815.00
Price: Carbine, 45 or 54, 22" barrel $790.00

Cabela's Accura 9000

CABELA'S ACCURA 9000 MUZZLELOADER
Caliber: 50, 54.
Barrel: 27"; 1:54 twist.

Weight: About 7½ lbs. **Length:** 44" overall.
Stock: European walnut with Monte Carlo cheekpiece, checkered grip and forend.
Sights: Hooded front with interchangeable blades, open rear adjustable for windage and elevation.
Features: In-line ignition system with removable breech plug. Automatic safety and half-cock. Quick detachable sling swivels, schnabel forend tip, recoil pad. From Cabela's.
Price: Right or left-hand $399.95

CAUTION: PRICES CHANGE, CHECK AT GUNSHOP.

Cabela's Swivel-Barrel

CABELA'S SWIVEL-BARREL RIFLE
Caliber: 50, 54.
Barrel: 23.75".

Weight: 10 lbs. **Length:** 40" overall.
Stock: Checkered American walnut.
Sights: Blade front, open rear adjustable for windage and elevation; one set for each barrel.
Features: Barrel assembly rotates for second shot. Back action mechanism. Monte Carlo comb, rubber butt pad; checkered pistol grip and forend panels. Introduced 1992. From Cabela's.
Price: **$379.95**

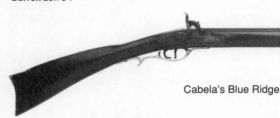

Cabela's Blue Ridge

CABELA'S TRADITIONAL HAWKEN'S
Caliber: 45, 50, 54, 58.
Barrel: 29".
Weight: About 9 lbs.
Stock: Walnut.
Sights: Blade front, open adjustable rear.
Features: Flintlock or percussion. Adjustable double-set triggers. Polished brass furniture, color case-hardened lock. Imported by Cabela's.
Price: Percussion, right-hand **$169.95**
Price: Percussion, right-hand, kit **$139.95**
Price: Percussion, left-hand **$174.95**
Price: Flintlock, right-hand **$189.95**
Price: Flintlock kit **$164.95**

CABELA'S TAOS RIFLE
Caliber: 45, 50.
Barrel: 28¼".
Weight: 6 lbs., 11 oz. **Length:** 43¼" overall.
Stock: Oil-finished walnut.

CABELA'S BLUE RIDGE RIFLE
Caliber: 36, 45, 50.
Barrel: 39".
Weight: 7¾ lbs. **Length:** 55⅛" overall.
Stock: American walnut.
Sights: Blade front, rear drift adjustable for windage.
Features: Brown-finished octagonal barrel; adjustable double-set triggers. Trigger guard and buttplate of polished brass, lock and fittings are color case-hardened. Imported by Cabela's.
Price: Percussion **$249.95**
Price: Flintlock **$269.95**

Cabela's Hawken's Hunter Rifle
Similar to the Traditional Hawken's except has more modern stock style with rubber recoil pad, blued furniture, sling swivels. Percussion only, in 45-, 50-, 54- or 58-caliber.
Price: Right-hand **$184.95**
Price: Left-hand **$189.95**

Sights: Blade front, rear adjustable for windage.
Features: Carbine version of the Pennsylvania rifle. Adjustable double-set triggers. Imported by Cabela's.
Price: Percussion **$229.95**
Price: Flintlock **$239.95**

Cook & Brother

COOK & BROTHER CONFEDERATE CARBINE
Caliber: 58.
Barrel: 24".

Weight: 7½ lbs. **Length:** 40½" overall.
Stock: Select walnut.
Features: Recreation of the 1861 New Orleans-made artillery carbine. Color case-hardened lock, browned barrel. Buttplate, trigger guard, barrel bands, sling swivels and nose cap of polished brass. From Euroarms of America.
Price: **$366.00**

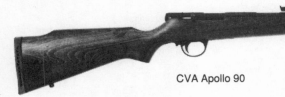

CVA Apollo 90

CVA Apollo 90 Shadow
Similar to the Apollo 90 except has black textured epoxicoat hardwood stock. Rifle length only with 27" barrel, 50- or 54- caliber.
Price: **$299.95**

CVA EXPRESS RIFLE
Caliber: 50, 54.
Barrel: 28", round.
Weight: 9 lbs.
Stock: Walnut-stained hardwood.
Sights: Bead and post front, adjustable rear.
Features: Double rifle with twin percussion locks and triggers, adjustable barrels. Hooked breech. Introduced 1989. From CVA.
Price: Finished **$489.95**

CVA APOLLO 90 PERCUSSION RIFLE
Caliber: 50, 54.
Barrel: 22", 27", round, tapered; 1:32" rifling. Chrome bore.
Weight: 7½ lbs. **Length:** 45" overall.
Stock: Laminated walnut. Monte Carlo comb with flutes, beavertail cheekpiece; ventilated rubber recoil pad, sling swivel studs.
Stock: Removable brass bead on ramp front, removable hunting-style open rear adjustable for windage and elevation.
Features: In-line percussion system with push-pull bolt block safety system. One-piece blued barrel and receiver. Receiver drilled and tapped for scope mounting, has loading window and spark protector cover. Vented for gas escape. Introduced 1990. Imported by CVA.
Price: Standard Grade **$439.95**
Price: Carbine, 22", laminated stock **$375.95**

CVA Apollo Sporter
Similar to the Apollo 90 except has walnut-stained hardwood stock, composition buttplate. Available only in 50-caliber, 25" barrel.
Price: **$255.95**

CVA Bushwacker

CVA BUSHWACKER RIFLE
Caliber: 50.
Barrel: 26", octagonal; $^{15}/_{16}$" flats; 1:48" twist.
Weight: 7.5 lbs. **Length:** 40" overall.
Stock: Walnut-stained hardwood.
Sights: Brass blade front, fixed semi-buckhorn open rear.
Features: Color case-hardened lockplate; single trigger with oversize blackened trigger guard; blued barrel, wedge plates. From CVA.
Price: Percussion only $159.95

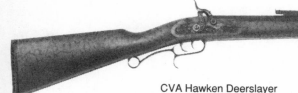

CVA Hawken Deerslayer

CVA Hawken Deerslayer Rifle/Carbine
Similar to the CVA Hawken except has non-glare black chrome furniture, schnabel forend tip, ventilated rubber recoil pad. Fully adjustable click rear sight. Over-sized trigger guard, blued wedge plates; 24" or 28" barrel; drilled and tapped for scope mounting. From CVA.
Price: Rifle or Carbine $249.95

CVA KENTUCKY RIFLE
Caliber: 50.
Barrel: 33½", rifled, octagon; $^{7}/_{8}$" flats.
Weight: 7½ lbs. **Length:** 48" overall.
Stock: Select hardwood.
Sights: Brass Kentucky blade-type front, fixed open rear.
Features: Available in percussion only. Stainless steel nipple included. From CVA.
Price: Percussion $249.95
Price: Percussion kit $189.95
Price: Kentucky Hunter (half-stock) $239.95

CVA PLAINSMAN RIFLE
Caliber: 50.
Barrel: 24" octagonal, $^{15}/_{16}$" flats; 1:48 rifling.
Weight: 6 lbs., 9 oz. **Length:** 40" overall.
Stock: Select hardwood.
Sights: Brass blade front, fixed semi-buckhorn rear.
Features: Color case-hardened lock plate; screw-adjustable sear engagement, V-type mainspring; single trigger with large guard; black trigger guard, wedge plate and thimble. Introduced 1990. Imported by CVA.
Price: Finished $229.95

CVA Stalker

CVA FRONTIER CARBINE
Caliber: 50.
Barrel: 24" octagon; $^{15}/_{16}$" flats.
Weight: 6½ lbs. **Length:** 40" overall.
Stock: Selected hardwood.
Sights: Brass blade front, fixed open rear.
Features: Color case-hardened lockplate, V-type mainspring. Early style brass trigger with tension spring. Brass buttplate, trigger guard, wedge plate, nose cap, thimble. From CVA.
Price: Percussion $195.95
Price: Flintlock rifle $208.95
Price: Percussion Carbine kit $129.95

CVA Frontier Hunter Carbine
Similar to the CVA Frontier Carbine except has conventional-style black rubber butt pad, black chrome furniture. Barrel is drilled and tapped for scope mounting. Fuully adjustable rear sight. Overall length 40", weight 7.5 lbs., 50-caliber only. From CVA.
Price: $195.95

CVA HAWKEN RIFLE
Caliber: 50, 54.
Barrel: 28", octagon; $^{15}/_{16}$" across flats; 1:66" twist.
Weight: 8 lbs. **Length:** 44" overall.
Stock: Select hardwood.
Sights: Beaded blade front, fully adjustable open rear.
Features: Fully adjustable double-set triggers; brass patch box, wedge plates, nosecap, thimbles, trigger guard and buttplate; blued barrel; color case-hardened, engraved lockplate. V-type mainspring. Percussion only. Hooked breech. Introduced 1981. From CVA.
Price: St. Louis Hawken, finished $229.95
Price: As above, combo kit (50-, 54-cal. bbls.) $229.95

CVA MOUNTAIN RIFLE
Caliber: 50, 54.
Barrel: 32" octagon; $^{15}/_{16}$" flats.
Weight: 9 lbs. **Length:** 48" overall.
Stock: European walnut with cheekpiece.
Sights: German silver blade front, adjustable open rear.
Features: Blued and engraved lockplate; bridle, fly, screw-adjustable sear engagement. Double-set triggers. Pewter nose cap, trigger guard, buttplate. From CVA.
Price: $259.95

CVA PENNSYLVANIA LONG RIFLE
Caliber: 50.
Barrel: 40", octagonal; $^{7}/_{8}$" flats.
Weight: 8 lbs., 3 oz. **Length:** 55¾" overall.
Stock: Select walnut.
Sights: Brass blade front, fixed semi-buckhorn rear.
Features: Color case-hardened lockplate, brass buttplate, toe plate, patchbox, trigger guard, thimbles, nosecap; blued barrel, double-set triggers; authentic V-type mainspring. Introduced 1983. From CVA.
Price: Finished, percussion $455.95
Price: Finished, flintlock $455.95

CVA STALKER RIFLE/CARBINE
Caliber: 50, 54.
Barrel: 24", 28"; octagonal; drilled and tapped for scope mounting; 1:32" twist.
Weight: 7.5 lbs. **Length:** 44" overall (rifle).
Stock: Walnut-stained hardwood with Monte Carlo comb, cheekpiece. Ventilated rubber recoil pad.
Sights: Beaded blade front, fully adjustable click rear.
Features: Color case-hardened lockplate; V-type mainspring; single modern-style trigger. From CVA.
Price: 50, 54 rifle $210.95
Price: 50, 54 carbine $210.95

Consult our Directory pages for the location of firms mentioned.

CVA Tracker

CVA TRACKER CARBINE
Caliber: 50.
Barrel: 21", half round, half octagon with ¹⁵⁄₁₆" flats; 1:32" twist.
Weight: 6.5 lbs. **Length:** 36" overall.
Stock: Matte finish walnut with straight grip; ventilated rubber recoil pad.
Sights: Beaded blade front, fully adjustable click rear.
Features: Color case-hardened lockplate, black-chromed furniture; drilled and tapped for scope mounting. From CVA.
Price: **$239.95**

DIXIE DELUX CUB RIFLE
Caliber: 40.
Barrel: 28".
Weight: 6½ lbs.
Stock: Walnut.
Sights: Fixed.
Features: Short rifle for small game and beginning shooters. Brass patchbox and furniture. Flint or percussion. From Dixie Gun Works.
Price: Finished **$335.00**
Price: Kit **$205.00**

CVA SQUIRREL RIFLE
Caliber: 36, 36/50 Combo.
Barrel: 25", octagonal; ⅞" flats.
Weight: 6 lbs. **Length:** 40¾" overall.
Stock: Hardwood.
Sights: Beaded blade front, fully adjustable hunting-style rear.
Features: Color case-hardened lockplate, brass buttplate, trigger guard, wedge plates, thimbles; double-set triggers; hooked breech; authentic V-type mainspring. From CVA.
Price: Finished, percussion, 36-cal. **$249.95**

CVA TROPHY CARBINE
Caliber: 50, 54.
Barrel: 24", half round, half octagon with ¹⁵⁄₁₆" flats; 1:32" twist.
Weight: 7.5 lbs. **Length:** 40" overall.
Stock: Walnut with Monte Carlo comb, cheekpiece.
Sights: White bead on blade front, fully adjustable click rear.
Features: Color case-hardened lockplate, blued barrel, thimble. Modern-style stock; modern rifle trigger with over-sized guard; drilled and tapped for scope mounting. From CVA.
Price: **$239.95**

Dixie Hawken

DIXIE HAWKEN RIFLE
Caliber: 45, 50, 54.
Barrel: 30".

DIXIE TENNESSEE MOUNTAIN RIFLE
Caliber: 32 or 50.
Barrel: 41½", 6-groove rifling, brown finish. **Length:** 56" overall.
Stock: Walnut, oil finish; Kentucky-style.
Sights: Silver blade front, open buckhorn rear.
Features: Recreation of the original mountain rifles. Early Schultz lock, interchangeable flint or percussion with vent plug or drum and nipple. Tumbler has fly. Double-set triggers. All metal parts browned. From Dixie Gun Works.

Weight: 8 lbs. **Length:** 46½" overall.
Stock: Walnut.
Sights: Blade front, adjustable rear.
Features: Blued barrel, double-set triggers, steel crescent buttplate. Imported by Dixie Gun Works.
Price: Finished **$250.00**
Price: Kit **$220.00**

Price: Flint or percussion, finished rifle, 50-cal. **$450.00**
Price: Kit, 50-cal. **$360.00**
Price: Left-hand model, flint or percussion **$450.00**
Price: Left-hand kit, flint or perc., 50-cal. **$360.00**
Price: Squirrel Rifle (as above except in 32-cal. with ¹³⁄₁₆" barrel flats), flint or percussion **$450.00**
Price: Kit, 32-cal., flint or percussion **$360.00**

Dixie Model 1816

DIXIE 1863 SPRINGFIELD MUSKET
Caliber: 58 (.570" patched ball or .575" Minie).
Barrel: 50", rifled.
Stocks: Walnut stained.
Sights: Blade front, adjustable ladder-type rear.
Features: Bright-finish lock, barrel, furniture. Reproduction of the last of the regulation muzzleloaders. Imported from Japan by Dixie Gun Works.
Price: Finished **$475.00**
Price: Kit **$330.00**

EUROARMS BUFFALO CARBINE
Caliber: 58.
Barrel: 26", round.
Weight: 7¾ lbs. **Length:** 42" overall.
Stock: Walnut.
Sights: Blade front, open adjustable rear.
Features: Shoots .575" round ball. Color case-hardened lock, blue hammer, barrel, trigger; brass furniture. Brass patchbox. Imported by Euroarms of America.
Price: **$407.00**

DIXIE U.S. MODEL 1816 FLINTLOCK MUSKET
Caliber: 69.
Barrel: 42", smoothbore.
Weight: 9.75 lbs. **Length:** 56.5" overall.
Stock: Walnut with oil finish.
Sights: Blade front.
Features: All metal finished "National Armory Bright"; three barrel bands with springs; steel ramrod with buttom-shaped head. Imported by Dixie Gun Works.
Price: **$695.00**

DIXIE U.S. MODEL 1861 SPRINGFIELD
Caliber: 58.
Barrel: 40".
Weight: About 8 lbs. **Length:** 55¹³⁄₁₆" overall.
Stock: Oil-finished walnut.
Sights: Blade front, step adjustable rear.
Features: Exact recreation of original rifle. Sling swivels attached to trigger guard bow and middle barrel band. Lockplate marked "1861" with eagle motif and "U.S. Springfield" in front of hammer; "U.S." stamped on top of buttplate. From Dixie Gun Works.
Price: **$450.00**
Price: Kit **$420.00**

Gonic GA-87

HARPER'S FERRY 1803 FLINTLOCK RIFLE
Caliber: 54 or 58.
Barrel: 35".
Weight: 9 lbs. **Length:** 59½" overall.
Stock: Walnut with cheekpiece.
Sights: Brass blade front, fixed steel rear.
Features: Brass trigger guard, sideplate, buttplate; steel patch box. Imported by Euroarms of America, Navy Arms (54-cal. only).
Price: $512.00
Price: 54-cal. (Navy Arms) $495.00

GONIC GA-87 M/L RIFLE
Caliber: 30, 38, 44, 45, 50, 54, 20-ga.
Barrel: 26".
Weight: 6 to 6½ lbs. **Length:** 43" overall (Carbine).
Stock: American walnut with checkered grip and forend, or laminated stock.
Sights: Optional bead front, open or peep rear adjustable for windage and elevation; drilled and tapped for scope bases (included).
Features: Closed-breech action with straight-line ignition. Modern trigger mechanism with ambidextrous safety. Satin blue finish on metal, satin stock finish. Introduced 1989. From Gonic Arms, Inc.
Price: Standard rifle, no sights $493.38
Price: As above, with sights, from $535.95
Price: Deluxe Rifle, no sights $526.06
Price: As above, with sights, from $568.64
Price: Accessory 24" carbine barrel, from ... $190.49

Hatfield Squirrel Rifle

HATFIELD SQUIRREL RIFLE
Caliber: 36, 45, 50.
Barrel: 39½", octagon, 32" on half-stock.
Weight: 7½ lbs. (32-cal.).
Stock: American fancy maple.
Sights: Silver blade front, buckhorn rear.
Features: Recreation of the traditional squirrel rifle. Available in flint or percussion with brass trigger guard and buttplate. From Hatfield Rifle Works. Introduced 1983.
Price: Full stock, percussion, Grade II $598.00
Price: As above, flintlock $620.00
Price: As above, Grade III, flint or percussion .. $700.00
Price: Mountain Rifle $665.00

ITHACA-NAVY HAWKEN RIFLE
Caliber: 50.
Barrel: 32" octagonal, 1" dia.
Weight: About 9 lbs.
Stocks: Walnut.
Sights: Blade front, rear adjustable for windage.
Features: Hooked breech, 1⅞" throw percussion lock. Attached twin thimbles

HAWKEN RIFLE
Caliber: 45, 50, 54 or 58.
Barrel: 28", blued, 6-groove rifling.
Weight: 8¾ lbs. **Length:** 44" overall.
Stock: Walnut with cheekpiece.
Sights: Blade front, fully adjustable rear.
Features: Coil mainspring, double-set triggers, polished brass furniture. From Armsport, Ellett Bros., Navy Arms, E.M.F.
Price: .... $245.00 to $345.00
Price: 50-, 54-cal., right-hand, percussion (Ellett Bros.) $289.95
Price: 50-, 54-cal., left-hand, percussion (Ellett Bros.) $299.95
Price: 50-cal., right-hand, flintlock (Ellett Bros.) $309.95
Price: 50-cal., left-hand, flintlock (Ellett Bros.) $389.95

and under-rib. German silver barrel key inlays, Hawken-style toe and buttplates, lock bolt inlays, barrel wedges, entry thimble, trigger guard, ramrod and cleaning jag, nipple and nipple wrench. Introduced 1977. From Navy Arms.
Price: Complete, percussion $400.00
Price: Kit, percussion $360.00

Knight MK-85 Hunter

Knight MK-85 Grand American Rifle
Similar to the MK-85 Hunter except comes with Shadow Black or Shadow Brown thumbhole stock. Comes with test target, hard gun case. Blue finish.
Price: $995.00
Price: As above except in stainless steel $1,095.00

KENTUCKY FLINTLOCK RIFLE
Caliber: 44, 45, or 50.
Barrel: 35".
Weight: 7 lbs. **Length:** 50" overall.
Stock: Walnut stained, brass fittings.
Sights: Fixed.
Features: Available in carbine model also, 28" bbl. Some variations in detail, finish. Kits also available from some importers. Imported by Navy Arms, The Armoury.
Price: About .... $217.95 to $345.00
Price: Percussion, 45 or 50-cal. (Navy Arms) $330.00

KNIGHT MK-85 HUNTER RIFLE
Caliber: 50, 54.
Barrel: 24".
Weight: 7 lbs.
Stock: Classic, walnut; recoil pad; swivel studs.
Sights: Hooded blade front on ramp, open adjustable rear.
Features: One-piece in-line bolt assembly with straight through Sure-Fire ignition system. Adjustable Timney Featherweight trigger. Drilled and tapped for scope mounting. Made in U.S. From Modern Muzzle Loading, Inc.
Price: $529.95
Price: Stalker (laminated, colored stock), 50 or 54 .... $579.95
Price: Predator (stainless steel, composition stock), 50 or 54 ... $649.95
Price: Grizzly PLB (50, 54, integral muzzle brake, brown laminated stock) $649.95
Price: Grizzly PLB Stainless (as above except all stainless steel, Autumn Brown, Black Composite or Shadow Black stock) $749.95
Price: Light Knight (20" barrel, walnut stock) $499.95
Price: Light Knight (20" barrel, black composite stock) ... $519.95
Price: BK-92 Black Knight (blued, hardwood Monte Carlo stock) .. $329.99
Price: As above with black synthetic-coated stock $319.99
Price: As above with composite stock $349.99

Kentucky Percussion Rifle
Similar to flintlock except percussion lock. Finish and features vary with importer. Imported by Navy Arms (45-cal.), The Armoury, CVA.
Price: About $259.95
Price: 50-cal. (Navy Arms) $330.00
Price: Kit, 50-cal. (CVA) $189.95

Navy Kodiak

KENTUCKIAN RIFLE & CARBINE
Caliber: 44.
Barrel: 35" (Rifle), 27½" (Carbine).
Weight: 7 lbs. (Rifle), 5½ lbs. (Carbine). **Length:** 51" overall (Rifle), 43" (Carbine).
Stock: Walnut stain.
Sights: Brass blade front, steel V-ramp rear.
Features: Octagon barrel, case-hardened and engraved lockplates. Brass furniture. Imported by Dixie Gun Works.
Price: Rifle or carbine, flint, about **$259.95**
Price: As above, percussion, about **$249.95**

LONDON ARMORY 3-BAND 1853 ENFIELD
Caliber: 58 (.577" Minie, .575" round ball, .580" maxi ball).
Barrel: 39".
Weight: 9½ lbs. **Length:** 54" overall.
Stock: European walnut.
Sights: Inverted "V" front, traditional Enfield folding ladder rear.
Features: Recreation of the famed London Armory Company Pattern 1862 Enfield Musket. One-piece walnut stock, brass buttplate, trigger guard and nose cap. Lockplate marked "London Armoury Co." and with a British crown. Blued Baddeley barrel bands. From Dixie Gun Works, Euroarms of America, Navy Arms.
Price: About . . . . **$350.00 to $485.00**
Price: Assembled kit (Dixie, Euroarms of America) **$425.00**

KODIAK MK. III DOUBLE RIFLE
Caliber: 54x54, 58x58, 50x50.
Barrel: 28", 5-groove, 1:48 twist.
Weight: 9½ lbs. **Length:** 43¼" overall.
Stock: Czechoslovakian walnut, hand-checkered.
Sights: Adjustable bead front, adjustable open rear.
Features: Hooked breech allows interchangeability of barrels. Comes with sling, swivels, bullet mould and bullet starter. Engraved lockplates, top tang and trigger guard. Locks and top tang polished, rest browned. Introduced 1976. Imported from Italy by Trail Guns Armory, Inc., Navy Arms.
Price: 50-, 54-, 58-cal. SxS . . . . **$650.00 to $680.00**
Price: Spare barrels, all calibers **$394.25**
Price: Spare barrels, 12-ga.x12-ga. **$295.00**

LONDON ARMORY 2-BAND ENFIELD 1858
Caliber: .577" Minie, .575" round ball.
Barrel: 33".
Weight: 10 lbs. **Length:** 49" overall.
Stock: Walnut.
Sights: Folding leaf rear adjustable for elevation.
Features: Blued barrel, color case-hardened lock and hammer, polished brass buttplate, trigger guard, nosecap. From Navy Arms, Euroarms of America, Dixie Gun Works.
Price: . . . . **$399.00 to $450.00**
Price: Assembled kit (Euroarms of America) **$364.00**

LONDON ARMORY ENFIELD MUSKETOON
Caliber: 58, Minie ball.
Barrel: 24", round.
Weight: 7-7½ lbs. **Length:** 40½" overall.
Stock: Walnut, with sling swivels.
Sights: Blade front, graduated military-leaf rear.
Features: Brass trigger guard, nose cap, buttplate; blued barrel, bands, lock-plate, swivels. Imported by Euroarms of America, Navy Arms.
Price: . . . . **$300.00 to $350.00**
Price: Kit **$250.00**

Lyman Deerstalker

Lyman Deerstalker Custom Carbine
Similar to the Deerstalker rifle except in 50-caliber only with 21" stepped octagon barrel; 1:24 twist for optimum performance with conical projectiles. Comes with Lyman 37MA front sight, Lyman 16A folding rear. Weighs 6¾ lbs., measures 38½" overall. Percussion or flintlock. Comes with Delrin ramrod, modern sling and swivels. Introduced 1991.
Price: Percussion **$349.95**
Price: Flintlock **$374.95**
Price: Percussion, left-hand **$349.95**

LYMAN DEERSTALKER RIFLE
Caliber: 50, 54.
Barrel: 24", octagonal; 1:48 rifling.
Weight: 7½ lbs.
Stock: Walnut with black rubber buttpad.
Sights: Lyman #37MA beaded front, fully adjustable fold-down Lyman #16A rear.
Features: Stock has less drop for quick sighting. All metal parts are blackened, with color case-hardened lock; single trigger. Comes with sling and swivels. Available in flint or percussion. Introduced 1990. From Lyman.
Price: 50- or 54-cal., percussion **$339.95**
Price: 50- or 54-cal., flintlock **$359.95**
Price: 50- or 54-cal., percussion, left-hand **$339.95**
Price: 50-cal., flintlock, left-hand **$359.95**

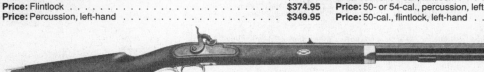

Lyman Trade Rifle

LYMAN TRADE RIFLE
Caliber: 50 or 54.
Barrel: 28" octagon, 1:48 twist.
Weight: 8¾ lbs. **Length:** 45" overall.
Stock: European walnut.
Sights: Blade front, open rear adjustable for windage or optional fixed sights.
Features: Fast twist rifling for conical bullets. Polished brass furniture with blue steel parts, stainless steel nipple. Hook breech, single trigger, coil spring percussion lock. Steel barrel rib and ramrod ferrules. Introduced 1980. From Lyman.
Price: Percussion **$309.95**
Price: Kit, percussion **$249.95**
Price: Flintlock **$339.95**
Price: Kit, flintlock **$284.95**

BLACKPOWDER MUSKETS & RIFLES

LYMAN GREAT PLAINS RIFLE
Caliber: 50- or 54-cal.
Barrel: 32", 1:66 twist.
Weight: 9 lbs.
Stock: Walnut.
Sights: Steel blade front, buckhorn rear adjustable for windage and elevation and fixed notch primitive sight included.
Features: Blued steel furniture. Stainless steel nipple. Coil spring lock, Hawken-style trigger guard and double-set triggers. Round thimbles recessed and sweated into rib. Steel wedge plates and toe plate. Introduced 1979. From Lyman.
Price: Percussion **$399.95**
Price: Flintlock **$429.95**
Price: Percussion kit **$324.95**
Price: Flintlock kit **$354.95**

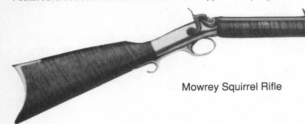

Mowrey Squirrel Rifle

MOWREY SQUIRREL RIFLE
Caliber: 32, 36 or 45.
Barrel: 28"; 13/16" flats; 1:66" twist.
Weight: About 7.5 lbs. **Length:** 43" overall.
Stock: Curly maple; crescent buttplate.
Sights: German silver blade front, semi-buckhorn rear.
Features: Brass or steel boxlock action; cut-rifled barrel. Steel rifles have browned finish, brass have browned barrel. Adjustable sear and trigger pull. Made in U.S. by Mowrey Gun Works.
Price: Brass or steel **$350.00**
Price: Kit **$300.00**

Mowrey Silhouette Rifle
Similar to the Squirrel Rifle except in 40-caliber with 32" barrel. Available in brass or steel frame.
Price: Brass frame **$350.00**
Price: Steel frame **$350.00**
Price: Kit, brass or steel **$300.00**

Mowrey Plains Rifle
Similar to the Squirrel Rifle except in 50- or 54-caliber with 32" barrel. Available in brass or steel frame.
Price: Brass frame **$350.00**
Price: Steel frame **$350.00**
Price: Rocky Mountain Hunter (as above except 28" bbl.), brass . . **$350.00**
Price: As above, steel frame **$350.00**
Price: All above in kit form, ea. **$300.00**

Mowrey 1 N 30 Conical Rifle
Similar to the Squirrel Rifle except in steel frame only, 45-, 50- or 54-caliber. Has special 1:24" twist barrel for conical- and sabot-style bullets. The 50- and 54-caliber barrels have 1" flats.
Price: **$350.00**
Price: Kit **$300.00**

J.P. MURRAY 1862-1864 CAVALRY CARBINE
Caliber: 58 (.577" Minie).
Barrel: 23".
Weight: 7 lbs., 9 oz. **Length:** 39" overall.
Stock: Walnut.
Sights: Blade front, rear drift adjustable for windage.
Features: Browned barrel, color case-hardened lock, blued swivel and band springs, polished brass buttplate, trigger guard, barrel bands. From Navy Arms, Euroarms of America.
Price: . . . . **$300.00 to $358.00**

NAVY ARMS 1777 CHARLEVILLE MUSKET
Caliber: 69.
Barrel: 44 5/8".
Weight: 10 lbs., 4 oz. **Length:** 59 3/4" overall.
Stock: Walnut.
Sights: Brass blade front.
Features: Exact copy of the musket used in the French Revolution. All steel is polished, in the white. Brass flashpan. Introduced 1991. Imported by Navy Arms.
Price: **$690.00**
Price: 1763 Standard Charleville Musket, finished **$575.00**
Price: As above, kit **$450.00**
Price: 1816 M.T. Wickham Musket **$690.00**

Navy Arms 1863

NAVY ARMS 1862 C.S. RICHMOND RIFLE
Caliber: 58.
Barrel: 40".
Weight: 10 lbs. **Length:** NA.
Stock: Walnut.
Sights: Blade front, adjustable rear.
Features: Copy of the three-band rifle musket made at Richmond Armory for the Confederacy. All steel polished bright. Imported by Navy Arms, Euroarms.
Price: **$550.00**
Price: From Euroarms **$647.15**

NAVY ARMS 1863 SPRINGFIELD
Caliber: 58, uses .575" Minie.
Barrel: 40", rifled.
Weight: 9 1/2 lbs. **Length:** 56" overall.
Stock: Walnut.
Sights: Open rear adjustable for elevation.
Features: Full-size three-band musket. Polished bright metal, including lock. From Navy Arms.
Price: Finished rifle **$550.00**
Price: Kit **$450.00**

Navy Arms Japanese Matchlock

NAVY ARMS JAPANESE MATCHLOCK RIFLE
Caliber: 50.
Barrel: 41".
Weight: 8 1/2 lbs. **Length:** 54 1/4" overall.
Stock: Stained hardwood.
Sights: Blade front, rear adjustable for windage.
Features: Replica of the matchlocks used by the Samurai. Brass lock, serpentine and trigger guard. Introduced 1991. Imported by Navy Arms.
Price: **$495.00**

BLACKPOWDER MUSKETS & RIFLES

NAVY ARMS MORTIMER FLINTLOCK RIFLE
Caliber: 54.
Barrel: 36".
Weight: 9 lbs. **Length:** 52¼" overall.
Stock: Checkered walnut.
Sights: Bead front, rear adjustable for windage.
Features: Waterproof pan, roller frizzen; sling swivels; browned barrel; external safety. Introduced 1991. Imported by Navy Arms.
Price: **$690.00**

NAVY ARMS PENNSYLVANIA LONG RIFLE
Caliber: 32, 45.
Barrel: 40½".
Weight: 7½ lbs. **Length:** 56½" overall.
Stock: Walnut.
Sights: Blade front, fully adjustable rear.
Features: Browned barrel, brass furniture, polished lock with double-set triggers. Introduced 1991. Imported by Navy Arms.
Price: Percussion **$395.00**
Price: Flintlock **$410.00**

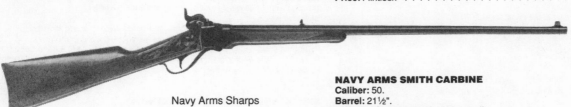

Navy Arms Sharps

NAVY ARMS SMITH CARBINE
Caliber: 50.
Barrel: 21½".
Weight: 7¾ lbs. **Length:** 39" overall.
Stock: American walnut.
Sights: Brass blade front, folding ladder-type rear.
Features: Replica of the breech-loading Civil War carbine. Color case-hardened receiver, rest blued. Cavalry model has saddle ring and bar, Artillery model has sling swivels. Introduced 1991. Imported by Navy Arms.
Price: Cavalry model **$600.00**
Price: Artillery model **$600.00**

NAVY ARMS SHARPS PERCUSSION CARBINE
Caliber: 54.
Barrel: 22".
Weight: 7¾ lbs. **Length:** 39" overall.
Stock: Walnut.
Sights: Blade front, military ladder-type rear.
Features: Color case-hardened action, blued barrel. Has saddle ring. Introduced 1991. Imported from Navy Arms.
Price: **$650.00**
Price: Sharps Plains rifle (28.5" barrel) **$650.00**

Parker-Hale 1853

PARKER-HALE ENFIELD 1853 MUSKET
Caliber: .577".
Barrel: 39", 3-groove cold-forged rifling.
Weight: About 9 lbs. **Length:** 55" overall.
Stock: Seasoned walnut.
Sights: Fixed front, rear step adjustable for elevation.
Features: Three-band musket made to original specs from original gauges. Solid brass stock furniture, color hardened lockplate, hammer; blued barrel, trigger. Made by Gibbs Rifle Co., distributed by Navy Arms.
Price: **$585.00**

PARKER-HALE ENFIELD PATTERN 1858 NAVAL RIFLE
Caliber: .577".
Barrel: 33".
Weight: 8½ lbs. **Length:** 48½" overall.
Stock: European walnut.
Sights: Blade front, step adjustable rear.
Features: Two-band Enfield percussion rifle with heavy barrel. Five-groove progressive depth rifling, solid brass furniture. All parts made exactly to original patterns. Made by Gibbs Rifle Co., distributed by Navy Arms.
Price: **$550.00**

PARKER-HALE ENFIELD 1861 MUSKETOON
Caliber: 58.
Barrel: 24".
Weight: 7 lbs. **Length:** 40½" overall.
Stock: Walnut.
Sights: Fixed front, adjustable rear.
Features: Percussion muzzleloader, made to original 1861 English patterns. Made by Gibbs Rifle Co., distributed by Navy Arms.
Price: **$450.00**

Consult our Directory pages for the location of firms mentioned.

Parker-Hale Whitworth

PARKER-HALE WHITWORTH MILITARY TARGET RIFLE
Caliber: 45.
Barrel: 36".
Weight: 9¼ lbs. **Length:** 52½" overall.
Stock: Walnut. Checkered at wrist and forend.
Sights: Hooded post front, open step-adjustable rear.
Features: Faithful reproduction of the Whitworth rifle, only bored for 45-cal. Trigger has a detented lock, capable of being adjusted very finely without risk of the sear nose catching on the half-cock bent and damaging both parts. Introduced 1978. Made by Gibbs Rifle Co., distributed by Navy Arms.
Price: **$815.00**

Parker-Hale Limited Edition Whitworth Sniping Rifle
Same as the Parker-Hale Whitworth Military Target Rifle except has replica of the Model 1860 brass telescope sight in fully adjustable mount. Made by Gibbs Rifle Co., distributed by Navy Arms.
Price: **$995.00**

PARKER-HALE VOLUNTEER RIFLE
Caliber: .451".
Barrel: 32".
Weight: 9½ lbs. **Length:** 49" overall.
Stock: Walnut, checkered wrist and forend.
Sights: Globe front, adjustable ladder-type rear.

Features: Recreation of the type of gun issued to volunteer regiments during the 1860s. Rigby-pattern rifling, patent breech, detented lock. Stock is glass bedded for accuracy. Made by Gibbs Rifle Co., distributed by Navy Arms.
Price: **$750.00**
Price: Three-band Volunteer **$815.00**

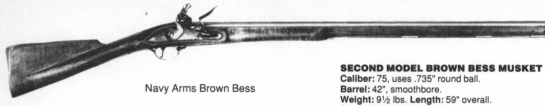

Navy Arms Brown Bess

PENNSYLVANIA FULL-STOCK RIFLE
Caliber: 45 or 50.
Barrel: 32" rifled, $1^5/_{16}$" dia.
Weight: 8½ lbs.
Stock: Walnut.
Sights: Fixed.
Features: Available in flint or percussion. Blued lock and barrel, brass furniture. Offered complete or in kit form. From The Armoury.
Price: Flint $250.00
Price: Percussion $225.00

SHARPS PERCUSSION RIFLES
Caliber: 54.
Barrel: 28".
Weight: 9 lbs. **Length:** 46" overall.
Stock: Checkered walnut.
Sights: Blade front, ladder-type adjustable rear.
Features: Blued barrel, color case-hardened receiver and buttplate. Imported from Italy by E.M.F.
Price: Rifle or carbine $860.00

SECOND MODEL BROWN BESS MUSKET
Caliber: 75, uses .735" round ball.
Barrel: 42", smoothbore.
Weight: 9½ lbs. **Length:** 59" overall.
Stock: Walnut (Navy); walnut-stained hardwood (Dixie).
Sights: Fixed.
Features: Polished barrel and lock with brass trigger guard and buttplate. Bayonet and scabbard available. From Navy Arms, Dixie Gun Works.
Price: Finished . . . . $475.00 to $850.00
Price: Kit (Dixie Gun Works, Navy Arms) . . . . $400.00 to $510.00
Price: Carbine (Navy Arms) $635.00

SHILOH SHARPS 1863 MILITARY RIFLE
Caliber: 54.
Barrel: 30", round.
Weight: 8 lbs., 12 oz.
Stock: Military-style butt, steel buttplate; patchbox optional. Standard-grade walnut.
Sights: Iron block front, Lawrence-style ladder rear.
Features: Recreation of the 1863 percussion rifle. Made in U.S. by Shiloh Rifle Mfg. Co.
Price: $940.00
Price: 1863 Military Carbine (as above except has 22" round bbl., band on military-style forend, saddle bar and ring) $860.00

Shiloh 1863 Sporting

Shiloh Sharps Model 1863 Sporting Rifle
Similar to the Military Carbine except has 30" octagon barrel, blade front and sporting rear sights, shotgun butt available, steel buttplate, schnabel forend. Standard-grade wood (semi-fancy available).
Price: $840.00

T/C Big Boar

THOMPSON/CENTER BIG BOAR RIFLE
Caliber: 58.
Barrel: 26" octagon; 1:48 twist.

Weight: 7¾ lbs. **Length:** 42½" overall.
Stock: American black walnut; rubber buttpad; swivels.
Sights: Bead front, fullt adjustable open rear.
Features: Percussion lock; single trigger with wide bow trigger guard. Comes with soft leather sling. Introduced 1991. From Thompson/Center.
Price: $340.00

T/C Hawken

THOMPSON/CENTER HAWKEN RIFLE
Caliber: 45, 50 or 54.
Barrel: 28" octagon, hooked breech.

Stocks: American walnut.
Sights: Blade front, rear adjustable for windage and elevation.
Features: Solid brass furniture, double-set triggers, button rifled barrel, coil-type mainspring. From Thompson/Center.
Price: Percussion model (45-, 50- or 54-cal.) $375.00
Price: Flintlock model (50-cal.) $385.00
Price: Percussion kit $275.00
Price: Flintlock kit $295.00

T/C High Plains

THOMPSON/CENTER HIGH PLAINS SPORTER
Caliber: 50.
Barrel: 24".

Weight: 7 lbs. **Length:** 41" overall.
Stock: Black walnut with pistol grip, rubber recoil pad, sling swivel studs.
Sights: Blade front with open hunting-style rear, or T/C hunting-style tang peep sight.
Features: Percussion lock only. Single hunting-style trigger with wide bow trigger guard. Color case-hardened lock plate. Introduced 1992. From Thompson/Center.
Price: With open sights $340.00
Price: With tang sight $345.00

CAUTION: PRICES CHANGE, CHECK AT GUNSHOP.

THOMPSON/CENTER NEW ENGLANDER RIFLE
Caliber: 50, 54.
Barrel: 28", round.
Weight: 7 lbs., 15 oz.
Stock: American walnut or Rynite.
Sights: Open, adjustable.
Features: Color case-hardened percussion lock with engraving, rest blued. Also accepts 12-ga. shotgun barrel. Introduced 1987. From Thompson/Center.
Price: Right-hand model **$270.00**
Price: As above, Rynite stock **$255.00**
Price: Left-hand model **$290.00**
Price: Accessory 12-ga. barrel, right-hand **$130.00**

THOMPSON/CENTER PENNSYLVANIA HUNTER RIFLE
Caliber: 50.
Barrel: 31", half-octagon, half-round.
Weight: About 7½ lbs. **Length:** 48" overall.
Stock: Black walnut.
Sights: Open, adjustable.
Features: Rifled 1:66 for round ball shooting. Available in flintlock or percussion. From Thompson/Center.
Price: Percussion **$320.00**
Price: Flintlock **$335.00**

T/C Pennsylvania Hunter

Thompson/Center Pennsylvania Hunter Carbine
Similar to the Pennsylvania Hunter except has 21" barrel, weighs 6.5 lbs., and has an overall length of 38". Designed for shooting patched round balls. Available in percussion or flintlock styles. Introduced 1992. From Thompson/Center.
Price: Percussion **$310.00**
Price: Flintlock **$325.00**
Price: Accessory barrels **$155.00**

THOMPSON/CENTER RENEGADE RIFLE
Caliber: 50 and 54.
Barrel: 26", 1" across the flats.
Weight: 8 lbs.
Stock: American walnut.
Sights: Open hunting (Patridge) style, fully adjustable for windage and elevation.
Features: Coil spring lock, double-set triggers, blued steel trim. From Thompson/Center.
Price: Percussion model **$335.00**
Price: Flintlock model, 50-cal. only **$345.00**
Price: Percussion kit **$245.00**
Price: Flintlock kit **$260.00**
Price: Left-hand percussion, 50- or 54-cal. **$345.00**

Thompson/Center Renegade Hunter
Similar to standard Renegade except has single trigger in a large-bow shotgun-style trigger guard, no brass trim. Available in 50- or 54-caliber. Color case-hardened lock, rest blued. Introduced 1987. From Thompson/Center.
Price: **$310.00**

THOMPSON/CENTER SCOUT RIFLE
Caliber: 50 and 54.
Barrel: 21", interchangeable, 1:20 twist.
Weight: 7 lbs., 4 oz. **Length:** 38⅝" overall.
Stocks: American black walnut stock and forend.
Sights: Bead front, adjustable semi-buckhorn rear.
Features: Patented in-line ignition system with special vented breech plug.

Patented trigger mechanism consists of only two moving parts. Interchangeable barrels. Wide grooved hammer. Brass trigger guard assembly, brass barrel band and buttplate. Ramrod has blued hardware. Comes with q.d. swivels and suede leather carrying sling. Drilled and tapped for standard scope mounts. Introduced 1990. From Thompson/Center.
Price: 50- or 54-cal. **$395.00**
Price: Extra barrel, 50- or 54-cal. **$160.00**

T/C Tree Hawk

THOMPSON/CENTER TREE HAWK CARBINE
Caliber: 50.
Barrel: 21".
Weight: 6.75 lbs. **Length:** 38" overall.
Stock: Rynite composition with choice of Realtree or Mossy Oak Bottomland camouflage.
Sights: Bead front, fully adjustable open hunting-style rear.
Features: All hardware (except sling swivels and barrel wedge) finished in camouflage, including the polymer-coated fiberglass ramrod. Single trigger, wide bow trigger guard, rubber recoil pad, camo sling. Introduced 1992. From Thompson/Center.
Price: 50-cal. percussion only **$340.00**
Price: Accessory 12-gauge barrel **$165.00**

THOMPSON/CENTER WHITE MOUNTAIN CARBINE
Caliber: 45, 50 and 54.
Barrel: 21", half-octagon, half-round.
Weight: 6½ lbs. **Length:** 38" overall.
Stock: American black walnut.
Sights: Open hunting (Patridge) style, fully adjustable rear.
Features: Percussion or flintlock. Single trigger, large trigger guard; rubber buttpad; rear q.d. swivel, front swivel mounted on thimble; comes with sling. Introduced 1989. From Thompson/Center.
Price: Percussion **$335.00**
Price: Flintlock **$355.00**

Traditions Buckskinner

TRADITIONS BUCKSKINNER CARBINE
Caliber: 50.
Barrel: 21", ¹⁵⁄₁₆" flats, half octagon, half round.

Weight: 6 lbs. **Length:** 36¼" overall.
Stock: Beech or black laminated.
Sights: Beaded blade front, hunting-style open rear click adjustable for windage and elevation.
Features: Uses V-type mainspring, single trigger. Non-glare hardware. Comes with leather sling. From Traditions, Inc.
Price: Percussion **$280.00**
Price: Percussion, left-hand **$297.00**
Price: Percussion, laminated stock **$327.00**
Price: Flintlock **$297.00**

Traditions Frontier

TRADITIONS FRONTIER RIFLE
Caliber: 45, 50.
Barrel: 28", ¹⁵/₁₆" flats.
Weight: 8 lbs. **Length:** 44¾" overall.
Stock: Beech.
Sights: Beaded blade front, hunting-style rear click adjustable for windage and elevation.
Features: Adjustable sear engagement with fly and bridle, V-type mainspring; double-set triggers. Brass furniture. From Traditions, Inc.
Price: Percussion **$254.00**
Price: Flintlock **$274.00**
Price: Kit, 50-caliber percussion **$175.00**

Traditions Frontier Carbine
Similar to the Frontier Rifle except has 24" barrel, is 40½" overall, weighs 6½ lbs. Available in 50-caliber percussion only. From Traditions, Inc.
Price: **$254.00**

TRADITIONS FRONTIER SCOUT RIFLE
Caliber: 36, 45, 50.
Barrel: 24" (36-cal.), 26" (45, 50); ⅞" flats.
Weight: 6 lbs. **Length:** 39⅛" overall (24" barrel).
Stock: Beech.
Sights: Blade Front, primitive-style adjustable rear.
Features: Scaled-down version of the Frontier rifle for smaller shooters. Percussion only. Color case-hardened lock plate. From Traditions, Inc.
Price: **$239.00**

TRADITIONS HAWKEN RIFLE
Caliber: 50, 54.
Barrel: 32¼"; 1" flats.
Weight: 9 lbs. **Length:** 50" overall.
Stock: Walnut with cheekpiece.
Sights: Hunting style, click adjustable for windage and elevation.
Features: Fiberglass ramrod, double-set triggers, polished brass furniture. From Traditions, Inc.
Price: Percussion **$412.00**

TRADITIONS PENNSYLVANIA RIFLE
Caliber: 45, 50.
Barrel: 40¼", ⅞" flats.
Weight: 9 lbs. **Length:** 57½" overall.
Stock: Walnut.
Sights: Blade front, adjustable rear.
Features: Brass patchbox and ornamentation. Double-set triggers. From Traditions, Inc.
Price: Flintlock **$495.00**
Price: Percussion **$467.00**

Traditions Hunter Rifle
Similar to the Hawken except has blackened and German silver furniture. Has 28¼" barrel with 1" flats.
Price: Percussion only, 50- or 54-cal. **$424.00**
Price: Hawken Woodsman (50- or 54-cal.) **$259.00**
Price: As above, kit **$200.00**

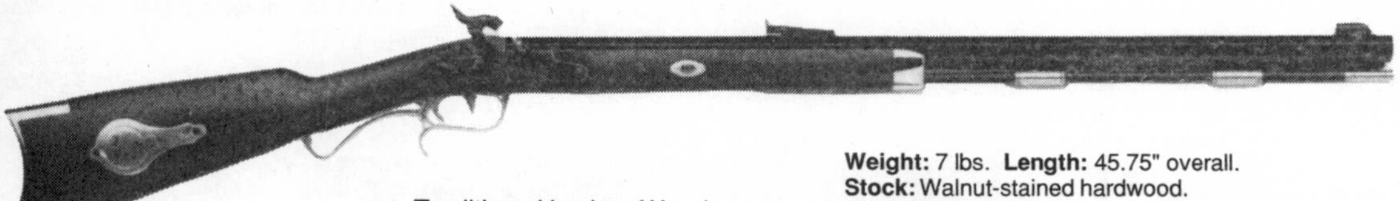

Traditions Hawken Woodsman

TRADITIONS HAWKEN WOODSMAN RIFLE
Caliber: 50 and 54.
Barrel: 28"; ¹⁵/₁₆" flats.

Weight: 7 lbs. **Length:** 45.75" overall.
Stock: Walnut-stained hardwood.
Sights: Beaded blade front, hunting-style open rear adjustable for windage and elevation.
Features: Percussion only. Brass patchbox and furniture. Double triggers. From Traditions, Inc.
Price: 50 or 54 . . . . **$292.00**
Price: 50-cal., left-hand **$309.00**

TRADITIONS PIONEER RIFLE/CARBINE
Caliber: 50, 54.
Barrel: 27¼"; ¹⁵/₁₆" flats.
Weight: 7 lbs. **Length:** 44" overall.
Stock: Beech with pistol grip, recoil pad.
Sights: German silver blade front, buckhorn rear with elevation ramp.
Features: V-type mainspring, adjustable single trigger; blackened furniture; color case-hardened lock; large trigger guard. From Traditions, Inc.
Price: Percussion only, rifle **$227.00**
Price: Carbine. 24" barrel, 50-cal. only **$227.00**

TRADITIONS TROPHY RIFLE
Caliber: 50, 54.
Barrel: 27¼", round.
Weight: 7 lbs. **Length:** 44¾" overall.
Stock: Walnut with full pistol grip and cheekpiece.
Sights: Patridge-style blade front, hunting-style rear click adjustable for windage and elevation.
Features: Engraved, color case-hardened lock with bridle, claw mainspring; single trigger. Sling swivels; fiberglass ramrod; recoil pad. From Traditions, Inc.
Price: Percussion only **$424.00**

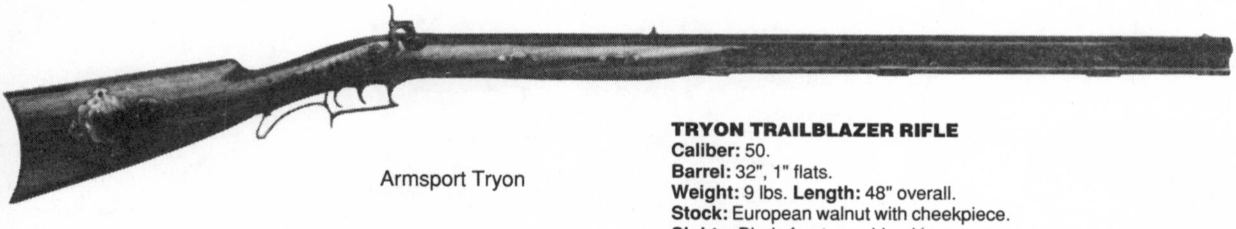

Armsport Tryon

TRYON TRAILBLAZER RIFLE
Caliber: 50.
Barrel: 32", 1" flats.
Weight: 9 lbs. **Length:** 48" overall.
Stock: European walnut with cheekpiece.
Sights: Blade front, semi-buckhorn rear.
Features: Reproduction of a rifle made by George Tryon about 1820. Double-set triggers, back action lock, hooked breech with long tang. From Armsport, Navy Arms.
Price: About **$375.00**
Price: 50-, 54-cal., 28", 30" bbl. (Armsport) **$775.00**
Price: Deluxe model with silver finish (Armsport) **$795.00**

> Consult our Directory pages for the location of firms mentioned.

CAUTION: PRICES CHANGE, CHECK AT GUNSHOP.

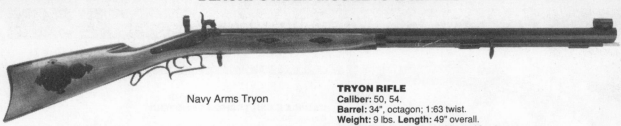

Navy Arms Tryon

TRYON RIFLE
Caliber: 50, 54.
Barrel: 34", octagon; 1:63 twist.
Weight: 9 lbs. **Length:** 49" overall.
Stock: European walnut with steel furniture.
Sights: Blade front, fixed rear.
Features: Reproduction of an American plains rifle with double-set triggers and back-action lock. Imported from Italy by Dixie Gun Works.
Price: **$435.00**
Price: Kit **$375.00**

Navy Arms Tryon Creedmoor Target Model
Similar to the standard Tryon rifle except 45-caliber only, 33" octagon barrel, globe front sight with inserts, fully adjustable match rear. Has double-set triggers, sling swivels. Imported by Navy Arms.
Price: **$680.00**

Ultra Light Model 90

ULTRA LIGHT ARMS MODEL 90 MUZZLELOADER
Caliber: 45, 50.
Barrel: 28", button rifled; 1:48 twist.
Weight: 6 lbs.
Stock: Kevlar/graphite, colors optional.
Sights: Hooded blade front on ramp, Williams aperture rear adjustable for windage and elevation.
Features: In-line ignition system with top loading port. Timney trigger; integral side safety. Comes with recoil pad, sling swivels and hard case. Introduced 1990. Made in U.S. by Ultra Light Arms.
Price: **$950.00**

UBERTI SANTA FE HAWKEN RIFLE
Caliber: 50 or 54.
Barrel: 32", octagonal.
Weight: 9.8 lbs. **Length:** 50" overall.
Stock: Walnut, with beavertail cheekpiece.
Sights: German silver blade front, buckhorn rear.
Features: Browned finish, color case-hardened lock, double triggers, German silver ferrule, wedge plates. Imported by Uberti USA.
Price: **$485.00**

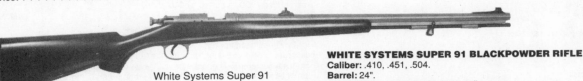

White Systems Super 91

WHITE SYSTEMS SUPER 91 BLACKPOWDER RIFLE
Caliber: .410, .451, .504.
Barrel: 24".
Weight: 8 lbs. **Length:** 43.5" overall.
Stock: Walnut, laminated birch or composite.
Sights: Bead front on ramp, fully adjustable open rear.
Features: Insta-Fire straight-line ignition system; all stainless steel construction; side-swing safety; fully adjustable trigger; full barrel under-rib with two ramrod thimbles. Introduced 1991. Made in U.S. by White Systems, Inc.
Price: Walnut stock **$675.00**
Price: Laminated or composite stock **$712.00**

White Systems Whitetail

WHITE SYSTEMS WHITETAIL RIFLE
Caliber: .410, .451, .504, 54.
Barrel: 20", 22".
Weight: 6.5 lbs. **Length:** 39.5" overall.
Stock: Hardwood or composite; classic style.
Sights: Bead front on ramp, fully adjustable open rear.
Features: Insta-Fire straight-line ignition; action and trigger safeties; adjustable trigger; stainless or blued chrome-moly steel. Introduced 1992. Made in U.S. by White Systems, Inc.
Price: Blue, hardwood stock **$325.00**
Price: Stainless, composite stock **$437.00**

Dixie Zouave

ZOUAVE PERCUSSION RIFLE
Caliber: 58, 59.
Barrel: 32½".
Weight: 9½ lbs. **Length:** 48½" overall.
Stock: Walnut finish, brass patchbox and buttplate.
Sights: Fixed front, rear adjustable for elevation.
Features: Color case-hardened lockplate, blued barrel. From CVA, Navy Arms, Dixie Gun Works, Euroarms of America (M1863), E.M.F.
Price: About . . . . **$325.00 to $540.00**
Price: CVA, 58-cal. **$334.95**
Price: Kit (Euroarms 58-cal. only) **$263.00**

Mississippi Model 1841 Percussion Rifle
Similar to Zouave rifle but patterned after U.S. Model 1841. Imported by Dixie Gun Works, Euroarms of America, Navy Arms.
Price: . . . . **$430.00 to $463.00**

CAUTION: PRICES CHANGE, CHECK AT GUNSHOP.

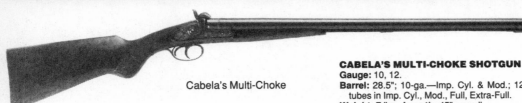

Cabela's Multi-Choke

CABELA'S 12-GAUGE SHOTGUN
Gauge: 12.
Barrel: 28".
Weight: 7½ lbs. **Length:** 44.1" overall.
Stock: Hand-checkered European walnut.
Features: Recreates an English muzzleloader. Color case-hardened lock, blued chrome-lined barrels. Imported by Cabela's.
Price: **$339.95**
Price: 10-gauge (30" barrels, engraved lockplates) **$389.95**

CABELA'S MULTI-CHOKE SHOTGUN
Gauge: 10, 12.
Barrel: 28.5"; 10-ga.—Imp. Cyl. & Mod.; 12-ga.—Imp.Cyl. & Mod. or choke tubes in Imp. Cyl., Mod., Full, Extra-Full.
Weight: 7 lbs. **Length:** 45" overall.
Stock: Checkered European walnut.
Features: Percussion only. Blued, chrome-lined barrels, engraved lockplates and hammers; double triggers. Introduced 1992. Imported by Cabela's.
Price: 10-gauge **$399.95**
Price: 12-gauge **$389.95**

CVA Classic Turkey

CVA CLASSIC TURKEY DOUBLE SHOTGUN
Gauge: 12.
Barrel: 28" (Imp. & Imp.).

CVA TRAPPER PERCUSSION
Gauge: 12.
Barrel: 28". Choke tubes (Imp. Cyl., Mod., Full).
Weight: NA.
Length: 46" overall.
Stock: English-style straight grip of walnut-finished hardwood.

Weight: 9 lbs. **Length:** 45" overall.
Stock: Select hardwood; classic English style with checkered straight grip, wrap-around forend with bottom screw attachment.
Sights: Bead front.
Features: Hinged double triggers; color case-hardened and engraved lock-plates, trigger guard and tang. Rubber recoil pad. Not suitable for steel shot. Introduced 1990. Imported by CVA.
Price: **$389.95**

Sights: Brass bead front.
Features: Single blued barrel; color case-hardened lockplate and hammer; screw adjustable sear engagements, V-type mainspring; brass wedge plates; color case-hardened and engraved trigger guard and tang. From CVA.
Price: Finished **$314.95**

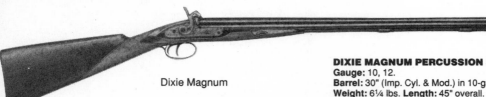

Dixie Magnum

EUROARMS DUCK SHOTGUN
Gauge: 8, 10, 12.
Barrel: 33".
Weight: 8½ lbs. **Length:** 49" overall.
Stock: Walnut.
Features: Color case-hardened lock; blue hammer, trigger, barrel; brass furniture. Imported by Euroarms of America.
Price: **$407.00**

DIXIE MAGNUM PERCUSSION SHOTGUN
Gauge: 10, 12.
Barrel: 30" (Imp. Cyl. & Mod.) in 10-ga.; 28" in 12-ga.
Weight: 6¼ lbs. **Length:** 45" overall.
Stock: Hand-checkered walnut, 14" pull.
Features: Double triggers, light hand engraving. Case-hardened locks in 12-ga.; polished steel in 10-ga. with sling swivels. From Dixie Gun Works.
Price: Upland **$399.00**
Price: 12-ga. kit **$350.00**
Price: 10-ga. **$425.00**
Price: 10-ga. kit **$375.00**

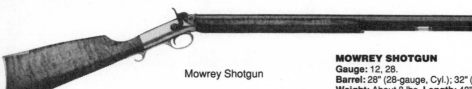

Mowrey Shotgun

NAVY ARMS STEEL SHOT MAGNUM SHOTGUN
Gauge: 10.
Barrel: 28" (Cyl. & Cyl.).
Weight: 7 lbs., 9 oz. **Length:** 45½" overall.
Stock: Walnut, with cheekpiece.
Features: Designed specifically for steel shot. Engraved, polished locks; sling swivels; blued barrels. Introduced 1991. Imported by Navy Arms.
Price: **$510.00**

MOWREY SHOTGUN
Gauge: 12, 28.
Barrel: 28" (28-gauge, Cyl.); 32" (12-gauge, Cyl.); octagonal.
Weight: About 8 lbs. **Length:** 48" overall (32" barrel).
Stock: Curly maple.
Sights: Bead front.
Features: Brass or steel frame; shotgun butt. Made in U.S. by Mowrey Gun Works.
Price: Finished **$350.00**
Price: Kit **$300.00**

BLACKPOWDER SHOTGUNS

Navy Arms Fowler

TRAIL GUNS KODIAK 10-GAUGE DOUBLE
Gauge: 10.
Barrel: 20", 30¾" (Cyl. bore).
Weight: About 9 lbs. **Length:** 47⅛" overall.
Stock: Walnut, with cheek rest. Checkered wrist and forend.
Features: Chrome-plated bores; engraved lockplates, brass bead front and middle sights; sling swivels. Introduced 1980. Imported from Italy by Trail Guns Armory, Inc.
Price: **$425.00**

NAVY ARMS FOWLER SHOTGUN
Gauge: 12.
Barrel: 28".
Weight: 7 lbs., 12 oz. **Length:** 45" overall.
Stock: Walnut-stained hardwood.
Features: Color case-hardened lockplates and hammers; checkered stock. Imported by Navy Arms.
Price: Fowler model, 12-ga. only **$325.00**

NAVY ARMS MORTIMER FLINTLOCK SHOTGUN
Gauge: 12.
Barrel: 36".
Weight: 7 lbs. **Length:** 53" overall.
Stock: Walnut, with cheekpiece.
Features: Waterproof pan, roller frizzen, external safety. Color case-hardened lock, rest blued. Introduced 1991. Imported by Navy Arms.
Price: **$670.00**

Navy Arms T&T

NAVY ARMS T&T SHOTGUN
Gauge: 12.
Barrel: 28" (Full & Full).
Weight: 7½ lbs.
Stock: Walnut.
Sights: Bead front.
Features: Color case-hardened locks, double triggers, blued steel furniture. From Navy Arms.
Price: **$480.00**

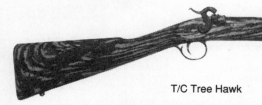

T/C Tree Hawk

THOMPSON/CENTER NEW ENGLANDER SHOTGUN
Gauge: 12.
Barrel: 28" (Imp. Cyl.), round.
Weight: 5 lbs., 2 oz.
Stock: Select American black walnut with straight grip.
Features: Percussion lock is color case-hardened, rest blued. Also accepts 26" round 50- and 54-cal. rifle barrel. Introduced 1986. From Thompson/Center.
Price: Right-hand **$270.00**
Price: Right-hand, Rynite stock **$255.00**
Price: Left-hand **$310.00**
Price: Accessory rifle barrel, right-hand, 50 or 54 . . . . . **$130.00**
Price: As above, left-hand **$140.00**

THOMPSON/CENTER TREE HAWK SHOTGUN
Gauge: 12.
Barrel: 28" (Full choke tube).
Weight: 6.75 lbs. **Length:** 45" overall.
Stock: Rynite composition with choice of Realtree or Mossy Oak Bottomland camouflage.
Sights: Bead front.
Features: All hardware (except sling swivels and barrel wedge) finished in camouflage, including the polymer-coated fiberglass ramrod. Single trigger, wide bow trigger guard, rubber recoil pad, camo sling. Accessory Imp. Cyl. and Mod. choke tubes available. Introduced 1992. From Thompson/Center.
Price: 12-gauge, percussion only **$345.00**
Price: Accessory 50-caliber barrel **$160.00**

AIRGUNS—HANDGUNS

Beeman Adder

BEEMAN ADDER AIR PISTOL
Caliber: 20, 25, single shot.
Barrel: 10.5"; 12-groove rifling.
Weight: 3 lbs. **Length:** 16.5" overall.
Power: Pre-charged pneumatic, internal air chamber.
Stocks: Smooth, select hardwood.
Sights: Micrometer click adjustable. Built-in scope dovetail.
Features: Two-stage trigger. Steel body, highly polished, blued and accented with solid brass. Introduced 1992. Imported by Beeman.
Price: 20-, 25-cal. **$479.95**

BEEMAN P1 MAGNUM AIR PISTOL
Caliber: 177, 5mm, 22, single shot.
Barrel: 8.4".
Weight: 2.5 lbs. **Length:** 11" overall.
Power: Top lever cocking; spring piston.
Stocks: Checkered walnut.
Sights: Blade front, square notch rear with click micrometer adjustments for windage and elevation. Grooved for scope mounting.
Features: Dual power for 177 and 20-cal.: low setting gives 350-400 fps; high setting 500-600 fps. Rearward expanding mainspring simulates firearm recoil. All Colt 45 auto grips fit gun. Dry-firing feature for practice. Optional wooden shoulder stock. Introduced 1985. Imported by Beeman.
Price: 177, 5mm, 22-cal. **$347.50**
Price: 177, 5mm, stainless/blue finish **$367.50**

Beeman P2 Match Air Pistol

Similar to the Beeman P1 Magnum except shoots only 177 or 5mm pellets; completely recoilless single-stroke pneumatic action. Weighs 2.2 lbs. Choice of thumbrest match grips or standard style. Introduced 1990.
Price: 177, 5mm, standard grip **$385.00**
Price: 177, 5mm, match grip **$409.95**

BEEMAN/FEINWERKBAU 65 MKII AIR PISTOL

Caliber: 177, single shot.
Barrel: 6.1" or 7.5", removable bbl. wgt. available.
Weight: 42 oz. **Length:** 13.3" or 14.1" overall.
Power: Spring, sidelever cocking.
Stocks: Walnut, stippled thumbrest; adjustable or fixed.
Sights: Front, interchangeable post element system, open rear, click adjustable for windage and elevation and for sighting notch width. Scope mount available.
Features: New shorter barrel for better balance and control. Cocking effort 9 lbs. Two-stage trigger, four adjustments. Quiet firing, 525 fps. Programs instantly for recoil or recoilless operation. Permanently lubricated. Steel piston ring. Special switch converts trigger from 17.6-oz. pull to 42-oz. let-off. Imported by Beeman.
Price: Right-hand **$998.50**
Price: Left-hand, 6.1" barrel **$1,045.00**
Price: Model 65 Mk. I (7.5" bbl.) **$965.00**

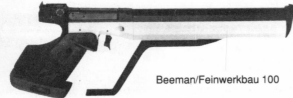

Beeman/Feinwerkbau 100

BEEMAN/FEINWERKBAU C5 CO_2 RAPID FIRE PISTOL

Caliber: 177.
Barrel: 7.25".
Weight: 2.42 lbs.
Power: NA.
Stocks: Anatomical match.
Sights: Match.
Features: Velocity 510 fps. Has special trigger shape with swivel action, longitudinal positioning. Introduced 1990. Imported by Beeman.
Price: Right-hand **$1,350.00**
Price: Left-hand **$1,425.00**

> Consult our Directory pages for
> the location of firms mentioned.

BEEMAN/FEINWERKBAU C25 CO_2 PISTOL

Caliber: 177, single shot.
Barrel: 10.1"; 12-groove rifling.
Weight: 2.5 lbs. **Length:** 16.5" overall.
Power: Vertical, interchangeable CO_2 bottles.
Stocks: Stippled walnut with adjustable palm shelf.
Sights: Blade front, rear micrometer adjustable. Notch size adjustable for width; interchangeable front blades.
Features: Fully adjustable trigger; can be set for dry firing. Separate gas chamber for uniform power. Short-barrel model (C25 Mini) also available. Introduced 1992. Imported by Beeman.
Price: Right-hand **$1,098.00**
Price: Left-hand **$1,160.00**
Price: C25 Mini **$1,098.00**

Beeman HW70

Beeman P2

BEEMAN/FEINWERKBAU 100 PISTOL

Caliber: 177, single shot.
Barrel: 10.1", 12-groove rifling.
Weight: 2.5 lbs. **Length:** 16.5" overall.
Power: Single-stroke pneumatic, underlever cocking.
Stocks: Stippled walnut with adjustable palm shelf.
Sights: Blade front, open rear adjustable for windage and elevation. Notch size adjustable for width. Interchangeable front blades.
Features: Velocity 460 fps. Fully adjustable trigger. Cocking effort 12 lbs. Introduced 1988. Imported by Beeman.
Price: Right-hand **$1,098.00**
Price: Left-hand **$1,160.00**

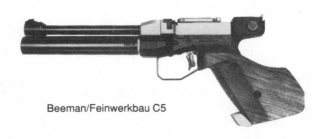

Beeman/Feinwerkbau C5

BEEMAN/FEINWERKBAU C20 CO_2 PISTOL

Caliber: 177, single shot.
Barrel: 10.1", 12-groove rifling.
Weight: 2.5 lbs. **Length:** 16" overall.
Power: Special CO_2 cylinder.
Stock: Stippled walnut with adjustable palm shelf.
Sights: Blade front, open rear adjustable for windage and elevation. Notch size adjustable for width. Interchangeable front blades.
Features: Fully adjustable trigger; can be set for dry firing. Separate gas chamber for uniform power. Cylinders interchangeable even when full. Short-barrel model also available. Introduced 1988. Imported by Beeman.
Price: Right-hand, regular or Mini **$1,025.00**
Price: Left-hand **$1,085.00**

BEEMAN HW70 AIR PISTOL

Caliber: 177, single shot.
Barrel: 6¼", rifled.
Weight: 38 oz. **Length:** 12¾" overall.
Power: Spring, barrel cocking.
Stocks: Plastic, with thumbrest.
Sights: Hooded post front, square notch rear adjustable for windage and elevation. HW70A has scope base.
Features: Adjustable trigger, 24-lb. cocking effort, 410 fps MV; automatic barrel safety. Imported by Beeman.
Price: HW70 (open sights) **$169.98**
Price: HW70A (open sights, scope base) **$189.98**

BEEMAN WOLVERINE PISTOL

Caliber: 177, 20, 25, single shot.
Barrel: 10.5"; 12-groove rifling.
Weight: 3 lbs. **Length:** 16.5" overall.
Power: Pre-charged pneumatic, internal air chamber.
Stocks: Stippled walnut.
Sights: Blade front, micrometer click adjustable rear. Built-in scope dovetail.
Features: Match trigger. Solid brass rear receiver cap. Introduced 1992. Imported by Beeman.
Price: 177, 20, 25 . . . . **$598.00**

Benjamin/Sheridan CO₂

BENJAMIN/SHERIDAN CO2 PELLET PISTOLS
Caliber: 177, 20, 22, single shot.
Barrel: 6⅜", rifled brass.
Weight: 28 oz. **Length:** 9" overall.
Power: 12-gram CO_2 cylinder.
Stocks: Walnut on nickeled model, simulated walnut on black guns.
Sights: High ramp front, fully adjustable notch rear.
Features: Velocity to 400 fps. Turn-bolt action with cross-bolt safety. Gives about 40 shots per CO_2 cylinder. Introduced 1991. Made in U.S. by Benjamin Sheridan Co.
Price: Black finish, EB17 (177), EB20 (20), EB22 (22) **$96.50**
Price: Nickel finish, E17 (177), E20 (20), E22 (22) **$109.50**

BENJAMIN/SHERIDAN PNEUMATIC PELLET PISTOLS
Caliber: 177, 20, 22, single shot.
Barrel: 9⅜", rifled brass.
Weight: 40 oz. **Length:** 12¼" overall.
Power: Under-lever pnuematic, hand pumped.
Stocks: Walnut stocks and pump handle.
Sights: High ramp front, fully adjustable notch rear.
Features: Velocity to 400 fps (variable). Bolt action with cross-bolt safety. Choice of black or nickel finish. Made in U.S. by Benjamin Sheridan Co.
Price: Black finish, HB17 (177), HB20 (20), HB22 (22) **$104.95**
Price: Nickel finish, H17 (177), H20 (20), H22 (22) **$111.50**

Benjamin/Sheridan Pneumatic

BSA SCORPION AIR PISTOL
Caliber: 177 or 22, single shot.
Barrel: 7¾".
Weight: 3½ lbs. **Length:** 15¾" overall.
Power: Spring piston, barrel cocking.
Stocks: Moulded synthetic with thumbrest.
Sights: Globe front, adjustable open rear.
Features: Velocity to 600 fps (177); 400 fps (22). Two-stage trigger. Barrel extension to ease cocking effort. Polished blue finish. Imported from England by Air Rifle Specialists.
Price: **$190.00**

BSA Scorpion

CROSMAN AUTO AIR II PISTOL
Caliber: BB, 17-shot magazine, 177 pellet, single shot.
Barrel: 8⅝" steel, smoothbore.
Weight: 13 oz. **Length:** 10¾" overall.
Power: CO_2 Powerlet.
Stocks: Grooved plastic.
Sights: Blade front, adjustable rear; highlighted system.
Features: Velocity to 480 fps (BBs), 430 fps (pellets). Semi-automatic action with BBs, single shot with pellets. Silvered finish. Introduced 1991. From Crosman.
Price: About **$39.99**

Crosman Auto Air II

CROSMAN MODEL 357 AIR PISTOL
Caliber: 177, 6- or 10-shot.
Barrel: 4" (Model 357-4), 6" (Model 357-6), rifled steel; 8" (Model 357-8), rifled brass.
Weight: 32 oz. (6"). **Length:** 11⅜" overall.
Power: CO_2 Powerlet.
Stocks: Checkered wood-grain plastic.
Sights: Ramp front, fully adjustable rear.
Features: Average 430 fps (Model 357-6). Break-open barrel for easy loading. Single or double action. Vent. rib barrel. Wide, smooth trigger. Two speed loaders come with each gun. Model 357-8 has matte gray finish, black grips. From Crosman.
Price: 4" or 6", about **$55.00**
Price: 8", about **$62.00**
Price: Model 1357 (same gun as above, except shoots BBs, has 6-shot clip), about **$55.00**

Crosman 357

CROSMAN MODEL 1008 REPEAT AIR
Caliber: 177, 8-shot clip.
Barrel: 4.25", rifled steel.
Weight: 17 oz. **Length:** 8.625" overall.
Power: CO_2 powerlet.
Stocks: Checkered plastic.
Sights: Post front, adjustable rear.
Features: Velocity about 400 fps. Break-open barrel for easy loading; single or double semi-automatic action; two 8-shot clips included. Optional carrying case available. Introduced 1992. From Crosman.
Price: About **$45.00**

CROSMAN MODEL 1322, 1377 AIR PISTOLS
Caliber: 177 (M1377), 22 (M1322), single shot.
Barrel: 8", rifled steel.
Weight: 39 oz. **Length:** 13⅝".
Power: Hand pumped.
Sights: Blade front, rear adjustable for windage and elevation.
Features: Moulded plastic grip, hand size pump forearm. Cross-bolt safety. Model 1377 also shoots BBs. From Crosman.
Price: About **$50.00**

Crosman 1322

Crosman SSP 250

CROSMAN MODEL SSP 250 PISTOL
Caliber: 177, 20, 22, single shot.
Barrel: 9⅞", rifled steel.
Weight: 3 lbs., 1 oz. **Length:** 14" overall.
Power: CO_2 Powerlet.
Stocks: Composition; black, with checkering.
Sights: Hooded front, fully adjustable rear.
Features: Velocity about 560 fps. Interchangeable accessory barrels. Two-stage trigger. High/low power settings. From Crosman.
Price: About **$47.00**

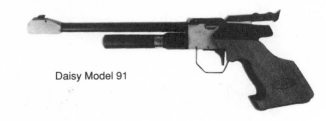

Daisy Model 91

DAISY MODEL 91 MATCH PISTOL
Caliber: 177, single shot.
Barrel: 10.25", rifled steel.
Weight: 2.5 lbs. **Length:** 16.5" overall.
Power: CO_2, 12-gram cylinder.
Stocks: Stippled hardwood; anatomically shaped and adjustable.
Sights: Blade and ramp front, changeable-width rear notch with full micrometer adjustments.
Features: Velocity to 476 fps. Gives 55 shots per cylinder. Fully adjustable trigger. Introduced 1991. Imported by Daisy Mfg. Co.
Price: About **$500.00**

Daisy/Power Line 45

DAISY MODEL 188 BB PISTOL
Caliber: BB.
Barrel: 9.9", steel smoothbore.
Weight: 1.67 lbs. **Length:** 11.7" overall.
Stocks: Copolymer; checkered with thumbrest.
Sights: Blade and ramp front, open fixed rear.
Features: 24-shot repeater. Spring action with under-barrel cocking lever. Grip and receiver of Nylafil-copolymer material. Introduced 1979. From Daisy Mfg. Co.
Price: About **$25.00**

DAISY/POWER LINE 45 AIR PISTOL
Caliber: 177, 13-shot clip.
Barrel: 5", rifled steel.
Weight: 1.25 lbs. **Length:** 8.5" overall.
Power: CO_2.
Stocks: Checkered plastic.
Sights: Fixed.
Features: Velocity 400 fps. Semi-automatic repeater with double-action trigger. Manually operated lever-type trigger block safety; magazine safety. Introduced 1990. From Daisy Mfg. Co.
Price: About **$69.00**
Price: Model 645 (nickel-chrome plated), about **$75.00**

DAISY/POWER LINE 44 REVOLVER
Caliber: 177 pellets, 6-shot.
Barrel: 6", rifled steel; interchangeable 4" and 8".
Weight: 2.7 lbs.
Power: CO_2.
Stocks: Moulded plastic with checkering.
Sights: Blade on ramp front, fully adjustable notch rear.
Features: Velocity up to 400 fps. Replica of 44 Magnum revolver. Has swingout cylinder and interchangeable barrels. Introduced 1987. From Daisy Mfg. Co.
Price: **$49.00**

Daisy/Power Line 93

DAISY/POWER LINE 93 PISTOL
Caliber: 177, BB, 15-shot clip.
Barrel: 5", steel.
Weight: 17 oz. **Length:** NA.
Power: CO_2.
Stocks: Checkered plastic.
Sights: Fixed.
Features: Velocity to 400 fps. Semi-automatic repeater. Manual lever-type trigger-block safety. Introduced 1991. From Daisy Mfg. Co.
Price: About **$60.00**
Price: Model 693 (nickel-chrome plated), about **$65.00**

DAISY/POWER LINE 717 PELLET PISTOL
Caliber: 177, single shot.
Barrel: 9.61".
Weight: 2.8 lbs. **Length:** 13½" overall.
Stocks: Moulded wood-grain plastic, with thumbrest.
Sights: Blade and ramp front, micro-adjustable notch rear.
Features: Single pump pneumatic pistol. Rifled steel barrel. Cross-bolt trigger block. Muzzle velocity 385 fps. From Daisy Mfg. Co. Introduced 1979.
Price: About **$68.00**

Daisy/Power Line 747 Pistol
Similar to the 717 pistol except has a 12-groove rifled steel barrel by Lothar Walther. Velocity of 360 fps. Manual cross-bolt safety.
Price: About **$109.00**

Daisy/Power Line 717

DAISY/POWER LINE MATCH 777 PELLET PISTOL
Caliber: 177, single shot.
Barrel: 9.61" rifled steel by Lothar Walther.
Weight: 32 oz. **Length:** 13½" overall.
Power: Sidelever, single pump pneumatic.
Stocks: Smooth hardwood, fully contoured with palm and thumbrest.
Sights: Blade and ramp front, match-grade open rear with adjustable width notch, micro. click adjustments.
Features: Adjustable trigger; manual cross-bolt safety. MV of 385 fps. Comes with cleaning kit, adjustment tool and pellets. From Daisy Mfg. Co.
Price: About **$236.00**

Daisy/Power Line 777

Daisy/Power Line 1200

MARKSMAN 17 AIR PISTOL
Caliber: 177, single shot.
Barrel: 7.5".
Weight: 46 oz. **Length:** 14.5" overall.
Power: Spring-air, barrel-cocking.
Stocks: Checkered composition with right-hand thumbrest.
Sights: Tunnel front, fully adjustable rear.
Features: Velocity of 360-400 fps. Introduced 1986. Imported from Spain by Marksman Products.
Price: **$56.00**

MARKSMAN 1010 REPEATER PISTOL
Caliber: 177, 18-shot repeater.
Barrel: 2½", smoothbore.
Weight: 24 oz. **Length:** 8¼" overall.
Power: Spring.
Features: Velocity to 200 fps. Thumb safety. Black finish. Uses BBs, darts or pellets. Repeats with BBs only. From Marksman Products.
Price: Matte black finish **$24.50**
Price: Model 1010X (as above except nickel-plated) **$33.50**

MARKSMAN 1015 SPECIAL EDITION AIR PISTOL
Caliber: 177, 24-shot repeater.
Barrel: 3.8", rifled.
Weight: 22 oz. **Length:** 10.3" overall.
Power: Spring-air.
Stocks: Checkered brown composition.
Sights: Fixed.
Features: Velocity about 230 fps. Skeletonized trigger, extended barrel with "ported compensator." Shoots BBs, pellets, darts or bolts. From Marksman Products.
Price: **$29.00**

RWS/DIANA MODEL 5G AIR PISTOL
Caliber: 177, single shot.
Barrel: 7".
Weight: 2¾ lbs. **Length:** 16" overall.
Power: Spring-air, barrel cocking.
Stocks: Plastic, thumbrest design.
Sights: Tunnel front, micro-click open rear.
Features: Velocity of 410 fps. Two-stage trigger with automatic safety. Imported from Germany by Dynamit Nobel-RWS, Inc.
Price: **$185.00**

RWS/DIANA MODEL 6M MATCH AIR PISTOL
Caliber: 177, single shot.
Barrel: 7".
Weight: 3 lbs. **Length:** 16" overall.
Power: Spring-air, barrel cocking.
Stocks: Walnut-finished hardwood with thumbrest.
Sights: Adjustable front, micro. click open rear.
Features: Velocity of 410 fps. Recoilless double piston system, movable barrel shroud to protect from sight during cocking. Imported from Germany by Dynamit Nobel-RWS, Inc.
Price: Right-hand **$400.00**
Price: Left-hand **$425.00**

DAISY/POWER LINE CO₂ 1200 PISTOL
Caliber: BB, 177.
Barrel: 10½", smooth.
Weight: 1.6 lbs. **Length:** 11.1" overall.
Power: Daisy CO_2 cylinder.
Stocks: Contoured, checkered moulded wood-grain plastic.
Sights: Blade ramp front, fully adjustable square notch rear.
Features: 60-shot BB reservoir, gravity feed. Cross-bolt safety. Velocity of 420-450 fps for more than 100 shots. From Daisy Mfg. Co.
Price: About **$39.00**

"GAT" AIR PISTOL
Caliber: 177, single shot.
Barrel: 7½" cocked, 9½" extended.
Weight: 22 oz.
Power: Spring piston.
Stocks: Cast checkered metal.
Sights: Fixed.
Features: Shoots pellets, corks or darts. Matte black finish. Imported from England by Stone Enterprises, Inc.
Price: **$21.95**

Marksman 17

Marksman 1015

RWS/Diana Model 5G

RWS/Diana Model 6G, 6GS Air Pistols
Similar to the Model 6M except does not have the movable barrel shroud. Has click micrometer rear sight, two-stage adjustable trigger, interchangeable tunnel front sight. Available in right- or left-hand models.
Price: Right-hand **$295.00**
Price: Left-hand **$320.00**

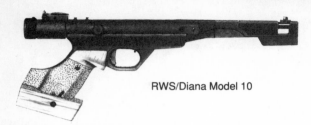

RWS/Diana Model 10

RWS GAMO FALCON AIR PISTOL
Caliber: 177, single shot.
Barrel: 7.1".
Weight: 2.8 lbs. **Length:** 14.9" overall.
Power: Underlever cocking, spring piston.
Stocks: Composition.
Sights: Blade front, adjustable open rear.
Features: Velocity to 430 fps. Cocking effort of 27 lbs. Manual safety; two-stage adjustable trigger. Imported from Spain by Dynamit Nobel-RWS, Inc.
Price: **$105.00**

RWS GAMO PR-45 AIR PISTOL
Caliber: 177, single shot.
Barrel: 8.3".
Weight: 25 oz. **Length:** 11" overall.
Power: Pre-compressed air.
Stocks: Composition.
Sights: Blade front, adjustable rear.
Features: Velocity to 430 fps. Recoilless and vibration free. Manual safety. Imported from Spain by Dynamit Nobel-RWS, Inc.
Price: **$130.00**
Price: Compact model (adjustable walnut grips, adjustable trigger, swiveling trigger shoe) **$200.00**

SHARP MODEL U-FP CO₂ PISTOL
Caliber: 177, single shot.
Barrel: 8", rifled steel.
Weight: 2.4 lbs. **Length:** 11.6" overall.
Power: 12-gram CO_2 cylinder.
Stocks: Smooth hardwood. Walnut target stocks available.
Sights: Post front, fully adjustable target rear.
Features: Variable power adjustment up to 545 fps. Adjustable trigger. Also available with adjustable field sight. Imported from Japan by Great Lakes Airguns.
Price: With target sights **$209.50**
Price: With field sights **$189.50**

STEYR CO₂ MATCH PISTOL
Caliber: 177, single shot.
Barrel: 9".
Weight: 38.7 oz. **Length:** 15.3" overall.
Power: Pre-compressed CO_2 cylinders.
Stocks: Fully adjustable Morini match with palm shelf; stippled walnut.
Sights: Interchangeable blade in 4mm, 4.5mm or 5mm widths, fully adjustable open rear with interchangeable 3.5mm or 4mm leaves.
Features: Velocity about 500 fps. Adjustable trigger, adjustable sight radius from 12.4" to 13.2". Imported from Austria by Nygord Precision Products.
Price: About **$1,050.00**

RWS/Diana Model 10 Match Air Pistol
Refined version of the Model 6M. Has special adjustable match trigger, oil-finished and stippled match grips, barrel weight. Also available in left-hand version, and with fitted case.
Price: Model 10 . . . . **$670.00**
Price: Model 10, left-hand **$735.00**
Price: Model 10, with case **$720.00**
Price: Model 10, left-hand, with case **$765.00**

RWS GAMO AF-10 AIR PISTOL
Caliber: 177 pellets or round balls, 15-shot repeater.
Barrel: 7".
Weight: 19 oz. **Length:** 9" overall.
Power: Pre-compressed air.
Stocks: Checkered composition.
Sights: Blade front, adjustable rear.
Features: Velocity 430 fps. Recoilless operation. Imported from Spain by Dynamit Nobel-RWS.
Price: **$115.00**

RWS Gamo Falcon

Sharp Model U-FP

WALTHER CP 3 AIR PISTOL
Caliber: 177, single shot.
Barrel: 9".
Weight: 40 oz. **Length:** 14¾" overall.
Power: CO_2.
Stocks: Full target-type stippled wood with adjustable hand shelf.
Sights: Target post front, fully adjustable target rear.
Features: Velocity of 520 fps, CO_2 powered; target-quality trigger; comes with adaptor for charging with standard CO_2 air tanks, case, and accessories. Introduced 1983. Imported from Germany by Interarms.
Price: **$960.00**
Price: Model CP-5 Match **$1,650.00**
Price: Model LPM-1 Match **$1,583.00**

AIRGUNS—LONG GUNS

AIR ARMS SM 100 AIR RIFLE
Caliber: 177, 22, single shot.
Barrel: 22", 12-groove Lothar Walther.
Weight: 8½ lbs. **Length:** 39½" overall.
Power: Pre-charged compressed air from diving tank.
Stock: Walnut-finished beech.
Sights: None furnished.
Features: Velocity to 1000 fps (177), 800 fps (22). PFTE-coated lightweight striker for consistent shots. Blued barrel and air chamber. Imported from England by Air Rifle Specialists.
Price: **$750.00**
Price: For left-hand stock add **$60.00**
Price: Model XM 100 (same as SM100 except walnut stock) **$940.00**
Price: For left-hand stock add **$60.00**

Air Arms TM 100 Air Rifle
Similar to the SM 100 except is target model with hand-picked barrel for best accuracy. Target-type walnut stock with adjustable cheekpiece and adjustable buttplate. Stippled grip and forend. Available in 177 or 22 (special order), right- or left-hand models. Variable power settings. Two-stage adjustable trigger; 22" barrel. Imported from England by Air Rifle Specialists.
Price: **$1,170.00**
Price: Left-hand **$1,230.00**

Air Arms NJR 100 Air Rifle
Similar to the SM 100 except designed for Field Target competition. Hand-picked Walther barrel for best accuracy. Walnut Field Target thumbhole stock has adjustable forend, cheekpiece and buttpad. Has lever-type bolt, straight blade trigger. Imported from England by Air Rifle Specialists, Beeman.
Price: **$1,670.00**
Price: Left-hand **$1,730.00**
Price: Right-hand (Beeman) **$1,795.00**
Price: Left-hand (Beeman) **$1,895.00**

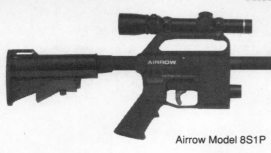

Airrow Model 8S1P

AIRROW MODEL 8SRB STEALTH AIR GUN
Caliber: 177, 22, 25, 38.
Barrel: 17", 23".
Weight: 5 lbs. **Length:** 31.5" overall.
Power: CO_2 or compressed air; variable power.
Stock: Telescoping CAR-15-type.
Sights: 1.5-5x variable power scope.
Features: Velocity 1100 fps in all calibers. Pneumatic air trigger. All aircraft aluminum and stainless steel construction. Mil-spec materials and finishes. Introduced 1992. From Swivel Machine Works, Inc.
Price: About **$1,599.00**

Sights: 1.5-5x variable power scope.
Features: Velocity to 650 fps with 260-grain arrow. Pneumatic air trigger. All aircraft aluminum and stainless steel construction. Mil-spec materials and finishes. Waterproof case. Introduced 1991. From Swivel Machine Works, Inc.
Price: About **$1,599.00**

AIRROW MODEL 8S1P STEALTH AIR GUN
Caliber: #2512 16" arrow.
Barrel: 16".
Weight: 4.3 lbs. **Length:** 30.1" overall.
Power: CO_2 or compressed air; variable power.
Stock: Telescoping CAR-15-type.

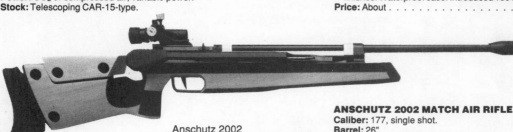

Anschutz 2002

ARS AR6 REPEATING AIR RIFLE
Caliber: 22, 6-shot repeater.
Barrel: 23¼".
Weight: 6¾ lbs. **Length:** 38¼" overall.
Power: Pre-compressed air from diving tank or CO_2.
Stock: Walnut with checkered grip; rubber buttpad.
Sights: Blade front, adjustable peep rear.
Features: Velocity to 1100 fps with 25-grain pellet. Receiver grooved for scope mounting. Imported from Korea by Air Rifle Specialists.
Price: **$550.00**

ANSCHUTZ 2002 MATCH AIR RIFLE
Caliber: 177, single shot.
Barrel: 26".
Weight: 10½ lbs. **Length:** 44½" overall.
Stock: European walnut; stippled grip and forend.
Sights: Globe front, #6824 Micro Peep rear.
Features: Balance, weight match the 1907 ISU smallbore rifle. Uses #5019 match trigger. Recoil and vibration free. Fully adjustable cheekpiece and buttplate. Introduced 1988. Imported from Germany by Precision Sales International.
Price: Right-hand **$1,953.00**
Price: Left-hand, hardwood stock **$1,989.00**
Price: Model 2002D RT (Running Target) **$2,059.00**

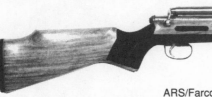

ARS/Farco Shotgun

ARS/FARCO CO_2 AIR SHOTGUN
Caliber: 51 (28-gauge).
Barrel: 30".
Weight: 7 lbs. **Length:** 48½" overall.
Power: 10-oz. refillable CO_2 tank.
Stock: Hardwood.
Sights: Bead front, fixed dovetail rear.
Features: Gives over 100 ft. lbs. energy for taking small game. Imported from Korea by Air Rifle Specialists.
Price: **$395.00**

BEEMAN AIR HUNTER AIR RIFLE
Caliber: 20, 25, single shot.
Barrel: 14"; 12-groove rifling.
Weight: 9.2 lbs. **Length:** 41.5" overall.
Power: Metal spring-piston, single stroke, underlever.
Stock: Walnut with satin finish. Designed for field use; high comb rollover cheekpiece and wide forend.
Sights: None furnished; grooved for scope mounting.
Features: Rotating piston. Special high-power breech. Imported by Beeman.
Price: **$495.00**

Beeman Air Hunter

BEEMAN AIR WOLF AIR RIFLE
Caliber: 177, 20, 22, 25, single shot.
Barrel: 21"; 12-groove rifling.
Weight: 5.7 lbs. **Length:** 37" overall.
Power: Pre-charged pneumatic, internal air chamber.
Stock: Select walnut, adult-scaled stock; hand checkered.
Sights: None furnished; grooved for scope mounting
Features: Up to 150 shots per air charge. Imported by Beeman.
Price: **$598.00**
Price: Wolf Pup (15.5" bbl., 5 lbs.) **$598.00**

Beeman Classic

BEEMAN CLASSIC MAGNUM AIR RIFLE
Caliber: 20, 25, single shot.
Barrel: 15"; 12-groove rifling.
Weight: 8.6 lbs. **Length:** 44.5" overall.
Power: Gas-spring; barrel cocking action. Adjustable power.
Stock: Walnut.
Sights: None furnished. Built-in base and 1" rings included.
Features: Two-stage adjustable trigger. Automatic safety. Also available in 22-caliber on special order. Imported by Beeman.
Price: $895.00

BEEMAN CROW MAGNUM AIR RIFLE
Caliber: 20, 25, single shot.
Barrel: 16"; 10-groove rifling.
Weight: 8.5 lbs. **Length:** 46" overall.
Power: Gas-spring; adjustable power to 32 foot pounds muzzle energy. Barrel-cocking.
Stock: Classic-style walnut; hand checkered.
Sights: For scope use only; built-in base and 1" rings included.
Features: Adjustable two-stage trigger. Automatic safety. Also available in 22-caliber on special order. Introduced 1992. Imported by Beeman.
Price: $1,095.00

Beeman Game Keeper

BEEMAN GAMEKEEPER AIR RIFLE
Caliber: 25, single shot.
Barrel: 15"; 12-groove rifling.

BEEMAN MANITOU FT MATCH RIFLE
Caliber: 177, single shot.
Barrel: 21"; 12-groove rifling.
Weight: 8.7 lbs. **Length:** 36.25" overall.
Power: Pre-charged pneumatic, internal air chamber.
Stock: Walnut; fully adjustable.

Weight: 7.9 lbs. **Length:** 36.3" overall.
Power: Pre-charged pneumatic, quick-change bottle, adjustable power.
Stock: Black pebble-finish mil-spec composition; or walnut.
Sights: None furnished; grooved for scope mounting.
Features: Interchangeable 177, 20, 22-caliber barrels, stocks and air bottles. Imported by Beeman.
Price: 25-caliber, composite stock $989.00
Price: 25-caliber, standard walnut stock $989.00
Price: 25-caliber, grade II walnut stock $1,098.00

Sights: Optional.
Features: Brass match trigger. Brass fittings. Left-hand stock on special order. Imported by Beeman.
Price: 177 . . . . $898.00
Price: 22 (special order) $925.00

Beeman Super 7

BEEMAN SUPER 7 AIR RIFLE
Caliber: 22, 7-shot repeater.
Barrel: 19"; 12-groove rifling.
Weight: 7.2 lbs. **Length:** 41" overall.
Power: Pre-charged pneumatic, external air reservoir.
Stock: Walnut; high cheekpiece; rubber buttpad.
Sights: None furnished; drilled and tapped; 1" ring scope mounts included.
Features: Two-stage adjustable trigger; 7-shot rotary magazine. Receiver of anodized aircraft aluminum. All working parts either hardened or stainless steel. Imported by Beeman.
Price: $1,560.00

Beeman/Feinwerkbau 300-S

BEEMAN/FEINWERKBAU 300-S SERIES MATCH RIFLE
Caliber: 177, single shot.
Barrel: 19.9", fixed solid with receiver.
Weight: Approx. 10 lbs. with optional bbl. sleeve. **Length:** 42.8" overall.
Power: Single stroke sidelever, spring piston.
Stock: Match model—walnut, deep forend, adjustable buttplate.
Sights: Globe front with interchangeable inserts. Click micro. adjustable match aperture rear. Front and rear sights move as a single unit.
Features: Recoilless, vibration free. Five-way adjustable match trigger. Grooved for scope mounts. Permanent lubrication, steel piston ring. Cocking effort 9 lbs. Optional 10-oz. barrel sleeve. Available from Beeman.
Price: Right-hand $1,095.00
Price: Left-hand $1,187.00
Price: Tyrolean, right-hand $1,295.00
Price: Tyrolean, left-hand $1,310.00

BEEMAN UL-7 AIR RIFLE
Caliber: 22, 7-shot repeater.
Barrel: 12"; 12-groove rifling.
Weight: 8.5 lbs. **Length:** 41.75" overall.
Power: Gas-spring; adjustable power; underlever cocking.
Stock: Checkered walnut.
Sights: None furnished. Built-in base and 1" rings included.
Features: Two-stage adjustable trigger. Automatic safety. Removable rotary 7-shot magazine. Imported by Beeman.
Price: $1,560.00

CAUTION: PRICES CHANGE, CHECK AT GUNSHOP.

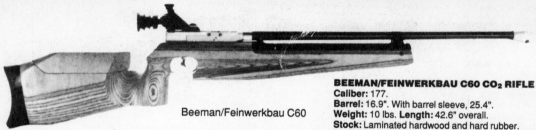

Beeman/Feinwerkbau C60

BEEMAN/FEINWERKBAU MODEL 601 AIR RIFLE
Caliber: 177, single shot.
Barrel: 16.6".
Weight: 10.8 lbs. **Length:** 43" overall.
Power: Single stroke pneumatic.
Stock: Special laminated hardwoods and hard rubber for stability.
Sights: Tunnel front with interchangeable inserts, click micrometer match apperture rear.
Features: Recoilless action; double supported barrel; special, short rifled area frees pellet from barrel faster so shooter's motion has minimum effect on accuracy. Fully adjustable match trigger. Trigger and sights blocked when loading latch is open. Imported by Beeman. Introduced 1984.
Price: Right-hand **$1,495.00**
Price: Left-hand **$1,635.00**
Price: Right-hand, walnut stock **$1,495.00**

Beeman/Feinwerkbau 601 Running Target
Similar to the standard Model 601. Has 16.9" barrel (33.7" with barrel sleeve); special match trigger, short loading gate which allows scope mounting. No sights—built for scope use only. Introduced 1987.
Price: Right-hand **$1,435.00**
Price: Left-hand **$1,595.00**
Price: Running target scope mounts **$159.95**

BEEMAN/FEINWERKBAU C60 CO$_2$ RIFLE
Caliber: 177.
Barrel: 16.9". With barrel sleeve, 25.4".
Weight: 10 lbs. **Length:** 42.6" overall.
Stock: Laminated hardwood and hard rubber.
Sights: Tunnel front with interchangeable inserts, quick release micro. click match aperture rear.
Features: Similar features, performance as Beeman/FWB 601. Virtually no cocking effort. Right- or left-hand. Running target version available. Introduced 1987. Imported from Germany by Beeman.
Price: Right-hand **$1,390.00**
Price: Left-hand **$1,530.00**
Price: Running Target, right-hand **$1,360.00**
Price: Running Target, left-hand **$1,490.00**
Price: Mini C60, right-hand **$1,390.00**

BEEMAN/FEINWERKBAU 300-S MINI-MATCH
Caliber: 177, single shot.
Barrel: 17⅛".
Weight: 8.8 lbs. **Length:** 40" overall.
Power: Spring piston, single stroke sidelever cocking.
Stock: Walnut. Stippled grip, adjustable buttplate. Scaled-down for youthful or slightly built shooters.
Sights: Globe front with interchangeable inserts, micro. adjustable rear. Front and rear sights move as a single unit.
Features: Recoilless, vibration free. Grooved for scope mounts. Steel piston ring. Cocking effort about 9½ lbs. Barrel sleeve optional. Left-hand model available. Introduced 1978. Imported by Beeman.
Price: Right-hand **$1,095.00**
Price: Left-hand **$1,198.00**

Beeman FX-1

BEEMAN FX-1 AIR RIFLE
Caliber: 177, single shot.
Barrel: 18", rifled.
Weight: 6.6 lbs. **Length:** 43" overall.
Power: Spring-piston, barrel cocking.
Stock: Walnut-stained hardwood.
Sights: Tunnel front with interchangeable inserts; rear with rotating disc to give four sighting notches.
Features: Velocity 680 fps. Match-type adjustable trigger. Receiver grooved for scope mounting. Imported by Beeman.
Price: **$169.50**

BEEMAN/HW50 LIGHT/SPORTER TARGET RIFLE
Caliber: 177, single shot.
Barrel: 18.4"; 12-groove rifling.
Weight: 6.9 lbs. **Length:** 43.1" overall.
Power: Spring piston; single-stroke barrel cocking.
Stock: Walnut-finished hardwood.
Sights: Blade front, adjustable rear.
Features: Velocity about 705 fps. Synthetic non-drying breech and piston seals. Double-jointed cocking lever. Introduced 1990. Imported by Beeman.
Price: **$199.98**

BEEMAN/HW30 AIR RIFLE
Caliber: 177, 22, single shot.
Barrel: 17" (177), 16.9" (20); 12-groove rifling.
Weight: 5.5 lbs.
Power: Spring piston; single-stroke barrel cocking.
Stock: Walnut-finished hardwood.
Sights: Blade front, adjustable rear.
Features: Velocity about 660 fps (177). Double-jointed cocking lever. Cast trigger guard. Synthetic non-drying breech and piston seals. Introduced 1990. Imported by Beeman.
Price: 177 . . . . **$179.98**
Price: 20 . . . . **$185.98**

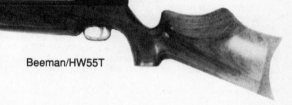

Beeman/HW55T

BEEMAN/HW55 TARGET RIFLES

Model	55SM	55MM	55T
Caliber:	177	177	177
Barrel:	18½"	18½"	18½"
Length:	43½"	43½"	43½"
Wgt. lbs.:	7.8	7.8	7.8
Rear sight:	All aperture		
Front sight:	All with globe and four interchangeable inserts.		
Power:	All spring (barrel cocking). 660-700 fps.		
Price:	$479.50	$559.50	$619.50

Features: Trigger fully adjustable and removable. Micrometer rear sight adjusts for windage and elevation in all. Pistol grip high comb stock with beavertail forend, walnut finish stock on 55SM. Walnut stock on 55MM, Tyrolean stock on 55T. Nylon piston seals in all. Imported by Beeman.

> Consult our Directory pages for the location of firms mentioned.

Beeman/HW77

BEEMAN/HW77 AIR RIFLE & CARBINE
Caliber: 177, 20 or 22, single shot.
Barrel: 14.5" or 18.5", 12-groove rifling.
Weight: 8.9 lbs. **Length:** 39.7" or 43.7" overall.
Power: Spring-piston; under-lever cocking.
Stocks: Walnut-stained beech; rubber buttplate, cut checkering on grip; cheekpiece.
Sights: Blade front, open adjustable rear.
Features: Velocity 830 fps. Fixed-barrel with fully opening, direct loading breech. Extended under-lever gives good cocking leverage. Adjustable trigger. Grooved for scope mounting. Carbine has 14.5" barrel, weighs 8.7 lbs., and

is 39.7" overall. Imported by Beeman.
Price: Right-hand, 177, 20, 22 . . . . **$469.95**
Price: Left-hand, 177, 20, 22 . . . . **$519.95**
Price: With Tyrolean walnut stock, right-hand **$599.95**

BEEMAN R1 CARBINE
Caliber: 177, 20, 22, 25, single shot.
Barrel: 16.1".
Weight: 8.6 lbs. **Length:** 41.7" overall.
Power: Spring-piston, barrel cocking.
Stock: Stained beech; Monte Carlo comb and checkpiece; cut checkered p.g.; rubber buttpad.
Sights: Tunnel front with interchangeable inserts, open adjustable rear; receiver grooved for scope mounting.
Features: Velocity up to 1050 fps (177). Non-drying nylon piston and breech seals. Adjustable metal trigger. Machined steel receiver end cap and safety. Right- or left-hand stock. Imported by Beeman.
Price: 177, 20, 22, 25, right-hand **$449.98**
Price: As above, left-hand **$499.98**

Beeman RX-1

BEEMAN RX-1 GAS-SPRING MAGNUM AIR RIFLE
Caliber: 177, 20, 22, 25, single shot.
Barrel: 19.6"; 12-groove rifling.
Weight: 8.8 lbs.
Power: Gas-spring piston air; single stroke barrel cocking.
Stock: Walnut-finished hardwood, hand checkered, with cheekpiece. Adjustable cheekpiece and buttplate.
Sights: Tunnel front, click-adjustable rear.
Features: Velocity adjustable to about 1200 fps. Uses special sealed chamber of air as a mainspring. Gas-spring cannot take a set. Introduced 1990. Imported by Beeman.
Price: 177 or 22, regular, right-hand **$487.50**
Price: 20 or 25, regular, right hand **$487.50**
Price: 177, 20, 22, 25 Field Target **$659.95**

BEEMAN/HARPER AIRCANE
Caliber: 22 and 25, single shot.
Barrel: 31½", rifled.
Weight: 1 lb. **Length:** 34" overall.
Features: Walking cane also acts as an airgun. Solid walnut handle with polished brass ferrule. Available in various hand-carved models. Intricate deep engraving on the ferrule. Uses rechargeable air "cartridges" loaded with pellets. Kit includes separate pump, extra cartridges and fitted case. Introduced 1987. Imported by Beeman.
Price: Basic set **$595.95**
Price: Goose, Labrador, Spaniel sets **$655.00**

Beeman C1

BEEMAN CARBINE MODEL C1
Caliber: 177 or 22, single shot.
Barrel: 14", 12-groove rifling.
Weight: 6¼ lbs. **Length:** 38" overall.
Power: Spring-piston, barrel cocking.
Stock: Walnut-stained beechwood with rubber buttpad.
Sights: Blade front, rear click-adjustable for windage and elevation.
Features: Velocity 830 fps. Adjustable trigger. Receiver grooved for scope mounting. Imported by Beeman.
Price: **$249.95**

BEEMAN R1 AIR RIFLE
Caliber: 177, 20 or 22, single shot.
Barrel: 19.6", 12-groove rifling.
Weight: 8.5 lbs. **Length:** 45.2" overall.
Power: Spring-piston, barrel cocking.
Stock: Walnut-stained beech; cut-checkered pistol grip; Monte Carlo comb and cheekpiece; rubber buttpad.
Sights: Tunnel front with interchangeable inserts, open rear click-adjustable for windage and elevation. Grooved for scope mounting.
Features: Velocity of 940-1050 fps (177), 860 fps (20), 800 fps (22). Non-drying nylon piston and breech seals. Adjustable metal trigger. Milled steel safety. Right- or left-hand stock. Available with adjustable cheekpiece and buttplate at extra cost. Custom and Super Laser versions available. Imported by Beeman.
Price: Right-hand, 177, 20, 22 . . . . **$449.98**
Price: Left-hand, 177, 20, 22 . . . . **$499.98**
Price: Field Target, right-hand, 177, 20 . . . . **$619.95**
Price: 177, 20, with Tyrolean walnut stock **$589.95**

Beeman R7 Air Rifle
Similar to the R8 model except has lighter ambidextrous stock, match-grade trigger block; velocity of 680-700 fps; barrel length 17"; weight 5.8 lbs. Milled steel safety. Imported by Beeman.
Price: 177, 20 . . . . **$279.98**

BEEMAN R1 LASER AIR RIFLE
Caliber: 177, 20, 22, 25, single shot.
Barrel: 16.1" or 19.6".
Weight: 8.4 lbs. **Length:** 41.7" overall (16.1" barrel).
Power: Spring-piston, barrel cocking.
Stock: Laminated wood with Monte Carlo comb and cheekpiece; checkered p.g. and forend; rubber buttpad.
Sights: Tunnel front with interchangeable inserts, open adjustable rear.
Features: Velocity up to 1150 fps (177). Special powerplant components. Built from the Beeman R1 rifle by Beeman.
Price: 177, 20, 22, 25 . . . . **$899.50**

BEEMAN R8 AIR RIFLE
Caliber: 177, single shot.
Barrel: 18.3".
Weight: 7.2 lbs. **Length:** 43.1" overall.
Power: Barrel cocking, spring-piston.
Stock: Walnut with Monte Carlo cheekpiece; checkered pistol grip.
Sights: Globe front, fully adjustable rear; interchangeable inserts.
Features: Velocity of 735 fps. Similar to the R1. Nylon piston and breech seals. Adjustable match-grade, two-stage, grooved metal trigger. Milled steel safety. Rubber buttpad. Imported by Beeman.
Price: **$349.98**

CAUTION: PRICES CHANGE, CHECK AT GUNSHOP.

BEEMAN R10 AIR RIFLES
Caliber: 177, 20, 22, single shot.
Barrel: 16.1"; 12-groove rifling.
Weight: 7.9 lbs. **Length:** 46" overall.
Power: Spring-piston, barrel cocking.
Stock: Standard—walnut-finished hardwood with Monte Carlo comb, rubber buttplate; Deluxe has white spacers at grip cap, buttplate, checkered grip, cheekpiece, rubber buttplate.
Sights: Tunnel front with interchangeable inserts, open rear click adjustable for

windage and elevation. Receiver grooved for scope mounting.
Features: Over 1000 fps in 177-cal. only; 26-lb. cocking effort; milled steel safety and body tube. Right- and left-hand models. Similar in appearance to the Beeman R8. Introduced 1986. Imported by Beeman.
Price: 177, 20 or 22 Standard **$359.98**
Price: 20, Standard **$359.98**
Price: 177, 20, 22, Deluxe, right-hand **$409.88**
Price: 177, 20, 22, Deluxe, left-hand **$459.98**

Benjamin CO₂

BENJAMIN CO₂ AIR RIFLES
Caliber: 177 or 22, single shot.
Barrel: 19⅜", rifled brass.
Weight: 5 lbs. **Length:** 36½" overall.
Power: 12-gram CO_2 cylinder.
Stock: Walnut with Monte Carlo comb.

Sights: High ramp front, fully adjustable notch rear or Williams peep.
Features: Velocity to 600 fps (177). Bolt action with ambidextrous push-pull safety. Gives about 40 shots per cylinder. Black or nickel finish. Introduced 1991. Made in the U.S. by Benjamin Sheridan Co.
Price: Black finish, open sight, Model G397 (177), Model G392 (22) **$114.50**
Price: As above with Williams peep, Model G397W (177), Model G392W (22) **$143.95**
Price: Nickel finish, open sight, Model GS397 (177), Model GS392 (22) **$122.00**
Price: As above with Williams peep, Model GS397W (177), GS392W (22) **$151.95**

Benjamin Pneumatic

BENJAMIN PNEUMATIC (PUMP-UP) AIR RIFLES
Caliber: 177 or 22, single shot.
Barrel: 19⅜", rifled brass.
Weight: 5½ lbs. **Length:** 36¼" overall.
Power: Under-lever pneumatic, hand pumped.
Stock: Walnut Monte Carlo stock and forend.

Sights: High ramp front, choice of fully adjustable notch rear or Williams peep.
Features: Variable velocity to 750 fps. Bolt action with ambidextrous push-pull safety. Black or nickel finish. Introduced 1991. Made in the U.S. by Benjamin Sheridan Co.
Price: Black finish, open sight, Model 397 (177), Model 392 (22) **$125.50**
Price: As above with Williams peep sight, Model 397W (177), Model 392W (22) **$155.00**
Price: Nickel finish, open sight, Model S397 (177), Model S392 (22) **$134.00**
Price: As above with Williams peep sight, Model S397W (177), Model S392W (22) **$163.75**

BSA SUPERSPORT AIR RIFLE
Caliber: 177, 22 or 25, single shot.
Barrel: 18½".
Weight: 7 lbs. **Length:** 41¾" overall.
Power: Spring piston or optional sealed gas Ram.
Stock: Walnut-stained European beech.
Sights: Globe front, adjustable open rear.
Features: Velocity up to 1010 fps (177); 830 fps (22); 700 fps (25). Adjustable two-stage trigger. Polished blue finish. Checkered pistol grip, rubber buttpad. Introduced 1991. Imported from England by Air Rifle Specialists.
Price: Spring piston model **$250.00**
Price: With sealed gas Ram **$375.00**

BSA Supersport

BSA SUPERSTAR AIR RIFLE
Caliber: 177 or 22, single shot.
Barrel: 18½".
Weight: 7¾ lbs. **Length:** 42½" overall.
Power: Under-lever cocking spring piston or optional sealed gas Ram.
Stock: Walnut-stained European beech; checkered grip, rubber buttpad.
Sights: Globe front, open adjustable rear.
Features: Velocity up to 1000 fps (177); 800 fps (22). Adjustable two-stage trigger. Polished blue finish. Introduced 1991. Imported from England by Air Rifle Specialists.
Price: Spring piston model **$385.00**
Price: With sealed gas Ram **$510.00**

CROSMAN MODEL 66 POWERMASTER
Caliber: 177 (single shot) or BB.
Barrel: 20", rifled steel.
Weight: 3 lbs. **Length:** 38½" overall.
Power: Pneumatic; hand pumped.
Stock: Wood-grained plastic; checkered p.g. and forend.
Sights: Ramp front, fully adjustable open rear.
Features: Velocity about 675 fps. Bolt action, cross-bolt safety. Introduced 1983. From Crosman.
Price: About **$42.00**
Price: Model 664X (as above, with 4x scope) **$47.00**

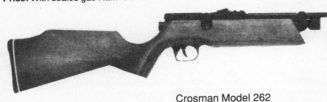

Crosman Model 262

CROSMAN MODEL 262 SPORTER AIR RIFLE
Caliber: 177 pellet, single shot.
Barrel: 21.75", rifled steel.
Weight: 4 lbs. 14 oz.
Power: CO_2 Powerlet.
Stock: Hardwood.
Sights: Fixed front, adjustable rear.
Features: Easy-loading pellet port, two-stage trigger. Also available as Youth model with overall length of 33.75". Introduced 1990. From Crosman.
Price: About **$69.00**

Crosman Model 760

CROSMAN MODEL 760 PUMPMASTER
Caliber: 177 pellets or BB, 200-shot.
Barrel: 19½", rifled steel.

CROSMAN MODEL 781 SINGLE PUMP
Caliber: 177, 5-shot pellet clip; 195-shot BB magazine.
Barrel: 19½"; steel.
Weight: 2 lbs., 14 oz. **Length:** 35.8" overall.
Power: Pneumatic, single pump.
Stock: Wood-grained plastic; checkered p.g. and forend.
Sights: Blade front, open adjustable rear.
Features: Velocity of 350-400 fps (pellets). Uses only one pump. Hidden BB reservoir holds 195 shots; pellets loaded via 5-shot clip. Introduced 1984. From Crosman.
Price: About $29.00

Weight: 2 lbs., 12 oz. **Length:** 33.5" overall.
Power: Pneumatic, hand pumped.
Features: Short stroke, power determined by number of strokes. Walnut-finished plastic checkered stock and forend. Post front sight and adjustable rear sight. Cross-bolt safety. Introduced 1966. From Crosman.
Price: About $30.00

CROSMAN MODEL 788 BB SCOUT RIFLE
Caliber: BB only, 20-shot magazine.
Barrel: 14", steel.
Weight: 2 lbs. 7 oz. **Length:** 31½" overall.
Power: Pneumatic; hand pumped.
Stock: Wood-grained ABS plastic, checkered p.g. and forend.
Sights: Blade on ramp front, open adjustable rear.
Features: Variable pump power—three pumps give MV of 330 fps, six pumps 437 fps, 10 pumps 465 fps (BBs, average). Steel barrel, cross-bolt safety. Introduced 1978. From Crosman.
Price: About $29.00

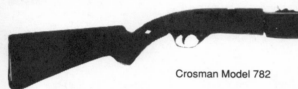

Crosman Model 782

CROSMAN MODEL 782 BLACK DIAMOND AIR RIFLE
Caliber: 177, 5-shot clip; BB, 195-shot magazine.
Barrel: 18", rifled steel.

Weight: 3 lbs.
Power: CO_2 Powerlet.
Stock: Wood-grained plastic; checkered grip and forend.
Sights: Blade front, open adjustable rear.
Features: Velocity up to 595 fps (pellets), 650 fps (BB). Black finish with white diamonds. Introduced 1990. From Crosman.
Price: About $39.95

Crosman Backpacker

CROSMAN MODEL 1389 BACKPACKER RIFLE
Caliber: 177, single shot.
Barrel: 14", rifled steel.
Weight: 3 lbs. 3 oz. **Length:** 31" overall.
Power: Hand pumped, pneumatic.
Stock: Composition, skeletal type.
Sights: Blade front, rear adjustable for windage and elevation.
Features: Velocity to 560 fps. Detachable stock. Receiver grooved for scope mounting. Metal parts blued. From Crosman.
Price: About $54.00

CROSMAN MODEL 2200 MAGNUM AIR RIFLE
Caliber: 22, single shot.
Barrel: 19", rifled steel.
Weight: 4 lbs., 12 oz. **Length:** 39" overall.
Stock: Full-size, wood-grained plastic with checkered p.g. and forend.
Sights: Ramp front, open step-adjustable rear.
Features: Variable pump power—three pumps give 395 fps, six pumps 530 fps, 10 pumps 595 fps (average). Full-size adult air rifle. Has white line spacers at pistol grip and buttplate. Introduced 1978. From Crosman.
Price: About $54.00

CROSMAN MODEL 2100 CLASSIC AIR RIFLE
Caliber: 177 pellets (single shot), or BBs, 200-shot BB magazine.
Barrel: 21", rifled.
Weight: 4 lbs., 13 oz. **Length:** 39¾" overall.
Power: Pump-up, pneumatic.
Stock: Wood-grained checkered ABS plastic.
Features: Three pumps give about 450 fps, 10 pumps about 755 fps (BBs). Cross-bolt safety; concealed reservoir holds over 200 BBs. From Crosman.
Price: About $54.00

Daisy Model 840

DAISY MODEL 840
Caliber: 177 pellet single shot; or BB 350-shot.
Barrel: 19", smoothbore, steel.

Weight: 2.7 lbs. **Length:** 36.8" overall.
Stock: Moulded wood-grain stock and forend.
Sights: Ramp front, open, adjustable rear.
Features: Single pump pneumatic rifle. Muzzle velocity 335 fps (BB), 300 fps (pellet). Steel buttplate; straight pull bolt action; cross-bolt safety. Forend forms pump lever. Introduced 1978. From Daisy Mfg. Co.
Price: About $38.00

Daisy Red Ryder

Weight: 2.2 lbs. **Length:** 35.4" overall.
Stock: Walnut stock burned with Red Ryder lariat signature.
Sights: Post front, adjustable V-slot rear.
Features: Walnut forend. Saddle ring with leather thong. Lever cocking. Gravity feed. Controlled velocity. One of Daisy's most popular guns. From Daisy Mfg. Co.
Price: About $41.00

DAISY 1938 RED RYDER CLASSIC
Caliber: BB, 650-shot repeating action.
Barrel: Smoothbore steel with shroud.

Daisy Model 1894

DAISY/POWER LINE 130 AIR RIFLE
Caliber: 177, single shot.
Barrel: 18", rifled steel.
Weight: 5.9 lbs. **Length:** 41" overall.
Power: Spring-air, barrel cocking.
Stock: European-style hardwood.
Sights: Hooded front with blade on ramp, micrometer adjustable open rear.
Features: Velocity up to 800 fps. Introduced 1990. Imported from Spain by Daisy Mfg. Co.
Price: About **$155.00**

DAISY/POWER LINE 753 TARGET RIFLE
Caliber: 177, single shot.
Barrel: 20.9", Lothar Walther.
Weight: 6.4 lbs. **Length:** 39.75" overall.
Power: Recoilless pneumatic, single pump.
Stock: Walnut with adjustable cheekpiece and buttplate.
Sights: Globe front with interchangeable inserts, diopter rear with micro. click adjustments.
Features: Includes front sight reticle assortment, web shooting sling. From Daisy Mfg. Co.
Price: About **$325.00**

DAISY MODEL 1894
Caliber: BB, 40-shot magazine.
Barrel: 17.5".
Weight: 2.2 lbs. **Length:** 39.5" overall.
Power: Spring air.
Stock: Moulded woodgrain plastic.
Sights: Blade on ramp front, adjustable open rear.
Features: Velocity 300 fps. Side loading port; slide safety; die-cast receiver. Made in U.S. From Daisy Mfg. Co.
Price: **$45.00**

DAISY/POWER LINE 853
Caliber: 177 pellets.
Barrel: 20.9"; 12-groove rifling, high-grade solid steel by Lothar Walther™, precision crowned; bore size for precision match pellets.
Weight: 5.08 lbs. **Length:** 38.9" overall.
Power: Single-pump pneumatic.
Stock: Full-length, select American hardwood, stained and finished; black buttplate with white spacers.
Sights: Globe front with four aperture inserts; precision micrometer adjustable rear peep sight mounted on a standard 3/8" dovetail receiver mount.
Features: Single shot. From Daisy Mfg. Co.
Price: About **$200.00**

Daisy/Power Line 860

DAISY/POWER LINE 860 PUMP-UP AIRGUN
Caliber: 177 (pellets), BB, 100-shot BB magazine.
Barrel: Rifled steel with shroud.

DAISY/POWER LINE 880 PUMP-UP AIRGUN
Caliber: 177 pellets, BB.
Barrel: Rifled steel with shroud.
Weight: 4.5 lbs. **Length:** 37¾" overall.
Power: Pneumatic pump-up.
Stock: Wood-grain moulded plastic with Monte Carlo cheekpiece.
Sights: Ramp front, open rear adjustable for elevation.
Features: Crafted by Daisy. Variable power (velocity and range) increase with pump strokes. 10 strokes for maximum power. 100-shot BB magazine. Cross-bolt trigger safety. Positive cocking valve. From Daisy Mfg. Co.
Price: About **$54.00**

Weight: 4.18 lbs. **Length:** 37.4" overall.
Power: Pneumatic pump-up.
Stock: Moulded wood-grain with Monte Carlo cheekpiece.
Sights: Ramp and blade front, open rear adjustable for elevation.
Features: Velocity from 315 fps (two pumps) to 650 fps (10 pumps). Shoots BBs or pellets. Heavy die-cast metal receiver. Cross-bolt trigger-block safety. Introduced 1984. From Daisy Mfg. Co.
Price: About **$52.00**

DAISY/POWER LINE 922
Caliber: 22, 5-shot clip.
Barrel: Rifled steel with shroud.
Weight: 4.5 lbs. **Length:** 37¾" overall.
Stock: Moulded wood-grained plastic with checkered p.g. and forend, Monte Carlo cheekpiece.
Sights: Ramp front, fully adjustable open rear.
Features: Muzzle velocity from 270 fps (two pumps) to 530 fps (10 pumps). Straight-pull bolt action. Separate buttplate and grip cap with white spacers. Introduced 1978. From Daisy Mfg. Co.
Price: About **$65.00**
Price: Models 970/920 (same as Model 922 except with hardwood stock and forend), about **$100.00**

Daisy/Power Line 7856

DAISY/POWER LINE EAGLE 7856 PUMP-UP AIRGUN
Caliber: 177 (pellets), BB, 100-shot BB magazine.
Barrel: Rifled steel with shroud.

Weight: 2¾ lbs. **Length:** 37.4" overall.
Power: Pneumatic pump-up.
Stock: Moulded wood-grain plastic.
Sights: Ramp and blade front, open rear adjustable for elevation.
Features: Velocity from 315 fps (two pumps) to 650 fps (10 pumps). Finger grooved forend. Cross-bolt trigger-block safety. Introduced 1985. From Daisy Mfg. Co.
Price: With 4x scope, about **$39.00**

Daisy Model 95

DAISY/YOUTH LINE RIFLES
Model:	95	111	105
Caliber:	BB	BB	BB
Barrel:	18"	18"	13½"
Length:	35.2"	34.3"	29.8"
Power:	Spring	Spring	Spring
Capacity:	700	650	400
Price: About	$37.00	$30.00	$25.00

Features: Model 95 stock and forend are wood; 105 and 111 have plastic stocks. From Daisy Mfg. Co.

El Gamo 126

"GAT" AIR RIFLE
Caliber: 177, single shot.
Barrel: 17¼" cocked, 23¼" extended.
Weight: 3 lbs.
Power: Spring piston.
Stock: Composition.
Sights: Fixed.
Features: Velocity about 450 fps. Shoots pellets, darts, corks. Imported from England by Stone Enterprises, Inc.
Price: **$34.95**

HAENEL MODEL 110 AIR RIFLE
Caliber: 177, single shot.
Barrel: 16.7".
Weight: 6.6 lbs.
Power: Spring-piston, barrel cocking.
Stock: Walnut-stained beech with cheekpiece and buttpad.
Sights: Hooded front, click rear adjustable for windage and elevation.
Features: Velocity 575 fps. Adjustable trigger, automatic safety. Imported from Germany by GSI, Inc.
Price: **$199.00**

EL GAMO 126 SUPER MATCH TARGET RIFLE
Caliber: 177, single shot.
Barrel: Match grade, precision rifled.
Weight: 10.6 lbs. **Length:** 43.8" overall.
Power: Single pump pneumatic.
Stock: Match-style, hardwood, with stippled grip and forend.
Sights: Hooded front with interchangeable elements, fully adjustable match rear.
Features: Velocity of 590 fps. Adjustable trigger; easy loading pellet port; adjustable buttpad. Introduced 1984. Imported from Spain by Daisy Mfg. Co.
Price: About **$650.00**

FAMAS SEMI-AUTO AIR RIFLE
Caliber: 177, 10-shot magazine.
Barrel: 19.2".
Weight: About 8 lbs. **Length:** 29.8" overall.
Power: 12 gram CO_2.
Stock: Synthetic bullpup design.
Sights: Adjustable front, aperture rear.
Features: Velocity of 425 fps. Duplicates size, weight and feel of the centerfire MAS French military rifle in caliber 223. Introduced 1988. Imported from France by Century International Arms.
Price: **$262.95**

Haenel Model 120

HAENEL MODEL 410 LEVER-ACTION AIR RIFLE
Caliber: 177 (BB), 12-shot magazine optional.
Barrel: 15.7".
Weight: 6.1 lbs. **Length:** 40.5" overall.
Power: Spring-piston, underlever cocking.
Stock: Walnut-stained beech.
Sights: Hooded front, click rear adjustable for windage and elevation.
Features: Blue finish. Has scope mount on receiver. Imported from Germany by GSI, Inc.
Price: **$275.00**

HAENEL MODEL 800 MATCH AIR RIFLE
Caliber: 177, single shot.
Barrel: 14.3".
Weight: 10.8 lbs. **Length:** 42.9" overall.
Power: Spring-piston, top lever cocking.
Stock: Match-type beech wood; stippled grip and forend; adjustable cheekpiece, adjustable buttpad.
Sights: Match-type globe front, fully adjustable aperture match rear.
Features: Conforms to UIT design regulations. Sight radius adjustable from 31.8" to 33.2". Imported from Germany by GSI, Inc.
Price: **$995.00**

HAENEL MODEL 120 AIR RIFLE
Caliber: 177, single shot.
Barrel: 19.6".
Weight: 8.1 lbs. **Length:** 46.6" overall.
Power: Spring-piston, barrel cocking.
Stock: Walnut-stained beech with Monte Carlo comb, cheekpiece.
Sights: Match type; detachable globe front with post, micrometer rear adjustable for windage and elevation.
Features: Velocity to 900 fps. Adjustable trigger, automatic safety, rubber recoil pad. Imported from Germany by GSI, Inc.
Price: **$359.00**
Price: Model 120S (as above except has checkered walnut stock) . **$429.00**

HAENEL MODEL 600 MATCH AIR RIFLE
Caliber: 177, single shot.
Barrel: 16.5".
Weight: 8.8 lbs. **Length:** 42.1" overall.
Power: Spring-piston, side lever cocking.
Stock: Match style of walnut-stained beech; Monte Carlo comb, stippled grip, adjustable rubber buttpad.
Sights: Match type; globe front, micrometer diopter rear adjustable for windage and elevation.
Features: Adjustable trigger; integral scope mount. Imported from Germany by GSI, Inc.
Price: **$439.00**

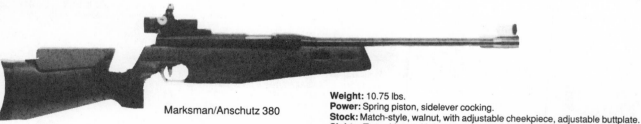

Marksman/Anschutz 380

MARKSMAN/ANSCHUTZ MODEL 380 MATCH AIR RIFLE
Caliber: 177, single shot.
Barrel: 20.75".

Weight: 10.75 lbs.
Power: Spring piston, sidelever cocking.
Stock: Match-style, walnut, with adjustable cheekpiece, adjustable buttplate.
Sights: Tunnel front with interchangeable inserts, match diopter rear.
Features: Velocity of 600-640 fps. Fully adjustable trigger. Recoilless and vibration free. Introduced 1990. Imported from Germany by Marksman Products.
Price: Right-hand **$1,000.00**
Price: Left-hand **$1,050.00**

AIRGUNS—LONG GUNS

MARKSMAN 28 INTERNATIONAL AIR RIFLE
Caliber: 177, single shot.
Barrel: 17".
Weight: 5¾ lbs.
Power: Spring-air, barrel cocking.
Stock: Hardwood.
Sights: Hooded front, adjustable rear.
Features: Velocity of 580-620 fps. Introduced 1989. Imported from Germany by Marksman Products.
Price: **$195.00**

MARKSMAN 56-FTS FIELD TARGET RIFLE
Caliber: 177, single shot.
Barrel: 19⅝".
Weight: 8.8 lbs.
Power: Spring-air, barrel cocking.
Stock: Hardwood with stippled grip; ambidextrous, with adjustable cheekpiece,

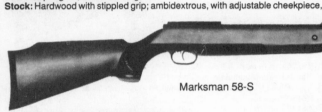

Marksman 58-S

MARKSMAN 58-S SILHOUETTE RIFLE
Caliber: 177, single shot.
Barrel: 16".

MARKSMAN MODEL 60 AIR RIFLE
Caliber: 177, single shot.
Barrel: 18.5", rifled.
Weight: 8.9 lbs. **Length:** 44.75" overall.
Power: Spring piston, under-lever cocking.
Stock: Walnut-stained beech with Monte Carlo comb, hand-checkered pistol grip, rubber butt pad.
Sights: Blade front, open, micro. adjustable rear.
Features: Velocity of 810-840 fps. Automatic button safety on rear of receiver. Receiver grooved for scope mounting. Fully adjustable Rekord trigger. Intro

MARKSMAN 70T AIR RIFLE
Caliber: 177, 20 or 22, single shot.
Barrel: 19.75".
Weight: 8 lbs. **Length:** 45.5" overall.
Power: Spring air, barrel cocking.
Stock: Stained hardwood with Monte Carlo cheekpiece, rubber buttpad, cut checkered p.g.
Sights: Hooded front, open fully adjustable rear.
Features: Velocity of 910-940 fps (177), 810-840 fps (20), 740-780 fps (22); adjustable Rekord trigger. Introduced 1988. Imported from Germany by Marksman Products.
Price: 177 (Model 70T) **$315.00**
Price: 20 (Model 72) **$325.00**
Price: (Model 71) **$270.00**

Marksman 55T Air Rifle
Similar to the Model 70T except has uncheckered hardwood stock, no cheekpiece, plastic buttplate. Adjustable Rekord trigger. Overall length is 45.25", weight is 7½ lbs. Available in 177-caliber only.
Price: **$270.00**
Price: Model 59T (as above, carbine) **$270.00**

Marksman 1790

MARKSMAN 40 INTERNATIONAL AIR RIFLE
Caliber: 177, single shot.
Barrel: 18⅜".
Weight: 7⅓ lbs.
Power: Spring-air, barrel cocking.
Stock: Hardwood.
Sights: Hooded front, adjustable rear.
Features: Velocity of 700-720 fps. Introduced 1989. Imported from Germany by Marksman Products.
Price: **$215.00**

adjustable buttplate.
Sights: None furnished.
Features: Velocity of 910-940 fps. Introduced 1989. Imported from Germany by Marksman Products.
Price: **$425.00**

Weight: 8.5 lbs.
Power: Spring-air, barrel cocking.
Stock: Hardwood with stippled grip; ambidextrous.
Sights: None furnished.
Features: Velocity 910-940 fps. Adjustable Rekord trigger. Removable full-length barrel sleeve. Introduced 1989. Imported from Germany by Marksman Products.
Price: **$375.00**

Marksman Model 60

duced 1990. Imported from Germany by Marksman Products.
Price: **$399.00**
Price: Model 61 Carbine (14.5" barrel) **$399.00**

MARKSMAN 1740 AIR RIFLE
Caliber: 177 or 18-shot BB repeater.
Barrel: 15½", smoothbore.
Weight: 5 lbs., 1 oz. **Length:** 36½" overall.
Power: Spring, barrel cocking.
Stock: Moulded high-impact ABS plastic.
Sights: Ramp front, open rear adjustable for elevation.
Features: Velocity about 450 fps. Automatic safety; fixed front, adjustable rear sight; positive feed BB magazine; shoots 177-cal. BBs, pellets and darts. From Marksman Products.
Price: **$47.00**
Price: Model 1780 (deluxe sights, rifled barrel, shoots only pellets) . . **$60.00**

MARKSMAN 1750 BB BIATHLON REPEATER RIFLE
Caliber: BB, 18-shot magazine.
Barrel: 15", smoothbore.
Weight: 4.7 lbs.
Power: Spring piston, barrel cocking.
Stock: Moulded composition.
Sights: Tunnel front, open adjustable rear.
Features: Velocity of 450 fps. Automatic safety. Positive Feed System loads a BB each time gun is cocked. Introduced 1990. From Marksman Products.
Price: **$53.50**

MARKSMAN 1790 BIATHLON TRAINER
Caliber: 177, single shot.
Barrel: 15", rifled.
Weight: 4.7 lbs.
Power: Spring-air, barrel cocking.
Stock: Synthetic.
Sights: Hooded front, match-style diopter rear.
Features: Velocity of 450 fps. Endorsed by the U.S. Biathlon Team. Introduced 1989. From Marksman Products.
Price: **$67.00**

RWS/DIANA MODEL 24 AIR RIFLE
Caliber: 177, 22, single shot.
Barrel: 17", rifled.
Weight: 6 lbs. **Length:** 42" overall.
Power: Spring air, barrel cocking.
Stock: Beech.
Sights: Hooded front, adjustable rear.
Features: Velocity of 700 fps (177). Easy cocking effort; blue finish. Imported from Germany by Dynamit Nobel-RWS, Inc.
Price: **$165.00**
Price: Model 24C **$165.00**

RWS/DIANA MODEL 36 AIR RIFLE
Caliber: 177, 22, single shot.
Barrel: 19", rifled.
Weight: 8 lbs. **Length:** 45" overall.
Power: Spring air, barrel cocking.
Stock: Beech.
Sights: Hooded front (interchangeable inserts avail.), adjustable rear.
Features: Velocity of 1000 fps (177-cal.). Comes with scope mount; two-stage adjustable trigger. Imported from Germnay by Dynamit Nobel-RWS, Inc.
Price: **$300.00**
Price: Model 38 (as above, walnut stock) **$345.00**
Price: Model 36S (as above except comes with sling, swivels, barrel weight, 4x20 scope) **$345.00**
Price: Model 36 Muzzlebrake (same as Model 36 except no sights, has muzzlebrake/barrel weight) **$275.00**
Price: Model 36 Carbine (same as Model 36 except has 15" barrel) **$300.00**

RWS/DIANA MODEL 45 AIR RIFLE
Caliber: 177, single shot.
Weight: 7¾ lbs. **Length:** 46" overall.
Power: Spring air, barrel cocking.
Stock: Walnut-finished hardwood with rubber recoil pad.
Sights: Globe front with interchangeable inserts, micro. click open rear with four-way blade.
Features: Velocity of 820 fps. Dovetail base for either micrometer peep sight or scope mounting. Automatic safety. Imported from Germany by Dynamit Nobel-RWS, Inc.
Price: **$250.00**

RWS/DIANA MODEL 70 MATCH AIR RIFLE
Caliber: 177, single shot.
Barrel: 13.5".
Weight: 4.5 lbs. **Length:** 33" overall.
Power: Spring air, barrel cocking.
Stock: Beech, match-type.
Sights: Tunnel front with interchangeable inserts, fully adjustable peep rear.
Features: Velocity of 450 fps. Adjustable trigger. Designed and scaled for junior shooters. Introduced 1990. Imported from Germany by Dynamit Nobel-RWS, Inc.
Price: **$190.00**

RWS/Diana Model 26 Air Rifle
Similar to the Model 24 except weighs 6.25 lbs., gives velocity of 750 fps (177), 500 fps (22). Automatic safety, scope rail, synthetic seals.
Price: 177 or 22 . . . . **$195.00**

RWS/Diana Model 28 Air Rifle
Similar to the Model 26 except has Monte Carlo stock with cheekpiece, rubber recoil pad and two-stage trigger. Velocity of 750 fps (177), 500 fps (22).
Price: 177 or 22 . . . . **$205.00**

RWS/Diana 38

RWS/Diana Model 34 Air Rifle
Similar to the Model 24 except has 19" barrel, weighs 7.5 lbs. Gives velocity of 1000 fps (177), 800 fps (22). Adjustable trigger, synthetic seals. Comes with scope rail.
Price: 177 or 22 . . . . **$220.00**

RWS/Diana 52

RWS/DIANA MODEL 52 AIR RIFLE
Caliber: 177, 22, single shot.
Barrel: 17", rifled.
Weight: 8½ lbs. **Length:** 43" overall.
Power: Spring air, sidelever cocking.
Stock: Beech, with Monte Carlo, cheekpiece, checkered grip and forend.
Sights: Ramp front, adjustable rear.
Features: Velocity of 1100 fps (177). Blue finish. Solid rubber buttpad. Imported from Germany by Dynamit Nobel-RWS, Inc.
Price: **$390.00**
Price: Model 48 (same as Model 52 except no Monte Carlo, cheekpiece or checkering) **$350.00**

RWS/Diana Model 72 Air Rifle
Similar to the Model 70 except has recoilless action. Introduced 1990.
Price: **$340.00**

> Consult our Directory pages for the location of firms mentioned.

RWS/Diana 75 T01

RWS/Diana Model 75S T01 Air Rifle
Similar to the Model 75 T01 except has beech stock specially shaped for standing and three-position shooting. Buttplate is vertically adjustable with curved and straight spacers for individual fit, adjustable cheekpiece. Introduced 1990.
Price: Right-hand **$935.00**
Price: Left-hand **$975.00**

RWS/DIANA MODEL 75 T01 MATCH AIR RIFLE
Caliber: 177, single shot.
Barrel: 19".
Weight: 11 lbs. **Length:** 43.7" overall.
Power: Spring air, sidelever cocking.
Stock: Oil-finished beech with stippled grip, adjustable buttplate, accessory rail. Conforms to ISU rules.
Sights: Globe front with five inserts, fully adjustable match peep rear.
Features: Velocity of 574 fps. Fully adjustable trigger. Model 75 HV has stippled forend, adjustable cheekpiece. Uses double opposing piston system for recoilless operation. Imported from Germany by Dynamit Nobel-RWS, Inc.
Price: Model 75 T01 . . . . **$850.00**

CAUTION: PRICES CHANGE, CHECK AT GUNSHOP.

RWS/Diana 100

RWS/DIANA MODEL 100 MATCH AIR RIFLE
Caliber: 177, single shot.
Barrel: 19".
Weight: 11 lbs. **Length:** 43" overall.
Power: Spring air, sidelever cocking.
Stock: Walnut.
Sights: Tunnel front, fully adjustable match rear.
Features: Velocity of 580 fps. Single-stroke cocking; cheekpiece adjustable for height and length; recoilless operation. Cocking lever secured against rebound. Introduced 1990. Imported from Germany by Dynamit Nobel-RWS, Inc.
Price: Right-hand only **$850.00**

RWS GAMO CF-20 AIR RIFLE
Caliber: 177, single shot.
Barrel: 17.7".
Weight: 6.6 lbs. **Length:** 43.3" overall.
Power: Barrel cocking, spring piston.
Stock: Hardwood.
Sights: Blade on ramp front, fully adjustable open rear.
Features: Velocity to 800 fps. Cocking effort of 33 lbs. Grooved receiver, synthetic seals, dual safeties; sdjustable two-stage trigger. Imported from Spain by Dynamit Nobel-RWS, Inc.
Price: **$190.00**

RWS Gamo CF-20

RWA GAMO HUNTER 440 AIR RIFLE
Caliber: 177, single shot.
Barrel: 18".
Weight: 6.75 lbs. **Length:** 43" overall.
Power: Spring piston, barrel cocking.
Stock: Hardwood.
Sights: Hooded blade on ramp front, fully adjustable rear.
Features: Velocity 1000 fps. Monte Carlo stock with cheekpiece; scope rail; dual safeties. Imported from Spain by Dynamit Nobel-RWS.
Price: **$205.00**

RWS GAMO EXPOMATIC 2000 AIR RIFLE
Caliber: 177, 25-shot magazine.
Barrel: 17.7".
Weight: 5.5 lbs. **Length:** 40.9" overall.
Power: Barrel cocking, spring piston.
Stock: Hardwood.
Sights: Blade front, fully adjustable open rear.
Features: Velocity to 600 fps. Cocking effort of 20 lbs. Dual safeties, grooved receiver, synthetic seals. Magazine tube holds 25 pellets, loads automatically. Imported from Spain by Dynamit Nobel-RWS, Inc.
Price: **$150.00**

RWS GAMO DELTA AIR RIFLE
Caliber: 177.
Barrel: 15.73".
Weight: 5.3 lbs. **Length:** 37" overall.
Power: Barrel cocking, spring piston.
Stock: Carbon fiber.
Sights: Blade front, fully adjustable open rear.
Features: Velocity to 565 fps. Has 20-lb. cocking effort. Synthetic seal; dual

RWS Gamo Delta

safeties; grooved for scope mounting. Imported from Spain by Dynamit Nobel-RWS, Inc.
Price: **$105.00**

Sheridan CO$_2$

SHERIDAN PNEUMATIC (PUMP-UP) AIR RIFLES
Caliber: 20 (5mm), single shot.
Barrel: 19⅜", rifled brass.
Weight: 6 lbs. **Length:** 36½" overall.
Power: Under-lever pneumatic, hand pumped.
Stock: Walnut with buttplate and sculpted forend.
Sights: High ramp front, fully adjustable notch rear or Williams peep.
Features: Variable velocity to 700 fps. Bolt action with ambidextrous push-pull safety. Blue finish (Blue Streak) or nickel finish (Silver Streak). Introduced 1991. Made in the U.S. by Benjamin Sheridan Co.
Price: Blue Streak, open sight, Model CB9 . . . . **$139.95**
Price: As above with Williams peep, Model CBW9 . . . . . . **$168.95**
Price: Silver streak, open sight, Model C9 . . . . **$148.50**
Price: As above with Williams peep, Model CW9 . . . . **$177.50**

SHERIDAN CO$_2$ AIR RIFLES
Caliber: 20 (5mm), single shot.
Barrel: 19⅜", rifled brass.
Weight: 5 lbs. **Length:** 36½" overall.
Power: 12-gram CO$_2$ cylinder.
Stock: Walnut, with buttplate.
Sights: High ramp front, fully adjustable notch rear or Williams peep.
Features: Velocity to 550 fps. Gives about 40 shots per cylinder. Bolt action with ambidextrous push-pull safety. Blue finish (Blue Streak) or nickel finish (Sliver Streak). Introduced 1991. Made in the U.S. by Benjamin Sheridan Co.
Price: Blue Streak, open sight, Model FB9 . . . . **$124.00**
Price: As above with Williams peep, Model FBW9 . . . . **$153.00**
Price: Silver Streak, open sight, Model F9 . . . . **$131.95**
Price: As above with Williams peep, Model FW9 . . . . **$161.00**

Sterling HR81

Weight: 9½ lbs. (HR81), 9¾ lbs. (HR83). **Length:** 42½" overall. (HR81).
Power: Spring piston with under-barrel lever.
Stock: American walnut (HR81); HR83 has walnut with checkpiece and hand-checkered grip. Rubber buttpad.
Features: Velocity to 700 fps (177). Spring-loaded bolt action with adjustable single stage match trigger. Introduced 1983. Made in the U.S. by Benjamin Sheridan Co.

STERLING SPRING PISTON AIR RIFLES
Caliber: 177, 20, 22, single shot.
Barrel: 18½", Lothar Walther, steel.

Price: Standard models, HR81-17 (177), HR81-20 (20), HR81-22 (22) **$341.95**
Price: Deluxe models, HR83-17 (177), HR83-20 (20), HR83-22 (22) **$481.95**

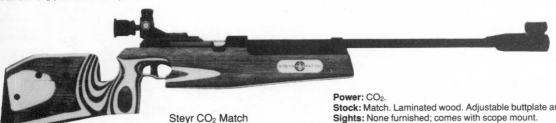

Steyr CO$_2$ Match

Power: CO$_2$.
Stock: Match. Laminated wood. Adjustable buttplate and cheekpiece.
Sights: None furnished; comes with scope mount.
Features: Velocity 577 fps. CO$_2$ cylinders are refillable; about 320 shots per cylinder. Designed for 10-meter shooting. Introduced 1990. Imported from Austria by Nygord Precision Products.

STEYR CO$_2$ MATCH AIR RIFLE MODEL 91
Caliber: 177, single shot.
Barrel: 23.75", (13.75" rifled).
Weight: 10.5 lbs. **Length:** 51.7" overall.

Price: About $1,300.00
Price: Left-hand, about $1,400.00
Price: Running Target Rifle, right-hand, about $1,325.00
Price: As above, left-hand, about $1,425.00

Theoben Classic

THEOBEN CLASSIC AIR RIFLE
Caliber: 177 or 22, single shot.
Barrel: 19½".
Weight: 7¾ lbs. **Length:** 44" overall.
Power: Gas ram piston. Variable power.
Stock: Walnut with checkered grip and forend.
Sights: None furnished. Comes with scope mount.
Features: Velocity to 1100 fps (177) and 900 fps (22). Barrel-cocking action. Polished blue finish on metal, oil-finished stock. Adjustable trigger. Imported from England by Air Rifle Specialists.
Price: $830.00
Price: For left-hand stock add $60.00
Price: Grand Prix model (same as Classic except has thumbhole stock with adjustable buttplate) $940.00
Price: For left-hand stock add $60.00

Theoben Eliminator Air Rifle
Similar to the Theoben Classic except has a longer, more sturdily built action with longer piston stroke for more power. Has walnut thumbhole stock with adjustable buttplate and comes with sling. Imported from England by Air Rifle Specialists.
Price: $1,500.00
Price: Left-hand stock, add $60.00

Theoben Imperator FT

THEOBEN IMPERATOR FT AIR RIFLE
Caliber: 177, single shot.
Barrel: 16".
Weight: 8½ lbs. **Length:** 42" overall.
Power: Under-lever cocking gas Ram piston. Variable power.
Stock: Hand-checkered European walnut, thumbhole design with adjustable forend block, roll-over cheekpiece, adjustable rubber buttpad.
Sights: None furnished. Comes with scope mount.
Features: Velocity up to 900 fps. Stippled grip and forend panels. Adjustable match-grade trigger. Imported from England by Air Rifle Specialists.
Price: $1,500.00

Theoben Imperator SLR 88 Air Rifle
Sporter version of the Theoben Imperator FT in 22-caliber only. Has conventional sporter stock of oil-finished walnut with checkered grip and forend. Has 7-shot clip. Velocity up to 725 fps. Imported from England by Air Rifle Specialists.
Price: $1,680.00

WALTHER CG90 AIR RIFLE
Caliber: 177, single shot.
Barrel: 18.9".
Weight: 10.2 lbs. **Length:** 44" overall.
Power: CO$_2$ cartridge.
Stock: Match type of European walnut; stippled grip.
Sights: Globe front, fully adjustable match rear.
Features: Uses tilting-block action. Introduced 1989. Imported from Germany by Interarms.
Price: $1,660.00

WALTHER LG-90 MATCH AIR RIFLE
Caliber: 177, single shot.
Barrel: 25.5".
Weight: 13 lbs. **Length:** 44¾" overall.
Power: Spring air, barrel cocking.
Stock: Walnut match design with stippled grip and forend, adjustable cheekpiece, rubber buttpad.
Features: Has the same weight and contours as the Walther U.I.T. rimfire target rifle. Comes complete with sights, accessories and muzzle weight. Imported from Germany by Interarms.
Price: $1,791.67

GZ SERIES 1000 PAINT BALL PISTOL
Caliber: 68.
Barrel: 6.5".
Weight: 1.5 lbs. **Length:** NA.
Power: 12-gram CO_2.
Stocks: DuPont Zytel.
Sights: V-groove sight rail.
Features: Velocity 260-290 fps. Feed port to accommodate bulk loaders. Single-action mechanism. Black or green color. From GZ Paintball Sports Products.
Price: **$89.95**

GZ CARBON SERIES 2000 PAINT BALL PISTOL
Caliber: 68.
Barrel: 6.5"; optional 8.5", 11".
Weight: 1.7 lbs. **Length:** NA.
Power: CO_2; 7-oz cannister or 12-gram capsule.
Stocks: Carbon graphite composites.
Sights: V-groove sight rail with raised front bead, dovetail rear.
Features: Velocity 260-300 fps. Feed port to accommodate bulk loaders. Double-action, semi-automatic. Black or green color. From GZ Paintball Sports Products.
Price: Quick-Change **$179.95**
Price: Constant-Air **$234.95**
Price: PRO model **$299.95**

GZ Series 1000

Model 85

Sheridan PG68-AT

Sheridan Paint Pistol

MODEL 85 PAINT BALL MACHINE PISTOL
Caliber: 9.5mm, 24-shot removable magazine.
Barrel: 5", rifled.
Weight: 25 oz. **Length:** 9⅜" overall.
Stocks: Resin.
Sights: Blade front, notch rear.
Features: Velocity of 440 fps, muzzle energy of 3.4 ft. lbs. Stainless steel impregnated in fiber-filled resin construction. Has a cyclic rate of 1200 rounds per minute; fires from open bolt; reloadable cartridges. Not a firearm by B.A.T.F. standards. Introduced 1987. Made in Canada. From Para-Ordnance, Inc.
Price: **$299.95**

SHERIDAN P68-AT PAINT PISTOL
Caliber: 68; capacity depends on ammo box size.
Barrel: 13".
Weight: About 4.7 lbs. **Length:** NA.
Power: 7-oz bulk CO_2 tank/valve combo.
Stocks: Textured composition.
Sights: None.
Features: Auto-trigger action allows pumping action slide while holding trigger to fire. Velocity reduction bolt, centerfire gas system; quick-change bolt for fast barrel cleaning. Introduced 1991. Manufactured by Benjamin Sheridan Co.
Price: **$273.95**

SHERIDAN VM68-MAGNUM PAINT PISTOL
Caliber: 68; capacity depends on ammo box size.
Barrel: 14".
Weight: About 5.9 lbs. **Length:** 25.25" overall.
Power: 3-oz. CO_2 bottle; optional rear CO_2 tank, up to 20-oz. size.
Stocks: Composition.
Sights: Optional; has sight rail with ⅜" and ¾" dovetails.
Features: Velocity from 200 to 325 fps. Semi-automatic blowback action; notch safety. Comes with one removable barrel, front 3-oz. tank, ammo box, velocity adjustment tool. Introduced 1991. Manufactured by Benjamin Sheridan Co.
Price: **$469.95**

CONSULT
Shooter's Marketplace
Page 225, This Issue

SHERIDAN PAINT PISTOL
Caliber: 68 (paint balls), 10-shot magazine.
Barrel: 6½".
Weight: 36 oz. **Length:** 9" overall.
Power: 12-gram CO_2.
Stocks: Smooth wood with thumbrest.
Sights: Bead front, adjustable rear.
Features: Shoots 68-cal. paint balls; uses gravity-feed magazine. Comes with Rapid Fire Pump Kit. Manufactured by Benjamin Sheridan Co.
Price: **$115.95**

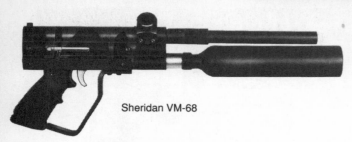

Sheridan VM-68

SHERIDAN VM 68 PAINT PISTOL
Caliber: 68, 45-shot capacity.
Barrel: 6⅜", 10".
Weight: 4 lbs., 8 oz. (6⅜" bbl.). **Length:** 14¾" overall (6⅜" bbl.).
Power: 12-gram CO_2 Quick Change, 3.5 or 7-oz. CO_2 tank.
Stock: Checkered black plastic; CAR-15 retractable stock and wire frame stock optional.
Sights: Optional.
Features: Four power settings from 200 to 325 fps. Semi-automatic blowback action. Notch safety. Comes with one removable barrel, one constant air tank, ammo box, velocity adjustment tool. Introduced 1991. Manufactured by Benjamin Sheridan Co.
Price: $379.95

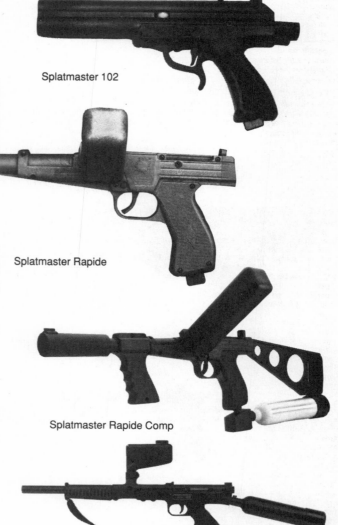

Splatmaster 102

Splatmaster Rapide

Splatmaster Rapide Comp

SPLATMASTER® 102 MARKING PISTOL
Caliber: 68 (paint balls), 10-shot magazine.
Barrel: 6½".
Weight: 1.9 lbs. **Length:** 13⅛" overall.
Power: 12.5-gram CO_2 cylinder.
Stocks: Checkered fiber reinforced plastic.
Sights: Open, fixed.
Features: Velocity about 260 fps. Shoots 68-cal. paint balls. Made of fiber reinforced plastic with an aluminum valve system. Moulded in green. Gives about 30 shots per CO_2 cylinder. Introduced 1983. From National Survival Game, Inc.
Price: $90.00

SPLATMASTER® RAPIDE™ SEMI-AUTO PISTOL
Caliber: 68, 20-shot spindle magazine.
Barrel: 6½".
Weight: 1.6 lbs. **Length:** 13" overall.
Power: 12-gram CO_2.
Stocks: Checkered fiber reinforced plastic.
Sights: Open, fixed.
Features: Velocity about 270 fps. New semi-automatic brass valve system. No cocking necessary. Made of fiber reinforced plastic moulded in green or blue. Gives about 20 shots per CO_2 capsule. Introduced 1988. From National Survival Game, Inc.
Price: $108.00

SPLATMASTER® RAPIDE™ COMP SEMI-AUTO PISTOL
Caliber: 68, 40-shot spindle magazine.
Barrel: 8½".
Weight: 4 lbs., 6 oz. **Length:** 26½" overall.
Power: 7-oz. refillable CO_2 cannister.
Stock: Checkered fiber reinforced plastic p.g. and foregrip.
Sights: Open, fixed.
Features: Velocity about 275 fps. Semi-automatic action. Gives about 350 shots per cannister. Barrel lined with brass for better accuracy. Brass valve system. Introduced 1989. From National Survival Game, Inc.
Price: $228.00

TIPPMANN MODEL 68-SPECIAL AUTO
Caliber: 68, 50-shot magazine.
Barrel: 11".
Weight: 4.8 lbs. **Length:** 32" overall.
Power: CO_2, 7-oz. siphon cylinder.
Stock: Cylinder forms stock.
Sights: Fixed.
Features: Velocity of about 250 fps. Semi-auto has cyclic rate of 300 r.p.m.; gives about 225 shots per CO_2 cylinder. From Tippmann Pneumatics, Inc.
Price: $389.00

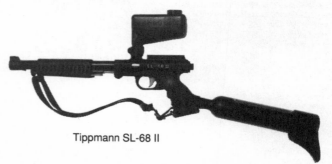

Tippmann 68-Special

Tippmann SL-68 II

TIPPMANN MODEL SL-68 II PUMP
Caliber: 68, 40+ shot magazine.
Barrel: 11".
Weight: 4 lbs. **Length:** 27" overall.
Power: CO_2, 7-oz. cylinder.
Stock: CO_2 cylinder forms stock.
Sights: Post front, notch rear grooved for spare mount.
Features: Velocity about 250 fps. Pump-action, gives about 300 shots per cylinder. From Tippmann Pneumatics, Inc.
Price: $275.00

CAUTION: PRICES CHANGE, CHECK AT GUNSHOP.

A

A.A. Arms, Inc. 4811 Persimmon Court, Monroe, NC 28110/704-289-5356/FAX: 704-289-5859

Accu-Tek, 4525 Carter Ct., Chino, CA 91710/714-627-2404

Accuracy Gun Shop, 1240 Hunt Ave., Columbus, GA 31907/404-561-6386

Accuracy Gun Shop, Inc., 5903 Boulder Highway, Las Vegas, NV 89122/702-458-3330

Accurate Plating & Weaponry, 1937 East Calumet St., Clearwater, FL 34625/813-449-9112

Action Arms Ltd., P.O. Box 9573, Philadelphia, PA 19124/215-744-0100

Adventure A.G.R., 3040 Sashabaw Rd., Waterford, MI 48329/313-673-3090

Ahlman's Custom Gun Shop, Inc., Rt. 1, Box 20, Morristown, MN 55052/507-685-4244

Aimpoint U.S.A., 580 Herndon Parkway, Suite 500, Herndon, VA 22070/703-471-6828

Aimtech Mount Systems, 101 Inwood Acres, Thomasville, GA 31792/912-226-4313

Air Arms (See Air Rifle Specialists)

Air Gun Rifle Repair, 6420 1st Ave. W., Sebring, FL 33870/813-655-0516

Air Gun Shop, The, 2312 Elizabeth St., Billings, MT 59102/406-656-2983

Air Rifle Specialists, 311 East Water St., Elmira, NY 14901/607-734-7340

Air Venture Air Guns, 9752 Flower St., Bellflower, CA 90706/213-867-6355

Airgun Centre, Ltd., 3230 Garden Meadow Dr., Lawrenceburg, IN 47025/812-637-1463

Airgun Repair Centre, Ltd., P.O. Box 6249, Cincinnati, OH 45206-0249/812-637-1463

Airgun Repair Specialists, 2709 S. Marshall St., Denver, CO 80227/303-980-9080

Airport Sports Shop, Inc., 585 Kelly Blvd., North Attleboro, MA 02760/617-695-7071

Alexander, Gunsmith, W.R., 3795 Forsythe Way, Tallahassee, FL 32308/904-893-1847

All Game Sport Center, 6076 Guinea Pike, Milford, OH 45150/513-575-0134

Allen County Gun Works, 900 E. Pettit Ave., Ft. Wayne, IN 46806/219-744-5690

Allen's, 412 Windsor Dr., Birmingham, AL 35209/205-879-6528

Allison & Carey Gun Works, 10218 S.E. Powell Blvd., Portland, OR 97266/503-760-3388

Alpine Arms Corp., 6716 Fort Hamilton Pkwy., Brooklyn, NY 11219/718-833-2228

RAI's Gun & Reel Shop, Inc., 318 E. Front St., North Platte, NE 69101/308-534-2660

A&M Sales, 23 W. North Ave., North Lake, IL 60164/708-562-8190

AMAC (American Military Arms Corp.), 2202 Redmond Rd., Jacksonville, AR 72076/501-982-1633

American Arms, Inc., 715 E. Armour Rd., N. Kansas City, MO 64116/816-474-3161/FAX: 816-474-3161

American Derringer Corp., 127 N. Lacy Dr., Waco, TX 76705/817-799-9111

Ammo Load, Inc., 1560 E. Edinger, Suite G, Santa Ana, CA 92705/714-558-8858

AMT (Arcadia Machine & Tool, Inc.), 6226 Santos Diaz St., Irwindale, CA 91702/818-334-6629

Anderson, Inc., Andy, 2125 Northwest Expressway, Oklahoma City, OK 73112/405-842-3305

Anderson Manufacturing Co., Inc., 2741 N. Crosby Rd., Oak Harbor, WA 98277/206-675-7300

Anschutz (See Precision Sales Intl., Inc.)

Apple Town Gun Shop, Rt. 104, Williamson, NY 14589/315-589-3311

Argonaut Gun Shop, 607 McHenry Ave., Modesto, CA 95350/209-522-5876

Arizaga (See Mandall Shooting Supplies)

Armadillo Air Gun Repair, 5892 Hampshire Rd., Corpus Christi, TX 78408/512-289-5458

Armes de Chasse, Phone: 215-388-1146 or FAX: 215-388-1147

Armoury, Inc., The, Route 202, New Preston, CT 06777/203-868-0001

Arms Corp. of America, Inc., 4424 John Ave., Baltimore, MD 21227/301-247-6200

Arms Corp. of the Phillipines (See Ruko Products)

Armsport, Inc. 3950 NW 49th St., Miami, FL 33142/305-635-7850

Armurie De L'Outaouqis, 28 Rue Bourque, Hull, Quebec, CANADA J84 181

Armurerie I.A.S. Gunshop, Inc., 470 St. Catherine St. E., Montreal Que, CANADA H1V 1Y5/514-252-1677

Arrieta (See Wingshooting Adventures)

ASI, 6226 Santos Diaz St., Irwindale, CA 91702/818-334-6629

A-Square Co., Inc., One Industrial Pk., Bedford, KY 40006/502-255-7456

Astra-Unceta Y Cia, S.A. (See Interarms)

ATIS, Armi S.A.S. (See E.A.A. Corp.)

Atlantic Guns, Inc., 944 Bonifant St., Silver Springs, MD 20910/301-585-4448/301-279-7963

Atlas Gun Repair, 4908 E. Judge Perez Dr., Violet, LA 70092/504-277-4229

Auto Electric & Parts, Inc., 24 W. Baltimore Ave., Media, PA 19063/215-565-2432

Auto-Ordnance Corp., Williams Ln., West Hurley, NY 12491/914-679-7225

Autumn Sales, Inc., 1320 Lake St., Fort Worth, TX 76102/817-335-1634

AYA (See Armes de Chasse)

B

Bachelder Master Gunmakers, 1229 Michigan N.E., Grand Rapids, MI 49503/616-459-3636

Badgers Shooters Supply, Inc., 106 S. Harding St., Owen, WI 54460/715-229-2101

Bain & Davis, 307 East Valley Blvd., San Gabriel, CA 91776/213-283-7449

Bait & Tackle Shop, The, Rt. 1, Box 5B, Fairmont, NC 26554/304-363-0183

Baity's Custom Gunworks, 414 Second St., North Wilksboro, NC 28659/919-667-8785

Baltimore Gunsmiths, 218 South Broadway, Baltimore, MD 21231/301-276-6908

Barrett Firearms Mfg., Inc., 8211 Manchester Hwy., Murfreesboro, TN 37133

Barton Sport Center, Bill, 7417 N. Milwaukee Ave., Niles, IL 60648/708-647-8585

Bausch & Lomb, Inc., 300 N. Lone Hill Ave., San Dimas, CA 91773

B&B Supply Co., 4501 Minnehaha Ave., Minneapolis, MN 56406/612-724-5230

Bear Archery Center, Inc., 440 Leonard N.W., Grand Rapids, MI 49504/616-458-2469

Beards Sport Shop, 811 Broadway, Cape Girardeau, MO 63701/314-334-2266

Bedlan's Sporting Goods, Inc., 1318 E. Street, P.O. Box 244, Fairbury, NE 68352/402-729-6112

Beeman Precision Arms, Inc., 3440-GD Airway Dr., Santa Rosa, CA 95403/707-578-7900

Bell's Gun & Sport Shop, Inc., 3309-19 Mannheim Rd., Franklin Park, IL 60131/708-678-1900

Belleplain Supply, Inc., Box 222, Handsmill Rd., Belleplain, NJ 08270/609-861-2345

Bellrose & Son, L.E., 21 Forge Pond Rd., Granby, MA 01033-0184/413-467-9695

Ben's Gun Shop, 1151 S. Cedar Ridge Rd., Duncanville, TX 75137/214-780-1807

Benchmark Guns, 1265 5th Ave., Yuma, AZ 85364/602-783-5161

Benelli Armi S.p.A. (See Sile Distributors)

Benjamin/Sheridan Co., 2600 Chicory Rd., Racine, WI 53403/414-554-7900

Benson Gun Shop, 35 Middle Country Rd., Coram L.I., NY 11727/516-736-0065

Beretta U.S.A., 17601 Beretta Dr., Accokeek, MD 20607/301-283-2191

Beretta U.S.A., c/o Bolsa Gunsmithing, 7404 Bolsa Ave., Westminster, CA 92683/714-894-9100 (California only)

Bernardelli SpA (See Magnum Research, Inc.)

Bernston Gun Shop, 925 Mississippi St., Fridley, MN 55432/612-571-1618

Bersa S.A. (See Eagle Imports)

Bethpage Bicycle Shop, Inc., 355 Broadway, Bethpage, NY 11714/516-935-9688

E. Arthur Brown, 3404 Pawnee Drive, Alexandria, MN 56308/612-762-8847

Bickford Arms, 127 N. Main St., Joplin, MO 64801/417-781-6440

Big Bear Arms, 2714 Fairmount St., Dallas, TX/214-871-7061/FAX: 214-754-0449

Billings Gunsmiths, 1940 Grand Ave., Billings, MT 59102/406-652-3104

Blaser Jagdwaffen GmbH (See Autumn Sales, Inc.)

Blue Ridge Outdoor Sports, Inc., 2314 Spartanburg Hwy., E. Flatrock, NC 28726/704-697-3006

Blount, Inc., Sporting Equipment Division, Outers/Weaver Operation, N5549 CTH "Z", Onalaska, WI 54650/608-781-3358/800-635-7656

Blythe's Sport Shop, Inc., 2810 N. Calmut Ave., Valparaiso, IN 46383/219-462-4412

Bob's Crosman Repair, 2510 E. Henry Ave., Cudahy, WI 53110/414-769-8256

Bob's Gun Shop, Georgia Manor Road, RFD #3, Milton, VT 05468/802-524-4906

Bob's Gun Shop, 8470 Edinboro Road, McKean, PA 16426/814-476-7523

Bob's Gun & Tackle Shop, (Blaustein & Reich, Inc.), 746 Granby St., Norfolk, VA 23510/804-627-8311/804-622-9786

Bob's Gunsmithing, 810 Charway Dr., Johnson City, TN 37601

Bob's Repair, 750 Contor, Idaho Falls, ID 83401/208-522-4959

Boggus Gun Shop, 1402 W. Hopkins St., San Marcos, TX 78666/512-392-3513

Bolsa Gunsmithing, 7404 Bolsa Ave., Westminster, CA 92683/714-894-9100

BOMAC Gunpar, Ltd., Postal Bag 8090, Lakefield, Ontario, CANADA K0L 2H0/705-748-4004

Boracci, E. John, Village Sport Center, 38-10 Merrick Rd., Seaford L.I., NY 11783/516-221-8229

Borgheresi, Enrique, 106 E. Tallalah, P.O. Box 8063, Greenville, SC 29604/803-271-2664

Boudreaux, Gunsmith, Preston, 412 W. School St., Lake Charles, LA 70605/318-478-8908

Bradys Sportsmans Surplus, P.O. Box 4166, Missoula, MT 59806/460-721-5500

Brazdas Top Guns, 307 Bertrand Dr., Lafayette, LA 70506/318-233-4137

Brenner Sport Shop, Charlie, 344 St. George Ave., Rahway, NJ 07065/201-382-4066

Bretton (See Mandall Shooting Supplies)

Bridge Sportsmen's Center, 1319 Spring St., Paso Robles, CA 93446/805-238-4407

BRNO (See Action Arms, Ltd.)

Broadway Arms, 4116 E. Broadway, N. Little Rock, AR 72203

Brock's Gunsmithing, Inc., North 2104 Division St., Spokane, WA 99207/509-328-9788

Browning (See page 451)

Bryco Arms, 17692 Cowan, Irvine, CA 92714/714-252-7621

Brunswick Gun Shop, 31 Bath Rd., Brunswick, ME 04011/207-729-8322

Brunton U.S.A., 620 E. Monroe Ave., Riverton, WY 82501/307-856-6559

Bryan & Associates, 201 S. Gossett St., Anderson, SC 29624/803-225-4475

Bryco Arms (See Jennings Firearms, Inc.)

BSA Guns Ltd. (See Air Rifle Specialists)

B-Square Co., 2708 St. Louis Ave., Fort Worth, TX 76110/817-923-0964

Budd's Custom Shop, Ed, 5100 Harlan Dr., El Paso, TX 79924

Buffalo Gun Center, Inc., 3385 Harlem Rd., Buffalo, NY 14225/716-833-2581

Bullseye Gun Works, 7949 E. Frontage Rd., Overland Park, KS 66204/913-648-4867

Burby, Inc. Guns & Gunsmithing, Rt. 7 South RR #3, Box 345, Middlebury, VT 05753/802-388-7365

Burgins Gun Shop, RD #1 Box 66, Sidney Center, NY 13839/607-829-8668

Burris (Canada Repairs), Harvey Trace Scope Repair, 11915-132nd Ave., Edmonton, Alberta TSE 1AB/403-454-1397

Burris Co., Inc., 331 E. 8th St., Greeley, CO 80631/303-356-1670

Burton Hardware, 200 N. Huntington, Sulphur, LA 70663/318-527-0794

Bushnell, 300 N. Lone Hill Ave., San Dimas, CA 91773/714-592-8000

B&W Gunsmithing, 505 Main Ave. N.W., Cullman, AL 35055/205-737-9595

C

Cabanas (See Mandall Shooting Supplies, Inc.)

Calico Light Weapon Systems, 405 E. 19th St., Bakersfield, CA 93305/805-323-1327

Cal's Customs, 110 E. Hawthorne, Fallbrook, CA 92028/619-728-5230

Camdex, Inc., 2330 Alger, Troy, MI 48083/313-528-2300

Cannon's Guns, Inc., 2387 Meridian Rd. Box 357, Victor, MT 59875/406-642-3937

Cape Oufitters, Rte. #2, Beuton Hill Rd., Cape Girardeau, MO 63701/314-335-1403

Capitol Sports & Western Wear, 1092 Helena Ave., Helena, MT 59601/406-443-2978

Carl's Gun Shop, Route 1, Box 131, El Dorado Springs, MO 64744/417-876-4168

Carpenters Gun Works, RD 1 Box 43D, Newton Rd., Proctorsville, VT 05153/802-226-7690

Carroll's Gun Shop, Inc., 1610 N. Alabama Rd., Wharton, TX 77488/409-532-3175

Carter's Country, 8925 Katy Freeway, Houston, TX 77024/713-461-1844

Casey's Gun Shop, 59 Des E Rables, P.O. Box 100, Rogersville, New Brunswick E0A 2T0 CANADA/506-775-6822

Catfish Guns, 900 Jeffco-Executive Park, Imperial, MO 63052/314-464-1217

CBC (See Magtech Recreational Products, Inc.)

Central Ohio Police Supply, c/o Wammes Guns, 225 South Main St., Bellefontaine, OH 43311

Century Gun Dist., Inc., 1467 Jason Rd., Greenfield, IN 46140/317-462-4524

Century Intl. Arms, Inc., 48 Lower Newton St., St. Albans, VT 05478/802-527-1252

C.G.& S. (Crescent), 2401 S. Clairbourn Ave., New Orleans, LA 70125/504-525-9752

C-H Tool & Die Corp. (See 4-D Die Co.)

Chaney Rifle Works, Tinker Street, Waldron, IN 46182/Phone and FAX: 317-525-6181

Chapuis Armes (See Armes de Chasse)

Charlie's Sporting Goods, Inc., 7401-H Menaul Blvd. N.E., Albuquerque, NM 87110/505-884-4545

Charlton Co., Ltd., M.D., Box 153, Brentwood Bay, B.C., CANADA V0S 1A0/604-652-5266

Charter Arms Corp. (CHARCO), 26 Beaver St., Ansonia, CT 06401/203-735-4686/FAX: 203-735-6569

Cheney Firearms Co., 915 E. 1050 N., Bountiful, UT 84010/801-295-4396

Cherry Corners, Inc., 11136 Congress Rd., P.O. Box 38, Lodi, OH 44254/216-948-1238

Chet Paulson Outfitters, 6409 South Sprague, Tacoma, WA 98409/206-475-4868

ChinaSports, Inc., 2010 S. Lynx Pl., Ontario, CA 91761/714-923-1411

Chipmunk (See Oregon Arms, Inc.)

Christopher Firearms Co., Inc., E., Rt. 128 & Ferry St., Miamitown, OH 45041/513-353-1321

Chung, Gunsmith, Mel, 8 Ing Rd., Kaunakakai, HI 96748/808-553-5888

Chuchill (See Ellett Brothers)

Cimarron Arms (See Uberti USA, Inc.)

Clapps Gun Shop, P.O. Box 578, Orchard Heights, VT 05301/802-254-4663

Claridge Hi-Tec, Inc., 19350 Business Ctr. Dr. Suite 200, Northridge, CA 91324/818-700-9093

Clark Custom Guns, Inc., 11462 Keatchie Rd., Keithville, LA 71047/318-925-0836

CMCI, Talcott Road, West Hartford, CT 06110/800-962-COLT

Colabaugh Gunsmith, Inc., Craig, R.D. 4, Box 4168 Gumm St., Stroudsburg, PA 18360/717-992-4499

Coleman, Inc., Ron, 1600 North I-35 #106, Carrollton, TX 75006/214-245-3030

Coliseum Gun Traders, Ltd., 1180 Hempstead Turnpike, Uniondale, NY 11553/718-833-2228

Colt Firearms (See page 451)

Colt Mfg., Inc., 150 Huyshope Ave., Hartford, CT 06010/203-236-6311

Conner, Bob, Gunsmith, 5550 South 900 East, Murray, UT 84107/801-263-3633

Cook's Shootist Supply, 1531 Mill St., Belle Fourche, SD 57717/605-892-6329

Coonan Arms, Inc., 830 Hampden Ave., St. Paul, MN 55114/612-646-6672

Cooper Arms, 4072 East Side Hwy., Stevensville, MT 59870/800-732-GUNS

Corbin Mfg. & Supply, Inc., 600 Industrial Circle, White City, OR 97503/503-826-5211

Colabaugh, Craig, R.D. #4, Box 4168, Gumm St., Stroudsburg, PA/717-992-4499

Cosmi (See Incor, Inc.)

Creekside Gun Shop, East Main Street, Holcomb, NY 14469/716-657-6131

Crosman Airguns (See page 451)

Crosman Corp., Rt. 5 and 20, E. Bloomfield, NY 14443/716-657-6161; FAX: 716-657-5405

Cumberland Arms, Rt. 1, Box 1150, Manchester, TN 37355

Cumberland Knife & Gun Works, 5661 Bragg Blvd., Fayetteville, NC 28303/919-867-0009

Custom Chronograph, Inc., 5305 Reese Hill Rd., Sumas, WA 98295/206-988-7801

Custom Firearms Shop, The, 1133 Indiana Ave., Sheboygan, WI 53081/414-457-3320

Custom Gun Service, 1104 Upas Ave., McAllen, TX 78501/512-686-4670

Custom Gun Shop, 10558 115 St., Edmonton, Alberta, CANADA T5H 3K6/403-426-4417

Custom Gun Works, 4952 Johnston St., Lafayette, LA 70503/318-984-0721

CVA (Connecticut Valley Arms Co.), Customer Service, 5988 Peachtree Corners East, Norcross, GA 30071/404-449-4687

Cylinder & Slide, Inc., 245 E. 4th St. Box 937, Fremont, NE 68025/402-721-4277

CZ (See Action Arms, Ltd.)

D

Daenzer, Charles E., 142 Jefferson Ave., Otisville, MI 48463/313-631-2415

Daewoo Precision Industries, Ltd. (See Firstshot, Inc.)

Daisy Mfg. Co., 2111 South 8th St., Rogers, AR 72756/501-636-1200

Dakota Arms, Inc., HC 55, Box 326, Sturgis, SD 57785/605-347-4686

Dale's Guns & Archery Center, 3915 Eighteenth Ave., S.W., Rochester, MN 55902/507-289-8308

Daly, Charles (See Outdoor Sports Headquarters, Inc.)

Danny's Gun Repair, 811 East Market St., Louisville, KY 40202/502-583-7100

Darnall's Gun Works, RR #3, Bloomington, IL 61704/309-379-4331

Daryl's Gun Shop, Inc., R.R. #2 Highway 30 West, State Center, IA 50247/515-483-2656

Davco Stores, 305 Broadway, Box 152, Monticello, NY 12701/914-794-5225

Davidson's Canada, 71 Princess Street, Peterborough, Ontario, CANADA K9J 6Z6/705-742-5408

Davis Industries, 15150 Sierra Bonita Ln., Chino, CA 91710/714-591-4726

D&D Sporting Goods, 108 E. Main, Tishomingo, OK 73460/405-371-3571

Dean's Place, Route 41, Box 61, Hockessin, DE 19707/302-239-5959

Deer Creek Rifle Co., Tinker Street, Waldron, IN 46182/317-525-6181

Delhi Small Arms, 22B Argyle Ave., Delhi, Ontario, CANADA N4B 1J3/519-582-0522

Delisle Thompsoon Sport Goods, Ltd., 1814A Loren Ave., Saskatoon, Saskatchewan, CANADA/306-653-2171

Denver Arms, Ltd., P.O. Box 4640, Pagosa Springs, CO 81157/303-731-2295

Denver Instrument Company, 6542 Fig St., Arvada, CO 80004/800-321-1135

Desert Industries, Inc., 3245 E. Patrick Ln., Suite H, Las Vegas, NV 89120/702-597-1066

Destination North Software, 804 Surry Rd., Wenatchee, WA 98801/501-662-6602

D&H Precision Tooling, 7522 Barnard Mill Rd., Ringwood, IL 60072/815-653-4011

Diana (See Dynamit Nobel-RWS, Inc.)

Dillon Precision Prods., Inc., 7442 E. Butherus Dr., Scottsdale, AZ 85260/602-948-8009

Dixie Gun Works, Inc., Hiway 51 S., Union City, TN 38261

D&J Coleman Service, 4811 Guadalupe Ave., Hobbs, NM 88240/505-392-5318

D&L Gunsmithing/Guns & Ammo, 3615 Summer Ave., Memphis, TN 38122/901-327-4384

D&L Shooting Supplies, 2663 W. Shore Rd., Warwick, RI 02886/401-738-1889

D Max Industries, 1701 W. Valley Hwy. N., Auburn, WA 98071/206-939-5137

Dollar Drugs, Inc., 15A West 3rd, Lee's Summit, MO 64063/816-524-7600

Don & Tim's Gun Shop, 3724 Northwest Loop 410 and Fredricksburg, San Antonio, TX 78229/512-736-0263

Don's Gun Sales, 8517 Perrin Bettel Road, San Antonio, TX 78217/512-657-4550

Don's Gun Shop, 1085 Tunnel Rd., Ashville, NC 28805/704-298-4867

Don's Sport Shop, Inc., 7803 E. McDowell Rd., Scottsdale, AZ 85257/602-946-5313

Dorn's Outdoor Center, 4388 Mercer University Drive, Macon, GA 31206/912-474-1991

Down Under Gunsmiths, 205 Driveway, Fairbanks, AK 99701/907-456-8500

Dress Ranch & Home, Inc., 1147 W. Broadway, Moses Lake, WA 98837/509-765-9231

Dubbs, Gunsmith, Dale R., Box 54, Route 1, Hwy. 90, Seminole, AL 36574/205-946-3245

Dynamit Nobel-RWS, Inc., 105 Stonehurst Ct., Northvale, NJ 07647/201-767-1995

E

Eagle Arms, Inc., 131 E. 22nd Ave., Coal Valley, IL 61240/309-799-5619

Eagle Gun Works, 15866 Main St., La Puente, CA 91744/818-333-4991

Eagle Imports, Inc., c/o Bolsa Gunsmithing, 7404 Bolsa Ave., Westminster, CA 92683/714-894-9100

Eagle Imports, Inc., c/o Walker Arms Co., 499 Dallas Road 820, Selma, AL 36701/205-872-6231

Ed's Gun & Tackle Shop, Inc., 2727 Canton Rd. (Hwy. 5), Marietta, GA 30066/404-425-8461

Elbe Arms Co., Inc., 610 East 27th St., Cheyenne, WY 82001/307-634-5731

Ellett Bros., Churchill Repairs, 201 Clark St., Chapin, SC 29036/803-345-2199

Emerging Technologies, Inc., 716 Main St., Little Rock, AR 72201

EMF Co., Inc., 1900 East Warner Ave. 1-D, Santa Ana, CA 92705/714-261-6611/FAX: 714-756-0133

Enstad & Douglas, 211 Hedges, Oregon City, OR 97045/503-655-3751

Epps, Ellwood, Highway 11 N. R.R. 3, Orillia, Ontario, CANADA L0K 1G0/705-689-5333

Erma Werke GmbH (See Mandall Shooting Supplies, Inc./PSI, Inc.)

Ernie's Gun Shop, Ltd., 1031 Marion St., Winnipeg, Manitoba, CANADA R2J 0L1/204-233-1928

Euroarms of America, Inc., 208 East Piccadilly, Winchester, VA, 22601/703-662-1863

E.A.A. (European American Armory Corp.), 4480 E. 11th Ave., Hialeah, FL 33013

European Arms Dist. Ltd., 275 Pemberton Ave., No. Vancouver, British Columbia, Canda V7P 2R4/604-984-9508/FAX:604-984-4435

Europtik, Ltd., 5437 Laurel Canyon Blvd., North Hollywood, CA 91617/818-761-1593

Eversull Gunsmith, Inc., K., 4800 Hwy. 121, Boyce, LA 71409/318-793-8728

Ewell Cross Gun Shop, Inc., 8240 Interstate 30W, Ft. Worth, TX 76108/817-246-4622

Eyster Heritage Gunsmiths, Inc., Ken, 6441 Bishop Rd., Centerburg, OH 43011/614-625-6131

F

Fabarm SpA (See St. Lawrence Sales, Inc.)

Fabrica D'Armi Sabatti S.R.L. (See E.A.A. Corp.)

Famas (See Century International Arms, Inc.)

FAS (See Mandall Shooting Supplies, Inc./Nygord Precision Products)

Fausti Stefano (See American Arms, Inc.)

F&D Guns, 5140 Westwood Drive, Harvester, MO 63303/314-441-5897

Feather Industries, Inc., 2300 Central Ave. #K, Boulder, CO 80301/303-442-7021

Federal Eng. Corp., 2335 S. Michigan Ave., Chicago, IL 60616/312-842-1063

Federal Firearms Co., Inc., Box 145, Thom's Run Rd., Oakdale, PA 15071/412-221-0300

Federal Ordnance, 1443 Potrero Ave., So. El Monte, CA 91733/818-350-4161

FEG (See K.B.I., Inc.)

Felton, James, Custom Gunsmith, 1033 Elizabeth St., Eugene, OR 97402/503-689-1687

FWB (Feinwerkbau) (See Beeman Precision Arms, Inc.)

FERLIB (See Moore & Company, William Larkin)

Fidler's Firearms, 12441-S 450 East, Lafayette, IN 47905/317-538-3770

Fiocchi of America, Nygord Precision Products, 15735 Starthern Unit 5, Van Nuys, CA 91406/818-352-3027

Firearms Co. Ltd./Alpine (See Mandall Shooting Supplies, Inc.)

Firearms Repair & Refinish Shoppe, 639 Hoods Mill Rd., Woodbine, MD 21797/301-795-5859

Firearms Service Center, 2140 Old Shepherdsville Rd., Louisville, KY 40218/502-458-1148

Firearms Unlimited, 4360 Corporate Square, Naples, FL 33942/813-643-2922

Firstshot, Inc., 4101 Far Green Rd., Harrisburg, PA 17110/717-238-2575

Fischer Gunsmithing, Inc., Steve, 4235 S.W. 75th Ave., Miami, FL 33155/305-261-1820

Fishing Corner, The, 14604 Pacific Hwy. S., Seattle, WA 98168/206-246-8653

Fix Gunshop, Inc., Michael D., R.D. 11, Box 192, Reading, PA 19607/215-775-2067

Flintrop Arms Corp., 4034 W. National Ave. West, Milwaukee, WI 53215/414-383-2626

FN Herstal (See GSI, Inc.)

Foothills Shooting Center, 7860 W. Jewell Ave., Lakewood, CO 80226/303-985-4417

Forster Products, Inc., 82 E. Lanark Ave., Lanark, IL 61046/815-493-6360/FAX: 815-493-2371

4-D Die Co./C-H Tool & Die, 711 N. Sandusky St., Mount Vernon, OH 43050/614-397-7214/FAX: 614-397-6600

Fox & Company, 2211 Dutch Valley Rd., Knoxville, TN 37918/615-687-7411

Francotte & CIE S.A., Auguste (See Armes de Chasse)

Franchi S.p.A., Luigi (See American Arms, Inc.)

Franklin Sports, Inc., 575 Hawthorne Ave., Athens, GA 30606/404-543-7803

Fred's Gun Shop, 1364 Ridgewood Dr., Mobile, AL 36608/205-344-1079

Freedom Arms Reworks Dept., #1 Freedom Ln., Freedom, WY 83120

Freeland Scope Stands, Inc., 3737 14th Ave., Rock Island, IL 61201/309-788-7440/309-788-7449

Freer's Gun Shop, Building B-1, 8928 Spring Branch Drve, Houston, TX 77080/713-467-3016

Fremont Tool Works, 1214 Praire, Ford, KS 67842/316-369-2338 (after 5 p.m.)

Fricano, Gunsmith, J., 15258 Moreland, Grand Haven, MI 49417/616-846-4458

Friedman's Army Surplus, 2617 Nolenville Rd., Nashville, TN 37211/615-244-1653

Frontier Gun & Sport, 9 Canbero Road West, Font Hill, Ontario, CANADA L0S 1E0/416-892-6962

Frontiersman's Sports, 6925 Wayzeta Blvd., Minneapolis, MN 55426/612-544-3775

G

Galaxy Imports Ltd., Inc., 303 Sherwood, Victoria, TX 77901

Gamba S.p.A., Renato (See Gamba U.S.A.)

Gamba U.S.A., 925 Wilshire Blvd., Santa Monica, CA 90401/310-917-2255/FAX: 310-917-2253

Gamo (See Daisy Mfg. Co./Dynamit Nobel-RWS, Inc.)

Gander Mountain, Inc., P.O. Box 128, Highway W, Wilmot, WI 53192/414-862-2331

Garbi, Armas Urki (See Moore & Co., William Larkin)

Garfield Gunsmithing, 237 Wessington Ave., Garfield, NJ 07026/201-478-0171

Garrett Gunsmiths, Inc., Peter, 838 Monmouth St., Newport, KY 41071-1821/606-261-1855

Gart Brothers Sporting Goods, 1000 Broadway, Denver, CO 80203/303-861-1122

Gary's Gun Shop, 700 S. Minnesota Ave., Sioux Falls, SD 57104/605-332-6119

Gateway Shooter Supply, 10145-103rd St., Jacksonville, FL 32210/904-778-2323

Gaucher Armes S.A. (See Mandall Shooting Supplies, Inc.)

Gemini Arms Ltd., 324 Jackson Ave., Syosset, NY 11791/516-921-0134

Gene's Gunsmithing, Box 34 GRP 326 R.R. 3, Selkirk, Manitoba, CANADA R1A 2A8/204-757-2003

Gene Taylor's Sportsman Supply, Inc., 445 W. Gunnison Ave., Grand Junction, CO 81505/303-242-8165

GFR Corp., Rt. 11, Andover, NH 03216/603-735-5300

G.H. Gun Shop, 323 W. "B" St., McCook, NE 69001/308-345-1250

Gibbs Rifle Company, Inc., R.R. #2, Box 214, Hoffman Rd., Cannon Hill Industrial Park, Martinsburg, WV 25401/304-274-0458

G.I. Loan Shop, 1004 W. Second St., Grand Island, NE 68801/308-382-9573

Gilman-Mayfield, 1552 N. 1st, Fresno, CA 93703/209-237-2500

Girard, Florent, Gunsmith, 598 Verreault, Chicoutimi, Quebec, CANADA G7H 2B8/418-696-3329

Glenn's Reel & Rod Repair, 2210 E. 9th St., Des Moines, IA 50316/515-262-2990

Glock, Gesell Schaft m.b.h., P.O. Box 50, A-2232 Deutsch-Wagram, Austria (International)

Glock, Inc., 6000 Highlands Pkwy, Smyrna, GA 30082/404-447-4466

Gonic Arms, Inc., 134 Flagg Rd., Gonic, NH 03867/603-332-8456

Gordon's Wigwam, 501 S. St. Francis, Wichita, KS 67202/316-264-5311

Gorenflo Gunsmithing, 1821 State St., Erie, PA 16501/814-452-4855

Great Lakes Airguns, 6175 S. Park Ave., Hamburg, NY 14075/716-648-6666

Great Northern Guns, 2920 Tudor Rd., Anchorage, AK 99515/907-563-3006

Green Acres Sporting Goods, Inc., 8774 Normandy Blvd., Jacksonville, FL 32221/904-786-5166

Greene, Sam, 45 Floral Dr., Monticello, NY 12701/914-794-7717

Greene's Gun Shop, 4778 Monkey Hill Rd., Oak Harbor, WA 98277/206-675-3421

Grenada Gun Works, Hwy. 8 East, Grenada, MS 38901/601-226-9272

Grendel, Inc., 550 St. Johns St., Cocoa, FL 32922

Grice Gun Shop, Inc., 216 Reed St., P.O. 2028, Clearfield, PA 16830/814-765-9273

Grulla Armes (See American Arms, Inc.)

Grundman's, Inc., 75 Wildwood Ave., Rio Dell, CA 95562/707-764-5744

G&S Gunsmithing, 220 N. Second St., Eldridge, IA 52748/319-285-4153

GSI, Inc., 108 Morrow Ave., Trussville, AL 35173/205-655-8299

G.U. Inc., 4325 S. 120th, Omaha, NE 68137/402-330-4492/FAX: 402-330-8029

Gun Ace, Rt. 1, Box 376, Buena Vista, VA 24416-9605/703-261-1412

Gun Center, The, 5733 Buckeystown Pike, Frederick, MD 21701/301-694-6887

Gun City, Inc., 212 West Main, Bismarck, ND 58501/701-223-2304

Gun City USA, Inc., 573 Murfreesboro Rd., Nashville, TN 37210/615-256-6127

Gun Corral, Inc., 2827 East College Ave., Decatur, GA 30030/404-299-0288

Gun Exchange, Inc., 5317 W. 65th St., Little Rock, AR 72209/501-562-4668

Gun Hospital, The, 45 Vineyard Ave., E. Providence, RI 02914/401-438-3495

Gun Parts Corp., P.O. Box 2, West Hurley, NY 12491/914-679-2417

Gun Rack, Inc., The, 213 Richland Ave., Aiken, SC 29801/803-648-7100

Gun Room, The, 201 Clark St., Chapin, SC 29036/803-345-2199

Gun Shop, Inc., The, 8945 Biscayne Blvd., Miami Shores, FL 33138/305-757-1422

Gun Shop, The, 5550 South 900 East, Salt Lake City, UT 84117/801-263-3633

Gun South, Inc. (See GSI, Inc.)

Gun & Stuff, Inc., 3055 N. Broadway, Wichita, KS 67219/316-838-2448

Gun & Tackle Store, The, 6041 Forrest Ln., Dallas, TX 75230/214-239-8181

Gun Works, The, 4325 S. 120th St., Omaha, NE 68127/402-339-2249

Gunsmith Co., The, 3435 S. State St., Salt Lake City, UT 84115/801-467-8244

Gunsmith, Inc., The, 1410 Sunset Blvd., West Columbia, SC 29169/803-791-0250

Gunsmithing Limited, 57 Unquowa Rd., Fairfield, CT 06430/203-254-0436

Gunsmithing Specialties, Co., 110 North Washington St., Papillion, NE 68046/402-339-1222

Gun World, 392 Fifth Street, Elko, NV 89801/702-458-3330

Gustaf, Carl (See PSI, Inc.)

H

Haenel (See GSI, Inc.)

Hagstrom, E.G., 2008 Janis Dr., Memphis, TN 38116/910-398-5333

Hall Brothers Sporting Goods, 1817 4th Ave., P.O. Box 1170, Jasper, AL 35501/205-384-3463

Hallberg, Inc., Fritz, 833 SW 30th, P.O. Box 322, Ontario, OR 97914/503-889-7052

Hallowell & Co., 340 West Putnum Ave., Greenwich, CT 006830/203-869-2190/FAX: 203-869-0692

Hal's Gun Supply, 505 Main Ave., Cullman, AL 35055/205-734-7546

Hammerli (See Beeman Precision Arms, Inc./Hammerli-U.S.A./Mandall Shooting Supplies, Inc.)

Hammerli-U.S.A., 19296 Oak Grove Circle, Groveland, CA 95321/209-962-5311

Hampel's, Inc., 710 Randolph, Traverse City, MI 49684/616-946-5485

Hanus, Bill (See Precision Sports)

Harrington & Richardson (See Gun Parts Corp./parts only)

Harry's Army & Navy Store, 691 NJSH Rt. 130, Robbinsville, NJ 08691/609-585-5450

Hart & Son, Robert W., 401 Montgomery Street, Nescopeck, PA 18635/717-752-3655

Hart's Gun Supply, Ed, U.S. Route 15 N., Bath, NY 14810/607-776-4228

Harvey Enterprises, Bob, Highway 2 & 52 West, Minot, ND 58701/701-852-6168

Haskell Mfg., Inc, 399 Lester Ave., Lima, OH 45801/419-225-8297

Hatfield International, Inc., 224 N. 4th St., St. Joseph, MO 64501/816-279-8688

Hawken Shop, The, P.O. Box 593, Oak Harbor, WA 98277/206-679-4657/FAX: 206-675-1114

Heckler & Koch, Inc., 21480 Pacific Blvd., Sterling, VA 22170/703-450-1900

Heckman Arms Company, Chagrin Valley Firearms, 32 N. Main St, Chagrin, OH 44022/216-289-9182

Helwan (See Interarms)

Hemlock Gun Shop, Box 149, Rt. 590 W., Lakeville, PA 18438/717-226-9410

Hemlock Gun Shop, Star Rt. 1, Box 128, Hawley, PA 18428/717-226-9410

Henry's Airguns, 1204 W. Locust, Belvidere, IL 61008/815-547-5091

Hermanos S.A., Zabala (See American Arms, Inc.)

Herold's Gun Shoppe, 1498 E. Main Street, Box 350, Waynesboro, PA 17268/717-762-4010

Heym GmbH & Co., Friedrich Wilh. (See Heckler & Koch, Inc.)

Hill's Hardware & Sporting Goods, 1304 S. Second St., Union City, TN 38261/901-885-1510

Hill's, Inc., 1720 North Blvd., Raleigh, NC 27604/919-833-4884

Hobb's Bicycle & Gun Sales, 406 E. Broadway, Hobbs, NM 88240/505-393-9815

Hodson & Son Pell Gun Repair, 4500 S. 100 E., Anderson, IN 46013/317-643-2055

Hoffman's Gun Center, Inc., 2600 Berlin Turnpike, Newington, CT 06111/203-666-8827

Hollywood Engineering (M&M Engineering), 10642 Arminta St., Sun Valley, CA 91352/818-842-8376

Holmes Firearms Corp., Bill Holmes, 1100 E. Township, Fayetteville, AR 72703

Horchler's Gun Shop, Ratlum Mt. Rd. RFD PO, Collinsville, CT 06022/203-379-1977

Hornady Manufacturing Co., 3625 Old Potash Hwy., Grand Island, NE 68802/308-382-1390/800-338-3220

Houma Gun Works, 1520 Grand Caillou Rd., Houma, LA 70363/504-872-2782

H&R 1871, Inc., Service Dept., Industrial Rowe, Gardner, MA 01440

H-S Precision, Inc., 1301 Turbine Dr., Rapid City, SD 57701/605-341-3006

Huntington Die Specialties, 601 Oro Dam Blvd., Oroville, CA 95965/916-534-1210/FAX: 916-534-1212

Huntington Sportsman's Store, 601 Oro Dam Blvd., P.O. Box 991, Oroville, CA 95965/916-534-8000

Hutchinson's Gun Repair, 507 Clifton St., Pineville, LA 71360/318-640-4315

Hutch's, 50 E. Main St., Lehi, UT 84043/801-768-3461

I

IAI (See AMT)

Iberia Firearms, Inc., 3929 S.R. 309, Galion, OH 44833/419-468-3746

IGA (See Stoeger Industries)

IMI/Desert Eagle (See Magnum Research, Inc.)

IMI/Galil, UZI (See Action Arms, Ltd.)

IMI/Jericho (See K.B.I., Inc.)

IMI/Timberwolf (See Action Arms, Ltd./Springfield Armory, Inc.)

Imatronic, Inc., 1275 Paramount Pkwy., Batavia, IL 60510/708-406-1920

Imbert & Smithers, Inc., 1148 El Camino Real, San Carlos, CA 94070/415-593-4207

Incor, Inc., P.O. Box 132, Addison, TX 75001/214-931-3500

INDESAL (See American Arms, Inc.)

Inland Pacific Distributors, d/b/a Inland Sports, 15404-114 Ave., Edmonton, Alberta, Canada T5M 3S8/403-451-6636/FAX: 403-451-2907

Interarmco (See Interarms)

Interarms, 10 Prince St., Alexandria, VA 22314/703-548-1400

Intermountain Arms & Tackle, Inc., 105 East Idaho St., Meridian, ID 83642/208-888-4911

Intratec, 12405 SW 130th St., Miami, FL 33186/FAX: 305-253-7207

Irwin, Gunsmith, C.H.,Hartland Blvd., East Hartland, CT 06027/203-653-3901

Ithaca Aquisition Corp./Ithaca Gun Co., 891 Route 34B, King Ferry, NY 13081/315-364-7171

Iver Johnson, 2202 Redmond Rd., Jacksonville, AR 72076/501-982-1633

J

Jackalope Gun Shop, 1048 South 5th St., Douglas, WY 82633/307-358-3441

Jack First Distributors, 44633 Sierra Highway, P.O. Box 542, Lancaster, CA 93534/805-945-6981

Jack's Lock & Gun Shop, 32 4th St., Fond Du Lac, WI 54935/414-922-4420

Jacobson's Gun Center, 607 Broad Street, Story City, IA 50248/515-733-2995

Jaeger, Inc., Paul, 1 Madison Ave., Grand Junction, TN 38039/901-764-6909

Jason Empire, Inc., 9200 Cody, Overland Park, KS 66214/913-888-0220

Jay's Sports, Inc., North 88 West 15263 Main St., Menomonee Falls, WI 53051/414-251-0550

Jennings Firearms, Inc. (See Bryco)

Jensen's Custom Ammunition/Lathrops Shooting Supplies, 5146 E. Pima, Tuscon, AZ 85712/602-325-3346

J&G Gunsmithing, 625 Vernon St., Roseville, CA 95678/916-782-7075

Jim's Gun & Service Center, 514 Tenth Ave. S.E., Aberdeen, SD 57401/605-225-9111

Jim's Trading Post, #10 Southwest Plaza, Pine Bluff, AR 71603/501-534-8591

J.O. Arms & Ammunition Co., 5709 Hartsdale, Huston, TX 77036/713-789-0745/FAX: 713-789-7513

Joe's Gun Shop, 4430 14th St., Dorr, MI 49323/616-877-4615

Joe's Gun Shop, 5215 W. Edgemont Ave., Phoenix, AZ 85035/602-233-0694

John Q's Quality Gunsmithing, 5165 Auburn Blvd., Sacramento, CA 95841/916-344-7669

John's Sporting Goods, 2655 Harrison Ave. S.W., Canton, OH 44706/216-456-9100

Johnson Gunsmithing, Don, N15515 Country Rd. 566, Powers, MI 49874/906-497-5757

Johnson, Iver (See AMAC)

Johnson Service, Inc., W., 3654 N. Adrian Rd., Adrian, MI 49221/517-265-2545

Jones Gun Shop, Inc., 741 Washington Ave., Greenville, MS 38701/601-332-3181

Jordan Gun & Pawn Shop, Rt. 3, Box 19, Tifton, GA 31794/912-382-4251

Jordan Gun Shop, 28 Magnolia Dr., Tifton, GA 31794/912-382-4251

Jovino Co., Inc., John, 5 Center Market Pl., New York, NY 10013/212-925-4881

JSL (See Rogers Ltd. International)

J.T. Gunshop, Inc., d/b/a Carolina Gun & Sports, 145 Dexter Ave., Beckley, WV 25801/304-256-1217

K

Kahles Scopes, c/o Swarovski Optik, One Wholesale Way, Cranston, RI 02920/401-942-3380

Karrer's Gunatorium, 5323 N. Argonne Rd., Spokane, WA 99212/509-924-3030

Kassnar (See K.B.I., Inc.)

K.B.I., Inc., 5398 Linglestown Rd., Harrisburg, PA 17112/717-540-4645/FAX: 717-540-5801

KDF, Inc., 2485 Hwy. 46 N., Seguin, TX 78155/512-379-8141

Keeley, John L., 679 Ridge Rd., Spring City, PA 19475/215-495-6874

Keidel's Gunsmithing Service, 927 Jefferson Ave., Washington, PA 15301/412-222-6379

Keller's Co., Inc., Rt. 4, Box 1257, Burlington, CT 06013/203-583-2220

Kemp Gun Shop, 7625 W. U.S. 20, Michigan City, IN 46360/219-872-7959

Keng's Firearms Specialty, Inc., 875 Wharton Drive SW, Atlanta, GA 30336/404-691-7611/FAX: 404-505-8445

Kesselring Gun Shop, 400 Pacific Hwy., 99 North, Burlington, WA 98233/206-724-3113

Kick's Sport Center, 300 Goodge St., Claxton, GA 30417/912-739-1734

Kimel Industries, P.O. Box 335, Matthews, NC 28106/704-821-7663

King's Gun Shop, Inc., Rt. 1 Box 78, Franklin, VA 23851/804-562-4725

Kintrek, Owensboro, KY/502-686-8137

Kirkpatrick, Gunsmith, Larry, 707 79th St., Lubbock, TX 79404/806-745-5308

Kirk's Gun Shop, Inc., 3333 Yarough, El Paso, TX 79925/915-592-6401

Klelon, Gunsmith, Dave, 57 Kittleberger Park, Webster, NY 14580/716-872-2256

Klondike Arms & Antiques, 10552 115th St., Edmonton, Alberta, T5H 3K6/403-422-2223

K&M Services, 2525 Primrose Lane, York, PA 17404/717-764-1461

Kopp, Professional Gunsmith, Terry K., Hwy. 13, Lexington, MO 64067/816-259-2636

Korth (See Mandall Shooting Supplies, Inc.)

Kotila Gun Shop, Rt. #2, Box 212, Cokato, MN 55321/612-286-5636

Kowa Optimed, Inc., 20001 S. Vermont Ave., Torrance, CA 90502/310-327-1913/800-966-5692

Krico/Kriegeskorte GmbH, A. (See Mandall Shooting Supplies, Inc.)

Krieghoff International, Inc., Customer Service Manager, 7528 Easton Road, Ottsville, PA 18942/215-847-5173

L

La Armeria Metropolitana In, Ave Dediego 799 Capparra, San Juan, Puerto Rico 00921/809-782-6378

Labs Air Gun Shop, 2307 N. 62nd St., Omaha, NE 68104/402-553-0990

Laibs Gunsmithing, North Hwy. 23, R.R. 1, Spicer, MN 56288/612-796-2686

Lakefield Arms Ltd., Taylors Service Center, RR #1, Box 112, Mokane, MO 65059/314-676-5675

Lakefield Arms Ltd., c/o The Gun Room, 201 Clark St., Chapin, SC 29036/803-345-2199

Lanber Armes S.A. (See American Arms, Inc.)

L.A.R. Manufacturing, Inc., 4133 W. Farm Rd., West Jordan, UT 84088/801-255-7106

L'Armurier Alain Bouchard, Inc., 293 Rue Notre Dame, St. Chryostome Quebec J0S 1R0 CANADA

Laser Devices, Inc., 2 Harris Ct., A4, Monterey, CA 93940

Laurona Armes S.A. (See Galaxy Imports Ltd., Inc.)

Lawsons Custom Firearms, Inc., Art, 313 S. Magnolia Ave., Ocala, FL 32671/904-629-7793

Lebeau-Courally (See New England Arms, Co.)

Lee Precision, Inc., 4275 Hwy. U, Hartford, WI 53027/414-673-3075

LeFever & Sons, Inc., Frank, RD 1, Lee Center, NY 13363/315-337-6722

Leo's Custom Stocks, 1767 Washington Ave., Library, PA 15129/412-835-4126

Les Gun & Tackle Shop, 1423 New Boston Rd., Texarkana, TX 75501/214-793-2201

Leupold & Stevens, Inc., 600 NW Meadow Dr., Beaverton, OR 97006/503-646-9171

Levan's Sport Goods, 433 N. Ninth St., Lebanon, PA 17042/717-273-3148

Lewis Arms at Riley's, 1575 Hooksett Rd., Hooksett, NH 03106/603-485-7334

Lew's Mountaineer Gunsmithing, Route 2, Box 330A, Charleston, WV 25314/304-344-3745

Ljutic Industries, Inc., 732 N. 16th Ave., Suite #22, Yakima, WA 98902/509-248-0476

Ljutic Industries, Inc., Paul's Gun Shop, 307 S. Riverview Dr., E. Peoria, IL 61611

Llama (See Stoeger Industries)

L&M Firing Line, Inc., 20 S. Potomac St., Aurora, CO 80012/303-363-0041

Lock Stock & Barrel Gun Repair, Rt. 3, Box 336, Crystal Springs, MS 39059/601-8992-1267

Lock Stock & Barrel, 775 S.E. 6th St. (rear), Grants Pass, OR 97526/503-474-0775

Loftin & Taylor, 2619 N. Main St., Jacksonville, FL 32206/904-353-9634

Log Cabin Sport Shop, 8010 Lafayette Rd., Rt. 1, Lodi, OH 44254/216-948-1082

Lolo Sporting Goods, 1026 Main St., Lewiston, ID 83501/208-743-1031

Lone Star Guns, Inc., 2452 Avenue "K", Plano, TX 75074/214-424-4501

Longacres, Inc., 358 Chestnut St., Abilene, TN 79602/915-672-9521

Long Beach Uniform Co., Inc., 2789 Long Beach Blvd., Long Beach, CA 90806/213-424-0220

Long Gunsmithing Ltd., W.R., 2007 Brook Rd. North, Coburg, Ontario CANADA K9A 4W4/416-372-5955

Longs Gunsmiths, Ltd., W.R., P.O. Box 876, Cobourg, CANADA K9A 4S3/416-372-5955

Lorcin Engineering Co., Inc., 10427 San Sevaine Way Unit A, Mira Loma, CA 91752/714-360-1406/FAX:714-360-0623

Lounsbury Sporting Goods, Bob, 104 North St., Middletown, NY 10940/914-343-1808

L&S Technologies, Inc., P.O. Box 223, 101 Inwood Acres, Thomasville, GA 31792/Phone and FAX: 912-226-4313

Lutter, Robert E., 3547 Auer Dr., Ft. Wayne, IN 46835/219-485-8319

Lyman (Blackpowder Products Only), Dixon Muzzle Loading, RD 1, Box 175, Kempton, PA 19529

Lyman Products Corp., 147 West St., Middlefield, CT 06455/203-349-3421

M

Mac-1, 13972 VanNess, Gardena, CA 90249/213-327-3581

Magasin Latulippe, Inc., 637 St. Vallier O, P.O. Box 395, Quebec, CANADA G1K 6W8/418-529-0024

Magma Engneering, ¼ Mile East of Ellsworth on Ocotillo Rd., Queen Creek, AZ 85242/602-987-9008

Magnum Research, Inc., 7110 University Ave. NE, Minneapolis, MN 55432/612-574-1868

Magtech Recreational Products, Las Vegas, NV 89119/702-795-7191

Mandall Shooting Supplies, 3616 N. Scottsdale Rd., Scottsdale, AZ 85252/602-945-2553

Mannlicher (See GSI, Inc.)

Marble Arms Corp., 420 Industrial Park, Gladstone, MI 49837/906-428-3710

Marksman Products, 5482 Argosy Dr., Huntington Beach, CA 92649/714-898-7535

Marlin Firearms Co., 100 Kenna Dr., North Haven, CT 06473

Marlin Service Dept., Howards Gun Shop, 100 E. International Airport Rd., Anchorage, AK 99501/907-562-3030

Marlin Service Dept., Mel Chung, Gunsmith, #8 Ing Rd., Kaunakaki, HI 96748/808-553-5888

Marocchi F.Ili S.p.A. (See PSI, Inc./Sile Distributors)

Marten's Sports Ltd, John, 1865 Burrows Ave., Winnipeg, Manitoba, Canada R2X 2V9/204-633-9740

Martin Gun Shop, Henry, 206 Kay Lane, Shreveport, LA 71115/318-797-1119

Martins Gun Shop, 3600 Laurel Ave., Natchez, MS 39120/601-442-0784

Mashburn Arms Co., Inc., 1218-20 North Pennsylvania Ave., Oklahoma City, OK 73107/405-236-5151

Master Gunsmiths, Inc., 21621 Ticonderoga, Houston, TX 77044/713-459-1631

Matt's 10K Gunsmithing, Inc., 5906 Castle Rd., Duluth, MN 55803/218-721-4210

Mauser-Werke (See Precision Imports, Inc.)

Maverick Arms, Inc., Industrial Blvd., Eagle Pass, TX 78853/512-773-9007

May & Company, Inc., P.O. Box 1111, 838 W. Capitol St., Jackson, MS 39209/601-354-5781

McBride's Guns, Inc., 2915 San Gabriel, Austin, TX 78705/512-472-3532

McClelland Gun Shop, 1533 Centerville Rd., Dallas, TX 75228-2597/214-321-0231

McDaniel Co., Inc., B., 8880 Pontiac Tr., P.O. Box 119, South Lyon, MI 48178/313-437-8989

McDonald Grothers & Chet Paulson, Inc., 6409 South Sprague,Tacoma, WA 98409/206-627-9195

McGuns, W.H., Central Ave. & 2215 Osborn St., Humboldt, TN 38343/901-784-5742

McMillan Gunworks, Inc., 302 W. Melinda Dr., Phoenix, AZ 85027/602-582-9627/FAX: 602-582-5178

MEC (Mayville Engineering Co.), 715 South St., Mayville, WI 53050/414-387-4500

Merkel Freres (See GSI, Inc.)

Merrill Pistol (See RPM)

Metro Rod & Reel, 236 S.E. Grand Ave., Portland, OR 97214/503-232-3193

Meydag Porter, 12114 East 16th, Tulsa, OK 74128/918-437-1928

Miclean, Bill, 499 Theta Ct., San Jose, CA 95123/408-224-1445

Midwest Sport Distributors, Box 129, Fayette, MO 65248

Midwest Sporting Goods Co., Inc., 8865 Plainfield Rd., Lyons, IL 60534/708-447-4848

Midwestern Shooters Supply, Inc., 150 Main St., Lomira, WI 53048/414-269-4995

Mike's Crosman Service, 5995 Renwood Dr., Winston-Salem, NC 27106/919-922-1031

Milarm Co., Ltd., 10769 99th St., Edmonton, Alberta, Canada T5H 4H6/403-424-5281

Millers Gun Shop, 915 23rd St., Gulfport, MS 39501/601-684-1765

Miller's Sport Shop, 2 Summit View Dr., Mountaintop, PA 18707/717-474-6931

Millie "D" Enterprises, 1241 W. Calle Concordia, Tucson, AZ 85737/602-297-4887

Milliken's Gun Shop, Rt. 4, Box 167, Elm Grove, WV 26003/304-242-0827

Mirador Optical Corp., 4051 Glencoe Ave., Marina Del Rey, CA 90292/310-821-5587

Miroku, B.C./Daly, Charles (See Outdoor Sports Headquarters)

Missoula Air Guns, 2 September Dr., Missoula, MT 59802/406-728-0189

Mitchell Arms, Inc., 3400-I W. MacArthur Blvd., Suite I, Santa Ana, CA 92704/714-957-5711 (Rifles only)

MK Arms, Inc., P.O. Box 16411, Irvine, CA 92713/714-261-2767

MKS Supply (See Stallard, Haskell, Iberia)

M&M Engineering (See Hollywood Engineering)

M.O.A. Corp., 175 Carr Dr., Brookville, OH 45309/513-833-5559

Moates Sport Shop, Bob, 10418 Hull St. Rd., Midlothian, VA 23113/804-276-2293

Modern Guncraft, 148 N. Branford Rd., Collinsville, CT 06492/203-265-1015

Modern Muzzleloading, Inc., 234 Airport Rd., Centerville, IA 52544/515-856-2623

Moneymaker Gun Craft, Inc., 1420 Minitary Ave., Omaha, NE 68131/402-556-0226

Montana Armory, Inc., 100 Centennial Dr., Big Timber, MT 59011/406-932-4353

Montana Gun Works, 3017 10th Ave. S., Great Falls, MT 59405/406-761-4346

Moore & Co., William Larkin, c/o Freddie Bruner, 1610 Friendship Lane, Escondido, CA 92026/619-738-8413

Moore & Co., William Larkin, c/o Ken Eversull, Tracemont Farms, 4800 Hwy 121, Boyce, LA 71409/318-793-8728

Moore & Co., William Larkin, c/o John F. Rowe, 2501 Rockwood Rd., Box 86, Enid, OK 73702/405-233-5942

Mooreheads Service & Repair, 8315 Division Rd., White City, OR 97503/503-826-3414

Moreau, Gunsmith, Pete, 1296 Orchard Rd., Essexvile, MI 48732

Morrison, Carl Bill, Middle Rd., Bradford, ME 04410/207-327-1116

Mossberg & Sons, O.F. (See page 451)

Mowrey Gun Works, Tinker Street, Waldron, IN 46182/Phone and FAX: 317-525-6181

Mueschke Manufacturing Co., 1003 Columbia St., Houston, TX 77008/713-869-7073

N

N.A. Guns, Inc., 10220 Florida Blvd., Baton Rouge, LA 70815/504-272-3620

Nagel Gun Shop, Inc., 6201 San Pedro Ave., San Antonio, TX 78216/512-342-5420/512-342-9893

Nusbaum Enterprises, Inc., 1364 Ridgewood Dr., Mobile, AL 38808/205-344-1079

Navy Arms Co., 689 Bergen Blvd., Ridgefield, NJ 07657/201-945-2500

Nelson's Engine Shop, 620 State St., Cedar Falls, IA 50613/319-266-4497

Nevada Air Guns, 3297 "J" Las Vegas Blvd. N., N. Las Vegas, NV 89115/702-643-8532

New Advantage Arms Corp., Inc., 7545 University Ave., La Mesa, CA 91941/619-589-8565

Newby, Stewart, Gunsmith, Main & Cross Streets, New Burgh, Ontario CANADA K0K 2S0/613-378-6613

New England Arms, Co., 60 Industrial Rowe, Gardner, MA 01440/508-632-9393 FAX: 508-632-2300

New England Firearms Co., Inc. (See H&R 1871)

New England Firearms, c/o Walker Arms, Highway 80 West-Route #2, Selma, AL 36701/205-872-6231

Nichols Dist., Inc., R., 372 Ste-Catherine W., Suite 410, Montreal, Quebec, Canada H3B 1A2/514-861-3391/FAX:514-861-9450

Nichols Sports Optics (See G.U. Inc.)

Nicholson's Gunsmithing, 35 Center St., Shelton, CT 06484/203-924-5635

Nikon, Inc., Repair Dept., 19601 Hamilton Ave., Torrance, CA 90502

Norckauer Assoc., 10220 Florida Blvd., Baton Rouge, LA 70815/504-272-3620

Norica (See American Arms, Inc./K.B.I., Inc.)

Norinco (See Century International Arms, Inc./China Sports, Inc./Interarms/Midwest Sport Distributors/Navy Arms Co./Sportarms of Florida)

Norm's Gun Shop, RFD 1 Box 59, Woodstock Rd., White River Junction, VT 05001/802-295-3364

North American Arms, 1800 North 300 West, Spanish Fork, UT 84660/801-798-7401

Northern Precision Airguns, 1161 Grove St., Tawas City, MI 48763/517-362-6949

Northern Virginia Gun Works, Inc., 7518-K Fullerton Road, Springfield, VA 22153/703-644-6504

Northland Sport Center, 1 Mile W. on U.S. 2, Bagley, MN 56621/218-694-2464

North Sylva Company, 18 Ripley Ave., Toronto, Ontario, Canada M6S 3N9/416-767-1196

Northwest Arms Service, 720 S. Second St., Atwood, KS 67730/913-626-3700

Nu-Line Guns, Inc., 1053 Caulks Hill Rd., Harvester, MO 63303/314-441-4500/314-447-4501

Nygord Precision Products, 6278 Hamilton Lane, La Crescenta, CA 91214/Phone and FAX: 818-352-3027

O

Oehler Research, Inc., 1308 Barclay, Austin, TX 78746/512-327-6900

Old West Arms, 7024 West ColFAX: Ave., Lakewood, CO 80215/303-232-1423

Old Western Scrounger, Inc., 12924 Hwy. A-12, Montague, CA 96064/916-459-5445

Olympic Arms, Inc. (See Safari Arms/SGW)

On Target Gunshop, Inc., 6984 West Main St., Kalamazoo, MI 49009/616-375-4570

Oregon Arms, Inc., 165 Schulz Rd., Central Point, OR 97502/503-664-5586

Oshman's Sporting Goods, Inc., 7729 Westheimer, Houston, TX 77029/713-780-3235

Ott's Gun Service, Rt. 2, Box 169A, Atmore, AL 36502/205-862-2588

Ott's Gunsmith Service, RR 1, Box 259, Decatur, IL 62526/217-875-3468

Outdoor America Store, 1925 N. MacArthur Blvd., Oklahoma City, OK 73127/405-789-0051

Outdoor Sports Headquarters, Inc., 967 Watertower Ln., Dayton, OH 45449/513-865-5855

Outdoorsman Sporting Goods Co., The, 105 W. State St., Geneva, IL 60134/312-232-4680

Outdoorsman, Inc., Village West Shopping Center, Fargo, ND 58103/701-282-0131

Outers Operation, N5549 CTH Z, P.O. Box 39, OnAlaska, WI 54650

Outpost, The, 2451 E. Maple Rapids Rd., Eureka, MI 58833/517-224-9562

Ozark Shooters, Inc., 1719 W. College St., Springfield, MO 65806/417-865-8500

P

Pachmayr, Ltd., 1875 South Mountain Ave., Monrovia, CA 91016/818-357-7771

Pacific International Service Co., Mountain Way, P.O. Box 3, Janesville, CA 96114/916-253-2218

P.A.C.T., Inc., P.O. Box 531525, Grand Prairie, TX 75050/214-641-0049

Paducah Shooters Supply, Inc., 3919 Cairo St., Paducah, KY 42001/502-443-3758

Para-Ordnance Mfg., Inc., C.S.G.S., Inc., Rd 1, Main Street, Holcomb, NY 14469/716-657-6131

Para-Ordnance Mfg., Inc., P.I.S.C.O., Inc., Mountain Way, Janesville, CA 96114/916-253-2218

Parker-Hale (See Navy Arms Co.)

Parker Reproductions, 124 River Rd., Middlesex, NJ 08846

Pasadena Gun Center, 206 East Shaw, Pasadena, TX 77506/713-472-0417

Pavillon Chasse & Peche, 440 Inc., 4,501 quest-Autoroute 440, Chomedey, Laval, Quebec, CANADA H7P 4W6/418-335-2020

Pedersoli Davide & C. (See Dixie Gun Works/EMF Co., Inc./Navy Arms Co./Trail Guns Armory Inc.)

Pederson & Son, C.R., 2717 S. U.S. 31, Ludington, MI 49431/616-843-2061

Pekin Gun & Sporting Goods, 1304 Derby St., Pekin, IL 61554/309-347-6060

Pelzer's Sport Shop, 2330 E. Monument St., Baltimore, MD 21205/301-675-3130

Pend Oreille Sport Shop, Rt. 1, Box 232, Sandpoint, ID 83864/208-263-2412

Penny's Hardware & Sporting Goods, 1800 N. Pace Blvd., Pensacola, FL 32505/904-438-9633/904-438-6624

Pentax Corp., 35 Inverness Dr. E., Englewood, CO 80112/303-799-8000

Perazzi U.S.A., Inc., 1207 S. Shamrock Ave., Monrovia, CA 91016/818-303-0068

Peregrine Industries, Inc., 7601 Woodwind Dr., Huntington Beach, CA 92647-1310/714-847-4700

Perry's of Wendell, Inc., P.O. Box 826, Wendell, NC 27591/919-365-6391

Perugini-Visini & Co. s.r.l. (See Moore & Co., William Larkin)

Peterborough Guns, Box 479, 71 Princess St., Peterborough, Ont., K9J 6Z6 CANADA/705-742-6408

Peters Pellet Place, 293 S. Yonge St., Ormond Beach, FL 32174/904-676-1353

Peters Stahl GmbH (See Federal Ordnance, Inc.)

Peterson Gun Shop, A.W., 4255 West Old U.S. 441, Mount Dors, FL 32757/904-383-4258/904-383-0595

Phelps Mfg. Co., Box 2266, Evansville, IN 47741

Phillips, D.J., Gunsmith, Rt. 1, N31-W22087 Shady Ln., Pewaukee, WI 53072/414-691-2165

Phoenix Arms, 1420 S. Archibald Ave., Ontario, CA 91761/714-947-4843

PHOXX Shooters Supply, 5813 Watt Ave., N. Highlands, CA 95660/916-348-9827

Pioneer Marketing & Research, 216 Haddon Ave., Westmont, NJ 08108/609-854-2424

Pioneer Sporting Goods, 622-5th Avenue, Belle Fourche, SD 57717/605-892-2822

Piotti (See Moore & Co., William Larkin)

Pittsburgh Handgun HQ., 1330 Center Ave., Pittsburgh, PA 15229/412-766-6100

Plaza Gunworks, Inc., 983 Gasden Highway, Birmingham, AL 35235/205-836-6206

Poly Technologies, Inc. (See Keng's Firearms Specialty, Inc.)

Ponsness-Warren, South 763, Hwy. 41, Rathdrum, ID 83858

Poor Borch's, Inc., 1204 E. College Dr., Marshall, MN 56258/507-532-4880

Potter Gunsmithing, 13960 Boxhorn Dr., Muskego, WI 53150/414-425-4830

Precision Airgun Sales, 31812 Bainbridge Rd., Solon, OH 44139/216-248-7550

Precision Arms & Gunsmithing Ltd., Hwy. 27 & King Road Box 809, Nobleton, Ontario, CANADA L0G-1N0

Precision Gunsmithing, 2723 W. 6th St., Amarillo, TX 79106/806-376-7223

Precision Gun Works, 4717 State Rd. 44, Oshkosh, WI 54904/414-233-2274

Precision Imports, Inc./Mauser, 5040 Space Center Drive, San Antonio, TX 78155/512-666-3033

Precision Reloading, Inc., 165 Crooked S Road, Stafford Springs, CT 06076/800-223-0900

Precision Sales Intl., Inc., c/o Pacific International Service Co., Box 3-Mountain Way, Janesville, CA 96114/916-253-2218

Precision Sales, c/o Uncle Fred's Gun Shop, 1 East St., Southampton, MA 01073/413-527-1660

Precision Sport Optics, 15571 Producer Ln., Unit G, Huntington Beach, CA 92649/714-891-1309/FAX: 714-892-6920

Precision Sports, Div. of Cortland Line Co., 3736 Kellogg Rd., Cortland, NY 13045/607-756-2851

Preuss Gun Shop, 4545 E. Shepherd, Clovis, CA 93612/209-299-6248

Professional Armaments, Inc., 4555 S. 300 West, Murray, UT 84107/801-268-2598

PSI, Inc., P.O. Box 1776, Westfield, MA 01086/413-562-5055/FAX: 413-562-5056

Q

Quality Arms, Inc., 2000 Dari Ashford Suite 490, Houston, TX 77077

Quality Firearms, Inc., 4530 NW 135 Street, Opa Locka, FL 33054

Quinn & Son, William, 681 Park Avenue, Route 33, Freehold, NJ 07728/908-462-0269

R

Rahn Gun Works, Inc., 3700 Anders Rd., Hastings, MI 49058/616-945-9894

Rajo Corporation, 2025 W. Franklin St., Evansville, IN 47712/812-422-6945

Ralph's Gun Shop, Box 662 Canora, Saskatoon, Saskatchewan, CANADA S0A 0L0/306-244-2023

Ram-Line, Inc., 10601 West 48 Ave., Wheatridge, CO 80033/303-467-0300

Randy's Gun Repair, P.O. Box 106, Tabustinac, N.B. CANADA E0C 2A0

Ranging, Inc., Routes 5 & 20, East Bloomfield, NY 14443/716-657-6161

Ransom Intl. Corp., 1040-A Sandretto Dr., Prescott, AZ 86302/602-778-7899/FAX: 602-778-7993

Rapids Gun Shop, 7811 Buffalo Ave., Niagra Falls, NY 14304/716-283-7873

Ray's Gunsmith Shop, 3199 Elm Ave., Grand Junction, CO 81504/303-434-6162

Ray's Liquor and Sporting Goods, 1956 Solano St., Box 677, Corning, CA 96021/916-824-5625

Ray's Rod & Reel Service, 414 Pattie St., Wichita, KS 67211/316-267-9462

Ray's Sport Shop, Inc., 559 Route 22 North, Plainfield, NJ 07060/908-561-4400

Ray's Sporting Goods, 730 Singleton Blvd., Dallas, TX 75212/214-747-7916

RCBS, 605 Oro Dam Blvd., Oroville, CA 95965/800-533-5000

R.D.P. Tool Co., Inc., 49162 McCoy Ave., East Liverpool, OH 43920/216-385-5129

Redding Reloading, Inc., 1089 Starr Rd., Cortland, NY 13045/607-753-3331

Redfield, Inc., 5800 E. Jewell Ave., Denver, CO 80224/303-757-6411/FAX: 303-756-2338

Red's Gunsmithing, 1230 E. 68th Ave. Suite #102, Ankorage, AK 99518/907-344-4867

Red Willow Tool & Armory, Inc., 4004 Highway 93 North, Stevensville, MT 59870/406-777-5401/FAX: 406-777-5402

Reliable Gun & Tackle, Ltd., 3227 Fraser St., Vancouver, British Columbia CANADA V5V 4B8/604-874-4710

Reloaders Specialty Mfg., 7602 Carlton Rd., Coopersburg, PA 18036/215-838-9507

Reloading & Ammo Shop, 2032 Airway Dr., Stockton, CA 95205/209-465-7415

Reloading Center, 515 W. Main St., Burley, ID 83318/208-678-5053

Remington Arms Co. (See page 451)

Reynolds Gun Shop, 314 N. Western Ave., Peoria, IL 61606/309-674-5790

Reynolds Gun Shop, Inc., 3502A S. Broadway, Tyler, TX 75702/214-592-1531

Richland Gun Shop, 207 Park St., Richland, PA 17087/717-866-4246

Richmond Gun Shop, 517 E. Main St., Richmond, VA 23219/804-644-7207

Rigby & Co., John (See Hallowell & Co.)

River Bend Sport Shop, 230 Farmsite Dr., Waupaca, WI 54981/715-258-3583

Rizzini, F.LLI (See Moore & Co., William Larkin)

Robinson's Sporting Goods, Ltd., 1307 Broad St., Victoria, British Columbia CANADA V8W 2A8/604-385-3429

Rogers Ltd. International, 891 Dixwell Ave., Hamden, CT 06514/203-865-8484/FAX: 800-847-7492

Ron's Gun Repair, 1517 E. 10th St., Sioux Falls, SD 57103/605-338-7398

Rossi S.A. Metalurgica E Municoes, Amadeo (See Interarms)

RPM (R&R Sporting Arms, Inc.), 15481 N. Twin Lakes Dr., Tucson, AZ 85337/602-725-1233

R&R Shooters Supply, W6553 North Rd., Mauston, WI 53948/608-847-4562

Rue's Gunsmithing, 427 Broadway, El Cajon, CA 92021/619-447-2169

Ruger (See Sturm Ruger & Co.)

Ruko Products, Suite 102, Walnutport, PA 18088/215-767-1339

Rusk Gun Shop, Inc., 6904 Watts Rd., Madison, WI 53719/608-274-8740

Russel's Sporting Goods, 6624 Centre St. S., Calgary, Alberta, CANADA T2H 0C6/403-269-5566

RWS (See Dynamit Nobel-RWS, Inc.)

S

Safari Arms/SGW (See Olympic Arms, Inc.)

Saffle Repair Service, 312 Briar Wood Dr., Jackson, MS 39206/601-956-4968

Sako, Ltd. (See Stoeger Industries)

Sanders Custom Gun Shop, P.O. Box 5967-2031, Bloomingdale Ave., Augusta, GA 30906/404-798-5220

Sanders Gun Shop, 3001 Fifth St., P.O. Box 4181, Meridian, MS 39301/601-485-5301

Sardius Industries, Ltd. (See Arms Corp. of America, Inc.)

Saskatoon Gunsmith Shoppe, Ltd., 2310 Avenue "C" N., Saskatoon, Saskatchewan, CANADA S7L·5X5/306-242-6747

Sauer (See G.U. Inc./Simmons Enterprises, Ernie/Simmons Gun Repair)

Savage Arms, Inc., Davidson's Canada, 584 Neal Drive, Peterborough, Ontario, CANADA K9J 6Z6/705-742-5408

Savage Arms, Inc., Randy's Gun Repair, P.O. Box 106, Tabusinac, NB, CANADA E0C 2A0/506-779-4768

Savage Arms, Inc., Red's Gunsmithing, 1230 East 68th Ave. #102, Anchorage, AK 99518/907-344-4867

Savage Arms, Inc., Repair Station, W.R. Longs Gunsmiths Ltd., Brook Road North, Coburg, Ontario, CANADA K9A 453/416-372-5955

Savage Arms, Inc., Shop 2, #8 Ing Road, Kaunakakai, HI 96748/808-553-5888

Savage Arms, Inc., Springdale Rd., Westfield, MA 01085/413-568-7001

Scalzo's Sporting Goods, 207 Odell Ave., Endicott, NY 13760/607-746-7586

Scattergun Technologies, 518 3rd Avenue South, Nashville, TN 37210/615-254-1441

Scharch Mfg., Inc., 10325 Co. Rd. 120 Unit "C", Salida, CO 81201/719-539-7242/FAX: 719-539-3021

Schmidt & Bender (See Jaeger, Inc., Paul)

Sea Gull Marina, 1400 Lake, Two Rivers, WI 54241/414-794-7533

Seecamp Co., Inc., L.W., 301 Brewster Rd., Milford, CT 06460

Selin Gunsmith, Ltd., Del, 2803 28th Street, Vernon, British Columbia, CANADA V1T 4Z5/604-545-6413

S.E.M. Gun Works, 3204 White Horse Rd., Greenville, SC 29611/803-295-2948

Shaler Eagle, R.R. 8 Box 407, Jonesbrough, TN 37659/615-753-7620

Shamburg's Wholesale Spt. Gds., 403 Frisco Ave., Clinton, OK 73601/405-323-0209

Shapel & Son, 1708 N. Liberty, Boise, ID 83704/208-375-6159

Sharps Arms Co., Inc., C., 100 Centennial Dr., Big Timber, MT 59011/406-932-4353

Shepherd Scope Ltd., RR 2 Box 23, Waterloo, NE 68069/402-779-2424

Sheridan Gun Shop, 1037 N. Main St, Sheridan, WY 82801/307-674-8360

Sheridan Products, Inc. (See Benjamin/Sheridan Co.)

Shiloh Rifle Mfg. Co., Inc., 201 Centennial Dr., Big Timber, MT 59011

Shockey, H., 204 E. Farmington Rd., Hanna City, IL 61536/309-565-4524

Shooters Supply, 1120 Tieton Dr., Yakima, WA 98902

Siegle's Gunshop, Inc., 508 W. MacArthur Blvd., Oakland, CA 94609/415-655-8789

Sievert's Guns 4107 W. Northern, Pueblo, CO 81005/719-564-0035

SIG (See Mandall Shooting Supplies Inc.)

SIG-Sauer (See Sigarms, Inc.)

Sigarms, Inc., Industrial Dr., Corporate Park, Exeter, NH 03833/603-722-2302

Sile Distributors, 8 Centre Market Place, New York, NY 10013

Sillman, Hal, Associated Services, 1514 NE 205 Terrace, Miami, FL 33170/305-651-4450

Simmons Enterprises, c/o The Gun Works, 8540 I St., Omaha, NE 68127/402-339-2249

Simmons Enterprises, Ernie, 709 East Elizabethtown Rd., Manheim, PA 17545/717-664-4040

Simmons Enterprises, Paul's Gun Shop, 307 S. Riverview Dr., East Peoria, IL 61611/309-822-8727

Simmons Gun Repair/Sauer, 700 S. Rodgers Rd., Olathe, KS 66083/913-782-3131

Simmons Outdoor Corp., 14530 SW 119 Ave., Miami, FL 33186/305-252-0477

Sipes Gun Shop, 919 High St, Little Rock, AR 72202/501-376-8940

SKB Arms Co. (See G.U. Inc./Simmons Enterprises Ernie)

Skeet's Gun Shop, Rt. 3, Box 235, Tahlequah, OK 74464/918-456-4749

Skeet Hill Gun Shop, R.L., 209 Raymond St., Verona, MS 38879/601-566-8353

S.K. Guns, Inc., 3041A Main Ave., Fargo, ND 58103/701-293-4867

Smith & Smith Gun Shop, Inc., 2589 Oscar Johnson Drive, Charleston Heights, SC 29405/803-744-2024

Smith & Wesson (See page 451)

Smith's Lawn & Marine Svc., 9100 Main St., Clarence, NY 14031/716-633-7868

Sodak Sport & Bait, 319 8th Ave. N.W., Aberdeen, SD 57401/605-225-2737

Solvay Home & Outdoor Center, 102 First St., Solvay, NY 13209/315-468-6285

Southland Gun Works, Inc., 1134 Hartsville Rd., Darlington, SC 29532/803-393-6291

Southwest Guns, 801 West Hatcher, Phoenix, AZ 85020/602-861-1275
Southwest Shooters Supply, Inc., 1940 Linwood Blvd., Oklahoma City, OK 73106/405-235-4476/405-235-7022
Sportarms of Florida, 5555 N.W. 36 Ave., Miami, FL 33142/305-635-2411
Sport Shop, The, 100 Will Roger Dr., Kingfisher, OK 73750/405-375-5130
Sport Shop, The, 707 Central Ave., Nebraska City, NE 68410/402-873-6020
Sportarms of Florida, 5555 NW 36 Ave., Miami, FL 33142/305-635-2411
Sporting Arms Mfg., Inc., 801 Hall Ave., Littlefield, TX 79339/806-385-5665
Sporting Goods, Inc., 232 North Lincoln St., Hastings, NE 68901/402-462-6132
Sports Mart, The, 828 Ford St., Ogdensburg, NY 13669/315-393-2865
Sports Shop, The, 8055 Airline Hwy., Baton Rouge, LA 70815/504-927-2600
Sports World, Inc., 5800 S. Lewis Ave., Suite 154, Tulsa, OK 74105/918-742-4027
Sportsman's Center, U.S. Hwy. 130, Box 731, Bordentown, NJ 08505/609-298-5300
Sportsman's Exchange, Inc., 560 South "C" St., Oxnard, CA 93030/805-483-1917
Sportsman's Haven, Rt. 4, Box 541, 14695 E. Pike Rd., Cambridge, OH 43725/614-432-7243
Sportsman's Paradise Gunsmith, 640 Main St., Pineville, LA 71360/318-443-6041
Sportsman's Shop, 101 W. Main St., New Holland, PA 17557/717-354-4311
Sportsman's Surplus, Trumpers Shopping Center, P.O. Box 4166, Missoula, MT 59806/406-721-5500
Sportsmen's Repair Ctr., Inc., 106 S. High St., Box 134, Columbus Groves, OH 45830/419-659-5818
Springfield Armory, Inc., 420 W. Main St., Geneseo, IL 61254/309-944-5631
Spradlin's, 113 Arthur, Pueblo, CO 81004/719-543-9462/fs
Stallard Arms, Inc., 728 FairFAX: Ave., Mansfield, OH 44906/419-747-6095
Stalwart Corp., 756 N. Garfield, Pocatello, ID 83204/208-232-7899
Star Bonifacio Echeverria S.A. (See Interarms)
Star Machine Works, 418 10th Ave., San Diego, CA 92101/619-232-3216
Starnes, Gunmaker, Ken, Rt. 1 Box 269, Scroggins, TX 75480/907-789-2680
Steel City Arms, Inc. (See Desert Industries, Inc.)
Stephen's Gun Shop, Inc., 901-6th Ave. North, Great Falls, MT 59401/406-761-2510
Steyr airguns (See Nygord Precision Products)
Steyr-Daimler-Puch (See GSI, Inc.)
Steyr Mannlicher (See GSI, Inc.)
St. Lawrence Sales, Inc., 12 West Fint St., Lake Orion, MI 48035/313-693-7760
Stocker's Shop, 5199 Mahoning Ave., Warren, OH 44483/216-847-9579
Stoeger Industries (See page 451)
Stratton Sporting Goods, Inc., 16 W. Rt. 70 Marlton Green, Marlton, NJ 08053/609-985-3676
Sturm, Ruger & Co., Guild Rd., Newport, NH 03773/603-863-3300
Sumner Sports, Inc., 405 Galilee Ave., Prontnac Industrial Park, Quebec, Quebec, Canada G1P 4M6/418-527-5031/FAX: 418-527-9715
Sundance Industries, Inc., 25163 W. Ave. Stanford, Valencia, CA 91355/805-257-4807
Surplus Center, 621 S.E. Cass, Roseburg, OR 97470/503-672-4312
Survival Arms, 4500 Pine Cone Place, Cocao, FL 32922/407-633-4880
Suter's Inc., 332 North Tejon Street, Colorado Springs, CO 80902/719-635-1475
Sutter's House of Guns, 332 N. Tejon St., Colorado Springs, CO 80903/719-635-1475
Swarovski Optik, One Wholesale Way, Cranston, RI 02920/401-942-3380
Swift Instruments, Inc., 952 Dorchester Ave., Boston, MA 02125
Swift Instruments, Inc., (West Coast Only), 1190 North 4th Street, San Jose, CA 95112
Swivel Machine Works, Inc., 167 Cherry St., Suite 286, Milford, CT 06460/203-926-1840

T

Tanfoglio S.r.l., Fratelli/Witness (See E.A.A. Corp.)
Tanner (See Mandall Shooting Supplies, Inc.)
Tapco, Inc., P.O. Box 818, Smyrna, GA 30081/404-435-9782
Tasco Sales, Inc., 7600 NW 26th St., Miami, FL 33122/305-591-3670
Taurus Firearms, Inc., 16175 NW 49th Ave., Miami, FL 33014/305-624-1115
Taylor's Sporting Goods, Gene, 445 W. Gunnison Ave., Grand Junction, CO 81505/303-242-8165
Taylor's Technical Gunsmithing Co., 14 Stalwart Industrial Drive, Gormely, Ontario CANADA L0H 1G0/416-888-9391
Taylor & Vadney, Inc., 303 Central Ave., Albany, NY 12206/518-472-9183
Techni-Mec (See Rahn Gunworks, Inc.)
Ted's Gun & Reel Repair, 311 Natchitoches St. Box 1635, W. Monroe, LA 71291/318-323-0661
Terry's Guns, 1429 Penna, Weirton, WV 26062/304-797-1470
Texas Longhorn Arms, Inc., 3830 FM 2218, Richmond, TX 77469/713-341-0775
The Way It Was Sporting, 620 Chestnut Street, Moorestown, NJ 08057/609-234-0212
Theoben Engineering (See Air Rifle Specialists)
Thom Co., Ltd., The, P.O. Box 1913, Honolulu, HI 96805/808-538-6764
Thompson/Center Arms (See page 451)
Thompson's Gunshop, Inc., 10254-84th St., Alto, MI 49302/616-868-6156
Thunder Mountain Arms, P.O. Box 593, Oak Harbor, WA 98277/206-679-4657/FAX: 206-675-1114
Tikka (See Stoeger Industries)
Tom Mason Guns & Ammo, 41 South Street, Danbury, CT 06810/203-778-6421
300 Gunsmith Service, 6850 South Yosemite Ct., Englewood, CO 80112/303-773-0300
Tony's Gun Shop, 2110 E. 14th St., Des Moines, IA 50316/515-262-6898
Traders, The, 685 E. 14th St., San Leandro, CA 94577/415-569-0555
Tradewinds, 2339 Tacoma Ave. S., Tacoma, WA 98402/206-272-4887
Trading Post, The, 412 Erie St. S., Massillon, OH 44646/216-833-7761
Traditions, Inc., 500 Main St., Deep River, CT 06417/203-526-9555
Trail Guns Armory, 1422 E. Main St., League City, TX 77573/713-332-5833/FAX: 713-332-5833
Treaster, Inc., Verne, 3604 West 16th St., Indianapolis, IN 46222/317-638-6921
Trident Ltd., 564 Kantz Rd., Springdale, AZ 72764/501-361-2803
Trijicon, Inc., 37716 Hills Tech Drive, Farmington Hills, MI 48331

U

Uberti USA (West Coast Only), Tabor Engineering, 527 San Mateo Ave., San Bruno, CA 94066
Uberti USA, Inc., 362 Limerock Rd., Lakeville, CT 06039/203-435-8068
Ultra Light Arms, Inc., 214 Price St., Granville, WV 26534/304-599-5687
Unertl Optical Co., John, 1224 Freedom Rd., Mars, PA 16046/412-776-9700
Ugartechea S.A., Ignacio (See Mandall Shooting Supplies, Inc.)
Unique/M.A.P.F. (See Nygord Precision Products)
Unique Sporting Goods, First United Federal Bldg., Edensburg, PA 15931/814-472-4123
Upper Missouri Trading Co., Inc., 304 Harold St., Crofton, NE 68730/402-388-4844
Upton's Gun Shop, 810 Croghan St., Fremont, OH 43420/419-332-1326
U.S. Repeating Arms Co. (See Winchester)

V

Valley Gun Shop, 7719 Hartford Rd., Baltimore, MD 21234/301-668-2171
Valley Gunsmithing, John A. Foster, 619 Second St., Webster City, IA 50595/515-832-5102
Valmet (See Stoeger Industries)
Van Burens Gun Shop, 2706 Sylvania Ave., Toledo, OH 43613/419-475-9526
Van's Gunsmith Service, Rt. 69A, Parish, NY 13131/315-625-7251
Varner Sporting Arms, Inc., P.O. Box 450421, Atlanta, GA 30345/404-491-1223
Vincent's, 1723 18th St., Bakersfield, CA 93301/805-327-9501
Voere (See Rahn Gun Works, Inc.)

W

Walker Arms Co., Inc., Hwy. 80 West, Rt. 2, Box 73, Selma, AL 36701/205-872-6231
Wallace Gatlin Gun Repair, Rt. 2, Box 73, Oxford, AL 36203/205-831-6993
Walther GmbH, Carl (See Interarms)
Way It Was Sporting Services, The, 620 Chestnut St., Moorestown, NJ 08057/609-234-0212
Weapon Works, The, 7017 N. 19th Ave., Phoenix, AZ 85021/602-995-3010
Weatherby, Inc. (See page 451)
Weaver Scope Repair Service, 1121 Larry Mahan Dr., Suite B, El Paso, TX 79925/915-593-1005
Webley & Scott, Ltd. (See Beeman Precision Arms, Inc.)
Weihrauch KG, Hermann (See Beeman Precision Arms, Inc./E.A.A. Corp.)
Wessel Gun Service, 4000 E. 9-Mile Rd., Warren, MI 48091/313-756-2660
Wesson Firearms Co., Inc., Attn: OSR, Maple Tree Industrial Center, Rt. 20, Wilbraham Rd., Palmer, MA 01069/413-267-4081
Western Ordnance Intl. Corp., 325 S. Westwood, Suite #1, Mesa, AZ 85210/602-964-1799
Westgate Gunsports, Inc., 10116-175th Street, Edmonton, Alberta, CANADA T5S 1A1
West Luther Gun Repair, R.R. #1, Conn, Ontario, CANADA/519-848-6260
Westley Richards & Co. (See New England Arms, Co.)
Wheeler Gun Shop, C., 1908 George Washington Way Bldg. F, Richland, WA 99352/509-946-4634
White Dog Gunsmithing, 62 Central Ave., Ilion, NY 13357/315-894-6211
White Systems, Inc., 810 W. 100 North, Roosevelt, UT 84066/Phone and FAX: 801-722-3085
Wichita Arms, Inc., 444 Ellis St., Wichita, KS 67211/316-265-0661/FAX: 316-265-0760
Wichita Guncraft, Inc., 4607 Barnett Rd., Wichita Falls, TX 76310/817-692-5622
Wilderness Sport & Electronics, 14430 S. Pulaski Rd., Midlothian, IL 60445/708-389-1776
Wildey, Inc., 458 Danbury Rd., New Milford, CT 06776/203-355-9000/FAX: 203-354-7759
Wilkinson Arms, 26884 Pearl Rd., Parma, ID 83660/208-722-6771
Willborn Outdoors & Feed, 505 Main Avenue N.W., Cullman, AL 35055/205-737-9595
Williams Gun Shop, 7389 Lapeer Rd., Davison, MI 48423/313-742-2120
Williams Gun Sight Co., 7389 Lapeer Rd., Davison, MI 48423/313-653-2131
Williams Gunsight & Outfitters, 7389 Lapeer Rd., Davison, MI 48423/313-653-2131
Williams Gunsmithing, 1480 Houlihan Rd., Saginaw, MI 48601/517-777-1240
Williamson-Pate Gunsmith Service, 117 West Pipeline Rd., Hurst, TX 76053/817-282-1464
Will's Gun Shop, 5603 N. Hubbard Lake Rd., Spruce, MI 48762/517-727-2500
Winchester (See page 451)
Windsor Gun Shop, 8410 Southeastern Ave., Indianapolis, IN 46239/317-862-2512
Wingshooting Adventures, 4320 Kalamazoo Ave. SE, Grand Rapids, MI 49508/616-455-7810/FAX: 616-455-5212
Wisner's Gun Shop, Inc., 287 NW Chehalis Ave., Chehalis, WA 98532/206-748-8942
Wolf Custom Gunsmithing, Gregory, c/o Albright's Gun Shop, 36 E. Dover St., Easton, MD 21601/301-820-8811
Wolfer Brothers, Inc., 1701 Durham, Houston, TX 77007/713-869-7640
Woodman's Sporting Goods, 223 Main Street, Norway, ME 04268/207-743-6602
Wortner Gun Works, Ltd., 433 Queen St., Chatham, Ont., M7M 5K5/519-352-0924
Wyoming Arms Mfg. Corp., 210 Hwy. 20 South, Thermopolis, WY 82443/307-864-5503

Y

Ye Olde Blk Powder Shop, 994 W. Midland Rd., Auburd, MI 48611/517-662-2271
Ye Olde Gun Shop, 12 Woodlawn Ave., Bradford, PA 16701/814-368-3034

Z

Zanes Gun Rack, 4167 N. High St., Columbus, OH 43214/614-263-0369
Zanoletti, Pietro (See Mandall Shooting Supplies, Inc.)
Zavodi Crvena Zastava (See Interarms)
Zeiss Optical, Inc., Carl, Sports Optics Repair Shop, 1015 Commerce St., Petersburg, VA 23803/804-861-0033/800-446-1807
Zoli USA, Inc., Antonio, 1426 E. Tillman Rd., Ft. Wayne, IN 46816

■BR=Browning ■CO=Colt ■CR=Crosman ■MO=Mossberg ■RE=Remington ■ST=Stoeger ■SW=Smith & Wesson ■TC=Thompson/Center
■WN=Winchester ■WE=Weatherby

ALABAMA

SERVICE CENTER	CITY	BR	CO	CR	MO	RE	ST	SW	TC	WN	WE
Allen's	Birmingham										
B&W Gunsmithing	Cullman			●							
Dubbs, Gunsmith, Dale R.	Seminole					●					
Fred's Gun Shop	Mobile					●					
Hal's Gun Supply	Cullman				●						
Hall Brothers Sporting Goods	Jasper	●	●								
Nusbaum Enterprises, Inc.	Mobile	●	●								
Ott's Gun Service	Atmore			●		●					
Plaza Gunworks, Inc.	Birmingham	●	●	●	●	●		●			●
Walker Arms Co., Inc.	Selma				●	●	●	●	●		●
Wallace Gatlin Gun	Oxford				●	●					
Wilborn Outdoors & Feed	Cullman										●

ALASKA

SERVICE CENTER	CITY	BR	CO	CR	MO	RE	ST	SW	TC	WN	WE
Down Under Gunsmiths	Fairbanks										●
Great Northern Guns	Anchorage	●	●		●	●					
Red's Gunsmithing	Anchorage	●	●		●	●		●			

ARIZONA

SERVICE CENTER	CITY	BR	CO	CR	MO	RE	ST	SW	TC	WN	WE
BenchMark Guns	Yuma	●	●		●	●					
Don's Sport Shop, Inc.	Scottsdale	●	●		●	●			●	●	●
Jensen's Custom Ammunition/Lathrops	Tucson	●	●						●	●	●
Joe's Gun Shop	Phoenix			●							
Millie "D" Enterprises	Tucson			●	●						
Southwest Guns	Phoenix										
Weapon Works, The	Phoenix					●					

ARKANSAS

SERVICE CENTER	CITY	BR	CO	CR	MO	RE	ST	SW	TC	WN	WE
Broadway Arms	Little Rock				●	●					●
Gun Exchange, Inc.	Little Rock				●	●		●			
Jim's Trading Post	Pine Bluff	●	●								
Sipes Gun Shop	Little Rock	●	●		●	●					

CALIFORNIA

SERVICE CENTER	CITY	BR	CO	CR	MO	RE	ST	SW	TC	WN	WE
Air Venture Air Guns	Bellflower			●							
Argonaut Gun Shop	Modesto		●								
Bain & Davis	San Gabriel			●		●					●
Beeman Precision Arms, Inc.	Santa Rosa			●							
Bolsa Gunsmithing	Westminster	●	●		●	●					●
Bridge Sportsman's Ctr.	Pasa Robles				●	●					
Cat's Customs	Fallbrook					●					
Eagle Gun Works	La Puente		●		●						
Gilman-Mayfield	Fresno										
Grundman's	Del Rio					●					

CALIFORNIA

SERVICE CENTER	CITY	BR	CO	CR	MO	RE	ST	SW	TC	WN	WE
Huntington Sportsman's Store	Oroville	●									
Imbert & Smithers, Inc.	San Carlos	●				●				●	
Jack First Distributors	Lancaster			●		●		●	●	●	●
J&G Gunsmithing	Roseville				●	●					
John Q's Quality Gunsmithing	Sacramento	●			●	●		●			
Long Beach Uniform Co., Inc.	Long Beach							●			
Mac-1	Gardena										
Miclean, Bill	San Jose	●	●		●	●		●	●		
Pacific International Service Co.	Janesville		●								
PHOXX Shooters Supply	N. Highlands			●							
Preuss Gun Shop	Clovis	●									
Ray's Liquor and Sporting Goods	Corning				●						
Reloading & Ammo Shop	Stockton										
Rue's Gunsmithing	El Cajon		●								
Siegle's Gunshop, Inc.	Oakland	●									
Sportsman's Exchange, Inc.	Oxnard	●			●						
Traders, The	San Leandro		●								
Vincent's	Bakersfield				●						

COLORADO

SERVICE CENTER	CITY	BR	CO	CR	MO	RE	ST	SW	TC	WN	WE
Airgun Repair Specialists	Denver			●							
Foothills Shooting Ctr.	Lakewood	●			●	●					
Gart Brothers Sporting Goods	Denver	●			●	●		●	●	●	
L&M Firing Line, Inc.	Aurora										
Old West Arms	Lakewood	●									
Ray's Gunsmith Shop	Grand Junction		●		●						
Sievert's Guns	Pueblo										
Spradlin's	Pueblo					●					
Sutter's Inc.	Colorado Springs	●									
Sutter's House of Guns	Colorado Springs										●
Taylor's Sporting Goods, Gene	Grand Junction					●				●	●
300 Gunsmith Service	Englewood									●	

CONNECTICUT

SERVICE CENTER	CITY	BR	CO	CR	MO	RE	ST	SW	TC	WN	WE
CMCI	West Hartford	●				●					
Gunsmithing Limited	Fairfield	●				●				●	
Hoffman's Gun Center, Inc.	Newington										
Horchler's Gun Shop	Collinsville		●								
Irwin, Gunsmith, C.H.	East Hartland					●				●	
Keller's Co., Inc.	Burlington										
Modern Guncraft	Collinsville		●			●					
Nicholson's Gunsmithing	Shelton					●					
Tom Mason Guns & Ammo	Danbury		●								

DELAWARE

SERVICE CENTER	CITY	BR	CO	CR	MO	RE	ST	SW	TC	WN	WE
Dean's Place	Hockessin					●					●

See page 445 for Service Center addresses.

■BR=Browning ■CO=Colt ■CR=Crosman ■MO=Mossberg ■RE=Remington ■ST=Stoeger ■SW=Smith & Wesson ■TC=Thompson/Center ■WN=Winchester ■WE=Weatherby

SERVICE CENTER	CITY	BR	CO	CR	MO	RE	ST	SW	TC	WN	WE
FLORIDA											
Accurate Plating & Weaponry	Clearwater		●								
Air Gun Rifle Repair	Sebring			●							
Alexander, Gunsmith, W.R.	Tallahassee					●					
Firearms Unlimited, Inc.	Naples							●			
Fischer Gunsmithing, Inc., Steve	Miami		●								
Gateway Shooter Supply	Jacksonville										●
Green Acres Sporting Goods, Inc.	Jacksonville	●		●				●			
Gun Shop, Inc., The	Miami Shores					●					
Lawsons Custom Firearms, Inc., Art	Ocala					●				●	
Loftin & Taylor	Jacksonville					●				●	
Penny's Hardware & Sporting Gds.	Pensacola	●		●							
Peters Pellet Place	Ormond Beach										
Peterson Gun Shop, A.W.	Mount Dors		●			●				●	
Sillman, Hal, Associated Services	Miami			●					●		
GEORGIA											
Accuracy Gun Shop	Columbus	●	●	●	●	●			●	●	
Dorn's Outdoor Center	Macon	●	●	●	●	●			●	●	
Ed's Gun & Tackle Shop, Inc.	Marietta	●	●	●							
Franklin Sports, Inc.	Athens	●		●	●	●		●	●		
Gun Corral, Inc.	Decatur	●			●	●					
Jordan Gun & Pawn Shop	Tifton	●			●	●					
Kick's Sport Center	Claxton			●		●			●	●	
Sanders Custom Gun Shop	Augusta										
HAWAII											
Chung, Gunsmith, Mel	Kaunakakai	●	●		●	●		●	●	●	●
Thom Co., Ltd., The	Honolulu			●		●					
IDAHO											
Bob's Repair	Idaho Falls		●		●	●					●
Intermountain Arms & Tackle, Inc.	Meridian		●			●				●	
Lolo Sporting Goods	Lewiston				●	●				●	
Pend Oreille Sport Shop	Sandpoint				●	●			●	●	
Quality Firearms	Nampa										●
Reloading Center	Burley				●	●					
Shapel & Son	Boise		●								
ILLINOIS											
A&M Sales	North Lake		●		●	●					
Barton Sport Center, Bill	Niles				●	●					●
Bell's Gun & Sport Shop, Inc.	Franklin Park				●	●					
Darnall's Gun Works	Bloomington				●	●				●	
Freeland Scope Stands, Inc.	Rock Island	●									
Henry's Airguns	Belvidere			●							
Midwest Sporting Goods Co., Inc.	Lyons		●			●					
Ott's Gunsmith Service	Decatur		●			●	●				
Outdoorsman Sporting Goods Co.	Geneva		●			●					
Pekin Gun & Sporting Goods	Pekin										
Reynolds Gun Shop	Peoria	●									
Shockey, H.	Hanna City	●									

SERVICE CENTER	CITY	BR	CO	CR	MO	RE	ST	SW	TC	WN	WE
Wilderness Sport & Electronics	Midlothian		●								
INDIANA											
Airgun Centre, Ltd.	Lawrenceburg		●								
Allen County Gun Works	Ft. Wayne					●				●	
Blythe's Sport Shop, Inc.	Valparaiso			●		●					
Fidler's Firearms	Lafayette				●	●					
Hodson & Son Pell Gun Repair	Anderson			●							
Kemp Gun Shop	Michigan City		●	●							
Lutter, Robert E.	Ft. Wayne		●	●							
Rajo Corporation	Evansville					●					
Treaster, Inc.	Indianapolis		●								
Windsor Gun Shop	Indianapolis				●	●					
IOWA											
Daryl's Gun Shop, Inc.	State Center		●			●					
Glenn's Reel & Rod Repair	Des Moines			●		●					
G&S Gunsmithing	Eldridge		●			●					
Jacobson's Gun Center	Story City										●
Nelson's Engine Shop	Cedar Falls			●							
Tony's Gun Shop	Des Moines			●							
Valley Gunsmithing, John A. Foster	Webster City				●	●					
KANSAS											
Bullseye Gun Works	Overland Park					●					
Gordon's Wigwam	Wichita	●									
Gun & Stuff, Inc.	Wichita										
Northwest Arms Service	Atwood					●					
Ray's Rod & Reel Service	Wichita		●			●					
Simmons Gun Repair	Olathe				●	●				●	
KENTUCKY											
Danny's Gun Repair, Inc.	Louisville		●			●				●	
Firearms Service Center	Louisville					●					
Garrett Gunsmiths, Inc.	Newport				●	●					
Paducah Shooters Supply, Inc.	Paducah				●	●					
LOUISIANA											
Atlas Gun Repair	Violet	●									
Boudreaux, Gunsmith	Lake Charles					●					
Brazdas Top Guns	Lafayette		●			●				●	
Burton Hardware	Sulphur					●					
C.G.&S. (Crescent)	New Orleans		●								
Clark Custom Guns, Inc.	Keithville		●					●			
Custom Gun Works	Lafayette				●	●					
Eversull Gunsmith, Inc., K.	Boyce	●				●					
Houma Gun Works	Houma	●									
Hutchinson's Gun Repair	Pineville		●			●					
Martin Gun Shop	Shreveport					●					
N.A. Guns, Inc.	Baton Rouge		●								
Norckauer Assoc.	Baton Rouge					●					
Sports Shop, The	Baton Rouge	●									
Sportsman's Paradise Gunsmith	Pineville										●

See page 445 for Service Center addresses.

Warranty Service Centers (cont.)

■BR=Browning ■CO=Colt ■CR=Crosman ■MO=Mossberg ■RE=Remington ■ST=Stoeger ■SW=Smith & Wesson ■TC=Thompson/Center ■WN=Winchester ■WE=Weatherby

SERVICE CENTER	CITY	BR	CO	CR	MO	RE	ST	SW	TC	WN	WE
Ted's Gun & Reel Repair	W. Monroe					●					
MAINE											
Brunswick Gun Shop	Brunswick		●		●	●		●		●	
Morrison, Carl Bill	Bradford				●	●				●	
Woodman's Sporting Goods	Norway					●					
MARYLAND											
Atlantic Guns, Inc.	Silver Springs	●	●		●	●		●		●	
Baltimore Gunsmiths	Baltimore		●		●						
Firearms Repair & Refinish Shoppe	Woodbine										●
Gun Center, The	Frederick			●							
Pelzer's Sport Shop	Baltimore			●							
Valley Gun Shop	Baltimore	●			●	●					
Wolf Custom Gunsmithing, Gregory, c/o Albright's Gun Shop	Easton	●				●					
MASSACHUSETTS											
Airport Sports Shop, Inc.	North Attleboro				●	●					
Bellrose & Son, L.E.	Granby			●							●
MICHIGAN											
Adventure A.G.R.	Waterford		●		●	●	●				
Bachelder Master Gunmakers	Grand Rapids				●	●	●	●		●	
Bear Archery Center, Inc.	Grand Rapids			●	●	●					
Daenzer, Charles E.	Otisville			●							
Fricano, Gunsmith, J.	Grand Haven			●							
Hampel's, Inc.	Traverse City				●	●					
Joe's Gun Shop	Dorr			●							
Johnson Gunsmithing, Don	Powers				●	●					
Johnson Service, Inc., W.	Adrian				●	●					
McDaniel Co., Inc., B.	South Lyon			●							
Moreau, Gunsmith, Pete	Essexvile		●		●	●					
Northern Precision Airguns	Tawas City			●							
On Target Gunshop, Inc.	Kalamazoo	●			●	●					
Outpost, The	Eureka			●		●					
Pederson & Son, C.R.	Ludington			●							
Thompson's Gunshop, Inc.	Alto			●							
Wessel Gun Service	Warren	●	●		●						
Williams Gun Sight Co.	Davison			●	●	●				●	
Williams Gunsight & Outfitters	Davison			●	●	●					
Williams Gunsmithing	Saginaw										
Will's Gun Shop	Spruce			●	●	●					●
Ye Olde Blk Powder Shop	Auburd								●		
MINNESOTA											
Ahlman's Custom Gun Shop, Inc.	Morristown	●	●		●	●		●		●	●
B&B Supply Co.	Minneapolis			●	●						
Bernston Gun Shop	Fridley			●	●						
Dale's Guns & Archery Center	Rochester				●	●		●		●	
Frontiersman's Sports	Minneapolis	●			●						
Kotila Gun Shop	Cokato				●	●		●		●	
Laibs Gunsmithing	Spicer				●	●					

SERVICE CENTER	CITY	BR	CO	CR	MO	RE	ST	SW	TC	WN	WE
Matt's 10K Gunsmithing, Inc.	Duluth					●					
Northland Sport Center	Bagley				●	●				●	
Poor Borch's, Inc.	Marshall				●	●					
MISSISSIPPI											
Grenada Gun Works	Grenada				●	●					
Jones Gun Shop, Inc.	Greenville				●	●					
Lock Stock & Barrel Gun Repair	Crystal Springs										●
Martins Gun Shop	Natchez			●							
May & Company, Inc.	Jackson			●							
Millers Gun Shop	Gulfport								●		
Saffle Repair Service	Jackson				●	●					
Sanders Gun Shop	Meridian				●	●					
Skeet Hill Gun Shop, R.L.	Verona							●		●	
MISSOURI											
Beards Sport Shop	Cape Girardeau				●	●					●
Bickford Arms	Joplin				●	●				●	●
Carl's Gun Shop	El Dorado Springs					●					
Catfish Guns	Imperial			●							
Dollar Drugs, Inc.	Lee's Summit			●							
F&D Guns	Harvester			●				●			
Kopp, Prof. Gunsmith, Terry K.	Lexington	●			●	●		●			
Nu-Line Guns, Inc.	Harvester	●	●		●	●		●			
Ozark Shooters, Inc.	Springfield			●				●			
MONTANA											
Air Gun Shop, The	Billings		●	●							
Billings Gunsmiths	Billings				●	●				●	
Bradys Sportsmans Surplus	Missoula				●	●		●			
Cannon's Guns, Inc.	Victor			●							
Capitol Sports & Western Wear	Helena	●	●		●	●					
Missoula Air Guns	Missoula			●							
Montana Gun Works	Great Falls					●		●			●
Sportsman's Surplus	Missoula			●							
Stephen's Gun Shop, Inc.	Great Falls				●	●					
NEBRASKA											
Al's Gun & Reel Shop, Inc.	North Platte				●	●				●	
Bedlan's Sporting Goods, Inc.	Fairbury	●			●	●					
Cylinder & Slide, Inc.	Fremont					●					
G.H. Gun Shop	McCook			●							
G.I. Loan Shop	Grand Island				●	●				●	●
Gun Works, The	Omaha			●	●	●					
Gunsmithing Specialties, Co.	Papillion	●								●	
Labs Air Gun Shop	Omaha			●						●	
Moneymaker Gun Craft, Inc.	Omaha			●	●						
Sport Shop, The	Nebraska City			●	●						
Sporting Goods, Inc.	Hastings				●	●		●	●		
Upper Missouri Trading Co., Inc.	Crofton				●	●			●		
NEVADA											
Accuracy Gun Shop, Inc.	Las Vegas				●	●				●	●

See page 445 for Service Center addresses.

47th EDITION, 1993 **453**

Warranty Service Centers (cont.)

■BR=Browning ■CO=Colt ■CR=Crosman ■MO=Mossberg ■RE=Remington ■ST=Stoeger ■SW=Smith & Wesson ■TC=Thompson/Center ■WN=Winchester ■WE=Weatherby

SERVICE CENTER	CITY	BR	CO	CR	MO	RE	ST	SW	TC	WN	WE
Gun World	Elko					●				●	
Nevada Air Guns	N. Las Vegas			●							
NEW HAMPSHIRE											
Lewis Arms at Riley's	Hooksett	●	●	●	●	●		●	●	●	●
NEW JERSEY											
Belleplain Supply, Inc.	Belleplain	●									
Brenner Sport Shop, Charlie	Rahway		●			●					
Garfield Gunsmithing	Garfield	●	●	●	●						
Harry's Army & Navy Store	Robbinsville	●		●						●	
Quinn & Son, William	Freehold		●		●	●					
Ray's Sport Shop, Inc.	Plainfield	●			●	●		●			
Sportsman's Center	Bordentown	●	●			●	●				
Stratton Sporting Goods, Inc.	Marlton	●		●							
The Way It Was Sporting	Moorestown	●		●							
Way It Was Sporting Services, The	Moorestown	●									
NEW MEXICO											
Charlie's Sporting Goods, Inc.	Albuquerque	●	●	●		●		●		●	●
D&J Coleman Service	Hobbs		●								
Hobb's Bicycle & Gun Sales	Hobbs	●				●					
NEW YORK											
Alpine Arms Corp.	Brooklyn	●	●								
Apple Town Gun Shop	Williamson		●	●		●					
Benson Gun Shop	Coram L.I.		●	●							
Bethpage Bicycle Shop, Inc.	Bethpage			●	●	●		●			
Boracci, E. John, Village Sport Ctr.	Seaford L.I.		●	●							
Buffalo Gun Center, Inc.	Buffalo		●			●					
Burgins Gun Shop	Sidney Center				●	●		●			
Coliseum Gun Traders, Ltd.	Uniondale			●							
Creekside Gun Shop	Holcomb	●				●		●			●
Davco Stores, 305 Broadway	Monticello		●	●	●	●					
Gemini Arms Ltd.	Syosset		●	●		●					
Greene, Sam	Monticello		●	●							
Hart's Gun Supply, Ed	Bath				●	●					
Jovino Co., Inc., John	New York		●					●			
Klelon, Gunsmith, Dave	Webster			●							
LeFever & Sons, Inc., Frank	Lee Center									●	
Lounsbury Sporting Goods, Bob	Middletown		●	●							
Rapids Gun Shop	Niagra Falls		●	●		●					
Scalzo's Sporting Goods	Endicott		●	●		●					
Smith's Lawn & Marine Svc.	Clarence			●							
Solvay Home & Outdoor Center	Solvay									●	
Sports Mart, The	Ogdensburg		●			●					
Taylor & Vadney, Inc.	Albany		●			●					
Van's Gunsmith Service	Parish			●	●	●		●			
White Dog Gunsmithing	Ilion					●					
NORTH CAROLINA											
Baity's Custom Gunworks	North Wilksboro	●									
Blue Ridge Outdoor Sports, Inc.	E. Flatrock							●	●	●	●

SERVICE CENTER	CITY	BR	CO	CR	MO	RE	ST	SW	TC	WN	WE
Cumberland Knife & Gun Works	Fayetteville									●	
Don's Gun Shop	Ashville		●	●							
Hill's, Inc.	Raleigh	●									
Mike's Crosman Service	Winston-Salem										●
Perry's of Wendell, Inc.	Wendell				●	●					
NORTH DAKOTA											
Gun City, Inc.	Bismarck	●	●								
Harvey Enterprises, Bob	Minot		●							●	
Outdoorsman, Inc.	Fargo	●			●	●					●
S.K. Guns, Inc.	Fargo				●	●					
OHIO											
Airgun Centre, Ltd.	Cincinnati		●								
All Game Sport Center	Milford		●								
Central Ohio Police Supply, c/o Wammes Guns	Bellefontaine								●		
Cherry Corners, Inc.	Lodi	●									
Eyster Heritage Gunsmiths, Ken	Centerburg					●					
Heckman Arms Company, Chagrin Valley Firearms	Chagrin							●			
John's Sporting Goods	Canton				●	●			●		
Log Cabin Sport Shop	Lodi										
Precision Airgun Sales	Solon										
Sportsman's Haven	Cambridge	●	●			●		●		●	●
Sportsmen's Repair Ctr., Inc.	Columbus Groves		●		●	●					
Stocker's Shop	Warren		●								
Trading Post, The	Massillon		●								
Upton's Gun Shop	Fremont		●					●			
VanBurnes Gun Shop	Toledo	●									
Zanes Gun Rack	Columbus					●					
OKLAHOMA											
Anderson, Inc., Andy	Oklahoma City	●									
D&D Sporting Goods	Tishomingo				●	●				●	
Mashburn Arms Co., Inc.	Oklahoma City	●			●	●		●			
Meydag, Peter	Tulsa										
Outdoor America Store	Oklahoma City							●			
Shamburg's Wholesale Spt. Gds.	Clinton		●		●						
Skeet's Gun Shop	Tahlequah										
Southwest Shooters Supply, Inc.	Oklahoma City	●	●			●		●			
Sport Shop, The	Kingfisher			●							
Sports World, Inc.	Tulsa	●				●				●	
OREGON											
Allison & Carey Gun Works	Portland	●	●			●				●	
Enstad & Douglas	Oregon City				●	●				●	●
Felton, James	Eugene								●		
Hallberg, Inc., Fritz	Ontario	●								●	●
Lock Stock & Barrel	Grants Pass										
Metro Rod & Reel	Portland										
Mooreheads Service & Repair	White City		●		●						
Surplus Center	Roseburg					●					

See page 445 for Service Center addresses.

Warranty Service Centers (cont.)

BR=Browning ■CO=Colt ■CR=Crosman ■MO=Mossberg ■RE=Remington ■ST=Stoeger ■SW=Smith & Wesson ■TC=Thompson/Center ■WN=Winchester ■WE=Weatherby

PENNSYLVANIA

SERVICE CENTER	CITY	BR	CO	CR	MO	RE	ST	SW	TC	WN	WE
Auto Electric & Parts, Inc.	Media										
Bob's Gun Shop	McKean		●								
Colabaugh Gunsmith, Inc., Craig	Stroudsburg		●								
Federal Firearms Co., Inc.	Oakdale			●	●	●					
Fix Gunshop, Inc., Michael D.	Reading				●	●					
Gorenflo Gunsmithing	Erie				●	●					
Grice Gun Shop, Inc.	Clearfield				●	●	●			●	
Hart & Son, Robert W.	Nescopeck							●			
Hemlock Gun Shop	Lakeville			●	●						
Hemlock Gun Shop	Hawley			●		●					
Herold's Gun Shoppe	Waynesboro	●								●	
Keeley, John L.	Spring City					●					
Keidel's Gunsmithing Service	Washington	●		●		●				●	
Leo's Custom Stocks	Library					●	●			●	
Levan's Sport Goods	Lebanon	●		●							
Miller's Sport Shop	Mountaintop										
Pittsburgh Handgun HQ.	Pittsburgh		●	●							
Richland Gun Shop	Richland			●		●					
Sportsman's Shop	New Holland	●		●		●					
Unique Sporting Goods	Edensburg			●		●	●				
Ye Olde Gun Shop	Bradford			●							

RHODE ISLAND

SERVICE CENTER	CITY	BR	CO	CR	MO	RE	ST	SW	TC	WN	WE
D&L Shooting Supplies	Warwick		●	●		●				●	
Gun Hospital, The	E. Providence			●							

SOUTH CAROLINA

SERVICE CENTER	CITY	BR	CO	CR	MO	RE	ST	SW	TC	WN	WE
Borgheresi, Enrique	Greenville		●								
Bryan & Associates	Anderson		●			●					
Gun Rack, Inc., The	Aiken		●								
Gun Room, The	Chapin										
Gunsmith, Inc., The	West Columbia		●			●		●			
S.E.M. Gun Works	Greenville				●	●					
Smith & Smith Gun Shop, Inc.	Charleston Hghts.	●		●							
Southland Gun Works, Inc.	Darlington					●					

SOUTH DAKOTA

SERVICE CENTER	CITY	BR	CO	CR	MO	RE	ST	SW	TC	WN	WE
Cook's Shootist Supply	Belle Fourche		●			●					
Gary's Gun Shop	Sioux Falls					●				●	
Jim's Gun & Service Center	Aberdeen									●	
Pioneer Sporting Goods	Belle Fourche										●
Ron's Gun Repair	Sioux Falls	●			●	●		●	●	●	
Sodak Sport & Bait	Aberdeen	●			●	●			●	●	

TENNESSEE

SERVICE CENTER	CITY	BR	CO	CR	MO	RE	ST	SW	TC	WN	WE
Bob's Gunsmithing	Johnson City					●			●	●	
D&L Gunsmithing/Guns & Ammo	Memphis	●	●		●	●		●	●	●	
Fox & Company	Knoxville				●	●		●	●	●	
Friedman's Army Surplus	Nashville	●			●	●		●	●	●	
Gun City USA, Inc.	Nashville	●			●	●		●	●	●	
Hagstrom, E.G.	Memphis										
Hill's Hardware & Sporting Goods	Union City										
McGuns, W.H.	Humboldt		●								●
Shaler Eagle	Jonesbrough										●

TEXAS

SERVICE CENTER	CITY	BR	CO	CR	MO	RE	ST	SW	TC	WN	WE
Armadillo Air Gun Repair	Corpus Christi		●			●					
Ben's Gun Shop	Duncanville		●			●					
Boggus Gun Shop	San Marcos					●				●	
Budd's Custom Shop, Ed	El Paso	●			●	●				●	
Carroll's Gun Shop, Inc.	Wharton	●				●					
Carter's Country	Houston					●					●
Coleman, Inc., Ron	Carrollton	●				●				●	
Custom Gun Service	McAllen										
Don & Tim's Gun Shop	San Antonio	●			●	●				●	
Don's Gun Sales	San Antonio		●			●				●	
Ewell Cross Gun Shop, Inc.	Ft. Worth	●	●			●		●		● ●	
Freer's Gun Shop	Houston	●				●	●	●			●
Gun & Tackle Store, The	Dallas										
Kirkpatrick, Gunsmith, Larry	Lubbock		●					●			
Kirk's Gun Shop, Inc.	El Paso										
Les Star & Tackle Shop	Texarkana										
Lone Star Guns, Inc.	Plano										
Longacres, Inc.	Abilene				●			●			
Master Gunsmiths, Inc.	Houston	●				●	●				
McBride's Guns, Inc.	Austin	●	●		●	●	●			●	
McClelland Gun Shop	Dallas	●				●				● ●	
Mueschke Manufacturing Co.	Houston	●									
Nagel Gun Shop, Inc.	San Antonio	●				●	●	●			●
Oshman's Sporting Goods, Inc.	Houston										
Pasadena Gun Center	Pasadena		●		●	●		●	●		
Precision Gunsmithing	Amarillo										
Ray's Sporting Goods	Dallas	●				●		●			
Reynolds Gun Shop, Inc.	Tyler				●						
Starnes, Gunmaker, Ken	Scroggins										
Wichita Guncraft, Inc.	Wichita Falls	●	●		●	●	●	●	●	●	●
Williamson-Pate Gunsmith Service	Hurst	●		●		●					
Wolfer Brothers, Inc.	Houston					●				●	

UTAH

SERVICE CENTER	CITY	BR	CO	CR	MO	RE	ST	SW	TC	WN	WE
Conner, Bob, Gunsmith	Murray					●					
Gun Shop, The	Salt Lake City	●			●	●				●	
Gunsmith Co., The	Salt Lake City					●				●	
Hutch's	Lehi										
Professional Armaments, Inc.	Murray				●	●				●	

VERMONT

SERVICE CENTER	CITY	BR	CO	CR	MO	RE	ST	SW	TC	WN	WE
Bob's Gun Shop	Milton									●	
Burby, Inc. Guns & Gunsmithing	Middlebury										
Carpenters Gun Works	Proctorsville										
Clapps Gun Shop	Orchard Heights			●							
Norm's Gun Shop	White River Junc.									●	

See page 445 for Service Center addresses.

Warranty Service Centers (cont.)

■BR=Browning ■CO=Colt ■CR=Crosman ■MO=Mossberg ■RE=Remington ■ST=Stoeger ■SW=Smith & Wesson ■TC=Thompson/Center ■WN=Winchester ■WE=Weatherby

SERVICE CENTER	CITY	BR	CO	CR	MO	RE	ST	SW	TC	WN	WE
VIRGINIA											
Bob's Gun & Tackle Shop, (Blaustein & Reich, Inc.)	Norfolk	•	•		•	•		•			•
Gun Ace	Buena Vista										
King's Gun Shop, Inc.	Franklin	•	•		•	•					
Moates Sport Shop, Bob	Midlothian	•	•		•	•					
Northern Virginia Gun Works, Inc.	Springfield		•			•					
Richmond Gun Shop	Richmond					•					
WASHINGTON											
Brock's Gunsmithing, Inc.	Spokane					•		•		•	
Chet Paulson Outfitters	Tacoma	•							•	•	
Dress Ranch & Home, Inc.	Moses Lake			•		•					
Fishing Corner, The	Seattle										
Greene's Gun Shop	Oak Harbor					•		•			
Karrer's Gunatorium	Spokane	•				•					
Kesseling Gun Shop	Burlington	•	•			•					
McDonald Grothers & Chet Paulson, Inc.	Tacoma					•					
Shooters Supply	Yakima										
Wisner's Gun Shop, Inc.	Chehalis	•	•		•	•			•	•	•
Wheeler Gun Shop, C.	Richland							•			•
WEST VIRGINIA											
Bait & Tackle Shop, The	Fairmont			•		•					
J.T. Gunshop, Inc., d/b/a Carolina Gun & Sports	Beckley										
Lew's Mountaineer Gunsmithing	Charleston					•					
Milliken's Gun Shop	Elm Grove			•						•	•
Terry's Guns	Weirton		•								
WISCONSIN											
Badgers Shooters Supply, Inc.	Owen					•					
Bob's Crosman Repair	Cudahy			•		•					
Custom Firearms Shop, The	Sheboygan	•				•					
Flintrop Arms Corp.	Milwaukee		•		•	•					
Gander Mountain, Inc.	Wilmot	•	•		•	•		•			
Jack's Lock & Gun Shop	Fond Du Lac	•									
Jay's Sports, Inc.	Menomonee Falls	•	•			•					
Midwestern Shooters Supply, Inc.	Lomira					•				•	
Phillips, D.J., Gunsmith	Pewaukee			•		•					
Potter Gunsmithing	Muskego					•					
Precision Gun Works	Oshkosh			•		•					
River Bend Sport Shop	Waupaca					•					
R&R Shooters Supply	Mauston			•							
Rusk Gun Shop, Inc.	Madison	•	•		•	•					
Sea Gull Marina	Two Rivers										
WYOMING											
Elbe Arms Co., Inc.	Cheyenne			•		•					
Jackalope Gun Shop	Douglas										
Sheridan Gun Shop	Sheridan										•

SERVICE CENTER	CITY	BR	CO	CR	MO	RE	ST	SW	TC	WN	WE
CANADA											
Armurie De L'Outaouis	Hull, PQ							•		•	
Armurerie I.A.S. Gunshop, Inc.	Montreal, PQ							•		•	
BOMAC Gunpar, Ltd.	Lakefield, ON	•	•			•				•	
Casey's Gun Shop	Rogersville, NB	•	•			•				•	
Charlton Co., Ltd.	Brentwood Bay, BC										
Custom Gun Shop	Edmonton, AB	•				•				•	•
Davidson's Canada	Peterborough, ON					•				•	
Delhi Small Arms	Delhi, ON										
Delisle Thompson Sport Goods	Saskatoon, SK					•				•	
Epps, Ellwood	Orilla, ON				•	•				•	
Ernie's Gun Shop, Ltd.	Winnipeg, MB								•		
European Arms Dist. Ltd.	N. Vancouver, BC		•						•		
Frontier Gun & Sport	Font Hill, ON										
Gene's Gunsmithing	Selkirk, MB										
Girard, Florent, Gunsmith	Chicoutimi, PQ		•								
Inland Sports	Edmonton, AB					•					
Klondike Arms & Antiques	Edmonton, AB										
L'Armurier Alain Bouchard, Inc.	St. Chryostome, PQ	•				•				•	
Long Gunsmithing Ltd., W.R.	Coburg, ON										
Magasin Latulippe, Inc.	Quebec, PQ	•				•		•		•	
Marten's Sports Ltd. John	Winnipeg, MB		•		•	•					
Milarm Co., Ltd.	Edmonton, AB		•		•	•					
Newby, Stewart, Gunsmith	New Burgh, ON				•	•					
Nichols Dist. Inc., R.	Montreal, PQ		•		•				•		
North Sylva Company	Toronto, ON					•					•
Pavillon Chasse & Peche	Laval, PQ										
Peterborough Guns	Peterborough, ON				•	•				•	
Precision Arms & Gunsmithing Ltd.	Nobleton, ON					•					
Ralph's Gun Shop	Saskatoon, SK					•				•	
Randy's Gun Repair	Tabustinac, NB				•	•				•	
Reliable Gun & Tackle, Ltd.	Vancouver, BC				•	•		•		•	
Robinson's Sporting Goods, Ltd.	Victoria, BC		•			•					
Russel's Sporting Goods	Calgary, AB							•			
Saskatoon Gunsmith Shoppe, Ltd.	Saskatoon, SK										
Selin Gunsmith, Ltd., Del	Vernon, BC									•	
Sumner Sports, Inc.	Quebec, PQ		•								
Taylor's Technical Gunsmithing Co.	Gormely, ON									•	•
Westgate Gunsports, Inc.	Edmonton, AB					•					
West Luther Gun Repair	Conn, ON					•		•		•	
Wortner Gun Works, Ltd.	Chatham, ON					•		•		•	
PUERTO RICO											
La Armeria Metropolitana In	San Juan		•								

See page 445 for Service Center addresses.

METALLIC SIGHTS

Sporting Leaf and Open Sights

BURRIS SPORTING REAR SIGHT Made of spring steel, supplied with multi-step elevator for coarse adjustments and notch plate with lock screw for finer adjustments.
Price: **$15.95**

LYMAN No. 16 Middle sight for barrel dovetail slot mounting. Folds flat when scope or peep sight is used. Sight notch plate adjustable for elevation. White triangle for quick aiming. 3 heights: A—.400" to .500", B—.345" to .445", C—.500" to .600".
Price: **$13.00**

MARBLE FALSE BASE #72, #73, #74 New screw-on base for most rifles replaces factory base. ⅜" dovetail slot permits installation of any folding rear sight. Can be had in sweat-on models also.
Price: **$6.50**

MARBLE CONTOUR RAMP #14R For late model Rem. 725, 740, 760, 742 rear sight mounting. ⁹⁄₁₆" between mounting screws. Accepts all sporting rear sights.
Price: **$13.95**

MARBLE FOLDING LEAF Flat-top or semi-buckhorn style. Folds down when scope or peep sights are used. Reversible plate gives choice of "U" or "V" notch. Adjustable for elevation.
Price: **$12.50**
Price: Also available with both windage and elevation adjustment . . . **$18.50**

MARBLE SPORTING REAR With white enamel diamond, gives choice of two "U" and two "V" notches or different sizes. Adjustment in height by means of double step elevator and sliding notch piece. For all rifles; screw or dovetail installation.
Price: . . . . **$12.50-$14.20**

MARBLE #20 UNIVERSAL New screw or sweat-on base. Both have .100" elevation adjustment. In five base sizes. Three styles of U-notch, square notch, peep. Adjustable for windage and elevation.
Price: Screw-on **$19.25**
Price: Sweat-on **$17.65**

MILLETT RIFLE SIGHT Open, fully adjustable rear sight fits standard ⅜" dovetail cut in barrel. Choice of white outline or target rear blades, .360". Front with white or orange bar, .343", .400", .430", .460", .500", .540".
Price: Rear sight **$52.95**
Price: Front sight **$11.75**

MILLETT SCOPE-SITE Open, adjustable or fixed rear sights dovetail into a base integral with the top scope-mounting ring. Blaze orange front ramp sight is integral with the front ring half. Rear sights have white outline aperture. Provides fast, short-radius, Patridge-type open sights on the top of the scope. Can be used with all Millett rings, Weaver-style bases, Ruger 77 (also fits Redhawk), Ruger Ranch Rifle, No. 1, No. 3, Rem. 870, 1100; Burris, Leupold and Redfield bases.
Price: Angle-Loc for Weaver-style bases, windage adjustable, low, medium, high **$44.95**
Price: Angle-Loc for Weaver-style bases, fully adj., low, med., high **$77.95**
Price: For Ruger 77 (also Redhawk), windage only, medium **$44.95**
Price: As above, fully adjustable **$77.95**
Price: For Ruger 77, No. 1, 3 (also Redhawk), windage only **$44.95**
Price: As above, fully adjustable **$77.95**
Price: For Rem. 870, 1100 shotguns, windage only **$43.95**
Price: As above, fully adjustable **$76.95**
Price: For Millett, Burris, Leupold, Redfield bases, windage only, low, medium, high **$43.95**
Price: As above, fully adjustable **$76.95**
Price: Scope-Site top only, windage only **$29.65**
Price: As above, fully adjustable **$62.95**
Price: Scope-Site Hi-Turret, fully adjustable, low, medium, high **$76.95**
Price: As above, Tops only (.410" rear blade, .540" rifle front) **$62.95**
Price: For Colt Python, Peacekeeper, Diamondback, fully adjustable . . . **$80.25**
Price: For Dan Wesson (through 357 Mag.), fully adj., two rings) **$80.25**
Price: As above, 41/44 Mag., three rings **$96.20**
Price: For Ruger Redhawk, windage only, medium **$44.95**
Price: As above, fully adjustable **$77.95**

WICHITA MULTI RANGE SIGHT SYSTEM Designed for silhouette shooting. System allows you to adjust the rear sight to four repeatable range settings, once it is pre-set. Sight clicks to any of the settings by turning a serrated wheel. Front sight is adjustable for weather and light conditions with one adjustment. Specify gun when ordering.
Price: Rear sight **$93.50**
Price: Front sight **$69.95**

WILLIAMS DOVETAIL OPEN SIGHT (WDOS) Open rear sight with windage and elevation adjustment. Furnished with "U" notch or choice of blades. Slips into dovetail and locks with gib lock. Heights from .281" to .531".
Price: With blade **$14.95**
Price: Less Blade **$9.35**

WILLIAMS GUIDE OPEN SIGHT (WGOS) Open rear sight with windage and elevation adjustment. Bases to fit most military and commercial barrels. Choice of square "U" or "V" notch blade, ³⁄₁₆", ¼", ⁵⁄₁₆", or ⅜" high.
Price: With blade **$19.95**
Price: Extra blades, each **$5.60**
Price: Less blade **$14.35**

WILLIAMS WGOS OCTAGON Open rear sight for 1" octagon barrels. Installs with two 6-48 screws and uses same hole spacing as most T/C muzzleloading rifles. Four heights, choice of square, U, V, B blade.
Price: **$19.95**

Micrometer Receiver Sights

BEEMAN/WEIHRAUCH MATCH APERTURE SIGHT Micrometer ¼-minute click adjustment knobs with settings indicated on scales.
Price: **$89.95**

BEEMAN/FEINWERKBAU MATCH APERTURE SIGHTS Locks into one of four eye-relief positions. Micrometer ¼-minute click adjustments; may be set to zero at any range. Extra windage scale visible beside eyeshade. Primarily for use at 5 to 20 meters.
Price: **$169.95**

BEEMAN SPORT APERTURE SIGHT Positive click micrometer adjustments. Standard units with flush surface screwdriver adjustments. Deluxe version has target knobs. For air rifles with grooved receivers.
Price: Standard **$34.98**
Price: Deluxe **$44.98**

FREELAND TUBE SIGHT Uses Unertl 1" micrometer mounts. For 22-cal. target rifles, including 52 Win., 37, 40X Rem. and BSA Martini.
Price: **$150.00**

LYMAN No. 57 ¼-minute clicks. Stayset knobs. Quick release slide, adjustable zero scales. Made for almost all modern rifles.
Price: **$64.00**

LYMAN No. 66 Fits close to the rear of flat-sided receivers, furnished with Stayset knobs. Quick release slide, ¼-min. adjustments. For most lever or slide action or flat-sided automatic rifles.
Price: **$64.00**

LYMAN No. 66U Light weight, designed for most modern shotguns with a flat-sided, round-top receiver. ¼-minute clicks. Requires drilling, tapping. Not for Browning A-5, Rem. M11.
Price: **$64.00**

LYMAN 90MJT RECEIVER SIGHT Mounts on standard Lyman and Williams FP bases. Has ¼-minute audible micrometer click adjustments, target knobs with direction indicators. Adjustable zero scales, quick release slide. Large ⅞" diameter aperture disk.
Price: **$75.00**

MILLETT ASSAULT RIFLE SIGHTS Fully adjustable, heat-treated nickel steel peep aperture receiver sights for AR-15, Mini-14. AR-15 rear sight has windage and elevation adjustments; non-glare replacement ramp-style front also available. Mini-14 sight has fine windage and elevation adjustments; replaces original.
Price: Rear sight for above guns **$51.45**
Price: Front and rear combo for AR-15 . . . . **$62.65**
Price: Front sight for AR-15 . . . . **$12.25**
Price: Front and rear combo for Mini-14 . . . . **$68.25**
Price: Front sight for Mini-14 . . . . **$17.85**

WILLIAMS FP Internal click adjustments. Positive locks. For virtually all rifles, T/C Contender, Heckler & Koch HK-91, Ruger Mini-14, plus Win., Rem. and Ithaca shotguns.
Price: From **$53.25**
Price: With Twilight Aperture **$54.85**
Price: With Target Knobs **$63.25**
Price: With Target Knobs & Twilight Aperture **$64.85**
Price: With Square Notched Blade **$56.00**
Price: With Target Knobs & Square Notched Blade **$66.15**
Price: FP-GR (for dovetail-grooved receivers, 22s and air guns) **$53.25**

WILLIAMS TARGET FP Similar to the FP series but developed for most bolt-action rimfire rifles. Target FP High adjustable from 1.250" to 1.750" above centerline of bore; Target FP Low adjustable from .750" to 1.250". Attaching bases for Rem. 540X, 541-S, 580, 581, 582 (#540); Rem. 510, 511, 512, 513-T, 521-T (#510); Win. 75 (#75); Savage/Anschutz 64 and Mark 12 (#64). Some rifles require drilling, tapping.
Price: High or Low, with Base **$84.10**
Price: As above, less Base **$72.00**
Price: Base only **$12.10**
Price: FP-T/C Scout rifle, from **$53.25**

WILLIAMS 5-D SIGHT Low cost sight for shotguns, 22s and the more popular big game rifles. Adjustment for windage and elevation. Fits most guns without drilling or tapping. Also for British SMLE, Winchester M94 Side Eject.
Price: **$29.95**
Price: With Twilight Aperture **$31.60**
Price: With Shotgun Aperture **$29.95**

WILLIAMS GUIDE (WGRS) Receiver sight for 30 M1 Carbine, M1903A3 Springfield, Savage 24s, Savage-Anschutz rifles and Weatherby XXII. Utilizes military dovetail; no drilling. Double-dovetail windage adjustment, sliding dovetail adjustment for elevation.
Price: **$29.95**
Price: With Twilight Aperture **$31.60**
Price: With Open Sight Blade **$27.55**

Front Sights

LYMAN HUNTING SIGHTS Made with gold or white beads $1/16$" to $3/32$" wide and in varying heights for most military and commercial rifles. Dovetail bases.
Price: **$8.95**

MARBLE STANDARD Ivory, red, or gold bead. For all American-made rifles, $1/16$" wide bead with semi-flat face which does not reflect light. Specify type of rifle when ordering.
Price: **$7.50**

MARBLE-SHEARD "GOLD" Shows up well even in darkest timber. Shows same color on different colored objects; sturdily built. Medium bead. Various models for different makes of rifles so specify type of rifle when ordering.
Price: **$9.50**

MARBLE CONTOURED Same contour and shape as Marble-Sheard but uses standard $1/16$" or $3/32$" bead, ivory, red or gold. Specify rifle type.
Price: **$8.65**

MARBLE PATRIDGE Gold-faced Patridge front sight is available in .250" or .34" widths and heights from .260" to .538".
Price: **$9.50**

POLY-CHOKE Rifle front sights available in six heights and two widths. Model A designed to be inserted into the barrel dovetail; Model B is for use with standard .350" ramp; both have standard $3/8$" dovetails. Gold or ivory color $1/16$" bead. From Marble Arms.
Price: **$6.00**

WILLIAMS RISER BLOCKS For adding .250" height to front sights when using a receiver sight. Two widths available: .250" for Williams Streamline Ramp or .340" on all standard ramps having this base width. Uses standard $3/8$" dovetail.
Price: **$4.95**

Globe Target Front Sights

FREELAND SUPERIOR Furnished with six 1" plastic apertures. Available in $4^1/2$"-$6^1/2$" lengths. Made for any target rifle.
Price: **$48.50**
Price: With six metal insert apertures **$51.60**
Price: Front base **$12.50**

FREELAND TWIN SET Two Freeland Superior Front Sights, long or short, allow switching from 50 yd. to 100 yd. ranges and back again without changing rear sight adjustment. Sight adjustment compensation is built into the set; just interchange and you're "on" at either range. Set includes six plastic apertures.
Price: **$67.00**
Price: With six metal apertures **$70.00**

FREELAND MILITARY Short model for use with high-powered rifles where sight must not extend beyond muzzle. Screw-on base; six plastic apertures.
Price: **$48.50**
Price: With six metal apertures **$51.60**
Price: Front base **$12.50**

LYMAN 20 MJT TARGET FRONT Has $7/8$" diameter, one-piece steel globe with $3/8$" dovetail base. Height is .700" from bottom of dovetail to center of aperture; height on 20 LJT is .750". Comes with seven Anschutz-size steel inserts—two posts and five apertures .126" through .177".
Price: 20 MJT or 20 LJT **$35.00**

LYMAN No. 17A TARGET Includes seven interchangeable inserts: four apertures, one transparent amber and two posts .50" and .100" in width.
Price: **$28.00**
Price: Insert set **$9.95**

Ramp Sights

LYMAN SCREW-ON RAMP Used with 8-40 screws but may also be brazed on. Heights from .10" to .350". Ramp without sight.
Price: **$15.50**

MARBLE FRONT RAMPS Available in either screw-on or sweat-on style, five heights: $3/16$", $5/16$", $3/8$", $7/16$", $9/16$". Standard $3/8$" dovetail slot.
Price: **$14.95**
Price: Hoods for above ramps **$3.25**

WILLIAMS SHORTY RAMP Companion to "Streamlined" ramp, about $1/2$" shorter. Screw-on or sweat-on. It is furnished in $1/8$", $3/16$", $9/32$", and $3/8$" heights without hood only.
Price: **$12.50**
Price: With dovetail lock **$14.85**

WILLIAMS STREAMLINED RAMP Hooded style in screw-on or sweat-on models. Furnished in $9/16$", $7/16$", $3/8$", $5/16$", $3/16$" heights.
Price: With hood **$18.45**
Price: Without hood **$14.95**

WILLIAMS STREAMLINED FRONT SIGHTS Narrow (.250" width) for Williams Streamlined ramps and others with $1/4$" top width; medium (.340" width) for all standard factory ramps. Available with white, gold or flourescent beads, $1/16$" or $3/32$".
Price: . . . . **$7.90 to $8.20**

Handgun Sights

BO-MAR DELUXE BMCS Gives $3/8$" windage and elevation adjustment at 50 yards on Colt Gov't 45; sight radius under 7". For GM and Commander models only. Uses existing dovetail slot. Has shield-type rear blade.
Price: **$65.95**

BO-MAR LOW PROFILE RIB & ACCURACY TUNER Streamlined rib with front and rear sights; $7^1/8$" sight radius. Brings sight line closer to the bore than standard or extended sight and ramp. Weight 5 oz. Made for Colt Gov't 45, Super 38, and Gold Cup 45 and 38.
Price: **$123.00**

BO-MAR COMBAT RIB For S&W Model 19 revolver with 4" barrel. Sight radius $5^3/4$", weight $5^1/2$ oz.
Price: **$110.00**

BO-MAR FAST DRAW RIB Streamlined full-length rib with integral Bo-Mar micrometer sight and serrated fast draw sight. For Browning 9mm, S&W 39, Colt Commander 45, Super Auto and 9mm.
Price: **$110.00**

BO-MAR WINGED RIB For S&W 4" and 6" length barrels—K-38, M10, HB 14 and 19. Weight for the 6" model is about $7^1/4$ oz.
Price: **$123.00**

BO-MAR COVER-UP RIB Adjustable rear sight, winged front guards. Fits right over revolver's original front sight. For S&W 4" M-10HB, M-13, M-58, M-64 & 65, Ruger 4" models SDA-34, SDA-84, SS-34, SS-84, GF-34, GF-84.
Price: **$117.00**

C-MORE SIGHTS Replacement front sight blades offered in two types and five styles. Made of Du Pont Acetal, they come in a set of five high-contrast colors: blue, green, pink, red and yellow. Easy to install. Patridge style for Colt Python (all barrels), Ruger Super Blackhawk ($7^1/2$"), Ruger Blackhawk ($4^5/8$"); ramp style for Python (all barrels), Blackhawk ($4^5/8$"), Super Blackhawk ($7^1/2$" and $10^1/2$"). From Mag-na-port Int'l.
Price: Per set **$19.95**

MMC COMBAT FIXED REAR SIGHT (Colt 1911-Type Pistols) This veteran MMC sight is well known to those who prefer a true combat sight for "carry" guns. Steel construction for long service. Choose from a wide variety of front sights.
Price: Combat Fixed Rear, plain **$18.45**
Price: As above, white outline **$23.65**
Price: Combat Front Sight for above, six styles, from **$5.15**

MMC M/85 ADJUSTABLE REAR SIGHT Designed to be compatible with the Ruger P-85 front sight. Fully adjustable for windage and elevation.
Price: M/85 Adjustable Rear Sight, plain **$52.45**
Price: As above, white outline **$57.70**

MMC STANDARD ADJUSTABLE REAR SIGHT Available for Colt 1911 type, Ruger Standard Auto, and now for S&W 469, and 659 pistols. No front sight change is necessary, as this sight will work with the original factory front sight.
Price: Standard Adjustable Rear Sight, plain leaf **$46.05**
Price: Standard Adjustable Rear Sight, white outline **$51.15**

MMC MINI-SIGHT Miniature size for carrying, fully adjustable, for maximum accuracy with your pocket auto. MMC's Mini-Sight will work with the factory front sight. No machining is necessary; easy installation. Available for Walther PP, PPK, and PPK/S pistols. Will also fit fixed sight Browning Hi-Power (P-35).
Price: Mini-Sight, plain **$58.45**
Price: Mini-Sight, white bar **$63.45**

MEPROLIGHT SIGHTS Replacement open sights for popular handguns and Uzi carbine, AR-15/M-16 rifles. Both front and rear sights have tritium inserts for illumination in low-light conditions. Inserts give constant non-glare green light for 5 years, even in cold weather. For most popular auto pistols, revolvers, some rifles and shotguns. Contact Hesco, Inc. for complete details.
Price: Universal front for revolvers **$24.95**
Price: Front and rear sights **$89.95**
Price: Shotgun bead **$24.95**

MILLETT BAR-DOT-BAR TRITIUM SIGHTS Combo set uses the Series 100 fully adjustable sight system with horizontal tritium inserts on the rear, a single insert on the front. Available for: Ruger P-85, SIG Sauer P220, P225/226, Browning Hi-Power, Colt GM, CZ/TZ, TA-90, Glock 17, 19, 20, 21, 22, 23, S&W (2nd, 3rd generations), Beretta 84, 85, 92SB, Taurus PT-92.
Price: **$135.00**
Price: Beretta, Taurus **$143.50**

MILLETT 3-DOT SYSTEM SIGHTS The 3-Dot System sights use a single white dot on the front blade and two dots flanking the rear notch. Fronts available in Dual-Crimp and Wide Stake-On styles, as well as special applications. Adjustable rear sight available for most popular auto pistols and revolvers.
Price: Front, from **$15.25**
Price: Adjustable rear, from . . . . **$46.96 to $68.25**

MILLETT SERIES 100 ADJUSTABLE SIGHTS   Replacement sights for revolvers and auto pistols. Positive click adjustments for windage and elevation. Designed for accuracy and ruggedness. Made to fit S&W, Colt, Beretta, SIG Sauer P220, P225, P226, Ruger P-85, Ruger GP-100 (and others), Glock 17, CZ-75, TZ-75, Dan Wesson, Browning, AMT Hardballer. Rear blades are available in white outline or positive black target. All steel construction and easy to install.
Price: . . . . **$46.95 to $75.35**

MILLETT MARK SERIES PISTOL SIGHTS   Mark I and Mark II replacement combat sights for government-type auto pistols, including H&K P7. Mark I is high profile, Mark II low profile. Both have horizontal light deflectors.
Price: Mark I, front and rear **$32.95**
Price: Mark II, front and rear **$46.95**
Price: For H&K P7 . . . . **$46.95**

MILLETT REVOLVER FRONT SIGHTS   All-steel replacement front sights with either white or orange bar. Easy to install. For Ruger GP-100, Redhawk, Security-Six, Police-Six, Speed-Six, Colt Trooper, Diamondback, King Cobra, Peacemaker, Python, Dan Wesson 22 and 15-2.
Price: **$15.25**

MILLETT DUAL-CRIMP FRONT SIGHT   Replacement front sight for automatic pistols. Dual-Crimp uses an all-steel two-point hollow rivet system. Available in eight heights and four styles. Has a skirted base that covers the front sight pad. Easily installed with the Millett Installation Tool Set. Available in Blaze Orange Bar, White Bar, Serrated Ramp, Plain Post.
Price: **$15.25**

MILLETT STAKE-ON FRONT SIGHT   Replacement front sight for automatic pistols. Stake-On sights have skirted base that covers the front sight pad. Easily installed with the Millet Installation Tool Set. Available in seven heights and four styles—Blaze Orange Bar, White Bar, Serrated Ramp, Plain Post.
Price: **$15.25**

OMEGA OUTLINE SIGHT BLADES   Replacement rear sight blades for Colt and Ruger single action guns and the Interarms Virginian Dragoon. Standard Outline available in gold or white notch outline on blue metal. From Omega Sales, Inc.
Price: **$8.95**

OMEGA MAVERICK SIGHT BLADES   Replacement "peep-sight" blades for Colt, Ruger SAs, Virginian Dragoon. Three models available—No. 1, Plain; No. 2, Single Bar; No. 3, Double Bar Rangefinder. From Omega Sales, Inc.
Price: Each **$6.95**

TRIJICON NIGHT SIGHTS   Three-dot sighting system uses tritium inserts in the front and rear sights. Tritium "lamps" are mounted in silicone rubber inside a metal cylinder. A polished crystal sapphire provides protection and clarity. Inlaid white outlines provide 3-dot aiming in daylight also. Available for most popular handguns with fixed or adjustable sights. From Trijicon, Inc.
Price: . . . . **$19.95 to $175.00**

THOMPSON/CENTER "ULTIMATE" SIGHTS   Replacement front and rear sights for the T/C Contender. Front sight has four interchangeable blades (.060", .080", .100", .120"), rear sight has four notch widths of the same measurements for a possible 16 combinations. Rear sight can be used with existing soldered front sights.
Price: Front sight **$35.00**
Price: Rear sight **$65.00**

WICHITA SERIES 70/80 SIGHT   Provides click windage and elevation adjustments with precise repeatability of settings. Sight blade is grooved and angled back at the top to reduce glare. Available in Low Mount Combat or Low Mount Target styles for Colt 45s and their copies, S&W 645, Hi-Power, CZ 75 and others.
Price: Rear sight, target or combat **$66.75**
Price: Front sight, Patridge or ramp **$10.45**

WICHITA GRAND MASTER DELUXE RIBS   Ventilated rib has wings machined into it for better sight acquisition. Made of stainless steel, sights blued. Uses Wichita Multi-Range rear sight, adjustable front sight. Made for revolvers with 6" barrel.
Price: Model 301 (adj. sight K-frames with custom bbl. of 1.000"-1.032" dia., L- and N-frames with 1.062"-1.100" bbl.) **$160.00**
Price: Model 302 (fixed sight K-frames; M10, 65, 13 with 1.000" bbl., N-frame with 1.062" bbl.) **$160.00**
Price: Model 303 (Model 29, 629 with factory bbl., adj. sight K-, L-, N-frames) **$160.00**

WICHITA DOUBLE MASTER RIB   Ventilated rib has wings machined on either side of fixed front post sight for better acquisition and is relieved for Mag-na-ports. Milled to accept Weaver See-Thru-style rings. Made of blued steel. Has Wichita Multi-Range rear sight system. Made for Model 29/629 with factory barrel, and all adjustable-sight K-, L- and N-frames.
Price: Model 403 . . . . **$140.00**

Shotgun Sights

ACCURA-SITE   For shooting shotgun slugs. Three models to fit most shotguns—"A" for vent. rib barrels, "B" for solid ribs, "C" for plain barrels. Rear sight has windage and elevation provisions. Easily removed and replaced. Includes front and rear sights.
Price: . . . . **$27.95 to $34.95**

FIRE FLY EM-109 SL SHOTGUN SIGHT   Made of aircraft-grade aluminum, this ¼-oz. "channel" sight has a thick, sturdy hollowed post between the side rails to give a Patridge sight picture. All shooting is done with both eyes open, allowing the shooter to concentrate on the target, not the sights. The hole in the sight post gives reduced-light shooting capability and allows for fast, precise aiming. For sport or combat shooting. Model EM-109 fits all vent. rib and double barrel shotguns and muzzleloaders with octagon barrel. Model MOC-110 fits all plain barrel shotguns without screw-in chokes. From JAS. Add $3 postage.
Price: **$29.95**

LYMAN   Three sights of over-sized ivory beads. No. 10 Front (press fit) for double barrel or ribbed single barrel guns...**$4.80**; No. 10D Front (screw fit) for non-ribbed single barrel guns (comes with wrench)...**$6.00**; No. 11 Middle (press fit) for double and ribbed single barrel guns...**$4.80**.

MMC M&P COMBAT SHOTGUN SIGHT SET   A durable, protected ghost ring aperture, combat sight made of steel. Fully adjustable for windage and elevation.
Price: M&P Sight Set (front and rear) **$73.45**
Price: As above, installed **$83.95**

MARBLE SHOTGUN BEAD SIGHTS   No. 214—Ivory front bead, 11/64", tapered shank...**$3.70**; No. 223—Ivory rear bead, .080", tapered shank...**$3.75**; No. 217—Ivory front bead, 11/64", threaded shank...**$4.00**; No. 223-T—Ivory rear bead, .080", threaded shank...**$5.30**. Reamers, taps and wrenches available from Marble Arms.

MILLET SHURSHOT SHOTGUN SIGHT   A sight system for shotguns with ventilated rib. Rear sight attaches to the rib, front sight replaces the front bead. Front has an orange face, rear has two orange bars. For 870, 1100 or other models.
Price: Front and rear **$20.95**
Price: Adjustable front and rear **$27.40**

POLY-CHOKE   Replacement front shotgun sights in four styles—Xpert, Poly Bead, Xpert Mid Rib sights, and Bev-L-Block. Xpert Front available in 3x56, 6x48 thread, ³⁄₃₂" or ⁵⁄₃₂" shank length, gold, ivory...**$4.50**; or Sun Spot orange bead...**$4.50**; Poly Bead is standard replacement ⅛" bead, 6x48...**$2.40**; Xpert Mid Rib in tapered carrier (ivory only) or 3x56 threaded shank (gold only)...**$3.50**; Hi and Lo Blok sights with 6x48 thread, gold or ivory...**$3.50** or Sun Spot Orange...**$4.50**. From Marble Arms.

SLUG SIGHTS   Made of non-marring black nylon, front and rear sights stretch over and lock onto the barrel. Sights are low profile with blaze orange front blade. Adjustable for windage and elevation. For plain-barrel (non-ribbed) guns in 12-, 16- and 20-gauge, and for shotguns with ⁵⁄₁₆" and ⅜" ventilated ribs. From Innovision Ent.
Price: **$11.95**

WILLIAMS GUIDE BEAD SIGHT   Fits all shotguns, ⅛" ivory, red or gold bead. Screws into existing sight hole. Various thread sizes and shank lengths.
Price: **$4.50**

WILLIAMS SLUGGER SIGHTS   Removable aluminum sights attach to the shotgun rib. High profile front, fully adjustable rear. Fits ¹⁵⁄₁₆" ribs.
Price: **$34.95**

Sight Attachments

FREELAND LENS ADAPTER   Fits 1⅛" O.D. prescription ground lens to all standard tube and receiver sights for shooting without glasses.
Price: Without lens **$66.50**
Price: Clear lens ground to prescription **$24.00**
Price: Yellow or green prescription lens **$24.00**

MERIT IRIS SHUTTER DISC   Eleven clicks give 12 different apertures. No. 3 Disc and Master, primarily target types, 0.22" to .125"; No. 4, ½" dia. hunting type, .025" to .155". Available for all popular sights. The Master Deluxe, with flexible rubber light shield, is particularly adapted to extension, scope height, and tang sights. All Merit Deluxe models have internal click springs; are hand fitted to minimum tolerance.
Price: Master Deluxe **$63.00**
Price: No. 3 Disc **$52.00**
Price: No. 4 Hunting Disc **$45.00**

MERIT LENS DISC   Similar to Merit Iris Shutter (Model 3 or Master) but incorporates provision for mounting prescription lens integrally. Lens may be obtained locally from your optician. Sight disc is ⁷⁄₁₆" wide (Model 3), or ¾" wide (Master). Model 3 Target.
Price: **$65.00**
Price: Master Deluxe **$75.00**

MERIT OPTICAL ATTACHMENT   For revolver and pistol shooters, instantly attached by rubber suction cup to regular or shooting glasses. Any aperture .020" to .156".
Price: Deluxe (swings aside) **$63.00**

WILLIAMS APERTURES   Standard thread, fits most sights. Regular series ⅜" to ½" O.D., .050" to .125" hole. "Twilight" series has white reflector ring. .093" to .125" inner hole.
Price: Regular series **$4.50**
Price: Twilight series **$6.15**
Price: Wide open ⁵⁄₁₆" aperture for shotguns fits 5-D or Foolproof sights (specify model) **$7.95**

CHOKES & BRAKES

Briley Screw-In Chokes

Installation of these choke tubes requires that all traces of the original choking be removed, the barrel threaded internally with square threads and then the tubes are custom fitted to the specific barrel diameter. The tubes are thin and, therefore, made of stainless steel. Cost of installation for single-barrel guns (pumps, autos), lead shot, 12-gauge, **$129.00**, 20-gauge **$139.00**; steel shot **$159.00** and **$169.00**, all with three chokes; un-single target guns run **$190.00**; over/unders and side-by-sides, lead shot, 12-gauge, **$340.00**, 20-gauge **$360.00**; steel shot **$390.00** and **$410.00**, all with five chokes. For 10-gauge auto or pump with two steel shot chokes, **$115.00**; over/unders, side-by-sides with three steel shot chokes, **$320.00**. For 16-gauge auto or pump, three lead shot chokes, **$159.00**; over/unders, side-by-sides with five lead shot chokes, **$420.00**. The 28 and 410-bore run **$159.00** for autos and pumps with three lead shot chokes, **$420.00** for over/unders and side-by-sides with five lead shot chokes.

Cellini Stabilizer System

Designed for handgun, rifle and shotgun applications, the Cellini Stabilizer System is available as a removable factory-installed accessory. Overall length is 1¾", weight is 2 oz., and is said to reduce muzzle jump to nearly zero, even for automatic weapons. If installed by the maker, cost starts at **$185.00** for rifles; double shotguns, **$180.00**; handguns **$165.00**; single barrel shotguns start at **$75.00**. From Vito Cellini.

Cutts Compensator

The Cutts Compensator is one of the oldest variable choke devices available. Manufactured by Lyman Gunsight Corporation, it is available with a steel body. A series of vents allows gas to escape upward and downward. For the 12-ga. Comp body, six fixed-choke tubes are available: the Spreader—popular with Skeet shooters; Improved Cylinder; Modified; Full; Superfull, and Magnum Full. Full, Modified and Spreader tubes are available for 12 or 20, and an Adjustable Tube, giving Full through Improved Cylinder chokes, is offered in 12 and 20 gauges. Cutts Compensator, complete with wrench, adaptor and any single tube **$69.80**; with adjustable tube **$91.00**. All single choke tubes **$22.00** each. No factory installation available.

Fabian Bros. Muzzle Stabilizer

A muzzlebrake/flash hider system that installs without gunsmithing on most military-type rifles, except Ruger Mini-14 and the Uzi Carbine. Adjustable for right- or left-handed shooters to eliminate muzzle rise and sideswing. No increase in sound level. Fabian Bros. offers a low-cost barrel threading service for the Mini-14 and Uzi Carbine. Available for most popular military-type rifles and carbines. Standard model, **$39.95**; Semi-Custom model (Cobray M11, MAC-10, Valmet), **$79.95**; Deluxe (M1A/M-14, M-60), **$79.95**; stainless steel, **$44.95**. All prices do not include shipping.

Gentry Quiet Muzzle Brake

Developed by gunmaker David Gentry, the "Quiet Muzzle Brake" is said to reduce recoil by up to 85 percent with no loss of accuracy or velocity. There is no increase in noise level because the noise and gasses are directed away from the shooter. The barrel is threaded for installation and the unit is blued to match the barrel finish. Price, installed, is **$150.00**. Add **$15.00** for stainless steel, **$25.00** for knurled cap to protect threads.

Intermountain Arms Recoil-Brake

Two models offered: Custom Compac and Custom Straight Line. Custom Compac is 1½" overall, increases barrel length by 1"; has 18 holes to direct gases away from shooter. Straight Line is 2¼" overall, adding 1¾" to barrel length; has 42 holes to direct gases. Both have expansion chambers. Said to reduce recoil by 50 percent. Price, blued, **$159.00**; stainless steel **$169.00**, installed. From Intermountain Arms.

KDF Slim Line Muzzle Brake

Works on the same principle as the KDF Recoil Arrestor except has 30 pressure ports, is closer to the carrel contour, and is made of a stronger steel. Price, installed, is **$179.00**. From KDF, Inc.

Lyman CHOKE

The Lyman CHOKE is similar to the Cutts Comp in that it comes with fixed-choke tubes or an adjustable tube, with or without recoil chamber. The adjustable tube version sells for **$47.95** with recoil chamber, in 12- or 20-gauge. Lyman also offers Single-Choke tubes at **$22.00**. This device may be used with or without a recoil-reduction chamber; cost of the latter is **$11.50** extra. Available in 12- or 20-gauge only. No factory installation offered.

Mag-na-port

Electrical Discharge Machining works on any firearm except those having non-conductive shrouded barrels. EDM is a metal erosion technique using carbon electrodes that control the area to be processed. The Mag-na-port venting process utilizes small trapezoidal openings to direct powder gases upward and outward to reduce recoil.

No effect is had on bluing or nickeling outside the Mag-na-port area so no refinishing is needed. Cost for the Mag-na-port treatment is **$65.00** for revolvers, **$90.00** for auto pistols, **$85.00** for rifles, not including shipping, handling and insurance.

Poly-Choke

Marble Arms Corp., manufacturer of the Poly-Choke adjustable shotgun choke, now offers two models in 12-, 16-, 20-, and 28-gauge—the Ventilated and Standard style chokes. Each provides nine choke settings including Xtra-Full and Slug. The Ventilated model reduces 20 percent of a shotgun's recoil, the company claims, and is priced at **$80.00**. The Standard Model is **$72.00**. Postage not included. Contact Marble Arms for more data.

Reed-Choke

Reed-Choke is a system of interchangeable choke tubes that can be installed in any single or double-barreled shotgun, including over/unders. The existing chokes are bored out, the muzzles over-bored and threaded for the tubes. A choice of three Reed-Choke tubes are supplied—Skeet, Imp. Cyl., Mod., Imp. Mod., or Full. Flush fitting, no notches exposed. Designed for thin-walled barrels. Made from 174 stainless steel. Cost of the installation is **$179.95** for single-barrel guns, **$229.95** for doubles. Extra tubes cost **$40.00** each. Postage and handling charges are **$8.50**.

Pro-port

A compound ellipsoid muzzle venting process similar to Mag-na-porting, only exclusively applied to shotguns. Like Mag-na-porting, this system reduces felt recoil, muzzle jump, and shooter fatigue. Very helpful for trap doubles shooters. Pro-Port is a patented process and installation is available in both the U.S. and Canada. Cost for the Pro-Port process is **$110.00** for over/unders (both barrels); **$80.00** for only the top or bottom barrel; and **$69.00** for single-barrel shotguns. Prices do not include shipping and handling. From Pro-port Ltd.

SSK Arrestor Brake

This is a true muzzlebrake with an expansion chamber. It takes up about 1 inch of barrel and reduces velocity accordingly. Some Arrestors are added to a barrel, increasing its length. Said to reduce the felt recoil of a 458 to that approaching a 30-06. Can be set up to give zero muzzle rise in any caliber, and can be added to most guns. For handgun or rifle. Prices start at **$75.00**. Contact SSK Industries for full data.

Techni-Port

The Techni-Port recoil compensation system is intended for revolvers, single shot pistols and rifles. This is a machined process which involves back-boring the muzzle (with a 30-degree internal crown) and cutting an oval port on each side of the barrel. The process is said to reduce muzzle jump up to 60 percent and felt recoil up to 50 percent, with no reduction in velocity or accuracy. Cost of the Techni-Port process is **$99.95**, plus **$6.00** for return freight and insurance. Available from Delta Vectors, Inc.

Walker Choke Tubes

This interchangeable choke tube system uses an adaptor fitted to the barrel without swaging. Therefore, it can be fitted to any single-barreled gun. The choke tubes use the conical-parallel system as used on all factory-choked barrels. These tubes can be used in Winchester, Mossberg, Smith & Wesson, Weatherby, or similar barrels made for the standard screw-in choke system. Available for 10-, 12-, 16- and 20-gauge. Factory installation (single barrel) with standard Walker choke tube is **$95.00**, **$190.00** for double barrels with two choke tubes. A full range of constriction is available. Contact Walker Arms for more data.

Walker Full Thread Choke Tubes

An interchangeable choke tube system using fully threaded inserts. No swaging, adaptor or change in barrel exterior dimensions. Available in 12- or 20-gauge. Factory installation cost: **$95.00** with one tube; extra tubes **$20.00** each. Contact Walker Arms Co. for more data.

Maker and Model	Magn.	Field at 100 Yds. (feet)	Relative Bright-ness	Eye Relief (in.)	Length (in.)	Tube Dia. (in.)	W&E Adjust-ments	Weight (ozs.)	Price	Other Data
ACTION ARMS										
Micro-Dot										
1.5-4.5x LER Pistol	1.5-4.5	80-26	—	12-24	8.8	1	Int.	9.5	$259.00	[1]56mm objective. Variable intensity LED red aiming dot. Average battery life 20 to 4500 hours. Waterproof, nitrogen-filled aluminum tube. Fits most standard 1" rings. Both Ultra Dot models avail. in black and satin chrome. Imported by Action Arms Ltd.
1.5-4.5x Rifle	1.5-4.5	80-26	—	3	9.8	1	Int.	10.5	259.00	
2-7x32	2-7	54-18	—	3	11	1	Int.	12.1	279.00	
3-9x40	3-9	40-14	—	3	12.2	1	Int.	13.3	309.00	
4x-12x[1]	4-12	—	—	3	14.3	1	Int.	18.3	415.00	
Ultra-Dot 25 1x	—	—	—	—	5.1	1	Int.	4.0	160.00	
Ultra-Dot 30 1x	—	—	—	—	5.1	30mm	Int.	3.9	195.00	
ADCO										
Mirage Ranger	0	—	—	—	5.5	1	Int.	5	129.00	Dot covers 1.5" at 100 yards. Black or nickel finish. Uses long-life lithium wafer battery that fits into the sight body—no battery appendage. [1]Multi-Color Dot changes from red to green color. 1" extension included. From ADCO.
Mirage Sportsman[1]	0	—	—	—	5.5	1	Int.	4.5	219.00	
Mirage Competitor[1]	0	—	—	—	5.5	30mm	Int.	5.4	249.00	
AIMPOINT										
Series 3000 Short[2]	0	—	—	—	5.5	1	Int.	5.5	249.95	Illuminates red dot in field of view. Noparallax (dot does not need to be centered). Unlimited field of view and eye relief. On/off, adj. intensity. Dot covers 3" @ 100 yds. Mounts avail. for all sights and scopes. [1]Comes with 30mm rings, battery, lens cloth. [2]Requires 1" rings. Black or stainless finish. 3x scope attachment (for rifles only), **$129.95**. [3]Projects red dot of visible laser light onto target. Black finish (LSR-2B) or stainless (LSR-2S); or comes with rings and accessories. Optional toggle switch, **$34.95**. Lithium battery life up to 15 hours. [4]Black finish (AP 5000-B) or stainless (AP 5000-S); avail. with regular 3-min. or 10-min. Mag Dot as B2 or S2. [5]Black finish; 2x magnification scope with floating dot. From Aimpoint.
Series 3000 Long[2]	0	—	—	—	6 7/8	1	Int.	5.8	259.95	
Laserdot[3]	—	—	—	—	4	1	Int.	4.0	329.95	
AP 5000[4]	0	—	—	—	5.5	30mm	Int.	5.8	309.95	
AP 5000/2x[1]	2	—	—	—	7	30mm	Int.	9	399.95	
AP 2P[5]	2	—	—	—	8.5	1	Int.	8.3	324.95	
APPLIED LASER SYSTEMS										
T2	—	—	—	—	2.8	—	Int.	2.2	210.00	Visible laser diode with 100,000 hour life. Class IIIa; deep red color; 80% of beam image in 1" square at 50ft.; 100-yd. effective range; all metal construction; over 2½-hour battery life at continuous duty. From Applied Laser Systems.
AR15	—	—	—	—	2	—	Int.	3	315.00	
Colt 1911	—	—	—	—	2	—	Int.	4	315.00	
Beretta 92F	—	—	—	—	2	—	Int.	4	315.00	
RM 870	—	—	—	—	3	—	Int.	3	315.00	
Glock	—	—	—	—	.75	—	Int.	.8	385.00	
ARMSON O.E.G.										
Standard	0	—	—	—	5 1/8	1	Int.	4.3	216.00	Shows red dot aiming point. No batteries needed. Standard model fits 1" ring mounts (not incl.). Other models available for many popular shotguns, para-military rifles and carbines. [1]Daylight Only Sight with 3/8" dovetail mount for 22s. Does not contain tritium. From Trijicon, Inc.
22 DOS[1]	0	—	—	—	3 3/4	—	Int.	3.0	121.00	
22 Day/Night	0	—	—	—	3 3/4	—	Int.	3.0	167.00	
M16/AR-15	0	—	—	—	5 1/8	—	Int.	5.5	250.00	
Colt Pistol	0	—	—	—	3 3/4	—	Int.	3.0	250.00	
BAUSCH & LOMB										
Target										
10x	10	11	—	3.1	13.75	1	Int.	21.8	1,852.95	All except Target scopes have ¼-minute click adjustments; Target scopes have ⅛-minute adjustments with standard turrets and expanded turret knobs. Target scopes come with sunshades, screw-on lens caps. [1]Matte finish **$596.95**. [2]Adj. obj. Matte finish **$666.95**. [3]Matte finish **$583.95**. [4]Silver finish. [5]Matte finish **$349.95**. [6]Matte finish **$367.95**. Contact Bushnell for details.
36x	36	3	—	3.2	15	1	Int.	17.6	719.95	
Balvar										
1.5-6x[1]	1.5-6	74-19	—	3.3	11.5	1	Int.	12.7	583.95	
2.5-10x[2]	2.5-10	44-12	—	3.3	13.8	1	Int.	18.9	652.95	
3-9x[3]	3-9	42-12	—	3.2	13.0	1	Int.	16.5	570.95	
6-24x	6-24	18-5	—	3.3	16.7	1	Int.	20.9	719.95	
Compact										
4x	4	24	—	3.3	9.7	1	Int.	10	362.95	
2-8x	2-8	53-13	—	3.5	10	1	Int.	11.6	479.95	
Handgun										
2x[4]	2	23	—	9-26	8.4	1	Int.	6.9	367.95	
4x[4]	4	8.7	—	10-20	8.4	1	Int.	6.9	381.95	
Scope Chief										
4x	4	30	—	3.0	12.5	1	Int.	10.8	306.95	
1.5-4.5x[5]	1.5-4.5	73-24	—	3.3	9.7	1	Int.	9.8	335.95	
2-7x	2-7	52-15	—	3.3	10.5	1	Int.	11.8	343.95	
3-9x[6]	3-9	35-12	—	3.3	12.6	1	Int.	13.9	354.95	
4-12x A.O.	4-12	30-9	—	3.2	13.2	1	Int.	15.4	397.95	
BEEMAN										
Blue Ring 20[1]	1.5	14	150	11-16	8.3	3/4	Int.	3.6	59.95	All scopes have 5-pt. reticle, all glass, fully coated lenses. [1]Pistol scope; cast mounts included. [2]Pistol scope; silhouette knobs. [3]Rubber armor coating; built-in double adj. mount, parallax-free setting. [4]Objective focus, built-in double-adj. mount. [5]Objective focus. [6]Also available with color reticle. [7]Includes cast mounts. [8]Objective focus; silhouette knobs; matte finish. [9]Also in "L" models with reticle lighted by ambient light or tiny add-on illuminator. Lighted models slightly higher priced. Imported by Beeman.
Blue Ribbon 25[2]	2	19	150	10-24	9 1/16	1	Int.	7.4	154.95	
SS-1[3,7]	2.5	30	61	3.25	5 1/2	1	Int.	7	198.50	
SS-2[4,6,7,8,9]	3	34.5	74	3.5	6.8	1.38	Int.	13.6	265.00	
Blue Ribbon 50R[5]	2.5	33	245	3.5	12	1	Int.	11.8	198.95	
Blue Ribbon 10	4	27	69	3.0	10.6	1	Int.	9.5	99.95	
Blue Ribbon 66R[6,8,9]	2-7	62-16	384-31	3	11.4	1	Int.	14.9	269.95	
Blue Ring 49R[5]	4	30	64	3	11.8	1	Int.	11.3	99.50	
Blue Ring 12	3-9	39-13	172-20	3.0	12.8	1	Int.	12.7	119.95	
SS-3[3,4]	1.5-4	44.6-24.6	172-24	3	5.75	7/8	Int.	8.5	279.95	
Blue Ribbon 68R	4-12	30.5-11	150-13.5	3	14.4	1	Int.	15.2	419.95	
Blue Ribbon 54R[5]	4	29	96	3.5	12	1	Int.	12.3	198.95	
SS-2[4,6,8]	4	24.6	41	5	7	1.38	Int.	13.7	298.50	
B-SQUARE										
BSL-1	—	—	—	—	2.75	.75	Int.	2.25	259.95	Blue or stainless finish. From B-Square.

Maker and Model	Magn.	Field at 100 Yds. (feet)	Relative Bright-ness	Eye Relief (in.)	Length (in.)	Tube Dia. (in.)	W&E Adjust-ments	Weight (ozs.)	Price	Other Data
BURRIS										
Fullfield										All scopes avail. in Plex reticle. Steel-on-steel click adjustments. [1]Dot reticle $13 extra. [2]Post crosshair reticle $13 extra. [3]Matte satin finish $20 extra. [4]Available with parallax adjustment $28 extra (standard on 10x, 12x, 4-12x, 6-12x, 6-18x, 6x HBR and 3-12x Signature). [5]Silver Safari finish $30 extra. [6]Target knobs $20 extra, standard on silhouette models, LER and XER with P.A., 6x HBR. [7]Sunshade avail. [8]Avail. with Fine Plex reticle. [9]Available with German three-post reticle.
1½x	1.6	62	—	3¼	10¼	1	Int.	9.0	223.95	
2½x	2.5	55	—	3¼	10¼	1	Int.	9.0	233.95	
4x[1,2,3]	3.75	36	—	3¼	11¼	1	Int.	11.5	249.95	
6x[1,3]	5.8	23	—	3¼	13	1	Int.	12.0	266.95	
10x[1,4,6,7,8]	9.8	12	—	3¼	15	1	Int.	15	307.95	
12x[1,4,6,7,8]	11.8	10.5	—	3¼	15	1	Int.	15	336.95	
1¾-5x[1,2]	1.7-4.6	66-25	—	3¼	10⅞	1	Int.	13	295.95	
2-7x[1,2,3]	2.5-6.8	47-18	—	3¼	12	1	Int.	14	322.95	
3-9x[1,2,3]	3.3-8.7	38-15	—	3¼	12⅝	1	Int.	15	331.95	
4-12x[1,4,8]	4.4-11.8	27-10	—	3¼	15	1	Int.	18	406.95	
6-18x[1,4,6,7,8]	6.5-17.6	16-7	—	3¼	15.8	1	Int.	18.5	422.95	
Mini Scopes										
4x[4,5]	3.6	24	—	3¾-5	8¼	1	Int.	7.8	201.95	
6x[1,4]	5.5	17	—	3¾-5	9	1	Int.	8.2	221.95	
6x HBR P.A.[1,5,8]	6.0	13	—	4.5	11¼	1	Int.	13.0	276.95	
2-7x	2.5-6.9	32-14	—	3¾-5	12	1	Int.	10.5	273.95	
3-9x[5]	3.6-8.8	25-11	—	3¾-5	12⅝	1	Int.	11.5	281.95	
4-12x[1,4,6]	4.5-11.6	19-8	—	3¾-4	15	1	Int.	15	372.95	
Signature Series										LER=Long Eye Relief; IER=Intermediate Eye Relief; XER=Extra Eye Relief. From Burris.
1.5-6x[2,3,5,9]	1.7-5.8	70-20	—	3½-4	10.8	1	Int.	13.0	384.95	
4x[3]	4.0	30	—	3	12⅛	1	Int.	14	325.95	
6x[3]	6.0	20	—	3	12⅛	1	Int.	14	340.95	
3-9x[3,5]	3.3-8.8	36-14	—	3	12⅞	1	Int.	15.5	455.95	
2½-10x[3,5]	2.7-9.5	37-10.5	—	3-3¾	14	1	Int.	19.0	514.95	
3-12x	3.3-11.7	34-9	—	3	14¼	1	Int.	21	571.95	
6-24x[1,3,5,6,8]	6.6-23.8	17-6	—	3-2½	16.0	1	Int.	22.7	600.95	
Handgun										
1½-4x LER[1,5]	1.6-3.8	16-11	—	11-25	10¼	1	Int.	11	308.95	
2½-7x LER[4,5]	2.7-6.7	12-7.5	—	11-28	12	1	Int.	12.5	303.95	
3-9x LER[4,5]	3.4-8.4	12-5	—	22-14	11	1	Int.	14	341.95	
1x LER[1]	1.1	27	—	10-24	8¾	1	Int.	6.8	190.95	
2x LER[4,5,6]	1.7	21	—	10-24	8¾	1	Int.	6.8	193.95	
3x LER[4,6]	2.7	17	—	10-20	8⅞	1	Int.	6.8	212.95	
4x LER[1,4,5,6]	3.7	11	—	10-22	9⅝	1	Int.	9.0	219.95	
5x LER[1,4,6]	4.5	8.7	—	12-22	10⅞	1	Int.	9.2	238.95	
7x IER[1,4,5,6]	6.5	6.5	—	10-16	11¼	1	Int.	10	244.95	
10x IER[1,4,6]	9.5	4	—	8-12	13½	1	Int.	14	301.95	
Scout Scope										
1½x XER[3,9]	1.5	22	—	7-18	9	1	Int.	7.3	193.95	
2¾x XER[3,9]	2.7	15	—	7-14	9⅜	1	Int.	7.5	201.95	
BUSHNELL										
Trophy										All have Multi-X reticle, one-piece tube, fully coated lenses. [1]Also matte silver, matte black **$240.95**. [2]Silver finish **$224.95**. [3]Silver finish **$274.95**. [4]For handguns, shotguns, blackpowder guns. [5]With 22 rings. [6]With 22 adj. obj. rings. **Only selected models shown.** Contact Bushnell for details.
4x	4	36	—	3.0	12.5	1	Int.	12.5	173.95	
2-7x W.A.	2-7	63-18	—	3.0	10.0	1	Int.	11.3	237.95	
3-9x W.A.[1]	3-9	42-14	—	3.0	11.7	1	Int.	13.2	226.95	
6-18x	6-18	17.3-6	—	3.0	14.8	1	Int.	17.9	370.95	
Trophy Handgun										
2x[2]	2	20	—	9-26	8.7	1	Int.	7.7	210.95	
2-6x[3]	2-6	21-7	—	9-26	9.1	1	Int.	9.6	261.95	
Illuminated Dot[4]	1	61	—	—	5.25	30mm	Int.	5.5	319.95	
Banner										
4x 22[5]	4	28	—	3.0	11.7	1	Int.	8.1	83.95	
3-9x BDC W.A.	3-9	42-14	—	3.3	12.0	1	Int.	13.1	162.95	
3-9x W.A.	3-9	39-13	—	3.0	12.0	1	Int.	12.5	466.95	
Lite-Site										
3-9x	3-9	36-13	—	3.1	12.8	1	Int.	15.5	386.95	
Sportview										
4x W.A.	4	34	—	3.0	12.5	1	Int.	11.7	109.95	
1.5-4.5	1.5-4.5	69-24	—	3.0	10.7	1	Int.	8.6	105.95	
3-9x	3-9	35-12	—	3.5	11.75	1	Int.	10.0	79.95	
4-12x A.O.	4-12	27-9	—	3.2	13.1	1	Int.	14.6	157.95	
Sportview Air Rifle										
4x[6]	4	31	—	4.0	11.7	1	Int.	11.2	109.95	
3-9x[6]	3-9	38-13	—	3.0	10.75	1	Int.	11.2	130.95	
CHARLES DALY										[1]Pistol scope. [2]Adj. obj. From Outdoor Sports Headquarters.
4x32	4	28	—	3.25	11.75	1	Int.	9.5	70.00	
4x32[2]	4	28	—	3	9	1	Int.	8.5	129.00	
4x40 WA	4	36	—	3.25	13	1	Int.	11.5	98.00	
2.5x20[1]	2.5	17	—	3	7.3	1	Int.	7.25	80.00	
2.5x32	2.5	47	—	3	12.25	1	Int.	10	80.00	
2-7x32 WA	2-7	56-17	—	3	11.5	1	Int.	12	125.00	
3-9x40	3-9	35-14	—	3	12.5	1	Int.	11.25	77.00	
3-9x40 WA	3-9	36-13	—	3	12.75	1	Int.	12.5	125.00	
4-12x40 WA	4-12	30-11	—	3	13.75	1	Int.	14.5	133.00	
2x20[1]	2	16	—	16-25	8.75	1	Int.	6.5	107.00	
GLOBAL INDUSTRIES										[1]With adj. obj.; [2]Also 4x40, 4x40 with adj. obj.; [3]Also with adj. obj.; [4]Also 2-7x40, 2-7x40 with adj. obj.; [5]Also 3-9x40, 3-9x40 with adj. obj.; [6]Also 4x30, 4x40; [7]Also 10x40.
30mm Superb Series WA										
1.5x20	1.5	78.73	69.64	3.9	9.4	1.18	Int.	12.3	300.53	
4x42	4	31.16	43.40	4.5	12.2	1.18	Int.	14.6	374.78	
6x42	6	19	19.29	3.7	12.2	1.18	Int.	14.6	385.39	

Maker and Model	Magn.	Field at 100 Yds. (feet)	Relative Bright- ness	Eye Relief (in.)	Length (in.)	Tube Dia. (in.)	W&E Adjust- ments	Weight (ozs.)	Price	Other Data
Global (cont.)										
8x56	8	13.12	19.29	3.7	13.5	1.18	Int.	19.0	424.28	**30mm Superb Series:** All models can be ordered with target or external knobs, magnifying reticle (European style), objective adjustment (O.A.), and choice of six reticles. Variables—IPC, extra-heavy construction of 6061 T-6 alloy. Fogproof, recoil-proof coated optics. **American Series:** Special reticles (12), target knobs, BDC objective lens adjustment feature can be added to any scope at extra cost. Sunshades also avail. 12x thru 24x can be made on special order. German-type speed focus avail. as option on all American Series scopes. Waterproof, fogproof, recoil-proof, fully coated. **European 1":** All wide angle with choice of 12 reticles, obj. adj. avail. on some models. BDC and target knobs avail. on all as options. Sunshades, locking lens covers, speed focus also optional. **Partial listing of models shown.** Contact Global Industries for full details.
15x56[1]	15	8.5	5.38	3.3	15.9	1.18	Int.	25.7	601.07	
30mm Variables										
1-4x20	1-4	101-30.1	157-9.8	4.3-3.3	9.4	1.18	Int.	11.1	434.89	
2-8x42	2-8	46.9-16	173-11	4.5-3.5	13.3	1.18	Int.	17.4	493.23	
2.5-10	2.5-10	42.6-13	111.1-69	4.3-3.3	13.3	1.18	Int.	17.4	510.91	
3-12x56	3-12	37.7-10.8	137-16	3.9-3.3	14.3	1.18	Int.	25.7	601.07	
4-20x42	4-20	26-6	40-4	3.3-3.0	17.7	1.18	Int.	23.8	664.71	
American 1" Series WA										
Adirondack 1x20	1	—	—	—	—	1	Int	—	159.10	
Raton 2.5x32	2.5	33.0	161	3.5	11.7	1	Int.	9.2	160.00	
Las Vegas 4x32[2]	4	29.0	64	3.3	11.7	1	Int.	9.2	162.64	
Kalispell 6x40[3]	6	18.5	45	3.2	13.0	1	Int.	10.2	187.07	
Pecos 8x40 O.A.	8	13.5	25	3.0	13.0	1	Int.	10.2	239.46	
San Antonio 10x40 O.A.	10	12.5	16	3.0	13.0	1	Int.	10.4	242.67	
Variables										
Abeline 1-3x20	1-3	—	—	—	—	1	Int.	—	224.51	
Shiloh 1.5-4.5x20	1.5-4.5	—	—	—	—	1	Int.	—	228.05	
Denver 2-7x32[4]	2-7	—	—	—	—	1	Int.	—	213.91	
Santa Fe 3-9x32[5]	3-9	43.5-15	114-13	3.3-3.0	12.2	1	Int.	12.0	210.37	
Sutter's Creek 4-12x40 O.A.	4-12	30.5-11	100-12.3	3.0	15.8	1	Int.	15.0	284.63	
European 1" Series										
Jutland 4x20[6]	4	33	25	3.2	11.0	1	Int.	10.5	197.00	
Grenoble 6x40	6	26	43.56	3	13.2	1	Int.	13.7	230.46	
Rhineland 8x56	8	20	49	3.2	13.5	1	Int.	17.2	292.50	
Hamburg 10x56 O.A.[7]	10	—	—	3.2	13.5	1	Int.	17.2	354.21	
Brunswick 15x56 O.A.	15	—	—	3.1	13.5	1	Int.	17.6	390.85	
INTERAIMS										
One V	0	—	—	—	4.5	1	Int.	4	139.95	Intended for handguns. Comes with rings. Dot size less than 1½" @ 100 yds. Waterproof. Battery life 50-10,000 hours. Black or nickel finish Imported by Stoeger.
One V	0	—	—	—	4.5	1	Int.	4	139.95	
AUS JENA										
ZF4x32-M	4	32	—	3.5	10.8	26mm	Int.	10	475.00	Fixed power scopes have 26mm alloy tubes, variables, 30mm alloy; rings avail. from importer. Also avail. with rail mount. Multi-coated lenses. Waterproof and fogproof. ⅓-min. clicks. Choice of nine reticles. Imported from Germany by Europtik, Ltd.
ZF6x42-M	6	22	—	3.5	12.6	26mm	Int.	13	510.00	
ZF8x56-M	8	17	—	3.5	14	26mm	Int.	17	580.00	
VZF1.5-6x42-M	1.5-6	67.8-22	—	3.5	12.6	30mm	Int.	14	635.00	
UZF3-12x56-M	3-12	30-11	—	3.5	15	30mm	Int.	18	710.00	
KASSNAR VISTASCOPES										
HI0405	4	26	—	4	12	1	Int.	9.1	NA	Waterproof, fogproof, shockproof. Four-post reticle. From K.B.I.
HI0413	3-9	28-12	—	3.4-2.9	12	1	Int.	9.8	NA	
HI0448	3-9	40-14	—	3.4-2.8	12.6	1	Int.	12.7	NA	
HI0480 Compact	4	21	—	4.1	9.9	1	Int.	9.1	NA	
HI0499 Pistol	4	9	—	14.5	9.5	1	Int.	9.5	NA	
HI0502 Pistol	2.5	12.6	—	13	8.9	1	Int.	9.1	NA	
KILHAM										
Hutson Handgunner II	1.7	8	—	5½	5	⅞	Int.	5.1	119.95	Unlimited eye relief; internal click adjustments; crosshair reticle. Fits Thompson/Center rail mounts, for S&W K, N, Ruger Blackhawk, Super, Super Single-Six, Contender.
Hutson Handgunner	3	8	—	10-12	6	⅞	Int.	5.3	119.95	
LASER AIM										
LA1[1]	—	—	—	—	3.50	.812	Int.	4	239.00	[1]LA1 Magnum has adjustable dot size, 1000-yard range, $259.00. [2]Mounts on top of scope; separate power module. [3]LA5 Magnum has 2.75" length, 1000-yard range. [4]For shotguns. Range 300 yards, 2" dot at 100 yards; LA6 Magnum has 2.75" length, 1000-yard range, $259.00. [5]Variable dot intensity, long battery life; includes battery, extender tube, fitter, eyepiece. [6]Intense red dot at crosshair intersection, adjustable intensity; electronic fiber optic lens system. Projects high intensity beam of laser light up to 300 yards. Dot size at 100 yards is 1". Adjustable for w. & e. Includes rings to mount on scope rail, battery charger plugs into cigarette lighter. Optional 110V charger, $19.00. From Emerging Technologies, Inc.
LA3[2]	—	—	—	—	1.15	1.94	Int.	1.5	259.00	
LA5[3]	—	—	—	—	1.9	.75	Int.	1.19	219.00	
LA6[4]	—	—	—	—	1.9	.75	Int.	1.19	239.00	
LA99 Illusion D.O.T.[5]	—	—	—	—	5.1	1	Adjustment	3.9	129.00	
LA27 Powerdot[6]	2-7	48.2-13.8	—	3-4	11.1	1	Int.	12	219.00	
LA39 Powerdot	3-9	37-12.5	—	2.7-3.2	12.3	1	Int.	13.4	219.00	
LA412 Powerdot	4-12	28.1-9.2	—	3	14.4	1	Int.	21	319.00	
LASER DEVICES										
He Ne FA-6	—	—	—	—	6.2	—	Int.	11	229.50	Projects high intensity beam of laser light onto target as an aiming point. Adj. for w. & e. [1]Diode laser system. From Laser Devices, Inc.
He Ne FA-9	—	—	—	—	12	—	Int.	16	299.00	
He Ne FA-9P	—	—	—	—	9	—	Int.	14	299.00	
FA-4[1]	—	—	—	—	4.5	—	Int.	3.5	299.00	
LASERSIGHT										
LS45	0	—	—	—	7.5	—	Int.	8.5	245.00	Projects a highly visible beam of concentrated laser light onto the target. Adjustable for w.& e. Visible up to 500 yds. at night. For handguns, rifles, shotguns. Uses two standard 9V batteries. From Imatronic Lasersight.
LS25	0	—	—	—	6	¾	Int.	3.5	270.00	
LS55	0	—	—	—	7	1	Int.	7	299.00	
LEATHERWOOD										
ART II	3.0-8.8	31-12	—	3.5	13.9	1	Int.	42	750.00	Compensates for bullet drop via external circular cam. Matte gray finish. Designed specifically for the M1A/M-14 rifle. Quick Detachable model for rifles with Weaver-type bases. From North American Specialties.
LEATHERWOOD-MEOPTA, INC.										
ART II	3.0-8.8	31-12	—	3.5	13.9	1	Int.	42	750.00	ART CZ-4 and CZ-6 have range-finding reticles with hold-over marks, multi-coated optics. Black or gray finish. From Leatherwood-Meopta, Inc.
ART CZ-4	4	32	—	—	11	1	Int.	13.4	257.90	
ART CZ-6	6	21	—	—	13.7	1	Int.	18.3	287.90	

Maker and Model	Magn.	Field at 100 Yds. (feet)	Relative Bright-ness	Eye Relief (in.)	Length (in.)	Tube Dia. (in.)	W&E Adjust-ments	Weight (ozs.)	Price	Other Data
LEUPOLD										
Vari-X III 3.5x10 STD Police[9]	3.5-10	29.5-10.7	—	3.6-4.6	12.5	1	Int.	13.5	610.70	Constantly centered reticles, choice of Duplex, tapered CPC, Leupold Dot, Crosshair and Dot. CPC and Dot reticles extra. [2]2x and 4x scopes have from 12"-24" of eye relief and are suitable for handguns, top ejection arms and muzzleloaders. [3]3x9 Compact, 6x Compact, 12x, 3x9, 3.5x10 and 6.5x20 come with adjustable objective. [3]Target scopes have 1-min. divisions with ¼-min. clicks, and adjustable objectives. 50-ft. Focus Adaptor available for indoor target ranges, $50.00. Sunshade available for all adjustable objective scopes, $17.90-26.80. [4]Also available in matte finish for about $20.00 extra. [5]Silver finish about $20.00 extra. [6]Matte finish with Multicoat 4, $391.10. [7]Matte finish. Partial listing shown. Contact Leupold for complete details.
M8-2X EER[1]	1.7	21.2	—	12-24	7.9	1	Int.	6.0	233.90	
M8-2X EER Silver[1]	1.7	21.2	—	12-24	7.9	1	Int.	6.0	255.40	
M8-4X EER[1]	3.7	9	—	12-24	8.4	1	Int.	7.0	296.40	
M8-4X EER Silver[1]	3.7	9	—	12-24	8.4	1	Int.	7.0	317.90	
M8-2.5X Compact	2.3	39.5	—	4.9	8.0	1	Int.	6.5	260.70	
M8-4X Compact	3.6	25.5	—	4.5	9.2	1	Int.	7.5	278.60	
2-7x Compact	2.5-6.6	41.7-16.5	—	5-3.7	9.9	1	Int.	8.5	355.40	
3-9x Compact	3.2-8.6	34-13.5	—	4.0-3.0	11-11.3	1	Int.	11.0	369.60	
M8-4X[4]	4.0	24	—	4.0	10.7	1	Int.	9.3	278.60	
M8-6X[7]	5.9	17.7	—	4.3	11.4	1	Int.	10.0	296.40	
M8-6x 42mm	6.0	17	—	4.5	12	1	Int.	11.3	369.60	
M8-8X[2]	7.8	14.3	—	3.9	12.4	1	Int.	13.0	400.00	
M8-12X[2]	11.6	9.1	—	4.2	13.0	1	Int.	13.5	408.90	
M8-12x A.O. Varmint	11.6	9.1	—	4.2	13.0	1	Int.	13.5	453.60	
6.5x20 Target A.O.[7]	6.5-19.2	14.2-5.5	—	5.3-3.6	14.2	1	Int.	17.5	628.60	
BR-24X[3]	24.0	4.7	—	3.2	13.8	1	Int.	15.3	766.10	
BR-36X[3]	36.0	3.2	—	3.4	14.1	1	Int.	15.6	801.80	
Vari-X 2.5-8 EER	2.5-8.0	13-4.3	—	11.7-12	9.7	1	Int.	10.9	482.10	
Vari-X 3-9x Compact EFR A.O.	3.8-8.6	34.0-13.5	—	4.0-3.0	11.0	1	Int.	11	407.10	
Vari-X-II 1x4	1.6-4.2	70.5-28.5	—	4.3-3.8	9.2	1	Int.	9.0	314.30	
Vari-X-II 2x7[4]	2.5-6.6	42.5-17.8	—	4.9-3.8	11.0	1	Int.	10.5	355.40	
Vari-X-II 3x9[1,4,5]	3.3-8.6	32.3-14.0	—	4.1-3.7	12.3	1	Int.	13.5	369.60	
Vari-X-II 3-9x50mm[4]	3.3-8.6	32.3-14	—	4.7-3.7	12	1	Int.	13.6	428.60	
Vari-X-II 4-12 A.O. Matte	4.4-11.6	22.8-11.0	—	5.0-3.3	12.3	1	Int.	13.5	487.50	
Vari-X-III 1.5x5	1.5-4.5	66.0-23.0	—	5.3-3.7	9.4	1	Int.	9.5	464.30	
Vari-X-III 1.75-6x 32	1.9-5.6	47-18	—	4.8-3.7	9.8	1	Int.	11	482.10	
Vari-X-III 2.5x8[4]	2.6-7.8	37.0-13.5	—	4.7-3.7	11.3	1	Int.	11.5	500.00	
Vari-X-III 3.5-10x50 A.O.	3.3-9.7	29.5-10.7	—	4.6-3.6	12.4	1	Int.	13.0	648.20	
Vari-X-III 3.5-10x50[2,4]	3.3-9.7	29.5-10.7	—	4.6-3.6	12.4	1	Int.	14.4	610.70	
Vari-X-III 3.5-10 A.O. Varmint	3.3-9.7	29.5-10.7	—	4.6-3.6	12.4	1	Int.	14.4	621.40	
Vari-X-III 6.5-20 A.O. Varmint	6.5-19.2	14.2-5.5	—	5.3-3.6	14.2	1	Int.	17.5	651.80	
Vari-X-III 6.5-20x Target EFR A.O.	6.5-19.2	—	—	5.3-3.6	14.2	1	Int.	16.5	680.40	
Mark 4 M1-10x[7]	10	11.1	—	3.6	13⅛	1	Int.	21	1,383.90	
Mark 4 M1-16x[7]	16	6.6	—	4.1	12⅞	1	Int.	22	1,383.90	
Mark 4 M3-10x[7]	10	11.1	—	3.6	13⅛	1	Int.	21	1,383.90	
Vari-X-III 6.5x20[2]	6.5-19.2	14.2-5.5	—	5.3-3.6	14.2	1	Int.	16.0	607.10	
Rimfire										
Vari-X-II 2-7x RF Special	3.6	25.5	—	4.5	9.2	1	Int.	7.5	355.40	
Shotgun										
M8 2x EER	1.7	21.2	—	12-24	7.9	1	Int.	6.0	257.10	
M8 4x	3.7	9.0	—	12-24	8.4	1	Int.	6.0	300.00	
Vari-X-II 1x4	1.6-4.2	70.5-28.5	—	4.3-3.8	9.2	1	Int.	9.0	337.50	
Vari-X-II 2x7	2.5-6.6	42.5-17.8	—	4.9-3.8	11.0	1	Int.	9.0	378.60	
MIRADOR										
RXW 4x40[1]	4	37	—	3.8	12.4	1	Int.	12	179.95	[1]Wide Angle scope. Multi-coated objective lens. Nitrogen filled; waterproof; shockproof. From Mirador Optical Corp.
RXW 1.5-5x20[1]	1.5-5	46-17.4	—	4.3	11.1	1	Int.	10	188.95	
RXW 3-9x40	3-9	43-14.5	—	3.1	12.9	1	Int.	13.4	251.95	
NICHOLS										
"Light" Series										
1.5-5x20 WA	1.5-5	80.8-24.2	—	3.2-4.5	9.5	1	Int.	10.1	264.00	[1]Matte finish; also avail. with high gloss. [2]Adj. obj. [3]Stainless; also 3-9x40, blue, $144.00. [4]50-yd. parallax, with 22 rings; also with adj. obj., $130.00. [5]Also in stainless. [6]50-yd. parallax, $90.00. [7]Also 3-9x40, $124.00. Imported by G.U., Inc.
2-7x32 WA	2-7	60.4-17.5	—	3.3-4.2	10.0	1	Int.	11.3	280.00	
3-9x40 WA	3-9	40.2-13.3	—	3.2-3.9	11.7	1	Int.	12.9	290.00	
3-10x44 WA	3-10	40.2-12.1	—	3.1-4.0	11.9	1	Int.	14.1	310.00	
4-12x44 WA A.O.	4-12	30.1-10	—	3.1-3.6	12.3	1	Int.	16.7	320.00	
"Magnum Target"										
12x44[2]	12	8.7	—	3.1	14.3	1	Int.	19.1	525.00	
24x44[2]	24	4.3	—	2.9	14.3	1	Int.	18.4	525.00	
6-20x44[2]	6-20	17.4-5.4	—	3.1-3.0	14.4	1	Int.	19.8	577.00	
"Classic"										
4x40 WA	4	37.0	—	3.8	13.0	1	Int.	11.6	140.00	
6x40 WA	6	24.5	—	3.3	13.0	1	Int.	11.6	142.00	
1.5-4.5x WA	1.5-4.5	54.0-22.0	—	3.4-3.3	11.5	1	Int.	10.9	163.00	
2-7x32 WA	2-7	36.7-15.8	—	2.8-2.6	11.7	1	Int.	10.9	163.00	
3-9x32 WA[3]	3-9	39.3-13.1	—	3.4-2.9	11.4	1	Int.	10.5	163.00	
4-12x40	4-12	30.0-11.0	—	3.9-3.2	12.3	1	Int.	12.3	170.00	
"Air Gun/Rimfire"										
4x32[4]	4	28.5	—	3.1	12.2	1	Int.	10.7	105.00	
2-7x32 WA A.O.	2-7	36.7-15.7	—	2.8-2.6	11.8	1	Int.	10.5	187.00	
"Classic Handgun"										
2x20[5]	2	17.0	—	8.6-19.5	7.4	1	Int.	7.5	135.00	
2-7x28[6]	2-7	40.0-9.7	—	8.9-19.5	9.0	1	Int.	9.0	260.00	
"Bullet"										
4x32[6]	4	28.5	—	3.1	12.2	1	Int.	10.7	82.00	
3-9x32[7]	3-9	34.5-23.6	—	3.1-3.0	12.6	1	Int.	11.2	118.00	

CAUTION: PRICES CHANGE, CHECK AT GUNSHOP.

Maker and Model	Magn.	Field at 100 Yds. (feet)	Relative Brightness	Eye Relief (in.)	Length (in.)	Tube Dia. (in.)	W&E Adjustments	Weight (ozs.)	Price	Other Data
NIKON										Super multi-coated lenses and blackening of all internal metal parts for maximum light gathering capability; positive 1/4-MOA; fogproof; waterproof; shockproof; luster and matte finish. From Nikon, Inc.
4x40	4	26.7	—	3.5	11.7	1	Int.	11.7	275.00	
1.5-4.5x20	1.5-4.5	67.8-22.5	—	3.7-3.2	10.1	1	Int.	9.5	361.00	
1.5-4.5x24 EER	1.5-4.4	13.7-5.8	—	24-18	8.9	1	Int.	9.3	361.00	
2-7x32	2-7	46.7-13.7	—	3.9-3.3	11.3	1	Int.	11.3	398.00	
3-9x40	3-9	33.8-11.3	—	3.6-3.2	12.5	1	Int.	12.5	404.00	
3.5-10x50	3.5-10	25.5-8.9	—	3.9-3.8	13.7	1	Int.	15.5	609.00	
4-12x40 A.O.	4-12	25.7-8.6	—	3.6-3.2	14	1	Int.	16.6	526.00	
4-12x50 A.O.	4-12	25.4-8.5	—	3.6-3.5	14.0	1	Int.	18.3	665.00	
6.5-20x44	6.5-19.4	16.2-5.4	—	3.5-3.1	14.8	1	Int.	19.6	609.00	
2x20 EER	2	22	—	26.4	8.1	1	Int.	6.3	218.00	
OAKSHORE ELECTRONICS										[1]Also 30mm tube, $199. [2]Variable intensity red dot appears in center of the duplex crosshair. Waterproof; nitrogen filled; coated lenses; 1/2-MOA dot at 100 yds. From Oakshore Electronic Sights, Inc.
UltraDOT[1]	0	—	—	—	5	1	Int.	3.9	139.00	
MicroDOT 1.5-4.5x LER[2]	1.5-4.5	14.9-6.9	—	12-24	9	1	Int.	10	259.00	
MicroDOT 1.5-4.5x[2]	1.5-4.5	73.8-24.6	—	3	9.8	1	Int.	10.5	259.00	
MicroDOT 2-7x[2]	2-7	48.2-13.8	—	3	11	1	Int.	12	279.00	
MicroDOT 3-9x[2]	3-9	37-12.5	—	3	12.3	1	Int.	13.4	299.00	
MicroDOT 4-12x[2]	1.5-4.5	28.1-9.2	—	3	14.4	1	Int.	21	399.00	
PENTAX										Multi-coated lenses, fogproof, waterproof, nitrogen-filled. Penta-Plex reticle. Click 1/3-1/2-MOA adjustments. Matte finish $20.00 extra. [1]Also in matte chrome $260.00. [2]Also in matte chrome $390.00. [3]ProFinish (matte) $500. [4]ProFinish (matte) $530.00; satin chrome $550.00. [5]Chrome-Matte finish $400.00. [6]ProFinish (matte) $460.00; satin chrome $480.00. Imported by Pentax Corp.
1.5-5x	1.5-5	66-25	—	3-3¼	11	1	Int.	13	310.00	
4x	4	35	—	3¼	11.6	1	Int.	12.2	280.00	
6x	6	20	—	3¼	13.4	1	Int.	13.5	310.00	
2-7x	2-7	42.5-17	—	3-3¼	12	1	Int.	14	360.00	
3-9x	3-9	33-13.5	—	3-3¼	13	1	Int.	15	380.00	
2-8x Lightseeker[6]	2-8	53-17	—	3.5	11⅞	1	Int.	14	450.00	
3-9x Lightseeker[4]	3-9	36-14	—	3	12.7	1	Int.	15	540.00	
3-9x Mini	3-9	26.5-10.5	—	3¾	10.4	1	Int.	13	320.00	
4-12x Mini[3]	4-12	19-8	—	3.75-4	11.3	1	Int.	11.3	410.00	
6-18x[3]	6-18	16-7	—	3-3.25	15.8	1	Int.	15.8	460.00	
Pistol										
2x LER[1]	2	21	—	10-24	8¾	1	Int.	6.8	240.00	
1.5-4x LER[2]	1.5-4	16-11	—	11-25	10	1	Int.	11	360.00	
2½-7x[5]	2.5-7	12.0-7.5	—	11-28	12	1	Int.	12.5	400.00	
RWS										Air gun scopes. All have Dyna-Plex reticle. Model 800 is for air pistols. Imported from Japan by Dynamit Nobel-RWS.
100	4	—	—	8	10½	¾	Int.	7	60.00	
300	4	—	—	8	12¾	1	Int.	11	130.00	
350	4	—	—	8	10	1	Int.	10	110.00	
400	2-7	—	—	8	12¾	1	Int.	12	135.00	
800	1.5	—	—	28	8¾	1	Int.	6	125.00	
CS-10	2.5	—	—	8	5¾	1	Int.	7	120.00	
REDFIELD										*Accutrac feature avail. on these scopes at extra cost. Traditionals have round lenses. 4-Plex reticle is standard. [1]"Magnum Proof." Specially designed for magnum and auto pistols. Uses "Double Dovetail" mounts. Also in nickel-plated finish, 2½x, $240.95, 4x, $253.95. [2]With matte finish $545.95. [3]Also available with matte finish at extra cost. [4]All Golden Five Star scopes come with Butler Creek flip-up lens covers. [5]Black anodized finish, also in nickel finish, $303.95. [6]56mm adj. objective; European #4 or 4-Plex reticle; comes with 30mm steel rings with Rotary Dovetail System. 1/4-min. click adj. Also in matte finish, $754.95. [7]Also available nickel-plated $329.95. [8]Also with RealTree camo finish $553.95. [9]With RealTree camo finish $407.95. [10]Also available with RealTree camo finish $187.95. [11]With RealTree camo finish $252.95. [12]Also with RealTree camo finish $395.95; with matte finish $386.95. [13]With RealTree camo finish $309.95.
Ultimate Illuminator 3-9x	3.4-9.1	27-9	—	3-3.5	15.1	30mm	Int.	20.5	652.95	
Ultimate Illuminator 3-12x[6]	2.9-11.7	27-10.5	—	3-3½	15.4	30mm	Int.	23	745.95	
Illuminator Trad. 3-9x	2.9-8.7	33-11	—	3½	12¾	1	Int.	17	482.95	
Illuminator Widefield 4x	4.2	28	—	3-3.5	11.7	1	Int.	13.5	359.95	
Illuminator Widefield 2-7x	2.0-6.8	56-17	—	3-3.5	11.7	1	Int.	13.5	475.95	
Illuminator Widefield 3-9x*[2,8]	2.9-8.7	38-13	—	3½	12¾	1	Int.	17	536.95	
Tracker 4x[3,10]	3.9	28.9	—	3½	11.02	1	Int.	9.8	162.95	
Tracker 6x[3]	6.2	18	—	3.5	12.4	1	Int.	11.1	182.95	
Tracker 2-7x[3]	2.3-6.9	36.6-12.2	—	3½	12.20	1	Int.	11.6	207.95	
Tracker 3-9x[3,11]	3.0-9.0	34.4-11.3	—	3½	14.96	1	Int.	13.4	233.95	
Traditional 4x ¾"	4	24½	27	3½	9⅜	¾	Int.	—	159.95	
Traditional 2½x	2½	43	64	3½	10¼	1	Int.	8½	159.95	
Golden Five Star 4x[4]	4	28.5	58	3.75	11.3	1	Int.	9.75	224.95	
Golden Five Star 6x[4]	6	18	40	3.75	12.2	1	Int.	11.5	244.95	
Golden Five Star 2-7x[4]	2.4-7.4	42-14	207-23	3-3.75	11.25	1	Int.	12	289.95	
Golden Five Star 3-9x[4,7]	3.0-9.1	34-11	163-18	3-3.75	12.50	1	Int.	13	310.95	
Golden Five Star 3-9x 50mm[4,12]	3.0-9.1	36.0-11.5	—	3-3.5	12.8	1	Int.	16	376.95	
Golden Five Star 4-12x A.O.*[4]	3.9-11.4	27-9	112-14	3-3.75	13.8	1	Int.	16	346.95	
Golden Five Star 6-18x A.O.*[4]	6.1-18.1	18.6	50-6	3-3.75	14.3	1	Int.	18	419.95	
I.E.R. 1-4x Shotgun[13]	1.3-3.8	48-16	—	6	10.2	1	Int.	12	290.95	
Compact Scopes										
Golden Five Star Compact 4x	3.8	28	—	3.5	9.75	1	Int.	8.8	216.95	
Golden Five Star Compact 6x	6.3	17.6	—	3.5	10.70	1	Int.	9.5	240.95	
Golden Five Star Compact 2-7x	2.4-7.1	40-16	—	3-3.5	9.75	1	Int.	9.8	286.95	
Golden Five Star Compact 3-9x	3.3-9.1	32-11.25	—	3-3.5	10.7	1	Int.	10.5	303.95	
Golden Five Star Compact 4-12x	4.1-12.4	22.4-8.3	—	3-3.5	12	1	Int.	13	383.95	
Pistol Scopes										
2½xMP[1]	2.5	9	64	14-19	9.8	1	Int.	10.5	224.95	
4xMP[1]	3.6	9	—	12-22	9¹¹⁄₁₆	1	Int.	11.1	239.95	
2-6x[5]	2-5.5	25-7	—	10-18	10.4	1	Int.	11	283.95	
Widefield Low Profile Compact										
Widefield 4xLP Compact	3.7	33	—	3.5	9.35	1	Int.	10	266.95	

Maker and Model	Magn.	Field at 100 Yds. (feet)	Relative Brightness	Eye Relief (in.)	Length (in.)	Tube Dia. (in.)	W&E Adjustments	Weight (ozs.)	Price	Other Data
Redfield (cont.)										
Widefield 3-9x LP Compact	3.3-9	37.0-13.7	—	3-3.5	10.20	1	Int.	13	339.95	
Low Profile Scopes										
Widefield 2¾xLP	2¾	55½	69	3½	10½	1	Int.	8	247.95	
Widefield 4xLP	3.6	37½	84	3½	11½	1	Int.	10	279.95	
Widefield 6xLP	5.5	23	—	3½	12¾	1	Int.	11	300.95	
Widefield 1¾x-5xLP	1¾-5	70-27	136-21	3½	10¾	1	Int.	11½	340.95	
Widefield 2x-7xLP*	2-7	49-19	144-21	3½	11¾	1	Int.	13	350.95	
Widefield 3x-9xLP*[9]	3-9	39-15	112-18	3½	12½	1	Int.	14	389.95	
SCHMIDT & BENDER										
Vari-M 1¼-4x20[1]	1¼-4	96-16	—	3¼	10.4	30mm	Int.	12.3	619.99	[1]All steel. 30-year warranty. All have ⅓-min. click adjustment, centered reticles, nitrogen filling. Most models avail. in aluminum with mounting rail. Imported from Germany by Paul Jaeger, Inc.
Vari-M 1½-6x42	1½-6	60-19.5	—	3¼	12.2	30mm	Int.	17.5	684.99	
Vari-M 2½-10x56	2½-10	37.5-12	—	3¼	14.6	30mm	Int.	21.9	804.99	
All Steel 4-12x42	4-12	34.7-12	—	3¼	13.25	30mm	Int.	23	736.99	
SHEPHERD										
3940-E	3-9	43.5-15	178-20	3.3	13	1	Int.	17	557.01	[1]Also avail. as 310-1, 310-E, **$434.28.** [2]Also avail. as 310-P1, 310-P2, 310-P3 with matte finish, click adj., **$434.28.** [3]Also avail. as 27-4 with 9" stadia circles, traj. for 22 rifles, **$355.00.** [4]Matte finish, click adj. for shotgun, carbine, blackpowder. All have Dual Reticle System with rangefinder-bullet drop compensation; multi-coated lenses, waterproof, shockproof, nitrogen filled. From Shepherd Scope, Ltd.
310-2[1,2]	3-10	35.3-11.6	178-16	3-3.75	12.8	1	Int.	18	434.28	
27-4[3]	2.5-7.5	42-14	164-18	2.5-3	11.6	1	Int.	16.3	355.00	
CBS[4]	1.5-5	82.5-27.5	45.5-40.9	2.5-3.25	11	1	Int.	14.9	500.00	
SIMMONS										
44 Mag										
M-1043	2-7	56-16	—	3.3	11.8	1	Int.	13	256.95	[1]Matte; also polished finish. [2]Silver; also black matte or polished. [3]Black polish finish. [4]Granite finish; black polish **$216.95;** silver $218.95; also with 50mm obj., black granite $336.95. [5]Camouflage. [6]Black polish. [7]With ring mounts. **Only selected models shown. Contact Simmons Outdoor Corp. for complete details.**
M-1044	3-10	36.2-10.5	—	3.4-3.3	13.1	1	Int.	16.3	268.95	
M-1045	4-12	27-9	—	3	12.6	1	Int.	19.5	280.95	
Prohunter										
7700[1]	2-7	58-17	—	3.25	11.6	1	Int.	12.4	131.95	
7710[2]	3-9	40-15	—	3	12.6	1	Int.	13.4	144.95	
7715[3]	4-12	—	—	—	—	1	Int.	—	168.95	
7720	6-18	38-13	—	2.5	12.5	1	Int.	13.5	168.95	
7725	4.5	26	—	3	9.9	1	Int.	9.9	84.95	
Whitetail Classic										
WTC10[4]	4	36.8	—	4	12.3	1	Int.	9.8	134.95	
WTC11[4]	1.5-5	80-23.5	—	3.4-3.2	12.6	1	Int.	11.8	169.95	
WTC12[4]	2.5-8	46.5-14.5	—	3.2-3	12.6	1	Int.	12.8	185.95	
WTC13[4]	3.5-10	35-12	—	3.2-3	12.4	1	Int.	12.8	204.95	
WTC14[4]	2-10	50-11	—	3	12.8	1	Int.	16.9	256.95	
Deerfield										
21006	4	28	—	4	12.0	1	Int.	9.1	74.95	
21010	3-9	38-12	—	3.4	12.6	1	Int.	12.3	91.95	
21029	3-9	32-11	—	3.4	12.6	1	Int.	12.3	104.95	
21031	4-12	28-11	—	3-2.8	13.9	1	Int.	14.6	104.95	
Gold Medal Silhouette										
23000	12	8.7	—	3.1-3	14.5	1	Int.	18.3	616.95	
23001	24	4.3	—	3	14.5	1	Int.	18.3	627.95	
23002	6-20	17.4-5.4	—	3	14.5	1	Int.	18.3	680.95	
Gold Medal Handgun										
22002[6]	2.5-7	9.7-4.0	—	8.9-19.4	9.25	1	Int.	9.0	326.95	
22004[6]	2	3.9	—	8.6-19.5	7.3	1	Int.	7.4	170.95	
22006[6]	4	8.9	—	9.8-18.7	9	1	Int.	8.8	226.95	
Shotgun										
21005	2.5	29	—	4.6	7.1	1	Int.	7.2	85.95	
7790	4	16	—	5.5	8.8	1	Int.	9.2	117.95	
Rimfire										
1022[7]	4	36	—	3.5	11.5	¾	Int.	10	74.95	
21007[7]	4	29	—	3.5	12.0	¾	Int.	11.5	108.95	
STEINER										
Penetrator										
6x42	6	20.4	—	3.1	14.8	26mm	Int.	14	889.00	Waterproof, fogproof, nitrogen filled, accordion-type eye cup. From Pioneer Marketing & Research, Inc.
1.5x6x42	1.5-6	64-21	—	3.1	12.8	30mm	Int.	17	1,099.00	
3-12x56	3-12	29-10	—	3.1	14.8	30mm	Int.	21	1,299.00	
SWAROVSKI HABICHT										
4x32	4	33	—	3¼	11.3	1	Int.	15	595.00	All models offered in either steel or lightweight alloy tubes. Weights shown are for lightweight versions. Choice of nine constantly centered reticles. Eyepiece recoil mechanism and rubber ring shield to protect face. American-style plex reticle available in 2.2-9x42 and 3-12x56 traditional European scopes. Imported by Swarovski Optik North America Ltd.
6x42	6	23	—	3¼	12.6	1	Int.	17.9	655.00	
8x56	8	17	—	3¼	14.4	1	Int.	23	765.00	
1.5-6x42	1.5-6	61-21	—	3¼	12.6	30mm	Int.	16	865.00	
2.2-9x42	2.2-9	39.5-15	—	3¼	13.3	30mm	Int.	15.5	995.00	
3-12x56	3-12	30-11	—	3¼	15.25	1	Int.	18	1,065.00	
AL Scopes										
4x32A	4	30	—	3.2	11.5	1	Int.	10.8	465.00	
6x36A	6	21	—	3.2	11.9	1	Int.	11.5	500.00	
1.5-4.5x20A	1.5-4.5	75-25.8	—	3.5	9.53	1	Int.	10.6	525.00	
3-9x36	3-9	39-13.5	—	3.3	11.9	1	Int.	13	600.00	
SWIFT										
600 4x15	4	16.2	—	2.4	11	¾	Int.	4.7	19.75	All Swift scopes, with the exception of the 4x15, have Quadraplex reticles and are fogproof and waterproof. The 4x15 has crosshair reticle and is non-waterproof. [1]Available in black or silver finish—same price. From Swift Instruments.
601 3-7x20	3-7	25-12	—	3-2.9	11	1	Int.	5.6	48.50	
650 4x32	4	29	—	3.5	12	1	Int.	9	75.00	
653 4x40WA[1]	4	35.5	—	3.75	12.25	1	Int.	12	96.50	

CAUTION: PRICES CHANGE, CHECK AT GUNSHOP.

Maker and Model	Magn.	Field at 100 Yds. (feet)	Relative Brightness	Eye Relief (in.)	Length (in.)	Tube Dia. (in.)	W&E Adjustments	Weight (ozs.)	Price	Other Data
Swift (cont.)										
654 3-9x32	3-9	35.75-12.75	—	3	12.75	1	Int.	13.75	94.50	
656 3-9x40WA[1]	3-9	42.5-13.5	—	2.75	12.75	1	Int.	14	103.50	
657 6x40	6	18	—	3.75	13	1	Int.	10	99.50	
660 4x20	4	25	—	4	11.8	1	Int.	9	79.50	
664 4-12x40[1]	4-12	27-9	—	3-2.8	13.3	1	Int.	14.8	140.00	
665 1.5-4.5x21	1.5-4.5	69-24.5	—	3.5-3	10.9	1	Int.	9.6	102.75	
666 Shotgun 1x20	1	113	—	3.2	7.5	1	Int.	9.6	98.00	
Pistol Scopes										
661 4x32	4	90	—	10-22	9.2	1	Int.	9.5	108.50	
662 2.5x32	2.5	14.3	—	9-22	8.9	1	Int.	9.3	102.50	
663 2x20[1]	2	18.3	—	9-21	7.2	1	Int.	8.4	103.50	
TASCO										
World Class										
WA4x40	4	36	100.0	3	13	1	Int.	11.5	128.00	
WA13.5x20[1,3,10]	1-3.5	115-31	400.0-32.4	3.5	9.75	1	Int.	10.2	183.00	
WA1.75-5x20[1,3]	1.75-5	72-24	129.9-16.0	3	10⅝	1	Int.	9.8	206.00	
WA27x32[1,3,9]	2-7	56-17	256.0-20.2	3.25	11.5	1	Int.	12	165.00	
WA39x40[1,3,6,11]	3-9	43.5-15	176.8-19.3	3⅛	12.75	1	Int.	12.5	159.00	
World Class Compact										
CW4x32LE	4	25	64	5	10.0	1	Int.	9.5	147.00	
CW28x32	2-8	55-16	—	3	10.5	1	Int.	11.5	171.00	
World Class Airgun										
AG4x40A	4	36	—	3	13	1	Int.	14	200.00	
AG39x50WA	3-9	41-14	—	3	15	1	Int.	17.5	336.00	
World Class Electronic										
ER39x40WA	3-9	41-14	176.8-19.3	3	12.75	1	Int.	16	368.00	
World Class Mag IV-44										
WC2510x44[6]	2.5-10	41-11	—	3.5	12.5	1	Int.	14.4	224.00	
World Class TS										
TS24x44	24	4.5	—	3	14	1	Int.	17.9	344.00	
TS624x44	6-24	15-4.5	—	3	14	1	Int.	18.5	408.00	
World Class TR										
TR39x40WA	3-9	41-14	—	3	12.75	1	Int.	12.5	196.00	
World Class Pistol										
PWC2x22[12]	2	25	—	11-20	8.75	1	Int.	7.3	147.00	
PWC4x28[12]	4	8	—	12-19	9.45	1	Int.	7.9	190.00	
Mag IV										
W312x40[1,2,4]	3-12	33-11	176.8-10.8	3	12⅛	1	Int.	12	147.00	
W416x40[1,2,4]	4-16	25.5-7	100.0-6.2	3	14.25	1	Int.	16.75	183.00	
W624x40	6-24	17-4	—	3	15.25	1	Int.	16.8	232.00	
Titan										
TT1.56x42	1.5-6	59-20	748-49	3.5-4	12	30mm	Int.	16.4	612.00	
TT39x42	3-9	37-13	196-22	3.5-4	12.5	30mm	Int.	16.8	587.00	
Golden Antler										
GA4x32TV	4	32	—	3	13	1	Int.	12.7	62.00	
GA2.510x44TV	2.5-10	35-9	—	3.5	12.5	1	Int.	14.4	171.00	
Silver Antler										
SA2.5x32	2.5	42	—	3¼	11	1	Int.	10	67.00	
SA4x40	4	32	—	3	12	1	Int.	12.5	77.00	
SA39x40	3-9	39-13	—	3	12.5	1	Int.	13	106.00	
Rubber Armored										
RC4x40A	4	27	—	3.25	12.5	1	Int.	14.2	160.00	
RC39x40A	3-9	35-12	—	3.25	12.5	1	Int.	14.3	176.00	
TR Scopes										
TR39x40WA	3-9	41-14	—	3	13	1	Int.	12.5	196.00	
TR416x40	4-16	26-7	—	3	14.25	1	Int.	16.8	208.00	
TR624x40	6-24	17-4	—	3	15.5	1	Int.	17.5	257.00	
Shotgun Scopes										
SG2.5x32[9]	2.5	42	163.8	3.25	11.75	1	Int.	15.7	98.00	
WA1.75-5x20[9]	1.75-5	74-24	—	3	10.5	1	Int.	10	208.00	
WA13.5x20[9]	1-3.5	103-31	—	3	9	1	Int.	12	183.00	
Airgun										
AG4x20	4	20	—	2.5	10.75	.75	Int.	5	38.00	
AG4x32	4	28	—	3	12	1	Int.	13	176.00	
AG39x50WA	3-9	27-9	—	3	15	1	Int.	17.5	336.00	
Rimfire										
RF4x15[8]	4	22.5	13.6	2.5	11	.75	Int.	4	13.00	
RF4x32	4	31	—	3	12.5	1	Int.	12.6	67.00	
RF37x20	3-7	24-11	—	2.5	11.5	.75	Int.	5.7	39.00	
P1.5x15	1.5	22.5	—	9.5-20.75	8.75	.75	Int.	3.25	30.00	
Propoint										
PDP2[10,12]	1	25-12	—	—	5	30mm	Int.	5.5	208.00	
PDP3[10,12]	1	40	—	—	5	30mm	Int.	5.5	294.00	
PB1[13]	3	35	—	3	5.5	30mm	Int.	6.3	147.00	
PB3	2	30	—	—	1.25	30mm	Int.	2.6	171.00	
Proclass										
P2x22S[14]	2	23-18	—	10-24	6.5	30mm	Int.	7.7	171.00	
P3x22[14,17]	3	13-6	—	12-24	8.25	30mm	Int.	8.5	196.00	
ER2x22P	2	25-15	—	8-20	8.75	30mm	Int.	9.4	245.00	
ER4x30P	4	7-6	—	12-24	9.75	30mm	Int.	12	269.00	

[1]Water, fog & shockproof; fully coated optics; ¼-min. click stops; haze filter caps; lifetime warranty. [2]30/30 range finding reticle. [3]World Class Wide Angle; Supercon multi-coated optics; Opti-Centered® 30/30 range finding reticle; lifetime warranty. [4]⅓ greater zoom range. [5]Trajectory compensating scopes, Opti-Centered® stadia reticle. [6]Anodized finish. [7]True one-power scope. [8]Coated optics; crosshair reticle; ring mounts included to fit most 22, 10mm receivers. [9]Fits Remington 870, 1100, 11-87. [10]Electronic dot reticle with rheostat; coated optics; adj. for windage and elevation; waterproof, shockproof, fogproof; Lithium battery; 3x power booster avail.; matte black or matte aluminum finish; dot or T-3 reticle. [11]TV view. [12]Also matte aluminum finish. [13]Also with crosshair reticle. [14]Also 30/30 reticle. [15]Dot size 1.5" at 100 yds.; waterproof. **Contact Tasco for details on complete line.**

Maker and Model	Magn.	Field at 100 Yds. (feet)	Relative Brightness	Eye Relief (in.)	Length (in.)	Tube Dia. (in.)	W&E Adjustments	Weight (ozs.)	Price	Other Data
Tasco (cont.)										
World Class Plus										
WCP4x44	4	32	—	3¼	12.75	1	Int.	13.5	**248.00**	
WCP3.510x50	3.5-10	30-10.5	—	3¾	13	1	Int.	17.1	**440.00**	
WCP6x44	6	21	—	3.25	12.75	1	Int.	13.6	**248.00**	
WCP39x44	3-9	39-14	—	3.5	12.75	1	Int.	15.8	**296.00**	
LaserPoint[15]	—	—	—	—	2	5/8	Int.	.75	**329.00**	
THOMPSON/CENTER RECOIL PROOF PISTOL SCOPES										[1]Also silver finish, **$265.00** (#8316); with rail mount, black, **$257.00** (#8317); with lighted reticle, black, **$295.00** (#8326); with rail, lighted reticle, black, **$300.00** (#8327). [2]With lighted reticle, **$225.00** (#8322); silver, **$235.00** (#8323); with lighted reticle, rail mount, black, **$235.00** (#8320). [3]With lighted reticle, **$295.00** (#8626). [4]With rail mount, lighted reticle, **$170** (#8640). From Thompson/Center.
8312 Compact Rail[2]	2.5	15	64	9-21	7.25	1	Int.	6.6	**160.00**	
8315 Compact[1]	2.5-7	15-5	125-16	8-21	9.25	1	Int.	9.2	**250.00**	
Rifle Scopes										
8621 Compact	1.5-5	61-20	177-16	3	10	1	Int.	8.5	**190.00**	
8623 Compact WA[3]	3-9	33-11	113-13	3	10.75	1	Int.	9.9	**210.00**	
8624 Compact[4]	4	26	64	3	10	1	Int.	8.2	**155.00**	
TRIJICON SPECTRUM										[1]Self-luminous low-light reticle glows in poor light; allows choice of red, amber or green via a selector ring on objective end. [2]Advanced Combat Optical Gunsight for AR-15, M-16, with integral mount. [3]Reticle glows only red in poor light. From Trijicon, Inc.
4x40[1]	4	38	—	3.0	12.2	1	Int.	15.0	**513.00**	
6x56[1]	6	24	—	3.0	14.1	1	Int.	20.3	**579.00**	
1-3x20[1]	1-3	94-33	—	3.7-4.9	9.6	1	Int.	13.2	**594.00**	
3-9x40[1]	3-9	35-14	—	3.3-3.0	13.1	1	Int.	16.0	**569.00**	
3-9x56[1]	3-9	35-14	—	3.3-3.0	14.2	1	Int.	21.5	**649.00**	
ACOG[2]	4	37	—	1.5	5.8	—	Int.	9.7	**695.00**	
4x32 Red[3]	4	29	—	3.3	11.6	1	Int.	10.2	**298.00**	
UNERTL										[1]Dural ¼-MOA click mounts. Hard coated lenses. Non-rotating objective lens focusing. [2]¼-MOA click mounts. [3]With target mounts. [4]With calibrated head. [5]Same as 1" Target but without objective lens focusing. [6]Price with ¼-MOA click mounts. [7]With new Posa mounts. [8]Range focus unit near rear of tube. Price is with Posa or standard mounts. Magnum clamp. From Unertl.
1" Target	6,8,10	16-10	17.6-6.25	2	21½	¾	Ext.	21	**233.00**	
1¼" Target[1]	8,10,12,14	12-16	15.2-5	2	25	¾	Ext.	21	**302.00**	
1½" Target	8,10,12,14, 16,18,20	11.5-3.2	—	2¼	25½	¾	Ext.	31	**326.00**	
2" Target[2]	8,10,12,14, 16,18,24, 30,36	8	22.6-2.5	2¼	26¼	1	Ext.	44	**431.00**	
Varmint, 1¼"[3]	6,8,10,12	1-7	28-7.1	2½	19½	7/8	Ext.	26	**296.00**	
Ultra Varmint, 2"[4]	8,10,12,15	12.6-7	39.7-11	2½	24	1	Ext.	34	**420.00**	
Small Game[5]	4,6	25-17	19.4-8.4	2¼	18	¾	Ext.	16	**175.00**	
Vulture[6]	8	11.2	29	3-4	15⅝	1	Ext.	15½	**333.00**	
	10	10.9	18½	—	16⅛	1				
Programmer 200[7]	8,10,12,14, 16,18,20, 24,30,36	11.3-4	39-1.9	—	26½	1	Ext.	45	**532.00**	
BV-20[8]	20	8	4.4	4.4	17⅞	1	Ext.	21¼	**390.00**	
WEATHERBY										Lumiplex reticle in all models. Blue-black, nonglare finish. From Weatherby.
Supreme 1¾-5x20	1.7-5	66.6-21.4	—	3.4	10.7	1	Int.	11	**281.00**	
Supreme 2-7x34	2.1-6.8	59-16	—	3.4	11¼	1	Int.	10.4	**291.00**	
Supreme 4x44	3.9	32	—	3	12½	1	Int.	11.6	**291.00**	
Supreme 3-9x44	3.1-8.9	36-13	—	3.5	12.7	1	Int.	11.6	**341.00**	
WEAVER										Micro-Trac adjustment system with ¼-minute clicks on all models. All have Dual-X reticle. One-piece aluminum tube, satin finish, nitrogen filled, multi-coated lenses, waterproof. From Weaver.
K2.5	2.5	35	—	3.7	9.5	1	Int.	7.3	**133.00**	
K4	3.7	26.5	—	3.3	11.3	1	Int.	10	**144.22**	
K6	5.7	18.5	—	3.3	11.4	1	Int.	10	**157.11**	
V3	1.1-2.8	88-32	—	3.9-3.7	9.2	1	Int.	8.5	**174.33**	
V9	2.8-8.7	33-11	—	3.5-3.4	12.1	1	Int.	11.1	**188.11**	
V10	2.2-9.6	38.5-9.5	—	3.4-3.3	12.2	1	Int.	11.2	**199.77**	
KT15	14.6	7.5	—	3.2	12.9	1	Int.	14.7	**314.60**	
WILLIAMS										[1]Matte or glossy black finish. TNT models from Williams Gunsight Co.
Twilight Crosshair TNT	1½-5	57¾-21	177-16	3½	10¾	1	Int.	10	**206.65**	
Twilight Crosshair TNT	2½	32	64	3¾	11¼	1	Int.	8½	**146.25**	
Twilight Crosshair TNT	4	29	64	3½	11¾	1	Int.	9½	**152.90**	
Twilight Crosshair TNT	2-6	45-17	256-28	3	11½	1	Int.	11½	**206.65**	
Twilight Crosshair TNT	3-9	36-13	161-18	3	12¾	1	Int.	13½	**217.15**	
Guideline II										
4x[1]	4	29	64	3.6	11¾	1	Int.	9½	**222.00**	
1.5-5x[1]	1.5-5	57¾-21	177-16	3.5	10¾	1	Int.	10	**267.00**	
2-6x[1]	2-6	45½-10¾	256-28	3	11½	1	Int.	11½	**267.00**	
3-9x[1]	3-9	36½-12¾	161.2-17.6	3.1-2.9	12¾	1	Int.	13½	**296.00**	
Pistol Scopes										
Twilight 1.5x TNT	1.5	19	177	18-25	8.2	1	Int.	6.4	**151.25**	
Twilight 2x TNT	2	17.5	100	18-25	8.5	1	Int.	6.4	**153.50**	
ZEISS										All scopes have ¼-minute click-stop adjustments. Choice of Z-Plex or fine crosshair reticles. Rubber armored objective bell, rubber eyepiece ring. Lenses have T-Star coating for highest light transmission. Z-Series scopes offered in non-rail tubes with duplex reticles only; 1" and 30mm. Imported from Germany by Carl Zeiss Optical, Inc.
Diatal C 4x32	4	30	—	3.5	10.6	1	Int.	11.3	**680.00**	
Diatal C 6x32	6	20	—	3.5	10.6	1	Int.	11.3	**715.00**	
Diatal C 10x36	10	12	—	3.5	12.7	1	Int.	14.1	**835.00**	
Diatal Z 6x42	6	22.9	—	3.5	12.7	1.02 (26mm)	Int.	13.4	**910.00**	
Diatal Z 8x56	8	18	—	3.5	13.8	1.02 (26mm)	Int.	17.6	**1,015.00**	
Diavari C 1.5-4.5	1.5-4.5	72-27	—	3.5	11.8	1	Int.	13.4	**930.00**	
Divari Z 2.5x10x48	2.5-10	33-11.7	—	3.2	14.5	30mm	Int.	24	**1,405.00**	
Diavari C 3-9x36	3-9	36-13	—	3.5	11.2	1	Int.	15.2	**975.00**	
Diavari ZA 1.5-6x42	1.5-6	65.5-22.9	—	3.5	12.4	1.18 (30mm)	Int.	18.5	**1,230.00**	
Diavari Z 3-12x56	3-12	27.6-9.9	—	3.2	15.3	1.18 (30mm)	Int.	25.8	**1,405.00**	

Hunting scopes in general are furnished with a choice of reticle—crosshairs, post with crosshairs, tapered or blunt post, or dot crosshairs, etc. The great majority of target and varmint scopes have medium or fine crosshairs but post or dot reticles may be ordered. W—Windage E—Elevation MOA—Minute of angle or 1" (approx.) at 100 yards, etc.

SCOPE MOUNTS

Maker, Model, Type	Adjust.	Scopes	Price
ACTION ARMS	No	1" split rings	**From $16.00**
For UZI, Galil, Ruger Mk. II, Mini-14, Win. 94, AR-15, Rem. 870, Ithaca 37, and many other popular rifles, handguns. From Action Arms.			
AIMPOINT	No	1"	49.95-89.95
Laser Mounts[1]	No	1", 30mm	51.95
Mounts/rings for all Aimpoint sights and 1" scopes. For many popular revolvers, auto pistols, shotguns, military-style rifles/carbines, sporting rifles. Most require no gunsmithing. [1]Mounts Aimpoint Laser-dot below barrel; many popular handguns, military-style rifles. Contact Aimpoint.			
AIMTECH			
Handguns			
AMT Auto Mag II, III	No	1"	56.99-64.95
Auto Mag IV	No	1"	64.95
Astra revolvers	No	1"	63.25
Beretta/Taurus auto	No	1"	63.25
Browning Buck Mark/Challenger II	No	1"	56.99
Browning Hi-Power	No	1"	63.25
Glock 17, 17L, 19, 22, 23	No	1"	63.25
Govt. 45 Auto	No	1"	63.25
Rossi revolvers	No	1"	63.25
Ruger Blackhawk/Super	No	1"	63.25
Ruger Mk I, Mk II	No	1"	49.95
S&W K,L,N frame	No	1"	63.25
S&W Model 41 Target	No	1"	63.25
S&W Model 52 Target	No	1"	63.25
S&W 45, 9mm autos	No	1"	56.99
S&W 422/622/2206	No	1"	56.99
Taurus revolvers	No	1"	63.25
TZ/CZ/P9 9mm	No	1"	63.25
Rifles			
AR-15	No	1"	21.95
Knight MK85	No	1"	21.95
Shotguns			
Benelli Super 90	No	1"	37.95
Ithaca 37	No	1"	37.95
Mossberg 500	No	1"	37.95
Mossberg 835 Ultimag	No	1"	37.95
Mossberg 5500	No	1"	37.95
Remington 870/1100	No	1"	37.95
Winchester 1300/1400	No	1"	37.95
Mount scopes, lasers, electronic sights using Weaver-style base. All mounts allow use of iron sights; no gunsmithing. Available in satin black or satin stainless finish. **Partial listing shown.** Contact maker for full details. From L&S Technologies, Inc.			
A.R.M.S.			
Beretta AR-70	No	—	59.00
FN FAL LAR	No	Weaver-type rail	98.00
FN FAL LAR Para.	No	—	120.00
M21/14	No	—	135.00
M16A1/A2/AR-15	No	Weaver-type rail	59.95
Multibase Weaver Rail[1]	No	—	59.95
Ring Inserts	No	30mm to 1"	29.00
Swan G-3	No	Weaver-type	165.00
STANAG Rings	No	30mm	65.00
Throw Lever Weaver Rings	No	1"	78.75
#19 Weaver/STANAG Throw Lever Rail	No	—	140.00
[1]For rifles with detachable carry handle, other Weaver rails. From A.R.M.S., Inc.			
ARMSON			
AR-15[1]	No	1"	39.00
Mini-14[2]	No	1"	56.00
H&K[3]	No	1"	74.00
UZI[4]	No	1"	74.00
[1]Fastens with one nut. [2]Models 181, 182, 183, 184, etc. [3]Claw mount. [4]Claw mount, bolt cover still easily removable. From Trijicon, Inc.			
ARMSPORT			
100 Series[1]	No	1" rings. Low, med., high	10.75
104 22-cal.	No	1"	10.75
201 See-Thru	No	1"	13.00
1-Piece Base[2]	No	—	5.50
2-Piece Base[2]	No	—	2.75
[1]Weaver-type rings. [2]Weaver-type base; most popular rifles. Made in U.S. From Armsport.			
B-SQUARE			
Pistols			
Beretta/Taurus 92/99[6]	—	1"	69.95
Browning Buck Mark[6]	No	1"	49.95
Colt 45 Auto	E only	1"	69.95

Maker, Model, Type	Adjust.	Scopes	Price
B-SQUARE (cont.)			
Colt Python/MkIV, 4",6",8"[1,6]	E	1"	59.95
Daisy 717/722 Champion	No	1"	39.95
Dan Wesson Clamp-On[2,6]	E	1"	59.95
Ruger 22 Auto Mono-Mount[3]	No	1"	49.95
Ruger Single-Six[4]	No	1"	49.95
Ruger Blackhawk, Super B'hwk[8]	W&E	1"	59.95
Ruger GP-100[9]	No	1"	59.95
Ruger Redhawk[8]	W&E	1"	59.95
S&W 422/2206[9]	No	1"	59.95
Taurus 66[9]	No	1"	59.95
S&W K, L, N frame[2,6]	No	1"	59.95
T/C Contender (Dovetail Base)	W&E	1"	49.95
Rifles			
Charter AR-7	No	1"	49.95
Mini-14 (dovetail/NATO Stanag)[5,6]	W&E	1"	59.95
M-94 Side Mount	W&E	1"	49.95
RWS, Beeman/FWB Air Rifles	E only	—	69.95
Ruger 77[6]	W&E	1"	69.95
SMLE Side Mount with rings	W&E	1"	69.95
Rem. Model Seven, 600, 660, etc.[6]	No	1" One-piece base	9.95
Military			
AK-47/AKM/AKS/SKS-56[10]	No	1"	59.95
AK-47, SKS-56[11]	No	1"	69.95
M1-A[7]	W&E	1"	99.50
AR-15/16[7]	W&E	1"	59.95
FN-LAR/FAL[6,7]	E only	1"	149.50
HK-91/93/94[6,7]	E only	1"	99.50
Shotguns[6]			
Browning A-5[6]	No	1"	59.95
Ithaca 37[6]	No	1"	49.95
Mossberg 500, 712, 5500[6]	No	1"	49.95
Rem. 870/1100 (12 & 20 ga.)[6]	No	1"	49.95
Rem. 870, 1100 (and L.H.)[6]	No	1"	49.95
BSL Laser Mounts			
Scope Tube Clamp[12,13,16]	No	—	39.95
45 Auto[12,13,16]	No	—	69.95
SIG P226[12,13,16]	No	—	69.95
Beretta 92F/Taurus PT99[12,13,16]	No	—	69.95
Colt King Cobra, Python, MkV[12,13,16]	No	—	39.95
S&W L Frame[13,16]	No	—	39.95
Taurus 66/69[12,14,16]	No	—	69.95
S&W K,L,N Frames[12,14,16]	No	—	69.95
Beretta 92F/Taurus PT99[12,15,16]	No	—	79.95
Glock 17[15,16]	No	—	79.95
Ruger P85[12,15,16]	No	—	79.95
S&W 4006, 1006[15,16]	No	—	89.95
S&W 5904[15,16]	No	—	79.95
S&W 5906[15,16]	No	—	89.95
[1]Clamp-on, blue finish; stainless finish **$59.95**. [2]Blue finish; stainless finish **$59.95**. [3]Clamp-on, blue; stainless finish **$59.95**. [4]Dovetail; stainless finish **$59.95**. [5]No gunsmithing, no sight removal; blue; stainless finish **$79.95**. [6]Weaver-style rings. Rings not included with Weaver-type bases; stainless finish add $10. [7]NATO Stanag dovetail model, **$99.50**. [8]Blue; stainless **$69.95**. [9]stainless **$69.95**. [10]Handguard mounts. [11]Receiver mounts. [12]Stainless finish add $10. [13]Under-barrel mount, no gunsmithing. [14]Ejector rod mount. [15]Guide rod mount. [16]Used with B-Square BSL-1 Laser Sight only. Mounts for many shotguns, airguns, military and law enforcement guns also available. **Partial listing of mounts shown here. Contact B-Square for more data.**			
B-Square makes mounts for the following military rifles: AK47/AKS, Egyptian Hakim, French MAS 1936, M91 Argentine Mauser, Model 98 Brazilian and German Mausers, Model 93, Spanish Mauser (long and short), Model 1916 Mauser, Model 38 and 96 Swedish Mausers, Model 91 Russian (round and octagon receivers), Chinese SKS 56, SMLE No. 1, Mk. III, 1903 Springfield, U.S. 30-cal. Carbine, and others. Those following replace gun's rear sight: AK47/AKS, P14/1917 Enfield, FN49, M1 Garand, M1-A/M14 (no sight removal), SMLE No. 1, Mk III/No. 4 & 5, Mk. 1, 1903/1903-A3 Springfield, Beretta AR 70 (no sight removal).			
BAUSCH & LOMB	No	1"	42.95
Rem. 700, 7400/7600, Ruger 77, Browning A-Bolt, Browning BBR, Savage 110, Win. 70, Marlin 336. Contact Bushnell for details.			
BEEMAN			
Double Adjustable	W&E	1"	29.98
Deluxe Ring Mounts	No	1"	29.98
Professional Mounts	W&E	1"	149.95
All grooved receivers and scope bases on all known air rifles and 22-cal. rimfire rifles (½" to ⅝"—6mm to 15mm).			
BOCK			
Swing ALK[1]	W&E	1", 26mm, 30mm	224.00
Safari KEMEL[2]	W&E	1", 26mm, 30mm	149.00
Claw KEMKA[3]	W&E	1", 26mm, 30mm	224.00

Maker, Model, Type	Adjust.	Scopes	Price
BOCK (cont.)			
ProHunter Fixed[4]	No	1", 26mm, 30mm	95.00
Dovetail 22[5]	No	1", 26mm	59.00

[1]Q.D.; pivots right for removal. For Steyr-Mannlicher, Win. 70, Rem. 700, Mauser 98, Dakota, Sako, Sauer 80, 90. Magnum has extra-wide rings, same price. [2]Heavy-duty claw-type; reversible for front or rear removal. For Steyr-Mannlicher rifles. [3]True claw mount for bolt-action rifles. Also in extended model. For Steyr-Mannlicher, Win. 70, Rem. 700. Also avail. as Gunsmith Bases—bases not drilled or contoured—same price. [4]Extra-wide rings. [5]Fit most 22 rimfires with dovetail receivers. Imported from Germany by GSI, Inc.

Maker, Model, Type	Adjust.	Scopes	Price
BUEHLER			
One Piece (T)[1]	W only	1" split rings, 3 heights	Complete— 86.50
		1" split rings, engraved	Rings only— 135.00
		26mm split rings, 2 heights	Rings only— 59.00
		30mm split rings, 1 height	Rings only— 74.00
One Piece Micro Dial (T)[1]	W&E	1" split rings	Complete— 110.50
Two Piece (T)[1]	W only	1" split rings	Complete— 86.50
Two Piece Dovetail (T)[2]	W only	1" split rings	Complete— 106.00
One Piece Pistol (T)[3]	W only	1" split rings	Complete— $86.50
One Piece Pistol Stainless (T)[1]	W only	1" stainless rings	Complete— 111.00
One Piece Ruger Mini-14 (T)[4]	W only	1" split rings	Complete— 106.00
One Piece Pistol M83 Blue[4,5]	W only	1" split rings	Complete— 98.50
One Piece Pistol M83 Silver[4,5]	W only	1" stainless rings	Complete— 114.00

[1]Most popular models. [2]Sako dovetail receivers. [3]15 models. [4]No drilling & tapping. [5]Aircraft alloy, dyed blue or to match stainless; for Colt Diamondback, Python, Trooper, Ruger Blackhawk, Single-Six, Security-Six, S&W K-frame, Dan Wesson.

Maker, Model, Type	Adjust.	Scopes	Price
BURRIS			
Supreme One Piece (T)[1]	W only	1" split rings, 3 heights	1 piece base— 25.95
Trumount Two Piece (T)	W only	1" split rings, 3 heights	2 piece base— 23.95
Trumount Two Piece Ext.[9]	W only	1" split rings	29.95
Browning Auto Mount[2]	No	1" split rings	19.95
Rings Mounts[3]	No	1" split rings	1" rings— 20.95
L.E.R. Mount Bases[4]	W only	1" split rings	23.95
L.E.R. No Drill-No Tap Bases[4,7,8]	W only	1" split rings	37.95-48.95
Extension Rings[5]	No	1" scopes	41.95-48.95
Ruger Ring Mount[6]	W only	1" split rings	36.95-41.95
Std. 1" Rings	—	Low, medium, high heights	33.95-41.95
Zee Rings	—	Fit Weaver bases; medium and high heights	27.95-35.95

[1]Most popular rifles. Universal rings, mounts fit Burris, Universal, Redfield, Leupold and Browning bases. Comparable prices. [2]Browning Standard 22 Auto rifle. [3]Grooved receivers. [4]Universal dovetail; accept Burris, Universal, Redfield, Leupold rings. For Dan Wesson, S&W, Virginian, Ruger Blackhawk, Win. 94. [5]Medium standard front, extension rear, per pair. Low standard front, extension rear, per pair. [6]Mini scopes, scopes with 2" bell, for M77R. [7]Selected rings and bases available with matte Safari or silver finish. [8]For S&W K,L,N frames, Colt Python, Dan Wesson with 6" or longer barrels. [9]For long scope tubes; Rem. 700, Win. 70A, FN.

Maker, Model, Type	Adjust.	Scopes	Price
BUSHNELL			
Detachable (T) mounts only[1]	W only	1" split rings, uses Weaver base	Rings—21.95
22 mount	No	1" only	Rings—9.95

[1]Most popular rifles. Includes windage adjustment.

Maker, Model, Type	Adjust.	Scopes	Price
CAPE OUTFITTERS			
Quick Detachable	No	1" split rings, lever quick detachable	99.95

Double rifles; Sauer, Win. Model 70, Rem. 700, Browning Safari, Mauser 98, grooved receiver 22s. All steel; returns to zero. From Cape Outfitters.

Maker, Model, Type	Adjust.	Scopes	Price
CLEAR VIEW			
Universal Rings, Mod. 101[1]	No	1" split rings	21.95
Standard Model[2]	No	1" split rings	21.95
Broad View[3]	No	1"	21.95
22 Model[4]	No	3/4", 7/8", 1"	13.95
SM-94 Winchester[5]	No	1" split rings	23.95
94 EJ[6]	No	1" split rings	21.95

[1]Most rifles by using Weaver-type base; allows use of iron sights. [2]Most popular rifles; allows use of iron sights. [3]Most popular rifles; low profile, wide field of view. [4]22 rifles with grooved receiver. [5]Side mount. [6]For Winchester Angle Eject. From Clear View Mfg.

Maker, Model, Type	Adjust.	Scopes	Price
CONETROL			
Huntur[1]	W only	1", 26mm, 26.5mm solid or split rings, 3 heights	59.91
Gunnur[2]	W only	1", 26mm, 26.5mm solid or split rings, 3 heights	74.91
Custum[3]	W only	1", 26mm, 26.5mm solid or split rings, 3 heights	89.91
One Piece Side Mount Base[4]	W only	1", 26mm, 26.5mm solid or split rings, 3 heights	—
Daptar Bases[5]	W only	1", 26mm, 26.5mm solid or split rings, 3 heights	—
Pistol Bases, 2 or 3-ring[6]	W only	1" scopes	—
Fluted Bases[7]	W only	Standard Conetrol rings	99.99
30mm Rings[8]	W only	30mm	49.98-69.96

[1]All popular rifles, including metric-drilled foreign guns. Price shown for base, two rings. Matte finish. [2]Gunnur grade has mirror-finished rings, satin-finish base. Price shown for base, two rings. [3]Custum grade has mirror-finished rings and mirror-finished, streamlined base. Price shown for base, two rings. [4]Win. 94, Krag, older solid-bridge Mannlicher-Schoenauer, Mini-14, etc. Prices same as above. [5]For all popular guns with integral mounting provision, including Sako, BSA, Ithacagun, Ruger, Tikka, H&K, BRNO—$29.97-$44.97—and many others. Also for grooved-receiver rimfires and air rifles. Prices same as above. [6]For XP-100, T/C Contender, Colt SAA, Ruger Blackhawk, S&W. [7]Sculptured two-piece bases as found on fine custom rifles. Price shown is for base alone. Also available unfinished—$74.91, or finished but unfluted—$87.95. [8]30mm rings made in projectionless style, medium height only. Three-ring mount available for T/C Contender and other pistols in Conetrol's three grades.

Maker, Model, Type	Adjust.	Scopes	Price
COOPER ARMS RINGS			
Rings for grooved receivers	No	1"	79.95
Double Lever Q.D.[1]	No	1"	109.95
Rings for bases[2]	No	1"	79.95
Scope Mount Bases[3]	No	—	9.50

[1]For grooved receivers. [2]30mm $95.95; 30mm Double Lever bases for bases $124.95. [3]For Kimber and many popular rifles. High and low semi-detachable rings for Kimber grooved receivers or Kimber 89 Squarebridge. Rings fit other popular rifles by using Kimber-style two-piece screw-on bases. Double Lever Q.D. rings in medium height for same applications. All avail. in bright blue, matte blue or stainless. From Cooper Arms.

Maker, Model, Type	Adjust.	Scopes	Price
EAW			
Quick Detachable Top Mount	W&E	1",26mm	259.99
	W&E	1"/26mm with front extension ring	259.99
	W&E	30mm	279.99
	W&E	30mm with front extension ring.	279.99

Also 30mm rings to fit Burris, Redfield or Leupold-type bases, low and high, **$112.00**; 1" or 26mm rings only, **$95.00** Most popular rifles. Elevation adjusted with variable-height sub-bases for rear ring. Imported by Paul Jaeger, Inc.

Maker, Model, Type	Adjust.	Scopes	Price
GENTRY			
Feather-Light Rings	No	1", 30mm	75.00

One-piece rings in matte blue or matte stainless. From David Gentry.

Maker, Model, Type	Adjust.	Scopes	Price
GRIFFIN & HOWE			
Standard Double Lever (S)	No	1" or 26mm split rings.	305.00

All popular models (Garand **$215**). All rings **$75**. Top ejection rings available. Price installed for side mount.

Maker, Model, Type	Adjust.	Scopes	Price
HOLDEN			
Wide Ironsighter™	No	1" split rings	26.95
Ironsighter Center Fire[1]	No	1" split rings	26.95
Ironsighter S-94	No	1" split rings	31.95
Ironsighter 22-Cal. Rimfire			
Model #500[2]	No	1" split rings	14.95
Model #600[3]	No	7/8" split rings also fits 3/4"	14.95
Series #700[5]	No	1" split rings	26.95
Model 732, 777[6]	No	1" split rings	56.95
Ironsighter Handguns[4]	No	1" split rings	31.95-56.95
Blackpowder Mount[7]	No	1"	26.95-56.95

[1]Most popular rifles, including Ruger Mini-14, H&R M700, and muzzleloaders. Rings have oval holes to permit use of iron sights. [2]For 1" dia. scopes. [3]For 3/4" or 7/8" dia. scopes. [4]For 1" dia. extended eye relief scopes. [5]702—Browning A-Bolt; 709—Marlin 39A. [6]732—Ruger 77/22 R&RS, No. 1, Ranch Rifle; 777 fits Ruger 77R, RS. Both 732, 777 fit Ruger integral bases. [7]Fits most popular blackpowder rifles; one model for Holden Ironsighter mounts, one for Weaver rings. Adj. rear sight is integral.

Maker, Model, Type	Adjust.	Scopes	Price
KENPATABLE MOUNT			
Shotgun Mount	No	1", laser or red dot device	49.95

Wrap-around design; no gunsmithing required. Models for Browning BPS, A-5 12-ga., Sweet 16, 20, Rem. 870/1100 (LTW and L.H.), S&W 916, Mossberg 500, Ithaca 37 & 51 12-ga., S&W 1000/3000, Win. 1400. From KenPatable Ent.

Maker, Model, Type	Adjust.	Scopes	Price
KRIS MOUNTS			
Side-Saddle[1]	No	1", 26mm split rings	12.98
Two Piece (T)[2]	No	1", 26mm split rings	8.98
One Piece (T)[3]	No	1", 26mm split rings	12.98

[1]One-piece mount for Win. 94. [2]Most popular rifles and Ruger. [3]Blackhawk revolver. Mounts have oval hole to permit use of iron sights.

Maker, Model, Type	Adjust.	Scopes	Price
KWIK-SITE			
KS-See-Thru[1]	No	1"	25.95
KS-22 See-Thru[2]	No	1"	22.95
KS-W94[3]	No	1"	30.95
Imperial Bench Rest	No	1"	30.95
KS-WEV	No	1"	21.95
KS-WEV-HIGH	No	1"	21.95
KS-T22 1"[4]	No	1"	22.95
KS-FL Flashlite[5]	No	Mini or C cell flashlight	49.95
KS-T88[6]	No	1"	10.95
KS-T89	No	30mm	14.95
KSN 22 See-Thru	No	1", 7⁄8"	19.95
KSN-T22	No	1", 7⁄8"	19.95
KSN-M16 See-Thru	No	1"	99.95
KSB Base Set	—	—	5.65
Combo Bases & Rings	No	1"	26.75

[1]Most rifles. Allows use of iron sights. [2]22-cal. rifles with grooved receivers. Allows use of iron sights. [3]Model 94, 94 Big Bore. No drilling or tapping. Also in adjustable model $49.95. [4]Non-see-through model for grooved receivers. [5]Allows Mag Lite or C or D, Mini Mag Lites to be mounted atop See-Thru mounts. [6]Fits any Redfield, Tasco, Weaver or universal-style Kwik-Site dovetail base. Bright blue, black matte or satin finish. Standard, high heights.

Maker, Model, Type	Adjust.	Scopes	Price
LASER AIM	No	Laser Aim	29.00-69.00

Mounts Laser Aim above or below barrel. Avail. for most popular handguns, rifles, shotguns, including militaries. From Emerging Technologies, Inc.

Maker, Model, Type	Adjust.	Scopes	Price
LASERSIGHT	No	LS45 only	29.95-149.00

For the LS45 Lasersight. Allows LS45 to be mounted alongside any 1" scope. Universal adapter attaches to any full-length Weaver-type base. For most popular military-type rifles, Mossberg, Rem. shotguns, Python, Desert Eagle, S&W N frame, Colt 45ACP. From Imatronic Lasersight.

Maker, Model, Type	Adjust.	Scopes	Price
LEUPOLD			
STD 7⁄8" Rings[10]	—	7⁄8"	32.00
STD Bases[1]	W only	One- or two-piece bases	22.90
STD Rings[2]	—	1" super low, low, medium, high	32.00
STD Handgun mounts[3]	No	—	57.90
Dual Dovetail Bases[1,4]	No	—	22.90
Dual Dovetail Rings[11]	—	1", super low, low	32.00
Ring Mounts[5,6,7]	No	7⁄8", 1"	81.10
22 Rimfire[11]	No	7⁄8", 1"	60.00
Gunmaker Base[8]	W only	1"	16.00
Gunmaker Ring Blanks[9]	—	1"	22.00
Quick Release Rings	—	1", low, med., high	32.00
Quick Release Bases[12]	No	1", one- or two-piece	66.00
Airgun Ringmount[13]	No	1"	92.00

[1]Rev. front and rear combinations; matte finish $22.90. [2]Avail. polished, matte or silver (low, med. only) finish. [3]Base and two rings; Casull, Ruger, S&W, T/C; add $5.00 for silver finish. [4]Rem. 700, Win. 70-type actions. [5]For Ruger No. 1, 77, 77/22; interchangeable with Ruger units. [6]For dovetailed rimfire rifles. [7]Sako; high, medium, low. [8]Must be drilled, tapped for each action. [9]Unfinished bottom, top completed; sold singly. [10]Fit all Leupold STD one-, two-piece bases. [11]Most dovetail-receiver 22s. [12]BSA Monarch, Rem. 40X, 700, 721, 725, Ruger M77, S&W 1500, Weatherby Mark V, Vanguard, Win M70. [13]Receiver grooves 9.5mm to 11.0mm; matte finish.

Maker, Model, Type	Adjust.	Scopes	Price
LEATHERWOOD			
Bridge Bases[1]	No	ART II or all dovetail rings	15.00
M1A/M-14 Q.D.	No	ART II or all dovetail rings	105.00
AR-15/M-16 Base	No	ART II or all dovetail rings	25.00
FN-FAL Base	No	ART II or all dovetail rings	100.00
FN Para. Base	No	ART II or all dovetail rings	110.00
Steyr SSG Base	No	ART II or all dovetail rings	55.00

[1]Many popular bolt actions. Mounts accept Weaver or dovetail-type rings. From North American Specialties.

Maker, Model, Type	Adjust.	Scopes	Price
MARLIN			
One Piece QD (T)	No	1" split rings	14.95

Most Marlin lever actions.

Maker, Model, Type	Adjust.	Scopes	Price
MILLETT			
Black Onyx Smooth		1", low, medium, high	29.65

Maker, Model, Type	Adjust.	Scopes	Price
MILLETT (cont.)			
Chaparral Engraved	—	engraved	43.95
One-Piece Bases[6]	Yes	1"	23.95
Universal Two-Piece Bases			
700 Series	W only	Two-piece bases	23.95
FN Series	W only	Two-piece bases	23.95
70 Series[1]	W only	1", two-piece bases	23.95
Angle-Loc Rings[2]	W only	1", low, medium, high	30.65-44.95
Ruger 77 Rings[3]	—	1"	44.95
Shotgun Rings[4]	—	1"	26.95
Handgun Bases, Rings[5]	—	1"	32.95-61.35
30mm Rings[7]	—	30mm	35.95
Extension Rings[8]	—	1"	33.95

[1]Rem. 40X, 700, 722, 725, Ruger 77 (round top), Weatherby, FN Mauser, FN Brownings, Colt 57, Interarms Mark X, Parker-Hale, Sako (round receiver), many others. Fits Win. M70, 70XTR, 670, Browning BBR, BAR, BLR, A-Bolt, Rem. 7400/7600, Four, Six, Marlin 336, Win. 94 A.E., Sav. 110. [2]To fit Weaver-type bases. [3]Engraved. Smooth $30.65. [4]For Rem. 870, 1100; smooth. [5]Two and three-ring sets for Colt Python, Trooper, Diamondback, Peacekeeper, Dan Wesson, Ruger Redhawk, Super Redhawk. [6]Turn-in bases and Weaver-style for most popular rifles and T/C Contender, XP-100 pistols. [7]Both Weaver and turn-in styles; three heights. [8]Med. or high; ext. front—std. rear, ext. rear—std. front, ext. front—ext. rear; $38.95 for double extension. Some models available in nickel at extra cost. From Millett Sights.

Maker, Model, Type	Adjust.	Scopes	Price
OAKSHORE			
Handguns			
Browning Buck Mark	No	1"	29.00
Colt Cobra, Diamondback, Python, 1911	No	1"	38.00-52.00
Ruger 22 Auto, GP100	No	1"	33.00-49.00
S&W N Frame	No	1"	45.00-60.00
S&W 422	No	1"	35.00-38.00
Rifles			
Colt AR-15	No	1"	26.00-34.00
H&K 91, 93, 94, MP-5, G-3	No	1"	56.00
Galil	No	1"	75.00
Marlin 336 & 1800 Series	No	1"	21.00
Win. 94	No	1"	39.00
Shotguns			
Mossberg 500	No	1"	40.00
Rem. 870, 1100	No	1"	33.00-52.00
Rings	No	1", med., high	5.20-9.80

See Through offered in some models. Black or silver finish; 1" rings also avail. for 3⁄8" grooved receivers (See Through). From Oakshore Electronic Sights, Inc.

Maker, Model, Type	Adjust.	Scopes	Price
RAM-LINE			
Mini-14 Mount	Yes	1"	24.97

No drilling or tapping. Use std. dovetail rings. Has built-in shell deflector. Made of solid black polymer. From Ram-Line, Inc.

Maker, Model, Type	Adjust.	Scopes	Price
REDFIELD			
American Rings[8]	No	1", low, med., high	16.95
American Bases[8]	No	—	3.95-5.95
American Widefield See-Thru[9]	No	1"	16.95
JR-SR (T)[1]	W only	3⁄4", 1", 26mm, 30mm	JR—22.95-52.95 SR—22.95-23.95
Ring (T)[2]	No	3⁄4" and 1"	27.95
Three-Ring Pistol System SMP[3]	No	1" split rings (three)	58.95-65.95
Midline Base & Rings[4]	No	1", low, medium, high	13.95
Widefield See-Thru Mounts	No	1"	16.95
Ruger Rings[4]	No	1", med., high	35.95
Ruger 30mm[5]	No	1"	46.95
Midline Ext. Rings	No	1"	18.95
Steel "WS" Rings[6]	W	1", 30mm	26.95
Steel 22 Ring Mount, Base[7]	No	3⁄4", 1"	13.95-29.95

[1]Low, med. & high, split rings. Reversible extension front rings for 1". 2-piece bases for Sako. Colt Sauer bases $39.85. Med. Top Access JR rings nickel-plated, $29.95. SR two-piece ABN mount nickel-plated, $23.95; RealTree Camo rings, med. & high $33.95; RealTree Camo JR bases $26.95; RealTree bases $26.95. [2]Split rings for grooved 22s. See-Thru mounts $16.95. [3]Used with MP scopes for: S&W K, L or N frame, XP-100, T/C Contender, Ruger receivers. [4]For Ruger Model 77 rifles, medium and high; medium only for M77/22. [5]For Model 77. Also in matte finish $44.95. [6]Nickel-plated, $33.95; with RealTree camo finish $30.95. [7]For 22 rifles with grooved receivers. Fits all radius dovetails. [8]Aluminum 22 groove mount $11.95; base and medium rings $17.95. [9]Fits American or Weaver-style base.

Maker, Model, Type	Adjust.	Scopes	Price
S&K			
Insta-Mount (T) bases and rings[1]	W only	Use S&K rings only	25.00-99.00
Conventional rings and bases[2]	W only	1" split rings	From 50.00
Skulptured Bases, Rings[2]	W only	1", 26mm, 30mm	From 50.00

[1]1903, A3, M1 Carbine, Lee Enfield #1, Mk. III, #4, #5, M1917, M98 Mauser, FN Auto, AR-15, AR-180, M-14, M-1, Ger. K-43, Mini-14, M1-A, Krag, AKM, AK-47, Win. 94, SKS Type 56, Daewoo, H&K. [2]Most popular rifles already drilled and tapped. Horizontally and vertically split rings, matte or high gloss.

SSK INDUSTRIES

Maker, Model, Type	Adjust.	Scopes	Price
T'SOB	No	1"	**65.00-145.00**
Quick Detachable	No	1"	**From 160.00**

Custom installation using from two to four rings (included). For T/C Contender, most 22 auto pistols, Ruger and other S.A. revolvers, Ruger, Dan Wesson, S&W, Colt DA revolvers. Black or white finish. Uses Kimber rings in two- or three-ring sets. In blue or SSK Khrome. For T/C Contender or most popular revolvers. Standard, non-detachable model also available, from **$65.00.**

SAKO

Maker, Model, Type	Adjust.	Scopes	Price
QD Dovetail	W only	1" only	**67.00-125.00**

Sako, or any rifle using Sako action, 3 heights available. Stoeger, importer.

SIMMONS

Maker, Model, Type	Adjust.	Scopes	Price
1460[1]	No	1"	**17.95**
1462[2]	No	1"	**17.95**
1465[3]	No	1"	**17.95**
1466[4]	No	1"	**17.95**
1469[5]	No	1"	**17.95**
1471[6]	No	1"	**17.95**
21000[7]	No	1"	**38.95**
SRB01[8]	No	1"	**43.95**
SRB02[9]	No	1"	**43.95**
SRB04[10]	No	1"	**43.95**
SRB08[11]	No	1"	**43.95**

[1]Browning Auto. [2]Marlin 336, 444, 36, 62, Glenfield 30. [3]Rem. 700 SA/Seven. [4]Rem. 700 L.A. [5]Win. 70A. [6]Sav. 110. [7]Rem. 870, 1100, 11-87. [8]Rem. Seven, 700 LA/SA; two-piece, med. rings. [9]Rem. Four, Six, 7400/7600, two-piece, med. rings. [10]Win. 70A LA/SA, two-piece, med. rings. [11]Sav. 110, two-piece, med. rings. Contact Simmons Outdoor Corp. for complete list of models and applications.

TASCO

Maker, Model, Type	Adjust.	Scopes	Price
World Class			
Universal "W" Ringmount[1]	No	1", 30mm	**27.00-59.00**
Ruger[2]	No	1", 30mm	**35.00-59.00**
22, Air Rifle[3]	No	1", 30mm	**28.00-66.00**
Center-Fire Ringmount[4]	No	1", 26mm, 30mm	**46.00-66.00**
Desert Eagle Ringmount[5]	No	1", 30mm	**51.00-72.00**
Ringsets[6]	No	1", 26mm, 30mm	**26.00-56.00**
Bases[7]	Yes	—	**26.00-46.00**
Pro-Mount Handgun Base[8]	No	—	**9.00-37.00**

[1]Steel; low, high only; also high-profile see-through; fit Tasco, Weaver, other universal bases; black gloss or satin chrome. [2]Low, high only; for Redhawk and Super, No.1, Mini-14 & Thirty, 77, 77/22; blue or stainless. [3]Low, med., high; 3⁄8" grooved receivers; black or satin chrome. [4]Low, med., high; for Tasco W.C. bases, some dovetail; black gloss only. [5]For Desert Eagle pistols, 22s, air rifles with deep dovetails. [6]Low, med., high; black gloss, matte satin chrome; also Traditional Ringsets **$31.00** (1"), **$42.00** (26mm), **$53.00** (30mm). [7]For popular rifles and shotguns; one-piece, two-piece, Q.D., long and short action, extension. Handgun bases have w&e adj. [8]For many popular handguns, blue or stainless. From Tasco.

THOMPSON/CENTER

Maker, Model, Type	Adjust.	Scopes	Price
Contender 9746[1]	No	T/C Lobo	**17.00**
Contender 9741[2]	No	2½, 4 RP	**17.00**
Contender 7410	No	Bushnell Phantom, 1.3-2.5x	**17.00**
S&W 9747[3]	No	Lobo or RP	**17.00**
Ruger 9748[4]	No	Lobo or RP	**17.00**
Hawken 9749[5]	No	Lobo or RP	**17.00**
Hawken/Renegade 9754[6]	No	Lobo or RP	**17.00**
Cherokee/Seneca 9756[7]	No	Lobo or RP	**17.00**
New Englander 9757	No	Lobo or RP	**17.00**
TCR '87 Base 9760[8]	Yes	—	**38.00**
Detachable Rings[9]	—	1"	**46.50**
T/C Base[10]	Yes	1"	**38.00**
Quick Release System[11]	No	1"	**Rings 48.00** **Base 24.50**

[1]All Contenders except vent. rib. [2]T/C rail mount scopes; all Contenders except vent. rib. [3]All S&W K and Combat Masterpiece, Hi-Way Patrolman, Outdoorsman, 22 Jet, 45 Target 1955. Requires drilling, tapping. [4]Blackhawk, Super Blackhawk, Super Single-Six. Requires drilling, tapping. [5]45 or 50 cal.; replaces rear sight. [6]Rail mount scopes; 54-cal. Hawken, 50, 54, 56-cal. Renegade. Replaces rear sight. [7]Cherokee 32 or 45 cal., Seneca 36 or 45 cal. Replaces rear sight. Carbine mount #9743 for Short Tube scope #8640, **$13.75**. [8]For T/C "Short Tube" scope #8630; matte blue; also #9710 base for std. scope; no gunsmithing. [9]Also silver finish, **$46.50**. [10]For Contender Carbine, pistol, Scout; silver finish, **$38.00**. [11]For Contender pistol, Carbine, Scout, all M/L long guns. From Thompson/Center.

UNERTL

Maker, Model, Type	Adjust.	Scopes	Price
1⁄4 Click[1]	Yes	3⁄4", 1" target scopes	**Per set 115.00**

[1]Unertl target or varmint scopes. Posa or standard mounts, less bases. From Unertl

WARNE

Maker, Model, Type	Adjust.	Scopes	Price
Quick Detachable Thumb Knob	No	1", 3 heights	**56.50**
		26mm 1 height	**68.50**
		30mm 2 heights	**68.55**
Double Lever	No	1", 3 heights	**79.50**
		26mm 1 height	**91.50**
		30mm 2 heights	**91.50**

WARNE (cont.)

Maker, Model, Type	Adjust.	Scopes	Price
Grooved Receivers[1]	No	1", 3 heights	**56.50**
BRNO (ZZK-series action)	No	1", 3 heights	**59.50**
		30mm 2 heights	**71.50**
SAKO[2]	No	1", 4 heights	**59.50**
Ruger[3]	No	M77 1", 2 heights	**59.50**
		M77 30mm, 2 heights	**71.50**
		All other 1", 3 heights	**59.50**
		All other 30mm, 3 heights	**71.50**
Two-Piece Bases (pr.)	—	—	**22.00**
One-Piece Base	—	—	**28.50**

Vertically split rings with dovetail clamp, precise repeat to zero. Fit most popular rifles, handguns. Regular blue, matte blue, silver finish. BRNO, Sako not q.d. [1]For 22-cal. dovetailed receivers. [2]For all action lengths. [3]Q.D. thumb knob version only. From Warne Mfg. Co.

WEAVER

Maker, Model, Type	Adjust.	Scopes	Price
Detachable Mounts			
Top Mount[1]	No	7⁄8", 1"	**25.48-26.51**
Side Mount[2]	No	1", 1" Long	**29.97-35.44**
Pivot Mount[3]	No	1"	**38.00-42.00**
Tip-Off Mount[4]	No	7⁄8", 1"	**21.82-27.82**
		1"	**27.82**
See-Thru Mount			
Traditional[5]	No	1"	**NA**
Symmetrical[6]	No	1"	**23.22-26.71**
Detachable[5]	No	1"	**26.51**
Tip-Off[4]	No	1", 7⁄8"	**19.11-26.51**
Pro View[6]	No	1"	**NA**
Mount Base System[7]			
Blue Finish	No	1"	**73.75**
Stainless Finish	No	1"	**103.17**
Shotgun Converta-Mount System[8]	No	1"	**73.75**
Rifle Mount System[9]	No	1"	**32.71**
Paramount Mount Systems[10]			
Bases, pair	Yes	1"	**25.33**
Rings, pair	No	1"	**32.91**

[1]Nearly all modern rifles. Low, med., high. 1" extension **$30.95**. 1" med. stainless steel **$40.53**. [2]Nearly all modern rifles, shotguns. [3]Most modern big bore rifles; std., high. [4]22s with 3⁄8" grooved receivers. [5]Nearly all modern rifles. 1" See-Thru extension **$30.95.** [6]Most modern big bore rifles. [7]No drilling, tapping. For Colt Python, Trooper, 357, Officer's Model, Ruger Blackhawk & Super, Mini-14, Security-Six, 22 auto pistols, Redhawk, Blackhawk SRM 357, S&W current K, L with adj. sights. [8]For Rem. 870, 1100, 11-87, Browning A-5, BPS, Ithaca 37, 87, Beretta A303, Winchester 1200-1500, Mossberg 500. [9]For some popular sporting rifles. [10]Dovetail design mount for Rem. 700, Win. 70, FN Mauser, low, med., high rings; std., extension bases. From Weaver.

WIDEVIEW

Maker, Model, Type	Adjust.	Scopes	Price
Premium 94 Angle Eject	No	1"	**24.00**
Premium See-Thru	No	1"	**22.00**
22 Premium See-Thru	No	3⁄4", 1"	**16.00**
Universal Ring Angle Cut	No	1"	**24.00**
Universal Ring Straight Cut	No	1"	**22.00**
Solid Mounts			
Lo Ring Solid[1]	No	1"	**16.00**
Hi Ring Solid[1]	No	1"	**16.00**
SR Rings	—	1", 30mm	**16.00**
22 Grooved Receiver	No	1"	**16.00**
94 Side Mount	No	1"	**26.00**
Blackpowder Mounts[2]	No	1"	**30.00**

[1]For Weaver-type bases. Models for many popular rifles. Low ring, high ring and grooved receiver types. [2]No drilling, tapping; for T/C Renegade, Hawken, CVA guns; for guns drilled and tapped, **$16.00**. From Wideview Scope Mount Corp.

WILLIAMS

Maker, Model, Type	Adjust.	Scopes	Price
Sidemount with HCO Rings[1]	No	1", split or extension rings.	**69.25**
Sidemount, offset rings[2]	No	Same	**57.00**
Sight-Thru Mounts[3]	No	1", 7⁄8" sleeves	**23.95**
Streamline Mounts	No	1" (bases form rings).	**23.95**
Guideline Handgun[4]	No	1" split rings.	**79.95**
Quick Detachable Top Mount[5]	No	1"	**57.00**

[1]Most rifles, Br. S.M.L.E. (round rec.) **$7.80** extra. [2]Most rifles including Win. 94 Big Bore. [3]Many modern rifles, including CVA Apollo, others with 1" octagon barrels. [4]No drilling, tapping required; heat treated alloy. For Ruger Blackhawk, Super Blackhawk, Redhawk; S&W N frame, M29 with 10⅝" barrel (**$79.95**); S&W K, L frames; Colt Python, King Cobra; Ruger MkII Bull Barrel; Streamline Top Mount for T/C Contender, Scout Rifle, CVA Apollo (**$39.95**), High Top Mount with sub-base (**$49.95**). [5]For T/C muzzleloaders; removes for cleaning gun. From Williams Gunsight Co.

YORK

Maker, Model, Type	Adjust.	Scopes	Price
M-1 Garand	Yes	1"	**39.95**

Centers scope over the action. No drilling, tapping or gunsmithing. Uses standard dovetail rings. From York M-1 Conversions.

(S)—Side Mount (T)—Top Mount; 22mm=.866"; 25.4mm=1.024"; 26.5mm=1.045"; 30mm=1.81"

SPOTTING SCOPES

Mirador SRA 25x60mm

Pentax 30x60 HG

BAUSCH & LOMB DISCOVERER—15x to 60x zoom, 60mm objective. Constant focus throughout range. Field at 1000 yds. 38 ft (60x), 150 ft. (15x). Comes with lens caps. Length 17½"; weight 48.5 oz.
Price: **$439.95**
BAUSCH & LOMB ELITE—15x to 45x zoom, 60mm objective. Field at 1000 yds., 119-62 ft. Length is 12.2"; weight, 26.5 oz. Waterproof, armored. Tripod mount. Comes with black case.
Price: **$769.95**
BAUSCH & LOMB 77MM ELITE—20x, 30x or 20-60x zoom, 77mm objective. Field of view at 1000 yds. 175 ft. (20x), 78 ft. (30x), 108-62 ft. (zoom). Weight 51 oz. (20x, 30x), 54 oz. (zoom); length 16.8". Interchangeable bayonet-style eyepieces. Built-in peep sight.
Price: **$852.95**
Price: 20-60x zoom eyepiece 466.95
Price: 30x eyepiece 306.95
Price: 20x eyepiece 333.95
BURRIS 20x SPOTTER—20x, 50mm objective. Straight type. Field at 100 yds. 15 ft. Length 10"; weight 21 oz. Rubber armor coating, multi-coated lenses, 22mm eye relief. Recessed focus adjustment. Nitrogen filled. Retractable sunshade.
Price: 20x 50mm **$478.95**
Price: 24x 60mm **$507.95**
Price: 30x 60mm **$536.95**
BUSHNELL BANNER SENTRY—18-36x zoom, 50mm objective. Field at 1000 yds. 115-78 ft. Length 14.5". Weight 27 oz. Black rubber armored. Built-in peep sight. Comes with tripod.
Price: **$237.95**
BUSHNELL COMPACT COMPETITOR—20x, 40mm objective. Field at 1000 yds. 141 ft. Focuses down to 40 ft. for indoor use. Tripod mount. Length 10.5"; weight 14.5 oz. Comes with tripod.
Price: **$157.95**
BUSHNELL SPACEMASTER—15x-45x zoom. Rubber armored, prismatic. 60mm objective. Field at 1000 yds. 125-65 ft. Minimum focus 20 ft. Length with caps 11.6"; weight 38.4 oz.
Price: With tripod and carrying case **$572.95**
Price: Interchangeable eyepieces—15x, 20x, 25x, 60x, each **$61.95**
Price: 22x Wide Angle **$96.95**
Price: 15-45x zoom eyepiece **$173.95**
BUSHNELL STALKER—10x to 30x zoom, 50mm objective. Field at 1000 yds. 142 ft. (10x) to 86 ft. (30x). Length 10.5"; weight 16 oz. Camo armored. Comes with tripod.
Price: **$450.95**
KOWA TSN-1-45°—Offset-type. 77mm objective, 25x, fixed and zoom eyepieces; field at 1000 yds. 94 ft.; relative brightness 9.6; length 15.4"; weight 48.8 oz. Lens shade and caps. Straight-type (TSN-2) also available with similar specs and prices.
Price: Without eyepiece **$519.90**
Price: 20x-60x zoom eyepiece **$209.90**
Price: 20x eyepiece (wide angle) **$176.90**
Price: 25x, 40x eyepiece **$108.90, $123.90**
Price: 25x LER eyepiece **$167.90**
Price: 30x eyepiece (wide angle) **$184.90**
Price: 60x eyepiece **$174.90**
Price: 77x eyepiece **$179.90**
Price: TSN-2 (straight), no eyepiece **$499.90**

KOWA TS-601—45° off-set type. 60mm multi-coated objective, 25x fixed and zoom eyepieces; field at 1000 yds. 93 ft.; relative brightness 5.8; length 14.8"; weight 37 oz. Comes with lens shade and caps. Straight-type also available (TS-602).
Price: Without eyepiece **$416.90**
Price: 25x eyepiece **$86.90**
Price: 20x eyepiece (wide angle) **$101.90**
Price: 40x eyepiece **$89.90**
Price: 25x-60x zoom eyepiece **$186.90**
Price: 25x LER eyepiece **$167.90**
KOWA TS-9C—Straight-type. 50mm objective, 20x compact model; fixed power eyepieces; objective focusing down to 17 ft.; field at 1000 yds. 157 ft.; relative brightness 6.3; length 9.65"; weight 22.9 oz. Lens caps.
Price: With 20x eyepiece **$184.80**
Price: 15x, 20x eyepieces, each **$33.90, $31.90**
Price: 11x-33x zoom eyepiece **$106.90**
Price: As above, rubber armored, 20x (TS-9R) **$208.80**
Price: TS-9B (45° offset), 20x **$224.80**
LEATHERWOO-MEOPTA C-Z SPOTTING SCOPE—25x, 70mm objective. Field at 1000 yards 101 ft. Length 13.7", weight 2.4 lbs. Comes with soft case.
Price: **$199.50**
LEUPOLD 20x50 COMPACT—50mm objective, 20x. Field at 100 yards 11.5 ft.; eye relief 1"; length 9.4"; weight 20.5 oz.
Price: Armored model **$533.90**
Price: Packer Tripod **$83.90**
LEUPOLD 25x50 COMPACT—50mm objective, 25x. Field at 100 yards 8.3 ft.; eye relief 1"; length overall 9.4"; weight 20.5 oz.
Price: Armored model **$569.60**
Price: Armored, with reticle **$587.50**
Price: Packer Tripod **$83.90**
LEUPOLD 30x60 COMPACT—60mm objective, 30x. Field at 100 yds. 6.4 ft.; eye relief 1"; length overall 12.9"; weight 26 oz.
Price: Armored model **$587.50**
Price: Packer Tripod **$83.90**
MIRADOR TTB SERIES—Draw tube armored spotting scopes. Available with 75mm or 80mm objective. Zoom model (28x-62x, 80mm) is 11⅞" (closed), weighs 50 oz. Field at 1000 yds. 70-42 ft. Comes with lens covers.
Price: 28-62x80mm **$953.95**
Price: 32x80mm **$809.95**
Price: 26-58x75mm **$863.95**
Price: 30x75mm **$719.95**
MIRADOR SSD SPOTTING SCOPES—60mm objective, 15x, 20x, 22x, 25x, 40x, 60x, 20-60x; field at 1000 yds. 37 ft.; length 10¼"; weight 33 oz.
Price: 25x **$548.95**
Price: 22x Wide Angle **$557.95**
Price: 20-60x Zoom **$701.95**
Price: As above, with tripod, case **$854.95**

MIRADOR SIA SPOTTING SCOPES—Similar to the SSD scopes except with 45° eyepiece. Length 12¼"; weight 39 oz.
Price: 25x $701.95
Price: 22x Wide Angle $710.95
Price: 20-60x Zoom $854.95
MIRADOR SSA SPOTTING SCOPES—Lightweight, slender version of the SSD series with 50mm objective. Length 11⅛"; weight 28 oz.
Price: 20x $413.95
Price: 18x Wide Angle $422.95
Price: 16-48x Zoom $566.95
MIRADOR SSR SPOTTING SCOPES—50mm or 60mm objective. Similar to SSD except rubber armored in black or camouflage. Length 11⅛"; weight 31 oz.
Price: Black, 20x $449.95
Price: Black, 18x Wide Angle $458.95
Price: Black, 16-48x Zoom $602.95
Price: Black, 20x, 60mm, EER $611.95
Price: Black, 22x Wide Angle, 60mm $602.95
Price: Black, 20-60x Zoom $746.95
MIRADOR SSF FIELD SCOPES—Fixed or variable power, choice of 50mm, 60mm, 75mm objective lens. Length 9¾"; weight 20 oz. (15-32x50).
Price: 20x50mm $287.95
Price: 25x60mm $341.95
Price: 30x75mm $413.95
Price: 15-32x50mm Zoom $449.95
Price: 18-40x60mm Zoom $503.95
Price: 22-50x75mm Zoom $575.95
MIRADOR SRA MULTI ANGLE SCOPES—Similar to SSF Series except eyepiece head rotates for viewing from any angle.
Price: 20x50mm $449.95
Price: 25x60mm $512.95
Price: 30x75mm $566.95
Price: 15-32x50mm Zoom $611.95
Price: 18-40x60mm Zoom $674.95
Price: 22-50x75mm Zoom $728.95
MIRADOR SIB FIELD SCOPES—Short-tube, 45° scopes with porro prism design. 50mm and 60mm objective. Length 10¼"; weight 18.5 oz. (15-32x50mm); field at 1000 yds. 129-81 ft.
Price: 20x50mm $359.95
Price: 25x60mm $422.95
Price: 15-32x50mm Zoom $521.95
Price: 18-40x60mm Zoom $584.95
NICHOLS "BACKPACKER" COMPACT—25x, 50mm objective. Field at 1000 yds. 101.2 ft. Overall length 8.76"; weight 20.6 oz. Gray finish. Comes with tripod.
Price: $157.00
NICHOLS "GRANDSLAM"—25x, 50mm objective. Field at 1000 yds. 91.6 ft. Overall length 12.2"; weight 24.7 oz. Gray finish. Comes with tripod.
Price: $255.00
Price: 17x-52x Zoom, with 25x lens, tripod $443.00
PENTAX 30x60 HG—60mm objective lens, 30x. Field of view 86 ft. at 1000 yds. Length 12.1"; weight 35 oz. Waterproof, rubber armor, multi-coated lenses. Comes with lens cap, case, neck strap.
Price: $600.00
REDFIELD 25x WATERPROOF SPOTTER—60mm objective, 25x fixed power. Black rubber armor coat. Field at 1000 yds. 100 ft. Length 12.5"; weight 24 oz. Comes with lens covers, vinyl carrying case.
Price: $416.95
Price: As above, with adjustable tripod, aluminum carrying case with shoulder strap $576.95
REDFIELD WATERPROOF 20-45x SPOTTER—60mm objective, 20-45x. Field at 1000 yds. 45-63 ft. Length 12.5"; weight 23 oz. Black rubber armor coat. With vinyl carrying case.
Price: $462.95
Price: As above, with adjustable tripod, aluminum carrying case with shoulder strap $613.95
REDFIELD REGAL II—Regal II has 60mm objective, interchangeable 25x and 18x-40x zoom eyepieces. Field at 1000 yds. •125 ft. (25x). Dual rotation of eyepiece and scope body. With aluminum carrying case, tripod.
Price: $718.95
REDFIELD REGAL IV—Conventional straight through viewing. Regal IV has 60mm objective and interchangeable 25x and 20x-60x zoom eyepieces. Field at 1000 yds. 94 ft. (25x). With tripod and aluminum carrying case.
Price: Regal IV with black rubber Armorcoat $755.95
REDFIELD REGAL VI—60mm objective, 25x fixed and 20x-60x interchangeable eyepieces. Has 45° angled eyepiece, front-mounted focus ring, 180° tube rotation. Field at 1000 yds. 94 ft. (25x); length 12¼"; weight 40 oz. Comes with tripod, aluminum carrying case.
Price: Regal VI $793.95

SIMMONS 1204 COMPACT—50mm objective, 12-36x zoom. Camouflage rubber armored finish. Ocular focus and variable power magnification.
Price: With tripod $267.95
Price: Model 1205 (black non-armored finish) ... $243.95
SIMMONS 1207 COMPACT—50mm objective, 25x fixed power. Ocular focus. Green rubber-armored finish.
Price: With tripod $202.95
Price: Model 1206 (black rubber-armored finish) . $202.95
SIMMONS 1208 COMPACT—50mm objective, 25x fixed power. Ocular focus. Non-reflective finish.
Price: With tripod $181.95
SIMMONS 1221—56.5mm objective, 20x. Has built-in electronic finder scope that requires two AAA batteries. Field at 1000 yds. 150 ft. Length 11½"; weight 33 oz.
Price: $466.95
SIMMONS 1299 15-60x ZOOM—60mm objective, 15-60x zoom. Field at 1000 yds. 156-40 ft. Slide-out sunshade. Has 3x finder scope. Photo adaptable and comes with a photo adapter tube. Black finish. Tripod not included.
Price: $551.95
SWAROVSKI HABICHT HAWK 30x75S TELESCOPE—75mm objective, 30x. Field at 1000 yds. 90 ft. Minimum focusing distance 90 ft. Length: closed 13", extended 20½"; weight 47 oz. Precise recognition of smallest details even at dusk. Leather or rubber covered, with caps and carrying case.
Price: $825.00
SWAROVSKI 25-40x75 TELESCOPE—75mm objective, variable power from 25x to 40x with a field of 98 ft. (25x) and 72 ft. (40x). Minimum focusing distance 66 ft. Length: closed 14.3", extended 21.7"; weight 46.8 oz. Rubber covered.
Price: Standard $1,025.00
SWIFT STALKER M838—40mm objective, 25x. Eye relief of 15mm. Field at 1000 yds. 80 ft. Length 10.25"; weight with tripod 26.2 oz. Comes with low-level tripod, lens covers.
Price: $115.00
SWIFT TELEMASTER M841—60mm objective. 15x to 60x variable power. Field at 1000 yds. 160 feet (15x) to 40 feet (60x). Weight 3.4 lbs.; length 17.6" overall.
Price: $399.50
SWIFT M700R—10x-40x, 40mm objective. Field of 210 feet at 10x, 70 feet at 40x. Length 16.3", weight 21.4 oz.
Price: $183.00
SWIFT SEARCHER M839—60mm objective, 20x, 40x. Field at 1000 yds. 118 ft. (30x), 59 ft. (40x). Length 12.6"; weight 3 lbs. Rotating eyepiece head for straight or 45° viewing.
Price: $398.00
Price: 30x, 50x eyepieces, each $45.00
Price: Tripod $38.00
TASCO CW50T COMPACT SPOTTING SCOPE—50mm objective, 25x. Field at 100 yds. 11 ft. Also available as CW50TBR with black rubber armor and tripod.
Price: CW50T $134.00
Price: CW50TBR $153.00
TASCO 17EB SPOTTING SCOPE—60mm objective lens, 20-60x zoom with black metal tripod, micro-adjustable elevation control. Built-in sights.
Price: $171.00
TASCO 20EB SPOTTING SCOPE—50mm objective lens, 15-45x zoom. Field at 1000 yds. 95-42 ft.; includes tripod with pan-head lever. Built-in sights.
Price: $92.00
TASCO 9002T WORLD CLASS SPOTTING SCOPE—60mm objective lens, 15-60x zoom. Field at 1000 yds. 160 ft. (15x). Fully multi-coated optics, includes camera adaptor, camera case, tripod with pan-head lever.
Price: $490.00
UNERTL "FORTY-FIVE"—54mm objective. 20x (single fixed power). Field at 100 yds. 10',10"; eye relief 1"; focusing range infinity to 33 ft. Weight about 32 oz.; overall length 15¾". With lens covers.
Price: With multi-layer lens coating $390.00
Price: With mono-layer magnesium coating $325.00
UNERTL RIGHT ANGLE—63.5mm objective, 24x. Field at 100 yds., 7 ft. Relative brightness, 6.96. Eye relief ½". Weight 41 oz.; length closed 19". Push-pull and screw-focus eyepiece. 16x and 32x eyepieces **$70.00** each.
Price: $350.00
UNERTL STRAIGHT PRISMATIC—Same as Unertl Right Angle except straight eyepiece and weight of 40 oz.
Price: $290.00
UNERTL 20x STRAIGHT PRISMATIC—54mm objective, 20x. Field at 100 yds. 8.5 ft. Relative brightness 6.1. Eye relief ½". Weight 36 oz.; length closed 13½". Complete with lens covers.
Price: $270.00
UNERTL TEAM SCOPE—100mm objective. 15x, 24x, 32x eyepieces. Field at 100 yds. 13 to 7.5 ft. Relative brightness, 39.06 to 9.79. Eye relief 2" to 1½". Weight 13 lbs.; length 29⅞" overall. Metal tripod, yoke and wood carrying case furnished (total weight 80 lbs.).
Price: $1,500.00

PERIODICAL PUBLICATIONS

Action Pursuit Games Magazine (M)
CFW Enterprises, Inc., 4201 W. Vanowen Pl., Burbank, CA 91505. $2.95 single copy U.S., $3.50 Canada. Editor: Randy Kamiya, 818-845-2656. World's leading magazine of paintball sports.

Airgun World
10 Sheet St., Windsor, Berks., SL4 1BG, England. £18.00 (£26.00 overseas) for 12 issues. Monthly magazine catering exclusively to the airgun enthusiast.

Alaska Magazine
Alaska Publishing Properties Inc., 808 E St., Suite 200, Anchorage, AK 99501. $26.00 yr. Hunting, Fishing and Life on the Last Frontier articles of Alaska and western Canada. Outdoors Editor, Ken Marsh.

American Airgunner (Q)
P.O. Box 1459, Abilene, TX 79604-1459. $15 yr. Anything and everything about airguns.

American Firearms Industry
Nat'l. Assn. of Federally Licensed Firearms Dealers, 2455 E. Sunrise Blvd., Ft. Lauderdale, FL 33304. $25.00 yr. For firearms retailers, distributors and manufacturers.

American Handgunner*
591 Camino de la Reina, Suite 200, San Diego, CA 92108. $16.75 yr. Articles for handgun enthusiasts, competitors, police and hunters.

American Hunter (M)
National Rifle Assn., 1600 Rhode Island Ave., NW, Washington, DC 20036. Publications Div., 470 Spring Park Pl., Suite 1000, Herndon, VA 22070. $25.00 yr. Wide scope of hunting articles.

American Rifleman (M)
National Rifle Assn., 1600 Rhode Island Ave., NW, Washington, DC 20036. Publications Div., 470 Spring Park Pl., Suite 1000, Herndon, VA 22070. $25.00 yr. Firearms articles of all kinds.

American Survival Guide
McMullen and Yee Publishing, Inc., 2145 West La Palma Ave., Anaheim, CA 92801. 12 issues $26.95/714-778-5773; FAX: 714-533-9979.

American West*
American West Management Corp., 7000 E. Tanque Verde Rd., Suite #30, Tucson, AZ 85715. $15.00 yr.

Angler & Hunter
Ontario's Wildlife Magazine, P.O. Box 1541, Peterborough, Ont. K9J 7H7, Canada. $23.49 yr. Canada; all others $28.95 yr. for 10 issues (includes Canadian Hunting annual and Canadian Fishing annual).

Arms Collecting (Q)
Museum Restoration Service, P.O. Drawer 390, Bloomfield, Ont., Canada K0K 1G0 and P.O. Box 70, Alexandria Bay, NY 13607. $15.00 yr.; $41.50 3 yrs.; $75.00 5 yrs.

Australian Gunsports*
Action Publishing Pty Ltd, P.O. Box 16, Alexandria, NSW 2015, Australia. $3.95 Aust. per issue. Hunting, shooting articles.

Australian Shooters' Journal
Sporting Shooter's Assn. of Australia, P.O. Box 2066, Kent Town SA 5071, Australia. $40.00 yr. locally; $50.00 yr. overseas surface mail only. Hunting and shooting articles.

The Backwoodsman Magazine
P.O. Box 627, Westcliffe, CO 81252. $14.00 for 6 issues per yr.; $26.00 for 2 yrs.; sample copy $2.50. Subjects include muzzle-loading, woodslore, primitive survival, trapping, homesteading, blackpowder cartridge guns, 19th century how-to.

Black Powder Times
P.O. Box 842, Mount Vernon, WA 98273. $15.00 yr.; add $2 per year for Canada, $5 per year other foreign. Tabloid newspaper for blackpowder activities; test reports.

The Blade Magazine*
P.O. Box 22007, Chattanooga, TN 37422. $14.99 for 6 issues. Add $13.00 for foreign subscription. A magazine for all enthusiasts of the edged blade.

The Caller (Q) (M)
National Wild Turkey Federation, P.O. Box 530, Edgefield, SC 29824. Tabloid newspaper for members; 4 issues per yr.

The Cast Bullet*(M)
Official journal of The Cast Bullet Assn. Director of Membership, 4103 Foxcraft Dr., Traverse City, MI 49684. Annual membership dues $14, includes 6 issues.

Combat Handguns*
Harris Publications, Inc., 1115 Broadway, New York, NY 10010. Single copy $2.95 U.S.A.; $3.25 Canada.

Deutsches Waffen Journal
Journal-Verlag Schwend GmbH, Postfach 100340, D7170 Schwäbisch Hall, Germany/0791-404-500; FAX:0791-42920. DM85.00 yr. plus DM16.80 for postage. Antique and modern arms. German text.

The Engraver (M) (Q)
P.O. Box 312, Evansville, IN 47702. Mike Dubber, editor. The journal of firearms engraving.

Ducks Unlimited, Inc. (M)
1 Waterfowl Way, Memphis, TN 38120

The Field
6 Sheet Street, Windsor, Berkshire, SL4 1BG, England. £35.00 sterling U.S. (approx. $70.00) yr. Hunting and shooting articles, and all country sports.

Field & Stream
Times Mirror Magazines, Two Park Ave., New York, NY 10016. $11.94 yr. Articles on firearms, plus hunting and fishing.

FIRE
Euro-Editions, Boulevard Du Triomphe 132, B1160 Brussels, Belgium. Belg. Franc 1500 for 6 issues. Arms, shooting, ammunition. French text.

Fur-Fish-Game
A.R. Harding Pub. Co., 2878 E. Main St., Columbus, OH 43209. $15.95 yr. "Gun Rack" column by Don Zutz.

Gray's Sporting Journal
Gray's Sporting Journal, Inc., P.O. Box 1207, Augusta, GA 30903. $34.95 per yr. for 6 consecutive issues. Hunting and fishing journals.

Gun List
700 E. State St., Iola, WI 54990. $24.95 yr. (26 issues); $46.50 2 yrs. (52 issues). Indexed market publication for firearms collectors and active shooters; guns, supplies and services.

The Gun Report
World Wide Gun Report, Inc., Box 38, Aledo, IL 61231-0038. $29.95 yr. For the antique and collectable gun dealer and collector.

Gunmaker (M)†
ACGG, P.O. Box 812, Burlington, IA 52601-0812. The journal of custom gunmaking.

The Gunrunner
Div. of Kexco Publ. Co. Ltd., Box 565G, Lethbridge, Alb., Canada T1J 3Z4. $23.00 yr. Monthly newspaper, listing everything from antiques to artillery.

Gun Show Calendar (Q)
700 E. State St., Iola, WI 54990. $12.95 yr. (4 issues). Gun shows listed chronologically by date, and alphabetically by state.

Gun Tests
11 Commerce Blvd., Palm Coast, FL 32142. The consumer resource for the serious shooter. Write for information.

Gun Week†
Second Amendment Foundation, P.O. Box 488, Station C, Buffalo, NY 14209. $32.00 yr. U.S. and possessions; $40.00 yr. other countries. Tabloid paper on guns, hunting, shooting and collecting.

Gun World
Gallant/Charger Publications, Inc., 34249 Camino Capistrano, Capistrano Beach, CA 92624. $20.00 yr. For the hunting, reloading and shooting enthusiast.

Guns & Ammo
Petersen Publishing Co., 8490 Sunset Blvd., Los Angeles, CA 90069. $21.94 yr. Guns, shooting, and technical articles.

Guns
Guns Magazine, P.O. Box 85201, San Diego, CA 92138. $19.95 yr. In-depth articles on a wide range of guns, shooting equipment and related accessories for gun collectors, hunters and shooters.

Guns Review
Ravenhill Publishing Co. Ltd., Box 35, Standard House, Bonhill St., London EC 2A 4DA, England. £20.00 sterling (approx. U.S. $38 USA & Canada) yr. For collectors and shooters.

Handgun Quarterly (Q)
PJS Publications, News Plaza, P.O. Box 1790, Peoria, IL 61656. Cover price $3.95; subscriptions $17.95 for 6 issues. Various recreational uses of handguns; hunting, silhouette, practical pistol and target shooting.

Handloader*
Wolfe Publishing Co., 6471 Airpark Dr., Prescott, AZ 86301. $19.00 yr. The journal of ammunition reloading.

HUNT Magazine*
TimberLine-B, Inc., P.O. Box 58069, Renton, WA 98058. $19.97 yr.; Canadian and foreign countries add U.S. $12 for postage. Geared to the serious hunter, with action hunting articles.

Hunting Horizons
Wolfe Publishing Co., 6471 Airpark Dr., Prescott, AZ 86301. $17.00 yr. Dedicated to the finest pursuit of the hunt.

The Insider Gun News
The Gunpress Publishing Co., 1347 Webster St. NE, Washington, DC 20017. Editor, John D. Aquilino. $50.00 yr. (12 issues). Newsletter by former NRA communications director.

INSIGHTS*
NRA, 1600 Rhode Island Ave., NW, Washington, DC 20036. Editor, John E. Robbins. $10.00 yr., which includes NRA junior membership; $9.00 for adult subscriptions (12 issues). Plenty of details for the young hunter and target shooter; emphasizes gun safety, marksmanship training, hunting skills.

International Shooting Sport*/UIT Journal
International Shooting Union (UIT), Bavariaring 21, D-8000 Munich 2, Fed. Rep. of Germany. Europe: (Deutsche Mark) DM44.00 yr.; outside Europe: DM50.00 yr. (air mail postage included.) For international sport shooting.

Internationales Waffen-Magazin
Habegger-Verlag Zürich, Postfach CH-8036 Zürich, Switzerland. SF 88.50 (approx. U.S. $60.00) surface mail for 10 issues. Modern and antique arms. German text; English summary of contents.

The Journal of the Arms & Armour Society (M)
E.J.B. Greenwood (Hon. Sec.), Field House, Upper Dicker, Hailsham, East Sussex, BN27 3PY, England. $20.00 yr. Articles for the historian and collector.

Journal of the Historical Breechloading Smallarms Assn.
Published annually. Imperial War Museum, Lambeth Road, London SE1 6HZ, England. $12.00 yr. Articles for the collector plus mailings of lecture transcripts, short articles on specific arms, reprints, newsletters, etc.; a surcharge is made for airmail.

Knife World
Knife World Publications, P.O. Box 3395, Knoxville, TN 37927. $15.00 yr.; $25.00 2 yrs. Published monthly for knife enthusiasts and collectors. Articles on custom and factory knives; other knife-related interests.

Law and Order
Law and Order Magazine, 1000 Skokie Blvd., Wilmette, IL 60091. $20.00 yr. Articles for law enforcement professionals.

Machine Gun News
Lane Publishing, P.O. Box 759, Dept. GD, Hot Springs, AR 71902/501-623-4951. $29.95 yr.; $3.50 sample copy. The magazine for full-auto enthusiasts, full-auto news, how to solve functioning problems, machinegun shoots from around the country and free classifieds for subscribers.

Man At Arms*
P.O. Box 460, Lincoln, RI 02865. $24.00 yr., plus $8.00 for foreign subscribers. The N.R.A. magazine of arms collecting-investing, with excellent brief articles for the collector of antique arms and militaria.

MAN/MAGNUM
S.A. Man (1982) (Pty) Ltd., P.O. Box 35204, Northway, Durban 4065, Republic of South Africa. SA Rand 70.00 for 12 issues. Africa's only publication on hunting, shooting, firearms, bushcraft, knives, etc.

The Marlin Collector (M)
R.W. Paterson, 407 Lincoln Bldg., 44 Main St., Champaign, IL 61820.

Muzzle Blasts (M)
National Muzzle Loading Rifle Assn., P.O. Box 67, Friendship, IN 47021. $30.00 yr. For the blackpowder shooter.

Muzzleloader Magazine*
Rebel Publishing Co., Inc., Dept. Gun, Route 5, Box 347-M, Texarkana, TX 75501. $14.00 U.S.; $17.00 U.S. for foreign subscribers a yr. The publication for blackpowder shooters.

National Defense (M)*
American Defense Preparedness Assn., Two Colonial Place, Suite 400, 2101 Wilson Blvd., Arlington, VA 22201-3061/703-522-1820; FAX: 703-522-1885. $35.00 yr. Articles on both military and civil defense field, including weapons, materials technology, management.

National Knife Magazine (M)
Natl. Knife Coll. Assn., 7201 Shallowford Rd., P.O. Box 21070, Chattanooga, TN 37421. Membership $29 yr.; $64.00 International yr.

National Rifle Assn. Journal (British) (Q)
Natl. Rifle Assn. (BR.), Bisley Camp, Brookwood, Woking, Surrey, England. GU24, OPB. £15.50 Sterling including air postage.

National Wildlife*
Natl. Wildlife Fed., 1400 16th St. NW, Washington, DC 20036. $16.00 yr. (6 issues); *International Wildlife*, 6 issues, $16.00 yr. Both, $22.00 yr., includes all membership benefits. Write attn.: Membership Services Dept., for more information.

New Zealand GUNS*
Waitekauri Publishing, P.O. 45, Waikino 2950, New Zealand. $NZ90.00 (6 issues) yr. Covers the hunting and firearms scene in New Zealand.

New Zealand Wildlife (Q)
New Zealand Deerstalkers Assoc., Inc., P.O. Box 6514, Wellington, N.Z. $30.00 (N.Z.). Hunting, shooting and firearms/game research articles.

North American Hunter* (M)
P.O. Box 3401, Minnetonka, MN 55343. $18.00 yr. (7 issues). Articles on all types of North American hunting.

Outdoor Life
Times Mirror Magazines, Two Park Ave., New York, NY 10016. Special 1-yr. subscription, $11.97. Extensive coverage of hunting and shooting. Shooting column by Jim Carmichel.

Paintball Magazine
CFW Enterprises, Inc., 4201 W. Vanowen Place, Burbank, CA 91505/818-845-2656. $3.00 single copy U.S.; $3.50 Canada. The complete guide to paintball airgun games.

La Passion des Courteaux (Q)
Phenix Editions, 25 rue Mademoiselle, 75015 Paris, France. French text.

Passion for Knives (Q)
P.O. Box 4822, Scottsdale, AZ 85261. English text. Write f. subscription prices. About blades, historical, sporting, collection knives and swords.

Petersen's HUNTING Magazine
Petersen Publishing Co., 8490 Sunset Blvd., Los Angeles, CA 90069. $19.94 yr.; Canada $29.34 yr.; foreign countries $29.94 yr. Hunting articles for all game; test reports.

Point Blank
Citizens Committee for the Right to Keep and Bear Arms (sent to contributors), Liberty Park, 12500 NE 10th Pl., Bellevue, WA 98005

POINTBLANK (M)
Natl. Firearms Assn., Box 4384 Stn. C, Calgary, AB T5T 5N2, Canada. Official publication of the NFA.

The Police Marksman*
6000 E. Shirley Lane, Montgomery, AL 36117. $17.95 yr. For law enforcement personnel.

Police Times (M)
Membership Records, 3801 Biscayne Blvd., Miami, FL 33137.

Popular Mechanics
Hearst Corp., 224 W. 57th St., New York, NY 10019. $15.94 yr. Firearms, camping, outdoor oriented articles.

Precision Shooting
Precision Shooting, Inc., 37 Burnham St., East Hartford, CT 06108. $22.00 yr. Journal of the International Benchrest Shooters, and target shooting in general. Also considerable coverage of varmint shooting.

Rifle*
Wolfe Publishing Co., 6471 Airpark Dr., Prescott, AZ 86301. $19.00 yr. The sporting firearms journal.

Rod & Rifle Magazine
Lithographic Serv. Ltd., P.O. Box 38-138, Petone, New Zealand. $50.00 yr. (6 issues). Hunting, shooting and fishing articles.

Safari* (M)
Safari Magazine, 4800 W. Gates Pass Rd., Tucson, AZ 85745/602-620-1220. $30.00 (6 times). The journal of big game hunting, published by Safari Club International.

Second Amendment Reporter
Second Amendment Foundation, James Madison Bldg., 12500 NE 10th Pl., Bellevue, WA 98005. $15.00 yr. (non-contributors).

Shooting Industry
Publisher's Dev. Corp., 591 Camino de la Reina, Suite 200, San Diego, CA 92108. $50.00 yr. To the trade $25.00.

Shooting Sports Retailer*
SSR Publishing, Inc., P.O. Box 25, Cuba, NY 14727-0025/716-968-3858. 6 issues yr. Free to qualifying retailers, wholesalers, manufacturers, distributors; $30 annually for all other subscribers; $35 for foreign subscriptions; single copy $5.

Shooting Sports USA
National Rifle Assn. of America, 1600 Rhode Island Ave., NW, Washington, DC 20036. $10 yr. for any non-active shooter. Covering events, techniques and personalities in competitive shooting.

The Shooting Times & Country Magazine (England)†
10 Sheet St., Windsor, Berkshire SL4 1BG, England. £57.20 (approx. $98.00) yr.; £71.20 yr. overseas (52 issues). Game shooting, wild fowling, hunting, game fishing and firearms articles. Britain's best selling field sports magazine.

Shooting Times
PJS Publications, News Plaza, P.O. Box 1790, Peoria, IL 61656. $17.97 yr. Guns, shooting, reloading; articles on every gun activity.

The Shotgun News‡
Snell Publishing Co., Box 669, Hastings, NE 68902. $20.00 yr.; all other countries $100.00 yr. Sample copy $3.00. Gun ads of all kinds.

Shotgun Sports
P.O. Box 6810, Auburn, CA 95603/916-889-2220; FAX:916-889-9106. $26.00 yr. Trapshooting how-to's, shotshell reloading, shotgun patterning, shotgun tests and evaluations, Sporting Clays action, waterfowl/upland hunting and the official publication for the United States Sporting Clays Association.

The Sixgunner (M)
Handgun Hunters International, P.O. Box 357, MAG, Bloomingdale, OH 43910

The Skeet Shooting Review
National Skeet Shooting Assn., P.O. Box 680007, San Antonio, TX 78268. $15.00 yr. (Assn. membership of $20.00 includes mag.) Competition results, personality profiles of top Skeet shooters, how-to articles, technical, reloading information.

Soldier of Fortune
Subscription Dept., P.O. Box 348, Mt. Morris, IL 61054. $24.95 yr.; $34.95 Canada; $45.95 foreign.

Sporting Clays Magazine*
21 Airport Rd., Suite 21-J, Hilton Head Island, SC 29926. $24.00 yr. (6 issues).

Sporting Goods Business
Miller Freeman, Inc., 1515 Broadway, New York, NY 10036. Trade journal.

Sporting Goods Dealer
Two Park Ave., New York, NY 10016. $100.00 yr. Sporting goods trade journal.

Sporting Gun
Bretton Court, Bretton, Peterborough PE3 8DZ, England. £24.00 (approx. U.S. $36.00), airmail £33.00 yr. For the game and clay enthusiasts.

Sports Afield
The Hearst Corp., 250 W. 55th St., New York, NY 10019. $13.97 yr. Tom Gresham on firearms, ammunition; Grits Gresham on shooting and Thomas McIntyre on hunting.

The Squirrel Hunter
P.O. Box 368, Chireno, TX 75937. $14.00 yr. Articles about squirrel hunting.

TACARMI
Via E. De Amicis, 25; 20123 Milano, Italy. $120.00 yr. approx. Antique and modern guns. (Italian text.)

Trap & Field
1200 Waterway Blvd., Indianapolis, IN 46202. $22.00 yr. Official publ. Amateur Trapshooting Assn. Scores, averages, trapshooting articles.

Turkey Call* (M)
Natl. Wild Turkey Federation, Inc., P.O. Box 530, Edgefield, SC 29824. $20.00 with membership (6 issues per yr.)

The U.S. Handgunner* (M)
U.S. Revolver Assn., 96 West Union St., Ashland, MA 01721. $8.00 yr. General handgun and competition articles. Bi-monthly sent to members.

The Varmint Hunter Magazine (Q)
The Varmint Hunters Assn., Box 730, Lone Grove, TX 73443/405-657-3098. $22.00 yr.

VDB-Aktuell (Q)
GFI-Verlag, Theodor-Heuss-Ring 62, 5000 Koln 1, Germany. For hunters, target shooters and outdoor people. (German text.)

Wild Sheep (M) (Q)
Foundation for North American Wild Sheep, 720 Allen Ave., Cody, WY 82414. Official journal of the foundation.

Women & Guns
P.O. Box 488, Sta. C, Buffalo, NY 14209. $24.95 yr. U.S.; (12 issues). Only magazine edited by and for women gun owners.

---

*Published bi-monthly †Published weekly ‡Published three times per month. All others are published monthly.
M=Membership requirements; write for details. Q=Published Quarterly.

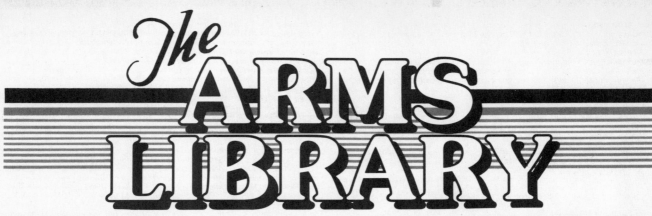

FOR COLLECTOR · HUNTER · SHOOTER · OUTDOORSMAN

BALLISTICS and HANDLOADING

ABC's of Reloading, 4th Edition, by Dean A. Grennell, DBI Books, Inc., Northbrook, IL, 1988. 288 pp., illus. Paper covers. $16.95.

An all-new book with everything from a discussion of the basics up through and including advanced techniques and procedures.

*ABC's of Reloading, 5th Edition, by Dean A. Grennell, DBI Books, Inc., Northbrook, IL. 288 pp., illus. Paper covers.

(January 1993)

*Ammunition Making, by George E. Frost, National Rifle Association of America, Washington, D.C., 1990. 160 pp., illus. Paper covers. $17.95.

Reflects the perspective of "an insider" with half a century's experience in successful management of ammunition manufacturing operations.

Ballistic Science for the Law Enforcement Officer, by Charles G. Wilber, Ph.D., Charles C. Thomas, Springfield, IL, 1977. 309 pp., illus. $80.00.

A scientific study of the ballistics of civilian firearms.

Basic Handloading, by George C. Nonte, Jr., Outdoor Life Books, New York, NY, 1982. 192 pp., illus. Paper covers. $6.95.

How to produce high-quality ammunition using the safest, most efficient methods known.

*Black Powder Guide, 2nd Edition, by George C. Nonte, Jr., Stoeger Publishing Co., So. Hackensack, NJ, 1991. 288 pp., illus. Paper covers. $12.95.

How-to instructions for selection, repair and maintenance of muzzleloaders, making your own bullets, restoring and refinishing, shooting techniques.

Black Powder Loading Manual, Revised Edition, DBI Books, Inc., Northbrook, IL, 1991, 320 pp., illus. Paper covers. $15.95.

Revised and expanded edition of this landmark loading book first published in 1982. Covers 600 loads for 120 of the most popular blackpowder rifles, handguns and shotguns.

Big Bore Rifles And Cartridges, Wolfe Publishing Co., Prescott, AZ, 1991. Paper cover. $26.00.

This book covers cartridges from 8mm to .600 Nitro with over 60 chapters containing loading tables and commentary.

The Bullet Swage Manual. MDSU/I, by Ted Smith, Corbin Manufacturing and Supply Co., White City, OR, 1988. 45 pp., illus. Paper covers. $10.00.

A book that fills the need for information on bullet swaging.

Cartridge Case Measurements, by Dr. Arthur J. Mack, Amrex Enterprises, Vienna, VA, 1990. 300 pp., illus. Paper covers. $49.95.

Lists over 5000 cartridges of all kinds. Gives basic measurements (rim, head, shoulder, neck, length, plus bullet diameter) in both English and Metric. Hundreds of experimental and wildcats.

Cartridges of the World, 6th Edition, by Frank C. Barnes, DBI Books, Inc., Northbrook, IL, 1989. 448 pp., illus. Paper covers. $19.95.

Completely revised edition of the general purpose reference work for which collectors, police, scientists and laymen reach first for answers to cartridge identification questions.

Cast Bullets, by Col. E. H. Harrison, A publication of the National Rifle Association of America, Washington, DC, 1979. 144 pp., illus. Paper covers. $12.95.

An authoritative guide to bullet casting techniques and ballistics.

Complete Guide to Handloading, by Philip B. Sharpe, Wolfe Publishing Co., Prescott, AZ, 1988. 465;229 pp., illus. $60.00.

A limited edition reprint of Sharpe's most sought-after classic. Includes the supplement.

The Complete Handloader, by John Wootters, Stackpole Books, Harrisburg, PA, 1989. 224 pp., illus. $29.95.

One of the deans of gun writers shares a lifetime of experience and recommended procedures on handloading for rifles, handguns, and shotguns.

The Complete Handloader for Rifles, Handguns and Shotguns, by John Wootters, Stackpole Books, Harrisburg, PA, 1988. 214 pp., $29.95.

Loading-bench know-how.

Discover Swaging, by David R. Corbin, Stackpole Books, Harrisburg, PA, 1979. 283 pp., illus. $18.95.

A guide to custom bullet design and performance.

Extended Ballistics for the Advanced Rifleman, by Art Blatt, Pachmayr, Inc., Los Angeles, CA, 1986. 379 pp. Spiral bound. $15.95.

Enhanced data on all factory centerfire rifle loads from Federal, Hornady, Norma, Remington, Weatherby, and Winchester.

Firearms Pressure Factors, by Dr. Lloyd Brownell, Wolfe Publishing Co., Prescott, AZ, 1990. 200 pp., illus. $14.00.

The only book available devoted entirely to firearms and pressure. Contains chapters on secondary explosion effect, modern pressure measuring techniques in revolvers and rifles, and Dr. Brownell's series on pressure factors.

*Gibbs' Cartridges and Front Ignition Loading Technique, by Roger Stowers, Wolfe Publishing Co., Prescott, AZ, 1991. 64 pp., illus. Paper covers. $14.95.

The story of this innovative gunsmith who designed his own wildcat cartridges known for their flat trajectories, high velocity and accuracy.

The Gun Digest Black Powder Loading Manual, Revised Edition, by Sam Fadala, DBI Books, Inc., Northbrook, IL, 1991. 320 pp., illus. Paper covers. $15.95.

Revised and expanded edition of this landmark loading book first published in 1982. Covers 600 loads for 120 of the most popular blackpowder rifles, handguns and shotguns.

The Gun Digest Book of Handgun Reloading, by Dean A. Grennell and Wiley M. Clapp, DBI Books, Inc., Northbrook, IL, 1987. 256 pp., illus. Paper covers. $14.95.

Detailed discussions of all aspects of reloading for handguns, from basic to complex. New loading data.

Handbook of Bullet Swaging No. 7, by David R. Corbin, Corbin Manufacturing and Supply Co., White City, OR, 1986. 199 pp., illus. Paper covers. $10.00.

This handbook explains the most precise method of making quality bullets.

Handbook for Shooters and Reloaders, by P.O. Ackley, Salt Lake City, UT, 1970, (Vol. I), 567 pp., illus. (Vol. II), a new printing with specific new material. 495 pp., illus. $15.95 each.

Handbook of Metallic Cartridge Reloading, by Edward Matunas, Winchester Press, Piscataway, NJ, 1981. 272 pp., illus. $19.95.

Up-to-date, comprehensive loading tables prepared by four major powder manufacturers.

Handloader's Digest, 12th Edition, edited by Ken Warner, DBI Books, Inc., Northbrook, IL, 1990. 384 pp., illus. Soft covers. $19.95.

This expanded edition offers something for any shooter. Includes over 200 pages of catalog covering all currently available loading tools, components, chronographs and accessories.

Handloader's Guide, by Stanley W. Trzoniec, Stoeger Publishing Co., So. Hackensack, NJ, 1985. 256 pp., illus. Paper covers. $14.95.

The complete step-by-step fully illustrated guide to handloading ammunition.

Handloader's Manual of Cartridge Conversions, by John J. Donnelly, Stoeger Publishing Co., So. Hackensack, NJ, 1986. Unpaginated. $34.95.

From 14 Jones to 70-150 Winchester in English and American cartridges, and from 4.85

U.K. to 15.2x28R Gevelot in metric cartridges. Over 900 cartridges described in detail.

Handloading, by Bill Davis, Jr., NRA Books, Wash., D.C., 1980. 400 pp., illus. Paper covers. $15.95.

A complete update and expansion of the NRA Handloader's Guide.

Handloading for Hunters, by Don Zutz, Winchester Press, Piscataway, NJ, 1977. 288 pp., illus. $30.00.

Precise mixes and loads for different types of game and for various hunting situations with rifle and shotgun.

***Hatcher's Notebook,** by S. Julian Hatcher, Stackpole Books, Harrisburg, PA, 1992. 488 pp., illus. $29.95.

A standard reference work for shooters, gunsmiths, ballisticians, historians, hunters and collectors.

Hodgdon Powder Data Manual No. 25, Hodgdon Powder Co., Inc., Shawnee Mission, KS, 1986. 544 pp., illus. $22.95.

For the first time includes data for Hercules, Winchester, and DuPont powders.

The Home Guide to Cartridge Conversions, by Maj. George C. Nonte Jr., The Gun Room Press, Highland Park, NJ, 1976. 404 pp., illus. $22.95.

Revised and updated version of Nonte's definitive work on the alteration of cartridge cases for use in guns for which they were not intended.

Hornady Handbook of Cartridge Reloading, Hornady Mfg. Co., Grand Island, NE, 1981. 650 pp., illus. $15.95.

New edition of this famous reloading handbook. Latest loads, ballistic information, etc.

***The Ideal Handbook of Useful Information for Shooters, No. 15,** originally published by Ideal Manufacturing Co., reprinted by Wolfe Publishing Co., Prescott, AZ, 1991. 142 pp., illus. Paper covers. $10.95.

A facsimile reprint of one of the early Ideal Handbooks.

The Identification of Firearms and Forensic Ballistics, by Major Gerald Burrard, Wolfe Publishing Co., Prescott, AZ, 1990. 220 pp., illus. $38.00.

The first part of this book is confined solely to forensic ballistics.... The second part deals with the problem of the identification of individual arms.

Lyman Cast Bullet Handbook, 3rd Edition, edited by C. Kenneth Ramage, Lyman Publications, Middlefield, CT, 1980. 416 pp., illus. Paper covers. $18.95.

Information on more than 5000 tested cast bullet loads and 19 pages of trajectory and wind drift tables for cast bullets.

Lyman Black Powder Handbook, ed. by C. Kenneth Ramage, Lyman Products for Shooters, Middlefield, CT, 1975. 239 pp., illus. Paper covers. $14.95.

The most comprehensive load information ever published for the modern black powder shooter.

Lyman Pistol & Revolver Handbook, edited by C. Kenneth Ramage, Lyman Publications, Middlefield, CT, 1978. 280 pp., illus. Paper covers. $14.95.

An extensive reference of load and trajectory data for the handgun.

Lyman Reloading Handbook No. 46, edited by C. Kenneth Ramage, Lyman Publications, Middlefield, CT, 1982. 300 pp., illus. $18.95.

A large and comprehensive book on reloading. Extensive list of loads for jacketed and cast bullets.

Lyman Shotshell Handbook, 3rd Edition, edited by C. Kenneth Ramage, Lyman Publications, Middlefield, CT, 1984. 312 pp., illus. Paper covers. $18.95.

Has 2000 loads, including slugs and buckshot, plus feature articles and a full color I.D. section.

Manual of Pistol and Revolver Cartridges, Volume 2, Centerfire U.S. and British Calibers, by Hans A. Erlmeier and Jakob H. Brandt, Journal-Verlag, Wiesbaden, Germany, 1981. 270 pp., illus. $34.95.

Catalog system allows cartridges to be traced by caliber or alphabetically.

Metallic Cartridge Reloading, 2nd Edition, by Edward A. Matunas, DBI Books, Inc., Northbrook, IL., 1988. 320 pp., illus. Paper covers. $16.95.

A true reloading manual with a wealth of invaluable technical data provided by a recognized expert.

Modern Handloading, by Maj. Geo. C. Nonte, Winchester Press, Piscataway, NJ, 1972. 416 pp., illus. $15.00.

Covers all aspects of metallic and shotshell ammunition loading, plus more loads than any book in print.

Modern Practical Ballistics, by Art Pejsa, Pejsa Ballistics, Minneapolis, MN, 1990. 150 pp., illus. $24.95.

Covers all aspects of ballistics and new, simplified methods. Clear examples illustrate new, easy but very accurate formulas.

Nosler Reloading Manual No. 3, edited by Gail Root, Nosler Bullets, Inc., Bend, OR, 1989. 516 pp., illus. $21.95.

All-new book. New format including featured articles and cartridge introductions by well-known shooters, gun writers and editors.

The Paper Jacket, by Paul Matthews, Wolfe Publishing Co., Prescott, AZ, 1991. Paper covers. $13.50.

Up-to-date and accurate information about paper-patched bullets.

Pet Loads, by Ken Waters, Wolfe Publishing Co., Prescott, AZ, 3rd edition, 1986. 2 volumes of 636 pp. Limp fabricoid covers. $34.95.

Ken Water's favorite loads that have appeared in "Handloader" magazine.

Practical Dope on the .22, by F.C. Ness, Wolfe Publishing Co., Prescott, AZ, 1989. 313 pp., illus. $39.00.

A limited edition reprint. Much information on 22 rifles, actions, loads, test firing, etc.

Practical Handgun Ballistics, by Mason Williams, Charles C. Thomas, Publisher, Springfield, IL, 1980. 215 pp., illus. $55.00.

Factual information on the practical aspects of ammunition performance in revolvers and pistols.

Precision Handloading, by John Withers, Stoeger Publishing Co., So. Hackensack, NJ, 1985. 224 pp., illus. Paper covers. $12.95.

An entirely new approach to handloading ammunition.

Propellant Profiles New and Expanded, 3rd Edition, Wolfe Publishing Co., Prescott, AZ, 1991. Paper covers. $16.95.

Rediscover Swaging, by David R. Corbin, Corbin Manufacturing and Supply, Inc., Phoenix, OR, 1983. 240 pp., illus. $18.50.

A new textbook on the subject of bullet swaging.

Reloader's Guide, 3rd Edition, by R.A. Steindler, Stoeger Publishing Co., So. Hackensack, NJ, 1984. 224 pp., illus. Paper covers. $11.95.

Complete, fully illustrated step-by-step guide to handloading ammunition.

Reloading for Shotgunners, 2nd Edition, edited by Robert S.L. Anderson, DBI Books, Inc., Northbrook, IL, 1985. 256 pp., illus. Paper covers. $14.95.

The very latest in reloading information for the shotgunner.

Sierra Handgun Manual, 3rd Edition, edited by Kenneth Ramage, Sierra Bullets, Santa Fe Springs, CA, 1990. 704 pp., illus. 3-ring binder. $19.95.

New listings for XP-100 and Contender pistols and TCU cartridges...part of a new single shot section. Covers the latest loads for 10mm Auto, 455 Super Mag, and Accurate powders.

Sierra Rifle Manual, 3rd Edition, edited by Kenneth Ramage, Sierra Bullets, Santa Fe Springs, CA, 1990. 856 pp., illus. 3-ring binder. $24.95.

Updated load information with new powder listings and a wealth of inside tips.

Sixgun Cartridges and Loads, by Elmer Keith, The Gun Room Press, Highland Park, NJ, 1986. 151 pp., illus. $19.95.

A manual covering the selection, uses and loading of the most suitable and popular revolver cartridges. Originally published in 1936. Reprint.

Small Arms Design and Ballistics, Volume 1, by Col. Townsend Whelen, Wolfe Publishing Co., Prescott, AZ, 1991. 352 pp., illus. $45.00.

Reprinting of this sought-after book dealing with small arms in general; barrels in general; breech actions; stocks and sights; ammunition, etc.

Small Arms Design and Ballistics, Volume 2, by Col. Townsend Whelen, Wolfe Publishing Co., Prescott, AZ, 1991. 314 pp., illus. $45.00.

Covers interior and exterior ballistics; trajectories; wounding effects; pressures and velocities; recoil, jump and vibration; shotgun ballistics; handloading ammunition, etc.

Speer Reloading Manual Number 11, edited by members of the Speer research staff, Omark Industries, Lewiston, ID, 1987. 621 pp., illus. $13.95.

Reloading manual for rifles and pistols.

***The Sporting Ballistics Book,** by Charles W. Matthews, Bill Matthews, Inc., Lakewood, CO, 1992. 182 pp. Wirebound. $19.95.

A useful book for those interested in doing their own exterior-ballistic calculations without the aid of a computer.

Why Not Load Your Own? by Col. T. Whelen, A. S. Barnes, New York, 1957, 4th ed., rev. 237 pp., illus. $10.95.

A basic reference on handloading, describing each step, materials and equipment. Loads for popular cartridges are given.

Wildcat Cartridges, Volume I, Wolfe Publishing Company, Prescott, AZ, 1992. 125 pp. Soft cover. $16.95.

From the pages of *Handloader* magazine, the more popular and famous wildcats are profiled.

Yours Truly, Harvey Donaldson, by Harvey Donaldson, Wolfe Publ. Co., Inc., Prescott, AZ, 1980. 288 pp., illus. $19.50.

Reprint of the famous columns by Harvey Donaldson which appeared in "Handloader" from May 1966 through December 1972.

COLLECTORS

The American Cartridge, by Charles R. Suydam, Borden Publishing Co., Alhambra, CA, 1986. 184 pp., illus. $12.50.

An illustrated study of the rimfire cartridge in the United States.

American .22 Rimfire Boxes, by Robert T. Buttweiler, Robert T. Buttweiler, Ltd., Houston, TX, 1990. 192 pp., illus. Paper covers. $29.95.

Provides the collector with a wealth of information concerning not only the specific boxes, but also basic types and styles as well as the companies which produced them.

Antique Guns: The Collector's Guide, by John E. Traister, Stoeger Publishing Co., So. Hackensack, NJ, 1988. 320 pp., illus. Paper covers. $16.95.

Covers all categories, history, craftsmanship, firearms components, gunmakers and values on the gun-trading market.

Arms & Accoutrements of the Mounted Police 1873-1973, by Roger F. Phillips and Donald J. Klancher, Museum Restoration Service, Ont., Canada, 1982. 224 pp., illus. $49.95.

A definitive history of the revolvers, rifles, machine guns, cannons, ammunition, swords, etc. used by the NWMP, the RNWMP and the RCMP during the first 100 years of the Force.

Arms Makers of Eastern Pennsylvania: The Colonial Years to 1790, by James B. Whisker and Roy F. Chandler, Acorn Press, Bedford, PA, 1984. Unpaginated. $10.00.

Definitive work on Eastern Pennsylvania gunmakers.

Arms Makers of Maryland, by Daniel D. Hartzler, George Shumway, York, PA, 1975. 200 pp., illus. $45.00.

A thorough study of the gunsmiths of Maryland who worked during the late 18th and early 19th centuries.

Astra Automatic Pistols, by Leonardo M. Antaris, FIRAC Publishing Co., Sterling, CO, 1989. 248 pp., illus. $45.00.

Charts, tables, serial ranges, etc. The definitive work on Astra pistols.

Backbone of the Wehrmacht: The German K98k Rifle, 1934-1945, by Richard D. Law, edited by R. Blake Stevens, 400 pp., illus. $60.00.

The first-ever in-depth study of the most-produced bolt-action rifle in history—the German K98k.

Basic Documents on U.S. Marital Arms, commentary by Col. B. R. Lewis, reissue by Ray Riling, Phila., PA, 1956 and 1960. *Rifle Musket Model 1855.* The first issue rifle of musket caliber, a muzzle loader equipped with the Maynard Primer, 32 pp. $2.50. *Rifle Musket Model 1863.* The typical Union muzzle-loader of the Civil War, 26 pp. $1.75. *Breech-Loading Rifle Musket Model 1866.* The first of our 50-caliber breechloading rifles, 12 pp. $1.75. *Remington Navy Rifle Model 1870.* A commercial type breech-loader made at Springfield, 16 pp. $1.75. *Lee Straight Pull Navy Rifle Model 1895.* A magazine cartridge arm of 6mm caliber. 23 pp. $3.00. *Breech-Loading Arms* (five models) 27 pp. $2.75. *Ward-Burton Rifle Musket 1871*-16 pp. $2.50. *U.S. Magazine Rifle and Carbine (cal. 30) Model 1892* (the Krag rifle) 36 pp. $3.00.

Beretta Automatic Pistols, by J.B. Wood, Stackpole Books, Harrisburg, PA, 1985. 192 pp., illus. $24.95.

Only English-language book devoted entirely to the Beretta line. Includes all important models.

Blacksmith Guide to Ruger Flat-top & Super Blackhawks, by H.W. Ross, Jr., Blacksmith Corp., Chino Valley, AZ, 1990. 96 pp., illus. Paper covers. $9.95.

A key source on the extensively collected Ruger Blackhawk revolvers.

Blue Book of Gun Values, 12th edition, compiled by S.P. Fjestad, Investment Rarities, Inc., Minneapolis, MN, 1990. 621 pp., illus. Soft covers. $19.95.

Uses percentage grading system to determine each gun's value based on its unique condition.

The Book of the Springfield, by Edward C. Crossman and Roy F. Dunlap, Wolfe Publishing Co., Prescott, AZ, 1990. 567 pp., illus. $49.00.

A textbook covering the military, sporting and target rifles chambered for the caliber 30 Model 1906 cartridge; their metallic and telescopic sights and ammunition used in them.

*Boy's Single-Shot Rifles, by James J. Grant, Wolfe Publishing Co., Prescott, AZ, 1991. 597 pp., illus. $36.00.

The bible for those single shots that became the prized possessions of boys growing up in the early part of the century.

Breech-Loading Carbines of the United States Civil War Period, by Brig. Gen. John Pitman, Armory Publications, Tacoma, WA, 1987. 94 pp., illus. $29.95.

The first in a series of previously unpublished manuscripts originated by the late Brigadier General John Putnam. Exploded drawings showing parts actual size follow each sectioned illustration.

The Bren Gun Saga, by Thomas B. Dugelby, Collector Grade Publications, Toronto, Canada, 1986. 300 pp., illus. $50.00.

Contains information on all models of Bren guns used by all nations.

The Browning Connection, by Richard Rattenbury, Buffalo Bill Historical Center, Cody, WY, 1982. 71 pp., illus. Paper covers. $10.00.

Patent prototypes in the Winchester Museum.

Browning Dates of Manufacture, compiled by George Madis, Art and Reference House, Brownsboro, TX, 1989. 48 pp. $5.00.

Gives the date codes and product codes for all models from 1824 to the present.

Bullard Arms, by G. Scott Jamieson, The Boston Mills Press, Ontario, Canada, 1989. 244 pp., illus. $35.00.

The story of a mechanical genius whose rifles and cartridges were the equal to any made in America in the 1880s.

*Burning Powder, compiled by Major D.B. Wesson, Wolfe Publishing Company, Prescott, AZ, 1992. 110 pp. Soft cover. $10.95.

A rare booklet from 1932 for Smith & Wesson collectors.

The Burnside Breech Loading Carbines, by Edward A. Hull, Andrew Mowbray, Inc., Lincoln, RI, 1986. 95 pp., illus. $16.00.

No. 1 in the "Man at Arms Monograph Series." A model-by-model historical/technical examination of one of the most widely used cavalry weapons of the American Civil War based upon important and previously unpublished research.

California Gunsmiths 1846-1900, by Lawrence P. Sheldon, Far Far West Publ., Fair Oaks, CA, 1977. 289 pp., illus. $29.65.

A study of early California gunsmiths and the firearms they made.

Carbines of the Civil War, by John D. McAulay, Pioneer Press, Union City, TN, 1981. 123 pp., illus. Paper covers. $7.95.

A guide for the student and collector of the colorful arms used by the Federal cavalry.

Cartology Savalog, by Gerald Bernstein, Gerald Bernstein, St. Louis, MO, 1976. 177 pp., illus. Paper covers. $8.95.

An infinite variations catalog of small arms ammunition stamps.

Cartridges for Breechloading Rifles, by A. Mattenheimer, Armory Publications, Oceanside, CA, 1989. 90 pp. with two 15"x19" color lithos containing 163 drawings of cartridges and firearms mechanisms. $29.95.

Reprinting of this German work on cartridges. Text in German and English.

Cartridges of the World, 6th Edition, by Frank C. Barnes, DBI Books, Inc., Northbrook, IL, 1989. 448 pp., illus. Paper covers. $19.95.

Completely revised edition of the general purpose reference work for which collectors, police, scientists and laymen reach first for answers to cartridge identification questions.

*Cast Iron Toy Guns and Capshooters, by Samuel H. Logan, and Charles W. Best, Samuel Logan, Davis, CA, 1991. 251 pp., illus. $55.00.

Covers 1860s to 1950 with some 1,250 toys shown with brief descriptions, estimated dates of production and indication of rarity.

A Catalog Collection of 20th Century Winchester Repeating Arms Co., compiled by Roger Rule, Alliance Books, Inc., Northridge, CA, 1985. 396 pp., illus. $29.95.

Reflects the full line of Winchester products from 1901-1931 with emphasis on Winchester firearms.

*Civil War Breech Loading Rifles, by John D. McAulay, Andrew Mowbray, Inc., Lincoln, RI, 1991. 144 pp., illus. Paper covers. $15.00.

All the major breech-loading rifles of the Civil War and most, if not all, of the obscure types are detailed, illustrated and set in their historical context.

Civil War Carbines, by A.F. Lustyik, World Wide Gun Report, Inc., Aledo, IL, 1962. 63 pp., illus. Paper covers. $3.50.

Accurate, interesting summary of most carbines of the Civil War period, in booklet form, with numerous good illus.

*Civil War Carbines Volume 2: The Early Years, by John D. McAulay, Andrew Mowbray, Inc., Lincoln, RI, 1991. 144 pp., illus. Paper covers. $15.00.

Covers the carbines made during the exciting years leading up to the outbreak of war and used by the North and South in the conflict.

*A Collector's Guide to Winchester in the Service, by Bruce N. Canfield, Andrew Mowbray, Inc., Lincoln, RI, 1991. 192 pp., illus. $38.00.

The firearms produced by Winchester for the national defense. From Hotchkiss to the M14, each firearm is examined and illustrated.

A Collector's Guide to the M1 Garand and the M1 Carbine, by Bruce N. Canfield, Andrew Mowbray, Inc., Publisher, Lincoln, RI, 1988. 144 pp., illus. $35.00.

A comprehensive guide to the most important and ubiquitous American arms of WWII and Korea.

A Collector's Guide to the '03 Springfield, by Bruce N. Canfield, Andrew Mowbray Inc, Lincoln, RI, 1989. 160 pp., illus. $35.00.

A comprehensive guide follows the '03 through its unparalleled tenure of service. Covers all of the interesting variations, modifications and accessories of this highly collectible military rifle.

*Collector's Illustrated Encyclopedia of the American Revolution, by George C. Neumann and Frank J. Kravic, Rebel Publishing Co., Inc., Texarkana, TX, 1989. 286 pp., illus. $29.95.

A showcase of more than 2,300 artifacts made, worn, and used by those who fought in the War for Independence.

Collecting Antique Firearms, by Dr. Martin Kelvin, Stanley Paul, London, 1987. 181 pp., illus. $55.00.

A book to add to the treasure store of any antique gun collector.

Collecting Shotgun Cartridges, by Ken Rutherford, Stanley Paul, London, 1987. 139 pp., illus. $45.00.

An illustrated catalog of all the major known suppliers and designs in Britain and Ireland.

Colonial Frontier Guns, by T.M. Hamilton, Pioneer Press, Union City, TN, 1988. 176 pp., illus. Paper covers. $13.95.

A complete study of early flint muskets of this country.

The Colt-Burgess Magazine Rifle, by Samuel L. Maxwell Sr., Samuel L. Maxwell,

Bellvue, WA, 1985. 176 pp., illus. $35.00.

Serial numbers, engraved arms, newly discovered experimental models, etc.

Colt Cavalry, Artillery and Militia Revolvers 1873-1903, by Keith Cochran, Cochran Publishing Co., Rapid City, SD, 1988. 288 pp., illus. $45.00.

A history and text book of the Colt Cavalry Model revolver with a complete analysis, nearly every variation and mark illustrated.

*Colt Firearms, by James E. Serven, Wolfe Publishing, Prescott, AZ, 1991. 400 pp., illus. $45.00.

An illustrated history of the Colt company and its firearms including the story of the Gatling gun and an outline of Colt automatic weapons.

Colt Firearms from 1836, by James E. Serven, new 8th edition, Stackpole Books, Harrisburg, PA, 1979. 398 pp., illus. Deluxe ed. $69.95.

Excellent survey of the Colt company and its products. Updated with new SAA production chart and commemorative list.

Colt Heritage, by R.L. Wilson, Simon & Schuster, 1979. 358 pp., illus. $75.00.

The official history of Colt firearms 1836 to the present.

Colt Peacemaker British Model, by Keith Cochran, Cochran Publishing Co., Rapid City, SD, 1989. 160 pp., illus. $35.00.

Covers those revolvers Colt squeezed in while completing a large order of revolvers for the U.S. Cavalry in early 1874, to those magnificent cased target revolvers used in the pistol competitions at Bisley Commons in the 1890s.

*Colt Peacemaker Collector Pocket Compendium, by Keith Cochran, Cochran Publishing Co., Rapid City, SD, 1991. 48 pp., illus. Paper covers. $7.50.

A ready source of information for the gun show or auction.

Colt Peacemaker Encyclopedia, by Keith Cochran, Keith Cochran, Rapid City, SD, 1986. 434 pp., illus. $59.95.

A must book for the Peacemaker collector.

Colt Peacemaker Ready-Reference Handbook, by Keith Cochran, Cochran Publishing Co., Rapid City, SD, 1985. 76 pp., illus. Paper covers. $12.95.

A must book for the SAA collector.

Colt Peacemaker Yearly Variations, by Keith Cochran, Keith Cochran, Rapid City, SD, 1987. 96 pp., illus. $17.95.

A definitive, precise listing for each year the Peacemaker was manufactured from 1873-1940.

Colt Pistols 1836-1976, by R.L. Wilson in association with R.E. Hable, Jackson Arms, Dallas, TX, 1976. 380 pp., illus. $125.00.

A magnificently illustrated book in full color featuring Colt firearms from the famous Hable collection.

Colt Revolvers and the Tower of London, by Joseph G. Rosa, Royal Armouries of the Tower of London, London, England, 1988. 72 pp., illus. Soft covers. $15.00.

Details the story of Colt in London through the early cartridge period.

Colt Revolvers and the U.S. Navy 1865-1889, by C. Kenneth Moore, Dorrance and Co., Bryn Mawr, PA, 1987. 140 pp., illus. $29.95.

The Navy's use of all Colt handguns and other revolvers during this era of change.

Colt Single Action Army Revolvers and the London Agency, by C. Kenneth Moore, Andrew Mowbray Publishers, Lincoln, RI, 1990. 144 pp., illus. $35.00.

Drawing on vast documentary sources, this work chronicles the relationship between the London Agency and the Hartford home office.

The Colt U.S. General Officers' Pistols, by Horace Greeley IV, Andrew Mowbray Inc., Lincoln, RI, 1990. 199 pp., illus. $38.00.

These unique weapons, issued as a badge of rank to General Officers in the U.S. Army from WWII onward, remain highly personal artifacts of the military leaders who carried them. Includes serial numbers and dates of issue.

Colt's Dates of Manufacture 1837-1978, by R.L. Wilson, published by Maurie Albert, Coburg, Australia; N.A. distributor I.D.S.A. Books, Hamilton, OH, 1983. 61 pp. $10.00.

An invaluable pocket guide to the dates of manufacture of Colt firearms up to 1978.

Colt's SAA Post War Models, George Garton, revised edition, Gun Room Press, Highland Park, NJ, 1987. 166 pp., illus. $29.95.

The complete facts on Colt's famous post war single action army revolver using factory records to cover types, calibers, production numbers and many variations of this popular firearm.

The Colt Whitneyville-Walker Pistol, by Lt. Col. Robert D. Whittington, Brownlee Books, Hooks, TX, 1984. 96 pp., illus. Limited edition. $20.00.

A study of the pistol and associated characters 1846-1851.

The Complete Kalashnikov Family of Assault Rifles, by Duncan Long, Paladin Press, Boulder, CO, 1989. 192 pp., illus. Soft covers. $14.00.

The scoop on this international collection of rifles from one of America's most trusted firearms writers.

Confederate Revolvers, by William A. Gary, Taylor Publishing Co., Dallas, TX, 1987. 174 pp., illus. $45.00.

Comprehensive work on the rarest of Confederate weapons.

*Coykendall's Sporting Collectibles Price Guide, by Ralf Coykendall, Jr., Lyons & Burford, Publishers, New York, NY, 1991. 325 pp., illus. Paper covers. $16.95.

A broad based up-to-date book that records the latest available prices for scores of prominent sporting antiques based on auction records and catalog offerings.

Dance & Brothers; Texas Gunmakers of the Confederacy, by Gary Wiggins, Moss Publications, Orange, VA, 1986. 151 pp., illus. $29.95.

Presents a thorough and detailed study of the legendary Texas gunmakers, Dance & Brothers.

The Deringer in America, Volume 1, The Percussion Period, by R.L. Wilson and L.D. Eberhart, Andrew Mowbray Inc., Lincoln, RI, 1985. 271 pp., illus. $48.00.

A long awaited book on the American percussion deringer.

*Description & Rules for the Management of the Springfield Rifle, Carbine and Army Revolver Caliber .45, originally published by the U.S. Ordnance Department, reprinted by Wolfe Publishing, Co., Prescott, AZ, 1991. 69 pp., illus. Paper covers. $10.50.

Reprint of the 1898 government manual giving complete directions, dimensions, care and use for these guns.

Development of the Henry Cartridge and Self-Contained Cartridges for the Toggle-Link Winchesters, by R. Bruce McDowell, A.M.B., Metuchen, NJ, 1984. 69 pp., illus. Paper covers. $10.00.

From powder and ball to the self-contained metallic cartridge.

Early Indian Trade Guns: 1625-1775, by T.M. Hamilton, Museum of the Great Plains, Lawton, OK, 1968. 34 pp., illus. Paper covers. $7.95.

Detailed descriptions of subject arms, compiled from early records and from the study of remnants found in Indian country.

*Encyclopedia and Price Guide of American Paper Shotshells, compiled by Dick Iverson, prices by Bob Strauss, Circus Promotions Corp., Spring, TX, 1991. 436 pp., illus. Paper covers. $25.00.

Pages of headstamps, head types, dimensions, color listed, and 3,100 individual prices.

English Pistols: The Armories of H.M. Tower of London Collection, by Howard L. Blackmore, Arms and Armour Press, London, England, 1985. 64 pp., illus. Soft covers. $14.95.

All the pistols described and pictured are from this famed collection.

European Firearms in Swedish Castles, by Kaa Wennberg, Bohuslaningens Boktryckeri AB, Uddevalla, Sweden, 1986. 156 pp., illus. $45.00.

The famous collection of Count Keller, the Ettersburg Castle collection, and others. English text.

Evolution of the Winchester, by R. Bruce McDowell, Armory Publications, Tacoma, WA, 1986. 200 pp., illus. $37.50.

Historic lever-action, tubular-magazine firearms.

Fifteen Years in the Hawken Lode, by John D. Baird, The Gun Room Press, Highland Park, NJ, 1976. 120 pp., illus. $19.95.

A collection of thoughts and observations gained from many years of intensive study of the guns from the shop of the Hawken brothers.

*Firearms and Tackle Memorabilia, by John Delph, Schiffer Publishing, Ltd., West Chester, PA, 1991. 124 pp., illus. $39.95.

A collector's guide to signs and posters, calendars, trade cards, boxes, envelopes, and other highly sought after memorabilia. With a value guide.

Firepower from Abroad: The Confederate Enfield and the LeMat Revolver, by Wiley Sword, Andrew Mowbray, Inc., Lincoln, RI, 1986. 119 pp., illus. $16.00.

No. two in the "Man at Arms Monograph Series." With new data on a variety of Confederate small arms.

Flayderman's Guide to Antique American Firearms...and Their Values, 5th Edition, by Norm Flayderman, DBI Books, Inc., Northbrook, IL, 1990. 624 pp., illus. Soft covers. $27.95.

Updated edition of this bible of the antique gun field.

*The .45-70 Springfield, by Joe Poyer and Craig Riesch, North Cape Publications, Tustin, CA, 1991. 112 pp., illus. Soft covers. $14.95.

A definitive work on the 45-70 Springfield. Organized by serial number and date of production to aid the collector in identifying models and rifle parts.

The 45/70 Trapdoor Springfield Dixie Collection, compiled by Walter Crutcher and Paul Oglesby, Pioneer Press, Union City, TN, 1975. 600 pp., illus. Paper covers. $9.95.

An illustrated listing of the 45-70 Springfields in the Dixie Gun Works Collection. Little known details and technical information is given, plus current values.

Frank and George Freund and the Sharps Rifle, by Gerald O. Kelver, Gerald O. Kelver, Brighton, CO, 1986. 60 pp., illus. Paper covers. $12.00.

Pioneer gunmakers of Wyoming Territory and Colorado.

French Military Weapons, 1717-1938, Major James E. Hicks, N. Flayderman & Co., Publishers, New Milford, CT, 1973. 281 pp., illus. $24.95.

Firearms, swords, bayonets, ammunition, artillery, ordnance equipment of the French army.

George Schreyer, Sr. and Jr., Gunmakers of Hanover, Pennsylvania, by George Shumway, George Shumway Publishers, York, PA, 1990. 160pp., illus. $45.00.

This monograph is a detailed photographic study of almost all known surviving long rifles and smoothbore guns made by highly regarded gunsmiths George Schreyer, Sr. and Jr.

The German Assault Rifle 1935-1945, by Peter R. Senich, Paladin Press, Boulder, CO, 1987. 328 pp., illus. $49.95.

A complete review of machine carbines, machine pistols and assault rifles employed by Hitler's Wehrmacht during WWII.

*German Military Pistols 1904-1930, by Fred A. Datig, Michael Zomber Co., Culver City, CA, 1990. 88 pp., illus. Paper covers. $14.95.

Monograph #2 in the series "The Luger Pistol Its History & Development from 1893-1945."

German Military Rifles and Machine Pistols, 1871-1945, by Hans Dieter Gotz, Schiffer Publishing Co., West Chester, PA, 1990. 245 pp., illus. $35.00.

This book portrays in words and pictures the development of the modern German weapons and their ammunition including the scarcely known experimental types.

German Pistols and Holsters 1934-1945, Vol. 2, by Robert Whittington, Brownlee Books, Hooks, TX, 1990. 312 pp., illus. $45.00.

This volume addresses pistols only: military (Heer, Luftwaffe, Kriegsmarine & Waffen-SS), captured, commercial, police, NSDAP and government.

German 7.9mm Military Ammunition, by Daniel W. Kent, Daniel W. Kent, Ann Arbor, MI, 1991. 244 pp., illus. $35.00.

The long-awaited revised edition of a classic among books devoted to ammunition.

*German Pistols and Holsters, 1934-1945, Volume 4, by Lt. Col. Robert D. Whittington, 3rd, U.S.A.R., Brownlee Books, Hooks, TX, 1991. 208 pp. $30.00.

Pistols and holsters issued in 412 selected armed forces, army and Waffen-SS units including information on personnel, other weapons and transportation.

The Government Models: The Development of the Colt Model of 1911, by William H.D. Goddard, Andrew Mowbray, Inc., Publishers, Lincoln, RI, 1988. 223 pp., illus. $58.50.

An authoritative source on the world's most popular military sidearm.

*Guide to Ruger Single Action Revolvers Production Dates, 1953-73, by John C. Dougan, Blacksmith Corp., Chino Valley, AZ, 1991. 22 pp., illus. Paper covers. $9.95.

A unique pocket-sized handbook providing production information for the popular Ruger single-action revolvers manufactured during the first 20 years.

Gun Collecting, by Geoffrey Boothroyd, Sportsman's Press, London, 1989. 208 pp., illus. $29.95.

The most comprehensive list of 19th century British gunmakers and gunsmiths ever published.

Gun Collector's Digest, 5th Edition, edited by Joseph J. Schroeder, DBI Books, Inc., Northbrook, IL, 1989. 224 pp., illus. Paper covers. $15.95.

The latest edition of this sought-after series.

The Gun Digest Book of Modern Gun Values, 8th Edition, by Jack Lewis, DBI Books, Inc., Northbrook, IL, 1991. 528 pp., illus. Paper covers. $18.95.

Updated and expanded edition of the book that has become the standard for valuing modern firearms.

*The Gun Digest Book of Modern Gun Values, 9th Edition, by Jack Lewis, DBI Books, Inc., Northbrook, IL. 528 pp., illus. Paper covers.

(February 1993)

Gunmakers of London 1350-1850, by Howard L. Blackmore, George Shumway Publisher, York, PA, 1986. 222 pp., illus. $35.00.

A listing of all the known workmen of gun making in the first 500 years, plus a history of the guilds, cutlers, armourers, founders, blacksmiths, etc. 260 gunmarks are illustrated.

*The Gunsmiths of Manhattan, 1625-1900: A Checklist of Tradesmen, by Michael H. Lewis, Museum Restoration Service, Bloomfield, Ont., Canada, 1991. 40 pp., illus. Paper

covers. $4.95.

This listing of more than 700 men in the arms trade in New York City prior to about the end of the 19th century will provide a guide for identification and further research.

Gunsmiths of Ohio—18th & 19th Centuries: Vol. I, Biographical Data, by Donald A. Hutslar, George Shumway, York, PA, 1973. 444 pp., illus. $45.00.

An important source book, full of information about the old-time gunsmiths of Ohio.

The Handgun, by Geoffrey Boothroyd, David and Charles, North Pomfret, VT, 1989. 566 pp., illus. $60.00.

Every chapter deals with an important period in handgun history from the 14th century to the present.

The Hawken Rifle: Its Place in History, by Charles E. Hanson, Jr., The Fur Press, Chadron, NE, 1979. 104 pp., illus. Paper covers. $6.00.

A definitive work on this famous rifle.

Hawken Rifles, The Mountain Man's Choice, by John D. Baird, The Gun Room Press, Highland Park, NJ, 1976. 95 pp., illus. $19.95.

Covers the rifles developed for the Western fur trade. Numerous specimens are described and shown in photographs.

*High Standard: A Collector's Guide to the Hamden & Hartford Target Pistols, by Tom Dance, Andrew Mowbray, Inc., Lincoln, RI, 1991. 192 pp., illus. Paper covers. $24.00.

From Citation to Supermatic, all of the production models and specials made from 1951 to 1984 are covered according to model number or series.

Historic Pistols: The American Martial Flintlock 1760-1845, by Samuel E. Smith and Edwin W. Bitter, The Gun Room Press, Highland Park, NJ, 1986. 353 pp., illus. $45.00.

Covers over 70 makers and 163 models of American martial arms.

Historical Hartford Hardware, by William W. Dalrymple, Colt Collector Press, Rapid City, SD, 1976. 42 pp., illus. Paper covers. $5.50.

Historically associated Colt revolvers.

The History and Development of Small Arms Ammunition, Volume 1, by George A. Hoyem, Armory Publications, Oceanside, CA, 1991. 230 pp., illus. $75.00.

Military musket, rifle, carbine and primitive machine gun cartridges of the 18th and 19th centuries, together with the firearms that chambered them.

The History and Development of Small Arms Ammunition, Volume 2, by George A. Hoyem, Armory Publications, Oceanside, CA, 1991. 303 pp., illus. $65.00.

Covers the blackpowder military centerfire rifle, carbine, machine gun and volley gun ammunition used in 28 nations and dominions, together with the firearms that chambered them.

*The History and Development of Small Arms Ammunition (British Sporting Rifle) Volume 3, by George A. Hoyem, Armory Publications, Oceanside, CA, 1991. 300 pp., illus. $60.00.

Concentrates on British sporting rifle cartridges that run from the 4-bore through the .600 Nitro to the .297/.230 Morris.

The History of Smith and Wesson, by Roy G. Jinks, Willowbrook Enterprises, Springfield, MA, 1988. 290 pp., illus. $23.95.

Revised 10th Anniversary edition of the definite book on S&W firearms.

History of Winchester Firearms 1866-1980, by Duncan Barnes, et al, Winchester Press, Piscataway, NJ, 1985. 256 pp., illus. $19.95.

A most complete and authoritative account of Winchester firearms.

How to Buy and Sell Used Guns, by John Traister, Stoeger Publishing Co., So. Hackensack, NJ, 1984. 192 pp., illus. Paper covers. $10.95.

A new guide to buying and selling guns.

Illustrations of United States Military Arms 1776-1903 and Their Inspector's Marks, compiled by Turner Kirkland, Pioneer Press, Union City, TN, 1988. 37 pp., illus. Paper covers. $4.95.

Reprinted from the 1949 Bannerman catalog. Valuable information for both the advanced and beginning collector.

An Introduction the Civil War Small Arms, by Earl J. Coates and Dean S. Thomas, Thomas Publishing Co., Gettysburg, PA, 1990. 96 pp., illus. Paper covers. $6.95.

The small arms carried by the individual soldier during the Civil War.

Iver Johnson's Arms & Cycle Works Handguns, 1871-1964, by W.E. "Bill" Goforth, Blacksmith Corp., Chino Valley, AZ, 1991. 160 pp., illus. Paper covers. $12.95.

Covers all of the famous Iver Johnson handguns from the early solid-frame pistols and revolvers to optional accessories, special orders and patents.

James Reid and His Catskill Knuckledusters, by Taylor Brown, Andrew Mowbray Publishers, Lincoln, RI, 1990. 288 pp., illus. $24.95.

A detailed history of James Reid, his factory in the picturesque Catskill Mountains, and the pistols which he manufactured there.

Japanese Handguns, by Frederick E. Leithe, Borden Publishing Co., Alhambra, CA, 1985. 160 pp., illus. $19.95.

An identification guide to all models and variations of Japanese handguns.

The Kentucky Rifle: A True American Heritage in Picture, by The Kentucky Rifle Association, The Forte Group of Creative Companies, Inc., Alexandria, VA, second edition, 1985. 110 pp., illus. $27.50.

This classic essay reveals both the beauty and the decorative nature of the Kentucky by providing detailed photographs of some of the most significant examples of American rifles, pistols, and accoutrements.

Kentucky Rifles and Pistols 1756-1850, compiled by members of the Kentucky Rifle Association, Wash., DC, Golden Age Arms Co., Delaware, OH, 1976. 275 pp., illus. $45.00.

Profusely illustrated with more than 300 examples of rifles and pistols never before published.

Know Your Broomhandle Mausers, by R.J. Berger, Blacksmith Corp., Southport, CT, 1985. 96 pp., illus. Paper covers. $9.95.

An interesting story on the big Mauser pistol and its variations.

Krag Rifles, by William S. Brophy, The Gun Room Press, Highland Park, NJ, 1980. 200 pp., illus. $35.00.

The first comprehensive work detailing the evolution and various models, both military and civilian.

The Krieghoff Parabellum, by Randall Gibson, Midland, TX, 1988. 279 pp., illus. $40.00.

A comprehensive text pertaining to the Lugers manufactured by H. Krieghoff Waffenfabrik.

Levine's Guide to Knives And Their Values, 2nd Edition, by Bernard Levine, DBI Books, Inc., Northbrook, IL, 1989. 480 pp., illus. Paper covers. $22.95.

An important guide to today's knife values and collecting them.

*Levine's Guide to Knives And Their Values, 3rd Edition, by Bernard Levine, DBI Books, Inc., Northbrook, IL. 480 pp., illus. Paper covers.

(January 1993)

Longrifles of North Carolina, by John Bivens, George Shumway Publisher, York, PA, 1988. 256 pp., illus. $45.00.

Covers art and evolution of the rifle, immigration and trade movements. Committee of Safety gunsmiths, characteristics of the North Carolina rifle.

Longrifles of Pennsylvania, Volume 1, Jefferson, Clarion & Elk Counties, by Russel H. Harringer, George Shumway Publisher, York, PA, 1984. 200 pp., illus. $45.00.

First in series that will treat in great detail the longrifles and gunsmiths of Pennsylvania.

Lugers at Random, by Charles Kenyon, Jr., Handgun Press, Glenview, IL, 1990. 420 pp., illus. $39.95.

A new printing of this classic and sought-after work on the Luger pistol. A boon to the Luger collector/shooter.

*Luger: The Multi-National Pistol, by Charles Kenyon, Jr., Richard Ellis Publications, Moline, IL, 1991. 192 pp., illus. $69.95 (hardcover); $150.00 (leather bound).

A fresh approach to this historical handgun. A must for the serious collector.

*The Luger Book, by John Walter, Sterling Publishing Co., New York, NY, 1991. 287 pp., illus. $19.95.

The encyclopedia of the Borchardt and Borchardt-Luger handgun 1885-1985.

Marlin Firearms: A History of the Guns and the Company That Made Them, by Lt. Col. William S. Brophy, USAR, Ret., Stackpole Books, Harrisburg, PA, 1989. 672 pp., illus. $59.95.

The definitive book on the Marlin Firearms Co. and their products.

Massachusetts Military Shoulder Arms 1784-1877, by George D. Moller, Andrew Mowbray Publisher, Lincoln, RI, 1989. 250 pp., illus. $24.00.

A scholarly and heavily researched study of the military shoulder arms used by Massachusetts during the 90-year period following the Revolutionary War.

Mauser Bolt Rifles, by Ludwig Olson, F. Brownell & Son, Inc., Montezuma, IA, 1976. 364 pp., illus. $47.50.

The most complete, detailed, authoritative and comprehensive work ever done on Mauser bolt rifles.

Mauser Rifles and Pistols, by Walter H.B. Smith, Wolfe Publishing Co., Prescott, AZ, 1990. 234 pp., illus. $30.00.

A handbook covering Mauser history and the amrs Mauser manufactured.

*Military Pistols of Japan, by Fred L. Honeycutt, Jr., Julin Books, Palm Beach Gardens, FL, 1991. 168 pp., illus. $31.00.

Covers every aspect of military pistol production in Japan through WWII.

*The Military Remington Rolling Block Rifle, by George Layman, Wolfe Publishing Company, Prescott, AZ, 1992. 250 pp., illus. Soft cover. $21.00.

A reference work for the collector, tracing the history of this military rifle and disclosing previously unpublished data.

Military Rifles of Japan, 3rd Edition, by F.L. Honeycutt, Julin Books, Lake Park, FL, 1989. 208 pp., illus. $37.00.

A new revised and updated edition. Includes the early Murata-period markings, etc.

Military Small Arms of the 20th Century, 6th Edition, by Ian V. Hogg, DBI Books, Inc., Northbrook, IL, 1991. 352 pp., illus. Paper covers. $18.95.

Fully revised and updated edition of the standard reference in its field.

Modern Guns Identification and Values, 1991 revised 8th edition, by Russell and Steve Quertermous, Collector Books, Paducah, KY, 1991. 464 pp., illus. Paper covers. $12.95.

This updated edition features current values for over 2700 models of rifles, shotguns and handguns with over 1800 illustrations.

M1 Carbine, by Larry Ruth, Gunroom Press, Highland Park, NJ, 1987. 291 pp., illus. Cloth $24.95; Paper $17.95.

The origin, development, manufacture and use of this famous carbine of World War II.

The M1 Garand: Post World War, by Scott A. Duff, Scott A. Duff, Export, PA, 1990. 139 pp., illus. Soft covers. $17.95.

A detailed account of the activities at Springfield Armory through this period. International Harvester, H&R, Korean War production and quantities delivered. Serial numbers.

More Single Shot Rifles, by James C. Grant, The Gun Room Press, Highland Park, NJ, 1976. 324 pp., illus. $25.00.

Details the guns made by Frank Wesson, Milt Farrow, Holden, Borchardt, Stevens, Remington, Winchester, Ballard and Peabody-Martini.

*The Muzzle-Loading Cap Lock Rifle, by Ned H. Roberts, reprinted by Wolfe Publishing Co., Prescott, AZ, 1991. 432 pp., illus. $30.00.

Originally published in 1940, this fascinating study of the muzzle-loading cap lock rifle covers rifles on the frontier to hunting rifles, including the famous Hawken.

The Navy Luger, by Joachim Gortz and John Walter, Handgun Press, Glenview, IL, 1988. 128 pp., illus. $24.95.

The 9mm Pistole 1904 and the Imperial German Navy. A concise illustrated history.

The Northwest Gun, by Charles E. Hanson, Jr., Nebraska State Historical Society, Lincoln, NE, 1976. 85 pp., illus., paper covers. $6.00.

Number 2 in the Society's "Publications in Anthropology." Historical survey of rifles which figured in the fur trade and settlement of the Northwest.

The P-08 Parabellum Luger Automatic Pistol, edited by J. David McFarland, Desert Publications, Cornville, AZ, 1982. 20 pp., illus. Paper covers. $8.00.

Covers every facet of the Luger, plus a listing of all known Luger models.

The P.38 Pistol, Volume 3, by Warren H. Buxton, Ucross Books, Los Alamos, NM, 1991. 270 pp., illus. $54.50.

The postwar distribution of the P.38 pistol.

Paterson Colt Pistol Variations, by R.L. Wilson and R. Phillips, Jackson Arms Co., Dallas, TX, 1979. 250 pp., illus. $35.00.

A tremendous book about the different models and barrel lengths in the Paterson Colt story.

Pennsylvania Longrifles of Note, by George Shumway, George Shumway, Publisher, York, PA, 1977. 63 pp., illus. Paper covers. $10.00.

Illustrates and describes samples of guns from a number of Pennsylvania rifle-making schools.

*Pistols of the World, 3rd Edition, by Ian Hogg and John Weeks, DBI Books, Inc., Northbrook, IL, 1992. 320 pp., illus. Paper covers. $18.95.

A totally revised edition of one of the leading studies of small arms.

The Pitman Notes on U.S. Martial Small Arms and Ammunition, 1776-1933, Volume 2, Revolvers and Automatic Pistols, by Brig. Gen. John Pitman, Thomas Publications, Gettysburg, PA, 1990. 192 pp., illus. $29.95.

A most important primary source of information on United States military small arms and ammunition.

The Plains Rifle, by Charles Hanson, Gun Room Press, Highland Park, NJ, 1989. 169 pp., illus. $24.95.

All rifles that were made with the plainsman in mind, including pistols.

Proving Ground History of the Carbine Caliber .30, M1, by G.P. Grant, Desert Publications, Cornville, AZ, 1990. 21 pp., illus. Paper covers. $5.00.

Reprint of the Addenda to Volume 2, Historical Data, Aberdeen Proving Ground, MD. Added to this is "Weapons Usage in Korea" by S.L.A. Marshall.

The Rare and Valuable Antique Arms, by James E. Serven, Pioneer Press, Union City, TN, 1976. 106 pp., illus. Paper covers. $4.95.

A guide to the collector in deciding which direction his collecting should go, investment value, historic interest, mechanical ingenuity, high art or personal preference.

Reloading Tools, Sights and Telescopes for Single Shot Rifles, by Gerald O. Kelver, Brighton, CO, 1982. 163 pp., illus. Paper covers. $12.00.

A listing of most of the famous makers of reloading tools, sights and telescopes with a brief description of the products they manufactured.

Revolvers of the British Services 1854-1954, by W.H.J. Chamberlain and A.W.F. Taylerson, Museum Restoration Service, Ottawa, Canada, 1989. 80 pp., illus. $27.50.

Covers the types issued among one or more of the United Kingdom's naval, land or air services.

*Rhode Island Arms Makers & Gunsmiths, by William O. Archibald, Andrew Mowbray, Inc., Lincoln, RI, 1990. 108 pp., illus. $16.50.

A serious and informative study of an important area of American arms making.

The Rimfire Cartridge in the United States and Canada 1857-1984, by John L. Barber, Armory Publications, Tacoma, WA, 1987. 221 pp., illus. $39.95.

An illustrated history of its manufacturers and their patents.

The Royal Gunroom at Sandringham, by David Baker, Paidon, Christie's Ltd., Oxford, England, 1989. 160 pp., illus. $150.00.

The British Royal Family's collection of rifles, shotguns and pistols housed at Sandringham is of unique historical importance. Includes the finest items in this collection.

*Ruger, edited by Joseph Roberts, Jr., the National Rifle Association of America, Washington, D.C., 1991. 109 pp. illus. Paper covers. $14.95.

The story of Bill Ruger's indelible imprint in the history of sporting firearms.

Ruger Rimfire Handguns 1949-1982, by J.C. Munnell, G.D.G.S. Inc., McKeesport, PA, 1982. 189 pp., illus. Paper covers. $13.50.

Updated edition with additional material on the semi-automatic pistols and the New Model revolvers.

Scottish Arms Makers, by Charles E. Whitelaw, Arms and Armour Press, London, England, 1982. 363 pp., illus. $29.95.

An important and basic addition to weapons reference literature.

Service Handguns: A Collector's Guide, by Klaus-Peter Konig and Martin Hugo, David and Charles, N. Pomfret, NH, 1989. 264 pp., illus. $34.95.

Over 200 pistols and revolvers are detailed, most of which have been introduced into the military and police service in Europe since 1850.

Sharps Firearms, by Frank Seller, Frank M. Seller, Denver, CO, 1982. 358 pp., illus. $45.00.

Traces the development of Sharps firearms with full range of guns made including all martial variations.

Shot Shell Boxes: Prices Realized at Auction 1985-1990 compiled by Bob Strauss, Circus Promotions Corp., Spring, TX, 2nd edition, 1990. 148 pp., illus. Paper covers. $12.00.

Actual prices realized at all major cartridge and other auctions over the past five years.

The Shotshell in the United States, by Richard J. Iverson, Circus Promotions Corp., Jefferson, ME, 1988. 193 pp., illus. Paper covers. $35.00.

Lists manufacturers, distributors, trade brands, headstamps, gauges, shot sizes, colors and configurations.

Simeon North: First Official Pistol Maker of the United States, by S. North and R. North, The Gun Room Press, Highland Park, NJ, 1972. 207 pp., illus. $9.95.

Reprint of the rare first edition.

*Small Arms of the World, 12th Edition, fully updated and revised, by Edward C. Ezell, Marboro Book Corp., New York, NY, 1990. 894 pp., illus. $16.95.

An encyclopedia of global weapons with over 3,500 entries.

Southern Derringers of the Mississippi Valley, by Turner Kirkland, Pioneer Press, Tenn., 1971. 80 pp., illus., paper covers. $5.00.

A guide for the collector, and a much-needed study.

Soviet Russian Postwar Military Pistols and Cartridges, by Fred A. Datig, Handgun Press, Glenview, IL, 1988. 152 pp., illus. $29.95.

Thoroughly researched, this definitive sourcebook covers the development and adoption of the Makarov, Stechkin and the new PSM pistols. Also included in this source book is coverage on Russian clandestine weapons and pistol cartridges.

*Sporting Collectibles, by Jim and Vivian Karsnitz, Schiffer Publishing Ltd., West Chester, PA, 1992. 160 pp., illus. Paper covers. $29.95.

The fascinating world of hunting related collectibles presented in an informative text.

The Springfield 1903 Rifles, by Lt. Col. William S. Brophy, USAR, Ret., Stackpole Books Inc., Harrisburg, PA, 1985. 608 pp., illus. $49.95.

The illustrated, documented story of the design, development, and production of all the models, appendages, and accessories.

Springfield Shoulder Arms 1795-1865, by Claud E. Fuller, S. & S. Firearms, Glendale, NY, 1986. 76 pp., illus. Paper covers. $15.00.

Exact reprint of the scarce 1930 edition of one of the most definitive works on Springfield flintlock and percussion muskets ever published.

Still More Single Shot Rifles, by James J. Grant, Pioneer Press, Union City, TN, 1979. 211 pp., illus. $17.50.

A sequel to the author's classic works on single shot rifles.

The Sumptuous Flaske, by Herbert G. Houze, Andrew Mowbray, Inc., Lincoln, RI, 1989. 158 pp., illus. Soft covers. $35.00.

Catalog of a recent show at the Buffalo Bill Historical Center bringing together some of the finest European and American powder flasks of the 16th to 19th centuries.

Textbook of Automatic Pistols, by R.K. Wilson, Wolfe Publishing Co., Prescott, AZ, 1990. 349 pp., illus. $54.00.

Reprint of the 1943 classic being a treatise on the history, development and functioning of modern military self-loading pistols.

Thoughts on the Kentucky Rifle in its Golden Age, by Joe Kindig, George Shumway, Publisher, York, PA, 1984. 561 pp., illus. $85.00.

A new printing of the classic work on Kentucky rifles.

The Trapdoor Springfield, by M.D. Waite and B.D. Ernst, The Gun Room Press, Highland Park, NJ, 1983. 250 pp., illus. $35.00.

The first comprehensive book on the famous standard military rifle of the 1873-92 period.

UK and Commonwealth FALS, by R. Blake Stevens, Collector Grade Publications, Toronto, Canada, 1987. 260 pp., illus. $36.00.

The complete story of the L1A1 in the UK, Australia and India.

Underhammer Guns, by H.C. Logan, Stackpole Books, Harrisburg, PA, 1965. 250 pp., illus. $20.00.

A full account of an unusual form of firearm dating back to flintlock days. Both

American and foreign specimens are included.

United States Martial Flintlocks, by Robert M. Reilly, Andrew Mowbray, Inc., Lincoln, RI, 1986. 263 pp., illus. $39.50.

A comprehensive illustrated history of the flintlock in America from the Revolution to the demise of the system.

*U.S. Breech-Loading Rifles and Carbines, Cal. 45, by Gen. John Pitman, Thomas Publications, Gettysburg, PA, 1992. 192 pp., illus. $29.95.

The third volume in the Pitman Notes on U.S. Martial Small Arms and Ammunition, 1776-1933. This book centers on the "Trapdoor Springfield" models.

U.S. Military Arms Dates of Manufacture from 1795, by George Madis, David Madis, Dallas, TX, 1989. 64 pp. Soft covers. $5.00.

Lists all U.S. military arms of collector interest alphabetically, covering about 250 models.

U.S. Military Small Arms 1816-1865, by Robert M. Reilly, The Gun Room Press, Highland Park, NJ, 1983. 270 pp., illus. $35.00.

Covers every known type of primary and secondary martial firearms used by Federal forces.

U.S. Naval Handguns, 1808-1911, by Fredrick R. Winter, Andrew Mowbray Publishers, Lincoln, RI, 1990. 128 pp., illus. $26.00.

The story of U.S. Naval Handguns spans an entire century—included are sections on each of the important naval handguns within the period.

Walther Models PP and PPK, 1929-1945, by James L. Rankin, assisted by Gary Green, James L. Rankin, Coral Gables, FL, 1974. 142 pp., illus. $30.00.

Complete coverage on the subject as to finish, proofmarks and Nazi Party inscriptions.

Walther P-38 Pistol, by Maj. George Nonte, Desert Publications, Cornville, AZ, 1982. 100 pp., illus. Paper covers. $9.95.

Complete volume on one of the most famous handguns to come out of WWII. All models covered.

Walther Volume II, Engraved, Presentation and Standard Models, by James L. Rankin, J.L. Rankin, Coral Gables, FL, 1977. 112 pp., illus. $35.00.

The new Walther book on embellished versions and standard models. Has 88 photographs, including many color plates.

Walther, Volume III, 1908-1980, by James L. Rankin, Coral Gables, FL, 1981. 226 pp., illus. $35.00.

Covers all models of Walther handguns from 1908 to date, includes holsters, grips and magazines.

Webley Revolvers, by Gordon Bruce and Christien Reinhart, Stocker-Schmid, Zurich, Switzerland, 1988. 256 pp., illus. $69.50.

A revised edition of Dowell's "Webley Story."

Westley Richards Guns and Rifles, a reprint of the Westley Richards firm's centennial catalog of 1912, by Armory Publications, Oceanside, CA, 1988. 211 pp., illus. Paper covers. $27.95.

A century of gun and rifle manufacture, 1812-1912.

The Whitney Firearms, by Claud Fuller, Standard Publications, Huntington, WV, 1946, 334 pp., many plates and drawings, $40.00.

An authoritative history of all Whitney arms and their maker. Highly recommended. An exclusive with Ray Riling Arms Books Co.

*Winchester: An American Legend, by R.L. Wilson, Random House, New York, NY, 1991. 403 pp., illus. $65.00.

The official history of Winchester firearms from 1849 to the present.

The Winchester Book, by George Madis, David Madis Gun Book Distributor, Dallas, TX, 1986. 650 pp., illus. $45.50.

A new, revised 25th anniversary edition of this classic book on Winchester firearms. Complete serial ranges have been added.

Winchester Catalogue of 1899, reprinted by Wolfe Publishing Co., Prescott, AZ, 1990. 158 pp., illus. Paper covers. $10.50

More than just a price list! This text contains explanations of parts, assembly and disassembly, testing techniques, and evaluations of selected models.

Winchester Dates of Manufacture 1849-1984, by George Madis, Art & Reference House, Brownsboro, TX, 1984. 59 pp. $5.95.

A most useful work, compiled from records of the Winchester factory.

Winchester Engraving, by R.L. Wilson, Beinfeld Books, Springs, CA, 1989. 500 pp., illus. $115.00.

A classic reference work, of value to all arms collectors.

The Winchester Handbook, by George Madis, Art & Reference House, Lancaster, TX, 1982. 287 pp., illus. $19.95.

The complete line of Winchester guns, with dates of manufacture, serial numbers, etc.

Winchester's 30-30, Model 94, by Sam Fadala, Stackpole Books, Inc., Harrisburg, PA, 1986. 223 pp., illus. $24.95.

The story of the rifle America loves.

World War 2 Small Arms, by John Weeks, Chartwell Books, Inc., Secaucus, NJ, 1989. 144 pp., illus. $10.95.

Assesses the weapons of each of the major combatant nations, their production, history, design and features.

EDGED WEAPONS

*A.G. Russell's Knife Trader's Guide, by A.G. Russell, Paul Wahl Corp., Bogata, NJ, 1991. 160 pp., illus. Paper covers. $10.00.

Recent sales prices of many popular collectible knives.

The American Eagle Pommel Sword: The Early Years 1793-1830, by Andrew Mowbray, Publisher, Lincoln, RI, 1988. 224 pp., illus. $45.00.

Provides an historical outline, a collecting structure and a vast new source of information for this rapidly growing field.

American Knives; The First History and Collector's Guide, by Harold L. Peterson, The Gun Room Press, Highland Park, NJ, 1980. 178 pp., illus. $19.95.

A reprint of this 1958 classic. Covers all types of American knives.

*American Military Swords: An Annotated Bibliography, by Leonard J. Garigliano, Parsonsburg, MD, 1991. 189 pp. Limited, numbered and signed edition. Spiral bound. $19.50.

This bibliography attempts to include all of what has been written about American swords through December 31, 1986.

American Primitive Knives 1770-1870, by G.B. Minnes, Museum Restoration Service, Ottawa, Canada, 1983. 112 pp., illus. $19.95.

Origins of the knives, outstanding specimens, structural details, etc.

American Socket Bayonets and Scabbards, by Robert M. Reilly, Andrew Mowbray, Inc., Lincoln, RI, 1990. 209 pp., illus. $40.00.

A comprehensive illustrated history of socket bayonets, scabbards and frogs in America from the Colonial period through the Civil War period.

The American Sword, 1775-1945, by Harold L. Peterson, Ray Riling Arms Books, Co., Phila., PA, 1980. 286 pp. plus 60 pp. of illus. $45.00.

1977 reprint of a survey of swords worn by U.S. uniformed forces, plus the rare "American Silver Mounted Swords, (1700-1815)."

Blacksmithing for the Home Craftsman, by Joe Pehoski, Joe Pehoski, Washington, TX, 1973. 44 pp., illus. Paper covers. $5.00.

This informative book is chock-full of drawings and explains how to make your own forge.

Blades and Barrels, by H. Gordon Frost, Wallon Press, El Paso, TX, 1972. 298 pp., illus. $19.95.

The first full scale study about man's attempts to combine an edged weapon with a firearm.

The Book of the Sword, by Richard F. Burton, Dover Publications, New York, NY, 1987. 199 pp., illus. Paper covers.

Traces the swords origin from its birth as a charged and sharpened stick through diverse stages of development.

*Borders Away, Volume 1: With Steel, by William Gilkerson, Andrew Mowbray, Inc., Lincoln, RI, 1991. 184 pp., illus. $48.00.

A comprehensive study of naval armament under fighting sail. This first voume covers axes, pikes and fighting blades in use between 1626-1826.

*The Bowie Knife, by Raymond Thorp, Phillips Publications, Wiliamstown, NJ, 1992. 167 pp., illus. $9.95.

After forty-five years, the classic work on the Bowie knife is once again available.

Bowie Knives, by Robert Abels, Sherwood International Corp., Northridge, CA, 1988. 30 pp., illus. Paper covers. $14.95.

Reprint of the classic work on Bowie knives.

Collecting the Edged Weapons of Imperial Germany, by Thomas M. Johnson and Thomas T. Wittmann, Johnson Reference Books, Fredricksburg, VA, 1989. 363 pp., illus. $39.50.

An in-depth study of the many ornate military, civilian, and government daggers and swords of the Imperial era.

*Collector's Handbook of World War 2 German Daggers, by LtC. Thomas M. Johnson, Johnson Reference Books, Fredericksburg, VA, 2nd edition, 1991. 252 pp., illus. Paper covers. $20.00.

Concise pocket reference guide to Third Reich daggers and accoutrements in a convenient format. With value guide.

Commando Dagger, by Leroy Thompson, Paladin Press, Boulder, CO, 1984. 176 pp., illus. $29.95.

The complete illustrated history of the Fairbairn-Sykes fighting knife.

The Complete Bladesmith: Forging Your Way to Perfection, by Jim Hrisoulas, Paladin Press, Boulder, CO, 1987. 192 pp., illus. $25.00.

Novice as well as experienced bladesmith will benefit from this definitive guide to smithing world-class blades.

*The Craft of the Japanese Sword, by Leon & Hiroko Kapp, Yoshindo Yoshihara, Kodanska Interantional, Tokyo, Japan, 1990. 167 pp., illus. $34.95.

The first book in English devoted entirely to contemporary sword manufacturing in Japan.

Custom Knifemaking,*55D by Tim McCreight, Stackpole Books, Inc., Harrisburg, PA, 1985. 224 pp., illus. $14.95.

Ten projects from a master craftsman.

The Gun Digest Book of Knifemaking, by Jack Lewis and Roger Combs, DBI Books, Inc., Northbrook, IL, 1989. 256 pp., illus. Paper covers. $14.95.

All the ins and outs from the world of knifemaking in a brand new book.

*The Gun Digest Book of Knives, 4th Edition, by Jack Lewis and Roger Combs, DBI Books, Inc., Northbook, IL, 1992. 256 pp., illus. Paper covers. $15.95.

All new edition covers practically every aspect of the knife world.

How to Make Knives, by Richard W. Barney & Robert W. Loveless, Beinfeld Publ., Inc., No. Hollywood, CA, 1977. 178 pp., illus. $17.95.

A book filled with drawings, illustrations, diagrams, and 500 how-to-do-it photos.

The Japanese Sword, by Kanzan Sato, Kodansha International Ltd. and Shibundo, Tokyo, Japan, 1983. 210 pp., illus. $27.95.

The history and appreciation of the Japanese sword, with a detailed examination of over a dozen of Japan's most revered blades.

Kentucky Knife Traders Manual No. 6, by R.B. Ritchie, Hindman, KY, 1980. 217 pp., illus. Paper covers. $10.00.

Guide for dealers, collectors and traders listing pocket knives and razor values.

Knife and Tomakawk Throwing: The Art of the Experts, by Harry K. McEvoy, Charles E. Tuttle, Rutland, VT, 1989. 150 pp., illus. Soft covers. $7.95.

The first book to employ side-by-side the fascinating art and science of knives and tomahawks.

Knife Throwing a Practical Guide, by Harry K. McEvoy, Charles E. Tuttle Co., Rutland, VT, 1973. 108 pp., illus. Paper covers. $5.00.

If you want to learn to throw a knife this is the "bible."

*Knives '93, 13th Edition, by Ken Warner, DBI Books, Inc., Northbrook, IL, 1992. 288 pp., illus. Paper covers. $15.95.

Covers trends and technology for both custom and factory knives.

Levine's Guide to Knives And Their Values, 2nd Edition, by Bernard Levine, DBI Books, Inc., Northbrook, IL, 1989. 480 pp., illus. Paper covers. $22.95.

An important guide to today's knife values and collecting them.

*Levine's Guide to Knives And Their Values, 3rd Edition, by Bernard Levine, DBI Books, Inc., Northbrook, IL. 480 pp., illus. Paper covers.
(January 1993)

*The Master Bladesmith: Advanced Studies in Steel, by Jim Hrisoulas, Paladin Press, Boulder, CO, 1990. 296 pp., illus. $45.00.

The author reveals the forging secrets that for centuries have been protected by guilds.

Military Swords of Japan 1868-1945, by Richard Fuller and Ron Gregory, Arms and Armour Press, London, England, 1986. 127 pp., illus. $27.50.

A wide-ranging survey of the swords and dirks worn by the armed forces of Japan until the end of World War II.

*On Damascus Steel, by Dr. Leo S. Figiel, Atlantis Arts Press, Atlantis, FL, 1991. 145 pp., illus. $68.00.

The historic, technical and artistic aspects of Oriental and mechanical Damascus. Persian and Indian sword blades, from 1600-1800, which have never been published, are illustrated.

Rice's Trowel Bayonet, reprinted by Ray Riling Arms Books, Co., Phila., PA, 1968. 8 pp., illus. Paper covers. $3.00.

A facsimile reprint of a rare circular originally published by the U.S. government in 1875 for the information of U.S. troops.

The Samurai Sword, by John M. Yumoto, Charles E. Tuttle Co., Rutland, VT, 1958. 191 pp., illus. $12.50.

A must for anyone interested in Japanese blades, and the first book on this subject written in English.

Scottish Swords from the Battlefield at Culloden, by Lord Archibald Campbell, The Mowbray Co., Providence, RI, 1973. 63 pp., illus. $15.00.

A modern reprint of an exceedingly rare 1894 privately printed edition.

Secrets of the Samurai, by Oscar Ratti and Adele Westbrook, Charles E. Tuttle Co., Rutland, VT, 1983. 483 pp., illus. $35.00.

A survey of the martial arts of feudal Japan.

Survival/Fighting Knives, by Leroy Thompson, Paladin Press, Boulder, CO, 1986. 104 pp., illus. Paper covers. $14.00.

Covers utility blades, hollow-handled survival knives—both commercial and custom-made—survival kits, folders, combat and street-fighting knives, and knife specs and evaluations.

Switchblade: The Ace of Blades, by Ragnar Benson, Paladin Press, Boulder, Co, 1989. 104 pp., illus. Soft covers. $10.00.

Types of switchblades and their operating mechanisms; how to use switchblade, butterfly, and gravity knives; unusual collector's models; federal and state laws.

Sword of the Samurai, by George R. Parulski, Jr., Paladin Press, Boulder, CO, 1985. 144 pp., illus. $34.95.

The classical art of Japanese swordsmanship.

Swords for the Highland Regiments 1757-1784, by Anthony D. Darling, Andrew Mowbray, Inc., Publisher, Lincoln, RI, 1988. 62 pp., illus. $18.00.

The basket-hilted swords used by private highland regiments in the 18th century British army.

Swords from Public Collections in the Commonwealth of Pennsylvania, edited by Bruce S. Bazelon, Andrew Mowbray Inc., Lincoln, RI, 1987. 127 pp., illus. Paper covers. $12.00.

Contains new information regarding swordmakers of the Philadelphia area.

Swords of Germany 1900/1945, by John R. Angolia, Johnson Reference Books, Fredericksburg, VA, 1990. 460 pp., illus. $37.95.

If you have an interest in edged weapons of Imperial and Nazi Germany, this is a highly recommended book.

*The Scottish Dirk, by James D. Forman, Museum Restoration Service, Bloomfield, Ont., Canada, 1991. 60 pp., illus. Paper covers. $4.95.

More than 100 dirks are illustrated with a text that sets the dirk and Sgian Dubh in their socio-historic content following design changes through more than 300 years of evolution.

*Swords and Blades of the American Revolution, by George C. Neumann, Rebel Publishing Co., Inc., Texarkana, TX, 1991. 288 pp., illus. $35.95.

The encyclopedia of bladed weapons—swords, bayonets, spontoons, halberds, pikes, knives, daggers, axes—used by both sides, on land and sea, in America's struggle for independence.

Tomahawks Illustrated, by Robert Kuck, Robert Kuck, New Knoxville, OH, 1977. 112 pp., illus. Paper covers. $15.00.

A pictorial record to provide a reference in selecting and evaluating tomahawks.

World Bayonets, 1800 to the Present, by Anthony Carter, Sterling Publishing Co., New York, NY, 1990. 72 pp., illus. $24.95.

An incredible bayonet-fancier's buying encyclopedia. Includes buying and selling prices, plus over 250 closeup photos.

GENERAL

Advanced Muzzleloader's Guide, by Toby Bridges, Stoeger Publishing Co., So. Hackensack, NJ, 1985. 256 pp., illus. Paper covers. $14.95.

The complete guide to muzzle-loading rifles, pistols and shotguns—flintlock and percussion.

Air Gun Digest, 2nd Edition, by J.I. Galan, DBI Books, Inc., Northbrook, IL, 1988. 256 pp., illus. Paper covers. $15.95.

Everything from A to Z on air gun history, trends and technology.

The AK47 Story, by Edward Ezell, Stackpole Books, Harrisburg, PA, 1988. 256 pp., illus. $12.95.

Evolution of the Kalashnikov weapons.

American Gunsmiths, by Frank M. Sellers, The Gun Room Press, Highland Park, NJ, 1983. 349 pp. $39.95.

A comprehensive listing of the American gun maker, patentee, gunsmith and entrepreneur.

American and Imported Arms, Ammunition and Shooting Accessories, Catalog No. 18 of the Shooter's Bible, Stoeger, Inc., reprinted by Fayette Arsenal, Fayetteville, NC, 1988. 142 pp., illus. Paper covers. $10.95.

A facsimile reprint of the 1932 Stoeger's Shooter's Bible.

*America's Great Gunmakers, by Wayne van Zwoll, Stoeger Publishing Co., So. Hackensack, NJ, 1992. 288 pp., illus. Paper covers. $16.95.

This book traces in great detail the evolution of guns and ammunition in America and the men who formed the companies that produced them.

Archer's Digest, 5th Edition, edited by Roger Combs, DBI Books, Inc., Northbrook, IL, 1990. 256 pp., illus. Paper covers. $15.95.

Authoritative information on all facets of the archer's sport.

Armed and Female, by Paxton Quigley, E.P. Dutton, New York, NY, 1989. 237 pp., illus. $16.95.

The first complete book on one of the hottest subjects in the media today, the arming of the American woman.

Arms and Equipment of the British Army, 1886, edited by John Walter, Presidio Press, Novato, CA, 1991. $30.00.

Victorian military equipment from the Enfield to the Snider.

*Arsenal of Freedom, The Springfield Armory, 1890-1948: A Year-by-Year Account Drawn from Official Records, compiled and edited by Lt. Col. William S. Brophy, USAR Ret., Andrew Mowbray, Inc., Lincoln, RI, 1991. 400 pp., illus. $36.00.

A "must buy" for all students of American military weapolns, equipment and accoutrements.

Assault Pistols, Rifles and Submachine Guns, by Duncan Long, Paladin Press, Boulder, CO, 1986. 152 pp., illus. Paper covers. $21.95.

A detailed guide to modern military, police and civilian combat weapons, both foreign and domestic.

The Australian Guerilla: Sniping, by Ion L. Idriess, Paladin Press, Boulder, CO, 1989. 104 pp. Paper covers. $8.00.

This classic reprint by Ion Idriess, one of Australia's greatest snipers, covers the art of sniping down to its most esoteric detail.

Be an Expert Shot with Rifle or Shotgun, by Clair Rees, Winchester Press, Piscataway, NJ, 1984. 192 pp., illus. $19.95.

The illustrated self-coaching method that turns shooters into fine marksmen.

Beginner's Guide to Guns and Shooting, Revised Edition, by Clair F. Rees, DBI Books, Inc., Northbrook, IL, 1988. 224 pp., illus. Paper covers. $14.95.

The "how to" book for beginning shooters. The perfect teaching tool for America's youth, the future of our sport, for novices of any age.

*A Bibliography of American Sporting Books, compiled by John C. Phillips, James Cummins, Bookseller, New York, NY, 1991. 650 pp. Edition limited to 250 numbered copies. $75.00.

A reprinting of the very scarce 1930 edition originally published by the Boone & Crockett Club.

Black Powder Loading Manual, Revised Edition, by Sam Fadala, DBI Books, Inc., Northbrook, IL, 1991. 320 pp., illus. Paper covers. $15.95.

Revised and expanded edition of this landmark loading book first published in 1982. Covers 600 loads for 120 of the most popular blackpowder rifles, handguns and shotguns.

*Bows and Arrows of the Native Americans, by Jim Hamm, Lyons & Burford Publishers, New York, NY, 1991. 156 pp., illus. $19.95.

A complete step-by-step guide to wooden bows, sinew-backed bows, composite bows, strings, arrows and quivers.

Cartridges of the World, 6th Edition, by Frank C. Barnes, DBI Books, Inc., Northbrook, IL, 1989. 448 pp., illus. Paper Covers. $19.95.

Completely revised edition of the general purpose reference work for which collectors, police, scientists and laymen reach first for answers to cartridge identification questions.

Civil War Chief of Sharpshooters Hiram Berdan, Military Commander and Firearms Inventor, by Roy M. Marcot, Northwood Heritage Press, Irvine, CA, 1990. 400 pp., illus. $59.95.

Details the life and career of Col. Hiram Berdan and his U.S. Sharpshooters.

Colonial Riflemen in the American Revolution, by Joe D. Huddleston, George Shumway Publisher, York, PA, 1978. 70 pp., illus. $25.00.

This study traces the use of the longrifle in the Revolution for the purpose of evaluating what effects it had on the outcome.

*Combat Ammunition of the 21st Century, by Duncan Long, Paladin Press, Boulder, CO, 1991. 216 pp., illus. Paper covers. $30.00.

An exhaustive evaluation of the stopping power of modern rifle, pistol, shotgun and machine gun rounds based on actual case studies of shooting incidents.

Competitive Shooting, by A.A. Yuryev, introduction by Gary L. Anderson, NRA Books, The National Rifle Assoc. of America, Wash., DC, 1985. 399 pp., illus. $29.95.

A unique encyclopedia of competitive rifle and pistol shooting.

The Complete Black Powder Handbook, Revised Edition, by Sam Fadala, DBI Books, Inc., Northbrook, IL, 1990. 320 pp., illus. Soft covers. $16.95.

Expanded and refreshed edition of the definitive book on the subject of blackpowder.

Complete Book of Shooting: Rifles, Shotguns, Handguns, by Jack O'Connor, Stackpole Books, Harrisburg, PA, 1983. 392 pp., illus. $24.95.

A thorough guide to each area of the sport, appealing to those with a new or ongoing interest in shooting.

The Complete Book of U.S. Sniping, by P.R. Senich, Paladin Press, Boulder, CO, 1988. 280 pp., illus. $39.95.

U.S. sniping material from its infancy to the current sophisticated systems in use today.

The Complete Guide to Game Care and Cookery, Revised Edition, by Sam Fadala, DBI Books, Inc., Northbrook, IL, 1989. 320 pp., illus. Paper covers. $15.95.

Over 500 detailed photos and hundreds of tested recipes anyone can master.

Crossbows, Edited by Roger Combs, DBI Books, Inc., Northbrook, IL, 1986. 192 pp., illus. Paper covers. $13.95.

Complete, up-to-date coverage of the hottest bow going—and the most controversial.

Death from Above: The German FG42 Paratrooper Rifle, by Thomas B. Dugelby and R. Blake Stevens, Collector Grade Publications, Toronto, Canada, 1990. 147 pp., illus. $39.95.

The first comprehensive study of all seven models of the FG42.

The Devil's Paintbrush, by Dolf L. Goldsmith, Collector Grade Publications, Toronto, Canada, 1989. 367 pp., illus. $60.00.

A comprehensive and long overdue treatise on the world's first machine gun and Sir Hiram Maxim's gun.

The Emma Gees, by Herbert W. McBride, Lancer Publications, Mt. Ida, AR, 1988. 218 pp., illus. $18.95.

The author's service with the Machine Gun Section of the 21st Battalion Canadian Expeditionary Force in World War I.

Encyclopedia of Modern Firearms, Vol. 1, compiled and publ. by Bob Brownell, Montezuma, IA, 1959. 1057 pp. plus index, illus. $60.00. Dist. By Bob Brownell, Montezuma, IA 50171.

Massive accumulation of basic information of nearly all modern arms pertaining to "parts and assembly." Replete with arms photographs, exploded drawings, manufacturers' lists of parts, etc.

Firearms Engraving as Decorative Art, by Dr. Fredric A. Harris, Barbara R. Harris, Seattle, WA, 1989. 172 pp., illus. $95.00.

The origin of American firearms engraving motifs in the decorative art of the Middle East. Illustrated with magnificent color photographs.

Firearms for Survival, by Duncan Long, Paladin Press, Boulder, CO, 1988. 144 pp., illus. Paper covers. $16.95.

First complete work on survival firearms for self-defense, hunting, and all-out combat.

Flayderman's Guide to Antique American Firearms...and Their Values, 5th Edition, by Norm Flayderman, DBI Books, Inc., Northbrook, IL, 1990. 624 pp., illus. Soft covers. $27.95.

Updated edition of this bible of the antique gun field.

The Frontier Rifleman, by H.B. LaCrosse Jr., Pioneer Press, Union City, TN, 1989. 183 pp., illus. Soft covers. $14.95.

The Frontier rifleman's clothing and equipment during the era of the American Revolution, 1760-1800.

The Gargantuan Gunsite Gossip, by Jeff Cooper, Gunsite Press, Paulden, AZ, 1990. 702

pp., illus. Paper covers. $25.00.

All the items that appeared in the *Gunsight Newsletter* and in a column in the *Guns & Ammo* magazine is in this book.

***The Gatling Gun: 19th Century Machine Gun to 21st Century Vulcan,** by Joseph Berk, Paladin Press, Boulder, CO, 1991. 136 pp., illus. $29.95.

Here is the fascinating on-going story of a truly timeless weapon, from its beginnings during the Civil War to its current role as a state-of-the-art modern combat system.

The German Sniper, 1914-45, by Peter R. Senich, Paladin Press, Boulder, CO, 1982. 468 pp., illus. $60.00.

The development and application of Germany's sniping weapons systems and tactics traced from WWI through WWII.

Good Friends, Good Guns, Good Whiskey: The Selected Works of Skeeter Skelton, by Skeeter Skelton, PJS Publications, Peoria, IL, 1989. 347 pp. $21.95.

A guidebook to the world of Skeeter Skelton.

Good Guns, by Stephen Bodio, Nick Lyons Books, New York, NY, 1986. 128 pp., illus. $14.95.

A celebration of fine sporting guns.

***Great Shooters of the World,** by Sam Fadala, Stoeger Publishing Co., So. Hackensack, NJ, 1991. 288 pp., illus. Paper covers. $18.95.

This book offers gun enthusiasts an overview of the men and women who have forged the history of firearms over the past 150 years.

Guerrilla Warfare Weapons, by Terry Gander, Sterling Publishing Co., Inc., 1990. 128 pp., illus. Paper covers. $9.95.

The latest and deadliest sophisticated armaments of the modern underground fighter's armory.

***Gun Digest, 1993, 47th Edition,** edited by Ken Warner, DBI Books, Inc., Northbrook, IL, 1992. 528 pp., illus. Paper Covers. $19.95.

The latest edition of "The World's Greatest Gun Book."

The Gun Digest Book of Assault Weapons, 2nd Edition, edited by Jack Lewis, DBI Books, Inc., Northbrook, IL, 1989. 256 pp., illus. Paper covers. $15.95.

An in-depth look at the history and uses of these arms.

***The Gun Digest Book of Assault Weapons, 3rd Edition,** edited by Jack Lewis, DBI Books, Inc., Northbrook, IL. 256 pp., illus. Paper covers.

(April 1993)

*** The Gun Digest Book of Combat Handgunnery, 3rd Edition,** by Chuck Karwan, DBI Books, Inc., Northbrook, IL, 1992. 256 pp., illus. Paper covers. $15.95.

This all-new edition looks at real world combat handgunnery from three different perspectives–military, police and civilian.

The Gun Digest Book of Metallic Silhouette Shooting, 2nd Edition, by Elgin Gates, DBI Books, Inc., Northbrook, IL, 1988. 256 pp., illus. Paper covers. $15.95.

Examines all aspects of this fast growing sport including history, rules and meets.

The Gun Digest Book of Modern Gun Values, 8th Edition, by Jack Lewis, DBI Books, Inc., Northbrook, IL, 1991. 528 pp., illus. Paper covers. $19.95.

Updated and expanded edition of the book that's become the standard for valuing modern firearms.

***The Gun Digest Book of Modern Gun Values, 9th Edition,** by Jack Lewis, DBI Books, Inc., Northbrook, IL. 528 pp., illus. Paper covers.

(February 1993)

***Gunshot Injuries: How They Are Inflicted, Their Complications and Treatment,** by Col. Louis A. La Garde, 2nd revised edition, Lancer Militaria, Mt. Ida, AR, 1991. 480 pp., illus. $34.95.

A classic work which was the standard textbook on the subject at the time of World War I.

***Guns Illustrated, 1993, 25th Edition,** edited by Harold A. Murtz, DBI Books, Inc., Northbrook, IL, 1992. 320 pp., illus. Paper covers. $17.95.

The latest edition of this much acclaimed annual.

***Guns of the Empire,** by George Markham, Arms & Armour Press, London, England, 1991. 160 pp., illus. $29.95

The firearms that carved out the worldwide British Empire come together in a riveting display of handguns, rifles, and automatics.

***Guns of the Wild West,** by George Markham, Arms & Armour Press, London, England, 1991. 160 pp., illus. $19.95.

The handguns, longarms and shotguns of the Gold Rush, the American Civil War, and the Armed Forces.

Gun Talk, edited by Dave Moreton, Winchester Press, Piscataway, NJ, 1973. 256 pp., illus. $9.95.

A treasury of original writing by the top gun writers and editors in America. Practical advice about every aspect of the shooting sports.

The Gun That Made the Twenties Roar, by Wm. J. Helmer, rev. and enlarged by George C. Nonte, Jr., The Gun Room Press, Highland Park, NJ, 1977. Over 300 pp., illus. $21.95.

Historical account of John T. Thompson and his invention, the infamous "Tommy Gun."

The Gunfighter, Man or Myth? by Joseph G. Rosa, Oklahoma Press, Norman, OK, 1969. 229 pp., illus. (including weapons). Paper covers. $11.95.

A well-documented work on gunfights and gunfighters of the West and elsewhere. Great treat for all gunfighter buffs.

The Gunfighters, by Dale T. Schoenberger, The Caxton Printers, Ltd., Caldwell, ID, 1971. 207 pp., illus. $18.95.

Startling expose of our foremost Western folk heroes.

Gunproof Your Children/Handgun Primer, by Massad Ayoob, Police Bookshelf, Concord, NH, 1989. Paper covers. $4.95.

Two books in one. The first, keeping children safe from unauthorized guns in their hands; the second, a compact introduction to handgun safety.

Guns & Shooting: A Selected Bibliography, by Ray Riling, Ray Riling Arms Books Co., Phila., PA, 1982. 434 pp., illus. Limited, numbered edition. $75.

A limited edition of this superb bibliographical work, the only modern listing of books devoted to guns and shooting.

Guns and Shooting Yearbook 1990, edited by Jim Carmichel, Stackpole Books, Harrisburg, PA, 1990. 190 pp., illus. $19.95.

A compilation of the best and most informative articles written on guns and shooting during the preceding year, selected from numerous magazines.

Guns, Loads, and Hunting Tips, by Bob Hagel, Wolfe Publishing Co., Prescott, AZ, 1986. 509 pp., illus. $19.95.

A large hardcover book literally packed with shooting, hunting and handloading wisdom.

Guns of the Elite, by George Markham, Arms and Armour Press, Poole, England, 1987. 184 pp., illus. $24.95.

Special Forces firearms, 1940 to the present.

Guns of the First World War, Rifle, Handguns and Ammunition from the Text Book of Small Arms, 1909, edited by John Walter, Presidio Press, Novato, CA, 1991. $30.00.

Here are the details of the Austro-Hungarian Mannlichers, French Lebels, German Mausers, U.S. Springfields, etc.

Guns of the Reich, by George Markham, Arms & Armour Press, London, England, 1989. 175 pp., illus. $24.95.

The pistols, rifles, submachine guns, machineguns and support weapons of the German armed forces, 1939-1945.

Gunshot Wounds, by Vincent J.M. DiMaio, M.D., Elsevier Science Publishing Co., New York, NY, 1985. 331 pp., illus. $70.00.

Practical aspects of firearms, ballistics, and forensic techniques.

"Hell, I Was There!," by Elmer Keith, Petersen Publishing Co., Los Angeles, CA, 1979. 308 pp., illus. $24.95.

Adventures of a Montana cowboy who gained world fame as a big game hunter.

Hidden Threat, a Guide to Covert Weapons, by Mark Smith, Paladin Press, Boulder, CO, 1989. 168 pp., illus. Soft covers. $12.00.

Intended for use by law enforcement personnel to enhance their knowledge and security when searching subjects, vehicles or premises; provides a fascinating glimpse into the darker side of police work.

***Jim Dougherty's Guide to Bowhunting Deer,** by Jim Dougherty, DBI Books, Inc., Northbrook, IL, 1992. 256 pp., illus. Paper covers. $15.95

Dougherty sets down some important guidelines for bowhunting and bowhunting equipment.

Kill or Get Killed, by Col. Rex Applegate, new rev. and enlarged ed. Paladin Press, Boulder, CO, 1976. 421 pp., illus. $29.95.

For police and military forces. Last word on mob control.

The Last Book: Confessions of a Gun Editor, by Jack O'Connor, Amwell Press, Clinton, NJ, 1984. 247 pp., illus. $30.00.

Jack's last book. Semi-autobiographical.

The Law Enforcement Book of Weapons, Ammunition and Training Procedures, Handguns, Rifles and Shotguns, by Mason Williams, Charles C. Thomas, Publisher, Springfield, IL, 1977. 496 pp., illus. $135.00.

Data on firearms, firearm training, and ballistics.

The Lewis Gun, by J. David Truby, Paladin Press, Boulder, CO, 1988. 206 pp., illus. $39.95.

The development and employment of this much loved and trusted weapon throughout the early decades of this century.

Machine Guns, a Pictorial, Tactical & Practical History, by Jim Thompson, Paladin Press, Boulder, CO, 1989. 248 pp., illus. $49.95.

The historical development of each weapon, useful information on how it shoots and exhaustive advice on ammunition, combined with the rules and regulations governing machinegun ownership in this country.

The Manufacture of Gunflints, by Sydney B.J. Skertchly, facsimile reprint with new introduction by Seymour de Lotbiniere, Museum Restoration Service, Ontario, Canada, 1984. 90 pp., illus. $24.50.

Limited edition reprinting of the very scarce London edition of 1879.

Master Tips, by J. Winokur, Potshot Press, Pacific Palisades, CA, 1985. 96 pp., illus. Paper covers. $11.95.

Basics of practical shooting.

Meditations on Hunting, by Jose Ortega y Gasset, Charles Scribner's Sons, New York, NY, 1985. 132 pp. Paper covers. $9.95.

Anticipates with profound accuracy the direction and basic formations of discipline which does not yet exist, a true ecology of men. A new printing of this 1942 classic.

Military Rifle & Machine Gun Cartridges, by Jean Huon, Paladin Press, Boulder, CO, 1990. 392 pp., illus. $34.95.

Describes the primary types of military cartridges and their principal loadings, as well as their characteristics, origin and use.

Military Small Arms of the 20th Century, 6th Edition, by Ian V. Hogg, DBI Books, Inc., Northbrook, IL, 1991. 352 pp., illus. Paper covers. $18.95.

Fully revised and updated edition of the standard reference in its field.

Modern Law Enforcement Weapons & Tactics, 2nd Edition, by Tom Ferguson, DBI Books, Inc., Northbrook, IL, 1991. 256 pp., illus. Paper covers. $16.95.

An in-depth look at weapons and equipment used by law enforcement agencies of today.

Modern Sporting Guns, by Jan Stevensen, Outlet Books, New York, NY, 1988. 208 pp., illus. $14.98.

Complete guide to target and sporting weapons. Illustrated with cutaway drawings, detailed diagrams and full-color plates.

***The More Complete Cannoneer,** by M.C. Switlik, Museum & Collectors Specialties Co., Monroe, MI, 1990. 199 pp., illus. $19.95.

Compiled agreeably to the regulations for the U.S. War Department, 1861, and containing current observations on the use of antique cannon.

No Second Place Winner, by Wm. H. Jordan, publ. by the author, Shreveport, LA (Box 4072), 1962. 114 pp., illus. $15.95.

Guns and gear of the peace officer, ably discussed by a U.S. Border Patrolman for over 30 years, and a first-class shooter with handgun, rifle, etc.

NRA Firearms Fact Book, by the editors of NRA, National Rifle Association, Wash., DC, 1991. 330 pp., illus. Paper covers. $10.95.

The second, revised edition of the classic *NRA Firearms and Ammunition Fact Book.* Covers gun collecting, firearms safety, ballistics and general references.

Outdoor Life Gun Data Book, by F. Philip Rice, Outdoor Life Books, New York, NY, 1987. 412 pp., illus. $27.95.

All the facts and figures that hunters, marksmen, handloaders and other gun enthusiasts need to know.

The Police Sniper, by Burt Rapp, Paladin Press, Boulder, CO, 1989. 200 pp., illus. Paper covers. $14.95.

An all-new work that covers this specialized topic unlike any other book.

E.C. Prudhomme, Master Gun Engraver, A Retrospective Exhibition: 1946-1973, intro. by John T. Amber, The R. W. Norton Art Gallery, Shreveport, LA, 1973. 32 pp., illus. Paper covers. $5.00.

Examples of master gun engravings by Jack Prudhomme.

A Rifleman Went to War, by H. W. McBride, Lancer Militaria, Mt. Ida, AR, 1987. 398 pp., illus. $19.95.

The classic account of practical marksmanship on the battlefields of World War I.

***Second to None,** edited by John Culler and Chuck Wechsler, Live Oak Press, Inc., Camden, SC, 1988. 227 pp., illus. $39.95.

The most popular articles to appear in *Sporting Classics* magazine on great sporting firearms.

Shooter's Bible, 1940, Stoeger Arms Corp., Stoeger, Inc., So. Hackensack, NJ, 1990. 512

pp., illus. Soft covers. $16.95.
Reprint of the Stoeger Arms Corp. catalog No. 33 of 1940.

***Shooter's Bible 1993, No. 84,** edited by William S. Jarrett, Stoeger Publishing Co., So. Hackensack, NJ, 1992. 576 pp., illus. Paper covers. $19.95.
Latest edition of the world's standard firearms reference book.

Shooting, by Edward A. Matunas, Stackpole Books, Harrisburg, PA, 1986. 416 pp., illus. $31.95.
How to become an expert marksman with rifle, shotgun, handgun, muzzle loader and bow.

***Shots Fired in Anger,** by Lt. Col. John George, The National Rifle Association of America, Washington, D.C., 2nd printing, 1991. 535 pp., illus. $19.95.
A rifleman's view of the war in the Pacific, 1942-45.

Small Arms Today, 2nd Edition, by Edward C. Ezell, Stackpole Books, Harrisburg, PA, 1988. 479 pp., illus. Paper covers. $19.95.
Latest reports on the world's weapons and ammunition.

The SPIW: Deadliest Weapon that Never Was, by R. Blake Stevens, and Edward C. Ezell, Collector Grade Publications, Inc., Toronto, Canada, 1985. 138 pp., illus. $29.95.
The complete saga of the fantastic flechette-firing Special Purpose Individual Weapon.

Steindler's New Firearms Dictionary, by R.A. Steindler, Stackpole Books, Inc., Harrisburg, PA, 1985. 320 pp., illus. $24.95.
Completely revised and updated edition of this standard work.

The Street Smart Gun Book, by John Farnam, Police Bookshelf, Concord, NH, 1986. 45 pp., illus. Paper covers. $11.95.
Weapon selection, defensive shooting techniques, and gunfight-winning tactics from one of the world's leading authorities.

Stress Fire, Vol. 1: Stress Fighting for Police, by Massad Ayoob, Police Bookshelf, Concord, NH, 1984. 149 pp., illus. Paper covers. $9.95.
Gunfighting for police, advanced tactics and techniques.

The Terrifying Three-Uzi, Ingram and Intratec Weapons Families, by Duncan Long, Paladin Press, Boulder, CO, 1989. 136 pp., illus. Soft covers. $20.00.
Discover everything you wanted to know about submachine guns in general, and the "terrifying three" in particular, including specifications for the models and their variants.

Thompson Guns 1921-1945, Anubis Press, Houston, TX, 1980. 215 pp., illus. Paper covers. $11.95.
Facsimile reprinting of five complete manuals on the Thompson submachine gun.

To Ride, Shoot Straight, and Speak the Truth, by Jeff Cooper, Paladin Press, Boulder, CO, 1988. 384 pp., illus. $26.00.
Cooper, a combat pistol shooting master and the nation's foremost instructor of defensive weaponcraft, squarely faces the facts of modern life and concludes that the armed citizen is the correct answer to the armed sociopath.

The Trappers Handbook, by Rick Jamison, DBI Books, Inc., Northbrook, IL, 1983. 224 pp., illus. Paper covers. $13.95.
Gives the ins and outs of successful trapping from making scent to marketing the pelts. Tips and solutions to trapping problems.

A Treasury of Modern Small Arms, by Jacob Burk, Gallery Books, New York, NY, 1988. 192 pp., illus. $17.95.
A carefully detailed volume with over 200 clear, close-up photos of the best-loved small arms in the world today.

A Treasury of Outdoor Life, edited by William E. Rae, Stackpole Books, Harrisburg, PA, 1983. 520 pp., illus. $24.95.
The greatest hunting, fishing, and survival stories from America's favorite sportman's magazine.

Triggernometry, by Eugene Cunningham, Caxton Printers Ltd., Caldwell, ID, 1970. 441 pp., illus. $17.95.
A classic study of famous outlaws and lawmen of the West—their stature as human beings, their exploits and skills in handling firearms. A reprint.

***U.S. Marine Corp Rifle and Pistol Marksmanship, 1935,** reprinting of a government publication, Lancer Militaria, Mt. Ida, AR, 1991. 99 pp., illus. Paper covers. $11.95.
The old corps method of precision shooting.

U.S. Marine Corps Scout/Sniper Training Manual, Lancer Militaria, Mt. Ida, AR, 1989. Soft covers. $14.95.
Reprint of the original sniper training manual used by the Marksmanship Training Unit of the Marine Corps Development and Education Command in Quantico, Virginia.

U.S. Marine Corps Sniping, Lancer Militaria, Mt. Ida, AR, 1989. Irregular pagination. Soft covers. $14.95.
A reprint of the official Marine Corps FMFM1-3B.

Unrepentant Sinner, by Charles Askins, Tejano Publications, San Antonio, TX, 1985. 322 pp., illus. Soft covers. $17.95.
The autobiography of Colonel Charles Askins.

Vietnam Weapons Handbook, by David Rosser-Owen, Patrick Stephens, Wellingborough, England, 1986. 136 pp., illus. Paper covers. $9.95.
Covers every weapon used by both sides.

Warsaw Pact Weapons Handbook, by Jacques F. Baud, Paladin Press, Boulder, CO, 1989. 168 pp., illus. Soft covers. $20.00.
The most complete handbook on weapons found behind the Iron Curtain.

Weapons of the Waffen-SS, by Bruce Quarrie, Sterling Publishing Co., Inc., 1991. 168 pp., illus. $24.95.
An in-depth look at the weapons that made Hitler's Waffen-SS the fearsome fighting machine it was.

The Winchester Era, by David Madis, Art & Reference House, Brownsville, TX, 1984. 100 pp., illus. $14.95.
Story of the Winchester company, management, employees, etc.

With British Snipers to the Reich, by Capt. C. Shore, Lander Militaria, Mt. Ida, AR, 1988. 420 pp., illus. $24.95.
One of the greatest books ever written on the art of combat sniping.

You Can't Miss, by John Shaw and Michael Bane, John Shaw, Memphis, TN, 1983. 152 pp., illus. Paper covers. $12.95.
The secrets of a successful combat shooter; how to better defensive shooting skills.

GUNSMITHING

The Art of Engraving, by James B. Meek, F. Brownell & Son, Montezuma, IA, 1973. 196 pp., illus. $33.95.
A complete, authoritative, imaginative and detailed study in training for gun engraving. The first book of its kind—and a great one.

Artistry in Arms, The R. W. Norton Gallery, Shreveport, LA, 1970. 42 pp., illus. Paper covers. $5.00.
The art of gunsmithing and engraving.

***Barrels & Actions,** by Harold Hoffman, H&P Publishers, San Angelo, TX, 1990. 309 pp., illus. Sprial bound. $24.95.
A manual on barrel making.

Checkering and Carving of Gun Stocks, by Monte Kennedy, Stackpole Books, Harrisburg, PA, 1962. 175 pp., illus. $34.95.
Revised, enlarged cloth-bound edition of a much sought-after, dependable work.

The Colt .45 Automatic Shop Manual, by Jerry Kuhnhausen, VSP Publishers, McCall, ID, 1987. 200 pp., illus. Paper covers. $19.95.
Covers repairing, accurizing, trigger/sear work, action tuning, springs, bushings, rebarreling, and custom .45 modification.

The Colt Double Action Revolvers: A Shop Manual, Volume 1, by Jerry Kuhnhausen, VSP Publishers, McCall, ID, 1988. 224 pp., illus. Paper covers. $22.95.
Covers D, E, and I frames.

The Colt Double Action Revolvers: A Shop Manual, Volume 2, by Jerry Kuhnhausen, VSP Publishers, McCall, ID, 1988. 156 pp., illus. Paper covers. $17.95.
Covers J, V, and AA models.

The Complete Rehabilitation of the Flintlock Rifle and Other Works, by T.B. Tyron, Limbo Library, Taos, NM, 1972. 112 pp., illus. Paper covers. $6.95.
A series of articles which first appeared in various issues of the "American Rifleman" in the 1930s.

Do-It-Yourself Gunsmithing, by Jim Carmichel, Outdoor Life-Harper & Row, New York, NY, 1977. 371 pp., illus. $16.95.
The author proves that home gunsmithing is relatively easy and highly satisfying.

Firearms Assembly 3: The NRA Guide to Rifle and Shotguns, NRA Books, Wash., DC, 1980. 264 pp., illus. Paper covers. $11.50.
Text and illustrations explaining the takedown of 125 rifles and shotguns, domestic and foreign.

Firearms Assembly 4: The NRA Guide to Pistols and Revolvers, NRA Books, Wash., DC, 1980. 253 pp., illus. Paper covers. $11.50.
Text and illustrations explaining the takedown of 124 pistol and revolver models, domestic and foreign.

Firearms Bluing and Browning, By R.H. Angier, Stackpole Books, Harrisburg, PA. 151 pp., illus. $14.95.
A world master gunsmith reveals his secrets of building, repairing and renewing a gun, quite literally, lock, stock and barrel. A useful, concise text on chemical coloring methods for the gunsmith and mechanic.

First Book of Gunsmithing, by John E. Traister, Stackpole Books, Harrisburg, PA, 1981. 192 pp., illus. $18.95.
Beginner's guide to gun care, repair and modification.

The Gun Digest Book of Exploded Firearms Drawings, 3rd Edition, edited by Harold A. Murtz, DBI Books, Inc., Northbrook, IL, 1990. 480 pp., illus. Paper covers. $16.95.
Back by popular demand, includes 470 exploded or isometric drawings for over 400 firearms.

***The Gun Digest Book of Exploded Handgun Drawings,** edited by Harold A. Murtz, DBI Books, Inc., Northbrook, Il, 1992. 512 pp., illus. Paper covers. $19.95.
Exploded or isometric drawings for 494 of the most popular handguns.

***The Gun Digest Book of Exploded Long Gun Drawings,** edited by Harold A. Murtz, DBI Books, Inc., Northbrook, IL. 512 pp., illus. Paper covers.
(February 1993)

The Gun Digest Book of Firearms Assembly/Disassembly, Part I: Automatic Pistols, Revised Edition, by J.B. Wood, DBI Books, Inc., Northbrook, IL, 1990. 480 pp., illus. Soft covers. $17.95.
Covers 58 popular autoloading pistols plus nearly 200 variants of those models integrated into the text and completely cross-referenced in the index.

The Gun Digest Book of Firearms Assembly/Disassembly Part II: Revolvers, Revised Edition, by J.B. Wood, DBI Books, Inc., Northbrook, IL, 1990. 480 pp., illus. Soft covers. $17.95.
Covers 49 popular revolvers plus 130 variants. The most comprehensive and professional presentation available to either hobbyist or gunsmith.

The Gun Digest Book of Firearms Assembly/Disassembly Part III: Rimfire Rifles, by J. B. Wood, DBI Books, Inc., Northbrook, IL, 1980. 288 pp., illus. Paper covers. $14.95.
A most comprehensive, uniform, and professional presentation available for disassembling and reassembling most rimfire rifles.

The Gun Digest Book of Firearms Assembly/Disassembly Part IV: Centerfire Rifles, Revised Edition, by J.B. Wood, DBI Books, Inc., Northbrook, IL, 1991. 480 pp., illus. Paper covers. $17.95.
Covers 54 popular centerfire rifles plus 300 variants. The most comprehensive and professional presentation available to either hobbyist or gunsmith.

***The Gun Digest Book of Firearms Assembly/Disassembly, Part V: Shotguns, Revised Edition** by J.B. Wood, DBI Books, Inc., Northbrook, IL, 1992. 480 pp., illus. Paper covers. $17.95.
Covers 46 popular shotguns plus over 250 variants. The most comprehensive and professional presentation available to either hobbyist or gunsmith.

The Gun Digest Book of Firearms Assembly/Disassembly Part VI: Law Enforcement Weapons, by J.B. Wood, DBI Books, Inc., Northbrook, IL, 1981. 288 pp., illus. Paper covers. $14.95.
Step-by-step instructions on how to completely dismantle and reassemble the most commonly used firearms found in law enforcement arsenals.

***The Gun Digest Book of Pistolsmithing, 2nd Edition** by Paul Hantke, DBI Books, Inc., Northbrook, IL, 1992. 256 pp., illus. Paper covers. $15.95.
An expert's guide to the operation of each of the handgun actions with all the major functions of pistolsmithing explained.

The Gun Digest Book of Riflesmithing, by Jack Mitchell, DBI Books, Inc., Northbrook, IL, 1982. 256 pp., illus. Paper covers. $14.95.
The art and science of rifle gunsmithing. Covers tools, techniques, designs, finishing wood and metal, custom alterations.

The Gun Digest Book of Shotgun Gunsmithing, by Ralph Walker, DBI Books, Inc., Northbrook, IL, 1983. 256 pp., illus. Paper covers. $14.95.
The principles and practices of repairing, individualizing and accurizing modern shotguns by one of the world's premier shotgun gunsmiths.

Gun Owner's Book of Care, Repair & Improvement, by Roy Dunlap, Outdoor Life-Harper & Row, NY, 1977. 336 pp., illus. $12.95.
A basic guide to repair and maintenance of guns, written for the average firearms owner.

Guns and Gunmaking Tools of Southern Appalachia, by John Rice Irwin, Schiffer Publishing Ltd., 1983. 118 pp., illus. Paper covers. $9.95.

The story of the Kentucky rifle.

Gunsmith Kinks, by F.R. (Bob) Brownell, F. Brownell & Son, Montezuma, IA, 1st ed., 1969. 496 pp., well illus. $18.95.

A widely useful accumulation of shop kinks, short cuts, techniques and pertinent comments by practicing gunsmiths from all over the world.

Gunsmith Kinks 2, by Bob Brownell, F. Brownell & Son, Publishers, Montezuma, IA, 1983. 496 pp., illus. $18.95.

An incredible collection of gunsmithing knowledge, shop kinks, new and old techniques, shortcuts and general know-how straight from those who do them best—the gunsmiths.

Gunsmithing, by Roy F. Dunlap, Stackpole Books, Harrisburg, PA, 1990. 742 pp., illus. $29.95.

A manual of firearm design, construction, alteration and remodeling. For amateur and professional gunsmiths and users of modern firearms.

Gunsmithing at Home, by John E. Traister, Stoeger Publishing Co., So. Hackensack, NJ, 1985. 256 pp., illus. Paper covers. $14.95.

Over 25 chapters of explicit information on every aspect of gunsmithing.

Gunsmithing With Simple Hand Tools, by Andrew Dubino, Stackpole Books, Harrisburg, PA, 1987. 205 pp., illus. $19.95.

How to repair, improve, and add a touch of class to the guns you own.

The Gunsmith's Manual, by J.P. Stelle and Wm. B. Harrison, The Gun Room Press, Highland Park, NJ, 1982. 376 pp., illus. $19.95.

For the gunsmith in all branches of the trade.

How to Build Your Own Flintlock Rifle or Pistol, by George Lauber, The John Olson Co., Paramus, NJ, 1976. Paper covers. $12.50.

The second in Mr. Lauber's three-volume series on the art and science of building muzzle-loading blackpowder firearms.

***The Mauser M91 Through M98 Bolt Actions: A Shop Manual,** by Jerry Kuhnhausen, VSP Books, McCall, ID, 1991. 224 pp., illus. Paper covers. $22.95.

An essential book if you work on or plan to work on a Mauser action.

The NRA Gunsmithing Guide—Updated, by Ken Raynor and Brad Fenton, National Rifle Association, Wash., DC, 1984. 336 pp., illus. Paper covers. $15.95.

Material includes chapters and articles on all facets of the gunsmithing art.

Pistolsmithing, by George C. Nonte, Jr., Stackpole Books, Harrisburg, PA, 1974. 560 pp., illus. $29.95.

A single source reference to handgun maintenance, repair, and modification at home, unequaled in value.

Practical Gunsmithing, by Edward A. Matunas, Stackpole Books, Harrisburg, PA, 1989. 352 pp., illus. $31.95.

A complete guide to maintaining, repairing, and improving firearms.

Recreating the American Longrifle, by William Buchele, et al., George Shumway, Publisher, York, PA, 1983. 175 pp., illus. Paper covers. $20.00.

Includes full-scale plans for building a Kentucky rifle.

Respectfully Yours H.M. Pope, compiled and edited by G.O. Kelver, Brighton, CO, 1976. 266 pp., illus. $19.00.

A compilation of letters from the files of the famous barrelmaker, Harry M. Pope.

Ruger Double Action Revolvers, Vol. 1, Shop Manual, by Jerry Kuhnhausen, VSP Publishers, McCall, ID, 1989. 176 pp., illus. Soft covers. $18.95.

Covers the Ruger Six series of revolvers: Security-Six, Service-Six, and Speed-Six. Includes step-by-step function checks, disassembly, inspection, repairs, rebuilding, reassembly, and custom work.

The S&W Revolver: A Shop Manual, by Jerry Kuhnhausen, VSP Publishers, McCall, ID, 1987. 152 pp., illus. Paper covers. $17.95.

Covers accurizing, trigger jobs, action tuning, rebarreling, barrel setback, forcing cone angles, polishing and rebluing.

Survival Gunsmithing, by J.B. Wood, Desert Publications, Cornville, AZ, 1986. 92 pp., illus. Paper covers. $9.95.

A guide to repair and maintenance of many of the most popular rifles, shotguns and handguns.

The Trade Gun Sketchbook, by Charles E. Hanson, The Fur Press, Chadron, NE, 1979. 48 pp., illus. Paper covers. $4.00.

Complete full-size plans to build seven different trade guns from the Revolution to the Indian Wars and a two-thirds size for your son.

The Trade Rifle Sketchbook, by Charles E. Hanson, The Fur Press, Chadron, NE, 1979. 48 pp., illus. Paper covers. $4.00.

Includes full-scale plans for 10 rifles made for Indian and mountain men; from 1790 to 1860, plus plans for building three pistols.

HANDGUNS

American Police Handgun Training, by Charles R. Skillen and Mason Williams, Charles C. Thomas, Springfield, IL, 1980. 216 pp., illus. $50.00.

Deals comprehensively with all phases of current handgun training procedures in America.

Askins on Pistols and Revolvers, by Col. Charles Askins, NRA Books, Wash., DC, 1980. 144 pp., illus. Paper covers. $14.95.

A book full of practical advice, shooting tips, technical analysis and stories of guns in action.

Automatics, Fast Firepower, Tactical Superiority, by Duncan Long, Paladin Press, Boulder, CO, 1986. 136 pp., illus. Paper covers. $18.00.

The pluses and minuses of dozens of automatic pistols are presented. Field stripping procedures for various pistol models are given.

Blue Steel and Gun Leather, by John Bianchi, Beinfeld Publishing, Inc., No. Hollywood, CA, 1978. 200 pp., illus. $14.95.

A complete and comprehensive review of holster uses plus an examination of available products on today's market.

Browning Hi-Power Pistols, Desert Publications, Cornville, AZ, 1982. 20 pp., illus. Paper covers. $9.00.

Covers all facets of the various military and civilian models of the Browning Hi-Power pistol.

***Business Partners: The Best Pistol/Ammo Combination for Personal Defense,** by Peter Alan Kasler, Paladin Press, Boulder, CO, 1991. 200 pp., illus. Paper covers. $22.95.

A no-nonsense critique of the wounding capabilities of handguns and ammunition designed for "business" situations.

Colt Automatic Pistols, by Donald B. Bady, Borden Publ. Co., Alhambra, CA, 1974, 368 pp., illus. $19.95.

The rev. and enlarged ed. of a key work on a fascinating subject. Complete information on every automatic marked with Colt's name.

The Colt .45 Auto Pistol, compiled from U.S. War Dept. Technical Manuals, and reprinted by Desert Publications, Cornville, AZ, 1978. 80 pp., illus. Paper covers. $9.95.

Covers every facet of this famous pistol from mechanical training, manual of arms, disassembly, repair and replacement of parts.

The Combat .45 Automatic, by Bill Wilson, Wilson's Gun Shop, Tampa, FL, 1988. 241 pp., illus. Soft covers. $14.95.

A guide to purchasing, modifying and using the .45 automatic.

***Combat Handgun Shooting,** by James D. Mason, Charles C. Thomas Publisher, Springfield, IL, 1990. 280 pp., illus. $47.00.

The most detailed and exciting book on this sport to date.

Combat Pistols, by Terry Gander, Sterling Publishing Co., Inc., 1991. Paper covers. $9.95.

The world's finest and deadliest pistols are shown close-up, with detailed specifications, muzzle velocity, rate of fire, ammunition, etc.

Combat Revolvers: The Best (and Worst) Modern Wheelguns, by Duncan Long, Paladin Press, Boulder, CO, 1989. 115 pp., illus. Soft covers. $18.95.

A no-holds-barred look at the best and worst combat revolvers available today.

The Complete Book of Combat Handgunning, by Chuck Taylor, Desert Publications, Cornville, AZ, 1982. 168 pp., illus. Paper covers. $16.95.

Covers virtually every aspect of combat handgunning.

Competitive Pistol Shooting, by Laslo Antal, A&C Black, Cambs, England, 1989. 176 pp., illus. Soft covers. $17.50.

Covers free pistol, air pistol, rapid fire, etc.

The CZ-75 Family: The Ultimate Combat Handgun, by J.M. Ramos, Paladin Press, Boulder, CO, 1990. 100 pp., illus. Soft covers. $16.00.

And in-depth discussion of the early-and-late model CZ-75s, as well as the many newest additions to the Czech pistol family.

Experiments of a Handgunner, by Walter Roper, Wolfe Publishing Co., Prescott, AZ, 1989. 202 pp., illus. $37.00.

A limited edition reprint. A listing of experiments with functioning parts of handguns, with targets, stocks, rests, handloading, etc.

Fast and Fancy Revolver Shooting, by Ed. McGivern, Anniversary Edition, Winchester Press, Piscataway, NJ, 1984. 484 pp., illus. $17.95.

A fascinating volume, packed with handgun lore and solid information by the acknowledged dean of revolver shooters.

***.45 ACP Super Guns,** by J.M. Ramos, Paladin Press, Boulder, CO, 1991. 144 pp., illus. Paper covers. $20.00.

Modified .45 automatic pistols for competition, hunting and personal defense.

***The Gun Digest Book of Combat Handgunnery, 3nd Edition,** by Chuck Karwan, DBI Books, Inc., Northbrook, IL, 1992. 256 pp., illus. Paper covers. $15.95.

This all-new edition looks at real world combat handgunnery from three different perspectives—military, police and civilian.

The Gun Digest Book of Firearms Assembly/Disassembly, Part I: Automatic Pistols, Revised Edition, by J.B. Wood, DBI Books, Inc., Northbrook, IL, 1990. 480 pp., illus. Soft covers. $17.95.

Covers 58 popular autoloading pistols plus nearly 200 variants of those models integrated into the text and completely cross-referenced in the index.

The Gun Digest Book of Firearms Assembly/Disassembly Part II: Revolvers, Revised Edition, by J.B. Wood, DBI Books, Inc., Northbrook, IL, 1990. 480 pp., illus. Soft covers. $17.95.

Covers 49 popular revolvers plus 130 variants. The most comprehensive and professional presentation available to either hobbyist or gunsmith.

The Gun Digest Book of Handgun Reloading, by Dean A. Grennell and Wiley M. Clapp, DBI Books, Inc., Northbrook, IL, 1987. 256 pp., illus. Paper covers. $15.95.

Detailed discussions of all aspects of reloading for handguns, from basic to complex. New loading data.

The Gun Digest Book of Metallic Silhouette Shooting, 2nd Edition, by Elgin Gates, DBI Books, Inc., Northbrook, IL, 1988. 256 pp., illus. Paper covers. $15.95.

All about the rapidly growing sport. With a history and rules of the International Handgun Metallic Silhouette Association.

The Gun Digest Book of 9mm Handguns, by Dean A. Grennell and Wiley Clapp, DBI Books, Inc., Northbrook, IL, 1986. 256 pp., illus. Paper covers. $15.95.

The definitive book on the 9mmP pistol.

***The Gun Digest Book of Pistolsmithing, 2nd Edition** by Paul Hantke, DBI Books, Inc., Northbrook, IL, 1992. 256 pp., illus. Paper covers. $15.95.

An expert's guide to the operation of each of the handgun actions with all the major functions of pistolsmithing explained.

The Gun Digest Book of the .45, by Dean A. Grennell, DBI Books, Inc., Northbrook, IL, 1989. 256 pp., illus. Paper covers. $15.95.

Definitive work on one of America's favorite calibers.

Hallock's .45 Auto Handbook, by Ken Hallock, The Mihan Co., Oklahoma City, OK, 1981. 178 pp., illus. Paper covers. $11.95.

For gunsmiths, dealers, collectors and serious hobbyists.

Handgun Digest, 2nd Edition, by Dean A. Grennell, DBI Books, Inc., Northbrook, IL, 1991. 256 pp., illus. Paper covers. $15.95.

Full coverage of all aspects of handguns and handgunning from a highly readable, knowledgeable author.

***Handgun Stopping Power, the Definitive Study,** by Evan P. Marshall & Edwin J. Sanow, Paladin Press, Boulder, CO, 1992. 240 pp., illus. $39.95.

What really happens when a bullet meets a man.

***Handguns '93, 5th Edition,** edited by Jack Lewis, DBI Books, Inc., Northbrook, IL, 1992. 320 pp., illus. Paper covers. $17.95

An informative annual giving a complete overview of handguns.

***Handguns of the World,** by Edward C. Ezell, Marboro Book, Corp., Rockleigh, NJ, 1991. 704 pp., illus. $16.95.

A comprehensive international guide to military revolvers and self-loaders.

High Standard Automatic Pistols 1932-1950, by Charles E. Petty, The Gunroom Press, Highland Park, NJ, 1989. 124 pp., illus. $16.95.

A definitive source of information for the collector of High Standard arms.

Hunting for Handgunners, by Larry Kelly and J.D. Jones, DBI Books, Inc., Northbrook, IL, 1990. 256 pp., illus. Paper covers. $15.95.

Covers the entire spectrum of hunting with handguns in an amusing, easy-flowing manner that combines entertainment with solid information.

Instinct Combat Shooting, by Chuck Klein, Chuck Klein, The Goose Creek, IN, 1989. 49 pp., illus. Paper covers. $10.95.

Defensive handgunning for police.

Know Your Czechoslovakian Pistols, by R.J. Berger, Blacksmith Corp., Chino Valley, AZ, 1989. 96 pp., illus. Soft covers. $9.95.

A comprehensive reference which presents the fascinating story of Czech pistols.

Know Your 45 Auto Pistols—Models 1911 & A1, by E.J. Hoffschmidt, Blacksmith Corp., Southport, CT, 1974. 58 pp., illus. Paper covers. $9.95.

A concise history of the gun with a wide variety of types and copies.

Know Your Walther P.38 Pistols, by E.J. Hoffschmidt, Blacksmith Corp., Southport, CT, 1974. 77 pp., illus. Paper covers. $9.95.

Covers the Walther models Armee, M.P., H.P., P.38—history and variations.

Know Your Walther PP & PPK Pistols, by E.J. Hoffschmidt, Blacksmith Corp., Southport, CT, 1975. 87 pp., illus. Paper covers. $9.95.

A concise history of the guns with a guide to the variety and types.

*****Luger: The Multi-National Pistol,** by Charles Kenyon, Jr., Richard Ellis Publications, Moline, IL, 1991. 192 pp. $69.95 (hardcover); $150.00 (leather bound).

A fresh approach to this most historical handgun.

Luger Variations, by Harry E. Jones, Harry E. Jones, Torrance, CA, 1975. 328 pp., 160 full page illus., many in color. $45.00.

A rev. ed. of the book known as "The Luger Collector's Bible."

The Mauser Self-Loading Pistol, by Belford & Dunlap, Borden Publ. Co., Alhambra, CA. Over 200 pp., 300 illus., large format. $24.95.

The long-awaited book on the "Broom Handles," covering their inception in 1894 to the end of production. Complete and in detail: pocket pistols, Chinese and Spanish copies, etc.

Modern American Pistols and Revolvers, by A.C. Gould, Wolfe Publishing Co., Prescott, AZ, 1988. 222 pp., illus. $37.00.

A limited edition reprint. An account of the development of those arms as well as the manner of shooting them.

Modern Handguns, by Robert Adams, Book Sales, Secaucus, NJ, 1989. 128 pp., illus. $10.98.

History and technical discussion of collectible pistols.

The M1911A1 Automatic Pistol: Proud American Legend, edited by the American Historical Foundation, Richmond, VA, 1985. 240 pp., illus. Paper covers. $11.95.

Contains reprints of rare governmental manuals, combat photographs and original works by the foundation staff.

The New Handbook of Handgunning, by Paul B. Weston, Charles C. Thomas, Publisher, Springfield, IL, 1980. 102 pp., illus. $35.00.

A step-by-step, how-to manual of handgun shooting.

Pistol & Revolver Guide, 3rd Ed., by George C. Nonte, Stoeger Publ. Co., So. Hackensack, NJ, 1975. 224 pp., illus. Paper covers. $11.95.

The standard reference work on military and sporting handguns.

The Pistol Book, by John Walter, 2nd edition, 1991. Sterling Publishing Co., Inc., 1991. 176 pp., illus. $29.95.

Beretta, Colt, Mauser—plus a wealth of information and specs on other worldwide manufacturers of pistols and ammunition.

*****Pistol Guide,** by George C. Nonte, Jr., Stoeger Publishing Co., So. Hackensack, NJ, 1991. 280 pp., illus. Paper covers. $13.95.

Covers handling and marksmanship, care and maintenance, pistol ammunition, how to buy a used gun, military pistols, air pistols and repairs.

*****Pistols of the World, 3rd Edition,** by Ian Hogg and John Weeks, DBI Books, Inc., Northbrook, IL, 1992. 320 pp., illus. Paper covers. $18.95.

A totally revised edtion of one of the leading studies of small arms.

Police Handgun Manual, by Bill Clede, Stackpole Books, Inc., Harrisburg, PA, 1985. 128 pp., illus. $15.95.

How to get street-smart survival habits.

Powerhouse Pistols—The Colt 1911 and Browning Hi-Power Source

book, by Duncan Long, Paladin Press, Boulder, CO, 1989. 152 pp., illus. Soft covers. $19.95.

The author discusses internal mechanisms, outward design, test-firing results, maintenance and accessories.

Report of Board on Tests of Revolvers and Automatic Pistols. From the Annual Report of the Chief of Ordnance, 1907. Reprinted by J.C. Tillinghast, Marlow, NH, 1969. 34 pp., 7 plates, paper covers. $9.95.

A comparison of handguns, including Luger, Savage, Colt, Webley-Fosbery and other makes.

*****Revolver Guide,** by George C. Nonte, Jr., Stoeger Publishing Co., So. Hackensack, NJ, 1991. 288 pp., illus. Paper covers. $10.95.

A detailed and practical encyclopedia of the revolver, the most common handgun to be found.

The Ruger .22 Automatic Pistol, Standard/Mark I/Mark II Series, by Duncan Long, Paladin Press, Boulder, CO, 1989. 168 pp., illus. Paper covers. $12.00.

The definitive book about the pistol that has served more than 1 million owners so well.

The Semiautomatic Pistols in Police Service and Self Defense, by Massad Ayoob, Police Bookshelf, Concord, NH, 1990. 25 pp., illus. Soft covers. $9.95.

First quantitative, documented look at actual police experience with 9mm and 45 police service automatics.

Shoot a Handgun, by Dave Arnold, PVA Books, Canyon County, CA, 1983. 144 pp., illus. Paper covers. $11.95.

A complete manual of simplified handgun instruction.

Shoot to Win, by John Shaw, Blacksmith Corp., Southport, CT, 1985. 160 pp., illus. Paper covers. $11.95.

The lessons taught here are of interest and value to all handgun shooters.

Sixgun Cartridges and Loads, by Elmer Keith, reprint edition by The Gun Room Press, Highland Park, NJ, 1984. 151 pp., illus. $19.95.

A manual covering the selection, use and loading of the most suitable and popular revolver cartridges.

*****Sixguns,** by Elmer Keith, Wolfe Publishing Company, Prescott, AZ, 1992. 336 pp. Hardcover. $34.95.

The history, selection, repair, care, loading, and use of this historic frontiersman's friend—the one-hand firearm.

Skeeter Skelton on Handguns, by Skeeter Skelton, PJS Publications, Peoria, IL, 1980. 122 pp., illus. Soft covers. $5.00.

A treasury of facts, fiction and fables.

Successful Pistol Shooting, by Frank and Paul Leatherdale, The Crowood Press, Ramsbury, England, 1988. 144 pp., illus. $34.95.

Easy-to-follow instructions to help you achieve better results and gain more enjoyment from both leisure and competitive shooting.

Textbook of Pistols & Revolvers, by Julian Hatcher, Wolfe Publishing Co., Prescott, AZ, 1988. 533 pp., illus. $65.00.

A limited edition reprint. Hatcher wrote this shooters' bible in 1935 and it remains a classic full of invaluable information.

World's Deadliest Rimfire Battleguns, by J.M. Ramos, Paladin Press, Boulder, CO, 1990. 184 pp., illus. Paper covers. $14.00.

This heavily illustrated book shows international rimfire assault weapon innovations from World War II to the present.

HUNTING

NORTH AMERICA

Advanced Deer Hunting, by John Weiss, Stackpole Books, Harrisburg, PA, 1988. 352 pp., illus. $28.95.

New strategies based on the latest studies of whitetail behavior.

Advanced Wild Turkey Hunting & World Records, by Dave Harbour, Winchester Press, Piscataway, NJ, 1983. 264 pp., illus. $19.95.

The definitive book, written by an authority who has studied turkeys and turkey calling for over 40 years.

After Your Deer is Down, by Josef Fischl and Leonard Lee Rue, III, Winchester Press, Piscataway, NJ, 1981. 160 pp., illus. Paper covers. $10.95.

The care and handling of big game, with a bonus of venison recipes.

Alaska Safari, by Harold Schetzle, Great Northwest Publishing and Distributing Co., Inc., Anchorage, AK, 1990. 366 pp., illus. $35.00.

The most comprehensive and up-to-date guide to Alaska big game hunting available anywhere.

Alaska Wilderness Hunter, by Harold Schetzle, Great Northwest Publishing and Distributing Co., Anchorage, AK, 1987. 224 pp., illus. $35.00.

A superb collection of Alaska hunting adventures by master guide Harold Schetzle.

Alaskan Yukon Trophies Won and Lost, by G.O. Young, Wolfe Publishing Co., Prescott, AZ, 1989. 273 pp., illus. $35.00.

A new printing of the classic book on Alaskan big game hunting.

All About Bears, by Duncan Gilchrist, Stoneydale Press Publishing Co., Stevensville, MT, 1989. 176 pp., illus. $19.95.

Covers all kinds of bears—black, grizzly, Alaskan brown, polar and leans on a lifetime of hunting and guiding experiences to explore proper hunting techniques.

All About Deer in America, edited by Robert Elman, Winchester Press, Piscataway, NJ, 1976. 256 pp., illus. $15.95.

Twenty of America's great hunters share the secrets of their hunting success.

All About Varmint Hunting, by Nick Sisley, The Stone Wall Press, Inc., Wash., DC, 1982. 182 pp., illus. Paper covers. $12.95.

The most comprehensive up-to-date book on hunting common varmints found throughout North America.

All-American Deer Hunter's Guide, edited by Jim Zumbo and Robert Elman, Winchester Press, Piscataway, NJ, 1983. 320 pp., illus. $29.95.

The most comprehensive, thorough book yet published on American deer hunting.

All Season Hunting, by Bob Gilsvik, Winchester Press, Piscataway, NJ, 1976. 256 pp., illus. $14.95.

A guide to early-season, late-season and winter hunting in America.

*****American Duck Shooting,** by George Bird Grinnell, Stackpole Books, Harrisburg, PA, 1991. 640 pp., illus. Paper covers. $17.95.

First published in 1901 at the height of the author's career. Describes 50 species of waterfowl, and discusses hunting methods common at the turn of the century.

The Bear Hunter's Century, by Paul Schullery, Stackpole Books, Harrisburg, PA, 1989. 240 pp., illus. $19.95.

Thrilling tales of the bygone days of wilderness hunting.

Bear Hunting, by Jerry Meyer, Stackpole Books, Harrisburg, PA, 1983. 224 pp., illus. $16.95.

First complete guide on the how-to's of bear hunting. Information on every type of bear found in the U.S. and Canada.

Bear in Their World, by Erwin Bauer, an Outdoor Life Book, New York, NY, 1985. 254 pp., illus. $32.95.

Covers all North American bears; including grizzlies, browns, blacks, and polars.

The Best of Babcock, by Havilah Babcock, selected and with an introduction by Hugh Grey, The Gunnerman Press, Auburn Hills, MI, 1985. 262 pp., illus. $19.95.

A treasury of memorable pieces, 21 of which have never before appeared in book form.

The Best of Nash Buckingham, by Nash Buckingham, selected, edited and annotated by George Bird Evans, Winchester Press, Piscataway, NJ, 1973. 320 pp., illus. $17.95.

Thirty pieces that represent the very cream of Nash's output on his whole range of outdoor interests—upland shooting, duck hunting, even fishing.

Big Game, Big Country, by Dr. Chauncey Guy Suits, Great Northwest Publishing and Distributing Co., Anchorage, AK, 1987. 224 pp., illus. $29.50.

Chronicles more than a decade of high-quality wilderness hunting by one of this country's more distinguished big game hunters.

Big Game of North America, Ecology and Management, by Wildlife Management Institute, Stackpole Books, Harrisburg, PA, 1983. 512 pp., illus. $34.95.

An outstanding reference for professionals and students of wildlife management.

Big Game Trails in the Far North, by Col. Philip Neuweiler, Great Northwest Publishing and Distributing Co., Inc., Anchorage, AK, 1990. 320 pp., illus. $35.00.

This book is the result of 50 years hunting big game in the Far North.

Bird Hunting with Dalrymple, by Byron W. Dalrymple, Stackpole Books, Harrisburg, PA, 1987. 256 pp., illus. $24.95.

The rewards of shotgunning across North America.

The Bobwhite Quail Book, Compiled by Lamar Underwood, Amwell Press, Clinton, NJ, 1981. 442 pp., illus. $25.00.

An anthology of the finest stories on Bobwhite quail ever assembled under one cover.

Bowhunter's Digest, 3rd Edition, by Chuck Adams, DBI Books, Inc., Northbrook, IL, 1990. 288 pp., illus. Soft covers. $15.95.

All-new edition covers all the necessary equipment and how to use it, plus the fine points on how to improve your skill.

Brown Feathers, by Steven J. Julak, Stackpole Books, Harrisburg, PA, 1988. 224 pp., illus. $16.95.

Waterfowling tales and upland dreams.

Bugling for Elk, by Dwight Schuh, Stoneydale Press Publishing Co., Stevensville, MT, 1983. 162 pp., illus. $18.95.

A complete guide to early season elk hunting.

Call of the Quail: A Tribute to the Gentleman Game Bird, by Michael McIntosh, et al., Countrysport Press, Traverse City, MI, 1990. 175 pp., illus. $39.50.

A new anthology on quail hunting.

***Calling All Elk,** by Jim Zumbo, Jim Zumbo, Cody, WY, 1989. 169 pp., illus. Paper covers. $14.95.

The only book on the subject of elk hunting that covers every aspect of elk vocalization.

Campfires and Game Trails: Hunting North American Big Game, by Craig Boddington, Winchester Press, Piscataway, NJ, 1985. 295 pp., illus. $23.95.

How to hunt North America's big game species.

***Come October,** by Gene Hill et al, Countrysport Press, Inc., Traverse City, MI, 1991. 176 pp., illus. $39.50.

A new and all-original anthology on the woodcock and woodcock hunting.

The Complete Book of Hunting, by Robert Elman, Abbeville Press, New York, NY, 1982. 320 pp., illus. $29.95.

A compendium of the world's game birds and animals, handloading, international hunting, etc.

The Complete Book of Hunting: A Guide to Game Hunting, Wildfowling and Competition Shooting, edited by David Petzal, W.H. Smith, Publishers, New York, NY, 1988. 192 pp., illus. $14.98.

Equipment, game and dogs, plus techniques and reading the land.

The Complete Book of the Wild Turkey, by Roger M. Latham, Stackpole Books, Harrisburg, PA, 1978. 228 pp., illus. $14.95.

A new revised edition of the classic on American wild turkey hunting.

The Complete Guide to Bowhunting Deer, by Chuck Adams, DBI Books, Inc., Northbrook, IL, 1984. 256 pp., illus. Paper covers. $14.95.

Plenty on equipment, bows, sights, quivers, arrows, clothes, lures and scents, stands and blinds, etc.

The Complete Guide to Game Care and Cookery, Revised Edition, by Sam Fadala, DBI Books, Inc., Northbrook, IL, 1989. 320 pp., illus. Paper covers. $15.95.

Over 500 detailed photos and hundreds of tested recipes anyone can master.

The Complete Smoothbore Hunter, by Brook Elliot, Winchester Press, Piscataway, NJ, 1986. 240 pp., illus. $16.95.

Advice and information on guns and gunning for all varieties of game.

The Complete Turkey Hunt, by William Morris Daskal, El-Bar Enterprises Publishers, New York, NY, 1982. 129 pp., illus. Paper covers. $7.95.

Covers every aspect of turkeys and turkey hunting, by an expert.

Complete Turkey Hunting, by John Phillips, Stackpole Books, Harrisburg, PA, 1988. 320 pp., illus. $24.95.

The definitive work on hunting America's largest game bird.

Confessions of an Outdoor Maladroit, by Joel M. Vance, Amwell Press, Clinton, NJ, 1983. $20.00.

Anthology of some of the wildest, irreverent, and zany hunting tales ever.

The Corey Ford Sporting Treasury, by Corey Ford, Willow Creek Press, Wautoma, WI, 1987. 351 pp. $25.00.

Minutes of the "Lower Forty" and other treasured Corey Ford stories return to print.

Covey Rises and Other Pleasures, by David H. Henderson, Amwell Press, Clinton, NJ, 1983. 155 pp., illus. $17.50.

A collection of essays and stories concerned with field sports.

Coveys and Singles: The Handbook of Quail Hunting, by Robert Gooch, A.S. Barnes, San Diego, CA, 1981. 196 pp., illus. $11.95.

The story of the quail in North America.

Deer and Deer Hunting: The Serious Hunter's Guide, by Dr. Robert Wegner, Stackpole Books, Harrisburg, PA, 1984. 384 pp., illus. $24.95.

In-depth information from the editor of "Deer & Deer Hunting" magazine. Major bibliography of English language books on deer and deer hunting from 1838-1984.

Deer and Deer Hunting Book 2, by Dr. Robert Wegner, Stackpole Books, Harrisburg, PA, 1987. 400 pp., illus. $29.95.

Strategies and tactics for the advanced hunter.

Deer and Deer Hunting, Book 3, by Dr. Robert Wegner, Stackpole Books, Harrisburg, PA, 1990. 368 pp., ilus. $29.95.

This comprehensive volume covers natural history, deer hunting lore, profiles of deer hunters, and discussion of important issues facing deer hunters today.

The Deer Book, edited by Lamar Underwood, Amwell Press, Clinton, NJ, 1982. 480 pp., illus. $25.00.

An anthology of the finest stories on North American deer ever assembled under one cover.

Deer Hunter's Guide to Guns, Ammunition, and Equipment, by Edward A. Matunas, an Outdoor Life Book, distributed by Stackpole Books, Harrisburg, PA, 1983. 352 pp., illus. $24.95.

Where to hunt for North American deer. An authoritative guide that will help every deer hunter get maximum enjoyment and satisfaction from his sport.

Deer Hunting, by R. Smith, Stackpole Books, Harrisburg, PA, 1978. 224 pp., illus. Paper covers. $14.95.

A professional guide leads the hunt for North America's most popular big game animal.

Deer Hunting Coast to Coast, by C. Boddington and R. Robb, Safari Press, Long Beach, CA, 1989. 248 pp., illus. $24.95.

Join the authors as they hunt whitetail deer in eastern woodlot, southern swamps, midwestern prairies, and western river bottom; mule deer in badland, deserts, and high alpine basins; blacktails in oak grasslands and coastal jungles.

Deer in Their World, by Erwin Bauer, Stackpole Books, Harrisburg, PA, 1984. 256 pp., illus. $29.95.

A showcase of more than 250 natural habitat deer photographs. Substantial natural history of North American deer.

The Deer of North America, edited by Leonard Lee Rue, Stackpole Books, Harrisburg, PA, 1989. 544 pp., illus. $32.95.

Updated and expanded edition of this definitive work on North American deer.

The Desert Bighorn, its Life History, Ecology, and Management, edited by Gale Monson and Lowel Sumner, University of Arizona Press, Tucson, AZ, 1985. 370 pp., illus. Paper covers. $14.95.

There is nothing else around that can tell you anywhere near as much about desert sheep.

Dove Hunting, by Charley Dickey, Galahad Books, NY, 1976. 112 pp., illus. $10.00.

This indispensable guide for hunters deals with equipment, techniques, types of dove shooting, hunting dogs, etc.

***Doves and Dove Shooting,** by Byron Dalrymple, New Win Publishing, Inc., Hampton, NJ, 1991. 256 pp., illus. $17.95.

The classic book on the subject in a new printing.

Drummer in the Woods, by Burton L. Spiller, Stackpole Books, Harrisburg, PA, 1990. 240 pp., illus. Soft covers. $16.95.

Twenty-one wonderful stories on grouse shooting by "the Poet Laureate of Grouse."

Duck Decoys and How to Rig Them, by Ralf Coykendall, revised by Ralf Coykendall, Jr., Nick Lyons Books, New York, NY, 1990. 137 pp., illus. Paper covers. $12.95.

Sage and practical advice on the art of decoying ducks and geese.

The Duck Hunter's Handbook, by Bob Hinman, revised, expanded, updated edition, Winchester Press, Piscataway, NJ, 1985. 288 pp., illus. $15.95.

The duck hunting book that has it all.

The Duck-Huntingest Gentlemen, by Keith C. Russell et al., Winchester Press, Piscataway, NJ, 1980. 284 pp., illus. $17.95.

A collection of stories on waterfowl hunting.

Ducks of the Mississippi Flyway, ed. by John McKane, North Star Press, St. Cloud, MN, 1969. 54 pp., illus. Paper covers. $10.00.

A duck hunter's reference. Full color paintings of some 30 species, plus descriptive text.

Early American Waterfowling, 1700's-1930, by Stephen Miller, Winchester Press, Piscataway, NJ, 1986. 256 pp., illus. $27.95.

Two centuries of literature and art devoted to the nation's favorite hunting sport.

Eastern Upland Shooting, by Dr. Charles C. Norris, Countrysport Press, Traverse City, MI, 1990. 424 pp., illus. $29.50.

A new printing of this 1946 classic with a new, original Foreword by the author's friend and hunting companion, renowned author George Bird Evans.

The Education of Pretty Boy, by Havilah Babcock, The Gunnerman Press, Auburn Hills, MI, 1985. 160 pp., illus. $19.95.

Babcock's only novel, a heartwarming story of an orphan boy and a gun-shy setter.

Elk and Elk Hunting, by Hart Wixom, Stackpole Books, Harrisburg, PA, 1986. 288 pp., illus. $29.95.

Your practical guide to fundamentals and fine points of elk hunting.

Elk Hunting in the Northern Rockies, by Ed. Wolff, Stoneydale Press, Stevensville, MT, 1984. 162 pp., illus. $18.95.

Helpful information about hunting the premier elk country of the northern Rocky Mountain states—Wyoming, Montana and Idaho.

Fair Chase, by Jim Rikhoff, Amwell Press, Clinton, NJ, 1984. 323 pp., illus. $25.00.

A collection of hunting experiences from the Arctic to Africa, Mongolia to Montana, taken from over 25 years of writing.

Field Dressing Big Game, by James Churchill, Stackpole Books, Harrisburg, PA, 1989. 88 pp., illus. Soft covers. $10.95.

Dressing, caping, skinning and butchering instructions.

Field Dressing Small Game and Fowl, by James Churchill, Stackpole Books, Harrisburg, PA, 1987. 112 pp., illus. Paper covers. $10.95.

The illustrated guide to dressing 20 birds and animals.

Field Judging Trophy Animals, by William Shuster, Stackpole Books, Harrisburg, PA, 1987. 132 pp., illus. Paper covers. $8.95.

Expert advice and practical suggestions.

Firelight, by Burton L. Spiller, Gunnerman Press, Auburn Hills, MI, 1990. 196 pp., illus. $19.95.

Enjoyable tales of the outdoors and stalwart companions.

Fireside Waterfowler, edited by David E. Wesley and William G. Leitch, A Ducks Unlimited Book, Stackpole Books, Harrisburg, PA, 1987. 357 pp., illus. $29.95.

Fundamentals of duck and goose hunting.

For Whom the Ducks Toll, by Keith C. Russell, et al., Winchester Press, Piscataway, NJ, 1984. 288 pp., illus. Slipcased, limited and signed edition. $30.00. Trade edition, $16.95.

A select gathering of memorable waterfowling tales by the author and 68 of his closest friends.

The Formidable Game, by John H. Batten, Amwell Press, Clinton, NJ. 1983. 264 pp., illus. $175.00.

Deluxe, limited, signed and numbered edition. Big game hunting in India, Africa and North America by a world famous hunter.

Fur Trapping In North America, by Steven Geary, Winchester Press, Piscataway, NJ, 1985. 160 pp., illus. Paper covers. $10.95.

A comprehensive guide to techniques and equipment, together with fascinating facts about fur bearers.

A Gallery of Waterfowl and Upland Birds, by Gene Hill, with illustrations by David Maass, Petersen Prints, Los Angeles, CA, 1978. 132 pp., illus. $44.95.

Gene Hill at his best. Liberally illustrated with 51 full-color reproductions of David Maass' finest paintings.

Game in the Desert Revisited, by Jack O'Connor, Amwell Press, Clinton, NJ, 1984. 306 pp., illus. $27.50.

Reprint of a Derrydale Press classic on hunting in the Southwest

Getting the Most Out of Modern Waterfowling, by John O. Cartier, St. Martin's Press, NY, 1974. 396 pp., illus. $22.50.

The most comprehensive, up-to-date book on waterfowling imaginable.

The Gordon MacQuarrie Trilogy, by Gordon MacQuarrie, compiled and edited by Zack Taylor, Willow Creek Press, Oshkosh, WI, 1985. A three book, slip-cased set. $45.00.

Three-volume set comprising: **Stories of the Old Duck Hunters and Other Drivel, More Stories of the Old Duck Hunters, Last Stories of the Old Duck Hunters.**

The Grand Passage: A Chronicle of North American Waterfowling, by Gene Hill, et al., Countrysport Press, Traverse City, MI, 1990. 175 pp., illus. $39.50.

A new original anthology by renowned sporting authors on our world of waterfowling.

The Grand Spring Hunt for America's Wild Turkey Gobbler, by Bart Jacob with Ben Conger, Winchester Press, Piscataway, NJ, 1985. 176 pp., illus. $15.95.

The turkey book for novice and expert alike.

Grizzlies Don't Come Easy, by Ralph Young, Winchester Press, Piscataway, NJ, 1981. 200 pp., illus. $15.95.

The life story of a great woodsman who guided famous hunters such as O'Connor, Keith, Fitz, Page and others.

Grizzly Country, by Andy Russell, A.A. Knopf, NYC, 1973, 302 pp., illus. $15.95.

Many-sided view of the grizzly bear and his world, by a noted guide, hunter and naturalist.

Grouse and Grouse Hunting, by Frank Woolner, Nick Lyons Books, N.Y., NY, 1987. 192 pp., illus. $18.95.

An authoritative and affectionate portrait of one of America's greatest game birds.

Grouse of North America, by Tom Huggler, NorthWord Press, Inc., Minocqua, WI, 1990. 160 pp., illus. $29.95.

A cross-continental hunting guide.

Grouse Hunter's Guide, by Dennis Walrod, Stackpole Books, Harrisburg, PA, 1985. 192 pp., illus. $16.95.

Solid facts, observations, and insights on how to hunt the ruffed grouse.

***Gun Clubs & Decoys of Back Bay & Currituck Sound,** by Archie Johnson and Bud Coppedge, CurBac Press, Virginia Beach, VA, 1991. 224 pp., illus. $40.00.

This book identifies and presents a photographic history of over 100 hunting clubs and lodges on Back Bay, VA and Currituck Sound, NC.

Gunning for Sea Ducks, by George Howard Gillelan, Tidewater Publishers, Centreville, MD, 1988. 144 pp., illus. $14.95.

A book that introduces you to a practically untouched arena of waterfowling.

Horned and Antlered Game, by Erwin Bauer, Stackpole Books, Harrisburg, PA, 1987. 256 pp., illus. $32.95.

This book features spectacular color photographs and text brimming with animal lore.

Horns in the High Country, by Andy Russell, Alfred A. Knopf, NY, 1973. 259 pp., illus. Paper covers. $12.95.

A many-sided view of wild sheep and their natural world.

How to Get Your Deer, by John O. Cartier, Stackpole Books, Harrisburg, PA, 1986. 320 pp., illus. $24.95.

An authoritative guide to deer hunting that shows you how to match wits with your quarry and win.

How to Hunt, by Dave Bowring, Winchester Press, Piscataway, NJ, 1982. 208 pp., illus. Paper covers. $10.95; cloth, $15.00.

A basic guide to hunting big game, small game, upland birds, and waterfowl.

*****Hunt High,** by Duncan Gilchrist, Outdoor Expeditions & Books, Cowallis, MT, 1992. 192 pp., illus. Limited, signed edition. $34.95.

High country lore and how-to information on hunting Rocky Mountain Goats, Bighorn Sheep, Chamois, and Tahr.

The Hunters and the Hunted, by George Laycock, Outdoor Life Books, New York, NY, 1990. 280 pp., illus. $34.95.

The pursuit of game in America from Indian times to the present.

A Hunter's Fireside Book, by Gene Hill, Winchester Press, Piscataway, NJ, 1972. 192 pp., illus. $16.95.

An outdoor book that will appeal to every person who spends time in the field—or who wishes he could.

The Hunter's Shooting Guide, by Jack O'Connor, Outdoor Life Books, New York, NY, 1982. 176 pp., illus. Paper covers. $5.95.

A classic covering rifles, cartridges, shooting techniques for shotguns/rifles/handguns.

The Hunter's World, by Charles F. Waterman, Winchester Press, Piscataway, NJ, 1983. 250 pp., illus. $29.95.

A classic. One of the most beautiful hunting books that has ever been produced.

Hunting America's Game Animals and Birds, by Robert Elman and George Peper, Winchester Press, Piscataway, NJ, 1975. 368 pp., illus. $16.95.

A how-to, where-to, when-to guide—by 40 top experts—covering the continent's big, small, upland game and waterfowl.

Hunting and Stalking Deer Throughout the World, by Kenneth G. Whitehead, Batsford Books, London, 1982. 336 pp., illus. $35.00.

Comprehensive coverage of deer hunting areas on a country-by-country basis, dealing with every species in any given country.

Hunting Ducks and Geese, by Steven Smith, Stackpole Books, Harrisburg, PA, 1984. 160 pp., illus. $15.95.

Hard facts, good bets, and serious advice from a duck hunter you can trust.

Hunting for Handgunners, by Larry Kelly and J.D. Jones, DBI Books, Inc., Northbrook, IL, 1990. 256 pp., illus. Soft covers. $15.95.

A definitive work on an increasingly popular sport.

Hunting Fringeland Deer, by David Richey, Stackpole Books, Harrisburg, PA, 1987. 208 pp., illus. $24.95.

Tactics for trail watching, stillhunting and driving whitetails in farmlands, edge country and populated areas.

Hunting in Many Lands, edited by Theodore Roosevelt and George Bird Grinnell, et al., Boone & Crockett Club, Dumphries, VA, 1990. 447 pp., illus. $40.00.

A limited edition reprinting of the original Boone & Crockett Club 1895 printing.

Hunting in the Rockies, by Jack O'Connor, Safari Press, Long Beach, CA, 1988. 297 pp., illus. $29.95.

This new revised edition of Jack O'Connor's hard-to-find book on the game animals of the Rockies includes tips for hunting throughout the entire Rocky Mountain region.

Hunting in the Southlands, edited by Lamar Underwood, Amwell Press, Clinton, NJ, 1987. 565 pp., illus. $35.00.

An anthology of the best stories of southern hunts including dove, turkey, waterfowl, deer, quail and more.

Hunting North America's Big Game, by Bob Hagel, Stackpole Books, Harrisburg, PA, 1987. 220 pp., illus. $27.95.

Complete and reliable coverage on how to approach, track, and shoot game in different terrains.

Hunting Open-Country Mule Deer, by Dwight Schuh, Sage Press, Nampa, ID, 1989. 180 pp., illus. $18.95.

A guide taking Western bucks with rifle and bow.

Hunting Predators for Hides and Profits, by Wilf E. Pyle, Stoeger Publishing Co., So. Hackensack, NJ, 1985. 224 pp., illus. Paper covers. $11.95.

The author takes the hunter through every step of the hunting/marketing process.

Hunting the Alaskan Brown Bear, by John Eddy, Wolfe Publishing Co., Prescott, AZ, 1988. 253 pp., illus. $47.00.

A limited edition reprint of the best book on the big brown bear of the North.

Hunting the American Wild Turkey, by Dave Harbour, Stackpole Books, Harrisburg, PA, 1975. 256 pp., illus. $14.95.

The techniques and tactics of hunting North America's largest, and most popular, woodland game bird.

Hunting the Southwest, by Jack Samson, The Amwell Press, Clinton, NJ, 1985. 172 pp., illus. In slipcase $27.50.

The most up-to-date look at one of the most difficult and diverse hunting areas in the world today.

Hunting Superbucks, by Kathy Etling, Grolier Book Clubs, Danbury, CT, 1989. 444 pp., illus. $32.95.

How to find and hunt today's trophy mule and whitetail deer.

Hunting Trips in North America, by F.C. Selous, Wolfe Publishing Co., Prescott, AZ, 1988. 395 pp., illus. $52.00.

A limited edition reprint. Coverage of caribou, moose and other big game hunting in virgin wilds.

Hunting Trophy Deer, by John Wootters, Winchester Press, Piscataway, NJ, 1983. 265 pp., illus. $15.95.

All the advice you need to succeed at bagging trophy deer.

Hunting Upland Gamebirds, by Steve Smith, Stackpole Books, Harrisburg, PA, 1987. 176 pp., illus. $16.95.

What the wingshooter needs to know about the birds, the game, and the new clay games.

Hunting Wild Turkeys in the Everglades, by Frank P. Harben, Harben Publishing Co., Safety Harbor, FL, 1983. 341 pp., illus. Paper covers. $8.95.

Describes techniques, ways and means of hunting this wary bird.

Hunting Wild Turkeys with Ray Eye, by Michael Pearce and Ray Eye, Stackpole Books, Harrisburg, PA, 1990. 208 pp., illus. $22.95.

Whether you hunt in spring or fall, with a gun or bow and arrow, alone or with a partner, you will find in this book a wealth of practical information.

I Don't Want to Shoot an Elephant, by Havilah Babcock, The Gunnerman Press, Auburn Hills, MI, 1985. 184 pp., illus. $19.95.

Eighteen delightful stories that will enthrall the upland gunner for many pleasurable hours.

In Search of the Wild Turkey, by Bob Gooch, Greatlakes Living Press, Ltd., Waukegan, IL, 1978. 182 pp., illus. $9.95.

A state-by-state guide to wild turkey hot spots, with tips on gear and methods for bagging your bird.

Indian Hunts and Indian Hunters of the Old West, by Dr. Frank C. Hibben, Safari Press, Long Beach, CA, 1989. 228 pp., illus. $24.95.

Tales of some of the most famous American Indian hunters of the Old West as told to the author by an old Navajo hunter.

Instinctive Shooting, by G. Fred Asbell, Stackpole Books, Harrisburg, PA, 1988. 132 pp., illus. Paper covers. $13.95.

Expert advice on applying instinctive shooting to bowhunting. Written by the president of the Pope & Young Club.

*****Jack O'Connor's Gun Book,** by Jack O'Connor, Wolfe Publishing Company, Prescott, AZ, 1992. 208 pp. Hardcover. $26.00.

Jack O'Connor imparts a cross-section of his knowledge on guns and hunting. Brings back some of his writings that have here-to-fore been lost.

Jaybirds Go to Hell on Friday, by Havilah Babcock, The Gunnerman Press, Auburn Hills, MI, 1985. 149 pp., illus. $19.95.

Sixteen jewels that reestablish the lost art of good old-fashioned yarn telling.

*****Jim Dougherty's Guide to Bowhunting Deer,** by Jim Dougherty, DBI Books, Inc., Northbrook, IL, 1992. 256 pp., illus. Paper covers. $15.95.

Dougherty sets down some important guidelines for bowhunting and bowhunting equipment.

A Listening Walk...and Other Stories, by Gene Hill, Winchester Press, Piscataway, NJ, 1985. 208 pp., illus. $15.95.

Vintage Hill. Over 60 stories.

Making Game: An Essay on Woodcock, by Guy De La Valdene, Willow Creek Press, Oshkosh, WI, 1985. 202 pp., illus. $35.00.

The most delightful book on woodcock yet published.

Marsh Tales, by William N. Smith, Tidewater Publishers, Centreville, MD, 1985. 228 pp., illus. $15.95.

Market hunting, duck trapping, and gunning.

Matching the Gun to the Game, by Clair Rees, Winchester Press, Piscataway, NJ, 1982. 272 pp., illus. $17.95.

Covers selection and use of handguns, blackpowder firearms for hunting, matching rifle type to the hunter, calibers for multiple use, tailoring factory loads to the game.

Measuring and Scoring North American Big Game Trophies, by Wm. H. Nesbitt and Philip L. Wright, The Boone and Crockett Club, Alexandria, VA, 1986. 176 pp., illus. $15.00.

The Boone and Crockett Club official scoring system, with tips for field evaluation of trophies.

Meat on the Table: Modern Small-Game Hunting, by Galen Geer, Paladin Press, Boulder, CO, 1985. 216 pp., illus. $16.95.

All you need to know to put meat on your table from this comprehensive course in modern small-game hunting.

Mixed Bag, by Jim Rikhoff, National Rifle Association of America, Wash., DC, 1981. 284 pp., illus. Paper covers. $9.95.

Reminiscences of a master raconteur.

Modern Pheasant Hunting, by Steve Grooms, Stackpole Books, Harrisburg, PA, 1982. 224 pp., illus. Paper covers. $10.95.

New look at pheasants and hunters from an experienced hunter who respects this splendid gamebird.

Modern Waterfowl Guns and Gunning, by Don Zutz, Stoeger Publishing Co., So. Hackensack, NJ, 1985. 224 pp., illus. Paper covers. $11.95.

Up-to-date information on the fast-changing world of waterfowl guns and loads.

Montana: Land of Giant Rams, by Duncan Gilchrist, Stoneydale Press Publishing Co., Stevensville, MT, 1990. 208 pp., illus. $19.95.

Latest information on Montana bighorn sheep and why so many Montana bighorn rams are growing to trophy size.

More Alaska Bear Tales, by Larry Kamut, Alaska Northwest Books, Bothell, WA, 1991. 295 pp., illus. Paper covers. $12.95.

Action-packed stories for everyone with an interest in the most powerful animal roaming the North American wilderness.

More and Better Pheasant Hunting, by Steve Smith, Winchester Press, Piscataway, NJ, 1986. 192 pp., illus. $15.95.

Complete, fully illustrated, expert coverage of the bird itself, the dogs, the hunt, the guns, and the best places to hunt.

More Grouse Feathers, by Burton L. Spiller, Crown Publ., NY, 1972. 238 pp., illus. $25.00.

Facsimile of the original Derrydale Press issue of 1938. Guns and dogs, the habits and shooting of grouse, woodcock, ducks, etc. Illus. by Lynn Bogue Hunt.

More Stories of the Old Duck Hunter, by Gordon MacQuarrie, Willow Creek Press, Oshkosh, WI, 1983. 200 pp., illus. $15.00.

Collection of 18 treasured stories of The Old Duck Hunters originally published in major magazines of the 1930s and '40s.

More Than a Trophy, by Dennis Walrod, Stackpole Books, Harrisburg, PA, 1983. 256 pp., illus. Paper covers. $12.95.

Field dressing, skinning, quartering, and butchering to make the most of your valuable whitetail, blacktail or mule deer.

Mostly Huntin', by Bill Jordan, Everett Publishing Co., Bossier City, LA, 1987. 254 pp., illus. $21.95.

Jordan's hunting adventures in North America, Africa, Australia, South America and Mexico.

Mostly Tailfeathers, by Gene Hill, Winchester Press, Piscataway, NJ, 1975. 192 pp., illus. $15.95.

An interesting, general book about bird hunting.

Movin' Along with Charley Dickey, by Charlie Dickey, Winchester Press, Piscataway,

NJ, 1985. 224 pp., illus. $14.95.

More wisdom, wild tales, and wacky wit from the Sage of Tallahassee.

"Mr. Buck": The Autobiography of Nash Buckingham, by Nash Buckingham, Countrysport Press, Traverse City, MI, 1990. 288 pp., illus. $39.50.

A lifetime of shooting, hunting, dogs, guns, and Nash's reflections on the sporting life, along with previously unknown pictures and stories written especially for this book.

Murry Burnham's Hunting Secrets, by Murry Burnham with Russell Tinsley, Winchester Press, Piscataway, NJ, 1984. 244 pp., illus. $17.95.

One of the great hunters of our time gives the reasons for his success in the field.

The Muzzleloading Hunter, by Rick Hacker, Stackpole Books, Harrisburg, PA, 1989. 295 pp., illus. $19.95.

The book for anyone interested in the rapidly growing sport of hunting with a muzzleloader.

My Health is Better in November, by Havilah Babcock, University of S. Carolina Press, Columbia, SC, 1985. 284 pp., illus. $19.95.

Adventures in the field set in the plantation country and backwater streams of South Carolina.

My Lost Wilderness: Tales of an Alaskan Woodsman, by Ralph Young, Winchester Press, Piscataway, NJ, 1983. 193 pp., illus. $22.50.

True tales of an Alaskan hunter, guide, fisherman, prospector, and backwoodsman.

New England Grouse Shooting, by William Harnden Foster, Willow Creek Press, Oshkosh, WI, 1983. 213 pp., illus. $45.00.

A new release of a classic book on grouse shooting.

North American Big Game Animals, by Byron W. Dalrymple and Erwin Bauer, Outdoor Life Books/Stackpole Books, Harrisburg, PA, 1985. 258 pp., illus. $29.95.

Complete illustrated natural histories. Habitat, movements, breeding, birth and development, signs, and hunting.

North American Elk: Ecology and Management, edited by Jack Ward Thomas and Dale E. Toweill, Stackpole Books, Harrisburg, PA, 1982. 576 pp., illus. $39.95.

The definitive, exhaustive, classic work on the North American elk.

The North American Waterfowler, by Paul S. Bernsen, Superior Publ. Co., Seattle, WA, 1972. 206 pp. Paper covers. $4.95.

The complete inside and outside story of duck and goose shooting. Big and colorful, illus. by Les Kouba.

Northeast Upland Hunting Guide, by Jim Capossela, Stackpole Books, Harrisburg, PA, 1991. 120 pp., illus. Paper covers. $12.95.

Useful strategies and techniques for bagging all the region's most popular upland game.

Of Bears and Man, by Mike Cramond, University of Oklahoma Press, Norman, OK, 1986. 433 pp., illus. $29.95.

The author's lifetime association with bears of North America. Interviews with survivors of bear attacks.

The Old Man and the Boy and The Old Man Grows Older, by Robert Ruark, Stackpole Books, Harrisburg, PA, 1989. 620 pp., illus. Soft covers. $17.95.

Two novels in one volume. Classic tales of the coming of age of a boy and young man as he is nurtured and educated by his remarkable sportsman grandfather.

The Old Pro Turkey Hunter, by Gene Nunnery, Gene Nunnery, Meridian, MS, 1980. 144 pp., illus. $12.95.

True facts and old tales of turkey hunters.

1001 Hunting Tips, by Robert Elman, Winchester Press, Piscataway, NJ, 1983. 544 pp., illus. $22.95.

New edition, updated and expanded. A complete course in big and small game hunting, wildfowling and hunting upland birds.

The Only Good Bear is a Dead Bear, by Jeanette Hortick Prodgers, Falcon Press, Helena, MT, 1986. 204 pp. Paper covers. $7.95.

A collection of the West's best bear stories.

Opening Shots and Parting Lines: The Best of Dickey's Wit, Wisdom, and Wild Tales for Sportsmen, by Charley Dickey, Winchester Press, Piscataway, NJ, 1983. 208 pp., illus. $14.95.

Selected by the writer who has entertained millions of readers in America's top sporting publications—49 of his best pieces.

The Outdoor Life Bear Book, edited by Chet Fish, an Outdoor Life book, distributed by Stackpole Books, Harrisburg, PA, 1983. 352 pp., illus. $26.95.

All-time best personal accounts of terrifying attacks, exciting hunts, and intriguing natural history.

The Outdoor Life Deer Hunter's Encyclopedia, by John Madson, et al., Stackpole Books, Harrisburg, PA, 1985. 800 pp., illus. $49.95.

The largest, most comprehensive volume of its kind ever published.

Outdoor Life Deer Hunter's Yearbook 1991 compiled by George H. Haas, Meredith Press, Des Moines, IA, 1990. 192 pp., illus. $19.95.

A selection of the best deer hunting stories that appeared in the preceding year of *Outdoor Life* magazine.

***Outdoor Life Deer Hunters Yearbook 1992, 10th Anniversary Edition,** compiled by George Haas, Stackpole Books, Harrisburg, PA, 1991. 192 pp., illus. $21.95.

The most exciting deer hunting book of the year.

Outdoor Yarns & Outright Lies, by Gene Hill and Steve Smith, Stackpole Books, Harrisburg, PA, 1984. 168 pp., illus. $16.95.

Fifty or so stories by two good sports.

The Outlaw Gunner, by Harry M. Walsh, Tidewater Publishers, Cambridge, MD, 1973. 178 pp., illus. $13.50.

A colorful story of market gunning in both its legal and illegal phases.

Pheasant Hunter's Harvest, by Steve Grooms, Lyons & Burford Publishers, New York, NY, 1990. 180 pp. $18.95.

A celebration of pheasant, pheasant dogs and pheasant hunting. Practical advice from a passionate hunter.

Picking Your Shots, by Steve Smith, Stackpole Books, Harrisburg, PA, 1986. 160 pp., illus. $16.95.

Stories of dogs and birds, and guns and days afield.

Pinnell and Talifson: Last of the Great Brown Bear Men, by Marvin H. Clark, Jr., Great Northwest Publishing and Distributing Co., Spokane, WA, 19880. 224 pp., Illus. $39.95

The story of these famous Alaskan guides and some of the record bears taken by them.

The Practical Hunter's Handbook, by Anthony J. Acerrano, Winchester Press, Piscataway, NJ, 1978. 224 pp., illus. Paper covers. $12.95.

How the time-pressed hunter can take advantage of every edge his hunting situation affords him.

Predator Caller's Companion, by Gerry Blair, Winchester Press, Piscataway, NJ, 1981. 280 pp., illus. $18.95.

Predator calling techniques and equipment for the hunter and trapper.

Predators of North America, by Erwin Bauer, Stackpole Books, Harrisburg, PA, 1988. 256 pp., illus. $34.95.

Pronghorn, North America's Unique Antelope, by Charles L. Cadieux, Stackpole Books, Harrisburg, PA, 1986. 256 pp., illus. $24.95.

The practical guide for hunters.

Quail Hunting in America, by Tom Huggler, Stackpole Books, Harrisburg, PA, 1987. 288 pp., illus. $19.95.

Tactics for finding and taking bobwhite, valleys, Gambel's Mountain, scaled-blue, and Mearn's quail by season and habitat.

Radical Elk Hunting Strategies, by Mike Lapinski, Stoneydale Press Publishing Co., Stevensville, MT, 1988. 161 pp., illus. $18.95.

Secrets of calling elk in close.

Ranch Life and the Hunting Trail, by Theodore Roosevelt, Readex Microprint Corp., Dearborn, MI, 1966. 186 pp. With drawings by Frederic Remington. $22.50.

A facsimile reprint of the original 1899 Century Co. edition. One of the most fascinating books of the West of that day.

Records of North American Big Game 1932, by Prentis N. Grey, Boone and Crockett Club, Dumfries, VA, 1988. 178 pp., illus. $79.95.

A reprint of the book that started the Club's record keeping for native North American big game.

Records of North American Big Game, 9th Edition, 1988, edited by William H. Nesbitt and Jack Reneau, Boone and Crockett Club, Dumfries, VA, 1989. 512 pp., illus. $49.95.

A special Centennial Year edition of useful statistics and good reading about our native big game animals. With a special full-color section.

Records of North American Whitetailed Deer, by the editors of the Boone and Crockett Club, Dumfries, VA, 1987. 256 pp., illus. Flexible covers. $15.00.

Contains data on 1293 whitetail trophies over the all-time record book minimum, listed and ranked by state or province and divided into typical and non-typical categories.

Ridge Runners & Swamp Rats, by Charles F. Waterman, Amwell Press, Clinton, NJ, 1983. 347 pp., illus. $25.00.

Tales of hunting and fishing.

***The Rifles, the Cartridges, and the Game,** by Clay Harvey, Stackpole Books, Harrisburg, PA, 1991. 254 pp., illus. $29.95.

Engaging reading combines with exciting photos to present the hunt with an intense level of awareness and respect.

Ringneck! Pheasants & Pheasant Hunting, by Ted Janes, Crown Publ., NY, 1975. 120 pp., illus. $15.95.

A thorough study of one of our more popular game birds.

Ruffed Grouse, edited by Sally Atwater and Judith Schnell, Stackpole Books, Harrisburg, PA, 1989. 370 pp., illus. $59.95.

Everything you ever wanted to know about the ruffed grouse. More than 25 wildlife professionals provided in-depth information on every aspect of this popular game bird's life. Lavishly illustrated with over 300 full-color photos.

Shadows of the Tundra, by Tom Walker, Stackpole Books, Harrisburg, PA, 1990. 192 pp., illus. $19.95.

Alaskan tales of predator, prey, and man.

Charles Sheldon Trilogy, by Charles Sheldon, Amwell Press, Clinton, NJ, 1983. 3 volumes in slipcase. **The Wilderness of the Upper Yukon,** 363 pp., illus.; **The Wilderness of the North Pacific Coast Islands,** 246 pp., illus.; **The Wilderness of Denali,** 412 pp., illus. Deluxe edition. $205.00.

Custom-bound reprinting of Sheldon's classics, each signed and numbered by the author's son, William G. Sheldon.

***Shorebirds: The Birds, The Hunters, The Decoys,** by John M. Levinson & Somers G. Headley, Tidewater Publishers, Centreville, MD, 1991. 160 pp., illus. $49.95.

A thorough study of shorebirds and the decoys used to hunt them. Photographs of more than 200 of the decoys created by prominent carvers are shown.

Shots at Big Game, by Craig Boddington, Stackpole Books, Harrisburg, PA, 1989. 198 pp., illus. $24.95.

How to shoot a rifle accurately under hunting conditions.

Small Game & Varmint Hunting, by Wilf E. Pyle, Stoeger Publishing Co., So. Hackensack, NJ, 1989. 288 pp., illus. Soft covers. $16.95.

Provides information on modern techniques and methods needed for successful hunting of small game.

Sport and Travel; East and West, by Frederick Courteney Selous, Wolfe Publishing Co., Prescott, AZ, 1988. 311 pp., illus. $29.00.

A limited edition reprint. One of the few books Selous wrote covering North American hunting. His daring in Africa is equalled here as he treks after unknown trails and wild game.

Spring Turkey Hunting, by John M. McDaniel, Stackpole Books, Harrisburg, PA, 1986. 224 pp., illus. $21.95.

The serious hunter's guide.

Squirrels and Squirrel Hunting, by Bob Gooch. Tidewater Publ., Cambridge, MD, 1973. 148 pp., illus. $9.95.

A complete book for the squirrel hunter, beginner or old hand. Details methods of hunting, squirrel habitat, management, proper clothing, care of the kill, cleaning and cooking.

The Still-Hunter, by Theodore S. Van Dyke, reprinted by the Gunnerman Press, Auburn Hills, MI, 1988. 390 pp., illus. $21.95.

Covers each aspect of this fine sport in such complete detail that both the novice and the experienced hunter will profit from its reading.

Strayed Shots and Frayed Lines, edited by John E. Howard, Amwell Press, Clinton, NJ, 1982. 425 pp., illus. $25.00.

Anthology of some of the finest, funniest stories on hunting and fishing ever assembled.

Successful Goose Hunting, by Charles L. Cadieux, Stone Wall Press, Inc., Washington, DC, 1986. 223 pp., illus. $24.95.

Here is a complete book on modern goose hunting by a lifetime waterfowler and professional wildlifer.

Successful Handgun Hunting, by Phil W. Johnson. The Shooting Sports Press, Minneapolis, MN, 1988. 216 pp., illus. $19.95.

The definitive work on the most exciting sport in America.

Supreme Duck Shooting Stories, by William Hazelton, The Gunnerman Press, Auburn Hills, MI, 1989. 160 pp. $19.95.

Originally published in 1931, this is about duck hunting as it was.

Taking Big Bucks, by Ed Wolff, Stoneydale Press, Stevensville, MT, 1987. 169 pp., illus. $18.95.

Solving the whitetail riddle.

Tales of Alaska's Big Bears, by Jim Rearden, Wolfe Publishing Co., Prescott, AZ, 1989. 125 pp., illus. Soft covers. $12.95.

A collection of bear yarns covering nearly three-quarters of a century.

Tales of Quails 'n Such, by Havilah Babcock, University of S. Carolina Press, Columbia, SC, 1985. 237 pp. $19.95.

A group of hunting stories, told in informal style, on field experiences in the South in quest of small game.

They Left Their Tracks, by Howard Coperhaver, Stoneydale Press Publishing Co., Stevensville, MT, 1990. 190 pp., illus. $18.95.

Recollections of 60 years as an outfitter in the Bob Marshall Wilderness.

Timberdoodle, by Frank Woolner, Nick Lyons Books, N. Y., NY, 1987. 168 pp., illus. $18.95.

The classic guide to woodcock and woodcock hunting.

Track of the Kodiak, by Marvin H. Clark, Great Northwest Publishing and Distributing Co., Anchorage, AK, 1984. 224 pp., illus. $39.95.

A full perspective on Kodiak Island bear hunting.

Tracking Wounded Deer, by Richard P. Smith, Stackpole Books, Harrisburg, PA, 1988. 159 pp., illus. Paper covers. $15.95.

How to find and tag deer shot with bow or gun.

Trail and Campfire, edited by George Bird Grinnel and Theodore Roosevelt, The Boone and Crockett Club, Dumfries, VA, 1989. 357 pp., illus. $39.50.

Reprint of the Boone and Crockett Club's 3rd book published in 1897.

***Trail of the Eagle,** by Bud Conkle, as told to Jim Rearden, Great Northwest Publishing & Distributing Co., Anchorage, AK, 1991. 280 pp., illus. $29.50.

Hunting Alaska with master guide Bud Conkle.

Tranquillity, by Col. H.P. Sheldon, Willow Creek Press, Oshkosh, WI, 1986. In slipcase with its acclaimed companion volumes. **Tranquillity Revisited** and **Tranquillity Regained.** The 3 volume set. $45.00.

A reprint of this 1936 Derrydale Press classic set.

Trophy Hunter in Asia, by Elgin T. Gates, Charger Productions Inc., Capistrano Beach, CA, 1982. 272 pp., illus. $19.95.

Fascinating high adventure with Elgin Gates, one of America's top trophy hunters.

Trophy Rams of the Brooks Range Plus Secrets of a Sheep and Mountain Goat Guide, by Duncan Gilchrist, Pictorial Histories Publishing Co., Missoula, MT, 1984. 176 pp., illus. $19.95.

Covers hunting a remote corner of the Brooks Range for virgin herds of dall rams.

The Turkey Hunter's Book, by John M. McDaniel, Amwell Press, Clinton, NJ, 1980. 147 pp., illus. Paper covers. $9.95.

One of the most original turkey hunting books to be published in many years.

Turkey Hunter's Digest, by Dwain Bland, DBI Books, Inc., Northbrook, IL, 1986. 256 pp., illus. Paper covers. $14.95.

Describes and pictures all varieties of turkey. Offers complete coverage on calls, calling techniques, appropriate guns, bows, cameras and other equipment.

Turkey Hunter's Guide, by Byron W. Dalrymple, et al., a publication of The National Rifle Association, Washington, DC, 1979. 96 pp., illus. Paper covers. $9.95.

Expert advice on turkey hunting hotspots, guns, guides, and calls.

Turkey Hunting, Spring and Fall, by Doug Camp, Outdoor Skills Bookshelf, Nashville, TN, 1983. 165 pp., illus. Paper covers. $12.95.

Practical turkey hunting, calling, dressing and cooking, by a professional turkey hunting guide.

***Turkey Hunting with Gerry Blair,** by Gerry Blair, Krause Publications, Iola, WI, 1991. 280 pp., illus. $19.95.

Turkey types, guns, camouflage, calls, bowhunting, field care, spring tactics and fall tactics.

The Upland Gunner's Book, edited by George Bird Evans, The Amwell Press, Clinton, NJ, 1985. 263 pp., illus. In slipcase. $27.50.

An anthology of the finest stories ever written on the sport of upland game hunting.

The Waterfowl Gunner's Book, edited by F. Phillips Williamson, The Amwell Press, Clinton, NJ, 1986. 282 pp., illus. In slipcase. $27.50. An anthology of the finest duck hunting stories ever gathered under one cover.

Western Hunting Guide, by Mike Lapinski, Stoneydale Press Publishing Co., Stevensville, MT, 1989. 168 pp., illus. $18.95.

A complete where-to-go and how-to-do-it guide to Western hunting.

White-Tailed Deer: Ecology and Management, by Lowell K. Halls, Stackpole Books, Harrisburg, PA, 1984. 864 pp., illus. $59.95.

The definitive work on the world's most popular big game animal.

***Whitetails,** by Leonard Lee Rue III, Stackpole Books, Harrisburg, PA, 1991. 320 pp., illus. $32.95.

Answers to all your questions on life cycle, feeding patterns, antlers, scrapes and rubs, behavior during the rut, and habitat.

The Wild Bears, by George Laycock, Outdoor Life Books, N. Y., NY, 1987. 272 pp., illus. Soft covers. $19.95.

The story of the grizzly, brown and black bears, their conflicts with man, and their chances of survival in the future.

The Wild Turkey Book, edited and with special commentary by J. Wayne Fears, Amwell Press, Clinton, NJ, 1982. 303 pp., illus. $22.50.

An anthology of the finest stories on wild turkey ever assembled under one cover.

Wilderness Hunting and Wildcraft, by Townsend Whelen, Wolfe Publishing Co., Prescott, AZ, 1988. 338 pp., illus. $39.00.

A limited edition reprint. Plentiful information on sheep and mountain hunting with horses and on life histories of big game animals.

The Wildfowler's Quest, by George Reiger, Lyons & Burford, Publishers, New York, NY, 1989. 320 pp., illus. $24.95.

A richly evocative look into one man's passionate pursuit of ducks, geese, turkey, woodcock, and other wildfowl all over the world.

***Wind on the Water,** as told to Jim Rearden, Great Northwest Publishing & Distributing Co., Anchorage, AK, 1991. 280 pp., illus. $19.95.

The true-life account of a pioneering couple, Bud and Lenora Conkle, in the wilds. Hunting stories as well as takes of the trapline, winter hardship and wilderness life in the far North.

The Wings of Dawn, by George Reiger, Lyons & Burford, Publishers, New York, NY, 1989. 320 pp., illus. Soft covers. $15.95.

This memorable and rich portrait of the waterfowler's world includes the history of the sport, natural history of all types of ducks and geese, useful hunting advice, and more.

Woodchucks and Woodchuck Rifles, by Charles Landis, Wolfe Publishing Co., Prescott, AZ, 1988. 402 pp., illus. $42.00.

A limited edition reprint of the most complete text on the subject.

Woodcock, by John Alden Knight, Gunnerman Press, Auburn Hills, MI, 1989. 160 pp., illus. $21.95.

A new printing of one of the finest books ever written on the subject.

Woodcock Shooting, by Steve Smith, Stackpole Books, Inc., Harrisburg, PA, 1988. 142 pp., illus. $16.95.

A definitive book on woodcock hunting and the characteristics of a good woodcock dog.

AFRICA/ASIA

African Game Trails, by Theodore Roosevelt, St. Martin's Press, New York, NY, 1988. 583 pp., illus. $19.95.

The 1908 safari of President Teddy Roosevelt and his son Kermit to East Africa.

African Hunter, by James Mellon, Safari Press, Long Beach, CA, 1988. 522 pp., illus. $100.00.

The most ardent and intricately detailed book on African game hunting to appear in 50 years.

African Hunter, by Baron Bror von Blixen-Finecke, St. Martin's Press, New York, NY, 1986. 284 pp., illus. $14.95.

Reprint of the scarce 1938 edition. An African hunting classic.

African Hunting and Adventure, by William Charles Baldwin, Books of Zimbabwe, Bulawayo, 1981. 451 pp., illus. $75.00.

Facsimile reprint of the scarce 1863 London edition. African hunting and adventure from Natal to the Zambezi.

African Rifles & Cartridges, by John Taylor, The Gun Room Press, Highland Park, NJ, 1977. 431 pp., illus. $29.95.

Experiences and opinions of a professional ivory hunter in Africa describing his knowledge of numerous arms and cartridges for big game. A reprint.

The African Safari, by P. Jay Fetner, St. Martin's Press, Inc., N. Y., NY, 1987. 700 pp., illus. $70.00.

A lavish, superbly illustrated, definitive work that brings together the practical elements of planning a safari with a proper appreciation for the animals and their environment.

After Big Game in Central Africa, by Edouard Foa, St. Martin's Press, New York, NY, 1989. 400 pp., illus. $16.95.

Reprint of the scarce 1899 edition. This sportsman covered 7200 miles, mostly on foot—from Zambezi delta on the east coast to the mouth of the Congo on the west.

Bell of Africa, compiled and edited by Townsend Whelen, Safari Press, Huntington Beach, CA, 1990. 236 pp., illus. $24.95.

The autobiography of W.D.M. Bell compiled and edited by his lifetime friend from Bell's own papers.

The Big Game Hunters, by Michael Brander, St. Martin's Press, New York, NY, 1989. 192 pp., illus. $24.95.

The adventures of 19 sportsmen of yore in Asia, Africa, and America.

Big Game Hunting and Collecting in East Africa 1903-1926, by Kalman Kittenberger, St. Martin's Press, New York, NY, 1989. 496 pp., illus. $16.95.

One of the most heart stopping, charming and funny accounts of adventure in the Kenya Colony ever penned.

Big Game Hunting Around the World, by Bert Klineburger and Vernon W. Hurst, Exposition Press, Jericho, NY, 1969. 376 pp., illus. $30.00.

The first book that takes you on a safari all over the world.

Big Game Hunting in North-Eastern Rhodesia, by Owen Letcher, St. Martin's Press, New York, NY, 1986. 272 pp., illus. $15.95.

A classic reprint and one of the very few books to concentrate on this fascinating area, a region that today is still very much safari country.

The Book of the Lion, by Sir Alfred E. Pease, St. Martin's Press, New York, NY, 1986. 305 pp., illus. $15.95.

Reprint of the finest book ever published on the subject. The author describes all aspects of lion history and lion hunting, drawing heavily on his own experiences in British East Africa.

Cats!, edited by Jim Rikhoff, The Amwell Press, Clinton, NJ, 1990. 600 pp., illus. $47.50.

An anthology of the finest stories ever compiled on hunting the world's largest wild cats.

Claws of Africa, by Roger Courtney, Trophy Room Books, Agoura, CA, 1990. 272 pp., illus. $65.00.

A classic account of the experiences of a professional "White Hunter," one of a carefully selected band of men who acted as official guides to hunters and shooting parties throughout Equatorial Africa in the 1940s and 1950s.

Death in a Lonely Land, by Peter Capstick, St. Martin's Press, New York, NY, 1990. 284 pp., illus. $19.95.

Twenty-three stories of hunting as only the master can tell them.

Death in the Dark Continent, by Peter Capstick, St. Martin's Press, New York, NY, 1983. 238 pp., illus. $15.95.

A book that brings to life the suspense, fear and exhilaration of stalking ferocious killers under primitive, savage conditions, with the ever present threat of death.

Death in the Long Grass, by Peter Hathaway Capstick, St. Martin's Press, New York, NY, 1977. 297 pp., illus. $15.95.

A big game hunter's adventures in the African bush.

Death in the Silent Places, by Peter Capstick, St. Martin's Press, New York, NY, 1981. 243 pp., illus. $15.95.

The author recalls the extraordinary careers of legendary hunters such as Corbett, Karamojo Bell, Stigand and others.

East Africa and its Big Game, by Captain Sir John C. Willowghby, Wolfe Publishing Co., Prescott, AZ, 1990. 312 pp., illus. $52.00.

A deluxe limited edition reprint of the very scarce 1889 edition of a narrative of a sporting trip from Zanzibar to the borders of the Masai.

East of the Sun and West of the Moon, by Theodore and Kermit Roosevelt, Wolfe Publishing Co., Prescott, AZ, 1988. 284 pp., illus. $25.00.

A limited edition reprint. A classic on Marco Polo sheep hunting. A life experience unique to hunters of big game.

Elephant, by Commander David Enderby Blunt, The Holland Press, London, England, 1985. 260 pp., illus. $35.00.

A study of this phenomenal beast by a world-leading authority.

Elephant Hunting in East Equatorial Africa, by Arthur H. Neumann, Books of Zimbabwe, Bulawayo, 1982. 455 pp., illus. $85.00.

Facsimile reprint of the scarce 1898 London edition. An account of three years ivory hunting under Mount Kenya.

Elephant Hunting in Portuguese East Africa, by Jose Pardal, Safari Press, Huntington Beach, CA, 1990. 256 pp., illus. $60.00.

This book chronicles the hunting-life story of a nearly vanished breed of man—those who single-handedly hunted elephants for prolonged periods of time.

Elephants of Africa, by Dr. Anthony Hall-Martin, New Holland Publishers, London, England, 1987. 120 pp., illus. $75.00.

A superbly illustrated overview of the African elephant with reproductions of paintings by the internationally acclaimed wildlife artist Paul Bosman.

Ends of the Earth, by Roy Chapman Andrews, Wolfe Publishing Co., Prescott, AZ, 1988. 230 pp., illus. $27.00.

A limited edition reprint. Includes adventures in China and hunting in Mongolia. Andrews was a distinguished hunter and scout.

First Wheel, by Bunny Allen, Amwell Press, Clinton, NJ, 1984. Limited, signed and numbered edition in the NSFL "African Hunting Heritage Series." 292 pp., illus. $100.00.

A white hunter's diary, 1927-47.

Green Hills of Africa, by Ernest Hemingway. Charles Scribner's Sons, NY, 1963. 285 pp., illus. Paper covers. $11.95.

A famous narrative of African big game hunting, that was first published in 1935.

Gun and Camera in Southern Africa, by H. Anderson Bryden, Wolfe Publishing Co., Prescott, AZ, 1989. 201 pp., illus. $37.00.

A limited edition reprint. The year was 1893 and author Bryden wandered for a year in Bechuanaland and the Kalahari Desert hunting the white rhino, lechwe, eland, and other animals.

Horn of the Hunter, by Robert Ruark, Safari Press, Long Beach, CA, 1987. 315 pp., illus. $35.00.

Ruark's most sought-after title on African hunting, here in reprint.

The Hunter is Death, by T. V. Bulpin, Safari Press, Long Beach, CA, 1987. 348 pp., illus. $30.00.

This is the life story of George Rushby, professional ivory hunter who killed the man-eating lions of the Njombe district.

Hunting Big Game, 2 volumes, by Townsend Whelen, Wolfe Publishing Co., Prescott, AZ, 1989. Volume I, Africa and Asia, 339 pp., illus.; Volume 2, The America's, 282 pp., illus. $90.00.

A limited edition reprint. Articles and stories by F.C. Selous, Sir Samuel Baker, Arthur H. Neumann, Theodore Roosevelt and others.

Hunting in Many Lands, by Theodore Roosevelt and George Bird Grinnel, The Boone and Crockett Club, Dumfries, VA, 1987. 447 pp., illus. $40.00.

Limited edition reprint of this 1895 classic work on hunting in Africa, India, Mongolia, etc.

***Hunting in Tanzania, An Anthology,** by Tony Sanchez-Arino, Safari Press, Huntington Beach, CA, 1991. 416 pp., illus. Limited, signed and numbered edition, in a slipcase. $125.00.

The finest selection of hunting stories ever compiled on that great East African game country, Tanzania.

Hunting the Elephant in Africa, by Captain C.H. Stigand, St. Martin's Press, New York, NY, 1986. 379 pp., illus. $14.95.

A reprint of the scarce 1913 edition; vintage Africana at its best.

The Ivory Trail, by Tom Bulpin, Safari Press, Long Beach, CA, 1988. 235 pp., illus. $27.50.

The uproarious adventures of "Bvekenya," the greatest of all ivory poachers and a legend of the South African bush.

Jaguar Hunting in the Mato Grosso and Bolivia, by T. Almedia, Safari Press, Long Beach, CA, 1989. 256 pp., illus. $35.00.

Not since Sacha Siemel has there been a book on jaguar hunting like this one.

***The Jim Corbett Collection,** by Jim Corbett. Safari Press, Huntington, CA, 1991. 1124 pp., illus., five volumes in slipcase. $105.00.

This slip-cased set of Jim Corbett's works includes: *Jungle Lore, The Man-Eating Leopard of Rudraprayag, My India, Man-Eaters of Kumaon, Tree Tops,* and *Temple Tiger.*

Karamojo Safari, by W.D.M. Ball, Safari Press, Huntington Beach, CA, 1990. 288 pp., illus. $24.95.

The story of Bell's caravan travels through Karamojo, his exciting elephant hunts, and his life among the uncivilized and uncorrupted natives.

Lake Ngami, by Charles Anderson, New Holland Press, London, England, 1987. 576 pp., illus. $35.00.

Originally published in 1856. Describes two expeditions into what is now Botswana, depicting every detail of landscape and wildlife.

Last Horizons: Hunting, Fishing and Shooting on Five Continents, by Peter Capstick, St. Martin's Press, New York, NY, 1989. 288 pp., illus. $19.95.

The first in a two volume collection of hunting, fishing and shooting tales from the selected pages of The American Hunter, Guns & Ammo and Outdoor Life.

The Last Ivory Hunter: The Saga of Wally Johnson, by Peter Capstick, St. Martin's Press, New York, NY, 1988. 220 pp., illus. $18.95.

A grand tale of African adventure by the foremost hunting author of our time. Wally Johnson spent half a century in Mozambique hunting white gold—ivory.

Last of the Ivory Hunters, by John Taylor, Safari Press, Long Beach, CA, 1990. 354 pp., illus. $29.95.

Reprint of the classic book "Pondoro" by one of the most famous elephant hunters of all time.

The Man-Eaters of Tsavo, by Lt. Col. J.H. Patterson, St. Martin's Press, New York, NY, 1986. 346 pp., illus. $14.95.

A reprint of the scarce original book on the man-eating lions of Tsavo.

Memories of an African Hunter, by Denis D. Lyell, St. Martin's Press, New York, NY, 1986. 288 pp., illus. $15.95.

A reprint of one of the truly great writers on African hunting. A gripping and highly readable account of Lyell's many years in the African bush.

The Mighty Nimrod: A Life of Fredrick Courteney Selous African Hunter and Adventurer 1851-1917, by Stephen Taylor, William Collins Sons and Co., Ltd., 1989. $40.00.

The story of one of the greatest big game hunters of them all.

Peter Capstick's Africa: A Return to the Long Grass, by Peter Hathaway Capstick, St. Martin's Press, N. Y., NY, 1987. 213 pp., illus. $29.95.

A first-person adventure in which the author returns to the long grass for his own dangerous and very personal excursion.

The Recollections of an Elephant Hunter 1864-1875, by William Finaughty, Books of Zimbabwe, Bulawayo, Zimbabwe, 1980. 244 pp., illus. $85.00.

Reprint of the scarce 1916 privately published edition. The early game hunting exploits of William Finaughty in Matabeleland and Nashonaland.

***Robert Ruark's Africa,** by Robert Ruark, Countrysport Press, Inc., Traverse City, MI, 1991. 256 pp., illus. $29.50.

A new release of previously uncollected stories of the wanderings through Africa of this giant in American sporting literature.

Safari: A Chronicle of Adventure, by Bartle Bull, Viking/Penguin, London, England, 1989. 383 pp., illus. $40.00.

The thrilling history of the African safari, highlighting some of Africa's best-known personalities.

Safari Rifles: Double, Magazine Rifles and Cartridges for African Hunting, by Craig Boddington, Safari Press, Huntington Beach, CA, 1990. 416 pp., illus. $37.50.

A wealth of knowledge on the safari rifle. Historical and present double-rifle makers, ballistics for the large bores, and much, much more.

Safari: The Last Adventure, by Peter Capstick, St. Martin's Press, New York, NY, 1984. 291 pp., illus. $15.95.

A modern comprehensive guide to the African Safari.

***Sands of Silence,** by Peter H. Capstick, Saint Martin's Press, New York, NY, 1991. 224 pp., illus. $35.00.

Join the author on safari in Nambia for his latest big-game hunting adventures.

The Shamba Raiders: Memories of a Game Warden, by Bruce Kinlock, Safari Press, Long Beach, CA, 1988. 405 pp., illus. $35.00.

Thrilling stories of encounters with rogue elephants, buffalo and other dangerous animals.

Sourdough and Swahili, by Bud Branham, The Amwell Press, Clinton, NJ, 1990. 265 pp., illus. $35.00.

A professional hunter's experiences on two continents.

South Pacific Trophy Hunter, by Murray Thomas, Safari Press, Long Beach, CA, 1988. 181 pp., illus. $37.50.

A record of a hunter's search for a trophy of each of the 15 major game species in the South Pacific region.

Tales of the Big Game Hunters, selected and introduced by Kenneth Kemp, The Sportsman's Press, London, 1986. 209 pp., illus. $15.00.

Writings by some of the best known hunters and explorers, among them: Frederick Courteney Selous, R.G. Gordon Cumming, Sir Samuel Baker, and elephant hunters Neumann and Sutherland.

Tanzania Safari, by Brian Herne, Amwell Press, Clifton, NJ, 1982. 259 pp., illus. Limited, signed and numbered edition. $125.00.

The story of Tanzania and hunting safaris, professional hunters, and a little history, too.

Uganda Safaris, by Brian Herne, Winchester Press, Piscataway, NJ, 1979. 236 pp., illus. $12.95.

The chronicle of a professional hunter's adventures in Africa.

The Wanderings of an Elephant Hunter, by W.D.M. Bell, Safari Press, Huntington Beach, CA, 1990. 187 pp., illus. $24.95.

The greatest of elephant books by the greatest-of-all elephant hunter.

A White Hunters Life, by Angus MacLagan, an African Heritage Book, published by Amwell Press, Clinton, NJ, 1983. 283 pp., illus. Limited, signed, and numbered deluxe edition, in slipcase. $100.00.

True to life, a sometimes harsh yet intriguing story.

Wild Ivory, by Horace S. Mazet, Nautulus Books, No. Plainfield, NJ, 1971. 280 pp., illus. $30.00.

The true story of the last of the old elephant hunters.

Wild Sports of Southern Africa, by William Cornwallis Harris, New Holland Press, London, England, 1987. 376 pp., illus. $35.00.

Originally published in 1863, describes the author's travels in Southern Africa.

With a Rifle in Mongolia, by Count Hoyos-Sprizenstein, Safari Press, Long Beach, CA, 1987. 144 pp., illus. In slipcase. $85.00.

First English edition of the author's 1911 expedition to Mongolia and China.

RIFLES

***The Accurate Varmint Rifle,** by Boyd Mace, Precision Shooting, Inc., Whitehall, NY, 1991. 184 pp., illus. $19.95.

A long overdue and long needed work on what factors go into the selection of components for and the susequent assembly of...the accurate varmint rifle.

The AK-47 Assault Rifle, Desert Publications, Cornville, AZ, 1981. 150 pp., illus. Paper covers. $10.00.

Complete and practical technical information on the only weapon in history to be produced in an estimated 30,000,000 units.

The AR-15/M16, A Practical Guide, by Duncan Long. Paladin Press, Boulder, CO, 1985. 168 pp., illus. Paper covers. $16.95.

The definitive book on the rifle that has been the inspiration for so many modern assault rifles.

AR-15/M16 Super Systems, by Duncan Long, Paladin Press, Boulder, CO, 1989. 144 pp., illus. Soft covers. $19.95.

Taking up where other AR-15 books leave off, this book shows you how to customize this reliable firearm into a super system suited to your needs.

The Big-Bore Rifle, by Michael McIntosh, Countrysport Press, Traverse City, MI, 1990. 224 pp., illus. $39.50.

The book of fine magazine and double rifles 375 to 700 calibers.

Big Game Rifles and Cartridges, by Elmer Keith, reprint edition by The Gun Room Press, Highland Park, NJ, 1984. 161 pp., illus. $24.95.

Reprint of Elmer Keith's first book, a most original and accurate work on big game rifles and cartridges.

The Black Rifle, M16 Retrospective, R. Blake Stevens and Edward C. Ezell, Collector Grade Publications, Toronto, Canada, 1987. 400 pp., illus. $47.50.

The complete story of the M16 rifle and its development.

The Bolt Action, Volume 2, by Stuart Otteson, Wolfe Publishing Co., Inc. Prescott, AZ, 1985. 289 pp., illus. $22.50.

Covers 17 bolt actions from Newton to Ruger.

Bolt Action Rifles, revised edition, by Frank de Haas, DBI Books, Inc., Northbrook, IL, 1984. 448 pp., illus. Paper covers. $17.95.

A revised edition of the most definitive work on all major bolt-action rifle designs. Detailed coverage of over 110 turnbolt actions, including how they function, takedown and assembly, strengths and weaknesses, dimensional specifications.

The Book of the Garand, by Maj.-Gen. J.S. Hatcher, The Gun Room Press, Highland Park, NJ, 1977. 292 pp., illus. $24.95.

A new printing of the standard reference work on the U.S. Army M1 rifle.

The Book of the Rifle, by T.F. Fremantle, Wolfe Publishing Co., Prescott, AZ, 1988. 558 pp., illus. $54.00.

A limited edition reprint. This book records the point of the rifle's evolution at the opening of the 19th century.

The Book of the Twenty-Two: The All American Caliber, by Sam Fadala, Stoeger Publishing Co., So. Hackensack, NJ, 1989. 288 pp., illus. Soft covers. $16.95.

The All American Caliber from BB caps up to the powerful 226 Barnes. It's about ammo history, plinking, target shooting, and the quest for the one-hole group.

The Breech-Loading Single-Shot Rifle, by Major Ned H. Roberts and Kenneth L. Waters, Wolfe Publishing Co., Prescott, AZ, 1987. 333 pp., illus. $32.50.

A comprehensive history of the evolution of Scheutzen and single shot rifles.

Combat Rifles of the 21st Century, by Duncan Long, Paladin Press, Boulder, CO, 1991. 115 pp., illus. Paper covers. $15.00.

An inside look at the U.S. Army's program to develop a super advanced combat rifle to replace the M16.

The Fighting Rifle, by Chuck Taylor, Paladin Press, Boulder, CO, 1983. 184 pp., illus. Paper covers. $16.95.

The difference between assault and battle rifles and auto and light machine guns.

F.N.-F.A.L. Auto Rifles, Desert Publications, Cornville, AZ, 1981. 130 pp., illus. Paper covers. $13.95.

A definitive study of one of the free world's finest combat rifles.

A Forgotten Heritage; The Story of a People and the Early American Rifle, by Harry P. Davis, The Gun Room Press, Highland Park, NJ, 1976. 199 pp., illus. $9.95.

Reprint of a very scarce history, originally published in 1941, the Kentucky rifle and the people who used it.

The Golden Age of Single-Shot Rifles, by Edsall James, Pioneer Press, Union City, TN, 1975. 33 pp., illus. Paper covers. $2.75.

A detailed look at all of the fine, high quality sporting single shot rifles that were once the favorite of target shooters.

The Gun Digest Book of Assault Weapons, 2nd Edition, edited by Jack Lewis, DBI Books, Inc., Northbrook, IL, 1989. 256 pp., illus. Paper covers. $15.95

The Gun Digest Book of Assault Weapons, 3rd Edition, edited by Jack Lewis, DBI Books, Inc., Northbrook, IL. 256 pp., illus. Paper covers.

(April 1993)

The Gun Digest Book of Firearms Assembly/Disassembly Part III: Rimfire Rifles, by J.B. Wood, DBI Books, Inc., Northbrook, IL, 1980. 288 pp., illus. Paper covers. $14.95.

A most comprehensive, uniform, and professional presentation available for disassembling and reassembling most rimfire rifles.

The Gun Digest Book of Firearms Assembly/Disassembly Part IV: Centerfire Rifles, Revised Edition, by J.B. Wood, DBI Books, Inc., Northbrook, IL, 1991. 480 pp., illus. Paper covers. $17.95.

Covers 54 popular centerfire rifles plus 300 variants of those models integrated into the text and completely cross-referenced in the index.

The Gun Digest Book of Riflesmithing, by Jack Mitchell, DBI Books, Inc., Northbrook, IL, 1982. 256 pp., illus. Paper covers. $14.95.

Covers major and minor gunsmithing operations for rifles—locking systems, triggers, safeties, rifling, crowning, scope mounting, and more.

***The History and Development of the M16 Rifle and Its Cartridge,** by David R. Hughes, Armory Publications, Oceanside, CA, 1990. 294 pp., illus. $49.95.

Study of small caliber rifle development culminating in the M16 with encyclopedic coverage of the .223/5.56mm cartridge.

***Hunting Rifles and Cartridges,** by Finn Aagaard, the National Rifle Association, Washington, D.C., 1991. 203 pp., illus. Paper covers. $15.95.

A collection of informative articles reprinted from 10 years of *American Rifleman* and *American Hunter* magazines.

Jim Carmichel's Book of the Rifle, by Jim Carmichel, an Outdoor Life Book, New York, NY, 1985. 564 pp., illus. $34.95.

The most important book of the author's career, and the most comprehensive ever published on the subject.

Keith's Rifles for Large Game, by Elmer Keith, The Gun Room Press, Highland Park, NJ, 1986. 406 pp., illus. $39.95.

Covers all aspects of selecting, equipping, use and care of high power rifles for hunting big game, especially African.

Know Your M1 Garand, by E. J. Hoffschmidt, Blacksmith Corp., Southport, CT, 1975, 84 pp., illus. Paper covers. $9.95.

Facts about America's most famous infantry weapon. Covers test and experimental models, Japanese and Italian copies, National Match models.

Know Your Ruger 10/22 Carbine, by William E. Workman, Blacksmith Corp., Chino Valley, AZ, 1991. 96 pp., illus. Paper covers. $9.95.

The story and facts about the most popular 22 autoloader ever made.

***Legendary Sporting Rifles,** by Sam Fadala, Stoeger Publishing Co., So. Hackensack, NJ, 1992. 288 pp., illus. Paper covers. $16.95.

This book covers a vast span of time and technology beginning with the Kentucky Long-rifle.

The M-14 Rifle, facsimile reprint of FM 23-8, Desert Publications, Cornville, AZ, 50 pp., illus. Paper $7.95.

In this well illustrated and informative reprint, the M-14 and M-14E2 are covered thoroughly.

Military and Sporting Rifle Shooting, by Captain E.C. Crossman, Wolfe Publishing Co., Prescott, AZ, 1988. 449 pp., illus. $45.00.

A limited edition reprint. A complete and practical treatise covering the use of rifles.

The Mini-14, by Duncan Long, Paladin Press, Boulder, CO, 1987. 120 pp., illus. Paper covers. $10.00.

History of the Mini-14, the factory-produced models, specifications, accessories, suppliers, and much more.

Modern Military Bullpup Rifles, by T.B. Dugelby, Collector Grade Publications, Toronto, Canada, 1984. 97 pp., illus. $20.00.

The EM-2 concept comes to age.

Modern Sniper Rifles, by Duncan Long, Paladin Press, Boulder, CO, 1988. 120 pp., illus. Paper covers. $16.95.

An in-depth look at the variety of rifles currently on the market that are suitable for long-distance precision shooting.

Modern Sportsman's Gun and Rifle, by J.H. Walsh ("Stonehenge"), Wolfe Publishing Co., Prescott, AZ, 1988. In two volumes, Vol. 1, 459 pp., Vol. 2, 546 pp., illus. $110.00.

A limited edition reprint. An extremely rare set of books first published in 1880s. Covers game, sporting and match rifles, and revolvers.

M1 Carbine Owner's Manual, M1, M2 & M3 .30 Caliber Carbines, Firepower Publications, Cornville, AZ, 1984. 102 pp., illus. Paper covers. $9.95.

The complete book for the owner of an M1 Carbine.

More Single Shot Rifles and Actions, by Frank de Haas, Frank de Haas, Orange City, IA, 1989. 146 pp., illus. Soft covers. $29.95.

A definitive book with in-depth studies, illustrations, drawings and descriptions of over 45 obsolete single shot rifles and actions.

The Pennsylvania Rifle, by Samuel E. Dyke, Sutter House, Lititz, PA, 1975. 61 pp., illus. Paper covers. $5.00.

History and development, from the hunting rifle of the Germans who settled the area. Contains a full listing of all known Lancaster, PA, gunsmiths from 1729 through 1815.

The Remington 700, by John F. Lacy, Taylor Publishing Co., Dallas, TX, 1990. 208 pp., illus. $44.95.

Covers the different models, limited editions, chamberings, proofmarks, serial numbers, military models, and much more.

The Revolving Rifles, by Edsall James, Pioneer Press, Union City, TN, 1975. 23 pp., illus. Paper covers. $2.50.

Valuable information on revolving cylinder rifles, from the earliest matchlock forms to the latest models of Colt and Remington.

Rifle and Marksmanship, by Judge H.A. Gildersleeve, reprinted by W.S. Curtis, Buckinghamshire, England, 1986. 131 pp., illus. $25.00.

Reprint of a book first published in 1878 in New York, catering to the shooter of early breechloaders and late muzzleloaders.

***The Rifle Book,** by John Walter, Arms & Armour Press, London, England, 1990. 158 pp. illus. $29.95.

The comprehensive one-volume guide to the world's shoulder guns.

Rifle Guide, by Robert A. Steindler, Stoeger Publishing Co., South Hackensack, NJ, 1978. 304 pp., illus. Paper covers. $9.95.

Complete, fully illustrated guide to selecting, shooting, caring for, and collecting rifles of all types.

The Rifle in America, by Philip B. Sharpe, Wolfe Publishing Co., Prescott, AZ, 1988. 641 pp., illus. $59.00.

A limited edition reprint. A marvelous volume packed with information for the man who is interested in rifles, from the man whose life was guns.

Rifle Shooting as a Sport, by Bernd Klingner, A.S. Barnes and Co., Inc., San Diego, CA, 1980. 186 pp., illus. Paper covers. $15.00.

Basic principles, positions and techniques by an international expert.

Rifleman's Handbook: A Shooter's Guide to Rifles, Reloading & Results, by Rick Jamison, NRA Publications, Washington, DC, 1990. 303 pp., illus. $21.95.

Helpful tips on precision reloading, how to squeeze incredible accuracy out of an "everyday" rifle, etc.

Ned H. Roberts and the Schuetzen Rifle, edited by Gerald O. Kelver, Brighton, CO, 1982. 99 pp., illus. $12.00.

A compilation of the writings of Major Ned H. Roberts which appeared in various gun magazines.

Schuetzen Rifles, History and Loading, by Gerald O. Kelver, Gerald O. Kelver, Publisher, Brighton, CO, 1972. Illus. $12.00.

Reference work on these rifles, their bullets, loading, telescopic sights, accuracy, etc. A limited, numbered ed.

Semi-Auto Rifles: Data and Comment, edited by Robert W. Hunnicutt, The National Rifle Association, Washington, DC, 1988. 156 pp., illus. Paper covers. $12.95.

A book for those who find military-style self-loading rifles interesting for their history, intriguing for the engineering that goes into their design, and a pleasure to shoot.

***Single Shot Actions, Their Design and Construction,** by Frank and Mark DeHaas, Dehaas Books, Orange City, IA, 1991. 247 pp. illus. $35.00.

Covers the best single shot rifles of the past plus a potpourri of modern single shot rifle actions.

***Single-Shot Rifle Finale,** by James Grant, Wolfe Publishing Co., Prescott, AZ, 1992. 556 pp., illus. $36.00.

The master's 5th book on the subject and his best.

Single Shot Rifle Notes, Yesterday and Today, by Gerald O. Kelver, Brighton, CO, 1988. 254 pp., illus. Paper covers. $16.00.

A mixing of old traditions and those of today with regard to single shot rifle shooting.

Single Shot Rifles and Actions, by Frank de Haas, Orange City, IA, 1990. 352 pp., illus. Soft covers. $25.00.

The definitive book on over 60 single shot rifles and actions. Covers history, parts, design and construction.

The Springfield Rifle M1903, M1903A1, M1903A3, M1903A4, Desert Publications, Cornville, AZ, 1982. 100 pp., illus. Paper covers. $10.00.

Covers every aspect of disassembly and assembly, inspection, repair and maintenance.

***Sixty Years of Rifles,** by Paul A. Matthews, Wolfe Publishing Co., Prescott, AZ, 1991. 224 pp., illus. $19.50.

About rifles and the author's experience and love affair with shooting and hunting.

The Sturm, Ruger 10/22 Rifle and .44 Magnum Carbine, by Duncan Long, Paladin Press, Boulder, CO, 1988. 108 pp., illus. Paper covers. $12.00.

An in-depth look at both weapons detailing the elegant simplicity of the Ruger design. Offers specifications, troubleshooting procedures and ammunition recommendations.

***.22 Caliber Varmint Rifles,** by Charles Landis, Wolfe Publishing Co., Prescott, AZ, 1991. 531 pp., illus. $32.00.

From the history of 22-caliber varmint rifles through various cartridges of different design to tests and opinions, with incidental relative material.

The Ultimate in Rifle Accuracy, by Glenn Newick, Benchrest and Bucks, Houston, TX, 1989. 200 pp., illus. $34.95.

Getting the most out of your equipment and yourself.

***U.S. Rifle M14–From John Garand to the M21,** by R. Blake Stevens, Collector Grade Publications, Inc., Toronto, Canada, revised second edition, 1991. 350 pp., illus. $47.50.

A classic, in-depth examination of the development, manufacture and fielding of the last wood-and-metal ("lock, stock, and barrel") battle rifle to be issued to U.S. troops.

***The Winchester Model 94: The First 100 Years,** by Robert C. Renneberg, Krause Publications, Iola, WI, 1991. 207 pp., illus. $34.95.

Covers the design and evolution from the early years up to the many different editions that exist today.

SHOTGUNS

The American Shotgun, by Charles Askins, Wolfe Publishing Co., Prescott, AZ, 1988. 321 pp., illus. $39.00.

A limited edition reprint. Askins covers shotguns and patterning extremely well.

The American Shotgun, by David F. Butler, edited by C. Kenneth Ramage, Lyman Publications, Middlefield, CT, 1973. 243 pp., illus. Paper covers. $14.95.

A comprehensive history of the American smoothbore's evolution from Colonial times to the present day.

American Shotgun Design and Performance, by L.R. Wallack, Winchester Press, Piscataway, NJ, 1977. 184 pp., illus. $16.95.

An expert lucidly recounts the history and development of American shotguns and explains how they work.

The American Single Barrel Trap Gun, by Frank F. Conley, Frank F. Conley, Carmel Valley, CA, 1989. 241 pp., illus. $39.95.

History, serial numbers, collecting and how they were made. Covers Baker, Fox, Ithaca, Levefer, Meriden, Parker, L.C. Smith, etc.

Best Guns, by Michael McIntosh, Countrysport, Inc., Traverse City, MI, 1989. 288 pp., illus. $39.50.

Devoted to the best shotguns ever made in the United States and the best presently being made in the world.

The British Shotgun, Volume 1, 1850-1870, by I.M. Crudington and D.J. Baker, Barrie & Jenkins, London, England, 1979. 256 pp., illus. $59.95.

An attempt to trace, as accurately as is now possible, the evolution of the shotgun during its formative years in Great Britain.

The British Shotgun, Volume 2, 1871-1890, by I.M. Crudginton and D.J. Baker, Ashford Press, Southampton, England, 1989. 250 pp., illus. $59.95.

The second volume of a definitive work on the evolution and manufacture of the British shotgun.

*****Clay Pigeon Shooting for Beginners and Enthusiasts,** by John King, The Sportsman's Press, London, England, 1991. 94 pp., illus. $24.95.

John King has devised this splendid guide to clay pigeon shooting in the same simple, direct, and person-to-person style in which he teaches at his popular Barbury Shooting School near Swindon.

*****Clay Shooting,** by Peter Croft, Ward Lock, London, England, 1990. 160 pp., illus, $29.95.

A complete guide to Skeet, trap and sporting shooting.

Clay Target Shooting, by Paul Bentley, A&C Black, London, England, 1987. 144 pp., illus. $25.00.

Practical book on clay target shooting written by a very successful international competitor, providing valuable professional advice and instruction for shooters of all disciplines.

Cradock on Shotguns, by Chris Cradock, Banford Press, London, England, 1989. 200 pp., illus. $45.00.

A definitive work on the shotgun by a British expert on shotguns.

The Defensive Shotgun, by Louis Awerbuck, S.W.A.T. Publications, Cornville, AZ, 1989. 77 pp., illus. Soft covers. $12.95.

This book cuts through the maze of myths concerning the shotgun and its attendant ballistic effects.

The Double Shotgun, by Don Zutz, Winchester Press, Piscataway, NJ, 1985. 304 pp., illus. $19.95.

Revised, updated, expanded edition of the history and development of the world's classic sporting firearms.

Field, Cover and Trap Shooting, by Adam H. Bogardus, Wolfe Publishing Co., Prescott, AZ, 1988. 446 pp., illus. $43.00.

A limited edition reprint. Hints for skilled marksmen as well as young sportsmen. Includes haunts and habits of game birds and waterfowl.

*****Finding the Extra Target,** by Coach John R. Linn & Stephen A. Blumenthal, Shotgun Sports, Inc., Auburn, CA, 1989. 126 pp., illus. Paper covers. $14.95.

The ultimate training guide for all the clay target sports.

The Golden Age of Shotgunning, by Bob Hinman, Wolfe Publishing Co., Inc., Prescott, AZ, 1982. $17.95.

A valuable history of the late 1800s detailing that fabulous period of development in shotguns, shotshells and shotgunning.

The Gun Digest Book of Firearms Assembly/Disassembly, Part V: Shotguns, Revised Edition, by J.B. Wood, DBI Books, Inc., Northbrook, IL, 1992. 480 pp., illus. Paper covers. $17.95.

Covers 46 popular shotguns and over 250 variants of those models integrated into the text and completely cross-referenced in the index. The most professional presentation available to either hobbyist or gunsmith.

The Gun Digest Book of Shotgun Gunsmithing, by Ralph Walker, DBI Books, Inc., Northbrook, IL, 1983. 256 pp., illus. Paper covers. $14.95.

The principles and practices of repairing, individualizing and accurizing modern shotguns by one of the world's premier shotgun gunsmiths.

The Gun Digest Book of Sporting Clays, by Jack Lewis, DBI Books, Inc., Northbrook, IL, 1991. 224 pp., illus. Paper covers. $15.95.

A superb introduction to the fastest growing gun game in America.

The Gun Digest Book of Trap & Skeet Shooting, 2nd Edition, by Art Blatt, DBI Books, Inc., Northbrook, IL, 1989. 288 pp., illus. Paper covers. $15.95.

This new edition contains lots of valuable information for the intermediate and advanced competition shooter.

Hartman on Skeet, By Barney Hartman, Stackpole Books, Harrisburg, PA, 1973. 143 pp., illus. $14.95.

A definitive book on Skeet shooting by a pro.

*****The Ithaca Gun Company From the Beginning,** by Walter Claude Snyder, Cook & Uline Publishing Co., Spencerport, NY, 1991. 256 pp., illus. $59.95.

The entire "family" of Ithaca Gun Company products is described together with a photo gallery section containing many previously unpublished photographs of the gun makers.

L.C. Smith Shotguns, by Lt. Col. William S. Brophy, The Gun Room Press, Highland Park, NJ, 1979. 244 pp., illus. $35.00.

The first work on this very important American gun and manufacturing company.

Lefever: Guns of Lasting Fame, by Robert W. (Bob) Elliot and Jim Cobb, Robert W. (Bob) Elliot, Lindale, TX, 1986. 174 pp., illus. $35.00.

Hundreds of photographs, patent drawings and production figures are given on this famous maker's shotguns.

A Manual of Clayshooting, by Chris Cradock, Hippocrene Books, Inc., New York, NY, 1983. 192 pp., illus. $39.95.

Covers everything from building a range to buying a shotgun, with lots of illustrations and diagrams.

The Modern Shotgun, by Major Sir Charles Burrard, Ashford Press, Southampton, England, 1986 reprint of this 3-volume set. The set, $125.00.

Reprinting of the most classic and informative work on the shotgun.

The Mysteries of Shotgun Patterns, by George G. Oberfell and Charles E. Thompson, Oklahoma State University Press, Stillwater, OK, 1982. 164 pp., illus. Paper covers. $25.00.

Shotgun ballistics for the hunter in non-technical language, with information on improving effectiveness in the field.

The Orvis Wing-Shooting Handbook, by Bruce Bowlen, Nick Lyons Books, New York, NY, 1985. 83 pp., illus. Paper covers. $8.95.

Proven techniques for better shotgunning.

Plans and Specifications of the L.C. Smith Shotgun, by Lt. Col. William S. Brophy, USAR Ret., F. Brownell & Son, Montezuma, IA, 1982. 247 pp., illus. $19.95.

The only collection ever assembled of all the drawings and engineering specifications on the incomparable and very collectable L.C. Smith shotgun.

Police Shotgun Manual, by Bill Clede, Stackpole Books, Harrisburg, PA, 1986. 128 pp., illus. $15.95.

Latest shotgun techniques for tough situations.

Purdey's, the Guns and the Family, by Richard Beaumont, David and Charles, Pomfert, VT, 1984. 248 pp., illus. $39.95.

Records the history of the Purdey family from 1814 to today, how the guns were and are built and daily functioning of the factory.

Recreating the Double Barrel Muzzle-Loading Shotgun, by William R. Brockway, George Shumway Publisher, York, PA, 1985. 198 pp., illus. Paper covers. $20.00.

Treats the making of double guns of classic type.

Reloading for Shotgunners, 2nd Edition, edited by Robert S.L. Anderson, DBI Books, Inc., Northbrook, IL, 1985. 256 pp., illus. Paper covers. $14.95.

The very latest in reloading information for the shotgunner.

Robert Churchill's Game Shooting, edited by MacDonald Hastings, Countrysport Press, Traverse City, MI, 1990. 252 pp., illus. $29.50.

A new revised edition of the definitive book on the Churchill method of instinctive wingshooting for game and Sporting Clays.

75 Years with the Shotgun, by C.T. (Buck) Buckman, Valley, Publ., Fresno, CA, 1974. 141 pp., illus. $10.00.

An expert hunter and trapshooter shares experiences of a lifetime.

*****Shooting at Clays,** by Alan Jarrett, Stanley Paul, London, England, 1991. 176 pp., illus. $34.95.

This comprehensive book unravels the complexities of clay pigeon shooting, with clear descriptions of each discipline.

The Shooting Field with Holland & Holland, by Peter King, Quiller Press, London, England, new & enlarged edition, 1990. 184 pp., illus. $49.95.

The story of a company which has produced a high degree of excellence in all aspects of gunmaking.

The Shotgun in Combat, by Tony Lesce, Desert Publications, Cornville, AZ, 1979. 148 pp., illus. Paper covers. $10.00.

A history of the shotgun and its use in combat.

Shotgun Digest, 3rd Edition, edited by Jack Lewis, DBI Books, Inc., Northbrook, IL, 1986. 256 pp., illus. Paper covers. $14.95.

A new look at shotguns.

*****Shotgun Digest, 4th Edition,** edited by Jack Lewis, DBI Books, Inc., Northbrook, IL. 256 pp., illus. Paper covers.
(March 1993)

*****Shotgun Stuff,** by Don Zutz, Shotgun Sports, Inc., Auburn, CA, 1991. 172 pp., illus. Paper covers. $19.95.

This book gives shotgunners all the "stuff" they need to achieve better performance and get more enjoyment from their favorite smoothbore.

Shotgunner's Notebook: The Advice and Reflections of a Wingshooter, by Gene Hill, Countrysport Press, Traverse City, MI, 1990. 192 pp., illus. $24.50.

Covers the shooting, the guns and the miscellany of the sport.

Shotgunning: The Art and the Science, by Bob Brister, Winchester Press, Piscataway, NJ, 1976. 321 pp., illus. $17.95.

Hundreds of specific tips and truly novel techniques to improve the field and target shooting of every shotgunner.

Shotgunning Trends in Transition, by Don Zutz, Wolfe Publishing Co., Prescott, AZ, 1990. 314 pp., illus. $29.50.

This book updates American shotgunning from those post WWII transitional years to the high-tech present.

Shotguns and Cartridges for Game and Clays, by Gough Thomas, edited by Nigel Brown, A & C Black, Ltd., Cambs, England, 1989. 256 pp., illus. Soft covers. $24.95.

Gough Thomas' well-known and respected book for game and clay pigeon shooters in a thoroughly up-dated edition.

Shotguns by Keith, by Elmer Keith, Wolfe Publishing Co., Prescott, AZ, 1988. 305 pp., illus. $39.00.

A limited edition reprint. The master reveals his knowledge again.

*****Sidelocks & Boxlocks,** by Geoffrey Boothroyd, Sand Lake Press, Amity, OR, 1991. 271 pp., illus. $29.95.

The story of the classic British shotgun.

The Sporting Clay Handbook, by Jerry Meyer, Lyons and Burford Publishers, New York, NY, 1990. 140 pp., illus. Soft covers. $14.95.

Introduction to the fastest growing, and most exciting, gun game in America.

*****Sporting Clays,** by Michael Pearce, Stackpole Books, Harrisburg, PA, 1991. 192 pp., illus. $16.95.

Expert techniques for every kind of clays course.

Sporting Clays, by A.J. "Smoker" Smith, Willowcreek Press, Wautoma, WI, 1989. 150 pp., illus. $19.50.

The author reveals techniques that led him to win almost every major sporting clays competition in England, where the sport originated.

*****The Story of the Sporting Gun,** by Ranulf Rayner, Trafalgar Square, North Pomfret, VT, 1991. 96 pp., illustrated. $75.00.

This magnificent volume traces the story of game shooting from the early development of the shotgun to the present day.

U.S. Shotguns, All Types, reprint of TM9-285, Desert Publications, Cornville, AZ, 1987. 257 pp., illus. Paper covers. $9.95.

Covers operation, assembly and disassembly of nine shotguns used by the U.S. armed forces.

The Winchester Model Twelve, by George Madis, David Madis, Dallas, TX, 1984. 176 pp., illus. $19.95.

A definitive work on this famous American shotgun.

The Winchester Model 42, by Ned Schwing, Krause Publications, Iola, WI, 1990. 159 pp., illus. $39.95.

Behind-the-scenes story of the model 42's invention and its early development. Production totals and manufacturing dates; reference work.

Winchester Shotguns and Shotshells, by Ronald W. Stadt, Armory Publications, Tacoma, WA, 1984. 184 pp., illus. $45.00.

From the hammer and double guns to the Model 59.

*****Winchester's Finest, the Model 21,** by Ned Schwing, Krause Publicatons, Inc., Iola, WI, 1990. 360 pp., illus. $49.95.

The classic beauty and the interesting history of the Model 21 Winchester shotgun.

Wing & Shot, by R.G. Wehle, Country Press, Scottsville, NY, 1967. 190 pp., illus. $24.95.

Step-by-step account on how to train a fine shooting dog.

The World's Fighting Shotguns, by Thomas F. Swearengen, T. B. N. Enterprises, Alexandria, VA, 1979. 500 pp., illus. $34.95.

The complete military and police reference work from the shotgun's inception to date, with up-to-date developments.

ARMS ASSOCIATIONS

UNITED STATES

ALABAMA

Alabama Gun Collectors Assn.
Secretary, P.O. Box 6080, Tuscaloosa, AL 35405

ALASKA

Alaska Gun Collectors Assn., Inc.
Gereth Stillman, Pres., 1554 Myrtle, Eagle River, AK 99577

ARIZONA

Arizona Arms Assn.
Don DeBusk, President, 4837 Bryce Ave., Glendale, AZ 85301

CALIFORNIA

California Waterfowl Assn.
4630 Northgate Blvd., #150, Sacramento, CA 95834
Greater Calif. Arms & Collectors Assn.
Donald L. Bullock, 8291 Carburton St., Long Beach, CA 90808-3302
Los Angeles Gun Ctg. Collectors Assn.
F.H. Ruffra, 20810 Amie Ave., Apt. #9, Torrance, CA 90503

COLORADO

Colorado Gun Collectors Assn.
L.E.(Bud) Greenwald, 2553 S. Quitman St., Denver, CO 80219/303-935-3850

CONNECTICUT

Ye Connecticut Gun Guild, Inc.
Dick Fraser, P.O. Box 425, Windsor, CT 06095

FLORIDA

Tampa Bay Arms Collectors' Assn.
John Tuvell, 2461-67th Ave., S., St., Petersburg, FL 33712
Unified Sportsmen of Florida
P.O. Box 6565, Tallahassee, FL 32314

GEORGIA

Georgia Arms Collectors Assn., Inc.
Michael Kindberg, President, P.O. Box 277, Alpharetta, GA 30239-0277

ILLINOIS

Illinois State Rifle Assn.
P.O. Box 27, Kankakee, IL 60901
Illinois Gun Collectors Assn.
T.J. Curl, Jr., P.O. Box 971, Kankakee, IL 60901
Mississippi Valley Gun & Cartridge Coll. Assn.
Bob Filbert, P.O. Box 61, Port Byron, IL 61275/309-523-2593
Sauk Trail Gun Collectors
Gordell M. Matson, P.O. Box 1113, Milan, IL 61264
Wabash Valley Gun Collectors Assn., Inc.
Jerry D. Holycross, RR #6, Box 341, Danville, IL 61832

INDIANA

Indiana Sportsmen's Council-Legislative
Maurice Latimer, P.O. Box 93, Bloomington, IN 47402
Indiana State Rifle & Pistol Assn.
Thos. Glancy, P.O. Box 552, Chesterton, IN 46304
Southern Indiana Gun Collectors Assn., Inc.
Sheila McClary, 309 W. Monroe St., Boonville, IN 47601/812-897-3742

IOWA

Central States Gun Collectors Assn.
Avery Giles, 1104 S. 1st Ave., Marshtown, IA 50158

KANSAS

Kansas Cartridge Collectors Assn.
Bob Linder, Box 84, Plainville, KS 67663

KENTUCKY

Kentuckiana Arms Collectors Assn.
Ralph Handy, President, Box 1776, Louisville, KY 40201
Kentucky Gun Collectors Assn., Inc.
Ruth Johnson, Box 64, Owensboro, KY 42302

LOUISIANA

Washitaw River Renegades
Sandra Rushing, P.O. Box 256, Main St., Grayson, LA 71435

MARYLAND

Baltimore Antique Arms Assn.
Stanley I. Kellert, 8340 Dubbs Dr., Severn, MD 21144

MASSACHUSETTS

Bay Colony Weapons Collectors, Inc.
John Brandt, Box 111, Hingham, MA 02043
Massachusetts Arms Collectors
John J. Callan, Jr., 1887 Main St., Leicester, MA 01524-1943/508-892-3837

MISSISSIPPI

Mississippi Gun Collectors Assn.
Jack E. Swinney, P.O. Box 16323, Hattiesburg, MS 39402

MISSOURI

Mineral Belt Gun Collectors Assn.
D.F. Saunders, 1110 Cleveland Ave., Monett, MO 65708
Missouri Valley Arms Collectors Assn., Inc.
L.P Brammer II, Membership Secy., P.O. Box 33033, Kansas City, MO 64114

MONTANA

Montana Arms Collectors Assn.
Lewis E. Yearout, 308 Riverview Dr. East, Great Falls, MT 59404
The Winchester Arms Collectors Assn.
Richard Berg, P.O. Box 6754, Great Falls, MT 59406

NEW HAMPSHIRE

New Hampshire Arms Collectors, Inc.
Frank H. Galeucia, Rt. 28, Box 44, Windham, NH 03087

NEW JERSEY

Englishtown Benchrest Shooters Assn.
Michael Toth, 64 Cooke Ave., Carteret, NJ 07008
Jersey Shore Antique Arms Collectors
Joe Sisia, P.O. Box 100, Bayville, NJ 08721
New Jersey Arms Collectors Club, Inc.
Angus Laidlaw, President, 230 Valley Rd., Montclair, NJ 07042/201-746-0939

NEW YORK

Empire State Arms Collectors Assn.
P.O. Box 2328, Rochester, NY 14623
Iroquois Arms Collectors Assn.
Bonnie Robinson, Show Secy., P.O. Box 142, Ransomville, NY 14131/716-791-4096
Mid-State Arms Coll. & Shooters Club
Jack Ackerman, 24 S. Mountain Terr., Binghamton, NY 13903

NORTH CAROLINA

North Carolina Gun Collectors Assn.
Jerry Ledford, 3231-7th St. Dr. NE, Hickory, NC 28601

OHIO

Ohio Gun Collectors Assn.
P.O. Box 24 F, Cincinnati, OH 45224
The Start Gun Collectors, Inc.
William I. Gann, 5666 Waynesburg Dr., Waynesburg, OH 44688

OKLAHOMA

Indian Territory Gun Collector's Assn.
P.O. Box 4491, Tulsa, OK 74159

OREGON

Oregon Arms Collectors Assn., Inc.
Phil Bailey, P.O. Box 25103, Portland, OR 97225
Oregon Cartridge Collectors Assn.
Gale Stockton, 133 NW 12th, Gresham, OR 97030

PENNSYLVANIA

Presque Isle Gun Collectors Assn.
James Welch, 156 E. 37 St., Erie, PA 16504

SOUTH CAROLINA

Belton Gun Club, Inc.
J.K. Phillips, 195 Phillips Dr., Belton, SC 29627
South Carolina Shooting Assn.
P.O. Box 12658, Columbia, SC 29211-2658
Membership Div.: William Strozier, Secretary, P.O. Box 70, Johns Island, SC 29457-0070

SOUTH DAKOTA

Dakota Territory Gun Coll. Assn., Inc.
Curt Carter, Castlewood, SD 57223

TENNESSEE

Smoky Mountain Gun Coll. Assn., Inc.
Hugh W. Yabro, President, P.O. Box 23225, Knoxville, TN 37933
Tennessee Gun Collectors Assn., Inc.
M.H. Parks, 3556 Pleasant Valley Rd., Nashville, TN 37204

TEXAS

Houston Gun Collectors Assn., Inc.
P.O. Box 741429, Houston, TX 77274-1429
Texas Cartridge Collectors Assn., Inc.
James C. Sartor, Sec./Tres., 5606 Duxbury St., Houston, TX 77035
Texas Gun Collectors Assn.
85 Wells Fargo Trail, Austin, TX 78737
Texas State Rifle Assn.
P.O. Drawer 710549, Dallas, TX 75371

WASHINGTON

Washington Arms Collectors, Inc.
J. Dennis Cook, P.O. Box 7335, Tacoma, WA 98407

WISCONSIN

Great Lakes Arms Collectors Assn., Inc.
Edward C. Warnke, 2913 Woodridge Lane, Waukesha, WI 53188
Wisconsin Gun Collectors Assn., Inc.
Lulita Zellmer, P.O. Box 181, Sussex, WI 53089

WYOMING

Wyoming Weapons Collectors
P.O. Box 284, Laramie, WY 82070

NATIONAL ORGANIZATIONS

Amateur Trapshooting Assn.
601 W. National Rd., Vandalia, OH 45377

American Coon Hunters Assn.
Opal Johnston, P.O. Cadet, Route 1, Box 492, Old Mines, MO 63630

American Custom Gunmakers Guild
Jan Billeb, Exec. Director, P.O. Box 812, Burlington, IA 52601-0812/319-752-6114

American Defense Preparedness Assn.
Two Colonial Place, 2101 Wilson Blvd., Suite 400, Arlington, VA 22201-3061

American Pistolsmiths Guild
Hamilton S. Bowen, President, P.O. Box 67, Louisville, TN 37777

American Police Pistol & Rifle Assn.
3801 Biscayne Blvd., Miami, FL 33137

American Single Shot Rifle Assn.
L.B. Thompson, 987 Jefferson Ave., Salem, OH 44460

American Society of Arms Collectors
George E. Weatherly, P.O. Box 2567, Waxahachie, TX 75165

Association of Firearm and Toolmark Examiners
Eugenia A. Bell, Secy., 7857 Esterel Dr., LaJolla, CA 92037; Membership Secy., Andrew B. Hart, 80 Mountain View Ave., Rensselaer, NY 12144

Boone & Crockett Club
241 South Fraley Blvd., P.O. Box 547, Dumfries, VA 22026

Browning Collectors Assn.
Bobbie Hamit, P.O. Box 526, Aurora, NE 68818/402-694-6602

The Cast Bullet Assn., Inc.
Ralland J. Fortier, Membership Director, 4103 Foxcraft Dr., Traverse City, MI 49684

Citizens Committee for the Right to Keep and Bear Arms
Natl. Hq., Liberty Park, 12500 NE Tenth Pl., Bellevue, WA 98005

Colt Collectors Assn.
3200 Westminster, Dallas, TX 75205

Ducks Unlimited, Inc.
One Waterfowl Way, Memphis, TN 38120

Fifty Caliber Shooters Assn.
11469 Olive St. Rd., Suite 50, St. Louis, MO 63141

Firearms Coalition
Box 6537, Silver Spring, MD 20906/301-871-3006

Firearms Engravers Guild of America
Robert Evans, Secy., 332 Vine St., Oregon City, OR 97045

Foundation for North American Wild Sheep
720 Allen Ave., Cody, WY 82414

Garand Collectors Assn.
P.O. Box 181, Richmond, KY 40475

Golden Eagle Collectors Assn.
Chris Showler, 11144 Slate Creek Rd., Grass Valley, CA 95945

Gun Owners of America
8001 Forbes Place, Suite 102, Springfield, VA 22151/703-321-8585

Handgun Hunters International
J.D. Jones, Director, P.O. Box 357 MAG, Bloomingdale, OH 43910

Harrington & Richardson Gun Coll. Assn.
George L. Cardet, 525 NW 27th Ave., Suite 201, Miami, FL 33125

International Benchrest Shooters
Joan Borden, RD 1, Box 244A, Tunkhannock, PA 18657

International Cartridge Coll. Assn., Inc.
Charles Spano, P.O. Box 5297, Ormond Beach, FL 32174-5297

IHMSA (Intl. Handgun Metallic Silhouette Assn.)
Frank Scotto, 127 Winthrop Terr., Meriden, CT 06450

IPPA (International Paintball Players Assn.)
P.O. Box 90974, Los Angeles, CA 90009/310-322-3107

Jews for the Preservation of Firearms Ownership (JPFO)
2872 S. Wentworth Ave., Milwaukee, WI 53207/414-769-0760

The Mannlicher Collectors Assn.
Rev. Don L. Henry, Secy., P.O. Box 7144, Salem, OR 97303

Marlin Firearms Collectors Assn., Ltd.
Dick Paterson, Secy., 407 Lincoln Bldg., 44 Main St., Champaign, IL 61820

Miniature Arms Collectors/Makers Society, Ltd.
Donald A. Beck, Secretary, 3329 Palm St., Granite City, IL 62040/618-877-5284

M1 Carbine Collectors Assn. (M1-CCA)
P.O. Box 4895, Stateline, NV 89449

National Association of Buckskinners
Tim Pray, 1981 E. 94th Ave., Thornton, CO 80229

National Assn. of Federally Licensed Firearms Dealers
Andrew Molchan, 2455 E. Sunrise, Ft. Lauderdale, FL 33304

National Association to Keep and Bear Arms
P.O. Box 78336, Seattle, WA 98178

National Automatic Pistol Collectors Assn.
Tom Knox, P.O. Box 15738, Tower Grove Station, St. Louis, MO 63163

National Bench Rest Shooters Assn., Inc.
Pat Baggett, 2027 Buffalo, Levelland, TX 79336

National Firearms Assn.
P.O. Box 160038, Austin, TX 78716

National Muzzle Loading Rifle Assn.
Box 67, Friendship, IN 47021

National Reloading Manufacturers Assn.
One Centerpointe Dr., Suite 300, Lake Oswego, OR 97035

National Rifle Assn. of America
1600 Rhode Island Ave., NW, Washington, DC 20036

National Shooting Sports Foundation, Inc.
Robert T. Delfay, Exec. Director, 555 Danbury Rd., Wilton, CT 06897/203-762-1320

National Skeet Shooting Assn.
Mike Hampton, Exec. Director, P.O. Box 680007, San Antonio, TX 78268-0007

National Sporting Clays Association
P.O. Box 680007, San Antonio, TX 78268/800-877-5338

National Wild Turkey Federation, Inc.
P.O. Box 530, Edgefield, SC 29824

North American Hunting Club
P.O. Box 3401, Minnetonka, MN 55343

North-South Skirmish Assn., Inc.
Stevan F. Meserve, Exec. Secretary, 204 W. Holly Ave., Sterling, VA 22170-4006

Remington Society of America
Leon W. Wier Jr., President, 22526 Leyte Dr., Torrance, CA 90505

Rocky Mountain Elk Foundation
P.O. Box 8249, Missoula, MT 59807-8249

Ruger Collector's Assn., Inc.
P.O. Box 1441, Yazoo City, MS 39194

Safari Club International
Philip DeLone, Admin. Dir., 4800 W. Gates Pass Rd., Tucson, AZ 85745/602-620-1220

Sako Collectors Assn., Inc.
Karen Reed, 1725 Woodhill Ln., Bedford, TX 76021

Second Amendment Foundation
James Madison Building, 12500 NE 10th Pl., Bellevue, WA 98005

Smith & Wesson Collectors Assn.
George Linne, 133 S. 11th St., Chouteau Ctr., Suite 400, St. Louis, MO 63102

The Society of American Bayonet Collectors
P.O. Box 234, East Islip, NY 11730-0234

Southern California Schuetzen Society
Dean Lillard, 34657 Ave. E., Yucaipa, CA 92399

Sporting Arms & Ammunition Manufacturers Institute (SAAMI)
555 Danbury Rd., Wilton, CT 06897

The Thompson/Center Assn.
Joe Wright, President, Box 792, Northboro, MA 01532/508-393-3834

USPSA/IPSC
Dave Stanford, P.O. Box 811, Sedro Woolley, WA 98284/206-855-2245

U.S. Revolver Assn.
Chick Shuter, 96 West Union St., Ashland, MA 01721

U.S. Sporting Clays Assn.
Glynne Moseley, Membership Services Mgr., 50 Briar Hollow, Suite 490 East, Houston, TX 77027/713-622-8043

The Varmint Hunters Assn., Inc.
Box 730, Lone Grove, OK 73443/405-657-3098

Weatherby Collectors Assn., Inc.
P.O. Box 128, Moira, NY 12957

Winchester Arms Collectors Assn.
Richard Berg, Executive Secy., P.O. Box 6754, Great Falls, MT 59406

AUSTRALIA

Sporting Shooters Assn. of Australia, Inc.
P.O. Box 2066, Kent Town, SA 5071, Australia

CANADA

ALBERTA

Canadian Historical Arms Society
P.O. Box 901, Edmonton, Alb., Canada T5J 2L8

National Firearms Assn.
Natl. Hq: P.O. Box 1779, Edmonton, Alb., Canada T5J 2P1

ONTARIO

Tri-County Antique Arms Fair
P.O. Box 122, RR #1, North Lancaster Ont., Canada K0C 1Z0

EUROPE

ENGLAND

Arms and Armour Society
E.J.B. Greenwood, Field House, Upper Dicker, Hailsham, East Sussex, BN27 3PY, England

Historical Breechloading Smallarms Assn.
D.J. Penn M.A., Imperial War Museum, Lambeth Rd., London SE 1 6HZ, England.
Journal and newsletter are $12 a yr., plus surcharge for airmail.

National Rifle Assn.
(Great Britain) Bisley Camp, Brookwood, Woking Surrey GU24 OPB, England/0483.797777

FRANCE

Syndicat National de l'Auquebuserie du Commerce de l'Arme Historique
B.P. No. 3, 78110 Le Vesinet, France

GERMANY

Deutscher Schützenbund
Lahnstrasse 120, W-6200 Wiesbaden-Klarenthal, Germany

NEW ZEALAND

New Zealand Deerstalkers Assn.
Michael Watt, P.O. Box 6514, Wellington, New Zealand

SOUTH AFRICA

Historical Firearms Soc. of South Africa
P.O. Box 145, 7725 Newlands, Republic of South Africa

DIRECTORY
OF THE
ARMS TRADE

The **Product Directory** contains a total of 53 product categories. This year we have changed Guns, Foreign to **Guns, Foreign—Manufacturers** and have added a new category **Guns, Foreign—Importers**. The two are cross-referenced to aid you in finding the U.S. importers of any foreign-manufactured firearm.

Also note in the Product Directory, a black bullet preceeding the manufacturer's name indicates the availability of a Warranty Service Center address, which can be found on page 445.

The **Manufacturer's Directory** lists the manufacturers alphabetically, their addresses, phone numbers and FAX numbers.

DIRECTORY OF THE ARMS TRADE INDEX

PRODUCT DIRECTORY **498-511**

AMMUNITION, COMMERCIAL 498
AMMUNITION, CUSTOM 498
AMMUNITION, FOREIGN 498
AMMUNITION COMPONENTS—BULLETS, POWDER,
   PRIMERS 498
ANTIQUE ARMS DEALERS 499
APPRAISERS—GUNS, ETC. 499
AUCTIONEERS—GUNS, ETC 499
BOOKS (Publishers and Dealers) 499
BULLET AND CASE LUBRICANTS 499
BULLET SWAGE DIES AND TOOLS 499
CARTRIDGES FOR COLLECTORS 499
CASES, CABINETS AND RACKS—GUN 499
CHOKE DEVICES, RECOIL ABSORBERS
   AND RECOIL PADS 500
CHRONOGRAPHS AND PRESSURE TOOLS 500
CLEANING AND REFINISHING SUPPLIES 500
COMPUTER SOFTWARE—BALLISTICS 500
CUSTOM GUNSMITHS 500
CUSTOM METALSMITHS 502
DECOYS 502
ENGRAVERS, ENGRAVING TOOLS 502
GAME CALLS 502
GUN PARTS, U.S. AND FOREIGN 503
GUNS, AIR 503
GUNS, FOREIGN—MANUFACTURERS 503
GUNS, FOREIGN—IMPORTERS 504
GUNS, U.S.-MADE 504
GUNS AND GUN PARTS, REPLICA
   AND ANTIQUE 504
GUNS, SURPLUS—PARTS AND AMMUNITION 504

GUNSMITHS, CUSTOM (See Custom Gunsmiths)
GUNSMITHS, HANDGUN (See Pistolsmiths)
GUNSMITH SCHOOLS 505
GUNSMITH SUPPLIES, TOOLS, SERVICES 505
HANDGUN ACCESSORIES 505
HANDGUN GRIPS 505
HEARING PROTECTORS 506
HOLSTERS AND LEATHER GOODS 506
HUNTING AND CAMP GEAR, CLOTHING, ETC. 506
KNIVES AND KNIFEMAKER'S SUPPLIES— FACTORY
   AND MAIL ORDER 506
LABELS, BOXES, CARTRIDGE HOLDERS 507
LOAD TESTING AND PRODUCT TESTING
   (Chronographing, Ballistic Studies) 507
MISCELLANEOUS 507
MUZZLE-LOADING GUNS, BARRELS AND EQUIP. ... 508
PISTOLSMITHS 508
REBORING AND RERIFLING 508
RELOADING TOOLS AND ACCESSORIES 508
RESTS—BENCH, PORTABLE—AND ACCESSORIES ... 509
RIFLE BARREL MAKERS (See also Muzzle-Loading
   Guns, Barrels and Equipment) 509
SCOPES, MOUNTS, ACCESSORIES, OPTICAL
   EQUIPMENT 509
SHOOTING/TRAINING SCHOOLS 510
SIGHTS, METALLIC 510
STOCKS (Commercial and Custom) 510
TARGETS, BULLET AND CLAYBIRD TRAPS 511
TAXIDERMY 511
TRAP AND SKEET SHOOTER'S EQUIPMENT 511
TRIGGERS, RELATED EQUIPMENT 511

MANUFACTURERS' DIRECTORY **512-528**

PRODUCT DIRECTORY

AMMUNITION, COMMERCIAL

Action Arms Ltd.
ACTIV Industries, Inc.
A-Square Co., Inc.
American Ballistics Co., Inc. (9mm subsonic, ball ammo)
Atlanta Discount Ammo
Behlert Precision
Black Hills Ammunition
Blammo Ammo
Blount, Inc. Sporting Equipment Division
California Magnum
CBC
ChinaSports, Inc.
Cor-Bon Bullet & Ammo Co.
Crosman Corp.
Daisy Mfg. Co.
Dakota Arms, Inc.
Denver Bullets, Inc.
DKT, Inc.
Dynamit Nobel-RWS, Inc.
Eley Ltd.
Elite Ammunition
Enguix Import-Export
Estate Cartridge, Inc.
Federal Cartridge Co.
FN Herstal
Garrett Cartridges, Inc.
GDL Enterprises
Glaser Safety Slug, Inc.
Hansen Cartridge Co.
Hartmann & Weiss GmbH

Horizons Unlimited
Hornady Mfg. Co.
ICI-America
IMI
Kent Cartridge Mfg. Co. Ltd.
K.B.I., Inc.
Lapua Ltd.
Lever Arms Service Ltd.
M&D Munitions Ltd.
Maionchi - L.M.I.
MagSafe Ammo Co.
MAGTECH Recreational Products, Inc.
Men—Metallwerk Elisenhuette, GmbH
New England Ammunition Co.
Old Western Scrounger
Omark Industries
Paragon Sales & Services, Inc.
PMC/Eldorado Cartridge Corp.
Precision Delta Corp.
Precision Prods. of Wash., Inc.
Pro Load Ammunition, Inc.
Remington Arms Co.
Safari Gun Co.
Speer Products
Star Reloading Co., Inc.
3-D Ammunition & Bullets
USAC
Weatherby, Inc.
Winchester Div., Olin Corp.
Zero Ammunition Co., Inc.

AMMUNITION, CUSTOM

AFSCO Ammunition (blanks)
A-Square Co., Inc.
Atlanta Discount Ammo
Ballistica Maximus North
Ballistica Maximus South
Beeman Precision Arms, Inc. (for airguns)
Black Hills Ammunition
Cartridges Unlimited
Country Armourer, The
Cubic Shot Shell Co., Inc.
Custom Hunting Ammo & Arms
Custom Tackle & Ammo
C.W. Cartridge Co.
DKT, Inc.
Elite Ammunition
Elko Arms
Ellis Sport Shop, E.W.
Enguix Import-Export
Epps "Orillia" Ltd., Ellwood
Estate Cartridge, Inc. (shotshell)
Freedom Arms, Inc.
Gammog, Gregory B. Gally
GDL Enterprises
"Gramps" Antique Cartridges
Hardin Specialty Distributors
Hindman, Ace
Hornady Mfg. Co.
Jensen's Custom Ammunition
Jett & Co., Inc.

Kaswer Custom, Inc.
Keeler, R.H.
Kent Cartridge Mfg. Co. Ltd.
L.A.R. Manufacturing, Inc.
Lindsley Arms Cartridge Co.
Lomont Precision Bullets, Kent (cast only)
MagSafe Ammo Co.
McConnellstown Reloading & Cast Bullets, Inc.
M&D Munitions Ltd.
Mountain Arms
Mountain South
Naval Ordnance Works
Newman Gunshop
Old Western Scrounger
Personal Protection Systems Ltd. (high-performance handgun loads)
Pony Express Reloaders
Precision Delta Corp.
Precision Munitions, Inc. (reloaded ammo)
Professional Hunter Supplies
Randco UK
Sanders Custom Gun Service
Spence, George W.
State Arms Gun Co.
Three-Ten Corp.
Thunderbird Cartridge Co., Inc.
Worthy Products, Inc.

AMMUNITION, FOREIGN

Action Arms Ltd.
AFSCO Ammunition
Atlanta Discount Ammo
Brenneke KG, Wilhelm
Cartridges Unlimited
Century International Arms, Ltd.
CBC
Champion's Choice, Inc.
Cubic Shot Shell Co., Inc.
DKT, Inc.
Dynamit Nobel-RWS, Inc.
Estate Cartridge, Inc.
Fiocchi of America, Inc.
FN Herstal
Gibbs Rifle Company, Inc.
"Gramps" Antique Cartridges
Hansen Cartridge Co.
Hirtenberger Patronen-, Zundhutchen- & Metallwarenfabrik
IMI

Jaeger, Inc., Paul (RWS centerfire ammo)
Lapua Ltd.
Maionchi - L.M.I.
MAGTECH Recreational Products, Inc.
M&D Munitions Ltd.
Merkuria Ltd.
Navy Arms Company
New England Arms Co.
Nygord Precision Products
Old Western Scrounger
Paragon Sales & Services, Inc.
Pragotrade
Precision Delta Corp.
R.E.T. Enterprises
Safari Gun Co.
Samco Global Arms, Inc.
Spence, George W.
Su-Press-On, Inc.
T.F.C. S.p.A.

AMMUNITION COMPONENTS—BULLETS, POWDER, PRIMERS

Accuracy Unlimited (50-, 54-caliber hunting bullets)

Accurate Arms Company, Inc. (powders)
ACTIV Industries, Inc.

Ahlman Guns
Allred Bullet Co. (custom bullets)
American Bullets
A-Square Co., Inc. (custom bullets; brass)
American Products Co. (12-ga. shot wad)
Armfield Custom Bullets
Atlanta Discount Ammo
Ballard Built Custom Bullets
Ballistic Products, Inc. (shotgun powders, primers)
Barnes Bullets, Inc.
Behlert Precision
Belding & Mull, Inc.
Berger Bullets (benchrest, varmint bullets)
Bertram Bullet Co.
Bitterroot Bullet Co.
Black Hills Shooters Supply
Black Mountain Bullets (custom Fluid King match bullets)
Blount, Inc. Sporting Equipment Division
Blue Mountain Bullets (custom)
Brenneke KG, Wilhelm
BRP, Inc. (cast bullets)
Bruno Shooters Supply (22, 6mm benchrest bullets)
Buffalo Bullet Co., Inc. (ML bullets)
Buffalo Rock Shooters Supply
Bullet Swaging Supply, Inc.
Bull-X, Inc.
Buzztail Brass (brass)
Calhoon Mfg., James (varmint bullets)
Cartridges Unlimited (cast bullets)
CFVentures ("soft gas checks")
Champion's Choice, Inc.
Cheddite France S.A. (empty shotshells)
CheVron Bullets
CBC
Competition Bullets, Inc.
Competitor Corporation, Inc.
Cor-Bon Bullet & Ammo Co. (375, 44, 45 solid brass partition bullets)
Crawford Co., Inc., R.M.
Creative Cartridge Co.
Denver Bullets, Inc. (hardcast bullets)
Dixie Gun Works
DKT, Inc. (bullets)
DuPont
Dynamit Nobel-RWS, Inc. (RWS percussion caps)
Enguix Import-Export
Excaliber Wax, Inc. (wax bullets)
Federal Cartridge Co. (primers)
Fiocchi of America, Inc. (primers; shotshell cases)
Fitz Pistol Grip Co.
4-D Custom Die Co.
Fowler Bullets (benchrest bullets)
Freedom Arms, Inc.
GOEX, Inc. (blackpowder only)
Golden Powder International Sales, Inc. (Golden Powder/blackpowder)
Green Bay Bullets (cast lead bullets)
Grizzly Bullets (custom)
Gun City
Gusty Winds Corp.
Hardin Specialty Distributors (casings)
Harris Enterprises (custom bullets)
Harrison Bullet Works (swaged 41 mag. bullets)
Hart & Son, Inc., Robert W.
Hawk Co. (bullets)
Hercules, Inc. (smokeless powder)
Hornady Mfg. Co.
Huntington Die Specialties
IMR Powder Co.
IMI
Jensen Bullets
Jensen's Custom Ammunition
Kaswer Custom, Inc.
K.B.I., Inc.
Keith's Bullets
Kent Cartridge Mfg. Co. Ltd.
Kodiak Custom Bullets
Lachaussee, S.A.
Lage Uniwad, Inc.
Lane Bullets (custom cast handgun bullets)
Lapua Ltd.
Lindsley Arms Cartridge Co. (brass)
Lomont Precision Bullets, Kent (cast)

Mack's Sport Shop (custom bullets)
Maionchi - L.M.I.
MCC
McConnellstown Reloading & Cast Bullets, Inc.
McMurdo, Lynn (50-cal. custom bullets)
M&D Munitions Ltd.
MEC (non-toxic steel shot kits)
Merkuria Ltd.
Michael's Antiques
Midway Arms, Inc.
MoLoc Bullets
Mountain Arms
Mushroom Express Bullet Co. (ML bullets)
Naval Ordnance Works
Necromancer Industries, Inc.
Norma
Northern Precision Custom Swaged Bullets (.416)
Nosler, Inc.
O'Connor Rifle Products Co., Ltd. (steelhead cartridge cases)
Old Western Scrounger
Omark Industries
Orion Bullets (partitioned, bonded bullets)
Pace Marketing, Inc.
Jaro Mfg.
Patchbox, The
Patriot Manufacturing (custom bullets)
Pattern Control (plastic wads)
PMC/Eldorado Cartridge Corp.
Polywad, Inc. (Spred-Rs for shotshells)
Pomeroy, Robert (obsolete cases, bullets)
Pony Express Reloaders
Precision Components & Guns
Precision Delta Corp.
Precision Munitions, Inc. (cast bullets)
Precision Reloading, Inc.
Professional Hunter Supplies (408, 375, 308, 510 custom bullets)
Randco UK
Red Willow Tool & Armory, Inc.
Remington Arms Co.
Renner Co., R.J. (x-ring rubber bullets)
R.I.S. Co., Inc.
Rolston, Jr., Fred (cast bullets only)
Rossi S.A. Metalurgica E Municoes, Amadeo
Rubright Bullets (custom 22, 6mm benchrest bullets)
Sandia Die & Cartridge Co.
Scot Powder Co. of Ohio, Inc. (smokeless powder)
Shappy Bullets (swaged and cast lead bullets)
Shell Shack
Southern Ammunition Co., Inc.
Specialty Gunsmithing
Speer Products
Sport Flite Mfg., Inc. (zinc bases, lead wire, copper jackets)
Star Reloading Co., Inc. (bullets)
Stevi Machine, Inc. (cases)
Swift Bullet Co. (375 big game, 224 custom)
Taracorp Industries (Lawrence Brand lead shot)
T.F.C. S.p.A.
3-D Ammunition & Bullets
Thompson Precision (bullets)
Thunderbird Cartridge Co., Inc. (powder)
TMI Products
Trophy Bonded Bullets, Inc.
True Flight Bullet Co.
USAC (bullets)
Vihtavuori Oy
Vitt/Boos (aerodynamic shotgun slug)
Warren Muzzleloading Co., Inc.
Watson Trophy Match Bullets (22, 6mm, 243, 30 custom benchrest bullets)
Whitestone Lumber Corp.
Widener's Reloading & Shooting Supply
Winchester Div., Olin Corp.
Windjammer Tournament Wads, Inc. (shotshell wads)
Woodland Bullets (bullets)
Worthy Products, Inc. (slug loads)
Wosenitz, William B. (slug loads)
Zero Ammunition Co., Inc.

ANTIQUE ARMS DEALERS

Ad Hominem
Ahlman Guns
Ammunition Consulting Services, Inc.
Antique American Firearms
Antique Arms Co.
Aplan Antiques & Art, James O.
Beeman Precision Arms, Inc. (airguns only)
Bondini Paolo
Boggs, Wm.
British Arms Co. Ltd.
Buckskin Machine Works
Cape Outfitters
Carlson, Douglas R.
Century International Arms, Ltd.
Chadick's Ltd.
Condon, Inc., David
Corry, John (English guns)
Delhi Gun House
Dilliott Gunsmithing, Inc.
Dixie Gun Works
Dyson & Son Ltd., Peter
Ed's Gun House
Epps "Orillia" Ltd., Ellwood
Fagan & Co., William
Flayderman & Co., N.
Flintlock Muzzle Loading Gun Shop, The
Frielich Police Equipment
Fulmer's Antique Firearms, Chet
Glass, Herb
Goergen Gun Shop, Inc.
Golden Age Arms Co.
Griffin's Guns & Antiques
Guncraft Sports, Inc.
Gun Parts Corporation, The
Gun Works, The
Hallowell & Co.
Hansen & Co.

Hansen Cartridge Co.
Hunkeler, A.
Kelley's
Lever Arms Service Ltd.
Liberty Antique Gunworks
Log Cabin Sport Shop
Markell, Inc.
Martin's Gun Shop
McKee, Arthur (Rem. double shotguns)
Mendez, John A.
Michael's Antiques
Montana Outfitters
Museum of Historical Arms, Inc.
Muzzleloaders Etcetera, Inc.
Navy Arms Company
New England Arms Co.
New Orleans Arms Co.
Paragon Sales & Services, Inc.
Patchbox, The
Pioneer Guns
Pony Express Sport Shop, Inc.
P.S.M.G. Gun Co.
Retting, Inc., Martin B.
Rutgers Gun & Boat Center
San Francisco Gun Exchange
Safari Outfitters Ltd.
Semmer, Charles
Sherwood Intl. Export Corp.
S&S Firearms
Steves House of Guns
Stott's Creek Armory, Inc.
Track of the Wolf, Inc.
Trail Guns Armory, Inc.
Vintage Arms, Inc.
Ward & Van Valkenburg
Wiest, M.C.
Yearout, Lewis E.

APPRAISERS—GUNS, ETC.

Ahlman Guns
Ammunition Consulting Services, Inc.
Aplan Antiques & Art, James O.
Arms, Peripheral Data Systems
Beeman Precision Arms, Inc. (airguns only)
Behlert Precision
Billings Gunsmiths, Inc.
Blue Book Publications
Bustani Appraisers, Leo
Butterfield & Butterfield
Cameron's
Camilli, Lou
Chadick's Ltd.
Christie's East
Christopher Firearms Co., Inc., E.
Clements' Custom Leathercraft, Chas
Condon, Inc., David
Custom Tackle & Ammo
Dixie Gun Works
Dixon Muzzleloading Shop, Inc.
D.O.C. Specialists, Inc.
Ed's Gun House
Ellis Sport Shop, E.W.
Epps "Orillia" Ltd., Ellwood
Eversull Co., Inc., K.
Flayderman & Co., Inc., N.
Forgett, Valmore J., Jr.
Fredrick Gun Shop
Goergen's Gun Shop, Inc.
Golden Age Arms Co.
Gonzalez Guns, Ramon B.
Goodwin, Fred
Greenwald, Leon E. "Bud"
Griffin & Howe, Inc.
Guncraft Sports, Inc.
Gun Works, The
Hallowell & Co.
Hansen & Co.
Hansen Cartridge Co.
Holland, Dick
Hughes, Steven Dodd

Irwin, Campbell H.
Jaeger, Inc., Paul
Jonas Appraisals & Taxidermy, Jack (animal trophies)
Kelley's
Ledbetter Airguns, Riley
Liberty Antique Gunworks
Martin's Gun Shop
Montana Outfitters
Museum of Historical Arms, Inc.
Muzzleloaders Etcetera, Inc.
Navy Arms Company
New England Arms Co.
Oakland Custom Arms, Inc.
Orvis Co., The
Perazzi U.S.A., Inc.
Pony Express Sport Shop, Inc.
P.S.M.G. Gun Co.
Rahn Gun Works, Inc.
R.E.T. Enterprises
Richards, John
Riggs, Jim
Sarco, Inc.
Shooting Gallery, The
Silver Ridge Gun Shop
S.K. Guns, Inc.
Stott's Creek Armory, Inc.
Strawbridge, Victor W.
Tillinghast, James C.
Ulrich, Doc & Bud
Unick's Gunsmithing
Vic's Gun Refinishing
Vintage Industries, Inc.
Walker Arms Co., Inc.
Wardrop, R. Alex
Wayne Firearms for Collectors and Investors, James
Whildin & Sons Ltd., E.H.
Whitestone Lumber Corp.
Wiest, M.C.
Williamson Precision Gunsmithing
Yearout, Lewis E.

AUCTIONEERS—GUNS, ETC.

Ammunition Consulting Services, Inc.
Bourne Co., Inc., Richard A.
Butterfield & Butterfield
Christie's East
Fagan & Co., William
Goodwin, Fred

Kelley's
"Little John's" Antique Arms
Parke-Bernet
Silver Ridge Gun Shop
Sotheby's
Tillinghast, James C.

BOOKS (Publishers and Dealers)

Ackley Rifle Barrels, P.O.
American handgunner Magazine
Aplan Antiques & Art, James O.

Armory Publications
Arms & Armour Press, Ltd.
Ballistic Products, Inc. (reloading, hunting)

Beeman Precision Arms, Inc. (airguns only)
Belding & Mull, Inc.
Bellm Contenders (P.O. Ackley)
Blacksmith Corp.
Blacktail Mountain Books
Blue Book Publications
British Arms Co. Ltd.
Brownell's, Inc.
Bruno Shooters Supply
Calibre Press, Inc. (police survival books)
Colorado Sutlers Arsenal
Corbin Manufacturing & Supply, Inc.
DBI Books, Inc.
Dixie Gun Works
Flores Publications, J.
Fortress Publications, Inc.
Golden Age Arms Co.
"Gramps" Antique Cartridges
Gun City
Guncraft Books
Gun Hunter Books
Gun Room Press, The
Guns Magazine
Gunnerman Books
Gun Works, The
Handgun Press
H and P Publishing
Ironside International Publishers, Inc.
K-D, Inc.
Krause Publications
Lane Publishing
Lyman Products Corporation
King & Co.

Madis, David
Magma Engineering Co.
Matthews, Inc., Bill
McKee Publications
Mitchell Arms, Inc.
Mountain South
NgraveR Co., The
October Country
Outdoorsman's Bookstore, The
Paladin Press
Pejsa Ballistics
Petersen Publishing Co.
Pettinger Books, Gerald
Police Bookshelf
Pranger, Ed G.
Riling Arms Books Co., Ray
Rutgers Book Center
Safari Press, Inc.
Stackpole Books
Stoeger Industries
Su-Press-On, Inc.
Survival Books/The Larder
Tank's Rifle Shop
Thomas, Charles C.
Threat Management Institute
Trafalgar Square
Trotman, Ken
Vintage Industries, Inc.
VSP Publishers (gunsmithing)
Wahl Corp., Paul
Weisz Antique Gun Parts
Wilderness Sound Productions Ltd.
Winchester Press
Wolfe Publishing Co.

BULLET AND CASE LUBRICANTS

American Gas & Chemical Co., Ltd.
Armite Laboratories
Belding & Mull, Inc.
Blackhawk East
Blackhawk Mountain
Blackhawk West
Blount, Inc. Sporting Equipment Division
BRP, Inc. Cast Bullets
Bruno Shooters Supply
Clenzoil Corp.
Cooper-Woodward (Perfect Lube)
Corbin Manufacturing & Supply, Inc.
Dillon Precision Prods., Inc.
Enguix Import-Export
Fitz Pistol Grip Co.
4-D Custom Die Co.
Guardsman Products
Hollywood Engineering
Hornady Mfg. Co.
Huntington Die Specialties
Javelina Products (Alox 2138F beeswax)
Lane Bullets, Inc.
LBT
LeClear Industries

Lee Precision, Inc.
Lighthouse Mfg. Co., Inc.
Lithi Bee Bullet Lube
Lyman Products Corporation (Size-Ezy)
Magma Engineering Co.
Micro-Lube
Midway Arms, Inc.
M&N Bullet Lube
NEI (Ten X-Lube; mould prep.)
Old Western Scrounger
Ox-Yoke Originals, Inc.
RCBS
Reardon Products
Redding Reloading, Inc.
SAECO
Sandia Die & Cartridge Co.
Shooters Accessory Supply
Shootin' Accessories Ltd.
Slipshot MTS Group
Tamarack Products, Inc. (bullet lube)
TDP Industries, Inc.
Thompson Bullet Lube Co.
Watson Trophy Match Bullets
Young Country Arms

BULLET SWAGE DIES AND TOOLS

Belding & Mull, Inc.
Blount, Inc. Sporting Equipment Division
Bruno Shooters Supply
Bullet Swaging Supply, Inc.
Corbin Manufacturing & Supply, Inc.
Fitz Pistol Grip Co.
4-D Custom Die Co.
Hawk Co. (jackets)

Hollywood Engineering
Lachaussee, S.A.
Necromancer Industries, Inc.
Rorschach Precision Products
Seneca Run Iron Works, Inc. (muzzle-loading round ball)
Sport Flite Mfg., Inc.
Swagease

CARTRIDGES FOR COLLECTORS

Ad Hominem
Ammunition Consulting Services, Inc.
Baekgaard Ltd.
Cameron's
Campbell, Dick
Competitor Corporation, Inc.
Delhi Gun House
Duffy, Chas. E.
Epps "Orillia" Ltd., Ellwood
Excaliber Wax, Inc.
Fiocchi of America, Inc.
First Distributors, Inc., Jack
Fitz Pistol Grip Co.
Forty Five Ranch

"Gramps" Antique Cartridges
Griffin's Guns & Antiques
Hansen Cartridge Co.
Idaho Ammunition Service (ammunition)
Kelley's
Keokuk Kollectors Kartridges
Montana Outfitters
MCC
Paragon Sales & Services, Inc.
Ramos, Jesse
San Francisco Gun Exchange
Tillinghast, James C.
Ward & Van Valkenburg
Yearout, Lewis

CASES, CABINETS AND RACKS—GUN

A&B Industries, Inc. (cases)
Abel Safe & File, Inc. (gun safes)
Airmold/W.R. Grace & Co.-Conn.
Alco Carrying Cases (aluminum)
Allen Co.. Bob (carrying cases)
Allen Co., Inc.
American Import Co., The
American Security Products Co.
Americase

Arizona Custom Case
Arkfeld Mfg. & Dist. Co., Inc. (security steel cabinets)
Art Jewel Enterprises Ltd. (cases)
Ashby Turkey Calls
Big Sky Racks, Inc.
Big Spring Enterprises "Bore Stores" (synthetic cases)
Black Sheep Brand

Boyt Co. (cases)
Brauer Bros. Mfg. Co.
British Arms Co. Ltd.
Browning Arms Co.
Bucheimer, J.M.
Bushmaster Hunting & Fishing
Cannon Safe, Inc.
Cascade Fabrication (aluminum cases)
Chipmunk
Crane & Crane Ltd.
Dara-Nes, Inc.
Deepeeka Exports Pvt. Ltd. (cases & racks)
Detroit-Armor Corp. (Saf-Gard steel gun safe)
Doskocil Mfg. Co., Inc. (Gun Guard carrying)
DTM International, Inc. (cases)
Elk River, Inc. (cases)
EMF Co., Inc.
English Co., A.G. (gun safes)
Enhanced Presentations, Inc. (hardwood and leather cases)
Epps "Orillia" Ltd., Ellwood (custom gun cases)
Eversull Co., Inc., K.
Flambeau Products Corp.
Fort Knox Security Products (safes)
Gould & Goodrich
Gun-Ho Sports Cases
Gun Vault, Inc.
Gusdorf Corp. (gun cabinets)
Hafner Enterprises, Inc. (cases)
Hall Plastics, Inc., John (cases)
Hansen Cartridge Co.
Harrison-Hurtz Enterprises, Inc. (custom hardwood cases)
Huey Gun Cases, Marvin (handbuilt leather cases)
Hugger Hooks Co.
Hunting Classics Ltd.
Impact Case Company
Jaeger, Inc., Paul
Jumbo Sports Products
Kane Products, Inc.
KMP (aluminum boxes)
Knock on Wood Antiques (gun & security cabinets)
Kolpin Mfg., Inc.

Lakewood Products, Inc.
Maloni, Russ
McGuire, Bill (custom)
McWelco Products (gun safes)
Michael's of Oregon Co.
National Security Safe Company, Inc.
Nesci Enterprises, Inc. (firearms security chests)
New England Arms Co.
Nielsen & Co. (handgun only)
Oregon Arms, Inc.
Otto, Tim (custom cases)
Outa-Site Gun Carriers
Outdoor Connection, Inc., The
Pendleton Royal
Penguin Industries, Inc.
Perazzi U.S.A., Inc.
Pflumm Gun Mfg. Co.
PistolPAL Products
Powell & Son Ltd., William
Protecto Plastics (carrying cases)
Quality Arms, Inc.
Rahn Gun Works, Inc. (leather trunk cases)
Red Head, Inc.
Russwood Custom Pistol Grips
San Angelo Sports Products, Inc.
Savana Sports, Inc.
Schulz Industries (carrying cases)
Shell Shack
Sonderman, Robert B. (handgun cases)
Sportsman's Communicators
SSK Industries (wooden cases)
Sweet Home, Inc.
Tinks & Ben Lee Hunting Products
Tread Corp. (security gun chest)
Unick's Gunsmithing
Verdemont Fieldsports
Waller & Son, Inc., W.
WAMCO, Inc. (wooden display cases)
Weather Shield Sports Equipment, Inc.
Wellington Outdoors
Wilson Case, Inc.
Woodstream
Zanotti Armor (safes)
Ziegel Engineering (aluminum cases)

CHOKE DEVICES, RECOIL ABSORBERS AND RECOIL PADS

Action Products, Inc. (recoil shock eliminator)
Arms Ingenuity Co. (Jet-Away)
Armsport, Inc. (choke devices)
Baker, Stan (shotgun specialist)
Bob's Gun Shop
Boyds' Gunstock Industries, Inc.
B-Square Co.
Briley Mfg., Inc. (choke tubes)
C&H Research (Mercury recoil suppressor)
Cellini, Inc., Vito Francesca (recoil reducer; muzzlebrake)
Clark Custom Guns, Inc.
Clinton River Gun Serv., Inc. (Reed Choke)
Colonial Arms, Inc. (invector-style screw-in choke tubes)
Danuser Machine Co. (recoil absorbers)
Delta Vectors, Inc. (Techni-Port recoil compensation)
Dever Co., Jack
Fabian Bros. Sporting Goods, Inc. (DTA Muzzle Mizer recoil absorber; MIL/brake)
FAPA Corp.
Frank Custom Gun Service, Ron
Gentry Custom Gunmaker, David (muzzlebrakes)
Great 870 Co., The
Griggs Products
Gun Parts Corporation, The
Harper, William E.
Hastings Barrels
I.N.C., Inc. (Kick-Eez recoil pad)

Intermountain Arms (Gunner's Choice muzzlebrake)
Jaeger, Inc., Paul
Jeffredo Gunsight
Jenkins Recoil Pads, Inc.
KDF, Inc. (muzzlebrake)
LaRocca Gun Works, Inc.
London Guns Ltd.
Mag-Na-Port International, Inc. (muzzlebrake system)
Marble Arms Corporation (Poly Choke)
McGowen Rifle Barrels
Mittermeier, Inc., Frank
Moneymaker Guncraft Corp.
Nelson/Weather-rite
Nu-Line Guns, Inc.
Oakland Custom Arms, Inc.
One Of A Kind
Pachmayr Ltd. (recoil pads)
Palsa Outdoor Products
P.A.S.T. Corp. (recoil reducer shield)
Pendleton Royal
Pro-Port Ltd.
Protektor Model Co. (shoulder recoil pad)
Shootin' Accessories Ltd.
Shotguns Unlimited (custom shotgun choke work)
Silhouette Arms Custom 45 Shop, Inc.
Sipes Gun Shop
S.K. Guns, Inc.
Trevallion Gunstocks
Trulock Tool
Upper Missouri Trading Co.
Walker Arms Co., Inc.
Williamson Precision Gunsmithing

CHRONOGRAPHS AND PRESSURE TOOLS

Behlert Precision
Bruno Shooters Supply
Canons Delcour
Competition Electronics, Inc.
•Custom Chronograph, Inc.
•D&H Precision Tooling (pressure testing receiver)

•H-S Precision, Inc. (pressure barrels)
Lachaussee, S.A.
•Oehler Research, Inc.
•P.A.C.T., Inc. (Precision chronograph)
Shooting Chrony, Inc.
Su-Press-On, Inc. (chronographs)
Tepeco (Speed-Meter)

CLEANING AND REFINISHING SUPPLIES

Acculube II, Inc. (lubricants/cleaners)
Accupro Gun Care (chemical bore cleaner)
Accuracy Products S.A. (solvent gun cleaner)
ADCO
Alsa Corp., The (ALLGUN Universal gun care kit)
American Gas & Chemical Co., Ltd. (TSI gun lube)
Armite Laboratories (pen oiler)
Armoloy Company of Ft. Worth (refinishing)
Art's Gun & Sport Shop, Inc.
Behlert Precision
Belding & Mull, Inc.
Belltown, Ltd. (gun cleaning cloth kit)
Beretta, Dr. Franco
Big 45 Frontier Gun Shop
Bill's Gun Repair (rust, bluing solutions)
Birchwood Casey
Blount, Inc. Sporting Equipment Division
Bondini Paolo
Break-Free (lubricants)
Brobst, Jim (J-B Cleaning Compound)
Brownell's, Inc.
Browning Arms Co.
Bruno Shooters Supply
Butler Creek Corporation
Chopie Mfg., Inc. (Black-Solve gun cleaner)
Clenzoil Corp.
Corbin Manufacturing & Supply, Inc.
Crane & Crane Ltd.
Creedmoor Sports, Inc.
Crouse's Country Cover (scented lubes and cleaners)
Deepeeka Exports Pvt. Ltd. (cleaning kits)
Delhi Gun House
Dewey Mfg. Co., Inc., J. (one-piece gun cleaning rod)
DMG Technologies, Inc.
Dri-Slide, Inc.
Du-Lite Corp.
Dutchman's Firearms, Inc., The
Dykstra, Doug (lubricants/dry film)
Eezox, Inc. (synthetic lubricant)
E&L Mfg., Inc.
Enguix Import-Export
Faith Associates, Inc. (brushes)
Fitz Pistol Grip Co.
Flex Gun Rods Co., Inc.
Flitz International Ltd.
Flouramics, Inc. (lubricant-gun coat)
Force 10, Inc. (anti-rust protectant)
Forster Products
Forty-Five Ranch
4-D Custom Die Co.
Frontier Products Co.
FTI, Inc.
G96 Products Co., Inc.
Golden Age Arms Co.
Gozon Corp.
Graves Co.
Greene's Machine Carving (flexible cleaning rod)
Guardsman Products
Gun Works, The
Hafner Enterprises, Inc.
Half Moon Rifle Shop
Heatbath Corp.
Hoppe's Div.

Iosso Marine Products
Jantz Supply
J-B Bore Cleaner
Johnston Bros.
Jonad Corporation (lubricators)
Kleen-Bore, Inc.
Kopp, Terry K. (stock rubbing compound; rust preventative grease)
LEM Gun Specialties
LPS Chemical Prods.
LT Industries, Inc. (airguns—flexible cleaning rods/felt cleaning pellets)
Marble Arms Corporation
Marsh, Mike
Micro Sight Co. (stock bedding compound)
Mountain View Sports, Inc.
Muscle Products Corp./Firepower Lubricants
Nesci Enterprises, Inc.
Northern Precision Custom Swaged Bullets
Oakland Custom Arms, Inc.
Old World Oil Products (gun stock finish)
Omark Industries
Outers Laboratories, Div. of Blount
Ox-Yoke Originals, Inc. (dry lubrication patches)
Parker Gun Finishes
Pendleton Royal
P&M Sales and Service
Precision Sports
Prolix
Pro-Shot Products
Radiator Specialty Co.
R&S Industries Corp. (Miracle All Purpose polishing cloth)
Rice, Keith
Rice Protective Gun Coatings
Richards Classic Oil Finish (gunstock oils, wax)
RIG Products
Rusteprufe Laboratories
Rusty Duck Premium Gun Care Products
San Angelo Sports Products, Inc.
Sandia Die & Cartridge Co.
Scott, Inc., Tyler (muzzle-loading black solvent; patch lube)
Seacliff International, Inc. (portable parts washer)
Sheffield Knifemakers Supply
Shootin' Accessories Ltd.
Slipshot MTS Group
Sports Support Systems, Inc.
Su-Press-On, Inc.
TDP Industries, Inc.
Texas Platers Supply Co.
T.F.C. S.p.A.
Treso, Inc. (Durango Gun Rod)
United States Products Co. (Gold Medallion bore cleaner/conditioner)
Van Gorden & Son, Inc., C.S. (Van's Instant Blue)
Venco Industries, Inc. (Shooter's Choice bore cleaner and conditioner)
Verdemont Fieldsports
Watson Trophy Match Bullets
WD-40 Co.
White Rock Tool & Die
Williams Shootin' Iron Service (Lynx Line)
Young Country Arms (Wood Love)
Z-Coat Co.

COMPUTER SOFTWARE—BALLISTICS

ADC, Inc.
AmBr Software Group Ltd.
Ballistics Program Co., Inc., The
Barnes Bullets, Inc.
Blount, Inc. Sporting Equipment Division
Canons Delcour
Corbin Applied Technology
Corbin Manufacturing & Supply, Inc.
Country Armourer, The
Destination North Software
Exe, Inc.
HomeCraft
Hutton Rifle Ranch

J.I.T. Ltd.
Lachaussee, S.A.
Lee Precision, Inc.
Load From A Disk
Magma Engineering Co.
Maionchi - L.M.I.
Midway Arms, Inc.
Pejsa Ballistics
Peripheral Data Systems
Regional Associates
Sierra Bullets
Vancini, Carl

CUSTOM GUNSMITHS

Accuracy Gun Shop
Accuracy Unlimited
Accurate Plating & Weaponry, Inc.
Ackley Rifle Barrels, P.O.
Adair Custom Shop, Bill
Ad Hominem

Ahlman Guns
Ahrends, Kim
Aldis Gunsmithing & Shooting Supply
Alpine Precision Gunsmithing & Indoor Range
American Custom Gunmakers Guild

•See page 445 for Warranty Service Center Addresses

Amrine's Gun Shop
Answer Products Co.
Apel, Dietrich
Armament Gunsmithing Co., Inc.
Arms Craft Gunsmithing (rebluing, restorations)
Arms Ingenuity Co.
Armurier Hiptmayer
Arrieta, S.L.
A&W Repair (stock restoration)
Bain & Davis, Inc.
Baity's Custom Gunworks
Barnes Bullets, Inc.
Barta's Gunsmithing
Baumannize, Inc.
Beeman Precision Arms, Inc. (airguns only)
Behlert Precision (custom)
Beitzinger, George
Belding's Custom Gun Shop
Bellm Contenders
Benchmark Guns
Bengtson Arms Co., L.
Biesen, Al
Biesen, Roger
Billeb, Stephen L.
Billings Gunsmiths, Inc.
Billingsley & Brownell (custom rifles)
Bill's Gun Repair
Bolden's (rust bluing)
Boltin, John M.
Border Guns & Leather
Borovnik KG, Ludwig
Bowerly, Kent
Brace, Larry D.
Brgoch, Frank
Briganti & Co., A. (rust bluing)
Brown Precision, Inc. (rifles)
Brown Products, Ed
Bruno Shooters Supply
Buckhorn Gun Works
Buckskin Machine Works
Budin, Dave
Burgess and Son Gunsmiths, R.W.
Burkhart Gunsmithing, Don (rifles)
Bustani Appraisers, Leo
Cache La Poudre Rifleworks (muzzleloaders)
CAM Enterprises
Camilli, Lou (muzzleloaders)
Campbell, Dick
Carter's Gun Shop
Caywood, Shane J.
Champlin Firearms, Inc.
Christopher Firearms Co., Inc., E.
Chuck's Gun Shop
Clark Custom Guns, Inc.
Classic Arms Corp.
Classic Guns
Clinton River Gun Service, Inc.
Cloward's Gun Shop
Coffin, Charles H.
Competitive Pistol Shop, The
Conrad, C.A.
Cook, John
Corkys Gun Clinic
Costa, David
Cox, C. Ed
Creekside Gun Shop, Inc. (color case hardening, bone charcoal bluing)
Cumberland Knife & Gun Works (muzzleloaders)
Custom Checking Service
Custom Firearms
Custom Gun Products
Custom Gunsmiths
Custom Gun Stocks
Custom Shop, The
Dangler, Homer L. (Kentucky rifles)
Darlington Gun Works, Inc.
Davis Service Center, Bill
D.D. Custom Rifles
D&D Gunsmiths, Ltd.
Delorge, Ed
Dever Co., Jack
Devereaux, R.H. "Dick"
DGS, Inc.
Dilliott Gunsmithing, Inc.
D.O.C. Specialists, Inc.
Donnelly, C.P.
Dowtin Gunworks (double shotguns)
Dressel Jr., Paul G.
Duffy, Charles E.
Duncan's Gun Works, Inc.
Dyson & Son Ltd., Peter
Eckelman Gunsmithing
Echols & Co., D'Arcy

Eggleston, Jere D.
EMF Co., Inc.
Emmons, Bob
Erhardt, Dennis
European American Armory Corp.
Eversull Co., Inc., K.
Eyster Heritage Gunsmiths, Inc., Ken
Fanzoj GmbH
Farmer-Dressell, Sharon
Fautheree, Andy
Fellowes, Ted (muzzleloaders)
Ferris Firearms, Gregg
First Distributors, Inc., Jack
Fish, Marshall F.
Fisher, Jerry
Flaig's
Flint Creek Arms Co. (bluing; repairs)
Flynn's Custom Guns
Fogle, James W.
Forster, Larry L.
Forthofer's Gunsmithing & Knifemaking
Forty-Niner Trading Co.
Francesca Stabilizer's, Inc.
Frank Custom Gun Service, Ron
Frazier Brothers Enterprises
Fredrick Gun Shop
Freeland's Scope Stands, Inc.
Frontier Arms Co.
Furr Arms
Gander Mountain, Inc.
Garrett Accur-Lt. D.F.S. Co.
Gator Guns & Repair
Genecco Gun Works, K.
Gentry Custom Gunmaker, David
Gillmann, Edwin
Gilman-Mayfield
Giron, Robert E.
Goens, Dale W.
Goode, A.R.
Goodling's Gunsmithing
Goodwin, Fred
Gordie's Gun Shop
Grace, Charles E.
Granger, Georges
Graybill's Gun Shop
Green, Roger M.
Greg Gunsmithing Repair
Griffin & Howe, Inc.
Guncraft, Inc.
Gun Doctor, The
Gun Shop, The
Guns
Gunsite Gunsmithy
Gunsmithing Ltd.
Gun Works, The (muzzleloaders)
Gutridge, Inc.
Hagn Rifles & Actions, Martin (s.s. actions & rifles)
Hammans, Charles E.
Hanson's Gun Center, Dick
Hardison, Charles
Hart & Son, Inc., Robert W. (actions, stocks)
Hartmann & Weiss GmbH
Hecht, Hubert J.
Heilmann, Stephen
Heinie Specialty Products
Hensley, Darwin
Heppler, Keith
High Bridge Arms, Inc.
Hiptmayer, Klaus
H&L Gun Works
Hoag, James W.
Hobaugh, Wm.
Hobbie Gunsmithing, Duane A.
Hodgson, Richard
Hoenig & Rodman
Hofer Jagdwaffen, P.
Holland, Dick
Hollis Gun Shop
Horst, Alan K.
H-S Precision, Inc.
Huebner, Corey O.
Hughes, Steven Dodd (muzzleloaders)
Hunkeler, Al (muzzleloaders)
Huntington Die Specialties
Hyper-Single, Inc. (precision single shot rifles)
Intermountain Arms
Irwin, Campbell H.
Ivanoff, Thomas G.
Jackalope Gun Shop
Jaeger, Inc., Paul
Jarrett Rifles, Inc. (rifles)
Johnson Gunsmithing, Inc., Neal G.
Juenke, Vern
Jurras, L.E.

Kartak Gun Works
K-D, Inc.
KDF, Inc.
Keith's Custom Gunstocks
Ken's Gun Specialties
Kilham & Co.
Klein Custom Guns, Don
Kleinendorst, K.W.
Kneiper Custom Rifles, Jim (rifles)
Kopp, Terry K.
Korzinek Riflesmith, J.
LaFrance Specialties
Lair, Sam (single shots)
Lampert, Ron
LaRocca Gun Works, Inc.
Lawson Co., Harry
Lawson, John G.
Lebeau-Courally
Lee's Red Ramps
Lee Supplies, Mark
LeFever & Sons, Inc., Frank
Liberty Antique Gunworks
Lilja Precision Rifle Barrels
Lind Custom Guns, Al
Linebaugh Custom Sixguns
Lofland, James W. (single shot rifles)
Logan, Harry M.
London Guns Ltd.
Long Island Gunsmith, Inc.
Mag-Na-Port International, Inc.
Mahoney, Philip Bruce
Makinson, Nicholas (English guns)
Mandarino, Monte (Penn. rifles)
Manley Shooting Supplies, Lowell
Martin's Gun Shop
Martz, John V. (Lugers and P-38s only)
Masker, Seely
Mathews & Son, Inc., Geo. E.
Mazur Restoration, Pete (double-barrel rifles, shotguns)
McCament, Jay
McCann's Muzzle-Gun Works (blackpowder)
McCormick's Custom Gun Bluing
McFarland, Stan (custom rifles)
McGowen Rifle Barrels
McGuire, Bill
Mercer Custom Stocks, R.M.
Mid-America Recreation, Inc.
Miller Arms, Inc.
Miller Co., David (rifles)
Miller, Tom
Mills Jr., Hugh B.
Moeller, Steve
Monell Custom Guns
Moneymaker Guncraft Corp.
Moore & Co., Wm. Larkin
Morrison Custom Rifles, J.W.
Morrow, Bud
Mountain Bear Rifle Works, Inc.
Mowreys Guns & Supplies
Mullis Guncraft
Mustra's Custom Guns, Inc., Carl
Nelson, Stephen E.
Nettestad Gun Works
New England Arms Co.
New England Custom Gun Service
Newman Gunshop (muzzleloaders)
Nickels, Paul R.
Nicklas, Ted
Nolan, Dave
Norman Custom Gunstocks, Jim
North Fork Custom Gunsmithing
Nu-Line Guns, Inc.
Oakland Custom Arms, Inc.
Old World Gunsmithing
Olson, Vic
Orvis Co., The
Ottmar, Maurice
Pace Marketing, Inc.
Pachmayr Ltd.
Pagel Gun Works, Inc. (custom gunmaking and refinishing)
Parker Gun Finishes
Pasadena Gun Center
Paterson Gunsmithing
Pell, John T.
Pence Precision Barrels
Penrod Precision
Pentheny de Pentheny
Peterson Gun Shop, Inc., A.W. (muzzleloaders)
Powell & Son Ltd., William
Power Custom, Inc.
Professional Gunsmiths of America, Inc.
Pro-Port Ltd.
P&S Gun Service

Quality Firearms of Idaho, Inc.
Randco UK
R&J Gun Shop
Rice, Keith
Ries, Chuck
Rifle Shop, The
Rizzini Battista
RMS Custom Gunsmithing
Robar Co.'s, Inc., The
Roberts Jr., Wm. A. (muzzleloaders)
Robinson, Don (air rifle stocks)
Rocky Mountain Rifle Works Ltd.
Rogers Gunsmithing, Bob
Royal Arms
Russell's Rifle Shop
Ryan, Chad L.
Sanders Custom Gun Service
Sandy's Custom Gunshop
Schaefer, Roy V.
Schiffman, Curt
Schiffman, Mike
Schiffman, Norman
Schumakers Gun Shop, William
Schwartz Custom Guns, David W.
Schwartz Custom Guns, Wayne E.
Scott Fine Guns, Inc., Thad
Scott (Gunmakers) Ltd., W&C
Scott/McDougall Custom Gunsmiths
Shane's Gunsmithing
Shaw, Inc., E.R.
Shaw's Finest in Guns
Shell Shack (muzzleloaders)
Sherk, Dan A.
Shilen Rifles, Inc.
Shiloh Rifle Mfg.
Shockley, Harold H. (hot bluing & plating)
Shootin' Shack, Inc. (smithing services)
Shooting Gallery, The
Shotgun Shop, The
Silhouette Arms Custom 45 Shop, Inc.
Silver Ridge Gun Shop
Singletary, Kent
Sipes Gun Shop
Sight Shop, The
Siskiyou Gun Works
S.K. Guns, Inc.
Sklany, Steve (Ferguson rifle)
Slezak, Jerome F.
Small Arms Mfg. Co.
Smith, Art
Snapp's Gunshop
Spencer Reblue Service (electroless nickel plating)
Sportsmen's Equipment Co.
Sportsmen's Exchange & Western Gun Traders, Inc.
Spradlin's
Springfield Armory, Inc.
SSK Industries
Starnes, Ken
Steelman's Gun Shop
Steffens, Ron
Stott's Creek Armory, Inc.
Strawbridge, Victor W.
Stroup, Earl R. (rifles)
Sunora Gun Shop
Swann, D.J. (makers of falling block rifle)
Swenson's 45 Shop, A.D.
300 Gunsmith Service, Inc.
Talmage, William G.
Tank's Rifle Shop
Taylor & Robbins
Tennessee Valley Mfg.
Ten-Ring Precision, Inc.
Tertin, James A.
Thompson, Larry R.
Thurston Sports, Inc.
Tom's Gun Repair
Tom's Gunshop
Trapper Gun, Inc.
Trevallion Gunstocks
T.S.W. Conversion, Inc.
Ulrich, Doc & Bud
Unick's Gunsmithing
Upper Missouri Trading Co.
Vais Arms
Van Epps, Milton
Van Horn, Gil (safari rifles)
Van Patten, J.W.
Vest, John
Vic's Gun Refinishing
Vintage Arms, Inc.
Volquartsen Custom Ltd.
Waffen-Weber Custom Gunsmithing
Walker Arms Co., Inc.
Wallace's
Wardell Precision Handguns Ltd.

Wardrop, R. Alex
Weatherby, Inc.
Weaver Arms Corp.
Weaver's Gun Shop
Weems, Cecil
Wells, R.A.
Wells Sport Store
Werth, T.W.
Wessinger Custom Guns & Engraving
West, Robert G.
Western Design
Western Gunstock Mfg. Co.

Western Ordnance Int'l Corp.
White Rock Tool & Die
Wiebe, Duane
Williams Shootin' Iron Service
Williamson Precision Gunsmithing
Wilson's Gun Shop
Winter, Robert M.
Wisner's Gun Shop, Inc.
Wood, Frank
Yankee Gunsmith
Zeeryp, Russ

CUSTOM METALSMITHS

Accuracy Unlimited
Ackley Rifle Barrels, P.O.
Ahlman Guns
Aldis Gunsmithing & Shooting Supply
Alpine Precision Gunsmithing & Indoor Range
Amrine's Gun Shop
Apel, Dietrich
Armurier Hiptmayer
Baron Technology, Inc.
Barta's Gunsmithing
Beitzinger, George
Benchmark Guns
Bengtson Arms Co., L.
Biesen, Al
Brace, Larry D.
Briganti & Co., A.
Brown Precision, Inc.
Buckhorn Gun Works
Bustani Appraisers, Leo
Campbell, Dick
Carter's Gun Shop
Champlin Firearms, Inc.
Checkmate Refinishing (electroplating)
Chuck's Gun Shop
Classic Guns
Clinton River Gun Serv., Inc.
Condor Mfg. Co.
Costa, David
Craftguard (bluing, plating, Parkerizing)
Crandall Tool & Machine Company
Cullity Restoration, Daniel
Custom Gun Products
Custom Gunsmiths
Custom Products
D&D Gunsmiths, Ltd.
Dever Co., Jack
D&H Precision Tooling
Duncan's Gunworks, Inc.
Dyson & Son Ltd., Peter
Eversull Co., Inc., K.
Eyster Heritage Gunsmiths, Inc., Ken
Farmer-Dressel, Sharon
First Distributors, Inc., Jack
Flaig's
Flint Creek Arms Co.
Forster, Larry L.
Francesca Stabilizer's, Inc.
Frank Custom Gun Service, Ron
Fullmer, Geo. M.
Gentry Custom Gunmaker, David
Giron, Robert E.
Goens, Dale W.
Goodwin, Fred
Gordie's Gun Shop
Graybill's Gun Shop
Green, Roger M.
Griffin & Howe, Inc.
Gun Doctor, The
Guns
Gutridge, Inc.
Hagn Rifles & Actions, Martin
Hecht, Hubert J.
Heilmann, Stephen
Heppler's Machining
Hoenig & Rodman
Highline Machine Co.
Hiptmayer, Klaus
Hobaugh, Wm. H.
H-S Precision, Inc.
Hyper-Single, Inc.
Intermountain Arms
Ivanoff, Thomas G.
Jaeger, Inc., Paul
Jamison's Forge Works
Jones, Neil
Jurras, L.E.
Kartak Gun Works

Kilham & Co.
Klein Custom Guns, Don
Kleinendorst, K.W.
Kopp, Terry K.
Lampert, Ron
Lawson Co., Harry
Lee Supplies, Mark
Logan, Harry M.
Martin's Gun Shop
Martz, John V. (Lugers and P-38s only)
McCament, Jay
McFarland, Stan
Mid-America Recreation, Inc.
Miller Arms, Inc.
Morrison Custom Rifles, J.W.
Morrow, Bud
Mountain Bear Rifle Works, Inc.
Mullis Guncraft
Nettestad Gun Works
New England Custom Gun Service
Noreen, Peter H.
North Fork Custom Gunsmithing
Oakland Custom Arms, Inc.
Pace Marketing, Inc.
Pagel Gun Works, Inc.
Pasadena Gun Center
Patchbox, The
Penrod Precision
Pentheny de Pentheny
Precise Metal Finishing
Precise Metalsmithing Enterprises
Precision Specialties
P&S Gun Service
Rice, Keith
Rifle Shop, The
Rogers Gunsmithing, Bob
Shaw, Inc., E.R.
Shirley Co. Gun & Riflemakers Ltd., J.A.
Shockley, Harold H.
Shooter Shop, The
Silhouette Arms Custom 45 Shop, Inc.
Silver Ridge Gun Shop
Sipes Gun Shop
S.K. Guns, Inc.
Small Arms Mfg. Co.
Snapp's Gunshop
Sportsmen's Exchange & Western Gun Traders, Inc.
Spradlin's
Strawbridge, Victor W.
Steffens, Ron (bluing barrels w/o bluing bore)
Talley, Dave
Ten-Ring Precision, Inc.
Tom's Gun Repair
Thompson, Randall
T.S.W. Conversions, Inc.
Unick's Gunsmithing
Van Horn, Gil
Van Patten, J.W.
Vic's Gun Refinishing
Vintage Arms, Inc.
Waldron, Herman
Wallace's
Wells Sport Store
Werth, T.W.
Wessinger Custom Guns & Engraving
West, Robert G.
Western Design
White Rock Tool & Die (rebarreling action mods.)
Wiebe, Duane
Williamson Precision Gunsmithing
Williams Shootin' Iron Service
Wisner's Gun Shop, Inc.
Westrom, John
Wood, Frank

DECOYS

A&M Waterfowl, Inc. (motorized ducks, geese)
Ammunition Consulting Services, Inc.

Baekgaard Ltd.
Burnham Bros.
Carry-Lite, Inc.

Deer Me Products Co. (anchors)
Fair Game International (Enticer duck decoys)
Farm Form, Inc. (goose)
Feather Flex Decoys
Flambeau Products Corp.
G&H Decoys, Inc.
Herter's Manufacturing, Inc.
Hiti-Schuch, Atelier Wilma
Iron Mountain Knife Co.
Jaeger, Inc., Paul

Klingler Woodcarving
North Wind Decoys Co. (goose, duck windsock)
Penn's Woods Products, Inc.
Quack Decoy Corp.
Royal Arms (wooden, duck)
Sports Innovations, Inc.
Tanglefree Industries
Waterfield Sports, Inc.
Woods Wise Products

ENGRAVERS, ENGRAVING TOOLS

Adair Custom Shop, Bill
Adams, John J.
Ahlman Guns
Alfano, Sam
Allard, Gary
Anthony and George Ltd.
Armurier Hiptmayer
Baron Technology, Inc.
Bates Engraving, Billy
Bell Originals, Sid
Bledsoe, Weldon
Bleile, C. Roger
Boessler, Erich
Bone Engraving, Ralph
Bratcher, Dan
Brgoch, Frank
Brooker, Dennis
Brownell's, Inc. (engraving tools)
Burgess, Byron
CAM Enterprises
Christopher Firearms Co., Inc., E.
Churchill, Winston
Clark Firearms Engraving
Clark, Frank
Coffey, Barbara
Creek Side Metal & Woodcrafters
Custom Gun Engraving
Davidson, Jere
Delorge, Ed
Dolbare, Elizabeth
Drain, Mark
Dubber, Michael W.
Dyson & Son Ltd., Peter
Engraving Artistry
Evans Engraving, Robert
Eversull Co., Inc., K.
Eyster Heritage Gunsmiths, Inc., Ken
Fanzoj GesmbH
Favre, Jacqueline
Firearms Engraver's Guild of America
Flannery Engraving Co., Jeff W.
Floatstone Mfg. Co.
Fogle, James W.
Fountain Products
Francolini, Leonard
Frank Knives
Gene's Custom Guns
George, Tim and Christy
Glimm, Jerome C.
Golden Age Arms Co.
Gournet, Geoffroy
Grant, Howard V.
Griffin & Howe, Inc.
GRS Corp. (Gravermeister tool)
Gun Room, The
Gurney Engraving Method Ltd.
Guns
Gwinnell, Bryson J.
Hale, Peter
Hand Engravers Supply Co.
Harris Hand Engraving, Paul A.
Harwood, Jack O.
Hendricks, Frank E.
Hiptmayer, Heidemarie
Horst, Alan K.
Ingle, Ralph W.
Johns, Bill
Kamyk, Steven
Kehr, Roger
Kelly, Lance
Klingler Woodcarving (gun stocks)
Koevenig's Engraving Service
Kudlas, John M.

Lebeau-Courally
Leibowitz, Leonard (etcher)
Letschnig, Franz
Lindsay, Steve
London Guns Ltd.
Mains Enterprises
Maki School of Engraving, Robert E.
Marek, George
Master Engravers, Inc.
McDonald, Dennis
McKenzie, Lynton
Mele, Frank
Mid-America Recreation, Inc.
Mittermeier, Inc., Frank (tool)
Moschetti, Mitchell R.
Mountain States Engraving
Nelson, Gary K.
New Orleans Arms Co.
New Orleans Jewelers Supply Co. (magnifying tools)
NgraveR Co., The (MagnaGraver tool)
Oker's Engraving
Old Dominion Engravers
Pachmayr Ltd.
Palmgren Steel Products
Patchbox, The
Pedersen & Son, C.R.
Pilkington, Scott
Piquette, Paul R.
Potts, Wayne E.
Pranger, Ed G.
P&S Gun Service
Rabeno, Martin
Reed, Dave
Reno, Wayne & Karen (scrimshanders)
Riggs, Jim (handguns)
Roberts, J.J.
Rohner, Hans and John
Rosser, Bob
Rundell's Gun Shop
Runge, Robert P.
Sampson, Roger
Schiffman, Mike
Schiffman, Norman
Shaw's Finest in Guns
Sheffield Knifemakers Supply
Sherwood, George
Sinclair, W.P.
Singletary, Kent
Skaggs, R.E.
Smith, Mark A.
Smith, Ron
Smokey Valley Rifles
Theis, Terry
Thiewes, George W.
Thirion, Denise
Valade, Robert
Vest, John
Viramontez, Ray
Vorhes, David
Wagoner, Vernon G.
Wallace's
Wallace, Terry
Warenski, Julie
Warren, Kenneth W.
Welch, Sam
Wells, Rachel
Wessinger Custom Guns & Engraving
Willig, Claus
Wolfe, Bernie (engraving, plating, scrimshawing)
Wood, Mel

GAME CALLS

Adventure Game Calls
Arkansas Mallard Duck Calls
Ashby Turkey Calls (turkey)
Baekgaard Ltd.
Blakemore Game Calls, Jim
Bostick Wildlife Calls, Inc.
Burnham Bros.
Carter's Wildlife Calls, Inc., Garth
Cedar Hill Game Call Co.

Crawford Co., Inc., R.M.
D-Boone Ent., Inc.
Deepeeka Exports Pvt. Ltd.
Dr. O's Products Ltd.
Duck Call Specialists
Faulk's Game Call Co., Inc.
Fibron Products, Inc.
Flow-Rite of Tennessee, Inc.
Green Head Game Call Co.

Hally Caller
Haydel's Game Calls, Inc.
Hunter's Specialties, Inc.
Jaeger, Inc., Paul
Keowee Game Calls
Kingyon, Paul L.
Knight & Hale Game Calls
Lohman Mfg. Co., Inc.
Mallardtone Game Calls
Marsh, Johnny (duck & goose calls)
Moss Double Tone, Inc.
Mountain Hollow Game Calls
Oakman Turkey Calls
Olt Co., Philip S.
Penn's Woods Products, Inc.
Preston Pittman Game Calls, Inc.
(diaphragm turkey calls)
Primos Wild Game Calls, Inc.
Quaker Boy, Inc.
Rickard, Inc., Pete

Robbins Scent, Inc.
Safari Gun Co.
Salter Calls, Inc., Eddie
San Angelo Sports Products, Inc.
Savana Sports, Inc.
Sceery Company, E.J.
Scobey Duck & Goose Calls, Glynn
Scotch Hunting Products Co., Inc.
Scruggs' Game Calls, Stanley
Stewart Game Calls, Inc., Johnny
Sure-Shot Game Calls, Inc.
Tanglefree Industries
Tink's & Ben Lee Hunting Products
Tink's Safariland Hunting Corp.
Wellington Outdoors
Wilderness Sound Productions Ltd.
Wittasek, Dipl.-Ing. Norbert
Woods Wise Products
Wyant's Premium Outdoor Products, Inc.,
Roger

GUN PARTS, U.S. AND FOREIGN

Ahlman Guns
Amherst Arms (U.S. Military)
Armes de Chasse
Armsport, Inc.
Aztec International Ltd.
B&D Trading Co., Inc.
Badger Shooters Supply, Inc.
Behlert Precision (handgun parts)
Bill's Gun Repair
Bob's Gun Shop
Border Guns & Leather
British Arms Co. Ltd.
Brown Products, Ed
Bustani Appraisers, Leo
Butler Creek Corporation (rifle magazines)
Cadre Supply
Can Am Enterprises
Caspian Arms
Century International Arms, Ltd.
Clark Custom Guns, Inc.
Colonial Repair
Concorde Arms, Inc.
Condor Mfg. Co. (rifle magazines)
Dakota Arms, Inc.
Defense Moulding Enterprises (plastic
cartridge magazines)
Delta Arms Ltd.
Dibble, Derek A. (magazines)
Dixie Gun Works
Duffy, Charles E.
Eagle International, Inc.
E&L Mfg. Inc.
Ed's Gun House
EMF Co., Inc.
Enguix Import-Export
Essex Arms (45 1911A1 frames & slides)
European American Armory Corp.
Fabian Bros. Sporting Goods, Inc.
FAPA Corp.
Federal Ordnance, Inc.
First Distributors, Inc., Jack
Forrest, Inc., Tom
Galati International
Greider Precision Products
Gun Parts Corporation, The
Gun Shop, The
Hansen Cartridge Co.
Hart & Son, Inc., Robert W.
Hastings Barrels
Jaeger, Inc., Paul
J.O. Arms & Ammunition
Keng's Firaarms Specialty, Inc.
Kimber Parts
Kopp, Terry K.

Kopec Enterprises, John (Colt Model P
only)
Krico/Kriegeskorte GmbH, A.
L.A.R. Manufacturing, Inc.
Liberty Antique Gunworks (S&W only)
Lodewick, Walter H. (Winchester parts)
Markell, Inc.
Martz, John V. (Lugers and P-38s only)
Masen Co., John
McCormick Corp., Chip
MEC-GAR S.R.L. (magazines)
Merkuria Ltd.
Miller Gun Woods (rifle magazines)
Morrow, Bud
N.C. Ordnance Co.
Nu-Line Guns, Inc.
Olympic Arms, Inc.
Pace Marketing, Inc.
Para-Ordnance Mfg., Inc. (frames only)
Peacemaker Specialists
Perazzi U.S.A., Inc.
Pre-Winchester Parts Co.
Quality Parts Co.
Rahn Gun Works, Inc.
Ram-Line, Inc. (magazines)
Ranch Products
Retting, Inc., Martin B.
Rizzini Battista
Safari Arms, Inc./SGW
Sarco, Inc.
Scherer (rifle, pistol magazines)
Sherwood Intl. Export Corp.
Smires, Clifford L. (Mauser rifle parts)
Southern Ammunition Co., Inc.
Southern Armory, The
Springfield Sporters, Inc.
Su-Press-On, Inc.
Tank's Rifle Shop
Tapco, Inc.
Taurus, S.A., Forjas
Tradewinds, Inc.
Triple-K Mfg. Co., Inc. (magazines, gun
parts)
T&S Industries, Inc.
T.S.W. Conversions, Inc.
Twin Pine Armory
Vintage Industries, Inc.
Wardell Precision Handguns Ltd.
Weaver's Gun Shop
Weisz Antique Gun Parts
Westfield Engineering
Wisner's Gun Shop, Inc.
Wolff Co., W.C. (springs only)
Zoli USA, Inc., Antonio

GUNS, AIR

•Action Arms Ltd.
•Airgun Repair Centre
•Air Rifle Specialists
•Beeman Precision Arms, Inc. (FWB,
Weihrauch, Webley)
•Benjamin/Sheridan Co.
Brass Eagle, Inc. (paintball guns)
•BSA Guns Ltd.
Champion's Choice, Inc.
Component Concepts, Inc. (paintball)
Crawford Co., Inc., R.M.
Creedmoor Sports, Inc.
•Crosman Corp.
•Crosman Products of Canada Ltd.
•Daisy Mfg. Co.
•Dynamit Nobel-RWS, Inc. (Dianawerk)
•FWB
•Fiocchi of America, Inc.
Ford Ltd., J. and J.

•GFR Corp.
•Great Lakes Airguns
GZ Paintball Sports Products
Hebard Guns, Gil
Hy-Score Arms Co. Ltd.
•Interarms
I.S.S.
Ledbetter Airguns, Riley
•Mac-1 Distributors
•Marksman Products
Merkuria Ltd.
National Survival Game, Inc. (paintball
guns)
•Nygord Precision Products
Pardini Armi Commerciale Srl
Penguin Industries, Inc. (gas pistol)
PMI (paintball)
•PSI, Inc.
Precision Sport Optics

Savana Sports, Inc.
S.G.S. Sporting Guns Srl
•Steyr-Mannlicher
Stone Enterprises Ltd.
•Swivel Machine Works, Inc.

GUNS, FOREIGN—MANUFACTURERS (Importers)

•Air Arms (Air Rifle Specialists)
•Anschutz GmbH (PSI, Inc.)
•Ariziga (Mandall Shooting Supplies, Inc.)
•Arms Corp. of the Philippines (Ruko
Products)
•Arrieta, S.L. (Wingshooting Adventures)
•Astra-Unceta Y Cia, S.A. (Interarms)
•ATIS Armi S.A.S. (E.A.A. Corp.)
•AYA (Armes de Chasse)
•Benelli Armi S.p.A. (Heckler & Koch, Inc.;
Sile Distributors)
•Beretta Firearms, Pietro (Beretta U.S.A.
Corp.)
Beretta, Dr. Franco
•Bernardelli Vincenzo S.p.A. (Magnum
Research, Inc.)
•Bersa S.A. (Eagle Imports, Inc.)
•Blaser Jagdwaffen GmbH (Autumn
Sales, Inc.)
Bondini Paolo (blackpowder arms)
•Bretton (Mandall Shooting Supplies, Inc.)
•BRNO (Action Arms Ltd.)
•Browning Arms Co. (Browning Arms Co.)
•BSA Guns Ltd. (Air Rifle Specialists)
•Cabanas (Mandall Shooting Supplies,
Inc.)
•CBC (MAGTECH Recreational Products,
Inc.)
•Chapuis Armes (Armes de Chasse)
•Churchill (Ellett Bros.)
•Cosmi Americo & Figlio s.n.c. (Incor, Inc.)
•CVA (blackpowder arms)
•Daewoo Precision Industries Ltd.
(Firstshot, Inc.)
•Dakota (EMF Co., Inc.)
•Diana (Dynamit Nobel-RWS, Inc.)
Dumoulin, Ernest
Elko Arms
•Erma Werke GmbH (Mandall Shooting
Supplies, Inc.; PSI, Inc.)
•Euroarms of America, Inc. (blackpowder
arms)
•Fabarm S.p.A. (St. Lawrence Sales, Inc.)
•Fabrica D'Armi Sabatti S.R.L. (E.A.A.
Corp.)
•Famas (Century International Arms, Ltd.)
•FAS (Mandall Shooting Supplies, Inc.;
Nygord Precision Products)
•Fausti, Stefano (American Arms, Inc.)
•FEG (K.B.I., Inc.)
•FERLIB (Moore & Co., Wm. Larkin)
•Firearms Co. Ltd./Alpine (Mandall
Shooting Supplies, Inc.)
•FN Herstal
Frankonia Jagd
•Francotte & Cie S.A., Auguste (Armes de
Chasse)
•Franchi S.p.A, Luigi (American Arms, Inc.)
•FWB (Beeman Precision Arms, Inc.)
•Gamba S.p.A., Renato (Gamba U.S.A.)
•Gamo (Daisy Mfg. Co.; Dynamit
Nobel-RWS, Inc.)
•Garbi, Armas Urki (Moore & Co., Wm.
Larkin)
•Gaucher Armes S.A. (Mandall Shooting
Supplies, Inc.)
•Glock GmbH (Glock, Inc.)
•Grulla Armes (American Arms, Inc.)
•Gustaf, Carl (PSI, Inc.)
•Haenel (GSI, Inc.)
•Hammerli (Beeman Precision Arms, Inc.;
Hammerli USA; Mandall Shooting
Supplies, Inc.)
•Hanus, Bill (Precision Sports)
•Heckler & Koch, GmbH (Heckler & Koch,
Inc.)
•Helwan (Interarms)
•Hermanos S.A., Zabala (American Arms,
Inc.)
•Heym GmbH & Co., Friedrich Wilh.
(Heckler & Koch, Inc.)
Holland & Holland Ltd.
•Howa Machinery Ltd. (Interarms)
•IGA (Stoeger Industries)
•IMI/Desert Eagle (Magnum Research,
Inc.)
•IMI/Galil (Action Arms Ltd.)
•IMI/Jericho (K.B.I., Inc.)
•IMI/Timberwolf (Action Arms Ltd.;
Springfield Armory, Inc.)

•Taurus, S.A., Forjas
Tippman Pneumatics, Inc.
•Webley and Scott Limited
•Weihrauch KG, Hermann

•IMI/UZI (Action Arms Ltd.)
•INDESAL (American Arms, Inc.)
•Interarms (Interarms)
•J.O. Arms & Ammunition Co. (J.O. Arms
& Ammunition Co.)
•JSL Ltd. (Rogers Ltd.)
•Kassnar (K.B.I., Inc.)
•K.B.I., Inc. (K.B.I., Inc.)
•Korth (Mandall Shooting Supplies, Inc.)
•Krieghoff Gun Co., H. (Krieghoff
International, Inc.)
•Krico/Kriegeskorte GmbH, A. (Mandall
Shooting Supplies, Inc.)
Korth (Mandall Shooting Supplies, Inc.)
•Lakefield Arms Ltd. (Ellett Bros.)
•Lanber Armes S.A. (American Arms, Inc.)
•Laurona Armes S.A. (Galaxy Imports
Ltd., Inc.)
•Lebeau-Courally (New England Arms Co.)
•Llama Gabilondo Y Cia (Stoeger
Industries)
•Marocchi F.lli S.p.A. (PSI, Inc.; Sile
Distributors)
•Mauser-Werke (Precision Imports, Inc.)
•Merkel Freres (GSI, Inc.)
•Miroku, B.C./Daly, Charles (Outdoor
Sports Headquarters)
•Mitchell Arms, Inc. (Mitchell Arms, Inc.)
•Norica (American Arms, Inc.; K.B.I., Inc.)
•Norinco (Century International Arms, Ltd.;
ChinaSports, Inc.; Interarms; Midwest
Sport Distributors; Navy Arms
Company; Sportarms of Florida)
•Para-Ordnance Mfg., Inc.
•Parker Reproductions (Parker
Reproductions)
•Pedersoli Davide & C. (Dixie Gun Works;
EMF Co., Inc.; Navy Arms Company;
Trail Guns Armory, Inc.)
•Perazzi m.a.p. S.p.A. (Perazzi U.S.A.,
Inc.)
•Perugini-Visini & Co. s.r.l. (Moore & Co.,
Wm. Larkin)
•Piotti (Moore & Co., Wm. Larkin)
•Peters Stahl GmbH (Federal Ordnance,
Inc.)
•Poly Technologies, Inc. (Keng's Firearms
Specialty, Inc.)
Powell & Son Ltd., William
Pragotrade
Purdey & Sons Ltd., James
•Rigby & Co., John (Hallowell & Co.)
•Rizzini, F.LLI (Moore & Co., Wm. Larkin)
•Rossi S.A. Metalurgica E Municoes,
Amadeo (Interarms)
•RWS (Dynamit Nobel-RWS, Inc.)
•Sako Ltd. (Stoeger Industries)
•Sardius Industries Ltd. (Armscorp. of
America, Inc.)
•Sauer (G.U., Inc.; Simmons Enterprises,
Ernie)
•SIG (Mandall Shooting Supplies, Inc.)
•SIG-Sauer (Sigarms, Inc.)
•SKB Arms Co. (G.U., Inc.; Simmons
Enterprises, Ernie)
•Springfield Armory, Inc. (Springfield
Armory, Inc.)
•Star Bonifacio Echeverria S.A. (Interarms)
•Steyr airguns (Nygord Precision Products)
•Steyr-Daimler-Puch (GSI, Inc.)
•Steyr-Mannlicher (GSI, Inc.)
•Tanfoglio S.r.l., Fratelli/Witness (E.A.A.
Corp.)
•Tanner (Mandall Shooting Supplies, Inc.)
•Taurus International Firearms (Taurus
Firearms, Inc.)
•Techni-Mec (Rahn Gun Works, Inc.)
T.F.C. S.p.A.
•Theoben Engineering (Air Rifle
Specialists)
•Tikka (Stoeger Industries)
•Uberti, Aldo (Cimarron Arms; Navy Arms
Company; Uberti USA, Inc.)
•Ugartechea S.A., Ignacio (Mandall
Shooting Supplies, Inc.)
•Unique/M.A.P.F. (Nygord Precision
Products)
•Voere (Rahn Gun Works, Inc.)
•Walther GmbH, Carl (Interarms)
•Weatherby, Inc. (Weatherby, Inc.)

- Weihrauch KG, Hermann (Beeman Precision Arms, Inc.; E.A.A. Corp.)
- Westley Richards & Co. (New England Arms Co.)

- Zanoletti, Pietro (Mandall Shooting Supplies, Inc.)
- Zoli, Antonio (E.A.A. Corp.; Mandall Shooting Supplies, Inc.; Zoli USA, Inc., Antonio)

- Intratec
- Ithaca Aquisition Corp./Ithaca Gun Co.
- Jennings Firearms, Inc.
- J.O. Arms & Ammunition
- Johnson, Iver
- K.B.I., Inc.
- KDF, Inc.
- Kimel Industries
- Kintrek, Inc.
- L.A.R. Manufacturing, Inc.
- Ljutic Industries, Inc.
- Lorcin Engineering Co., Inc.
- Magnum Research, Inc.
- Marlin Firearms Co.
- Maverick Arms, Inc.
- McMillan Gunworks, Inc.
- Mitchell Arms, Inc.
- MK Arms, Inc. (semi-auto carbines)
- M.O.A. Corp. (Maximum pistol)
- Modern MuzzleLoading, Inc.
- Montana Armory, Inc.
- Mossberg & Sons, O.F.
- Navy Arms Company
- New Advantage Arms Corp.
- New England Arms Co.
- New England Firearms Co.
- North American Arms
- Olympic Arms, Inc.
- Oregon Arms, Inc.
- Parker-Hale
- Peregrine Industries, Inc.
- Phelps Mfg. Co.
- Phoenix Arms
- QFI
- Rahn Gun Works, Inc.

- Ram-Line, Inc.
- Red Willow Tool & Armory, Inc.
- Remington Arms Co.
- RPM
- Safari Arms/SGW
- Savage Arms, Inc.
- Scattergun Technologies, Inc.
- Seecamp Co., Inc., L.W.
- Sharps Arms Co., Inc., C.
- Shiloh Rifle Mfg.
- Smith & Wesson
- Sporting Arms Mfg., Inc. (Night Charmer/Snake Charmer II)
- Springfield Armory, Inc.
- Sturm, Ruger & Co., Inc.
- Sundance Industries, Inc. (Model A-25 pistol)
- Survival Arms, Inc.
- Taurus Firearms, Inc.
- Texas Longhorn Arms, Inc. (single-action sixgun)
- Thompson/Center Arms
- TMI Products
- Trail Guns Armory, Inc. (muzzleloaders)
- Ultra Light Arms, Inc.
- U.S. Arms Corp.
- U.S. Repeating Arms Co. (Winchester)
- Varner Sporting Arms, Inc.
- Weatherby, Inc.
- Wesson Firearms Co., Inc.
- Wichita Arms, Inc.
- Wildey, Inc.
- Wilkinson Arms
- Wyoming Armory, Inc.
- Wyoming Arms Mfg. Corp.

GUNS, FOREIGN—IMPORTERS (Manufacturers)

Action Arms Ltd. (BRNO; IMI/Galil, Timber Wolf, UZI)
Air Rifle Specialists (BSA Guns Ltd., Theoben Engineering)
American Arms, Inc. (Fausti, Stefano; Franchi S.p.A., Luigi; Grulla Armes; Hermanos S.A., Zabala; INDESAL; Lanber Armes S.A.; Norica)
Armes de Chasse (AYA; Chapuis Armes; Francotte & Cie S.A., Auguste)
Armoury, The (blackpowder arms)
Armscorp. of America, Inc. (Sardius Industries Ltd.)
Armsport, Inc. (blackpowder arms)
Autumn Sales, Inc. (Blaser Jagdwaffen GmbH)
Beeman Precision Arms, Inc. (FWB; Hammerli; Weihrauch KG, Hermann)
Beretta U.S.A. Corp. (Beretta Firearms, Pietro)
Browning Arms Co. (Browning Arms Co.)
Cape Outfitters (blackpowder arms)
Century International Arms, Ltd. (Famas, Norinco)
ChinaSports, Inc. (Norinco)
Cimarron Arms (Uberti, Aldo; blackpowder arms)
CVA (blackpowder arms)
Daisy Mfg. Co. (Gamo)
Dixie Gun Works (Pedersoli Davide & C.; blackpowder arms)
Dynamit Nobel-RWS, Inc. (Diana, Gamo, RWS)
E.A.A. Corp. (ATIS Armi S.A.S.; Fabrica D'Armi Sabatti S.R.L.; Tanfoglio S.r.l., Fratelli/Witness; Weihrauch KG, Hermann; Zoli, Antonio)
Eagle Imports, Inc. (Bersa S.A.)
Ellett Bros. (Churchill, Lakefield Arms Ltd.)
EMF Co., Inc. (Dakota, Pedersoli Davide & C.; blackpowder arms)
Euroarms of America, Inc. (blackpowder arms)
Federal Ordnance, Inc. (Peters Stahl GmbH)
Firstshot, Inc. (Daewoo Precision Industries Ltd.)
Galaxy Imports Ltd., Inc. (Laurona Armes)
Gamba U.S.A. (Gamba S.p.A., Renato)
Glock, Inc. (Glock GmbH)
Great Lakes Airguns (Sharp airguns)
GSI, Inc. (Haenel, Merkel Freres, Steyr-Daimler-Puch, Steyr-Mannlicher)
G.U., Inc. (Sauer, SKB Arms Co.)
Hallowell & Co. (Rigby & Co., John)
Hammerli USA (Hammerli)
Heckler & Koch, Inc. (Benelli Armi S.p.A.; Heckler & Koch, GmbH; Heym GmbH & Co., Friedrich Wilh.)
Incor, Inc. (Cosmi Americo & Figlio s.n.c.)
Interarms (Astra-Unceta Y Cia, S.A.; Helwan; Howa Machinery Ltd.; Interarms; Norinco; Rossi, Amadeo; Star Bonifacio Echeverria S.A.; Walther GmbH, Carl)
J.O. Arms & Ammunition Co. (J.O. Arms & Ammunition Co.)

K.B.I., Inc. (FEG, IMI/Jericho, Kassnar, K.B.I., Inc., Norica)
Keng's Firearms Specialty, Inc. (Poly Technologies, Inc.)
Krieghoff International, Inc. (Krieghoff Gun Co., H.)
Magnum Research, Inc. (Bernardelli Vincenzo S.p.A.; IMI/Desert Eagle)
MAGTECH Recreational Products, Inc. (CBC)
Mandall Shooting Supplies, Inc. (Ariziga; Bretton; Cabanas; Erma Werke GmbH; FAS; Firearms Co. Ltd./Alpine; Gaucher Armes S.A.; Hammerli; Korth; Krico/Kriegeskorte GmbH, A.; SIG; Tanner; Ugartechea S.A., Ignacio; Zanoletti, Pietro; Zoli, Antonio)
Midwest Sport Distributors (Norinco)
Mitchell Arms, Inc. (Mitchell Arms, Inc.)
Moore & Co., Wm. Larkin (FERLIB; Garbi, Armas Urki; Perugini-Visini & Co. s.r.l.; Piotti; Rizzini, F.LLI)
Navy Arms Company (Norinco; Pedersoli Davide & C.; Uberti, Aldo; blackpowder)
New England Arms Co. (Lebeau-Courally, Westley Richards & Co.; premium high-grade shotguns)
Nygord Precision Products (FAS, Steyr airguns, Unique/M.A.P.F.)
Outdoor Sports Headquarters, Inc. (Miroku, B.C./Daly, Charles)
Parker Reproductions (Parker Reproductions)
Perazzi U.S.A., Inc. (Perazzi m.a.p. S.p.A.)
Precision Imports, Inc. (Mauser-Werke)
PSI, Inc. (Anschutz GmbH; Erma Werke GmbH; Gustaf, Carl; Marocchi F.lli S.p.A.)
Precision Sports (Hanus, Bill)
Rahn Gun Works, Inc. (Techni-Mec, Voere)
Rogers Ltd. (JSL Ltd.)
Ruko Products (Arms Corp. of the Philippines)
Sigarms, Inc. (SIG-Sauer)
Sile Distributors (Benelli Armi S.p.A., Marocchi F.lli S.p.A.)
Simmons Enterprises, Ernie (Sauer, SKB Arms Co.)
Sportarms of Florida (Norinco)
St. Lawrence Sales, Inc. (Fabarm S.p.A.)
Springfield Armory, Inc. (IMI/Timber Wolf; Springfield Armory, Inc.)
Stoeger Industries (IGA, Llama Gabilondo Y Cia, Sako Ltd., Tikka)
Stone Enterprises Ltd. (air guns)
Taurus Firearms, Inc. (Taurus International Firearms)
Tradewinds, Inc.
Traditions, Inc. (blackpowder arms)
Trail Guns Armory, Inc. (Pedersoli Davide & C.; blackpowder arms)
Uberti USA, Inc. (Uberti, Aldo; blackpowder arms)
Weatherby, Inc. (Weatherby, Inc.)
Wingshooting Adventures (Arrieta, S.L.)
Zoli U.S.A., Inc., Antonio (Zoli, Antonio)

GUNS AND GUN PARTS, REPLICA AND ANTIQUE

Antique Arms Co.
Armi San Paolo
Armsport, Inc.
Bob's Gun Shop
Border Guns & Leather
British Arms Co. Ltd.
Buckskin Machine Works
Cache La Poudre Rifleworks
Champlin, R. MacDonald
Colonial Repair
Cumberland Arms
Dangler, Homer L.
Day & Sons, Inc., Leonard
Dayton Traister
Delhi Gun House
Delta Arms Ltd.
Dilliott Gunsmithing, Inc.
Dixie Gun Works
Dixon Muzzleloading Shop, Inc.
Dwyer, Dan (obsolete and antique parts)
Dyson & Son Ltd., Peter
Ed's Gun House
EMF Co., Inc.
Essex Arms
Federal Ordnance, Inc.
First Distributors, Inc., Jack
Furr Arms
Golden Age Arms Co.
Goodwin, Fred (Win. rings & studs)
Gun Parts Corporation, The
Guns
Gun Works, The
Hansen Cartridge Co.
House of Muskets, Inc., The (ML supplies)
Hunkeler, A.
Kopec Enterprises, John (Colt Model P only)
Kopp, Terry K. (1890 and 1906 Win.)

Liberty Antique Gunworks (S&W only)
Log Cabin Sport Shop
Lucas, Edw. E. (45/70 Springfield parts; some Sharps, Spencer parts)
Martz, John V. (Lugers and P-38s only)
McKee, Arthur (Remington only)
Mitchell Arms, Inc.
Munsch Gunsmithing, Tommy (Win. obsolete and Marlin parts only)
Muzzleloaders Etcetera, Inc.
Navy Arms Company
N.C. Ordnance Co.
OMR Feinmechanik, Jagd-und Sportwaffen, GmbH
Patchbox, The
Peacemaker Specialists (Colt Model P only)
Pedersoli Davide & C.
Precise Metalsmithing Enterprises
Pre-Winchester Parts Co.
Ram-Line, Inc.
Sarco, Inc.
Shiloh Rifle Mfg. (Sharps)
Silver Ridge Gun Shop
Sklany, Steve
S&S Firearms
Stott's Creek Armory, Inc.
Taylor's & Co., Inc.
Track of the Wolf, Inc.
Trail Guns Armory, Inc.
Upper Missouri Trading Co.
Vintage Industries, Inc.
Wayne Firearms for Collectors & Investors, James
Wescombe (Rem. rolling block parts)
Winchester Sutler, Inc.

GUNS, U.S.-MADE

- A.A. Arms, Inc.
- Accu-Tek
- AMAC
- American Arms, Inc.
- American Derringer Corp.
- AMT
- A-Square Co., Inc.
- Auto-Ordnance Corp.
- Barrett Firearms Mfg., Inc. (Light Fifty)
- Beretta U.S.A. Corp.
- Brown Mfg., E.A.
- Browning Arms Co. (Parts & Service)
- Bryco Arms
- Calico Light Weapon Systems
- Cape Outfitters
- Century Gun Dist., Inc. (Century Model 100 SA rev.)
- Charter Arms
- Claridge Hi-Tec, Inc.
- Colt's Mfg. Co., Inc.

- Coonan Arms, Inc. (357 Mag. auto)
- Cooper Arms
- CVA
- Dakota Arms, Inc. (bolt-action rifles)
- Davis Industries (derringers; 32 auto pistol)
- Desert Industries, Inc.
- Dixie Gun Works
- D Max Industries
- Eagle Arms, Inc.
- EMF Co., Inc.
- Feather Industries, Inc.
- Federal Engineering Corp.
- Freedom Arms, Inc. (mini and Casull revolvers)
- Gibbs Rifle Company, Inc.
- Gonic Arms, Inc.
- Grendel, Inc.
- H&R 1871, Inc.
- IAI

GUNS, SURPLUS—PARTS AND AMMUNITION

Ammunition Consulting Services, Inc.
Aztec International Ltd.
Ballistica Maximus North
Ballistica Maximus South
Bob's Gun Shop
Braun, M.
British Arms Co. Ltd.
Century International Arms, Ltd.
ChinaSports, Inc.
Concorde Arms, Inc.
Delhi Gun House
Delta Arms Ltd.
Federal Ordnance, Inc.
First Distributors, Inc., Jack
Forrest, Inc., Tom
Garcia National Gun Traders, Inc.
Gibbs Rifle Company, Inc.
Gun Parts Corporation, The
Hansen Cartridge Co.
Keng's Firearms Specialty, Inc.

Kimber Parts
Kimel Industries
Lever Arms Service Ltd.
Navy Arms Company
Paragon Sales & Services, Inc. (ammunition)
Pre-Winchester Parts Co.
Randall Firearms Research
Ruvel & Co., Inc.
Samco Global Arms, Inc.
Sarco, Inc. (military surplus ammo)
Sherwood Intl. Export Corp.
Southern Ammunition Co., Inc.
Southern Armory, The (modern military parts)
Springfield Sporters, Inc.
T.F.C. S.p.A.
U.S. Arms Corp.
Westfield Engineering
Whitestone Lumber Corp.

•See page 445 for Warranty Service Center Addresses

GUNSMITHS, CUSTOM (see Custom Gunsmiths)

GUNSMITHS, HANDGUN (see Pistolsmiths)

GUNSMITH SCHOOLS

Colorado School of Trades
Forster Products
Lassen Community College
Modern Gun Repair School
(correspondence school only)
Montgomery Community College (also
1-yr. engraving school)
Murray State College
North American Correspondence
Schools

Pennsylvania Gunsmith School
Piedmont Community College
Pine Technical College
Professional Gunsmiths of America, Inc.
(Technical training ctr.)
Southeastern Community College
Trinidad State Junior College
Yavapai College

GUNSMITH SUPPLIES, TOOLS, SERVICES

Adair Custom Shop, Bill
Alley Supply Co. (JET line lathes, mills,
etc.)
Atlantic Mills, Inc. (gun cleaners, patches,
shop wipes)
Bald Eagle Precision Machine Co.
Baron Technology, Inc. (chemical
etching, plating)
Behlert Precision
Belding & Mull, Inc.
Bell Originals, Sid (floorplate decoration)
Belltown, Ltd.
Bengtson Arms Co., L.
Biesen, Al (grip caps, buttplates)
Biesen, Roger
Bill's Gun Repair
Blue Ridge Machinery & Tools, Inc.
(gunsmithing lathe, mills and shop
supplies)
Bob's Gun Shop
Briganti & Co., A. (cold rust bluing, hand
polishing, metal work)
Brownell's, Inc.
Brownell Checkering Tools, W.E.
Brown Products, Ed
B-Square Co.
Buehler Scope Mounts
Can Am Enterprises
Chapman Manufacturing Company, The
Choate Machine & Tool Company, Inc.
(tools)
Chopie Mfg., Inc.
Clymer Manufacturing Company, Inc.
(reamers, etc.)
Colonial Arms, Inc.
Corbin Manufacturing & Supply, Inc.
Crouse's Country Cover (Masking Gun
Oil)
Custom Checkering Service
Custom Gun Products
Dakota Arms, Inc.
Davidson Products, Inc.
Decker Shooting Products
Delhi Gun House
Dem-Bart Hand Checkering Tools, Inc.
de Treville, Stan (checkering patterns)
Dremel Mfg. Co. (grinders)
Duffy, Charles E.
Du-Lite Corp.
The Dutchman's Firearms, Inc.
Edmund Scientific Co.
Eilan S.A.L.
FERLIB di Ferraglio Libero & Co.
First Distributors, Inc., Jack
Fisher, Jerry
Flashette Co. (bore illuminator gun
cleaning aid)
Flex Gun Rods Co., Inc.
Flitz International Ltd.
Foredom Electric Co.
Forster Products
Frank Custom Gun Service, Ron
Garrett Accur-Lt. D.F.S. Co.
Grace Metal Products
Graybill's Gun Shop
GRS Corp. (Gravermeister; Grave Max
tools)
Gunline Tools
Gun-Tec (files)
Gutridge, Inc. (pin takedown tool, S&W
action tool)
Hastings Barrels
Henriksen Tool Co., Inc. (reamers)
Iosso Marine Products
Ivanoff, Thomas G. (black anodizing)
Jantz Supply
JGS Precision Tool Mfg.

Kasenit Co., Inc. (surface hardening
compound)
Kimber Parts
Kleinendorst, K.W.
Kopp, Terry K. (stock rubbing compound;
rust preventive grease)
Korzinek Riflesmith, J. (stainless steel
bluing)
LaRocca Gun Works, Inc.
Lawson, John G.
Lea Mfg. Co.
Lee Supplies, Mark
Liberty Antique Gunworks (spl. S&W
tools)
Lock's Philadelphia Gun Exchange
London Guns Ltd.
Lortone, Inc.
Lyman Products Corporation
Marble Arms Corporation (shotgun,
handgun ribs)
Marsh, Mike (accessories)
Masen Co., John
McMillan Rifle Barrels (services)
MDS, Inc. (bore lights)
Metalife Industries
Millenium Safety Products, Inc.
MMC (screwdriver grinding fixtures)
Mittermeier, Inc., Frank
Moreton/Fordyce Enterprises
NGraveR Co., The
Nitex, Inc. (custom metal finish)
N&J Sales (screw drivers)
Novak's .45 Shop
Nowlin Custom Barrels Mfg.
Pace Marketing, Inc.
Palmgren Steel Products (vises, etc.)
Panavise Products, Inc.
Power Custom, Inc.
Precise Metal Finishing
Precision Specialties
Prolix
Reardon Products
Redman's Rifling & Reboring (barrel
liners)
Robar Co.'s, Inc., The
Roto/Carve (tool)
Russell Knives, Inc., A.G. (Arkansas
oilstones)
Scott/McDougall Custom Gunsmiths
Seacliff International, Inc. (portable parts
washer)
Shaw's Finest in Guns
Shirley Co. Gun & Riflemakers Ltd.,
J.A.
Silhouette Arms Custom 45 Shop, Inc.
Sight Shop, The
S.K. Guns, Inc.
Slipshot MTS Group (metal treatment
system)
Smith Whetstone, Inc.
Starrett Co., L.S.
Stuart Products, Inc. (Sight-Vise)
Sure Shot of LA, Inc.
Swift River Gunworks, Inc.
Texas Platers Supply (plating kit)
Tom's Gun Repair
Unick's Gunsmithing
Washita Mountain Whetstone Co.
Weaver Arms Corp. (action wrenches &
transfer punches)
Weaver's Gun Shop (tools)
Westfield Engineering
Westrom, John
Will-Burt Co. (vises)
Williams Gun Sight Co.
Williams Shootin' Iron Service
Wolff Co., W.C. (springs)

HANDGUN ACCESSORIES

A.A. Arms, Inc.
Action Arms Ltd.
ADCO (speed loaders)
Adventurer's Outpost
Ajax Custom Grips, Inc.
Allen Co., Bob
American Bullets
American Gas & Chemical Co., Ltd.
(cleaning lube)
Answer Products Co. (Accu-Comfort
Magnum Pistol Glove)
Armsport, Inc.
Bar-Sto Precision Machine (barrels)
Baumannize, Inc.
Behlert Precision
Bellm Contenders (contenders only)
Belltown, Ltd.
Bob's Gun Shop
Bob's Tactical Indoor Shooting Range &
Gun Shop
Boonie Packer Products (speedloaders)
Brown Products, Ed
B-Square Co.
Centaur Systems, Inc. (Quadra-Lok
barrels)
Central Specialties Co. (trigger locks only)
Champion's Choice, Inc.
Clark Custom Guns, Inc.
Cobra Gunskin
Conetrol Scope Mounts
Crane & Crane Ltd.
C3 Systems (speedloaders)
Dade Screw Machine Products (Dade
speed loaders)
Doskocil Mfg. Co., Inc (Gun Guard cases)
Eagle Imports, Inc.
Eagle International, Inc.
E&L Mfg., Inc.
EMF Co., Inc.
Enguix Import-Export
Essex Arms (45 Auto frames)
European American Armory Corp.
Feminine Protection, Inc. (holster
handbags)
Fitz Pistol Grip Co.
Frielich Police Equipment (cases)
Galati International
Glaser Safety Slug, Inc.
Glock, Inc.
Greider Precision Products
Gremmel Enterprises (conversion units)
Guncraft Sports, Inc.
Gunfitters, The
Gun-Ho Sports Cases
Gun Parts Corporation, The
Hafner Enterprises, Inc.
Hebard Guns, Gil
Heinie Specialty Products
Hill Speed Leather, Ernie
H.K.S. Products (revolver speed loaders)
I.N.C., Inc.
Jarvis Gunsmithing, Inc.
Jeffredo Gunsight
Jett & Co., Inc.
J.O. Arms & Ammunition
Keller Co., The
King's Gun Works
K&K Ammo Wrist Band
KLP, Inc.

Kopp, Terry K.
Korth
Lakewood Products, Inc.
La Prade (full moon clips)
LaRocca Gun Works, Inc.
Lee's Red Ramps (ramp insert, spring
kits)
Liberty Antique Gunworks (shims for
S&W revolvers)
Lighthouse Mfg. Co., Inc.
Linebaugh Custom Sixguns
Loch Leven Industries
Lomont Precision Bullets, Kent (Auto Mag
only)
Lone Star Gunleather
L.P.A. Snc
Mag-Na-Port International, Inc.
Magnum Research, Inc.
Mag-Pack Corp.
Mahony, Philip Bruce
Maloni, Russ
M.A.M. Products, Inc. (free standing
brass catcher for all auto pistols and/or
semi-auto rifles)
Markell Inc.
Masen Co., John
McCormick Corp., Chip
Menck, Thomas W.
Merit Corporation
Merkuria Ltd.
Michael's of Oregon Co.
MTM Molded Products Company
Mustra's Custom Guns, Inc., Carl
Noble Co., Jim
No-Sho Mfg. Co.
Oakland Custom Arms, Inc.
Owen, Harry
Pace Marketing, Inc.
Pachmayr Ltd.(cases)
Pardini Armi Commerciale Srl
Pflumm Gun Mfg. Co. (pistol cases)
PistolPAL Products
Police Bookshelf
Ranch Products (third-moon clips)
Randco UK
Ransom International Corp.
Rupert's Gun Shop
Russwood Custom Pistol Grips
Shooter Shop, The
Shurkatch Corp.
Sile Distributors
Sonderman, Robert
Southwind Sanctions
Sport Specialties
Sportsmen's Equipment Co.
SSK Industries
Su-Press-On, Inc.
Tapco, Inc.
Taurus, S.A., Forjas
T.F.C. S.p.A.
Triple-K Mfg. Co.
Tyler Mfg.-Dist., Melvin (grip adaptor)
Volquartsen Custom Ltd.
Wardell Precision Handguns Ltd. (grip
adaptor)
Whitestone Lumber Corp.
Williams Gun Sight Co.
Wilson's Gun Shop
Wichita Arms, Inc.

HANDGUN GRIPS

African Import Co.
Ahrends, Kim (exotic wood grips for
1911-frame pistols)
Ajax Custom Grips, Inc.
Altamont Co.
American Gripcraft
Art Jewel Enterprises Ltd. (Eagle Grips)
Barami Corp. (Hip-Grip)
Bear Hug Grips, Inc. (custom)
Behlert Precision
Bob's Gun Shop
Boone's Custom Ivory Grips, Inc.
Boyds' Gunstock Industries, Inc.
CAM Enterprises
Champion's Choice, Inc.
Cobra Gunskin
Cole-Grip
Colonial Repair
Custom Firearms
Custom Gun Grips
DeSantis Holster & Leather Goods
Eagle Imports, Inc.
EMF Co., Inc.
Enguix Import-Export

European American Armory Corp.
Eyears
Fitz Pistol Grip Co.
Forrest, Inc., Tom
Greene's Machine Carving (45 ACP grips)
Gun Parts Corporation, The
Harrison-Hurtz Enterprises, Inc.
Herrett's Stocks, Inc.
Hogue Grips
Holster Shop, The
H-S Precision, Inc.
Logan Security Products Co.
Maloni, Russ
Markell, Inc.
Marple & Associates, Dick (inserts)
Michael's of Oregon Co.
Monte Kristo Pistol Grip Co.
N.C. Ordnance Co.
Newell, Robert H. (custom stocks)
Oakland Custom Arms, Inc.
Pace Marketing, Inc.
Pachmayr Ltd.
Pardini Armi Commerciale Srl
Randco UK

Renner Co., R.J. (Radical Grips)
Rosenberg & Sons, Jack A.
Russwood Custom Pistol Grips (custom exotic woods)
Safari Gun Co.
Safariland Ltd., Inc.
Savana Sports, Inc.
Sile Distributors
Sonderman, Robert B.

Spegel, Craig
Taurus, S.A., Forjas
Taurus Firearms, Inc.
Tyler Mfg.-Dist., Melvin
Vintage Industries, Inc.
Volquartsen Custom Ltd.
Wallace's (custom only)
Wayland Precision Wood Products ("Classic" & "Double Diamond" grips)

HEARING PROTECTORS

Bausch & Lomb, Inc.
Behlert Precision
Belding & Mull, Inc.
Bilsom Int., Inc. (ear plugs, muffs)
Blount, Inc. Sporting Equipment Division
Champion's Choice, Inc.
Clark Co., Inc., David
Cobra Gunskin
E-A-R, Inc.
Fitz Pistol Grip Co.
Flents Products Co., Inc.
Jaeger, Inc., Paul
Marble Arms Corporation

Markell, Inc.
North Consumer Prods. Div. (Lee Sonic ear valves)
Peltor, Inc. (ear muffs, electronic hearing protectors)
Pendleton Royal
Police Bookshelf
R.E.T. Enterprises
Safari Gun Co.
Safariland Ltd., Inc.
Safety Direct (Silencio)
Smith & Wesson
Willson Safety Prods. Div. (Ray-O-Vac)

HOLSTERS AND LEATHER GOODS

A.A. Arms, Inc.
A&B Industries, Inc.
Adventurer's Outpost
Aker Leather Products
Alessi Holsters, Inc.
Allen Co., Bob
American Import Co., The
American Sales & Mfg. Co.
Ansen Enterprises (Hide-A-Gun)
Arratoonian, Andy
Atsko/Sno-Seal, Inc. (leather waterproofing)
Baker's Leather Goods, Roy (belts, accessories)
Bandcor Industries
Barami Corp.
Beeman Precision Arms, Inc. (airguns only)
Behlert Precision
Bianchi International, Inc.
Blocker's Custom Holsters, Ted
Bob's Tactical Indoor Shooting Range & Gun Shop
Border Guns & Leather (Old West custom)
Boyt Co.
Brauer Bros. Mfg. Co.
Browning Arms Co.
Bruno Shooters Supply
Bucheimer, J.M.
Carvajal Belts & Holsters
Cathey Enterprises, Inc.
Chace Leather Products
Clements' Custom Leathercraft, Chas
Cobra Gunskin
Cobra Sport
Colonial Repair
Concorde Arms, Inc. (ammo pouches)
Crane & Crane Ltd.
Crawford Co., Inc., R.M.
Creedmoor Sports, Inc.
Dakota Corp. (leather gloves)
Davis Leather Co., G. Wm.
Delhi Gun House
DeSantis Holster & Leather Goods
Easy Pull/Outlaw Products
Ekol Leather Care (leather care products)
El Paso Saddlery Co.
Emerging Technologies, Inc.
EMF Co., Inc.
Epps "Orillia" Ltd., Ellwood (custom made)
Eutaw Co., Inc., The
Faust, Inc., T.G.
Fitz Pistol Grip Co.
Fobus International Ltd.
Galati International
GALCO International Ltd.
Glock, Inc. (holsters)
GML Products, Inc.
Gould & Goodrich
Gunfitters, The (custom holsters)
Gun Leather Limited
Gun Parts Corporation, The
Gusty Winds Corp.
Gun Works, The
Hafner Enterprises, Inc.
Hebard Guns, Gil
Henigson & Associates, Steve
High North Products, Inc.
Hill Speed Leather, Ernie
Holster Outpost
Holster Shop, The

Horseshoe Leather Products
Hoyt Holster Co., Inc.
Hume, Don
Hunter Co., Inc.
J.O. Amrs & Ammunition
John's Custom Leather (leather repair)
Jumbo Sports Products
Kane Products, Inc. (GunChaps)
Kirkpatrick Leather Co.
KLP, Inc.
Kolpin Mfg., Inc.
Korth
L.A.R. Manufacturing, Inc.
Lawrence Leather Co.
Leather Arsenal (belts)
Lone Star Gunleather
Magnolia Sports, Inc.
Markell, Inc.
Marple & Associates, Dick
Michael's of Oregon Co.
Mitchell Arms, Inc.
Mixson Leathercraft, Inc.
Nelson Combat Leather, Bruce
Noble Co., Jim
North American Arms
No-Sho Mfg. Co.
Null Holsters Ltd., K.L.
October Country
Ojala Holsters, Arvo
Oklahoma Leather Products, Inc.
Old West Reproductions, Inc.
Pace Marketing, Inc.
Pathfinder Sports Leather
Pendleton Royal
Police Bookshelf
Pony Express Sport Shop, Inc.
Proline Handgun Leather, Inc.
Randco UK
Red Head, Inc.
Red River Frontier Outfitters (clothing)
Renegade
Ringler Custom Leather Co.
Rybka Custom Leather Equipment, Thad
Safari Gun Co.
Safariland Ltd., Inc.
Safety Speed Holster, Inc.
Savana Sports, Inc.
Schulz Industries
Shadow Concealment Systems
Shoemaker & Sons, Inc., Tex
Shootin' Accessories Ltd.
Shurkatch Corp.
Sile Distributors
Silhouette Leathers (custom holsters)
Smith Saddlery, Jesse W.
Southwind Sanctions
Sparks, Milt
Stalker, Inc.
Strong Holster Co.
Tabler Marketing (cincher)
Taylor's & Co., Inc.
Torel, Inc.
Triple-K Mfg. Co.
Tyler Mfg.-Dist., Melvin
Venus Industries
Viking Leathercraft, Inc.
Walt's Custom Leather
Whinnery, Walt
Wild Bill's Originals (antique holstermaker)
Whitestone Lumber Corp.
Winchester Sutler, Inc. (military only)

HUNTING AND CAMP GEAR, CLOTHING, ETC.

Ace Sportswear, Inc.
Adventure 16, Inc. (accessories)
All Weather Outerwear
Allen Co., Bob
American Import Co., The (compasses, hand warmers)
Armor
Atsko/Sno-Seal, Inc.
Barbour, Inc.
Bauer, Eddie
Bausch & Lomb, Inc. (Ray Ban shooting glasses)
Bean, L.L.
Bear Archery (Himalayan backpack)
Bell Originals, Sid
Better Concepts Co. (for geese)
Bilsom Intl., Inc. (shooting glasses)
Boss Manufacturing Company (hunting gloves and mitts)
Brell Mar Products
Browning Arms Co.
Brunton U.S.A. (compasses)
Buck Stop Lure Co., Inc.
Cabela's
Camofare Company (camouflage accessories)
Camp-Cap Products
Carhartt, Inc.
Catoctin Cutlery
Chameleon Camouflage Systems (camouflage accessories)
Coulston Int. Corp. (Duranon tick repellent; Perma-Kill)
Chimere, Inc.
Chippewa Shoe Co. (boots)
Churchill Glove Co., James (shooting gloves)
Clarkfield Enterprises, Inc. (camouflage clothing)
Cobra Gunskin
Coghlan's Ltd.
Crawford Co., Inc., R.M. (clothing)
Creedmoor Sports, Inc. (shooting coats)
Coleman Co., Inc.
Counter Assault
Dakota Corp. (leather gloves)
Danner Shoe Mfg. Co. (boots)
Deer Me Products
Dr. O's Products Ltd.
Dunham Co. (boots)
Duofold, Inc. (clothing)
Duxbak, Inc.
Dynalite Products, Inc. (flashlights)
E-A-R, Inc. (shooting glasses)
Erickson's Mfg., Inc., C.W.
Faith Associates, Inc. (shooting glasses)
Feather Flex Decoys
Finerty, Raymond F. (Medalist apparel)
Fish-N-Hunt, Inc.
Forrest Tool Co.
Fox River Mills, Inc.
Frankonia Jagd
Game Winner, Inc. (camouflage suits; orange vests)
Gander Mountain, Inc.
Gerber Legendary Blades
Glacier Glove (neoprene gloves)
Gozon Corp.
Gun Club Sportswear
Hawken Shop, The
Herrett's Stocks, Inc. (belt buckles)
Hinman Outfitters, Bob
Hodgman, Inc.
Houtz & Barwick
Hunter's Specialties, Inc.
Hunting Classics Ltd.

Jaeger, Inc., Paul
Joy Enterprises
Just Brass, Inc. (belt buckles)
Kamik Outdoor Footwear
K&M Industries, Inc.
LaCrosse Footwear, Inc.
Langenberg Hat Co.
Lectro Science, Inc. (spotlights)
Liberty Trouser Co.
MAG Instrument, Inc.
Marathon Rubber Prods. Co., Inc. (rain gear)
Melton Shirt Co., Inc.
Molin Ind./Tru-Nord Division
Nelson/Weather-Rite
Newbern Glove (hunting/shooting gloves)
Northlake Boot Co. (Durango)
Original Mink Oil, Inc.
Orvis Co., The (fishing gear; clothing)
Palsa Outdoor Products
Partridge Sales Ltd., John
P.A.S.T. Corp. (shooting shirts)
Pendleton Woolen Mills (clothing)
Porta Blind, Inc. (ground blinds)
Precise International
Primos Wild Game Calls, Inc.
Pro-Mark (shooting/hunting gloves)
Pyromid, Inc. (portable camp stoves)
Ranger Footwear
Ranger Mfg. Co., Inc. (camouflage suits)
Rattlers Brand (snake-proof chaps)
Red Ball (boots)
Red Head, Inc.
Refrigiwear, Inc.
Re-Heater, Inc. (reusable portable heat packs)
Remington Footwear Co.
Rocky (boots, shoes)
Rocky Mountain High Sports Glasses (shooting glasses)
R.V.I. (Fire 'n Five Starter Kit)
Safari Gun Co.
Safesport Manufacturing Co. (safety garments, snowshoes)
Saf-T-Bak, Inc.
San Angelo Sports Products, Inc.
Savana Sports, Inc.
Scansport, Inc. (wool hunting packs)
Servus Footwear Co.
Shurkatch Corp.
Shell Shack
Smith Whethstone, Inc.
Streamlight, Inc.
Survival Books/The Larder
Swanndri New Zealand (pure wool hunting clothing)
Torel, Inc.
Trail Timer Co.
Teledyne, Inc.
10-X Products Group
Thompson, Norm
Tink's Safariland Hunting Corp. (camouflage rain gear)
Torel, Inc.
Traq, Inc.
Venus Industries
Wakina
Walker Shoe Co. (boots)
Walls Industries
Willson Safety Prods. Div. (shooting glasses)
Woodstream
Wolverine Boots & Shoes Div. (footwear)
Woolrich Woolen Mills
Wyoming Knife Corp. (saw)
Yellowstone Wilderness Supply

KNIVES AND KNIFEMAKER'S SUPPLIES—FACTORY AND MAIL ORDER

Adventure 16, Inc.
African Import Co.
Aitor-Cuchilleria Del Norte, S.A.
American Import Co., The
American Target Knives
Aristocrat Knives
Art Jewel Enterprises Ltd.
Atlanta Cutlery Corp. (mail order, supplies)
B&D Trading Co., Inc.
Baker's Leather Goods, Roy
Barteaux Machete
Bean, L.L. (mail order)
Benchmark Knives
Blackjack Knives
Blue Ridge Knives

Boker USA, Inc.
Bowen Knife Co.
Browning Arms Co.
Brunton U.S.A.
Buck Knives, Inc.
Buster's Custom Knives
CAM Enterprises
Camillus Cutlery Co.
Campbell, Dick
Case & Sons Cutlery Co., W.R.
Catoctin Cutlery
Chicago Cutlery Co.
Christopher Firearms Co., Inc., E. (supplies)
Clements' Custom Leathercraft, Chas (exotic sheaths)

Coast Cutlery Co.
Cold Steel, Inc.
Coleman Co., Inc.
Collins Brothers Div.
Colonial Knife Co. (Master Brand)
Compass Industries, Inc.
Crawford Co., Inc., R.M.
Creative Craftsman, Inc., The
 (sharpening equipment)
Crosman Blades
Custom Knifemaker's Supply
Cutco Cutlery
Cutlery Shoppe
Damascus-U.S.A.
Dan's Whetstone Co., Inc. (sharpening
 stones, abrasives)
Degen Knives
Edgecraft Corp. (sharpeners)
Ek Commando Knife Co.
Empire Cutlery Corp.
Eze-Lap Diamond Prods. (knife
 sharpeners)
Fibron Products, Inc.
Fitz Pistol Grip Co.
Forrest Tool Company (Max Multipurpose
 Ax)
Forthofer's Gunsmithing & Knifemaking
Fortune Products, Inc. (knife sharpeners)
Frank Knives
Frost Cutlery Co.
Gerber Legendary Blades
Golden Age Arms Co.
Gutmann Cutlery Co., Inc.
Hawken Shop, The
H&B Forge Co. (throwing knives,
 tomahawks)
Harrington Cutlery, Inc., Russell (Dexter,
 Green River Works)
Henckels Zwillingswerk, Inc., J.A.
High North Products, Inc.
Hubertus Schneidwarenfabrik
Hunting Classics Ltd.
Hy-Score Arms Co. Ltd.
Ibberson (Sheffield) Ltd., George
Iron Mountain Knife Co.
J.A. Blades, Inc. (supplies)
Jaeger, Inc., Paul
Jantz Supply
Jenco Sales, Inc.
Joy Enterprises (Fury sporting knives)
KA-BAR Knives
Kasenit Co., Inc.
Kellogg's Professional Products

Kelly, Lance
Ken's Finn Knives
Kershaw Knives
Koval Knives, Inc.
Lamson & Goodnow Mfg. Co.
Lansky Sharpeners & Crock Stick
 (sharpening devices)
Leatherman Tool Group, Inc.
Lebeau-Courally
Linder Solingen Knives
Marble Arms Corporation
Mar Knives, Inc., Al
Marple & Associates, Dick
Matthews Cutlery
Molin Ind./Tru-Nord Division
Murphy Co., Inc., R. (StaySharp)
Normark Corp.
Outdoor Edge Cutlery Corp.
Plaza Cutlery, Inc. (mail order)
Police Bookshelf
Precise International
Queen Cutlery Co.
Randall-Made Knives
R&C Knives & Such (custom only)
Reno, Wayne and Karen
Russell Knives, Inc., A.G.
Safesport Manufacturing Co.
Sanders Custom Gun Service (importer)
Scansport, Inc.
Schiffman, Mike
Schrade Cutlery Corp.
Sheffield Knifemakers Supply
Smith & Wesson
Smith Saddlery, Jesse W. (sheathmakers)
Smith Whetstone, Inc.
Spyderco, Inc.
Survival Books/The Larder
Swiss Army Knives, Inc.
T.F.C. S.p.A.
Thompson/Center Arms
Tru-Balance Knife Co.
United Cutlery Corp.
Utica Cutlery Co. (Kutmaster)
Valor Corp.
Venus Industries
Walt's Custom Leather
Washita Mountain Whetstone Co.
Weber Jr., Rudolf
Wenoka/Seastyle
Whinnery, Walt (sheathmaker)
White Owl Enterprises
Wostenholm
Wyoming Knife Corp.

LABELS, BOXES, CARTRIDGE HOLDERS

Accuracy Products S.A. (plastic ammo
 boxes)
Anderson Manufacturing Co., Inc.
Arkfeld Mfg. & Dist. Co., Inc.
Belding & Mull, Inc.
Cabinet Mtn. Outfitter (cartridge holders)
Corbin Manufacturing & Supply, Inc.
Del Rey Products
DeSantis Holster and Leather Goods
Fitz Pistol Grip Co.
Flambeau Products Corp.
Gould & Goodrich

Hunter Co., Inc.
KLP, Inc.
Kolpin Mfg., Inc.
K&T Co.
Lakewood Products, Inc.
Lyman Products Corporation
Midway Arms, Inc.
Pendleton Royal
Peterson Instant Targets Co. (cartridge
 box labels; Targ-Dots)
Shootin' Accessories Ltd.
Shurkatch Corp.

LOAD TESTING AND PRODUCT TESTING,
(Chronographing, Ballistic Studies)

Ballistic Research (ballistic studies,
 pressure and velocity)
Bustani Appraisers, Leo
Clerke Co., J.A.
Corbin Applied Technology
D&D Gunsmiths, Ltd.
D&H Precision Tooling (pressure testing
 equipment)
H-S Precision, Inc.
Hutton Rifle Ranch (ballistic studies)
Jensen Bullets
Lachaussee, S.A.
Lomont Precision Bullets, Kent
 (handguns, handgun ammunition)
Lyman Products Corporation
Maionchi - L.M.I.

McMurdo, Lynn
Neutralizer Police Munitions
Pejsa Ballistics
Plum City Ballistic Range
Professional Hunter Supplies
Rupert's Gun Shop
Russell's Rifle Shop (load testing and
 chronographing to 300 yds.)
Schumakers Gun Shop, William
Scot Powder Co. of Ohio, Inc.
Shooting Chrony, Inc.
Specialty Gunsmithing
SSK Industries
Thunderbird Cartridge Co., Inc.
Vancini, Carl A.
White Laboratory, Inc., H.P.

MISCELLANEOUS

Actions
 Left-hand (Gentry Custom Gunmaker,
  David)
 Mauser-style only (Crandall Tool &
  Machine Company)
 Rifle, stainless steel (Hall Manufacturing)

Rifle, falling block (Miller Arms, Inc.)
Accurizing, rifle (Stoney Baroque
 Shooters Supply)
Adapters
 Cartridge (Alex, Inc.)
 Cartridge (Owen, Harry)

Shotshell, Plummer 410 converter (PC
 Co.)
Shotshell, 12-ga./410 converter
 (Ramos, Jesse)
Airgun Accessories
 Beeman Pell seat, Pell Size (Beeman
  Precision Arms, Inc.)
 BSA Guns Ltd.
Art, old gun industry (Hansen Cartridge
 Co.)
Assault Rifle Accessories
 Feather Industries, Inc.
 Ram-Line, Inc.
Bedding kit, Tru-Set (Fenwal, Inc.)
Body Armor
 A&B Industries, Inc.
 Faust, T.G.
 Second Chance Body Armor
Bore collimator, Sweany Site-A-Line
 optical collimator (Alley Supply Co.)
Bore illuminator, gun cleaning aid
 (Flashette Co.)
Bore lights (MDS, Inc.)
Brass catcher, free standing for all auto
 pistols and/or semi-auto rifles (M.A.M.
 Products, Inc.)
Bullets, rubber (CIDCO)
Cannons, miniature replicas
 Furr Arms
 R.G.-G., Inc.
Consultant, firearms (Puccinelli, Leonard)
Convert-A-Pell (Jett & Co., Inc.)
Dehumidifiers
 Buenger Enterprises
 Hydrosorbent Products
Deer Drag (D&H Prods. Co., Inc.)
Dryers
 Thermo-electric (Golden Rod
  Dehumidifier Co., Inc.)
 Electric boot, shoe, hip, chest wader
  (Peet Shoe Dryer, Inc.)
E-Z Loader, for 22-cal. rifles (Del Rey
 Products)
Firearms Restoration
 Adair Custom Shop, Bill (lettering)
 Art's Gun & Sport Shop, Inc.
 Kneiper Custom Rifles, Jim
 Mazur Restoration, Pete
 Moeller, Steve
 Pentheny de Pentheny
FFL Record Keeping
 Basics Information Systems, Inc.
 R.E.T. Enterprises
Flares (Aztec International Ltd.)
Gatling guns (Furr Arms)
Jewelry
 Sportsmen's (Bell Originals, Sid)
 Sportsmen's (Mains Enterprises, Inc.)
Hunting Trips
 Safaris, African (Professional Hunter
  Specialties)
 World hunting information (J/B
  Adventures & Safaris, Inc.)
Hypodermic rifles and
 pistols—slaughtering pistols
 (Multipropulseurs)
Indoor range (Guncraft Sports, Inc.)
Insert barrels (Owen, Harry/Sport
 Specialties)
IR detection systems (GTS Enterprises,
 Inc.)
Locks, Gun
 Brown Manufacturing
 Master Lock Co.
Military equipment and accessories
 (Alpha 1 Drop Zone)
Monte Carlo pad (Hoppe's Div.)
Photographers, Gun
 Bilal, Mustafa
 Hanusin, John
 Macbean, Stan
 Payne Photodesign, Robert
 Semmer, Charles
 Smith, Michael
 Weyer International
Racks, gun (All Rite Products, Inc.)
Record books, for dealers and collectors
 (PFRB Co.)
Saddle rings, studs (Goodwin, Fred/Silver
 Ridge Gun Shop)
Safety Devices
 Gun safety cover (Gun-Alert/Master
  Products, Inc.)
 P&M Sales and Service

Safeties, for Rem. 870P (Harper,
 William E./The Great 870 Co.)
Safeties, side lever for rifle (Taylor &
 Robbins)
Scents and Lures
 Buck Stop Lure Co., Inc.
 Cabinet Mtn. Outfitter
 Dr. O's Products Ltd.
 Mountain Hollow Game Calls
 Rickard, Inc., Pete
 Robbins Scent, Inc.
 Tink's Safariland Hunting Corp.
 Wildlife Research Center, Inc.
Scrimshaw
 Boone's Custom Ivory Grips, Inc.
 Dolbare, Elizabeth
 Gun Room, The
 Marek, George
 Reno, Wayne and Karen
 Sherwood, George
Scoring plug, RIG and NRA (RIG
 Products)
Self-defense sprays (Counter Assault)
Shell catcher (Condor Mfg. Co.)
Shooting range equipment (Caswell
 International Corp.)
Silencers
 AWC Systems Technology
 Blaylock Gun Works
 Ciener, Jonathan Arthur
 Developmental Concepts
 DLO Mfg.
 Fleming Firearms
 Norrell Arms, John
 Precision Arms International, Inc.
 S&H Arms Mfg. Co.
 Sound Technology
 South Central Research Corp.
 Ward Machine
Speedloader, shotgun (Armstec, Inc.)
Slings and Swivels
 Baker's Leather Goods, Roy
 Boonie Packer Products
 DTM International, Inc.
 Johanssons Vapentillbehor, Bert
 Michael's of Oregon Co.
 Palsa Outoor Products
 Rifle (Bianchi International, Inc.)
 Rifle (Butler Creek Corporation)
 Rifle (Leather Arsenal)
 Rifle (Pathfinder Sports Leather)
 Rifle (Schulz Industries)
 Sile Distributors
 Slings 'N Things, Inc.
 Supersound (Edmund Scientific Co.)
 Torel, Inc.
Snap caps (Armsport, Inc.)
Springs (Wolff Co., W.C.)
Rotary flexible shaft power tools
 (Foredom Electric Co.)
Shell dispenser (Loadmaster)
Treestands and Steps
 A&J Products
 Amacker International, Inc.
 Apache Products
 Dr. O's Products Ltd.
 Silent Hunter
 Summit Specialties, Inc.
 Trax America, Inc.
 Treemaster
 Warren & Sweat Mfg. Co.
Trophies
 Blackinton & Co., Inc., V.H.
 Marple & Associates, Dick
Trap and Skeet (Favre, Jacqueline)
Ventilation, filtration for indoor ranges
 (ScanCo Environmental Systems)
Video Tapes
 Foothills Video Productions, Inc.
 Gunsmithing (VSP Publishers)
 Kentucky rifles (Dangler, Homer L.)
 Outdoor adventure (Eastman Products,
  R.T.)
 Paladin Press
 Police survival (Calibre Press, Inc.)
 Muzzle-loading (New Historians
  Productions, The)
 Wilderness Sound Productions Ltd.
Vise, gun (Pflumm Gun Mfg. Co.)
Xythos-Miniature revolver (Andres &
 Dworsky)

MUZZLE-LOADING GUNS, BARRELS AND EQUIPMENT

Accuracy Unlimited (stainless steel
ramrods; tips and short-starters)
Adkins, Luther (breech plugs)
•American Arms, Inc.
•Anderson Manufacturing Co., Inc.
(Accra-Shot)
Armi San Paolo
•Armoury, Inc., The
•Armsport, Inc.
Beaver Lodge (custom ML)
Bentley, John
Blackhawk East (blackpowder)
Blackhawk Mountain (blackpowder)
Blackhawk West (blackpowder)
•Blount, Inc. Sporting Equipment Division
Bridgers Best
Buckskin Machine Works
Buffalo Bullet Co., Inc. (bullets, balls and
sabots)
Burgess and Son Gunsmiths, R.W.
Butler Creek Corporation
Cache La Poudre Rifleworks (custom
muzzleloaders)
Chopie Mfg., Inc. (nipple wrenches)
CONKKO
Cumberland Arms
•Cumberland Knife & Gun Works
Cureton Powder Horns (powder horns)
•CVA (muzzleloaders, kits)
Dangler, Homer L.
Day & Sons, Inc., Leonard
deHaas Barrels
Delhi Gun House
Denver Arms, Ltd.
DGS, Inc.
•Dixie Gun Works
Dixon Muzzleloading Shop, Inc.
•EMF Co., Inc.
•Euroarms of America, Inc.
Eutaw Co., Inc., The
Fautheree, Andy
Fellowes, Ted
Fish, Marshall F. (antique ML repairs)
Flintlock Muzzle Loading Gun Shop, The
Flintlocks, Etc.
•Forster Products
Frank Custom Gun Service, Ron
Frontier
Getz Barrel Co. (barrels)
•Gibbs Rifle Company, Inc.
Golden Age Arms Co.
•Gonic Arms, Inc.
Goode, A.R. (ML rifle barrels)
Green Bay Bullets
Guncraft, Inc.
Gun Parts Corporation, The
•Gun Works, The (supplies)
Hart & Son, Inc., Robert W.
Hastings Barrels
•Hatfield International, Inc. (squirrel rifle)
•Hawken Shop, The
Hege Jagd-u. Sporthandels, GmbH
Hornady Mfg. Co.
House of Muskets, Inc., The (ML barrels
and supplies)
Hughes, Steven Dodd (custom guns)
Hunkeler, A. (muzzle-loading guns)
Jamison's Forge Works
•K.B.I., Inc.
K&M Industries, Inc.
Kolpin Mfg., Inc.

Kwik-Site Co.
•Lee Precision, Inc.
Lite Tek International
Log Cabin Sport Shop
•Lyman Products Corporation
McCann's Muzzle-Gun Works
Michael's Antiques
Michael's of Oregon Co. (recoil pads)
•Mitchell Arms, Inc.
•Modern MuzzleLoading, Inc.
•Montana Armory, Inc.
Mountain State Muzzleloading Supplies
•Mowrey Gun Works
MMP
Mt. Alto Outdoor Products
Muzzleloaders Etcetera, Inc.
•Navy Arms Company
Neumann GmbH
Newman Gunshop (custom ML rifles)
October Country
Oklahoma Leather Products, Inc.
Ox-Yoke Originals, Inc. (dry lube patches)
Patchbox, The
•Pedersoli Davide & C.
Peterson Gun Shop, Inc., A.W.
Phyl-Mac
Redman's Rifling & Reboring (barrels
only)
R.V.I. (high-grade BP accoutrements)
Scott, Inc., Tyler (bore cleaner)
Selsi Co., Inc.
Safari Gun Co.
S&B Industries
•Sharps Arms Co., Inc., C.
Sheridan USA, Inc., Austin
•Shiloh Rifle Mfg. Co.
•Sile Distributors
Siler Locks (flintlocks)
Single Shot, Inc.
Slipshot MTS Group
Smokey Valley Rifles
South Bend Replicas, Inc. (artillery)
Southern Bloomer Mfg. Company (cotton
gun cleaning patches)
SPG Bullet Lubricant
Stratco, Inc.
•Sturm, Ruger & Co., Inc.
Taylor's & Co., Inc.
TDP Industries, Inc.
Tennessee Valley Mfg. (powderhorns)
•Thompson/Center Arms
•Thunder Mountain Arms
Tom's Gunshop
Track of the Wolf, Inc.
•Traditions, Inc. (guns, kits, accessories)
•Trail Guns Armory, Inc.
•Uberti USA, Inc.
•Ultra Light Arms, Inc.
•Upper Missouri Trading Co.
Venco Industries, Inc.
Warren Muzzleloading Co., Inc.
(blackpowder accessories)
Wescombe (parts)
White Owl Enterprises
•White Systems, Inc.
•Williams Gun Sight Co.
Winchester Sutler, Inc. (haversacks)
Winter & Associates (Olde Pennsylvania
ML accessories)
Young Country Arms (paste lube)

PISTOLSMITHS

Accuracy Unlimited
Accurate Plating & Weaponry, Inc.
Aldis Gunsmithing & Shooting Supply
Alpha Precision, Inc.
Alpine Precision Gunsmithing & Indoor
Range
American Pistolsmiths Guild
Armament Gunsmithing Co., Inc.
Bain & Davis, Inc.
Baity's Custom Gunworks
Banks, Ed
Bar-Sto Precision Machine (single-shot
barrels for 45 ACP)
Barta's Gunsmithing
Baumannize, Inc.
Behlert Precision (short actions)
Bengtson Arms Co., L.
Bill's Gun Repair
Border Guns & Leather
Bowen Classic Arms Corp.
Brian, C.T.
Briley Mfg., Inc.

Brown Products, Ed
Buckhorn Gun Works
Campbell, Dick
Cannon's Guns
Caraville Manufacturing
Cellini, Inc., Vito Francesca
Chesire & Perez Dist.
Chuck's Gun Shop
Clark Custom Guns, Inc.
Classic Guns
Colonial Repair
Combat Shop, The
Corkys Gun Clinic
Costa, David
Curtis Custom Shop
Custom Gunsmiths
Cylinder & Slide, Inc.
Darlington Gun Works, Inc.
Davis Service Center, Bill
Dayton Traister
D&D Gunsmiths, Ltd.
Dilliott Gunsmithing, Inc.

D&L Sports
DMG Technologies, Inc.
D.O.C. Specialists, Inc.
Duncan's Gunworks, Inc.
Dwyer, Dan
EMF Co., Inc.
First Distributors, Inc., Jack
Fisher Custom Firearms
Francesca Stabilizer's, Inc.
Frielich Police Equipment
Garthwaite, Jim
Giron, Robert E.
Greider Precision Products
Guncraft Sports, Inc.
Gunsite Gunsmithy
Gunsmithing Ltd.
Gutridge, Inc.
Hamilton, Keith
Hammond Custom Guns Ltd., Guy
Hank's Gun Shop
Hanson's Gun Center, Dick
Hardison, Charles
Hart & Son, Inc., Robert W.
Hebard Guns, Gil
Heinie Specialty Products
High Bridge Arms, Inc.
Highline Machine Co.
Hindman, Ace
Hoag, James W.
Irwin, Campbell H.
Ivanoff, Thomas G.
Jarvis Gunsmithing, Inc.
Jones, J.D.
Jungkind, Reeves C.
Jurras, L.E.
Kilham & Co.
Kimball, Gary
King's Gun Works
Kopec Enterprises, John (Colt Model P only)
Kopp, Terry K. (rebarreling, conversions)
La Clinique du .45
LaFrance Specialties
LaRocca Gun Works, Inc.
Laughridge, William R.
Lawson, John G.
Lee's Red Ramps
Linebaugh Custom Sixguns
Lomont Precision Bullets, Kent (Auto Mag
only)
Long, George F.
Mac's .45 Shop
Mag-Na-Port International, Inc.
Mahony, Phillip Bruce
Marent, Rudolf (Hammerli)
Marvel, Alan
Mid-America Recreation, Inc.
Miller Custom
Mitchell's Accuracy Shop
MJK Gunsmithing, Inc.
Moran, Jerry
Mountain Bear Rifle Works, Inc.
Mullis Guncraft
Mustra's Custom Guns, Inc., Carl

Nastoff's 45 Shop (1911 conversions)
North Fork Custom Gunsmithing
Novak's .45 Shop, Wayne
Nowlin Custom Barrels Mfg.
Nu-Line Guns, Inc.
Oglesby & Oglesby Gunmakers, Inc.
Old West Reproductions
Pace Marketing, Inc.
Pachmayr Ltd.
Pacific Pistolcraft
Pardini Armi Commercial Srl
Paris, Frank J.
Paterson Gunsmithing
Peacemaker Specialists
Performance Specialists
Phillips & Bailey, Inc.
Pierce Pistols
Plaxco, J. Michael
Power Custom, Inc.
Practical Tools, Inc.
Precision Specialties
P&S Gun Service
Randco UK
Ries, Chuck
Robar Co.'s, Inc., The
Rogers Gunsmithing, Bob (custom)
Sanders Custom Gun Service
Scott/McDougall Custom Gunsmiths
Seecamp Co., Inc., L.W.
Shooter Shop, The
Silhouette Arms Custom 45 Shop, Inc.
Sipes Gun Shop
Sight Shop, The
S.K. Guns, Inc.
Slings & Arrows
Spokhandguns, Inc.
Sportsmen's Equipment Co. (specialty
limiting trigger motion in autos)
SSK Industries
Steger, James R.
Strawbridge, Victor W.
Stroup, Earl R.
Swenson's 45 Shop, A.D.
300 Gunsmith Service, Inc.
Ten-Ring Precision, Inc.
Thompson, Randall
Tom's Gun Repair
Trapper Gun, Inc.
T.S.W. Conversions, Inc.
Ulrich, Doc & Bud
Unick's Gunsmithing
Vic's Gun Refinishing
Volquartsen Custom Ltd.
Walker Arms Co., Inc.
Wallace's
Walters Industries
Wardell Precision Handguns Ltd.
Wessinger Custom Guns & Engraving
Western Design
Wichita Arms, Inc.
Williamson Precision Gunsmithing
Wood, Frank
Woods Pistolsmithing

REBORING AND RERIFLING

Ackley Rifle Barrels, P.O.
Barnes Bullets, Inc.
Bellm Contenders (rifle only)
Chuck's Gun Shop
Darlington Gun Works, Inc.
DKT, Inc.
Francotte & Cie S.A., Auguste
Goode, A.R.
Hart & Son, Inc., Robert W.
H&S Liner Service
Irwin, Campbell H.
Ivanoff, Thomas G.
Jaeger, Inc., Paul
K-D, Inc.
Kopp, Terry K. (Invis-A-Line bbl.; relining)
LaBounty Precision Reboring

Matco, Inc.
Mid-America Recreation, Inc.
Pence Precision Barrels
P&S Gun Service
Redman's Rifling & Reboring
Ridgetop Sporting Goods
Rogers Gunsmithing, Bob
Shaw, Inc., E.R.
Small Arms Mfg. Co.
Snapp's Gunshop
Stratco, Inc.
300 Gunsmith Service, Inc.
Tom's Gun Repair
Van Patten, J.W.
West, Robert G. (barrel relining)

RELOADING TOOLS AND ACCESSORIES

Advance Car Mover Co., Inc. (bottom
pour lead casting ladles)
American Products Co. (12-ga. shot wad)
•Ammo Load, Inc.
•AMT (Autoscale)
•ASI (Autoscale)
Bald Eagle Precision Machine Co.
Ballisti-Cast, Inc.
Ballistic Products, Inc. (for shotguns)
Barlett, J.
Belding & Mull, Inc.
Ben's Gun Shop
Berdon Machine Co. (metallic press)
•Blount, Inc. Sporting Equipment Division

Bruno Shooters Supply
C&D Special Products (Claybuster Wads)
•Camdex, Inc.
Carbide Die & Mfg. Co., Inc.
•C-H Tool & Die Co.
CheVron Case Master
Coats, Mrs. Lester (lead wire core cutter)
Colorado Shooter's Supply (Hoch custom
bullet moulds)
Competitor Corporation, Inc.
CONKKO
•Corbin Manufacturing & Supply, Inc.
•Cumberland Arms
Custom Products (decapping tool, dies)

•See page 445 for Warranty Service Center Addresses

•Denver Instrument Company
•Destination North Software
Dewey Mfg. Co., Inc., J.
•Dillon Precision Prods., Inc.
Efemes Enterprises (Berdan decapper)
E&L Mfg., Inc.
Engineered Accessories
  (Reload-A-Stand, portable)
Enguix Import-Export
Fitz Pistol Grip Co.
Flambeau Products Corp.
•Forster Products
4-D Custom Die Co.
•Fremont Tool Works
"Gramps" Antique Cartridges
Green, Arthur S. (metals, fluxes, ladles)
Hanned Line, The
Hart & Son, Inc., Robert W.
Hensley & Gibbs (bullet moulds)
Hindman, Ace (Reloader's Logbook)
Hi-West Sales
Hodgdon Powder Co.
•Hollywood Engineering
Hornady Mfg. Co.
•Huntington Die Specialties (compact press)
Iosso Marine Products
Jeffredo Gunsight
Jones, Neil
King & Co.
•K&M Services
Lachaussee, S.A. (ammunition loading
  machines)
Lage Uniwad, Inc. (Universal shotshell
  wad)
LBT
•Lee Precision, Inc.
Lighthouse Mfg. Co., Inc.
Lite Tek International
Lock's Philadelphia Gun Exchange
Lortone, Inc. (tumblers, metal polishing
  media)
•Lyman Products Corporation
Magma Engineering Co.
MCC
McKillen & Heyer, Inc. (case gauge)
MCS, Inc.
•MEC
Midway Arms, Inc. (cartridge boxes)
Millenium Safety Products, Inc. (face mask)
MMP (Tri-Cut trimmer; powder trickler)
Mountain South
MTM Molded Products Company
Multi-Scale Charge Ltd.
Necromancer Industries, Inc. (Compucaster
  automated bullet casting machine)

NEI (bullet mould)
Omark Industries
Pattern Control (shotshell wads)
•Pend Oreille Sport Shop
Plum City Ballistic Range
•Ponsness/Warren
Precision Castings & Equipment, Inc.
•Precision Reloading, Inc.
Quinetics Corporation (kinetic bullet puller)
Rapine Bullet Mould Mfg. Co.
•RCBS
•R.D.P. Tool Co., Inc. (progressive loader)
•Redding Reloading, Inc.
•Reloaders Specialty Mfg.
Roberts Products (Pak-Tool)
Rochester Lead Works, Inc. (lead wire)
Rooster Laboratories
Rorschach Precision Products (carboloy
  bullet dies)
SAECO
Safari Gun Co.
Sandia Die & Cartridge Co.
•Scharch Mfg., Inc.
Shooters Accessory Supply
Shootin' Accessories Ltd.
Sierra Bullets
Simmons, Jerry
Slipshot MTS Group
Sport Flite Mfg., Inc. (swaging dies)
Sportsman Supply Co.
Speer Products
•Stalwart Corp. (wooden loading blocks)
Star Machine Works
Sunora Gun Shop
Taracorp Industries
Thompson Bullet Lube Co.
Trammco, Inc. (Electra-Jacket bullet
  plater)
Tru-Square Metal Products (Thumbler's
  tumbler case polishers; Ultra Vibe 18)
T&S Industries, Inc.
VibraShine, Inc.
Vibra-Tek Co. (brass polisher; Brite
  Rouge)
•Weatherby, Inc.
Webster Scale Mfg. Co.
Westfield Engineering
Whitestone Lumber Corp.
Whitetail Design & Engineering Ltd.
Widener's Reloading & Shooting Supply
William's Gun Shop, Ben (brass sorters,
  sizing machines)
Wilson, Inc., L.E.
Young Country Arms (accessories)

RESTS—BENCH, PORTABLE—AND ACCESSORIES

Armor Metal Products (portable shooting
  bench)
Bald Eagle Precision Machine Co.
Blount, Inc. Sporting Equipment Division
Bruno Shooters Supply
B-Square Co. (handgun)
Champion's Choice, Inc.
Clift Mfg., L.R.
Clifton Arms, Inc.
Cravener's Gun Shop
Davidson Products, Inc. (accessories)
Decker Shooting Products (rifle rests)
Desert Mountain Mfg. (Benchmaster rifle
  rest)
Harris Engineering, Inc. (bipods)
Hart & Son, Inc., Robert W.
Hidalgo, Tony (adjustable shooting seat)
Holden Company, J.B.

Hoppe's Div. (benchrests and bags)
Houtz & Barwick (shooting stools)
Millett Sights
Pease Accuracy, Bob
Protektor Model Co. (sandbags)
Ransom International Corp.
Sinclair International, Inc.
Sportsman Supply Co. (portable bench
  rest)
Sports Support Systems, Inc.
Sure Shot of LA, Inc.
Ultra Light Arms, Inc.
Verdemont Fieldsports
Wichita Arms, Inc.
World of Targets (shooting bench—Porta
  Bench)

RIFLE BARREL MAKERS (See also Muzzle-Loading Guns, Barrels and Equipment)

Ackley Rifle Barrels, P.O.
American Bullets
Answer Products Co.
Bellm Contenders
Borovnik KG, Ludwig
Bruno Shooters Supply
Bustani Appraisers, Leo (Win. 92
  takedown; Trapper 357-44 magnum
  barrels)
Canons Delcour
Carter's Gun Shop
Cation
Clark Custom Guns, Inc.
Clerke Co., J.A.
Competition Limited
DKT, Inc.
Donnelly, C.P.
Douglas Barrels, Inc.

Federal Ordnance, Inc.
Getz Barrel Co.
Goode, A.R.
Graybill's Gun Shop (chambering barrels)
Green Mountain Rifle Barrel Co., Inc.
H-S Precision, Inc.
Half Moon Rifle Shop
Hart Rifle Barrels, Inc.
Hastings Barrels (shotguns only)
Jackalope Gun Shop
Jarvis Gunsmithing, Inc.
K-D, Inc.
KOGOT (octagonal)
Kopp, Terry K. (22-cal. blanks)
Krieger Barrels, Inc.
LaBounty Precision Reboring
Lilja Precision Rifle Barrels
Marquart Precision Co., Inc.

Matco, Inc.
McGowen Rifle Barrels
McMillan Rifle Barrels
Mid-America Recreation, Inc.
Nowlin Custom Barrels Mfg.
Obermeyer Rifled Barrels
Olympic Arms, Inc.
Pell, John T. (custom octagon)
Pence Precision Barrels
Rocky Mountain Rifle Works Ltd.
Safari Arms, Inc./SGW
Sanders Custom Gun Service (importer)
Schneider Rifle Barrels, Inc., Gary

Sharon Rifle Barrel Co.
Shaw, Inc., E.R. (also shotgun barrels)
Shilen Rifles, Inc.
Shiloh Rifle Mfg.
Small Arms Mfg. Co.
Siskiyou Gun Works
Societa Armi Bresciane Srl
Stratco, Inc.
Strutz Rifle Barrels, Inc., W.C.
Unique/M.A.P.F.
Verney-Carron
Wilson Arms Co., The

SCOPES, MOUNTS, ACCESSORIES, OPTICAL EQUIPMENT

•Action Arms Ltd.
ADCO (Inter-Aims Mark V sight)
Adventurer's Outpost (shotgun
  lasersights)
•Aimpoint (electronic sight)
•Aimtech Mount Systems
Alley Supply Co.
Alpec TEam, Inc.
•Anderson Manufacturing Co., Inc. (lens
  caps: Storm King, Storm Queen)
Apel GmbH, Ernst
Applied Case Systems, Inc.
A.R.M.S., Inc. (mounts)
•Armsport, Inc.
Armurier Hiptmayer
•Bausch & Lomb, Inc.
Beaver Park Products, Inc.
•Beeman Precision Arms, Inc. (for airguns)
Behlert Precision
Belding & Mull, Inc.
•Blount, Inc. Sporting Equipment Division
Brown Products, Ed
Bruno Shooters Supply
Brunton U.S.A.
•B-Square Co.
Buehler Scope Mounts
•Burris Company, Inc.
•Bushnell
Butler Creek Corporation (lens caps)
California Grips (mounts for auto
  handguns)
Canons Delcour
Celestron International (spotting scope)
•Clark Custom Guns, Inc.
Clearview Mfg. Co., Inc. (See-Thru mounts)
Compass Industries, Inc.
Conetrol Scope Mounts
•Cooper Arms
Creedmoor Sports, Inc.
•Crosman Corp.
Del-Sports, Inc. (EAW mounts)
D&H Prods. Co., Inc. (lens covers)
•Dynamit Nobel-RWS, Inc. (Laser sight &
  mounts)
Ednar, Inc.
Eggleston, Jere D.
•Emerging Technologies, Inc. (Laseraim
  sights)
•Europtik, Ltd.
Farr Studio, Inc. (Farrsight)
Flaig's
Ford Ltd., J. and J.
•Freeland's Scope Stands, Inc.
Fujinon, Inc. (binoculars)
Global Industries
Greenwood & Gryphon Ltd.
•GSI, Inc. (Bock mounts)
Griffin & Howe, Inc.
•G.U., Inc.
Hakko Co. Ltd.
Hermann Leather Co., H.J. (lens caps)
Hertel & Reuss
Hiptmayer, Klaus
Holden Company, J.B. (mounts)
•H-S Precision, Inc.
•Imatronic, Inc. (Laser Sights)
Innovision Enterprises
•Jaeger, Inc., Paul
•Jason Empire, Inc.
Jeffredo Gunsight
Kahles of America
•K.B.I., Inc.
KenPatable Ent., Inc.
•Kesselring Gun Shop
Kilham & Co.
Kimber Parts
Kmount
•Kowa Optimed, inc.
Kris Mounts
KVH Industries, Inc.
Kwik Mount Corp.
Kwik-Site Co.

•L&S Technologies, Inc.
•Laser Devices, Inc. (Laser sight)
Leatherwood-Meopta, Inc.
Lee Supplies, Mark
Leica USA, Inc. (binoculars)
•Leupold & Stevens, Inc.
Lite Tek International
London Guns Ltd.
Mag-Na-Port International, Inc.
McKee, Arthur
Michael's of Oregon Co. (QD scope covers)
Military Armament Corp. (Leatherwood)
Millett Sights (mounts)
•Mirador Optical Corp.
Muzzle-Nuzzle Co.
New Democracy, Inc. (Auto-Ranging
  telescopes)
•New England Arms Co.
•Nichols Sports Optics
Night Vision Equipment Co., Inc. (Night
  vision optics)
•Nikon, Inc.
North American Specialties
Oakshore Electronic Sights, Inc. (Micro
  DOT, Ultra DOT)
Olympic Optical Co.
OMR Feinmechanik, Jagd-und
  Sportwaffen, GmbH
Optolyth-USA, Inc.
Orchard Park Enterprise (Saddleproof
  mounts only)
Outdoor Connection, Inc., The
Pace Marketing, Inc.
Pachmayr Ltd.
PECAR Herbert Schwarz GmbH
•Pentax Corp. (riflescopes, pistol scopes)
Pilkington Gun Co. (QD mount)
Precise Metalsmithing Enterprises
Precision Sport Optics
Premier Reticles (Dot reticles in Leupold)
•Ram-Line, Inc. (see-thru mount for Mini-14)
Ranch Products
•Ranging, Inc.
•Redfield, Inc.
Schmidt & Bender
Seattle Binocular & Scope Repair Co.
Selsi Co., Inc. (spotting scopes,
  binoculars)
Shepherd Scope Ltd.
Sherwood Intl. Export Corp. (mounts)
•Shooters Supply (mount for M14/M1A
  rifles)
•Simmons Enterprises, Ernie
•Simmons Outdoor Corp.
S&K Mfg. Co. (Insta-Mount)
Societa Armi Bresciane Srl.
SSK Industries (bases, rings)
•Stoeger Industries
Supreme Lens Covers (lens caps)
Sure Shot of LA, Inc. (rifle sighting device)
•Swift Instruments, Inc.
•Tapco, Inc.
•Tasco Sales, Inc.
Taylor's & Co., Inc.
Tele-Optics
Tele-Optics, Inc. (spotting scopes)
•Thompson/Center Arms
Traq, Inc. (optics)
•Trijicon, Inc. (rifle scopes)
•Unertl Optical Co., John
United Binocular Co.
•United States Optics Technologies, Inc.
Wardrop, R. Alex
Warne Manufacturing Company
WASP Shooting Systems
•Weatherby, Inc.
•Weaver Products
Westfield Engineering
Wideview Scope Mount Corp.
•Williams Gun Sight Co.
York M-1 Conversions
•Zeiss Optical, Inc., Carl

SHOOTING/TRAINING SCHOOLS

Alpine Precision Gunsmithing & Indoor Range
American Pistol Institute
American Small Arms Academy
Auto Arms
Bob's Tactical Indoor Shooting Range & Gun Shop
Bilsom International, Inc.
Chapman Academy of Practical Shooting
Chelsea Gun Club of New York City, Inc.
CQB Training
Daisy Mfg. Co.
Defense Training International, Inc.
Dowtin Gunworks
Executive Protection Institute
Eversull Co., Inc., K.
Firearm Training Center, The
Firearms Academy of Seattle
Francesca Stabilizer's, Inc.
G.H. Enterprises Ltd.
Guardian Group International
Guncraft Sports, Inc.
Gunfitters, The
Holster Shop, The
H-S Precision, Inc.
Insights Training Center, Inc.
International Shootists, Inc.
Lethal Force Institute
Mendez, John A.
National Guild of Shotgun Shooting Instructors
Northeast Training Institute, Inc.
Pacific Pistolcraft
Quigley's Personal Protection Strategies, Paxton
Reeves Sporting Clays Academy, Dan
Robar Co.'s, Inc., The
Rossi S.A. Metalurgica E Municoes, Amadeo
Security Awareness & Firearms Education (civilian/police instruction)
Shooter's World
Shotgun Shop, The
Slings & Arrows
Starlight Training Center, Inc.
S.W.I.F.T.
Tactical Training Center
Threat Management Institute
Western Missouri Shooters Alliance
Yavapai Firearms Academy Ltd.

SIGHTS, METALLIC

Alley Supply Co.
All's, The Jim J. Tembelis Co., Inc. (shotgun Accura-Sites)
Behlert Precision
Belding & Mull, Inc.
Bob's Gun Shop
Bo-Mar Tool & Mfg. Co.
Bradley Gunsight Co. (shotgun sight)
British Arms Co. Ltd.
Burris Company, Inc.
Cape Outfitters
Carter's Gun Shop
Champion's Choice, Inc.
Clark Custom Guns, Inc.
Colonial Repair
Competitor Corporation, Inc.
Daigmont Industries, Inc. (shotgun)
DGS, Inc.
Engineered Accessories
Fautheree, Andy ("California Sight" for ML)
Francesca Stabilizer's, Inc.
Frank Custom Gun Service, Ron
Freeland's Scope Stands, Inc.
Guardian Group International
Gun Doctor, The (Hunt Saver Sight Systems)
Gun Parts Corporation, The
Gun Works, The
Heinie Specialty Products
Hesco-Meprolight (tritium illuminated sights)
Imatronic, Inc.
Innovision Enterprises
Jaeger, Inc., Paul
J.O. Amrs & Ammunition
Kiss Sights
Kopp, Terry K.
Lee's Red Ramps
Lofland, James W. (single shot replica)
London Guns Ltd.
L.P.A. Snc
Lyman Products Corporation
Marble Arms Corporation
McKee, Arthur
MCS, Inc.
Meier Works (Express sights)
Merit Corporation
Mid-America Recreation, Inc.
Millett Sights
MMC
Novak's .45 Shop, Wayne
Omega Sales, Inc.
OMR Feinmechanik, Jagd-und Sportwaffen, GmbH
Pachmayr Ltd.
RPM
Slug Site Co.
Tanfoglio S.r.l., Fratelli
T.F.C. S.p.A.
Trijicon, Inc.
Varner Sporting Arms, Inc.
Walker Arms Co., Inc.
Williams Gun Sight Co.

STOCKS (Commercial and Custom)

Adair Custom Shop, Bill
Adventurer's Outpost
Amrine's Gun Shop
Angelo & Little Custom Gun Stock Blanks (wood blanks only)
Apel, Dietrich
Arms Ingenuity Co.
Armurier Hiptmayer
Bain & Davis, Inc. (custom)
Balickie, Joe
Barta's Gunsmithing
Bartlett, Don
Barton, Michael D.
Beaver Lodge
Beeman Precision Arms, Inc. (airguns only)
Belding's Custom Gun Shop
Bell & Carlson, Inc. (commercial)
Benchmark Guns
Biesen, Al
Biesen, Roger
Billeb, Stephen L.
Billings Gunsmiths, Inc.
Bishop, E.C.
Bob's Gun Shop
Boltin, John M.
Borovnik KG, Ludwig
Bowerly, Kent (custom)
Boyds' Gunstock Industries, Inc. (commercial)
Brace, Larry D.
Brgoch, Frank
Briganti & Co., A.
Brown Precision, Inc.
Bruno Shooters Supply
Buckhorn Gun Works
Burkhart Gunsmithing, Don
Burres, Jack (English, Claro, Bastogne Paradox walnut blanks only)
Butler Creek Corporation
Cali'co Hardwoods, Inc. (blanks)
Camilli, Lou
Campbell, Dick (custom)
Cape Outfitters
Caywood, Shane J. (custom)
Champlin Firearms, Inc.
Churchill, Winston
Classic Guns
Clifton Arms, Inc.
Clinton River Gun Serv., Inc.
Cloward's Gun Shop (custom)
Coffin, Charles H.
Coffin, Jim
Conrad, C.A. (custom)
Costa, David (custom)
Crane Sales Co., George S. (extensions)
Creedmoor Sports, Inc. (commercial)
Custom Gun Products
Custom Gun Stocks
Dahl's Custom Stocks (custom checkering)
Dakota Arms, Inc.
Dangler, Homer L.
Darlington Gun Works, Inc.

D&D Gunsmiths, Ltd. (custom)
Dever Co., Jack
DGS, Inc.
Dillon, Ed (Circassian walnut blanks)
Dowtin Gunworks (custom for double shotguns)
Dressel Jr., Paul G. (custom)
Duane Custom Stocks, Randy
Dutchman's Firearms, Inc., The
Duncan's Gunworks, Inc. (custom)
Eggleston, Jere D. (custom)
Emmons, Bob (custom)
Erhardt, Dennis
Eversull Co., Inc., K.
Eyster Heritage Gunsmiths, Inc., Ken (custom)
Fajen, Inc., Reinhart
Farmer-Dressel, Sharon (custom)
Fellowes, Ted (custom ML)
Fiberpro Rifle Stocks
Fibron Products (commercial)
Fisher, Jerry
Flaig's
Folks, Donald E. (custom)
Forster, Larry L.
Francotte & Cie S.A., Auguste
Frank Custom Gun Service, Ron
Freeland's Scope Stands, Inc.
Game Haven Gunstocks (Kevlar rifle stocks)
Garrett Accur-Lt. D.F.S. Co. (fiberglass)
Gene's Custom Guns (custom)
Gentry Custom Gunmaker, David
Gilman-Mayfield
Glaser Safety Slug, Inc.
Goens, Dale W.
Golden Age Arms Co.
Gordie's Gun Shop
Goudy Classic Stocks, Gary (custom)
Grace, Charles E.
Green, Roger M. (custom)
Greene's Machine Carving (stock duplicating; blanks)
Griffin & Howe, Inc.
Guncraft, Inc.
Gun Parts Corporation, The (commercial)
Guns
Gun Shop, The
Gunsmithing Ltd.
Gun Works, The
Halstead, Rick
Hank's Gun Shop
Hanson's Gun Center, Dick
Harper's Custom Stocks
Hart & Son, Inc., Robert W. (custom)
Hecht, Hubert J. (custom)
Heilmann, Stephen (custom)
Hensley, Darwin (custom)
Heppler, Keith M. (custom rifle)
Heydenberk, Warren R.
Hillmer Custom Gunstocks, Paul D.
Hi-West Sales
Hiptmayer, Klaus
Hoenig & Rodman (stock duplicating machines)
H-S Precision, Inc. (Fiberglass)
Huebner, Corey O. (custom)
Hughes, Steven Dodd (custom)
Intermountain Arms (custom)
Ivanoff, Thomas G.
Jaeger, Inc., Paul
Jarrett Rifles, Inc. (custom)
Johnson Gunsmithing, Inc., Neal G.
Johnson Wood Products (blanks only)
Kartak Gun Works (custom)
Keith's Custom Gunstocks
Ken's Rifle Blanks
Kimber Parts
Klein Custom Guns, Don
Kneiper Custom Rifles, Jim
Knippel, Richard (custom)
Kopp, Terry K.
Lawson Co., Harry
LeFever & Sons, Inc., Frank
Lind Custom Guns, Al (custom)
Lynn's Custom Gunstocks
Makinson, Nicholas
Mandarino, Monte
Manley Shooting Supplies, Lowell
Marple & Associates, Dick
McCullough, Ken
McCament, Jay
McDonald, Dennis (custom)
McFarland, Stan
McGuire, Bill (custom)
McMillan Fiberglass Stocks, Inc.
Mercer Custom Stocks, R.M. (custom)

Mid-America Recreation, Inc.
Miller Gun Woods
Millett Sights
Milliron Gunstocks, Earl
Morrison Custom Rifles, J.W.
Morrow, Bud
MPI Stocks (fiberglass)
Muzzelite Corp. (bullpup)
Nettestad Gun Works
New England Arms Co.
New England Custom Gun Service
Nickels, Paul R.
Nicklas, Ted (custom)
Norman Custom Gunstocks, Jim
North Fork Custom Gunsmithing
Oakland Custom Arms, Inc.
Old World Gunsmithing
One Of A Kind
Or-Ün (walnut gunstock blanks)
Orvis Co., The
Ottmar, Maurice
Pachmayr Ltd. (blanks and custom obs)
Pagel Gun Works, Inc.
Pasadena Gun Center
Paulsen Gunstocks (blanks)
Pentheny de Pentheny
Perazzi U.S.A., Inc.
P&S Gun Service
Rahn Gun Works, Inc.
Reiswig, Wallace E. (California walnut blanks)
Richards Micro-Fit Stocks
R&J Gun Shop (custom)
RMS Custom Gunsmithing
Robinson, Don (blanks only)
Robinson Firearms Mfg. Ltd.
Rogers Gunsmithing, Bob
Royal Arms
Ryan, Chad L. (custom)
Samco Global Arms, Inc.
Sanders Custom Gun Service (rifle blanks)
Schaefer, Roy V. (commercial blanks)
Schiffman, Curt (custom)
Schiffman, Mike (custom)
Schiffman, Norman (custom)
Schwartz Custom Guns, David W.
Schwartz Custom Guns, Wayne E.
Shaw's Finest in Guns (custom only)
Shell Shack
Sherk, Dan A. (custom)
Shooting Gallery, The
Sile Distributors
Sinclair International, Inc.
Six Enterprises (fiberglass)
Snider Stocks, Walter S.
Speedfeed, Inc.
Speiser, Fred D.
Sportsmen's Equipment Co. (carbine conversions)
Stott's Creek Armory, Inc.
Strawbridge, Victor W.
Swan, D.J. (custom)
Talmage, William G.
Tapco, Inc.
Taylor's & Co., Inc.
Tecnolegno S.p.A.
T.F.C. S.p.A.
Tiger-Hunt (curly maple stock blanks)
Tirelli
Tom's Gun Repair
Tom's Gun Shop
Trevallion Gunstocks
Tucker, James C. (custom)
Unick's Gunsmithing
Vest, John (classic rifles)
Vic's Gun Refinishing
Vintage Industries, Inc.
Waffen-Weber Custom Gunsmithing
Wallace's (custom)
Weatherby, Inc.
Weems, Cecil
Werth, T.W. (custom)
West, Robert G.
Western Gunstock Mfg. Co.
Westminster Arms Ltd. (Bull-Pup kits)
Windish, Jim (walnut blanks)
Winter, Robert M.
Wisner's Gun Shop, Inc.
Wood, Frank
Wright's Hardwood Sawmill (blanks only)
Yee, Mike
York M-1 Conversions
Zeeryp, Russ

TARGETS, BULLET AND CLAYBIRD TRAPS

Abbott Industries
Action Target, Inc. (automated and static
   range equipment)
Aldis Gunsmithing & Shooting Supply
   (target shooting accessories)
American Whitetail Target Systems
Armor Metal Products
Aztec International Ltd. (Exploding
   Bullseye targets)
Birchwood Casey
Blount, Inc. Sporting Equipment Division
Caswell International Corp. (target
   carriers; commercial shooting ranges)
Champion's Choice, Inc.
Champion Target Company (clay targets)
Clay Target Enterprises (clay target
   launching equipment)
Crosman Corp.
Dapkus Co., J.G. (live bullseye targets)
Datumtech Corporation (electronic target
   systems)
Detroit-Armor Corp. (shooting ranges)
Dutchman's Firearms, Inc., The
Epps "Orillia" Ltd., Ellwood (hand traps)
Feather Flex Decoys
Federal Champion Target Co.
Freeman Animal Targets
G.H. Enterprises Ltd.
Hiti-Schuch, Atelier Wilma
Hunterjohn
Innovision Enterprises
Jaeger, Inc., Paul

KK Awards Mfg.
Kleen-Bore, Inc.
Littler Sales Co.
Lyman Products Corporation
Maki Industries (X-Spand Target System)
MTM Molded Products Company
National Target Co.
Nu-Teck (electronic ranges)
Outers Laboratories (claybird traps)
Ox-Yoke Originals, Inc.
Pease Accuracy, Bob
Peterson Instant Targets, Inc. (paste-ons;
   Targ-Dots)
Primos Wild Game Calls, Inc.
Randco UK
Red Star Target Co.
Remington Arms Co. (claybird traps)
Rockwood Corp.
Rocky Mountain Target Co. (Data-Targ)
R-Tech Corporation (targets)
Schaefer Shooting Sports (shooting
   games)
Seligman Shooting Products
Shooting Arts Ltd.
Shotgun Shop, The
Thompson Target Technology (firearms
   and archery targets)
Trius Products, Inc. (claybird, can thrower)
Verdemont Fieldsports
White Flyer
White Flyer Targets
World of Targets (targets)

TAXIDERMY

Jonas Appraisals & Taxidermy, Jack
Kulis Freeze Dry Taxidermy
Parker, Mark D.

Piedmont Community College
Shooting Arts Ltd. (kits)
World Trek, Inc.

TRAP AND SKEET SHOOTER'S EQUIPMENT

Barsotti, Bruce
Blount, Inc. Sporting Equipment Division
Briley Mfg., Inc. (choke tubes)
Cape Outfitters
Caswell International Corp.
C&H Research
Crane & Crane Ltd.
D&H Prods. Co., Inc. (snap shell)
Euroarms of America, Inc.
European American Armory Corp.
Eyster Heritage Gunsmiths, Inc., Ken
   (shotgun competition choking)
Ganton Manufacturing Ltd. (clothing)
G.H. Enterprises Ltd.
Great 870 Company, The
Griggs Products
Hall Plastics, Inc., John
Harper, William E.
Hoppe's Div. (Monte Carlo pad)
Hunter Co., Inc.
I.N.C., Inc.
Jenkins Recoil Pads, Inc.
KK Awards Mfg.
Krieghoff Gun Co., H.
K&T Co.

Loadmaster
Lynn's Custom Gunstocks
Magnum Research, Inc.
Maionchi - L.M.I.
Meadow Industries
Moneymaker Guncraft Corp.
   (free-floating, ventilated ribs)
MTM Molded Products Company
   (claybird thrower)
Noble Co., Jim
Outers Laboratories (trap, claybird)
Perazzi U.S.A., Inc.
Pro-Port Ltd.
Protektor Model Co.
Remington Arms Co. (trap, claybird)
Rhodeside, Inc.
Shootin' Accesories Ltd.
Shooting Specialties
Shotgun Shop, The
Titus, Daniel
Trius Products, Inc.
T&S Industries, Inc.
Universal Clay Pigeon Traps
Winchester Div., Olin Corp. (trap, claybird)

TRIGGERS, RELATED EQUIPMENT

Belding & Mull, Inc.
B.M.F. Activator, Inc.
Bob's Gun Shop
Boyds' Gunstock Industries, Inc.
Brownell's, Inc.
Brown Products, Ed
Bruno Shooters Supply
Canjar Co., M.H. (triggers)
Central Specialties Co. (trigger locks only)
Clark Custom Guns, Inc.
Custom Products
Cycle Dynamics, Inc.
Dayton Traister (triggers)
Electronic Trigger Systems, Inc.
European American Armory Corp.
Flaig's (trigger shoes)

Hart & Son, Inc., Robert W.
Hi-West Sales
Jaeger, Inc., Paul
Jones, Neil
Mid-America Recreation, Inc.
Midway Arms, Inc.
Miller Single Trigger Mfg. Co.
Pace Marketing, Inc.
Pachmayr Ltd. (trigger shoe)
Penrod Precision (triggers for Ruger #1,3)
Perazzi U.S.A., Inc.
Randco UK
S&B Industries
Taurus, S.A., Forjas
Timney Mfg., Inc. (triggers)
Tyler Mfg.-Dist., Melvin (trigger shoe)

MANUFACTURERS' DIRECTORY

A

A&B Industries, Inc., 7920-28 Hamilton Ave., Cincinnati, OH 45231/513-522-2992, 800-346-6699; FAX: 513-522-0916
A&J Products, Inc., 5791 hall Rd., Muskegon, MI 49442-1964
A&M Waterfowl, Inc., 301 Burke Dr., Ripley, TN 38063/901-635-4003; FAX: 901-635-2320
A&W Repair, 2930 Schneider Dr., Arnold, MO 63010/314-287-3725
A.A. Arms, Inc., 4811 Persimmon Ct., Monroe, NC 28110/704-289-5356; FAX: 704-289-5859
Abbott Industries, 3368 Miller St., Philadelphia, PA 19134/215-426-3435; FAX: 215-426-1718
Abel Safe & File, Inc., 124 West Locust St., Fairbury, IL 61739/815-692-2131; FAX: 815-692-3350
Accu-Tek, 4525 Carter Ct., Chino, CA 91710/714-627-2404; FAX: 714-627-7817
Acculube II, Inc., 22261 68th Ave. S., Kent, WA 98032-1914/206-395-7171
Accupro Gun Care, Div. of RTI Research Ltd., 15512-109 Ave., Surrey, BC U3R 7E8, Canada/604-583-7807
Accuracy Gun Shop, 3651 University Ave., San Diego, CA 92104/619-282-8500
Accuracy Products, S.A., 14 rue de Lawsanne, Brussels, 1060 Belgium/32-2-539-34-42; FAX: 32-2-539-39-60
Accuracy Unlimited, 7479 S. Dewpew St., Littleton, CO 80123
Accuracy Unlimited, 16036 N. 49 Ave., Glendale, AZ 85306/602-978-9089
Accurate Arms Company, Inc., Rt. 1, Box 167, McEwen, TN 37101/615-729-4207; FAX 615-729-4217
Accurate Plating & Weaponry, Inc., 1937 Calumet St., Clearwater, FL 34625/813-449-9112
Ace Sportswear, Inc., 700 Quality Rd., Fayetteville, NC 28306/919-323-1223
Ackley Rifle Barrels, P.O. (See K-D, Inc.)
Action Ammo Ltd. (See Action Arms Ltd.)
Action Arms Ltd., P.O. Box 9573, Philadelphia, PA 19124/215-744-0100; FAX: 215-533-2188
Action Products, Inc., 22 N. Mulberry St., Hagerstown, MD 21740/301-797-1414
Action Target, Inc., P.O. Box 636, Provo, UT 84603/801-377-8033; FAX: 801-377-8096
ACTIV Industries, Inc., 1000 Zigor Rd., P.O. Box 339, Kearneysville, WV 25430/304-725-0451; FAX: 304-725-2080
Ad Hominem, RR 3, Orillia, Ont. L3V 6H3, Canada/705-689-5303
Adair Custom Shop, Bill, 2886 Westridge, Carrollton, TX 75006
Adams, John J., P.O. Box 167, Corinth, VT 05039/802-439-5904
ADC, Inc., 32654 Coal Creek Rd., Scappoose, OR 97056/503-543-5088; FAX: 503-543-5990
ADCO, 1 Wyman St., Woburn, MA 01801/617-935-1799; FAX: 617-932-4807
Adkins, Luther, P.O. Box 281, Shelbyville, IN 46176/317-392-3795
Advance Car Mover Co., Inc., Rowell Div., P.O. Box 1181, 112 N. Outagamie St., Appleton, WI 54912/414-734-1878
Adventure 16, Inc., 4620 Alvarado Canyon Rd., San Diego, CA 92120/619-283-6314
Adventure Game Calls, R.D. #1, Leonard Rd., Spencer, NY 14883/607-589-4611
Adventurer's Outpost, P.O. Box 70, Cottonwood, AZ 86326/800-762-7471; FAX: 602-634-8781
African Import Co., 20 Braunecker Rd., Plymouth, MA 02360/508-746-8552
AFSCO Ammunition, 731 W. Third St., P.O. Box L, Owen, WI 54460/715-229-2516
Ahlman Guns, Rt. 1, Box 20, Morristown, MN 55052/507-685-4243; FAX: 507-685-4247
Ahrends, Kim, Custom Firearms, Box 203, Clarion, IA 50525/515-532-3449
Aimpoint, 580 Herndon Parkway, Suite 500, Herndon, VA 22070/703-471-6828; FAX: 703-689-0575
Aimtech Mount Systems, P.O. Box 223, Thomasville, GA 31799/912-226-4313; FAX: 912-226-4313
Air Rifle Specialists, 311 East Water St., Elmira, NY 14901/607-734-7340
Air Venture, 9752 E. Flower St., Bellflower, CA 90706/213-867-6344
Airgun Repair Centre, 3230 Garden Meadows, Lawrenceburg, IN 47025/812-637-1463
Airmold/W.R. Grace & Co.-Conn., Becker Farms Industrial Park, P.O. Box 610, Roanoke Rapids, NC 27870/919-536-2171; FAX: 919-536-2201
Airrow (See Swivel Machine Works, Inc.)
Aitor-Cuchilleria Del Norte, S.A., Izelaieta, 17, 48260 Ermua (Vizcaya), Spain/43-17-08-50; FAX: 43-17-00-01
Ajax Custom Grips, Inc., Div. of A. Jack Rosenberg & Sons, 11311 Stemmons, Suite #5, Dallas, TX 75229/214-241-6302
Aker Leather Products, 2248 Main St., Suite 6, Chula Vista, CA 91911/619-423-5182
Alcas Cutlery Corp. (See Cutco Cutlery)
Alco Carrying Cases, 601 W. 26th St., New York, NY 10001/212-675-5820
Aldis Gunsmithing & Shooting Supply, 502 S. Montezuma St., Prescott, AZ 86303/602-445-6723; FAX: 602-445-6763
Alessi Holsters, Inc., 2465 Niagara Falls Blvd., Amherst, NY 14228-3527/716-691-5615
Alex, Inc., Box 3034, Bozeman, MT 59772/406-282-7396; FAX: 406-282-7396
Alfano, Sam, 36180 Henry Gaines Rd., Pearl River, LA 70452/504-863-3364
All Rite Products, Inc., 1001 W. Cedar Knolls South, Cedar City, UT 84720/801-586-7100
All Weather Outerwear, 1270 Broadway, Rm 1005, New York, NY 10001/212-244-2690
All's, The Jim J. Tembelis Co., Inc., 280 E. Fernau Ave., Oshkosh, WI 54901/414-426-1080; FAX: 414-426-1080
Allard, Gary, Creek Side Metal & Woodcrafters, Fishers Hill, VA 22626/703-465-3903
Allen Co., Bob, 214 SW Jackson, Des Moines, IA 50315/515-283-2191; 800-247-8048
Allen Co., Inc., 525 Burbank St., Broomfield, CO 80020/303-469-1857
Alley Supply Co., P.O. Box 848, Gardnerville, NV 89410/702-782-3800
Allred Bullet Co., 932 Evergreen Dr., Logan, UT 84321/801-752-6983
Alpec Team, Inc., 55 Oak Ct., Suite 205, Danville, CA 94526/510-820-1763; FAX: 510-820-8738

Alpha 1 Drop Zone, 2121 N. Tyler, Wichita, KS 67212/316-729-0800
Alpha Precision, Inc., 2765 Preston Rd. NE, Good Hope, GA 30641/404-267-6163
Alpine Precision Gunsmithing & Indoor Range, 2401 Government Way, Coeur D'Alene, ID 83814/208-765-3559
Alsa Corp., The, 1245 McClellan, Suite 204, Los Angeles, CA 90025/213-207-4005
Altamont Co., 901 N. Church St., P.O. Box 309, Thomasboro, IL 61878/217-643-3125; FAX: 217-643-7973
AMAC, Iver Johnson, 2202 Redmond Rd., Jacksonville, AR 72076/501-982-1633
Amacker International, Inc., 1212 Main St., Amacker Park, Delhi, LA 71232/318-878-9061; FAX: 318-878-5532
AmBr Software Group Ltd., The, 2205 Maryland Ave., Baltimore, MD 21218/301-243-7717; FAX: 301-366-8742
American Arms, Inc., 715 E. Armour Rd., N. Kansas City, MO 64116/816-474-3161; FAX: 816-474-1225
American Ballistics Co., Inc., P.O. Box 1410, Marietta, GA 30061/404-426-5311
American Bullets, 2190 C Coffee Rd., Lithonia, GA 30058
American Custom Gunmakers Guild, P.O. Box 812, Burlington, IA 52601/319-752-6114
American Derringer Corp., P.O. Box 8983, Waco, TX 76714/817-799-9111
American Gas & Chemical Co., Ltd., 220 Pegasus Ave., Northvale, NJ 07647/201-767-7300
American Gripcraft, 3230 S. Dodge #2, Tucson, AZ 85713/602-790-1222
American Handgunner Magazine, 591 Camino de la Reina, Suite 200, San Diego, CA 92108/619-297-5350; FAX: 619-297-5353
American Import Co., The, 1453 Mission St., San Francisco, CA 94103/415-863-1506
American Military Arms Corp. (See AMAC)
American Pistol Institute, P.O. Box 401, Paulden, AZ 86334/602-636-4565; FAX: 602-636-1236
American Pistolsmiths Guild, 3922 Madonna Rd., Jarrettsville, MD 21084/301-557-6545
American Products Co., 14729 Spring Valley Rd., Morrison, IL 61270/815-772-3336; FAX: 815-772-7921
American Sales & Mfg. Co., P.O. Box 677, Laredo, TX 78042/512-723-6893; FAX: 512-725-0672
American Security Products Co., 11925 Pacific Ave., Fontana, CA 92335/714-685-9680, 800-421-6142
American Small Arms Academy, P.O. Box 12111, Prescott, AZ 86304/602-778-5623
American Target Knives, 1030 Brownwood NW, Grand Rapids, MI 49504/616-453-1998
American Whitetail Target Systems, P.O. Box 41, 106 S. Church St., Tennyson, IN 47637/812-567-4527
Americase, P.O. Box 271, Waxahachie, TX 75165/800-972-2737
Amherst Arms, P.O. Box 658, Mt. Airy, MD 21771/301-829-9544
Ammo Load, Inc., 1560 E. Edinger, Suite G, Santa Ana, CA 92705/714-558-8858; FAX: 714-569-0319
Ammunition Consulting Services, Inc., P.O. Box 1303, St. Charles, IL 60174/708-377-4625; FAX: 708-377-4680
Amrine's Gun Shop, 937 La Luna, Ojai, CA 93023/805-646-2376
AMT, 6226 Santos Diaz, Irwindale, CA 91702/818-334-6629; FAX: 818-969-5247
Anderson Manufacturing Co., Inc., P.O. Box 2640, 2741 N. Crosby Rd., Oak Harbor, WA 98277/206-675-7300
Andres & Dworsky, Bergstrasse 18, A-3822 Karlstein/Thaya, Austria, Europe/0 28 44-285
Angelo & Little Custom Gun Stock Blanks, Chaffin Creek Rd., Darby, MT 59829/406-821-4530
Anschutz GmbH, Postfach 1128, D-7900 Ulm/Donau, France (U.S. importer—PSI, Inc.)
Ansen Enterprises, 1506 228th St., Torrance, CA 90501-1506/213-534-1837
Answer Products Co., 1519 Westbury Dr., Davison, MI 48423/313-653-2911
Anthony and George Ltd., Rt. 1, P.O. Box 45, Evington, VA 24550/804-821-8117
Antique American Firearms (See Carlson, Douglas R.)
Antique Arms Co., 1110 Cleveland Ave., Monett, MO 65708/417-235-6501
AO Safety Products, Div. of American Optical Corp. (See E-A-R, Inc.)
Apache Products, 2208 Mallory Place, Monroe, LA 71201/318-325-1761; FAX: 318-325-4873
Apel GmbH, Ernst, Am Kirschberg 3, D-8708 Gerbrunn, Germany/0(9 31)-70 71 91; FAX: 0(9 31)70 71 92
Apel, Dietrich, New England Custom Gun Service, RR 2, Box 122W, Brook Rd., W. Lebanon, NH 03784/603-469-3565; FAX: 603-469-3471
Aplan Antiques & Art, James O., HC 80, Box 793-25, Piedmont, SD 57769/605-347-5016
Applied Case Systems, Inc., 2160 NW Vine St., Bldg. A, Grants Pass, OR 97526/503-479-0484; FAX: 503-476-5105
Arcardia Machine & Tool, Inc. (See AMT)
Aristocrat Knives, 9608 Van Nuys Blvd. #104, Panorama City, CA 91402/818-892-6534; FAX: 818-830-7333
Arizaga (See U.S. importer—Mandall Shooting Supplies, Inc.)
Arizona Custom Case, 1015 S. 23rd St., Phoenix, AZ 85034/602-273-0220
Arkansas Mallard Duck Calls, Rt. Box 182, England, AR 72046/501-842-3597
Arkfeld Mfg. & Dist. Co., Inc., P.O. Box 54, Norfolk, NE 68702-0054/402-371-9430; 800-533-0676
Armament Gunsmithing Co., Inc., 525 Rt. 22, Hillside, NJ 07205/908-686-0960
Armes de Chasse, P.O. Box 827, Chadds Ford, PA 19317/215-388-1146
Armfield Custom Bullets, 4775 Caroline Dr., San Diego, CA 92115/619-582-7188
Armi San Paolo, via Europa 172-A, I-25062 Concesio, Italy 030-2751725
Armite Laboratories, 1845 Randolph St., Los Angeles, CA 90001/213-587-7768; FAX: 213-587-5075
Armoloy Company of Ft. Worth, 204 E. Daggett St., Fort Worth, TX 76104/817-332-5604; FAX: 817-335-6517
Armor (See Buck Stop Lure Co., Inc.)
Armor Metal Products, P.O. Box 4609, Helena, MT 59604/406-442-5560

Armory Publications, P.O. Box 4206, Oceanside, CA 92052-4206/619-757-3930; FAX: 619-722-4108
Armoury, Inc., The, Rt. 202, Box 2340, New Preston, CT 06777/203-868-0001
A.R.M.S., Inc., 375 West St., West Bridgewater, MA 02379/508-584-7816
Arms & Armour Press, Ltd., Villiers House, 41/47 Strand, London WC2N 5JE England
Arms Corp. of the Philippines, 550E Delos Santos Ave., Cubau, Quezon City, Phillipines (U.S. importer—Ruko Products)
Arms Craft Gunsmithing, 1106 Linda Dr., Arroyo Grande, CA 93420/805-481-2830
Arms Ingenuity Co., P.O. Box 1, 51 Canal St., Weatogue, CT 06089/203-658-5624
Arms, Peripheral Data Systems, 15110 SW Boones Ferry Rd., #225, P.O. Box 1526, Lake Oswego, OR 97035/503-697-0533
Armscor Precision, 225 Lindbergh St., San Mateo, CA 94403/415-347-9556
Armscorp. of America, Inc., 4424 John Ave., Baltimore, MD 21227/301-247-6200
Armsport, Inc., 3950 NW 49th St., Miami, FL 33142/305-635-7850
Armstec, Inc., 339 East Ave., Rochester, NY 14604/800-262-2832
Armurier Hiptmayer, RR 112 #750, P.O. Box 136, Eastman, Quebec JOE 1P0, Canada/514-297-2492
Arratoonian, Andy (See Horseshoe Leather Products)
Arrieta, S.L., Morkaiko, 5, Elgoibar, E-20870, Spain/(43) 74 31 50; FAX: (43) 74 31 54 (U.S. importer—Wingshooting Adventures)
Art Jewel Enterprises Ltd., Eagle Business Ctr., 460 Randy Rd., Carol Stream, IL 60188/708-260-0400
Art's Gun & Sport Shop, Inc., 6008 Hwy. Y, Hillsboro, MO 63050
A-Square Co., Inc., One Industrial Park, Bedford, KY 40006/502-255-7456
Ashby Turkey Calls, HCR 5, Box 345, Houston, MO 65483/417-967-3787
ASI, 6226 Santos Diaz St., Irwindale, CA 91702/818-334-6629
Astra-Unceta Y Cia, S.A., Apartado 3, 48300 Guernica, Espagne, Spain (U.S. importer—Interarms)
ATIS Armi S.A.S., via Gussalli 24, Zona Industriale-Loc. Fornaci, 25020 Brescia, Italy (U.S. importer—E.A.A. Corp.)
Atlanta Cutlery Corp., 2143 Gees Mill Rd., Box 839XE, Conyers, GA 30207/800-241-3595
Atlanta Discount Ammo, P.O. Box 258, Clarkesville, GA 30523/404-754-9000
Atlantic Mills, Inc., 1325 Washington Ave., Asbury Park, NJ 07712/201-774-4882
Atlantic Research Marketing Systems (See A.R.M.S., Inc.)
Atsko/Sno-Seal, Inc., 2530 Russell SE, Orangeburg, SC 29115/803-531-1820; FAX: 803-531-2139
Auto Arms, 738 Clearview, San Antonio, TX 78228/512-434-5450
Auto-Ordnance Corp., Williams Lane, West Hurley, NY 12491/914-679-7225
Automatic Weaponry (See Scattergun Technologies, Inc.)
Autumn Sales, Inc., 1320 Lake St., Fort Worth, TX 76102/817-335-1634
AWC Systems Technology, P.O. Box 41938, Phoenix, AZ 85080-1938/602-780-1050
AYA (See U.S. importer—Armes de Chasse)
Aztec International Ltd., P.O. Box 1384, Clarkesville, GA 30523/404-754-8282

B

B&C (See Bell & Carlson, Inc.)
B&D Trading Co., Inc., 3935 Fair Hill Rd., Fair Oaks, CA 95628/916-967-9366
Badger Shooters Supply, Inc., 202 N. Harding, Owen, WI 54460/715-229-2101; FAX: 715-229-2332
Baekgaard Ltd., 1855 Janke Dr., Northbrook, IL 60062/708-498-3040; FAX: 708-493-3106
Bain & Davis, Inc., 307 E. Valley Blvd., San Gabriel, CA 91776-3522/818-573-4241
Baity's Custom Gunworks, 414 2nd St., N. Wilkesboro, NC 28659/919-667-8785
Baker's Leather Goods, Roy, P.O. Box 893, Magnolia, AR 71753/501-234-0344
Baker, Stan, 10,000 Lake City Way, Seattle, WA 98125/206-522-4575
Bald Eagle Precision Machine Co., 101 Allison St., Lock Haven, PA 17745/717-748-6772; FAX: 717-748-4443
Balickie, Joe, 408 Trelawney Lane, Apex, NC 27502/919-362-5185
Ballard Built Custom Bullets, P.O. Box 1443, Kingsville, TX 78364/512-592-0853
Ballisti-Cast, Inc., P.O. Box 383, Pershall, ND 58770/701-862-3324
Ballistic Products, Inc., P.O. Box 408, 2105 Daniels St., Long Lake, MN 55356/612-473-1550; FAX: 612-473-2981
Ballistic Research, 1108 W. May Ave., McHenry, IL 60050/815-385-0037
Ballistica Maximus North, 107 College Park Plaza, Johnstown, PA 15904/814-266-8380
Ballistica Maximus South, 3242 Mary St., Suite S-318, Miami, FL 33133/305-446-5549
Ballistics Program Co., Inc., The, 2417 N. Patterson St., Thomasville, GA 31792/912-228-1961
Bandcor Industries, Div. of Man-Sew Corp., 6108 Sherwin Dr., Port Richey, FL 34668/813-848-0432
Bang-Bang Boutique (See Holster Shop, The)
Banks, Ed, 2762 Hwy. 41 N., Ft. Valley, GA 31030/912-987-4665
Bar-Sto Precision Machine, 73377 Sullivan Rd., P.O. Box 1838, Twentynine Palms, CA 92277/619-367-2747; FAx: 619-367-2407
Barami Corp., 6250 E. 7 Mile Rd., Detroit, MI 48234/313-891-2536
Barbour, Inc., 55 Meadowbrook Dr., Milford, NH 03055/603-673-1313; FAX: 603-673-6510
Barlett, J., 6641 Kaiser Ave., Fontana, CA 92336-3265
Barnes Bullets, Inc., P.O. Box 215, American Fork, UT 84003/801-756-4222
Barnett International, P.O. Box 934, 1967 Gunn Highway, Odessa, FL 33556/813-920-2241
Baron Technology, 62 Spring Hill Rd., Trumbull, CT 06611/203-452-0515; FAX: 203-452-0663
Barrett Firearms Mfg., Inc., P.O. Box 1077, Murfreesboro, TN 37133/615-896-2938
Barsotti, Bruce (See River Road Sporting Clays)
Barta's Gunsmithing, 10231 US Hwy. 10, Cato, WI 54206/414-732-4472
Barteaux Machete, P.O. Box 66464, Portland, OR 97266/503-665-2577
Bartlett, Don, P.O. Box 9657, Spokane, WA 99209/206-839-3167
Barton, Michael D. (See Tiger-Hunt)
Basics Information Systems, Inc., 2730 University Blvd., Suite 309, Wheaton, MD 20902/301-949-1070
Bates Engraving, Billy, 2905 Lynnwood Circle SW, Decatur, AL 35603/205-355-3690
Bauer, Eddie, 15010 NE 36th St., Redmond, WA 98052
Baumannize, Inc., 7484 Sunrise Hwy., Bohemia, NY 11716/800-472-4387; FAX: 516-567-0001
Bausch & Lomb Sports Optics Div. (See Bushnell)
Bausch & Lomb, Inc., 42 East Ave., Rochester, NY 14603/800-828-5423
Bean, L.L., 386 Main St., Freeport, ME 04032/207-865-3111
Bear Archery, RR 4, 4600 Southwest 41st Blvd., Gainesville, FL 32601/904-376-2327
Bear Hug Grips, Inc., 17230 County Rd. 338, Buena Vista, CO 81211/800-232-7710
Beaver Lodge (See Fellowes, Ted)
Beaver Park Products, Inc., 840 J St., Penrose, CO 81240/719-372-6744
Beeman Precision Arms, Inc., 3440 Airway Dr., Santa Rosa, CA 95403/707-578-7900
Behlert Precision, RD 2, Box 63, Pipersville, PA 18947/215-766-8681; FAX: 215-766-8681
Beitzinger, George, 116-20 Atlantic Ave., Richmond Hill, NY 11419/718-847-7661
Belding & Mull, Inc., P.O. Box 428, 100 N. 4th St., Philipsburg, PA 16866/814-342-0607
Belding's Custom Gun Shop, 10691 Sayers Rd., Munith, MI 49259/517-596-2388
Bell & Carlson, Inc., 509 N. 5th St., Atwood, KS 67730/913-626-3204; FAX: 913-626-9602
Bell Originals, Sid, RR 2, Box 219, Tully, NY 13159/607-842-6431
Bellm Contenders (See K-D, Inc.)
Belltown, Ltd., 11 Camps Rd., Kent, CT 06757/203-354-5750
Ben's Gun Shop, 1151 S. Cedar Ridge, Duncanville, TX 75137/214-780-1807
Benchmark Guns, 1265 5th Ave., Yuma, AZ 85364/602-783-5161
Benchmark Knives (See Gerber Legendary Blades)
Benelli Armi, S.p.A., Via della Stazione, 61029 Urbino, Italy (U.S. importers—Heckler & Koch, Inc.; Sile Distributors)
Bengtson Arms Co., L., 6345-B E. Akron St., Mesa, AZ 85205/602-981-6375
Benjamin Air Rifle Co. (See Benjamin/Sheridan Co.)
Benjamin/Sheridan Co., 2600 Chicory Rd., Racine, WI 53403/414-554-7900
Bentley, John, 128-D Watson Dr., Turtle Creek, PA 15145
Berdon Machine Co., 2011 W. Washington Ave., Yakima, WA 98902/509-453-0374
Beretta Firearms, Pietro, 25063 Gardone V.T., Italy (U.S. importer—Beretta U.S.A. Corp.)
Beretta U.S.A. Corp., 17601 Beretta Drive, Accokeek, MD 20607/301-283-2191
Beretta, Dr. Franco, via Rossa, 4, Concesio (BC), Italy I-25062/030-2751955; FAX: 030-218-0414
Berger Bullets, 4234 N. 63rd Ave., Phoenix, AZ 85033/602-846-5791; FAX: 602-848-0780
Bernardelli Vincenzo S.p.A., Via Matteotti 125, Gardone V.T., Italy I-25063/30-8912851-2-3 (U.S. importer—Magnum Research, Inc.)
Bersa S.A., Las Heras 892, 1704 Rengs Mejia Bs.As, Republic of Argentina (U.S. importer—Eagle Imports, Inc.)
Bertram Bullet Co., P.O. Box 313, Seymour, Victoria 3660, Australia (057) 92 2912
Better Concepts Co., 663 New Castle Rd., Butler, PA 16001/412-285-9000
Bianchi International, Inc., 100 Calle Cortez, Temecula, CA 92590/714-676-5621
Biesen, Al, 5021 Rosewood, Spokane, WA 99208/509-328-9340
Biesen, Roger, 5021 W. Rosewood, Spokane, WA 99208/509-328-9340
Big 45 Frontier Gun Shop, 515 Cliff Ave., Valley Springs, SD 57068/605-757-6248; FAX: 605-757-6248
Big Sky Racks, Inc., P.O. Box 729, Bozeman, MT 59771-0729/406-586-9393
Big Spring Enterprises "Bore Stores," P.O. Box 1115, Yellville, AR 72687/501-449-5297; FAX: 501-449-5297
Bilal, Mustafa, 5429 Russell Ave. NW, Suite 202, Seattle, WA 98107/206-782-4164
Bill's Gun Repair, 1007 Burlington St., Mendota, IL 61342/815-539-5786
Billeb, Stephen L., 1100 N. 7th St., Burlington, IA 52601/319-753-2110
Billings Gunsmiths, Inc., 1940 Grand Ave., Billings, MT 59102/406-652-3104
Billingsley & Brownell, P.O. Box 25, Dayton, WY 82836/307-655-9344
Bilsom Intl., Inc., 109 Carpenter Dr., Sterling, VA 22170/703-834-1070
Birchwood Casey, 7900 Fuller Rd., Eden Prairie, MN 55344/612-937-7933; FAX: 612-937-7979
Birchwood Laboratories, Inc. (See Birchwood Casey)
Bishop, E.C., P.O. Box 7, Warsaw, MO 65355/816-438-5121; FAX: 816-4387-2201
Bitterroot Bullet Co., P.O. Box 412, Lewiston, ID 83501-0412/208-743-5635
Black Hills Ammunition, P.O. Box 5070, Rapid City, SD 57709/605-348-5150; FAX: 605-348-9827
Black Hills Shooters Supply, P.O. Box 4220, Rapid City, SD 57709/605-348-4477; FAX: 605-348-5037
Black Mountain Bullets, Rt. 7, P.O. Box 297, Warrenton, VA 22186/703-347-1199
Black Sheep Brand, 3220 W. Gentry Parkway, Tyler, TX 75702/214-592-3853
Blackhawk East, P.O. Box 2274, Loves Park, IL 61131
Blackhawk Mountain, P.O. Box 210, Conifer, CO 80433
Blackhawk West, P.O. Box 285, Hiawatha, KS 66434
Blackinton & Co., Inc., V.H., 221 John L. Dietsch, Attleboro Falls, MA 02763-0300/508-699-4436; FAX: 508-695-5349
Blackjack Knives, 7210 Jordan Ave., #D72, Canoga Park, CA 91303/818-902-9853
Blacksmith Corp., 830 North Road #1 East, P.O. Box 1752, Chino Valley, AZ 86323/602-636-4456; FAX: 602-636-4457
Blacktail Mountain Books, 42 First Ave. West, Kalispell, MT 59901/406-257-5573
Blakemore Game Calls, Jim, P.O. Box 10, Rt. 1, McClure, IL 62957-0010/618-661-1624
Blammo Ammo, P.O. Box 1677, Seneca, SC 29679/803-882-1768
Blaser Jagdwaffen GmbH, D-7972 Isny Im Allgau, R.F.A. (U.S. importer—Autumn Sales, Inc.)
Blaylock Gun Works, Rt. 3, Box 103-A Lot 25, Victoria, TX 77901/512-573-2744
Blaylock Gun Works, Rt. 3, Box 103-A Lot 25, Victoria, TX 77901/512-573-2744
Bledsoe, Weldon, 6812 Park Place Dr., Fort Worth, TX 76118/817-589-1704
Bleile, C. Roger, 5040 Ralph Ave., Cincinnati, OH 45238/513-251-0249
Blocker's Custom Holsters, Ted, 5360 NE 112th, Portland, OR 97220/503-254-9950
Blount, Inc. Sporting Equipment Division, 2299 Snake River Ave., Lewiston, ID 83501/208-746-2351
Blue and Gray Products, Inc. (See Ox-Yoke Originals, Inc.)
Blue Book Publications, 1 Appletree Square, Suite 1086, Minneapolis, MN 55425/800-877-4867; FAX: 612-853-1486
Blue Moutain Bullets, HCR 77, Box 23I, John Day, OR 97845/503-820-4594
Blue Ridge Knives, Rt. 6, Box 185, Marion, VA 24354/703-783-6143; FAX: 703-783-9298
Blue Ridge Machinery and Tools, Inc., P.O. Box 536-GDAT, Hurricane, WV 25526/304-562-3538; FAX: 304-562-5311
B.M.F. Activator, Inc., P.O. Box 262364, Houston, TX 77207/713-477-8442
Bo-Mar Tool & Mfg. Co., Rt. 12, P.O. Box 405, Longview, TX 75605/903-759-4784
Bob's Gun Shop, P.O. Box 200, Royal, AR 71968/501-767-1970
Bob's Tactical Indoor Shooting Range & Gun Shop, 122 Lafayette Rd., Salisbury, MA 01952/508-465-5561
Boessler, Erich, Am Vogeltal 3, 8732 Munnerstadt, W. Germany/9733-9443
Boggs, Wm., 1816 Riverside Dr. #C, Columbus, OH 43212/614-486-6965
Boker USA, Inc., 14818 West 6th Ave., Suite #17A, Golden, CO 80401-5045/303-279-5997; FAX: 303-279-5919
Bolden's, 1295 Lassen Dr., Hanford, CA 93230/209-582-6937
Boltin, John M., P.O. Box 644, Estill, SC 29918/803-625-2185
Bondini Paolo, Via Sorrento, 345, San Carlo di Cesena, Italy I-47020/0547-663 240
Bone Engraving, Ralph, 718 N. Atlanta, Owasso, OK 74055/918-272-9745

Boone's Custom Ivory Grips, Inc., 562 Coyote Rd., Brinnon, WA 98320/206-796-4330
Boonie Packer Products, P.O. Box 12204, Salem, OR 97309/800-477-3244
Border Guns & Leather, P.O. Box 1423, 110 E. Spruce St., Deming, NM 88031
Borovnik KG, Ludwig, 9170 Ferlach, Bahnhofstrasse 7, Austria
Boss Manufacturing Company, 221 W. First St., Kewanee, IL 61443/309-852-2131
Bostick Wildlife Calls, Inc., P.O. Box 728, Estill, SC 29918/803-625-2210, 803-625-4512
Bourne Co., Inc., Richard A., P.O. Box 141, Hyannis Port, MA 02647/508-775-0797
Bowen Classic Arms Corp., P.O. Box 67, Louisville, TN 37777/615-984-3583
Bowen Knife Co., P.O. Box 590, Blackshear, GA 31516/912-449-4794
Bowerly, Kent, HCR Box 1903, Camp Sherman, OR 97730/503-595-6028
Boyds' Gunstock Industries, Inc., 3rd & Main, Box 305, Geddes, SD 57342/605-337-2123; FAX: 605-337-3363
Boyt Co., Div. of Welsh Sporting Goods, 509 Hamilton, P.O. Drawer 668, Iowa Falls, IA 50126/515-648-4826
Brace, Larry D., 771 Blackfoot Ave., Eugene, OR 97404/503-688-1278
Bradley Gunsight Co., P.O. Box 140, Plymouth, VT 05056/203-589-0531; FAX: 203-582-6294
Brass Eagle, Inc., 7050A Bramalea Rd., Unit 19, Mississauga, Ont. L4Z 1C7, Canada/416-848-4844
Bratcher, Dan, 311 Belle Air Pl., Carthage, MO 64836/417-358-1518
Brauer Bros. Mfg. Co., 2020 Delmar Blvd., St. Louis, MO 63112/314-231-2864; FAX: 314-249-4952
Braun, M., 32, rue Notre-Dame, 2440 Luxembourg, Luxembourg
Break-Free, P.O. Box 25020, Santa Ana, CA 92799/714-953-1900
Brell Mar Products, Inc., 5701 Hwy. 80 West, Jackson, MS 39209
Brenneke KG, Wilhelm, Ilmenauweg 2, P.O. Box 16 46, D-3012 Langenhagen, Germany/511-772288
Bretton, 19 rue Victor Grignard, Z.I. Montreynaud, 42-St. Etienne, France (U.S. importer—Mandall Shooting Supplies, Inc.)
Brgoch, Frank, 1580 S. 1500 East, Bountiful, UT 84010/801-295-1885
Brian, C.T., 1101 Indiana Ct., Decatur, IL 62521/217-429-2290
Bridgers Best, P.O. Box 1410, Berthoud, CO 80513
Briganti & Co., A., 475 Rt. 32, Highland Mills, NY 10930/914-928-9573
Briley Mfg., Inc., 1085-B Gessner, Houston, TX 77055/713-932-6995
British Arms Co. Ltd., P.O. Box 7, Latham, NY 12110/518-783-0773
BRNO (See U.S. importer—Action Arms Ltd.)
Brobst, Jim, 299 Poplar St., Hamburg, PA 19526/215-562-2103
Brooker, Dennis, Rt. 1, Box 12A, Derby, IA 50068/515-533-2103
Brown Manufacturing, P.O. Box 9219, Akron, OH 44305/800-837-GUNS
Brown Mfg., E.A., 3404 Pawnee Dr., Alexandria, MN 56308/612-762-8847
Brown Precision, Inc., 7786 Molinos Ave., Los Molinos, CA 96055/916-384-2506; FAX: 916-384-1638
Brown Products, Ed, Rt. 2, Box 2922, Perry, MO 63462/314-565-3261; FAX: 565-2791
Brown, H.R. (See Silhouette Leathers)
Brownell Checkering Tools, W.E., 3356 Moraga Place, San Diego, CA 92117/619-276-6146
Brownell's, Inc., 222 W. Liberty, Montezuma, IA 50171/515-623-5401
Browning Arms Co. (Gen. Offices), Rt. 1, Morgan, UT 84050/801-876-2711
Browning Arms Co. (Parts & Service), 3005 Arnold Tenbrook Rd., Arnold, MO 63010-9406/314-287-6800; FAX: 314-287-9751
BRP, Inc. Cast Bullets, 1210 Alexander Rd., Colorado Springs, CO 80909/719-633-0658
Bruno Shooters Supply, P.O. Box 2501, Hazleton, PA 18201/717-455-2211; FAX: 717-455-2211
Brunton U.S.A., 620 E. Monroe Ave., Riverton, WY 82501/307-856-6559; FAX: 307-856-1840
Bryco Arms (See U.S. distributor—Jennings Firearms, Inc.)
BSA Guns Ltd., Armoury Rd. Small Heath, Birmingham, England B11 2PX/(011)21 772 8543; FAX: (011)21 773-0845 (U.S. importer—Air Rifle Specialists)
B-Square Co., P.O. Box 11281, Ft. Worth, TX 76110/817-923-0964; FAX: 817-926-7012
Bucheimer, J.M., Jumbo Sports Products, 721 N. 20th St., St. Louis, MO 63103/314-241-1020
Buck Knives, Inc., 1900 Weld Blvd., El Cajon, CA 92020/619-449-1100, 800-854-2557; FAX: 619-562-5774
Buck Stop Lure Co., Inc., 3600 Grow Rd. NW, P.O. Box 636, Stanton, MI 48888/517-762-5091; FAX: 517-762-5124
Buckhorn Gun Works, Rt. 6, Box 324, Rapid City, SC 57702/605-787-6289
Buckskin Machine Works, A. Hunkeler, 3235 S. 358th St., Auburn, WA 98001/206-927-5412
Budin, Dave, Main St., Margaretville, NY 12455/914-568-4103; FAX: 914-586-4105
Buehler Scope Mounts, 17 Orinda Way, Orinda, CA 94563/510-254-3201; FAX: 510-254-2499
Buenger Enterprises, Box 5286, Oxnard, CA 93031/805-985-0541
Buffalo Bullet Co., Inc., 12637 Los Nietos Rd. Unit A, Santa Fe Springs, CA 90670/310-944-0322; FAX: 310-944-5054
Buffalo Rock Shooters Supply, RR 1, Ottawa, IL 61350/815-433-2471
Bull-X, Inc., 520 N. Main St., Farmer City, IL 61842/309-928-2574
Bullet Swaging Supply, Ltd., P.O. Box 1056, 303 McMillan Rd., West Monroe, LA 71291/318-387-7257; FAX: 318-387-7779
Burgess & Son Gunsmiths, R.W., P.O. Box 3364, Warner Robins, GA 31099/912-328-7487
Burgess, Byron, 1816 Gathe Dr., San Luis Obispo, CA 93405/805-543-7744
Burkhart Gunsmithing, Don, P.O. Box 852, Rawlins, WY 82301/307-324-6007
Burnham Bros., P.O. Box 669, 912 Hi-way 1431 West, Marble Falls, TX 78654/512-693-3112
Burres, Jack, 10333 San Fernando Rd., Pacoima, CA 91331/818-899-8000
Burris Company, Inc., P.O. Box 1747, Greeley, CO 80632/303-356-1670; FAX: 303-356-8702
Bushmaster Hunting & Fishing, 451 Alliance Ave., Toronto, Ont. M6N 2J1 Canada/416-763-4040; FAX: 416-763-0623
Bushnell, Bausch & Lomb Sports Optics Div., 9200 Cody, Overland Park, KS 66214/913-888-0220
Bushwacker Backpack & Supply Co. (See Counter Assault)
Bustani Appraisers, Leo, P.O. Box 8125, W. Palm Beach, FL 33407/305-622-2710
Buster's Custom Knives, P.O. Box 214, Richfield, UT 84701/801-896-5319
Butler Creek Corporation, 290 Arden Dr., Belgrade, MT 59714/406-388-1356; FAX: 406-388-7204
Butterfield & Butterfield, 220 San Bruno Ave., San Francisco, CA 94103/415-861-7500
Buzztail Brass, P.O. Box 656, 10905 Needle Dam Rd., Keno, OR 97627/503-884-1072

C

C3 Systems, Box 485, N. Scituate, RI 02857
C&D Special Products, 309 Sequoya Dr., Hopkinsville, KY 42240/800-922-6287, 800-284-1746
C&H Research, 115 Sunnyside Dr., Box 351, Lewis, KS 67552/316-324-5445
Cabanas (See U.S. importer—Mandall Shooting Supplies, Inc.)
Cabela's, 812-13th Ave., Sidney, NE 69160/308-254-5505
Cabinet Mtn. Outfitter, P.O. Box 766, Plains, MT 59859/406-826-3970
Cache La Poudre Rifleworks, 140 N. College, Ft. Collins, CO 80524/303-482-6913
Cadre Supply, P.O. Box 22074, Memphis, TN 38122/901-526-4986
Calhoon Mfg., James, 6035 Penworth Rd. SE, Calgary, AB T2A 4E9 Canada/403-235-2959
Cali'co Hardwoods, Inc., 1648 Airport Blvd., Windsor, CA 95492/707-546-4045; FAX: 707-546-4027
Calibre Press, Inc., 666 Dundee Rd., Suite 1607, Northbrook, IL 60062-2760/800-323-0037; FAX: 708-498-6869
Calico Light Weapon Systems, 405 E. 19th St., Bakersfield, CA 93305/805-323-1327; FAX: 805-323-7844
California Grip, 1323 Miami Ave., Clovis, CA 93612/209-299-1316
California Magnum, 20746 Dearborn St., Chatsworth, CA 91313/818-341-7302; FAX: 818-341-7304
California Sight, P.O. Box 4607, Pagosa Springs, CO 81157/303-731-5003
CAM Enterprises, 5090 Iron Springs Rd., Box 2, Prescott, AZ 86301/602-776-9640
Camdex, Inc., 2330 Alger, Troy, MI 48083/313-528-2300
Cameron's, 16690 W. 11th Ave., Golden, CO 80401/303-279-7365; FAX: 303-628-5527
Camilli, Joe, 4700 Oahu Dr. NE, Albuquerque, NM 87111/505-293-5259
Camillus Cutlery Co., 54 Main St., Camillus, NY 13031/315-672-8111, 800-344-0456; FAX: 315-672-8832
Camofore Company, 712 Main St. 2800, Houston, TX 77002/713-229-9253
Camp-Cap Products, P.O. Box 173, Chesterfield, MO 63006/314-532-4340
Campbell, Dick, 20,000 Silver Ranch Rd., Conifer, CO 80433/303-697-0150
Can Am Enterprises, Box 27, Fruitland, Ont. LOR ILO, Canada/416-643-4357
Canjar Co., M.H., 500 E. 45th Ave., Denver, CO 80216/303-295-2638
Cannon Safe, Inc., 9358 Stephens St., Pico Rivera, CA 90660/213-692-0636, 800-242-1055, 800-222-1055 (CA)
Cannon's Guns, P.O. Box 357, 2387 Meridian, Victor, MT 59875/406-642-3644
Canons Delcour, 287 Rue F. Roosevelt, 4870 Fraipont, Belgium/(+32)87.26.85.81; FAX: (+32)87.26.72.89
Cape Outfitters, Rt. 2, Box 437C, Cape Girardeau, MO 63701/314-335-4103; FAX: 314-335-1555
Caraville Manufacturing, P.O. Box 4545, Thousand Oaks, CA 91359/805-499-1234
Carbide Die & Mfg. Co., Inc., 15615 E. Arrow Hwy., Irwindale, CA 91706/818-337-2518
Carhartt, Inc., P.O. Box 600, Dearborn, MI 48121/800-358-3825; FAX: 313-271-3455
Carlson, Douglas R., Antique American Firearms, P.O. Box 71035, Des Moines, IA 50325/515-224-6552
Carry-Lite, Inc., 5203 W. Clinton Ave., Milwaukee, WI 53223/414-355-3520
Carter's Gun Shop, 225 G St., Penrose, CO 81240/719-372-6240
Carter's Wildlife Calls, Inc., Garth, P.O. Box 821, Cedar City, UT 84720/801-586-7639
Cartridges Unlimited, 190 Bull's Bridge Rd., South Kent, CT 06785/203-927-3053
Carvajal Belts & Holsters, 422 Chestnut, Unit #4, San Antonio, TX 78202/512-222-8262; FAX: 512-222-0118
Cascade Fabrication, 1090 Bailey Hill Rd. Unit A, Eugene, OR 97402/503-485-3433; FAX: 503-485-3543
Case & Sons Cutlery Co., W.R., Owens Way, Bradford, PA 16701/814-368-4123; FAX: 814-362-4877
Caspian Arms, 14 North Main St., Hardwick, VT 05843/802-472-6454
Caswell International Corp., 1221 Marshall St. NE, Minneapolis, MN 55413/612-379-2000
Cathey Enterprises, Inc., P.O. Box 2202, Brownwood, TX 76804/915-643-2553; FAX: 915-643-3653
Cation, 32360 Edward, Madison Heights, MI 48071/313-588-0160
Catoctin Cutlery, 17 S. Main St., P.O. Box 188, Smithburg, MD 21783/301-824-7416; FAX: 301-824-6138
Caywood, Shane J., P.O. Box 321, Minocqua, WI 54548
CBC, Avenida Industrial, 3330, Santo Andre-SP-Brazil 09080/11-449-5600, (U.S. importer—MAGTECH Recreational Products, Inc.)
CCI (See Blount, Inc. Sporting Equipment Division)
Cedar Hill Game Call Co., Rt. 2, Box 236, Downsville, LA 71234/318-982-5632
Celestron International, P.O. Box 3587, Torrance, CA 90503
Cellini, Inc., Vito Francesca, 3115 Old Ranch Rd., San Antonio, TX 78217/512-826-2584
Centaur Systems, Inc., 6849 Hwy. 89 NW, Bemidji, MN 56601/218-751-8609
Central Specialties Co., 200 Lexington Dr., Buffalo Grove, IL 60089/708-537-3300; FAX: 708-537-3615
Century Gun Dist., Inc., 1467 Jason Rd., Greenfield, IN 46140/317-462-4524
Century International Arms, Ltd., 48 Lower Newton St., St. Albans, VT 05478/802-527-1252; FAX: 802-524-5631
CFVentures, 509 Harvey Dr., Bloomington, IN 47403
C-H Tool & Die Corp. (See 4-D Custom Die Co.)
Chace Leather Products, 507 Alden St., Fall River, MA 02722/508-678-7556; FAX: 675-9666
Chadick's Ltd., P.O. Box 100, Terrell, TX 75160/214-563-7577
Chameleon Camouflage Systems, 15199 S. Maplelane Rd., Oregon City, OR 97045/503-657-2266
Champion Target Company, 232 Industrial Parkway, Richmond, IN 47374/800-441-4971
Champion's Choice, Inc., 223 Space Park South, Nashville, TN 37211/615-834-6666; FAX: 615-831-2753
Champlin Firearms, Inc., P.O. Box 3191, Woodring Airport, Enid, OK 73701/405-237-7388; FAX: 405-242-6922
Champlin, R. MacDonald, P.O. Box 693, Manchester, NH 03105/603-483-8557
Chapman Academy of Practical Shooting, 4350 Academy Rd., Hallsville, MO 65255/314-696-5544; FAX: 314-696-2266
Chapman Manufacturing Company, The, 471 New Haven Rd., P.O. Box 250, Durham, CT 06422/203-349-9228; FAX: 203-349-0084
Chapuis Armes, 21 La Gravoux, BP15, 42380 St. Bonnet-le-Chateau, France/(33)77.50.06.96 (U.S. importer—Armes de Chasse)
CHARCO, 26 Beaver St., Ansonia, CT 06401/203-735-4686

Charter Arms (See CHARCO)
Checkmate Refinishing, 8232 Shaw Rd., Brooksville, FL 34602/904-799-5774
Cheddite France, S.A., 99 Route de Lyon, F-26500 Bourg Les Valence, France/75 56 45 45; FAX: 75 56 98 89
Chelsea Gun Club of New York City, Inc., 237 Ovington Ave., Apt. D53, Brooklyn, NY 11209/718-836-9422, 718-833-2704
Cherokee Gun Accessories (See Glaser Safety Slug, Inc.)
Chesapeake Importing & Distributing Company (See CIDCO)
Chesire & Perez Dist., 425 W. Allen Ave., San Dimas, CA 91773-1485
CheVron Bullets, RR 1, Ottawa, IL 61350/815-433-2471
CheVron Case Master (See CheVron Bullets)
Chicago Cutlery Co., 5420 N. County Rd. 18, Minneapolis, MN 55428/612-533-0472
Chimere, Inc., 4406 Exchange Ave., Naples, FL 33942/813-643-4222
ChinaSports, Inc., 2010 S. Lynx Place, Ontario, CA 91761/714-923-1411; FAX: 714-923-0775
Chipmunk (See Oregon Arms, Inc.)
Chippewa Shoe Co., P.O. Box 2521, Ft. Worth, TX 76113/817-332-4385
Choate Machine & Tool Company, Inc., P.O. Box 218, Bald Knob, AR 72010/501-724-6193
Chopie Mfg., Inc., 700 Copeland Ave., LaCrosse, WI 54603/608-784-0926
Christie's East, 219 E. 67th St., New York, NY 10021/212-606-0400
Christopher Firearms Co., Inc., E., Route 128 & Ferry St., Miamitown, OH 45041/513-353-1321
Chuck's Gun Shop, P.O. Box 597, Waldo, FL 32694/904-468-2264
Churchill (See U.S. importer—Ellett Bros.)
Churchill Glove Co., James, P.O. Box 298, Centralia, WA 98531
Churchill, Winston, Twenty Mile Stream Rd., RFD P.O. Box 29B, Proctorsville, VT 05153/802-226-7772
CIDCO, 21480 Pacific Blvd., Sterling, VA 22170/703-444-5353
Ciener, Inc., Jonathan Arthur, 8700 Commerce St., Cape Canaveral, FL 32920/407-868-2200
Cimarron Arms, 1106 Wisterwood #G, Houston, TX 77043/713-468-2007
Claridge Hi-Tec, Inc., P.O. Box 7309, Northridge, CA 91324/818-700-9093
Clark Co., Inc., David, P.O. Box 15054, Worcester, MA 01615-0054/508-756-6216; FAX: 508-753-5827
Clark Custom Guns, Inc., P.O. Box 530, 11462 Keatchie Rd., Keithville, LA 71047/318-925-0836; FAX: 318-925-9425
Clark Firearms Engraving, P.O. Box 80746, San Marino, CA 91118/818-287-1652
Clark, Frank, 3714-27th St., Lubbock, TX 79410/806-799-1187
Clarkfield Enterprises, Inc., 1032 10th Ave., Clarkfield, MN 56223/612-669-7140
Classic Arms Corp., P.O. Box 106, Dunsmuir, CA 96025-0106/916-235-2000
Classic Guns, Frank Wood, 3230 Madlock Ridge Rd., Suite 14, Norcross, GA 30092/404-242-7944
Clay Target Enterprises, 300 Railway Ave., Campbell, CA 95008/408-379-4829
Clearview Mfg. Co., Inc., 413 South Oakley St., Fordyce, AR 71742/501-352-8557
Clements' Custom Leathercraft, Chas, 1741 Dallas St., Aurora, CO 80010-2018/303-364-0403
Clenzoil Corp., P.O. Box 80226, Canton, OH 44708/216-833-9758
Clerke Co., J.A., P.O. Box 627, Pearblossom, CA 93553-0627/805-945-0713
Clift Mfg., L.R., P.O. Box 2334, Marysville, CA 95901/916-755-3390; FAX: 916-755-3393
Clifton Arms, Inc., P.O. Box 531258, Grand Prairie, TX 75053/214-647-2500; FAX: 214-647-8200
Clinton River Gun Serv., Inc., 30016 S. River Rd., Mt. Clemens, MI 48045/313-468-1090
Cloward's Gun Shop, 4023 Aurora Ave. N, Seattle, WA 98103/206-632-2072
Clymer Manufacturing Co., Inc., 1645 W. Hamlin Rd., Rochester Hills, MI 48309/313-853-5555; FAX: 313-853-1530
Coast Cutlery Co., 609 SE Ankeny, Portland, OR 97214/503-234-4545
Coats, Mrs. Lester, 300 Luman Rd., Space 125, Phoenix, OR 97535/503-535-1611
Cobra Gunskin, 133-30 32nd Ave., Flushing, NY 11354/718-762-8181; FAX: 718-762-0890
Cobra Sport, s.n.c. Di Leto A&C, Via Caduti Del Lager 1, S. Romano (PISA) Italy/0039-571-450490
Coffey, Barbara, Rt. 1, P.O. Box 208, Amherst, VA 24521/804-435-2259, 804-922-7249
Coffin, Charles H., 3719 Scarlet Ave., Odessa, TX 79762/915-366-4729
Coffin, Jim, 250 Country Club Lane, Albany, OR 97321/503-928-4391
Coghlan's Ltd., 121 Irene St., Winnipeg, Man., Canada R3T 4C7/204-284-9550
Cold Steel, Inc., 2128 Knoll Dr., Unit D, Ventura, CA 93003/800-255-4716, 800-624-2363
Cole-Grip, 16135 Cohasset St., Van Nuys, CA 91406/818-782-4424
Coleman Co., Inc., 250 N. St. Francis, Wichita, KS 67201
Collins Brothers Div. (See Bowen Knife Co.)
Colonial Arms, Inc., P.O. Box 636, Selma, AL 36702-0636/205-872-9455; FAX: 205-872-9540
Colonial Knife Co., P.O. Box 3327, Providence, RI 02909/401-421-1600; FAX: 401-421-2047
Colonial Repair, P.O. Box 372, Hyde Park, MA 02136-9998/617-469-2991
Colorado School of Trades, 1575 Hoyt St., Lakewood, CO 80215/800-234-4594; FAX: 303-233-4723
Colorado Shooter's Supply, 138 S. Plum, P.O. Box 132, Fruita, CO 81521/303-858-9191
Colorado Sutlers Arsenal, Box 991, Granby, CO 80446/303-887-2813
Colt's Mfg. Co., Inc., P.O. Box 1868, Hartford, CT 06101/203-236-6311
Combat Shop, The, Rt. 1, P.O. Box 112-C, Surry, VA 23883/804-357-0881
Companhia Brasileira de Cartuchos (See CBC)
Compass Industries, Inc., 104 East 25th St., New York, NY 10010/212-473-2614
Competition Bullets, Inc., 9996-29 Ave., Edmonton, Alb. T6N 1A2, Canada/403-463-2817
Competition Electronics, Inc., 3469 Precision Dr., Rockford, IL 61109/815-874-8001; FAX: 815-874-8181
Competition Limited, 1664 S. Research Loop Rd., Tucson, AZ 85710/602-722-6455
Competitive Pistol Shop, The, 5233 Palmer Dr., Ft. Worth, TX 76117-2433/817-834-8479
Competitor Corporation, Inc., P.O. Box 244, 293 Townsend Rd., West Groton, MA 01472/508-448-3521; FAX: 603-673-4540
Component Concepts, Inc., 10240 SW Nimbus Ave.., Suite L-8, Portland, OR 97223/503-684-9262; FAX: 503-620-4285
Concorde Arms, Inc., 27820 Fremont Ct. #3, Valencia, CA 91355/805-257-1955
Condon, Inc., David, P.O. Box 312, 14502-G Lee Rd., Chatilly, VA 22021/703-631-7748 or 109 E. Washington St., Middleburg, VA 22117/703-687-5642
Condor Mfg. Co., 418 W. Magnolia Ave., Glendale, CA 91204/818-240-3173
Conetrol Scope Mounts, Hwy. 123 South, Seguin, TX 78155/512-379-3030
CONKKO, P.O. Box 40, Broomall, PA 19008/215-356-0711
Connecticut Valley Arms Co. (See CVA)

Conrad, C.A., 3964 Ebert St., Winston-Salem, NC 27127/919-788-5469
Continental Kite & Key Co. (See CONKKO)
Coonan Arms, Inc., 830 Hampden Ave., St. Paul, MN 55114/612-646-6672; FAX: 612-646-0902
Cooper Arms, P.O. Box 114, Stevensville, MT 59870/800-732-GUNS
Cooper-Woodward, 8073 Canyon Ferry Rd., Helena, MT 59601/406-375-3321
Cor-Bon Bullet & Ammo Co., 4828 Michigan Ave., Detroit, MI 48210/313-894-2373
Corbin Applied Technology, P.O. Box 2171, White City, OR 97503/503-826-5211
Corbin Manufacturing & Supply, Inc., 600 Industrial Circle, P.O. Box 2659, White City, OR 97503/503-826-5211; FAX: 503-826-8669
Corkys Gun Clinic, 111 North 11th Ave., Greeley, CO 80631/303-330-0516
Corry, John, 861 Princeton Ct., Neshanic Station, NJ 08853/308-369-8019
Cosmi Americo & Figlio s.n.c., Via Flaminia 307, Ancona, Italy I-60020/071-888208; FAX: 071-887008 (U.S. importer—Incor, Inc.)
Costa, David, P.O. Box 428, Island Pond, VT 05844
Coulston Int. Corp., P.O. Box 30, Eaaston, PA 18044-0030/215-253-0167; FAX: 215-252-1511
Counter Assault, Box 4721, Missoula, MT 59806/406-728-6241; FAX: 406-728-8800
Country Armourer, The, P.O. Box 308, Ashby, MA 01431/508-386-7789
Cox, C. Ed, RD 2, Box 192, Prosperity, PA 15329/412-228-4984
CQB Training, P.O. Box 1739, Manchester, MO 63011
Craftguard, 3624 Logan Ave., Waterloo, IA 50703/319-232-2959
Crandall Tool & Machine Company, 1545 N. Mitchell St., P.O. Box 569, Cadillac, MI 49601/616-775-5562
Crane & Crane Ltd., 105 N. Edison Way #6, Reno, NV 89502-2355/702-856-1516; FAX: 702-856-1616
Crane Sales Co., George S., P.O. Box 385, Van Nuys, CA 91409/818-505-8337
Cravener's Gun Shop, 1627-5th Ave., Ford City, PA 16226/412-763-8312
Crawford Co., Inc., R.M., P.O. Box 277, Everett, PA 15537/814-652-6536; FAX: 814-652-9526
Creative Cartridge Co., 56 Morgan Rd., Canton, CT 06019/203-693-2529
Creative Craftsman, Inc., The, 95 Highway 29 North, P.O. Box 331, Lawrenceville, GA 30246/404-963-2112
Creedmore Sports, Inc., P.O. Box 1040, Oceanside, CA 92051/619-757-5529
Creek Side Metal & Woodcrafters (See Allard, Gary)
Creekside Gun Shop, Inc., Main St., Holcomb, NY 14469/716-657-6131
Crosman Blades (See Coleman Co., Inc.)
Crosman Corp., Rt. 5 and 20, E. Bloomfield, NY 14443/716-657-6161; FAX: 716-657-5405
Crosman Products of Canada Ltd., 1173 N. Service Rd. West, Oakville, Ontario, LCM2V9 Canada/416-827-1822
Crouse's Country Cover, P.O. Box 160, Storrs, CT 06268/203-423-0702
Cubic Shot Shell Co., Inc., 98 Fatima Dr., Campbell, OH 44405/216-755-0349; FAX: 216-755-0349
Cullity Restoration, Daniel, 209 Old County Rd., East Sandwich, MA 02537/508-888-1147
Cumberland Arms, Rt. 1, Box 1150, Manchester, TN 37355
Cumberland Knife & Gun Works, 5661 Bragg Blvd., Fayetteville, NC 28303/919-867-0009
Cureton Powder Horns, Rt. 2, Box 388 Willoughby Rd., Bulls Gap, TN 37711/615-235-2854
Curtis Custom Shop, 26 Novak Dr., Stafford, VA 22554/703-659-4265
Custom Checkering Service, 2124 SE Yamhill St., Portland, OR 97214/503-236-5874
Custom Chronograph, Inc., 5305 Reese Hill Rd., Sumas, WA 98295/206-988-7801
Custom Firearms (See Ahrends, Kim)
Custom Gun Engraving, 3645 N. 71 Ave., Phoenix, AZ 85033/602-848-6685
Custom Gun Grips, 101 Primrose Lane, Lynchburg, VA 24501/804-385-6667
Custom Gun Products, 5021 W. Rosewood, Spokane, WA 99208/509-328-9340
Custom Gun Stocks, Rt. 6, P.O. Box 177, McMinnville, TN 37110/615-668-3912
Custom Gunsmiths, 4303 Friar Lane, Colorado Springs, CO 80907/719-599-3366
Custom Hunting Ammo & Arms, 2900 Fisk Rd., Howell, MI 48843/517-546-9498
Custom Knifemaker's Supply, P.O. Box 308, Emory, TX 75440/903-473-3330
Custom Products, Neil A. Jones, RD #1, P.O. Box 483A, Saegertown, PA 16433/814-763-2769
Custom Shop, The, 890 Cochrane Crescent, Peterborough, Ont. K9H 5N3 Canada/705-742-6693
Custom Tackle & Ammo, P.O. Box 1886, Farmington, NM 87499/505-632-3539
Cutco Cutlery, P.O. Box 810, Olean, NY 14760/716-372-3111
Cutlery Shoppe, 5461 Kendall St., Boise, ID 83706-1248/800-231-1272
CVA, 5988 Peachtree Corners East, Norcross, GA 30071/404-449-4687
C.W. Cartridge Co., 242 Highland Ave., Kearny, NJ 07032/201-998-1030
Cycle Dynamics, Inc., 74 Garden St., Feeding Hills, MA 01030/413-786-0141
Cylinder & Slide, Inc., William R. Laughridge, 245 E. 4th St., Fremont, NE 68025/402-721-4277

D

D&D Gunsmiths, Ltd., 363 E. Elmwood, Troy, MI 48083/313-583-1512
D&H Precision Tooling, 7522 Barnard Mill Rd., Ringwood, IL 60072/815-653-4011
D&H Prods. Co., Inc., 465 Denny Rd., Valencia, PA 16059/412-898-2840
D&L Sports, P.O. Box 651, Gillette, WY 82717/307-686-4008
Dade Screw Machine Products, 2319 NW 7th Ave., Miami, FL 33127/305-573-5050
Daewoo Precision Industries Ltd., 34-3 Yeoeuido-Dong, Yeongdeungpo-GU, 15th Fl., Seoul, Korea (U.S. importer—Firstshot, Inc.)
Dahl's Custom Stocks, Rt. 4, P.O. Box 558, Lake Geneva, WI 53147/414-248-2464
Daigmont Industries, Inc., 422 E. Main St., Suite 207, Nacogdoches, TX 75961/409-560-4367
Daisy Mfg. Co., P.O. Box 220, Rogers, AR 72756/501-636-1200; FAX: 501-636-1601
Dakota (See U.S. importer—EMF Co., Inc.)
Dakota Arms, Inc., HC 55, Box 326, Sturgis, SD 57785/605-347-4686; FAX: 605-347-5227
Dakota Corp., P.O. Box 543, Rutland, VT 05702/800-451-4167; FAX: 802-773-3919
Daly, Charles (See Miroku, B.C./Daly, Charles)
Damascus-U.S.A., Rt. 3, Box 39A Wildcat Rd., Edenton, NC 27932/919-482-4992; FAX: 919-482-4703
Dan's Whetstone Co., Inc., 109 Remington Terrace, Hot Springs, AK 71913/501-767-9598; FAX: 501-767-9598
Dangler, Homer L., Box 254, Addison, MI 49220/517-547-6745
Danner Shoe Mfg. Co., 12722 NE Airport Way, Portland, OR 97230/503-251-1100; FAX: 503-251-1119
Danuser Machine Co., 550 E. Third St., P.O. Box 368, Fulton, MO 65251/314-642-2246; FAX: 314-642-2240

Dapkus Co., J.G., P.O. Box 180, Cromwell, CT 06416/203-632-2308
Dara-Nes, Inc. (See Nesci Enterprises, Inc.)
Darlington Gun Works, Inc., P.O. Box 698, 516 S. 52 Bypass, Darlington, SC 29532/803-393-3931
Datumtech Corporation, 8575 Roll Rd., Clarence Center, NY 14032/716-741-4405
Davidson Products, Inc., 2020 Huntington Dr., Las Cruces, NM 88001/505-522-5612
Davidson's, P.O. Box 5387, Greensboro, NC 27435/800-367-4867
Davidson, Jere, Rt. 1, Box 132, Rustburg, VA 24588/804-821-3637
Davis Industries, 15150 Sierra Bonita Lane, Chino, CA 91710/714-597-4726
Davis Leather Co., G. Wm., 3990 Valley Blvd., Unit D, Walnut, CA 91789/714-598-5620
Davis Service Center, Bill, 10173 Croydon Way #9, Sacramento, CA 95827/916-369-6789
Day & Sons, Inc., Leonard, P.O. Box 122, Flagg Hill Rd., Heath, MA 01346/413-337-8369
Dayton Traister, P.O. Box 593, Oak Harbor, WA 98277/206-679-4657; FAX:206-675-1114
DBASE Consultants (See Peripheral Data Systems)
DBI Books, Inc., 4092 Commercial Ave., Northbrook, IL 60062/708-272-6310; FAX: 708-272-2051
D-Boone Ent., Inc., 5900 Colwyn Dr., Harrisburg, PA 17109
D.D. Custom Rifles, R.H. "Dick" Devereaux, 5240 Mule Deer Dr., Colorado Springs, CO 80919/719-548-8468
de Treville & Co., Star, 4129 Normal St., San Diego, CA 92103/619-298-3393
Decker Shooting Products, 1729 Laguna Ave., Schofield, WI 54476/715-359-5873
Deepeeka Exports Pvt. Ltd., D-78, Saket, Meerut, India 250-006/0121-74483
Deer Me Products Co., Box 34, 1208 Park St., Anoka, MN 55303/612-421-8971; FAX: 612-422-0536
Defense Moulding Enterprises, 16781 Daisey Ave., Fountain Valley, CA 92708/714-842-5062
Defense Training International, Inc., 6565 Gunpark Dr., Suite 150-4, Boulder, CO 80301/303-530-7106
Degen Knives, 9608 Van Nuys Blvd., #104, Panorama City, CA 91402/818-892-6534; FAX: 818-830-7333
deHaas Barrels, RR #3, Box 77, Ridgeway, MO 64481/816-872-6308
Del Rey Products, P.O. Box 91561, Los Angeles, CA 90009/213-823-0494
Del-Sports, Inc., Box 685, Main St., Margaretville, NY 12455/914-586-4103; FAX: 914-586-4105
Delhi Gun House, 1374 Kashmere Gate, Delhi, India 110 006/23735-2917344; FAX: 91-11-6411711
Delorge, Ed, 2231 Hwy. 308, Thibodaux, LA 70301/504-447-1633
Delta Arms Ltd., P.O. Box 68, Sellers, SC 29592-0068/803-752-7426, 800-677-0641; 800-274-1611
Delta Vectors, Inc., 7119 W. 79th St., Overland Park, KS 66204/913-642-0307
Dem-Bart Checkering Tools, Inc., 6807 Hwy. #2, Bickford Ave., Snohomish, WA 98290/206-568-7356; FAX: 206-334-8455
Denver Arms, Ltd., P.O. Box 4640, Pagosa Springs, CO 81157/303-731-2295
Denver Bullets, Inc., 1811 W. 13th Ave., Denver, CO 80204/303-893-3146
Denver Instrument Company, 6542 Fig St., Arvada, CO 80004/800-321-1135
DeSantis Holster & Leather Goods, P.O. Box 2039, New Hyde Park, NY 11040-0701/516-354-8000; FAX: 516-354-7501
Desert Industries, Inc., 3245 E. Patrick Ln., Suite H, Las Vegas, NV 89120/702-597-1066
Desert Mountain Mfg., P.O. Box 184, Coram, MT 59913/406-387-5381
Destination North Software, 804 Surry Rd., Wenatchee, WA 98801/509-662-6602
Detroit-Armor Corp., 720 Industrial Dr. #112, Cary, IL 60013/708-639-7666
Developmental Concepts, Rt. 4, New Henderson Rd., Clinton, TN 37716/615-945-1428
Dever Co., Jack, 8590 NW 90, Oklahoma City, OK 73132/405-721-6393
Devereaux, R.H. "Dick" (See D.D. Custom Rifles)
Dewey Mfg. Co., Inc., J., P.O. Box 2014, Southbury, CT 06488/203-598-7912
DGS, Inc., 1117 E. 12th, Casper, WY 82601/307-237-2414
Diana (See U.S. importer—Dynamit Nobel-RWS, Inc.)
Dibble, Derek A., 555 John Downey Dr., New Britain, CT 06051/203-224-2630
Dilliott Gunsmithing, Inc., 657 Scarlett Rd., Dandridge, TN 37725/615-397-9204
Dillon Precision Prods., Inc., 7442 E. Butherus Dr., Scottsdale, AZ 85260/602-948-8009
Dillon, Ed, 6304 Rabbit Ears Circle, Colorado Springs, CO 80919/719-598-4929; FAX: 719-598-4929
Dixie Gun Works, Hwy. 51 South, Union City, TN 38261/901-885-0700; FAX: 901-885-0440
Dixon Muzzleloading Shop, Inc., RD 1, Box 175, Kempton, PA 19529/215-756-6271
DKT, Inc., 14623 Vera Dr., Union, MI 49130/616-641-7120; FAX: 616-641-2015
DLO Mfg., 415 Howe Ave., Shelton, CT 06484/203-924-2952
D Max Industries, 17700 147th St. SE, Bldg. G, Monroe, WA 98272/206-794-7754
DMG Technologies, Inc., 931 Cumberland St., Lakeland, FL 33801/813-646-8888
Dolbare, Elizabeth, 39 Dahlia, Casper, WY 82604/307-266-5924
Donnelly, C.P., 405 Kubli Rd., Grants Pass, OR 97527/503-846-6604
Doskocil Mfg. Co., Inc., P.O. Box 1246, Arlington, TX 76004/817-467-5116
Douglas Barrels, Inc., 5504 Big Tyler Rd., Charleston, WV 25313-1398/304-776-1341; FAX: 304-776-8560
Dowtin Gunworks, Rt. 4, Box 930A, Flagstaff, AZ 86001/602-779-1898
Dr. O's Products Ltd., P.O. Box 111, Niverville, NY 12130/518-784-3333; FAX: 518-784-2800
Drain, Mark, SE 3211 Kamilche Point Rd., Shelton, WA 98584/206-426-5452
Dremel Mfg. Co., 4915-21st St., Racine, WI 53406
Dressel Jr., Paul G., 209 N. 92nd Ave., Yakima, WA 98908/509-966-9233
Dri-Slide, Inc., 411 N. Darling, Fremont, MI 49412/616-924-3950
DTM International, Inc., 40 Joslyn Rd., P.O. Box 5, Lake Orion, MI 48035/313-693-6670
D.O.C. Specialists, Inc., Doc & Bud Ulrich, 2209 S. Central Ave., Cicero, IL 60650/708-652-3606; FAX: 708-652-2516
Du-Lite Corp., 171 River Rd., Middletown, CT 06457/203-347-2505
Duane Custom Stocks, Randy, 110 W. North Ave., Winchester, VA 22601/703-667-9461; FAX: 703-722-3993
Dubber, Michael W., P.O. Box 312, Evansville, IN 47702/812-424-9000; FAX: 812-424-6551
Duck Call Specialists, P.O. Box 124, Jerseyville, IL 62052/618-498-4692
Duffy, Charles E., Williams Lane, West Hurley, NY 12491/914-679-2997
Dumoulin, Ernest, Rue Florent Boclinville 8-10, 13-4041 Votten, Belgium/41 27 78 92
Duncan's Gun Works, Inc., 1619 Grand Ave., San Marcos, CA 92069/619-727-0515
Dunham Co., P.O. Box 813, Brattleboro, VT 05301/802-254-2316
Duofold, Inc., 120 W. 45th St., 15th Floor, New York, NY 10036
DuPont (See IMR Powder Co.)
Dutchman's Firearms, Inc., The, 4143 Taylor Blvd., Louisville, KY 40215/502-366-0555
Duxbak, Inc., 903 Woods Rd., Cambridge, MD 21613/301-228-2990, 800-334-1845

Dwyer, Dan, 915 W. Washington St., San Diego, CA 92103/619-296-1501
Dykstra, Doug, 411 N. Darling, Fremont, MI 49412/616-924-3950
Dynalite Products, Inc., 215 S. Washington St., Greenfield, OH 45123/513-981-2124
Dynamit Nobel-RWS, Inc., 81 Ruckman Rd., Closter, NJ 07624/201-767-1995
Dyson & Son Ltd., Peter, 29-31 Church St., Honley, Huddersfield, W. Yorkshire HD7 2AH, England/0484-661062; FAX: 0484 663709

E

E&L Mfg., Inc., 39042 N. School House Rd., Cave Creek, AZ 85331/602-488-2598; FAX: 602-488-0813
E.A.A. Corp., P.O. Box 3498 Bright Station, Hialeah, FL 33013/305-688-4442; FAX: 305-688-5656
Eagle Arms, Inc., 131 E. 22nd Ave., P.O. Box 457, Coal Valley, IL 61240/309-799-5619
Eagle Imports, Inc., 1907 Highway 35, Ocean, NJ 07712/908-531-8375; FAX: 908-531-1520
Eagle International, Inc., 5195 W. 58th Ave., Suite 300, Arvada, CO 80002/303-426-8100
E-A-R, Inc., Div. of Cabot Safety Corp., 5457 W. 79th St., Indianapolis, IN 46268/800-327-3431; FAX: 800-488-8007
East Enterprises, Inc. (See Apache Products)
Eastman Products, R.T., P.O. Box 1531, Jackson, WY 83001
Easy Pull/Outlaw Products, 316 1st St. East, Polson, MT 59860/406-883-6822
Echols & Co., D'Arcy, 164 W. 580 S., Providence, UT 84332/801-753-2367
Eckelman Gunsmithing, Rt. 1, Box 73A, Fort Ripley, MN 56449/218-829-3176
Ed's Gun House, Rt. 1, Box 62, Minnesota City, MN 55959/507-689-2925
Edgecraft Corp., P.O. Box 3000, Avondale, PA 19311/215-268-0500; FAX: 215-268-3545
Edmund Scientific Co., 101 E. Gloucester Pike, Barrington, NJ 08033/609-543-6250
Ednar, Inc., 2-4-8 Kayabacho, Nihonbashi, Chuo-ku, Tokyo, Japan/81(Japan)-3-3667-1651
Eezox, Inc., P.O. Box 772, Waterford, CT 06385-0772/203-447-8282; FAX: 203-447-3484
Efemes Enterprises, P.O. Box 691, Colchester, VT 05446
Eggleston, Jere D., 400 Saluda Ave., Columbia, SC 29205/803-799-3402
Eilan S.A.L., Paseo San Andres N8, Eibar, Spain 20600/(34)43118916; FAX: (34)43 114038
Ek Commando Knife Co., 601 N. Lombardy St., Richmond, VA 23220/804-257-7272
Ekol Leather Care, P.O. Box 2652, West Lafayette, IN 47906/317-463-2250; FAX: 317-463-7004
El Paso Saddlery Co., P.O. Box 27194, El Paso, TX 79926/915-544-2233; FAX: 915-544-2535
Eldorado Cartridge Corp. (See PMC/Eldorado Cartridge Corp.)
Electronic Trigger Systems, Inc., 4124 Thrushwood Lane, Minnetonka, MN 55345/612-935-7829
Eley Ltd., P.O. Box 705, Wilton, Birmingham, B6 7UT, England/21-356-8899; FAX: 21-331-4173
Elite Ammunition, P.O. Box 3251, Oakbrook, IL 60522/708-366-9006
Elk River, Inc., 1225 Paonia St., Colorado Springs, CO 80915/719-574-4407
Elko Arms, Dr. L. Kortz, 28 rue Ecole Moderne, B-7060 Soignies, Belgium/(32)67-33-29-34
Ellett Bros., 267 Columbia Ave., Chapin, SC 29036/803-345-3751
Ellis Sport Shop, E.W., RD 1, Route 9N, P.O. Box 315, Corinth, NY 12822/518-654-6444
Emerging Technologies, Inc., P.O. Box 3548, Little Rock, AR 72203/501-375-2227; FAX: 501-372-1445
EMF Co., Inc., 1900 E. Warner Ave. Suite 1-D, Santa Ana, CA 92705/714-261-6611; FAX: 714-956-0133
Emmons, Bob, 11748 Robson Rd., Grafton, OH 44044/216-458-5890
Empire Cutlery Corp., 12 Kruger Ct., Clifton, NJ 07013/201-472-5155; FAX: 201-779-0759
Engineered Accessories, 1307 W. Wabash Ave., Effingham, IL 62401/217-347-7700; FAX: 217-347-7737
English, Inc., A.G., 708 S. 12th St., Broken Arrow, OK 74012/918-251-3399
Englishtown Sporting Goods Co., Inc., David J. Maxham, 38 Main St., Englishtown, NJ 07726/201-446-7717
Engraving Artistry, 36 Alto Rd., RFD #2, Burlington, CT 06013/203-673-6837
Enguix Import-Export, Alpujarras 58, Alzira, Valencia, Spain 46600/(96) 241 43 95; FAX: (96) 241 43 95
Enhanced Presentations, Inc., 5929 Market St., Wilmington, NC 28405/919-799-1622; FAX: 919-799-5004
Epps "Orillia" Ltd., Ellwood, RR 3, Hwy. 11 North, Orillia, Ont. L3V 6H3, Canada/705-689-5333
Erhardt, Dennis, 3280 Green Meadow Dr., Helena, MT 59601/406-442-4533
Erickson's Mfg., Inc., C.W., Rt. 6, Box 202, Buffalo, MN 55313-9762/612-682-3665; FAX: 612-682-4328
Erma Werke GmbH, Johan Ziegler St., 13/15/FeldigISt., D-8060 Dachau, R.F.A. (U.S. importers—Mandall Shooting Supplies, Inc.; PSI, Inc.)
Essex Arms, P.O. Box 345, Island Pond, VT 05846/802-723-4313
Estate Cartridge, Inc., 2778 FM 830, Willis, TX 77378/409-856-7277; FAX: 409-856-5486
Euroarms of America, Inc., 208 E. Piccadilly St., Winchester, VA 22601/703-662-1863; FAX: 703-662-4464
European American Armory Corp. (See E.A.A. Corp.)
Europtik Ltd., P.O. Box 319, Dunmore, PA 18512/717-347-6049; FAX: 717-969-4330
Eutaw Co., Inc., The, P.O. Box 608, U.S. Hwy. 176 West, Holly Hill, SC 29059/803-496-3341
Evans Engraving, Robert, 332 Vine St., Oregon City, OR 97045/503-656-5693
Eversull Co., Inc., K., 1 Tracemont, Boyce, LA 71409/318-793-8728; FAX: 318-793-5483
Excaliber Wax, Inc., 14344 County Rd. 140, Kenton, OH 43326/419-673-0512
Exe, Inc., 18830 Partridge Circle, Eden Prairie, MN 55346
Executive Protection Institute, North Mountain Pine Training Center, Rt. 2, Box 3645, Berryville, VA 22611/703-955-1128
Eyears Insurance, 4926 Annhurst Rd., Columbus, OH 43228-1341
Eyster Heritage Gunsmiths, Inc., Ken, 6441 Bishop Rd., Centerburg, OH 43011/614-625-6131
Eze-Lap Diamond Prods., P.O. Box 2229, 15164 Weststate St., Westminster, CA 92683/714-847-1555

F

4-D Custom Die Co., 711 N. Sandusky St., P.O. Box 889, Mt. Vernon, OH 43050-0889/614-397-7214; FAX: 614-397-6600
Fabarm S.p.A., Via G. Zola N.33, Brescia, Italy 25136/(030)2004805; FAX: (030)2004816 (U.S. importer—St. Lawrence Sales, Inc.)

Fabian Bros. Sporting Goods, Inc., 1510 Morena Blvd., Suite "G," San Diego, CA 92110/619-275-0816
Fabrica D'Armi Sabatti S.R.L., via Dante 179, 25068 Sarezzo, Brescia, Italy (U.S. importer—E.A.A. Corp.)
Fagan & Co., William, 22952 15 Mile Rd., Mt. Clemens, MI 48043/313-465-4637; FAX: 313-792-6996
Fair Game International, P.O. Box 77234-34053, Houston, TX 77234/713-941-6269
Faith Associates, Inc., 1139 S. Greenville Hwy., Hendersonville, NC 28792/704-692-1916; FAX: 704-697-6827
Fajen, Inc., Reinhart, 1000 Red Bud Dr., P.O. Box 338, Warsaw, MO 65355/816-438-5111; FAX: 816-438-5175
Falling Block Works, Inc., P.O. Box 3087, Fairfax, VA 22038/703-476-0043
Famas (See U.S. importer—Century Intl. Arms, Inc.)
Fanzoj GmbH, Griesgasse 1, 9170 Ferlach, Austria 9170/(43) 04227-2283; FAX: (43) 04227-2867
FAPA Corp., P.O. Box 1439, New London, NH 03257/603-735-5652; FAX: 603-735-5154
Farm Form, Inc., 7730 Chantilly, Galveston, TX 77551/409-744-0762
Farmer-Dressel, Sharon, 209 N. 92nd Ave., Yakima, WA 98908/509-966-9233
Farr Studio, Inc., 1231 Robinhood Rd., Greeneville, TN 37743/615-638-8825
FAS, Via E. Fermi, 8, 20019 Settimo Milanese, Milano, Italy (U.S. importers—Mandall Shooting Supplies, Inc.; Nygord Precision Products)
Faulk's Game Call Co., Inc., 616 18th St., Lake Charles, LA 70601/318-436-9726
Faust, Inc., T.G., 544 Minor St., Reading, PA 19602/215-375-8549; FAX: 215-375-4488
Fausti, Stefano, Via Parte, 33, 25060 Marcheno, Brescia, Italy (U.S. importer—American Arms, Inc.)
Fautheree, Andy, P.O. Box 4607, Pagosa Springs, CO 81157/303-731-5003
Favre, Jacqueline, 3111 S. Valley View Blvd., Suite B-214, Las Vegas, NV 89102/702-876-6278
Feather Flex Decoys, 1655 Swan Lake Rd., Bossier City, LA 71111/318-746-8596; FAX: 318-742-4815
Feather Industries, Inc., 2500 Central Ave. K, Boulder, CO 80301/303-442-7021
Federal Cartridge Co., 900 Ehlen Dr., Anoka, MN 55303/612-422-2840
Federal Champion Target Co., 232 Industrial Parkway, Richmond, IN 47374/800-441-4971; FAX: 317-966-7747
Federal Engineering Corp., 2335 S. Michigan Ave., Chicago, IL 60616/312-842-1063
Federal Ordnance, Inc., 1443 Potrero Ave., S. El Monte, CA 91733/818-350-4161
FEG, Budapest, Soroksariut 158, H-1095 Hungary (See U.S. importer—K.B.I., Inc.)
Feinwerkbau Westinger & Altenburger GmbH & Co. KG (See FWB)
Fellowes, Ted, Beaver Lodge, 9245 16th Ave. SW, Seattle, WA 98106/206-763-1698
Feminine Protection, Inc., 10514 Shady Trail, Dallas, TX 75220/214-351-4500
Fenwal, Inc., Resins Systems Div., 50 Main St., Ashland, MA 01721/508-881-2000 Ext. 2372
FERLIB di Ferraglio Libero & C., Via Costa 46, 25063 Gardone V.T. (Brescia), Italy/30 89 12 586; FAX: 30 89 12 586 (U.S. importer—Moore & Co., Wm. Larkin)
Ferris Firearms, Gregg, 1827 W. Hildebrand, San Antonio, TX 78201/512-734-0304
Fiberpro Rifle Stocks, Div. of Fibers West, 10977 San Diego Mission Rd., San Diego, CA 92108/619-282-4211; FAX: 619-282-0598
Fibron Products, Inc., 170 Florida St., Buffalo, NY 14208/716-886-2378; FAX: 716-886-2394
Finerty, Raymond F., 803 N. Downing St., P.O. Box 914, Piqua, OH 45356/800-543-8952
Fiocchi of America, Inc., Rt. 2, P.O. Box 90-8, Ozark, MO 65721/417-725-4118; FAX: 417-725-1039
Firearm Training Center, The, 9555 Blandville Rd., West Paducah, KY 42086/502-554-5886
Firearms Academy of Seattle, P.O. Box 6691, Lynnwood, WA 98036/206-827-0533
Firearms Co. Ltd./Alpine (See U.S. importer—Mandall Shooting Supplies, Inc.)
Firearms Engraver's Guild of America, 332 Vine St., Oregon City, OR 97045/503-656-5693
First Distributors, Inc., Jack, 44633 Sierra Hwy., Lancaster, CA 93534/805-945-6981; FAX: 805-942-0844
Firstshot, Inc., 4101 Far Green Rd., Harrisburg, PA 17110/717-238-2575
Fish, Marshall F., Rt. 22 N., P.O. Box 2439, Westport, NY 12993/518-962-4897
Fish-N-Hunt, Inc., 5651 Beechnut St., Houston, TX 77096/713-777-3285; FAX: 713-777-9884
Fisher Custom Firearms, 2199 S. Kittredge Way, Aurora, CO 80013/303-755-3710
Fisher, Jerry, P.O. Box 652, Dubois, WY 82513/307-455-2722
Fitz Pistol Grip Co., P.O. Box 610, Douglas City, CA 96024/916-778-3136
Flaig's, 2220 Evergreen Rd., Millvale, PA 15209/412-821-1717
Flambeau Products Corp., P.O. Box 97, Middlefield, OH 44062/216-632-1631; FAX: 216-632-1581
Flannery Engraving Co., Jeff W., 11034 Riddles Run Rd., Union, KY 41091/606-384-3127 (color catalog $5)
Flashette Co., 4725 S. Kolin Ave., Chicago, IL 60632/312-927-1302
Flayderman & Co., N., P.O. Box 2446, Ft. Lauderdale, FL 33303/305-761-8855
Fleming Firearms, 7720 E. 126 St. N., Collinsville, OK 74021/918-371-3624
Flents Products Co., Inc., P.O. Box 2109, Norwalk, CT 06852/203-866-2581; FAX: 203-854-9322
Flex Gun Rods Co., Inc., P.O. Box 202, Dearborn, MI 48121/313-271-2595
Flint Creek Arms Co., P.O. Box 205, 136 Spring St., Philipsburg, MT 59858/406-859-3877
Flintlock Muzzle Loading Gun Shop, The, 1238 "G" S. Beach Blvd., Anaheim, CA 92804/714-821-6655
Flintlocks, Etc., 38 Gamwell Ave., Pittsfield, MA 01201
Flitz International Ltd., 821 Mohr Ave., Waterford, WI 53185/414-534-5898; FAX: 414-534-2991
Floatstone Mfg. Co., 106 Powder Mill Rd., P.O. Box 765, Canton, CT 06019/203 -693-1977
Flores Publications, J., P.O. Box 163001, Miami, FL 33116/305-559-4652
Flouramics, Inc., 103 Pleasant Ave., Upper Saddle River, NJ 07458/201-825-8110
Flow-Rite of Tennessee, Inc., 107 Allen St., Bruceton, TN 38317/901-586-2271; FAX: 901-586-2300
Flynn's Custom Guns, P.O. Box 7461, Alexandria, LA 71306/318-455-7130
FN Herstal, Voie de Liege 33, Herstal 4040, Belgium/(32)41/40.82.83; FAX: (32)40.86.79
Fobus International Ltd., Kfar Hess, Israel 40692/FAX: 972-52-911716
Fogle, James W., RR 2, P.O. Box 258, Herrin, IL 62948/618-988-1795
Folks, Donald E., 205 W. Lincoln St., Pontiac, IL 61764/815-844-7901
Foothills Video Productions, Inc., P.O. Box 651, Spartanburg, SC 29304/803-573-7023,800-782-5358
Force 10, Inc., 50 Revere St. #A, Boston, MA 02114-4342

Ford Ltd., J. and J., 16 Summer St., Leighton Buzzard, Bedfordshire, LU7 8HT England/0525-381638
Foredom Electric Co., Rt. 6, 16 Stony Hill Rd., Bethel, CT 06801/203-792-8622
Forgett, Valmore J., Jr., 689 Bergen Blvd., Ridgefield, NJ 07657/201-945-2500
Forrest Tool Company, P.O. Box 768, 44380 Gordon Lane, Mendocino, CA 95460/707-937-2141; FAX: 717-937-1817
Forrest, Inc., Tom, P.O. Box 326, Lakeside, CA 92040/619-561-5800; FAX: 619-561-0227
Forster Products, 82 E. Lanark Ave., Lanark, IL 61046/815-493-6360; FAX: 815-493-2371
Forster, Larry L., P.O. Box 212, 220 First St. NE, Gwinner, ND 58040-0212/701-678-2475
Fort Knox Security Products, 1051 N. Industrial Park Rd., Orem, UT 84057/801-224-7233
Forthofer's Gunsmithing & Knifemaking, 711 Spokane Ave., Whitefish, MT 59937/406-862-2674
Fortress Publications, Inc., P.O. Box 9241, Stoney Creek, Ont. L8G 3X9, Canada/416-662-3505
Fortune Products, Inc., Box 1308, Friendswood, TX 77546/713-996-0729; FAX: 713-996-1034
Forty-Five Ranch, Box 1080, Miami, OK 74355-1080/918-542-5875
Forty-Niner Trading Co., P.O. Box 792, Manteca, CA 95336/209-823-7263
Fountain Products, 492 Prospect Ave., West Springfield, MA 01089/413-781-4651; FAX: 413-733-8217
Fowler Bullets, 4003 Linwood Rd., Gastonia, NC 28052/704-867-3259
Fox River Mills, Inc., P.O. Box 298, 227 Poplar St., Osage, IA 50461/515-732-3798; FAx: 515-732-5128
Francesca Stabilizer's, Inc., 3115 Old Ranch Rd., San Antonio, TX 78217/512-826-2584
Franchi S.p.A., Luigi, Via del Serpente, 12, 25020 Fornaci, Italy (U.S. importer—American Arms, Inc.)
Francolini, Leonard, 106 Powder Mill Rd., P.O. Box 765, Canton, CT 06019/203-693-1977
Francotte & Cie S.A., Auguste, rue du Trois Juin 109, 4400 Herstal-Liege, Belgium/41-48.13.18 (U.S. importer—Armes de Chasse)
Frank Custom Gun Service, Ron, 7131 Richland Rd., Ft. Worth, TX 76118/817-284-4426
Frank Knives, Box 984, Whitefish, MT 59937/406-862-2681; FAX: 906-862-2681
Frankonia Jagd, Hofmann & Co., P.O. Box 6780, D-8700 Wurzburg 1, Germany/09302-200; FAX: 09302-20200
Frazier Brothers Enterprises, 1118 N. Main St., Franklin, IN 46131/317-736-4000; FAX: 317-736-4000
Fredrick Gun Shop, 10 Elson Dr., Riverside, RI 02915/401-433-2805
Freedom Arms, Inc., P.O. Box 1776, Freedom, WY 83120/307-883-2468
Freeland's Scope Stands, Inc., 3737 14th Ave., Rock Island, IL 61201/309-788-7449
Freeman Animal Targets, 8237 Indy Lane, Indianapolis, IN 46214/317-271-5314; FAX: 317-271-9106
Fremont Tool Works, 1214 Prairie, Ford, KS 67842/316-369-2338
Frielich Police Equipment, 211 East 21st St., New York, NY 10010/212-254-3045
Frontier Arms Co., Inc., 401 W. Rio Santa Cruz, Green Valley, AZ 85614-3932
Frontier Cartridge Division (See Hornady Mfg. Co.)
Frontier Products Co., 164 E. Longview Ave., Columbus, OH 43202/614-262-9357
Frontier, 2910 San Bernardo, Laredo, TX 78040/512-723-5409
Frost Cutlery Co., P.O. Box 21353, Chattanooga, TN 37421/615-894-6079; FAX: 615-894-9576
FTI, Inc., 1812 Margaret Ave., Annapolis, MD 21401/410-268-6451; FAX: 410-268-8377
Fujinon, Inc., 10 High Point Dr., Wayne, NJ 07470/201-633-5600
Fullmer, Geo. M., 2499 Mavis St., Oakland, CA 94601/510-533-4193
Fulmer's Antique Firearms, Chet, P.O. Box 792, Rt. 2 Buffalo Lake, Detroit Lakes, MN 56501/218-847-7712
Furr Arms, 91 N. 970 W., Orem, UT 84057/801-226-3877; FAX: 801-226-0085
FWB, Neckarstrabe 43, 7238 Oberndorf a. N., Germany/07423-814-0; FAX: 07423-814-89 (U.S. importer—Beeman Precision Arms, Inc.)

G

G96 Products Co., Inc., 237 River St., Paterson, NJ 07524/201-684-4050; FAX: 201-684-3848
G&H Decoys, Inc., P.O. Box 1208, Hwy. 75 North, Henryetta, OK 74437/918-652-3314
Galati International, P.O. Box 326, Catawissa, MO 63015/314-257-4837; FAX: 314-257-2268
Galaxy Imports Ltd., Inc., P.O. Box 3361, Victoria, TX 77903/512-573-4867; FAX: 512-576-9622
GALCO International Ltd., 2019 W. Quail Ave., Phoenix, AZ 85027/602-258-8295; FAX: 602-582-6854
Gamba S.p.A., Renato, P.O. Box 48, Via Artigiani n.89, I-25063 Gardone V.T. (Brescia), Italy (U.S. importer—Gamba U.S.A.)
Gamba U.S.A., 925 Wilshire Blvd., Santa Monica, CA 90401/310-917-2255; FAX: 310-917-2253
Game Haven Gunstocks, 13750 Shire Rd., Wolverine, MI 49799/616-525-8257
Game Winner, Inc., 2625 Cumberland Parkway, Suite 220, Atlanta, GA 30339/404-434-9210; FAX: 404-434-9215
Gammog, Gregory B.Gally, 16009 Kenny Rd., Laurel, MD 20707/301-725-3838
Gamo (See U.S. importers—Daisy Mfg. Co.; Dynamit Nobel-RWS, Inc.)
Gander Mountain, Inc., P.O. Box 128, Hwy. "W," Wilmot, WI 53192/414-862-2331, Ext. 6425
Ganton Manufacturing Ltd., Depot Lane, Seamer Rd., Scarborough, North Yorkshire, Y012 4EB England/(0723)371910; FAX: (0723)501671
Garbi, Armas Urki, #12-14, 20.600 Eibar (Guipuzcoa) Spain/43-11 38 73 (U.S. importer—Moore & Co., Wm. Larkin)
Garcia National Gun Traders, Inc., 225 SW 22nd Ave., Miami, FL 33135/305-642-2355
Garrett Accur-Lt. D.F.S. Co., P.O. Box 8675, 1413B East Olive Ct., Ft. Collins, CO 80524/303-224-3067
Garrett Cartridges, Inc., P.O. Box 178, Chehalis, WA 98532/206-736-0702
Garthwaite, Jim, Rt. 2, Box 310, Watsontown, PA 17777/717-538-1566
Gator Guns & Repair, 6255 Spur Hwy., Kenai, AK 99611/907-283-7947
Gaucher Armes, S.A., 46, rue Desjoyaux, 42000 Saint-Etienne, France/77 33 38 92 (U.S. importer—Mandall Shooting Supplies, Inc.)
GDL Enterprises, 409 Le Gardeur, Slidell, LA 70460/504-649-0693
Gene's Custom Guns, 3890 Hill Ave., White Bear Lake, MN 55110/612-429-5105
Genecco Gun Works, K., 10512 Lower Sacramento Rd., Stockton, CA 95210/209-951-0706
Gentry Custom Gunmaker, David, 314 N. Hoffman, Belgrade, MT 59714/406-388-4867
George, Tim and Christy, Rt. 1, P.O. Box 45, Evington, VA 24550/804-821-8117

Gerber Legendary Blades, 14200 SW 72nd Ave., Portland, OR 97223/503-639-6161; FAX: 503-684-7008
Getz Barrel Co., P.O. Box 88, Beavertown, PA 17813/717-658-7263
GFR Corp., P.O. Box 430, Andover, NH 03216/603-735-5300
G.H. Enterprises Ltd., Bag 10, Okotoks, Alberta T0L 1T0 Canada/403-938-6070
Gibbs Rifle Company, Inc., Cannon Hill Industrial Park, Rt. 2, Box 214 Hoffman Rd., Martinsburg, WV 25401/304-274-0458; FAX: 304-274-0078
Gilbert Equipment Co., Inc., 960 Downtowner Rd., Mobile, AL 36609/205-344-3322
Gillmann, Edwin, 33 Valley View Dr., Hanover, PA 17331/717-632-1662
Gilman-Mayfield, 1552 N. 1st, Fresno, CA 93703/209-237-2500
Giron, Robert E., 1328 Pocono St., Pittsburgh, PA 15218/412-731-6041
Glacier Glove, 4890 Aircenter Circle #206, Reno, NV 89502/702-825-8225; FAX: 702-825-6544
Glaser Safety Slug, Inc., P.O. Box 8223, Foster City, CA 94404/415-345-7677; FAX:415-345-0327
Glass, Herb, P.O. Box 25, Bullville, NY 10915/914-361-3021
Glimm, Jerome C., 19 S. Maryland, Conrad, MT 59425/406-278-3574
Global Industries, 1501 E. Chapman Ave., #306, Fullerton, CA 92631/714-879-8922
Glock GmbH, P.O. Box 50, A-2232 Deutsch Wagram, Austria (U.S. importer—Glock, Inc.)
Glock, Inc., 6000 Highlands Parkway, Smyrna, GA 30082/404-432-1202
GML Products, Inc., 1634-A Montgomery Hwy., Suite 196, Birmingham, AL 35216/205-979-4867
Goens, Dale W., P.O. Box 224, Cedar Crest, NM 87008/505-281-5419
Goergen's Gun Shop, Inc., Rt. 2, Box 182BB, Austin, MN 55912/507-433-9280
GOEX, Inc., 1002 Springbrook Ave., Moosic, PA 18507/717-457-6724; FAX: 717-457-1130
Golden Age Arms Co., 115 E. High St., Ashley, OH 43003/614-747-2488
Golden Powder International Sales, Inc., 8300 Douglas Ave., Suite 729, Dallas, TX 75225/214-373-3350
Gonic Arms, Inc., 134 Flagg Rd., Gonic, NH 03867/603-332-8456
Gonzalez Guns, Ramon B., P.O. Box 370, Monticello, NY 12701/914-794-4515
Goode, A.R., 4125 NE 28th Terr., Ocala, FL 32670/904-622-9575
Goodling's Gunsmithing, R.D. #1, Box 1097, Spring Grove, PA 17362/717-225-3350
Goodwin, Fred, Silver Ridge Gun Shop, Sherman Mills, ME 04776/207-365-4451
Gordie's Gun Shop, 1401 Fulton St., Streator, IL 61364/815-672-7202
Goudy Classic Stocks, Gary, 263 Hedge Rd., Menlo Park, CA 94025-1711/415-322-1338
Gould & Goodrich, P.O. Box 1479, Lillington, NC 27546/919-893-2071; FAX: 919-893-4742
Gournet, Geoffroy, 820 Paxinosa Ave., Easton, PA 18042/215-559-0710
Gozon Corporation, P.O. Box 6278, Folsom, CA 95630/FAX: 916-983-9500
Grace & Co.-Conn., W.R. (See Airmold/W.R. Grace & Co.-Conn.)
Grace Metal Products, Inc., P.O. Box 67, Elk Rapids, MI 49629/616-264-8133
Grace, Charles E., 10144 Elk Lake Rd., Williamsburg, MI 49690/616-264-9483
"Gramps" Antique Cartridges, Ellwood Epps, Box 341, Washago, Ont. L0K 2B0 Canada/705-689-5348
Granger, Georges, 66 cours Fauriel, 42100 Saint Etienne, France/(77)25 14 73
Grant, Howard V., Hiawatha 15, Woodruff, WI 54568/715-356-7146
Graves Co., 1800 Andrews Av., Pompano Beach, FL 33069/800-327-9103; FAX: 305-960-0301
Graybill's Gun Shop, 1035 Ironville Pike, Columbia, PA 17512/717-684-6220
Great 870 Company, The, William E. Harper, P.O. Box 6309, El Monte, CA 91734
Great Lakes Airguns, 6175 S. Park Ave., Hamburg, NY 14075/716-648-6666
Green Bay Bullets, P.O. Box 10446, 1860 Burns Ave., Green Bay, WI 54303/414-499-1393
Green Head Game Call Co., RR 1, Box 33, Lacon, IL 61540/309-246-2155
Green Mountain Rifle Barrel Co., Inc., RFD #2, Box 8, Center Conway, NH 03813/603-356-2047; FAX: 603-356-2048
Green, Arthur S., 485 S. Robertson Blvd., Suite 5, Beverly Hills, CA 90211/310-274-1283
Green, Roger M., P.O. Box 984, 435 E. Birch, Glenrock, WY 82637/307-436-9804
Greene's Machine Carving, 17200 W. 57th Ave., Golden, CO 80403/303-279-2383
Greenwald, Leon E. "Bud", 2553 S. Quitman St., Denver, CO 80219/303-935-3850
Greenwood & Gryphon Ltd., 123 Massasolt Ave., Barrington, RI 02806/401-245-4461
Greg Gunsmithing Repair, 3732 26th Ave. North, Robbinsdale, MN 55422/612-529-8103
Greider Precision, 431 Santa Marina Ct., Escondido, CA 92029/619-480-8892
Gremmel Enterprises, 271 Sterling Dr., Eugene, OR 97404/503-688-3319
Grendel, Inc., P.O. Box 560909, Rockledge, FL 32956-0909
Griffin & Howe, Inc., 33 Claremont Rd., Bernardsville, NJ 07924/908-766-2287; FAX: 908-766-1068
Griffin & Howe, Inc., 36 W. 44th St., Suite 1011, New York, NY 10036/212-921-0980
Griffin's Guns & Antiques, RR 4, Peterboro, Ont., Canada K9J 6X5/705-745-7022
Grifon, Inc., 58 Guinam St., Waltham, MS 02154
Griggs Products, P.O. Box 789, 270 S. Main St., Suite #103, Bountiful, UT 84010/801-295-9696
Grizzly Bullets, 2137 Hwy. 200, Trout Creek, MT 59874/406-847-2627
GRS Corp., Glendo, P.O. Box 1153, 900 Overlander St., Emporia, KS 66801/316-343-1084
Grulla Armes, Apartado 453, Avda Otaloa, 12, Eiber, Spain (U.S. importer—American Arms, Inc.)
GSI, Inc., 108 Morrow Ave., P.O. Box 129, Trussville, AL 35173/205-655-8299
GTS Enterprises, Inc., Dynaray Marketing Div., 50 W. Hillcrest Dr., Suite 215, Thousand Oaks, CA 91360/805-373-0921
G.U., Inc., 4325 S. 120th St., P.O. Box 37669, Omaha, NE 68137/402-330-4492
Guardian Group International, 21 Warren St., Suite 3E, New York, NY 10007/212-619-3838
Guardsman Products, 411 N. Darling, Fremont, MI 49412/616-924-3950
Gun City, 212 W. Main Ave., Bismarck, ND 58501/701-223-2304
Gun Club Sportswear, P.O. Box 477, Des Moines, IA 50302
Gun Doctor, The, 435 East Maple, Roselle, IL 60172/708-894-0668
Gun Doctor, The, P.O. Box 39242, Downey, CA 90242
Gun Hunter Books, Div. of Gun Hunter Trading Co., 5075 Heisig St., Beaumont, TX 77705/409-835-3006
Gun Leather Limited, 116 Lipscomb, Ft. Worth, TX 76104/817-334-0225, 800-247-0609
Gun Parts Corporation, The, Williams Lane, West Hurley, NY 12491/914-679-2417; FAX: 914-679-5849
Gun Room Press, The, 127 Raritan Ave., Highland Park, NJ 08904/201-545-4344
Gun Room, The, 1121 Burlington, Muncie, IN 47302/317-282-9073; FAX: 317-282-9073
Gun Shop, The, 5550 S. 900 East, Salt Lake City, UT 84117/801-263-3633
Gun South, Inc. (See GSI, Inc.)
Gun Vault, Inc., 200 Larkin Dr., Unit E, Wheeling, IL 60090/708-215-6606; FAX: 708-215-7550
Gun Works, The, 236 Main St., Springfield, OR 97477/503-741-4118

Gun-Alert/Master Products, Inc., 1010 N. Mallay Ave., San Fernando, CA 91340/818-365-0864; FAX: 818-365-1308
Gun-Ho Sports Cases, 110 E. 10th St., St. Paul, MN 55101/612-224-9491
Gun-Tec, P.O. Box 8125, W. Palm Beach, FL 33407
Guncraft Books, 10737 Dutchtown Rd., Knoxville, TN 37932/615-966-4501
Guncraft Sports, Inc. (See Guncraft Books)
Guncraft, Inc., 117 W. Pipeline, Hurst, TX 76053/817-282-1464
Gunfitters, The, P.O. 426, Cambridge, WI 53523-0426/608-764-8128
Gunline Tools, 2970 Saturn St. "F", Brea, CA 92621/714-528-5252; FAX: 714-572-4128
Gunnerman Books, P.O. Box 214292, Auburn Hills, MI 48321/313-879-2779
GUNS Magazine, 591 Camino de la Reina, Suite 200, San Diego, CA 92108/619-297-5350; FAX: 619-297-5353
Guns Unlimited, Inc. (See G.U., Inc.)
Guns, 81 E. Streetsboro St., Hudson, OH 44236/216-650-4563
Gunsite Gunsmithy, P.O. Box 451, Paulden, AZ 86334/602-636-4565; FAX: 602-636-1236
Gunsmithing Ltd., 57 Unquowa Rd., Fairfield, CT 06430/203-254-0436
Gurney Engraving Method Ltd., Box 13, Sooke, BC V0S 1N0 Canada/604-642-5282
Gusdorf Corp., 11440 Lackland Rd., St. Louis, MO 63146/314-567-5249
Gustav, Carl (See U.S. importer—PSI, Inc.)
Gusty Winds Corp., 2950 Bear St., Suite 120, Costa Mesa, CA 92626/714-536-3587
Gutmann Cutlery Co., Inc., 120 S. Columbus Ave., Mt. Vernon, NY 10553/914-699-4044
Gutridge, Inc., 2143 Gettler St., Dyer, IN 46311/219-865-8617
Gwinnell, Bryson J., P.O. Box 248C, Maple Hill Rd., Rochester, VT 05767/802-767-3664
GZ Paintball Sports Products, P.O. Box 430, Andover, NH 03216/603-735-5300; FAX: 603-735-5154

H

H&B Forge Co., Rt. 2 Geisinger Rd., Shiloh, OH 44878/419-895-1856
H&L Gun Works, 817 N. Highway 90 #1109, Sierra Vista, AZ 85635/602-452-0702
H&P Publishing, 7174 Hoffman Rd., San Angelo, TX 76905/915-655-5953
H&R 1871, Inc., 60 Industrial Rowe, Gardner, MA 01440/508-632-9393; FAX: 508-632-2300
H&S Liner Service, 515 E. 8th, Odessa, TX 79761/915-332-1021
Haenel (See U.S. importer—GSI, Inc.)
Hafner Enterprises, Inc., Rt. 1, P.O. Box 248A, Lake City, FL 32055/904-755-6481
Hagn Rifles & Actions, Martin, P.O. Box 444, Cranbrook, B.C. VIC 4H9, Canada/604-489-4861
Hakko Co. Ltd., 5F Daini-Tsunemi Bldg., 1-13-12, Narimasu, Itabashiku Tokyo 175/(03)5997-7870-2
Hale, Peter, 800 E. Canyon Rd., Spanish Fork, UT 84660/801-798-8215
Half Moon Rifle Shop, 490 Halfmoon Rd., Columbia Falls, MT 59912/406-892-4409
Hall Manufacturing, 1801 Yellow Leaf Rd., Clanton, AL 35045/205-755-4094
Hall Plastics, Inc., John, P.O. Box 1526, Alvin, TX 77512/713-489-9709
Hallowell & Co., 340 W. Putnam Ave., Greenwich, CT 06830/203-869-2190; FAX: 203-869-0692
Hally Caller, 443 Wells Rd., Doylestown, PA 18901/215-345-6354
Halstead, Rick, P.O. Box 63, Grinnell, IA 50112/515-236-5904
Hamilton, Keith, P.O. Box 871, Gridley, CA 95948/916-846-2316
Hammans, Charles E., P.O. Box 788, 2022 McCracken, Stuttgart, AR 72106/501-673-1388
Hammerli USA, 19296 Oak Grove Circle, Groveland, CA 95321/209-962-5311; FAX: 209-962-5311
Hammerli, CH-5600 Lenzbourg, Switzerland (U.S. importers—Beeman Precision Arms, Inc.; Hammerli USA; Mandall Shooting Supplies, Inc.)
Hammond Custom Guns Ltd., Guy, 619 S. Pandora, Gilbert, AZ 85234/602-892-3437
Hand Engravers Supply Co., 601 Springfield Dr., Albany, GA 31707/912-432-9683
Handgun Press, P.O. Box 406, Glenview, IL 60025/708-657-6500
HandiCrafts Unltd. (See Clements' Custom Leathercraft, Chas)
Hank's Gun Shop, Box 370, 50 West 100 South, Monroe, UT 84754/801-527-4456
Hanned Line, The, P.O. Box 161565, Cupertino, CA 95016-1565
Hanned Precision (See Hanned Line, The)
Hansen & Co., 244-246 Old Post Rd., Southport, CT 06490/203-789-7337
Hansen Cartridge Co., 244 Old Post Rd., Southport, CT 06490/203-259-6222
Hanson's Gun Center, Dick, 521 S. Circle Dr., Colorado Springs, CO 80910/719-634-4220
Hanus, Bill, P.O. Box 80, Pinos Altos, NM 88053/505-536-9383
Hanusin, John, 3306 Commercial, Northbrook, IL 60062/708-564-2706
Hardin Specialty Dist., P.O. Box 338, Radcliff, KY 40159-0338/502-351-6649
Hardison, Charles, P.O. Box 356, 200 W. Baseline Rd., Lafayette, CO 80026-0356/303-666-5171
Harper's Custom Stocks, 928 Lombrano St., San Antonio, TX 78207/512-732-5780
Harper, William E. (See Great 870 Co., The)
Harrington & Richardson (See H&R 1871, Inc.)
Harrington Cutlery, Inc., Russell, Subs. of Hyde Mfg. Co., 44 River St., Southbridge, MA 01550/617-765-0201
Harris Engineering, Inc., Barlow, KY 42024/502-334-3633; FAX: 502-334-3000
Harris Enterprises, P.O. Box 105, Bly, OR 97622/503-353-2625
Harris Hand Engraving, Paul A., 10630 Janet Lee, San Antonio, TX 78230/512-391-5121
Harrison Bullet Works, 6437 E. Hobart, Mesa, AZ 85205/602-985-7844
Harrison-Hurtz Enterprises, Inc., P.O. Box 268, Wymore, NE 68466/402-645-3378; FAX: 402-645-3606
Hart & Son, Inc., Robert W., 401 Montgomery St., Nescopeck, PA 18635/717-752-3655; FAX: 717-752-1088
Hart Rifle Barrels, Inc., RD 2, Apulia Rd., P.O. Box 182, Lafayette, NY 13084/315-677-9841
Hartmann & Weiss GmbH, Rahlstedter Bahnhofstr. 47, 2000 Hamburg 73, Germany/(40) 677 55 85; FAX: (40) 677 55 92
Harwood, Jack O., 1191 S. Pendlebury Lane, Blackfoot, ID 83221/208-785-5368
Hastings Barrels, 320 Court St., Clay Center, KS 67432/913-632-3169; FAX: 913-632-6554
Hatfield International, Inc., 224 N. 4th St., St. Joseph, MO 64501/816-279-8688; FAX: 816-279-2716
Hawk Co., P.O. Box 1843, Glenrock, WY 82637
Hawken Shop, The (See Dayton Traister)
Hawkeye West, 3442 E. Kleindale Rd., Tucson, AZ 85716/602-326-7951
Haydel's Game Calls, Inc., 5018 Hazel Jones Rd., Bossier City, LA 71111/318-746-3586; FAX: 318-746-3711
Heatbath Corp., P.O. Box 2978, Springfield, MA 01101/413-543-3381
Hebard Guns, Gil, 125-129 Public Square, Knoxville, IL 61448
Hecht, Hubert J., Waffen-Hecht, P.O. Box 2635, Fair Oaks, CA 95628/916-966-1020

Heckler & Koch GmbH, Postfach 1329, D-7238 Oberndorf, Neckar, Germany (U.S. importer—Heckler & Koch, Inc.)
Heckler & Koch, Inc., 21480 Pacific Blvd., Sterling, VA 22170/703-450-1900; FAX: 703-450-8160
Hege Jagd-u. Sporthandels, GmbH, P.O. Box 101461, W-7770 Ueberling a. Bodensee, Germany
Heilmann, Stephen, P.O. Box 657, Grass Valley, CA 95945/916-272-8758
Heinie Specialty Products, 323 W. Franklin St., Havana, IL 62644/309-543-4535; FAX: 309-543-2521
Helwan (See U.S. importer—Interarms)
Henckels Zwillingswerk, Inc., J.A., 9 Skyline Dr., Hawthorne, NY 10532/914-592-7370
Hendricks, Frank E., Master Engravers, Inc., HC03, Box 434, Dripping Springs, TX 78620/512-858-7828
Henigson & Associates, Steve, 2049 Kerwood Ave., Los Angeles, CA 90025/213-305-8288
Henriksen Tool Co., Inc., 8515 Wagner Creek Rd., Talent, OR 97540/503-535-2309
Hensley & Gibbs, P.O. Box 10, Murphy, OR 97533/503-862-2341
Hensley, Darwin, P.O. Box 179, Brightwood, OR 97011/503-622-5411
Heppler's Machining, 2238 Calle Del Mundo, Santa Clara, CA 95054/408-748-9166; FAX: 408-988-7711
Heppler, Keith M., Keith's Custom Gunstocks, 540 Banyan Circle, Walnut Creek, CA 94598/510-934-3509
Hercules, Inc., 1313 N. Market St., Wilmington, DE 19894/302-594-5000
Hermann Leather Co., H.J., Rt. 1, P.O. Box 525, Skiatook, OK 74070/918-396-1226
Hermanos S.A., Zabala, P.O. Box 97, Eibar, Spain 20600 (U.S. importer—American Arms, Inc.)
Herrett's Stocks, Inc., P.O. Box 741, Twin Falls, ID 83303/208-733-1498
Hertel & Reuss, Werk für Optik und Feinmechanik GmbH, Quellhofstrabe 67, 3500 Kassel, Fed. Rep. of Germany/0561-83006; FAX: 0561-893308
Herter's Manufacturing, Inc., 111 E. Burnett St., P.O. Box 518, Beaver Dam, WI 53916/800-654-3825; FAX: 414-887-1608
Hesco-Meprolight, 2821 Greenville Rd., LaGrange, GA 30240/404-884-7967; FAX: 404-882-4683
Heydenberk, Warren R., 1059 W. Sawmill Rd., Quakertown, PA 18951/215-538-2682
Heym GmbH & Co., Friedrich Wilh., Wehrtechnik, Coburger Str. 8, D-8732 Munn, R.F.A. (U.S. importer—Heckler & Koch, Inc.)
Hi-West Sales, P.O. Box 2016, Cut Bank, MT 59427/406-873-5634
Hidalgo, Tony, 12701 SW 9th Pl., Davie, FL 33325/305-476-7645
High Bridge Arms, Inc., 3185 Mission St., San Francisco, CA 94110/415-282-8358
High North Products, Inc., P.O. Box 2, Antigo, WI 54409
Highline Machine Co., 654 Lela Place, Grand Junction, CO 81504/303-434-4971
Hill Speed Leather, Ernie, 4507 N. 195th Ave., Litchfield Park, AZ 85340/602-853-9222; FAX: 602-853-9235
Hillmer Custom Gunstocks, Paul D., 7251 Hudson Heights, Hudson, IA 50643/319-988-3941
Hindman, Ace, 1880 1/2 Upper Turtle Creek Rd., Kerrville, TX 78028/512-257-4290
Hinman Outfitters, Bob, 1217 W. Glen, Peoria, IL 61614/309-691-8132
Hiptmayer, Heidemarie, RR 112 #750, P.O. Box 136, Eastman, Quebec J0E 1P0, Canada/514-297-2492
Hiptmayer, Klaus, RR 112 #750, P.O. Box 136, Eastman, Quebec J0E 1P0, Canada/514-297-2492
Hirtenberger Patronen-, Zundhutchen- & Metallwarenfabrik, A.G., Leobersdorfer Str. 33, A2552 Hirtenberg, Austria
Hiti-Schuch, Atelier Wilma, A-8863 Predlitz, Pirming Y1 Austria/0353418278
H.K.S. Products, 7841 Foundation Dr., Florence, KY 41042/606-342-7841
Hoag, James W., 8523 Canoga Ave., Suite C, Canoga Park, CA 91304/818-998-1510
Hobaugh, Wm. H. (See Rifle Shop, The)
Hobbie Gunsmithing, Duane A., 2412 Pattie Ave., Wichita, KS 67216/316-264-8266
Hodgdon Powder Co., Inc., 6231 Robinson, Shawnee Mission, KS 66202/913-362-9455; FAX: 913-362-1307
Hodgman, Inc., 1750 Orchard Rd., Montgomery, IL 60538/708-897-7555; FAX: 708-897-7558
Hodgson, Richard, 9081 Tahoe Lane, Boulder, CO 80301
Hoenig & Rodman, 6521 Morton Dr., Boise, ID 83704/208-375-1116
Hofer Jagdwaffen, P., Buchsenmachermeister, F.-Lange Strabe 13, A-9170 Ferlach, Austria/04227-3683
Hogue Grips, P.O. Box 2038, Atascadero, CA 93423/FAX: 805-466-7329
Holden Company, J.B., P.O. Box 320, Plymouth, MI 48170/313-455-4850; FAX: 313-455-4212
Holland, Dick, 422 NE 6th St., Newport, OR 97365/503-265-7556
Hollis Gun Shop, 917 Rex St., Carlsbad, NM 88220/505-835-3782
Hollywood Engineering, 10642 Arminta St., Sun Valley, CA 91352/818-842-8376
Holster Outpost, 950 Harry St., El Cajon, CA 92020/619-588-1222
Holster Shop, The, 720 N. Flagler Dr., Ft. Lauderdale, FL 33304/305-463-7910; FAX: 305-761-1483
HomeCraft, P.O. Box 974, Tualatin, OR 97062/503-692-3732; FAX: 503-692-0382
Hoppe's Div., Penguin Industries, Inc., Airport Industrial Mall, Coatesville, PA 19320/251-384-6000
Horizons Unlimited, 8351 Roswell Rd., Suite 168, Atlanta, GA 30350/404-683-1269; FAX: 404-993-9770
Hornady Mfg. Co., P.O. Box 1848, Grand Island, NE 68801/308-382-1390
Horseshoe Leather Products, Andy Arratoonian, The Cottage Sharow, Ripon HG4 5BP England/0765-605858
Horst, Alan K., 3221 2nd Ave. N., Great Falls, MT 59401/406-545-1831
Horton Dist. Co., Inc., Lew, 15 Walkup Dr., Westboro, MA 01581/508-872-9242
House of Muskets, Inc., The, P.O. Box 4640, Pagosa Springs, CO 81157/303-731-2295
Houtz & Barwick, P.O. Box 435, W. Church St., Elizabeth City, NC 27909/919-335-4191; FAX: 919-335-1152
Howa Machinery Ltd., Shinkawa-Chonear, Nagoya 452, Japan (U.S. importer—Interarms)
Hoyt Holster Co., Inc., P.O. Box 69, Coupeville, WA 98239-0069/206-678-6640; FAX: 206-678-6549
H-S Precision, Inc., 1301 Turbine Dr., Rapid City, SD 55701/605-341-3006; FAX: 605-342-8964
Hubertus Schneidwarenfabrik, P.O. Box 180 106, Solingen, Germany, D-W-5650/01149-212-59-19-94; FAX: 01149-212-59-19-92
Huebner, Corey O., P.O. Box 2074, Missoula, MT 59804/406-721-9647
Huey Gun Cases, Marvin, P.O. Box 22456, Kansas City, MO 64113/816-444-1637
Hugger Hooks Co., 3900 Easley Way, Golden, CO 80403/303-279-0600

Hughes, Steven Dodd, P.O. Box 11455, Eugene, OR 97440/503-485-8869
Hume, Don, P.O. Box 351, Miami, OK 74355/918-542-6604
Hunkeler, A. (See Buckskin Machine Works)
Hunter Co., Inc., 3300 W. 71st Ave., Westminster, CO 80030/303-427-4626
Hunter's Specialties, Inc., 5285 Rockwell Dr. NE, Cedar Rapids, IA 52402/319-395-0321
Hunterjohn, P.O. Box 477, St. Louis, MO 63166/314-531-7250
Hunting Classics Ltd., P.O. Box 2089, Gastonia, NC 28053/704-867-1307; FAX: 704-867-0491
Huntington Die Specialties, Tom Miller, 601 Oro Dam Blvd., Oroville, CA 95965/916-534-1210; FAX: 916-534-1212
Hutton Rifle Ranch, P.O. Box 45236, Boise, ID 83711/208-345-8781
Hy-Score Arms Co. Ltd., 40 Stonar Industrial Estate, Sandwich, Kent CT13 9LN, England/0304-61.12.21
Hydrosorbent Products, P.O. Box 437, Ashley Falls, MA 01222/413-229-2967; FAX: 413-229-8743
Hyper-Single, Inc., 520 E. Beaver, Jenks, OK 74037/918-299-2391

I

IAI, 6226 Santos Diaz St., Irwindale, CA 91702/818-334-1200
Ibberson (Sheffield) Ltd., George, 25-31 Allen St., Sheffield, S3 7AW England/0742-766123; FAX: 0742-738465
ICI-America, P.O. Box 751, Wilmington, DE 19897/302-575-3000
Idaho Ammunition Service, 2816 Mayfair Dr., Lewiston, ID 83501/208-743-0270
IGA (See U.S. importer—Stoeger Industries)
Imatronic, Inc., 1275 Paramount Pkwy., P.O. Box 520, Batavia, IL 60510/708-406-1920; FAX: 708-879-6749
IMI, P.O. Box 1044, Ramat Hasharon 47100, Israel/972-3-5485222 (U.S. importers—Action Arms Ltd.; K.B.I., Inc.; Magnum Research, Inc.; Springfield Armory)
Impact Case Company, P.O. Box 9912, Spokane, WA 99209-0912/509-467-3303; FAX: 509-326-5436
IMR Powder Co., Box 247E, Xplo Complex, RTS, Plattsburgh, NY 12901/518-561-9530; FAX: 518-563-0044
I.N.C., Inc., P.O. Box 12767, Wichita, KS 67277/316-721-9570; FAX: 316-721-5260
Incor, Inc., P.O. Box 132, Addison, TX 75001/214-931-3500
INDESAL, P.O. Box 233, Eibar, Spain 20600/43-751800; FAX: 43-751962 (U.S. importer—American Arms, Inc.)
Industria de la Escopeta S.A.L. (See INDESAL)
Ingle, Ralph W., #4 Missing Link, Rossville, GA 30741/404-866-5589
Innovision Enterprises, 728 Skinner Dr., Kalamazoo, MI 49001/616-382-1681; FAX: 616-382-1830
Insights Training Center, Inc., 240 NW Gilman Blvd., Issaquah, WA 98027/206-391-4834
Interarms, 10 Prince St., Alexandria, VA 22314/703-548-1400
Intermountain Arms & Tackle, Inc., 105 E. Idaho St., Meridian, ID 83642/208-888-4911; FAX: 208-888-4981
International Shooters Service (See I.S.S.)
International Shootists, Inc., P.O. Box 5354, Mission Hills, CA 91345/818-891-1723
Intratec, 12405 SW 130th St., Miami, FL 33186/FAX: 305-253-7207
Iosso Marine Products, 1485 Lively Blvd., Elk Grove, IL 60007/708-437-8400
Iron Mountain Knife Co., P.O. Box 2146, Sparks, NV 89432-2146/702-356-3632
Ironside International Publishers, Inc., P.O. Box 55, 800 Slaters Lane, Alexandria, VA 22313/703-684-6111; FAX: 703-683-5486
Irwin, Campbell H., 140 Hartland Blvd., East Hartland, CT 06027/203-653-3901
Irwindale Arms, Inc. (See IAI)
Israel Military Industries Ltd. (See IMI)
I.S.S., P.O. Box 185234, Ft. Worth, TX 76181/817-595-2090
Ithaca Aquisition Corp./Ithaca Gun Co., 891 Route 34B, King Ferry, NY 13081/315-364-7171
Ivanoff, Thomas G. (See Tom's Gun Repair)

J

J.A. Blades, Inc. (See Christopher Firearms Co., Inc., E.)
Jackalope Gun Shop, 1048 S. 5th St., Douglas, WY 82633/307-358-3441
Jaeger, Inc., Paul, P.O. Box 449, 1 Madison Ave., Grand Junction, TN 38039/800-223-8667; FAX: 901-764-6503
Jamison's Forge Works, 4527 Rd. 6.5 NE, Moses Lake, WA 98837/509-762-2659
Jantz Supply, P.O. Box 584-GD, Davis, OK 73030/405-369-2316; FAX: 405-369-3082
Jaro Manufacturing (See Pasadena Gun Center)
Jarrett Rifles, Inc., 383 Brown Rd., Jackson, SC 29831/803-471-3616
Jarvis Gunsmithing, Inc., 1123 Cherry Orchard Lane, Hamilton, MT 59840/406-961-4392
Jason Empire, Inc., 9200 Cody, Overland Park, KS 66214-3259/913-888-0220; FAX: 913-888-0222
Javelina Products, P.O. Box 337, San Bernardino, CA 92402/714-882-5847; FAX: 714-434-6937
J/B Adventures & Safaris, Inc., P.O. Box 3397, Englewood, CO 80155/303-771-0977
J-B Bore Cleaner, 299 Poplar St., Hamburg, PA 19526/215-562-2103
Jeffredo Gunsight, P.O. Box 669, San Marcos, CA 92079/619-728-2695
Jenco Sales, Inc., P.O. Box 1000, Manchaca, TX 78652/512-282-2800; FAX: 512-282-7504
Jenkins Recoil Pads, Inc., RR #2, P.O. Box 471, Olney, IL 62450/618-395-3416
Jennings Firearms, Inc., 3680 Research Way #1, Carson City, NV 89706/702-882-4007
Jensen Bullets, 86 N., 400 W., Blackfoot, ID 83221/208-785-5590
Jensen's Custom Ammunition, 5146 E. Pima, Tucson, AZ 85712/602-325-3346; FAX: 602-322-5704
Jett & Co., Inc., RR #3 P.O. Box 167-B, Litchfield, IL 62056/217-324-3779
JGS Precision Tool Mfg., 1141 S. Sumner Rd., Coos Bay, OR 97420/503-267-4331
Jim's Gun Shop (See Spradlin's)
J.I.T. Ltd., P.O. Box 749, Glenview, IL 60025/708-998-0937
J.O. Arms & Ammunition Co., 5709 Hartsdale, Houston, TX 77036/713-789-0745; FAX: 713-789-7513
Johanssons Vapentillbehor, Bert, S-430 20 Veddige, Sweden
John's Custom Leather, 523 S. Liberty St., Blairsville, PA 15717/412-459-6802
Johns, Bill, 1412 Lisa Rae, Round Rock, TX 78664/512-255-8246
Johnson Gunsmithing, Inc., Neal G., 111 Marvin Dr., Hampton, VA 23666/804-838-8091; FAX: 804-838-8157
Johnson Wood Products, RR #1, Strawberry Point, IA 52076/319-933-4930

Johnson, Iver (See AMAC)
Johnston Bros., 1889 Rt. 9, Unit 22, Toms River, NJ 08755/908-240-6873; FAX: 908-505-1969
Jonad Corporation, 2091 Lakeland Ave., Lakewood, OH 44107/216-226-3161
Jonas Appraisals & Taxidermy, Jack, 1625 S. Birch, Suite 708, Denver, CO 80222/303-757-7347
Jones, J.D., 721 Woodvue Lane, Wintersville, OH 43952/614-264-0176
Jones, Neil (See Custom Products)
Joy Enterprises, 801 Broad Ave., Ridgefield, NJ 07657/201-943-5920; FAX: 201-943-1579
JSL (Hereford) Ltd., 35 Church St., Hereford HR1 2LR England/0432-355416; FAX: 0432-355242 (U.S. importer—Rogers Ltd. International)
Juenke, Vern, 25 Bitterbush Rd., Reno, NV 89523/702-345-0225
Jumbo Sports Products (See Bucheimer, J.M.)
Jungkind, Reeves C., 5001 Buckskin Pass, Austin, TX 78745/512-442-1094
Jurras, L.E., P.O. Box 680, Washington, IN 47501/812-254-7698
Just Brass, Inc., 121 Henry St., P.O. Box 112, Freeport, NY 11520/516-378-8588

K

K&K Ammo Wrist Band, R.D. #1, P.O. Box 448-CA18, Lewistown, PA 17044/717-242-2329
K&M Industries, Inc., Box 66, 510 S. Main, Troy, ID 83871/208-835-2281; FAX: 208-835-5211
K&M Services, 2525 Primrose Lane, York, PA 17404/717-764-1461
K&T Co., 1027 Skyview Dr., W. Carrollton, OH 45449/513-859-8414
KA-BAR Knives, 31100 Solon Rd., Solon, OH 44139/216-248-7000, 800-321-9336; FAX: 216-248-8651
Kahles of America, Main St., Margaretville, NY 12455
Kalispel Metal Products (See KMP)
Kamik Outdoor Footwear, 554 Montee de Liesse, Montreal, Quebec, H4T 1P1 Canada/514-341-3950
Kamyk Engraving Co., Steve, 9 Grandview Dr., Westfield, MA 01085/413-568-0457
Kane Products, Inc., 5572 Brecksville Rd., Cleveland, OH 44131/216-524-9962
Kartak Gun Works, 7525 S. Coast Hwy., South Beach, OR 97366/503-867-4951
Kasenit Co., Inc., 13 Park Ave., Highland Mills, NY 10930/914-928-9595; FAX: 914-928-7292
Kassnar (See U.S. importer—K.B.I., Inc.)
Kaswer Custom, Inc., 13 Surrey Dr., Brookfield, CT 06804/203-775-0564; FAX: 203-775-6872
Kayusoft Intl., Star Route, Spray, OR 97874/503-462-3934
K.B.I., Inc., P.O. Box 6346, Harrisburg, PA 17112/717-540-8518; FAX: 717-540-8567
K-D, Inc., 665 W. 300 South, Price, UT 84501/801-637-9062
KDF, Inc., 2485 Hwy. 46 N., Seguin, TX 78155/512-379-8141
Keeler, R.H., 817 N St., Port Angeles, WA 98362/206-457-4702
Kehr, Roger, 7810 B Samurai Dr. SE, Olympia, WA 98503/206-456-0831
Keith's Bullets, 942 Twisted Oak, Algonquin, IL 60102/708-658-3520
Keith's Custom Gunstocks (See Heppler, Keith M.)
Keller Co., The, 4215 McEwen Rd., Dallas, TX 75244/214-788-4254
Kelley's, P.O. Box 125, Woburn, MA 01801/617-935-3389
Kellogg's Professional Products, 325 Pearl St., Sandusky, OH 44870/419-625-6551; FAX: 419-625-6167
Kelly, Lance, 1723 Willow Oak Dr., Edgewater, FL 32132/904-423-4933
Ken's Finn Knives, Rt. 1, Box 338, Republic, MI 49879/906-376-2132
Ken's Gun Specialties, Rt. 1, Box 147, Lakeview, AR 72642/501-431-5606
Ken's Rifle Blanks, Ken McCullough, Rt. 2, P.O. Box 85B, Weston, OR 97886/503-566-3879
Keng's Firearms Specialty, Inc., 875 Wharton Dr. SW, Atlanta, GA 30336/404-691-7611; FAX: 404-505-8445
KenPatable Ent., Inc., P.O. Box 19422, Louisville, KY 40259/502-239-5447
Kent Cartridge Mfg. Co. Ltd., Unit 16, Branbridges Industrial Estate, East Peckham, Tonbridge, Kent, TN12 5HF England/622-872255; FAX: 622-873645
Keokuk Kollectors Kartridges, 1342 S. Poplar, Casper, WY 82601
Keowee Game Calls, 608 Hwy. 25 North, Travelers Rest, SC 29690/803-834-7204
Kershaw Knives, 25300 SW Parkway Ave., Wilsonville, OR 97070/503-682-1966; FAX: 503-682-7168
Kesselring Gun Shop, 400 Hwy. 99 North, Burlington, WA 98233/206-724-3113; FAX: 206-724-7003
Kilham & Co., Main St., Lyme, NH 03768/603-795-4112
Kimball, Gary, 1526 N. Circle Dr., Colorado Springs, CO 80909/719-634-1274
Kimber Parts, 16709 NE Union Rd., Ridgefield, WA 98642/206-573-4783
Kimel Industries, P.O. Box 335, Matthews, NC 28106/704-821-7663
King & Co., P.O. Box 1242, Bloomington, IL 61701/309-473-3964
King's Gun Works, 1837 W. Glenoaks Blvd., Glendale, CA 91201/818-956-6010
Kingyon, Paul L., 607 N. 5th St., Burlington, IA 52601/319-752-4465
Kintrek, Inc., P.O. Box 72, Owensboro, KY 42302/502-686-8137
Kirkpatrick Leather Co., 1910 San Bernardo, Laredo, TX 78040/512-723-6631; FAX: 512-725-0672
Kiss Sights, 355 N. Lantana Ave., Suite 505, Camarillo, CA 93010/805-492-4007
KK Awards Mfg., P.O. Box 1586, Lomita, CA 90717-5586/310-325-0102; FAX: 310-325-0298
Kleen-Bore, Inc., 20 Ladd Ave., Northampton, MA 01060/413-586-7240; FAX: 413-586-0236
Klein Custom Guns, Don, 433 Murray Park Dr., Ripon, WI 54971/414-748-2931
Kleinendorst, K.W., RR #1, Box 1500, Hop Bottom, PA 18824/717-289-4687; FAX: 717-289-4687
Klingler Woodcarving, P.O. Box 141, Thistle Hill, Cabot, VT 05647/802-426-3811
KLP, Inc., 215 Charles Dr., Holland, MI 49424/616-396-2575; FAX: 616-396-1287
Kmount, P.O. Box 19422, Louisville, KY 40259/502-239-5447
KMP, P.O. Box 267, Cusick, WA 99119/509-445-1121
Kneiper Custom Rifles, Jim, RR 1, Box 103, Jay, NY 12941/518-946-7944
Knife Importers, Inc., P.O. Box 1000, Manchaca, TX 78652/512-282-6860
Knight & Hale Game Calls, Box 468 Industrial Park, Cadiz, KY 42211/502-522-3651; FAX: 502-522-0211
Knippel, Richard, 5924 Carnwood, Riverbank, CA 95367/209-869-1469
Knock on Wood Antiques, 355 Post Rd., Darien, CT 06820/203-655-9031
Kodiak Custom Bullets, 8261 Henry Circle, Anchorage, AK 99507/907-349-2282
Koevenig's Engraving Service, Box 55 Rabbit Gulch, Hill City, SD 57745/605-574-2239
KOGOT, 410 College, Trinidad, CO 81082/719-846-9406

Kolpin Mfg., Inc., P.O. Box 107, 205 Depot St., Fox Lake, WI 53933/414-928-3118; FAX: 414-928-3687
Kopec Enterprises, John (See Peacemaker Specialists)
Kopp Publishing Co., Div. of Koppco Industries, 1301 Franklin, Lexington, MO 64067/816-259-2636
Kopp, Terry K., 1301 Franklin, Lexington, MO 64067/816-259-2636
Korth, Robert-Bosch-Str. 4, P.O. Box 1320, 2418 Ratzeburg, Germany/0451-4991497; FAX: 0451-4993230 (U.S. importer—mandall Shooting Supplies, Inc.)
Korzinek Riflesmith, J., RD #2, Box 73, Canton, PA 17724/717-673-8512
Koval Knives, 460 D Schrock Rd., Columbus, OH 43229/614-888-6486; FAX: 614-888-8218
Kowa Optimed, Inc., 20001 S. Vermont Ave., Torrance, CA 90502/310-327-1913
Krause Publications, 700 E. State St., Iola, WI 54990/715-445-2214; FAX: 715-445-4087
Krico/Kriegeskorte GmbH, A., Kronacherstr. 63, 85 W. Fürth-Stadeln, D-8510 Germany/0911-796092; FAX: 0911-796074 (U.S. importer—Mandall Shooting Supplies, Inc.)
Krieger Barrels, Inc., N114 W18697 Clinton Dr., Germantown, WI 53022/414-255-9593; FAX: 414-255-9586
Kriegeskorte GmbH., A. (See Krico/Kriegeskorte GmbH., A.)
Krieghoff Gun Co., H., Bosch Str. 22, 7900 Ulm, Germany (U.S. importer—Krieghoff International, Inc.)
Krieghoff International, Inc., P.O. Box 549, Ottville, PA 18942/215-847-5173
Kris Mounts, 108 Lehigh St., Johnstown, PA 15905/814-539-9751
Kudlas, John M., 622 14th St. SE, Rochester, MN 55904/507-288-5579
Kulis Freeze Dry Taxidermy, 725 Broadway Ave., Bedford, OH 44146/216-232-8352; FAX: 216-232-7305
KVH Industries, Inc., 110 Enterprise Center, Middletown, RI 02840/401-847-3327; FAX: 401-849-0045
Kwik Mount Corp., P.O. Box 19422, Louisville, KY 40259/502-239-5447
Kwik-Site Co., 5555 Treadwell, Wayne, MI 48184/313-326-1500; FAX: 313-326-4120

L

L&S Technologies, Inc. (See Aimtech Mount Systems)
La Clinique du .45, 1432 Rougemont, Chambly, Quebec, J3L 2L8 Canada/514-658-1144
La Prade, Rt. 5, P.O. Box 240A, Tazewell, TN 37879
LaBounty Precision Reboring, P.O. Box 186, 7968 Silver Lk. Rd., Maple Falls, WA 98266/206-599-2047
Lachaussee, S.A., 29 Rue Kerstenne, Ans, B-4430 Belgium/041-63 88 77
LaCrosse Footwear, Inc., P.O. Box 1328, La Crosse, WI 54602/608-782-3020
LaFrance Specialties, P.O. Box 178211, San Diego, CA 92117/619-293-3373
Lage Uniwad, Inc., P.O. Box 446, Victor, IA 52327/319-647-3232
Lair, Sam, 520 E. Beaver, Jenks, OK 74037/918-299-2391
Lakefield Arms Ltd., 248 Water St., Lakefield, Ont. K0L 2H0, Canada/705-652-6735; FAX: 705-652-8431 (U.S. importer—Ellett Bros.)
Lakewood Products, Inc., P.O. Box 1527, 1445 Eagle St., Rhinelander, WI 54501/715-369-3445
Lampert, Ron, Rt. 1, Box 177, Guthrie, MN 56461/218-854-7345
Lamson & Goodnow Mfg. Co., 45 Conway St., Shelburne Falls, MA 03170/413-625-6331
Lanber Armes S.A., Calle Zubiaurre 5, Zaldibar, Spain (U.S. importer—American Arms, Inc.)
Lane Bullets, Inc., 1011 S. 10th St., Kansas City, KS 66105/913-621-6113
Lane Publishing, P.O. Box 759, Hot Springs, AR 71902/501-623-4951; FAX: 501-623-9832
Langenberg Hat Co., P.O. Box 1860, Washington, MO 63090/800-428-1860; FAX: 314-239-3151
Lansky Sharpeners & Crock Stick, P.O. Box 800, Buffalo, NY 14231/716-877-7511; FAX: 716-877-6955
Lapua Ltd., P.O. Box 5, Lapua, Finland SF-62101/64-310111
L.A.R. Manufacturing, Inc., 4133 W. Farm Rd., West Jordan, UT 84088/801-255-7106; FAX: 801-569-1972
LaRocca Gun Works, Inc., 51 Union Place, Worcester, MA 01608/508-754-2887; FAX: 508-754-2887
Larry's Gun Shop (See Thompson, Larry R.)
Laser Aim, Inc. (See Emerging Technologies, Inc.)
Laser Devices, Inc., 2 Harris Ct. A4, Monterey, CA 93940/408-373-0701; FAX: 408-373-0903
Lassen Community College, Gunsmithing Dept., P.O. Box 3000, Hwy. 139, Susanville, CA 96130/916-257-6181 ext. 109; FAX: 916-257-8964
Laughridge, William R. (See Cylinder & Slide, Inc.)
Laurona Armas S.A., Apartado 260, Avda Otaloa 25, Eibar, Spain (U.S. importer—Galaxy Imports Ltd., Inc.)
Lawrence Leather Co., P.O. Box 1479, Lillington, NC 27546/919-893-2071; FAX: 919-893-4742
Lawson Co., Harry, 3328 N. Richey Blvd., Tucson, AZ 85716/602-326-1117
Lawson, John G. (See Sight Shop, The)
LBT, HCR 62, Box 145, Moyie Springs, ID 83845/208-267-3588
Lea Mfg. Co., 237 E. Aurora St., Waterbury, CT 06720/203-753-5116
Lead Bullets Technology (See LBT)
Leather Arsenal, 27549 Middleton Rd., Middleton, ID 83644/208-585-6212
Leatherman Tool Group, Inc., P.O. Box 20595, Portland, OR 97220/503-253-7826; FAX: 503-253-7830
Leatherwood-Meopta, Inc., 719 Ryan Plaza, Suite 103, Arlington, TX 76011/817-965-3253
Lebeau-Courally, Rue St. Gilles, 386, 4000 Liege, Belgium/047 52 48 43; FAX: 047 52 20 08 (U.S. importer—New England Arms Co.)
LeClear Industries, 1126 Donald Ave., P.O. Box 484, Royal Oak, MI 48068/313-588-1025
Lectro Science, Inc., 6410 W. Ridge Rd., Erie, PA 16506/814-833-6487; FAX: 814-833-0447
Ledbetter Airguns, Riley, 1804 E. Sprague St., Winston Salem, NC 27107-3521/919-784-0676
Lee Precision, Inc., 4275 Hwy. U, Hartford, WI 53027/414-673-3075
Lee Supplies, Mark, 9901 France Ct., Lakeville, MN 55044/612-461-2114
Lee's Red Ramps, P.O. Box 1249, Phelan, CA 92371/619-868-5731
LeFever & Sons, Inc., Frank, RD #2, P.O. Box 31, Lee Center, NY 13363/315-337-6722
Legacy, Ltd., S.F., P.O. Box 1589, Bridgeport, MI 48722-1589/517-777-5200
Leibowitz, Leonard, 1205 Murrayhill Ave., Pittsburgh, PA 15217/412-361-5455
Leica USA, Inc., 156 Ludlow Ave., Northvale, NJ 07647/201-767-7500; FAX: 201-767-8666
LEM Gun Specialties, P.O. Box 97031, College Park, GA 30337

Lethal Force Institute (See Police Bookshelf)
Letschnig, Franz, RR 1, Martintown, Ont. K0C IS0, Canada/613-528-4843
Leupold & Stevens, Inc., P.O. Box 688, Beaverton, OR 97075/503-646-9171
Lever Arms Service Ltd., 2131 Burrard St., Vancouver, B.C. V6J 3H7
    Canada/604-736-0004; FAX: 604-738-3503
Liberty Antique Gunworks, 19 Key St., P.O. Box 183, Eastport, ME 04631/207-853-2327
Liberty Trouser Co., 2301 First Ave. North, Birmingham, AL 35203/205-251-9143
Lighthouse Mfg. Co., Inc., P.O. Box 948, West Palm Beach, FL 33408/407-626-9122
Lilja Precision Rifle Barrels, P.O. Box 372, Plains, MT 59859/406-826-3084; FAX:
    406-826-3083
Lind Custom Guns, Al, 7821 76th Ave. SW, Tacoma, WA 98498/206-584-6361
Linder Solingen Knives, 4401 Sentry Dr., Tucker, GA 30084/404-939-6915
Lindsay, Steve, RR 2 Cedar Hills, Kearney, NE 68847/308-236-7885
Lindsley Arms Cartridge Co., P.O. Box 757, Henniker, NH 03242/603-428-3127
Linebaugh Custom Sixguns, P.O. Box 1263, Cody, WY 82414/307-645-3162
Lite Tek International, 133-30 32nd Ave., Flushing, NY 11354/718-463-0650; FAX:
    718-762-0890
Lithi Bee Bullet Lube, 2161 Henry St., Muskegon, MI 49441/616-755-4707
"Little John's" Antique Arms, 1740 W. Laveta, Orange, CA 92668
Littler Sales Co., 20815 W. Chicago, Detroit, MI 48228/313-273-6888; FAX: 313-273-1099
Ljutic Industries, Inc., 732 N. 16th Ave., Yakima, WA 98902/509-248-0476
Llama Gabilondo Y Cia, Apartado 290, E-01080, Victoria, Spain (U.S. importer—Stoeger
    Industries)
Load From A Disk, 9826 Sagedale, Houston, TX 77089/713-484-0935
Loadmaster, P.O. Box 1209, Warminster, Wilts. BA12 9XJ England/(0985)218544; FAX:
    (0985)214111
Loch Leven Industries, P.O. Box 2751, Santa Rosa, CA 95405/707-573-8735
Lock's Philadelphia Gun Exchange, 6700 Rowland Ave., Philadelphia, PA
    19149/215-332-6225; FAX: 215-332-4800
Lodewick, Walter H., 2816 NE Halsey St., Portland, OR 97232/503-284-2554
Lofland, James W., 2275 Larkin Rd., Boothwyn, PA 19061/215-485-0391
Log Cabin Sport Shop, 8010 Lafayette Rd., Lodi, OH 44254/216-948-1082
Logan Security Products Co., 4926 Annhurst Rd., Columbus, OH 43228-1341
Logan, Harry M., Box 745, Honokaa, HI 96727/808-776-1644
Lohman Mfg. Co., Inc., 4500 Doniphan Dr., P.O. Box 220, Neosho, MO
    64850/417-451-4438; FAX: 417-451-2576
Lomont Precision Bullets, Kent, 4236 West 700 South, Poneto, IN 46781/219-694-6792
London Guns Ltd., Box 3750, Santa Barbara, CA 93130/805-683-4141; FAX:
    805-683-1712
Lone Pine Trading Post (See Ed's Gun House)
Lone Star Gunleather, 1301 Brushy Bend Dr., Round Rock, TX 78681/512-255-1805
Long Island Gunsmith, Inc., 552 Walt Wittman Rd., Huntington, NY 11747/516-427-4867
Long, George F., 1500 Rogue River Hwy., Ste. F, Grants Pass, OR 97527/503-476-7552
Lorcin Engineering Co., Inc., 10427 San Sevaine Way, Ste. A, Mira Loma, CA
    91752/714-360-1406; FAX: 714-360-0623
Lortone, Inc., 2856 NW Market St., Seattle, WA 98107/206-789-3100
L.P.A. Snc, Via V. Alfieri #26, Gardone V.T. BS, Italy 25063/(30)8911481; FAX:
    (30)8910951
LPS Chemical Prods., Holt Lloyd Corp., 4647 Hugh Howell Rd., P.O. Box 3050, Tucker,
    GA 30084/404-934-7800
LT Industries, Inc., 31812 Bainbridge Rd., Solon, OH 44139/216-248-7550
Lucas, Edw. E., 32 Garfield Ave., East Brunswick, NJ 08816/201-251-5526
Lyman Products Corporation, Rt. 147 West St., Middlefield, CT 06455/203-349-3421; FAX:
    203-349-3586
Lynn's Custom Gunstocks, RR 1, Brandon, IA 52210/319-474-2453

M

M&D Munitions Ltd., 127 Verdi St., Farmingdale, NY 11735/516-752-1038; FAX:
    516-752-1905
M&M Engineering (See Hollywood Engineering)
M&N Bullet Lube, P.O. Box 495, 151 NE Jefferson St., Madras, OR 97741/503-255-3750
Mac-1 Distributors, 13972 Van Ness Ave., Gardena, CA 90249/310-327-3582
Mac's .45 Shop, P.O. Box 2028, Seal Beach, CA 90740/213-438-5046
Macbean, Stan, 754 North 1200 West, Orem, UT 84057/801-224-6446
Mack's Sport Shop, P.O. Box 1155, Kodiak, AK 99615/907-486-4276
Madis, David, 2453 West Five Mile Pkwy., Dallas, TX 75233/214-330-7169
MAG Instrument, Inc., 1635 S. Sacramento Ave., Ontario, CA 91761/714-947-1006; FAX:
    714-947-3116
Mag-Na-Port International, Inc., 41302 Executive Dr., Mt. Clemens, MI
    48045-3446/313-469-6727; FAX: 313-469-0425
Mag-Pack Corp., P.O. Box 846, Chesterland, OH 44026
Magma Engineering Co., P.O. Box 161, Queen Creek, AZ 85242/602-987-9008; FAX:
    602-987-0148
Magnolia Sports, Inc., 211 W. Main, Magnolia, AR 71753/800-530-7816; FAx:
    501-234-8117
Magnum Research, Inc., 7110 University Ave., Minneapolis, MN 55432/612-574-1868;
    FAX: 612-574-0109
MagSafe Ammo Co., 2725 Friendly Grove Rd. NE, Olympia, WA 98506/206-357-6383
MAGTECH Recreational Products, Inc., 5030 Paradise Rd., Suite C211, Las Vegas, NV
    89119/702-795-7191; FAX: 702-795-2769
Mahony, Phillip Bruce, 67 White Hollow Rd., Lime Rock, CT 06039-2418/203-435-9341
Mains Enterprises, Inc., 3111 S. Valley View Blvd., Suite B120, Las Vegas, NV
    89102-7790/702-876-6278; FAX: 702-876-1269
Maionchi-L.M.I., Via Di Coselli—Zona Industriale Di Guamo, Lucca, Italy 55060/011
    39-583 94291
Maki Industries, 26-10th St. SE, Medicine Hat, AB T1A 1P7 Canada/403-526-7997
Maki School of Engraving, Robert E., P.O. Box 947, Northbrook, IL 60065/708-724-8238
Makinson, Nicholas, RR #3, Komoka, Ont. N0L 1R0 Canada/519-471-5462
Mallardtone Game Calls, 2901 16th St., Moline, IL 61265/309-762-8089
Maloni, Russ (See Russwood Custom Pistol Grips)
M.A.M. Products, Inc., 153 B Cross Slope Court, Englishtown, NJ 07726/908-536-7268
Mandall Shooting Supplies, Inc., 3616 N. Scottsdale Rd., Scottsdale, AZ
    85252/602-945-2553; FAX: 602-949-0734
Mandarino, Monte, 205 Fifth Ave. East, Kalispell, MT 59901/406-257-6208
Manley Shooting Supplies, Lowell, 3684 Pine St., Deckerville, MI 48427/313-376-3665
Manufacture D'Armes Des Pyrenees Francaises (See Unique/M.A.P.F.)

Mar Knives, Inc., Al, 5755 SW Jean Rd., Suite 101, Lake Oswego, OR
    97035/503-635-9229
Marathon Rubber Prods. Co., Inc., 510 Sherman St., Wausau, WI 54401/715-845-6255
Marble Arms Corporation, 420 Industrial Park, P.O. Box 111, Gladstone, MI
    49837/906-428-3710; FAX: 906-428-3711
Marek, George, 55 Arnold St., Westfield, MA 01085/413-562-5673
Marent, Rudolf, 9711 Tiltree St., Houston, TX 77075/713-946-7028
Markell, Inc., 422 Larkfield Center #235, Santa Rosa, CA 95403/707-573-0792; FAX:
    707-573-9867
Marksman Products, 5482 Argosy Dr., Huntington Beach, CA 92649/714-898-7535; FAX:
    714-891-0782
Marlin Firearms Co., 100 Kenna Dr., New Haven, CT 06473/203-239-5621; FAX:
    203-234-7991
Marocchi F.lli S.p.A., Via Galileo Galilei, I-25068 Zanano di Sarezzo, Italy (U.S.
    importers—PSI, Inc.; Sile Distributors)
Marple & Associates, Dick, 21 Dartmouth St., Hooksett, NH 03106/603-627-1837; FAX:
    603-641-4837
Marquart Precision Co., Inc., P.O. Box 1740, Prescott, AZ 86302/602-445-5646
Marsh, Johnny, 1007 Drummond Dr., Nashville, TN 37211/615-834-2103
Marsh, Mike, Croft Cottage, Main St., Elton, Derbyshire DE4 2BY, England/0629 650 669
Martin's Gun Shop, 937 S. Sheridan Blvd., Lakewood, CO 80226/303-922-2184
Martz, John V., 8060 Lakeview Lane, Lincoln, CA 95648/916-645-2250
Marvel, Alan, 3922 Madonna Rd., Jarretsville, MD 21084/301-557-6545
Masen Co., John, P.O. Box 5050, Suite 165, Lewisville, TX 75028/817-430-8732
Masker, Seely, 54 Woodshire S., Getzville, NY 14068/716-689-8894
Master Engravers, Inc. (See Hendricks, Frank E.)
Master Lock Co., 2600 N. 32nd St., Milwaukee, WI 53245/414-444-2800
Master Products, Inc. (See Gun-Alert/Master Products, Inc.)
Matco, Inc., 1003-2nd St., N. Manchester, IN 46962/219-982-8282
Mathews & Son, Inc., Geo. E., 10224 S. Paramount Blvd., Downey, CA
    90241/310-862-6719
Matthews Cutlery, 4401 Sentry Dr., Tucker, GA 30084
Matthews, Inc., Bill, P.O. Box 26727, Lakewood, CO 80226/303-922-0055
Mauser-Werke Oberndorf, P.O. Box 1349, 7238 Oberndorf/Neckar, Germany (U.S.
    importer—Precision Imports, Inc.)
Maverick Arms, Inc., Industrial Blvd., P.O. Box 586, Eagle Pass, TX 78853/512-773-9007
Mayville Engineering Co. (See MEC)
Mazur Restoration, Pete, 13083 Drummer Way, Grass Valley, CA 95949/916-268-2412
MCC, 214 E. Third St., Mt. Vernon, NY 10550/914-664-1311
McCament, Jay, 1730-134th St. Ct. S., Tacoma, WA 98444/206-531-8832
McCann's Muzzle-Gun Works, 76 Old York Rd., New Hope, PA 18938/215-862-9180
McConnellstown Reloading & Cast Bullets, Inc., P.O. Box 476, Huntingdon, PA
    16652-0476/814-627-5402
McCormick Corp., Chip, 1825 Fortview Rd. #115, Austin, TX 78704/512-462-0004; FAX:
    512-462-0009
McCormick's Custom Gun Bluing, 609 NE 104th Ave., Vancouver, WA
    98664/206-896-4232
McCullough, Ken (See Ken's Rifle Blanks)
McDonald, Dennis, 8359 Brady St., Peosta, IA 52068/319-556-7940
McFarland, Stan, 2221 Idella Ct., Grand Junction, CO 81505/303-243-4704
McGowen Rifle Barrels, 5961 Spruce Lane, St. Anne, IL 60964/815-937-9816; FAX:
    815-937-4024
McGuire, Bill, 1600 N. Eastmont Ave., East Wenatchee, WA 98802/509-884-6021
McKee Publications, 121 Eatons Neck Rd., Northport, NY 11768/516-575-8850
McKee, Arthur, 121 Eatons Neck Rd., Northport, NY 11768/516-757-8850
McKenzie, Lynton, 6940 N. Alvernon Way, Tucson, AZ 85718/602-299-5090
McKillen & Heyer, Inc., 5551B Ivy Ct., Willoughby, OH 44094/216-942-2491
McMillan Fiberglass Stocks, Inc., 21421 N. 14th Ave., Phoenix, AZ 85027/602-582-9635
McMillan Gunworks, Inc., 302 W. Melinda Dr., Phoenix, AZ 85027/602-582-9627; FAX:
    602-582-5178
McMillan Rifle Barrels, U.S. International, P.O. Box 3427, Bryan, TX 77805/409-846-3990
McMurdo, Lynn (See Specialty Gunsmithing)
MCS, Inc., 34 Delmar Dr., Brookfield, CT 06804/203-775-1013; FAX: 203-775-9462
McWelco Products, 6730 Santa Fe Ave., Hesperia, CA 92345/619-244-8876; FAX:
    619-244-9398
MDS, Inc., 1640 Central Ave., St. Petersburg, FL 33712/813-894-3512
Meadow Industries, P.O. Box 754, Locust Grove, VA 22508/703-972-2175
MEC, 715 South St., Mayville, WI 53050/414-387-4500
MEC-Gar S.R.L., Via Madonnina 64, Gardone V.T. (BS) Italy 25063/39-30-8911719; FAX:
    39-30-8910065
Meier Works, Box 328, Canyon, TX 79015/806-655-9443
Mele, Frank, Rt. 1 P.O. Box 349, Springfork Rd., Granville, TN 38564/615-653-4414
Melton Shirt Co., Inc., 56 Harvester Ave., Batavia, NY 14020/716-343-8750
Men—Metallwerk Elisenhuette, GmbH, P.O. Box 1263, W-5408 Nassau,
    Germany/2604-7819
Menck, Thomas W., 5703 S. 77th St., Ralston, NE 68127-4201
Mendez, John A., P.O. Box 1534, Radio City Station, New York, NY 10019/212-315-2580
Meprolight (See Hesco-Meprolight)
Mercer Custom Stocks, R.M., 216 S. Whitewater Ave., Jefferson, WI 53549/414-674-3839
Merit Corporation, Box 9044, Schenectady, NY 12309/518-346-1420
Merkel Freres, Strasse 7 October, 10, Suhl, R.D.A. (U.S. importer—GSI, Inc.)
Merkuria Ltd., Argentinska 38, 17005 Praha 7, Czechoslovakia/422-875117; FAX:
    422-809152
Metalife Industries, Box 53 Mong Ave., Reno, PA 16343/814-436-7747; FAX:
    814-676-5662
Metallic Casting & Copper Corp. (See MCC)
Michael's Antiques, P.O. Box 591, Waldoboro, ME 04572
Michaels of Oregon Co., P.O. Box 13010, Portland, OR 97213/503-255-6890; FAX:
    503-255-0746
Micro Sight Co., 242 Harbor Blvd., Belmont, CA 94002/415-591-0769
Micro-Lube, Rt. 2, P.O. Box 201, Deming, NM 88030/505-546-9116
Mid-America Recreation, Inc., 1328 5th Ave., Moline, IA 52807/309-764-5089; FAX:
    309-764-2722
Midway Arms, Inc., P.O. Box 1483, Columbia, MO 65205/314-445-6363; FAX:
    214-446-1018
Midwest Gun Sport, 1108 Herbert Dr., Zebulon, NC 27597/919-269-5570
Midwest Sport Distributors, Box 129, Fayette, MO 65248

Military Armament Corp., P.O. Box 120, Mt. Zion Rd., Lingleville, TX 76461/817-965-3253
Millenium Safety Products, Inc., P.O. Box 9802-916, Austin, TX 78766-0802/512-346-3876
Miller Arms, Inc., P.O. Box 260 Purl St., St. Onge, SD 57779/605-578-1790
Miller Co., David, 3131 E. Greenlee Rd., Tucson, AZ 85716/602-326-3117
Miller Custom, 210 E. Julia, Clinton, IL 61727/217-935-9362
Miller Gun Woods, 1440 Peltier Dr., Point Roberts, WA 98281/206-945-7014
Miller Single Trigger Mfg. Co., R.D. 1, P.O. Box 99, Millersburg, PA 17061/717-692-3704
Miller, Tom (See Huntington's Die Specialties)
Millett Sights, 16131 Gothard St., Huntington Beach, CA 92647/714-842-5575; FAX: 714-843-5707
Milliron Gunstocks, Earl, 1249 NE 166th Ave., Portland, OR 97230/503-252-3725
Mills Jr., Hugh B., 3615 Canterbury Rd., New Bern, NC 28560/919-637-4631
Miniature Machine Co. (See MMC)
Mirador Optical Corp., 4051 Glencoe Ave., Marina Del Rey, CA 90292/310-821-5587; FAX: 310-305-0386
Miroku, B.C./Daly, Charles (See U.S. importer—Outdoor Sports Headquarters)
Mitchell Arms, Inc., 3400 W. MacArthur Blvd., Suite 1, Santa Ana, CA 92704/714-957-5711; FAX: 714-957-5732
Mitchell's Accuracy Shop, 68 Greenridge Dr., Stafford, VA 22554/703-659-0165
Mittermeier, Frank, P.O. BNox 2G, 3577 E. Tremont Ave., Bronx, NY 10465/212-828-3843
Mixson Leathercraft, Inc., 7435 W. 19th Ct., Hialeah, FL 33014/305-821-5190; FAX: 305-558-9318
MJK Gunsmithing, Inc., 417 N. Huber Ct., E. Wenatchee, WA 98802/509-884-7683
MK Arms, Inc., P.O. Box 16411, Irvine, CA 92713/714-261-2767
MKS Supply, Inc., 1015 Springmill Rd., Mansfield, OH 44906/419-747-1088
MMC, 606 Grace Ave., Ft. Worth, TX 76111/817-831-0837
MMP, RR 6, Box 384, Harrison, AR 72601/501-741-5019; FAX: 501-741-3104
M.O.A. Corp., 175 Carr Dr., Brookville, OH 45309/513-833-5559
Modern Gun Repair School, 2538 N. 8th St., P.O. Box 5338, Phoenix, AZ 85010/602-990-8346
Modern MuzzleLoading, Inc., 234 Airport Rd., P.O. Box 130, Centerville, IA 52544/515-856-2623
Moeller, Steve, 1213 4th St., Fulton, IL 61252/815-589-2300
Molin Industries/Tru-Nord Division, P.O. Box 365, 204 North 9th St., Brainerd, MN 56401/218-829-2870
MoLoc Bullets, P.O. Box 2810, Turlock, CA 95381/209-874-4322
Monell Custom Guns, Red Mill Road, Pine Bush, NY 12566/914-744-3021
Moneymaker Guncraft Corp., 1420 Military Ave., Omaha, NE 68131/402-556-0226
Montana Armory, Inc., 100 Centennial Dr., Big Timber, MT 59011/406-932-4353
Montana Outfitters, Lewis E. Yearout, 308 Riverview Dr. E., Great Falls, MT 59404/406-761-0859
Monte Kristo Pistol Grip Co., P.O. Box 85, Whiskeytown, CA 96095/916-623-4019
Montgomery Community College, P.O. Box 787, Troy, NC 27371/919-572-3691
Moore & Co., Wm. Larkin, 31360 Via Colinas, Suite 109, Westlake Village, CA 91360/818-889-4160
Moran, Jerry, P.O. Box 357, Mt. Morris, MI 45458-0357
Moreton/Fordyce Enterprises, P.O. Box 940, Saylorsburg, PA 18353/717-992-5742
Morrison Custom Rifles, J.W., 4015 W. Sharon, Phoenix, AZ 85029/602-978-3754
Morrow, Bud, 11 Hillside Lane, Sheridan, WY 82801-9729/307-674-8360
Mo's Competitor Supplies (See MCS)
Moschetti, Mitchell R., P.O. Box 27065, Denver, CO 80227/303-733-9593
Moss Double Tone, Inc., P.O. Box 1112, 2101 S. Kentucky, Sedalia, MO 65301/816-827-0827
Mossberg & Sons, Inc., O.F., 7 Grasso Ave., N. Haven, CT 06473/203-288-6491; FAX: 203-288-2404
Mountain Arms, Rt. 3, P.O. Box 297, Warrenton, VA 22186/703-347-1199
Mountain Bear Rifle Works, Inc., 100 B Ruritan Rd., Sterling, VA 22170/703-430-0420
Mountain Hollow Game Calls, Box 121, Cascade, MD 21719/301-241-3282
Mountain South, P.O. Box 381, Barnwell, SC 29812/FAX: 803-259-3227
Mountain State Muzzleloading Supplies, Box 154-1, Rt. 2, Williamstown, WV 26187/304-375-7842; FAX: 304-375-3737
Mountain States Engraving, Kenneth W. Warren, P.O. Box 2842, Wenatchee, WA 98802/509-663-6123
Mountain View Sports, Inc., Box 188, Troy, NH 03465/603-357-9690; FAX: 603-357-9691
Mowrey Gun Works, P.O. Box 246, Waldron, IN 46182/317-525-6181
Mowreys Guns & Supplies, RD 1, Box 82, Canajoharie, NY 13317/518-673-3483
MPI Stocks, P.O. Box 83266, Portland, OR 97283-0266/503-226-1215
Mt. Alto Outdoor Products, Rt. 735, Howardsville, VA 24562
MTM Molded Products Company, P.O. Box 14117, Dayton, OH 45414/513-890-7461; FAX: 513-890-1747
Mullis Guncraft, 3523 Lawyers Road E., Monroe, NC 28110/704-283-6683
Multi-Scale Charge Ltd., 3269 Niagara Blvd., N. Tonwanda, NY 14120/416-566-1255; FAX: 416-276-6292
Multipropulseurs, La Bertrandiere, 42580 L'Etrat, France/77 74 01 30; FAX: 77 93 19 34
Munger, Robert D. (See Rusteprufe Laboratories)
Munsch Gunsmithing, Tommy, Rt. 2, P.O. Box 248, Little Falls, MN 56345/612-632-6695
Murphy Co., Inc., R., 13 Groton-Harvard Rd., P.O. Box 376, Ayer, MA 01432/617-772-3481
Murray State College, 100 Faculty Dr., Tishomingo, OK 73460/405-371-2371
Muscle Products Corp./Firepower Lubricants, 188 Freeport Rd., Butler, PA 16001/412-283-0567
Museum of Historical Arms, Inc., 1038 Alton Rd., Miami Beach, FL 33139/305-672-7480
Mushroom Express Bullet Co., 3147 W. U.S. 40, Greenfield, IN 46140/317-462-9390
Mustra's Custom Guns, Inc., Carl, 1002 Pennsylvania Ave., Palm Harbor, FL 34683/813-785-1403
Muzzle-Nuzzle Co., 609 N. Virginia Ave., Roswell, NM 88201/505-624-1260
Muzzlelite Corp., P.O. Box 100, Junction City, WI 54443/715-457-2431
Muzzleload Magnum Products (See MMP)
Muzzleloaders Etcetera, Inc., 9901 Lyndale Ave. S., Bloomington, MN 55420/612-884-1161

N

N&J Sales, Lime Kiln Rd., Northford, CT 06472/203-484-0247
Nastoff's 45 Shop, Steve, 1057 Laverne Ave., Youngstown, OH 44511/216-799-8870
National Guild of Shotgun Shooting Instructors, 4017 Emerald St., Torrance, CA 90503/310-371-1128; FAX: 310-542-5226
National Security Safe Company, Inc., P.O. Box 39, 620 S. 380 E., American Fork, UT 84003/801-756-7706

National Survival Game, Inc.. P.O. Box 1439, New London, NH 03257/603-735-6165; FAX: 603-735-5154
National Target Co., 4690 Wyaconda Rd., Rockville, MD 20852/301-770-7060; FAX: 301-770-7892
Nationwide Airgun Repairs (See Airgun Repair Centre)
Naval Ordnance Works, 14702 Old National Pike, Clejar Spring, MD 21722/301-582-0204
Navy Arms Company, 689 Bergen Blvd., Ridgefield, NJ 07657/201-945-2500; FAX: 201-945-6859
N.C. Ordnance Co., P.O. Box 3254, Wilson, NC 27895/919-237-2440
Necromancer Industries, Inc., 14 Communications Way, West Newton, PA 15089/412-872-8722
NEI, 9330 NE Halsey, Portland, OR 97220/206-260-0182
Nelson Combat Leather, Bruce, P.O. Box 8691 CRB, Tucson, AZ 85738/602-825-9047
Nelson, Gary K., 975 Terrace Dr., Oakdale, CA 95361/209-847-4590
Nelson, Stephen, 7365 NW Spring Creek Dr., Corvallis, OR 97330/503-745-5232
Nelson/Weather-Rite, 14760 Santa Fe Trail Dr., Lenexa, KS 66215/913-492-3200
Nesci Enterprises, Inc., P.O. Box 119, Summit St., East Hampton, CT 06424/203-267-2588
Nettestad Gun Works, RR 1, Box 160, Pelican Rapids, MN 56572/218-863-4301
Neumann GmbH, Untere Ringstr. 17, 8506 Langenzenn, Germany/09101-8258
Neutralizer Police Munitions, 5029 Middle Rd., Horseheads, NY 14845-9568/607-739-8362; FAX: 607-594-3900
New Advantage Arms Corp., 2843 N. Alvernon Way, Tucson, AZ 85712/602-881-7444; FAX: 602-323-0949
New Democracy, Inc., 719 Ryan Plaza, Suite 103, Arlington, TX 76011
New England Ammunition Co., 1771 Post Rd. East, Suite 223, Westport, CT 06880/203-254-8048
New England Arms Co., Box 278, Lawrence Lane, Kittery Point, ME 03905/207-439-0593; FAX: 207-439-6726
New England Custom Gun Service (See Apel, Dietrich)
New England Firearms Co., 60 Industrial Rowe, Gardner, MA 01440/508-632-9393; FAX: 508-632-2300
New Historians Productions, The, 131 Oak St., Royal Oak, MI 48067/313-544-7544
New Orleans Arms Co., 1001 Treasure St., New Orleans, LA 70186/504-944-3371
New Orleans Jewelers Supply Co., 206 Charters St., New Orleans, LA 70130/504-523-3839
Newbern Glove, 301 Jefferson St., Newbern, TN 38059/901-627-2557
Newell, Robert H., 55 Coyote, Los Alamos, NM 87544/505-662-7135
Newman Gunshop, Rt. 1, Box 90F, Agency, IA 52530/515-937-5775
NgraveR Co., The, 67 Wawecus Hill Rd., Bozrah, CT 06334/203-823-1533
Nichols Sports Optics, P.O. Box 37669, Omaha, NE 68137/402-339-3530
Nickels, Paul R., 4789 Summerhill Rd., Las Vegas, NV 89121/702-435-5318
Nicklas, Ted, 5504 Hegel Rd., Goodrich, MI 48438/313-797-4493
Nielsen & Co., P.O. Box 26297, Las Vegas, NV 89126/702-878-5611; FAX: 702-877-4433
Night Vision Equipment Co., Inc., P.O. Box 266, Emmaus, PA 18049/215-391-9101
Nikon, Inc., 1300 Walt Whitman Rd., Melville, NY 11747/516-547-4200
Nitex, Inc., P.O. Box 1706, Uvalde, TX 78801/512-278-8843
No-Sho Mfg. Co., 10727 Glenfield Ct., Houston, TX 77096/713-723-5332
Noble Co., Jim, 1305 Columbia St., Vancouver, WA 98660/206-695-1309
Nolan, Dave, Fox Valley Range, P.O. Box 155, Dundee, IL 60118/708-426-5921
Noreen, Peter H., 5075 Buena Vista Dr., Belgrade, MT 59714
Norica, Avnda Otaola, 16, Apartado 68, 20600 Eibar, Spain (U.S. importers—American Arms, Inc.; K.B.I., Inc.)
Norinco, 7A, Yun Tan N Beijing, China (U.S. importers—Century Intl. Arms, Inc.; ChinaSports, Inc.; Interarms; Midwest Sport Distributors; Navy Arms Co.; Sportarms of Florida)
Norma (See U.S. importer—Paul Co., The)
Norman Custom Gunstocks, Jim, 14281 Cane Rd., Valley Center, CA 92082/619-749-6252
Normark Corp., 1710 E. 78th St., Minneapolis, MN 55423/612-869-3291
Norrell Arms, John, 2608 Grist Mill Rd., Little Rock, AR 72207/501-225-7864
North American Arms, 1800 North 300 West, Spanish Fork, UT 84660/800-821-5783; FAX: 801-798-9418
North American Correspondence Schools, The Gun Pro School, Oak & Pawnee St., Scranton, PA 18515/717-342-7701
North American Specialties, 25422 Trabuco Rd. #105-328, El Toro, CA 92630/714-979-4867; FAX: 714-979-1520
North Consumer Prods. Div., 2664-B Saturn St., Brea, CA 92621/714-524-1665
North Fork Custom Gunsmithing, 428 Del Rio Rd., Roseburg, OR 97470/503-673-4467
North Mountain Pine Training Center (See Executive Protection Institute)
North Wind Decoys Co., 1005 N. Tower Rd., Fergus Falls, MN 56537/218-736-4378; FAX: 218-736-4378
Northeast Industrial, Inc. (See NEI)
Northeast Training Institute, Inc., 1142 Rockland St., Suite 380, Reading, PA 19604/215-373-1940
Northern Precision Custom Swaged Bullets, 337 S. James St., Carthage, NY 13619/315-493-3456
Northlake Boot Co., 1810 Columbia Ave., Franklin, TN 37064/615-794-1556
Nosler, Inc., P.O. Box 671, Bend, OR 97709/503-382-3921; FAX: 503-388-4667
Novak's .45 Shop, Wayne, 1206 1/2 30th St., P.O. Box 4045, Parkersburg, WV 26101/304-485-9295
Nowlin Custom Barrels Mfg., Rt. 1, Box 308, Claremore, OK 74017/918-342-0689; FAX: 918-342-0624
Nu-Line Guns, Inc., 1053 Caulks Hill Rd., Harvester, MO 63303/314-441-4500; FAX: 314-447-5018
Nu-Teck, 30 Industrial Park Rd., Box 37, Centerbrook, CT 06409/203-767-3573; FAX: 203-767-9137
Null Holsters Ltd., K.L., Hill City Station, Resaca, GA 30735/404-625-5643; FAX: 404-625-9392
Nygord Precision Products, P.O. Box 8394, La Crescenta, CA 91224/818-352-3027; FAX: 818-352-3027

O

Oakland Custom Arms, Inc., 9191 Pine Knob Rd., Clarkston, MI 48348/313-625-1150
Oakman Turkey Calls, RD 1, P.O. Box 825, Harrisonville, PA 17228/717-485-4620
Oakshore Electronic Sights, Inc., P.O. Box 4470, Ocala, FL 32678-4470/904-629-7112; FAX: 904-629-1433
Obermeyer Rifled Barrels, 23122 60th St., Bristol, WI 53104/414-843-3537; FAX: 414-843-2129

O'Connor Rifle Products Co., Ltd., 2008 Maybank Hwy., Charleston, SC 29412/803-795-8590
October Country, P.O. Box 969, Hayden Lake, ID 83835/208-772-2068
Oehler Research, Inc., P.O. Box 9135, Austin, TX 78766/512-327-6900
Oglesby & Oglesby Gunmakers, Inc., RR #5, Springfield, IL 62707/217-487-7100
Ojala Holsters, Arvo, P.O. Box 98, N. Hollywood, CA 91603/503-669-1404
Oker's Engraving, 365 Bell Rd., P.O. Box 126, Shawnee, CO 80475/303-838-6062
Oklahoma Leather Products, Inc., 402 Newman Rd., Miami, OK 74354/918-542-6651
Old Dominion Engravers, 100 Progress Drive, Lynchburg, VA 24502/804-237-4450
Old West Reproductions, Inc., 446 Florence S. Loop, Florence, MT 59833/406-273-2615
Old Western Scrounger, 12924 Hwy. A-12, Montague, CA 96064/916-459-5445; FAX: 916-459-3944
Old World Gunsmithing, 2901 SE 122nd, Portland, OR 97236-3205/503-760-7681
Old World Oil Products, 3827 Queen Ave. N., Minneapolis, MN 55412/612-522-5037
Olson, Vic, 5002 Countryside Dr., Imperial, MO 63052/314-296-8086
Olt Co., Philip S., P.O. Box 550, Pekin, IL 61554/309-348-3633; FAX: 309-348-3300
Olympic Arms, Inc., 624 Old Pacific Hwy. SE, Olympia, WA 98503/206-456-3471; FAX: 206-491-3447
Olympic Optical Co., P.O. Box 752377, Memphis, TN 38175-2377/901-794-3890
Omark Industries (See Blount, Inc., Sporting Equipment Division)
Omega Sales, Inc., P.O. Box 1066, Mt. Clemens, MI 48046
OMR Feinmechanik, Jagd-und Sportwaffen, GmbH, Postfach 1231, Schutzenstr. 20, D-5400 Koblenz, Germany/0261-31865-15351
One Of A Kind, 15610 Purple Sage, San Antonio, TX 78255/512-695-3364
Optolyth-USA, Inc., 18805 Melvista Lane, Hillsboro, OR 97123/503-628-0246; FAX: 503-628-0797
Orchard Park Enterprise, P.O. Box 563, Orchard Park, NY 14227/616-656-0356
Oregon Arms, Inc., P.O. Box 1104, Medford, OR 97501/503-664-5586
Original Mink Oil, Inc., P.O. Box 20191, 11021 NE Beach St., Portland, OR 97220/503-255-2814
Orion Bullets, P.O. Box 264, Franklin, ID 83237/208-646-2373
Or-Ün, Tahtakale Menekse Han 18, Istanbul, Turkey 34460/901-522-5912; FAX: 901-522-7379
Orvis Co., The, Rt. 7, Manchester, VT 05254/802-362-3622 ext. 283; FAX: 802-362-3525
Ottmar, Maurice, Box 657, 113 E. Fir, Coulee City, WA 99115/509-632-5717
Otto, Tim, 320 Fairhaven Rd., Alameda, CA 94501-5963
Outa-Site Gun Carriers, 219 Market, Laredo, TX 78040/512-722-4678; FAX: 512-726-4858
Outdoor Connection, Inc., The, 201 Douglas, P.O. Box 7751, Waco, TX 76712/800-533-6076, 817-772-5575; FAX: 817-776-6076
Outdoor Edge Cutlery Corp., 2888 Bluff St., Suite 130, Boulder, CO 80301/303-530-3855; FAX: 303-530-3855
Outdoor Sports Headquarters, Inc., 967 Watertower Lane, Dayton, OH 45449/513-865-5855
Outdoorsman's Bookstore, The, Llangorse, Brecon, County Powys LD3 7UE, U.K./44-87484-660; FAX: 44-87484-650
Outers Laboratories, Div. of Blount, Inc., Route 2, Onalaska, WI 54650/608-781-5800
Owen, Harry, Sport Specialties, 100 N. Citrus Ave. #412, W. Covina, CA 91791-1614
Ox-Yoke Originals, Inc., 34 Main St., Milo, ME 04463/800-231-8313; FAX: 207-943-2416

P

P&M Sales and Service, 5724 Gainsborough Pl., Oak Forest, IL 60452/708-687-7149
P&S Gun Service, 2138 Old Shepardsville Rd., Louisville, KY 40218/502-456-9346
Pace Marketing, Inc., 9474 NW 48th St., Sunrise, FL 33351-5137/305-741-4361; FAX: 305-741-2901
Pachmayr Ltd., 1875 S. Mountain Ave., Monrovia, CA 91016/818-357-7771
Pacific Pistolcraft, 1810 E. Columbia Ave., Tacoma, WA 98404/206-474-5465
P.A.C.T., Inc., P.O. Box 531525, Grand Prairie, TX 75053/214-641-0049
Pagel Gun Works, 1407 4th St. NW, Grand Rapids, MN 55744/218-326-3003
Paladin Press, P.O. Box 1307, Boulder, CO 80306/303-443-7250; FAX: 303-442-8741
Palmer Metal Products, 2930 N. Campbell Ave., Chicago, IL 60618/800-788-7725; FAX: 312-267-8080
Palmgren Steel Products, 8383 S. Chicago Ave., Chicago, IL 60617/312-721-9675; FAX: 312-721-9739
Palsa Outdoor Products, P.O. Box 81336, Lincoln, NE 68501/800-456-9281; FAX: 402-488-5288
Panavise Products, Inc., 1485 Southern Way, Sparks, NV 89431/702-353-2900; FAX: 702-353-2929
Para-Ordnance Mfg., Inc., 3411 McNicoll Ave., Unit #14, Scarborough, Ont. M1V 2V6, Canada/416-297-7855; FAX: 416-297-1289
Paragon Sales & Services, Inc., P.O. Box 2022, Joliet, IL 60434/815-725-9212; FAX: 815-725-8974
Pardini Armi Commerciale Srl, Via Italica 154, Lido Di Camaiore Lu, Italy 55043/584-90121; FAX: 584-90122 (Distributed by MCS, Inc.)
Paris, Frank J., 13945 Minock Dr., Redford, MI 48239/313-255-0888
Parke-Bernet (See Sotheby's)
Parker Gun Finishes, 9337 Smokey Row Rd., Strawberry Plains, TN 37871/615-933-3286
Parker Reproductions, 124 River Rd., Middlesex, NJ 08846/908-469-0100; FAX: 908-469-9692
Parker, Mark D., 1240 Florida Ave. #7, Longmont, CO 80501/303-772-0214
Parker-Case (See Case & Sons Cutlery Co, W.R.)
Parker-Hale (See U.S. distributor—Navy Arms Co.)
Partridge Sales Ltd., John, Trent Meadows, Rugeley, Staffordshire, WS15 2HS England/0889-584438
Pasadena Gun Center, 206 E. Shaw, Pasadena, TX 77506/713-472-0417; FAX: 713-472-1322
P.A.S.T. Corp., 210 Park Ave., Columbia, MO 65205/314-449-7278
Patchbox, The, 600 Farm Rd., Kalispell, MT 59901/406-756-8851
Paterson Gunsmithing, 438 Main St., Paterson, NJ 07502/201-345-4100
Pathfinder Sports Leather, 2920 E. Chambers St., Phoenix, AZ 85040/602-276-0016
Patriot Manufacturing, P.O. Box 50065, Lighthouse Point, FL 33074/305-783-4849
Pattern Control, 114 N. 3rd St., Garland, TX 75040/214-494-3551
Paul Co., The, Rt. 1, Box 177A, Wellsville, KS 66092/913-883-4444
Paulsen Gunstocks, Rt. 71, Box 11, Chinook, MT 59523/406-357-3403
Payne Photodesign, Robert, P.O. Box 141471, Austin, TX 78714/512-272-4554
PC Co., 5942 Secor Rd., Toledo, OH 43623/419-472-6222

Peacemaker Specialists, John Kopec Enterprises, P.O. Box 157, Whitmore, CA 96096/916-472-3438
Pease Accuracy, Bob, P.O. Box 310787, New Braunfels, TX 78131
PECAR Herbert Schwarz, GmbH, Kreuzbergstrasse 6, Berlin 61, 1000 Germany/004930-785-7383; FAX: 004930-785-1934
Pedersen & Son, C.R., 2717 S. Pere Marquette Hwy., Ludington, MI 49431/616-843-2061
Pedersoli Davide & C., Via Artigiani 53, Gardone V.T. (BS) Italy 25063/030-8912402; FAX: 030-8911019 (U.S. importers—Dixie Gun Works, EMF Co., Navy Arms Co., Trail Guns Armory, Inc.)
Peet Shoe Dryer, Inc., 130 S. 5th St., St. Maries, ID 83861/800-222-PEET; FAX: 208-245-5441
Pejsa Ballistics, 2120 Kenwood Pkwy., Minneapolis, MN 55405/612-374-3337; FAX: 612-374-3337
Pell, John T., 410 College, Trinidad, CO 81082/719-846-9406
Peltor, Inc., 63 Commercial Way, E. Providence, RI 02914/401-438-4800; FAX: 800-EAR-FAX1
Pence Precision Barrels, RR #2 , S. Whitley, IN 46787/219-839-4745
Pend Oreille Sport Shop, 3100 Hwy. 200 East, Sandpoint, ID 83864/208-263-2412
Pendleton Royal, 407 Highgate St., Birmingham, England B12 0X5/44 21 440 3060; FAX: 44 21 446 4165
Pendleton Woolen Mills, P.O. Box 3030, 220 N.W. Broadway, Portland, OR 97208/503-226-4801
Penguin Industries, Inc., Airport Industrial Mall, Coatesville, PA 19320/215-384-6000
Penn's Woods Products, Inc., 19 W. Pittsburgh St., Delmont, PA 15626/412-468-8311
Pennsylvania Gunsmith School, 812 Ohio River Blvd., Avalon, Pittsburgh, PA 15202/412-766-1812
Penrod Precision, 312 College Ave., P.O. Box 307, N. Manchester, IN 46962/219-981-8385
Pentax Corp., 35 Inverness Dr. E., Englewood, CO 80112/303-799-8000
Pentheny de Pentheny, 2352 Baggett Ct., Santa Rosa, CA 95401/707-573-1390
Perazzi m.a.p. S.P.A., Via Fontanelle 1/3, I-25080 Botticino Mattina, Italy (U.S. importer—Perazzi U.S.A., Inc.)
Perazzi U.S.A., Inc., 1207 S. Shamrock Ave., Monrovia, CA 91016/818-303-0068
Peregrine Industries, Inc., P.O. Box 1310, Huntington Beach, CA 92647-1310/714-847-4700
Performance Specialists, 308 Eanes School Rd., Austin, TX 78746/512-327-0119
Peripheral Data Systems (See Arms)
Personal Firearms Record Book Co. (See PFRB Co.)
Personal Protection Systems Ltd., Aberdeen Rd., RD #5 P.O. Box 5027-A, Moscow, PA 18444/717-842-1766
Perugini Visini & Co. s.r.l., Via Camprelle, 126, 25080 Nuvolera (Bs.), Italy (U.S. importer—Moore & Co., Wm. Larkin)
Peters Stahl GmbH, Stettiner Str. 42, D-4790 Paderborn, Germany/05251-750025-27; FAX: 05251-75611 (U.S. importer—Federal Ordnance, Inc.)
Petersen Publishing Co., 8490 Sunset Blvd., Los Angeles, CA 99069
Peterson Gun Shop, Inc., A.W., 4255 W. Old U.S. 441, Mt. Dora, FL 32757-3299/904-383-4258
Peterson Instant Targets, Inc. (See Lyman Products Corp.)
Pettinger Books, Gerald, Rt. 2, Russell, IA 50238/515-535-2239
Pflumm Gun Mfg. Co., 6139 Melrose Lane, Shawnee, KS 66203/800-888-4867
PFRB Co., P.O. Box 1242, Bloomington, IL 61701/309-473-3964
Phelps Mfg. Co., Box 2266, Evansville, IN 47714/812-476-8791
Phillips & Bailey, Inc., 815A Yorkshire St., Houston, TX 77022/713-699-4288
Phoenix Arms Co. Ltd. (See Hy-Score Arms Co. Ltd.)
Phoenix Arms, 1420 S. Archibald Ave., Ontario, CA 91761/714-947-4843
Phyl-Mac, 609 NE 104th Ave., Vancouver, WA 98664/206-256-0579
Piedmont Community College, P.O. Box 1197, Roxboro, NC 27573/919-599-1181
Pierce Pistols, 2326 E. Hwy. 34, Newnan, GA 30263/404-253-8192
Pilgrim Pewter, Inc. (See Bell Originals, Sid)
Pilkington Gun Co., P.O. Box 1296, Muskogee, OK 74402/918-683-9418
Pilkington, Scott, Little Trees Ramble, P.O. Box 97, Monteagle, TN 37356/615-924-3475; FAX: 615-924-3442
Pine Technical College, 1100 4th St., Pine City, MN 55063/800-521-7463; FAX: 612-629-6766
Pioneer Guns, 5228 Montgomery Rd., Norwood, OH 45212/513-631-4871
Piotti (See U.S. importer—Moore & Co., Wm. Larkin)
Piquette, Paul R., 80 Bradford Dr., Feeding Hills, MA 01030/413-781-8300, Ext. 682
PistolPAL Products, 2930 N. Campbell Ave., Chicago, IL 60618/800-788-7725; FAX: 312-267-8080
Plaxco, J. Michael, Rt. 1, P.O. Box 203, Roland, AR 72135/501-868-9787
Plaza Cutlery, Inc., 3333 Bristol, #161, South Coast Plaza, Costa Mesa, CA 92626/714-549-3932
Plum City Ballistic Range, N2162 80th St., Plum City, WI 54761/715-647-2539
PMC/Eldorado Cartridge Corp., P.O. Box 62508, 12801 U.S. Hwy. 95 S., Boulder City, NV 89006-2508/702-294-0025; FAX: 702-294-0121
PMI, 1935 Techny Rd., Unit 16, Northbrook, IL 60062/708-272-4765; FAX: 708-272-3697
Police Bookshelf, p.O. Box 122, Concord, NH 03301/603-224-6814; FAX: 603-226-3554
Poly Technologies, Inc. (See U.S. distributor—PTK International, Inc.; U.S. importer—Keng's Firearms Specialty, Inc.)
Polywad, Inc., P.O. Box 7916, Macon, GA 31209/912-477-0669
Pomeroy, Robert, RR 1, P.O. Box 50, East Corinth, ME 04427/207-285-7721
Ponsness/Warren, P.O. Box 8, Rathdrum, ID 83858/208-687-2231; FAX: 208-687-2233
Pony Express Reloaders, 608 E. Co. Rd. D, Suite #3, St. Paul, MN 55117/612-483-9406
Pony Express Sport Shop, Inc., 16606 Schoenborn St., Sepulveda, CA 91343/818-895-1231
Porta Blind, Inc., 2700 Speedway, Wichita Falls, TX 76308/800-842-5545
Potts, Wayne E., 912 Poplar St., Denver, CO 80220/303-355-5462
Powell & Son Ltd., William, 35-37 Carrs Lane, Birmingham B4 7SX England/21-643-0689; FAX: 21-631-3504
Power Custom, Inc., RR 2, P.O. Box 756AB, Gravois Mills, MO 65037/314-372-5684
Practical Tools, Inc., P.O. Box 63, Rd #2, Rt. 611, Pipersville, PA 18947/215-766-8681
Pragotrade, 307 Humberline Dr., Rexdale, Ontario, Canada M9W 5V1/416-675-1322
Pranger, Ed G., 1414 7th St., Anacortes, WA 98221/206-293-3488
Pre-Winchester Parts Co., P.O. Box 8125, W. Palm Beach, FL 33407
Precise International, 15 Corporate Dr., Orangeburg, NY 10962/914-365-3500
Precise Metalsmithing Enterprises, 146 Curtis Hill Rd., Chehalis, WA 98532/206-748-3743; FAX: 206-748-8102

Precision Arms International, Inc., Rt. 17, Box 456, Saluda, VA 23149/804-758-5233
Precision Castings & Equipment, Inc., P.O. Box 326, Jasper, IN 47547-0326/812-634-9167
Precision Components & Guns, Rt. 55, P.O. Box 337, Pawling, NY 12564/914-855-3040
Precision Delta Corp., P.O. Box 128, Ruleville, MS 38771/601-756-2810; FAX: 601-756-2590
Precision Imports, Inc., 5040 Space Center Dr., San Antonio, TX 78218/512-666-3033
Precision Metal Finishing, John Westrom, P.O. Box 3186, Des Moines, IA 50316/515-288-8680; FAX: 515-288-8680
Precision Munitions, Inc., P.O. Box 326, Jasper, IN 47547
Precision Prods. of Wash., Inc., N. 311 Walnut Rd., Spokane, WA 99206/509-928-0604
Precision Reloading, Inc., P.O. Box 122, Stafford Springs, CT 06076/203-684-7979; FAX: 203-684-6788
Precision Sales International, Inc. (See PSI, Inc.)
Precision Small Parts, Inc., 155 Carlton Rd., Charlottesville, VA 22902/804-293-6124
Precision Specialties, 131 Hendom Dr., Feeding Hills, MA 01030/413-786-3365; FAX: 413-786-3365
Precision Sport Optics, 15571 Producer Lane, Unit G, Huntington Beach, CA 92649/714-891-1309; FAX: 714-892-6920
Precision Sports, 3736 Kellogg Rd., P.O. Box 5588, Cortland, NY 13045-5588/607-756-2851;800-847-6787
Premier Reticles, Rt. 3, P.O. Box 369, Wardensville, WV 26851/304-874-3917
Preston Pittman Game Calls, Inc., Rt. 1, Box 837, Sumrall, MS 39402
Primos Wild Game Calls, Inc., P.O. Box 12785, Jackson, MS 39236-2785/601-366-1288; FAX: 601-362-3274
Pro Load Ammunition, Inc., 1120 S. Varney St., Burbank, CA 91502/800-729-6978; FAX: 818-842-6141
Pro-Mark, Div. of Wells Lamont, 6640 W. Touhy, Chicago, IL 60648/312-647-8200
Pro-Port Ltd., 41302 Executive Dr., Mt. Clemens, MI 48045-3448/313-469-7323; FAX: 313-469-0425
Pro-Shot Products, P.O. Box 763, Taylorville, IL 62568/217-824-9133; FAX: 217-824-8861
Professional Gunsmiths of America, Inc., 1301 Franklin, P.O. Box 224E, Lexington, MO 64067/816-259-2636
Professional Hunter Supplies, P.O. Box 608, 468 Main St., Ferndale, CA 95536/707-786-4040;FAX:707-786-9117
Proline Handgun Leather, P.O. Box 112154, Tacoma, WA 98411/206-564-6652
Prolix, 15578 Mojave Dr. #D, Victorville, CA 92392/619-243-3129; FAX: 619-241-0148
Protecto Plastics, Div. of Penguin Ind., Airport Industrial Mall, Coatesville, PA 19320/215-384-6000
Protektor Model Co., 7 Ash St., Galeton, PA 16922/814-435-2442
PSI, Inc., P.O. Box 1776, Westfield, MA 01086/413-562-5055; FAX: 413-562-5056
P.S.M.G. Gun Co., 10 Park Ave., Arlington, MA 02174/617-646-8845; FAX: 617-646-2133
PTK International, Inc., 2814 New Spring Rd. 340, Atlanta, GA 30339
Puccinelli, Leonard, 5580 La Jolla Blvd., Suite 323, La Jolla, CA 92037
Pursuit Marketing, Inc. (See PMI)
Pyramid, Inc., 3292 S. Highway 97, Redmond, OR 97786

Q

QFI, 4530 NW 135 St., Opa Locka, FL 33054/305-685-5966; FAX: 305-687-6721
Quack Decoy Corp., 4 Mill St., Cumberland, RI 02864/401-723-8202
Quaker Boy, Inc., 5455 Webster Rd., Orchard Parks, NY 14127/716-662-3979
Quality Arms, Inc., Box 19477, Dept. GD, Houston, TX 77224/713-870-8377; FAX: 713-870-8524
Quality Firearms of Idaho, Inc., 114 13th Ave. S., Nampa, ID 83651/208-466-1631
Quality Firearms, Inc. (See QFI)
Quality Parts Co., 999 Roosevelt Trail, Bldg. 3, Windham, ME 04062/800-556-SWAT
Queen Cutlery Co., 507 Chestnut St., Titusville, PA 16354/800-222-5233
Quigley's Personal Protection Strategies, Paxton, 9903 Santa Monica Blvd., #300, Beverly Hills, CA 90212/310-281-1762
Quinetics Corporation, P.O. Box 13237, San Antonio, TX 78213/512-684-8561; FAX: 512-684-2912

R

R&C Knives & Such, P.O. Box 1047, Manteca, CA 95336/209-239-3722
R&J Gun Shop, 133 W. Main St., John Day, OR 97845/503-575-2130
R&R Sporting Arms, Inc. (See RPM)
R&S Industries Corp., 8255 Brentwood Industrial Dr., St. Louis, MO 63144/314-781-5400
Rabeno, Martin, Box 37F, RD #1, Spook Hole Rd., Ellenville, NY 12428/914-647-4567
Radiator Specialty Co., 1900 Wilkinson Blvd., P.O. Box 34689, Charlotte, NC 28234/800-438-6947; FAX: 800-421-9525
Rahn Gun Works, Inc., 3700 Anders Rd., Hastings, MI 49058
Ram-Line, Inc., 10601 W. 48th Ave., Wheat Ridge, CO 80033/303-467-0300
Ramos, Jesse, P.O. Box 7105, La Puente, CA 91744/818-369-6384
Ranch Products, P.O. Box 145, Malinta, OH 43535/313-277-3118; FAX: 313-565-8536
Randall Firearms Research, P.O. Box 1586, Lomita, CA 90717-5586/310-325-0102; FAX: 310-325-0298
Randall-Made Knives, P.O. Box 1988, Orlando, FL 32802/407-855-8075
Randco UK, 286 Gipsy Rd., Welling, Kent DA16 1JJ, England/44 81 303 4118
Ranger Footwear, 1100 E. Main St., Endicott, NY 13760/800-688-6148
Ranger Mfg. Co., Inc., 1536 Crescent Dr., Augusta, GA 30919/404-738-3469
Ranging, Inc., Routes 5 & 20, East Bloomfield, NY 14443/716-657-6161
Ransom International Corp., P.O. Box 3845, 1040-A Sandretto Dr., Prescott, AZ 86302/602-778-7899; FAX: 602-778-7993
Rapine Bullet Mould Mfg. Co., P.O. Box 1119, East Greenville, PA 18041/215-679-5413
Rattlers Brand, P.O. Box 311, Thomaston, GA 30286/800-652-1341; FAX: 404-647-2742
RCBS, Div. of Blount, Inc., 605 Oro Dam Blvd., Oroville, CA 95965/916-533-5191
R.D.P. Tool Co., Inc., 49162 McCoy Ave., East Liverpool, OH 43920/216-385-5129
Re-Heater, Inc., 15828 S. Broadway, #C, Gardena, CA 90248
Reagent Chemical and Research, Inc. (See Calico Hardwoods, Inc.)
Reardon Products, P.O. Box 126, Morrison, IL 61270/815-772-3155
Red Ball, 100 Factory St., Nashua, NH 03060/603-881-4420
Red Head, Inc., P.O. Box 7100, Springfield, MO 65801/417-864-5430
Red River Frontier Outfitters, P.O. Box 241, Tujunga, CA 91043/818-352-6426
Red Star Target Co., 4519 Brisebois Dr. NW, Calgary, Alberta, Canada T2L2G3/403-289-7939; FAX: 403-289-3215

Red Willow Tool & Armory, Inc., 4004 Hwy. 93 N., Stevensville, MT 59870/406-777-5401; FAX: 406-777-5402
Redding Reloading, Inc., 1089 Starr Rd., Cortland, NY 13045/607-753-3331; FAX: 607-756-8445
Redfield, Inc., 5800 E. Jewell Ave., Denver, CO 80224/303-757-6411
Redman's Rifling & Reboring, Rt. 3, Box 330A, Omak, WA 98841/509-826-5512
Reed, Dave, Rt. 1, Box 374, Minnesota City, MN 55959/507-689-2944
Reeves Sporting Clays Academy, Dan (See National Guild of Shotgun Shooting Instructors)
Refrigiwear, Inc., 71 Inip Dr., Inwood, Long Island, NY 11696
Regional Associates, P.O. Box 9849, Alexandria, VA 22304/703-461-9140
Reiswig, Wallace E., Claro Walnut Gunstock Co., 1235 Stanley Ave., Chico, CA 95928/916-342-5188
Reloaders Specialty Mfg., 7602 Carlton Rd., Coopersburg, PA 18036/215-838-9507
Remington Arms Co., 1007 Market St., Wilmington, DE 19898/302-773-5291
Remington Footwear Co., 1810 Columbia Ave., Franklin, TN 37604/800-332-2688
Renegade, P.O. Box 31546, Phoenix, AZ 85046/602-482-6777
Renner Co., R.J., 8774 Sepulveda Blvd., Suite 1, Sepulveda, CA 91343/818-892-8008; FAX: 818-892-9188
Reno, Wayne and Karen, 2808 Stagestop Rd., Jefferson, CO 80456/719-836-3452
R.E.T. Enterprises, 2608 S. Chestnut, Broken Arrow, OK 74012/918-251-GUNS; FAX: 918-251-0587
Retting, Inc., Martin B., 11029 Washington, Culver City, CA 90232/213-837-2412
R.G.-G., Inc., P.O. Box 1261, Conifer, CO 80433-1261
Rhodeside, Inc., 1704 Commerce Dr., Piqua, OH 45356/513-773-5781
Rice Protective Gun Coatings, 1320 S. Hartle Rd., Clermont, FL 34711-9571
Rice, Keith (See White Rock Tool & Die)
Richards Classic Oil Finish, John Richards, Rt. 2, Box 325, Bedford, KY 40006/502-255-7222
Richards Micro-Fit Stocks, 8331 N. San Fernando Rd., P.O. Box 1066, Sun Valley, CA 91352/818-767-6097
Richards, John (See Richards Classic Oil Finish)
Rickard, Inc., Pete, RD 1, Box 292, Crommie Rd., Cobleskill, NY 12043/518-234-3758; FAX: 518-234-2454
Ridgetop Sporting Goods, P.O. Box 306, 42907 Hilligoss Ln. East, Eatonville, WA 98328/206-832-6422
Ries, Chuck, 415 Ridgecrest Dr., Grants Pass, OR 97527/503-476-5623
Rifle Shop, The, Wm. H. Hobaugh, P.O. Box M, Philipsburg, MT 59858/406-859-3515
RIG Products, 87 Coney Island Dr., Sparks, NV 89431/703-331-5666
Rigby & Co., John, 66 Great Suffolk St., London SE1 0BU, Angleterre, England (U.S. importer—Hallowell & Co.)
Riggs, Jim, 206 Azalea, Boerne, TX 78006/512-249-8567
Riling Arms Books Co., Ray, 6844 Gorsten St., P.O. Box 18925, Philadelphia, PA 19119/215-438-2456
Ringler Custom Leather Co., P.O. Box 206, Cody, WY 82414/307-645-3255
R.I.S. Co., Inc., 718-C Timberlake Circle, Richardson, TX 75080/214-235-0933
River Road Sporting Clays, Bruce Barsotti, P.O. Box 3016, Gonzales, CA 93926/408-675-2473
Rizzini Battista, Via 2 Giugno 7/7Bis-25060 Marcheno (Brescia), Italy
Rizzini, F.LLI (See U.S. importer—Moore & Co., Wm. Larkin)
RMS Custom Gunsmithing, 4120 N. Bitterroot, Prescott Valley, AZ 86314/602-772-7626
Robar Co.'s, Inc., The, 21438 N. 7th Ave., Suite B, Phoenix, AZ 85027/602-581-2648; FAX: 602-582-0059
Robbins Scent, Inc., P.O. Box 779, Connellsville, PA 15425/412-628-2529; FAX: 412-628-9598
Roberts Jr., Wm. A., Rt. 14, P.O. Box 75, Athens, AL 35611/205-232-7027
Roberts Products, 25238 SE 32nd, Issaquah, WA 98027/206-392-8172
Roberts, J.J., 166 Manassas Dr., Manassas Park, VA 22111/703-330-0448
Robinson Firearms Mfg. Ltd., RR2, Suite 51, Comp. 24, Winfield, BC Canada V0H 2C0/604-766-5353
Robinson, Don, Pennsylvania Hse., 36 Fairfax Crescent, Southowram, Halifax, W. Yorkshire HX3 9SQ, England/0422-364458
Rochester Lead Works, Inc., 76 Anderson Ave., Rochester, NY 14607/716-442-8500
Rockwood Corp., 136 Lincoln Blvd., Middlesex, NJ 08846/908-560-7171
Rocky Fork Enterprises, P.O. Box 427, 878 Battle Rd., Nolensville, TN 37135/615-941-1307
Rocky Mountain High Sports Glasses, 8121 N. Central Park Ave., Skokie, IL 60076/708-679-1012; FAX: 708-679-0184
Rocky Mountain Rifle Works Ltd., 1707 14th St., Boulder, CO 80302/303-443-9189
Rocky Mountain Target Co., P.O. Box 700, Blackhawk, SD 57718/605-787-5946
Rocky, Div. of Wm. Brooks Shoe Co., 294 Harper St., Nelsonville, OH 45764/614-753-1951; FAX: 614-753-4042
Rogers Gunsmithing, Bob, P.O. Box 305, 344 S. Walnut St., Franklin Grove, IL 61031/815-456-2685; FAX: 815-288-7142
Rogers Ltd., 891 Dixwell Ave., Hamden, CT 06514/203-865-8484; FAX: 800-847-7492
Rohner, Hans and John, 710 Sunshine Canyon, Boulder, CO 80302/303-444-3841
Rolston, Jr., Fred, 210 E. Cummins, Tecumseh, MI 49286/517-423-6002
Rooster Laboratories, P.O. Box 412514, Kansas City, MO 64141/816-474-1622; FAX: 816-474-1307
Rorschach Precision Products, P.O. Box 151613, Irving, TX 75015/214-790-3487
Rosenberg & Sons, Jack A., 12229 Cox Lane, Dallas, TX 75234/214-241-6302
Rosser, Bob, 142 Ramsey Dr., Albertville, AL 35950/205-878-5388
Rossi S.A. Metalurgica E Municoes, Amadeo, Rua Amadeo Rossi, 143, Sao Leopoldo, RS, Brazil 93 030/0512-92-5566 (U.S. importer—Interarms)
Roto/Carve, 6509 Indian Hills Rd., Minneapolis, MN 55435/612-944-5150
Royal Arms, 1934 John Towers Ave. #A, El Cajon, CA 92020/619-448-5466
RPM, 15481 N. Twin Lakes Dr., Tucson, AZ 85737/602-825-1233; FAX: 602-825-1233
R-Tech Corporation, P.O. Box 1281, Cottage Grove, OR 97424/503-942-5126
Rubright Bullets, 1008 S. Quince Rd., Walnutport, PA 18088/215-767-1339
Ruger (See Sturm, Ruger & Co.)
Ruko Products, Suite 102, 2245 Kenmore Ave., Buffalo, NY 14207/716-874-2707
Rundell's Gun Shop, 6198 Frances Rd., Clio, MI 48420/313-687-0559
Runge, Robert P., 94 Grove St., Ilion, NY 13357/315-894-3036
Rupert's Gun Shop, 2202 Dick Rd., Suite B, Fenwick, MI 48834/517-248-3252
Russell Knives, Inc., A.G., 1705 Hwy. 71 North, Springdale, AR 72764/501-751-7341
Russell's Rifle Shop, Rt. 5, P.O. Box 92, Georgetown, TX 78626/512-778-5338
Russwood Custom Pistol Grips, Russ Maloni, 455 Olean Rd., P.O. Box 460, East Aurora, NY 14052/716-652-7131

Rusteprufe Laboratories, Robert D. Munger, 1319 Jefferson Ave., Sparta, WI 54656/608-269-4144

Rusty Duck Premium Gun Care Products, 7785 Foundation Dr., Florence, KY 41042/606-342-5553

Rutgers Book Center, 127 Raritan Ave., Highland Park, NJ 08904/908-545-4344

Rutgers Gun & Boat Center, 127 Raritan Ave., Highland Park, NJ 08904/908-545-4344

Ruvel & Co., Inc. 4128 W. Belmont Ave., Chicago, IL 60641/312-286-9494

R.V.I., P.O. Box Q-1, 925 Boblett St., Blaine, WA 98230/206-595-2933

RWS (See U.S. importer—Dynamit Nobel-RWS, Inc.)

Ryan, Chad L., RR 3, Box 72, Cresco, IA 52136/319-547-4384

Rybka Custom Leather Equipment, Thad, 32 Havilah Hill, Odenville, AL 35120

S

S&B Industries, 11238 McKinley Rd., Montrose, MI 48457/313-639-5491

S&H Arms Mfg. Co., Rt. 3, Box 689, Berryville, AR 72616/501-545-3511

S&K Mfg. Co., P.O. Box 247, Pittsfield, PA 16340/814-563-7808; FAX: 814-563-7808

S&S Firearms, 74-11 Myrtle Ave., Glendale, NY 11385/718-497-1100

SAECO (See Redding Reloading, Inc.)

Saf-T-Bak, Inc., 201 Cayuga Ave., Altoona, PA 16602

Safari Arms/SGW (See Olympic Arms, Inc.)

Safari Gun Co., 6410 Brandon Ave., Springfield, VA 22150/703-569-1097

Safari Outfitters Ltd., 71 Ethan Allan Hwy., Ridgefield, CT 06877/203-544-9505

Safari Press, Inc., 15621 Chemical Lane #B, Huntington Beach, CA 92649/714-894-9080; FAX: 714-894-4949

Safariland Ltd., Inc., 3120 E. Mission Blvd., P.O. Box 51478, Ontario, CA 91761/714-923-7300; FAX: 714-923-7400

Safesport Manufacturing Co., 1100 W. 45th Ave., Denver, CO 80211/303-433-6506; FAX: 303-433-4112

Safety Direct, 56 Coney Island Dr., Sparks, NV 89431/702-354-4451

Safety Speed Holster, Inc., 910 S. Vail Ave., Montebello, CA 90640/213-723-4140; FAX: 213-726-6973

Sako Ltd., P.O. Box 149, SF-11101, Riihimaki, Finland (U.S. importer—Stoeger Industries)

Salter Calls, Inc., Eddie, Hwy. 31 South-Brewton Industrial Park, Brewton, AL 36426/205-867-2584; FAX: 206-867-9005

Samco Global Arms, Inc., 6995 NW 43rd St., Miami, FL 33166/305-593-9782

Sampson, Roger, 430 N. Grove, Mora, MN 55051/612-679-4868

San Angelo Sports Products, Inc., 909 W. 14th St., San Angelo, TX 76903/915-655-7126; FAX: 915-653-6720

San Francisco Gun Exchange, 124 Second St., San Francisco, CA 94105/415-982-6097

Sanders Custom Gun Service, 2358 Tyler Lane, Louisville, KY 40205/502-454-3338

Sandia Die & Cartridge Co., 37 Atancacio Rd. NE, Albuquerque, NM 87123/505-298-5729

Sandy's Custom Gunshop, Rt. #1, P.O. Box 4, Rockport, IL 62370/217-437-4241

Sarco, Inc., 323 Union St., Stirling, NJ 07980/908-647-3800

Sardius Industries Ltd., 72 Rokach St., Ramat Gan, Israel 52542/972-3-7521353 (U.S. importer—Arms Corp. of America, Inc.)

Sauer (See U.S. importers—G.U., Inc.; Simmons Enterprises, Ernie)

Sauer Sporting Rifles, P.O. Box 37669, Omaha, NE 68137

Savage Arms, Inc., Springdale Rd., Westfield, MA 01085/413-568-7001

Savana Sports, Inc., 5763 Ferrier St., Montreal, Quebec, Canada/514-739-1753; FAX: 514-739-1755

Scanco Environmental Systems, 5000 Highlands Parkway, Suite 180, Atlanta, GA 30082/404-431-0025; FAX: 404-431-0028

Scansport, Inc., P.O. Box 700, Enfield, NH 03748/603-632-7654

Scattergun Technologies, Inc., 518 3rd Ave. S., Nashville, TN 37210/615-254-1441

Sceery Company, E.J., 1949 Osage Lane, Sante Fe, NM 87501/505-983-2125

Schaefer Shooting Sports, 2280 Grand Ave., Baldwin, NY 11510/516-379-4900; FAX: 516-379-6701

Schaefer, Roy V., 101 Irving Rd., Eugene, OR 97404/503-688-4333

Scharch Mfg., Inc., 10325 Co. Rd. 120, Unit C, Salida, CO 81201/719-539-7242

Scherer, Box 250, Ewing, VA 24248/615-733-2615; FAX: 615-733-2073

Schiffman, Curt, 3017 Kevin Cr., Idaho Falls, ID 83402/208-524-4684

Schiffman, Mike, 8233 S. Crystal Springs, McCammon, ID 83250/208-254-9114

Schiffman, Norman, 3017 Kevin Cr., Idaho Falls, ID 83402/208-524-4684

Schmidt & Bender (See U.S. importer—Jaeger, Inc., Paul)

Schneider Rifle Barrels, Inc., Gary, 12202 N. 62nd Pl., Scottsdale, AZ 85254/602-948-2525

Schrade Cutlery Corp., Rt. 209 North, Ellenville, NY 12428/914-647-7600

Schulz Industries, 16247 Minnesota Ave., Paramount, CA 90723/213-439-5903

Schumakers Gun Shop, William, 512 Prouty Corner Lp. #A, Colville, WA 99114/509-684-4848

Schwartz Custom Guns, David W., 2505 Waller St., Eau Claire, WI 54703/715-832-1735

Schwartz Custom Guns, Wayne E., 970 E. Britton Rd., Morrice, MI 48857/517-625-4079

Scobey Duck & Goose Calls, Glynn, Rt. 3, Box 37, Newbern, TN 38059/901-643-6241

Scot Powder Co. of Ohio, Inc., 430 Powder Plant Rd., McArthur, OH 45651/614-596-2704; FAX: 614-596-4050

Scotch Hunting Products Co., Inc., 6619 Oak Orchard Rd., Elba, NY 14058/716-757-9958; FAX: 716-757-9066

Scott (Gunmakers) Ltd., W&C, Premier Works, Tame Rd., Witton, Birmingham, B6 7HS England/021-328-4107

Scott Fine Guns, Inc., Thad, P.O. Box 412, Indianola, MS 38751/601-887-5929

Scott, Inc., Tyler, 313 Rugby Ave., Terrace Park, OH 45174/513-831-7603

Scott/McDougall Custom Gunsmiths, 880 Piner Rd., Suite 50, Santa Rosa, CA 95403/707-546-2264

Scruggs' Game Calls, Stanley, Rt. 1, Hwy. 661, Cullen, VA 23934/804-542-4241, 800-323-4828

Seacliff International, Inc., 2210 Santa Anita, S. El Monte, CA 91733/818-350-0515

Seattle Binocular & Scope Repair Co., P.O. Box 46094, Seattle, WA 98146/206-932-3733

Second Chance Body Armor, P.O. Box 578, Central Lake, MI 49622/616-544-5721; FAX: 616-544-9824

Security Awareness & Firearms Education, P.O. Box 864, Post Falls, ID 83854/208-773-3624

Seecamp Co., Inc., L.W., P.O. Box 255, New Haven, CT 06502/203-877-3429

Seligman Shooting Products, Box 133, Seligman, AZ 86337/602-422-3607

Selsi Co., Inc., 40 Veterans Blvd., Carlstadt, NJ 07072-0497/201-935-5851

Semmer, Charles, 7885 Cyd Dr., Denver, CO 80221/303-429-6947

Seneca Run Iron Works, Inc., "Swagease," P.O. Box 3032, Greeley, CO 80633/303-352-1425

Servus Footwear Co., 1136 2nd St., Rock Island, IL 61204-3610/309-786-7741; FAX: 309-786-9808

S.G.S. Sporting Guns Srl., F1 Milanofiori, Assago, 20090 Italy/2-8241144-5; FAX: 2-8254644

Shadow Concealment Systems, P.O. Box 3952, Dept. GD, Wilmington, NC 28406/919-791-6656

Shane's Gunsmithing, P.O. Box 321, Hwy. 51 S., Minocqua, WI 54548/715-356-5414

Shappy Bullets, 76 Milldale Ave., Plantsville, CT 06479/203-621-3704

Sharon Rifle Barrel Co., 14396 D. Tuolumne Rd., Sonora, CA 95370/209-532-4139

Sharps Arms Co., Inc., C. (See Montana Armory, Inc.)

Shaw's Finest in Guns, 1255 N. Broadway #351, Escondido, CA 92026-2858

Shaw, Inc., E.R. (See Small Arms Mfg. Co.)

Sheffield Knifemakers Supply, P.O. Box 141, Deland, FL 32721/904-775-6453; FAX: 904-774-5754

Shell Shack, 113 E. Main, Laurel, MT 59044/406-628-8986

Shepherd Scope Ltd., Box 189, Waterloo, NE 68069/402-779-2424; FAX: 402-779-4010

Sheridan Products, Inc. (See Benjamin/Sheridan Co.)

Sheridan USA, Inc., Austin, P.O. Box 577, Durham, CT 06422

Sherk, Dan A., 1311-105 AVe., Dawson Creek, B.C. V1G 2L9, Canada/604-782-3720

Sherwood Intl. Export Corp., 18714 Parthenia St., Northridge, CA 91324/818-349-7600

Sherwood, George, 46 N. River Dr., Roseburg, OR 97470/503-672-3159

Shilen Rifles, Inc., P.O. Box 1300, 205 Metro Park Blvd., Ennis, TX 75119/214-875-5318; FAX: 214-875-1442

Shiloh Rifle Mfg., 201 Centennial Dr., Big Timber, MT 59011/406-932-4454; FAX: 406-932-5627

Shirley Co. Gun & Riflemakers Ltd., J.A., P.O. Box 368, High Wycombe, Bucks. HP13 6YN, England/0494-446883; FAX: 0494-463685

Shockley, Harold H., 204 E. Farmington Rd., Hanna City, IL 61536/309-565-4524

Shoemaker & Sons, Inc., Tex, 714 W. Cienega Ave., San Dimas, CA 91750/714-592-2071; FAX: 714-592-2378

Shooter Shop, The, 514 N. Main, Butte, MT 59701/406-723-3842

Shooter's World, 3828 N. 28th Ave., Phoenix, AZ 85017/602-266-0170

Shooters Accessory Supply (See Corbin Mfg. & Supply, Inc.)

Shooters Supply, 1120 Tieton Dr., Yakima, WA 98902/509-452-1181

Shootin' Accessories Ltd., P.O. Box 6810, Auburn, CA 95604/916-889-2220

Shootin' Shack, Inc., 1065 Silver Beach Rd., Riviera Beach, FL 33403/407-842-0990

Shooting Arts Ltd., Box 621399, Littleton, CO 80162/303-933-2539

Shooting Chrony, Inc., 2480 Cawthra Rd., Unit 22, Mississauga, Ont. L5A 2X2, Canada/416-276-6292

Shooting Gallery, The, 8070 Southern Blvd., Boardman, OH 44512/216-726-7788

Shooting Specialties (See Titus, Daniel)

Shotgun Shop, The, 14145 Proctor Ave., Suite 3, Industry, CA 91746/818-855-2737; FAX: 818-855-2735

Shotguns Unlimited, 2307 Fon Du Lac Rd., Richmond, VA 23229/804-752-7115

Shurkatch Corp., P.O. Box 850, Richfield Springs, NY 13439/315-858-1470; FAX: 315-858-2969

Sierra Bullets, 1400 W. Henry St., Sedalia, MO 65301/816-827-6300; FAX: 816-827-4999

SIG, CH-8212 Neuhausen, Switzerland (U.S. importer—Mandall Shooting Supplies, Inc.)

SIG-Sauer (See U.S. importer—Sigarms, Inc.)

Sigarms, Inc., Industrial Drive, Exeter, NH 03833/603-772-2302

Sight Right Co. (See Crosman Corp.)

Sight Shop, The, John G. Lawson, 1802 E. Columbia Ave., Tacoma, WA 98404/206-474-5465

Sile Distributors, 7 Centre Market Pl., New York, NY 10013/212-925-4389

Silent Hunter, 1100 Newton Ave., W. Collingswood, NJ 08107/609-854-3276

Siler Locks, 7 Acton Woods Rd., Candler, NC 28715/704-667-9991

Silhouette Arms Custom 45 Shop, Inc., P.O. Box 3431, N. Fort Myers, FL 33918-3431/813-656-2639

Silhouette Leathers, P.O. Box 280202, Memphis, TN 38124/901-372-5731

Silver Ridge Gun Shop (See Goodwin, Fred)

Simmons Enterprises, Ernie, 709 East Elizabethtown Rd., Manheim, PA 17545/717-664-4040

Simmons Outdoor Corp., 14530 SW 119 Ave., Miami, FL 33186/305-252-0477

Simmons, Jerry, 715 Middlebury St., Goshen, IN 46526/219-533-8546

Sinclair International, Inc., 718 Broadway, New Haven, IN 46774/219-493-1858

Sinclair, W.P., Box 1209, Warminster, Wiltshire BA12 9XJ, England/01044-985-218544; FAX: 01044-985-214111

Single Shot, Inc. (See Montana Armory, Inc.)

Singletary, Kent, 14020 N. Black Canyon #1071, Phoenix, AZ 85023/602-789-6004

Sipes Gun Shop, 919 High St., Little Rock, AR 72202/501-376-8940

Siskiyou Gun Works (See Donnelly, C.P.)

Six Enterprises, 320-D Turtle Creek Ct., San Jose, CA 95125/408-999-0201; FAX: 408-999-0216

Skaggs, R.E., P.O. Box 34, 1217 S. Church, Princeton, IL 61356/815-875-8207

SKB Arms Co., C.P.O. Box 1401, Tokyo, Japan (U.S. importers—G.U., Inc.; Simmons Enterprises, Ernie)

S.K. Guns, Inc., 3041A Main Ave., Fargo, ND 58103/701-293-4867; FAX: 701-232-0001

Sklany, Steve, 566 Birch Grove Dr., Kalispell, MT 59901/406-755-4257

Slezak, Jerome F., 1290 Marlowe, Lakewood (Cleveland), OH 44107/216-221-1668

Slings & Arrows, RD 1, Box 91A, Barnet, VT 05821/802-633-3314; FAX: 802-684-1108

Slings 'N Things, Inc., 8909 Bedford Circle, Suite 11, Omaha, NE 68134/402-571-6954; FAX: 402-571-7082

Slipshot MTS Group, P.O. Box 5, Postal Station D, Etobicoke, Ont., Canada M9A 4X1/416-762-0962

Slug Site Co., Ozark Wilds, Rt. 2, P.O. Box 158, Versailles, MO 65084/314-378-6430

Small Arms Mfg. Co., 611 Thoms Run Rd., Bridgeville, PA 15017/412-221-4343; FAX: 412-221-8443

Smires, Clifford L., RD 1, Box 100, Columbus, NJ 08022/609-298-3158

Smith & Wesson, 2100 Roosevelt Ave., Springfield, MA 01102/413-781-8300

Smith Saddlery, Jesse W., N. 1325 Division, Spokane, WA 99202/509-325-0622

Smith Whetstone, Inc., 1500 Sleepy Valley Rd., Hot Springs, AR 71901/501-321-2244; FAX: 501-321-9232

Smith, Art, 4124 Thrushwood Lane, Minnetonka, MN 55345/612-935-7829

Smith, Mark A., 200 N. 9th, Sinclair, WY 82334/307-324-7929

Smith, Michael, 620 Nye Circle, Chattanooga, TN 37405/615-267-8341

Smith, Ron, 5869 Straley, Ft. Worth, TX 76114/817-732-6768

Smokey Valley Rifles, E. 1998 Smokey Valley Rd., Scandinavia, WI 54977/715-467-2674

Snapp's Gunshop, 6911 E. Washington Rd., Clare, MI 48617/517-386-9226
Snider Stocks, Walter S., Rt. 2 P.O. Box 147, Denton, NC 27239
Sno-Seal (See Atsko/Sno-Seal)
Societa Armi Bresciane Srl., Via Artigiani 93, Gardone Val Trompia, Italy 25063/30-8911640, 30-8911648
Sonderman, Robert, 735 Kenton Dr., Charleston, IL 61920/217-345-5429
Sotheby's, 1334 York Ave. at 72nd St., New York, NY 10021
Sound Technology, P.O. Box 1132, Kodiak, AK 99615/907-486-8448
South Bend Replicas, Inc., 61650 Oak Rd., South Bend, IN 46614/219-289-4500
South Central Research Corp., P.O. Box 660, Kary, TX 77492-0660/713-492-6332
Southeastern Community College, 1015 S. Gear Ave., West Burlington, IA 52655/319-752-2731
Southern Ammunition Co., Inc., Rt. 1, Box 6B, Latta, SC 29565-9701/803-752-7751; FAX: 803-752-2022
Southern Armory, The, Rt. 2, Box 134, Woodlawn, VA 24381/703-236-7835; FAX: 703-236-3714
Southern Bloomer Mfg. Company, P.O. Box 1621, Bristol, TN 37620/615-878-6660
Southwest Institute of Firearms Training (See S.W.I.F.T.)
Southwind Sanctions, P.O. Box 445, Aledo, TX 76008/817-441-8917
Sparks, Milt, P.O. Box 187, Idaho City, ID 83631/208-392-6695
Specialized Weapons, Inc. (See Tapco, Inc.)
Specialty Gunsmithing, Lynn McMurdo, P.O. Box 404, Afton, WY 83110/307-886-5535
Speedfeed, Inc., P.O. Box 258, Lafayette, CA 94549/510-284-2929; FAX: 510-284-2879
Speer Products, Div. of Blount, Inc., P.O. Box 856, Lewiston, ID 83501/208-746-2351
Spegel, Craig, P.O. Box 108, Bay City, OR 97107/503-377-2697
Speiser, Fred D., 2229 Dearborn, Missoula, MT 59801/406-549-8133
Spence, George W., 115 Locust St., Steele, MO 63877/314-695-4926
Spencer Reblue Service, 1820 Tupelo Trail, Holt, MI 48842/517-694-7474
SPG Bullet Lubricant, Box 761, Livingston, MT 59047
Spokhandguns, Inc., 1206 Fig St., Benton City, WA 99320/509-588-5255
Sport Flite Mfg., Inc., P.O. Box 1082, Bloomfield Hills, MI 48303/313-647-3747
Sport Specialties (See Owen, Harry)
Sportarms of Florida, 5555 NW 36 Ave., Miami, FL 33142/305-635-2411
Sporting Arms Mfg., Inc., 801 Hall Ave., Littlefield, TX 79339/806-385-5665; FAX: 806-385-3394
Sports Innovations, Inc., P.O. Box 5181, 8505 Jacksboro Hwy., Wichita Falls, TX 76307/817-723-6015
Sports Shack (See Quality Firearms of Idaho, Inc.)
Sports Support Systems, Inc., 28416 Pacheco, Mission Viejo, CA 92692/714-367-0343
Sportsman Supply Co., 714 E. Eastwood, P.O. Box 650, Marshall, MO 65340
Sportsman's Communicators, 588 Radcliffe Ave., Pacific Palisades, CA 90272
Sportsmen's Equipment Co., 915 W. Washington, San Diego, CA 92103/619-296-1501
Sportsmen's Exchange & Western Gun Traders, Inc., 560 S. "C" St., Oxnard, CA 93030/805-483-1917
Spradlin's, 113 Arthur St., Pueblo, CO 81004/719-543-9462
Springfield Armory, Inc., 420 W. Main St., Geneseo, IL 61254/309-944-5631; FAX: 309-944-3676
Springfield Sporters, Inc., RD 1, Penn Run, PA 15765/412-254-2626; FAX: 412-254-9173
Spyderco, Inc., P.O. Box 800, Golden, CO 80402/800-525-7770
SSK Co., 220 N. Belvidere Ave., York, PA 17404/717-854-2897
SSK Industries, 721 Woodvue Lane, Wintersville, OH 43952/614-264-0176; FAX: 614-264-2257
St. Lawrence Sales, Inc., 12 W. Fint St., Lake Orion, MI 48035/313-693-7760; 313-693-7718
Stackpole Books, P.O. Box 1831, Harrisburg, PA 17105/717-234-5041; FAX: 717-234-1359
Stalker, Inc., P.O. Box 21, Fishermans Wharf Rd., Malakoff, TX 75148/903-489-1010
Stalwart Corp., P.O. Box 357, 756 N. Garfield, Pocatello, ID 83204/208-232-7899
Star Bonifacio Echeverria S.A., Torrekva 3, Eibar, Spain 20600/43-117340; FAX: 43-111524 (U.S. importer—Interarms)
Star Machine Works, 418 10th Ave., San Diego, CA 92101/619-232-3216
Star Reloading Co., Inc., 5520 Rock Hampton Ct., Indianapolis, IN 46268/317-872-5840
Starlight Training Center, Inc., Rt. 1, P.O. Box 88, Bronaugh, MO 64728/417-843-3555
Starnes, Ken, 1733 W. Peralta Ave., Mesa, AZ 85202/602-730-0980
Starrett Co., L.S., 121 Crescent St., Athol, MA 01331/617-249-3551
State Arms Gun Co., 815 S. Division St., Waunakee, WI 53597/608-849-5800
Steelman's Gun Shop, 10465 Beers Rd., Swartz Creek, MI 48473/313-735-4884
Steffens, Ron, 18396 Mariposa Creek Rd., Willits, CA 95490/707-485-0873
Steger, James R., 1131 Dorsey Pl., Plainfield, NJ 07062
Steves House of Guns, Rt. 1, Minnesota City, MN 55959/507-689-2573
Stevi Machine, 4004 Highway 93 North, Stevensville, MT 59870/406-777-5401
Stewart Game Calls, Inc., Johnny, P.O. Box 7954, 5100 Fort Ave., Waco, TX 76714/817-772-3261
Steyr Mannlicher, Mannlicherstrabe 1, P.O. Box 1000, A-4400 Steyr, Austria/0043-7252-67331; FAX: 0043-7252-68621 (U.S. importer—GSI, Inc.)
Steyr-Daimler-Puch, Schonauerstrasse 5, A-4400 Steyr (U.S. importer—GSI, Inc.)
Stoeger Industries, 55 Ruta Ct., S. Hackensack, NJ 07606/201-440-2700; FAX: 201-440-2707
Stoeger Publishing Co. (See Stoeger Industries)
Stone Enterprises Ltd., Rt. 609, P.O. Box 335, Wicomico Church, VA 22579/804-580-5114
Stoney Baroque Shooters Supply, Rt. 2, Box 325, Bedford, KY 40006/502-255-7222
Stott's Creek Armory, Inc., RR1, Box 70, Morgantown, IN 46160/317-878-5489
Stratco, Inc., 343 1st Ave. W., Suite 204, Kalispell, MT 59901/406-755-4034; FAX: 406-257-4753
Strawbridge, Victor W., 6 Pineview Dr., Dover, NH 03820/603-742-0013
Streamlight, Inc., 1030 W. Germantown Pike, Norristown, PA 19403/215-631-0600
Strong Holster Co., 105 Maplewood Ave., Gloucester, MA 01930/508-281-3300; FAX: 508-281-6321
Stroup, Earl R., 30506 Flossmoor Way, Hayward, CA 94544/415-471-1549
Strutz Rifle Barrels, Inc., W.C., P.O. Box 611, Eagle River, WI 54521/715-479-4766
Stuart Products, Inc., P.O. Box 1587, Easley, SC 29641/803-859-9360
Sturm, Ruger & Co., Inc., Lacey Place, Southport, CT 06490/203-259-7843
Su-Press-On, Inc., P.O. Box 09161, Detroit, MI 48209/313-842-4222
Summit Specialties, Inc., P.O. Box 786, Decatur, AL 35602/205-353-0634
Sundance Industries, Inc., 25163 W. Avenue Stanford, Valencia, CA 91355/805-257-4807
Sunora Gun Shop, 22935 Watkins St., Buckeye, AZ 85326/602-386-3193; FAX: 602-386-6372
Sure Shot of LA, Inc., 103 Coachman Dr., Houma, LA 70360/504-876-6709

Sure-Shot Game Calls, Inc., P.O. Box 816, 6835 Capitol, Groves, TX 77619/409-962-1636; FAX: 409-962-5465
Survival Arms, Inc., 4500 Pine Cone Place, Cocoa, FL 32922/407-633-4880; FAX: 407-633-4975
Survival Books/The Larder, 11106 Magnolia Blvd., North Hollywood, CA 91601/818-763-0804
Swageease (See Seneca Run Iron Works, Inc.)
Swampfire Shop, The (See Peterson Gun Shop, Inc., A.W.)
Swann, D.J., 5 Orsova Close, Eltham North, Vic. 3095, Australia/03-431-0323
Swanndri New Zealand, 152 Elm Ave., Burlingame, CA 94010/415-347-6158
Swarovski Optik (See Greenwood & Gryphon Ltd.)
Sweet Home, Inc., P.O. Box 900, Orrville, OH 44667-0900
Swenson's 45 Shop, A.D., P.O. Box 606, Fallbrook, CA 92028
S.W.I.F.T., 4610 Blue Diamond Rd., Las Vegas, NV 89118/702-897-1100
Swift Bullet Co., 201 Main St., P.O. Box 27, Quinter, KS 67752/913-754-3959
Swift Instruments, Inc., 952 Dorchester Ave., Boston, MA 02125/617-436-2960; FAX: 617-436-3232
Swift River Gunworks, Inc., 450 State St., Belchertown, MA 01007/413-323-4052
Swiss Army Knives, Inc., 151 Long Hill Crossroads, 37 Canal St., Shelton, CT 06484/800-243-4032
Swivel Machine Works, Inc., 167 Cherry St., Suite 286, Milford, CT 06460/203-926-1840
Szweda, Robert (See RMS Custom Gunsmithing)

T

3-D Ammunition & Bullets, 112 Plum St., P.O. Box J, Doniphan, NE 68832/402-845-2285; FAX: 402-815-6546
10-X Products Group, 2915 Lyndon B. Johnson Freeway, Suite 133, Dallas, TX 75234/214-243-4016
300 Gunsmith Service, Inc., 6850 S. Yosemite Ct., Englewood, CO 80112/303-773-0300
T&S Industries, Inc., 1027 Skyview Dr., W. Carrollton, OH 45449-1640/513-859-8414
Tabler Marketing, 2554 Lincoln Blvd. #555, Marina Del Rey, CA 90291-5082/818-366-7485; FAX: 818-994-7696
Tactical Training Center, 574 Miami Bluff Ct., Loveland, OH 45140/513-677-8229
Talley, Dave, P.O. Box 821, Glenrock, WY 82637/307-436-8724
Talmage, William G., 540 W. Phantom Creek Dr., Meadview, AZ 86444/602-564-2380
Tamarack Products, Inc., P.O. Box 625, Wauconda, IL 60084/708-526-9333
Tanfoglio S.r.l., Fratelli, via Valtrompia 39/41, 25068 Gardone V.T., Brescia, Italy/30-8910361; FAX: 30-8910183 (Imported by E.A.A. Corp.)
Tanglefree Industries, 16102 Duggans Rd., Grass Valley, CA 95949
Tank's Rifle Shop, 1324 Ohio St., P.O. Box 474, Fremont, NE 68025/402-727-1317
Tanner (See U.S. importer—Mandall Shooting Supplies, Inc.)
Tapco, Inc., P.O. Box 546, Smyrna, GA 30081/404-435-9782; 404-333-9782
Taracorp Industries, 16th & Cleveland Blvd., Granite City, IL 62040/618-451-4400
Tasco Sales, Inc., 7600 NW 84th Ave., Miami, FL 33015/305-591-3670; FAX: 305-592-5895
Taurus Firearms, Inc., 16175 NW 49th Ave., Miami, FL 33014/305-624-1115; FAX: 305-623-7506
Taurus International Firearms (See U.S. importer—Taurus Firearms, Inc.)
Taurus, S.A., Forjas, Avenida Do Forte 511, Porto Alegre, Brazil 91360/55 512-40 22 44
Taylor & Robbins, P.O. Box 164, Rixford, PA 16745/814-966-3233
Taylor's & Co., Inc., 1180 Broad Ave., Winchester, VA 22601/703-722-2017; FAX: 703-722-2018
T.D. Arms, 32464 #2 23 Mile Rd., New Baltimore, MI 48047/313-949-1890
TDP Industries, Inc., 603 Airport Blvd., Doylestown, PA 18901/215-345-8687
Techni-Mec, Via Gitti s.n., 25060 Marcheno, Italy (U.S. importer—Rahn Gun Works, Inc.)
Tecnolegno S.p.A., Via A. Locatelli, 6/10, 24019 Zogno, Italy/0345-91114
Tele-Optics, 5514 W. Lawrence Ave., Chicago, IL 60630/312-283-7757
Tele-Optics, Inc., P.O. Box 176, 219 E. Higgins Rd., Gilberts, IL 60136/708-426-7444
Teledyne Co., 290 E. Prairie St., Crystal Lake, IL 60014
Ten-Ring Precision, Inc., 1449 Blue Crest Lane, San Antonio, TX 78232/512-494-3063; FAX: 512-494-3066
Tennessee Valley Mfg., P.O. Box 1175, Corinth, MS 38834/601-286-5014
Tepeco, P.O. Box 342, Friendswood, TX 77546/713-482-2702
Tertin, James A. (See Jaeger, Inc., Paul)
Texas Longhorn Arms, Inc., P.O. Box 703, Richmond, TX 77469/713-341-0775; FAX: 713-660-0493
Texas Platers Supply, 2453 W. Five Mile Parkway, Dallas, TX 75233/214-330-7168
T.F.C. S.p.A., Via G. Marconi 118/B, Villa Carcina, Brescia 25069, Italy/030-881271; FAX: 030-881826
Theis, Terry, P.O. Box 535, Fredericksburg, TX 78624/512-997-6778
Theoben Engineering (See U.S. importer—Air Rifle Specialists)
Thiewes, George W., 1846 Allen Lane, St. Charles, IL 60174/708-584-1383
Thirion, Denise, P.O. Box 408, 3240 Edison St., Graton, CA 95444/707-829-1876
Thomas, Charles C., 2600 S. First St., Springfield, IL 62794/217-789-8980; FAX: 217-789-9130
Thompson Bullet Lube Co., P.O. Box 472343, Garland, TX 75047-2343/214-271-8063; FAX: 214-840-6743
Thompson Precision, 110 Mary St., P.O. Box 251, Warren, IL 61087/815-745-3625
Thompson Target Technology, 618 Roslyn Ave., SW, Canton, OH 44710/216-453-7707
Thompson, Larry R., Larry's Gun Shop, 521 E. Lake Ave., Watsonville, CA 95076/408-724-5328
Thompson, Norm, 18905 NW Thurman St., Portland, OR 97209
Thompson, Randall (See Highline Machine Co.)
Thompson/Center Arms, Farmington Rd., P.O. Box 5002, Rochester, NH 03867/603-332-2394
Threat Management Institute, 1 St. Francis Place #2801, San Francisco, CA 94107/415-777-0303
Three-Ten Corp., P.O. Box 269, Feeding Hills, MA 01030/413-789-2086
Thunder Mountain Arms, P.O. Box 593, Oak Harbor, WA 98277/206-679-4657; FAX: 206-675-1114
Thunderbird Cartridge Co., Inc., P.O. Box 302, Phoenix, AZ 85001/602-237-3823
Thurston Sports, Inc., RD #3 Donovan Rd., Auburn, NY 13021/315-253-0966
Tiger-Hunt, Michael D. Barton, Box 379, Beaverdale, PA 15921/814-487-7956
Tikka (See U.S. importer—Stoeger Industries)
Tillinghast, James C., P.O. Box 405DG, Hancock, NH 03449/603-525-4049

Timney Mfg., Inc., 3065 W. Fairmont Ave., Phoenix, AZ 85017/602-274-2999; FAX: 602-240-0361

Tink's Safariland Hunting Corp., P.O. Box 244, Madison, GA 30650/404-342-4915

Tinks & Ben Lee Hunting Products (See Wellington Outdoors)

Tippman Pneumatics, Inc., 3518 Adams Center Rd., Fort Wayne, IN 46825/219-749-6619

Tirelli, Snc Di Tirelli Primo E.C., Via Matteotti No. 359, Gardone V.T., Brescia, Italy 25063/030-8912819; FAX: 030-832240

Titus, Daniel, Shooting Specialties, 872 Penn St., Bryn Mawr, PA 19010/215-525-8829

TMI Products, 930 S. Plumer Ave., Tucson, AZ 85719/602-792-1075; FAX: 602-792-0093

Tom's Gun Repair, Thomas G. Ivanoff, 76-6 Rt. Southfork Rd., Cody, WY 82414/307-587-6949

Tom's Gunshop, 3601 Central Ave., Hot Springs, AR 71913/501-624-3856

Torel, Inc., 1053 N. South St., P.O. Box 592, Yoakum, TX 77995/512-293-2341; FAX: 512-293-3413

Totally Dependable Products (See TDP Industries, Inc.)

Track of the Wolf, Inc., P.O. Box 6, Osseo, MN 55369-0006/612-424-2500; FAX: 612-424-9860

Tradewinds, Inc., P.O. Box 1191, 2339-41 Tacoma Ave. S., Tacoma, WA 98401/206-272-4887

Traditions, Inc., 500 Main St., P.O. Box 235, Deep River, CT 06417/203-526-9555; FAx: 203-526-4564

Trafalgar Square, P.O. Box 257, N. Pomfret, VT 05053/802-457-1911

Trail Guns Armory, Inc., 1422 E. Main St., League City, TX 77573/713-332-5833

Trail Timer Co., 1992-A Suburban Ave., P.O. Box 19722, St. Paul, MN 55119/612-738-0925

Trammco, Inc., P.O. Box 1258, Bellflower, CA 90706/213-428-5250

Trapper Gun, Inc., 18717 East 14 Mile Rd., Fraser, MI 48026/313-792-0134

Traq, Inc., 1444 Kansas Ave., Kansas City, KS 66105/913-371-9630

Trax America, Inc., P.O. Box 898, 1150 Eldridge, Forrest City, AR 72335/800-232-2327

Tread Corp., 1764 Granby St. NE, Roanoke, VA 24012/703-982-6881

Treemaster, P.O. Box 247, Guntersville, AL 35976/205-878-3597

Treso, Inc., P.O. Box 4640, Pagosa Springs, CO 81157/303-731-2295

Trevallion Gunstocks, 9 Old Mountain Rd., Cape Neddick, ME 03902/207-361-1130

Trijicon, Inc., P.O. Box 2130, Farmington Hills, MI 48333/313-553-4960; FAX: 313-553-6129

Trinidad State Junior College, 600 Prospect St., Trinidad, CO 81082/719-846-5631; FAX: 719-846-5667

Triple-K Mfg. Co., Inc., 2222 Commercial St., San Diego, CA 92113/619-232-2066; FAX: 619-232-7675

Trius Products, Inc., P.O. Box 25, 221 S. Miami Ave., Cleves, OH 45002/513-941-5682; FAX: 513-941-7970

Trophy Bonded Bullets, Inc., 900 S. Loop W., Suite #190, Houston, TX 77054/713-645-4499; FAX: 713-741-6393

Trotman, Ken, 135 Ditton Walk, Unit 11, Cambridge CB5 8QD, England/0223-211030; FAX: 0223-212317

Tru-Balance Knife Co., 2155 Tremont Blvd. NW, Grand Rapids, NI 49504/616-453-3679

Tru-Square Metal Products, 640 First St. SW, P.O. Box 585, Auburn, WA 98001/206-833-2310

True Flight Bullet Co., 421 N. Pennsylvania Ave., Wilkes-Barre, PA 18702/717-821-5644; FAX: 717-823-8925

Trulock Tool, Broad St., Whigham, GA 31797/912-762-4678

T.S.W. Conversions, Inc., E. 115 Crain Rd., Paramus, NJ 07650-4017/201-265-1618

Tucker, James C., P.O. Box 38790, Sacramento, CA 95838/916-662-0571

Turnbull Restoration, Doug, 6562 County Rd. 30, Holcomb, NY 14469/716-657-6338

Twin Pine Armory, P.O. Box 58, Hwy. 6, Adna, WA 98522/206-748-4590; FAX: 205-748-7011

Tyler Mfg.-Dist., Melvin, 1326 W. Britton Rd., Oklahoma City, OK 73114/405-842-8044

U

Uberti USA, Inc., 362 Limerock Rd., P.O. Box 469, Lakeville, CT 06039/203-435-8068

Uberti, Aldo, Casella Postale 43, I-25063 Gardone V.T., Italy (U.S. importer—Uberti USA, Inc.)

Ugartechea S.A., Ignacio, Chonta 26, Eibar, Spain 20600/43-121257; FAX: 43-121669 (U.S. importer—Mandall Shootinag Supplies, Inc.)

Ulrich, Doc & Bud (See D.O.C. Specialists, Inc.)

Ultra Light Arms, Inc., P.O. Box 1270, 214 Price St., Granville, WV 26534/304-599-5687

Uncle Mike's (See Michaels of Oregon Co.)

Unertl Optical Co., John, 1224 Freedom Rd., Mars, PA 16046/412-776-9700

Unick's Gunsmithing, 5005 Center Rd., Lowellville, OH 44436/216-536-8015

Unique/M.A.P.F., 10, Les Allees, 64700 Hendaye, France 64700/33-59 20 71 93 (U.S. importer—Nygord Precision Products)

United Binocular Co., 9043 S. Western Ave., Chicago, IL 60620

United Cutlery Corp., 1425 United Blvd., Sevierville, TN 37862/615-428-2532

United States Ammunition Co. (See USAC)

United States Optics Technologies, Inc., 15936 Downey Ave., Paramount, CA 90723/310-220-2616; FAX: 310-220-2627

United States Products Co., 518 Melwood Ave., Pittsburgh, PA 15213/412-621-2130

Universal Clay Pigeon Traps, Unit 5, Dalacre Industrial Estate, Wilbarston, England LE16 8QL/011-44536771625; FAX: 011-44536771625

Upper Missouri Trading Co., 304 Harold St., Crofton, NE 68730/402-388-4844

USAC, 4500-15th St. East, Tacoma, WA 98424/206-922-7589

U.S. Arms Corp., 444 Brickell Ave., Suite P-26, Miami, FL 33131/305-371-7211

U.S. Repeating Arms Co., Inc., 275 Winchester Ave., New Haven, CT 06511/203-789-5000; FAX: 203-789-5071

Utica Cutlery Co., 820 Noyes St., Utica, NY 13503/315-733-4663

V

Vais Arms, George Vais, 4120 Willowbend, Houston, TX 77025

Valade, Robert, 931 3rd Ave., Seaside, OR 97138/503-738-7672

Valmet (See Tikka)

Valor Corp., 5555 NW 36th Ave., Miami, FL 33142/305-633-0127

Van Epps, Milton, Rt. 69-A, Parish, NY 13131/315-625-7251

Van Gorden & Son, Inc., C.S., 1815 Main St., Bloomer, WI 54724/715-568-2612

Van Horn, Gil, P.O. Box 207, Llano, CA 93544

Van Patten, J.W., P.O. Box 145, Foster Hill, Milford, PA 18337/717-296-7069

Vancini, Carl A., P.O. Box 4354, Stamford, CT 06907/203-978-1551; FAX: 203-978-0796

Varner Sporting Arms, Inc., P.O. Box 450421, Atlanta, GA 30345/404-491-1223

Venco Industries, Inc., 16770 Hilltop Park Place, Chagrin Falls, OH 44022/216-543-8808; FAX: 216-543-8811

Venus Industries, P.O. Box 246, Sialkot-1, Pakistan/ FAX: 92 432 85579

Verdemont Fieldsports, P.O. Box 9337, San Bernardino, CA 92427/714-880-8255; FAX: 714-880-8255

Verney-Carron, B.P. 72, 54 Boulevard Thiers, 42002 St. Etienne Cedex 1, France/33-77791500; FAX: 33-77790702

Vest, John, P.O. Box 1552, Susanville, CA 96130/916-257-7228

Vibra-Tek Co., 1844 Arroya Rd., Colorado Springs, CO 80906/719-634-8611; FAX: 719-632-8331

VibraShine, Inc., Rt. 1, P.O. Box 64, Mt. Olive, MS 39119/601-733-5614; FAX: 601-733-2226

Vic's Gun Refinishing, 6 Pineview Dr., Dover, NH 03820/603-742-0013

Vihtavuori Oy, 41330 Vihtavuori, Finland/358-41-779211

Viking Leathercraft, Inc., 1579A Jayken Way, Chula Vista, CA 91911/800-262-6666; FAX: 619-429-8268

Vintage Arms, Inc., 6003 Saddle Horse, Fairfax, VA 22030/703-968-0779

Vintage Industries, Inc., P.O. Box 872, Casselberry, FL 32718-0872; FAX: 407-699-4919; FAX: 407-699-8419

Viramontez, Ray, 601 Springfield Dr., Albany, GA 31707/912-432-9683

Vitt/Boos, 2178 Nichols Ave., Stratford, CT 06497/203-375-6859

Voere, P.O. Box 416, A-6333 Kufstein/Tirol, Austria/05372-62547; FAX: 5372-65752 (U.S. importer—Rahn Gun Works, Inc.)

Volquartsen Custom Ltd., RR 1, Box 33A, P.O. Box 271, Carroll, IA 51401/712-792-4238; FAX: 712-792-2542

Vorhes, David, 3042 Beecham St., Napa, CA 94558/707-226-9116

VSP Publishers, P.O. Box 887, McCall, ID 83638/208-634-4104

W

Waffen-Frankonia (See Frankonia Jagd)

Waffen-Weber Custom Gunsmithing, #4-1691 Powick Rd., Kelowna, B.C. Canada V1X 4L1/604-762-7575; FAX: 604-861-3655

Wagoner, Vernon G., 2325 E. Encanto, Mesa, AZ 85213/602-835-1307

Wahl Corp., Paul, P.O. Box 500, Bogota, NJ 07603-0500/201-261-9245; FAX: 201-487-9329

Wakina, 28150 Avenue Crocker #226, Newhall, CA 91355/805-295-8194

Waldron, Herman, Box 475, 80 N. 17th St., Pomeroy, WA 99347/509-843-1404

Walker Arms Co., Inc., 499 County Rd. 820, Selma, AL 36701/205-872-6231

Walker Shoe Co., P.O. Box 1167, Asheboro, NC 27203-1167/919-625-1380

Wallace's, Star Rt.1, Box 76, Grandin, MO 63943/314-593-4773

Wallace, Terry, 385 San Marino, Vallejo, CA 94589/707-642-7041

Waller & Son, Inc., W., 142 New Canaan Ave., Norwalk, CT 06850/203-838-4083

Walls Industries, P.O. Box 98, Cleburne, TX 76031/817-645-4366

Walt's Custom Leather, Walt Whinnery, 1947 Meadow Creek Dr., Louisville, KY 40218/502-458-4361

Walters Industries, 6226 Park Lane, Dallas, TX 75225/214-691-6973

Walther GmbH, Carl, B.P. 4325, D-7900 Ulm, Germany (U.S. importer—Interarms)

WAMCO, Inc., Mingo Loop, P.O. Box 337, Oquossoc, ME 04964-0337/207-864-3344

Ward & Van Valkenburg, 114 32nd Ave. N., Fargo, ND 58102/701-232-2351

Ward Machine, 5620 Lexington Rd., Corpus Christi, TX 78412/512-992-1221

Wardell Precision Handguns Ltd., 48851 N. Fig Springs Rd., New River, AZ 85027/602-465-7995

Wardrop, R. Alex, Box 245, 409 E. Marble St., Mechanicsburg, PA 17055/717-766-9663

Warenski, Julie, 590 E. 500 N., Richfield, UT 84701/801-896-5319; FAX: 801-896-5319

Warne Manufacturing Company, 9039 SE Jannsen Rd., Clackamas, OR 97015/503-657-5590; FAX: 503-657-5695

Warren & Sweat Mfg. Co., 38051 State Road 19, Umatilla, FL 32784/904-669-3166; FAX: 904-669-7272

Warren Muzzleloading Co., Inc., Hwy. 21 North, Ozone, AR 72854/501-292-3268

Warren, Kenneth W. (See Mountain States Engraving)

Washita Mountain Whetstone Co., P.O. Box 378, Lake Hamilton, AR 71951/501-525-3914

WASP Shooting Systems, Rt. 1, Box 147, Lakeview, AR 72642/501-431-5606

Waterfield Sports, Inc., 13611 Country Lane, Burnsville, MN 55337/612-435-8339

Watson Trophy Match Bullets, 2404 Wade Hampton Blvd., Greenville, SC 29615/803-244-7948

Wayland Precision Wood Products, P.O. Box 1142, Mill Valley, CA 94942/415-381-3543

Wayne Firearms for Collectors and Investors, James, 2608 N. Laurent, Victoria, TX 77901/512-578-1258; FAX: 512-578-3559

WD-40 Co., P.O. Box 80607, San Diego, CA 92138/619-275-1400; FAX: 619-275-5823

Weather Shield Sports Equipment, Inc., Rt. #3, Petoskey Rd., Charlevoix, MI 49720

Weatherby, Inc., 2781 Firestone Blvd., South Gate, CA 90280/213-569-7186

Weaver Arms Corp., P.O. Box 8, Dexter, MO 63841/314-568-3800

Weaver Products, Div. of Blount, Inc., P.O. Box 39, Onalaska, WI 54650/800-635-7656

Weaver Scope Repair Service, 1121 Larry Mahan Dr., Suite B, El Paso, TX 70025/915-593-0847

Weaver's Gun Shop, P.O. Box 8, Dexter, MO 63841/314-568-3101

Weber Jr., Rudolf, P.O. Box 160106, D-5650 Solingen, Germany/0212-592136

Webley and Scott Ltd., Frankley Industrial Park, Tay Rd., Rubery Rednal, Birmingham B45 OPA, United Kingdom/021-453-1864; FAX: 021-457-7846

Webster Scale Mfg. Co., P.O. Box 188, Sebring, FL 33870/813-385-6362

Weems, Cecil, P.O. Box 657, Mineral Wells, TX 76067/817-325-1462

Weihrauch KG, Hermann, Industriestrabe 11, 8744 Mellrichstadt, Germany/09776-497-498 (U.S. importers—Beeman Precision Arms, Inc.; E.A.A. Corp.)

Weisz Antique Gun Parts, P.O. Box 311, Arlington, VA 22210/703-243-9161

Welch, Sam, CVSR 2110, Moab, UT 84532/801-259-8131

Wellington Outdoors, P.O. Box 244, Madison, GA 30650/404-342-4915; FAX: 404-342-4656

Wells Sport Store, ¹10 N. Summit St., Prescott, AZ 86301/602-445-3655

Wells, R.A., 3452 1st Ave., Racine, WI 53402/414-639-5223

Wells, Rachel, 110 N. Summit St., Prescott, AZ 86301/602-445-3655

Wenoka/Seastyle, P.O. Box 8238, West Palm Beach, FL 33407/407-845-6155; FAX: 407-842-4247

Werth, T.W., 1203 Woodlawn Rd., Lincoln, IL 62656/217-732-1300

Wescombe, P.O. Box 488, Glencoe, CA 95232/209-293-7010

Wessinger Custom Guns & Engraving, 268 Limestone Rd., Chapin, SC 29036/803-345-5677

Wesson Firearms Co., Inc., Maple Tree Industrial Center, Rt. 20, Wilbraham Rd., Palmer, MA 01069/413-267-4081

West, Robert G., 3973 Pam St., Eugene, OR 97402/503-344-3700

Western Design, 1629 Via Monserate, Fallbrook, CA 92028/619-723-9279

Western Gunstock Mfg. Co., 550 Valencia School Rd., Aptos, CA 95003/408-688-5884

Western Missouri Shooters Alliance, P.O. Box 11144, Kansas City, MO 64119/816-597-3950; FAX: 816-229-7350

Western Ordnance Int'l Corp., 325 S. Westwood St. #1, Mesa, AZ 85210/602-964-1799

Westfield Engineering, 6823 Watcher St., Commerce, CA 90040; FAX: 213-928-8270

Westley Richards & Co., 40 Grange Rd., Birmingham, England B29 6AR/010-214722953 (U.S. importer—New England Arms Co.)

Westminster Arms Ltd., P.O. Box 60260, Reno, CA 89506/916-827-2179

Westrom, John (See Precise Metal Finishing)

Weyer International, 333-14th St., Toledo, OH 43624/419-241-5454

Whildin & Sons Ltd., E.H., 76 Autumn Dr., Tolland, CT 06084/203-870-8713

Whinnery, Walt (See Walt's Custom Leather)

White Flyer Targets, 124 River Rd., Middlesex, NJ 08846/908-469-0100; FAX: 908-469-9692

White Flyer, Div. of Reagent Chemical & Research, Inc., 9139 W. Redfield Rd., Peoria, AZ 85381/800-647-2898

White Laboratory, Inc., H.P., 3114 Scarboro Rd., Street, MD 21154/410-838-6550; FAX: 410-838-2802

White Owl Enterprises, Rt. 4, Box 266 GD, Abilene, KS 67410/913-263-1926; FAX: 913-263-1426

White Rock Tool & Die, Keith Rice, 6400 N. Brighton Ave., Kansas City, MO 64119/816-454-0478

White Systems, Inc., 810 W. 100 N., Roosevelt, UT 84066/801-722-3085; FAX: 801-722-3085

Whitestone Lumber Corp., 148-02 14th Ave., Whitestone, NY 11357/718-746-4400; FAX: 718-767-1748

Whitetail Design & Engineering Ltd., 9421 E. Mannsiding Rd., Clare, MI 48617/517-386-3932

Wichita Arms, Inc., 444 Ellis St., P.O. Box 11371, Wichita, KS 67211/316-265-0661; FAX: 316-265-0760

Widener's Reloading & Shooting Supply, Inc., P.O. Box 3009 CRS, Johnson City, TN 37602/615-282-6786; FAX: 615-282-6651

Wideview Scope Mount Corp., 26110 Michigan Ave., Inkster, MI 48141/313-274-1238; FAX: 313-274-2814

Wicbe, Duane, Casper Mt. Rt., Box 40, Casper, WY 82601/307-237-0615; FAX: 307-266-4143

Wiest, M.C., 10737 Dutchtown Rd., Knoxville, TN 37932/615-966-4545

Wild Bill's Originals, 25734 Bates Walk S.W., Vashon, WA 98070/206-463-5738

Wilderness Sound Products Ltd., 4015 Main St. #A, Springfield, OR 97478/503-741-0263; FAX: 503-741-7648

Wildey, Inc., P.O. Box 475, Brookfield, CT 06804/203-355-9000; FAX: 203-354-7759

Wildlife Research Center, Inc., 4345 157th Ave. NW, Anoka, MN 55304/612-427-3350

Wilkinson Arms, 26884 Pearl Rd., Parma, ID 83660/208-722-6771

Will-Burt Co., 169 S. Main, Orrville, OH 44667

William's Gun Shop, Ben, 1151 S. Cedar Ridge, Duncanville, TX 75137/214-780-1807

Williams Gun Sight Co., 7389 Lapeer Rd., Davison, MI 48423/313-653-2131; FAX: 313-658-2140

Williams Shootin' Iron Service, 8857 Bennett Hill Rd., Central Lake, MI 49622/616-544-6615

Williamson Precision Gunsmithing, 117 W. Pipeline, Hurst, TX 76053/817-285-0064

Willig, Claus, Siedlerweg 17, 8720 Schweinfurt, West Germany/01149-9721-41446

Willson Safety Prods. Div., P.O. Box 622, Reading, PA 19603

Wilson Arms Co., The, 63 Leetes Island Rd., Branford, CT 06405/203-488-7297; FAx: 203-488-0135

Wilson Case, Inc., P.O. Box 1106, Hastings, NE 68902-1106/800-322-5493; FAX: 402-463-5276

Wilson's Gun Shop, Box 578, Rt. 3, Berryville, AR 72616/501-545-3635; FAX: 501-545-3310

Wilson, Inc., L.E., P.O. Box 324, 404 Pioneer Ave., Cashmere, WA 98815/509-782-1328

Winchester (See U.S. Repeating Arms Co., Inc.)

Winchester Div., Olin Corp., 427 N. Shamrock, E. Alton, IL 62024/618-258-3566; FAX: 618-258-3180

Winchester Press, 220 Old New Brunswick Rd., Piscataway, NJ 08854/201-981-0820

Winchester Sutler, Inc., HC 38 Box 1000, Winchester, VA 22601/703-888-3595

Windish, Jim, 2510 Dawn Dr., Alexandria, VA 22306/703-765-1994

Windjammer Tournament Wads, Inc., 750 W. Hampton Ave., Suite 170, Englewood, CO 80110/303-781-6329

Wingshooting Adventures, 4320 Kalamazoo Ave. SE, Grand Rapids, MI 49508/616-455-7810; FAX: 616-455-5212

Winter & Associates, 239 Hillary Dr., Verona, PA 15147/412-795-4124

Winter, Robert M., RR 2, P.O. Box 484, Menno, SD 57045/605-387-5322

Wisner's Gun Shop, Inc., 287 NW Chehalis Ave., Chehalis, WA 98532/206-748-8942; FAX: 206-748-7011

Wittasek, Dipl.-Ing. Norbert, Seilergasse 2, Wien, 1010 Austria/0222-513-7001

Wolfe Publishing Co., 6471 Airpark Dr., Prescott, AZ 86301/602-445-7810; FAX: 602-778-5124

Wolfe, Bernie, 2025 E. Yandall, El Paso, TX 79903

Wolff Co., W.C., P.O. Box I, Newtown Square, PA 19073/215-359-9600

Wolverine Boots & Shoes Div., Wolverine World Wide, 9341 Courtland Dr., Rockford, MI 49351/616-866-1561

Wood, Frank (See Classic Guns)

Wood, Mel, P.O. Box 1255, Sierra Vista, AZ 85636/602-455-5541

Woodland Bullets, 638 Woodland Dr., Manheim, PA 17545/717-665-4332

Woods Pistolsmithing, 3840 Dahlgren Ct., Ellicott City, MD 21042/410-465-7979

Woods Wise Products, P.O. Box 681552, 2200 Bowman Rd., Franklin, TN 37064/800-735-8182; FAX: 615-790-8775

Woodstream, P.O. Box 327, Lititz, PA 17543/717-626-2125; FAX: 717-626-1912

Woolrich Woolen Mills, Mill St., Woolrich, PA 17779/717-769-6464

World of Targets, Div. of Steidle Corp., 9200 Floral Ave., Cincinnati, OH 45242/513-791-0917; FAX: 513-792-0004

World Trek, Inc., 2648 McCormick Ave., Pueblo CO 81001/719-546-2121; FAX: 719-543-6886

Worthy Products, Inc., RR I, P.O. Box 213, Martville, NY 13111

Wosenitz, William B., 341 NE 2nd Ct., Dania, FL 33004/305-923-3748

Wostenholm (See Ibberson [Sheffield] Ltd., George)

Wright's Hardwood Sawmill, 8540 SE Kane Rd., Gresham, OR 97080/503-666-1705

Wyant's Premium Outdoor Products, Inc., Roger, P.O. Box 1325, Harrisonburg, VA 22801-1325/FAX: 702-833-4021

Wyoming Armory, Inc., Rt. 1, Afton, WY 83110/307-886-9024

Wyoming Arms Mfg. Corp., 210 Hwy. 20 South, Thermopolis, WY 82443/307-864-5503

Wyoming Knife Corp., 101 Commerce Dr., Ft. Collins, CO 80524/303-224-3454

Y

Yankee Gunsmith, 1306 Oak Hill Dr., Copperas Cove, TX 76522/817-547-8433

Yavapai College, 1100 E. Sheldon St., Prescott, AZ 86301/602-776-2359; FAX: 602-776-2193

Yavapai Firearms Academy Ltd., P.O. Box 27290, Prescott Valley, AZ 86312/602-772-8262

Yearout, Lewis E. (See Montana Outfitters)

Yee, Mike, 29927 56 Pl. S., Auburn, WA 98001/206-839-3991

Yellowstone Wilderness Supply, P.O. Box 129, W. Yellowstone, MT 59758/406-646-7613

York M-1 Conversions, P.O. Box 262364, Houston, TX 77217/800-527-2881

Young Country Arms, P.O. Box 3615, Simi Valley, CA 93093

Z

Zanoletti, Pietro, Via Monte Gugielpo, 4, I-25063 Gardone V.T., Italy (U.S. importer—Mandall Shooting Supplies, Inc.)

Zanotti Armor, 123 W. Lone Tree Rd., Cedar Falls, IA 50613/319-232-9650

Z-Coat Co., 3915 U.S. Hwy. 98 S., Lakeland, FL 33801/813-665-1734

Zeeryp, Russ, 1601 Foard Dr., Lynn Ross Manor, Morristown, TN 37814/615-586-2357

Zeiss Optical, Inc., Carl, 1015 Commerce St., Petersburg, VA 23803/804-861-0033; FAX: 804-862-3734

Zero Ammunition Co., Inc., 1601 22nd St. SE, P.O. Box 1188, Cullman, AL 35055-1188/800-545-9376; FAX: 205-739-4683

Ziegel Engineering, 2108 Lomina Ave., Long Beach, CA 90815/310-596-9481; FAX: 310-598-4734

Zoli USA, Inc., Antonio, P.O. Box 6190, Fort Wayne, IN 46896/219-447-4603

Zoli, Antonio, Via Zanardelli 39, Casier Postal 21/23, I-25063 Gardone V.T., Italy (U.S. importers—E.A.A. Corp.; Mandall Shooting Supplies, Inc.; Zoli USA, Inc., Antonio)